CORNERSTONE
BIBLICAL
COMMENTARY

General Editor
Philip W. Comfort
D. Litt. et Phil., University of South Africa;
Tyndale House Publishers;
Coastal Carolina University.

Consulting Editor, Old Testament
Tremper Longman III
PhD, Yale University;
Robert H. Gundry Professor of Biblical Studies, Westmont College.

Consulting Editor, New Testament
Grant Osborne
PhD, University of Aberdeen;
Professor of New Testament, Trinity Evangelical Divinity School.

Associate Editors
Jason Driesbach
MA, Biblical Exegesis and Linguistics, Dallas Theological Seminary;
Tyndale House Publishers.

Mark R. Norton
MA, Theological Studies, Wheaton Graduate School;
Tyndale House Publishers.

James A. Swanson
MSM, Multnomah Biblical Seminary;
MTh, University of South Africa;
Tyndale House Publishers.

CORNERSTONE BIBLICAL COMMENTARY

The Book of Psalms

Mark D. Futato

The Book of Proverbs

George M. Schwab

GENERAL EDITOR

Philip W. Comfort

featuring the text of the

NEW LIVING TRANSLATION

TYNDALE HOUSE PUBLISHERS, INC. CAROL STREAM, ILLINOIS

Cornerstone Biblical Commentary, Volume 7

Visit Tyndale online at www.tyndale.com and www.newlivingtranslation.com.

Designed by Luke Daab and Timothy R. Botts.

Library of Congress Cataloging-in-Publication Data

Cornerstone biblical commentary.
p. cm.
Includes bibliographical references and index.
ISBN-13: 978-0-8423-3433-4 (hc : alk. paper)
1. Bible—Commentaries. I. Futato, Mark D. II. Schwab, George M.
BS491.3.C67 2006
220.7′7—dc22
2005026928

23 22 21 20
8 7 6 5 4 3

CONTENTS

CONTRIBUTORS TO VOLUME 7

Psalms: Mark D. Futato
BA, Geneva College;
MDiv, Westminster Theological Seminary;
MA, The Catholic University of America;
PhD, The Catholic University of America;
Robert L. Maclellan Professor of Old Testament, Reformed Theological Seminary

Proverbs: George M. Schwab
BS, Drexel University;
MDiv, Westminster Theological Seminary;
PhD, Westminster Theological Seminary;
Professor of Old Testament, Erskine Theological Seminary

GENERAL EDITOR'S PREFACE

The *Cornerstone Biblical Commentary* is based on the second edition of the New Living Translation (2007). Nearly 100 scholars from various church backgrounds and from several countries (United States, Canada, England, and Australia) participated in the creation of the NLT. Many of these same scholars are contributors to this commentary series. All the commentators, whether participants in the NLT or not, believe that the Bible is God's inspired word and have a desire to make God's word clear and accessible to his people.

This Bible commentary is the natural extension of our vision for the New Living Translation, which we believe is both exegetically accurate and idiomatically powerful. The NLT attempts to communicate God's inspired word in a lucid English translation of the original languages so that English readers can understand and appreciate the thought of the original writers. In the same way, the *Cornerstone Biblical Commentary* aims at helping teachers, pastors, students, and laypeople understand every thought contained in the Bible. As such, the commentary focuses first on the words of Scripture, then on the theological truths of Scripture—inasmuch as the words express the truths.

The commentary itself has been structured in such a way as to help readers get at the meaning of Scripture, passage by passage, through the entire Bible. Each Bible book is prefaced by a substantial book introduction that gives general historical background important for understanding. Then the reader is taken through the Bible text, passage by passage, starting with the New Living Translation text printed in full. This is followed by a section called "Notes," wherein the commentator helps the reader understand the Hebrew or Greek behind the English of the NLT, interacts with other scholars on important interpretive issues, and points the reader to significant textual and contextual matters. The "Notes" are followed by the "Commentary," wherein each scholar presents a lucid interpretation of the passage, giving special attention to context and major theological themes.

The commentators represent a wide spectrum of theological positions within the evangelical community. We believe this is good because it reflects the rich variety in Christ's church. All the commentators uphold the authority of God's word and believe it is essential to heed the old adage: "Wholly apply yourself to the Scriptures and apply them wholly to you." May this commentary help you know the truths of Scripture, and may this knowledge help you "grow in your knowledge of God and Jesus our Lord" (2 Pet 1:2, NLT).

PHILIP W. COMFORT
GENERAL EDITOR

ABBREVIATIONS

GENERAL ABBREVIATIONS

b. Babylonian Gemara
bar. baraita
c. *circa*, around, approximately
cf. *confer*, compare
ch, chs chapter, chapters
contra in contrast to
DSS Dead Sea Scrolls
ed. edition, editor
e.g. *exempli gratia*, for example
et al. *et alli*, and others
fem. feminine
ff following (verses, pages)
fl. flourished
Gr. Greek
Heb. Hebrew
ibid. *ibidem*, in the same place
i.e. *id est*, the same
in loc. *in loco*, in the place cited
lit. literally
LXX Septuagint
M Majority Text
m. Mishnah
masc. masculine
mg margin
ms manuscript
mss manuscripts
MT Masoretic Text
n.d. no date
neut. neuter
no. number
NT New Testament
OL Old Latin
OS Old Syriac
OT Old Testament
p., pp. page, pages
pl. plural
Q Quelle ("Sayings" as Gospel source)
rev. revision
sg. singular
t. Tosefta
TR Textus Receptus
v., vv. verse, verses
vid. *videtur*, it seems
viz. *videlicet*, namely
vol. volume
y. Jerusalem Gemara

ABBREVIATIONS FOR BIBLE TRANSLATIONS

ASV American Standard Version
CEV Contemporary English Version
ESV English Standard Version
GW God's Word
HCSB Holman Christian Standard Bible
JB Jerusalem Bible
KJV King James Version
NAB New American Bible
NASB New American Standard Bible
NCV New Century Version
NEB New English Bible
NET The NET Bible
NIV New International Version
NIrV New International Reader's Version
NJB New Jerusalem Bible
NJPS The New Jewish Publication Society Translation (*Tanakh*)
NKJV New King James Version
NRSV New Revised Standard Version
NLT New Living Translation
REB Revised English Bible
RSV Revised Standard Version
TEV Today's English Version
TLB The Living Bible

ABBREVIATIONS FOR DICTIONARIES, LEXICONS, COLLECTIONS OF TEXTS, ORIGINAL LANGUAGE EDITIONS

ABD *Anchor Bible Dictionary* (6 vols., Freedman) [1992]

ANEP *The Ancient Near East in Pictures* (Pritchard) [1965]

ANET *Ancient Near Eastern Texts Relating to the Old Testament* (Pritchard) [1969]

BAGD *Greek-English Lexicon of the New Testament and Other Early Christian Literature*, 2nd ed. (Bauer, Arndt, Gingrich, Danker) [1979]

BDAG *Greek-English Lexicon of the New Testament and Other Early Christian Literature*, 3rd ed. (Bauer, Danker, Arndt, Gingrich) [2000]

BDB *A Hebrew and English Lexicon of the Old Testament* (Brown, Driver, Briggs) [1907]

BDF *A Greek Grammar of the New Testament and Other Early Christian Literature* (Blass, Debrunner, Funk) [1961]

BHS *Biblia Hebraica Stuttgartensia* (Elliger and Rudolph) [1983]

CAD *Assyrian Dictionary of the Oriental Institute of the University of Chicago* [1956]

COS *The Context of Scripture* (3 vols., Hallo and Younger) [1997–2002]

DBI *Dictionary of Biblical Imagery* (Ryken, Wilhoit, Longman) [1998]

DBT *Dictionary of Biblical Theology* (2nd ed., Leon-Dufour) [1972]

DCH *Dictionary of Classical Hebrew* (5 vols., D. Clines) [2000]

DLNTD *Dictionary of the Later New Testament and Its Development* (R. Martin, P. Davids) [1997]

DJD *Discoveries in the Judean Desert* [1955–]

DJG *Dictionary of Jesus and the Gospels* (Green, McKnight, Marshall) [1992]

DOTP *Dictionary of the Old Testament: Pentateuch* (T. Alexander, D.W. Baker) [2003]

DPL *Dictionary of Paul and His Letters* (Hawthorne, Martin, Reid) [1993]

DTIB *Dictionary of Theological Interpretation of the Bible* (Vanhoozer) [2005]

EDNT *Exegetical Dictionary of the New Testament* (3 vols., H. Balz, G. Schneider. ET) [1990–1993]

GKC *Gesenius' Hebrew Grammar* (Gesenius, Kautzsch, trans. Cowley) [1910]

HALOT *The Hebrew and Aramaic Lexicon of the Old Testament* (L. Koehler, W. Baumgartner, J. Stamm; trans. M. Richardson) [1994–1999]

IBD *Illustrated Bible Dictionary* (3 vols., Douglas, Wiseman) [1980]

IDB *The Interpreter's Dictionary of the Bible* (4 vols., Buttrick) [1962]

ISBE *International Standard Bible Encyclopedia* (4 vols., Bromiley) [1979–1988]

KBL *Lexicon in Veteris Testamenti libros* (Koehler, Baumgartner) [1958]

LCL Loeb Classical Library

L&N *Greek-English Lexicon of the New Testament: Based on Semantic Domains* (Louw and Nida) [1989]

LSJ *A Greek-English Lexicon* (9th ed., Liddell, Scott, Jones) [1996]

MM *The Vocabulary of the Greek New Testament* (Moulton and Milligan) [1930; 1997]

NA26 *Novum Testamentum Graece* (26th ed., Nestle-Aland) [1979]

NA27 *Novum Testamentum Graece* (27th ed., Nestle-Aland) [1993]

NBD *New Bible Dictionary* (2nd ed., Douglas, Hillyer) [1982]

NIDB *New International Dictionary of the Bible* (Douglas, Tenney) [1987]

NIDBA *New International Dictionary of Biblical Archaeology* (Blaiklock and Harrison) [1983]

NIDNTT *New International Dictionary of New Testament Theology* (4 vols., C. Brown) [1975–1985]

NIDOTTE *New International Dictionary of Old Testament Theology and Exegesis* (5 vols., W. A. VanGemeren) [1997]

PGM *Papyri graecae magicae: Die griechischen Zauberpapyri.* (Preisendanz) [1928]

PG *Patrologia Graecae* (J. P. Migne) [1857–1886]

TBD *Tyndale Bible Dictionary* (Elwell, Comfort) [2001]

TDNT *Theological Dictionary of the New Testament* (10 vols., Kittel, Friedrich; trans. Bromiley) [1964–1976]

TDOT *Theological Dictionary of the Old Testament* (8 vols., Botterweck, Ringgren; trans. Willis, Bromiley, Green) [1974–]

TLNT *Theological Lexicon of the New Testament* (3 vols., C. Spicq) [1994]

TLOT *Theological Lexicon of the Old Testament* (3 vols., E. Jenni) [1997]

TWOT *Theological Wordbook of the Old Testament* (2 vols., Harris, Archer) [1980]

UBS3 *United Bible Societies' Greek New Testament* (3rd ed., Metzger et al.) [1975]

UBS4 *United Bible Societies' Greek New Testament* (4th corrected ed., Metzger et al.) [1993]

WH *The New Testament in the Original Greek* (Westcott and Hort) [1882]

ABBREVIATIONS FOR BOOKS OF THE BIBLE

Old Testament

Gen	Genesis	Deut	Deuteronomy	1 Sam	1 Samuel
Exod	Exodus	Josh	Joshua	2 Sam	2 Samuel
Lev	Leviticus	Judg	Judges	1 Kgs	1 Kings
Num	Numbers	Ruth	Ruth	2 Kgs	2 Kings

1 Chr	1 Chronicles
2 Chr	2 Chronicles
Ezra	Ezra
Neh	Nehemiah
Esth	Esther
Job	Job
Ps, Pss	Psalm, Psalms
Prov	Proverbs
Eccl	Ecclesiastes
Song	Song of Songs
Isa	Isaiah
Jer	Jeremiah
Lam	Lamentations
Ezek	Ezekiel
Dan	Daniel
Hos	Hosea
Joel	Joel
Amos	Amos
Obad	Obadiah
Jonah	Jonah
Mic	Micah
Nah	Nahum
Hab	Habakkuk
Zeph	Zephaniah
Hag	Haggai
Zech	Zechariah
Mal	Malachi

New Testament

Matt	Matthew
Mark	Mark
Luke	Luke
John	John
Acts	Acts
Rom	Romans
1 Cor	1 Corinthians
2 Cor	2 Corinthians
Gal	Galatians
Eph	Ephesians
Phil	Philippians
Col	Colossians
1 Thess	1 Thessalonians
2 Thess	2 Thessalonians
1 Tim	1 Timothy
2 Tim	2 Timothy
Titus	Titus
Phlm	Philemon
Heb	Hebrews
Jas	James
1 Pet	1 Peter
2 Pet	2 Peter
1 John	1 John
2 John	2 John
3 John	3 John
Jude	Jude
Rev	Revelation

Deuterocanonical

Bar	Baruch
Add Dan	Additions to Daniel
Pr Azar	Prayer of Azariah
Bel	Bel and the Dragon
Sg Three	Song of the Three Children
Sus	Susanna
1–2 Esdr	1–2 Esdras
Add Esth	Additions to Esther
Ep Jer	Epistle of Jeremiah
Jdt	Judith
1–2 Macc	1–2 Maccabees
3–4 Macc	3–4 Maccabees
Pr Man	Prayer of Manasseh
Ps 151	Psalm 151
Sir	Sirach
Tob	Tobit
Wis	Wisdom of Solomon

MANUSCRIPTS AND LITERATURE FROM QUMRAN

Initial numerals followed by "Q" indicate particular caves at Qumran. For example, the notation 4Q267 indicates text 267 from cave 4 at Qumran. Further, 1QS 4:9-10 indicates column 4, lines 9-10 of the *Rule of the Community*; and 4Q166 1 ii 2 indicates fragment 1, column ii, line 2 of text 166 from cave 4. More examples of common abbreviations are listed below.

CD	Cairo Geniza copy of the *Damascus Document*
1QH	*Thanksgiving Hymns*
1QIsa[a]	Isaiah copy [a]
1QIsa[b]	Isaiah copy [b]
1QM	*War Scroll*
1QpHab	*Pesher Habakkuk*
1QS	*Rule of the Community*
4QLam[a]	Lamentations
11QPs[a]	Psalms
11QTemple[a,b]	*Temple Scroll*
11QtgJob	*Targum of Job*

IMPORTANT NEW TESTAMENT MANUSCRIPTS

(all dates given are AD; ordinal numbers refer to centuries)

Significant Papyri (𝔓 = Papyrus)

𝔓1 Matt 1; early 3rd
𝔓4+𝔓64+𝔓67 Matt 3, 5, 26; Luke 1–6; late 2nd
𝔓5 John 1, 16, 20; early 3rd
𝔓13 Heb 2–5, 10–12; early 3rd
𝔓15+𝔓16 (probably part of same codex) 1 Cor 7–8, Phil 3–4; late 3rd
𝔓20 Jas 2–3; 3rd
𝔓22 John 15–16; mid 3rd
𝔓23 Jas 1; c. 200
𝔓27 Rom 8–9; 3rd
𝔓30 1 Thess 4–5; 2 Thess 1; early 3rd
𝔓32 Titus 1–2; late 2nd
𝔓37 Matt 26; late 3rd
𝔓39 John 8; first half of 3rd
𝔓40 Rom 1–4, 6, 9; 3rd

𝔓45 Gospels and Acts; early 3rd
𝔓46 Paul's Major Epistles (less Pastorals); late 2nd
𝔓47 Rev 9–17; 3rd
𝔓49+𝔓65 Eph 4–5; 1 Thess 1–2; 3rd
𝔓52 John 18; c. 125
𝔓53 Matt 26, Acts 9–10; middle 3rd
𝔓66 John; late 2nd
𝔓70 Matt 2–3, 11–12, 24; 3rd
𝔓72 1–2 Peter, Jude; c. 300
𝔓74 Acts, General Epistles; 7th
𝔓75 Luke and John; c. 200
𝔓77+𝔓103 (probably part of same codex) Matt 13–14, 23; late 2nd
𝔓87 Philemon; late 2nd
𝔓90 John 18–19; late 2nd
𝔓91 Acts 2–3; 3rd
𝔓92 Eph 1, 2 Thess 1; c. 300
𝔓98 Rev 1:13-20; late 2nd
𝔓100 Jas 3–5; c. 300
𝔓101 Matt 3–4; 3rd
𝔓104 Matt 21; 2nd
𝔓106 John 1; 3rd
𝔓115 Rev 2–3, 5–6, 8–15; 3rd

Significant Uncials

א (Sinaiticus) most of NT; 4th
A (Alexandrinus) most of NT; 5th
B (Vaticanus) most of NT; 4th
C (Ephraemi Rescriptus) most of NT with many lacunae; 5th
D (Bezae) Gospels, Acts; 5th
D (Claromontanus), Paul's Epistles; 6th (different MS than Bezae)
E (Laudianus 35) Acts; 6th
F (Augensis) Paul's Epistles; 9th
G (Boernerianus) Paul's Epistles; 9th
H (Coislinianus) Paul's Epistles; 6th
I (Freerianus or Washington) Paul's Epistles; 5th
L (Regius) Gospels; 8th
Q (Guelferbytanus B) Luke, John; 5th
P (Porphyrianus) Acts—Revelation; 9th
T (Borgianus) Luke, John; 5th
W (Washingtonianus or the Freer Gospels) Gospels; 5th
Z (Dublinensis) Matthew; 6th
037 (Δ; Sangallensis) Gospels; 9th
038 (Θ; Koridethi) Gospels; 9th
040 (Ξ; Zacynthius) Luke; 6th
043 (Φ; Beratinus) Matthew, Mark; 6th
044 (Ψ; Athous Laurae) Gospels, Acts, Paul's Epistles; 9th
048 Acts, Paul's Epistles, General Epistles; 5th
0171 Matt 10, Luke 22; c. 300
0189 Acts 5; c. 200

Significant Minuscules

1 Gospels, Acts, Paul's Epistles; 12th
33 All NT except Rev; 9th
81 Acts, Paul's Epistles, General Epistles; 1044
565 Gospels; 9th
700 Gospels; 11th
1424 (or Family 1424—a group of 29 manuscripts sharing nearly the same text) most of NT; 9th-10th
1739 Acts, Paul's Epistles; 10th
2053 Rev; 13th
2344 Rev; 11th
f^{1} (a family of manuscripts including 1, 118, 131, 209) Gospels; 12th-14th
f^{13} (a family of manuscripts including 13, 69, 124, 174, 230, 346, 543, 788, 826, 828, 983, 1689, 1709—known as the Ferrar group) Gospels; 11th-15th

Significant Ancient Versions

SYRIAC (SYR)

syr^{c} (Syriac Curetonian) Gospels; 5th
syr^{s} (Syriac Sinaiticus) Gospels; 4th
syr^{h} (Syriac Harklensis) Entire NT; 616

OLD LATIN (IT)

it^{a} (Vercellenis) Gospels; 4th
it^{b} (Veronensis) Gospels; 5th
it^{d} (Cantabrigiensis—the Latin text of Bezae) Gospels, Acts, 3 John; 5th
it^{e} (Palantinus) Gospels; 5th
it^{k} (Bobiensis) Matthew, Mark; c. 400

COPTIC (COP)

cop^{bo} (Boharic—north Egypt)
cop^{fay} (Fayyumic—central Egypt)
cop^{sa} (Sahidic—southern Egypt)

OTHER VERSIONS

arm (Armenian)
eth (Ethiopic)
geo (Georgian)

TRANSLITERATION AND NUMBERING SYSTEM

Note: For words and roots from nonbiblical languages (e.g., Arabic, Ugaritic), only approximate transliterations are given.

HEBREW/ARAMAIC

Consonants

א	*aleph*	= '	מ, ם	*mem*	= *m*
בּ, ב	*beth*	= *b*	נ, ן	*nun*	= *n*
גּ, ג	*gimel*	= *g*	ס	*samekh*	= *s*
דּ, ד	*daleth*	= *d*	ע	*ayin*	= '
ה	*he*	= *h*	פּ, פ, ף	*pe*	= *p*
ו	*waw*	= *w*	צ, ץ	*tsadhe*	= *ts*
ז	*zayin*	= *z*	ק	*qoph*	= *q*
ח	*heth*	= *kh*	ר	*resh*	= *r*
ט	*teth*	= *t*	שׁ	*shin*	= *sh*
י	*yodh*	= *y*	שׂ	*sin*	= *s*
כּ, כ, ך	*kaph*	= *k*	תּ, ת	*taw*	= *t, th* (spirant)
ל	*lamedh*	= *l*			

Vowels

ַ	*patakh*	= *a*	ָ	*qamets khatuf*	= *o*
חַ	*furtive patakh*	= *a*	ֹ	*holem*	= *o*
ָ	*qamets*	= *a*	וֹ	*full holem*	= *o*
ָה	*final qamets he*	= *ah*	ֻ	*short qibbuts*	= *u*
ֶ	*segol*	= *e*	ֻ	*long qibbuts*	= *u*
ֵ	*tsere*	= *e*	וּ	*shureq*	= *u*
ֵי	*tsere yod*	= *e*	ֲ	*khatef patakh*	= *a*
ִ	*short hireq*	= *i*	ֳ	*khatef qamets*	= *o*
ִ	*long hireq*	= *i*	ְ	*vocalic shewa*	= *e*
ִי	*hireq yod*	= *i*	ַי	*patakh yodh*	= *a*

GREEK

α	*alpha*	= *a*	ι	*iota*	= *i*
β	*beta*	= *b*	κ	*kappa*	= *k*
γ	*gamma*	= *g, n* (before γ, κ, ξ, χ)	λ	*lamda*	= *l*
			μ	*mu*	= *m*
δ	*delta*	= *d*	ν	*nu*	= *n*
ε	*epsilon*	= *e*	ξ	*ksi*	= *x*
ζ	*zeta*	= *z*	ο	*omicron*	= *o*
η	*eta*	= *ē*	π	*pi*	= *p*
θ	*theta*	= *th*	ρ	*rho*	= *r* (ῥ = *rh*)

σ, ς	*sigma*	= *s*	ψ	*psi*	= *ps*
τ	*tau*	= *t*	ω	*omega*	= *ō*
υ	*upsilon*	= *u*	ʽ	*rough breathing mark*	= *h (with vowel or diphthong)*
φ	*phi*	= *ph*			
χ	*chi*	= *ch*			

THE TYNDALE-STRONG'S NUMBERING SYSTEM

The Cornerstone Biblical Commentary series uses a word-study numbering system to give both newer and more advanced Bible students alike quicker, more convenient access to helpful original-language tools (e.g., concordances, lexicons, and theological dictionaries). Those who are unfamiliar with the ancient Hebrew, Aramaic, and Greek alphabets can quickly find information on a given word by looking up the appropriate index number. Advanced students will find the system helpful because it allows them to quickly find the lexical form of obscure conjugations and inflections.

There are two main numbering systems used for biblical words today. The one familiar to most people is the Strong's numbering system (made popular by the *Strong's Exhaustive Concordance to the Bible*). Although the original Strong's system is still quite useful, the most up-to-date research has shed new light on the biblical languages and allows for more precision than is found in the original Strong's system. The Cornerstone Biblical Commentary series, therefore, features a newly revised version of the Strong's system, the Tyndale-Strong's numbering system. The Tyndale-Strong's system brings together the familiarity of the Strong's system and the best of modern scholarship. In most cases, the original Strong's numbers are preserved. In places where new research dictates, new or related numbers have been added.[1]

The second major numbering system today is the Goodrick-Kohlenberger system used in a number of study tools published by Zondervan. In order to give students broad access to a number of helpful tools, the Commentary provides index numbers for the Zondervan system as well.

The different index systems are designated as follows:

TG	Tyndale-Strong's Greek number	ZH	Zondervan Hebrew number
ZG	Zondervan Greek number	TA/ZA	Tyndale/Zondervan Aramaic number
TH	Tyndale-Strong's Hebrew number	S	Strong's Aramaic number

So in the example, "love" *agapē* [TG26, ZG27], the first number is the one to use with Greek tools keyed to the Tyndale-Strong's system, and the second applies to tools that use the Zondervan system.

The indexing of Aramaic terms differs slightly from that of Greek and Hebrew. Strong's original system mixed the Aramaic terms in with the Hebrew, but the Tyndale-Strong's system indexes Aramaic with a new set of numbers starting at 10,000. Since Tyndale's system for Aramaic diverges completely from original Strong's, the original Strong's number is listed separately so that those using tools keyed to Strong's can locate the information. This number is designated with an S, as in the example, "son" *bar* [TA/ZA10120, S1247].

1. Generally, one may simply use the original four-digit Strong's number to identify words in tools using Strong's system. If a Tyndale-Strong's number is followed by a capital letter (e.g., TG1692A), it generally indicates an added subdivision of meaning for the given term. Whenever a Tyndale-Strong's number has a number following a decimal point (e.g., TG2013.1), it reflects an instance where new research has yielded a separate, new classification of use for a biblical word. Forthcoming tools from Tyndale House Publishers will include these entries, which were not part of the original Strong's system.

The Book of Psalms

MARK D. FUTATO

INTRODUCTION TO
Psalms

PSALMS IS A BOOK OF PRAISES. A crescendo of praise overwhelms the reader at the grand finale of the book of Psalms:

> Praise the LORD!
>
> Praise God in his sanctuary;
> praise him in his mighty heaven!
> Praise him for his mighty works;
> praise his unequaled greatness!
> Praise him with a blast of the ram's horn;
> praise him with the lyre and harp!
> Praise him with the tambourine and dancing;
> praise him with strings and flutes!
> Praise him with a clash of cymbals;
> praise him with loud clanging cymbals.
> Let everything that breathes sing praises to the LORD!
>
> Praise the LORD!

Harmonizing with the Psalter, Luther opens his own "Preface to the Psalter" with chords of praise:

> *Many of the holy fathers prized and praised the Psalter above all the other books of the Scripture. To be sure, the work itself gives praise enough to its author; nevertheless we must give evidence of our own praise and thanks. . . . The Psalter ought to be a precious and beloved book, if for no other reason than this: it promises Christ's death and resurrection so clearly—and pictures his kingdom and the condition and nature of all Christendom—that it might well be called a little Bible. In it is comprehended most beautifully and briefly everything that is in the entire Bible. It is really a fine enchiridion or handbook. In fact, I have a notion that the Holy Spirit wanted to take the trouble Himself to compile a short Bible and book of examples of all Christendom or all saints, so that anyone who could not read the whole Bible would here have anyway an entire summary of it, comprised in one little book.* (Luther 1960:254)

Similar praise of the Psalter resounds throughout the history of the church, as a few examples make clear.

> *I believe that a man can find nothing more glorious than these Psalms; for they embrace the whole life of man, the affections of his mind, and the motions of his soul. To praise and glorify God, he can select a psalm suited to every occasion,*

and thus will find that they were written for him. (Athanasius, quoted in Bushell 1980:94)

The Law instructs, history informs, prophecy predicts, correction censures, and morals exhort. In the book of Psalms you find all of these, as well as a remedy for the salvation of the soul. The Psalter deserves to be called the praise of God, the glory of man, the voice of the church, and the most beneficial confession of faith. (Ambrose, quoted in Bushell 1980:94)

I have been accustomed to call this book, I think not inappropriately, "An Anatomy of all the Parts of the Soul"; for there is not an emotion of which anyone can be conscious that is not here represented as in a mirror. Or rather, the Holy Spirit has here drawn to the life all the griefs, sorrows, fears, doubts, hopes, cares, perplexities, in short, all the distracting emotions, with which the minds of men are wont to be agitated . . . in short, there is no other Book in which we are more perfectly taught the right manner of praising God, or in which we are more powerfully stirred up to the performance of this religious exercise. (Calvin 1979:1.xxxvi-xxxvii)

The Psalter is a theatre, where God allows us to behold both Himself and His works; a most pleasant green field, a vast garden, where we see all manner of flowers: a paradise, having the most delicious flowers and fruits; a great sea in which are hid costly pearls: a heavenly school, where we have God for our teacher: a compend of all Scripture: a mirror of divine grace, reflecting the face of our heavenly Father: and the anatomy of our souls. (Paul Gerhard, quoted in Bushell 1980:95)

Such a concert of praise well suits the book of Psalms, whose Hebrew title is *seper tehillim* [TH5612/8416, ZH6219/9335] (Book of Praises).[1] However, this book is not predominantly exhilarating. The dominant mood of the Psalter is characterized by disorientation, sorrow, and perplexity—as the following examples show:

O LORD, why do you stand so far away?
  Why do you hide when I am in trouble? (10:1)

O LORD, how long will you forget me? Forever?
  How long will you look the other way?
How long must I struggle with anguish in my soul,
  with sorrow in my heart every day?
  How long will my enemy have the upper hand? (13:1-2 [2-3])[2]

My God, my God, why have you abandoned me?
  Why are you so far away when I groan for help? (22:1 [2])

How can "Book of Praises" be the title, when such psalms of negativity outnumber hymns of praise? Simply put, praise is the *final* word (Crenshaw 1986:293; Miller 1986:66). Praise is the final word even in the vast majority of the psalms of negativity (Pss 44 and 88 being exceptions). Praise is also the final word in each of the five major divisions of the Psalter (41:13 [14]; 72:18-19 [19-20]; 89:52 [53]; 106:48; 150). And praise is the final word of the Psalter as a whole (Westermann 1981:250-258). While psalms of negativity dominate the beginning of the Psalter (Pss 3–7, 10–13, etc.), resounding praise concludes the work (Pss 146–150) with the final line of the final psalm issuing the command: "Let everything that breathes sing *praises* to the LORD!" (150:6; my italics).

As Luther said, "So, then, let us see to it that we thank God for all these unspeakable blessings. Let us receive them and use them diligently and carefully, exercising ourselves in them to the praise and honor of God" (1960:257).

AUTHORS

In order to determine the various authors of the psalms, it is first necessary to understand that many of the titles to different psalms include the name of the author. Out of 150 psalms, 116 have titles. Some titles are as brief as that to Psalm 15, "A psalm of David," while others are as full as that to Psalm 60, "For the choir director: A psalm of David useful for teaching, regarding the time David fought Aram-naharaim and Aram-zobah, and Joab returned and killed 12,000 Edomites in the Valley of Salt. To be sung to the tune 'Lily of the Testimony.'" A given title may contain information on the author, the historical background, or matters related to the use of the psalm in worship.

Can we trust that the titles are giving us accurate information about the author of a particular psalm? Even among evangelical scholars there is no consensus on this issue. (For example, compare the views in Craigie 1983:31, Kidner 1973a:32-33, and Young 1949:307.) Dillard and Longman indicate that the "nature and origin of the titles are tricky issues that must be handled with care and scholarly humility" (2006:214). My position is that the preponderance of evidence leads to the conclusion that the titles should be considered canonical. They are as much a part of the Hebrew text as are the titles in 2 Samuel 22:1, Isaiah 38:9, and Habakkuk 3:1, or the editorial notes in Proverbs 10:1, 22:17, and 24:23. The ancient tradition of the Masoretes accents the titles along with the text and thus does not separate the titles from the rest of the text. And the New Testament is at times willing to base a theological argument on information in a title (see Acts 2:29-31). Authenticity does not, however, require a given title to have been written by the original poet (Kidner 1973a:33 and Longman 1995:208 n. 22), any more than it requires Deuteronomy 34:5-8 to have been written by Moses. Authenticity as used here means the titles record accurate information with regard to the particular psalm.

Problems remain in our understanding of some information in several titles. For example, David's concern for the well-being of Absalom in 2 Samuel 18:5, 12, 33 seems to be at odds with his animosity toward his enemies in Psalm 3, written "regarding the time David fled from his son Absalom." And how a song of thanksgiving for restoration from sickness (Ps 30) served as "a song for the dedication of the Temple" also remains problematic.

Many titles contain the prepositional Lamedh followed by a proper name, e.g., *ledawid* [TH3807.1/1732, ZH4200/1858] (David). While some regard this construction as ambiguous (Craigie 1983:34 and VanGemeren 1991:19-20), the prevailing view is that authorship is indicated (Rendtorff 1986:247; Sawyer 1970:26; Waltke 1991:586). "In the headings . . . the connection between *ledawid* and the description of the situation that follows immediately is so close that it is impossible to construe the lamed in *ledawid* as anything else than the *l auctoris*" (Kraus 1988:22).

Other evidence supports this conclusion. The expansion of *ledawid* with, "He sang this song to the LORD on the day the LORD rescued him from all his enemies and from Saul" (Ps 18) argues for *ledawid* as "by David" (Dillard and Longman 2006:216), especially in light of the fact that this same poem is embedded in the historical narrative at 2 Samuel 22:1. The title to the psalm in Habakkuk 3 reads *lakhabaqquq* [TH3807.1/2265, ZH4200/2487], which in context must mean "by Habakkuk." Hezekiah's hymn is likewise introduced in Isaiah 38:9 with *lekhizqiyahu* [TH3807.1/2396A, ZH4200/2625] ("by Hezekiah"; see Childs 1971:140). Moreover, Jesus posited an argument for his own identity in the Davidic authorship of Psalm 110 (Mark 12:35-37), and Luke posited an argument for the resurrection of Christ in the Davidic authorship of Psalm 16 (Acts 13:25-37).

DATE AND OCCASION OF WRITING

When considering the date and occasion of the Psalms, a distinction must be made between the individual psalms and the collection as a whole. The various individual psalms were composed over a long period of time, spanning the preexilic, exilic, and postexilic eras (Crenshaw 1986:293). Approximately one thousand years separates Psalms 90 and 137. The presence of psalms like Psalm 137 demonstrates that the book as a whole could not have reached its final form before the postexilic period. The book of Psalms as we have it was probably completed by the end of the fourth century BC (Craigie 1983:31; Kraus 1988:20). The theological rationale for the final shape will be explored below.

Only 14 psalms contain historical information in their titles, and all of these are related to the life of David. The specific occasion that gave rise to most psalms is unknown to us. Owing to the frequency of figurative and formulaic language in the psalms, it is often impossible to reconstruct the historical background of a given psalm based on its content. Rather than being a liability, however, this lack of historical specificity has always been an asset in the ongoing use of the Psalms. "The psalms are historically nonspecific so that they may be continually used in Israel's corporate and individual worship of God" (Dillard and Longman 2006:216). Given the difference of our own historical situation from that of the ancient psalmist, our own ability to appropriate these ancient texts is enhanced by their historical nonspecificity.

AUDIENCE

The immediate recipients of the psalms were the musicians and singers who performed them, as well as the congregation of Israel who was also encouraged to sing the praises of the psalms to their God. Many of our 150 psalms were composed to be used in the public worship of God, as is clear from the content of numerous psalms. For example, 100:2, 4 summons the nations with these words:

> Worship the LORD with gladness.
> Come before him, singing with joy.
>
> Enter his gates with thanksgiving;
> go into his courts with praise.

Psalm 68:24-26 [25-27] describes a liturgical procession that culminates in God's people gathering for worship:

> Your procession has come into view, O God—
> the procession of my God and King as he goes into the sanctuary.
> Singers are in front, musicians behind;
> between them are young women playing tambourines.
> Praise God, all you people [congregation] of Israel;
> praise the LORD, the source of Israel's life.

Psalm 35:18 also envisions the assembled community in public worship:

> Then I will thank you in front of the great assembly.
> I will praise you before all the people.

USE OF THE PSALMS

Numerous elements of the titles are intended to provide information on the use of the psalms in worship, but the precise meaning of many of these terms is unknown. Only the frequent terms are discussed here. Terms that occur only a time or two will be treated as they occur. (For a comprehensive discussion of this material see Kraus 1988:21-32. For an excellent summary of music in Old Testament worship see Eaton 1986:72-101.)

A title at times provides information on the type of psalm that follows. The general terms *shir* [TH7892, ZH8877] (song) and *mizmor* [TH4210, ZH4660] (psalm) must have held some distinction between them, but their precise meaning cannot be determined. Perhaps the denotation of *shir* is "vocal song," while that of *mizmor* is "song accompanied by instrumentation" (Kraus 1988:21-22; TDOT 4.93, 96-97). Lyrics may not always be in view in the verbal uses of the root *zamar* [TH2167, ZH2376] (see TWOT 1.245), from which *mizmor* is derived. On the other hand, *mizmor* may simply be more specific than *shir,* since it is used only in the Psalter exclusively for religious compositions (Sawyer 1970:32). The expression *shir hamma'aloth* [TH7892/4609A, ZH8877/5092] (song of ascents) occurs in the titles of Psalms 120–134. Psalm 121 is a song for pilgrimage and Psalm 132 has a procession in view. Accordingly, *shir hamma'aloth* is best taken to refer to a song sung by pilgrims as they made their way up to Jerusalem to worship God at the Temple. The meaning of *miktam* [TH4387, ZH4846] is not known.[3]

The term *maskil* [TH4905, ZH5380] occurs for the first time in 32:TITLE. Given that the same root is used in the same stem (Hiphil, meaning "to guide") in the same psalm (32:8), the same sense ("guide/instruct") may be involved: A *maskil* may be a didactic poem. Such a sense would be quite appropriate in 32:TITLE and 78:TITLE, but not all *maskil* psalms are explicitly didactic (e.g., Pss 42, 45, 89, 142). The term *tepillah* [TH8605, ZH9525] (prayer) is used exclusively for "prayer of lament" in psalm titles.

A title may also provide liturgical information. The term *lamenatseakh* [TH5329A, ZH5904] has traditionally been translated "for the choir director," and that is probably correct based on the use of the corresponding infinitive in 1 Chronicles 15:21, though the precise sense in which a given psalm is "for the choir director" is not known.[4] That *lamenatseakh* has a liturgical referent is seen not only in the use of the infinitive in a liturgical context (1 Chr 15:21) but also in the frequently accompanying phrase *bineginoth* [TH5058, ZH5593]. *Bineginoth,* used only following *lamenatseakh,* means "[played] on stringed instruments."[5] While not occurring in a title, the ubiquitous *selah* [TH5542, ZH6138] is also apparently a liturgical note, though the meaning of this term is also unknown.[6]

CANONICITY AND TEXTUAL HISTORY

The canonicity of the book of Psalms is readily seen in the use of "Psalms" for the title to the third division of the Hebrew canon. Jesus said, "When I was with you before, I told you that everything written about me in the law of Moses and the prophets and in the Psalms must be fulfilled" (Luke 24:44). Philo also referred to "Laws, and Oracles given by inspiration through Prophets, and Psalms" (*De Vita Contemplativa* 25). In texts like Luke 24:44 and Philo, "Psalms" was probably used as part for the whole (Crenshaw 1986:292), i.e., "Psalms" represented the whole third division of the Hebrew Bible, because of the Psalter's importance and initial position in the third division (Beckwith 1985:111-112).[7]

The Hebrew text of the book of Psalms is in relatively good condition (Harrison 1969:999). Irregularities exist, however. For example, Psalms 9 and 10 together form one alphabetic acrostic, indicating that the two were probably a single psalm originally (also, the absence of Mem, Nun, and Samekh lines in Psalm 10 indicate that the text has been damaged in transmission). Similarly, the threefold refrain in Psalms 42 and 43 is evidence for the accidental division of a single original psalm. Moreover, a comparison of Psalm 18 and 2 Samuel 22 or Psalms 14 and 53 gives evidence of other textual irregularities—some transmissional, others editorial. While maintaining general confidence in the Masoretic Text, this commentary will deal with textual problems as they are encountered (see Kraus 1988:13-16).

LITERARY STYLE

Poetry. Readers of the Psalms face special difficulties, one of which is the poetic nature of the text (Longman 1993:10). Evidence of this difficulty is found in the fact that numerous introductions to the literature of the Bible find it necessary to provide a special introduction to the poetry of the Bible but not to the prose (Petersen and Richards 1992:1-2). Accordingly, an overview of poetry is included here. (See Berlin 1985, Fokkelman 2001, Longman 1993, Miller 1994, and Schokel 1988 for more detailed treatments of the material covered here.) Some scholars deny the usefulness of using the category of poetry for the Hebrew Bible (Kugel 1981), but most affirm that a difference exists between prose and poetry. In most current discussions, prose and poetry are said to be different points on a continuum: At the extremes the difference is obvious (compare Gen 12 and Ps 34), but the boundary is at times fuzzy (e.g., Is the book of Haggai prose or poetry?). So rather than defining poetry in terms of its unique features over against prose, scholars now list the features that indicate the presence of poetry when these features occur in high concentration (Berry 1995; Longman 1993; Miller 1994b; Petersen and Richards 1992). Before surveying these features, I need to introduce some basic terminology.

A *poem* is "an independent unit of poetry" (Watson 2005:14; see Jonah's thanksgiving poem in Jonah 2:2-9). Subdivisions of a poem include the stanza, strophe, line, and colon. A *line* (not always equated with a biblical verse) is usually made up of *two* cola (plural of *colon*), and is thus called a *bi*colon; 111:2 provides an example:

Colon A: How amazing are the deeds of the LORD!

Colon B: All who delight in him should ponder them.

Alternatively, a line may be made up of a single colon (monocolon), three cola (tricolon), or even four cola (tetracolon). A variety of devices (such as refrains, *inclusios,* repeated key words, chiasms, and acrostics) are used to batch a group of lines together into a *strophe.* So, for example, Psalm 119 is broken into 22 strophes, based on the 22 letters in the Hebrew alphabet. In some poems a group of strophes can be batched together into a larger unit that I will call a *stanza.*[8]

Now we can survey the features of Hebrew poetry under four interrelated headings. (For more detailed and differently arranged discussions, see Miller 1994b and Longman 1993.)

1. Terseness. Poetic sentences are consistently terse, owing to a variety of factors. A poetic sentence is short, usually having two to five words per colon. The features mentioned in the following three headings contribute to the terseness of Hebrew poetry.

2. Parallelism. This refers to correspondence between the cola of a poetic line. While one initially may think of the correspondence as semantic (a correspondence in meaning), grammatical (phonological, morphological, syntactical) correspondences are abundant (Berlin 1985). Previous generations understood this correspondence in terms of equivalence: saying the same thing twice with different words. Robert Alter argues, however, that "good poetry at all times is an intellectually robust activity to which such laziness is alien" (Alter 1992:179). Alter goes on to say that "the ancient Hebrew poets are constantly advancing their meanings where the casual ear catches mere repetition" (Alter 1992:179). Not a correspondence of equivalency but a correspondence with development is now understood to be the essence of parallelism (Longman 1993:83). Take 2:4-5 as a simple illustration:

But the one who rules in heaven laughs.
  The Lord scoffs at them.
Then in anger he rebukes them,
  terrifying them with his fierce fury.

Notice the growing intensity in the progression: "laugh," "scoff," "rebuke," "terrify." Parallelism accounts for the symmetry that characterizes poetic lines as well as the frequent use of word pairs. In poetry, word pairs, like "heaven and earth," are typically broken up, one word occurring in each colon, e.g., 73:25:

Whom have I in heaven but you?
  I desire you more than anything on earth.

3. Figures of thought. "Poetry is a language of images" (Ryken 1984:89). Images are concrete and sensory: "The poets of the Bible constantly put us into a world of water and sheep and lions and rocks and arrows and grass" (Ryken 1984:90). The high frequency of concrete word pictures is one key factor that has made the message of the Psalms accessible to readers throughout history. Because the text is concrete, we readily relate to it, and because the images are usually metaphoric, we can apply them to a variety of analogous situations in our own lives.

An image is "a figure of speech expressing some similarity or analogy" (Watson 2005:251). The reader must compare the topic at hand with the word picture that is drawn and then determine the point of similarity, if it is not explicit. In 51:7 [9] forgiveness is similar to the whiteness of snow: "Purify me from my sins, and I will be clean; wash me, and I will be whiter than snow." And in 68:14 [15] the scattered enemies are similar to scattered flakes of snow: "The Almighty scattered the enemy kings like a blowing snowstorm on Mount Zalmon."

A wide variety of figures of thought fills the pages of the Psalter: simile, metaphor, metonymy, synecdoche, hyperbole, personification, etc. Numerous works discuss these and other particular images in detail (Beekman and Callow 1974:124-150; Bullinger 1968; Caird 1980; Ryken 1984:88-103; Watson 2005:251-272).

4. Grammar. The grammar of poetry sets it apart from prose. Again, however, we are speaking of a continuum based on the frequency of grammatical features, rather than a set of features unique to poetry. One delimiter of poetry is the relative absence of the definite article, the direct object marker, and the relative pronoun (Freedman 1987). Along with this is the broader paratactic nature of poetry, i.e., "the juxtaposition of clauses without syntactical indicators" (Miller 1994b:222), as in "I saw the shirt you bought" instead of "I saw the shirt *that* you bought," and the frequent use of ellipsis, particularly of the verb, where words are left out and are to be supplied by the reader, as in "She is taller than you [are tall]." Also, the alternation of the perfect and the imperfect in parallel cola for stylistic rather than semantic reasons is typical in poetry (Berlin 1985:36).

So why poetry? An ultimate answer cannot be given, but two perspectives can be offered.[9] Poetry is *pleasurable.* Prose narrative has one kind of beauty, poetry another. The symmetrical lines filled with images is simply a pleasure to read. Poetry is *powerful.* Poetry powerfully informs the intellect. Whether at the crossing of the Red Sea (Exod 15) or the incarnation of Christ (Luke 1:46-55, 68-79), God seems to use poetry when he "has something important to say" (Frame 1986:1). The power of poetry makes it memorable so that virtually all key events in redemptive history are commemorated in poetry. Poetry also powerfully moves the feelings and the will (Longman 1993:81), in particular through the pictures it paints: "The LORD is my shepherd" (23:1); "God is our refuge and strength" (46:1 [2]); "The hillsides blossom with joy" (65:12 [13]); "Instead, I have calmed and quieted myself, like a weaned child who no longer cries for its mother's milk" (131:2).

God wants us to be overwhelmed by his truth. It is not enough to agree; we must be shaken. We must see the earthshaking importance of what he is telling us (Frame 1986:2). As we learn more about Hebrew poetry, we are better equipped to surmount the difficulties and experience the pleasure and power of the Psalms.

Genre. Another inescapable literary category is genre. Without using the term, we have already had to employ the concept. In saying that the Psalms are poetry, not prose, we are saying the Psalms are one genre and not another.

Written materials can be organized into a variety of groups, based on features they share. A genre is a group of texts with common characteristics (Woodward and

Travers 1995:29) or more simply a category (Fisher 1980:291). Genres ought not to be thought of as rigid categories, however (Giese 1995:16; Longman 1985:56-58), as the discussion of the prose and poetry genres has already made clear. As we will see, whether a psalm is a hymn or a thanksgiving song is at times difficult to say, for it is a matter of degree. In addition, the same psalm may be studied, for example, in the context of both creation hymns and wisdom psalms.

Our concern with genre "is not so much to classify as to clarify" (Frye 1971:247-248). Our work is not done when we have put all of the psalms into genre boxes. Genre analysis is one part of a holistic approach to interpretation. Recognizing the genre provides the reader with a reading strategy and thereby shapes the interpretation (Longman 1985:67; Longman 1988:21-23). For example, by knowing the genre, a reader will be aided in determining whether to understand a particular text literally or figuratively.

What genres are found in the Psalms? Based on the work of Claus Westermann, it has become customary to group most psalms into one of two genres: lament or praise (Clines 1969; Giese 1995; Murphy 1959).[10] The genre of praise, however, is regularly divided in two, resulting in three basic genres: lament, thanksgiving, and hymn. In general terms the lament articulates the troubles of life in all their variety, the thanksgiving song expresses gratitude for deliverance from such trouble, and the hymn offers praise for a well-ordered world (Brueggemann 1984).

1. Lament. The words of 90:10 resonate deep within the human soul:

Seventy years are given to us!
  Some even live to eighty.
But even the best years are filled with pain and trouble.

"Filled with pain and trouble" characterizes human existence in a world filled with sin and its misery. Rather than denying this dark side of life, the Psalms bring it into full view through the laments. Almost half of the psalms fall into this category (Longman 1995:203).

The lament is a psalm of disorientation (Brueggemann 1984:51-57), an expressing of the sorrow, distress, fear, anger, guilt, or perplexity of life. The lament articulates our agonizing questions:

O LORD, why do you stand so far away?
  Why do you hide when I am in trouble? (10:1)

O LORD, how long will you forget me? Forever?
  How long will you look the other way? (13:1 [2])

Lord, where is your unfailing love?
  You promised it to David with a faithful pledge. (89:49 [50])

The lament voices our stinging assertions:

All this has happened though we have not forgotten you.
  We have not violated your covenant. (44:17 [18])

You have taken away my companions and loved ones.
  Darkness is my closest friend. (88:18 [19])

Such expressions are not indications of doubt but affirmations of faith (Brueggemann 1984:52). In commenting on the agonizing questions of 13:1-2 [2-3], Calvin said that David thereby exercised great faith: "Had it been otherwise, how could [David] direct his groanings and prayers to [God]?" (Calvin 1979). All of our dark emotions come to expression in the laments (Allender and Longman 1994). Yet the laments are not typically unmitigated darkness, as their common structure makes clear. The fundamental movement in the lament is from plea to praise. The plea typically begins with an address to God and an initial cry for help. Then follows the recounting of the distress in terms of a complaint about one's circumstances, one's enemies, or God himself, joined by a confession of sin or innocence, depending on the circumstances. The heart of the plea is the petition for God to act in a saving way on behalf of the psalmist. The final note, however, is usually praise[11] in the form of a concise hymn of praise or a vow to praise or a statement of confidence in being heard. The laments are not literature of despair, but ultimately of hope (see Coetzee 1992 for a survey of research on the laments).

2. Thanksgiving Song. The thanksgiving song is the reflex of the lament, as singing the thanksgiving song is one aspect of the paying of the vow made when the psalmist was in trouble. The psalmist does not give thanks by saying, "Thank you," but by confessionally acknowledging who God is and what he has done in delivering him from distress (Brueggemann 1984:125).

The thanksgiving song typically begins with an expression of the intention to praise and perhaps a brief and general summary of the previous distress and deliverance, as in 30:1-5 [2-6]:

I will exalt you, LORD, for you rescued me.
  You refused to let my enemies triumph over me.
O LORD my God, I cried to you for help,
  and you restored my health.
You brought me up from the grave, O LORD.
  You kept me from falling into the pit of death.

Sing to the LORD, all you godly ones!
  Praise his holy name.
For his anger lasts only a moment,
  but his favor lasts a lifetime!
Weeping may last through the night,
  but joy comes with the morning.

The heart of the thanksgiving psalm follows with a recounting of the distress, the petition, and the deliverance, as in 30:6-10 [7-12]:

When I was prosperous, I said,
  "Nothing can stop me now!"
Your favor, O LORD, made me as secure as a mountain.
  Then you turned away from me, and I was shattered.

I cried out to you, O LORD.
  I begged the Lord for mercy, saying,

"What will you gain if I die,
  if I sink into the grave?
Can my dust praise you?
  Can it tell of your faithfulness?
Hear me, LORD, and have mercy on me.
  Help me, O LORD."

This recounting is the act of thanksgiving proper. A vow to continue giving thanks forever or a call for others to join in the thanksgiving often concludes the song, as in 30:11-12 [13]:

You have turned my mourning into joyful dancing.
  You have taken away my clothes of mourning and clothed me with joy,
that I might sing praises to you and not be silent.
  O LORD my God, I will give you thanks forever!

3. Hymn. The life reflected in the hymn is neither the troubled life of the lament nor the life of one recently delivered from trouble. It is, rather, "the well ordered life intended by God" (Brueggemann 1984:25). A text like 16:5-8 provides a good example of this happy state of affairs:

LORD, you alone are my inheritance, my cup of blessing.
  You guard all that is mine.
The land you have given me is a pleasant land.
  What a wonderful inheritance!

I will bless the LORD who guides me;
  even at night my heart instructs me.
I know the LORD is always with me.
  I will not be shaken, for he is right beside me.

The response to such circumstances is praise. The frequent "Praise the LORD" is not so much an exclamation as it is an imperative. The proper response to the command is not a corresponding "Praise the LORD!" but is a "recalling [of] God's marvelous attributes, reporting how he manifests and expresses those attributes through his mighty and redemptive acts for his people" (Barker 1995:217).

I will exalt you, my God and King,
  and praise your name forever and ever.
I will praise you every day;
  yes, I will praise you forever.
Great is the LORD! He is most worthy of praise!
  No one can measure his greatness.

Let each generation tell its children of your mighty acts;
  let them proclaim your power.
I will meditate on your majestic, glorious splendor
  and your wonderful miracles.
Your awe-inspiring deeds will be on every tongue;
  I will proclaim your greatness.

Everyone will share the story of your wonderful goodness;
they will sing with joy about your righteousness.

The LORD is merciful and compassionate,
slow to get angry and filled with unfailing love.
The LORD is good to everyone.
He showers compassion on all his creation.

As 145:1-9 illustrates, "The act of praise . . . means to acknowledge and confess who God is and in so doing render honor and glory to the one who is the object of praise" (Miller 1986:70). Typically a hymn opens with a call to praise God, and a variety of worshipers are in view: the congregation of Israel (113:1), the nations (117:1), the angelic host (29:1), the self (103:1), or the whole created realm (Ps 148).

The praise proper is frequently introduced by a *ki* [TH3588, ZH3954] clause, as in 33:1-7:

Let the godly sing for joy to the LORD;
it is fitting for the pure to praise him.
Praise the LORD with melodies on the lyre;
make music for him on the ten-stringed harp.
Sing a new song of praise to him;
play skillfully on the harp, and sing with joy.
For [*ki*] the word of the LORD holds true,
and we can trust everything he does.
He loves whatever is just and good;
the unfailing love of the LORD fills the earth.

The LORD merely spoke,
and the heavens were created.
He breathed the word,
and all the stars were born.
He assigned the sea its boundaries
and locked the oceans in vast reservoirs.

An echo of the opening call to praise is often heard at the finale to the hymn, as in 103:20-22:

Praise the LORD, you angels,
you mighty ones who carry out his plans,
listening for each of his commands.
Yes, praise the LORD, you armies of angels
who serve him and do his will!
Praise the LORD, everything he has created,
everything in all his kingdom.

Let all that I am praise the LORD.

In reference to the hymns in particular Brueggemann (1984:28) has said,

The Psalms bespeak a healthy, oriented life—that is, anticipated, even if not yet experienced. There moves in these psalms a deep conviction that God's purpose for

the world is resilient. That purpose will not yield until creation is brought to fullness. The Psalms assert that the creation finally is committed to and will serve the Creator. The Psalms thus are anticipatory of what surely will be.

Themes and Genres. A variety of themes run through the hymns: God as creator, sustainer, king, deliverer, etc. When a given theme dominates a group of hymns, a subgenre emerges, such as creation hymns and kingship hymns. Let us take, for example, kingship hymns.

The reign of God is celebrated in a group of hymns that we could call kingship songs or enthronement psalms (see Pss 29, 47, 93, 95–99). These psalms proclaim that the God of Israel reigns over the nations and the whole of creation. His reign has been established through his victory over all opposing forces. Those forces may be in the creation, as in 29:3, 10:

> The voice of the LORD echoes above the sea.
> The God of glory thunders.
> The LORD thunders over the mighty sea.
>
> The LORD rules over the floodwaters.
> The LORD reigns as king forever.

Or they may be the nations, as in 47:2-3 [3-4]:

> For the LORD Most High is awesome.
> He is the great King of all the earth.
> He subdues the nations before us,
> putting our enemies beneath our feet.

So the nations and the creation are called upon to worship the Lord.

> The LORD is king!
> Let the nations tremble!
> He sits on his throne between the cherubim.
> Let the whole earth quake!
> The LORD sits in majesty in Jerusalem,
> exalted above all the nations.
> Let them praise your great and awesome name.
> Your name is holy! (99:1-3)
>
> The LORD is king!
> Let the earth rejoice!
> Let the farthest coastlands be glad. (97:1)

These psalms would have liturgically reenacted the enthronement of God.

> God has ascended with a mighty shout.
> The LORD has ascended with trumpets blaring.
> Sing praises to God, sing praises;
> sing praises to our King, sing praises! (47:5-6 [6-7])

"Ascended" refers to God's ascent to his throne after the victory (Brueggemann 1984:150). And the festal setting in all likelihood would have been the Festival of Shelters, as indicated by the convergence of fall meteorological imagery and the kingship motif in these psalms (Futato 1984:252-254; see, for example, the commentary on Ps 29). Just as Israel at the Festival of Shelters looked back to past victories and forward to future victories, so these psalms anticipate the coming of God's reign in the future, even as they celebrate his victories in the past.

MAJOR THEMES

The individual psalms have many themes, as was already seen in our discussion of the various genres in the Psalms. The major themes that pertain to theological matters are discussed in the next section. In this section, I think it would serve the reader well to understand how the recent interpreters of Psalms have attempted to view the book as a unit that has one overall message—or at least a message that pervades the individual psalms.

Since the pioneering work of Herman Gunkel and Sigmund Mowinckel, the key contexts for interpreting psalms have been the text's genre and its function in the priestly cult of Judaism. The form-critical and cult-functional approaches will, no doubt, continue to play a role in the study of the Psalter. However, since the publication of Brevard Childs's *Introduction to the Old Testament as Scripture,* interest has been growing in the canonical book of Psalms as the key context for interpreting an individual psalm. Some have even suggested that form-critical and cult-functional questions must now be subordinated to what has been called "the book-as-context" approach (Mays 1987:12). The idea that the Psalms are a random anthology[12] is being replaced by the conviction that the Psalter has been intentionally shaped, so that the whole communicates a message that is crucial for interpreting the parts. (For a survey of the development of the book-as-context approach, see Howard 1993.) Numerous indicators of intentional shaping are evident in various psalms (see Wilson 1992:130-136 and Wilson 1993:72-75). First I will summarize the indicators, then I will draw out the significance for the purpose of the book of Psalms as a whole.

Claus Westermann (Westermann 1980) drew our attention to an initial indicator of shaping when he pointed out the movement from lamentation at the beginning of the Psalter to praise at its end. Thus it is the final shape of the Psalter, not the content of individual psalms, that justifies the title, "The Book of Praises." A second indicator is the division of the Psalter into five books (Pss 1–41, 42–72, 73–89, 90–106, 107–150). Earlier and once-independent collections of psalms are still evident in the Psalter: Davidic (Pss 3–41, 51–72), Korahite (Pss 42–49, 84–88), Asaphic (Pss 73–83), Psalms of Ascent (Pss 120–134), and Hallelujah Psalms (Pss 111–118, 146–150). Though the process of shaping these collections into books is not fully understood, the final shape of the Psalter as a whole is clearly that of five books, with the end of each book signaled by a doxology.

A third indicator of shaping is the presence of an introduction and a conclusion (Miller 1993:83). Psalms 1 and 2 serve to introduce the whole; they are differentiated from Book 1 by the absence of titles, and they are joined to each other by various literary links (Brennan 1980): (1) the *inclusio* formed by the repetition of *'ashre* [TH835A, ZH897] ("happy," "joy"; 1:1 and 2:12), (2) the contrast of the righteous meditating (*hagah* [TH1897, ZH2047]; 1:2) on God's law and the nations plotting (*hagah;* 2:1) against God's rule, (3) the wordplay on the righteous not joining in (*yashab* [TH3427, ZH3782], "sit"; 1:1) with scoffers and the Lord ruling (*yashab;* 2:4) in heaven, and (4) the repeated motif of the "perishing way" (*'abad* [TH6, ZH6] + *derek* [TH1870, ZH2006]; 1:6 and 2:12). And, like any well-crafted book, the book of Psalms has a conclusion (Pss 146–150) that articulates the telos of the work as a whole, as we have already seen.

One more indicator can be mentioned: The book of Psalms is comprised of two parts (Books 1–3 and Books 4–5) marked out by differing organizational techniques (Wilson 1992:131 and Wilson 1993:73-74). Books 1–3 primarily use the author from the titles to organize the material, whereas Books 4–5 are built around the genres of "Thanksgiving Psalms" and "Hallelujah Psalms."

The final shape of the book of Psalms answers the question of the book's purpose and message. Varying opinions have been expressed with regard to the primary purpose of the book of Psalms. Some have argued for a private and devotional use (Young 1949:309). Hermann Gunkel has said, "this collection has been assembled with the intention of creating a devotional and house book for pious lay people" (cited in Zenger 1994:44). Others argue for a public and liturgical use (Longman 1988:46-48). Each of these views has captured one side of the Psalter's "dual identity of liturgy and literature" (Mays 1993b:17). The final shape of the Psalter leads to the conclusion that the overarching category that best captures the purpose of the book as a whole is *instructional* (McCann 1993b).

Psalm 1 teaches that to be happy and prosperous one must take pleasure in and continually meditate on "the *torah* [TH8451, ZH9368] of the LORD." Torah is "teaching" (78:1; Prov 1:8b); Torah is instruction (Zorell 1963:893). Where would postexilic readers of the completed Psalter have turned to meditate on "the *torah* of the LORD"? They would have turned to "the Book of the Torah of the LORD" (see 2 Chr 17:9; 34:14; Neh 9:3), which is "the Book of the Torah of Moses" (cf. Neh 8:1 and 9:3) or "the Five Books of Moses" (see Williamson 1985:xxxvii-xxxix for a concise discussion of the issue; see also Terrien 1993:57). Psalm 1, however, is an introduction, not to "the Five Books of Moses," but to "the Five Books of the Psalms." The reason for the fivefold division of the book of Psalms now becomes clear, and the tradition found in *Midrash Tehillim* makes sense: "Moses gave Israel the five books, and David gave Israel the five Books of Psalms" (Braude 1959:1.5). The position and focus of Psalm 1 lead to the conclusion that just as "the Five Books of Moses" are an instance of "the *torah* of the LORD," so are "the Five Books of the Psalms." *Torah* captures the overarching purpose of "the Five Books of the Psalms."

Whereas Psalm 1 provides insight into the overall purpose of the Psalms, Psalm 2 sets forth the overall message: The Lord reigns. More will be said about this theme below under Theological Concerns, but here we can consider several facets of this theme as set forth in Psalm 2. First, the Lord reigns from heaven (2:4), showing his supremacy over all other rulers (2:1-3). Second, the Lord reigns through his royal son (2:6-7) to whom he promises the nations (2:8-9). Third, the Lord reigns with the goal of blessing all who take refuge in him (2:12b). The nations are given the choice between the foolish path that leads to perishing and the wise path that leads to blessing—the same choice set forth in Psalm 1. God's purpose for the nations (Ps 2) is the same as for Israel (Ps 1) from creation on: "But what joy for all who take refuge in him!" (2:12). How the Lord's reign plays out in the book as a whole can be seen in the following and final discussion of the shape of the Psalter.

Further insight into the final shape of the Psalter has been gained by examining the psalms that occur at the seams of the Five Books (McCann 1993a; Wilson 1985). A story line emerges. Book 1 begins and ends on the same note, "Oh, the joys of those . . ." (1:1 and 41:1). The joyful person in both cases is David (note the title to Ps 41, "A psalm of David"). According to Psalm 2, David had enemies who wanted him to die (41:5 [6]), as if he were among the wicked of 1:6 and 2:12. Though David had sinned (41:4 [5]), he was not a "sinner" in terms of Psalm 1 but was innocent of that charge (41:12 [13]). In other words, he knew that he had taken "pleasure" (*khepets* [TH2656, ZH2914]) in God's instruction as 1:2 would have had him to do, so he knew that God was pleased (*khapets* [TH2654, ZH2911]) with him (41:11a), would give him victory over his enemies (41:11b), as promised in Psalm 2, and would bless him (*'ashre* [TH835A, ZH897]; 41:2), according to the *'ashre* formula of 1:1. Book 1 thus opens with the inauguration of the royal covenant made with David, including the promise that David would inherit the nations (Ps 2), and Book 1 ends with the initial confirmation of this covenant in Psalm 41—David experiencing the pleasure of God and gaining victory over his enemies. All is proceeding according to plan.

The covenant with David included provisions for dynastic succession, but could the covenant be effectively transferred to a son of David? Book 2 says yes. Psalm 72 closes out Book 2, and though Book 2 as a whole can be called, "the prayers of David son of Jesse" (72:20), this final psalm is "of Solomon." Three features of Psalm 72 are pertinent here. (1) Verses 12-14 echo 41:1, but now Solomon, not David, is the king who cares for the weak. (2) Verses 8-11 echo Psalm 2, but now Solomon, not David, is the king who is ruling the nations with foreign kings in submission. (3) Verses 15-17 echo Psalm 1, but now Solomon, not David, is the joyful man whose reign is described in terms of agricultural bounty. By the end of Book 2, the covenant has been successfully transferred to David's son. All is going according to plan.

Will this idyllic situation last forever? Book 3 raises doubts. Psalm 89 ends Book 3 with a recitation of the covenant made with David. This recitation ends with a most emphatic articulation of the unconditional nature of the promise made to David (89:35-37):

I have sworn an oath to David,
  and in my holiness I cannot lie:
His dynasty will go on forever;
  his kingdom will endure as the sun.
It will be as eternal as the moon,
  my faithful witness in the sky!

In stark contrast to this stands the rest of the psalm (89:38-51 [39-52]) with its litany of defeats suffered by the "anointed king." These verses accuse God of disdaining the covenant made with David and raise the agonizing question:

Lord, where is your unfailing love?
  You promised it to David with a faithful pledge. (89:49)

As postexilic readers of the book of Psalms came to the end of Book 3, one burning theological question came to expression: Has the covenant with David been aborted? There was no son of David ruling over Judah, let alone ruling over the nations. How should the postexilic community respond to the apparent failure of the Davidic covenant? How should they live in the absence of the messianic king?

Books 4–5 answer such questions. Book 4 opens with Psalm 90, "A prayer of Moses, the man of God." Psalm 90 is the only psalm "of Moses." "Moses" occurs only eight times in the Psalter, and seven of the eight occurrences are in Book 4. This piling up of references to Moses in Book 4, together with the framing effect of one occurrence of "Moses" in the title of the opening psalm and three occurrences in the closing Psalm 106 (Wilson 1993:76), demonstrates a Mosaic orientation in Book 4. What is the point of this preoccupation with Moses at this juncture in the Psalter? The point seems to be that the Lord had been Israel's dwelling place long before there was a covenant with David. Though in the postexilic era there was no messianic king in whom to take *refuge* (*khasah* [TH2620, ZH2879]; see 2:12), the Lord was still Israel's dwelling place (90:1; 91:1) and would continue to be the *refuge* (*makhseh* [TH4268, ZH4726]) in whom Israel could trust (91:2). But there is more.

It is surely not coincidental that six of the seven enthronement psalms (Pss 93, 95–99) are found in Book 4. Immediately after the agonizing question has been raised of the failure of the covenant made with the messianic king, Book 4 reverberates with the refrain, "The LORD is king!" The Psalter was shaped to teach the postexilic community how to live in the absence of the messianic king: They were to trust (91:2) that the Lord who had always been their royal refuge continued to reign, in spite of geopolitical evidence to the contrary. The Lord who sat on his throne at the time of the inauguration of the David covenant (2:4) still reigns in the postexilic era, though no messianic king is on the scene.

Whereas Book 4 has a clear Mosaic orientation, Book 5 (Pss 107–150) is oriented once again toward David. Fifteen of the 44 psalms in Book 5 are "of David" (compared to only two in Book 4), and David is mentioned six times in the body of the psalms in Book 5 (compared to none in Book 4). Though there is no son of David ruling over the postexilic community, David's presence can still be felt in three themes in Book 5.

First, David is the joyful person who follows the law of the Lord. Book 5 is composed of three sections (Pss 107–117, 118–135, 136–145), each of which begins with the exhortation "give thanks" (*hodu* [TH3034, ZH3344]). Psalm 119 stands at the center (Wilson 1993:79). It begins with a double echo of Psalm 1: "Joyful are people of integrity, who follow the instructions of the LORD" (119:1). "Joyful" (*'ashre* [TH835A, ZH897]) echoes 1:1, "Oh, the joys of" (*'ashre*), and "the instructions of the LORD" (*torath yhwh* [TH8451/3068, ZH9368/3378]) echoes 1:2, "the law of the LORD" (*torath yhwh*). As David is the "joyful" person of Psalm 1, David is the "joyful" person of Psalm 119, the centerpiece of Davidically oriented Book 5. Though neither David nor his heir was reigning, the postexilic community had David's example, an example of one who followed God's *torah*/instruction and experienced God's "joyfulness." If the postexilic community would but follow David's example, they too would experience the "joyfulness" held out in Psalm 1.

Second, David lived to worship the Lord. That Book 5 focuses on worship is clear from the "Give thanks" and "Praise the LORD" frames that surround the three segments of the book. In addition, "Praise the LORD" resounds throughout Book 5 (111:1; 112:1; 113:1, 9; 115:18; 116:19; 117:2), and Psalms 146–150, which form a grand doxology to Book 5 and to the book of Psalms as a whole, all begin and end with "Praise the LORD." This means that the "final psalm" of Book 5 is Psalm 145, which is "A psalm of praise of David." This psalm gives us a glimpse into the heart of David, for example, in 145:1-2, 21:

I will exalt you, my God and King,
  and praise your name forever and ever.
I will praise you every day;
  yes, I will praise you forever.

I will praise the LORD,
  and may everyone on earth bless his holy name
  forever and ever.

David knew that the Lord God was the true King and that David's own reason for being was to worship his "God and King." Thus, the postexilic community should also follow David's example of living for the praise of God in order to experience the happiness of Psalm 1.

Is this, however, the complete response to the haunting question of 89:49?

Lord, where is your unfailing love?
  You promised it to David with a faithful pledge.

Is it only that the postexilic community should know that the Lord reigns and that they can trust him to be their refuge, a trust that manifests itself in following his instructions in general and living for his praise in particular? The question remains: Has the covenant with David been aborted?[13]

The third theme that demonstrates David's presence in Book 5 is that David's son will come to reign. Not only is David present in Book 5 in general terms, as noted above, but the question of the Davidic covenant is raised explicitly in Psalm 132. Psalm 132 is about a place, Zion (132:13), and a person, David the anointed/messianic king (132:10). Through his self-denial (132:3-4), David secured God's dwelling among his people (132:5-8, 13-14). Psalm 132 contains a prayer and a promise: a prayer that God would remember David's suffering and not reject his descendants (132:1-10) and a promise that this prayer would be answered (132:11-18). In unequivocal terms the pilgrims who used this psalm affirmed that God would keep his promise to David (132:11-12) and place a powerful and glorious anointed/messianic heir of David on the throne (132:17-18). "The place and person presented in Psalm 2 as the institution of heaven's reign in the world are here the subjects of hope" (Mays 1994:106). This hope was realized in Jesus Christ (see Luke 1:69, which alludes to 132:17), who through self-denial secured the dwelling of God among his people.

From the beginning, the royal psalms, like Psalm 132, portrayed the Davidic king in idealized terms (Day 1995:97). The reality was never fully realized in the monarchy. After the Exile, these psalms were read prophetically, predictively, eschatologically, and messianically (Rendtorff 1986:249 and Waltke 1981:15). The New Testament is the end point of this process, wherein psalms like Psalm 2 were applied to Christ (Acts 4:25-27; 13:32-33).

The final shape of the Psalter raises the question: How should we live in the absence of the messianic king? A central aspect of the answer is: In anticipation, for the Messiah will come. Not just this or that psalm, but the book of Psalms as a whole creates hope that the place, God's dwelling among his people, will be secured by the person, God's anointed king. Jesus Christ is the place (John 1:14) and that person (Matt 1:1).

THEOLOGICAL CONCERNS

The heart of the theology of the book of Psalms has already been touched on in the previous discussion of the shape of the book as a whole. Here the basics of this theology will be amplified in a more systematic form. (For a broader discussion of the theology of the Psalms, see Kraus 1979.) The following topics will be addressed: Yahweh; "Yahweh is King" (*yhwh malak* [TH3068/4427, ZH3378/4887]); "Yahweh is King" and History; "Yahweh is King" and Liturgy; "Yahweh is King" and Eschatology; and "Yahweh is King" and Refuge.

Yahweh. The book of Psalms begins by telling us that ultimately it is the care of Yahweh (*yhwh* [TH3068, ZH3378], "the LORD") that underlies the joyous and prosperous life of the righteous (Ps 1) and that his care is reliable, because he rules over the tumultuous world in which we live (Ps 2). The book of Psalms ends with a crescendo of praise to Yahweh in the repeated *halelu-yah* [TH1984A/3050, ZH2146/3363] of Pss 146–150. The book of Psalms is thus a book about Yahweh from beginning to end. But it is not a book about Yahweh in the abstract. Rather, the book of Psalms is about Yahweh in relation to his people. In the Psalms we meet Yahweh watching over his people (Ps 1), reigning for the sake of his people (Ps 2), and receiving the praise of his people (Pss 146–150). In other words, the book of Psalms is covenantal.

While in a narrow sense only 11 psalms refer explicitly to the covenant between God and his people,[14] and only two of these have covenant as a dominant motif,[15] it is nonetheless true that in a broad sense all of the psalms are covenantal, since the "core of the covenant idea is relationship" (Longman 1988:56) and the Psalms are about Yahweh's relationship with his people.

> *The theological richness of the psalms emerges out of a profound knowledge of God rooted in relationship; at bottom, the framework for all dimensions of that relationship is provided by the covenant. Thus the psalmists are covenant writers, whether their perspective is individual, national, or that of Israel's cult. And their knowledge of God is rooted in the covenant; they respond to God in prayer, in praise, or in particular life situations because of an already existing covenant relationship which makes such a response possible. In this broad sense, all the psalms may be related to this central concept of the covenant. (Craigie 1983:40)*

> *[The psalmists] are people who speak to God and about God on the basis of being in a covenant relationship with him. Thus, covenant is a concept which ties together many strands of the theology of the Psalms. (Longman 1988:57)*

The Psalms enable God's people to maintain their relationship with him in all the variegated circumstances of life (Kline 1972:63). When all is going well, we bring to Yahweh hymns of praise as part of our obligatory tribute to the great king. When life is full of trouble and sorrow, we bring to him our laments and plead with him to provide us with the protection that is his obligation as the great king. When he delivers, we bring our songs of thanksgiving as grateful gifts to the great king. Since all the psalms are instructional, they teach us how to live in relation to our covenant king.

"Yahweh Is King" (*yhwh malak*). "The LORD is king!" summarizes the message of the book of Psalms (Mays 1994:232-233; McCann 1993b:41-43). "The psalms are the poetry of the reign of the Lord" (Mays 1989:30). Both Psalm 2 and the flow of the Five Books of the Psalms warrant this conclusion. Though Psalm 2 is a royal coronation psalm (Craigie 1983:64-65), the Davidic king is not the primary focus of the text—the Lord is. The ultimate king is the Lord, who reigns in heaven, terrifies enemies with his fierce fury, installs the Davidic king on Mount Zion, grants the nations as an inheritance, and is served with fear. The Davidic king who is rebelled against, who is crowned, who receives the promise of possessing the nations, and to whom all must submit is the agent through whom the Lord's reign is established on earth. Psalm 2 thus teaches that the Lord reigns through his anointed/messianic king.

The covenant relationship that underlies the book of Psalms is thus not any relationship in general, but the relationship between the great king and his servant people (Longman 1988:57). So the book of Psalms is not just about Yahweh in general; the book is about Yahweh as king in particular. As we have seen, the Psalms begin with the proclamation of Yahweh's kingship (Ps 2). The Psalms also end with the celebration of Yahweh's kingship:

> I will exalt you, my God and King,
> and praise your name forever and ever. (145:1)
>
> The LORD will reign forever.
> He will be your God, O Jerusalem, throughout the generations. (146:10)
> Praise the LORD!
>
> Sing to the LORD a new song.
> Sing his praises in the assembly of the faithful.
>
> O Israel, rejoice in your Maker.
> O people of Jerusalem, exult in your King. (149:1-2)

This last text reminds us that the center of the book of Psalms (Book 4) calls us to sing a new song to Yahweh (96:1; 98:1) and draws our attention to the kingship of Yahweh (93:1; 95:3; 96:10; 97:1; 98:6; 99:1). From the beginning, through the middle, and to the end, the book of Psalms focuses on Yahweh as king in a way that no other book in the Old Testament does (Whitelam 1992:4.43).

It is not an overstatement to say that the message of the book of Psalms is encapsulated in the repeated sentence *yhwh malak* [TH3068/4427, ZH3378/4887] ("the LORD reigns"; 93:1; 96:10; 97:1; 99:1) and the related *malak 'elohim* [TH4427/430, ZH4887/466] ("God reigns"; 47:8 [9]). There have been a variety of proposals as to the best way to translate *yhwh malak* (see Eaton 1995:117 for suggestions made in the commentaries). All major English translations use a present tense—"the LORD reigns" ("reigneth," KJV; cf. NKJV, RSV, NASB, and NIV) or "the LORD is king" (NRSV and NLT). This is somewhat odd, because this verb form is usually translated with a past tense (e.g., "was king" or "has become king"). First Kings 1:13 and 14:21 are typical: "Why then has Adonijah become king [*malak*]?" "Meanwhile, Rehoboam son of Solomon was king [*malak*] in Judah. He was forty-one years old when he became king, and he reigned [*malak*] seventeen years in Jerusalem." Moreover, the Septuagint, an ancient Greek translation of the Hebrew Bible, consistently translates *yhwh malak* with a past tense (*ho kurios ebasileusen* [TG2962/936, ZG3261/996]).

Before the work of Sigmund Mowinckel, there was a virtual consensus among the commentators that *yhwh malak* has "an inchoative sense, even if a continuing state were denoted: Yahweh *has become king* and now reigns" (Eaton 1995:117; emphasis added). The present reticence among scholars to acknowledge the inchoative, or incipient, sense seems to stem primarily from a negative reaction to Mowinckel's methodology[16] and the nagging question as to how Yahweh, who has always been king, could become king (Whitelam 1992:4.43). Perhaps the latter was operative in the minds of those involved in the major translations. Whether or not we translate the sentence with "is king" or "has become king," it is clear that *yhwh malak* has an event in view, not just a state of sovereignty in general.[17] So, for example, when the NLT translates *malak yehu'* with "Jehu is king" (2 Kgs 9:13), it is nonetheless clear that the crowd is proclaiming that Jehu *has now become king* (see Goldingay 2007:80).

That an event is in view is clear from the repeated sentence "Sing a new song to the LORD" (96:1; 98:1). The new song presumes that something new has taken place, which worshipers are to sing about (Day 1995:79). But what has taken place? An event in history? A ritual in liturgy? Or is *yhwh malak* a proleptic proclamation about the eschatological future? The details will be presented throughout the commentary to show that *yhwh malak* is historical, liturgical, and eschatological in reference; a summary is provided here.

"Yahweh Is King" (*yhwh malak*) and History. The proclamation *yhwh malak* has historical events in view, two in particular: the Creation and the Exodus.

The affirmation that Yahweh is king is made in the context of his victory at creation. In 93:1 and 96:10, there is reference to the world being firmly established and not able to be shaken, a clear reference to God's work at creation (see 104:5). In 93:3 we hear echoes of God's victory over the sea at the time of creation (see 74:12-17; 104:7). In 95:4-5 Yahweh's kingship is directly connected with his work of creation, and in 96:5, the proof of the supremacy of Yahweh's kingship is his work of creation. When God created the heavens and the earth, he became king of creation.

The affirmation that Yahweh is king is also made in the context of his victory in the Exodus/Red Sea/Wilderness event. Psalm 95 celebrates Yahweh's kingship in creation and re-creation. "The LORD our maker" (95:6) is a reference to the (re)creation of Israel as the people of God through the Exodus/Red Sea/Wilderness event, as is clear from 95:7-11. Psalm 99:6-8 also brings into view God's victory at the Exodus/Red Sea/Wilderness. And sandwiched in between Psalms 95 and 99, 98:1-3 begs to be read as a reference to the Exodus, especially since the victory in view was seen by the nations (98:2). When Yahweh created his people Israel by vanquishing enemy Egypt, he became king in a new sense.

"Yahweh Is King" (*yhwh malak*) and Liturgy. Major events in history made their way into the liturgy of the worshiping community (Westermann 1980:13-16). The *yhwh malak* psalms were no doubt used in the liturgy of the Temple (TDOT 8.371-372). Evidence for the liturgical use of these psalms is found in Psalm 47 in particular. This psalm looks back in celebration to Yahweh's victory over the nations/Canaanites and the distribution of the land in the days of Joshua (47:1-4 [2-5]). God is then pictured as ascending with a mighty shout and with trumpets blaring (47:5 [6]). A liturgical procession is in view, as in Pss 24, 68, and 132. The Ark being carried into the Temple would have been the symbol of God's entrance into his palace, as was the case when David brought the Ark to Jerusalem in a festal procession that included the singing of Psalm 96 (see 1 Chr 16:1-6, 23-33). God's kingship over all the earth is then announced (47:7 [8]), as God is enthroned to begin his rule over the nations (47:8 [9]).

The *yhwh malak* psalms may have been used in the liturgy of the Temple in a variety of situations. For example, they would have been appropriate as victory songs after any major battle (Longman 1988:34). But numerous pieces of evidence point to the Festival of Shelters as the primary occasion for their use (for the best concise and recent summary of the evidence, see Day 1995). The Festival of Shelters was celebrated in the fall at the end of one agricultural year (Exod 23:16; 34:22) and the beginning of another. This festival was celebrated at the end of the dry season when the final crops were harvested, but this was also the beginning of the rainy season when, as a result of the softening effects of the early rains (65:10 [11]), the ground was able once again to be plowed and planted for the new year. We will see in the course of the commentary that the meteorological context of the *yhwh malak* psalms, and other psalms that focus on Yahweh's kingship, is the end of one agricultural/meteorological year and the beginning of another, for it is as king that Yahweh created and sustains the agricultural/seasonal cycle in general (see Pss 65 and 104) and the fall rains in particular (see Ps 29).[18]

It is this meteorological situation, in autumn, that Zechariah has in view when he proclaims that the nations who fail to come to Jerusalem to worship Yahweh at the Festival of Shelters "will have no rain" (Zech 14:17). In the context, Yahweh, having just won the final eschatological battle (Zech 14:1-8), has finally become the sole king over all the earth (Zech 14:9). Accordingly, the survivors come to Jerusalem not to worship Yahweh in general, but to worship Yahweh as "the King" in particular (Zech 14:16-17). Zechariah 14 brings together meteorological imagery from the fall, the Festival of Shelters, and the kingship of Yahweh, because the Festival of Shelters, celebrated at the turn of the agricultural year, was the festival par excellence for the celebration of Yahweh's kingship. This was so because in ancient Israelite thought, the coming of the fall *rain* was proof of Yahweh's *reign*.

"Yahweh Is King" (*yhwh malak*) and Eschatology. The *yhwh malak* psalms served not only to enable worshipers to look back on Yahweh's victories in the past, they also served to enable the worshiping community to look expectantly into the future, when Yahweh would come to consummate his kingship.

Surely, God has been king from all eternity (93:2), and yet he became king in a new sense at the Creation and again at the Exodus (as well as at other major victories over his enemies). In keeping with this trajectory, Jesus began his ministry by proclaiming, "The time promised by God has come at last! . . . The Kingdom of God is near!" (Mark 1:15). But the Kingdom had been here in some sense at least since the establishment of the theocracy at Sinai. Jesus was announcing that the Kingdom was near *in a new sense,* because the king had come *in a new sense.* At a later point in his ministry, Jesus encountered the expectation "that the Kingdom of God would begin right away" (Luke 19:11). Jesus corrected this expectation not by teaching that the Kingdom had begun with Creation or the Exodus or the establishment of the monarchy, but by teaching that the Kingdom (which had been here all along in some sense) would begin *in a new sense* at some point in the future. This future point is envisioned by John when he hears the 24 elders singing,

> We give thanks to you, Lord God, the Almighty,
> the one who is and who always was,
> for now you have assumed your great power
> and have begun to reign. (Rev 11:17)

Psalms 96:11-12 and 98:7-8 in particular, but all the *yhwh malak* psalms in general, anticipate this eschatological day. The commentary will show that these texts look to the future when the king will come to begin his reign by judging the earth—that is, by coming to put all things in right order. When he does, the whole creation will rejoice. The creation will rejoice as at the fall rains, when the rains rejuvenate the land that has languished during months of drought. The creation will rejoice, since the God who will consummate his kingship by putting his whole creation back into right order is the God who inaugurated his kingship by creating the heavens and the earth in the beginning.

But the eschaton, the final day, is not yet here, so what would the book of Psalms have us do in light of the fact that Yahweh is king? More than anything, it would have us take refuge in him as the king.

"Yahweh Is King" (*yhwh malak*) and Refuge. We have already seen that "poetry is a language of images" (Ryken 1984:89). The most pervasive image of Yahweh in the Psalter is the metaphor of Yahweh as refuge.[19] The primary words for Yahweh as refuge is the noun *makhseh* [TH4268, ZH4726] (refuge) and its related verb *khasah* [TH2620, ZH2879] (seek refuge). But many other words belong to the same semantic domain as refuge: *sether* [TH5643, ZH6260] (refuge, hiding place), *tsel* [TH6738, ZH7498] (shade, protection), *magen* [TH4043, ZH4482] (shield), *ma'oz* [TH4581, ZH5057] (mountain stronghold, place of refuge), *ma'on* [TH4583A, ZH5061] (den, dwelling), *miplat* [TH4655, ZH5144] (place of refuge), *metsudah* [TH4686A, ZH5181] (mountain stronghold), *sagab* [TH7682, ZH8435] (be inaccessible), *misgab* [TH4869, ZH5369] (high spot, refuge), *'oz* [TH5797.1, ZH6437] (fortress), *sela'* [TH5553, ZH6152] (rock), *tsur* [TH6697, ZH7446] (large rock), *migdal* [TH4026, ZH4463] (tower), and *manos* [TH4498, ZH4960] (place of refuge). In addition there are other closely associated words: *batakh* [TH982, ZH1053] (trust), *qawah* [TH982, ZH7747] (wait for), *yakhal* [TH3176, ZH3498] (wait), and *khakah* [TH2442, ZH2675] (wait for). Jerome Creach (1996) has made a fairly convincing case that the refuge metaphor played a primary role in the final shaping of the Psalter as a whole; at a minimum he has shown that the refuge metaphor is highly significant for the message of the book of Psalms.

The NLT at times uses the language of "refuge" (e.g., 46:1), but at other times uses the language of "protection," for example: "He is a shield for all who look to him for protection" (*khasah* [TH2620, ZH2879], 18:30). Protection captures the sense of the metaphor very well. The metaphor stems from literal uses such as seeking protection from inclement weather (see Job 24:8 and Isa 4:6). The bridge between the literal and the metaphorical is found in texts like the following: "But you are a tower of refuge (*ma'oz* [TH4581, ZH5057]) to the poor, O LORD, a tower of refuge to the needy in distress. You are a refuge (*makhseh* [TH4268, ZH4726]) from the storm and a shelter (*tsel* [TH6738, ZH7498]) from the heat" (Isa 25:4). "[The king] will be like a shelter (*sather* [TH5643, ZH6260]) from the wind and a refuge from the storm, like streams of water in the desert and the shadow (*tsel* [TH6738, ZH7498]) of a great rock (*sela'* [TH5553, ZH6152]) in a parched land" (Isa 32:2).

This last text also connects the image of refuge with the king, for one function of the king was to provide protection for his subjects. This latter idea comes to expression in Jotham's fable, when the thornbush said, "If you truly want to make me your king, come and take shelter in my shade" (Judg 9:15). There is thus a logical connection between the motif of Yahweh as king and Yahweh as refuge, for it is as king that Yahweh is refuge.

Psalm 2 creates the expectation that the refuge metaphor will be programmatic for the book as a whole by ending on the note that since Yahweh is king, all who take refuge in him will experience total well-being. This introductory note is amplified in Book 1, which has a higher concentration of words in the semantic domain of refuge than any other book in the Psalter.

"Book one of the Psalter seems to be a collected portrait of the one who is godly. One of the primary ways of describing those devoted to the Deity is the expression, 'those who seek refuge in Yahweh'" (Creach 1996:92). Books 2 and 3 continue this theme of seeking refuge in Yahweh but add two other themes: misplaced trust and Yahweh's rejection of those who claim to have taken refuge in him. Book 2 opens with the first Korahite collection (Pss 42–49), which begins with the struggle over Yahweh's rejection of his people (43:2 and 44:10) and ends with concern over misplaced trust (49:6-7). These twin themes crop up repeatedly in the second Davidic collection (Pss 51–72). Consider, for example, 52:7:

> Look what happens to mighty warriors
>   who do not trust in God [lit., "make God their refuge"].
> They trust their wealth instead
>   and grow more and more bold in their wickedness.

Book 3 opens with the tension between taking refuge in Yahweh and experiencing his rejection:

> But as for me, how good it is to be near God!
>   I have made the Sovereign LORD my shelter. (73:28a)

> O God, why have you rejected us so long? (74:1a)

Then it becomes explicit in Psalm 78 that Yahweh's rejection of Israel is owing to Israel's misplaced trust and their failure to live out the reality of making him their refuge:

> Yes, his anger rose against Israel,
> for they did not believe God
> or trust him to care for them. (78:21b-22)
>
> Then they remembered that God was their rock,
> that God Most High was their redeemer.
> But all they gave him was lip service. (78:35-36a)
>
> When God heard them, he was very angry,
> and he completely rejected Israel. (78:59)
>
> But he rejected Joseph's descendants;
> he did not choose the tribe of Ephraim. (78:67)

Psalms 88 and 89 together with Psalms 42–43 and 44 form an *inclusio* around Book 3 by ending on the same note with which Book 3 begins:

> O LORD, why do you reject me? (88:14a [15a])
>
> But now you have rejected him. (89:38a [39a])

Books 2 and 3 thus mark a shift in the flow of the Psalms from a dominant focus on the faithful believer in Book 1 to a focus on the struggle over Yahweh's rejection of those who claim him as refuge (Creach 1996:92). Whereas the center of Book 4 (Pss 90–106) focuses on Yahweh as king (Pss 93, 95–99), Book 4 opens with psalms that focus our attention on Yahweh as refuge (Pss 90–92, 94):

> Lord, through all the generations
> you have been our home! (90:1)
>
> If you make the LORD your refuge,
> if you make the Most High your shelter,
> no evil will conquer you;
> no plague will come near your home. (91:9-10)
>
> But the LORD is my fortress;
> my God is the mighty rock where I hide [lit., rock of my refuge]. (94:22)

These refuge psalms (Pss 90–92, 94) have been tied to the kingship-of-Yahweh psalms (Pss 93, 95–99) by a variety of techniques (Howard 1997), two of which will be mentioned here: (1) The apparently reversed order of Psalms 93 and 94 serves as an "interlocking mechanism" (Wilson 1993:75) that ties the refuge psalms to the kingship psalms. (2) Psalm 94 is tied to Psalm 95 by the repetition of "rock" in 94:22 and 95:1. The heart of the Psalter articulates the same message as the introductory Psalm 2: Yahweh is king, so take refuge in him.

While words in the same semantic domain as "refuge" do not have as high a profile in Book 5 as they have in Books 1–4, the domain is well represented (Creach 1996:100). Here are a few examples from near the end of Book 5:

I look to you for help, O Sovereign LORD.
You are my refuge; don't let them kill me. (141:8)

Then I pray to you, O LORD.
I say, "You are my place of refuge." (142:5a [6a])

Praise the LORD, who is my rock.
He trains my hands for war
and gives my fingers skill for battle.
He is my loving ally and my fortress,
my tower of safety, my rescuer.
He is my shield, and I take refuge in him.
He makes the nations submit to me. (144:1-2)

Quite a dramatic accumulation of words for refuge! It is fair to say that the book of Psalms does not disappoint the reader. Having created the expectation that Yahweh as refuge would be a dominant motif (Ps 2), the book of Psalms plays on this motif from beginning to end. Psalms 93:1 and 2:12 adequately summarize the basic theology of the book of Psalms:

The LORD is king!
What joy for all who take refuge in him!

ENDNOTES

1. The English title "Book of Psalms" derives from the Latin title *Liber Psalmorum,* which derives from the Greek title *biblos psalmoi. Psalmos* is not the translation-equivalent to *tehillah* [TH8416, ZH9335] (praise), but to *mizmor* [TH4210, ZH4660] ("song" [accompanied by instruments]).
2. At times there is a difference between the verse numbers in the Hebrew Bible and the NLT because the Hebrew Bible includes the title in the versification but the NLT (along with all other English translations) does not. The NLT verse number will be given first, followed by the Hebrew in brackets.
3. For a brief survey of opinions and a defense of the meaning "inscriptional poem," see Craigie 1983:154.
4. Sawyer (1970:35-36) argues for "to be recited by the official in charge."
5. Originally, *lamenatseakh* + optional prepositional phrase (e.g., *bineginoth*) was probably a postscript to the preceding psalm, rather than being part of the superscript (Waltke 1991).
6. For a full discussion and bibliography see Kraus 1988:27-29.
7. In the Talmudic tradition, the book of Ruth heads the third division, but Ruth, with its David genealogy, probably served as an introduction to the Psalter (Beckwith 1985:112; Childs 1979:502).
8. As with the prose-poetry distinction, some would deny the presence of strophes and stanzas in Hebrew poetry (G. Anderson 1973). But given the qualification that strophes and stanzas may be variable rather than uniform (Abrams 1985:177) and the fact that readers segment poems into units as they read (Petersen and Richards 1992:60), we are justified in segmenting poems into strophes and stanzas and in using this nomenclature.
9. For another approach to this question, see Miller 1994b.
10. Note that one recent guide to genres in the Old Testament (Sandy and Giese 1995) contains a chapter on lament and praise but nothing on other psalm genres.
11. Psalms 44 and 88 are the true exceptions, as they end bleakly. Psalms 38 and 39 also end on fairly negative notes.

12. Consider the following quotations, cited in Zenger 1994:37-38: (1) The Psalter is "only a heap of individual elements formlessly juxtaposed" (Walter Zimmerli), and (2) "In my opinion it is the right and duty of the exegete of the psalms to counteract the lack of intrinsic structure of the total volume of material by providing a suitable ordering principle. . . . We have arranged the psalms according to *literary-historical* types" (Willy Staerk).
13. Wilson (1993:81) and McCann (1993b:43) say yes.
14. Psalms 25:10, 14; 44:17 [18]; 50:5, 16; 74:20; 78:10; 89:3 [4], 28 [29], 34 [35], 39 [40]; 103:18; 105:8, 10; 106:45; 111:5, 9; 132:12. Psalms 55:20 [21] and 83:5 [6] also use the word *berith* [TH1285, ZH1382].
15. Psalms 89 and 132. See Longman 1988:57.
16. Mowinckel is typically criticized for importing the Babylonian *akitu* festival into the OT. But a more accurate reading shows that Mowinckel used the Babylonian material as a supplemental confirmation of what he found in the OT and not as a methodological basis for his position (Day 1995:69).
17. The best concise and recent defense of the incipient sense, which indicates the initial stage of a situation, is found in Day 1995:75-82, which is summarized here. (1) On philological grounds "became king," "reigned," or "has become king" are possible and attested elsewhere, but "is king" in an ongoing sense has no certain attestation. The first two possibilities are obviously to be dismissed on contextual grounds. Moreover, contrary to the opinion of some, the word order is irrelevant, since both subject + verb (1 Kgs 1:18; 16:29; 2 Kgs 15:13) and verb + subject (1 Kgs 15:1, 9) are found with the incipient sense. (2) Psalm 47:3-4 [4-5] clearly has an event, a victory, in view, after which God ascends the throne to the sound of the horn (47:5-7 [6-8]). Psalm 47 finds nice conceptual parallels in 2 Sam 15:10 and 2 Kgs 9:13, where the enthronement of a new king is accompanied by the sounding of the horn. (3) The new song presumes that something new has taken place, which worshipers are to sing about. (4) Zechariah 14:9 has in view Yahweh becoming king over all the earth in a different sense than that in which he is currently king. (5) The New Testament shares this concept of God beginning to reign in a new sense at the consummation of history (Rev 11:17; 19:6). Two other considerations should be added: (1) The Greek of Rev 11:17, 19:6, and 20:4 is the same as the Greek translation of Pss 93:1, 96:10, 97:1, and 99:1—*ebasileusen*, an incipient aorist. (2) In the Psalms *yhwh malak* is a speech act: lit., "Say among the nations, the LORD has become king" (96:10). The closest parallels are texts like 2 Kgs 9:13, where there is the speech act "Jehu is king" in the context of the beginning of the king's reign.
18. Note that Ps 29, which celebrates the kingship of Yahweh in the context of a fall rainstorm (see Futato 1984), is associated with the Festival of Shelters in the Septuagint by means of the title.
19. The present discussion draws heavily on Creach 1996.

COMMENTARY ON

Psalms

◆ I. Book One: Psalms 1–41

A. Psalm 1

[1]Oh, the joys of those who do not
follow the advice of the wicked,
or stand around with sinners,
or join in with mockers.
[2]But they delight in the law of the
LORD,
meditating on it day and night.
[3]They are like trees planted along
the riverbank,
bearing fruit each season.
Their leaves never wither,
and they prosper in all they do.
[4]But not the wicked!
They are like worthless
chaff, scattered by the
wind.
[5]They will be condemned at the time
of judgment.
Sinners will have no place among
the godly.
[6]For the LORD watches over the path
of the godly,
but the path of the wicked leads
to destruction.

NOTES

1:1 ***Oh, the joys of those who.*** The first word of the psalm, *'ashre* [TH835A, ZH897] (traditionally translated "blessed"), is a key word that runs through the Psalter from beginning to end. No single English word captures the full sense of *'ashre.* Those who are *'ashre* are in a state of total well-being: They lack nothing (34:8-10 [9-11]), are delivered from trouble (41:1-2 [2-3]; 94:12-13), and are wealthy and have successful children (112:1-3; 128:1-4; 144:12-15). No wonder they are so happy! The Psalms are about how to experience this profound happiness (Mays 1989:40): Yahweh must be your God (33:12; 144:15; 146:5), and you must trust him (40:4 [5]; 84:12 [13]) and delight in obeying his teaching (94:12; 106:3; 112:1; 119:1). Jesus' teaching in the Beatitudes complements what the Psalms express with *'ashre.* This opening clause stands outside the poetic structure (Petersen and Richards 1992:92; see also Miller 1986:82).

not follow the advice of. The word translated "advice" (*'etsah* [TH6098, ZH6783]) can also mean "counsel," but the exact expression "walk in the *'etsah* of" occurs in 2 Chr 22:5, and the phrase *'atsath resha'im* [TH6098/7563A, ZH6783/8401] occurs in Job 10:3, 21:16, and 22:18, establishing the meaning "follow the advice of."

not follow . . . or stand . . . or join. Lit., "not walk . . . not stand . . . not sit." The *'ashre* formula is characteristically followed by a positive description; here the threefold negative perspective keeps the formula from being a cliche and creates dramatic tension by delaying the expected positive note until 1:2 (Gitay 1996:234). The negative description connotes moral decline that begins with taking the wrong advice ("walk"), proceeds to acting the wrong way ("stand"), and results in becoming the wrong kind of person ("sit"); for the reversal of this decline, see Rom 12:2.

1:2 *delight.* The Lord's instruction is not burdensome (see 119:1-2, 14, 16, 45, 47).

law. Heb. *torah* [TH8451, ZH9368], here translated "law," has the broad sense of teaching (see Introduction and McCann 1992:27). The teaching in view is in written form (see Josh 1:8 and Mays 1989:41), and can be found, for example, in the Five Books of Moses or, closer at hand, the Five Books of the Psalms (see "Major Themes" in the Introduction). The poet focuses our attention on the "teaching" of Yahweh by using the term twice in one line, the usual poetic convention being to use a term once, followed by a synonym (Gitay 1996:235). The expression *torath yhwh* [TH8451/3068, ZH9368/3378] occurs in the Psalms only here, in 19:7 [8], and in 119:1.

meditating. Heb. *hagah* [TH1897, ZH2047] and its cognates are used for a low sound like the cooing of a dove (Isa 38:14) or the growling of a lion (Isa 31:4), so meditating on the word of God may have involved an intoned reading of the text (TWOT 1.205 and Craigie 1983:58). The imperfect verb contrasts with the perfect verbs of 1:1, and stresses the enduring nature of the pious (Gitay 1996:235).

day and night. Not just once during the day and once during the night, but continually (see 32:4; 42:3 [4]; 55:10 [11]; Isa 60:11). The Lord's instruction must govern the whole of life (see Deut 6:4-9).

1:3 *They are like trees.* The poet introduces a metaphor at this point to give concrete form to the more abstract concept of being *'ashre.* Whereas a tree in the steppe or desert may live but not thrive, this tree intentionally planted by an irrigation canal will always be productive.

they prosper in all they do. This prosperity includes material prosperity, but success in the sense of attaining one's goals is the broader meaning (see 1 Kgs 22:12).

1:4 *not the wicked!* The terseness emphasizes the brevity of the wicked's life. This is also underscored by the relative brevity of the chaff metaphor (6 words in Hebrew) over against the tree metaphor (17 words).

chaff, scattered by the wind. This is a prevalent image of divine judgment (see Isa 17:13; 29:5; 40:23-24; Jer 13:24; Hos 13:3). Zephaniah 2:2 makes explicit what is implicit elsewhere: The image of chaff driven before the wind is an image associated with the day of the Lord.

1:6 *the LORD watches over.* This expresses the Lord's intimate knowledge of and care for his people and is the ultimate basis of the experience of being blessed.

path. The word "path" is a frequent metaphor in the Wisdom Literature for the life one lives. There are two such paths: that of the righteous/wise and that of the wicked/fool. Each leads to its own inevitable destiny (cf. Matt 7:13-14).

destruction. As the last word in the Hebrew text, *to'bed* [TH6, ZH6] serves as a fitting antonym of *'ashre* [TH835A, ZH897].

COMMENTARY

The main message of this wisdom psalm can be articulated in two ways: (1) the pious experience total well-being, but the wicked perish, or (2) the pious prosper, but the wicked do not. This message is communicated by the form of the poem, as well as by its content. First, note that the opening word, *ashre* [TH835A, ZH897] (joy), begins with the first letter of the Hebrew alphabet, while the closing word, *to'bed* [TH6, ZH6] (destruction), begins with the last letter of the alphabet (see Ps 112 for this same poetic device). The psalm is thus an "incipient acrostic" (Petersen and Richards

1992:94), articulating the diametric opposition between life and death: The two are as far apart as Aleph and Taw. Second, note the chiastic structure of the whole:

Summarizing Introduction (1:1)
A. Description of the Righteous; key terms: wicked, sinners, not stand, advice (1:1-2)
  B. Metaphor for the Righteous; key phrase: like trees (1:3a)
    C. Fruition of the Righteous; key term: prosper (1:3b)
    C'. Fruition of the Wicked; key term: not (1:4a)
  B'. Metaphor for the Wicked; key phrase: like chaff (1:4b)
A'. Description of the Wicked; key terms: wicked, sinners, not stand (NLT, "be condemned"), no place (1:4-5)
Summarizing Conclusion (1:6)

This structure focuses our attention on the central point (see Petersen and Richards 1992:95-96): "They prosper in all they do. But not the wicked!" (1:3b-4a).

How does one come to enjoy the prosperity of the righteous? Whereas the Psalms as a whole provide a full answer to this question (see the first note above for a summary), Psalm 1 focuses on a key aspect of the answer: Live in the light of the Lord's teaching.[1] This means not giving heed to teaching that is contrary to the Lord's, for that would lead to wrong actions and attitudes. Rather, you must delight in the Lord's teaching and study it thoroughly. And, in fact, the Psalms provide you with the Lord's teaching from A to Z (or perhaps we should say Aleph to Taw).

If taken out of the context of the book of Psalms as a whole, Psalm 1 could be misunderstood in two critical ways. First, it could be taken as an expression of self-righteousness: If *I* do not follow the wrong advice and if *I* delight in doing everything the Lord wants and if *I* think about his teaching all the time, then *I* will be joyfully prosperous. Such a self-righteous reading of the psalm, however, ignores parallel texts like 40:4 [5], "Oh, the joys of those who trust the LORD" and 84:12 [13], "O LORD of Heaven's Armies, what joy for those who trust in you" (see also Jer 17:7-8), and goes against the grain of the wholesale critique of misplaced trust developed in the book (see Introduction).

Second, Psalm 1 could be taken as articulating a simple recipe for ensuring an easy life: If I just do what is right, then I will be blessed—*automatically*. Such a "health-and-wealth" reading of the psalm ignores the tension that arises when 1:3b-4a, "They prosper in all they do. But not the wicked," is read in the context of texts like 37:7b, "Don't worry about *evil people who prosper*" and 73:3 "For I envied the proud when I saw them *prosper despite their wickedness*" (italics mine). "The poet, who sought to be a true believer, notices the 'real world' turns upside down his own religious view" (Gitay 1996:236). Reading in context precludes a simplistic understanding of the text and life itself.

The teaching of Psalm 1 is idealistic (VanGemeren 1991:52) but true nonetheless: The righteous will be joyfully prosperous, but the wicked will not. This is true in part in this life, but in fullness only in the life to come. So as David thought about the prosperity of the wicked, his mind turned to the way their *lives will end up* (37:9, 10, 12-13). So, too, Psalm 1 points us forward to the time of judgment beyond this life (see Day 1995:44). Psalm 1 thus gives the Psalter an eschatological orientation from the start.

We are responsible to delight in and think about the Lord's teaching and to put that teaching into practice. But we are not to trust in any of this activity for our happiness in this life or the life to come. Rather, we are to trust in the Lord who watches over all our steps (1:6), whether those steps are on the heights of prosperity (23:2) or in the valley of adversity (23:4), knowing that ultimately he will bless us (94:12-15).

ENDNOTES

1. For the centrality of the *torah* [TH8451, ZH9368] in this psalm, see Botha 1991.

◆ B. Psalm 2

1 Why are the nations so angry?
Why do they waste their time with futile plans?
2 The kings of the earth prepare for battle;
the rulers plot together
against the LORD
and against his anointed one.
3 "Let us break their chains," they cry,
"and free ourselves from slavery to God."

4 But the one who rules in heaven laughs.
The Lord scoffs at them.
5 Then in anger he rebukes them,
terrifying them with his fierce fury.
6 For the Lord declares, "I have placed my chosen king on the throne
in Jerusalem,* on my holy mountain."

7 The king proclaims the LORD's decree:
"The LORD said to me, 'You are my son.*
Today I have become your Father.*
8 Only ask, and I will give you the nations as your inheritance,
the whole earth as your possession.
9 You will break* them with an iron rod
and smash them like clay pots.'"

10 Now then, you kings, act wisely!
Be warned, you rulers of the earth!
11 Serve the LORD with reverent fear,
and rejoice with trembling.
12 Submit to God's royal son,* or he will become angry,
and you will be destroyed in the midst of all your activities—
for his anger flares up in an instant.
But what joy for all who take refuge in him!

2:6 Hebrew *on Zion.* **2:7a** Or *Son;* also in 2:12. **2:7b** Or *Today I reveal you as my son.* **2:9** Greek version reads *rule.* Compare Rev 2:27. **2:12** The meaning of the Hebrew is uncertain.

NOTES

2:1 *angry.* The verb *ragash* [TH7283, ZH8093] occurs only here; related nouns occur in 55:14 [15] (*regesh* [TH7285, ZH8094]; see NASB, "throng") and 64:2 [3] (*rigshah* [TH7285A, ZH8095]), with the sense "uproar" (Zorell 1963:757), which may be positive (55:14 [15]) or negative (64:2 [3]). The verb carries a negative connotation in 2:1.

they. "They" translates the Hebrew word *le'om* [TH3816, ZH4211], which means "people" (HALOT 2.513), contra Craigie (1983:63), who proposed that it means "warriors." Hebrew dictionaries do not recognize "warrior" as a gloss for *le'om,* which is elsewhere, as here, parallel with terms for "people" (see, e.g., 44:2 [3]; 105:44; Gen 25:23; Isa 34:1).

futile plans. The verb underlying this phrase is the same verb used in 1:2, where it has the sense "think/meditate." In 2:1 it has the sense "plan/plot/conspire," as in 38:12 [13] and Prov 24:2. A contrast is thus drawn between those who "think" about the Lord in order to submit to him and those who "plot" to rebel against him.

2:2 ***against the LORD and against his anointed one.*** The conspiracy is explicitly against both the Lord and his anointed king. For "anointed one" in reference to the human king, see 18:50 [51] and 20:6 [7] (see also 1 Sam 10:1 and 16:6).

2:3 ***break their chains . . . from slavery.*** The Hebrew text speaks of "chains" and "ropes." The picture is that of oxen whose yokes are tied together (see Jer 27:2). The NLT captures the import of this picture with the word "slavery," because the "chains" and "ropes" refer to the servitude imposed upon a vanquished foe (see Isa 52:2 and Jer 27:2-8; see Keel 1997:302-303 for graphic representations). "Breaking chains" can be a positive symbol of freedom from slavery (see Jer 2:20) or a negative symbol of rebellion against authority (Jer 5:5); in 2:3 it is negative. The pronoun "their" refers to the Lord and his anointed one and shows the close association of the two (VanGemeren 1991:67).

2:4 ***the one who rules.*** Lit., "the one who sits," but when it is a king who sits, the sense is "rules" (Zorell 1968:334; see 29:10). There are two kinds of sitting at the opening of the Psalms: the "sitting" of scoffers ("join in"; 1:1, NLT) and the "sitting" of the LORD (2:4). Those who sit to scoff do so at the sitting/ruling of the LORD.

laughs . . . scoffs. There is movement from the general "laughs" to the specific "scoffs." This movement continues in 2:5.

2:5 ***rebukes . . . terrifying.*** The scoffing becomes a rebuke. Terror follows the rebuke.

2:6 ***I have placed my chosen king on the throne.*** The Hebrew is *wa'ani nasakti malki* [TH5258A/4428, ZH5820/4889]. The precise sense of the verb *nasakti* is in doubt. There have been numerous suggestions: (1) from *nasak* [TH5258, ZH5818] (pour out), meaning "dedicate by means of a libation" (Kraus 1988:129) or "pour out," "pour wide and firm," "set firmly in place" (Delitzsch 1982:94); revocalized as a Niphal, meaning "be consecrated by a drink offering" (HALOT 2.703); (2) from *nasak* II [TH5259, ZH5820] (constitute)—so Zorell 1968:520; (3) revocalized as a Niphal from *suk* [TH5480, ZH6057], meaning "be anointed" (Dahood 1965:10). All suggestions orbit around the general idea of the installation of the king, which is undoubtedly what the context requires.

2:7 ***proclaims the LORD's decree.*** The use of the verb *sapar* [TH5608, ZH6218] with the preposition *'el* [TH413, ZH448] instead of the direct object marker is unusual, but it does occur in 69:26 [27] with a similar sense as here ("tell of the pain," NASB). The "LORD's decree" refers to the royal covenant made with David and his descendants, and the central content is provided by the rest of 2:7b-9: the sonship of the anointed king (2:7; see 89:26-27 [27-28] and 2 Sam 7:14) and the promise of universal dominion (2:8-9; see 89:25 [26]; see also 2 Sam 7:16 for the analogous promise of an enduring dynasty). There may be a reference here to a copy of the decree/covenant given to the king at his coronation (see 2 Kgs 11:12).

2:9 ***You will break them.*** The NLT accurately translates the Heb. *tero'em* [TH7489A, ZH8318]. Revelation 2:27, 12:5, and 19:15, however, use a word meaning "rule," in keeping with the LXX; these Greek translations point to a Heb. *tir'em* [TH7462, ZH8286] ("shepherd," "rule"; Zorell 1968:783). The two alternatives are not unrelated because "the promise that the Davidic king can break and smash the nations is conventional royal language for the power to rule" (Mays 1994:47). The same Hebrew verb for "shepherd" is used in Ezek 34:23 for the future Davidic king.

2:10 ***Now then.*** The Heb. *we'attah* [TH6258, ZH6964] introduces an exhortation to take a wise course of action (VanGemeren 1991:71; see Job 42:8; Prov 5:7; 7:24; 8:32).

2:11 ***rejoice with trembling.*** This expression creates tension in the mind of a modern reader, but "the tension between the rejoice at the Lord [*sic*] and the fear of him seems to be integrated in the OT experience of God" (Vang 1995:176); "rejoice" is used in the context of celebrating the Lord's kingship (see 97:1, 8-9; 149:2; 1 Chr 16:31), and this rejoicing is at times coupled with trembling (97:1, 4). "Rejoice with trembling" makes sense in the context of foreign kings being terrified, on the one hand (2:5), and being invited to join the joyous ranks of the righteous, on the other (2:12).

2:12 ***Submit to God's royal son.*** Lit., "kiss [the] son," which is problematic on two counts: (1) the Aramaic word *bar* [TA/ZA10120, S1247] is used for "son" instead of the Heb. *ben* [TH1121, ZH1201], as in 2:7, and (2) there are no precise parallels for kissing the king as an act of submission. (See, however, Keel 1997:268 for a picture of vanquished Elamite nobles about to kiss the feet of the Assyrian king.)

what joy. This provides an *inclusio* with 1:1 and thus brings the introduction to the Psalms to a close.

COMMENTARY

"Why are the nations so angry?" sounds rather dissonant against the harmonious, "They are like trees planted along the riverbank, bearing fruit each season" (1:3). In Psalm 2 the reality of hostility resounds in the believer's ears. The nations are raging against the Lord and his anointed king (2:2b). There is a conspiracy afoot (2:2a), and the goal of this conspiracy is autonomy: liberation from God's authority, and that means from the authority of his anointed king (2:3). The Davidic kings were certainly the objects of this raging from time to time and to varying degrees, but this raging reached its climax when "Herod Antipas, Pontius Pilate the governor, the Gentiles, and the people of Israel were all united against Jesus, [the Lord's] holy servant, whom [he had] anointed" (Acts 4:27). The raging of the nations against the Lord Jesus entailed the raging of the nations against his disciples in the apostolic church: "And now, O Lord, hear their threats" (Acts 4:29)—a prayer offered in the wake of Peter and John being arrested for preaching that "There is salvation in no one else! God has given no other name under heaven by which we must be saved" (Acts 4:12). This raging continues in our own day, whether in the form of physical or political or social attempts to silence those who would proclaim Jesus Christ as the exclusive way to God (John 14:6).

To God, however, such raging is ultimately a colossal waste of time (2:1). So certain is his sovereign rule over the nations that he can "sit" in heaven and laugh. But eventually his laughing changes to scoffing, and his scoffing gives way to angry rebuking, until finally he is found to be "terrifying them with his fierce fury" (2:5). Now, what could possibly strike terror in the hearts of the raging nations? The declaration that God's "chosen king [is] on the throne" (2:6)!

Yes, the Lord reigns, but he exercises his reign through his anointed king. The Davidic king at his coronation would have declared his exalted position as son of the Father, his destiny as ruler of the nations, and ruler of the ends of the earth. But the Davidic king was only a shadow of the true King Jesus, who became Son of the Father in a special sense when he was raised from the dead (Acts 13:32-33). After his resurrection, when he entered into his messianic sonship, he could say, "I have been given all authority in heaven and on earth" (Matt 28:18).

Though the day will come when Jesus will use his authority to "break them with an iron rod and smash them like clay pots" (2:9; see Rev 19:15), this is not that day. Presently, while warning them of the destruction that lies ahead, he invites them to take the wise course of action and submit to God's authority, which is not a path to slavery but to true freedom (see 119:45 and John 8:32). To his disciples today he still says, "I have been given all authority in heaven and on earth. Therefore, go and make disciples of all the nations" (Matt 28:18-19).

The concluding beatitude is addressed not only to believers who need protection from the raging of the nations but also to the people of the nations who need protection from the fierce fury of the king: "But what joy for all who take refuge in him!" (2:12).

◆ C. Psalm 3

A psalm of David, regarding the time David fled from his son Absalom.

1 O LORD, I have so many enemies;
so many are against me.
2 So many are saying,
"God will never rescue him!"
Interlude*

3 But you, O LORD, are a shield around me;
you are my glory, the one who holds my head high.
4 I cried out to the LORD,
and he answered me from his holy mountain. ***Interlude***

5 I lay down and slept,
yet I woke up in safety,
for the LORD was watching over me.
6 I am not afraid of ten thousand enemies
who surround me on every side.

7 Arise, O LORD!
Rescue me, my God!
Slap all my enemies in the face!
Shatter the teeth of the wicked!
8 Victory comes from you, O LORD.
May you bless your people.
Interlude

3:2 Hebrew *Selah*. The meaning of this word is uncertain, though it is probably a musical or literary term. It is rendered *Interlude* throughout the Psalms.

NOTES

3:TITLE *A psalm of David, regarding the time David fled from his son Absalom.* While David was the implicit joyous person of Ps 1 and king of Ps 2, he is now the explicit person praying in Ps 3. The apparently differing attitudes of David toward his enemies in Ps 3 and toward Absalom in 2 Sam 15–19 present us with a certain level of difficulty, but sufficient parallels exist between the psalm and the narrative to justify the title (Craigie 1983:73). The situation envisioned in Ps 3 is that of a besieged David asking the Divine Warrior for victory (Brettler 1993:14-42), but the language is general enough to have allowed other Davidic kings and even lay people to have used the psalm, as each faced a variety of "enemies" (Craigie 1983:72).

3:2 The NLT (following most commentators) separates 3:2 from 3:3, no doubt in part because of the *selah* [TH5542, ZH46138] (interlude), but *selah* does not always occur at the boundary between stanzas (see Craigie 1983:76).

3:3 ***you . . . are a shield.*** The *magen* [TH4043, ZH4482] was a small, round shield, as opposed to the *tsinnah* [TH6793A, ZH7558], which was a body-length shield (TDOT 8.74). In contrast to the small shield, which protects from only one side, the Lord "protects from every side" (Keel 1997:222-223). The image of God as *magen* (used 13 times in the Psalter: 3:3 [4]; 7:10 [11]; 18:2 [3], 30 [31]; 28:7; 33:20; 59:11 [12]; 84:11 [12]; 115:9, 10, 11; 119:114; 144:2) communicates the idea of protection, since the shield was a defensive part of the warrior's panoply and evokes the related image of God as warrior. As part of the "refuge" semantic domain (see Introduction), *magen* connects Ps 3 with 2:12.

you are my glory. Some have taken *kabod* [TH3519, ZH3883] as a divine title, "My Glorious One" (Dahood 1965:1.17; VanGemeren 1991:75; NIV). While this reading is not impossible, "glory" is better taken in reference to the psalmist with God being the source. "Glory" is something God gives someone in connection with being that person's shield (84:11 [12]) and is that which makes a person respectable (Kraus 1988:140). In the very next psalm (4:2 [3]) and in 7:5 [6] the same word is used in the sense of the psalmist's reputation/honor, and in 62:7 [8] God as the psalmist's glory (or honor) is used in conjunction with God being a rock, fortress, and refuge, as he is the psalmist's shield in 3:3 [4]. The sense of 3:3 is that the Lord will protect David on the one hand ("shield") and give him victory over his enemies on the other ("my glory" and "holds my head high").

3:4 ***cried out.*** The verb is an imperfect for repeated action in the past (Joüon and Muraoka 1991:§113e).

holy mountain. As the Lord had anointed David on his "holy mountain" (2:6), he answered his prayer from this same "holy mountain."

3:5 ***was watching.*** The verb is an imperfect for durative action in the past (Joüon and Muraoka 1991:§113f).

3:6 ***ten thousand enemies.*** These ten thousand people or enemies (*ribeboth* [TH7233, ZH8047]) are a particular instance of the "nations" and "people" of 2:1 who oppose the anointed king.

3:7 ***Arise, O Lord!*** This petition evokes Num 10:35, where Yahweh as Divine Warrior was summoned to arise and scatter his enemies. There is irony in Ps 3, however, since *ribeboth* [TH7233, ZH8047] refers to foes, whereas in Num 10:36 it refers to friends. Yahweh arising to rescue David provides a contrast with the many who were rising against him in 3:1 (VanGemeren 1991:77).

Slap. . . . Shatter the teeth. Wedged between the imperatives of 3:7a and the wish formula of 3:8, the perfects in 3:7b are precative, i.e., they express a prayer, often, as here, in the form of an imprecation or a curse (Waltke and O'Connor 1990:§30.5.4c-d). The idea of "shattering the teeth" is used with different vocabulary in 58:6 [7] and Job 4:10, 29:17. The exact cognate expression occurs in a thirteenth-century Akkadian legal document from Emar: "If they contest, this tablet will break their teeth" (Hackett and Huehnergard 1984:262). The expression originated in the ancient Near Eastern legal context of punishment for breach of contract and describes a talion-type punishment for verbal offense (Hackett and Huehnergard 1984:262-263, 273).

the wicked! Those who oppose the king are among the wicked of 1:1, 5.

COMMENTARY

How ironic that the David who is promised the nations in Psalm 2 is fleeing his son in Psalm 3! Delighting in the instruction (Ps 1) of the king who reigns in heaven

(Ps 2) is obviously no guarantee of a trouble-free life. So in Psalm 3 the psalmist puts the message of Psalm 2 into practice by praying to the Divine Warrior for protection from hostile forces. This prayer has a threefold focus.

Psalm 3:1-3 (second-person address) focuses on the psalmist's enemies: "so many . . . so many . . . so many." The vocative "O LORD" forms an *inclusio* around the whole. As the kings and rulers were "against the LORD and against his anointed one" in 2:2, "many are against" the king here. The hostile forces speak, as in 2:3, and this taunt against the king ("God will never rescue him!") is also an attack on God, since it presumes to limit what God can and cannot do (Mays 1994:52). Is the taunt true? The king does not believe so, as is clear from the contrastive, "But you, O LORD, are a shield around me." In 3:3 the psalmist confesses that "the one who rules in heaven" (2:4) is the Divine Warrior (Brettler 1993:140-142), who is always ready to protect and to grant victory over opposing forces.

Psalm 3:4-6 (third-person address) focuses on the psalmist himself: "I cried out. . . . I lay down and slept . . . I woke. . . . I am not afraid." In the evening the psalmist had repeatedly cried out to the Lord, until the Lord finally answered, perhaps through a priestly oracle. So the king was able to lie down and sleep through the night and then wake in safety the next morning, since his prayer had secured the watchful care of God through the night as a foreshadowing of his care for the day that lay ahead. Thus protected by God, the king could face the new day without fear, in spite of being surrounded by a myriad of enemies.

Psalm 3:7-8 (second-person address) focuses on the psalmist's God: "Arise. . . . Rescue. . . . Slap. . . . Shatter. . . . Victory comes from you . . . you bless." As in 3:1-3, the vocative "O LORD" forms an *inclusio* around the whole of 3:7-8. The request grows more intense as two terse petitions are followed by two longer petitions in 3:7. Not self-reliance, but prayer, is the path to finding protection (2:12) from otherwise insurmountable foes. Such prayer leads to the assurance that the Lord will grant "victory." This repetition "traces the psalmist's growing faith in Yahweh the warrior's ability to deliver him" (Brettler 1993:142), since "no trouble is beyond help and no human hostility can limit God's help" (Mays 1994:53).

While Psalm 1 promises joyous prosperity and Psalm 2 affirms the sovereign rule of God to guarantee such prosperity, Psalm 3 confronts us with the sobering truth that along "the path of the godly" (1:6) there will at times be seemingly overwhelming trouble. Thus "the path of the godly" must be the path of prayer. We should not be surprised at this, for this was the path that Jesus walked before us and for us:

> *While Jesus was here on earth, he offered prayers and pleadings, with a loud cry and tears, to the one who could rescue him from death. And God heard his prayers because of his deep reverence for God. . . . In this way, God qualified him as a perfect High Priest, and he became the source of eternal salvation for all those who obey him. (Heb 5:7, 9)*

Because Jesus prayed and God answered, we can pray knowing that God will answer by providing protection no matter what the problem.

◆ D. Psalm 4

For the choir director: A psalm of David, to be accompanied by stringed instruments.

1 Answer me when I call to you,
O God who declares me innocent.
Free me from my troubles.
Have mercy on me and hear
my prayer.

2 How long will you people ruin my
reputation?
How long will you make groundless
accusations?
How long will you continue your
lies? *Interlude*
3 You can be sure of this:
The LORD set apart the godly for
himself.
The LORD will answer when I call
to him.
4 Don't sin by letting anger control
you.
Think about it overnight and remain
silent. *Interlude*
5 Offer sacrifices in the right spirit,
and trust the LORD.

6 Many people say, "Who will show us
better times?"
Let your face smile on us, LORD.
7 You have given me greater joy
than those who have abundant
harvests of grain and new
wine.
8 In peace I will lie down and sleep,
for you alone, O LORD, will keep
me safe.

NOTES

4:1 ***O God who declares me innocent.*** Lit., "O God of my righteousness." In the context of groundless accusations and lies (4:2), the sense is "O God who vindicates me" (cf. Mal 2:17).

Free me from my troubles. The perfect-tense verb *hirkhabta* [TH7337, ZH8143] is taken as a precative, which expresses a prayer, in the context of the surrounding imperatives. The word for "troubles" (*tsar* [TH6862C, ZH7639]) is the adjective related to the noun (*tsar* [TH6862A, ZH7640]), which is translated "enemies" in 3:1 and serves to connect the two psalms.

4:2 ***you people.*** The repeated suggestion (Craigie 1983:80; Kraus 1988:148; VanGemeren 1991:82) that *bene 'ish* [TH1121/376, ZH1201/408] (lit., "sons of man") refers to influential people is attractive in light of 49:2 [3] and 62:9 [10], but Lam 3:33 casts a shadow of doubt.

my reputation. The Heb. *kebodi* [TH3519, ZH3883] (my glory), as in 3:3, refers to "the dignity and respect that belong to a person's position in relation to family, friends, and the community" (Mays 1994:55).

4:4 ***Think about it overnight and remain silent.*** To "think" is the established sense of the expression *amar bilebab* [TH559/3824, ZH606/4222] (lit., "say in heart"; DCH 324), but since this expression always introduces direct discourse, the text is suspect here where the expression does not introduce direct discourse (Barré 1995:59). Kselman (1987:104-105) proposed a dittography of Aleph and the emendation of *'amar* [TH559, ZH606] to *mar* [TH4751, ZH5253] (bitter) in light of the root's usage in mourning contexts (Isa 33:7; Ezek 27:30-31). (For the connection between "bitter" and weeping see Collins 1971.) But Kselman cannot account for the final vowel on *'imru,* and for additional reasons a better solution (Barré 1995:59) is to emend to the Hiphil of *marar* [TH4843, ZH5352] with the sense "grieve bitterly," as in Zech 12:10, where the verb is parallel with *sapad* [TH5594, ZH6199] (mourn). "Grieve bitterly" then finds a nice parallel in *dommu* [TH1826/1826A, ZH1957/1958] (NLT, "remain silent"), not in the sense "be silent" but in the sense "wail/moan" (DCH 2.51). The imperatives are calling for heartfelt repentance (Barré 1995:60; see 2:10-12): "Grieve bitterly in your hearts; really wail on your beds."

4:5 *Offer sacrifices in the right spirit.* Lit., "sacrifices of righteousness," which recalls "God of my righteousness" (see note on 4:1). By offering such sacrifices, David's opponents would be acknowledging God's righteous vindication of him (Kraus 1988:148).

4:6 *Many people say.* The Heb. *rabbim 'omrim* [TH7227/559, ZH8041/606] is the same phrase as in 3:2 [3], and serves to connect the two psalms. The Heb. *rabbim* is used 12 times in the Psalter in reference to humans; 10 of these refer to enemies of the psalmist (3:1, 2 [2, 3]; 4:6 [7]; 37:16; 55:18 [19]; 56:2 [3]; 71:7; 89:50 [51]; 119:157; 135:10. The word refers to the faithful in 40:3 [4]; 109:30), so the "many" here are not a third category, as Craigie (1983:81) implies.

Let your face smile on us. The Hebrew text form *nesah* is apparently a by-form of *nasa'* [TH5375, ZH5951] (BDB 650; HALOT 2.702). The prayer recalls the Aaronic benediction (Num 6:24-26).

4:7 *You have given me greater joy.* The Hebrew is better taken as a precative in the context of the previous imperative: "Give me greater joy" (Craigie 1983:79; VanGemeren 1991:85).

4:8 *I will lie down and sleep.* This recalls 3:5 and serves to connect the two psalms.

will keep me safe. This recalls the psalmist's exhortation to "trust" in the Lord (4:5).

COMMENTARY

There are three movements in this psalm: prayer (4:1), exhortation (4:2-5), and prayer (4:6-8). Surrounded once again by "many," David surrounds the "many" with prayer. In his prayer, David looks to a merciful God to deliver him from distress by vindicating him. He needs vindication from the groundless accusations and slanderous lies that are ruining his reputation, so he not only addresses God in prayer, but he also addresses his accusers with a fivefold exhortation:

1. *Turn from falsehood.* David exhorts his accusers to know the truth: He has been set apart by God (see 2:6), so God will surely answer his prayer for vindication.
2. *Turn from sinful anger.* In context, the anger of the accusers was far from righteous, so they should turn from it.
3. *Grieve over sin.* In contrast to formal, public grief, David calls for sincere remorse (Barré 1995:60).
4. *Restore relationships.* Through the sacrificial system, the accusers could be restored to rightness with God and with the offended party; eating the sacrificial meal together in the presence of God would be the fruit of restored relationships.
5. *Trust in the Lord.* Though mentioned last, trust comes first: The accusers had to begin the process of reconciliation by trusting that God's vindication of David was right.

In a concluding prayer David quotes the unbelief of the "many": "Who will show us better times?" (4:6). With contrasting trust David paraphrases the ancient Aaronic benediction by which God's blessing would come upon his people. David prays not only for God's smile, but also for the joy that comes from experiencing the smile, and not only for joy, but for the superabundant joy that exceeds even the joy of an abundant harvest. The smile of God from above and joy within are the fruits of faith in the Lord, faith that enables the psalmist to go to sleep in peace.

Psalm 4 reminds us of how fundamental faith in the Lord is for our well-being—our joy and peace in particular. When we are falsely accused and tempted to trust our own attempt at self-vindication, we must take refuge in prayer that trusts the Lord for vindication. In so doing we are following in the footsteps of Christ, who at times did not even reply to his accusers (Matt 27:12) and yet was fully vindicated by his resurrection from the dead. Following this path we will know profound joy and peace, even as we at times must wait long for our vindication.

And should you be the false accuser on some occasion, turn to Psalm 4 and read its fivefold prescription for repentance, trusting that Christ, who in your stead never once made a false accusation, is the sacrifice that restores you to a right relationship with God and with those you have offended.

◆ E. Psalm 5

For the choir director: A psalm of David, to be accompanied by the flute.

1 O LORD, hear me as I pray;
pay attention to my groaning.
2 Listen to my cry for help, my King and my God,
for I pray to no one but you.
3 Listen to my voice in the morning, LORD.
Each morning I bring my requests to you and wait expectantly.

4 O God, you take no pleasure in wickedness;
you cannot tolerate the sins of the wicked.
5 Therefore, the proud may not stand in your presence,
for you hate all who do evil.
6 You will destroy those who tell lies.
The LORD detests murderers and deceivers.

7 Because of your unfailing love, I can enter your house;
I will worship at your Temple with deepest awe.
8 Lead me in the right path, O LORD,
or my enemies will conquer me.
Make your way plain for me to follow.

9 My enemies cannot speak a truthful word.
Their deepest desire is to destroy others.
Their talk is foul, like the stench from an open grave.
Their tongues are filled with flattery.*
10 O God, declare them guilty.
Let them be caught in their own traps.
Drive them away because of their many sins,
for they have rebelled against you.

11 But let all who take refuge in you rejoice;
let them sing joyful praises forever.
Spread your protection over them,
that all who love your name may be filled with joy.
12 For you bless the godly, O LORD;
you surround them with your shield of love.

5:9 Greek version reads *with lies.* Compare Rom 3:13.

NOTES

5:TITLE *flute.* The word *nekhiloth* [TH5155, ZH5704] occurs only here, and "flute(s)," while not certain, is likely the sense. (See Kraus 1988:27 for a more detailed discussion.)

5:1 ***groaning.*** The Hebrew term (*hagig* [TH1901, ZH2052]) is used elsewhere only in 39:3 [4], where it refers to inaudible "thought" (so NLT), but in this context the term probably refers to audible groans (so DCH 488).

5:2 ***my King and my God.*** The exact expression occurs elsewhere only in 84:3 [4], but "my king" is used with "God" also in 44:4 [5]; 68:24 [25]; and 74:12. In 3:3, God is a "shield," a royal image; in Pss 3 and 4 the psalmist is looking to the divine king for protection.

5:3 ***Listen.*** An imperfect from *shama'* [TH8085, ZH9048] used as an imperative (Joüon and Muraoka 1991:§113m), which echoes "hear" in 4:1 (Brennan 1980:27).

I bring my requests to you. Lit., "I arrange before you," with no expressed object for the verb. Possible objects include: sacrifice (Lev 1:8, 12; Weiser 1962:125), words (Job 32:14; Craigie 1983:86), and case/charges (Job 13:18; 23:4; Ps 50:21; Dahood 1965:30). Words/requests is supported by 4:1-2.

5:4 ***take no pleasure.*** As the righteous "delight" (*khepets* [TH2656, ZH2914]) in the Lord's instruction (1:2), so the Lord does not "take pleasure" (*khapets* [TH2655, ZH2913]) in the wicked.

5:5 ***may not stand in your presence.*** This verb in the Hithpael (*yatsab* [TH3320, ZH3656], "take one's stand") is used elsewhere for assembling in the presence of God (Josh 24:1; 1 Sam 10:19; see Kraus 1988:155); see also 1:5.

you hate all who do evil. This is contrary to the popular oversimplification that God hates the sin but loves the sinner (see also 11:5).

5:6 ***You will destroy.*** The verb is the Piel of *'abad* [TH6, ZH6], the root used in 1:6 ("destruction") and 2:12 ("destroyed").

those who tell lies. The word for "lies" (*kazab* [TH3577, ZH3942]) is also found in 4:2 [3], and serves to connect the two psalms.

5:7 ***unfailing love.*** The Heb. *khesed* [TH2617, ZH2876] is related to "the godly" (*khasid* [TH2623A, ZH2883]) in 4:3 [4]. The NLT leaves *rob* [TH7230, ZH8044] (abundance of) untranslated. The "abundance of" the Lord's unfailing love contrasts with the "abundance of" (*rob;* 5:10 [11]) the sins of the "many" (*rabbim* [TH7227, ZH8041]; 3:2 [3] and 4:6 [7]) who rebel against him.

your house . . . your Temple. Kraus (1988:154) argues that the use of *bayith* [TH1004, ZH1074] (house) proves that the title's attribution of the psalm to David is spurious. But in Josh 6:24 and 2 Sam 12:20 (where David is on the scene) the Tabernacle is called *beth-yhwh* [TH1004/3068, ZH1074/3378]. See also 1 Sam 1:9, 2:22, and 3:3, where God's dwelling at Shiloh is variously called *hekal* [TH1964, ZH2121] (temple) and *'ohel* [TH168, ZH185] (tent); see Delitzsch 1982:124.

worship at your Temple. Lit., "bow down toward your holy Temple." The "holy Temple" was located on the "holy mountain." For prostrating oneself in prayer in the direction of the Temple, see 138:2, 1 Kgs 8:35, 38, 42, and Dan 6:10.

5:8 ***the right path.*** This is the "path of the godly" (1:6) in contrast to the "path of the wicked" (1:6; 2:12).

my enemies. This expression is used 5 times in the Psalms: 5:8 [9], 27:11; 54:5 [7]; 56:2 [3]; 59:10 [11].

5:10 ***O God, declare them guilty.*** This request contrasts with "O God who declares me innocent" in 4:1.

5:11 ***all who take refuge in you.*** This echoes the final blessing of 2:12.

Spread your protection over them. This is Hiphil of *sakak* [TH5526, ZH6114] (cover) and evokes the refuge metaphor; see 31:20 [21] for *sukkah* [TH5521, ZH6109] as "refuge, shelter."

5:12 ***For you . . . O LORD.*** This is the characteristic formula of lament, as in 4:8 [9] (Brennan 1980:27).

shield. Heb. *tsinnah* [TH6793A, ZH7558], which is a large body shield, as opposed to the small shield of 3:3 [4] (see Keel 1997:222-224).

love. Heb. *ratson* [TH7522, ZH8356] is used in the Psalms in the sense of desire or what pleases someone (see 145:16, 19) or "the pleasure that God takes in someone and makes clear through blessing" (HALOT 3.1283; see 30:5 [6], 7 [8]). Here the latter sense is intended. The English word "favor" has the same two senses: "friendly regard" (as in "I am the object of his favor") and "act of kindness," (as in, "Would you do me a favor?").

COMMENTARY

At the end of Psalm 4, David lay down in peace to sleep, and Psalm 5 is a prayer offered in the morning that follows. Psalm 5 is a bifid, which is comprised of a twofold prayer (5:1-7 [2-8] and 5:8-12 [9-13]), the structure of the second half mirroring that of the first. Each prayer is comprised of a request to the Lord (5:1-2a and 5:8; note the "O LORD" in the first line of each stanza), followed by reasons for the request (5:2b-7 and 5:9-12). Each reason is bifurcated into a shorter reason (5:2b-3 and 5:12; both introduced with *ki* [TH3588, ZH3954]) and a longer reason (5:4-7 and 5:9-11; both introduced with *ki*), the longer reasons containing a contrast between the wicked (5:4-6 and 5:9-10) and the righteous (5:7 and 5:11). Thus the structure:

PRAYER (5:1-7)	PRAYER (5:8-12)
Request (5:1-2a)	Request (5:8)
Reasons (5:2b-7)	Reasons (5:9-12)
Shorter reason (5:2b-3)	Longer reason (5:9-11)
Longer reason (5:4-7)	Shorter reason (5:12)

The request is quite general in 5:1-2a: "hear," "pay attention," "listen." And it is offered to "my King and my God," the human king articulating his dependence on the divine king who rules in heaven (2:4). The request becomes more specific in 5:8—"lead me," "make your way plain." The psalmist is asking the Lord for instruction (see 1:2) in the face of continuing opposition from "enemies" (see 3:1; 4:2; 5:8).

The bulk of the psalm is taken up with reasons as to why the Lord should answer the prayer. The first reason is short and simple: "for I pray to no one but you" (5:2). Prayer to the Lord denotes dependence on the Lord's answers. While praying, the psalmist waits expectantly (5:3). For what? The fourth reason, also short and simple, provides some detail: The king is waiting for the Lord to "bless the godly . . . surround[ing] them with [his] shield of love" (5:12). The appeal is to the truth that the divine king characteristically grants protection to those under his sovereign rule (1:6; 2:12; 3:3; 4:8)—i.e., the human king and his followers.

The second reason is longer: God detests sin and sinners, so they have no access to his beneficent presence. By way of contrast, the godly have access to the presence of God through his "unfailing love" (5:7). The verbal sins of 5:6 are amplified in the third, also longer, reason (5:9-11): The "enemies cannot speak a truthful word," "their talk is foul," and "their tongues are filled with flattery," all with "deepest desire . . . to destroy others" (5:9). In 5:10 imperatives replace the indicatives of

5:4-6, as the rebellion is not simply against the king and his followers but against God himself. The rebellion is verbal in particular, as has been the case in the previous psalms (2:3; 3:2; 4:2). By way of contrast, those who take refuge in the divine king use their mouths to "sing joyful praises forever" (5:11).

The opposition experienced by David was not unique but was owing to sinful human nature, so Paul can quote 5:9 [10] as true of people in all times and places (Rom 3:13). Jesus, however, is the exception. When Jesus' enemies told lies about him (e.g., Matt 26:57-61), he did not respond in kind but entrusted himself to his Father's protection, a protection which he experienced at his resurrection. So, too, we his followers can pray to our Father for protection and use our mouths to "sing joyful praises forever" (5:11), knowing that the divine King will bless us and surround us with the shield of his love for Jesus' sake.

◆ F. Psalm 6

*For the choir director: A psalm of David, to be accompanied by an eight-stringed instrument.**

1 O LORD, don't rebuke me in your anger
or discipline me in your rage.
2 Have compassion on me, LORD, for
I am weak.
Heal me, LORD, for my bones are
in agony.
3 I am sick at heart.
How long, O LORD, until you
restore me?

4 Return, O LORD, and rescue me.
Save me because of your unfailing
love.
5 For the dead do not remember you.
Who can praise you from the
grave?*
6 I am worn out from sobbing.
All night I flood my bed with
weeping,
drenching it with my tears.
7 My vision is blurred by grief;
my eyes are worn out because
of all my enemies.

8 Go away, all you who do evil,
for the LORD has heard my weeping.
9 The LORD has heard my plea;
the LORD will answer my prayer.
10 May all my enemies be disgraced
and terrified.
May they suddenly turn back
in shame.

6:TITLE Hebrew *with stringed instruments; according to the sheminith.* 6:5 Hebrew *from Sheol?*

NOTES

6:TITLE ***eight-stringed.*** The meaning of the Hebrew is not certain.

6:1 This verse finds an almost exact parallel in 38:1 [2]. The language is thus formulaic for situations where illness is owing to God's anger (contra Craigie 1983:92, who suggests that the plea is for God not to rebuke the psalmist for bringing the request).

6:2 ***weak.*** The predicate adjective occurs only here; the related verb is frequently used of fields, vines, figs, etc., withering (DCH 1.314).

6:3 ***sick.*** The same word is translated "agony" in 6:2 [3].

6:4 ***Save me.*** The same words are translated "rescue me" in 3:7 [8].

unfailing love. God's *khesed* [TH2617, ZH2876] is the basis of the petition, as in 5:7 [8].

6:5 ***grave.*** Heb. *she'ol* [TH7585, ZH8619] occurs 16 times in the Psalter. The NLT uses "grave" 13 times (see 6:5; 9:17; 16:10; 18:5; 30:3; 31:17; 49:14 [twice], 15; 55:15; 89:48;

116:3; 139:8), "burial" one time (141:7), and "death" twice (86:13; 88:3). In none of these texts does *she'ol* refer to a place where departed spirits go; the reference in all of them is to the "grave" (TDOT 2.892-893; see also Harrison 1986 and VanGemeren 1984).

6:6 ***All night.*** This echoes the motif of prayer and meditation at night, as in 3:4-5 and 4:4.

6:8 ***the LORD has heard my weeping.*** This answers to the request of 5:3 ("Listen to my voice").

6:9 ***has heard my plea . . . will answer my prayer.*** This answers to the request of 4:1 ("Have mercy on me and hear my prayer").

6:10 ***all my enemies.*** The same phrase occurs in 3:7 [8]. For the mention of "enemies" in prayers for healing, see Pss 31, 38, 41, and 102.

terrified. The same word is translated "agony" in 6:2 [3] and "sick" in 6:3 [4].

May they . . . turn back. The Heb. *yashubu* [TH7725, ZH8740] is a play on the request of 6:4 [5], *shubah* [TH7725, ZH8740] (return).

COMMENTARY

This prayer for deliverance from illness[1] and ill-treatment has three stanzas: (1) 6:1-4 [2-5] is a series of requests (note the volitives, i.e., verbs that express the will of the speaker) to the Lord (*yhwh* is used five times); (2) 6:5-7 [6-8] provides the reasons for the requests (note the indicatives and the absence of the divine name); and (3) 6:8-10 [9-11] is a series of requests (note the volitives) to and about those who have subjected David to ill-treatment during his illness, and the Lord is once again in view (*yhwh* is used three times).

"This prayer for help is a passionate, agonized appeal to the grace of God against the wrath of God" (Mays 1994:59). That David's heart was sick when his body was in agony shows the integration of body and soul and articulates the depth of agony experienced in prolonged illness, a depth that leads to the terse cry, "How long, O LORD?" Just as body and soul are not separated, so too David's illness and God's activity are not separated: The illness is owing to divine anger. True, David makes no confession of sin nor requests forgiveness (as he does in the related Pss 38, 41, and 102), but this is not unique. Psalm 88 is also a prayer for healing from illness that is owing to the anger of God, and it contains no confession of sin. Since all sickness is a result of humanity's (Adam's) rebellion against God, all sickness is in some sense owing to God's anger (see below on 90:3-11). Psalm 6 does not make explicit whether David was suffering because of some particular sin[2] or the general sinfulness of the human race. But we do know that in Psalm 6 David does not complain about the injustice of divine anger; rather, he pleads that God would turn from that anger and heal him. This is a plea for compassion flowing from the unfailing love of God.

Two reasons are offered in 6:5-7 to support the petitions just made. First is the loss of praise to God that would result from the psalmist's death (6:5). While at first glance this seems odd to us, this same reason is offered elsewhere in the Psalter (30:9 [10]; 88:10-12 [11-13]; 115:17). Dead bodies in the grave cannot praise the Lord, but the living can (115:17-18). Since God created us to praise him, sickness leading to death is contrary to his original purpose. Thus, the request for healing rooted in the praise of God makes perfect sense. Second is the intensity of the sickness (6:6-7), noted by such expressions as "worn out from sobbing," "flood my bed with weeping, drenching it with my tears," "my vision is blurred by grief," and "my eyes are worn out." These convey the intensity of the physical illness and the internal pain it caused, and these expressions stand in stark contrast to the joyful existence of the godly in 1:1, 3 and 2:12b. But the godly are part of a fallen creation. They must trust the Lord for protection (2:12; 5:11), a protection that should provide health (see note on 1:1), as well as security from the "enemies" (2:12; 4:2; 5:10-11). Such agony is not the way it should be, and the articulation of this agony in the presence of a compassionate God is intended to get him to respond.

The mood changes in 6:8-10. "After David has disburdened his griefs and troubles into the bosom of God, he now, as it were, assumes a new character" (Calvin 1979:1.73). He reverts to petitions, but this time with regard to those who have been opposing him. Perhaps they, like Job's friends, have been tormenting the psalmist with false accusations and lies (4:2; 5:9) that traced his sickness to some personal sin. Or maybe they were simply hoping for his demise as a result of disease, saying, "God will never rescue him!" (3:2). Whatever the nature of the opposition, David gained the confidence that his prayer had been received by the Lord and that the Lord would answer that prayer. With poetic irony we read that when the Lord would return from his anger (*shub* [TH7725, ZH8740] in 6:4 [5]), the enemies would "turn back in shame" (*shub* in 6:10 [11]), and instead of David being in "agony" and "sick" (*bahal* [TH926, ZH987] in 6:2 [3] and 6:3 [4]), all his enemies would be "terrified" (*bahal* in 6:10 [11]).

There is also irony in the fact that we can pray this "passionate, agonized appeal to the grace of God against the wrath of God," because Jesus did not! Echoing the language of 6:3, Jesus said, "Now my soul is deeply troubled" (John 12:27). But he went on to say, "Should I pray, 'Father, save me from this hour'?" Since Jesus endured the wrath of God, both for our personal sins and our sin in Adam, we can have confidence that God will hear and answer our prayers for healing. But just as David had to wait long for the answer, so we too may have to wait long. In fact, we may have to wait until the day of resurrection.

ENDNOTES

1. For other prayers for healing, see Pss 38, 41, 88, and 102. Psalms 13 and 31 may also be prayers for healing.
2. Read in the context of Ps 7, Ps 6 would be an example of the innocent sufferer.

◆ G. Psalm 7

A psalm of David, which he sang to the LORD concerning Cush of the tribe of Benjamin.

1 I come to you for protection, O LORD
my God.
Save me from my
persecutors—rescue me!
2 If you don't, they will maul me like
a lion,
tearing me to pieces with no one
to rescue me.
3 O LORD my God, if I have done wrong
or am guilty of injustice,
4 if I have betrayed a friend
or plundered my enemy without
cause,
5 then let my enemies capture me.
Let them trample me into the
ground
and drag my honor in the dust.
Interlude

6 Arise, O LORD, in anger!
Stand up against the fury of my enemies!
Wake up, my God, and bring justice!
7 Gather the nations before you.
Rule over them from on high.
8 The LORD judges the nations.
Declare me righteous, O LORD,
for I am innocent, O Most High!
9 End the evil of those who are wicked,
and defend the righteous.
For⌊you look deep within the mind and heart,⌋
O righteous God.

10 God is my shield,
saving those whose hearts are true and right.
11 God is an honest judge.
He is angry with the wicked every day.

12 If a person does not repent,
God* will sharpen his sword;
he will bend and string his bow.
13 He will prepare his deadly weapons
and shoot his flaming arrows.

14 The wicked conceive evil;
they are pregnant with trouble
and give birth to lies.
15 They dig a deep pit to trap others,
then fall into it themselves.
16 The trouble they make for others backfires on them.
The violence they plan falls on their own heads.

17 I will thank the LORD because he is just;
I will sing praise to the name of the LORD Most High.

7:12 Hebrew *he.*

NOTES

7:TITLE *A psalm.* The meaning of Heb. *shiggayon* [TH7692, ZH8710] is uncertain. The NLT is in keeping with *psalmos* of the LXX.

concerning Cush. The words *'al-dibre-* can mean "about/concerning" (see Deut 4:21; Jer 7:22; 14:1), but *dibre* [TH1697, ZH1821] usually has the meaning "words" or "achievements" when following *'al* [TH5921, ZH6584]. Second Samuel 3:8 is the only other occurrence of *'al-dibre-* + a personal name, and the sense there is "*because of* what X said" (see RSV, "over the words of Ish-bosheth"). So this agrees with Delitzsch (1982:138) and would render the Hebrew "concerning the words of Cush," especially in view of the verbal sins of the preceding psalms—false accusations (4:2), lying (5:6), and flattery (5:9). Psalms 3–7 form a group of laments bounded by the introductory Pss 1–2 and the hymn Ps 8. Psalms 3 and 7 are the only two in this group with historical information, thus forming an *inclusio.* I therefore conjecture that Cush was a person like Shimei son of Gera, who cursed David during Absalom's rebellion (2 Sam 16:5).

7:4 *plundered my enemy.* The word "plundered" (Piel of *khalats* [TH2502, ZH2740]) is the same as the word used in 6:4 [5], where the psalmist asks Yahweh to "rescue" him, and the word for "enemy" is the same as used in 6:7 [8].

without cause. Delitzsch (1982:140) is correct in having *reqam* [TH7387, ZH8200] modify "enemy" rather than "plundered" (see 25:3 and 69:4 [5] for the syntax). The "enemy without cause" (*reqam*) is one of those who "make groundless accusations" (*riq* [TH7385, ZH8198]; 4:2 [3]).

7:5 *then let my enemies capture me.* The NLT leaves *yiradop* [TH7291, ZH8103] (pursue) untranslated; the form mixes the vowels of both the Qal and the Piel (see Joüon and Muraoka 1991:§16g).

my honor. Based on the parallelism with *napshi* [TH5315, ZH5883] (my soul) and *khayyay* [TH2416, ZH2644] (my life), some translations take *kebodi* [TH3519, ZH3883] to refer to the psalmist's self (NIV, NRSV; so too A. Anderson 1972:95), but many commentators do not (e.g., Calvin 1979:80; Kraus 1988:171; VanGemeren 1991:103). The motif of concern for *kebodi* ("my glory" in 3:3 [4] and "my reputation" in 4:2 [3]) is resumed here and confirms the NLT's "my honor."

7:6 ***my God.*** The NLT (cf. RSV, NIV) either reads the Heb. *'elay* [TH413/2967.1, ZH448/3276], which typically means "to me," as a plural of the noun *'el* [TH410A, ZH446] (God) with the first-person sg. suffix, or it emends the MT to *'eli,* reading the singular of "God." In the first case the noun would be a plural of majesty (so Craigie 1983:98), but such plurals are in fact quite rare with *'el; 'el* consistently occurs in the singular with the first-person sg. suffix (e.g., *'eli* in 18:2 [3]; 22:1 [2]), hence the suggested emendation. "Awake for me" has also been suggested (cf. ASV, NKJV, ESV), based on *'urah liqra'thi* [TH5782/3807.1/7122, ZH6424/4200/7925] (awake to meet me) in 59:4 [5] (Delitzsch 1982:142 and Kraus 1988:167), but the parallel is not exact, and the verb *'ur* [TH5782, ZH6424] is not found elsewhere in combination with the preposition *'el* [TH413, ZH448], nor is this verb used with a noun like *mishpat* [TH4941, ZH5477] as the direct object. Thus, in this case, emending to *'eli* [TH410A, ZH446] is warranted.

7:7 ***Gather the nations before you.*** The nations (*le'ummim* [TH3816, ZH4211]) are the same as in 2:1. The NLT leaves *'adath* [TH5712, ZH6337] (assembly of) untranslated; this assembly is for the purpose of judgment, as is the case in 1:5, where the NLT also leaves *'adath* untranslated.

Rule over them. The verb *shubah* [TH7725, ZH8740] (return) is frequently emended to *shebah,* as if from *yashab* [TH3427, ZH3782] ("sit"; NLT, NIV, NRSV; Kraus 1988:167; VanGemeren 1991:103; McCann 1996:708). But "return" is understandable and even preferable in light of the same expression in 6:4 [5]. Just as God must "wake up" (never having fallen asleep), so must he "return" (never having left his place of judgment), for it is as if he were asleep and away.

7:8 ***The LORD judges.*** Though the form is not that of a jussive (*yadin* [TH1777, ZH1906] not the jussive *yaden*), it functions as one in the context of the imperatives in 7:6-9 [7-10]; "the jussive form is quite often neglected in cases where it could have been used" (Joüon and Muraoka 1991:§114g).

Declare me righteous. This echoes 4:1, "O God who declares me innocent."

7:9 ***mind and heart.*** The Heb. is *libboth* (hearts) and *kelayoth* (kidneys). This pair occurs 6 times in the MT (7:9 [10]; 26:2; 73:21; Jer 11:20; 17:10; 20:12). In all but one verse (73:21), the context is God's examination of our inner person: our thoughts (*leb* [TH3820, ZH4213]) and emotions (*kilyah* [TH362, ZH4000]).[1] The two stand for the whole person, perhaps by reference to the chest cavity and the abdominal cavity (TDOT 7.181).

7:10 ***God is my shield.*** Lit., "my shield is on God." Perhaps the picture is that of God as shield bearer (Craigie 1983:98), or perhaps the text should be emended to *'alay* [TH5921/2967.1, ZH6584/3276] ("above me"; Kraus 1988:168). At any rate, the motif of the Divine Warrior is resumed from 3:3 (see also 5:12).

7:17 ***I will thank the LORD.*** Heb. *'odeh yhwh* [TH3034A/3068, ZH3344/3378] answers to *bishe'ol mi yodeh-lak,* "Who can praise you from the grave?" in 6:5 [6] (Brennan 1980:27).

COMMENTARY

Psalm 7, comprised of two stanzas, is the song of a falsely accused person. The first stanza (7:1-9) is a prayer directed to the Lord (in predominantly second-person address), in which David asks for deliverance (7:1-2), pleads his innocence (7:3-5), and again asks for deliverance (7:6-7). The second stanza (7:10-17) is a confession (in predominantly third-person address), a confession about the outworking of the Lord's justice (7:10-13) and the enemies' wickedness and its outcome (7:14-16), followed by a concluding vow to thank God for his justice (7:17).

Once again we find David in prayer casting himself upon the Lord for "protection" (as in 2:12 and 5:11) and crying out, "Save me" (as in 3:7 and 6:4). In these opening verses David does not articulate that from which he needs protection (though the title has indicated it to be "the words of Cush"; see note). The seriousness of the need, however, is expressed in the language of being mauled and shredded by lions (7:2; for a pictorial representation, see Keel 1997:86).

In a form reminiscent of Job (see Job 31), David proceeds to plead his innocence as a way of protesting the treatment he has been receiving. It is implicit here that David needs protection from the charges that he is guilty of injustice, betrayal, and plunder. Should such charges be true, he would submit to just consequences, culminating in the loss of his honor. But David is certain that he is facing "enemies without cause" (see note on 7:4), that is, they have no just cause for their adversarial stance. David's protest, "If I have done wrong," must not be taken out of context and understood as a claim to self-righteousness; rather, it is a claim to innocence in this particular case (Mays 1994:63-64 and McCann 1996:70). Calvin (1979:84) says,

> *The subject here treated of is not how he should answer if God should demand from him an account of his whole life; but, comparing himself with his enemies, he maintains, and not without cause, that, in respect of them, he was righteous. But when each saint passes under the review of God's judgment, and his own character is tried upon its own merits, the matter is very different, for then the only sanctuary to which he can betake himself for safety is the mercy of God.*

All believers can be confident that they will receive this mercy because of the absolute innocence of Christ. And, following the pattern of Christ, they can be confident of receiving the grace needed to entrust themselves to God's justice when they are falsely accused (see the commentary on Ps 4).

Fully aware, then, of God's righteous and penetrating gaze, David was confident of his innocence and called for the divine judge to return to his judgment seat and convene the court (7:7 [8]). As in 3:7, David calls God to "arise" (7:6), and the "anger" he wished to avoid for himself (6:1) he here views as appropriate for his adversaries (McCann 1996:708) because of the injustice of their own "fury." Since he is in the right, he can call for justice, which would culminate in God declaring him "righteous" (7:8). This declaration would end the wickedness of the ungodly and help those who obey—that is, it would bring the truth of 1:6 to realization in this particular situation.

As the first stanza began with David coming to the Lord for protection and asking him to "save" (*hoshi'eni* [TH3467, ZH3828]; 7:1 [2]), the second stanza begins with a confession that God is the psalmist's shield (protection) and the one who "saves" (*moshia'* [TH3467, ZH3828] 7:10 [11]). And as David asked the Lord to declare him righteous (*shopteni yhwh ketsidqi* [TH8199/6664, ZH9149/7406]; 7:8 [9]), he now confesses that God is a "righteous judge" (*shopet tsaddiq* [TH8199/6662, ZH9149/7404]; 7:11 [12]).

Thus the second stanza begins with the related motifs of the Lord as warrior and judge (see Longman and Reid 1995:44). Psalm 7:12-13 shows how the Lord saves the psalmist and judges the enemy all in the same act, as is often the case. In the absence of repentance, the Divine Warrior prepares his offensive weapons to execute the enemy.

But the Lord does not have a literal sword or bow and arrows, so how is his judgment envisioned as working itself out? Here the Lord's judgment is worked out in the poetically just outworking of the wicked's own evil. Having conceived, carried to full term, and given birth to lies (7:14), that is, false accusations against the psalmist, the wicked get caught in their own trap (7:15-16). Calvin (1979:91) says,

> *There is a twofold use of this doctrine: In the first place, however skilled in craft our enemies may be, and whatever means of doing mischief they may have, we must nevertheless look for the issue which God here promises, that they shall fall by their own sword. And this is not a thing which happens by chance; but God, by the secret direction of his own hand, causes the evil which they intend to bring upon the innocent to return upon their own heads. In the second place, if at any time we are instigated by passion to inflict any injury upon our neighbours, or to commit any wickedness, let us remember this principle of retributive justice, which is often acted upon by the divine government, that those who prepare a pit for others are cast into it themselves; and the effect will be, that every one, in proportion as he would consult his own happiness and welfare, will be careful to restrain himself from doing any injury, even the smallest, to another.*

As is always the case, however, repentance (*yashub* [TH7725, ZH8740]; 7:12 [13]) is held out as the alternative to having sin come back upon (*yashub*; 7:16 [17]) one's own head.

As the first stanza ended on the note of God being righteousness (*tsaddiq* [TH6662, ZH7404]; 7:9 [10]), the second stanza ends with a vow to praise God for his justice (*ketsidqo* [TH6662, ZH7404] 7:17 [18]) in view of his declaration of the psalmist's innocence (*ketsidqi* [TH6664, ZH7406], 7:8 [9]). This vow to praise the name of the Lord will be fulfilled in the following psalm (Brennan 1980:28).

ENDNOTES

1. The word *leb* (heart) is used for both thoughts and emotions, whereas the word *kilyah* (kidneys) is used for emotions but not for thoughts. So the distinction here, presuming there is one, is between thoughts ("heart") and emotions ("kidney"). See the note at 16:7.

◆ H. Psalm 8

*For the choir director: A psalm of David, to be accompanied by a stringed instrument.**

[1] O LORD, our Lord, your majestic name
fills the earth!
Your glory is higher than the
heavens.

[2] You have taught children and infants
to tell of your strength,*
silencing your enemies
and all who oppose you.

[3]When I look at the night sky and see
the work of your fingers—
the moon and the stars you set
in place—
[4]what are mere mortals that you should
think about them,
human beings that you should care
for them?*
[5]Yet you made them only a little lower
than God*
and crowned them* with glory
and honor.
[6]You gave them charge of everything
you made,
putting all things under their
authority—
[7]the flocks and the herds
and all the wild animals,
[8]the birds in the sky, the fish in
the sea,
and everything that swims the
ocean currents.

[9]O LORD, our Lord, your majestic name
fills the earth!

8:TITLE Hebrew *according to the gittith.* **8:2** Greek version reads *to give you praise.* Compare Matt 21:16. **8:4** Hebrew *what is man that you should think of him, / the son of man that you should care for him?* **8:5a** Or *Yet you made them only a little lower than the angels;* Hebrew reads *Yet you made him* [i.e., man] *a little lower than Elohim.* **8:5b** Hebrew *him* [i.e., man]; similarly in 8:6.

NOTES

8:TITLE *a stringed instrument.* The meaning of Heb. *gittith* [TH1665, ZH1787], which occurs only here and in the titles of Pss 81 and 84, is uncertain.

8:1 *our Lord.* To address Yahweh as Lord (*'adon* [TH113, ZH123]) is to address him as king (see 97:5; VanGemeren 1991:110). The expression *'adonenu* occurs only 12 times: 2 times for a human master (1 Sam 25:14, 17), 4 times for a human king (1 Sam 16:16; 1 Kgs 1:11, 43, 47), and 6 times for Yahweh (8:1 [2], 9 [10]; 135:5; 147:5; Neh 8:10; 10:29 [30]). Psalm 8 has numerous connections with Ps 2; the use of *'adonenu* [TH113/5105.1, ZH123/5646] (8:1 [2]) and *'adonay* [TH136, ZH151] (2:4) is one of them.

name. Psalm 8 is the fulfilling of the vow made in 7:17 to "sing praise to the name of the LORD" (Brennan 1980:28).

Your glory is higher than the heavens. The first two words in Heb. (*'asher tenah* [TH834/5414, ZH889/5989]; "which" + "give!") are difficult. The form *tenah* is apparently an imperative, but the syntax of *'asher tenah* would be unparalleled; so too, if *tenah* is taken as an infinitive construct. Craigie (1983:105) follows Dahood (1965:1.49) in emending to *'asharetannah* ("I will adore/serve/worship"; Piel of *sharath* [TH8334, ZH9250] with an energic Nun). (For other suggested emendations, see Kraus 1988:178.) But the Piel of *sharath* never takes a word like *hod* [TH1935, ZH2086] (splendor, glory) as its object. The best solution is the proposal in BHS to emend to *'asher nathattah* (you who have put). The relative pronoun plus the perfect would be syntactically analogous to the participle with (or without) the definite article, which is frequent enough in hymnic praise (e.g., 103:3-6; 104:2-4). For *'asher* plus the perfect in hymnic praise, see 46:8 [9] and 71:19, 20. The closest text to Ps 8 in this regard is Ps 135, where Yahweh is addressed as *'adonenu* [TH136/5105.1, ZH151/5646] (135:5) and then praised with a hymnic participle (135:7a) and then with the relative *sha* [TH7578.7, ZH8611] plus a perfect (135:8, 10). The emended phrase from the MT *'asher natattah* begins the second stanza (8:1a [2a] being the first stanza) of the hymn, after the fashion of 103:3, and 8:1a [2a] and 8:9 [10] thus form a precisely parallel *inclusio* (contra Kraus 1988:185).

8:2 *to tell of your strength.* Lit., "you have founded strength." Since the word *'oz* [TH5797, ZH6437] means "strength" or a "stronghold," why do the LXX and NT (Matt 21:16) use *ainos* [TG136, ZG142] (praise), while the Latin Vulgate uses *laus* (praise)? Since *'oz* is often ascribed to God in praise (see 29:1; 59:16-17 [17-18]; 68:34 [35]; 96:7; 118:14), it appears that 8:2

[3] is a case of breviloquence,[1] a form of ellipsis: "You have established[2] [the praise of your] strength." The LXX, NT, and Latin Vulgate capture the part of the figure elided in the MT.

enemies. Two different words are used in 8:2 for "enemies:" *tsorer* [TH6887A, ZH7675] (as in 6:7 [8]; 7:4 [5], 6 [7]) and *'oyeb* [TH341, ZH367] (as in 3:7 [8]; 6:10 [11]; 7:5 [6]). The enemies in Ps 8 are not "the chaotic forces that God conquered and ordered in the sovereign act of creation" (McCann 1996:711) but are the king's adversaries encountered in Pss 3–7.

8:3 *night sky.* Heb. *shamayim* [TH8064, ZH9028], translated "heavens" in 8:1.

set in place. This is the same verb translated "prepare" in 7:13 [14]; the Divine Warrior who will "prepare" his weapons to fight for the psalmist is the Creator who has "set in place" the moon and stars.

8:4 *mere mortals.* Heb. *ben-adam* [TH1121/120, ZH1201/132] (lit., "son of man") is used for an individual person ("son of a person" according to DCH 128). If there is a difference between *'enosh* (NLT, "human beings") and *ben-adam* in Ps 8, the movement would be from the generic (humanity) to the specific (individual): "What are we as a race, not to mention as individuals, that you should have any concern for us?" On the other hand, *ben-adam* is used only two other times in the Psalter, and in both cases the *ben-adam* is a royal person (80:17 [18]; 146:3). So from one perspective the *ben-adam* is the *'ish* [TH376, ZH408] (NLT, "those") of Ps 1:1, but from another, he is the *melek* [TH4428, ZH4889] (king) of Ps 2:6 (see Miller 1993:92).

human beings. Heb. *'enosh* [TH582, ZH632] is used in the sense of an individual man, a frail mortal, and as a collective for the human race (DCH 334). Some have suggested that the second sense is activated here (e.g., Kraus 1988:182), but given that Ps 8 is looking back to Gen 1:26, the sense is not likely that of the *frail mortality* of humanity; rather, it is used here as a *generic term* for people.

8:5 *God.* The LXX, Syriac, Targums, Latin Vulgate, and NT (Heb 2:7) use terms for "angels" (Craigie 1983:108). Since Yahweh is being addressed in the psalm, we should presumably translate *'elohim* [TH430, ZH466] as "angels" (see Kraus 1988:183).

glory and honor. These are attributes of royalty, be it divine (24:7-10; 145:4-13) or human (21:5 [6]); see Futato 1984:13.

8:6 *You gave them charge.* The Heb. *mashal* [TH4910, ZH5440] signifies the exercise of royal dominion (see 1 Kgs 4:24 [5:1]).

everything you made. Lit., "the works of your hands." This expression echoes "the works of your fingers" in 8:3 [4]. The former refers to the earth, while the latter refers to the heavens.

8:7 *flocks and herds.* Heb. *tsoneh* [TH6792A, ZH7556] is an orthographic variant of *tso'nah* (HALOT 3.1037; Zorell 1963:696).

COMMENTARY

At its center, Psalm 8 raises a most fundamental question: How is it possible that "mere mortals" can be of any concern to God (8:4 [5])? What significance do people have? Where do we fit into the universal scheme of things? Why would God care about us or for us? The chiastic structure and the content of Psalm 8 provide two complementary answers.[3]

Human beings are the center of the universe! In the structure of the psalm the question pertaining to "mere mortals" stands in between the heavens above and the earth beneath. Psalm 8:1b-3 focuses on the heavens, as is clear from the *inclusio*-forming repetition of *shamayim* [TH8064, ZH9028] in 1:1b-3. The magnificence of the heavens on the one hand and the glory of the Lord that transcends the heavens on the other hand converge to evoke the question, "What are . . . human beings that you should care for them?" Psalm 8:5-8 focuses on the earth. The earth is the sphere where people, having been crowned with royal glory and honor, exercise their dominion over the sheep, cattle, wild animals, birds,[4] and fish. "The Creator and world ruler Yahweh assigns the world to the human being as to a king installed by God (cf. Ps. 2:8)" (Kraus 1988:183). By placing the question in between the heavens and the earth, the psalmist is providing an implicit answer to his own question: "Mere mortals" are the center of the universe! The heavens and the earth revolve around us. The explicit affirmation of human dominion underscores our uniqueness and central position in creation. As the center of the universe, we are the objects of God's thoughts and care. While we are the center, we are not thereby ultimate, however.

Human beings are not ultimate in the universe! The structure and content affirm that our glory and authority are derivative, not ultimate. For one thing, the Lord made us a little lower than the angels, the Lord gave us our glory and honor, and the Lord put us in charge of the earth. All that we are depends on him. Apart from him we are nothing. But we are not "apart from him." The central question is raised with the interrogative pronoun *mah* [TH4100, ZH4537], which is the same word used in 8:1 [2] and 8:9 [10] (*mah-'addir* [TH117, ZH129], traditionally translated "How majestic!"). This repetition of *mah* ties our identity as humans to God's and reinforces the answer to the question raised: Our glory and authority are not ultimate but are derived from the Lord's ultimate glory and authority. Our centrality in the poem and the universe is itself structurally surrounded by the majesty of the Lord's own name. Our glorious dominion has doxology as its beginning and its end. "*Doxology* gives *dominion* its context and legitimacy. Praise of God without human authority is abdication. But to use human power without the context of praise of God is to profane human regency over creation and so usurp more than has been granted" (Brueggemann 1984:37-38).

But how does 8:2 fit in? Does it not mar this beautiful portrait of divine majesty and human dignity? The theme of children giving God praise fits in well enough, but what of the silencing of the enemies? As indicated, Psalm 8 is the fulfilling of he vow made in 7:17 [18]. Psalm 7 is a prayer for protection against the "enemies" encountered in the previous psalms (3:7; 6:7, 10), as well as in Psalm 7 itself (7:4-6). The juxtaposition of Psalm 8 and Psalms 3–7 teaches that human suffering and glory are not mutually exclusive; more than that, it teaches that the path to glory is through suffering. The person crowned with glory and honor and given dominion over all things (Ps 8) is the person who still needs protection from enemies, especially from enemies who attack verbally (Pss 3–7). The Lord only needs an army of praise-wielding infant warriors to "silence" these enemies! Even the kings and rulers of "the earth" (2:2, 10) will be silenced by children praising him whose majestic name fills "the earth" (8:1, 9).

David understood that the glory and authority articulated in the psalm had not yet been realized in history. "The historical reality, according to Paul and the author of the Epistle to the Hebrews, is—and will be—fulfilled in the risen Christ" (Craigie 1983:110). "We have not yet seen all things put under their authority" says the author of Hebrews (Heb 2:8) about the truth of Psalm 8. "What we do see is Jesus, who was given a position 'a little lower than the angels'; and because he suffered death for us, he is now 'crowned with glory and honor'" (Heb 2:9). As "the Son of David" (Matt 21:15), he suffered verbal opposition (as in Pss 3–7) from his enemies, opposition that was silenced with the words, "You have taught children and infants to give you praise" (Matt 21:16). But more than that, he "suffered death for us" (Heb 2:9). But suffering was his path to "glory and honor." As surely as Jesus suffered and was crowned with glory and honor for us, we too will experience the glory and honor held out in Psalm 8, but only at the end of the path of the suffering of Psalms 3–7.

Psalm 8 is an interlude of glory during a cantata of suffering. It pointed David to the future; it pointed him to Christ. It points us to "the future world" (Heb 2:5); it points us to Christ—the truly royal human being who "radiates God's own glory and expresses the very character of God" (Heb 1:3).

ENDNOTES

1. For this figure of speech in general, see Bullinger 1968:47-51.
2. For the Piel of *yasad* [TH3245, ZH3569] in the sense "ordain, establish, assign," see Esth 1:8 and 1 Chr 9:22.
3. For a brief history of the interpretation of Ps 8 see Prinsloo 1995b:371-376.
4. In the biblical picture, the birds are part of the earth, not the heavens. The heavens are the *raqia'* [TH7549, ZH8385] (Gen 1:6; NLT, "space") and above, while the earth includes everything below the *raqia'*. Note that the birds fill the earth in Gen 1:22, and see the commentary on the structure of Ps 148.

◆ I. Psalms 9–10

For the choir director: A psalm of David, to be sung to the tune "Death of the Son."

1 I will praise you, LORD, with all my heart;
I will tell of all the marvelous things you have done.
2 I will be filled with joy because of you.
I will sing praises to your name, O Most High.

3 My enemies retreated;
they staggered and died when you appeared.
4 For you have judged in my favor;
from your throne you have judged with fairness.
5 You have rebuked the nations and destroyed the wicked;
you have erased their names forever.
6 The enemy is finished, in endless ruins;
the cities you uprooted are now forgotten.

7 But the LORD reigns forever,
executing judgment from his throne.
8 He will judge the world with justice
and rule the nations with fairness.
9 The LORD is a shelter for the oppressed,
a refuge in times of trouble.
10 Those who know your name trust in you,
for you, O LORD, do not abandon those who search for you.

11 Sing praises to the LORD who reigns in Jerusalem.*
Tell the world about his unforgettable deeds.
12 For he who avenges murder cares for the helpless.
He does not ignore the cries of those who suffer.

13 LORD, have mercy on me.
See how my enemies torment me.
Snatch me back from the jaws of death.

[14] Save me so I can praise you publicly
at Jerusalem's gates,
so I can rejoice that you have
rescued me.

[15] The nations have fallen into the pit
they dug for others.
Their own feet have been caught
in the trap they set.
[16] The LORD is known for his justice.
The wicked are trapped by their own
deeds. *Quiet Interlude**

[17] The wicked will go down to the grave.*
This is the fate of all the nations
who ignore God.
[18] But the needy will not be ignored
forever;
the hopes of the poor will not
always be crushed.

[19] Arise, O LORD!
Do not let mere mortals defy you!
Judge the nations!
[20] Make them tremble in fear, O LORD.
Let the nations know they are
merely human. *Interlude*

PSALM 10

[1] O LORD, why do you stand so far away?
Why do you hide when I am in
trouble?
[2] The wicked arrogantly hunt down the
poor.
Let them be caught in the evil they
plan for others.
[3] For they brag about their evil desires;
they praise the greedy and curse
the LORD.

[4] The wicked are too proud to seek God.
They seem to think that God is dead.
[5] Yet they succeed in everything they do.
They do not see your punishment
awaiting them.
They sneer at all their enemies.
[6] They think, "Nothing bad will ever
happen to us!
We will be free of trouble forever!"
[7] Their mouths are full of cursing, lies,
and threats.*
Trouble and evil are on the tips of
their tongues.
[8] They lurk in ambush in the villages,
waiting to murder innocent people.
They are always searching for
helpless victims.
[9] Like lions crouched in hiding,
they wait to pounce on the helpless.
Like hunters they capture the helpless
and drag them away in nets.
[10] Their helpless victims are crushed;
they fall beneath the strength of
the wicked.
[11] The wicked think, "God isn't
watching us!
He has closed his eyes and won't
even see what we do!"

[12] Arise, O LORD!
Punish the wicked, O God!
Do not ignore the helpless!
[13] Why do the wicked get away with
despising God?
They think, "God will never call us
to account."
[14] But you see the trouble and grief they
cause.
You take note of it and punish
them.
The helpless put their trust in you.
You defend the orphans.

[15] Break the arms of these wicked, evil
people!
Go after them until the last one is
destroyed.
[16] The LORD is king forever and ever!
The godless nations will vanish from
the land.
[17] LORD, you know the hopes of the
helpless.
Surely you will hear their cries and
comfort them.
[18] You will bring justice to the orphans
and the oppressed,
so mere people can no longer terrify
them.

9:11 Hebrew *Zion;* also in 9:14. **9:16** Hebrew *Higgaion Selah.* The meaning of this phrase is uncertain. **9:17** Hebrew *to Sheol.* **10:7** Greek version reads *cursing and bitterness.* Compare Rom 3:14.

NOTES

In reference to Psalms 9 and 10, A. F. Kirkpatrick (1902:42) said, "The two Psalms present an unsolved literary problem." The problem is whether or not Psalms 9 and 10 were originally one or two psalms. I treat the two as one. Others who treat Psalms 9–10 as a unit are Craigie (1983), Kraus (1988), Mays (1994), and McCann (1996); for the opposing view, see VanGemeren 1991. I think they comprise one psalm for the following reasons: (1) When combined, Psalms 9 and 10 form an acrostic.[1] (2) Many key terms and motifs are repeated in both psalms; I will mention a number of these in the notes below. (3) Psalms 9–10 form a chiastic, literary whole. (4) Psalm 10 has no title, which is unusual in Book 1.[2] (5) The LXX and some Hebrew manuscripts treat the two as one.

9:TITLE *the tune "Death of the Son."* The Heb. *'almuth labben* [TH4192B/1121, ZH6629/1201] is unexplainable. It may be related to *'al-muth* [TH5921/4191, ZH6584/4637] (until death) in 48:14 [15] or to the equally unexplainable *'al-'alamoth* [TH5921/5961, ZH6584/6628] (by alamoth) in 46:TITLE [1]. Here in Ps 9, the NLT presumes a redivision of the first word to *'al-muth* (concerning the death of) and understands *labben* as "to the son."

9:2 *your name, O Most High.* Praise of the "name" connects this psalm back to 8:1, 9; the collocation of "name" and "Most High" echoes 7:17.

9:4 *you have judged.* The word *mishpat* [TH4941, ZH5477] is repeated in 9:7 [8], 16 [17], and 10:5.

from your throne you have judged. The throne in view is that on which the king sits to judge (see 2:4). So also in 9:7 [8], the Lord is enthroned forever to execute judgment, and it is as king that he is so enthroned forever to judge (10:16, 18).

9:5 *rebuked the nations and destroyed the wicked.* The terms "nations" and "destroyed" (or "vanish") are repeated in 10:16. The term "wicked" is used repeatedly in Pss 9–10 (9:16 [17], 17 [18]; 10:2, 3, 4, 13, 15 [twice]).

their names forever. In contrast to the Lord's name, which is praised, the name of the wicked is wiped out. This wiping out is forever—in contrast to the Lord who reigns as king forever.

9:10 *do not abandon.* Since the Lord never abandons (*'azab* [TH5800, ZH6440]) those who search for him, they can trust him—in the (Hebrew) words of 10:14, they can "abandon" (*'azab*) themselves to the Lord.

9:12 *he who avenges.* Though the wicked think God will never "call us to account" (*darash* [TH1875, ZH2011]; 10:13), he will nevertheless "avenge" (*darash*); see also "Go after them" (*darash*) in 10:15.

He does not ignore the cries of those who suffer. Though there are nations that "ignore" (*shakakh*) God (9:17 [18]) and think that he will ignore (*shakakh* [TH7911, ZH8894]; 10:11) them when they afflict his people, he will not "ignore" (*shakakh*; 9:12 [13]) "the cries of those who suffer."

9:13 *See how my enemies torment me.* Here the psalmist asks the Lord to see his suffering, and in 10:14 he expresses confidence that the Lord does see his trouble and grief.

jaws of death. Lit., "gates of death." When saved from the gates of death, David will praise the Lord at the gates of Jerusalem (9:14).

9:15-18 *The nations have fallen.* Verses 13-20 [14-21] are a unit, bounded by the imperatives of 9:13 [14] and 9:19-20 [20-21]. In the context of these imperatives, it is best to understand the perfects of the main clauses in 9:15-16 [17-18] as precatives (forms that express a wish) and the imperfects of the main clauses in 9:17-18 [18-19] as jussives (verbs that make a wish). The entire section is a plea for deliverance.

9:15 ***the trap they set.*** These traps (*resheth* [TH7568, ZH8407]) are the "nets" (*resheth*) of 10:9. The rare relative particle *zu* [TH2098, ZH2306] occurs here and in 10:2, providing evidence for the original unity of Pss 9 and 10 (Craigie 1983:116).

9:16 ***trapped.*** The NLT correctly presumes the emendation of *noqesh* (Qal participle of *naqash* [TH5367, ZH5943]; "strike down") to *noqash* (Niphal perfect of *yaqash* [TH3369, ZH3704]; "be trapped").

9:17 ***grave.*** Heb. *she'ol* [TH7585, ZH8619]. See note at 6:5.

9:19 ***Arise, O LORD!*** This prayer, already expressed in 3:7 [8] and 7:6 [7], will be repeated in 10:12.

mere mortals. Heb. *'enosh* [TH582, ZH632] (repeated in 9:20 [21]) connects Ps 9 back to 8:4 [5] ("mortals") and forward to 10:18 ("people").

9:20 ***tremble in fear.*** The NLT correctly presumes the emendation of *morah* [TH4172A, ZH4624] (razor) to *mora'* [TH4172, ZH4616] (trembling).

10:1 ***when I am in trouble.*** See 9:9 and commentary.

10:3 ***evil desires.*** The "evil desires" (*ta'awath* [TH8378, ZH9294]) of the wicked contrast with the same word translated as the "hopes" (*ta'awath*) of the helpless (10:17).

10:5 ***they succeed.*** The Heb. *yakhilu* [TH2342B, ZH2656] is difficult but is probably from *khil* II ("be firm"; BDB 298).

10:7 ***Their mouths . . . their tongues.*** The wicked here are characterized by verbal sins, as was the case in Pss 3–7; see the commentary on 8:2.

10:8 ***They lurk.*** Lit., "they sit." The wicked "sit" with the intention of doing evil, but the Lord "sits" to judge such wickedness (9:4 [5], 7 [8], 11 [12]).

10:12 ***Punish the wicked, O God!*** Lit., "Lift up your hand." The Heb. *nasa'* + *yad* [TH5375/3027, ZH5951/3338] occurs 23 times in the MT: (1) as body language associated with swearing an oath (15 times: 106:26; Exod 6:8; Num 14:30; Deut 32:40; Ezek 20:5 [twice]; 20:6, 15, 23, 28, 42; 36:7; 44:12; 47:14; Neh 9:15), praying (twice: 28:2; 134:2), giving a blessing (once: Lev 9:22), and beckoning (once: Isa 49:22); and (2) as an idiom for rebellion (twice: 2 Sam 18:28; 20:21). While the sense in 10:12 could be "lift up your hand against the wicked to punish them," *nasa'* + *yad* is not used in this sense elsewhere in the OT. It is probably better to understand the sense as something like "lift up your hand as a sign of your blessing on or your oath to save the helpless."

COMMENTARY

Psalms 9–10 form a chiastic literary whole. The outer frame (9:1-12 and 10:16-18) consists of two hymns in praise of the divine king (see "the LORD reigns forever" in 9:7 and "The LORD is King forever and ever" in 10:16). As king, the Lord will not ignore the cry of the afflicted (9:12 and 10:17) but will destroy the nations that oppress his people (9:5 and 10:16). The inner frame (9:13-20 and 10:12-15) consists of two pleas for the Lord to come to the aid of his people (see "Arise, O LORD" in 9:19 and 10:12; note also the repetition of "see" in 9:13 and 10:14). The central section (10:1-11) is a lament concerning the wicked.

An agonizing "Why?" opens the central section (10:1-11). Why is God seemingly absent when it comes to dealing with wicked people? Psalm 1 promised that the wicked would not succeed but would be "like worthless chaff, scattered by the wind" (1:3-4). But in the real world (the psalmist's and ours) the wicked "succeed in everything they do" (10:5). Their success leads to blatant arrogance (10:2-3). In their arrogance the wicked imagine they will experience uninterrupted prosperity forever (10:6). This arrogance generates oppressive attitudes and actions toward the "poor" (10:2), the "helpless" who cannot stand up against the tyrannical onslaught of the wicked (10:8-10). Ultimately, this arrogance leads the wicked to curse God, to ignore him, and to consider him irrelevant. Why does the God of the promises in Psalm 1 tolerate such wickedness?

Psalms 9–10 does not directly answer the questions posed in 10:1-11. But surrounding this central lament are two pleas for the Lord to act (9:13-20 and 10:12-15). Twice the psalmist asks the Lord to arise. In 9:19 David asks the Lord to arise in order to judge the wicked. This request follows on the heels of 9:15-17, where the psalmist prays that the wicked experience poetic justice as the judgment of God (see also 10:15; see note on 9:15-18). Then in 10:12 David asks the Lord to arise in order to help the helpless. Confident that the Lord is not so far away that he cannot "see the trouble and grief" (10:14a), David affirms that faith in the Lord is the path the helpless should follow (10:14b), for the Lord is able to bring people from the gates of death to the gates of Jerusalem (9:13-14; see note on 9:13), where they can rejoice in his deliverance of them. Here, as elsewhere in the Bible, the destruction of the wicked and the salvation of the righteous go hand in hand.

Surrounding the two pleas for the Lord to arise and save the afflicted by destroying the wicked are two praise sections (9:1-12 and 10:16-18) that focus on the Lord's kingship. David brings the central theme of these sections to expression with the words "the LORD reigns forever" (9:7) and "The LORD is king forever and ever!" (10:16). As king, the Lord is judge and warrior (Longman and Reid 1995:44). As king, the Lord is judge, "executing judgment from his throne" (9:7). Of the judge we also read: "You have judged in my favor" (9:4a), "You have judged with fairness" (9:4b), "He will judge the world with justice" (9:8), and "You will bring justice to the orphans and the oppressed" (10:18). As king, the Lord is warrior, whose "enemies retreated; they staggered and died when [he] appeared" (9:3). Of the warrior we also read: "You have rebuked the nations and destroyed the wicked" (9:5), and "the godless nations will vanish from the land" (10:16). It may seem at times that the king, judge, and warrior is standing far away and hidden when his afflicted people need him to act. But the truth is that "He does not ignore the cries of those who suffer" (9:12) but "Surely [he] will hear their cries and comfort them" (10:17).

There are times in our lives when it seems as if God is far off. God often seems distant, uninvolved, and unconcerned "in times of trouble" (9:9 and 10:1). Our personal anguish can become even more intense when, "in times of trouble," we look around at those who have no time for God and who even despise God, yet they seem to be succeeding in every way. Psalms 9–10 teaches us how to respond in such situations. At the center of our response is our willingness to honestly pour out our heart to God, expressing to him exactly how we feel about his apparent distance and the apparent injustice of life. Such lamenting is not the complaining of ancient Israel in the wilderness, because surrounding this complaint is the plea for God to act. We may plead with the Lord in times of trouble. In spite of appearances, the Lord does see our trouble and grief. In his own time he will "arise" to help the helpless. With this assurance we can surround our sorrow with songs of praise.

Praise the Lord, because he does reign, even during our times of trouble. Praise him, because he is the warrior who will defeat all of his and our enemies. Praise him, because he is the judge who will bring justice. He has already judged our sin when he punished his Son on the cross in our place. On that dark day he stood far away from the Son and hid from him. But the day of resurrection came—the day of great reversal. So we can joyfully thank the Lord with all our heart and tell of all the marvelous things he has done, assured that he will not ultimately ignore us but will listen to our cry and comfort us.

ENDNOTES

1. The psalm was originally an acrostic written in couplets as can be seen in 9:1-17 and 10:12-18. This acrostic is the most damaged of any acrostic poem in the MT. For the amount of textual corruption in biblical acrostics see Gaebelein 1990. The text of Ps 10 is quite difficult in the verses where the acrostic pattern is no longer evident. For the reversal of the letters Pe and Ayin, see Lam 2, 3, and 4.
2. Psalm 33 is the only other psalm in Book 1 with no title, but Ps 33 is clearly joined to 32 by the repetition of vocabulary at the end of 32 and the beginning of 33.

◆ J. Psalm 11

For the choir director: A psalm of David.

1 I trust in the LORD for protection.
So why do you say to me,
"Fly like a bird to the mountains
for safety!
2 The wicked are stringing their
bows
and fitting their arrows on the
bowstrings.
They shoot from the shadows
at those whose hearts are right.
3 The foundations of law and order
have collapsed.
What can the righteous do?"

4 But the LORD is in his holy Temple;
the LORD still rules from heaven.
He watches everyone closely,
examining every person on earth.
5 The LORD examines both the righteous
and the wicked.
He hates those who love violence.
6 He will rain down blazing coals and
burning sulfur on the wicked,
punishing them with scorching
winds.
7 For the righteous LORD loves justice.
The virtuous will see his face.

NOTES

11:1 ***So why do you say.*** The speakers may be well-intentioned friends or the psalmist's adversaries (see 3:2).

Fly like a bird to the mountains. The Hebrew surrounding *tsippor* [TH6833, ZH7606] (bird) is difficult but not impossible. The often-suggested emendation from, "Flee, bird, to *your* mountain" (*harkem tsippor*) to "flee to the mountain(s) *as* a bird" (*har kemo tsippor* [TH3644, ZH4017]) has a good bit of support in the versions and may be correct but is not necessary; *tsippor* can be taken as a vocative.

11:2 ***They shoot.*** For an illustration of archers shooting at birds, see Keel 1997:95.

those whose hearts are right. See 7:10 [11] for this same expression (*yishre-leb* [TH3477/3820, ZH3838/4213]).

11:3 ***The foundations of law and order have collapsed.*** This sentence is introduced by *ki* [TH3588, ZH3954] (for), which may be emphatic (Craigie 1983:131). The word translated "foundations of law and order" (*shathoth* [TH8357, ZH9268]) occurs only here with the sense "the bases of common life and social order" (Mays 1994:75); see Ezek 30:4 for the same picture with the same verb (*haras* [TH2040, ZH2238]) and a typical word for "foundations" (*yesod* [TH3247, ZH3572]).

What can the righteous do? The perfect tense in *mah-pa'al* [TH4100/6466, ZH4537/7188] is difficult, since a modal nuance ("can") is not a use of the perfect. An emendation to the imperfect ("What will the righteous do?"; BHS) is possible, or the perfect following the previous imperfect may be used for action that is certain in the future (see Brockelmann 1965:§41f). It seems best, however, to understand the perfect as a stylistic variant, an example of perfect/imperfect grammatical parallelism (Berlin 1985:35-36), so the NLT is on target with "can . . . do," since the perfect here is functioning as a modal imperfect. The idea communicated, at any rate, is hopelessness (Kraus 1988:203) and impotence.

11:4 ***his holy Temple . . . from heaven.*** Heb. *hekal qodesh* [TH1964/6944, ZH2121/7731] (holy Temple) occurs only three other times in the Psalter (5:7 [8]; 79:1; 138:2), and in each case the earthly Temple is in view, so Craigie (1983:133; see also Keel 1997:77) is correct in seeing the immanence ("holy Temple") and transcendence ("rules from heaven") of God articulated in this verse (contra VanGemeren 1991:133).[1] In *yhwh bashamayim kis'o* [TH3678/8064, ZH4058/9028] (lit., "the LORD—his throne is in heaven") we have a case of *casus pendens* as an emphatic construction (Muraoka 1985:95).

examining. Heb. *bakhan* [TH974, ZH1043] has in view testing by means of a smelting process (see Zech 13:9; for the related noun see Jer 6:27); see Keel 1997:183-186 for illustrations and a description of the ancient process; see also 26:2.

11:5 ***The LORD examines both the righteous and the wicked.*** This is a possible translation, but the word order in Hebrew makes this unlikely. To arrive at this translation "a transposition is indispensable" (Kraus 1988:201). Since 11:7 mentions "the righteous LORD" (*yhwh tsaddiq* [TH3068/6662, ZH3378/7404]), it is better to take *tsaddiq* in relation to *yhwh*, either as an attributive, "Yahweh the Just" (Dahood 1965:68), or as a predicate ("the LORD is righteous"). The *we* [TH2050.1, ZH2256] on *werasha'* [TH7563A, ZH8401] (and the wicked) would then be emphatic.[2]

11:6 ***He will rain down blazing coals.*** "Blazing coals" correctly presumes an emendation of *pakhim 'esh* [TH6341, ZH7062] (bird-traps fire) to *pakham 'esh* [TH6352, ZH7073] (coal of fire) or *pakhame 'esh* (coals of fire).

punishing them. The Heb. *menath kosam* [TH4521/3563, ZH4987/3926] means "portion of their cup." There is a "cup of salvation" (116:13) but also a "cup of wrath" (75:8 [9]; see also Isa 51:17, 22-23; Jer 25:15-38; Lam 4:21; Ezek 23:32-33; Hab 2:16).

11:7 ***his face.*** Heb. *panemo* [TH6440, ZH7156] is most naturally translated as "their face(s)," but this makes no sense. For the suffix as third-person masc. sg., see Delitzsch 1982:191. For the motif of the face of God, see 9:3 [4], 19 [20]; 10:11.

COMMENTARY

What do you do when the moral fabric of church or society is being torn apart before your very eyes? Psalm 11 provides key answers to this question. Central to the answer is the affirmation that the Lord is in sovereign control of all things. Surrounding this central affirmation are two balanced sections: (1) faith, not flight and (2) fight, not flight.[3]

The opening strophe (11:1-3) presents us with a seemingly hopeless situation: The "foundations of law and order have collapsed" (11:3a), and the wicked have the upper hand (11:2). When such moral chaos confronts us, we cry out with the psalmist, "What can the righteous do?" (11:3b). Some would counsel, "Fly like a bird to the mountains for safety" (11:1b). "We may not literally be tempted to flee, but we are tempted to seek refuge in sheltered enclaves—perhaps in the latest home-security system or in the comfort of congregations that convince us that things are not really as bad as they seem" (McCann 1996:722).

But such advice should be as unthinkable to us as it was to the psalmist who retorted, "So why do you say to me, 'Fly like a bird to the mountains for safety!'" (11:1b). Such flight is a failure of faith. Such flight is failure to take refuge in the Lord. David drives us to faith, not flight, to take refuge not in ourselves in any way but in the Lord (11:1a; see 2:12).

The central strophe (11:4a) shows why refuge in the Lord is the only reasonable response: The Lord is our immanent and transcendent king. "The LORD is in his holy Temple." He is present with his people (see Josh 1:5, 9). He is "always ready to help in times of trouble" (46:1). But it is equally true that "the LORD still rules from heaven" (11:4). The Lord who is near is also the transcendent king who is enthroned in heaven. "God sits above the circle of the earth. The people below seem like grasshoppers to him!" (Isa 40:22). This immanence and transcendence meet in Jesus Christ, who is the dwelling of God among us (John 1:14), as well as the King of kings (Rev 19:16). Faith in this immanent and transcendent king is warranted, especially in times of moral decay.

The closing strophe (11:4b-7) calls us to fight, not flight. When immorality reigns, we are called to be righteous, "For the righteous LORD loves justice" (11:7). Just and right action is our calling in a world where there seems to be no justice at all. And justice will prevail, because the Lord "watches everyone closely," and "the LORD examines . . . the wicked" and hates their violence (11:4-5). The wicked will not endure the smelting furnace of God's discerning fire (see 1:6), so they will experience the blazing coals, burning sulfur, and scorching winds of his just judgment. Though the virtuous ones are the targets of the wicked, the virtuous will see the face of God (11:7). Seeing the face of him who sees all from his throne in heaven and who is yet near to us provides all the courage necessary for righteous action in a chaotic world.

This is my Father's world,
O let me ne'er forget
That though the wrong seems oft so strong,
God is the ruler yet.
This is my Father's world:
The battle is not done;
Jesus who died shall be satisfied,
And earth and heav'n be one. (*Maltbie Davenport Babcock*)

ENDNOTES

1. The other occurrences of *hekal qodesh* are Jonah 2:4, 7 [5, 8]; Mic 1:2; Hab 2:20.
2. With regard to emphatic Waw, Pope (1953:98) says, "The appearance of the *waw* in an unexpected position has the effect of calling special attention to the word to which it is attached and this adds emphasis to the whole sentence." See also Wernberg-Möller 1958 and Waltke and O'Connor 1990:§39.2.1b. Support for emphatic Waw in 11:5 is found in the other emphatic constructions in 11:3-4.
3. Balance is found in the repetitions of *nepesh* [TH5315, ZH5883] (11:1, 5), *rasha'* [TH7563A, ZH8401] (11:2, 5-6), *yashar* [TH3477A, ZH3838] (11:2 and 11:7), and *tsaddiq* [TH6662, ZH7404] (11:3, 5, 7). Both McCann 1996:721 and VanGemeren 1991:131 read Ps 11 as a chiasm with the Lord's kingship at the center, but their strophic divisions are different from mine.

◆ K. Psalm 12

*For the choir director: A psalm of David, to be accompanied by an eight-stringed instrument.**

1 Help, O LORD, for the godly are fast disappearing!
The faithful have vanished from the earth!
2 Neighbors lie to each other,
speaking with flattering lips and deceitful hearts.
3 May the LORD cut off their flattering lips
and silence their boastful tongues.
4 They say, "We will lie to our hearts' content.
Our lips are our own—who can stop us?"

5 The LORD replies, "I have seen violence done to the helpless,
and I have heard the groans of the poor.
Now I will rise up to rescue them,
as they have longed for me to do."
6 The LORD's promises are pure,
like silver refined in a furnace,
purified seven times over.
7 Therefore, LORD, we know you will protect the oppressed,
preserving them forever from this lying generation,
8 even though the wicked strut about,
and evil is praised throughout the land.

12:TITLE Hebrew *according to the sheminith.*

NOTES

12:TITLE *eight-stringed instrument.* This is a probable but uncertain interpretation of Heb. *sheminith* [TH8067, ZH9030].

12:1 *are fast disappearing.* Since the verb is perfect, a present perfect in English makes the point more graphic: "the godly have disappeared!"

from the earth! Lit., "from among the sons of man." "The sons of man" also occurs at the end of the last line of the psalm in the phrase, "among the sons of man," where it is translated "throughout the land" (12:8). The two occurrences form an *inclusio* around the entire psalm and focus our attention on the whole human race. Psalm 12 thus shares the same focus as Ps 11 (see 11:4).

12:2 *deceitful hearts.* The Heb. *leb waleb* [TH3820, ZH4213] (lit., "heart and heart") occurs only here and in 1 Chr 12:33 [34], where it is used in an opposite sense with the negative adverb and refers to "complete loyalty."

12:4 ***We will lie to our hearts' content.*** The Heb. *lileshonenu nagbir* [TH3956/1396, ZH4383/1504] is difficult. The LXX presumes *leshonenu* (our lips), and the Targum presumes *bileshonenu* [TH871.2, ZH928] (with our lips). The sense is "with our speech we can do anything."

Our lips are our own. Perhaps this is a perversion of a confession like "May the LORD our God be with us" (see 1 Kgs 8:57 and Mays 1994:77).

12:5 ***Now I will rise up to rescue them.*** In regard to the adverb "now" Calvin (1979:175) says,

> *There is also great emphasis in the adverb* now, *by which God intimates that, although our safety is in his hand, and, therefore, in secure keeping, yet he does not immediately grant deliverance from affliction; for his words imply that he had hitherto been, as it were, lying still and asleep, until he was awakened by the calamities and the cries of his people. When, therefore, the injuries, the extortions, and the devastations of our enemies leave us nothing but tears and groans, let us remember that now the time is at hand when God intends to rise up to execute judgment. This doctrine should also serve to produce in us patience, and prevent us from taking it ill, that we are reckoned among the number of the poor and afflicted, whose cause God promises to take into his own hand.*

have longed for. The Heb. *yapiakh lo* [TH6315A, ZH7032], usually translated along the lines of the NLT (see BDB 806), is difficult. See KBL 917 for a summary of options.

12:6 ***refined in a furnace, purified seven times over.*** The NLT leaves *la'arets* [TH776, ZH824] (to the earth) untranslated. It is perhaps best to emend *la'arets* to *kharuts* [TH2742, ZH3021] (gold), presuming a dittography of Lamedh from the previous word. The result would be "gold purified seven times over," which would provide a nice parallel to the previous colon (Craigie 1983:136-137). "Seven times over" expresses perfect purity.

12:8 ***the wicked.*** Heb. *rasha'* [TH7563A, ZH8401], as in 11:2, 5, 6.

COMMENTARY

Psalm 12 is a plea for help in view of the abysmal state of the human race: The psalm begins and ends on the note that the faithful have vanished "from the earth" (12:1) and that evil is praised "throughout the land" (12:8). The psalm is chiastically arranged.[1] Verses 1 and 7-8 form the outer frame: (1) Both refer to the entire earth, (2) both address the Lord in the second person, and (3) both bemoan the fact that the godly are nowhere to be found while the wicked are ubiquitous. The inner frame (12:2-4 and 6) is a third-person address and focuses on the valuation of speech—that of the wicked (12:2-4) and that of the Lord (12:6). The center (12:5) is a first-person address, where the Lord himself speaks.

A radical change takes place between the beginning of the psalm (12:1) with its plea for help in view of the disappearance of the godly from the human race and the end of the psalm (12:7-8) with its confidence that the Lord will help in spite of the pervasiveness of evil throughout the human race. David uses hyperbole in 12:1 to underscore the abysmal state of the race: "The godly are fast disappearing! The faithful have vanished." This sentiment flows directly out of the previous psalm, which bemoans the collapse of "law and order" (11:3) throughout human society (see 11:4). Part of the reason for this collapse is the rising tide of evil that has almost completely swept away godly and faithful people. Yet, in spite of the overwhelming odds, David is confident that the Lord will protect and preserve the godly.

What generated such confidence? Divine speech! The Lord's promise to help! The Lord immediately and explicitly answered the cry for help with a promise, "Now I will rise up to rescue them" (12:5). Though the helpless and the poor do not have the power to face their foe, they have the promise of the Divine Warrior—he will rescue them from their oppressors.

But is the Lord's promise reliable? Can the godly count on it? After all, not all speech is true and trustworthy. Human speech is all too often full of lies, flattery, hypocrisy, and arrogance: "Our lips are our own—who can stop us?" (12:4). Is divine speech any different? Yes! "The LORD's promises are pure, like silver refined in a furnace, purified seven times over" (12:6). In the previous psalm the Lord put people in the smelting furnace to test their integrity (11:4-5) and found much impurity that resulted in his just judgment. In Psalm 12 David puts the Lord's promises in the smelting furnace and finds a perfect purity that results in total confidence.

As we all know, it is one thing to confess that the Lord's promises are true in times of prosperity, but it is quite another to believe this when times are tough. So Calvin (1979:177) remarks, "It is, therefore, highly necessary for us to cut off the occasion of our distrust; and whenever any doubt respecting the faithfulness of God's promises steals in upon us, we ought immediately to lift up against it this shield, that the words of the Lord are pure." We have an even greater assurance than David did as to the fact that the word of the Lord is pure, for we know that the Word is pure. John tells us that "the Word became human and made his home among us. He was full of unfailing love and faithfulness" (John 1:14). And when he was put in the smelting furnace of obedience to the point of death on a cross, he was found to be without alloy (Phil 2:8; Heb 4:15).

In our own day it seems as if the godly have disappeared and the faithful have vanished. But "even though the wicked strut about, and evil is praised throughout the land" (12:8), we too can have confidence that the Lord will protect and preserve us. He has promised to rise up and rescue us, and his word is as reliable as his Word. We have confidence in his promise, because we have seen it fulfilled in part already. He has already risen up once "to take away the sins of many people," and he will rise up again "to bring salvation to all who are eagerly waiting for him" (Heb 9:28). So we wait, confidently trusting his pure promise.

ENDNOTES

1. For alternative chiastic arrangements see Brachter and Reyburn 1991:115 (who is followed by McCann 1996:724 and VanGemeren 1991:135). Kraus (1988:210) recognizes that 12:5 [6] is the center of the psalm, though he does not arrange the text chiastically.

◆ L. Psalm 13

For the choir director: A psalm of David.

[1] O LORD, how long will you forget me?
Forever?
How long will you look the other
way?

[2] How long must I struggle with
anguish in my soul,
with sorrow in my heart
every day?

How long will my enemy have the
upper hand?

[3]Turn and answer me, O LORD my God!
Restore the sparkle to my eyes, or
I will die.

[4]Don't let my enemies gloat, saying,
"We have defeated him!"

Don't let them rejoice at my
downfall.

[5]But I trust in your unfailing love.
I will rejoice because you have
rescued me.

[6]I will sing to the LORD
because he is good to me.

NOTES

13:1 *Forever?* Rather than being an independent question, the Heb. *netsakh* [TH5331, ZH5905] (forever) is an adverbial accusative intensifying the verb "forget," the sense being, "O LORD, how long will you go on and on forgetting us?" For similar uses of "forever," see 74:1 [2]; 79:5; 89:46 [47].

look the other way. Lit., "hide your face," an idiom connoting disdain, abandonment, and rejection.

13:2 *anguish.* The Heb. *'etsah* [TH6098, ZH6783] usually means "advice" or "plan." Here it must mean something like the NLT's "anguish" (TLOT 2.558). DCH (2.427) glosses it with "grief," based on its use in Sir 30:21, where it is parallel to *daon* (sadness).

have the upper hand? Lit., "How long will my enemy *rise* over me?" God's words in 12:5 [6], "Now I will rise up to rescue them," highlight the psalmist's perplexity with this situation in which an enemy has arisen and the psalmist does not yet see God as acting on his word in 12:5 and rising up to rescue him. McCann (1996:726) says, "In short, it seems to the psalmist that God has been displaced. The place to which one looks for help is occupied by the enemy. This is the worst possible news."

13:3 *Turn.* Lit., "Look," a request that answers to the question, "How long will you look the other way?" (13:1).

Restore the sparkle to my eyes. Lit., "Brighten my eyes," an idiom for the renewal of one's vigor. Out of energy, Jonathan ate some honey, then "he felt refreshed" (lit., "his eyes brightened"; cf. 1 Sam 14:27 mg, NLT).

13:5 *I will rejoice.* "I" translates *libbi* [TH3820, ZH4213] (my heart); the verb is a jussive. Sometimes the form of the jussive is impossible to explain (Joüon and Muraoka 1991:§114*l*), which may be the case here. Taken at face value, however, the language (volitive) expresses the will of the speaker; the jussive with "my heart" as the subject would be equivalent to a cohortative, and the sense would be that of resolve (Joüon and Muraoka 1991:§114c; Waltke and O'Connor 1990:§34.5.1a): "I *will* rejoice."

13:6 *I will sing.* The verb is a cohortative that expresses the speaker's resolve (Joüon and Muraoka 1991:§114c; Waltke and O'Connor 1990:§34.5.1a): "I *will* sing."

because he is good to me. The verb is in the perfect tense, which could be: (1) a present perfect (Waltke and O'Connor 1990:§30.5.2b), as in the NLT, (2) a prophetic/rhetorical perfect (Waltke and O'Connor 1990:§30.5.1e), "because he will most certainly be good to me," or (3) a future perfect (Waltke and O'Connor 1990:§30.5.2b), "when he will have been good to me." Is David asking for a joyful, singing heart because of God's goodness in the past or his goodness in the future? Certainty is not possible, but two reasons suggest the verb is a rhetorical perfect. First, Ps 142 is a similar lament that ends with the same colon as Ps 13, except that the verb is an imperfect, "because he will be good to me." Second, if the verb is a rhetorical perfect for certain action in the future, then a clear structure is evident:

Confidence: I trust
Resolve: I *will* rejoice
Resolve: I *will* sing
Confidence: He will be good to me.

COMMENTARY

The apostle Paul once said, "Our hearts ache, but we always have joy" (2 Cor 6:10). Agony and ecstasy at the same time! Is this true of you? Or do you typically get stuck in the mire of agony, so that the only prayer you can offer is, "O LORD, how long?" while the words "I will rejoice" strike not a single chord in your heart? Or in the name of "rejoicing always," do you at times live in denial of your misery? In the six brief verses of Psalm 13, David brings together the depths of human agony and the heights of ecstasy to show us the way to ache with joy.

David begins with a brutally honest cry of distress. This cry is built around a fourfold repetition of "how long?" that "reflects an ascent on a scale of intensity, the note of urgency pitched slightly higher with each repetition" (Alter 1985:65). "The questions do not seek information; they present distress" (Mays 1994:78). The distress is all-encompassing, having a theological, psychological, and sociological dimension (Westermann 1989:70).

The agony finds its ultimate source not in the self nor in the enemy but in God. The most poignant problem is that God seems (perhaps inadvertently) to have permanently forgotten David, and worse yet, has apparently with intention looked the other way while David suffered. David does not hide these thoughts and feelings, as if they were inappropriate in prayer, but begins his journey to ecstasy by expressing his sorrow.

> *Here [David] speaks not so much according to the opinion of others, as according to the feeling of his own mind, when he complains of being neglected by God. . . . When we are for a long time weighed down by calamities, and when we do not perceive any sign of divine aid, this thought unavoidably forces itself upon us, that God has forgotten us. . . . Thus, it seemed to David, so far as could be judged from beholding the actual state of his affairs, that he was forsaken of God. (Calvin 1979:181-182)*

But David's theological problem was at the same time a deeply personal problem: He had been experiencing anguish in his soul and sorrow in his heart not for a passing moment but for a protracted period of time. He was "for a long time weighed down by calamities." David did not describe the nature of his calamities, but he did point us to the immediate cause: his "enemy" (13:2). It is not important to know who the enemy was. What David was concerned to tell us is that the enemy had "the upper hand," which caused David personal pain because it created theological tension with the promises he had received as the Lord's anointed one (Ps 2).

In these two remarkable verses we discover that the path to ecstasy begins at the gate of honesty. "The one who laments his suffering to God does not remain in his lament. But before this point can be reached, the suffering must express itself, it must be put into words" (Westermann 1989:69).

The cry of distress lays the foundation for the plea for help. Three imperatives are bolstered by three reasons. The first and third imperatives, "turn" (lit., "look") and "restore the sparkle," are "obviously a prayer for the reversal of that awful hiding of the divine face invoked in line 1" (Alter 1985:65-66). The middle imperative, "answer," does more than seek an informational response to the questions raised earlier, because to "answer" is to cease to "look the other way" (69:17 [18]; 143:7). "The petitions seek the revival of life, appealing to God alone, who is the giver and protector of life. Without the salvation of the Lord there will be death" (Mays 1994:79).

So, the first reason given to move God to act is, "or I will die." The death of David leads immediately to the second and third reasons: The enemy would not simply have the upper hand for the moment but would ultimately triumph (Alter 1985:66) and would experience the joy reserved for those who serve the Lord (e.g., 2:11; 9:14 [15]; 14:7; 16:9), a consideration in and of itself that leads to anguish. The distress is a matter of life and death.

Just when "the white-hot point . . . of desperate need" comes to expression, David "swings away sharply into a concluding affirmation of faith, introduced by the strongly contrastive 'but I'" (Alter 1985:66). Ecstasy arrives! Confidence and firm resolve come alongside the cry. In spite of the enemy's upper hand, in spite of the anguish of soul, even in spite of the absence of God himself, David trusts—trusts that the unfailing love of God will eventually move God to be good to him.

> *The eyes of [David's] mind, guided by the light of faith, penetrated even to the grace of God, although it was hidden in darkness. When he saw not a single ray of good hope to whatever quarter he turned, so far as human reason could judge, constrained by grief, he cries out that God did not regard him . . . he gives evidence that faith enabled him to rise higher, and to conclude, contrary to the judgment of the flesh, that his welfare was secure in the hand of God. (Calvin 1979:182)*

In light of this confidence, David resolves to rejoice in and sing to the Lord, who will one day rescue him.

> *David, it is true, had not yet obtained what he earnestly desired, but being fully convinced that God was already at hand to grant him deliverance, he pledges himself to give thanks to him for it. And surely it becomes us to engage in prayer in such a frame of mind as at the same time to be ready to sing the praises of God; a thing which is impossible, unless we are fully persuaded that our prayers will not be ineffectual. We may not be wholly free from sorrow, but it is nevertheless necessary that this cheerfulness of faith rise above it, and put into our mouth a song on account of the joy which is reserved for us in the future, although not as yet experienced by us; just as we see David here preparing himself to celebrate in songs the grace of God, before he perceives the issue of his troubles. (Calvin 1979:187)*

Agony and ecstasy, at the same time! Is this true of you? Yes! For "we are simultaneously people of the cross and people of the resurrection" (McCann 1996:728). In this world you will have trouble (John 16:33); there will be crosses to bear (Matt 16:24). But "you have been raised to new life with Christ" and "your real life is hidden with Christ in God" (Col 3:1, 3). You also have the Holy Spirit "as the first installment that guarantees everything [God] has promised us" (2 Cor 1:22). "The agony and the ecstasy belong together as the secret of our identity" (Mays 1980:282). Luther said it well when he said that Psalm 13 speaks of the "state in which Hope despairs, and yet Despair hopes at the same time. . . . There is no one who understands who has not tasted it" (quoted in Perowne 1966:1.180). The apostle Paul understood Psalm 13: "Our hearts ache, but we always have joy" (2 Cor 6:10).

◆ M. Psalm 14

For the choir director: A psalm of David.

1 Only fools say in their hearts,
"There is no God."
They are corrupt, and their actions
are evil;
not one of them does good!

2 The LORD looks down from heaven
on the entire human race;
he looks to see if anyone is truly
wise,
if anyone seeks God.
3 But no, all have turned away;
all have become corrupt.*
No one does good,
not a single one!

4 Will those who do evil never learn?
They eat up my people like bread
and wouldn't think of praying to
the LORD.
5 Terror will grip them,
for God is with those who obey him.
6 The wicked frustrate the plans of the
oppressed,
but the LORD will protect his people.

7 Who will come from Mount Zion to
rescue Israel?
When the LORD restores his people,
Jacob will shout with joy, and Israel
will rejoice.

14:3 Greek version reads *have become useless*. Compare Rom 3:12.

NOTES

14:1 *fools say . . . "There is no God."* The Heb. *nabal* [TH5036A, ZH5572] is one of several terms for a "fool."[1] The word *nabal* is a rough synonym of *rasha'* [TH7563A, ZH8401] (wicked); both say, "There is no God" (10:4; TLOT 2.712).

They are corrupt. By using the verb *hishkhithu* [TH7843, ZH8845], the psalmist is probably alluding to the use of this verb in the flood story (Gen 6:12) and the story of the golden calf (Exod 32:7) to teach that the history of humanity and of Israel reveals the depravity of the race (McCann 1996:730).

14:2 *The LORD looks down . . . on the entire human race.* Previous psalms share this focus on the "entire human race" (*bene-'adam* [TH1121/120, ZH1201/132]; see 12:1 [2], 8 [9]; cf. 11:4). The Lord is the judge of the whole earth (Kraus 1988:222).

if anyone is truly wise. The Hiphil of *sakal* [TH7919, ZH8505] is used in 2:10 where it is defined in terms of submissive service to the Lord (2:11-12; McCann 1996:730).

14:3. At this point in the psalm the LXX has a number of lines not found in the MT. They seem to be an interpolation from Rom 3:10-18. Paul evidently put together a pastiche, a literary piece created by combining material from different sources of OT texts on human depravity. This pastiche was at some point included in the LXX as a marginal reference and then translated into Hebrew and incorporated into a minor textual tradition, as it is found in two manuscripts. (This common interpretation of the textual evidence apparently goes back to Briggs 1906:1.104.)

14:4-6 These verses are fraught with problems. An interpretation different from that of the NLT will be adopted here at several points, based on Irvine 1995. The Heb. *halo'*

[TH1886.2/3808, ZH2022/4202] "is sometimes used with a certain exclamatory nuance" (see Joüon and Muraoka 1991:§161c). The Heb. *yada'* [TH3045, ZH3359] can mean "consider/ reason" (see Isa 9:9 [8]; 44:19 and BDB 394, which cites Deut 4:39; 8:5; Judg 18:14; 2 Sam 24:13; 1 Kgs 20:7, 22).[2] The verb *yada'* is also used as a parallel term with the Piel of *khashab* [TH2803, ZH3108] (think) in 144:3. So the first statement can be rendered, "All those who do evil really think . . ."

14:4 *wouldn't think of praying to the* L*ORD*. If, as suggested by Irvine (1995:404), the verb is from *qara'* II [TH7122, ZH7925] (encounter), the sense is "they do not encounter the LORD." "Encounter" would have judgment in view, as in Amos 4:12. Verse 4 would then be translated, "Do all those who do evil, who consume my people as one consumes bread, really think they do not encounter the LORD?" Yes, they do, in keeping with their assertion that, "There is no God"!

14:6 *The wicked frustrate the plans of the oppressed, but.* The Hebrew text of 14:6 is quite difficult. After articulating his own solution to the problems, Dahood (1965:1.82) says, "This solution will be dispensed with when a better solution is proposed for this enigmatic verse." The Hebrew does speak of "frustrating the plans of," but this idea is usually expressed with the verb *parar* [TH6565, ZH7296] (2 Sam 17:14; Ezra 4:5; Neh 4:15 [9]), not *bosh* [TH954, ZH1017], the verb used here. The Heb. *ki* [TH3588, ZH3954] can mean "but," but only after a negative clause (HALOT 2.470 [3.]; BDB 474 [e.]; Joüon and Muraoka 1991:§172c). Given the parallel structure of 14:5-6 (verb with evildoers as the subject followed by a *ki* clause), we expect 14:6a to be a judgment against the evildoers with 14:6b providing the reason. The Heb. *tabishu* [TH954, ZH1017] can readily be taken as, "You will be ashamed" (HALOT 1.117; DCH 2.131). (The Hiphil may express the action of bringing shame on one's self rather than the state of being ashamed; TDOT 2.59-60.) If we understand *'atsath-'ani* [TH6098/6041, ZH6783/6714] (plan of the oppressed) "as a specification of circumstances in which the evildoers shall meet disaster" (Irvine 1995:465 n. 14), the sense is, "In your plan against the poor,[3] you will be ashamed, for the LORD will protect his people."

14:7 *rescue.* Heb. *yeshu'ah* [TH3444, ZH3802], as at the end of the previous psalm (13:5 [6]).

when the* L*ORD restores his people. "Restores his people" is used at times in reference to the return from captivity, but the meaning is broader: "Bring about a restoration" (NIDOTTE 4.58; see 53:6; 85:1; 126:1, 4); see TLOT 3.1314-1315 for a summary of opinions on this expression.

Jacob will shout. The verb is a jussive, as at the end of the previous psalm (13:5 [6]), so the sense is "Let Jacob shout." The verb that follows would also be jussive in meaning: "Let Israel rejoice."

COMMENTARY

The focus is on the fool in Psalm 14, which can be divided into two roughly equal halves: 14:1-3 (the fool's character) and 14:4-7 (the fool's fate). The first half is marked out by the fourfold repetition of *'ayin* [TH369, ZH401] ("there is not"; 2 times in 14:1 and 2 times in 14:3), while the second half is marked out by the *inclusio* formed by the repetition of *'am* [TH5971A, ZH6639] (people) in 14:4 and 14:7.

The first half of the psalm is given over to a description of the "fool" (*nabal* [TH5036A, ZH5572]). The foundational doctrine of the fool is, "There is no God" (14:1). This is not a confession of theoretical atheism, but of practical atheism. "There is no God" means there is no one to whom the fool is ultimately accountable, as is clear from 10:4, 13 (Mays 1994:81-82; McCann 1996:730). "They speak like that not in order to deny God but in order to evade His judgment and His claims upon them. . . . It is a practical atheism, as the sinner practices it; not a theoretical atheism" (Köhler 1957:19).

"Foolishness is not a lack of knowledge in general but a failure to acknowledge God in trustful obedience" (McCann 1996:729). So the confession, "There is no God," is amplified in 14:1 in terms of disobedience (Kraus 1988:221): "They are corrupt, and their actions are evil." David's assessment of the fool is summarized in the words "Not one of them does good."

The divine assessment of the fool is given in 14:2-3. As Calvin (1979:192) put it: "God himself is here introduced as speaking on the subject of human depravity, and this renders the discourse of David more emphatic than if he had pronounced the sentence in his own person." At times the Lord looks down from heaven to bless (102:19 [20]; Deut 26:15; Lam 3:50), and at times, to judge (Exod 14:24). But here he looks down to ascertain the state of affairs, so that he might know which course of action to take. He looks to find out if there are any who seek him and finds that none do. "*All* have turned away; *all* have become corrupt" (14:3). God's final word confirms David's initial assessment with an emphatic addition: "No one does good, *not a single one!*"

As we turn to the second half of the psalm, a certain tension arises at this point from two directions: (1) having affirmed that all are in the category of the corrupt, David goes on to speak of God's people who obey him, and (2) there are those who do "seek" God (9:10; 22:27; 24:6; 34:4; 69:33; 77:3; 78:34; 105:4; 119:2, 10). Aware of this tension, Calvin (1979:195) says,

> *It is, therefore, to be observed, that when David places himself and the small remnant of the godly on one side, and puts on the other the body of the people, in general, this implies that there is a manifest difference between the children of God who are created anew by his Spirit, and all the posterity of Adam, in whom corruption and depravity exercise dominion. Whence it follows, that all of us, when we are born, bring with us from our mother's womb this folly and filthiness manifested in the whole life, which David here describes, and that we continue such until God make us new creatures by his mysterious grace.*

In a similar manner Mays (1994:83) says,

> *Who would claim exemption from the psalmist's "all" by pretending always to live as if life were accountable to the* LORD*? Yet precisely for those who know they have come short, the* LORD *opens up by grace the way of taking refuge in the* LORD *and seeking the* LORD*. . . . Paul . . . maintained the tension: "All have sinned, but those who believe in Jesus Christ are justified by grace."*

But what fate awaits those who are not part of the people of God, but "who think no more of devouring God's people than they do of eating bread" (Brachter and Reyburn 1991:130) and who have persuaded themselves that they are not accountable to anyone, not even God, for such actions? The second half of the psalm answers this question.

They will be judged. Their judgment will bring terror and shame to them because of their plans against the poor. This is certain because the Lord is always present as a refuge for his people. The promise of 2:12 can be relied upon, "But what joy for all who take refuge in him!"

David concludes the psalm with a prayer that salvation would come from Zion for all Israel and that all Israel would be able to shout for joy when the Lord would restore them. He prays that God would reverse the situation of his people: Though the people are being devoured at present, the people will be shouting for joy in the future.

Today, fools still think there is no ultimate authority to which they are accountable. But there is. Practical atheism often leads to moral corruption and violence in practice. But there is a better way. If "foolishness is . . . a failure to acknowledge God in trustful obedience" (McCann 1996:729), then wisdom is the sincere acknowledgment of God in trustful obedience. The Lord Jesus Christ has shown us this better way, as he has become the wisdom of God for us (1 Cor 1:30). Christ lived in constant submission to the Father's authority and consequently lived a life without a trace of moral corruption. Rather than devouring God's people, he was devoured in our place that we might be restored. Having experienced restoration in part, we can now live not as fools but as wise people, acknowledging the Lord's authority with trustful obedience, even as we wait for the fullness of our restoration.

ENDNOTES

1. See Donald (1963) for the semantic domain of "fool"; see also Bennett (1975:16) and Kidner (1964:39-41) for brief summaries of the related terms.
2. The occurrences in Deuteronomy are used with "in your heart," as in the expression "say in your heart," meaning "think."
3. The Heb. *'etsah* [TH6098, ZH6783] (plan) is used in the construct 57 times in the MT, mostly with a subject genitive. There are a number of uses with an object genitive (119:24; Isa 40:13; 46:11; 47:13), though none with the precise sense "plan against."

◆ N. Psalm 15

A psalm of David.

1 Who may worship in your sanctuary,
LORD?
Who may enter your presence on
your holy hill?
2 Those who lead blameless lives and
do what is right,
speaking the truth from sincere
hearts.
3 Those who refuse to gossip
or harm their neighbors
or speak evil of their friends.
4 Those who despise flagrant
sinners,
and honor the faithful followers
of the LORD,
and keep their promises even when
it hurts.
5 Those who lend money without
charging interest,
and who cannot be bribed to lie
about the innocent.
Such people will stand firm forever.

NOTES

15:1 ***worship in your sanctuary.*** Lit., "sojourn in your tent." The verb *gur* [TH1481, ZH1591] carries the idea of being a resident alien or sojourner (see 61:4 [5] for another use of this verb in connection with the sanctuary). The original "tent" in view would have been the special tent that David had constructed for the Ark of the Covenant (see 2 Sam 6:17); the language would have been applied at a later date to the Temple built by Solomon.

enter your presence. Lit., "dwell in" (*shakan* [TH7931, ZH8905]; see 65:4 [5] for the use of this verb in connection with the sanctuary). The verb *yashab* [TH3427, ZH3782] (dwell) is used elsewhere for "dwelling" in God's presence (see 27:4; 84:4 [5]; 91:1 in light of 61:4 [5]; 101:6-8). Living in God's presence is elsewhere associated with safety (see 27:4-6; 61:1-5; 91:1-8; 101:6-8) and joy (27:4-6; 65:1-4; 84:1-4).

holy hill. The holy hill is the place where the king was anointed (2:6) and the place from where the Lord answered prayer (3:4). The "holy Temple" (11:4) was located on the holy hill.

15:2 ***lead blameless lives.*** This exact expression in Hebrew occurs three other times (84:11 [12]; 101:6; Prov 28:18). Men like Noah, Job, and David are examples of such "blamelessness" (see Gen 6:9; 1 Kgs 9:4; Job 1:1, 8; 2:3). "Blameless" refers not to perfection but to integrity, to "an attitude of the heart that is desirous of pleasing God" (VanGemeren 1991:150).

do. The Qal participle here translated "do" is used 18 times in the Psalter.[1] Sixteen of those occurrences refer to those "who do evil," as already encountered in 5:5 [6], 6:8 [9], and 14:4. One occurrence refers to God (74:12). Psalm 15:2 is the only use in reference to the righteous.

speaking the truth. The Qal participle here translated "speak" is used only 8 times in the Psalter. Seven times it is used for sinners (5:6 [7]; 15:2; 28:3; 31:18 [19]; 58:3 [4]; 63:11 [12]; 101:7; 109:20). Psalm 15:2 is the only use in reference to the righteous. Speaking the truth from a sincere heart contrasts with the insincere heart of 12:2 [3] (Craigie 1983:149). In 28:3, "those who do evil" also "speak friendly words to their neighbors while planning evil in their hearts." For those who speak lies being barred from the presence of God, see 101:7.

15:4 ***Keep their promises even when it hurts.*** The Heb. *nishba' lehara'* [TH7650/7489, ZH8678/8317] is most naturally translated "swears to do evil," but this cannot be correct (VanGemeren 1991:152). Craigie (1983:148) follows Dahood (1965:84) in taking the *le* [TH3807.1, ZH4200] as separative ("swears off doing evil"), but admits that "the form remains curious and the sense of the passage is uncertain."[2] Kraus (1988:226) is probably right in saying that "swears to one's own harm" (KJV, NASB, NIV, NLT) is not possible, but his own proposal of inserting a "not" before "swears" is not satisfactory. The best solution in my estimation is to follow the LXX, which reads the Hebrew consonants *lhr'* as *leharea'* [TH7453, ZH8276] (to the neighbor).[3] The "neighbor" has already been mentioned in 15:3 as the object of negative speech. In 15:4 the neighbor would be the receiver of positive speech, an oath. At any rate, the general point is clear enough—righteous people keep their word.

15:5 ***interest.*** The sense of *neshek* [TH5392, ZH5968] is probably usury—excessive interest (so Calvin 1979:212-214; Kraus 1988:230; VanGemeren 1991:152). In the ancient Near East interest up to 50 percent was charged at times (see Kraus 1988:230). Such interest was contrary to the intended function of the loan in view in the OT, viz., to aid those in financial distress. That business loans are in view is doubtful.

COMMENTARY

Psalm 15 is a wisdom poem that was based on an entrance liturgy (Craigie 1983:150; McCann 1996:732). This psalm is "a poem for instructional purposes to teach the congregation about the character of its relation to the Lord" (Mays 1994:85).

A threefold movement shapes the poem. Verse 1 invites us to contemplate whether our character matches that of those who live in the presence of God. Verses 2-5a describe that character. Verse 5b issues a wonderful promise to people of such character who live with God.

The invitation to contemplation uses striking language: not that of entering the sanctuary for a set period of worship, but that of residing in the sanctuary. While entrance into the sanctuary for worship is in view, the psalm has a broader purpose. Since laypeople did not live in the sanctuary, the language of dwelling in the sanctuary must contain a metaphorical dimension. "As a wisdom psalm its purpose is to guide God's people into a life of holiness, justice, and righteousness so that they may live in the presence of God, wherever they may reside" (VanGemeren 1991:149).

The two Hebrew verbs in 15:1 are rough synonyms "and may be interpreted metaphorically for communion with God" (VanGemeren 1991:148). There is probably some movement, however, from the first verb to the second. The first verb, being the language of the resident alien, may indicate that "those who enter the presence of God are like resident aliens; because they have no inherent right to be there, the privilege must be granted" (Mays 1994:84; see also McCann 1996:733), while the second verb has a more permanent nuance (see note on 15:1). The questions raised are, "Do you conduct your life in accordance with the covenant of Yahweh? Is Yahweh the Lord of your every day life?" (Kraus 1988:231).

The inner logic of 15:2-5a has been explained in a variety of ways (see McCann 1996:732-733).While none of the proposed schemas are entirely satisfactory, several general observations are valid. There is movement from the general to the specific between 15:2 with its participles and 15:3-5a with its finite verbs (Kraus 1988:228; Mays 1994:84). Verses 3-5a move from negative to positive to negative (Brachter and Reyburn 1991:133), stressing our need for active goodness and the absence of evil (Craigie 1983:151). The closing of the section is signaled by the shift from tricola in 15:2-4 to a bicolon in 15:5a.

"Those who lead blameless lives" stand in sharp contrast to the wicked in the previous psalms. Whereas the wicked are those "who do evil," those who live in communion with God "do righteousness." And whereas the wicked tell lies and use their mouths for evil, having insincere hearts (12:2), those who live in communion with God speak "the truth from sincere hearts."

The avoidance of evil speech is the focus in 15:3. Trapped between "gossip" and "speak evil," the "harm" probably means harmful speech.[4] Communion with the God of truth means avoiding all misuse of speech. Living with God means being like God, despising the wrong, honoring the right, and always keeping your promise. Verse 5 teaches that your attachment to money is a window to your soul. The godly do not greedily take advantage of others, whether through excessive interest, bribery, or any other means.

The psalm concludes with a promise: "Such people will stand firm forever." But are there any "such people"? Not according to the previous psalm! "The psalm, then, transcends the actual performance of the lives of those who come to the place of the Presence" (Mays 1994:86). All of us must admit that we fall short of this standard—all of us but one, of course.

> *When Psalm 15 states that only the* po'el tsedeq [TH6466/6664, ZH7188/7406] *(one doing right[eousness]) has access to the sanctuary of God, and when the "marks" of the* tsedeq, *as of a prototype, are portrayed as so supraindividual and exemplary, then we are to take note immediately that Christ is the fulfillment: He is "made our righteousness" by God (1 Cor. 1:30). In him the supraindividual and exemplary prototype of the OT* tsedeq *emerges. (Kraus 1988:232)*

By grace through faith in Jesus Christ the Son, those who fall short are viewed by God the Father as "such people." And "such people" actually become doers of the word (Jas 1:22-27; see Kraus 1988:232). Not perfectly, but truly. Not perfectly, but more and more.

The promise to such people is not one of security from all trouble, as is clear from the experiences of the psalmist in the previous psalms. The promise is that such people will not be shaken from residence in the divine presence, and in the divine presence there is an unshaken position that transcends the troubles of this life (Craigie 1983:152). This promise of standing firm forever forms an *inclusio* with the beginning of the psalm (Levenson 1985:173), for it is the hill/city/sanctuary that is not shaken even when the nations and the creation itself are. The invincibility of the mountain is effectively transferred to those who live there by faith (125:1-2),[5] by a faith that obeys (Ps 15). This invincibility derives ultimately not from the mountain but from the invincible presence of God on that mountain (46:5), or at any place where God is worshiped in spirit and in truth (John 4:23-24).

ENDNOTES

1. Pss 5:5 [6]; 6:8 [9]; 14:4; 15:2; 28:3; 36:12 [13]; 53:4 [5]; 59:2 [3]; 64:2 [3]; 74:12; 92:7 [8], 9 [10]; 94:4, 16; 101:8; 125:5; 141:4, 9.
2. Dahood's proposal has been less than persuasive; see VanGemeren (1991:152) and A. Anderson (1972:139).
3. Calvin (1979:210) notes that this solution "would agree very well with the scope of the passage" but opts to adhere to the Masoretic vocalization and the traditional understanding. Briggs (1906:114, 116) also notes that the LXX reading is well suited to the context.
4. See 10:6-7 for the use of *ra'* [TH7451, ZH8273] in the context of evil speech.
5. See 21:7 [8] for a portrayal of the king who trusts in God and is not shaken.

◆ O. Psalm 16

A psalm of David.*

1 Keep me safe, O God,
for I have come to you for refuge.

2 I said to the LORD, "You are my Master!
Every good thing I have comes from you."
3 The godly people in the land
are my true heroes!
I take pleasure in them!

4 Troubles multiply for those who chase after other gods.
I will not take part in their sacrifices of blood
or even speak the names of their gods.

5 LORD, you alone are my inheritance,
my cup of blessing.

You guard all that is mine.
[6]The land you have given me is
a pleasant land.
What a wonderful inheritance!

[7]I will bless the LORD who
guides me;
even at night my heart
instructs me.
[8]I know the LORD is always
with me.
I will not be shaken, for he is right
beside me.
[9]No wonder my heart is glad, and
I rejoice.*
My body rests in safety.
[10]For you will not leave my soul among
the dead*
or allow your holy one* to rot in the
grave.
[11]You will show me the way of life,
granting me the joy of your
presence
and the pleasures of living with
you forever.*

16:TITLE Hebrew *miktam*. This may be a literary or musical term. 16:9 Greek version reads *and my tongue shouts his praises*. Compare Acts 2:26. 16:10a Hebrew *in Sheol*. 16:10b Or *your Holy One*. 16:11 Greek version reads *You have shown me the way of life, / and you will fill me with the joy of your presence*. Compare Acts 2:28.

NOTES

16:TITLE *A psalm.* The meaning of Heb. *miktam* [TH4387, ZH4846] is uncertain. HALOT 2.583 suggests "inscription." Kraus (1988:25) proposes deriving *miktam* from the root *katham* [TH3799, ZH4187] ("to be indelible"; Jer 2:22) and suggests that a *miktam* "would be a poem or song that indelibly retains things that have happened" (similarly Craigie 1983:154). Perhaps Ps 16 originally circulated with Pss 56–60, all of which have *miktam* in the title (see VanGemeren 1991:155).

16:1 *refuge.* For this motif see 2:12; 5:11; 7:1; 11:1; 14:6. Trust in the Lord is the theme of this psalm.

16:2 *I said.* This translation correctly presumes an emendation of the verb from the second-person fem. sg. to the first-person common sg., an emendation for which there is some support in the Hebrew manuscripts and versions. The slight possibility exists that the fem. *nepesh* [TH5315, ZH5883] is the implicit subject of the verb; compare 103:1-2, where it is the explicit subject.

my Master. Heb., *'adonay* [TH136, ZH151] is probably the word *'adon* [TH113, ZH123] with an emphatic *-ay* [TH2967.1, ZH3276]; the sense is "Lord par excellence, Lord of all" (Waltke and O'Connor 1990:§7.4.3e; TDOT 1.70) with the emphasis on the universal authority of God (NIDOTTE 1.275).

Every good thing I have comes from you. The Hebrew is difficult, literally translated as "My good is not on you." The particle *bal* [TH1077/1077A, ZH1153] may not be a negative adverb, however, but may be an emphatic particle, "indeed" (DCH 2.174; HALOT 1.131). The sense would then be "My good is indeed [dependent] on you." The NLT captures this sense well.

16:3 *the godly people.* The Heb. *qedoshim* [TH6918, ZH7705] here refers to pious people, as in 34:9 [10] (so HALOT 3.1066).

my true heroes! The NLT correctly presumes an emendation from *'addire* [TH117A, ZH129] (heroes of) to *'addiray* (my heroes). The Waw preceding *'addiray* should probably be taken as emphatic (see note on 11:5) and *we'addiray* should be read with the preceding *hemmah* [TH1992, ZH2156] ("these"; in spite of the traditional MT accentuation, which starts a new phrase with *we'addire*). For the sense of *'addir* as something like "hero," see HALOT 1.14 and DCH 1.123.

16:4 *chase.* Though the NLT, along with other versions, takes the verb from *mahar* I [TH4116, ZH4554] (to be quick, swift), Zorell (1963:415), along with others, takes *maharu* from *mahar* II [TH4117, ZH4555] (pay a bride price) and renders the verb in our text "to take to yourself for some advantage."

16:5 *inheritance.* Heb. *menath-khelqi* [TH4521/2506, ZH4987/2750] means "portion of my share"; *kheleq* is used in Joshua (Josh 14:4; 15:13; 18:7; 19:9) in reference to the land, in Deut 32:9 in reference to Israel as the Lord's inheritance, and elsewhere (73:26; 119:57; 142:5 [6]; Num 18:20) in reference to God as his people's inheritance (see HALOT 1.323-324).

cup of blessing. Whereas the wicked will drink from the cup of wrath (see 11:6 and note), the Lord himself is the cup of blessing from which his people drink; he is the source of all good things (McCann 1996:736).

all that is mine. The Heb. *goral* [TH1486, ZH1598] means "lot" or "that which falls to one by lot" (see Num 36:3). DCH 2.337 says *goral* is sometimes used in reference to the "destiny" of people (16:5; Isa 17:14; Jer 13:25 are cited as examples). HALOT 1.185 is similar and cites 16:5, Isa 57:6 (both having *kheleq* [TH2506, ZH2750] as a parallel term), and Dan 12:13. The word *goral* is also used in Josh 18:6, 11 in reference to the land. It is difficult to be certain about the precise sense of the expression, but the NLT captures the general import.

16:6 *The land.* Heb. *khabalim* [TH2256A, ZH2475] means "rope" and then "territory (measured out by rope)" (DCH 3.151).

inheritance. On the basis of the LXX and Syriac, it is best to emend the difficult *nakhalath* [TH5159, ZH5709] (inheritance of) to *nakhalathi* (*my* inheritance; see HALOT 2.687); *nakhalah* is used throughout Joshua.

16:7 *at night.* Lit., "nights," which Briggs (1906:1.121) interprets as an intensive, citing 92:2 [3] and 134:1, but which HALOT (2.528) and Zorell (1963:397) interpret as "throughout the night." The latter seems to make the most sense. See VanGemeren (1991:158) for a survey of opinions.

my heart. Heb. *kilyothay* [TH3629, ZH4000] are the kidneys, which denote: (1) the organ itself (16 times in Exodus and Leviticus; once in Isa 34:6); (2) the seat of emotions (73:21; Job 16:13; Prov 23:16; Lam 3:13); (3) the inner being (16:7; 139:13; Job 19:27; Jer 12:2). That the kidneys could be "instructors" is without parallel in the OT (TDOT 7.180). Kraus (1988:239) is correct in understanding *kelayoth* here as the inner being: "The 'innermost being' constantly reminds the sufferer of the helpful revelation of Yahweh."

16:8 *I know.* Heb. *shiwwithi* [TH7737A, ZH8751] (I have set) expresses the psalmist's intentionality to live self-consciously in the Lord's presence.

not be shaken. See 13:4 for the fear of being shaken and 15:5 for the promise of not being shaken.

16:10 *the dead.* For *she'ol* [TH7585, ZH8619] see note on 6:5.

16:11 *pleasures.* The repetition of *na'im* [TH5273, ZH5833] from 16:6, where it is associated with being in the Lord's presence, underscores the point that the delight in 16:6 is primarily in the Lord and secondarily in the material gifts the Lord gives.

COMMENTARY

Psalm 16 displays the multifaceted nature of what it means to *trust in the Lord.* This psalm can be divided into five strophes. Each strophe is made up of two lines except the last, which has three.

To Trust Is to Rely on the Lord (16:1-2). David begins with a brief prayer that expresses his reliance on the Lord for protection by employing the "refuge" motif. He then confesses that the Lord is in fact his "Master" ("Lord of all") and the one on whom he is totally dependent for any and all good that he has. Reliance on the Lord excludes autonomous self-reliance.

To Trust Is to Be Devoted to the Lord (16:3-4). The heroes whom believers esteem supremely and take supreme pleasure in are the saints, and in so doing believers express their devotion to the Lord. Devotion also means disassociation from those who follow another lord. Realizing that those who follow another lord are on a path of pain, David refuses to associate with them, as anyone wishing to be truly happy does (see Ps 1). Such disassociation does not mean absolute separation (see 1 Cor 5:9-10); rather, it means not participating in their religious disloyalty to the Lord of all.

To Trust Is to Delight in the Lord (16:5-6). "Almost all of [the vocabulary of 16:5-6 is] unmistakably associated with the institution of the distribution of the land" in the book of Joshua (Kraus 1988:237). But the great delight of the psalmist here is not in the land itself. The language of the land is used to describe "the very relation to God . . . as the greatest benefit of the LORD's way with the servants of God" (Mays 1994:87). Calvin (1979:224, 226) captures the pathos of these two verses, saying:

> *This passage teaches us, that none are taught aright in true godliness but those who reckon God alone sufficient for their happiness. David, by calling God the portion of his lot, and his inheritance, and his cup, protests that he is so fully satisfied with him alone, as neither to covet any thing besides him, nor to be excited by any depraved desires. Let us therefore learn, when God offers himself to us, to embrace him with the whole heart, and to seek in him only all the ingredients and the fullness of our happiness. . . . Whenever, therefore, those things present themselves to us which would lead us away from resting in God alone, let us make use of this sentiment as an antidote against them, that we have sufficient cause for being contented, since he who has in himself an absolute fullness of all good has given himself to be enjoyed by us. In this way we will experience our condition to be always pleasant and comfortable; for he who has God as his portion is destitute of nothing which is requisite to constitute a happy life.*

To Trust Is to Learn from the Lord (16:7-8). Since the Lord is reliable, deserving of our devotion, and sufficient for our happiness, he is worthy of our praise, so this strophe begins, "I will bless the LORD." The praise, however, has a particular focus: learning from the Lord. Learning from the Lord is explicit in 16:7, where David expresses his openness to God's instruction (McCann 1996:737) in keeping with the essential nature of the Psalter (see Introduction and commentary on Ps 1). In 16:7b David is self-taught—that is, his inner being instructs him. This self-instruction is not autonomous but is carried out in submission to the Lord, as is indicated by the previous use of the verb *yasar* [TH3256, ZH3579] in 2:10 (McCann 1996:737), and the inner being can instruct us when it is "informed and guided by the praise of the LORD" (Mays 1994:87). The result of the Lord's direct teaching and our self-instruction is that we keep the Lord at the center of who we are and what we do. Submitting to the Lord's instruction by living in his presence results in a life of tremendous stability, as promised in 15:5.

To Trust Is Rejoicing in the Lord (16:9–11). The psalm ends with a strophe of joy, as is clear from the words "rejoice" and "joy" in the opening and closing lines. The final fruit of trust is joy. Reliance on, devotion to, delighting in, and learning from the Lord all culminate in great joy! This joy wells up from a spring deep down within the human soul and also expresses itself in physical well-being. Such joy is not rooted in a mindless mystical experience but in the personal knowledge that the Lord of all is our personal God who will never abandon us, not even in the hour of death. Even when we are facing death, he will be there to teach us the way to life—life that is full of abundant joy and that overflows with eternal pleasure in the Lord's presence.

David's confidence in neither being left among the dead nor allowed to rot in the grave was apparently a limited confidence in being kept from death in a certain situation (see the commentary on Ps 30). The limitations of this confidence have been removed by the resurrection of Jesus Christ from the dead. The language of 16:10 is pregnant with meaning that comes to full term in Jesus' resurrection. The apostles preached that the full significance of this language is realized not in David's being kept from dying, but in Jesus' resurrection (see Acts 2:25-31 and 13:35-37).

Ultimately, to trust is to believe in the Lord Jesus Christ, raised from the dead, as the one on whom we rely, to whom we are devoted, in whom we delight, from whom we learn, and in whom we rejoice. Because Jesus is at the Father's right hand, we will be also—forever!

◆ P. Psalm 17

A prayer of David.

1 O LORD, hear my plea for justice.
Listen to my cry for help.
Pay attention to my prayer,
for it comes from honest lips.
2 Declare me innocent,
for you see those who do right.

3 You have tested my thoughts and
examined my heart in the night.
You have scrutinized me and found
nothing wrong.
I am determined not to sin in what
I say.
4 I have followed your commands,
which keep me from following cruel
and evil people.
5 My steps have stayed on your path;
I have not wavered from following
you.

6 I am praying to you because I know
you will answer, O God.
Bend down and listen as I pray.
7 Show me your unfailing love in
wonderful ways.
By your mighty power you rescue
those who seek refuge from their
enemies.
8 Guard me as you would guard your
own eyes.*
Hide me in the shadow of your
wings.
9 Protect me from wicked people who
attack me,
from murderous enemies who
surround me.
10 They are without pity.
Listen to their boasting!

[11] They track me down and
surround me,
watching for the chance to throw
me to the ground.
[12] They are like hungry lions, eager to
tear me apart—
like young lions hiding in ambush.

[13] Arise, O LORD!
Stand against them, and bring them
to their knees!
Rescue me from the wicked with
your sword!
[14] By the power of your hand, O LORD,
destroy those who look to this world
for their reward.
But satisfy the hunger of your
treasured ones.
May their children have plenty,
leaving an inheritance for their
descendants.
[15] Because I am righteous, I will
see you.
When I awake, I will see you face
to face and be satisfied.

17:8 Hebrew *as the pupil of your eye.*

NOTES

17:1 ***hear my plea for justice.*** Heb. *shim'ah tsedeq* [TH8085/6664, ZH9048/7406] (hear righteousness) is an unparalleled expression. The imperative of *shama'* occurs with an object 17 times in the Psalter (the object usually referring to prayer). Since the objects almost always have the first-person common sg. suffix, the NLT's "my" seems warranted either as a textual emendation or as an implication from the following phrase ("my cry for help"), and since all of the objects refer to something audible, the sense of *tsedeq* must be something like "plea for justice" (see Dahood 1965:93 and Zorell 1963:683).

17:2 ***for you see those who do right.*** In the context of the preceding imperatives, I would interpret the imperfect verb as a volitive, as the NLT does in the previous colon, and render the Hebrew as "May your eyes see what is right." God's "eyes" are contrasted with the "eyes" of the wicked (17:11), but the psalmist is the apple of God's eye (17:8).

17:3 ***what I say.*** Lit., "my mouth"; see the wordplay on "mouth" in 17:10 (see note).

17:4 "There are almost as many different renditions of these lines as there are commentaries and translations" (Brachter and Reyburn 1991:152). A wooden translation is, "As for the deeds of man—by the word of your lips I have kept paths of a robber." The NLT's rendering suits the context of 17:3 and 17:5.

17:5 ***have stayed.*** For the use of an infinitive absolute as a finite verb, see GKC §113y-ff, Joüon and Muraoka 1991:§123u-w, and Waltke and O'Connor 1990:§35.5.2.a.

17:7 ***Show . . . in wonderful ways.*** NLT presumes an emendation from *hapleh* [TH6395, ZH7111] (distinguish) to *haple'* [TH6381, ZH7098] (astound, do wonders), for which there is ample manuscript support.

By your mighty power you rescue. "By your mighty power" translates *bimineka* [TH3225, ZH3545] (with your right [side]), which is more naturally read with *mimmithqomemim* [TH6965, ZH7756] (rise up [against]), resulting in, "Those who take refuge in you, you save from those who rebel against your authority."

17:8 ***Guard me.*** The Hebrew has no imperative here, which is an important point for the structure of the poem: 17:9 is better read with the descriptive section that follows (17:10-11) than the volitive section that precedes (17:6-8).

Hide me. The imperfect verb is used here as the equivalent to an imperative (Joüon and Muraoka 1991:§113m; Waltke and O'Connor 1990:§31.5.b) and marks the boundary of the unit (17:6-8) by terminating the series of imperatives.

17:10 ***They are without pity.*** Lit., "Their fatness they have closed up." Craigie (1983:160) is probably correct in interpreting this difficult colon as a metaphor for rebellion rather than pity, based on parallels with Deut 32:10-15, where we encounter "pupil of his eye" (Deut 32:10 mg), "protective wings" (Deut 32:11, as in 17:8b), and "fat" (Deut 32:15) in relation to rebellion. On the other hand, the NLT finds support in 119:70, where "fat" is used in a simile for callousness.[1]

Listen to their boasting! Lit., "with their mouth they speak arrogantly." The arrogant mouth of the wicked contrasts with the obedient mouth of the psalmist (17:3).

17:11 ***They track me down and surround me.*** The NLT presumes an emendation from *'ashurenu* [TH838, ZH892] (our steps) to *'isheruni* [TH833, ZH886] ("they track me down"; see Craigie 1983:161), and the correctness of the Kethiv, *sebabuni* [TH5437, ZH6015] (they surround me).

throw me to the ground. Lit., "They have set their eyes to stretch out the land." NLT follows Delitzsch (1982:240) in interpreting *natah* [TH5186, ZH5742] as transitive, "to incline to fall."

17:14 ***By the power of your hand, O Lord.*** Lit., "from people by your hand, O Lord, from people."

17:15 ***I will see you. . . . I will see you face to face.*** In the context of the other volitives in 17:13-14 and given the cohortative form of *'esbe'ah* [TH7646, ZH8425] (be satisfied), I would interpret these two finite verbs as cohortatives: "May I see . . . may I see."

COMMENTARY

McCann (1996:740) has pointed out the chiastic arrangement of Psalm 17; I have modified one boundary[2] and the descriptive language as follows:

- A. Prayer for vindication (17:1-2)
  - B. Affirmation of the psalmist's innocence (17:3-5)
    - C. Prayer for protection (17:6-8)
  - B'. Description of the psalmist's accusers (17:9-12)
- A'. Prayer for deliverance and blessing (17:13-15)[3]

The A and C strophes underscore the nature of this poem as a prayer, while the B strophes show us the nature of the psalmist's dilemma. Psalm 17 is a prayer for help that "reflects the situation of an innocent person under extreme pressure" (Craigie 1983:160).

The psalm opens with a prayer for vindication (17:1-2). Rapid-fire requests set the intense mood of the psalm: "hear," "listen," "pay attention." The deep desire for vindication permeates this opening strophe: "Hear my plea for justice," "Declare me innocent," "See those who do right." The daring affirmation of "honest lips," (i.e., "an honest heart") are a prelude to the second strophe.

The second strophe (17:3-5) starts with a bold declaration of innocence. This declaration of innocence is not a proclamation of perfection in all areas of life but is a protest of innocence in the particular situation envisioned in the psalm (Craigie 1983:162; Kraus 1988:247; McCann 1996:742; see my commentary on Ps 7). God himself had tested, examined, and scrutinized David but had found nothing culpable, in particular nothing culpable in the psalmist's speech, because of David's determination to be honest. Negatively, the psalmist's innocence was his avoidance of doing what was wrong. His innocence in action was owing to the operation of God's word and his own circumspection. Positively, David's innocence was his determined walk on the path of the godly (see Ps 1). Given the promise of 1:6, "The LORD watches over the path of the godly," we would not be surprised by an affirmation of assurance of being heard by God.

The central section (17:6-8) begins on just such a note of assurance: "I am praying to you because I know you will answer" (17:6a). "Bend down" and "listen" recall in reverse order the requests of the opening strophe, "hear" and "pay attention." David is aware that he is asking for an extraordinary display of God's unfailing love, but nothing is too wonderful for the Lord, who characteristically saves those who take refuge in him (see 2:12) by hiding in the shadow of his protective wings. Having guarded his own life from moral failure (17:4), David asks the Lord to guard him "as you would guard your own eyes" (17:8). And to be guarded is just what the psalmist needs, given the nature of his adversaries.

The fourth strophe (17:9-12) describes those from whom David needs to be delivered. They are wicked attackers and murderous enemies. Their weapons of destruction are their arrogant mouths, which contrast with the obedient mouth of the psalmist. And as a reward for the psalmist's tracking in the Lord's path, the enemies now track him down like the prey of ravenous beasts. Deliverance is needed in a most desperate way.

The psalm closes with a prayer for deliverance and blessing (17:13-14). The vicious nature of the attack warrants the plea for the Divine Warrior to arise with his sword and rescue his loyal subject by humbling the foe. In contrast to God's loyal subject who makes the Lord himself his "inheritance" (*kheleq* [TH2506, ZH2750]; 16:5) the enemies look for "their reward" (*kheleq*, 17:14) in this world. Finding satisfaction in material prosperity and passing that prosperity down to the next generation is not, however, an inherently evil activity to be left to the wicked but is a blessing sought after by the psalmist himself. But as in Psalm 16, the ultimate blessing sought after is the satisfaction that comes from seeing God face-to-face.

Psalm 17, like Psalm 7, is a source of great comfort and strength when one is falsely accused. This psalm provides us with clear instructions on how to live in God's presence when innocent. But most of us feel a certain discomfort in reading 17:1-5 in particular, for we know that we fall short of the ideal, the absolute innocence necessary to behold the face of God. On a deeper level, then:

> *The psalm shows us one who can lay himself open to the most holy Presence without terror, having a pure conscience and claiming a tender intimacy with the great God. From his beholding of God will follow the salvation of his people. There is a profound analogy here for Christian faith. Uniting themselves to the pure and beloved Son, the fulfillment of the Davidic ideal, his disciples can lay themselves down with confidence in the nearness of God. Into the last night also, the night of death, they go in sure hope to see the face and form of God as their Saviour and to be satisfied for ever. (Eaton 1967:61)*

ENDNOTES

1. The NLT interprets "fat" in 119:70 as a simile for stupidity. BDB (316) interprets 17:10 and 119:70 in terms of an unresponsive heart.
2. McCann reads 17:9 with 17:6-8; see my notes on 17:8 for my rationale in modifying McCann's schema.
3. Several key repetitions support this structure: (1) *tsedeq* [TH6664, ZH7406] (righteousness), the root *khazah* [TH7200, ZH8011] (see), and *paneh* [TH6440, ZH7156] (face) in 17:1-2 and 17:13-15, and (2) *peh* [TH6310, ZH7023] (mouth) and *'ashur* [TH838, ZH892] (steps) in 17:3-5 and 17:9-12. The use of verbs provides additional support: (1) a predominance of volitive verbs in 17:1-2, 6-7, and 13-15, and (2) the absence of volitive verbs in 17:3-4 and 17:9-12.

◆ Q. Psalm 18

For the choir director: A psalm of David, the servant of the LORD. He sang this song to the LORD on the day the LORD rescued him from all his enemies and from Saul. He sang:

1 I love you, LORD;
you are my strength.
2 The LORD is my rock, my fortress,
and my savior;
my God is my rock, in whom I
find protection.
He is my shield, the power that
saves me,
and my place of safety.
3 I called on the LORD, who is worthy
of praise,
and he saved me from my enemies.

4 The ropes of death entangled me;
floods of destruction swept over me.
5 The grave* wrapped its ropes
around me;
death laid a trap in my path.
6 But in my distress I cried out to
the LORD;
yes, I prayed to my God for help.
He heard me from his sanctuary;
my cry to him reached his ears.

7 Then the earth quaked and trembled.
The foundations of the mountains
shook;
they quaked because of his anger.
8 Smoke poured from his nostrils;
fierce flames leaped from his
mouth.
Glowing coals blazed forth from him.
9 He opened the heavens and came
down;
dark storm clouds were beneath
his feet.
10 Mounted on a mighty angelic being,*
he flew,
soaring on the wings of the wind.
11 He shrouded himself in darkness,
veiling his approach with dark rain
clouds.
12 Thick clouds shielded the brightness
around him
and rained down hail and burning
coals.*
13 The LORD thundered from heaven;
the voice of the Most High
resounded
amid the hail and burning coals.
14 He shot his arrows and scattered his
enemies;
his lightning flashed, and they were
greatly confused.
15 Then at your command, O LORD,
at the blast of your breath,
the bottom of the sea could be seen,
and the foundations of the earth
were laid bare.

16 He reached down from heaven and
rescued me;
he drew me out of deep waters.
17 He rescued me from my powerful
enemies,
from those who hated me and were
too strong for me.

18 They attacked me at a moment when
I was in distress,
but the LORD supported me.
19 He led me to a place of safety;
he rescued me because he delights
in me.
20 The LORD rewarded me for doing right;
he restored me because of my
innocence.
21 For I have kept the ways of the LORD;
I have not turned from my God to
follow evil.
22 I have followed all his regulations;
I have never abandoned his decrees.
23 I am blameless before God;
I have kept myself from sin.
24 The LORD rewarded me for doing
right.
He has seen my innocence.

25 To the faithful you show yourself
faithful;
to those with integrity you show
integrity.
26 To the pure you show yourself pure,
but to the wicked you show yourself
hostile.
27 You rescue the humble,
but you humiliate the proud.
28 You light a lamp for me.
The LORD, my God, lights up my
darkness.
29 In your strength I can crush an army;
with my God I can scale any wall.

30 God's way is perfect.
All the LORD's promises prove true.
He is a shield for all who look to
him for protection.
31 For who is God except the LORD?
Who but our God is a solid rock?
32 God arms me with strength,
and he makes my way perfect.
33 He makes me as surefooted as a deer,
enabling me to stand on mountain
heights.
34 He trains my hands for battle;
he strengthens my arm to draw
a bronze bow.
35 You have given me your shield of
victory.
Your right hand supports me;
your help has made me great.
36 You have made a wide path for
my feet
to keep them from slipping.

37 I chased my enemies and caught
them;
I did not stop until they were
conquered.
38 I struck them down so they could not
get up;
they fell beneath my feet.
39 You have armed me with strength for
the battle;
you have subdued my enemies
under my feet.
40 You placed my foot on their necks.
I have destroyed all who hated me.
41 They called for help, but no one came
to their rescue.
They even cried to the LORD, but he
refused to answer.
42 I ground them as fine as dust in the
wind.
I swept them into the gutter like
dirt.
43 You gave me victory over my
accusers.
You appointed me ruler over
nations;
people I don't even know now
serve me.
44 As soon as they hear of me, they
submit;
foreign nations cringe before me.
45 They all lose their courage
and come trembling from their
strongholds.

46 The LORD lives! Praise to my Rock!
May the God of my salvation be
exalted!
47 He is the God who pays back those
who harm me;
he subdues the nations under me
48 and rescues me from my enemies.
You hold me safe beyond the reach
of my enemies;
you save me from violent
opponents.

[49] For this, O LORD, I will praise you
among the nations;
I will sing praises to your name.
[50] You give great victories to your king;
you show unfailing love to your
anointed,
to David and all his descendants
forever.

18:5 Hebrew *Sheol.* **18:10** Hebrew *a cherub.* **18:12** Or *and lightning bolts;* also in 18:13.

NOTES

18:1 ***I love you.*** The Qal of *rakham* [TH7355, ZH8163] occurs only here and means "love"; see HALOT 3.1217 for a concise discussion of this verb.

18:3 ***who is worthy of praise.*** Heb. *mehullal* [TH1984A, ZH2146] occurs four other times in the Psalter (48:1 [2]; 96:4; 113:3; 145:3). The attributive use in 18:3 [4] is problematic, because all of the other occurrences are clearly predicate participles, and the clause-initial position with an intervening verb makes an attributive use unlikely; but perhaps this is a case of *casus pendens* to focus attention on the Lord's being "worthy of praise." A viable alternative is to emend to *mekholal* [TH2490A, ZH2726] ("pierced"; see Isa 53:5) and understand the psalmist as the referent (so Kraus 1988:255). The sense would then be, "As one who has been pierced, I will call on the Lord."

18:4 ***swept over me.*** The Piel of *ba'ath* [TH1204, ZH1286] means "terrify" or "overwhelm" (DCH 2.244; HALOT 1.147).

18:5 ***grave.*** See note on 6:5.

18:14 ***greatly confused.*** It is not at all likely that the word *rab* [TH7227, ZH8041] (great) modifies the verb "confused," the Waw relative imperfect that it precedes. Perhaps it is better to take *rab* as a transitive verb from *rabab* [TH7231, ZH8045], though the form is admittedly unusual, based on LXX's use of *eplēthunen* [TG4129, ZG4437] (he multiplied) (see Craigie 1983:169). The verb *wayhummem,* from the root *hamam* [TH2000, ZH2169] ("rout," "confuse"; DCH 2.571) is likewise transitive with God as the subject.

18:15 ***foundations.*** This repeats the word used in 18:7 [8] and forms an *inclusio* around the unit 18:7-15 [8-16].

18:18 ***attacked.*** This Piel of *qadam* [TH6923, ZH7709] echoes 18:5 [6], where the same verb is used but is translated "laid a trap."

18:20 ***my innocence.*** Lit., "innocence of my hands," as in 18:24 [25]. Along with the repetition of "for doing right," the repetition of "innocence of my hands" forms an *inclusio* around the unit 18:20-24 [21-25].

18:26 ***to the wicked you show yourself hostile.*** Lit., "to the crooked you show yourself tortuous" (HALOT 3.990).

18:29 ***I can crush an army.*** The meaning is uncertain. Given the parallel terms *shur* [TH7791, ZH8803] (wall) and the verb *ruts* [TH7323, ZH8132] (run), the noun *gedud* is more naturally taken as *gedud* [TH1417, ZH1521] (wall) and not *gedud* [TH1416, ZH1522] (army) (so HALOT 1.177 and DCH 2.317, but see BDB 151). The picture would be that of a runner on the wall of a fortress or city (HALOT 3.1208).

18:30 ***perfect.*** The Heb. *tamim* [TH8549, ZH9459] echoes 18:25 [26], where the same word is translated "integrity" and forms an *inclusio* around the unit 18:25-30 [26-31].

18:32 ***my way perfect.*** The Heb. *tamim darki* [TH8549/1870, ZH9459/2006] echoes *tamim darko* (his [God's] way [is] perfect) in 18:30 [31]. David's path is one of integrity, for he walks on the Lord's path of integrity.

18:34 ***trains my hands.*** The pure hands of 18:20, 24 here become hands prepared for battle.

18:35 ***your help.*** The NLT follows the emended *wa'anotheka* [TH6030, ZH6699] (your answer) in keeping with the use of *'anah* in 18:41 [42] and 2 Sam 22:36 (Kraus 1988:255; HALOT 2.852).

18:42 ***I swept them.*** The Heb. *'ariqem* [TH7324, ZH8197] means "I emptied them." Craigie (1983:171) may be correct in suggesting that we emend the text to read *'adiqqem* [TH1854, ZH1990] (I crushed them) in keeping with many Hebrew manuscripts, the LXX, and 2 Sam 22:43.

18:46 ***my Rock . . . my salvation.*** This echoes and forms an *inclusio* with "my rock . . . my savior" in 18:2 [3].

COMMENTARY

Psalm 18 is more like a flowing river than a series of connected lakes, and "while full confidence is not attainable" (Kuntz 1983:9), the stanzaic and strophic divisions are discernible. My own analysis approximates that of Craigie (1983:172) and Gerstenberger (1988:96). I divide the psalm into five concentric stanzas:

A. Opening praise of the Lord as refuge (18:1-3)
  B. What the Lord does for the king (18:4-19)
    C. Central praise of the Lord as refuge (18:20-30)
  B'. What the Lord does through the king (18:31-45)
A'. Concluding praise of the Lord as refuge (18:46-50).

As the structure indicates, this psalm is for experiencing the Lord as a saving refuge. It is the psalm of every believer who turns to the divine king for refuge in times of distress, though originally it was a plea of the human king to the divine king. Kraus (1988:265-266) explains the connection between the two uses of the psalm: "[The king's] distress is illustrated in images and conceptions that transcend all situations in the world. The king undergoes archetypal suffering. . . . The ordinary petitioner subsequently enters the area of royal statements and thereby places himself on the foundation of immovable saving acts that in his distress are received as effective" (Kraus 1988:265-266). As in Psalm 2, so also here, the universal reign of God is exercised through the agency of the messianic king. The universal and cosmic language of 18:7-15 in particular manifests the eschatological orientation of this psalm.

These hyperbolic descriptions obviously exceed the reality that any Israelite or Judean king actually experienced. In short, the descriptions affirm Israel's faith in God's rule amid circumstances that seem to deny it. Psalm 18, like the other royal psalms, functions eschatologically (McCann 1996:747; see also Gerstenberger 1988:99).

Opening Praise of the Lord as Refuge (18:1-3). These verses contain the "longest series of predicates for God found in the Psalter" (Mays 1994:91). Most of these predicates are part of the refuge motif: rock, fortress, rock, protection, shield, and stronghold. The king and all believers often find themselves in situations where they must trust the Lord for protection. Throughout life, as throughout this psalm, believers find in the Lord a faithful Savior. ("Salvation" is a key term in this psalm, as words from the root *yasha'* [TH3467/3468, ZH3828/3829] occur in 18:2, 3, 27, 35, 41, 46.)

What the Lord Does for the King (18:4-19). The second stanza is comprised of three strophes. Strophe one (18:4-6) describes, with language reminiscent of Jonah 2, the mortal danger experienced by the psalmist (18:4-5) and his distressed cry to the Lord, a cry that found entrance into the heavenly sanctuary (18:6). But before the description of David's personal salvation in the third strophe, we are provided a depiction of "salvation as a cosmic drama, not a personal subjective experience" (Mays 1994:91-92) in the second strophe (18:7-17). The saving, theophanic presence of the Lord penetrates to the very foundations of the mountains and the earth itself,[1] as the Divine Warrior descends (Longman and Reid 1995:75-76) to conquer his own foes. The Lord is so much the focus in this strophe that, whereas the first and third strophes abound with first-person pronouns in reference to the psalmist, this middle strophe contains not a single reference to the psalmist. The message is clear: "Salvation comes from the LORD alone" (Jonah 2:9), and this salvation is universal and cosmic in scope. Universal and cosmic do not, however, exclude the personal. The third strophe (18:16-19) records the Lord's saving response to the personal cry of David. The Lord "reached down from heaven" and saved David from David's own insuperable foes. When David was at his weakest he found in the Lord one on whom he could lean (18:18). The Lord rescued David, because the Lord delighted (*khapets* [TH2654, ZH2911]) in David (18:19). Given the use of *khepets* [TH2656, ZH2914] in Psalm 1, we might suspect that the Lord delighted in David because David delighted in the Lord. This theme is picked up in the next stanza.

Central Praise of the Lord as Refuge (18:20-30). This stanza climaxes on the note that the Lord "is a shield for all who look to him for protection" (18:30) and thus explicitly refocuses our attention on the opening theme of the Lord as refuge by repeating the language of protection and shield found in 18:2. The two strophes of this stanza unpack the significance of the refuge metaphor in this context in terms of the Lord's justice.

The first strophe (18:20-24) is chiastic with the boundaries clearly marked by the *inclusio* formed by the repetition of "for doing right" and "my innocence" (18:20, 24); this *inclusio* also brings to the fore the theme of God's justice. The inner frame (18:21, 23) stresses how David "kept" the ways of the Lord and "kept" himself from sin. At the center of the strophe (18:22) are references to the Lord's laws and principles. The logic is that the Lord rewarded David for doing what is right because David kept the ways of the Lord, for the Lord's laws were ever before him. "In short, the king is simply saying that he has been what God has intended and enabled him to be" (McCann 1996:748).

The second strophe (18:25-30) focuses on the Lord's "integrity" (*tamim* [TH8549, ZH9459] in 18:25 and 18:30 forming an *inclusio*) in his dealings not just with David but with all people in general. What is true of the Lord in his relationship with David (18:20-24) is true of his relationship with all (18:25-30); this point is underscored by the repetition in both strophes of *tamim* (18:23 and 18:25, 30). All who are humble will find the Lord to be a shield as they look to him for protection.

What the Lord Does through the King (18:31-45). The fourth stanza corresponds to the second stanza in that both have a high frequency of first-person pronouns in reference to the psalmist, and both describe victory. The two stanzas, while linked, are markedly different in one particular aspect. As we have seen, in stanza 2 victory is won by the Lord alone, whereas in stanza 4 victory is won by the Lord through the agency of the king: "I chased my enemies" (18:37), "I struck them down" (18:38), "I have destroyed all" (18:40), and "I ground them as fine as dust" (18:42). The king won this victory, however, only because the Lord was at work through him: "God arms me" (18:32), "He trains my hands for battle" (18:34), "He strengthens my arm to draw a bronze bow" (18:34), "You have given me your shield" (18:35), "You gave me victory" (18:43). Divine sovereignty exercised through human agency establishes the reign of God. The promise of Psalm 2 is being realized as the messianic king is appointed the ruler over nations (in 18:43, as in 2:7-9), which serve him (in 18:43, as in 2:11).

Concluding Praise of the Lord as Our Refuge (18:46-50). "Praise to my Rock!" (18:46) returns us to the opening of the psalm, "My God is my rock, in whom I find protection" (18:2), as does the reference to "my salvation" (18:2, 46). Because the Lord has rescued and held safe and saved the king and subdued his enemies under his feet, the king vows to praise the Lord among those vanquished nations (18:49). Because the Lord has granted "great victories" and "unfailing love" to the king, the anointed one, to David and his descendants (18:50), the Lord is truly worthy of praise (18:3) and love (18:1).

Psalm 18 begins with a reference to David as the servant (*pais* [TG3813, ZG4090], LXX) of the Lord and ends with a reference to David's descendants. This closing reference "is an epitaph for Israel's kings and at the same time an encouragement to the faithful who await the Davidic Messiah" (Gerstenberger 1988:99). Jesus is that Davidic Messiah. Jesus is the servant (*pais*) of the Lord from the royal line of David (Luke 1:69). Psalm 18 also praises the Lord as David's "mighty Savior" (*keras sōtērias* [TG2768/4991, ZG3043/5401]; 18:2 [3], LXX). Jesus is the Lord, the "mighty Savior" (*keras sōtērias;* Luke 1:69). In just one verse (Luke 1:69) we see Jesus both as the servant of the Lord from the house of David as well as the Lord and Savior of his people! As the servant, the Lord Jesus suffered in obedience: The ropes of death surrounded him, the grave wrapped its ropes around him, and death itself stared him in the face (18:4-5). Jesus experienced this language to the extreme, for he actually died in his service to the Lord. But then the Lord heard his cry (18:6) and raised him from the dead that he might be the mighty Savior for all who obey him (Heb 5:7-10). King Jesus has undergone not just "archetypal suffering" but substitutionary suffering for us. So we now sing the royal Psalm 18 and by faith place ourselves "on the foundation of immovable saving acts that in [our] distress are received as effective" (Kraus 1988:265-266).

ENDNOTES

1. See the *inclusio* formed by 18:7 [8] and 18:15 [16].

◆ R. Psalm 19

For the choir director: A psalm of David.

[1] The heavens proclaim the glory
of God.
The skies display his craftsmanship.
[2] Day after day they continue to speak;
night after night they make him
known.
[3] They speak without a sound or word;
their voice is never heard.*

4 Yet their message has gone
throughout the earth,
and their words to all the world.

God has made a home in the heavens
for the sun.
5 It bursts forth like a radiant
bridegroom after his wedding.
It rejoices like a great athlete eager
to run the race.
6 The sun rises at one end of the heavens
and follows its course to the other
end.
Nothing can hide from its heat.

7 The instructions of the LORD are
perfect,
reviving the soul.
The decrees of the LORD are
trustworthy,
making wise the simple.
8 The commandments of the LORD are
right,
bringing joy to the heart.
The commands of the LORD are clear,
giving insight for living.
9 Reverence for the LORD is pure,
lasting forever.
The laws of the LORD are true;
each one is fair.
10 They are more desirable than gold,
even the finest gold.
They are sweeter than honey,
even honey dripping from the
comb.
11 They are a warning to your servant,
a great reward for those who obey
them.

12 How can I know all the sins lurking
in my heart?
Cleanse me from these hidden
faults.
13 Keep your servant from deliberate sins!
Don't let them control me.
Then I will be free of guilt
and innocent of great sin.

14 May the words of my mouth
and the meditation of my heart
be pleasing to you,
O LORD, my rock and my redeemer.

19:3 Or *There is no speech or language where their voice is not heard.*

NOTES

19:1 ***The heavens proclaim the glory of God. The skies display his craftsmanship.*** This verse is a chiasm: (A) The heavens (B) proclaim (C) the glory of God. (C) His marvelous craftsmanship (B) display (A) the skies. The paralleling of the "glory of God" and "his craftsmanship" leads to the conclusion that the "glory of God" refers at least in part to "his craftsmanship," the heavens and the skies themselves as a manifestation of God's own intrinsic glory (Futato 1984:96-97). God's glory here is the visible manifestation in the creation of his otherwise invisible character. Similarly, in Isa 6:3 the glory of God that fills the whole earth is the visible manifestation of his otherwise invisible holiness (Futato 1984:97).

19:2 ***Day after day.*** Some understand the Heb. *yom leyom* [TH3117, ZH3427] to mean "day to day" in the sense that one day communicates with another (Kraus 1988:267; Mays 1989:97; NRSV). The expression, however, is better understood to mean "day after day," as in the NLT. The exact expression occurs nowhere else in the MT, but there are other analogous expressions that support the NLT rendering (1 Chr 12:22; 2 Chr 24:11).

continue to speak. The verb *yabbia'* [TH5042, ZH5580] is quite colorful and means "bubble" or "gush." The picture is that of words bubbling up, gushing up from a spring.

19:3 ***They speak without a sound or word; their voice is never heard.*** There are two different interpretations of this line. In one the point is that the speech of the heavens is inaudible (e.g., Craigie 1983:177-178; NLT, NASB). The point of the other is that the speech of the heavens is unlimited: "There is no speech or language where their voice is not heard" (NLT mg, NIV, NKJV). The latter is more likely for two reasons: (1) The next verse unpacks and amplifies this very point, and (2) when *beli* [TH1097, ZH1172] (without) is used elsewhere with a passive participle, it subordinates the following material to the previous (see 2 Sam 1:21 and Hos 7:8; see DCH 2.177), so it is best to understand 19:3b as a subordinate rather than coordinate clause.

19:4 *their message.* For a concise survey of ancient and modern interpretations of *qawwam* [TH6957/6957A, ZH7742/7743] (strange speech), see HALOT 3.1081. The frequently proposed emendation to *qolam* [TH6963, ZH7754] (their voice), based on LXX *phthongos* [TG5353, ZG5782] (sound) (so Craigie 1983:178) is not necessary according to Kraus (1988:268), who cites Isa 28:10, 13, where *qaw* probably means "sound" and is onomatopoetic, as are Greek *phthongos* (sound) and Latin *sonus* (sound).

home. This word renders what is expressed metaphorically in Hebrew by the word *'ohel* [TH168, ZH185] (tent), which is then played on in the following verse.

19:5 *after his wedding.* The simile in Hebrew is that the sun is like a radiant bridegroom bursting forth from his bridal chamber (*khuppatho* [TH2646, ZH2903]; NIDOTTE 2.229) after the wedding night. Based on this simile, the "tent" of the previous verse is probably not the daytime sky but the resting place of the sun during the night, from which the sun bursts forth in the morning. This interpretation finds support in the next verse, where David refers to the sun rising by using the word *motsa'* [TH4161, ZH4604], from the same root (*yatsa'* [TH3318, ZH3655]) as the verb "burst forth."

19:7 *perfect.* In context the sense is probably "all-encompassing" (McCann 1996:752); see commentary below.

reviving the soul. This may be a metaphor rooted in food restoring vitality to the body (so Clines 1974:8; see Lam 1:11, 19). The picture is that of God's instruction being "true soul-food," "imparting refreshment to the inner man" (Briggs 1906:1.169).

19:9 *Reverence for the LORD.* If "reverence for [or, "the fear of"] the LORD" is our subjective response to God's revelation (McCann 1996:152), then some think it is not a very good parallel term with the other words for "law" as objective revelation, and thus a variety of emendations have been proposed (e.g., Kraus 1988:268; see Craigie 1983:179 for a summary). But "the fear of the LORD" can refer to God's objective revelation; see Prov 1:29, where "the fear of the LORD" not being chosen is parallel to knowledge being hated, and Prov 2:5, where "the fear of the LORD" is understood and the "knowledge of God" is found. "The fear of the LORD" as objective revelation is a fine parallel with the other terms in the list.

19:12 *sins lurking in my heart.* The Heb. *shegi'oth* [TH7691, ZH8709] is apparently a biform of *shegagah* [TH7684, ZH8705] ("inadvertent or unintentional sin"; for the meaning of *shegagah* see NIDOTTE 4.42-44). Perhaps *shegi'oth* (19:12a) refers to actions that are known to the person though the sinfulness is not known, as opposed to the *nistaroth* [TH5641, ZH6259] (19:12b) that are completely unknown sins (so Milgrom 1967–1968:118).

19:14 *pleasing.* Heb. *ratson* [TH7522, ZH8356] is used elsewhere as "a technical term for qualified offerings to God at the sanctuary" (Mays 1994:100).[1] Here the "words" in praise of creation and instruction are the acceptable sacrifice (see Heb 13:15).

my redeemer. Heb. *go'ali* [TH1350B, ZH1457] "derives from family relationships, where it was the responsibility of family members to buy back, or 'redeem,' relatives who had fallen into slavery (see Lev 25:47-49). Thus redeemer connotes intimacy" (McCann 1996:753).

COMMENTARY

Psalm 19 has often been analyzed as a composite of two separate poems, but whether Psalm 19 is comprised of two originally separate poems or not, we are obligated to read it as a whole (Kraus 1988:269). Of this whole C. S. Lewis (1958:56) once said, "I take this to be the greatest poem in the Psalter and one of the greatest lyrics in the world."

I divide the poem in two: celebrating God's revelation in creation (19:1-6) and celebrating the Lord's revelation in Scripture (19:7-14). Each stanza is further divided into two strophes.

Celebrating God's Revelation in Creation (19:1-6). The first strophe (19:1-4a) tells us that the heavens display the radiant splendor of God. Specifically, this is the radiant splendor of the universal Creator—"his eternal power and divine nature" (Rom 1:20)—not the saving deeds of Yahweh (Mays 1994:98). This glory is made known every day and in every corner of the planet. Whenever and wherever the heavens are seen, God may be known in his glory.

In the second strophe (19:4b-6), the quintessential display of God's splendor is quite naturally said to be the sun. Like a bridegroom bursting forth from his wedding chamber the morning after and then like an Olympic runner sprinting to the finishing line, the sun rises in radiance, runs its course, and sets in magnificence. Not a nook or cranny in creation escapes the dazzling rays that reveal divine glory.

Celebrating the Lord's Revelation in Scripture (19:7-14). Pondering the sun produces connections between the two stanzas. "Just as the sun dominates the daytime sky, so too does Torah dominate human life" (Craigie 1983:183).[2] "While the sun, perfect in shape, revives the earth, Yahweh's instructions, perfect in their intent, reanimate humans in the depth of their being" (Terrien 1993:61).

The focus of the first strophe (19:7-11 [8-12]) is on the nature of revelation in Scripture. The revelation in Scripture is special. There is obvious movement between the first and second half of the poem, signaled by the shift from "God" (*'el* [TH410A, ZH446]) in the first stanza to *yhwh* [TH3068, ZH3378] ("the LORD") in the second. This movement parallels that in Genesis 1–2 and is a move from God's general revelation in creation to his special revelation in the Scriptures (Craigie 1983:182). The move is from the transcendent and cosmic God to the immanent and merciful Lord (Fishbane 1979:87). This movement shows that general revelation is not unimportant, since special revelation "works toward the fulfillment of God's creational purposes" (McCann 1996:754).

The revelation in Scripture is essential. "Though the vast firmament so high above us declares God's praise, it is the Torah of God that reveals to mankind that he has a place in the universal scheme of things" (Craigie 1983:183).

The revelation in Scripture is authoritative. "The creator of the universe is the LORD who gives Torah; the creator's authority is behind the law" (Mays 1994:98). This instruction is not only authoritative, but it is also all-encompassing, like the sun and the wide variety of terms used in reference to it; in short, the instruction of the Lord is presented as cosmic in scope (McCann 1996:752).

The second strophe (19:12-14) shifts to our response to this revelation in Scripture. While nothing can be *hidden* (*sathar* [TH5641, ZH6259]) from the heat of the sun (19:6 [7]), sins are often *hidden* (*sathar*) even from those who commit them (19:12 [13]). Our inability to be aware of all of our violations of Scripture leads to the conclusion that we cannot possibly be righteous through the law (Mays 1994:99). We are kept from life-dominating, willful rebellion by the Lord's grace and not through our own strength. "Only by God's forgiveness can [we] be blameless . . . and innocent of much transgression" (Mays 1994:99-100). Grace is our only hope of being "free of guilt" (*tamim* [TH8552, ZH9462]; 19:13 [14]) when the standard is a "perfect" (*tamim;* 19:7 [8]) law.

Grace produces gratitude. The sacrifice of praise from the heart is the fitting crescendo in this celebration of praise to the cosmic Creator who has drawn close to us as our kinsman-redeemer. The transcendent God and the immanent Lord meet in the Lord Jesus Christ, in whom we see the glory of God (John 1:14; Heb 1:3). He has revealed the Father (John 1:18). He has kept the law perfectly for us that we might be forgiven and receive the grace needed to escape the dominion of sin. "Therefore, let us offer through Jesus a continual sacrifice of praise to God, proclaiming our allegiance to his name" (Heb 13:15).

ENDNOTES

1. Heb. *ratson* [TH7522, ZH8356] at times refers to the favor one hopes to find in God through sacrifice (HALOT 3.1282); see Lev 1:3; 19:5; 22:19-21, 29; 23:11.
2. Sun imagery may be present in 19:8b [9b] and 19:9a [10a] in the words "clear" (*barah* [TH1249, ZH1338]) and "pure" (*tehorah* [TH2889, ZH3196]; cf. *tohar* [TH2892, ZH3198]) (see Exod 24:10) and in the yellow color of gold and honey (Glass 1987:154).

◆ S. Psalm 20

For the choir director: A psalm of David.

[1] In times of trouble, may the LORD
answer your cry.
May the name of the God of Jacob
keep you safe from all harm.
[2] May he send you help from his
sanctuary
and strengthen you from Jerusalem.*
[3] May he remember all your gifts
and look favorably on your burnt
offerings. *Interlude*

[4] May he grant your heart's desires
and make all your plans succeed.
[5] May we shout for joy when we hear
of your victory
and raise a victory banner in the
name of our God.
May the LORD answer all your
prayers.
[6] Now I know that the LORD rescues his
anointed king.
He will answer him from his holy
heaven
and rescue him by his great power.
[7] Some nations boast of their chariots
and horses,
but we boast in the name of the
LORD our God.
[8] Those nations will fall down and
collapse,
but we will rise up and stand firm.
[9] Give victory to our king, O LORD!
Answer our cry for help.

20:2 Hebrew *Zion.*

NOTES

20:1 ***answer.*** This is the first of three key uses of the verb *'anah* [TH6030, ZH6699] (answer); see also 20:6, 9.

the name. Heb. *shem* [TH8034, ZH9005] (name) is a key term in the psalm, as indicated by its repetition in 20:5 [6] and 20:7 [8].

keep you safe. The Piel of *sagab* [TH7682, ZH8435] means "protect" in the sense of "make high, be inaccessible" (HALOT 3.1306) and is part of the refuge semantic domain (see Introduction).

20:2 *send you help.* Lit., "send your help." For the dative use of the pronoun suffix, see Joüon and Muraoka 1991:§129h.

his sanctuary. "His" presumes emending the text by adding the suffix, which was probably lost through haplography (Craigie 1983:184). Based on the parallel "Zion/Jerusalem," the earthly sanctuary is in view here.

20:3 *look favorably.* Heb. *yedasheneh* is morphologically impossible. The NLT presumes a revocalization to *yedasheneha,* taken from *dashen* [TH1878, ZH2014], meaning "consider as fat" or "accept" (see HALOT 1.234). The suggestion in BHS, *yidreshennah* [TH1875, ZH2011] (seek it), is less likely.

20:5 *victory.* This is the first of four occurrences of words from the root *yasha'* [TH3467/3444, ZH3828/3802]; see also "rescues" (20:6a [7]), "rescue" (20:6b [7]), and "victory" (20:9 [10]).

raise a victory banner. The Heb. *nidgol* [TH1713A, ZH1839] is somewhat problematic, but the MT is understandable (see HALOT 1.213), and the NLT captures the sense of the MT well. An emendation to *nagil* [TH1523, ZH1635] (let us rejoice) would also make sense. The best option seems to be to read *negaddel* (from *gadal* [TH1431, ZH1540], "make great") for *nidgol.* This reading is suggested by the LXX, which translates the text with *megalunthēsomai* [TG3170, ZG3486] (we will boast). The Piel from *gadel* is used in Gen 12:2 with "name" as the direct object. Since some verbs in Hebrew take a direct object or an object mediated through a preposition, "in the name of our God" could be the direct object of the verb, and the sense would be "may we magnify the name of our God." This provides a fitting parallel for "May we shout for joy."

20:6 *rescues.* The verb is in the perfect tense and is used rhetorically for action that is sure to take place in the future (Craigie 1983:184).

his holy heaven. The reference is to the heavenly sanctuary.

20:7 *boast in the name of the LORD.* The Heb. *beshem . . . nazkir* [TH8034/2142, ZH9005/2349] ("in the name" + "mention") is difficult. The exact expression occurs two other times in the MT (Josh 23:7; Amos 6:10; see also Isa 48:1, which is quite similar), where the sense seems to be "invoke" (so DCH 3.109). But "invoke" does not make sense in Ps 20, especially with "chariots and horses." One solution would be to follow HALOT (1.270), which suggests "praise by mentioning the name of." The NLT's "boast" goes back to Driver (1967:53-54), who appeals to the LXX *megalunthēsometha* [TG3170, ZG3486] (we will boast).

COMMENTARY

Psalm 20 was originally composed for use before some particular battle, then could have been used before any battle, and finally came to be used in the face of any threatening danger (Calvin 1979:334). The psalm reflects a situation and sequence like that described in 2 Chronicles 20:5-19—a prayer before battle, oracle of salvation, and concluding praise (Craigie 1983:185). Going to the Temple was required *preparation* before *implementation.* Psalm 20 provides a window into these two key components of war.

• **Aspects of Preparation (20:1-5).** Preparing for war (or for any task, for that matter) has two aspects, one organizational and one spiritual (Craigie 1983:188). Getting prepared for victory begins with desire. "Your heart's desires" (20:4a) in this context is the desire for victory in battle. But desire is not enough. Desire must be directed by definite plans (20:4b). David would have followed the advice of the proverb that says, "Plans succeed through good counsel; don't go to war without wise advice" (Prov 20:18). But another proverb says, "Commit your actions to the LORD, and your plans will succeed" (Prov 16:3). All plans must be coupled with prayers (20:5).

"Before a campaign could commence, there must first be a retreat to the temple" (Craigie 1983:187). David would have made spiritual preparation by praying for the victory that he desired and planned for. Psalm 20 is not, however, a prayer by David. It is a prayer for David by others. In fact, it is primarily an indirect prayer offered on David's behalf in an address to David. The prayer is for protection, help, and strength as David goes to war. Sacrifices that were intended to procure the blessing of God would have accompanied this prayer. The prayer would have been offered in a spirit of eager anticipation of victory. This eager anticipation also anticipates the attitudes needed to implement the organizational and spiritual reparation.

Attitudes of Implementation (20:6-9). The dominant attitude that comes to expression in the second half of the psalm is that of confidence—not confidence in self (that is, in one's own preparation), but confidence in the Lord. The anticipation of "victory" (20:5) is here expressed as certainty: "Now I know that the LORD rescues his anointed king" (20:6). The prayerful hope that the Lord would respond to prayer (20:1) is likewise transformed into certainty: "He will answer" (20:6). Confidence is also expressed in boasting, not in one's own resources but in the Lord (20:7). The enemy will fall, but the people of God will stand (20:8).

Confidence is itself coupled with humility. Thus the second strophe and the psalm as a whole ends where it began, with dependence on the Lord in prayer: "Give victory to our king, O LORD! Answer our cry for help" (20:9). But we are not really where we began, for through the process of preparation we have become fully confident in the outcome.

In this psalm the king is not the savior but the saved one, and in his being saved lies the salvation of his people (Mays 1994:101). As David was answered, so Jesus was answered when he came forth from the grave in great victory over sin, the devil, and death. In this victory granted to Jesus lies the certainty of our own victory over all threatening dangers in this life. So we go forth in life with humble confidence in the Lord, a confidence that moves us to plan, to pray, and to anticipate victory all along the way.

◆ T. Psalm 21

For the choir director: A psalm of David.

1 How the king rejoices in your strength,
O LORD!
He shouts with joy because you give
him victory.
2 For you have given him his heart's
desire;
you have withheld nothing he
requested. *Interlude*

3 You welcomed him back with success
and prosperity.
You placed a crown of finest gold
on his head.
4 He asked you to preserve his life,
and you granted his request.
The days of his life stretch on
forever.

5 Your victory brings him great honor,
and you have clothed him with
splendor and majesty.
6 You have endowed him with eternal
blessings
and given him the joy of your
presence.
7 For the king trusts in the LORD.
The unfailing love of the
Most High will keep him from
stumbling.

8 You will capture all your enemies.
Your strong right hand will seize
all who hate you.
9 You will throw them in a flaming
furnace
when you appear.
The LORD will consume them in his
anger;
fire will devour them.
10 You will wipe their children from the
face of the earth;
they will never have descendants.
11 Although they plot against you,
their evil schemes will never
succeed.
12 For they will turn and run
when they see your arrows aimed
at them.
13 Rise up, O LORD, in all your power.
With music and singing we
celebrate your mighty acts.

NOTES

21:1 *the king . . . victory.* The king who rejoices in God's victory in 21:1 is the king for whom victory was requested in 20:9. Psalm 21 is thus a song of thanksgiving in response to the Lord's having answered the prayer offered in Ps 20.

21:2 *you have given him his heart's desire.* The prayer in 20:4 is, "May he grant your heart's desires," and the affirmation in 21:2 is that God has done just that.

21:3 *You welcomed him back.* The picture is that of the king returning to his capital, having won great victory in battle.

You placed a crown. For pictorial representations of a king being crowned by deity, see Keel 1997:259-260.

21:4 *He asked you to preserve his life.* "Asked" (*sha'al* [TH7592, ZH8626]) echoes "your prayers" (*mish'alotheka* [TH4862, ZH5399]) in 20:5 [6] and underscores the connection between the two psalms. The Lord spared the king's life in battle.

21:5 *honor.* For "honor" or "reputation" see 3:3; 4:2; 7:5.

splendor and majesty. Heb. *hod wehadar* [TH1935/1926, ZH2086/2077] may be abstract qualities in the figurative language of clothing or they may have a concrete reference to royal "robes of state." That this pair refers to clothing seems evident here ("clothed him with") and in Job 40:10; that the robes are royal is also clear from the context of Ps 20 and texts like 45:3 [4] and 96:6 (see also 104:1; 111:3; NIDOTTE 1.1013-1017; TDOT 3.337-338, 353-355; TLOT 2.353-356).

21:8 *You.* Does this portion of the psalm refer to the human or divine king? The text is ambiguous. Most commentators opt for the human king. See the commentary below.

right hand. See 20:6, where "power" translates the word for God's "right hand."

21:9 *The LORD will consume.* According to the accents in the MT, "the LORD" is to be read with the previous colon, "when you appear, LORD," and in this reading the Lord is thus the subject of the second-person verbs. The NLT, however, agrees with most other translations.

21:11 *plot.* Though the word is different, the concept is the same as in 2:2.

21:13 ***your power.*** This exact Hebrew expression (*be'uzzeka* [TH5797, ZH6437]) occurs in the opening line, where it is translated "in your strength." The repetition forms an *inclusio* around the whole that is the key to the focus of the psalm.

mighty acts. See 20:6 [7], where this same word (*geburah* [TH1369, ZH1476]) is rendered "great."

COMMENTARY

Psalm 21 is a song of thanksgiving in response to the victory God granted in response to the prayer offered in Psalm 20 (see notes for a variety of linguistic and conceptual connections). The psalm can be divided into two symmetrical halves, each half (21:1-7 and 21:8-13) being comprised of six primary lines plus a concluding line.

The King's Joy in the Lord's Strength (21:1-7). Psalm 20 ends with a prayer for God to give "victory" to the king. That prayer has now been answered. "Victory" has been granted, so the king "rejoices" and "shouts with joy." What the king "requested," "his heart's desire," has been granted. He requested that the Lord preserve his life in battle, but God did much more, as is clear in the Lord welcoming the king back into the city with great fanfare: "success and prosperity," "a crown of finest gold," "great honor," "splendor and majesty," "eternal blessings," and "the joy of [God's] presence." It is just like the Lord to give more than we would ever dare to ask or hope for (Eph 3:20).

All of the blessings enjoyed by the king were enjoyed through faith. Verse 7 concludes the first strophe by affirming both the king's faith in the Lord and the preserving effect of the Lord's unfailing love. The Lord's unfailing love kept the king from stumbling in battle, as the king trusted in the Lord. But this faith was a faith that worked, and the king's work in battle is the focus of the second strophe.

The King's Victory in the Lord's Strength (21:8-13). All of the main verbs in this strophe are imperfect verbs, which the NLT correctly renders with the future tense in English. So this second strophe is not a description of the recent victory, but based on that victory, the psalm looks with confidence into a future that will be characterized by the same kinds of victory, wherever the king will go. Victory in the future will come about only by trusting in the Lord's unfailing love, only because "the LORD will consume" David's enemies. But it is equally true that it is David's "strong right hand" that will seize his foes. David will destroy them. David will wipe out their descendants. As we saw in Psalm 18, so we see here: Divine sovereignty and human responsibility are two sides of the same coin. Faith in a sovereign Lord is faith that enters the battle in real time and space. Such faith is victorious faith.

Divine sovereignty and human responsibility are not, however, ultimately equal. This is clear from the final note of the psalm: praise to the Lord for his glorious power and celebration of his mighty acts, without which the king would have no victories. The psalm begins with rejoicing "in your strength" and ends with exalting "your mighty acts," for it is the Lord's strength that is the ultimately decisive factor in the battles of life.

There is a certain ambiguity throughout this second strophe. Is the subject of the main verbs the human king or the divine king? The ambiguity was eventually resolved when King Jesus was welcomed into this world, for in the Lord Jesus Christ the human king and the divine king are one.

◆ U. Psalm 22

For the choir director: A psalm of David, to be sung to the tune "Doe of the Dawn."

1 My God, my God, why have you
abandoned me?
Why are you so far away when
I groan for help?
2 Every day I call to you, my God, but
you do not answer.
Every night you hear my voice, but
I find no relief.

3 Yet you are holy,
enthroned on the praises of Israel.
4 Our ancestors trusted in you,
and you rescued them.
5 They cried out to you and were saved.
They trusted in you and were never
disgraced.

6 But I am a worm and not a man.
I am scorned and despised by all!
7 Everyone who sees me mocks me.
They sneer and shake their heads,
saying,
8 "Is this the one who relies on the LORD?
Then let the LORD save him!
If the LORD loves him so much,
let the LORD rescue him!"

9 Yet you brought me safely from my
mother's womb
and led me to trust you at my
mother's breast.
10 I was thrust into your arms at my
birth.
You have been my God from the
moment I was born.

11 Do not stay so far from me,
for trouble is near,
and no one else can help me.
12 My enemies surround me like a herd
of bulls;
fierce bulls of Bashan have hemmed
me in!
13 Like lions they open their jaws
against me,
roaring and tearing into their prey.
14 My life is poured out like water,
and all my bones are out of joint.
My heart is like wax,
melting within me.
15 My strength has dried up like
sunbaked clay.
My tongue sticks to the roof of
my mouth.
You have laid me in the dust and
left me for dead.
16 My enemies surround me like a pack
of dogs;
an evil gang closes in on me.
They have pierced my hands and
feet.
17 I can count all my bones.
My enemies stare at me and gloat.
18 They divide my garments among
themselves
and throw dice* for my clothing.

19 O LORD, do not stay far away!
You are my strength; come quickly
to my aid!
20 Save me from the sword;
spare my precious life from these
dogs.
21 Snatch me from the lion's jaws
and from the horns of these wild
oxen.

22 I will proclaim your name to my
brothers ~~and sisters~~.*
I will praise you among your
assembled people.
23 Praise the LORD, all you who fear him!
Honor him, all you descendants of
Jacob!

Show him reverence, all you
descendants of Israel!
24 For he has not ignored or belittled the
suffering of the needy.
He has not turned his back on them,
but has listened to their cries for
help.

25 I will praise you in the great assembly.
I will fulfill my vows in the presence
of those who worship you.
26 The poor will eat and be satisfied.
All who seek the LORD will praise
him.
Their hearts will rejoice with
everlasting joy.
27 The whole earth will acknowledge the
LORD and return to him.
All the families of the nations will
bow down before him.
28 For royal power belongs to
the LORD.
He rules all the nations.

29 Let the rich of the earth feast and
worship.
Bow before him, all who are
mortal,
all whose lives will end as dust.
30 Our children will also serve him.
Future generations will hear about
the wonders of the Lord.
31 His righteous acts will be told to those
not yet born.
They will hear about everything he
has done.

22:18 Hebrew *cast lots.* **22:22** Hebrew *my brothers.*

NOTES

22:1 ***help.*** The use of the root *yasha'* [TH3467/3444, ZH3828/3802] here and in 22:21 [22] ties this psalm to the previous two psalms (see 20:5-6 [6-7], 9 [1]; 21:1 [2], 5 [6]; McCann 1996:762).

22:2 ***answer.*** The use of the root *'anah* [TH6030, ZH6699] here and in 22:21 [22] ties this psalm to Ps 20 (see 20:1 [2], 6 [7], 9 [10]; McCann 1996:762)

relief. Here Heb. *dumiyah* [TH1747, ZH1875] probably means "silence" in the sense of "respite" (DCH 2.426) or "rest" (HALOT 1.217), but it may mean "silence" in the sense of "response" (DCH 2.426).

22:4 ***trusted.*** The use of the root *batakh* [TH982, ZH1053] here and in 22:5 [6], 9 [10] ties this psalm to Ps 21 (see 21:7 [8]; McCann 1996:762).

22:7 ***mocks.*** Whereas in 2:4 the Lord "scoffs" (*la'ag* [TH3932, ZH4352]) at the enemy, here the enemy "mocks" (*la'ag*) the Lord's anointed.

sneer. Lit., "open the lips," but a derisive gesture is in view (HALOT 3.925).

22:8 ***loves . . . rescue.*** The Heb. *khapets* [TH2654, ZH2911] ("loves" or "delights") was also used in connection with the verb "rescue" (*natsal* [TH5337, ZH5911]) in 18:17-19 [18-20], where David confessed that the Lord had "rescued" him because the Lord had "delighted" in him. David's experience in Ps 22 seems to be just the opposite: The Lord has not rescued him, apparently because the Lord does not delight in him.

22:10 ***my God.*** The exact expression as in 22:1.

22:11 ***so far.*** An adjective from this same root (*rakhaq* [TH7368, ZH8178]; cf. *rakhoq* [TH7350, ZH8158]) appears in 22:1 [2].

22:16 ***They have pierced.*** Heb. *ka'ari* [TH738, ZH787] means "like the lion" and may be correct, presuming the elision of a verb in this colon. The NLT presumes an emendation to *ka'ru* (from *karah* [TH3738, ZH4125]; see Delitzsch 1982:319). For a survey of opinions on this colon, see Vall 1997.

22:19 ***do not stay far away!*** In Hebrew, this repeats verbatim the request of 22:11.

my strength. Or, "my help" (DCH 1.213; HALOT 1.41).

aid. Heb., *'ezra* [TH5833, ZH6476], from the same root (*'azar* [TH5826, ZH6468]) rendered "help" in 22:11 [12].

22:22 ***your assembled people.*** Heb. *qahal* [TH6951, ZH7736] ("assembly"; see also 22:25a [26a]) has the community assembled for worship in view (see HALOT 3.1080).

22:29 ***Let the rich.*** The NLT takes the perfect tense as a precative, but in the context of the other future verbs in 22:27-31 [28-32] a rhetorical perfect would be a better choice (see Joüon and Muraoka 1991:§112h and Waltke and O'Connor 1990:§30.5.1e): "The rich of the earth will feast and worship."

Bow before him, all who are mortal. In the Hebrew the imperfect functions as a future, not a jussive: "All mortals will bow down."

22:30 ***Our children.*** Given the movement within the text from the congregation (22:22-26) to the world (22:27-31), the children in view are those from the whole earth.

COMMENTARY

"Psalm 22 traverses unimaginable dimensions" (Kraus 1988:300). It begins in the depths of an isolated individual suffering abandonment by God but ends in a worldwide assembly of peoples bowing before the LORD in worship. The psalm divides naturally into two stanzas: (1) pain in the face of unanswered prayer (22:1-21) and (2) praise in the light of answered prayer (22:22-31).[1]

Pain in the Face of Unanswered Prayer (22:1–21). The first stanza is comprised of two strophes. The first focuses on pain and trust (22:1-11). Pain and trust are juxtaposed in the opening strophe. "Why . . . Why" stands right beside "My God, my God" (22:1; Kraus 1988:300). The structure of the first two subsections of this strophe serves to magnify this tension (McCann 1996:762). Psalm 22:1-5 articulates the cry of pain (22:1-2) followed by an affirmation of the previous generations' faith, which begins with "Yet you" (22:3-5). Psalm 22:6-11 articulates the cry of pain (22:6-8), followed by an affirmation of the psalmist's faith, which begins with "Yet you" (22:9-11). Contrary to the pattern of the past, the psalmist has trusted in the LORD but has now been severely disappointed (McCann 1996:763). The position of Psalm 22 after Psalms 20–21 further emphasizes the pain, since in Psalms 20–21 we have just read of David's tremendous experience of answered prayer (McCann 1996:762). This first strophe ends with a brief subsection (22:11) that recalls the beginning of the strophe, "Do not stay so far from me." God is far away; trouble is near; there is no one to help.

The second strophe focuses on pain and prayer (22:12-21). The first two subsections focus on the pain. Psalm 22:12-15 describes the pain in terms of being attacked by wild animals (22:12-13) and in terms of pain in the body (22:14-15). Psalm 22:16-18 follows this same pattern (McCann 1996:763). Pain from attacking animals (22:16) is followed by pain in the body (22:17-18). But the pain is not restricted to the body, for the psalmist's "heart is like wax, melting within" (22:14; Kraus 1988:297). In the pain, prayer comes to expression (22:19-21). The prayer in Hebrew begins with *'attah* [TH859, ZH911] (you), recalling the faith of "Yet you" (22:3 [4], 9 [10]). The prayer repeats verbatim the request of 22:11 [12] (*'al-tirkhaq* [TH408/7368, ZH440/8178], "Do not stay so far from me"), and seeks a reversal of the opening question ("Why are you so far away?").

Praise in the Light of Answered Prayer (22:22-31). It is characteristic of psalms of lamentation to move with some abruptness from complaint to praise (Longman 1995:201), but the abruptness at 22:22 is most remarkable (see the discussion on Ps 13). Having been isolated and abandoned, David now declares the wonders of God's name within the worshiping congregation (22:22-26) and then throws open the doors of the feast to people from every nation (22:27-31). Community-wide praise is the theme of the first strophe (22:22-26) of this second stanza. David's own individual praise rings out in 22:22, 25, while the entire congregation's praise is called forth in 22:23, 26. The reason for the exuberant praise is expressed in the central line: The Lord has not ignored David's suffering and has not turned and walked away, but has listened to his cry for help (22:24). Though David had felt abandoned by God and in a sense had been abandoned by God, God had been there the whole time, sharing in the pain, supporting David's faith, and listening to his prayer. The heart that had been melting away (22:14) now rejoices with the congregation (22:26), as the congregation feasts with thanksgiving and celebrates the wonders of God's name.

Worldwide praise is the theme of the final strophe (22:27-31). The celebration bursts the borders of space and time (Davis 1992:96). The borders of Israel dissolve as worshipers from "the whole earth" and "all the nations" join the celebration. The borders of time dissolve as worshipers from future generations come onto the scene (22:30-31). The theme of the celebration is the central theme of the Psalter: "Royal power belongs to the LORD. He rules all the nations" (22:28).

Psalm 22 and Jesus' Passion. Psalm 22 "figures prominently in the passion" (McCann 1996:762) of Jesus Christ as recorded in the New Testament (see Matt 27:34-35, 43; Mark 15:24, 29; Luke 23:34; John 15:24; 19:28). There is an intensity in this psalm that drives the reader beyond the experience of David (Mays 1994:106-107) to that of Jesus Christ.

> *That David . . . had to traverse a path of suffering which resembles the suffering path of Jesus, the Son of David . . . and that this typical suffering of David is embodied for us in the Psalms as in the images reflected from a mirror, is an arrangement of divine power, mercy and wisdom. . . . David descends, with his complaint, into a depth that lies beyond the depth of his affliction, and rises, with his hopes, to a height that lies far beyond the height of the reward of his affliction. (Delitzsch 1982:306)*

The path that David traversed was the path of suffering that leads to glory. This was the path that Jesus traversed in the extreme. Because Jesus Christ has traversed this path for us, we too can traverse it. No, we *must* traverse it, for "if we are to share his glory, we must also share his suffering" (Rom 8:17). Psalm 22 is a remarkable guide along the way. It points us to the admixture of pain, faith, and prayer in this present age. It points us to the glory that is ours in the midst of the pain, as it points us to glory that awaits us in the future. It points us to the Lord Jesus Christ, who has gone before us and will go with us to the very end.

ENDNOTES

1. I basically follow McCann (1996:762) for the structure of Ps 22. For a discussion of the unity of Ps 22 and a slightly different analysis of the structure, see Prinsloo 1995a.

◆ V. Psalm 23

A psalm of David.

1 The LORD is my shepherd;
I have all that I need.
2 He lets me rest in green meadows;
he leads me beside peaceful
streams.
3 He renews my strength.
He guides me along right paths,
bringing honor to his name.
4 Even when I walk
through the darkest valley,*
I will not be afraid,
for you are close beside me.
Your rod and your staff
protect and comfort me.
5 You prepare a feast for me
in the presence of my enemies.
You honor me by anointing my head
with oil.
My cup overflows with blessings.
6 Surely your goodness and unfailing
love will pursue me
all the days of my life,
and I will live in the house of the
LORD forever.

23:4 Or *the dark valley of death.*

NOTES

23:1 ***my shepherd.*** In the OT the Lord is typically the shepherd of the community (e.g., 80:1), so here we are surprised by the personal nature of the metaphor—the Lord is "my" shepherd. As shepherd the Lord is also king, since in both the ancient Near East and the OT, "shepherd" is a royal metaphor (e.g., 95:1-7; Westermann 1989:129).

I have all that I need. Heb., *lo' 'ekhsar* [TH3808/2637, ZH4202/2893] (I will not lack). All of the verbs in 23:1-5a are imperfects and give the psalm an unmistakably future orientation (see commentary). There is only one other use of the verb *khaser* [TH2637, ZH2893] that is grammatically identical (used with neither an object nor an explicit subject and used with the negative adverb *lo'* [TH3808, ZH4202]); Neh 9:21 says of the wilderness generation, *lo' khaseru* (they lacked nothing). The connection with the wilderness generation in Neh 9:21 suggests the idea that 23:1 may have the wilderness experience in the background;[1] this is confirmed by comparison to a text like Deut 2:7, *lo' khasarta dabar* [TH3808/2637/1697, ZH4202/2893/1821] (you have lacked nothing).

23:2 ***green meadows . . . leads . . . peaceful streams.*** Each of these expressions is reminiscent of the Exodus and wilderness experience; for "meadows" (*ne'oth* [TH5116, ZH5661]) and "lead" (*nahal* [TH5095, ZH5633]) see Exod 15:13; for "peaceful" (*menukhoth* [TH4496, ZH4957]) see Num 10:33.

23:4 ***the darkest valley.*** The NLT mg reads, "the dark valley of death." Chaim Cohen (1996) has demonstrated that Heb. *tsalmaweth* [TH6757, ZH7516] is a word for "darkness" without any nuance of "death" in the word itself. It certainly remains the case, however, that death can be one dark valley through which a believer must walk.

Your rod and your staff. The rod was used to protect and the staff was used to guide. For a graphic representation of a shepherd with a rod and staff, see Keel 1997:229.

23:5 ***anointing my head.*** The verb here is a perfect for past time. The psalmist is a guest at a feast that will be spread before him in the near future, but he has already experienced the anointing with oil that was a customary expression of hospitality.

23:6 ***pursue.*** The word *radap* [TH7291, ZH8103] is usually used in the sense of "pursue to harm" (TWOT 2.2124; see also NIDOTTE 3.1057-1062), so the use of the verb here with "goodness and unfailing love" as the subject is as powerful as it is surprising.

and I will live. The Hebrew text reads *weshabti,* which is clearly a Qal Waw-relative perfect from *shub* [TH7725, ZH8740], meaning "I will return." The picture in view is that of the psalmist returning year after year to celebrate the feast. But the preposition that follows (*be* [TH871.2, ZH928], "in") is not at all what one would expect with *shub;* it is, however, the preposition one would expect with *yashab* [TH3427, ZH3782] (live). Delitzsch (1982:332) is no doubt correct in saying that this is a pregnant expression: "I will return for the purpose of dwelling" (see also Craigie 1983:204). In keeping with this the NLT, along with other translations, reads *shibti,* an infinitive construct with the first-person pronoun suffix from *yashab* (see Ps 27:4 for this same form in a similar context).

forever. The word *'orek yamim* [TH753/3117, ZH802/3427] means "length of days," an expression which has antecedents in the ancient Near East, e.g., Akkadian *umu arkutum* (long days, i.e., a long life; CAD A2. 285a). Given the Akkadian expression and the parallel Hebrew expression, *kol-yeme khayyay* [TH3605/3117/2416, ZH3972/3427/2644] (all the days of my life), it is not likely that "length of days" has eternity in view.

COMMENTARY

Psalm 23, perhaps the single most well-known biblical text, has a striking hold on popular American religion, no doubt for a number of reasons. Chief among them, it seems, is the surrounding and central motif of the psalm, the beneficent presence of a personal God. Someone once said, "You cannot get enough of what you do not want." There is some truth to this, though its rhetoric overstates the case. It is true that some seem to never have enough; we always want just a little more—a little more money, a little more recognition, a little more car, a little more house, a little more . . . , a little more. . . . Some want a little more of this stuff because this stuff alone is not what we *ultimately* want. As human beings we were created to live in the divine presence, and our souls are restless until they find rest in that presence. What we *ultimately* want is God himself—and when we have God, we find true joy and satisfaction in all of the other good things of life.

As the divine name (*yhwh*) surrounds the psalm (23:1, 6), so the divine presence surrounds all of life (Brueggemann 1984:154). Since the Lord is my shepherd, I will have everything I need (23:1); since the Lord's goodness and unfailing love will always pursue me, I will most assuredly return again and again to dwell in his presence (23:6); since the Lord is my shepherd (23:1a), I can be confident that his goodness and unfailing love will pursue me for the entirety of my life (23:6a); I will have everything I need (23:1b) as I return again and again to the divine presence (23:6b) (Tappy 1995:262). The central line of the psalm directs the soul to its chief passion, the divine presence: "You are close beside me" (23:4; McCann 1996:768 and Tappy 1995:260). The rest of the psalm fills in the details of this magnificent portrait of the beneficent presence of a personal God.

Daily Bread. Imagine yourself as a sheep near the end of the dry season. Grass has been as scarce as water for some time. You are emaciated and relatively lifeless from hunger and thirst. Your needs are basic: food and drink. Since the Lord is your shepherd, you will soon have everything you need. Your shepherd is the creator of heaven and earth who will send the rains to fill the stream and make the meadows green (see 104:10-14). Then he will lead you to those green meadows and peaceful streams where he will provide all the food and drink you need to renew your strength.

Daily Guidance. You are confident that your shepherd will guide you along the path that is just right to get you to the food and drink you need. As the rains subside and the grass and water decrease, your shepherd may lead you through some dark and dangerous ravines, where you may encounter thieves or voracious animals, or where you may face the danger of a false step along the narrow path upward, a step that could result in death. Your shepherd leads you on this path not to harm you but because it is the path of life, the path to higher ground where food and drink will be found. So you follow without fear because of the divine presence—his rod will keep away all predators and his staff will keep your foot from slipping. Your shepherd is motivated by what benefits you, but what benefits you is also what brings honor to his own name. Since your well-being is bound up with the honor of his name, you have rest, even when the way is dark. Whether you are in the dark valley or in the green meadow is not the issue; the issue is the truth that you are in the divine presence, for being there means that you will have everything you need.

Daily Bread. The shepherd metaphor falls away as you find yourself a guest in the home of the divine host. He will soon prepare a great feast for you. Since the time of year is the fall, just before the coming of the rains, the feast is the Festival of Tabernacles. This is the particular feast when you give thanks for being safely seen through another year and when you anticipate blessings in the year to come, blessings that will include freedom from preying enemies. In the anointing oil and the overflowing cup of wine you have a foretaste of future blessings. The shepherd and the host are one, as they provide you with daily bread (Tappy 1995:274).

The concluding verse "is more a beginning than a terminus. In it something is held in prospect" (Westermann 1981:39). What is held in prospect is the divine pursuit that culminates in your returning to and living in the divine presence. The divine shepherd becomes a human shepherd; the Lord who is your shepherd is the Lord Jesus Christ (John 10:11). He calls you to his presence, and you come to him because you recognize his voice (John 10:3-4). His purpose is never to "kill and destroy" but to give "a rich and satisfying life" (John 10:10). He will lead you to "good pastures" (John 10:9). He will not leave you when the wolves attack (John 10:12). In fact, he will pursue you into his presence at any cost, even the cost of his own life (John 10:11).

The fact that the good shepherd lays down his life that we might experience the beneficent presence of a personal God is itself "more a beginning than a terminus. In it something is held in prospect." For the shepherd has "other sheep, too, that are not in this sheepfold. . . . They will listen to [his] voice, and there will be one flock with one shepherd" (John 10:16). Human beings cannot get enough of what they do not want. They were created to live in the divine presence. They need to hear the shepherd's voice, so that they can come to him and say, "The LORD is *my* shepherd; I have all that I need" (italics added).

ENDNOTES

1. For the allusions cited here and below to the Exodus/Wilderness experience, see Milne (1974–1975), Freedman (1976), and Craigie (1983:205-208).

◆ W. Psalm 24

A psalm of David.

[1]The earth is the LORD's, and everything
in it.
The world and all its people belong
to him.
[2]For he laid the earth's foundation on
the seas
and built it on the ocean depths.

[3]Who may climb the mountain of
the LORD?
Who may stand in his holy
place?
[4]Only those whose hands and hearts
are pure,
who do not worship idols
and never tell lies.
[5]They will receive the LORD's
blessing
and have a right relationship
with God their savior.
[6]Such people may seek you
and worship in your presence,
O God of Jacob. *Interlude*

[7]Open up, ancient gates!
Open up, ancient doors,
and let the King of glory enter.
[8]Who is the King of glory?
The LORD, strong and mighty;
the LORD, invincible in battle.
[9]Open up, ancient gates!
Open up, ancient doors,
and let the King of glory enter.
[10]Who is the King of glory?
The LORD of Heaven's Armies—
he is the King of glory. *Interlude*

NOTES

24:2 *built it.* There is no need to emend the imperfect form of the verb to a perfect (contra Craigie 1983:210), as this is an example of perfect-imperfect parallelism (Berlin 1985:36).

ocean depths. Heb. *neharoth* [TH5104, ZH5643] (rivers) is a poetic parallel for *yammim* [TH3220, ZH3542] (seas), and the NLT's "ocean depths" captures the sense quite nicely (see VanGemeren 1991:220). This verse alludes to Baal's conquering of Yam and Nahar (Craigie 1983:212). The allusion to Canaanite mythology serves a polemical purpose (Longman and Reid 1995:76): the affirmation that Yahweh, not Baal or Marduk, is king over all creation.

24:3 *Who.* The interrogatory "who" occurs four times in the psalm, twice with regard to the identity of the worshipers and twice (24:8, 10) with regard to the identity of the one worshiped. This repetition serves to highlight the relationship between the people and the Lord (Botha 1994:363-364).

climb. The word *'alah* [TH5927, ZH6590] is used frequently for going up into Jerusalem, "the mountain of the LORD," in a context of worship (e.g., 47:5; 2 Sam 6:12, 15; 1 Kgs 8:4; Isa 2:3).

mountain . . . holy place. This language continues the motif encountered in 2:6; 3:4; 5:7; 11:4; 15:1.

24:4 *who do not worship idols.* Lit., "who does not lift up his soul to an idol." The language of "lifting the soul" will be repeated in 25:1, creating a link between the two psalms, which is essential for understanding Ps 24. To "lift one's soul" to God is to trust God, as is clear from the other occurrences (25:1; 86:4; 143:8), all of which use the expression in the context of trusting God (McCann 1996:777).

tell lies. Lit., "swear deceitfully"; Heb. *nishba'* [TH7650, ZH8678] echoes 15:4b, where the same verb occurs and is translated "keep their promises."

24:6 *Such people.* The word *zeh* [TH2088, ZH2296] (this, these) will be repeated two other times (24:8, 10) in the question as to the identity of the King of glory. This repetition serves to highlight the relationship between the people and the Lord (Botha 1994:364).

24:7 *Open up, ancient gates.* Lit., "Lift up your heads, O gates." This language echoes a Ugaritic text, where we read, "Lift up, O gods, your heads," in the context of Baal going to battle. The shout would have in all likelihood been used again when Baal returned victoriously from battle (Cross 1966:23-24). In Ps 24, the "gods" have been transformed into "gates," perhaps as metonymy for "gatekeepers" (Craigie 1983:212). The verb translated "lift up" (*nasa'* [TH5375, ZH5951]) occurs in four verses in the psalm, twice (24:4, 5)[1] with regard to the identity of the worshipers and twice (24:7, 9) with regard to the identity of the one worshiped. This repetition serves to highlight the relationship between the people and the Lord (Botha 1994:363).

24:8 *mighty . . . invincible.* The word *gibbor* [TH1368, ZH1475] stands behind both translations.

24:9 *Open up, ancient doors.* Verse 9 is a repetition of 24:7, but the second verb in 24:9 is a Qal, whereas the corresponding verb in 24:7 is a Niphal. An emendation to a Niphal is frequently suggested and may be correct, but Goldingay (1978:146-147) has argued that such variation within repetition is acceptable poetic style.

COMMENTARY

Psalm 24, more than most psalms, gives us a glimpse into the liturgical life of ancient Israel. In 42:4 the psalmist remembers what it was like to be "leading a great procession to the house of God" with singing and celebration. And in 68:24-25 we read,

> Your procession has come into view, O God—
> the procession of my God and King as he goes into the sanctuary.
> Singers are in front, musicians behind;
> between them are young women playing tambourines.

Psalm 24 is rooted in just such a procession of the divine king into his royal city. The psalm is comprised of three strophes[2] that progress from one to the other much as the procession itself moves to a climax.

Confessing the Creator-King (24:1-2). Psalm 24 begins with a confession that Yahweh is king because he is creator. The whole earth and everything in it, especially human beings, belong to the Lord, because he created it all. To create is to own, and to own is to have dominion over. Psalm 95:3-5 shares this same theological perspective:

> For the LORD is a great God,
> a great King above all gods.
> He holds in his hands the depths of the earth
> and the mightiest mountains.
> The sea belongs to him, for he made it.
> His hands formed the dry land, too.

The picture in 24:1-2 is that of the earth as a disc built and floating on top of a watery mass. This is related to the picture in Exodus 20:4, "You shall not make for yourself a carved image, or any likeness of anything that is in heaven above, or that is in the earth beneath, or that is in the water under the earth" (ESV). An earth floating on a watery mass would not be stable unless there were a solid foundation laid, and our text indicates that the Lord laid that very foundation (see also 93:1 and 96:10). This picture of an earth stabilized on water is not intended to teach us geology but theology. The "seas" and "ocean depths" evoked, in the ancient mind, images of Baal subduing Yam and Nahar, rival deities. In the Old Testament, however, the Lord does not subdue any rival deities in the process of creating the world, but the affirmation of a stable creation is the basis of the affirmation that the Lord is "a great King above all gods" (95:3). Psalm 24 begins by confessing that the God of Israel is the Creator-King who knows no rivals.

Approaching the Creator-King (24:3-6). All people belong to the Creator-King, but may all people approach him? His special presence is on a mountain, and this mountain is holy. What is required of those who would participate in a procession, climbing the mountain and entering his presence (24:3)? Verse 4 provides the answer. First, the worshiper must have purity. To the pure God shows himself pure (18:26). The purity required must be inward ("heart") as well as outward ("hands"). Second, the worshiper must have loyalty. To the loyal, God shows himself loyal (18:25). This loyalty excludes the worship of all rival deities. Third, the worshiper must have integrity. To those with integrity God shows integrity (18:25). Integrity between word and deed is essential in relating to God. Such people "will receive the LORD's blessing" (24:5) and have a right relationship with him.

The question in 24:3 may have been asked by a representative of those in the procession. The answer in 24:4 may have been given by a gatekeeper. Verse 6 would then have served as an affirmation that the people participating in the procession viewed themselves as qualified to proceed. But who can say, "I meet the requirements of the holy God?" We have already seen how this question was answered for Psalm 15 by the preceding Psalm 14. Here the answer will be given for Psalm 24 by the following Psalm 25, where David, fully aware of his failures to meet the requirements (see 25:7, 18), nevertheless confesses that he is one who lifts his soul to the Lord (25:1), not to idols (24:4), and who trusts in the Lord (25:2-3) for "compassion and unfailing love" (25:6). Anyone who comes by grace through faith may approach the Creator-King.

Welcoming the Creator-King (24:7-10). Climbing the mountain has no purpose if the Creator-King is not present. Moses once said to the Lord, "If you don't personally go with us, don't make us leave this place" (Exod 33:15). In Psalm 24 the procession of the people is joined with the procession of the Lord. A similar scenario is portrayed in 132:7-8:

> Let us go to the sanctuary of the LORD;
>   let us worship at the footstool of his throne.
> Arise, O LORD, and enter your resting place,
>   along with the Ark, the symbol of your power.

Since the participants in the procession meet the requirements, instructions are given to open the city gates that the "King of glory" may enter (24:7). But there were many claimants to the throne in the ancient world, so the question must be raised as to the identity of the deity who would presume to take the throne. Answer: "The LORD, strong and mighty; the LORD, invincible in battle" (24:8). The "battle" in view would have been some military battle in the history of Israel, but this battle was just one more demonstration that the Lord has been king since creation, when he "subdued" the seas and ocean depths (24:2; see also the commentary on 74:12-17). The question of identity is repeated in 24:10a, and the answer is repeated with variation in 24:10b: "The LORD of Heaven's Armies—he is the King of glory."

It does not take much imagination to envision a time when the Creator-King proceeded into Jerusalem on a donkey, surrounded by a throng of people shouting, "Praise God for the Son of David! Blessings on the one who comes in the name of the LORD!" (Matt 21:9). In fact, "the entire city of Jerusalem was in an uproar as he entered. 'Who is this?' they asked. And the crowds replied, 'It's Jesus'" (Matt 21:10-11). He is the King of glory. But soon the crowd would roar, "Crucify him!" (Matt 27:23), because without his substitutionary life and death none of the peoples of the earth could ever hope to approach the holy Creator-King. Because the Creator-King himself entered the city to atone for sin, whoever trusts in his unfailing love can approach the Creator-King with confidence (Heb 4:14-16). The day is coming when the Creator-King in all his glory will proceed with all the angels to enter his earth-sanctuary (Matt 25:31) so that his dominion might be established in its eternal fullness. On that day the shout will be heard, "Open up, ancient gates! Open up, ancient doors, and let the King of glory enter." Then will be heard the question, "Who is the King of glory?" The answer will resound throughout all space and time, "The LORD of Heaven's Armies—he is the King of glory."

ENDNOTES

1. The verb occurs in 24:4 in the phrase "who do not worship idols," (lit., "who does not lift up his soul to an idol"), and in 24:5, where it is translated "receive."
2. For a twofold division of the psalm, see Botha 1994. Botha offers numerous keen insights into Ps 24, but his twofold division is not convincing.

◆ X. Psalm 25*

A psalm of David.

1 O LORD, I give my life to you.
2 I trust in you, my God!
Do not let me be disgraced,
or let my enemies rejoice in my defeat.
3 No one who trusts in you will ever be disgraced,
but disgrace comes to those who try to deceive others.

4 Show me the right path, O LORD;
point out the road for me to follow.
5 Lead me by your truth and teach me,
for you are the God who saves me.
All day long I put my hope in you.
6 Remember, O LORD, your compassion and unfailing love,
which you have shown from long ages past.
7 Do not remember the rebellious sins of my youth.
Remember me in the light of your unfailing love,
for you are merciful, O LORD.

8 The LORD is good and does what is right;
he shows the proper path to those who go astray.
9 He leads the humble in doing right,
teaching them his way.

10 The LORD leads with unfailing love and
faithfulness
all who keep his covenant and obey
his demands.

11 For the honor of your name, O LORD,
forgive my many, many sins.
12 Who are those who fear the LORD?
He will show them the path they
should choose.
13 They will live in prosperity,
and their children will inherit the
land.
14 The LORD is a friend to those who
fear him.
He teaches them his covenant.
15 My eyes are always on the LORD,
for he rescues me from the traps of
my enemies.

16 Turn to me and have mercy,
for I am alone and in deep
distress.
17 My problems go from bad to worse.
Oh, save me from them all!
18 Feel my pain and see my trouble.
Forgive all my sins.
19 See how many enemies I have
and how viciously they hate me!
20 Protect me! Rescue my life from
them!
Do not let me be disgraced, for
in you I take refuge.
21 May integrity and honesty
protect me,
for I put my hope in you.

22 O God, ransom Israel
from all its troubles.

25 This psalm is a Hebrew acrostic poem; each verse begins with a successive letter of the Hebrew alphabet.

NOTES

25:1-2 ***O LORD, I give my life to you. I trust in you, my God!*** Psalm 25 is an alphabetic acrostic with each poetic line beginning with the succeeding letter of the alphabet, so we would expect the second line to begin with *beka* [TH43871.2/3509.2, ZH928/3870] (in you) and not with *'elohay* [TH430, ZH466] (my God). It appears that the poem is damaged at this point (see the discussion of damaged acrostics at Psalm 9–10). A variety of solutions have been proposed. The simplest solution is to presume that *'el* [TH413, ZH448] (to) has fallen out from in front of *'elohay* by means of haplography and that *napshi 'essa'* [TH5315/5375, ZH5883/5951] (I lift up my soul) serves as a hinge and is to be read with both the preceding and the following words: lit., "To you, O LORD, I lift my soul to my God." Then the second line would begin with the proper letter: "In you I trust."

25:3 ***trusts.*** Heb. *qawah* [TH6960, ZH7747] occurs again in 25:5 and 25:21, where it is translated "hope" (see also 39:7 [8]); *qawah* is semantically related to "trust" (*batakh* [TH982, ZH1053]) used in 25:2 (Creach 1996:31-34). Trust is a key theme in the psalm.

disgraced. The word *bosh* [TH954, ZH1017] is used three times in 25:2-3 and one more time in 25:20. A concern for honor is a key theme in the psalm.

those who try to deceive others. The word *bogedim* [TH898, ZH953] refers to those who are treacherous, traitors (DCH 2.90-91; HALOT 1.108; BDB 93). Following the affirmation of trust in God (25:3a) the *bogedim* are probably those who have deserted God (NIDOTTE 1.591). They are "senselessly faithless" (TDOT 1.199).

25:4 ***path.*** This noun (*derek* [TH1870, ZH2006]) is also used in 25:8b, 9b, 12b. A verb from the root *darak* [TH1869, ZH2005] is used in 25:5a and 25:9a. Note also the use of the synonym *'orakh* [TH734, ZH784] in 25:4b and 25:10a. Guidance on the right path is a key theme in the psalm.

25:8 ***those who go astray.*** This clause translates a single word (*khatta'im* [TH2400, ZH2629]) that is related to the word translated "sins" (*khatto'wth* [TH2403A, ZH2633]) in 25:7 and 25:18.

25:10 ***covenant and . . . demands.*** Covenant and decrees are not two separate ideas. This is hendiadys: "covenant stipulations" (Dahood 1965:157).

25:14 ***The Lord is a friend.*** The words *sod yhwh* [TH5475/3068, ZH6051/3378] occur only here and in Jer 23:18, 22. The sense is intimate companionship that includes confidential conversation (HALOT 2.754; BDB 691).

25:17 ***My problems go from bad to worse.*** Lit., "The distresses of my heart have made wide." The verb (*hirkhibu* [TH7337, ZH8143]) is problematic here. It is used in 4:1 [2] with a similar word for distress (*tsar* [TH6862, ZH7639]) as is used in 25:17 (*tsarah* [TH6869, ZH7650]). It is best to emend *hirkhibu* [TH7337, ZH8143] (perfect) to *harkheb* (imperative; see Joüon and Muraoka 1991:§54c for the spelling) and then to attach the Waw to the following word: "Take away the distresses of my heart and . . ." (Craigie 1983:217; Kraus 1988:318).

25:18 ***Feel . . . see.*** There is a single word in the Hebrew, *re'eh* [TH7200, ZH8011]. The word *re'eh* is probably a scribal mistake. According to the acrostic pattern we would expect a word that begins with a Qoph, and the following line also begins with *re'eh*. The best suggestion for a substitute comes from BHS: *qeshob* [TH7181, ZH7992] (pay attention).

25:22 ***ransom.*** The word *padah* [TH6299, ZH7009] begins the final line of the poem. It is somewhat odd that a Pe line is added after the Taw line. Leeman (1996) makes the case that the Pe line is a substitute for the missing Waw line, as the Pe corresponds to the Waw according to the atbash principle.[1] Leeman also notes that this same phenomenon occurs again in Ps 34.[2] Perhaps the poet wished to end with a line beginning with *padah* and to maintain 22 lines. The natural line to eliminate would have been the Waw line in light of the atbash principle and the fact that so few words begin with Waw.

COMMENTARY

Psalm 25 has a clear sequence of thought, contrary to the opinions of some (e.g., Craigie 1983:217). Based on change of address, the psalm can be divided into three stanzas: 25:1-7 address the Lord in the second person, 25:8-15 in the third, and 25:16-22 in the second; the one exceptional verse is 25:11, which is second person in the middle of a third-person stanza and thus stands in the middle of the middle stanza (McCann 1996:777). That 25:11 is the center of the poem finds further support in that the first stanza is comprised of two strophes (25:1-3 and 25:4-7), each of which are petitions; the third stanza is likewise comprised of two strophes (25:16-18 and 25:19-22), each of which are petitions; and the middle stanza is comprised of three strophes (25:8-10, 25:11, and 25:12-15) with 25:11 being a central petition surrounded by two strophes of assurance (Brachter and Reyburn 1991:244).[3] Several repetitions of key words also support this concentric pattern: *'elohim* [TH430, ZH466] (God) in 25:2 and 25:22; *bosh* [TH954, ZH1017] (disgrace) followed by *qawah* [TH6960, ZH7747] (hope) in 25:2-3 and 25:20-21; *'oyebay* [TH341, ZH367] (my enemies) in 25:2 and 25:19; and *khatto'wth* [TH2403A, ZH2633] (sins) in 25:7 and 25:18.[4] Seeing this structure enables us to see the five primary themes of Psalm 25 and the psalm's ultimate goal: honor, guidance, deliverance, forgiveness, faith.

Honor. Psalm 25 opens and closes with petitions that the psalmist not be disgraced (25:2-3 and 25:20). Concern for a good reputation or honor has been expressed repeatedly in previous psalms (3:3; 4:2; 7:5). Honor or a good reputation is to be highly valued (see, e.g., 91:15; 112:9; Prov 3:16, 35; 4:8; 8:18; 22:1, 4). Avoiding disgrace is a key theme in Psalm 25.

Guidance. To avoid disgrace in life, David needed guidance. Prayers for guidance play a prominent role in this psalm: "Show me the right path" (25:4), "Point out the road for me to follow" (25:4), and "Lead me . . . and teach me" (25:5). These petitions are based on the assurance that the Lord is a trustworthy and willing guide: "He shows the proper path" (25:8), "He leads . . . teaching them his way" (25:9), "The LORD leads with unfailing love" (25:10), and "He will show them the path" (25:12). Since David knows the Lord as his guiding shepherd (23:2-4), he can plead for and be assured of the guidance he needs to avoid disgrace.

Deliverance. Deliverance from enemies is hinted at in the opening strophe: "Do not let me be disgraced, or let my enemies rejoice in my defeat" (25:2). This concern becomes a dominant note in the final stanza: "Save me" (25:17), "See how many enemies I have" (25:19), "Rescue my life" (25:20), "Ransom Israel" (25:22). Disgrace would come through the mouths of the enemies, so deliverance from the enemies is deliverance from disgrace, which requires guidance for maneuvering down the right path.

Forgiveness. Forgiveness is the central concern of the psalm. The need for forgiveness comes to expression in the final line of the second strophe and the final line of the corresponding fourth strophe: "Do not remember the rebellious sins of my youth" (25:7) and "Forgive all my sins" (25:18). The need for forgiveness is also the concern of the central strophe of the central stanza: "Forgive my many, many sins" (25:11). Following the Lord's guidance and walking in his way, walking in his truth (25:5) and obeying his covenant stipulations (25:10) is the path of honor. Sin leads to disgrace as obedience leads to honor (119:5-6). So how can there be any hope of avoiding disgrace when we are not just aware of our sin (25:7, 18) but when we are aware of our many, many sins (25:11)? By God's forgiveness. But how can we hope for forgiveness from a just and holy God? By faith.

Faith. Faith is where the psalm begins: "I trust in you, my God! Do not let me be disgraced" (25:2) and "No one who trusts in you will ever be disgraced" (25:3). Faith is where the psalm ends: "Do not let me be disgraced, for in you I take refuge" (25:20) and "May integrity and honesty protect me, for I put my hope in you" (25:21). Through faith and hope in a God who is characterized by "unfailing love" (25:6, 7, 10), "compassion" (25:6), and mercy (25:7), we can experience the forgiveness needed to be delivered from disgrace that is the consequence of our sin. Through faith we can follow the guidance we receive and walk on the path that leads to honor.

Our forgiveness, deliverance, guidance, and honor are not, however, the ultimate goal of Psalm 25. These are means to a higher end—the highest end. This highest end occupies pride of place in the psalm, the first colon of the central line: "For the honor of your name, O LORD" (25:11). Forgiveness, deliverance, guidance, and honor—all legitimate concerns, all for the honor of God's own name.

ENDNOTES

1. Atbash is a code system "where the first letter of the alphabet is represented by the last, the second letter by the next to the last, and so on" (Leeman 1996:44). Atbash is used in Jer 25:26 where *sheshak* [TH8347, ZH9263] stands for *babel* [TH894, ZH951],

and in Jer 51:1 where *leb qamay* [TH3820A, ZH4214] stands for *kasdim* [TH3778, ZH4169] (see Thompson 1980:518, 747).
2. Zenger (1994) has shown that Pss 25 and 34 are an outside frame around the concentrically arranged subgroup, Pss 25–34.
3. I have modified their structure slightly by joining 25:1-3 into a single unit.
4. These nouns are positioned at the end of each of the strophes in the first and third stanzas. Note also the use of the synonym *'awon* [TH5771, ZH6411] (sins) in the central strophe (25:11).

◆ Y. Psalm 26

A psalm of David.

1 Declare me innocent, O LORD,
for I have acted with integrity;
I have trusted in the LORD without wavering.
2 Put me on trial, LORD, and cross-examine me.
Test my motives and my heart.
3 For I am always aware of your unfailing love,
and I have lived according to your truth.
4 I do not spend time with liars
or go along with hypocrites.
5 I hate the gatherings of those who do evil,
and I refuse to join in with the wicked.
6 I wash my hands to declare my innocence.
I come to your altar, O LORD,
7 singing a song of thanksgiving
and telling of all your wonders.
8 I love your sanctuary, LORD,
the place where your glorious presence dwells.

9 Don't let me suffer the fate of sinners.
Don't condemn me along with murderers.
10 Their hands are dirty with evil schemes,
and they constantly take bribes.
11 But I am not like that; I live with integrity.
So redeem me and show me mercy.
12 Now I stand on solid ground,
and I will publicly praise the LORD.

NOTES

26:1 *I have acted with integrity.* The word *bethummi halakti* [TH8537/1980, ZH9448/2143] ("blameless" + "walk") forms an *inclusio* with *bethummi 'elek* (I do what is right) in 26:11 (Mosca 1985:220-221). "Integrity" in 26:1 also links this psalm with the previous one, "May integrity and honesty protect me" (25:21).

I have trusted. The word *batakhti* [TH982, ZH1053] links this psalm with 25:2, "I trust (*batakhti*) in you."

without wavering. The NLT along with other translations (e.g., NIV and NRSV) take *lo' 'em'ad* [TH3808/4571, ZH4202/5048] as a circumstantial clause. It is preferable, however, to take it as an independent clause, "I will not waver." In 26:1 and 11-12 we have the sequence of integrity followed by having a firm place to stand, with a clear wordplay on *ma'ad* [TH4571, ZH5048] ("waver," 26:1) via *'amad* [TH5975, ZH6641] ("stand," 26:12). The sense in 26:1b is, "Since I have trusted in the LORD, I will not waver."

26:2 *trial. . . . Test.* While a court scene is no doubt in view, the words *bakhan* [TH974, ZH1043] and *tsarap* [TH6884, ZH7671] evoke an image of the smelting process (see note at 11:4). The NLT correctly chooses the Qere (*tsorpah* [TH6884, ZH7671]) over the Kethiv.

motives and my heart. For the word pair *kilyah* [TH3629, ZH4000] (emotions) and *leb* [TH3820, ZH4213] (thoughts) see the note at 7:9.

26:3 ***unfailing love . . . truth.*** The words *khesed* [TH2617, ZH2876] and *'emeth* [TH571, ZH622] link this psalm with the previous one (see 25:5-7, 10). "I have lived according to your truth" forms an *inclusio* with "I have acted with integrity" in 26:1. Verses 1-3 are thus the first strophe (Mosca 1985:223).

26:4 ***hypocrites.*** The word *na'alamim* [TH5956, ZH6623] means "those who conceal themselves," either in the sense of "hiding under a false appearance" (see BDB 761) or in the sense of "insidiously, craftily" (HALOT 2.834; see also Zorell 1963:603). The latter would fit well with the "treacherous" in 25:3 (see note).

26:5 ***I hate.*** "Hate" links this psalm with 25:19.

to join in with. The word *lo' 'esheb* [TH3808/3427, ZH4202/3782] forms an *inclusio* with *lo'-yashabti* (I do not spend time with) at the beginning of 26:4. Verses 4-5 are thus the second strophe (Mosca 1985:225).

26:7 ***singing.*** The NLT correctly follows the spelling of the MT here (Hiphil infinitive construct).

26:9 ***sinners.*** This word links this psalm with 25:8; see also 1:1, 5.

26:10 ***bribes.*** See 15:5.

26:11 ***redeem . . . show . . . mercy.*** "Redeem" links this psalm with 25:22 ("ransom"); "mercy" links this psalm with 25:16.

26:12 ***Now I stand.*** Since this clause forms an *inclusio* with the end of 26:1 (see note), it is better to interpret the perfect verb as rhetorical for action that is certain to take place in the future (Waltke and O'Connor 1990:§30.5.1e): "My foot will stand on level ground."

COMMENTARY

Psalm 26 is chiastically arranged in five strophes (Mosca 1985). Strophes 1 (26:1-3), 3 (26:6-8), and 5 (26:11-12) have the psalmist and the Lord in view,[1] while strophes 2 (26:4-5) and 4 (26:9-10) have the psalmist and sinners in view.[2] The *inclusio* (see note on 26:1) articulates the heart of the psalm: Because of David's integrity and innocence, he is certain of coming out on top in the situation he faces.

Like Psalms 7 and 17, Psalm 26 is the prayer of one who has been falsely accused (Kraus 1988:325-326 and Mays 1989:128), so the psalm begins, "Declare me innocent." David is willing to have the Lord test him in the deepest recesses of his soul and is confident that the Lord will find no sin (see 17:3). This claim to innocence is clearly not a claim to sinlessness for several contextual reasons: (1) Psalm 26 not only follows Psalm 25 but is closely connected to Psalm 25, as the notes have demonstrated. The innocent David of Psalm 26 is the David who needs forgiveness for "many, many sins" in 25:11. (2) As in Psalm 25, so in Psalm 26, David's relationship to the Lord is grounded in the Lord's unfailing love and mercy (see notes on 26:3 and 26:11). (3) Trust (25:1-2; 26:1) or dependence on God's grace, not the psalmist's goodness (see 14:1-3), underlies this relationship. (4) Like Psalms 7 and 17, Psalm 26 is not the prayer of a self-righteous person but of a person of real integrity who has been falsely accused in some particular situation.

The psalmist has, nonetheless, genuine integrity. Strophes 2 and 4 stress the practical nature of this integrity. In these strophes the psalmist separates himself from sinners. While self-righteous separation is an abomination (Luke 18:9-14), "there is a legitimate form of separatism" (McCann 1996:783; see 2 Cor 6:14-18). God "hates those who love violence" (11:5), so those who submit to his sovereignty "hate the gatherings of those who do evil" (26:5; see also Prov 8:13). We hate sinners in the sense that we do not choose their sinful ways.[3] There must be a real difference between the righteous and the wicked. Believers have not just been forgiven; believers have also been changed (1 Cor 6:9-11). In Psalm 26 David is saying that he conforms to the standard laid out in Psalms 1, 15, and 24. He conforms—not perfectly—but truly (with integrity).

So in this psalm David has great confidence as he prays for deliverance from false accusations. He knows he is a man of integrity in general and innocent in regard to the accusations brought against him in particular. Since God is just, David prays to be declared innocent. He prays with confidence: "I have trusted . . . without wavering" (26:1) and "Now I stand on solid ground" (26:12). Ultimately, however, David trusts not in his own integrity but in his Lord's merciful presence. The outside strophes underscore this truth: "I have trusted" (26:1) and "redeem me and show me mercy" (26:11). The central strophe brings this truth into sharp relief. In the sanctuary David finds an altar, a place of asylum from false accusations because it is a place where other sins have been atoned for. In the sanctuary David will sing songs of thanksgiving to the Lord, who has done marvelous things for him. In the sanctuary David will encounter God's glory that calls forth a response of love from David's own heart. This love shows itself to be genuine as it keeps the commandments by faith, faith in a God of unfailing love and mercy.

ENDNOTES

1. The divine name occurs only in these strophes.
2. Note also that strophes 2 and 4 begin with a negative adverb. For numerous other details that support this chiastic structure see Mosca 1985.
3. In Prov 1:29 hating is the same as not choosing (see also Rom 9:10-13).

◆ Z. Psalm 27

A psalm of David.

1 The LORD is my light and my salvation—
so why should I be afraid?
The LORD is my fortress, protecting me
from danger,
so why should I tremble?
2 When evil people come to devour me,
when my enemies and foes
attack me,
they will stumble and fall.
3 Though a mighty army surrounds me,
my heart will not be afraid.
Even if I am attacked,
I will remain confident.

4 The one thing I ask of the LORD—
the thing I seek most—
is to live in the house of the LORD all
the days of my life,
delighting in the LORD's perfections
and meditating in his Temple.
5 For he will conceal me there when
troubles come;
he will hide me in his sanctuary.
He will place me out of reach on
a high rock.
6 Then I will hold my head high
above my enemies who surround me.

At his sanctuary I will offer sacrifices
with shouts of joy,
singing and praising the LORD with
music.

7 Hear me as I pray, O LORD.
Be merciful and answer me!
8 My heart has heard you say, "Come
and talk with me."
And my heart responds, "LORD, I am
coming."
9 Do not turn your back on me.
Do not reject your servant in anger.
You have always been my helper.
Don't leave me now; don't abandon me,
O God of my salvation!
10 Even if my father and mother
abandon me,
the LORD will hold me close.
11 Teach me how to live, O LORD.
Lead me along the right path,
for my enemies are waiting
for me.
12 Do not let me fall into their
hands.
For they accuse me of things
I've never done;
with every breath they threaten me
with violence.
13 Yet I am confident I will see the LORD's
goodness
while I am here in the land of the
living.

14 Wait patiently for the LORD.
Be brave and courageous.
Yes, wait patiently for the LORD.

NOTES

27:2 ***evil people.*** The word *mere'im* [TH7489, ZH8317] occurs in 26:5 ("those who do evil"); false witnesses are in view in both psalms (see 27:12).

foes. The word *'oyebay* [TH341, ZH367] (see also 27:6) occurs in 25:2, 19 and links the two psalms.

will stumble. The perfect verb is used rhetorically here for action that is certain to take place in the future (Waltke and O'Connor 1990:§30.5.1e).

27:3 ***I will remain confident.*** The word *boteakh* [TH982, ZH1053] (trust) links Ps 27 with 26:1 and 25:2.

27:6 ***shouts of joy.*** The word *teru'ah* [TH8643, ZH9558] is a parallel term for *todah* [TH8426, ZH9343] in 26:7 (van Grol 1996:28; Delitzsch 1982:358).

27:7 ***Be merciful.*** The word *khonneni* [TH2603, ZH2858] is the same request made in 26:11 and 25:16 and links the three psalms.

27:8 ***My heart has heard you say, "Come and talk with me."*** The text is quite difficult here; an emendation is warranted. I propose emending to *lek 'amar libbi baqqesh panayw* ("Come," my heart said [to me], "seek his face"). For this kind of self-exhortation see 103:1-2.

27:9 ***O God of my salvation!*** The words *'elohe yish'i* [TH430/3468, ZH466/3829] occurs in 25:5 and links the two psalms.

27:11 ***Teach me how to live.*** The verb (Hiphil of *yarah* [TH3384E, ZH3723]) and the noun (*derek* [TH1870, ZH2006]) also occur together in 25:8, 12 and link the two psalms.

the right path. The word *'orakh mishor* links Ps 27 with Pss 25 and 26; *'orakh* [TH734, ZH784] occurs in 25:4, 10, and *mishor* [TH4334, ZH4793] in 26:12. *Mishor* occurs only three other times in the Psalter (45:6 [7]; 67:4 [5]; 143:10).

27:12 ***with every breath they threaten me with violence.*** The word translated "breath" (*yapeakh* [TH3307, ZH3641]) is best taken as a synonym of *'ed* [TH5707, ZH6332] (witness); see HALOT 2.424 and Pardee 1978. The form is a singular for a collective, and the sense is "violent witnesses" (Craigie 1983:230). The word *khamas* [TH2555, ZH2805] (violence) occurs in 25:19 ("how *viciously* they hate me").

27:13 *Yet.* The word *lule'* [TH3884, ZH4295] is problematic; it means "unless" and marks the protasis before an apodosis, which is absent in this line. In the absence of an apodosis, *lule'* may simply serve as a particle for absolute certainty (GKC §159ee and HALOT 2.524). But it should also be noted that the Masoretic scribes put extraordinary points, i.e., special dots above and below the letters of this word,[1] for one of a number of possible reasons. Kelly, Mynatt, and Crawford (1998:33) list four possible reasons: The text is (1) to be erased, (2) suspect, (3) the subject of special midrashic comment, or (4) doctrinally problematic.

27:14 *Wait.* The word *qawah* [TH6960, ZH7747] occurs in 25:3, 5, 21 and links the two psalms.

COMMENTARY

Psalm 27 is intertwined thematically with the two previous psalms. All three share the same foundation: trust in the Lord (25:2; 26:1; 27:3) and a plea for his mercy (25:16; 26:11; 27:7). In both Psalms 25 and 27 David expresses hope (25:3, 5, 21; 27:14) directed toward the God of his salvation (25:5; 27:9). Salvation is needed in view of the violence (25:19; 27:12) of the enemy (25:2, 19; 27:2, 6). Because David fears the Lord (25:12, 14), he does not fear his foes (27:1, 3). With confidence David looks to the Lord to teach him the best way to go (25:8, 12; 27:11).

Both Psalms 26 and 27 are prayers of one falsely accused (26:1-3; 27:12). The adversaries are those who do evil (26:5; 27:2). David prays that he not suffer the fate of the wicked (26:9) and is confident that the Lord will hold him close, even if all others forsake him (27:10). So David is confident that he will stand on level ground (26:12; 27:11).

Psalm 27, like Psalm 26, is comprised of five strophes. The psalm opens and closes on a note of confidence (27:1 and 27:13-14). The second strophe (27:2-3) brings the enemy into view, while the fourth strophe (27:7-12) is a prayer for mercy with false accusations of the enemy in view. The theme of the central strophe (27:4-6) is the same as that of the central strophe of Psalm 26: experiencing the presence of God in the sanctuary.

The central request—the one thing sought most—is to live in the presence of God, delighting in his perfections. In God's presence is safety; in God's presence is victory and joy. But surrounding this inner experience of God's presence, where all is well, are surrounding armies bent on destruction and enemies who would do violence to the psalmist. So he turns to God with a prayer for mercy. The obvious need is the mercy of deliverance from the foe, but there is a more foundational mercy sought as well—the mercy on one who has committed many, many sins (25:11) but who needs to enter into intimate communion with God (27:8). What does it ultimately profit if you are delivered from surrounding foes, but do not have the Lord holding you close?

Knowing that the Lord will hold us close means that the enemies who surround us are themselves surrounded by the Lord, who is our light and salvation, as well as our confidence and hope. On the inside we know the presence of God, so on the outside we are fearless and courageous—courageous with the confidence that the presence of God will have a practical outworking in this life.

Eaton (1967:87) points out that Jesus once said to Martha, "There is only one thing worth being concerned about. Mary has discovered it" (Luke 10:42). Psalm 27 asks, "Have you?"

ENDNOTES

1. It is the only word in the MT to have extraordinary points both above and below (Kelly, Mynatt, and Crawford 1998:140).

◆ AA. Psalm 28

A psalm of David.

1 I pray to you, O LORD, my rock.
Do not turn a deaf ear to me.
For if you are silent,
I might as well give up and die.
2 Listen to my prayer for mercy
as I cry out to you for help,
as I lift my hands toward your holy sanctuary.

3 Do not drag me away with the wicked—
with those who do evil—
those who speak friendly words to their neighbors
while planning evil in their hearts.
4 Give them the punishment they so richly deserve!
Measure it out in proportion to their wickedness.
Pay them back for all their evil deeds!
Give them a taste of what they have done to others.
5 They care nothing for what the LORD has done
or for what his hands have made.
So he will tear them down,
and they will never be rebuilt!

6 Praise the LORD!
For he has heard my cry for mercy.
7 The LORD is my strength and shield.
I trust him with all my heart.
He helps me, and my heart is filled with joy.
I burst out in songs of thanksgiving.

8 The LORD gives his people strength.
He is a safe fortress for his anointed king.
9 Save your people!
Bless Israel, your special possession.*
Lead them like a shepherd,
and carry them in your arms forever.

28:9 Hebrew *Bless your inheritance.*

NOTES

28:1 ***my rock.*** For the image of God as "my rock" see 18:2, 46, and 19:14. In 27:5 David was confident that the Lord would set him safely on a rock. "Rock" is part of the "refuge" semantic domain (see Introduction).

28:2 ***I lift my hands.*** The lifting of the hands is a gesture that may symbolize the receiving of something from God or the desire to be pulled out of the depths by God (see Keel 1997:321-322 for a brief discussion and graphic representations of hands lifted in prayer).

toward your holy sanctuary. The word *debir* [TH1687, ZH1808] has the inner sanctuary or Most Holy Place in view (see 1 Kgs 6:16; 8:6; HALOT 1.208).

28:3 ***evil.*** The word *ra'ah* [TH7451B, ZH8288] occurs in 27:5 ("trouble").

28:4 ***Give.*** The word *nathan* [TH5414, ZH5989] occurs in 27:12 ("fall").

28:5 ***rebuilt.*** The verb (*yibnem* [TH1129, ZH1215]) plays on the verb translated "care" (*yabinu* [TH1129, ZH1067]) in the previous line (McCann 1996:789); poetic justice is underscored by this play on words.

28:7 ***I trust.*** For this same verb (*batakh* [TH982, ZH1053]) see 25:2; 26:1; 27:3.

songs. The word "song" has the preposition *min* [TH4480, ZH4946] (from) attached to it, which presents a grammatical difficulty. Perhaps the text should be emended from *mishiri* [TH7892, ZH8877] (from my song) to the otherwise unattested *mshyry,* which would then be understood as a biform of *shir* [TH7891, ZH8876] ("song"; so Craigie 1983:236). The related verb is used in 27:6.

thanksgiving. For the somewhat odd form of the verb see Joüon and Muraoka 1991:§54b.

28:8 ***gives his people strength.*** The word *'oz* [TH5797, ZH6437] (strength) is part of the "refuge" semantic domain (see Introduction). The NLT apparently presumes an emendation from *lamo* [TH3807.1/4123.1, ZH4200/4564] (them) to *le'ammo* [TH5971A/2050.2, ZH6639/2257] (his people); see Craigie 1983:236.

safe fortress. Lit., "refuge of victories." The word *ma'oz* [TH4581, ZH5057] (refuge) is used in 27:1 (McCann 1996:790) and is part of the "refuge" semantic domain (see Introduction).

COMMENTARY

Psalm 28 is the third in a series of three psalms that express the prayers of one falsely accused (Craigie 1983:241; Kraus 1988:340; McCann 1996:789). A variety of lexical repetitions link Psalm 28 to Psalm 27 (see notes) and thereby to Psalm 26 (to which Ps 27 is linked). Implicit in David's request that he not be treated like the wicked (28:3) is an affirmation of his innocence.

Psalm 28 divides naturally into two strophes (28:1-5 and 28:6-9). The beginning of the second strophe (28:6) is marked by the words "he has heard my cry for mercy," which echoes "Listen to my prayer for mercy" in 28:2. The first strophe expresses the prayer, while the second celebrates a positive answer. Both strophes end with an odd line that can be scanned as a monocolon or a bicolon with a single word in the first colon; both of these lines contain two verbs, each having a third-person masculine plural suffix attached, a grammatical feature found nowhere else in the poem.

The first strophe is a prayer for justice with three main ideas:

1. Don't be silent (28:1-2). David begins by praying that the Lord as his rock/refuge not refuse to answer him by remaining silent. If God is silent, there is no hope. Rather, David would have the Lord listen to his prayer, as he directs that prayer toward the sanctuary (see, e.g., 1 Kgs 8:38-39).

2. Don't treat me like a sinner (28:3). David prays that he not be treated like the wicked, for that would be unjust, since David is innocent of the accusation being leveled against him. The accusation in particular may be that David has broken a covenant arrangement with someone, i.e., that he did not keep the "friendly words" he spoke under oath when making the agreement (Craigie 1983:239).

3. Treat them as they deserve (28:4-5). The prayer here is not for personal vengeance but for divine justice (McCann 1996:789). The poetic nature of the justice sought comes out in two ways. First, those who do evil will get the punishment they deserve, because they have not cared about what the Lord has done. Second, they will be paid back "for all their evil deeds" because they have not cared about what God's "hands have made."

The second strophe is a celebration of the answer to prayer with a twofold movement. First, it involves a prayer for himself that has been answered (28:6-7). The celebration begins with "Praise the LORD! For he has heard my cry for mercy." While it is possible that this is praise in anticipation of answered prayer (Gerstenberger 1988:129), it is more natural to presume a time lapse between the two strophes, wherein the Lord answered the prayer offered in strophe 1. The Lord has proven himself to be a trustworthy refuge. Since David trusted with all his heart, he now rejoices with all his heart. Second, it involves an offering of prayer for others (28:8-9). David concludes his celebration of answered prayer by offering a similar prayer for others. He prays that the Lord would be a refuge for the people as he has been for the king (see note on 28:8). As he has blessed (*barak* [TH1288A, ZH1385]) the Lord (28:6), so he asks that the Lord would bless (*barak*) the people (28:9a). As David has lifted (*nasa'* [TH5375, ZH5951]) his hands to the Lord (28:2), he concludes by asking the Lord to "carry" (*nasa'*) his people forever (28:9).

The destiny of the people is bound up with the destiny of the king (Eaton 1967:89). As the king has been saved through intercession, so will the people. Jesus prayed to the one who could save him from death, and his prayers were answered when he was raised from the dead (Heb 5:7). He is now able to save all who come to God through him, because he lives forever to plead with God on their behalf (Heb 7:25).

◆ BB. Psalm 29

A psalm of David.

1 Honor the LORD, you heavenly beings*;
honor the LORD for his glory and strength.
2 Honor the LORD for the glory of his name.
Worship the LORD in the splendor of his holiness.

3 The voice of the LORD echoes above the sea.
The God of glory thunders.
The LORD thunders over the mighty sea.
4 The voice of the LORD is powerful;
the voice of the LORD is majestic.
5 The voice of the LORD splits the mighty cedars;
the LORD shatters the cedars of Lebanon.
6 He makes Lebanon's mountains skip like a calf;
he makes Mount Hermon* leap like a young wild ox.
7 The voice of the LORD strikes with bolts of lightning.
8 The voice of the LORD makes the barren wilderness quake;
the LORD shakes the wilderness of Kadesh.
9 The voice of the LORD twists mighty oaks*
and strips the forests bare.
In his Temple everyone shouts, "Glory!"

10 The LORD rules over the floodwaters.
The LORD reigns as king forever.
11 The LORD gives his people strength.
The LORD blesses them with peace.

29:1 Hebrew *you sons of God.* **29:6** Hebrew *Sirion,* another name for Mount Hermon. **29:9** Or *causes the deer to writhe in labor.*

NOTES

29:2 *in the splendor of his holiness.* This phrase is often understood as referring to the appearance of the worshipers—their appropriate attire or attitude (e.g., McCann 1996:792). But it is better understood as a reference to the appearance of the Lord in the splendor of the storm described in 29:3-9 (Cross 1950:21 and Futato 1984:236).

29:3 *voice.* The voice of the Lord refers to thunder in this context ("the God of glory thunders"); for "voice" as thunder in the context of a rainstorm see 18:13 [14]. The repetition of *qol* [TH6963, ZH7754] (voice) reminds one of the rolling thunder of a storm as its follows its trek. The powerful and majestic voice (*qol*) of the Lord contrasts with the petitioning voice (*qol*) of the psalmist in 28:2, 6.

29:4 *is powerful.* For the preposition Beth of essence marking the predicate, see Joüon and Muraoka 1991:§133c. A wooden translation would be "The voice of the LORD in power," but Hebrew at times uses the preposition Beth ("in") where English uses the verb "is."

29:6 *skip.* The Mem on the end of the verb is probably an example of enclitic Mem (Hummel 1957). The enclitic Mem is an archaic grammatical particle of uncertain function but usually associated with the genitive function of nouns. For a full discussion see Waltke and O'Connor 1990:§9.8. Emerton (1996:325-326) denies the existence of enclitic Mem here, arguing for a pl. suffix *-m* [TH3963.1, ZH4392] with the trees of 29:5 as the antecedent, but this explanation is dubious, since it is difficult to imagine trees that were split and shattered now skipping like calves. The verb "skip" does not refer to joyful frolicking in this context but to awe and dread, as in 114:4-7.

Mount Hermon. As the NLT footnote indicates, Sirion is another name for Mount Hermon (see Deut 3:9).

29:7 *with bolts of lightning.* To communicate the idea "with," the preposition Beth [TH871.2, ZH928] is expected (see Isa 10:15), but not necessary. Compare the use of *ragam* [TH7275, ZH8083], ("to stone") with Beth in Deut 21:21 and without Beth in Josh 7:25.

29:9 *oaks.* The word *'ayyaloth* [TH355, ZH387] means "deer" (DCH 1.212 and HALOT 1.40), which is problematic on a number of counts (Futato 1984:221-222), especially the lack of congruency with the following colon (H. Cohen 1996:259). The emendation to *'eloth* [TH352A, ZH381] (oaks) is justifiable.[1]

Temple. "Temple" picks up the motif of the "sanctuary" from 28:2.

everyone. The word *kullo* [TH3605, ZH3972] can have the vague or general sense of "everyone" (Joüon and Muraoka 1991:§146j and BDB 482).

29:10 *floodwaters.* Heb. *mabbul* [TH3999, ZH4429] occurs only here and in the story of the flood in Noah's day. The *mabbul* probably refers to the celestial waters that are the source of the waters that fell at the time of the flood and that fall in every rainstorm.[2]

forever. The king who reigns forever is the Lord, who will carry his people forever (28:9).

29:11 *The LORD gives his people strength.* The words *yhwh 'oz le'ammo yitten* [TH5971A, ZH6639] are a clear echo of the beginning of 28:8 (*yhwh 'oz le'ammo*), presuming that the emendation suggested in 28:8 is correct (see note). The use of the verb "gives" (*nathan* [TH5414, ZH5989]) sets up a contrast with Ps 28, for in 28:4 the Lord is paying back (*nathan*) the wicked, whereas in 29:11 he is giving (*nathan*) strength to the faithful.

blesses them with peace. Psalm 28 ends with the Lord blessing (*barak* [TH1288A, ZH1385]) his people, as does Ps 29. The Lord is faithful to bless his people with peace (*shalom* [TH7965, ZH8934]), in contrast to the wicked who "speak friendly words" (*shalom*) while planning evil in their hearts (28:3).

COMMENTARY

Psalm 29 falls into three strophes: a call to worship (two lines; 29:1-2), a description of the Lord's theophanic presence in a thunderstorm (seven lines; 29:3-9), and an affirmation of the Lord's reign (two lines; 29:10-11). The central strophe is comprised of seven lines, a number that underscores the perfection of the theophanic presence, and each line begins with *qol* [TH6963, ZH7754] ("voice" or "thunder") except the central line.

In the first strophe (29:1-2), the angelic hosts are called upon to ascribe glory and strength to the Lord, when he appears in holy splendor. They are to ascribe glory and strength to the Lord when such glory and strength appear in a thunderstorm like the one that is described in the second strophe.

The second strophe (29:3-9) describes a typical thunderstorm of the Syro-Palestinian coastal strip (albeit in hyperbolic terms). The storm brews over the sea, "the mighty sea" (29:3), which is a reference to the Mediterranean, and the God who thunders in this storm is the God of glory. In 29:4 the thundering voice is both "powerful" and "majestic." The appearance of this glory and power and majesty will be the occasion of the ascription of glory and strength called for in 29:1-2.

The thundering voice of the storm is next heard over land, as the storm moves off of the Mediterranean and crosses the Lebanon range; the storm breaks the cedars of the Lebanon mountains as it passes on its way. So powerful is this storm that it makes the Lebanon range skip like a calf, as the storm crosses the Beqa Valley and passes over Mount Hermon in the Anti-Lebanon range. Magnificent lightning bolts accompany this storm in the mountains as it then makes its way out into the Syrian desert.

Having followed the path of the storm and having described the destruction left in its wake, the psalmist now sets the time of year in which the storm took place: the fall. The first powerful storms of the fall would have stripped the deciduous trees in the forest of any remaining foliage (Dalman 1928:1.98-100). With the reference to the leaves falling, the description of the storm is over, as is the first motivation for the angelic host to ascribe glory to the Lord.

The second motivation is found at the end of 29:9, where everyone in the Temple shouts, "Glory!" In the context of 29:1-2 the "temple" is the heavenly temple where the angelic host has always shouted, "There is the glory!" when the Lord's glory and power appeared in the first storms of the fall (Futato 1984:223). The angelic host is called upon in 29:1-2 to follow suit when the Lord's glory appears in the coming fall storms. Implicit is the call to worshipers in the earthly Temple to join the chorus.

The opening line of the third strophe is unique in that it begins with the divine name: "the LORD." In fact, the divine name occurs 18 times in these 11 verses. Such glorious and powerful thunderstorms as the one described in the previous strophe are evidence that Yahweh is the Lord of the rain, not Baal. It is Yahweh who controls the floodwaters as eternal king. The power manifest in the thunderstorm is not a power that will be used against the Lord's people. The Lord will, rather, give just such power to his people, and he will bless them with complete prosperity (*shalom* [TH7965, ZH8934]; 29:11).

The ultimate appearing of the Lord was not, however, in a thunderstorm but in the person of his Son, the Lord Jesus Christ. The "God of glory" became a human being, and the apostles saw his glory (John 1:14). He came in glory to accomplish everything necessary for the salvation of his people, and he will come again "on the clouds of heaven with power and great glory" (Matt 24:30) to bless his people with complete prosperity.

ENDNOTES

1. See Futato 1984:241 for an explanation of the odd fem. pl.
2. See the discussion at 104:3, 13. For a concise discussion of the issues involved in the word *mabbul* [TH3999, ZH4429] and a somewhat different approach to its use in 29:10 see NIDOTTE 2.835-837.

◆ CC. Psalm 30

A psalm of David. A song for the dedication of the Temple.

1 I will exalt you, LORD, for you
rescued me.
You refused to let my enemies
triumph over me.
2 O LORD my God, I cried to you for help,
and you restored my health.
3 You brought me up from the grave,*
O LORD.
You kept me from falling into the
pit of death.

4 Sing to the LORD, all you godly ones!
Praise his holy name.
5 For his anger lasts only a moment,
but his favor lasts a lifetime!
Weeping may last through the night,
but joy comes with the morning.

6 When I was prosperous, I said,
"Nothing can stop me now!"
7 Your favor, O LORD, made me as secure
as a mountain.
Then you turned away from me,
and I was shattered.

8 I cried out to you, O LORD.
I begged the Lord for mercy, saying,
9 "What will you gain if I die,
if I sink into the grave?
Can my dust praise you?
Can it tell of your faithfulness?
10 Hear me, LORD, and have mercy
on me.
Help me, O LORD."

11 You have turned my mourning into
joyful dancing.
You have taken away my clothes
of mourning and clothed me
with joy,
12 that I might sing praises to you and
not be silent.
O LORD my God, I will give you
thanks forever!

30:3 Hebrew *from Sheol.*

NOTES

30:TITLE ***A psalm of David. A song for the dedication of the Temple.*** The title to Ps 30 is problematic. Psalm 30 is a psalm of thanksgiving for recovery from illness, so how could it have been sung at "the dedication of the Temple"? This question is as poignant for those who hold that the title does not reflect the original use of the poem as for those who hold that it does. To what does *bayith* [TH1004, ZH1074] (temple) refer? The *bayith* could be the Solomonic Temple, if David provided the psalm for the dedication, as he provided lumber for the construction. The word *bayith* was used for the Tabernacle (Josh 6:24; Judg 18:31; 1 Sam 1:7) and may here refer to it or to the tent David built to house the Ark. Perhaps illness delayed the dedication, and therefore thanksgiving for recovery was part of the dedication. Kidner (1973b:1.128) suggests that "song for the dedication of the Temple" is a misplaced postscript to Ps 29. No completely satisfactory answer has been set forth as to the relation between the title and the content of the psalm.

30:1 ***rescued.*** The word *dalah* [TH1802, ZH1926] means "draw water" (DCH 2.4380) and is used for drawing up water from a well (Exod 2:16, 19).

30:2 ***I cried.*** This same verb (*shawa'* [TH7768, ZH8775]) is used in 28:2.

30:3 ***grave.*** For the word *she'ol* [TH7585, ZH8619] see note on 6:5.

falling into the pit of death. Lit., "those who go down to the pit"; also occurs in 28:1.

30:4 ***Praise his holy name.*** The Hiphil of *yadah* [TH3034A, ZH3344] is the key word of the psalm. It occurs again in 30:9 [10] and 30:12 [13], where it is translated "give you thanks"; this same verb occurs in 28:7. The noun here is *zeker* [TH2143, ZH2352] (remembrance) and is a frequent parallel to *shem* [TH8034, ZH9005] (name) in other contexts, so "name" is justifiable as the gloss for *zeker* in this text (cf. 106:47; 1 Chr 16:35, which are parallel to 30:4. For other close parallels see 122:4 and 140:13 [14]).

30:7 ***made me as secure as a mountain.*** The Hebrew is difficult. The closest grammatically parallel text is 105:10, which could be rendered, "He confirmed it to Jacob as a decree." So the sense here seems to be "you confirmed strength as my mountain." The NLT captures this sense.

30:8 ***I cried out.*** This verb (*'eqra'* [TH7121, ZH7924]) occurs in 28:1. The use of the imperfect indicates repeated action in the past (Joüon and Muraoka 1991:§113e).

30:10 ***Hear me.*** This verb (*shema'* [TH8085, ZH9048]) occurs in 28:2 (see also 28:6).

Help. The Niphal of this verb (*'azar* [TH5826, ZH6468]) occurs in 28:7.

30:12 ***that I might sing.*** "That" translates the word *lema'an* [TH3807.1/4616, ZH4200/5100], which here introduces a result clause, not a purpose clause (Joüon and Muraoka 1991:§169g). The NLT's "I" renders the word *kabod* [TH3519, ZH3883] (glory). The LXX adds a first-person sg. pronoun, hence, "my glory." Some understand *kabod* to mean "soul," based on the parallel with *nepesh* [TH5315, ZH5883] in 7:5 [6] (e.g., Craigie 1983:251), but see the note on that text. If the consonants in "my glory" are the original reading, they could be repointed to read *kebedi* [TH3516, ZH3879] (my liver). In 30:12 it is best to read *kebedi* as a self-reference, "I" (see 16:9).

forever. The word *le'olam* [TH3807.1/5769, ZH4200/6409] occurs at the end of 30:6 [7] and forms an *inclusio* around the second stanza (30:6-12 [7-13]).

COMMENTARY

Psalm 30 is a psalm of thanksgiving for recovery from illness. Psalm 30 pairs up with Psalm 28, a prayer for deliverance that has many links with Psalm 30 (see notes), to form a frame around the celebration of the Lord's kingship in Psalm 29 (Zenger 1994). This poem is comprised of two stanzas (30:1-5 and 30:6-12), each having two strophes. The strophes in the second stanza (30:6-10 and 30:11-12) unpack the content of the corresponding strophes in the first stanza (30:1-3 and 30:4-5).

David found himself in terrible trouble. The language is that of a life-threatening illness: David had one foot in the grave (30:3, 9). David's sickness had a cause: sin. David's sin was that of autonomous self-confidence (30:6). God's favor had resulted in prosperity for David. In that situation David used the language of confidence in God ("I will not be shaken"; see 16:8), but had twisted it into the language of confidence in self and the presumption of continual prosperity ("Nothing can stop me now!"; see also 10:6). David then reaped what he had sown. Believing he did not need God near him, he experienced God's absence and the bodily illness that was symptomatic of this spiritual absence. The punishment fit the crime: He who thought he was so immovable found himself slipping dangerously down to death (Craigie 1983:254).

Two concerns accompanied David's illness. He was concerned about enemies triumphing over him (30:1) and the loss of praise to God that would result should he die (30:9). These concerns are not unique to this psalm (see commentary on Ps 6).

Though the Lord had in a sense turned away from David (30:7), David believed the Lord was yet present to hear his cry for help and mercy (30:2, 8). And David's expression of faith was not in vain. The Lord healed him, bringing him up from the brink of death. "As water is drawn from a well in a bucket, so too the psalmist had been drawn from the pit of death by the divine hand" (Craigie 1983:253).

The second strophe of the first stanza and the second strophe of the second stanza begin and end with thanksgiving, which is the key word of the psalm even as it is the final word (Craigie 1983:252).Whereas David had once thought he would not be shaken "forever," by the end of the psalm he is vowing to give thanks to the Lord "forever." Whereas David had nearly slipped into the silence of death, by the end of the psalm he is vowing not to be silent but to sing praise.

David's thanksgiving had a cause: reversal. The Lord had reversed David's circumstances. Favor had replaced anger, and the joy of the morning had replaced the weeping of the night. Dancing had replaced mourning, and garments of joy had replaced clothes of mourning. Health had replaced sickness. Dependence on God had replaced autonomous self-confidence. God's presence had replaced his absence. As a sick body had been symptomatic of a sick soul, a healthy body now spoke of a healthy soul (see 3 John 2) focused on the praise of God.

This great reversal experienced by David was only possible because of an even greater reversal that David's greater Son would experience one day. Because our sins of autonomous self-confidence were transferred to him, Jesus experienced the ultimate absence of God (Mark 15:34) and slipped past the brink, falling headlong into the very pit of death itself (Mark 15:37). But God reversed his circumstances early one Sunday morning, when he raised Jesus from the dead (Mark 16). By God's favor and through our faith we are united to Christ in his reversal, and thus ours is secured (Col 3:1-3). We will experience absolute reversal of all of life's sin and misery in our own resurrection from the dead (1 Cor 15:42-44), and like David we can enjoy a foretaste of that reversal now. So our lives, like David's, must be lived with a focus on the praise of God, the great reverser.

◆ DD. Psalm 31

For the choir director: A psalm of David.

1 O LORD, I have come to you for
protection;
don't let me be disgraced.
Save me, for you do what is right.
2 Turn your ear to listen to me;
rescue me quickly.

Be my rock of protection,
a fortress where I will be safe.
3 You are my rock and my fortress.
For the honor of your name, lead me out of this danger.
4 Pull me from the trap my enemies set for me,
for I find protection in you alone.
5 I entrust my spirit into your hand.
Rescue me, LORD, for you are a faithful God.

6 I hate those who worship worthless idols.
I trust in the LORD.
7 I will be glad and rejoice in your unfailing love,
for you have seen my troubles,
and you care about the anguish of my soul.
8 You have not handed me over to my enemies
but have set me in a safe place.

9 Have mercy on me, LORD, for I am in distress.
Tears blur my eyes.
My body and soul are withering away.
10 I am dying from grief;
my years are shortened by sadness.
Sin has drained my strength;
I am wasting away from within.
11 I am scorned by all my enemies
and despised by my neighbors—
even my friends are afraid to come near me.
When they see me on the street,
they run the other way.
12 I am ignored as if I were dead,
as if I were a broken pot.
13 I have heard the many rumors about me,
and I am surrounded by terror.
My enemies conspire against me,
plotting to take my life.

14 But I am trusting you, O LORD,
saying, "You are my God!"
15 My future is in your hands.
Rescue me from those who hunt me down relentlessly.
16 Let your favor shine on your servant.
In your unfailing love,
rescue me.
17 Don't let me be disgraced, O LORD,
for I call out to you for help.
Let the wicked be disgraced;
let them lie silent in the grave.*
18 Silence their lying lips—
those proud and arrogant lips that accuse the godly.

19 How great is the goodness
you have stored up for those who fear you.
You lavish it on those who come to you for protection,
blessing them before the watching world.
20 You hide them in the shelter of your presence,
safe from those who conspire against them.
You shelter them in your presence,
far from accusing tongues.

21 Praise the LORD,
for he has shown me the wonders of his unfailing love.
He kept me safe when my city was under attack.
22 In panic I cried out,
"I am cut off from the LORD!"
But you heard my cry for mercy
and answered my call for help.

23 Love the LORD, all you godly ones!
For the LORD protects those who are loyal to him,
but he harshly punishes the arrogant.
24 So be strong and courageous,
all you who put your hope in the LORD!

31:17 Hebrew *in Sheol.*

NOTES

31:5 ***Rescue me.*** The verb is a rhetorical perfect for action that is certain to take place in the future (Joüon and Muraoka 1991:§112h).

31:7 ***I will be glad and rejoice.*** The two verbs are both cohortatives. Firm resolve to rejoice is the sense, "I *will* rejoice" (Joüon and Muraoka 1991:§114c).

31:13 ***surrounded by terror.*** In 27:6 David was surrounded by enemies.

conspire against me. The language here is the same as that found in 2:2. The irony is that in 2:2 the nations are conspiring against David, but here the conspirators are from within the covenant community.

31:16 ***Let your favor shine.*** The root of the verb (*'or* [TH215, ZH239]) is the same as that of the noun used in 27:1, which is translated "light."

31:18 ***lying lips.*** This phrase picks up the theme of false accusations found in 27:12 ("they accuse me of things I've never done").

31:19 ***goodness.*** The Lord's goodness (*tub* [TH2898, ZH3206]) is referred to in 27:13.

31:20 ***You hide them in the shelter of your presence.*** This echoes 27:5 ("he will hide me in his sanctuary").

You shelter them in your presence. This also echoes 27:5 ("he will conceal me there").

31:24 ***be strong and courageous, all you who put your hope in the Lord.*** This final encouragement echoes the final line of Ps 27 ("Be brave and courageous"), as does the reference to hoping in the Lord (see 27:14).

COMMENTARY

As Psalms 28 and 30 form a frame around Psalm 29, Psalms 27 and 31 form a frame around Psalms 28–30 (Zenger 1994:46-47). Psalms 27 and 31 have many characteristics in common.[1] At the core of each psalm is the concept of the Lord as the one who hides, conceals, and protects the psalmist from trouble when he has been falsely accused. Both psalms end with the same word of encouragement: Be strong and courageous. But the two psalms have a key difference: Psalm 27 is a prayer for deliverance from trouble, while Psalm 31 is thanksgiving for deliverance from trouble.[2]

Psalm 31 can be divided into two strophes: 31:1-18 articulates a prayer of trust for deliverance, while 31:19-24 articulates thanksgiving for answer to that prayer (Craigie 1983:259).[3]

Petition and Trust (31:1–18). Petition and trust are so interwoven in this strophe that these 18 verses defy being grouped into subunits.[4] *Petition* is powerful: "Don't let me be disgraced," "Save me," "Listen to me," "Rescue me," "Be my rock of protection," "Pull me from the trap," "Rescue me," etc. Equally powerful is the note of confident *trust:* "I have come to you for protection," "You do what is right," "You are my rock and my fortress," "I entrust my spirit into your hands," "You are a faithful God," "I trust in the Lord," etc. Deep "distress" demanded the petitions and the trust. The language is that of illness occasioned by sin (31:9-10),[5] which resulted in ostracism (31:11-13) and false accusations (31:17-18).

Thanksgiving and Encouragement (31:19–24). This strophe overflows with *thanksgiving* for a deliverance that has been experienced: "How great is [your] goodness," "You lavish it," "You hide them in the shelter of your presence," "You shelter them in your presence," "He has shown me . . . his unfailing love," "He kept me safe," "You heard my cry for mercy and answered my call for help." David's own deliverance from false accusation (31:20) leads him to give words of encouragement to others:[6] "Love the LORD," and "be strong and courageous."

At the heart of this psalm are the words, "I entrust my spirit into your hand" (31:5). These are not words of resignation but of great "confidence in God's ability to deliver and protect" (Craigie 1983:260). There are times in our lives as believers when all earthly support is gone and we have no recourse but to say to God, "I entrust my spirit into your hand." If David said these words with great confidence, how much more can we, because Jesus has said them for us. In the noontime darkness of distress, while dying on the cross, Jesus said, "Father, I entrust my spirit into your hands!" (Luke 23:46). Bearing not just our sickness because of our sin but also the death we deserved to die, Jesus entrusted himself to the care of his protecting Father.

Jesus did not entrust himself to his Father's care in vain, for his Father is "a faithful God" who has "stored up [goodness] for those who fear" him. And he proved this on the third day, when he delivered Jesus from the power of death through the Resurrection. Since Jesus has gone before us, we can entrust our lives to God's protecting care. We must love him, and we can be strong and courageous even when we have to say, "It is up to you, God, what becomes of me, and I am willing to have it so" (Mays 1994:144).

ENDNOTES

1. Only some of the lexical links between Ps 27 and 31 were mentioned in the notes.
2. Psalms 28 and 30 share this same technique of a prayer for deliverance matched by a song of thanksgiving. While some take Ps 31 to be a lament (e.g., Gerstenberger 1988:136-140), Kraus (1988:360) is no doubt correct when he says that Ps 31 is an "individual song of thanksgiving that has recourse to profound lamentation." In addition to Kraus's arguments from analogies with Pss 18, 30, and 102 is the argument from context: Ps 29 is the center of a concentric group of psalms with three prayers for deliverance preceding and three songs of thanksgiving following (Zenger 1994:45).
3. See Craigie 1983:262 for parallels between the two sections, that support this analysis.
4. A quick comparison of the divisions in any of several major commentaries will confirm this.
5. See also Ps 32, which is a song of thanksgiving for deliverance from illness that was a result of sin.
6. See Ps 32 for this same pattern.

◆ EE. Psalm 32

A psalm of David.*

[1]Oh, what joy for those
 whose disobedience is forgiven,
 whose sin is put out of sight!
[2]Yes, what joy for those
 whose record the LORD has cleared
 of guilt,*
 whose lives are lived in complete
 honesty!
[3]When I refused to confess
 my sin,
 my body wasted away,
 and I groaned all day long.

[4] Day and night your hand of discipline
was heavy on me.
My strength evaporated like water
in the summer heat. *Interlude*

[5] Finally, I confessed all my sins to you
and stopped trying to hide
my guilt.
I said to myself, "I will confess my
rebellion to the LORD."
And you forgave me! All my guilt
is gone. *Interlude*

[6] Therefore, let all the godly pray to you
while there is still time,
that they may not drown in the
floodwaters of judgment.
[7] For you are my hiding place;
you protect me from trouble.
You surround me with songs of
victory. *Interlude*

[8] The LORD says, "I will guide you along
the best pathway for your life.
I will advise you and watch over
you.
[9] Do not be like a senseless horse or
mule
that needs a bit and bridle to keep
it under control."

[10] Many sorrows come to the wicked,
but unfailing love surrounds those
who trust the LORD.
[11] So rejoice in the LORD and be glad, all
you who obey him!
Shout for joy, all you whose hearts
are pure!

32:TITLE Hebrew *maskil.* This may be a literary or musical term. **32:2** Greek version reads *of sin.* Compare Rom 4:7.

NOTES

32:TITLE *A psalm.* The word *maskil* [TH4905, ZH5380] may mean "a didactic poem" (see Introduction).

32:3 *When I refused to confess my sin.* The Hebrew text could be translated more tersely, "when I was silent." The silence was a form of denial regarding the presence of sin.

my body wasted away. Lit., "my bones were wasting away." The language is that of physical illness, as in 31:9-10.

32:4 *My strength.* The word *leshaddi* [TH3955, ZH4382] probably means "my moisture" (see Delitzsch 1982:396 and BDB 545). Some suggest emending the text to *leshoni* [TH3956, ZH4383] ("my tongue"; Craigie 1983:264; Kraus 1988:400), but the MT makes sense as is. Moisture drying up may be a metaphor for the loss of vitality in general.

32:5 *stopped trying to hide my guilt.* This verb (Piel of *kasah* [TH3680, ZH4059]) means "cover" and plays on the same verb (Qal of *kasah*) translated "put out of sight" in 32:1. Our sin can be covered (put out of sight) only if we do not try to hide it.

And you forgave me! The word *nasa'* [TH5375, ZH5951] ("lift up" or "carry") plus a word for sin is used in two ways: (1) to carry sin in the sense of taking upon oneself the consequences of it and (2) to carry away sin in the sense of forgiving it (HALOT 2.726). The Lord is able to carry away our sin in the sense of forgiving it, because Christ carried our sin when on the cross he took upon himself our sin and its consequences.

32:6 *while there is still time.* The Hebrew text is quite difficult at this point. The NLT seems to capture the sense well enough.

32:8 *The LORD says.* The NLT makes explicit what is probably implicit in the text: The Lord is the speaker at this point.

32:9 *that needs a bit and bridle to keep it under control.* The word *'edyo* [TH5716, ZH6344] may refer to some part of the harness, hence "bit and bridle," and *liblom* is an infinitive construct of *balam* [TH1102, ZH1178], which means "to restrain." The phrase *bal qerob 'eleka*

[TH7126, ZH7928] ("to keep it under control," NLT) could be translated "to bring it close to you." The idea is that one ought to avoid stubbornness, because it will result in the infliction of pain in order to keep one near to God.

COMMENTARY

A third level of framing around Psalm 29 is found in Psalms 26 and 32. These two psalms, however, are related to each other more by their differences than by their similarities. They are related by way of contrast (Zenger 1994:47). Psalm 26 is the plea of one who is facing the possibility of suffering the fate of sinners in spite of his innocence, whereas Psalm 32 is the thanksgiving of one who suffered as a result of his own sin but was then restored.

Psalm 32 shares features of the psalms of thanksgiving and wisdom psalms (Craigie 1983:265). The first stanza (32:1-5) is comprised of two strophes: a beatitude characteristic of wisdom psalms (32:1-2) and a recounting of distress and deliverance characteristic of psalms of thanksgiving (32:3-5). The second stanza (32:6-11) is comprised of three strophes: a call to prayer characteristic of psalms of thanksgiving (32:6-7), instruction characteristic of wisdom psalms (32:8-10), and a call to rejoice characteristic of psalms of thanksgiving (32:11).

The Joy of Forgiveness (32:1-5). "Oh, what joy" (*'ashre* [TH835A, ZH897]) reminds us of Psalm 1, where well-being is experienced by the righteous, who live according to God's instruction. That the righteous are not sinless is clear from Psalm 32, where this same well-being is experienced by those who have sinned and been forgiven (McCann 1996:802). That sin at times pervades the life of the righteous is made clear by the use of all three of the primary words for sin in 32:1-2: *pesha', khata'ah, 'awon* [TH6588/2401/5771, ZH7322/2631/6411]. Blessedness is experienced by those who receive comprehensive forgiveness by living in complete honesty. This honesty is not honesty in general but honesty with regard to the presence of sin in one's life, as the next strophe makes clear.

"If we claim we have no sin, we are only fooling ourselves and not living in the truth" (1 John 1:8). That is exactly what David did. He tried to deal with his sin by denying its presence in his life. While this may have seemed to be the easy way, it turned out to be the hard way. The results of denial were disastrous. David became ill: His bones were in agony,[1] he groaned all day long, and his vitality was reduced to nothing. Finally, David had a change of heart and direction. His confession was as comprehensive as his sin, for the same three words used for sin are repeated in 32:5. Upon confession David was forgiven. It was just that easy! The Lord is able to carry away our sin in the sense of forgiving it, because Christ carried our sin when on the cross he took upon himself our sin and its consequences.

Learning the Easy Way (32:6-11). In 32:6-7 David draws out of his experience a lesson for others. He encourages his fellow believers not to deny their sins but to confess them before they result in disaster; the floodwaters of divine discipline can be avoided through honest and comprehensive confession of sin. In effect, David is saying, "I learned the hard way. Learn from my mistake. That's a much easier way." He also testifies to the truth that God is our refuge in times of trouble. When we come to him confessing our sins, we find in him protection from trouble and victory in the face of defeat.

The psalms are for the most part our speech to God, but on occasion, as is the case in 32:8-9, God speaks directly in a psalm. The Lord's encouraging words are quite complimentary to those of David. The Lord promises to teach believers "the best pathway" (32:8; see 25:4-5, 8-10, 12) and "advise" them (see 16:7, where the same word is translated "guides"). His instruction is summarized in 32:9: Don't take the hard way. The Lord is committed to having his people near to him, so they will be kept near to him in the long run. There is a hard way to be kept near, the way of denial and discipline. But there is also an easy way, the way of confession and forgiveness. The Lord is not, however, presenting two ways in a neutral fashion. He shows us his heart's desire. His heart's desire is that we avoid the hard way and take the easy way. The easy way is "the best pathway." This encouragement is sealed with the promise that "unfailing love surrounds those who trust the LORD" (32:10). In Psalm 26 we are taught to trust the Lord when we are innocent of the charges against us. In Psalm 32 we are taught to trust the Lord when we are guilty of the charges against us. In all of life we are to trust the Lord and experience his unfailing love.

The psalm ends with a call to rejoice in the Lord (32:11). And we can rejoice in him because he is commited to have us in his presence. Nothing can separate us from him, not even our sin. For when we sin, he is there to forgive. Even if we choose the hard way, he is there to forgive and to teach us again that there is an easy way. There is an easy way for us, because Jesus has taken the hard way in our place. He bore in his own body all of our sin and all of its misery. And he calls us to trust in him. Jesus says, "Come to me all you who are weary and carry heavy burdens, and I will give you rest. Take my yoke upon you. Let me teach you, because I am humble and gentle, and you will find rest for your souls. For my yoke is easy, and the burden I give you is light" (Matt 11:28-30, author's translation).

ENDNOTE

1. For the effect of sin on the bones see Prov 14:30, which can be translated "jealousy rots the bones."

◆ FF. Psalm 33

1 Let the godly sing for joy to the LORD;
 it is fitting for the pure to praise
  him.
2 Praise the LORD with melodies on
  the lyre;
 make music for him on the
  ten-stringed harp.
3 Sing a new song of praise to him;
 play skillfully on the harp, and sing
  with joy.
4 For the word of the LORD holds true,
 and we can trust everything he does.
5 He loves whatever is just and good;
 the unfailing love of the LORD fills
  the earth.

6 The LORD merely spoke,
 and the heavens were created.
He breathed the word,
 and all the stars were born.
7 He assigned the sea its boundaries
 and locked the oceans in vast
  reservoirs.
8 Let the whole world fear the LORD,

and let everyone stand in awe of
him.
[9] For when he spoke, the world began!
It appeared at his command.

[10] The LORD frustrates the plans of the
nations
and thwarts all their schemes.
[11] But the LORD's plans stand firm
forever;
his intentions can never be shaken.

[12] What joy for the nation whose God
is the LORD,
whose people he has chosen as his
inheritance.

[13] The LORD looks down from heaven
and sees the whole human race.
[14] From his throne he observes
all who live on the earth.
[15] He made their hearts,
so he understands everything
they do.

[16] The best-equipped army cannot save a
king,
nor is great strength enough to save
a warrior.
[17] Don't count on your warhorse to give
you victory—
for all its strength, it cannot save
you.

[18] But the LORD watches over those who
fear him,
those who rely on his unfailing love.
[19] He rescues them from death
and keeps them alive in times of
famine.

[20] We put our hope in the LORD.
He is our help and our shield.
[21] In him our hearts rejoice,
for we trust in his holy name.
[22] Let your unfailing love surround us,
LORD,
for our hope is in you alone.

NOTES

33:1 ***Let the godly sing for joy.*** This vocabulary repeats that of 32:11 and thus links the two psalms together.

33:2 ***lyre . . . ten-stringed harp.*** The words *kinnor* [TH3658, ZH4036] and *nebel* [TH5035A, ZH5575] probably refer to two kinds of lyres (Keel 1997:346-349; NIDOTTE 2.666-667, 3.13-14).

33:3 ***new song.*** The words *shir khadash* [TH7892/2319, ZH8877/2543] occurs also in 40:3 [4]; 96:1; 98:1; 144:9; 149:1. In 96:1, 98:1, and 144:9 the "new song" is explicitly connected with the Lord's kingship, and 149:1-2 further connects the "new song" with the Lord as Creator-King. The "new song" is in particular a victory song of the Divine Warrior in creation (33:6-9) and redemption (33:10-19) (Longman and Reid 1995:45 and 191).

play . . . on the harp. No particular stringed instrument is in view in the text.

33:7 ***He assigned the sea its boundaries.*** The Heb. *kones kanned me hayyam* [TH5067, ZH5603] (he gathers as in a heap the waters of the sea) refers to the containment of the seas.

33:9 ***appeared.*** The verb *'amad* [TH5975, ZH6641] conveys permanence and endurance; this same verb is used of the Lord's plans in 33:11a.

33:11 ***intentions.*** The same word (*makhsheboth* [TH4284, ZH4742]) is translated "schemes" in 33:10. The repetition of "plans" and "thoughts" within the contrast between those of the nations and those of the Lord underscores the sovereignty of the Lord's will over all human affairs.

33:12 ***joy.*** The word *'ashre* [TH835A, ZH897] connects this psalm to 32:1.

33:15 ***He made their hearts.*** The NLT leaves the word *yakhad* [TH3162, ZH3480] (together) untranslated. The LXX translates *yakhad* with *kata monas* [TG2848/3868, ZG2596/3441] (alone), and this may be the sense here (Craigie 1983:270).

33:18 ***watches over.*** The word *'ayin* [TH5869, ZH6524] (eye) is found with this same sense of "watch over" in 32:8.

33:21 ***rejoice . . . trust.*** Ps 33 ends on the same notes as Ps 32 (32:10-11).

COMMENTARY

The internal structure of Psalm 33 indicates that it was originally an independent literary unit. In the context of the Psalter, however, Psalm 33 is bound to Psalm 32. The lack of a title[1] and the repetition of vocabulary in 32:11 and 33:1 serve to tie the two psalms closely together. Psalm 33 expresses the rejoicing in the Lord and the shouting for joy anticipated in 32:11.

Psalm 33 has been called an alphabetizing psalm (Craigie 1983:271). Since it has 22 lines, one for each letter of the Hebrew alphabet, we could also call it a modified acrostic. Given the position of *'ashre* [TH835A, ZH897] (joy) at 33:12, it would seem that the psalm should be divided into two strophes of equal length (33:1-11 and 33:12-22). The first strophe celebrates divine sovereignty, while the second expresses joyful human dependence.

Celebrating Divine Sovereignty (33:1-11). In the next to the last line of Psalm 32 we are told that "unfailing love surrounds those who trust the LORD." The first strophe of Psalm 33 celebrates just how trustworthy the Lord is. The celebration is grand: Skillfully played musical instruments accompany the joyful singing of a "new song." The new song celebrates what the Lord has done in restoring David (Ps 32).

The celebration is grounded in the trustworthy character of God. His trustworthiness is seen in his word and deed. Here his word and deed are not separated, for his deed is the creation of the heavens and the earth by his word. When God said, "Let there be light," there was light. What he said happened, so his word is obviously something we can rely on in life. When the Lord told David he was forgiven (Ps 32), David was forgiven. We can rely on the Lord's word. And the "we" is as wide as the world, for "the whole world" is called upon to "stand in awe" of this sovereign God, whose word and deed are utterly trustworthy.

The Lord is not only sovereign over creation, he is also sovereign over human history, and the latter sovereignty is grounded in the former (Craigie 1983:273). The nations do not, however, always stand in awe of this trustworthy God. Often they plan and scheme in rebellion against him, but such plans are futile (see 2:1), for the Lord shatters and thwarts them in his own time and way (33:10). Whereas rebellious human plans are not trustworthy, the Lord's are: His plans "stand firm forever" and "can never be shaken" (33:11).

Joyful Human Dependence (33:12-22). When the Lord shatters the plans of the nations, all is not lost. Should one of those nations follow David's and the Lord's advice (Ps 32), "what joy" it would experience (32:1; 33:12), having become part of the "people he has chosen as his inheritance." At that time, Israel was the chosen nation, but even then the Lord was looking "down from heaven" upon the "whole human race" and observing "all who live on the earth" (33:13-14). As their Creator, he understands everything about them. In particular, he knows that their own resources are insufficient to save them.

"Those who rely on his unfailing love" will find in God not one who shatters their plans, but one who "rescues them from death and keeps them alive in times of famine." So we must depend on the Lord alone to save us. And this dependence is a joyful dependence, "for we trust in his holy name" and his "unfailing love surround[s] us," as we put our hope in him (33:18-22). As we hope in him, we will never be disappointed, "for the word of the LORD holds true, and we can trust everything he does" (33:4).

ENDNOTES

1. Pss 10 and 33 are the only psalms among Pss 3–41 that lack titles. Since Ps 10 was originally part of Ps 9 (see notes to Pss 9–10), Ps 33 is the only independent psalm that lacks a title.

◆ GG. Psalm 34*

A psalm of David, regarding the time he pretended to be insane in front of Abimelech, who sent him away.

1 I will praise the LORD at all times.
I will constantly speak his praises.
2 I will boast only in the LORD;
let all who are helpless take heart.
3 Come, let us tell of the LORD's
greatness;
let us exalt his name together.

4 I prayed to the LORD, and he
answered me.
He freed me from all my fears.
5 Those who look to him for help will be
radiant with joy;
no shadow of shame will darken
their faces.
6 In my desperation I prayed, and the
LORD listened;
he saved me from all my troubles.
7 For the angel of the LORD is a guard;
he surrounds and defends all who
fear him.

8 Taste and see that the LORD is good.
Oh, the joys of those who take
refuge in him!
9 Fear the LORD, you his godly people,
for those who fear him will have all
they need.
10 Even strong young lions sometimes go
hungry,
but those who trust in the LORD will
lack no good thing.

11 Come, my children, and listen to me,
and I will teach you to fear the LORD.
12 Does anyone want to live a life
that is long and prosperous?
13 Then keep your tongue from
speaking evil
and your lips from telling lies!
14 Turn away from evil and
do good.
Search for peace, and work to
maintain it.

15 The eyes of the LORD watch over those
who do right;
his ears are open to their cries for
help.
16 But the LORD turns his face against
those who do evil;
he will erase their memory from
the earth.
17 The LORD hears his people when they
call to him for help.
He rescues them from all their
troubles.
18 The LORD is close to the
brokenhearted;
he rescues those whose spirits are
crushed.

19 The righteous person faces many
troubles,
but the LORD comes to the rescue
each time.
20 For the LORD protects the bones of
the righteous;
not one of them is broken!

[21] Calamity will surely overtake the wicked,
and those who hate the righteous will be punished.

[22] But the LORD will redeem those who serve him.
No one who takes refuge in him will be condemned.

34 This psalm is a Hebrew acrostic poem; each verse begins with a successive letter of the Hebrew alphabet.

NOTES

34:TITLE ***A psalm of David, regarding the time he pretended to be insane in front of Abimelech.*** The title connects Ps 34 to the story found in 1 Sam 21:10-15. The phrase "pretended to be insane" comes from 1 Sam 21:13. In 1 Samuel the king's name is Achish. "Abimelech" is not a mistake but was probably a title for Philistine kings, just as "Pharaoh" was for Egyptian kings (Craigie 1983:278; Delitzsch 1982:408).

34:1 Psalm 34 is an acrostic with alphabetical features that go beyond each line starting with a succeeding letter of the alphabet. When the vowel letters of this opening line are removed, Aleph is at the beginning, Lamedh is in the middle, and Pe is at the end (spelling the letter name Aleph). Thus an Aleph is embedded in the line (Ceresko 1985:100-101), as it is in the overall structure (see note on 25:1-2). In addition it can be noted that these consonants are the root letters of the verb *'alap*, which means "to learn."

34:2 ***let all who are helpless take heart.*** Lit., "Let all who are discouraged hear and rejoice." The idea is that those in circumstances similar to David's will hear his story and be glad.

34:6 ***desperation.*** This word is related to the word translated "helpless" in 34:2. Those who are helpless or discouraged will find encouragement from David, who was discouraged and then was delivered.

34:8 ***Taste.*** This verb comes from the same root as the noun translated "insane" in the title. The title could be rendered "when he changed his taste" (see commentary).

joys. The word *'ashre* [TH835A, ZH897] connects Ps 34 to 33:12 and 32:1.

34:11 ***teach.*** The line of the Hebrew letter Lamedh contains another alphabetical feature: The root of the final word is *lamad* [TH3925, ZH4340] (teach), which is a synonym of *'alap* [TH502, ZH544] ("learn" in the Qal and "teach" in the Piel; Ceresko 1985:100, 103).

34:15 ***eyes.*** The line of the Hebrew letter Ayin contains another alphabetical feature: The line contains the word *'ayin* [TH5869, ZH6524] ("eye"; Ceresko 1985:100).

34:18 ***he rescues.*** A synonymous verb was used in 34:6 [7] with David as the object. What was true of David was and will be true of others as well.

34:20 ***broken.*** Those who have a broken heart (34:18) will not have a broken bone; the verb in the Hebrew is the same.

COMMENTARY

Together with Psalm 25, Psalm 34 forms the outermost frame in a group of psalms that surround Psalm 29 (Zenger 1994). Both of these psalms are acrostic poems with two special features in common: the lack of the Waw line and an additional Pe line that starts with a verb from the root *padah* [TH6299, ZH7009]. Whereas Psalm 25 is a prayer of petition, Psalm 34 is a corresponding prayer of thanksgiving with significant influence from the wisdom tradition (Kraus 1988:383). Both psalms have the avoidance of shame as a theme (see 34:22).

Psalm 34 seems to be comprised of two stanzas of unequal length (Gaebelein

1990). Psalm 34:1-7 rehearses David's distress and deliverance, and 34:8-22 articulates David's advice based on his experience (see this same pattern in Ps 32).

David's Experience (34:1-7). In a fashion typical of the songs of thanksgiving, David begins by resolving to praise the Lord and by calling upon others to join in the celebration of his deliverance. David was aware that others in the congregation were discouraged as he was, and he was confident that as they heard his testimony, they would be able to rejoice not only in David's deliverance but also in anticipation of their own.

The language of the psalm itself provides us with little information on the nature of David's distress. Here, however, the title provides that information. While fleeing from Saul, David sought refuge in Gath, one of the five chief cities of Philistia. But he was received with some suspicion, because his reputation for killing thousands of Philistines had preceded him. David was afraid of what King Achish might do to him (34:4; 1 Sam 21:12), so he pretended to be insane (34:TITLE; 1 Sam 21:13). The Lord used David's charade to deliver him from Achish. David not only feigned insanity, however, he also cried out to the Lord (34:6). The Lord also used David's prayers to set him free. Together, the original story and the psalm demonstrate a balance of human ingenuity and dependence on divine aid. The whole of the Christian life is one of balance: being 100 percent faithful to carry out our responsibilities, while depending 100 percent on the Lord.

David's face must have been quite a sight with drool running down his beard (1 Sam 21:13). His face would have been characterized by shame, not honor. Having gone through that experience, he was confident that the faces of all who look to the Lord will not be darkened with shame, for if they fear the Lord, his angel will deliver them.

David's Instruction (34:8-22). In the first half of the psalm David provided some indirect advice (34:2, 5). The mood changes in 34:8, as David addresses his audience in the second person and with imperatives. The first instruction has to do with the Lord's goodness. "Taste and see that the LORD is good," advises David (34:8). The Lord is good, though his goodness is at times experienced in strange ways. David "tasted" the Lord's goodness by changing his taste (i.e., pretending to be insane!). We must be open to the unusual ways that the Lord may choose to demonstrate his goodness to us.

His goodness means total well-being (*'ashre* [TH835A, ZH897]; 34:8; see note at 1:1). Those who show reverence (*yare'* [TH3372, ZH3707]) for the Lord will in fact "have all they need" (34:9). The Lord is good to all he has made, including the animals (see 104:21; 145:9), but his goodness to his people exceeds his goodness to the rest of his creatures (Matt 6:25-33). Lions may go hungry, but since the Lord is good (*tob* [TH2896, ZH3202]; 34:8), we can be assured that we "will lack no good [*tob*] thing" (34:10).

David then instructs his readers to fear the Lord (34:11-16). "Come, my children, and listen to me" (34:11) sounds like a line straight from the book of Proverbs (see Prov 4:1). As a father instructs his children in the fear of the Lord (e.g., Prov 2:1-5), so David instructs the congregation. Like the goodness of the Lord, the fear of the Lord results in blessing—here, the blessing of a long and prosperous life (34:12).[1]

But the fear of the Lord also brings with it the responsibility to live in keeping with wisdom's principles. Examples of these principles include guarding your speech, turning from evil, and living at peace with others (34:13-14). As in the book of Proverbs, the promise is that the Lord will watch over those who keep these principles and will oppose those who do not (34:16-17).

The final set of instructions (34:17-22) returns to the opening themes of distress and deliverance, forming an envelope around the central wisdom instructions. The Lord's goodness and the fear of the Lord are not a guarantee of a trouble-free life. When speaking of the "righteous" (34:19), David refers to "all their troubles" (34:17) and the "many troubles" (34:19) they will face in life. But the overwhelming assurance is that we can face these troubles with the confidence that the Lord will deliver us from them all. On our part we must look to him with a humbled heart for protection (34:18, 22). If we have a broken heart (34:18), the Lord will be so near to us that we will not have a broken bone (34:20).

All of the benefits held out to us in this psalm are ours because of Jesus Christ. At the time of his crucifixion, soldiers broke the legs of the two who were crucified with Jesus. (They did this to speed up the process of the execution.) "But when they came to Jesus, they saw that he was already dead, so they didn't break his legs. . . . These things happened in fulfillment of the Scriptures that say, 'Not one of his bones will be broken'" (John 19:33, 36). Jesus tasted the bitter cup of God's wrath in our place, that we might taste and see that he is good.

ENDNOTES

1. See Estes 1997:80-84 for a good overview of the blessings entailed in "life" in the wisdom tradition.

◆ HH. Psalm 35

A psalm of David.

1 O LORD, oppose those who oppose me.
Fight those who fight against me.
2 Put on your armor, and take up your shield.
Prepare for battle, and come to my aid.
3 Lift up your spear and javelin against those who pursue me.
Let me hear you say,
"I will give you victory!"
4 Bring shame and disgrace on those trying to kill me;
turn them back and humiliate those who want to harm me.
5 Blow them away like chaff in the wind—
a wind sent by the angel of the LORD.
6 Make their path dark and slippery,
with the angel of the LORD pursuing them.
7 I did them no wrong, but they laid a trap for me.
I did them no wrong, but they dug a pit to catch me.
8 So let sudden ruin come upon them!
Let them be caught in the trap they set for me!
Let them be destroyed in the pit they dug for me.

9 Then I will rejoice in the LORD.
I will be glad because he rescues me.
10 With every bone in my body I will praise him:
"LORD, who can compare with you?

Who else rescues the helpless from
the strong?
Who else protects the helpless and
poor from those who rob them?"

11 Malicious witnesses testify against me.
They accuse me of crimes I know
nothing about.
12 They repay me evil for good.
I am sick with despair.
13 Yet when they were ill, I grieved for
them.
I denied myself by fasting for them,
but my prayers returned unanswered.
14 I was sad, as though they were my
friends or family,
as if I were grieving for my own
mother.
15 But they are glad now that I am in
trouble;
they gleefully join together
against me.
I am attacked by people I don't even
know;
they slander me constantly.
16 They mock me and call me names;
they snarl at me.

17 How long, O Lord, will you look on and
do nothing?
Rescue me from their fierce attacks.
Protect my life from these lions!
18 Then I will thank you in front of the
great assembly.
I will praise you before all the people.
19 Don't let my treacherous enemies
rejoice over my defeat.
Don't let those who hate me
without cause gloat over my
sorrow.
20 They don't talk of peace;
they plot against innocent people
who mind their own business.
21 They shout, "Aha! Aha!
With our own eyes we saw him
do it!"

22 O LORD, you know all about this.
Do not stay silent.
Do not abandon me now, O Lord.
23 Wake up! Rise to my defense!
Take up my case, my God and my
Lord.
24 Declare me not guilty, O LORD my God,
for you give justice.
Don't let my enemies laugh about
me in my troubles.
25 Don't let them say, "Look, we got what
we wanted!
Now we will eat him alive!"

26 May those who rejoice at my troubles
be humiliated and disgraced.
May those who triumph over me
be covered with shame and
dishonor.
27 But give great joy to those who came
to my defense.
Let them continually say, "Great is
the LORD,
who delights in blessing his servant
with peace!"
28 Then I will proclaim your justice,
and I will praise you all day long.

NOTES

35:2 ***armor . . . shield.*** These translate two different Hebrew words for shield, for which see note at 5:12.

35:4 ***Bring shame and disgrace . . . humiliate.*** The psalmist prays that his opponents will experience the shame (see also 35:26) that the righteous will not (34:5 [6]); additionally, the same word for "humiliate" (*khapar* [TH2659, ZH2917]) occurs also in 34:5b but is translated "shame" there.

35:5 ***the angel of the LORD.*** The angel of the Lord is referred to in the Psalter only here, in 35:6, and in 34:7 [8].

35:6 ***pursuing them.*** The angel of the Lord "pursues" (*radap* [TH7291, ZH8103]) the "pursuing enemies" (*radap;* 35:3) of the psalmist.

35:7 ***trap . . . pit.*** These two words occur in a construct relationship in the first colon: "pit of their trap/net." It seems best to move the *'athnach* back one word, placing one noun in each colon, and to reverse the order (as in the NLT), so that the trap/net is laid (see 35:8 for the identical language) and the pit is dug.

35:11 ***Malicious witnesses.*** This echoes the language of the false witnesses in 27:12.

35:12 ***I am sick with despair.*** The word *shekol* [TH7908, ZH8890] (cf. its related verb *shakal* [TH7921, ZH8897]) "refers, with one exception, to the parental loss of progeny through miscarriage or sword" (Janzen 1995:56); the parent involved in a great number of texts is the mother.

35:13 ***my prayers returned unanswered.*** Lit., "my prayer returned to my bosom," an appropriate metaphor in the context of the bereft and lamenting mother of 35:12 and 35:14.

35:14 ***as if I were grieving for my own mother.*** The NLT (so too the NIV and RSV) takes *ka'abel-'em* [TH57/517, ZH63/562] ("weeping" + "mother") as an object genitive construction. Janzen (1995:59) has made the case for a subject genitive construction: "like a lamenting mother." While either is possible, the latter is a more fitting parallel for the previous colon.

35:15 ***I am attacked.*** The Hebrew is difficult: *nekim* [TH5222, ZH5784] is a masc. pl. adjective that means "beaten"; the plural makes no sense if referring to the psalmist. Dahood (1965:213) revocalizes the MT written text to *nokim* ("strikers"; Qal masc. pl. participle from *nakah* [TH5221, ZH5782]); Craigie (1983:285) emends to *tokim* [TH8496, ZH9412] (oppressors).

35:16 ***They mock me and call me names.*** The meaning of the Hebrew text is uncertain: *bekhanpe la'age ma'og* [TH2611A/3933/4580, ZH2868/4353/5056] (with the godless of derisions of provisions). The NLT presumes an emendation to the internal accusative construction, *la'agu la'ag* [TH3932/3933, ZH4352/4353] ([they] mocked mockery) (similarly, see Craigie 1983:285). Perhaps the whole colon should be emended to *bekhanpi la'agu la'ag* [TH3382, ZH2867] ("When I was limping, they mocked me mercilessly"; see HALOT 1.335 and 2.532).

35:20 ***They don't talk of peace.*** This use of "peace" (*shalom* [TH7965, ZH8934]) is in contrast to 34:14 [15], where the righteous are called to "Search for peace [*shalom*], and work to maintain it" and to 35:27 where God enjoys giving his servant peace (*shalom*).

35:28 ***Then I will proclaim.*** The verb is *hagah* [TH1897, ZH2047] ("meditate"; see 1:2).

COMMENTARY

Psalm 35 uses powerful images of shields and spears, traps and pits, a bereft mother, and fierce lions to articulate the agony experienced in being falsely accused. The psalm can be divided into three strophes, each of which ends with praise (McCann 1996:818). The three strophes are well balanced: 35:1-10 has 12 lines and ends with three lines of joy and praise (35:9-10), 35:11-18 has 10 lines and ends with a single line of praise (35:18), and 35:19-28 has 12 lines and ends with 3 lines of joy and praise.

Call for the Divine Warrior to Do Battle (35:1-10). In the face of severe opposition, David calls upon the Lord as Divine Warrior to do battle on his behalf. David entreats the Divine Warrior to come in full armor, arrayed with shields and spear and javelin, and to assure David of victory. He wants to hear the promise, "I will give you victory!" (35:3). This victory will be experienced as the opposition retreats from the fray in humiliation and disgrace.

The agent of aid will be the angel of the Lord. Often the angel of the Lord is a messenger, but he is also at times the agent authorized to execute the divine will (TDOT 8.317-318). In one battle the angel of the Lord killed 185,000 Assyrian troops (2 Kgs 19:35), leading to the retreat of Sennacherib. In Psalm 35 the angel of the Lord will blast David's foes, blowing them away like chaff driven by the wind. With poetic justice he will pursue (*radap* [TH7291, ZH8103]) David's opponents (*radap*) who have been attacking him. The theme of poetic justice continues in 35:7-8, where in stereotypical language David prays for his enemies to be caught in the very traps they have set for him and to fall into the very pit they have dug for him (cf. 9:15).

David then anticipates the joy of victory and the praise of the victor (35:9-10). He vows to rejoice and be glad in the Lord, for it is the Lord who will rescue him. He also vows to praise the Lord, for the Lord is the incomparable defender of the defenseless.

Cry of the Betrayed Soul (35:11-18). Like Psalms 7, 17, 26 and 27, Psalm 35 is the cry of one falsely accused (35:11). The bitterness of the soul is exacerbated by a deep sense of betrayal: "They repay me evil for good" (35:12). The good that David had done was to enter into the suffering of others. He had grieved for them, fasted and prayed for them, and agonized over unanswered prayer for them. He grieved for them as one would grieve for the closest of friends or even family. More than that, he grieved like a mother grieving over a dead child.

How was David repaid? When he was in trouble, others did not enter into his suffering as he had entered into theirs. Instead, they rejoiced in attacking him with slander and mockery (35:15-16). Apparently, these attacks went on for a long time—long enough at least for David to have to cry out, "How long, O Lord?" The deeper pain came not from the words of the enemy but from the silence of the Lord: "How long, O Lord, will you look on and do nothing?" (35:17). David prays for the silence to be broken,[1] and vows to give thanks to the Lord in the presence of the worshiping community when the Lord will have delivered him from his foes.

Call for the Divine Judge to Give Justice (35:19-28). David prays that the rejoicing and gloating over his adversity would be put to a stop. His adversaries don't pursue peace, as the Lord has instructed his people to do (34:14). Rather, they stir up trouble by claiming to having seen (*ra'ah* [TH7200, ZH8011]) David sin (35:21). The Lord had been looking on (*ra'ah*) without taking any action to defend David (35:17), but the time came for the Lord to break his silence for he "know[s] all about" (*ra'ah*) what is going on (35:22).

David pleads for the Judge to wake up and rise to his defense, to vindicate David of the false accusations brought against him, and to silence the laughter of his adversaries (35:23-25). Picking up a motif from the first strophe, David prays for the humiliation and disgrace of those who have humiliated and disgraced him (35:26).

Echoing the end of the first strophe (35:9-10), David closes his prayer on the note of joy and praise (35:27-28). Here, however, he does not vow to rejoice, but prays that those who have stood by him would be able to rejoice in David's vindication. And then David vows once again to praise the Lord for his justice and goodness.

Jesus was the object of the same kind of hatred that David experienced. In reference to the hatred Jesus experienced, he said, "This fulfills what is written in their Scriptures: 'They hated me without cause'" (John 15:25—quoting Ps 35:19). This Scripture is also fulfilled when believers become the object of the world's hatred (John 15:18). As painful as that may be, it does not compare to the pain of being "hated" by those within the covenant community itself. Whether we experience hatred from the world or the church, however, we can bless those who persecute us, pray for those who abuse us, and love our enemies, because Jesus has overcome through his life, his death, and his resurrection (John 16:33).

ENDNOTES

1. Perhaps David had been ill. The Hebrew words *betsal'i* [TH6761, ZH7520] ("in my stumbling"; 35:15) and *bekhanpi* [TH3382, ZH2867] ("when I limped"; see note on 35:16) may indicate illness.

◆ II. Psalm 36

For the choir director: A psalm of David, the servant of the LORD.

1 Sin whispers to the wicked, deep
within their hearts.
They have no fear of God at all.
2 In their blind conceit,
they cannot see how wicked they
really are.
3 Everything they say is crooked and
deceitful.
They refuse to act wisely or do good.
4 They lie awake at night, hatching
sinful plots.
Their actions are never good.
They make no attempt to turn
from evil.

5 Your unfailing love, O LORD, is as vast
as the heavens;
your faithfulness reaches beyond
the clouds.
6 Your righteousness is like the mighty
mountains,
your justice like the ocean depths.
You care for people and animals alike,
O LORD.
7 How precious is your unfailing love,
O God!
All humanity finds shelter
in the shadow of your wings.
8 You feed them from the abundance of
your own house,
letting them drink from your river
of delights.
9 For you are the fountain of life,
the light by which we see.

10 Pour out your unfailing love on those
who love you;
give justice to those with honest
hearts.
11 Don't let the proud trample me
or the wicked push me around.
12 Look! Those who do evil have fallen!
They are thrown down, never to rise
again.

NOTES

36:1 ***Sin whispers to the wicked, deep within their hearts.*** The text is difficult. For a survey of opinions on the meaning of this colon see Craigie 1983:290 and Delitzsch 1982:3-4. The NLT is similar to Delitzsch's interpretation. Since the word *ne'um* [TH5002, ZH5536] is regularly followed by a subject genitive, *pesha'* [TH6588, ZH7322] (sin) is the speaker and "the wicked" are those spoken to. The MT's *libbi* [TH3820/2967.1, ZH4213/3276] (my heart) is then emended to *libbo* [TH3820/2050.2, ZH4213/2257] (his heart), based on some Hebrew mss and ancient versions.

36:3 ***They refuse.*** The word *khadal* [TH2308, ZH2532] means "stop" or "cease" (DCH 3.162).

36:5 ***beyond the clouds.*** The word *'ad-* [TH5704, ZH6330] means "as far as" (HALOT 2.786), and while *shekhaqim* [TH7834, ZH8836] is typically used for clouds, here in parallelism with "the heavens" it is used as a synonym for the heavens (NIDOTTE 4.83).

36:6 ***mighty mountains.*** Lit., "mountains of God," but *'el* [TH410A, ZH446] probably functions here to express the superlative (see Craigie 1983:290 and Thomas 1953:210; HALOT 1.50 suggests this as a possibility).

care for. This is a striking word to be used for God's care for humans and animals alike, for it is one of the primary words for God's saving activity (Hiphil of *yasha'* [TH3467, ZH3828]).

36:8 ***letting them drink from your river of delights.*** There is an allusion here to the Garden of Eden. "Your delights" (*'adaneka* [TH5730, ZH6358]) is a play on "Eden" (*'eden* [TH5731, ZH6359]), and the verb "drink" (Hiphil of *shaqah* [TH8248, ZH9197]) is used with the river that "watered" the garden (Gen 2:10).

36:10 ***those who love you.*** The word here is *yada'* [TH3045, ZH3359], which means "know." "To know God is to be in a right relationship with him, with characteristics of love, trust, respect, and open communication" (NIDOTTE 2.413).

COMMENTARY

Psalm 36 advances the thought of Psalm 35. Whereas a major motif in Psalm 35 is the opposition David experienced at the hands of his adversaries, Psalm 36 is a meditation on and a prayer for the unfailing love of God experienced in the midst of such opposition. There are three discernible strophes in this psalm: (1) 36:1-4 describes the attitudes and actions of the wicked (see *rasha'* [TH7563A, ZH8401] in 36:1 [2]); (2) 36:5-9 provides a contrasting meditation on the Lord's unfailing love; (3) 36:10-12 is a prayer for an outpouring of the Lord's unfailing love in the face of opposition from the wicked (see *rasha'* in 36:11 [12]).

The Attitudes and Actions of the Wicked (36:1-4). This opening strophe is reminiscent of 14:1-3 with its description of the character of the wicked. Both texts open with the wicked speaking in their hearts, and the initial utterance is "There is not." In 14:1, the fools say, "There is no God." In 36:1 the wicked in effect say, "There is no need to fear God." The same foundational point is made in both texts: God is not a force that needs to be reckoned with in life; we can live as if he does not exist. This arrogant autonomy is "blind conceit," a refusal to acknowledge and deal with the reality of sin in one's own life. Such an arrogant attitude results in corrupt speech and corrupt actions. The wickedness of Psalm 36 is the foolishness of Psalm 14, for the wicked in Psalm 36 refuse to act wisely. And just as there are none who do good in 14:1-3, the wicked refuse to do what is good in 36:3. In fact, "their actions are never good" (36:4). They are so corrupt, they "lie awake at night, hatching sinful plots" (36:4).

The Unfailing Love of God (36:5-9). Standing in stark contrast to this picture of the wicked is the magnificent portrait of the unfailing love of God. Other attributes of God are mentioned (faithfulness, righteousness, and justice), but these are surrounded by his unfailing love. The psalmist uses the immensity of the creation to describe God's unfailing love. The vastness of the heavens, the heights of the mountains, and the depths of the oceans provide beautiful word pictures to help us begin to grasp just how immense God's unfailing love and other attributes are.

This unfailing love is not just immense, it is also "precious" because of the way it manifests itself in God's care for the whole creation, "people and animals alike" (36:6). It is quite striking that God's "unfailing love," typically used in reference to his salvation of his people, is used in relation to God's general care for people and even animals (see 145:8-10). Here, however, we encounter a most remarkable contrast between Psalms 14 and 36. In 14:2-3 we find God looking down from heaven on "the entire human race" (*bene-'adam* [TH1121/120, ZH1201/132]) and finding that "all have become corrupt" and "no one does good, not a single one!" But in 36:7 we find that "all humanity" (*bene-'adam*) is the object of God's unfailing love, finding shelter in the shadow of his wings. As the language of salvation (typically used with reference to God's salvation of his people) is employed for God's general care for "people and animals alike," so too the language of shelter—feasting on the abundance of God's house, and experiencing his life and light (typically used for the privileges of the righteous)—is here used in reference to God's general care for "all humanity."

How do we as Christians relate to "all humanity"? Only from the perspective of Psalm 14? "All have turned away; all have become corrupt. No one does good, not a single one!" Do we share at all in the perspective of Psalm 36? "You care for people and animals alike, O LORD. How precious is your unfailing love, O God! All humanity finds shelter in the shadow of your wings." When we consider "the wicked"—and that is what they are—does God's unfailing love fill our hearts and flow out to them, or do we retreat into our churches to sit in smug judgment, saying, "I thank you, God, that I am not a sinner like everyone else" (Luke 18:11)? The portrait of God's unfailing love in Psalm 36 is a portrait of what we are to be like as his children.

We see this portrait in human flesh when we look at Jesus, "the one who is the true light, who gives light to everyone" (John 1:9). Any understanding of truth found anywhere in the world has its source in Jesus, who is the truth itself. Any beneficent care experienced by any creature in this fallen world has its source in Jesus. He is the fountain of life. We cannot, however, help but hear a deeper meaning in the words of 36:6-9. This language draws us through God's general care to his saving care of those who trust in him. By his grace, our general care for "the wicked" may be used by God to draw them to his saving care. This saving care is the focus of the final strophe.

The Outpouring of God's Unfailing Love (36:10-12). "Pour out your unfailing love on those who know you" (36:10; NLT, "those who love you"). All humanity should know God—"his eternal power and divine nature" (Rom 1:18-20), but all humanity does not know God. "This is the way to have eternal life—to know you, the only true God, and Jesus Christ, the one you sent to earth" (John 17:3). Not all know God in this way, being "in a right relationship with him, with characteristics of love, trust, respect, and open communication" (NIDOTTE 2.413). Those who do know him in this way experience his unfailing love in a way that others do not. One such way is protection from the proud and wicked who would "trample" and "push around" those who know God (36:11). If some choose to stand in opposition to God by opposing those who know him, they will find themselves "thrown down, never to rise again" (36:12). But for the moment, God is being "kind, tolerant, and patient," giving them the opportunity to turn from their sin (36:4; Rom 2:4) and to turn to him in faith, that they might experience his unfailing love and enjoy eternal life.

◆ JJ. Psalm 37*

A psalm of David.

1 Don't worry about the wicked
or envy those who do wrong.
2 For like grass, they soon fade away.
Like spring flowers, they soon withered.

3 Trust in the LORD and do good.
Then you will live safely in the land and prosper.
4 Take delight in the LORD,
and he will give you your heart's desires.

5 Commit everything you do to the LORD.
Trust him, and he will help you.
6 He will make your innocence radiate like the dawn,
and the justice of your cause will shine like the noonday sun.

7 Be still in the presence of the LORD,
and wait patiently for him to act.
Don't worry about evil people who prosper
or fret about their wicked schemes.

8 Stop being angry!
Turn from your rage!
Do not lose your temper—
it only leads to harm.
9 For the wicked will be destroyed,
but those who trust in the LORD will possess the land.

10 Soon the wicked will disappear.
Though you look for them, they will be gone.
11 The lowly will possess the land
and will live in peace and prosperity.

12 The wicked plot against the godly;
they snarl at them in defiance.
13 But the Lord just laughs,
for he sees their day of judgment coming.

14 The wicked draw their swords
and string their bows
to kill the poor and the oppressed,
to slaughter those who do right.
15 But their swords will stab their own hearts,
and their bows will be broken.

16 It is better to be godly and have little
than to be evil and rich.
17 For the strength of the wicked will be shattered,
but the LORD takes care of the godly.

18 Day by day the LORD takes care of the innocent,
and they will receive an inheritance that lasts forever.
19 They will not be disgraced in hard times;
even in famine they will have more than enough.

20 But the wicked will die.
The LORD's enemies are like flowers in a field—
they will disappear like smoke.

21 The wicked borrow and never repay,
but the godly are generous givers.
22 Those the LORD blesses will possess the land,
but those he curses will die.

23 The LORD directs the steps of the godly.
He delights in every detail of their lives.
24 Though they stumble, they will never fall,

for the LORD holds them by the
hand.

25 Once I was young, and now I am old.
Yet I have never seen the godly
abandoned
or their children begging for bread.
26 The godly always give generous loans
to others,
and their children are a blessing.

27 Turn from evil and do good,
and you will live in the land forever.
28 For the LORD loves justice,
and he will never abandon the
godly.

He will keep them safe forever,
but the children of the wicked
will die.
29 The godly will possess the land
and will live there forever.

30 The godly offer good counsel;
they teach right from wrong.
31 They have made God's law their own,
so they will never slip from his path.

32 The wicked wait in ambush for the
godly,
looking for an excuse to kill them.
33 But the LORD will not let the wicked
succeed
or let the godly be condemned when
they are put on trial.

34 Put your hope in the LORD.
Travel steadily along his path.
He will honor you by giving you the
land.
You will see the wicked destroyed.

35 I have seen wicked and ruthless
people
flourishing like a tree in its native
soil.
36 But when I looked again, they were
gone!
Though I searched for them, I could
not find them!

37 Look at those who are honest and
good,
for a wonderful future awaits those
who love peace.
38 But the rebellious will be destroyed;
they have no future.

39 The LORD rescues the godly;
he is their fortress in times of
trouble.
40 The LORD helps them,
rescuing them from the wicked.
He saves them,
and they find shelter in him.

37 This psalm is a Hebrew acrostic poem; each stanza begins with a successive letter of the Hebrew alphabet.

NOTES

37:1 *worry.* The sense of the Hithpael of *kharah* [TH2734, ZH3013] is something like "be upset," "be vexed" (DCH 3.314), or "get excited" (HALOT 1.351).

37:7 *wait patiently.* The MT reads *hithkholel* [TH2342, ZH2565], which BDB 297 glosses with "wait longingly," but the other occurrences of the Hithpolel mean "whirl" or "writhe in pain," so "wait longingly/patiently" seems to be forced. Perhaps the text should be emended to *hokhel* (from *yakhal* [TH3176, ZH3498]; see 38:15 [16]), which means "wait."

worry. See note on 37:1.

37:8 *Do not lose your temper.* This is the Hithpael of *kharah* [TH2734, ZH3013] (be upset), as in 37:1 and 37:7.

37:11 *will live in peace and prosperity.* This is the same verb that is translated "take delight" in 37:4. Those who take delight in the Lord will also take delight in prosperous security.

37:16 The contrast is quite striking: The little bit that one righteous person has is better than the abundance that many wicked people have.

37:20 *like flowers in a field.* The word *kiqar* [TH3509.1/3368, ZH3869/3701] means "like preciousness of" and may be a reference to flowers. On the other hand, *keyereq* [TH3509.1/3418, ZH3869/3764] (like flowers) occurs in 37:2 in the same image of the wicked not lasting long, so an emendation to *keyereq* here is feasible.

37:23 *in every detail of their lives.* Lit., "in their way."

37:28 *forever.* The text is damaged here, since this line should begin with an Ayin.[1] The simplest solution is to emend *le'olam* [TH3807.1/5769, ZH4200/6409] to *'ad-'olam* [TH5704, ZH6330] (until forever).

37:30 *they teach right from wrong.* Lit., "their tongues speak what is right."

37:40 *and they find shelter.* "For they find shelter" would capture the sense of the initial *ki* [TH3588, ZH3954].

COMMENTARY

Is Psalm 1 true? Psalm 1 paints a simple picture: The righteous are like fruitful trees, prospering in everything they do, but the wicked are like chaff, not prospering in what they do. The author of Psalm 37 looks at life and sees a different picture. He sees evil people prospering (37:7) and thriving like mighty trees (37:35). He also sees righteous people who are poor and oppressed (37:14), experiencing famine (37:19) and trouble (37:39), and needing to be rescued from the wicked (37:40). Quite a different picture.

Psalm 37 is an instructional poem from the wisdom tradition. The psalm is an alphabetic acrostic, written primarily in couplets, with the first word of each couplet beginning with successive letters of the alphabet. "There is little evidence of a logical progression of thought" in the psalm (VanGemeren 1991:297), but there is a cogency of thought when the psalm is read as an answer to the problem posed by the prosperity of the wicked and the suffering of the righteous.

The Prosperity of the Wicked. The wicked (*rasha'* [TH7563A, ZH8401]) are referred to 13 times in the psalm, so it is obvious that their lot in life is of central concern. Since Psalm 36 begins a description of the wicked (*rasha'* in 36:1), Psalm 37 is a natural follow-up. Psalm 37 is, in part, a record of what can be observed about the lives of the wicked and, in part, an affirmation of faith about the destiny of the wicked.

The wicked may prosper in the short run. But why would anyone be tempted to envy the wicked? We are tempted to envy the wicked because they, at times, have what we don't have. We are tempted to envy them when they are prospering in some way that we are not. But why would we get upset when the wicked prosper? We could get upset because we have read Psalm 1, which says the wicked will not prosper. But if we just open our eyes and look around, it is clear that wicked people are often "flourishing like a tree in its native soil" (37:35), in spite of the teaching of Psalm 1 that they are like chaff and the righteous are like trees. Facing the reality of the prosperity of the wicked can be quite painful and perplexing (see Ps 73). It will not do, however, to put our heads in the sand and pretend that the wicked do not prosper. And we cannot spiritualize the text and imagine that prosperity here is something other than what it is—prosperity.

The wicked will not prosper in the long run. This teaching is a consistent chorus throughout the psalm. Though they thrive like mighty trees, "they soon fade away . . .

they soon wither" (37:2), they "are like flowers in a field" that "will disappear like smoke" (37:20), and they will be cut down.[2] The wicked will eventually "disappear" (37:10). "Their day of judgment [is] coming" (37:13), and they will experience God's poetic justice, being killed by their own swords. "The wicked will die" (*'abad* [TH6, ZH6]; 37:20), just like Psalm 1 says (see *'abad* in 1:6, where it is translated "destruction"). They will be nowhere to be found (37:36). The bottom line is that "the rebellious will be destroyed; they have no future" (37:38). Psalm 1 is true—in the end.

The Suffering of the Righteous. The righteous (*tsaddiq* [TH6662, ZH7404]) are referred to nine times in the psalm. Though referred to fewer times than the wicked, the righteous are the focus of the psalm, for the psalm's purpose is to teach the righteous how to live in the face of the present prosperity of the wicked and their own suffering.

The righteous may suffer in the short run. Why would righteous people need to be exhorted to stop their anger and turn from their rage? Perhaps it is because they are suffering as a result of the "wicked schemes" of others (37:7). Or perhaps it is because their innocence is not seen at the present and the cause for which they stand is being maligned. Maybe it is because of the plots and the snarlings of the wicked who are attacking them ferociously. Maybe it is because they find themselves stumbling. Maybe they are the objects of great suspicion when there is no cause for such. Some of the preceding psalms have offered other potential reasons as to why the righteous might be angry. Perhaps they are angry because Psalm 1 seems to describe a life they are not experiencing: "They prosper in all they do."

The righteous will not suffer in the long run. This chord is struck again and again in the psalm. They "will live safely in the land and prosper" (37:3; see also 37:9, 11, 22, 27, 29). They will receive their heart's desires (37:4). Their innocence will "radiate like the dawn" (37:6). They will receive an eternal reward (37:18). "They will never slip from his path" (37:31). The bottom line is, they have a "wonderful future" ahead of them (37:37). Psalm 1 is true—in the end.

But how do we live in the present with all of its tensions? First, we live by faith. "Trust in the LORD" (37:3). "Trust him" (37:5). "Those who trust in the LORD will possess the land" (37:9). Faith is "the confidence that what we hope for will actually happen; it gives us assurance about things we cannot see" (Heb 11:1). Second, we live by a faith that obeys. "Trust in the LORD and do good" (37:3). "Turn from evil and do good" (37:27). "Travel steadily along his path" (37:34). Be "honest and good" and "love peace" (37:37). Third, we live in patient hope. "Be still in the presence of the LORD, and wait patiently for him to act" (37:7). "Put your hope in the LORD" (37:34).

Where can we find strength to live in obedient faith and hope? The Lord! "He will give you your heart's desires" (37:4). "He will help you" (37:5). "He will make your innocence radiate like the dawn" (37:6). "The LORD takes care of the godly" and the "innocent" (37:17-18). "The LORD rescues the godly; he is their fortress in times of trouble. The LORD helps them, rescuing them from the wicked. He saves them, and they find shelter in him" (37:39-40).

Psalm 37 teaches that Psalm 1 is true in the end. The end may be the end of the day. Or it may be the end of the week, month, or year. God's timetable is not like ours (90:4). The end may be the end of your life or it may even be the end of this present evil age. But the end will come, and Psalm 1 will be experienced as true, because Jesus has experienced the perplexities and sufferings of Psalm 37 in our place to the point of dying an unjust death. But the end came for him, and he was vindicated by being raised from the dead as the firstfruits of those who trust and obey and hope in him.

So delight in the Lord, and he will give you your heart's desires in the end.

ENDNOTES

1. For the extent of textual corruption in biblical acrostics, see Gaebelein 1990.
2. The Niphal of *karath* [TH3772, ZH4162] (cut) is used five times in this psalm to express the fate of the wicked: 37:9 ("be destroyed"), 37:22 ("will die"), 37:28 ("will die"), 37:34 ("destroyed"), and 37:38 ("be destroyed").

◆ KK. Psalm 38

A psalm of David, asking God to remember him.

1 O LORD, don't rebuke me in your anger
or discipline me in your rage!
2 Your arrows have struck deep,
and your blows are crushing me.
3 Because of your anger, my whole body
is sick;
my health is broken because of
my sins.
4 My guilt overwhelms me—
it is a burden too heavy to bear.
5 My wounds fester and stink
because of my foolish sins.
6 I am bent over and racked with pain.
All day long I walk around filled
with grief.
7 A raging fever burns within me,
and my health is broken.
8 I am exhausted and completely
crushed.
My groans come from an anguished
heart.

9 You know what I long for, Lord;
you hear my every sigh.
10 My heart beats wildly, my strength
fails,
and I am going blind.
11 My loved ones and friends stay away,
fearing my disease.
Even my own family stands at
a distance.
12 Meanwhile, my enemies lay traps
to kill me.
Those who wish me harm make
plans to ruin me.
All day long they plan their
treachery.

13 But I am deaf to all their threats.
I am silent before them as one who
cannot speak.
14 I choose to hear nothing,
and I make no reply.
15 For I am waiting for you, O LORD.
You must answer for me, O Lord
my God.
16 I prayed, "Don't let my enemies gloat
over me
or rejoice at my downfall."

17 I am on the verge of collapse,
facing constant pain.
18 But I confess my sins;
I am deeply sorry for what I have
done.
19 I have many aggressive enemies;
they hate me without reason.
20 They repay me evil for good
and oppose me for pursuing good.
21 Do not abandon me, O LORD.
Do not stand at a distance, my God.
22 Come quickly to help me,
O Lord my savior.

NOTES

38:2 ***your blows are crushing me.*** Lit., "your hand has come down on me." See 32:4 for this same picture of God's hand of discipline being on David; see also 39:10.

38:3 ***my whole body is sick; my health is broken.*** The first colon contains the word *basar* [TH1320, ZH1414] (flesh) and the second contains the word *'etsem* [TH6106, ZH6795] (bone). Together they indicate the pervasive nature of the illness.

38:6 ***All day long I walk around filled with grief.*** This same language occurs in 35:14 (see note).

38:10 ***I am going blind.*** The Hebrew text contains the words *gam-hem* [TH1571/1992, ZH1685/2156] (even they), which are problematic (Kraus 1988:410). The function of these two words is probably emphatic: literally, "The light of my eyes—even they (have been adversely affected)—is not with me." In 13:3 [4] the lack of light in the eyes is a metaphor for a general lack of health. The same is probably the case here (but see Kraus 1988:412). It is possible that "an actual loss of the ability to see" is in view here, or at least an impairment of vision owing to weeping, as in 6:6-7.

38:16 ***I prayed.*** Lit., "I said." Psalm 38:16-20 may not be a prayer to God but may be the psalmist's self-address (Kraus 1988:413).

38:19 ***I have many aggressive enemies.*** The text contains the word *khayyim* [TH2416A, ZH2645] (living), which the NLT translates as "aggressive." Craigie (1983:302) emends *khayyim* to *khinnam* [TH2600, ZH2855] (without cause) in keeping with 4QpPsa (see also Kraus 1988:410). The Hebrew text emphasizes the vigor of the attack, while the emended text focuses on its unjust nature. The concept of being unjustly opposed by enemies is found elsewhere in the Psalms. See 7:4 [5] and 35:19, which uses the word *sheqer* [TH8267, ZH9214] (treachery, lies), as in 38:19b [20b].

38:20 ***They repay me evil for good.*** See the discussion at 35:11-18.

COMMENTARY

The situation that gave birth to Psalm 38 was one of intense pain—physical, mental, and spiritual. David was suffering under the discipline of God (38:1), suffering as a result of his own sin (38:2-10) and suffering at the hands of friends who had become enemies (38:11-20). Having nowhere else to go, he turns to the Lord, his God and Savior, for the help he needs (38:21-22).

A Plea for Relief (38:1). Psalm 38:1 is almost identical to 6:1. In both texts suffering is experienced as an outworking of God's anger. The turning away of God's anger should thus entail relief from the suffering that is the result of that anger. The psalm opens with a plea for this relief, a plea for the cessation of the angry rebuke and discipline.

The Pain of Illness (38:2-10). The psalmist suffered extreme physical illness that pervaded his entire body. His skin had opened; he had putrefying wounds. He was bent over in pain and tormented by a "raging fever" (38:7). His energy was gone. His heart raced, while his strength failed. This is a pitiful picture of physical pain.

When there is pain in the body, there is often pain in the heart. Such is the case here. David's days were "filled with grief" (38:6), which came to expression in groans "from an anguished heart" (38:8). His "every sigh" (38:9) was the inarticulate cry of a heart that longed for relief from the pain that tortured both body and heart.

Pain of spirit was added to pain of body and heart. In this situation sickness had resulted from sin. The pain of body and heart was intensified to the point of being unbearable because of a conscience overwhelmed by guilt. The pain of a guilty conscience was exacerbated by the knowledge that all of this suffering was a concrete expression of God's anger toward him. God's beneficent presence was nowhere to be found.

The Pain of Alienation (38:11-20). Sadly, it is the case at times that those who are ill and need the comfort and support of the community find themselves alienated from that community. Illness, especially serious and prolonged illness, has the uncanny ability to put great distance between the one who suffers and even the closest of friends. Perhaps the distance is a result of the fear of contagion. Perhaps the discomfort is the result of illness confronting the healthy with their own mortality. This repulsion from illness may at times take the form of outright attack on the ill. Those in need of compassion become the recipients of human rage and even hatred. The pain that this evokes within the sufferer can be beyond words, especially when the sufferer has done nothing to warrant such treatment. It is not likely that in this case the enemies were saying that the psalmist's sickness was a result of sin, for the psalmist was more than willing to concede that point. No, there was some other reason, one left unarticulated in the poem, why the former friends were bent on the destruction of the ill person.

There is a benefit to this alienation. The alienation makes it absolutely clear that dependence on the Lord is the only course of action. Trying to answer the adversaries would not be beneficial. Contrite confession and patient waiting on the Lord to answer is the only option. And it is always the best option.

A Plea for Presence (38:21-22). Contrite confession in a spirit of dependence is the prerequisite for the final plea for presence. David had said that the Lord knew what David longed for. He certainly longed for healing from his illness and all of the concomitant misery. But before and behind that was the deepest longing of the human soul: the longing for the presence of God. "Do not abandon me, O LORD. Do not stand at a distance, my God" (38:21). Yes, the Lord was angry, but he was still "my God." David may not have had any present taste of the love and mercy of God, but he still believed that God was his God, full of unfailing love (36:5, 7, 10). The presence longed for was a helping presence, one that would entail restoration to life in all of its fullness. So the plea for the presence is followed by the plea for quick intervention by the Lord, whom David knew as his "savior" (38:22).

What must Jesus have felt when the crowd that cheered, "Praise God for the Son of David! Blessings on the one who comes in the name of the LORD!" (Matt 21:9), later shouted, "Crucify him!" (Matt 27:23)? What pain did he experience through the crown of thorns, the spear in his side, and the nails in his hands and feet, knowing all the while that he had done nothing against them and was being opposed because he had stood for what is right (38:19-20)? What pain did he endure under the hand of divine anger and rage, because his dying was the result of sin—not his own but ours? Jesus experienced the pain of Psalm 38 to depths that none other has or ever will. His Savior did not ultimately abandon him but came quickly to help him by raising him from the dead. And so he has become our Savior. By faith in him we can confess our sin and wait for God to act on our behalf should we experience the pain of Psalm 38. God will not ultimately abandon us, because in the Lord Jesus Christ he is our God and our Savior.

◆ LL. Psalm 39

For Jeduthun, the choir director: A psalm of David.

1 I said to myself, "I will watch what I do
and not sin in what I say.
I will hold my tongue
when the ungodly are around me."
2 But as I stood there in silence—
not even speaking of good things—
the turmoil within me grew worse.
3 The more I thought about it,
the hotter I got,
igniting a fire of words:
4 "LORD, remind me how brief my time
on earth will be.
Remind me that my days are
numbered—
how fleeting my life is.
5 You have made my life no longer than
the width of my hand.
My entire lifetime is just a moment
to you;
at best, each of us is but a breath."
Interlude

6 We are merely moving shadows,
and all our busy rushing ends in
nothing.
We heap up wealth,
not knowing who will spend it.
7 And so, Lord, where do I put my hope?
My only hope is in you.
8 Rescue me from my rebellion.
Do not let fools mock me.
9 I am silent before you; I won't say
a word,
for my punishment is from you.
10 But please stop striking me!
I am exhausted by the blows from
your hand.
11 When you discipline us for our sins,
you consume like a moth what is
precious to us.
Each of us is but a breath. *Interlude*

12 Hear my prayer, O LORD!
Listen to my cries for help!
Don't ignore my tears.
For I am your guest—
a traveler passing through,
as my ancestors were before me.
13 Leave me alone so I can smile again
before I am gone and exist no more.

NOTES

39:1 *I said.* The word *'amarti* [TH559, ZH606] occurs in 38:16 [17], where it is translated, "I prayed," but it is better understood as self-address, as is the case here.

I will watch. . . . I will hold. These two verbs are cohortatives used to express resolve (Joüon and Muraoka 1991:§114c). The second verb is a repetition of the first (*'eshmerah* [TH8104, ZH9068]; "guard") and is probably an error, since it is difficult to make sense of the word. An emendation to *'asimah* [TH7760, ZH8492] would result in, "I will put a muzzle on my mouth."

sin. The noun related to this verb is used in 38:3 [4], 18 [19].

39:2 *good things.* The word *tob* [TH2896, ZH3202] (good) recalls the "good" (*tob*) for which David had been repaid evil in 38:20 [21].

39:5 *to you.* The word *negdeka* [TH5048, ZH5584] means "before you"; it acknowledges the presence of God in the middle of the vanity of life.

each of us is but a breath. Lit., "Every breath is every person standing firm." The first "every" (*kol* [TH3605, ZH3972]) is probably the result of dittography (Craigie 1983:307); it is missing in many mss and in 39:11 [12], a parallel verse. The verb translated "standing firm" *nitsab* [TH5324, ZH5893] is also missing in 39:11 [12] and may not be part of the poetic line, but may be some sort of instruction like *selah* [TH5542, ZH6138] ("interlude"; see BHS). The word translated "breath" is *hebel* [TH1892, ZH2039] (meaningless), a key word in the book of Ecclesiastes.

39:6 *moving.* This Hithpael from *halak* [TH1980, ZH2143] recalls the use of the Piel from the same root in 38:6, where David walked about in mourning. Note also the use of the Qal in 39:13 [14]. All three uses express the idea of walking about in a negative situation.

our busy rushing. This translates the verb *yehemayun* [TH1993, ZH2159], which is problematic because it is plural in a sequence of singular verbs. If it is emended to *hamon* [TH1995, ZH2162] ("wealth"; see 37:16), the following verb ("heap up") has a direct object, which it is otherwise lacking (see Craigie 1983:307).

39:7 *My only hope is in you.* The noun translated "hope" (*tokheleth* [TH8431, ZH9347]) comes from the same root as the verb translated "waiting" in 38:15 [16] (McCann 1996:837).

39:9 *I am silent . . . I won't say a word.* The language echoes 38:13, where David is like a mute.

39:10 *please stop striking me!* Lit., "Remove your blow from me." The word for "blow" (*nega'* [TH5061, ZH5596]) occurs in 38:11 [12], where it is translated "disease."

your hand. God's "hand" of discipline is referred to in 38:2 [3].

39:11 *When you discipline us for our sins.* The NLT's "discipline" captures two words in the Hebrew, the verb *yissarta* [TH3256, ZH3579] and the noun *tokakhath* [TH8433A, ZH9350]. This verb here is used in 38:1 [2], where the verb from the root of *tokakhath* is also used. The noun for "sin" (*'awon* [TH5771, ZH6411]) is used in 38:4 [5], 18 [19].

COMMENTARY

The numerous lexical links between Psalm 39 and Psalm 38 (see notes) invite us to read Psalm 39 as an added perspective on the struggles that David endured in Psalm 38. There are three movements in the psalm: the inner turmoil of a silent sufferer (39:1-3), a seemingly despairing reflection on the fleeting nature of human existence (39:4-6), and a prayer of almost despairing hope (39:7-13).

The Inner Turmoil of a Silent Sufferer (39:1-3). The psalm begins with "I said," and the address is to the self, as in 38:16 (see note). David expresses a firm resolution not to sin in what he says. His resolution intensifies from watching what he says, to muzzling his mouth, to being absolutely silent (Alter 1985:70). The explicit reason for this resolution is the presence of the wicked. Should David complain about his circumstances or their response, for example, he would become the object of their criticism (Alter 1985:70). An implicit reason, however, is that David does not want to sin against the Lord, for all sin is against the Lord (51:4). So David chooses silence as the way to deal with his inner turmoil that is owing to the external turmoil around him. His silence goes to the extreme of not even speaking about good things, like the good things he has done for those who oppose him (35:11-14 and 38:20).

But silence would not suffice. The inner turmoil grew and grew until it reached the boiling point. Finally, David could no longer maintain his silence, and "a fire of words" was ignited (39:3). David's silence gave way to speech.

A Seemingly Despairing Reflection on the Fleeting Nature of Human Existence (39:4-6). This strophe is quite surprising. The buildup in 39:1-3 leads us to expect an outburst of anger or a severe complaint about David's suffering or his enemies or God's inactivity. Instead, David asks the Lord to remind him of the brevity of life and the vanity of life. Why reflect on the brevity and vanity of life in this situation?

First, though David's speech is in the form of a request in 39:4, he is not really looking for information. The information he is ostensibly seeking in 39:4 he reveals in 39:5. In these verses David is actually lamenting his situation (Mays 1994:166). More than that, David is placing his situation in the context of the plight of the whole human race. Life is fleeting. Life is but a breath. Life is frustrating. Life is meaningless. And David's particular situation is an intensification of what is more generally true of human existence (Mays 1994:166).

Second, there is a certain hope one can experience through accepting these facts of life. Denial will not generate hope, but acceptance can. This is not a passive acceptance in silence, however, but an active choice to speak out the negativity, to face and acknowledge the frustrating and meaningless side of life, to embrace it. Such an active acceptance of life may at times bring us close to the point of despair, but it will ultimately produce hope within.

A Prayer of Almost Despairing Hope (39:7-13). Silence gives way to speech, and speech gives way to hope (McCann 1996:839). If human existence is but a breath, where is hope to be found? "My only hope is in you," David says to the Lord (39:7). Who is this Lord? He is the one who punishes. He is the one who can crush people like moths. Where is there room for hope in him? If he can wound, he can also heal. He can rescue, and he can end the punishment. If life is only brief and frustrating and meaningless, then there is room only for despair. But life is not only these things. If life is also lived in the presence of a sovereign God (who can reverse the most negative circumstances of life; see Psalm 30), then there is room for hope in him.

So the prayer for relief can be offered: "Listen to my cries for help" and "Don't ignore my tears" (39:12), and "Leave me alone so I can smile again" (39:13). These requests are not, however, made from a stance of absolute confidence and hope. They are made with a certain resignation to the brevity and vanity of life. They are made by one who is not a permanent resident in this life, but by one who is a "guest—a traveler passing through" (39:12). He is not a unique traveler, however, but is one in a long train that reaches back to his ancestors. As such, his experience is typical.

His requests were also made in the face of the inevitability of death: "Leave me alone so I can smile again before I am gone and exist no more" (39:13). As in Ecclesiastes, so in Psalm 39, death is an inevitable fact of life with which we must deal. The tentacles of death at times reach back into our lives in a variety of forms of suffering and can almost eliminate all hope. Sometimes our hope burns brightly in the face of suffering and perplexity. At other times, our hope burns low and is more like a flickering torch than a blazing fire. But even then it is genuine hope, for it is born out of honest speech in the presence of a sovereign God. In those times of almost despairing hope we find comfort in knowing that our hope is not in the brightness of our hope. Our "only hope" is in the Lord, and even infinitesimal hope in him will never be disappointed. In fact, the almost despairing hope of Psalm 39 was not disappointed, as we will see in Psalm 40.

◆ MM. Psalm 40

For the choir director: A psalm of David.

1 I waited patiently for the LORD to help me,
and he turned to me and heard my cry.
2 He lifted me out of the pit of despair,
out of the mud and the mire.
He set my feet on solid ground
and steadied me as I walked along.
3 He has given me a new song to sing,
a hymn of praise to our God.
Many will see what he has done and be amazed.
They will put their trust in the LORD.

4 Oh, the joys of those who trust the LORD,
who have no confidence in the proud
or in those who worship idols.
5 O LORD my God, you have performed many wonders for us.
Your plans for us are too numerous to list.
You have no equal.
If I tried to recite all your wonderful deeds,
I would never come to the end of them.

6 You take no delight in sacrifices or offerings.
Now that you have made me listen,
I finally understand*—
you don't require burnt offerings or sin offerings.
7 Then I said, "Look, I have come.
As is written about me in the Scriptures:
8 I take joy in doing your will, my God,
for your instructions are written on my heart."

9 I have told all your people about your justice.
I have not been afraid to speak out,
as you, O LORD, well know.
10 I have not kept the good news of your justice hidden in my heart;
I have talked about your faithfulness and saving power.
I have told everyone in the great assembly
of your unfailing love and faithfulness.

11 LORD, don't hold back your tender mercies from me.
Let your unfailing love and faithfulness always protect me.
12 For troubles surround me—
too many to count!
My sins pile up so high
I can't see my way out.
They outnumber the hairs on my head.
I have lost all courage.

13 Please, LORD, rescue me!
Come quickly, LORD, and help me.
14 May those who try to destroy me
be humiliated and put to shame.
May those who take delight in my trouble
be turned back in disgrace.
15 Let them be horrified by their shame,
for they said, "Aha! We've got him now!"

16 But may all who search for you
be filled with joy and gladness in you.
May those who love your salvation
repeatedly shout, "The LORD is great!"
17 As for me, since I am poor and needy,
let the Lord keep me in his thoughts.
You are my helper and my savior.
O my God, do not delay.

40:6 Greek text reads *You have given me a body.* Compare Heb 10:5.

NOTES

40:1 *I waited patiently.* This same verb (*qiwwithi* [TH6960, ZH7747]) occurs in 39:7 [8] in the question, "Where do I put my hope?" Ps 40 is the sequel to Ps 39.

heard my cry. The Lord's hearing David's cry is a result of David having asked the Lord to hear his prayer and to listen to his cries in 39:12.

40:2 *despair.* The word *sha'on* I [TH7588, ZH8622] (desolation) is to be distinguished from *sha'on* II [TH7588A, ZH8623] (uproar) according to HALOT 4.1370. Zorell (1963:811) lists only one *sha'on* and glosses the occurrence in 40:2 [3] with "destruction."

40:3 *He has given me a new song to sing.* Lit., "He has put a new song in my mouth." In 39:1, David put a muzzle on his mouth, but after David waited patiently, albeit in almost despairing hope, the Lord put a new song in his mouth. The "new song" is in particular a victory song of the Divine Warrior in creation (33:6-9) and redemption (33:10-19) (Longman and Reid 1995:45 and 191). The focus in Ps 40 is on God's victories in redemption.

40:8 *I take joy.* This same verb (*khapets* [TH2654, ZH2911]) is translated "take . . . delight" in 40:6 [7].

40:13 *rescue me!* The use of this verb (Hiphil of *natsal* [TH5337, ZH5911]) repeats the request made in 39:8 [9].

Come quickly . . . and help me. "Come quickly" (*khushah* [TH2363, ZH2590]) and "help me" (*le'ezrathi* [TH5833, ZH6476]) repeat the request of 38:22 [23] with the same language.

COMMENTARY

Psalm 40 is seemly comprised of two disparate psalms: a thanksgiving psalm (40:1-10) and a lament (40:11-17).[1] But a comparison of Psalm 40 with other psalms shows that the movement from thanksgiving to lamentation is not unique to Psalm 40.[2] Moreover, the movement from thanksgiving to lamentation in Psalm 40 is theologically significant when Psalm 40 is read in the context of Psalms 38 and 39.

Thanksgiving for Hopes Realized and Prayers Answered (40:1-10). In Psalm 38 David was extremely ill, because he was under the discipline of the Lord as a result of his sin. To make matters worse, his family and friends had become his enemies. In that situation David put his hope in the Lord and prayed for help. In Psalm 39 David reveals more of his internal struggles in that situation, resolves to hope in the Lord, and asks for his cry to be heard. Psalm 40:1-10 is a song of thanksgiving in response to God's granting of help.

David had waited in hope (38:15; 39:7), asking God to hear his cry (39:12). His hope was not disappointed, and his cry was heard (40:1). The Lord delivered him from the despair he had experienced (39:4-6, 13; 40:2), and replaced the muzzle on his mouth (39:1) with a new song of salvation in his mouth (40:3).

One benefit of this whole ordeal would be that many who had been looking on would come away with a deeper faith in the Lord (40:3b). Those who would trust in the Lord and not in idols would experience complete well-being (see note on 1:1). David's praise expands from the wonderful things the Lord has recently done for him to the innumerable miracles that the Lord has done for the whole community.

David had come to realize that the Lord does not delight in bare and external religion; rather, he delights in those who listen to his instruction (*torah* [TH8451, ZH9368]) and delight in it. Such delight and obedience was the focus of his own life, in keeping with the instructions of Psalm 1. While all of God's instruction may be in view, the "Scriptures" in 40:7 (lit., "scroll") may have the instructions for the king in view in particular (Deut 17:14-20). David's chief responsibility as king was to have and read a copy of God's word, so that he could put that word into practice. In this way he would lead the people in covenant loyalty.

In 40:9-10, David carries out an aspect of his responsibility. He did not keep to himself all that the Lord had done for him. He told everyone assembled for worship just how faithful and full of unfailing love the Lord is, that they too might put their hope and trust in him. Were Psalm 40 to end here, it would be a marvelous song of thanksgiving, but the psalm does not end here, because David's troubles did not end here.

Prayer for Deliverance from New Troubles (40:11–17). The thanksgiving for deliverance that is offered in the first half of the psalm serves as the basis for the prayer for deliverance that is offered in the second half (Craigie 1983:313-314 and McCann 1996:842). Though the psalmist had been delivered, "no deliverance is final" in this life (McCann 1996:844). Life is like an onion: When one layer is removed, another layer becomes evident. Having been delivered, David finds himself needing to be delivered again. The unfailing love that he celebrated is needed once again, for he is surrounded by trouble, and his sin is piled up so high that he couldn't see his way out.

Just as he needed the Lord to come quickly to help him in the recent past (38:22), so he again needs the Lord to come quickly and help him in the present (40:13). Those who delight in David's trouble obviously do not delight in doing the Lord's will. They do not delight in the Lord, since their religion is external, as they are not attentive to the Lord's instruction. David prayed that they be put to shame. And just as David had prayed that those who had stood by him would be able to say, "Great is the LORD" (35:27), here he prays the same for those who, like him, seek the Lord and love him.

Though in terms of one aspect of his life David had been lifted out of the pit of despair, he was still "poor and needy." We are "perpetually needy and experiencing new life simultaneously" (McCann 1996:845). But the Lord is always there as our helper and Savior. We can always call on him in hope. Our hope, like David's, will never be disappointed. We live already experiencing the Lord's salvation, but not yet experiencing it fully, and so we live always in need of that experience in this life and in anticipation of the fullness of that experience in the life to come.

The fullness of this experience of new life, of absolute well-being, could not have been procured by David for himself, let alone for others, for he himself had sins piled sky high. He did not perfectly delight in doing God's will. So what was written in the scroll was not ultimately about David. It was about David's son, Jesus. Hebrews 10:3-10 teaches us that the scroll speaks of Jesus and his obedience unto death as the sacrifice that pleased the Father and procured our salvation. Because Jesus is our helper and Savior, we can live with the hope that God will not delay in delivering us in this life and in the life to come.

ENDNOTES

1. See Briggs 1906:350 and Kraus 1988:423-424; see Gerstenberger 1988:169 for additional bibliography in this regard. The most compelling argument for this position is the fact that 40:13-17 [14-18] is almost identical to Ps 70.
2. See Pss 9–10; 27; 44; and 89 (McCann 1996:842).

◆ NN. Psalm 41

For the choir director: A psalm of David.

1 Oh, the joys of those who are kind to
the poor!
The LORD rescues them when they
are in trouble.
2 The LORD protects them
and keeps them alive.
He gives them prosperity in the land
and rescues them from their
enemies.
3 The LORD nurses them when they
are sick
and restores them to health.

4 "O LORD," I prayed, "have mercy on me.
Heal me, for I have sinned against
you."
5 But my enemies say nothing but evil
about me.
"How soon will he die and be
forgotten?" they ask.
6 They visit me as if they were my
friends,
but all the while they gather gossip,
and when they leave, they spread it
everywhere.
7 All who hate me whisper about me,
imagining the worst.
8 "He has some fatal disease," they say.
"He will never get out of
that bed!"
9 Even my best friend, the one I trusted
completely,
the one who shared my food, has
turned against me.

10 LORD, have mercy on me.
Make me well again, so I can pay
them back!
11 I know you are pleased with me,
for you have not let my enemies
triumph over me.
12 You have preserved my life because
I am innocent;
you have brought me into your
presence forever.

13 Praise the LORD, the God of Israel,
who lives from everlasting to
everlasting.
Amen and amen!

NOTES

41:1 *are kind.* The Hiphil of *sakal* [TH7919, ZH8505] means "to understand," "to have insight," "to make wise," or "to succeed" (HALOT 3.1328-1329); "are considerate of" best captures the sense in this verse.

41:2 *rescues them.* The statement is cast in a negative form in the MT ("he does not hand them over to enemies"). The negative adverb is the one usually used with volitives (*'al* [TH408, ZH440]), but, especially in poetry, *'al* is at times used for *lo'* [TH3808, ZH4202] (Joüon and Muraoka 1991:§160f), so there is no need to emend the text (contra Craigie 1983:319).

41:3 *restores them to health.* Lit., "you turn over his whole bed in his illness." The idea may be that of changing bedding and or bedclothes and may thus refer to aiding one's healing (Eaton 1967:116; Gerstenberger 1988:174; Kraus 1988:431-432).

41:10 *pay them back!* "Pay them back" is a play on words, since this verb (*shalem* [TH7999, ZH8966]) is from the same root as the noun translated "my best friend" (*shalom* [TH7965, ZH8934]) in the previous verse.

41:13 ***Praise. . . . Amen and amen!*** Each boundary between the books of the Psalter is marked with a similar call to praise and a double "amen" (see 72:19 and 89:52).

COMMENTARY

Psalm 41 may be a lament, or it may be a song of thanksgiving. The imperative "Have mercy on me," repeated in 41:4 and 41:10, would lead to the conclusion that the psalm is lamenting current distress. But the expression "I prayed" at the beginning of 41:4 seems to indicate that the imperatives were past utterances, not present requests. While 41:11-12 could be expressing confidence in deliverance before the deliverance is experienced (Craigie 1983:322; see Ps 13), it is more likely that it expresses thanksgiving for deliverance experienced (McCann 1996:846-847).

Psalm 41 is comprised of three strophes: general instructions for receiving care (41:1-3), recounting of a prayer for healing (41:4-10), and confidence in God's pleasure (41:11-13).

Instructions for Receiving Care (41:1-3). "Oh, the joys of those who" (*'ashre* [TH835A, ZH897]) echoes the opening of the Psalter and provides closure for Book 1. In Psalm 1 (and elsewhere for that matter) blessedness is experienced by those who rightly relate to God. In Psalm 41 this same blessedness is experienced by those who rightly relate to other people—the poor, in particular. But of course, these two are inseparable. If we love God and God loves the poor, then we must love the poor. Love of God and love of neighbor stand together as the summary of the Christian life (Matt 22:37-40).

The joy of those who trust the Lord (40:4) is the joy of those who show their faith by their works, the work of caring for the poor in particular (41:1). Caring for poor people was the responsibility of all Israelites, but it was especially the responsibility of the king (see 72:12-14; Jer 22:16). And caring for the poor is a prerequisite for receiving care from the Lord. The Lord rescues those who care for the poor. By contrast, "Those who shut their ears to the cries of the poor will be ignored in their own time of need" (Prov 21:13). In the spirit of Psalm 41:1, Jesus declared that those who are merciful will be shown mercy, and in this way they will experience blessedness (Matt 5:7).

While general protection and prosperity are clearly in view in 41:1-3, the specific care in view is restoration from illness. The Lord "keeps them alive" (41:2) and nurses people back to health when they are sick (41:3). This general instruction on restoration to health is the backdrop against which the psalmist paints his testimony of being restored to health.

Prayer for Healing (41:4-10). In this strophe, David recounts his prayer for healing and the opposition he experienced at the hands of his enemies. David prayed, "Have mercy on me. Heal me, for I have sinned against you." Here as elsewhere in the Psalter (e.g., Pss 32 and 38), sin resulted in illness. David pleaded for mercy, and he desired that mercy would come in concrete form. Explicitly, he wanted the mercy of being healed from his sickness. Implicitly, he wanted the mercy of forgiveness.

As in Psalm 38, so too here, illness was the occasion for opposition. We do not know what brought about the opposition, but the expression of the opposition is clear: ungodly speech. The enemy spoke evil of David and wished for his death.

They visited David, not to comfort him, but to gather gossip, which they then spread far and wide. It is clear that these enemies could not have been counted among "those who are kind to the poor" (41:1), for they were rejoicing in his imminent demise (41:8). To make matters worse, David's best friend, his trusted companion with whom he had related intimately, had come under the influence of the enemy and had himself joined them in their opposition to David. His sickness was a source of pain. His sin was no doubt a source of grief. Opposition added insult to injury. But the deepest agony came from the sense of being abandoned by those who knew him well.

Jesus experienced the depths of this pain, when one of the Twelve, Judas Iscariot, became his betrayer. Jesus quoted 41:9 to express his agony (see John 13:18). Because Jesus was betrayed and died as a result, we can receive mercy to meet all our needs, whether those needs are for healing or forgiveness or strength to endure unjust opposition. In Jesus we have a best friend who will never betray us, but will always be there to give us mercy.

The strophe ends on the same note with which it began: "Have mercy on me" (41:10). And as in 41:4, the mercy desired was the mercy of restoration to health.

Confidence in God's Pleasure (41:11–13). In this final strophe, David gives thanks for receiving healing. That there is mercy to be healed proves that there is mercy to be forgiven. God proves that he is Lord and Savior over sin by remedying the sickness that results from that sin.

David knew that God was pleased with him, because his enemies were not permitted to triumph over him. They would have triumphed over him had he died. The defeat of his foes was experienced in the preservation of his life. He was preserved because he was innocent—better, he had "integrity," which captures the sense of the Hebrew word *tom* [TH8537, ZH9448] (NIDOTTE 4.306) better than "innocent." The idea is that the person of integrity is consistent and faithful (TLOT 3.1426), not morally perfect. David was a man of integrity. He was a godly man. But he still sinned and suffered as a result. In this regard, David was like Job, who was "blameless—a man of complete integrity" (*tam weyashar* [TH8535/3477, ZH9447/3838]; Job 1:1), but Job also sinned and needed the grace of repentance (Job 42:6). This grace comes from "the LORD, the God of Israel, who lives from everlasting to everlasting" and who is worthy to be praised. "Amen and amen!"

◆ II. BOOK TWO: Psalms 42–72
A. Psalms 42–43

For the choir director: A psalm of the descendants of Korah.*

1 As the deer longs for streams of water,
so I long for you, O God.
2 I thirst for God, the living God.
When can I go and stand before
him?
3 Day and night I have only tears
for food,
while my enemies continually
taunt me, saying,
"Where is this God of yours?"

4 My heart is breaking
as I remember how it used to be:
I walked among the crowds of
worshipers,

leading a great procession to the
house of God,
singing for joy and giving thanks
amid the sound of a great
celebration!

5 Why am I discouraged?
Why is my heart so sad?
I will put my hope in God!
I will praise him again—
my Savior and 6 my God!

Now I am deeply discouraged,
but I will remember you—
even from distant Mount Hermon, the
source of the Jordan,
from the land of Mount Mizar.
7 I hear the tumult of the raging seas
as your waves and surging tides
sweep over me.
8 But each day the LORD pours his
unfailing love upon me,
and through each night I sing his
songs,
praying to God who gives me life.

9 "O God my rock," I cry,
"Why have you forgotten me?
Why must I wander around in
grief,
oppressed by my enemies?"
10 Their taunts break my bones.
They scoff, "Where is this God
of yours?"
11 Why am I discouraged?
Why is my heart so sad?
I will put my hope in God!
I will praise him again—
my Savior and my God!

PSALM 43

1 Declare me innocent, O God!
Defend me against these ungodly
people.
Rescue me from these unjust liars.
2 For you are God, my only safe
haven.
Why have you tossed me aside?
Why must I wander around
in grief,
oppressed by my enemies?
3 Send out your light and your
truth;
let them guide me.
Let them lead me to your holy
mountain,
to the place where you live.
4 There I will go to the altar of God,
to God—the source of all my joy.
I will praise you with my harp,
O God, my God!

5 Why am I discouraged?
Why is my heart so sad?
I will put my hope in God!
I will praise him again—
my Savior and my God!

42:TITLE Hebrew *maskil*. This may be a literary or musical term.

NOTES

42:1 *deer.* The word *'ayyal* [TH354, ZH385] (masc. sg.) is to be emended to *'ayyeleth* [TH355, ZH387] (fem. sg.) in keeping with the gender of the verb; the Taw was probably omitted through haplography (the next word begins with a Taw; Craigie 1983:324).

42:4 *crowds of worshipers.* The word *sak* [TH5519, ZH6107] occurs only here; the meaning is obscure (HALOT 2.752).

leading. The word *'eddaddem* [TH1718, ZH1844] is apparently a Hithpael imperfect with a third-person masc. pl. object suffix ("walk with them"), but the text may be damaged.

42:5-6 *my Savior and my God.* Based on 42:11 and 43:5, it is clear that "my God" should be read at the end of 42:5 and that *yeshu'oth panayw 'elohay* [TH2050.2, ZH2257] (salvation of *his* face my God) should be emended to *yeshu'oth panay we'lohay* [TH2050.1, ZH2256] (salvation of *my* face *and* my God).

42:8 *pours.* The verb is an imperfect for repeated action in the past (Joüon and Muraoka 1991:§113e).

43:3 ***the place where you live.*** Lit., "your dwelling places," an intensive plural (VanGemeren 1991:336); this same form occurs with the same usage in 84:1 [2] (see also 46:4 [5]).

COMMENTARY

There is virtual consensus that Psalms 42 and 43 were originally one psalm, though there are no compelling explanations for how the psalm got separated into two poems. Numerous Hebrew manuscripts treat them as one. There is no title for Psalm 43, which is surprising in Book 2.[1] And the threefold refrain divides Psalms 42–43 into three relatively equal strophes. Psalm 42:1 contains the primary theme of the psalm: our longing for God. Each strophe amplifies this theme: longing expressed as thirst (42:1-5), longing expressed in discouragement (42:6-11), and longing expressed through prayer (43:1-5).

Longing Expressed as Thirst (42:1–5). As was mentioned earlier (see commentary on Ps 23), someone has said that you can't get enough of what you don't really want. Some people fill their lives with stuff—toys, activities, relationships, work, cars, vacations, food, books, recreation, church—but are not satisfied. They seem to never have enough and are driven to get just a little more. Some people can't get enough of what we don't *ultimately* want. What we ultimately want is God himself—and when we have God, we find true joy and satisfaction in all the other good stuff of life. In Psalms 42–43 the psalmist cries out both for God's presence and for particular good things that he wants from God.

"I long for you, O God," says the psalmist. Augustine said it well when he said our souls are restless until they find rest in God. This psalmist had one great advantage: He knew what was missing (Mays 1994:173). He knew that what he ultimately wanted was God.

When we are thirsty, the best food will not satisfy. Only drink will. Our souls thirst for the living God. He created us to drink of him, and nothing else will quench that thirst. "When can I go and stand before him?" (42:2) is the burning question. Experiencing his presence is our deepest need. But there are times when our only drink is our own bitter tears, bitter because of the agonizing question, "Where is this God of yours?" (42:3).

Our hearts break as we remember how it used to be. How we used to drink deeply of the presence of God in worship, surrounded by countless others, singing for joy and giving thanks in great celebration. These memories, which have the potential to provide great encouragement, now bring only perplexed discouragement: "Why am I discouraged?" (42:5).

Longing Expressed in Discouragement (42:6–11). "Now I am deeply discouraged," confesses the psalmist (42:6). So he calls to mind not his experience at worship but God himself: "I will remember you." This memory of God takes him to the lush area of the Jordan's headwaters. In contrast to the waterless situation of the first strophe, the psalmist now finds himself in the presence of abundant waters. These abundant waters are an image of the experience of the abundant presence of God. But the memory of these waters is not, at the present, a source of consolation. Ironically, they are an overwhelming deluge that threatens to sweep the psalmist away.

The memory of God's presence in the past only makes matters worse, for the contrast between the past and the present is so great. In the past the Lord had poured out his unfailing love on the psalmist time and time again (see note on 42:8), so that the psalmist's mouth was filled with songs and prayers throughout the night. But now what filled his mouth was the question, "Why have you forgotten me? Why must I wander around in grief, oppressed by my enemies? (42:9). Their oppression came in the form of the question we have already encountered, "Where is this God of yours?" (42:10). By reading 42:9-10 together we come to understand that what made the question of the enemies so painful is that it reveals that this was the psalmist's very own question. No wonder he repeats his first question, "Why am I discouraged?" (42:11). He is discouraged because he does not know where God is.

Longing Expressed through Prayer (43:1-5). The refrain has expressed profound discouragement and also at least a glimmer of hope. This hope begins to burn more brightly in the third strophe, where the psalmist moves from lamenting his situation to pleading with God in prayer to rectify that situation.

The request is twofold. This first dimension of the request is for vindication in relation to the enemies who have been taunting the psalmist. Down deep inside the psalmist knows that in their repeated question ("Where is this God of yours?") with its implied answer ("He is nowhere to be found"), they are liars. On one level, he knows that God is there as his "only safe haven," but on another level he has no sense of the presence of God, feeling as if he has been tossed aside to walk in darkness.

This drives him to the other dimension of his request. Only restoration to the presence of God will vindicate him, for restoration to the divine presence will silence the question of his enemy and that of his own heart. So he pleads for light and truth to lead him to the holy mountain where God lives, to Jerusalem and the Temple. There in the Temple he will come to the altar, where sacrifice is made and restoration to intimate fellowship with God is possible.

He is still discouraged and sad, for he has not yet experienced that which his soul longs for. But his hope is more sure, as he says twice, "I will praise" (43:4-5). His hope is sure, because the one to whom he prays is his Savior and God. He believes that God will save him from the worst of all possible fates: the absence of God. He believes that God will deliver him into God's very own presence.

People in the old covenant entered God's presence when they entered the Temple. But the Temple was only a shadow, not the reality itself (Heb 10:1). We can enter the reality of God's presence "because of the blood of Jesus" (Heb 10:19). "And since we have a great High Priest who rules over God's house, let us go right into the presence of God with sincere hearts fully trusting him" (Heb 10:21-22). We cannot enter unaided. God must send out his light and truth. Then we will enter his presence. Jesus is that light and truth that brings us to the Father.

ENDNOTES

1. See also the lack of a title for Ps 10 as an argument for the original unity of Pss 9 and 10.

◆ B. Psalm 44

For the choir director: A psalm of the descendants of Korah.*

1 O God, we have heard it with our
own ears—
our ancestors have told us
of all you did in their day,
in days long ago:
2 You drove out the pagan nations by
your power
and gave all the land to our ancestors.
You crushed their enemies
and set our ancestors free.
3 They did not conquer the land with
their swords;
it was not their own strong arm
that gave them victory.
It was your right hand and strong arm
and the blinding light from your
face that helped them,
for you loved them.

4 You are my King and my God.
You command victories for Israel.*
5 Only by your power can we push back
our enemies;
only in your name can we trample
our foes.
6 I do not trust in my bow;
I do not count on my sword to save
me.
7 You are the one who gives us victory
over our enemies;
you disgrace those who hate us.
8 O God, we give glory to you all day long
and constantly praise your name.
Interlude

9 But now you have tossed us aside in
dishonor.
You no longer lead our armies to
battle.
10 You make us retreat from our enemies
and allow those who hate us to
plunder our land.
11 You have butchered us like sheep
and scattered us among the nations.
12 You sold your precious people for a
pittance,
making nothing on the sale.
13 You let our neighbors mock us.
We are an object of scorn and
derision to those around us.
14 You have made us the butt of their
jokes;
they shake their heads at us in scorn.
15 We can't escape the constant
humiliation;
shame is written across our faces.
16 All we hear are the taunts of our
mockers.
All we see are our vengeful
enemies.

17 All this has happened though we have
not forgotten you.
We have not violated your covenant.
18 Our hearts have not deserted you.
We have not strayed from your
path.
19 Yet you have crushed us in the jackal's
desert home.
You have covered us with darkness
and death.
20 If we had forgotten the name of our
God
or spread our hands in prayer to
foreign gods,
21 God would surely have known it,
for he knows the secrets of every
heart.
22 But for your sake we are killed every
day;
we are being slaughtered like sheep.

23 Wake up, O Lord! Why do you sleep?
Get up! Do not reject us forever.
24 Why do you look the other way?
Why do you ignore our suffering
and oppression?
25 We collapse in the dust,
lying face down in the dirt.
26 Rise up! Help us!
Ransom us because of your
unfailing love.

44:TITLE Hebrew *maskil.* This may be a literary or musical term. **44:4** Hebrew *for Jacob.* The names "Jacob" and "Israel" are often interchanged throughout the Old Testament, referring sometimes to the individual patriarch and sometimes to the nation.

NOTES

44:2 ***crushed.*** The NLT apparently presumes an emendation from *tara'* [TH7489, ZH8317] ("do evil"; from *ra'a'* I) to *taroa'* [TH7489A, ZH8318] ("crush"; from *ra'a'* II); see HALOT 3.1271 and 2:9.

44:4 ***my God. You command.*** In the MT there is not a suffix for "my," and the form of the verb is an imperative, which is grammatically problematic (Kraus 1988:444). The NLT apparently presumes an emendation to a participle *metsawweh* [TH6680, ZH7422] ("commanding"; see the LXX and Syriac); the Mem of the participle could have been transferred backward to the preceding word, which would have been *e'lohay* [TH430/2967.1, ZH466/3276] ("my God"; see Syriac). This verb is used in the same sense in 42:8 [9] ("pours his unfailing love" is lit., "commands his unfailing love").

victories. The word *yeshu'oth* [TH3444, ZH3802] occurs in 42:5 [6], 11 [12] and 43:5, where it is translated, "Savior."

44:5-6 ***push back . . . trample . . . trust . . . count on . . . to save.*** The verbs in these verses are imperfects, signifying repeated action in the past (Joüon and Muraoka 1991:§113e); note the perfects for past time in 44:7 [8]. Psalm 44:1-3 [2-4] is about the distant past. Psalm 44:4-8 [5-9] is about the recent past of the psalmist's own day. Psalm 44:9 [10] brings us to the psalmist's present.

44:8 ***give glory . . . constantly praise.*** "Gave glory . . . constantly praised" in keeping with the note on 44:5-6.

44:9 ***tossed us aside.*** The word *zanakh* [TH2186, ZH2396] (reject) occurs in 43:2; see also 44:23 [24], where it is translated "reject."

44:16 ***mockers.*** The word *kharap* [TH2778, ZH3070] occurs in 42:10 [11].

enemies. The "enemies" are mentioned in 42:9 [10] and 43:2.

44:24 ***oppression.*** The word *lakhats* [TH3906, ZH4316] occurs in 42:9 [10] and 43:2; in 42:9 [10] it occurs in the context of God forgetting, as is also the case here in 44:24.

44:25 ***lying face down in the dirt.*** Lit., "Our belly clings to the ground."

COMMENTARY

The number of lexical connections between Psalms 42–43 and Psalm 44 (see notes) indicates that Psalm 44 can be read as a corporate articulation of the individual problem expressed in Psalms 42–43. Both texts articulate profound perplexity at God's rejecting (43:2; 44:10, 23) and forgetting (42:9; 44:24) his people, who are experiencing the oppression (42:9; 43:2; 44:24) of the enemy (42:9; 43:2; 44:16). Psalm 44 adds to the perplexity without solving it.

Psalm 44 can be divided into three stanzas: past victories through faith in God (44:1-8), present defeats in spite of faithfulness to God (44:9-22), and future salvation through the unfailing love of God (44:23-26).

Past Victories through Faith in God (44:1-8). The opening stanza is a record of covenant loyalty in the past, loyalty on the part of God and his people. The stanza is comprised of two strophes. The first strophe (44:1-3) records the covenant faithfulness of the distant past. "In days long ago" God dispossessed the Canaanites from the Promised Land and gave that land "to our ancestors." The ancestors did not conquer the land through dependence on their own resources but through dependence on the Lord and his favor. This all took place in accordance with the theology of Deuteronomy 28:1-2, 7: Covenant loyalty results in military victory.

The second strophe (44:4-8) records the covenant faithfulness of the recent past. The psalmist affirms that the same covenant loyalty experienced by his ancestors has been experienced by the community in the recent past. God was the one who "command[ed] victories," "[gave] us victory over our enemies," and "disgrace[d] those who hate us." On their part the people had acknowledged that these victories were "only by [God's] power" and "only in [his] name." Like their ancestors, they did not trust in their own resources but trusted in God. Thus, they were careful to give him the glory and praise. Their experience was like that of previous generations: Covenant faithfulness had resulted in military victories.

Present Defeats in Spite of Faithfulness to God (44:9-22). The middle stanza paints a radically different picture. This stanza is comprised of two strophes. The first strophe (44:9-16) provides the details of the present situation. God's people are in desperate straits, having experienced defeat after military defeat. The emphasis in this strophe is on the fact that these defeats are the Lord's doing. The Lord is the subject of the vast majority of the verbs: He has tossed his people aside, no longer leads their armies, made them retreat, allowed them to be plundered, treated them like sheep for slaughter, scattered them, sold them for nothing, placed no value on them, caused them to be mocked, and made them the butt of jokes.

Based on the theology implicit in 44:1-8 and explicit in Deuteronomy 28:15 and 25, we would expect the second strophe in this stanza to contain a confession of sin. So we are shocked that the second strophe contains a most vigorous protestation of innocence. "All this has happened though we have not forgotten you. We have not violated your covenant" (44:17). And this loyalty was not merely external. It was a loyalty from the heart. In spite of such loyalty, God's people had been "crushed" and "covered . . . with darkness and death" (44:19). The people admitted that God's actions would be understandable had they turned from God to idols. But such had not been the case. The people were not claiming sinlessness but only basic loyalty (Mays 1994:178)—the same kind of loyalty demonstrated by their ancestors in the distant past and by themselves in the recent past. In some way they were not suffering because of their sin but for God's sake. This profound perplexity did not lead to unbelief, however, but to prayer.

Future Salvation through the Unfailing Love of God (44:23-26). The prayer begins with three imperatives: "Wake up!" and "Get up!" and "Do not reject." It is as if God had been sleeping and needed to be aroused from his slumber. The prayer is for their present rejection to end.

Two lamenting interrogatives follow: "Why do you look the other way?" and "Why do you ignore our suffering and oppression?" God's people had not forgotten him (*shakakh* [TH7911, ZH8894] in 44:20 [21]), so why had he forgotten and ignored (*shakakh*) them (44:24 [25])? These two interrogatives are balanced by two lamenting indicatives: "We collapse in the dust" and "our belly clings to the ground" (see note on 44:25).

The mood returns to that of the beginning of the stanza with two final imperatives (in the MT): "Rise up!" and "Help us" (44:26). While it is true that the psalm ends on a mixed note of lamentation and petition, it is significant that the last word in the MT is *khesed* [TH2617, ZH2876]. The last word is not "why" but "unfailing love."

This final stanza is "prayer rooted in a faith deeper than reason," for "there is an immense mystery in God and his ways, but one must continue to trust and to pray" (Craigie 1983:335). Psalm 44 expresses a mysterious suffering in the service of the Kingdom. This suffering points forward to Christ and then to Romans 8:17-39 (Mays 1994:179-200), where Paul quotes 44:22, "For your sake we are killed every day; we are being slaughtered like sheep" (Rom 8:36). Throughout the history of the church, there have been faithful Christians who have suffered and have even been put to death at the hands of persecutors. They were called to share in Christ's suffering that they might also share in his glory (Rom 8:17). They could do so knowing, like the author of Psalm 44, that no suffering could ever separate them from God's unfailing love.

When we experience mysterious suffering in the service of the Kingdom, let us take full advantage of the freedom God has given us in Psalm 44, freedom to honestly admit our perplexity, to lament our situation, and to pray for help, depending all the while on God's unfailing love.

◆ C. Psalm 45

For the choir director: A love song to be sung to the tune "Lilies." A psalm of the descendants of Korah.*

1 Beautiful words stir my heart.
I will recite a lovely poem about the king,
for my tongue is like the pen of a skillful poet.

2 You are the most handsome of all.
Gracious words stream from your lips.
God himself has blessed you forever.

3 Put on your sword, O mighty warrior!
You are so glorious, so majestic!

4 In your majesty, ride out to victory,
defending truth, humility, and justice.
Go forth to perform awe-inspiring deeds!

5 Your arrows are sharp, piercing your enemies' hearts.
The nations fall beneath your feet.

6 Your throne, O God,* endures forever and ever.
You rule with a scepter of justice.

7 You love justice and hate evil.
Therefore God, your God, has anointed you,
pouring out the oil of joy on you more than on anyone else.

8 Myrrh, aloes, and cassia perfume your robes.
In ivory palaces the music of strings entertains you.

9 Kings' daughters are among your noble women.
At your right side stands the queen,
wearing jewelry of finest gold from Ophir!

10 Listen to me, O royal daughter; take to heart what I say.
Forget your people and your family far away.

11 For your royal husband delights in your beauty;
honor him, for he is your lord.

12 The princess of Tyre* will shower you with gifts.
The wealthy will beg your favor.

13 The bride, a princess, looks glorious in her golden gown.

14 In her beautiful robes, she is led to the king,
accompanied by her bridesmaids.

15 What a joyful and enthusiastic procession
as they enter the king's palace!

[16] Your sons will become kings like their
father.
You will make them rulers over
many lands.

[17] I will bring honor to your name in
every generation.
Therefore, the nations will praise
you forever and ever.

45:TITLE Hebrew *maskil.* This may be a literary or musical term. **45:6** Or *Your divine throne.* **45:12** Hebrew *The daughter of Tyre.*

NOTES

45:1 *poet.* The word *soper* [TH5608A, ZH6221] means "scribe," but a professional scribe is not necessarily in view, since *soper* is being used as a figure of speech (McCann 1996:861).

45:2 *You are the most handsome.* The form *yopyapitha* [TH3302, ZH3636] may be a dittography for *yapitha* (HALOT 2.423; Kraus 1988:451).

God himself. The NLT leaves *'al-ken* [TH5921/3651A, ZH6584/4027] (therefore) untranslated; *'al-ken* is used in 45:7 [8] (see also 45:17 [18]) in the same grammatical configuration as here: *'al-ken* + verb with second-person object suffix + God as the subject of the verb.

45:5 *Your arrows . . . your feet.* The MT is difficult. Lit., "Your arrows are sharp. Nations fall under you. In the heart of the king's enemies." The NLT interprets the first and third colas as a unit and thus reorders the cola for the English reader.

45:8 *the music of strings.* The NLT presumes an emendation from *minni* [TH4480/2967.1, ZH4946/3276] (from me) to *minnim* [TH4482, ZH4944] (harps).

45:9 *your noble women.* The word *yiqqerotheka* [TH3368, ZH3701] is difficult. The sense is "your precious ones" (BDB 430; Zorell 1963:326).

45:13 *The bride . . . looks glorious.* The word *kol-kebuddah* [TH3605/3519A, ZH3972/3884] means "every valuable thing" and may refer to the bride or to her regalia. Perhaps the phrase should be emended to *kol-yekkabbeduhah* [TH3513, ZH3877] (all will honor her).

COMMENTARY

Psalm 45 has a number of unique features in relation to other psalms. The primary unique feature is that the psalm is "A love song." It is similar in this regard to the Song of Songs, but Psalm 45 has a more profoundly royal nature. It was no doubt a royal wedding psalm that was in all likelihood used at the weddings of numerous Davidic kings,[1] even as Psalm 2 was used at their coronations. No other psalm contains such extensive praise of a human being. There are four strophes in this psalm: the poet's introduction (45:1), the praise of the king (45:2-9), the calling of the queen (45:10-15), and the poet's conclusion (45:16-17).

The Poet's Introduction (45:1). In no other psalm does the poet let his presence be known so directly as in Psalm 45. He has a poem overflowing from his heart. The tongue of the poet is likened to the pen of a scribe, as he recites his masterpiece to the king.

The Praise of the King (45:2-9). The king is a man of physical beauty. At the beginning of this strophe, he is "the most handsome of all" (45:2). At the end of the strophe we smell fragrant perfumes, see opulent ivories, and hear delightful music. As in the Song of Songs, so too here, the sensual is not denied but celebrated in its proper place in life.

The king is a man of military might. He wears his sword as a mighty warrior, riding out to victory. His sharp arrows pierce the hearts of his enemies, as the nations fall beneath his feet.

The king is a man of divine character (McCann 1996:861). Gracious words (or "grace," *khen* [TH2580, ZH2834]; 45:2 [3]) stream from his lips as one who has received such grace from the God (84:11) who is himself gracious (*khanan* [TH2603, ZH2858]; e.g., 41:4 [5], 10 [11]). The king, like God, is characterized as being glorious and majestic (*hod wehadar* [TH1935/1926, ZH2086/2077]; 45:3 [4]; see 104:1), as he goes forth to defend truth and justice. The king loves the right and hates the wrong. Because of this Godlike character, the king is addressed as "God" in the psalm,[2] though it is possible that deity is being referred to here. According to some ancient Near Eastern royal ideologies, especially that of Egypt, one would not have to choose between a divine referent and a human referent, because the king would have been viewed as divine. But such a divine-human king did not fit the worldview of ancient Israel. The human king was divine-like at best, which seems to be the case in this psalm. The New Testament likewise does not make us choose, as it reveals to us a human king (Jesus) who is at the same time God in the full sense of that term (Heb 1:8-9).

The king is a man in submission to authority. "God" is the king's God, and as the Lord's anointed, the king is under the Lord's authority (see Ps 2). It is as vice-regent of the divine king that the glory of the human king is celebrated on this, his wedding day.

The Calling of the Queen (45:10-15). While from one perspective the focus shifts to the bride in this strophe, from another the focus remains on the king, for the bride is portrayed in relation to the bridegroom. The bride may have been a non-Israelite, since she is called to forget her people. She is called to leave her father and to submit to her lord-king-husband. This submission will not result in degrading servitude but in matchless honor and prestige. She is called from her chamber to the king's side, accompanied by bridesmaids in a spectacular procession.

The Poet's Conclusion (45:16-17). The poet now draws our attention to one blessing that will flow from this union: children, sons in particular who will rule throughout the kingdom in their father's stead. The poet then concludes his lovely poem with a promise that this poem will honor the king's name throughout all time and space.

ENDNOTES

1. See Keel 1997:283-285 for graphic representations of events related to royal weddings.
2. See Exod 4:16 and 7:1, where "God" is used in reference to Moses. In both texts Moses is "God" and Aaron is his prophet. In the former text, the connection between Moses and "God" is indirect, as it is mediated through the preposition Lamedh, but in the latter the connection is direct as there is no preposition, resulting in a wooden translation, "I have made you God to Pharaoh," which all major translations soften to something like the NLT, "I will make you seem like God to Pharaoh."

D. Psalm 46

*For the choir director: A song of the descendants of Korah, to be sung by soprano voices.**

1 God is our refuge and strength,
always ready to help in times of trouble.
2 So we will not fear when earthquakes come
and the mountains crumble into the sea.
3 Let the oceans roar and foam.
Let the mountains tremble as the waters surge! *Interlude*

4 A river brings joy to the city of our God,
the sacred home of the Most High.
5 God dwells in that city; it cannot be destroyed.
From the very break of day, God will protect it.
6 The nations are in chaos,
and their kingdoms crumble!
God's voice thunders,
and the earth melts!
7 The LORD of Heaven's Armies is here among us;
the God of Israel* is our fortress. *Interlude*

8 Come, see the glorious works of the LORD:
See how he brings destruction upon the world.
9 He causes wars to end throughout the earth.
He breaks the bow and snaps the spear;
he burns the shields with fire.

10 "Be still, and know that I am God!
I will be honored by every nation.
I will be honored throughout the world."
11 The LORD of Heaven's Armies is here among us;
the God of Israel is our fortress. *Interlude*

46:TITLE Hebrew *according to alamoth.* **46:7** Hebrew *of Jacob;* also in 46:11. See note on 44:4.

NOTES

46:TITLE ***soprano voices.*** See the note to the title of Ps 9.

46:2 ***earthquakes.*** The word *hamir* is an infinitive construct of *mur* II [TH4171A, ZH4615] ("shake"; HALOT 2.560).

46:3 ***as the waters surge!*** Lit., "let the mountains tremble in its pride" (*ga'awah* [TH1346, ZH1452]). "Pride" is an abstract expression that refers to the waves of the sea. In Job 38:8-11, we read of God setting a boundary for the sea and then saying, "This far and no farther will you come. Here your proud (*ga'on* [TH1347, ZH1454]) waves must stop."

Interlude. While the word *selah* [TH5542, ZH6138] does not always occur at the end of a strophe or stanza, it does seem to divide Ps 46 into three strophes of roughly equal length. If the refrain (see 46:7, 11) is inserted here (so BHS and Kraus 1988:459), then the three strophes are each comprised of three lines plus the refrain.

46:4 ***the sacred home of the Most High.*** The phrase is difficult. Lit., "the holy one of the dwellings of the Most High." The plural "dwellings" could be an intensive (see notes on 43:3 and 84:1), and the singular in construct with a plural could be a superlative (Waltke and O'Connor 1990:§9.5.3j). The LXX presumes a different reading of the Hebrew: *qiddesh mishkeno 'elyon* [TH6942/4908/5945B, ZH7727/5438/6610] (the Most High has sanctified his dwelling).

46:6 ***the earth melts!*** The word *'erets* [TH776, ZH824] here refers to the inhabitants of the earth (cf. BDB 76), though there may also be a reference back to 46:2-3 [3-4] (Brettler 1993:145).

46:9 ***shields.*** The word *'agaloth* [TH5699, ZH6322] means "carts." The NLT presumes an emendation to *'agiloth* [TH5694.1, ZH6317] (round shields); this emended word (singular, *'agilah*) would occur only here in the MT, but would be related to the Aramaic *'agila'* ("shield"; HALOT 2.784) and finds support in the LXX.

COMMENTARY

Psalm 46 exudes confidence in God in the face of monumental troubles. The opening line and the refrain express the dominant theme of the psalm (Brettler 1993:143): God is present with us as our sufficient source of protection, no matter what troubles we face. The three strophes move from cosmic collapse (46:1-3) to national turmoil (46:4-7), then to divine intervention (46:8-11).

No Fear in spite of Cosmic Collapse (46:1-3). How would you respond if your whole world caved in? The psalmist's response was, "We will not fear" (46:2). What he describes in 46:2-3 is the world (as he knew it) being turned upside down.

The Bible at times describes the earth as founded on the seas (24:2) by being set on pillars.[1] Hypothetically, this would make the earth subject to tottering and falling over into the sea, with the sea then covering the earth. But the Bible also teaches that such tottering (*mot* [TH4131, ZH4572]) is not possible. "The world stands firm and cannot be shaken [*mot*]" (93:1; 96:10). "You placed the world on its foundation so it would never be moved [*mot*]" (104:5). The Bible also teaches that the sea, which covered the earth before the emergence of dry land, would never again be permitted to cover the earth. "Who kept the sea inside its boundaries as it burst from the womb? . . . I locked it behind barred gates, limiting its shores. I said, 'This far and no farther will you come. Here your proud waves must stop'" (Job 38:8, 10-11). "Then you set a firm boundary for the seas, so they would never again cover the earth" (104:9). "I, the LORD, define the ocean's sandy shoreline as an everlasting boundary that the waters cannot cross" (Jer 5:22).

It is against this biblical backdrop that we must hear the psalmist's words: We will not fear, even if the earth totters (*mot*) into the sea, as its waves threaten to cover the mountains themselves. We will not fear, he says, even if the world as we know it—more than that, the world as God has defined it—collapses before our very eyes. I know of no more radical profession of faith anywhere in the Scriptures.[2] Such faith, with its corresponding absence of fear, is built on the truth that "God is our refuge and strength, always ready to help in times of trouble" (46:1).

Flowing Joy in spite of National Upheaval (46:4-7). In this strophe it is not the waters that are roaring against God's people; it is the nations that are in such an uproar. The nations are threatening to destroy Jerusalem itself, the capital city. But in the face of such national upheaval, the city is full of joy. This joy flows throughout the city like a figurative multibranched river, evoking the multibranched river that supplied the Garden of Eden with all that it needed (Gen 2:10-14; see also Ezek 47:1-12 and Rev 22:1-2).

There is joy because the city is secure in spite of the threats. The city is secure, but not ultimately because of its many towers and fortified walls, which it certainly has (see 48:12-13). The city is secure because God is present there. The divine presence is the ultimate fortress (Brettler 1993:143; Kraus 1988:464). The "LORD of Heaven's Armies" is present as the Divine Warrior. He will be there at the break of day, the earliest time for battle (Brettler 1993:144), to protect the city from attack. He need only raise his thunderous voice, and the would-be attackers will melt away. There is flowing joy in spite of national upheaval, because "the LORD of Heaven's Armies is here among us; the God of Israel is our fortress" (46:7).

Peace because of Divine Intervention (46:8-11). Divine intervention into the threatening chaos of life, hinted at in the first strophe and introduced in the second, becomes the focus of attention in the final strophe. We are invited to "Come, see the glorious works of the LORD," his work of destruction in particular. The "destruction" is not, however, what we would expect (McCann 1996:866). The destruction is the destruction of war and all its weaponry. The destruction is the establishment of worldwide peace. We, and the nations, are summoned to stop all of our frenetic and rebellious activity and to know that the Lord is the true and living God. He is ultimate; we are not. His honor, not our own, is our ultimate reason for being. He pledges that he himself will be honored by every nation throughout the world.

Read in the context of 46:10, the final refrain, "The LORD of Heaven's Armies is here among us; the God of Israel is our fortress," is international in scope. In fact, in the context of the first strophe, it is a cosmic declaration. While the divine presence was in some special way located in the Temple in Jerusalem, the divine presence was never limited to that Temple. Isaiah knew that the whole cosmos is the dwelling of God (Isa 66:1-2). Jesus came as the true tabernacle (John 1:14). He is Immanuel, "God is with us" (Matt 1:23). He came to reconcile all to the Father—Jews and Gentiles; he came to make "peace with everything in heaven and on earth by means of [his] blood on the cross" (see Col 1:18-20). His redemption is cosmic because he is the Creator. He brings peace to the nations as he brings stability to the earth.

As the psalm envisioned Jerusalem having a multibranched river that supplied everything needed for life, so Jesus Christ offers "living water" (John 4:10). When partaken of, this living water "becomes a fresh, bubbling spring within them, giving them eternal life" (John 4:14). When drunk, this water becomes "rivers of living water" that flow out from within to give life to others (John 7:38). These rivers refer to the Holy Spirit (John 7:39). Through the Holy Spirit's presence within us, God "is able . . . to accomplish infinitely more than we might ask or think" for his own "glory . . . in the church and in Christ Jesus through all generations forever and ever!" (Eph 3:20-21).

ENDNOTES

1. The NLT uses the word "foundation" to translate the Hebrew word *'ammud* [TH5982, ZH6647] (pillar) in 75:3 [4] and Job 9:6. The *'ammud* is not a foundation in general but a particular component in the foundation, so the NLT is not too far off, even though it lacks some precision at this point.
2. The statements in Job 13:15 and Dan 3:16-18 are a close second and third in my estimation.

◆ E. Psalm 47

For the choir director: A psalm of the descendants of Korah.

1 Come, everyone! Clap your hands!
Shout to God with joyful praise!
2 For the LORD Most High is awesome.
He is the great King of all the earth.
3 He subdues the nations before us,
putting our enemies beneath our feet.
4 He chose the Promised Land as our inheritance,
the proud possession of Jacob's descendants, whom he loves.
Interlude

5 God has ascended with a mighty shout.
The LORD has ascended with trumpets blaring.
6 Sing praises to God, sing praises;
sing praises to our King, sing praises!
7 For God is the King over all the earth.
Praise him with a psalm.*
8 God reigns above the nations,
sitting on his holy throne.
9 The rulers of the world have gathered together
with the people of the God of Abraham.
For all the kings of the earth belong to God.
He is highly honored everywhere.

47:7 Hebrew *maskil.* This may be a literary or musical term.

NOTES

47:1 ***everyone.*** The word *'ammim* [TH5971A, ZH6639] (peoples) has the nations in view, in addition to Israel.

47:3 ***He subdues.*** The Hebrew imperfect verb here is not the long imperfect but the short imperfect, which is here used as a past tense (Waltke and O'Connor 1990:§31.1.1.d; see also Joüon and Muraoka 1991:§113h), the reference being to the conquest in the days of Joshua, as the following verse makes clear.

beneath our feet. Compare Josh 10:24 and see Keel 1997:293 for a graphic representation of a vanquished foe under the feet of the victor.

47:5 ***shout . . . trumpets blaring.*** The noun translated "shout" is from the same root as the verb translated "shout" in 47:1. "Trumpets blaring" translates *beqol shopar* [TH6963/7782, ZH7754/8795] (with voice of trumpet), which echoes *beqol rinnah* [TH6963/7440, ZH7754/8262] (joyful praise) in 47:1. Together these repetitions form a frame around the first strophe (47:1-5).

47:8 ***God reigns.*** The verb *malak* [TH4427, ZH4887] occurs with "God" or *yhwh* [TH3068, ZH3378] as the subject here and in 96:10 (cf. 1 Chr 16:31), 97:1, and 99:1. Since the days of Mowinckel (1962), the translation has been debated. Day (1995:75-82) has presented the best defense of the translation "has become king." The perfect can be translated "became king" (1 Kgs 16:23a), "reigned" (1 Kgs 16:23b), or "has become king" (2 Sam 15:10; 1 Kgs 1:11, 13, 18; 2 Kgs 9:13). Clear examples of "is king" are lacking. Contrary to common opinion, word order is not relevant, as the inceptive sense is found with the order subject + predicate (1 Kgs 16:29 and 2 Kgs 15:13) and the order predicate + subject (1 Kgs 15:1, 9). The context of the phrase in 47:8 [9] provides the best evidence for the inceptive rendering: God has just ascended, having won a great victory, and has taken his seat on his royal throne and begun to reign. While it is true that God has always been king, it is equally true that on specific occasions he became king in a new sense (Goldingay 2007:81). Vos (1972:342-343) says, "It will be remembered that the shout 'Absalom is King' was the shout of acclaim at his assumption of the kingship." In reference to the Lord becoming king, Vos goes on to say, "By this is meant a form of statement representing Jehovah as becoming, or revealing himself in the last crisis the victorious King of Israel. . . . The simple solution seems to lie in this: that 'kingship' is in the O.T. more a concept of action than of status. Jehovah becomes King = Jehovah works acts of deliverance. . . . The thought is not merely that Jehovah becomes King in order to save, but that through the salvation, as well as in other acts, He arrives at the acme of his royal splendor."

47:9 *have gathered together with the people of the God of Abraham.* The point is that the *'ammim* (nations) have become part of the people (*'am* [TH5971A, ZH6639]) of God. It is possible that *'im* [TH5973, ZH6640] (with) has fallen out of the text through haplography (so BHS and Craigie 1983:347).

kings. Lit., "shields," but the "shields" are here used metonymically for the "kings" (see 84:9 [10] and 89:18 [19] for this same usage), so there is no need to emend the text to *signe* [TH5461, ZH6036] (rulers) contra Craigie 1983:347.

COMMENTARY

Psalm 47 has been referred to as a "wild doxology" (Wharton 1993:163), as it celebrates in radical language the universal kingship of the God of Israel. Accordingly, Psalm 47 has a special place in the liturgy of Rosh Hashanah, which celebrates the sovereignty of God over the whole world (S. Cohen 1995:258). The psalm falls naturally into two stanzas: praise of the king who has conquered (47:1-5) and praise of the king who has begun to reign (47:6-9).

Praise the Conquering King (47:1–5). Not just Israel but "everyone," all the nations, are called upon in this psalm to praise the God of Israel. The reason is clear: "The LORD Most High is awesome. He is the great King of all the earth" (47:2). His universal kingship has been demonstrated in history. In the days of Joshua, the Lord subdued the Canaanites, putting them under the feet of his people, and then he granted the land of Canaan to them as their proud possession.

These awesome acts on behalf of Israel were at the same time a demonstration of the Lord's great love for his people. The Israelites were not chosen to take possession of the Promised Land because they were more righteous than the Canaanites (Deut 9:1-6). They were chosen because the Lord in his own mysterious way loved them (Deut 7:7-8).

The call to praise the Lord who has conquered was issued in the context of a liturgical procession during which the Lord "ascended with a mighty shout" and "with trumpets blaring" (47:5). A procession like that when David first brought the Ark of the Covenant to Jerusalem (2 Sam 6) is no doubt in view in this psalm. The language of the psalm as a whole, but particularly of 47:6, has made this psalm appropriate in the celebration of the ascension of Christ.

This first strophe could serve as a self-contained hymn of praise with its call to praise, which is bolstered by reasons for praise. But more worship is called for and more reasons are given (in the next verses) to celebrate the Lord's kingship.

Praise the Reigning King (47:6–9). Paralleling the first verse of the psalm, 47:6 issues a second call to praise the Lord, this time repeating the call to "sing praise" four times in one verse! All the nations are no doubt in view in this second call, as well.

Parallel to 47:2, which introduces the reason for the call in terms of the Lord being king over all the earth, 47:7 introduces the reasons to praise in the same language: "For God is the King over all the earth." This second strophe does not, however, merely repeat the reasons of the first strophe but advances them.

Having ascended into the city and the Temple, the Lord proceeds to take his seat on his royal throne and begin his newly established reign. Gathered before him are the rulers of the world, serving as representatives of the peoples of the world. Once enemies, the nations have become part of the worshiping community of God's people. In spite of their temporary attempts at autonomy (Ps 2), they "belong to God," who alone is highly exalted.

The scope of Psalm 47 matches that of Psalm 46. The universal peace of Psalm 46 is the setting for the universal worship of Psalm 47. While rooted in history, the language of Psalm 47 has not yet been fully realized in history. Psalm 47 drives us into the future in anticipation of the day when such universal celebration of the Lord's kingship will be reality. Zechariah (see Zech 14:9) envisioned the day when God will become king over all the earth in a way that he has not been and is not currently.

While the kingship of God has already been established through the person and work of the Lord Jesus Christ, this kingship is not yet fully realized. Thus Revelation 11:17 anticipates the future inauguration of the Lord's kingship in fullness with these words: "We give thanks to you, Lord God, the Almighty, the one who is and always was, for now you have assumed your great power and have begun to reign." And in another scene (Rev 15:3-4) we hear a song reminiscent of Psalm 47:

Great and marvelous are your works,
  O Lord God, the Almighty.
Just and true are your ways,
  O King of the nations.
Who will not fear you, Lord,
  and glorify your name?
  For you alone are holy.
All nations will come and worship before you,
  for your righteous deeds have been revealed.

As the church anticipates that glorious day when God arrives at the acme of his royal splendor, we labor with God's own heart, that "everyone" might join the people of God in worshiping the king of all the earth, who is to be highly honored everywhere.

◆ F. Psalm 48

A song. A psalm of the descendants of Korah.

1 How great is the LORD,
** how deserving of praise,**
in the city of our God,
** which sits on his holy mountain!**
2 It is high and magnificent;
** the whole earth rejoices to see it!**
Mount Zion, the holy mountain,*
** is the city of the great King!**
3 God himself is in Jerusalem's towers,
** revealing himself as its defender.**

4 The kings of the earth joined forces
** and advanced against the city.**
5 But when they saw it, they were
**   stunned;**

they were terrified and ran away.
6 They were gripped with terror
and writhed in pain like a woman
in labor.
7 You destroyed them like the mighty
ships of Tarshish
shattered by a powerful east wind.

8 We had heard of the city's glory,
but now we have seen it ourselves—
the city of the LORD of Heaven's
Armies.
It is the city of our God;
he will make it safe forever.
Interlude

9 O God, we meditate on your unfailing
love
as we worship in your Temple.
10 As your name deserves, O God,
you will be praised to the ends of
the earth.
Your strong right hand is filled with
victory.
11 Let the people on Mount Zion rejoice.
Let all the towns of Judah be glad
because of your justice.

12 Go, inspect the city of Jerusalem.*
Walk around and count the many
towers.
13 Take note of the fortified walls,
and tour all the citadels,
that you may describe them
to future generations.
14 For that is what God is like.
He is our God forever and ever,
and he will guide us until
we die.

48:2 Or *Mount Zion, in the far north;* Hebrew reads *Mount Zion, the heights of Zaphon.* **48:12** Hebrew *Zion.*

NOTES

48:2 ***high and magnificent.*** The NLT captures well the sense of *yepeh nop* [TH3303/5131, ZH3637/5679] (see HALOT 2.682).

the holy mountain. As the footnote indicates, the text reads, "the heights of Zaphon." In Ugaritic literature, "Zaphon" is used for the dwelling of Baal. Zaphon is the name of the mythological sacred dwelling of the gods (Clifford 1972:142-144 and Roberts 1973:334; see Craigie 1983:353 for a concise discussion of the issue). Hebrew poets at times used mythological language to make theological points with vividness (see Smick 1982). "The psalmist is borrowing the imagery and not the theology" (VanGemeren 1991:363; see commentary).

48:3 ***God himself is in Jerusalem's towers.*** Here the preposition ("in") may be the Beth of essence (Joüon and Muraoka 1991:§133c), used to mark the predicate. In this case the sense is, "God himself is Jerusalem's towers," not literally, of course. Support for this interpretation is found in the following colon, which could be translated, "He is known as a *fortress*" (*misgab* [TH4869, ZH5369]). The towers would be a symbol of the divine presence. The point is basically the same in both translations. While the NLT guards against misunderstanding, it loses rhetorical power (see note on 48:14).

48:10 ***the ends of the earth.*** Lit., "throughout the earth," in 46:9 [10].

48:11 ***the towns of Judah.*** Lit., "the daughters of Judah." This expression is a personification of the towns (see, for example, Josh 17:16; HALOT 1.166; Dobbs-Allsopp 1995).

48:13 ***the fortified walls.*** Lit., "her strength," emending the difficult *khelah* (a word that occurs nowhere else in the Hebrew Bible) to *khelahah* [TH2426/1886.3, ZH2658/2023], and understanding "strength" to refer to "sloping bank [glacis] outside the wall" (VanGemeren 1991:366).

tour. The verb *pasag* [TH6448, ZH7170] occurs only here; the meaning is uncertain (HALOT 3.946).

48:14 ***that is what God is like.*** Lit., "this is God." The NLT rightly understands the figurative nature of the sentence; the use of a simile ("is like") in English guards against misunderstanding but loses rhetorical power.

until we die. This is an attempt to make sense out of a most difficult phrase, *'al-muth* [TH5921/4191/4192B, ZH6584/4637/6629]. "About dying" is perhaps the sense of the MT. The NLT presumes an emendation to *'ad-muth* [TH5704/4191, ZH6330/4637] (until death) and supplies the subject "we" from the context. Alternatively, the consonants *'l-mwth* [TH5961, ZH6628] may be related to expressions found in the titles to Pss 9 and 46, and may, therefore, be displaced from the title of Ps 49. *Wa'ed* [TH5703, ZH6329] (forever) could then be read with *hu' yenahagenu* [TH1931/5090, ZH2085/5627] (he will guide us), but this would violate the Masoretic accents and *'olam wa'ed* (forever and ever) has already occurred as a fixed phrase in Pss 10:16 and 45:6 [7]. It seems to me that the reading of the NLT is the better option.

COMMENTARY

Psalm 48 continues the theme of God's universal reign found in Psalms 46 and 47. The "earth" is referred to 10 times in these three psalms. Psalm 46:9 and 48:10 envision God's sovereignty and praise reaching the ends of the earth, while 47:2, 7 and 48:2 see them reaching the whole earth. Like Psalm 46 in particular, but also like Psalm 47, the point of origination for God's sovereign rule is the city of God, Jerusalem. Psalm 48 praises God by praising the city from which he rules over the whole earth.

The City of the Great King (48:1-3). The psalm begins with the direct praise of God, "How great is the LORD, how deserving of praise." But this praise of God continues indirectly through the praise of "the city of our God" that is located on "his holy mountain." The city is "high and magnificent"; "the whole earth rejoices to see it!" (48:2). Hyperbole seems to be required in praise of the city (which is not all that high in elevation and which was not celebrated by the whole earth), but why? The city is great not because of its size or location. The city is great because it is "the city of the great King" (48:2). The real towers are not those of stone and earth but are God himself (see note on 48:3). God's presence gives the city its invincible character, as in 46:5. The presence of such a great God would make the most humble of cities great and worthy to be praised.

As is clear by now, the city is not just any city. This city, startling though the claim may be, is identified as Zaphon, the mythical meeting place of Canaanite deities where the palace of Baal was located. Why would the poet identify the city of God with the mountain of the gods? The Canaanites believed that deity, Baal in particular, was present on Mount Zaphon in the distant reaches of the north. To the extent that Israelites were influenced by Canaanite theology, they too believed this. In a rhetorically powerful way, "The psalmist affirms, in effect, that the aspirations of all peoples for a place on earth where God's presence could be experienced were fulfilled in Mount Zion, the true Zaphon" (Craigie 1983:353). Israelites need go no farther than Jerusalem to find the true location where God could be experienced and from where he truly ruled the earth. Zaphon was Jerusalem, a city for the whole earth to see.

Seeing the City through the Eyes of Fear (48:4-7). The second strophe describes the reaction of "the kings of the earth" upon seeing the city of God. They had apparently gathered to attack the city "together," as in 2:2. But before they attacked, upon seeing the city, "They were stunned . . . terrified and ran away" (48:5). The terror they experienced is compared to two things. They writhed in terror like a woman writhing with labor pains. And their terror was like that of sailors on a ship that is being shattered in a violent storm.

Such terror was not generated by the physical fortress of Jerusalem alone. The kings of the earth must have had some perception of the great king, some perception that God himself was the fortress, some perception that they had come to Zaphon. It was the divine presence that gripped them with terror. They were gripped with terror because they had joined together against the city. Had they come to Zaphon in humble submission to the great king, their response to seeing the city would have been quite different, as the following strophe makes clear.

Seeing the City through the Eyes of Faith (48:8–11). The "we" of 48:8 are apparently pilgrims who, like the kings of the earth, arrived at the city of God and, upon seeing it, responded. Their response, however, was not one of terrified withdrawal but one of joyful praise. Upon seeing the city, they saw not only the fortress but the God who "will make it safe forever" (48:8). Their response was positive, because they had not come to attack the great king's city but to meditate on his unfailing love as part of their worship in his Temple. They came to the city to offer praise, but the praise envisioned was not restricted to the city but would extend to the ends of the earth. Joy, not fear, filled their hearts, because they knew the great king to be just, his right hand filled with victory, and his protection permanent.

There was quite a contrast between what the kings saw and what the pilgrims saw, though both saw the same thing (Craigie 1983:353). The difference lay in the intention of the heart.

The City Is the Great King (48:12–14). Perhaps as part of their worship, the pilgrims participated in a procession around the city. As they walked around the city, they were encouraged to count the towers and to take note of the strength of the fortifications. One purpose was that the pilgrims would then be able to tell others about the magnificence of the city of the great king. But more important than that was that they themselves would gain a clearer picture of the nature of their God. He is the great king, a strong tower and sure defense, full of unfailing love, victory, and justice. And God is "our God forever and ever," the one who will guide us throughout life. This is what the pilgrims needed for their own faith, and this is what they would tell future generations.

In 587 BC Jerusalem was destroyed, demonstrating that the city and God were not one and the same. The city was a symbol, a shadow of another reality. That reality is God himself, dwelling with his people. Jesus Christ came as the great king, as the embodiment of the presence of God, to bring us into the presence of God. We experience that presence now through the Holy Spirit who lives within us. And we will experience that presence in fullness in the new heavens and new earth, when the glorious shout goes up, "Look, God's home is now among his people! He will live with them, and they will be his people. God himself will be with them" (Rev 21:3).

◆ G. Psalm 49

For the choir director: A psalm of the descendants of Korah.

1 Listen to this, all you people!
Pay attention, everyone in the world!
2 High and low,
rich and poor—listen!
3 For my words are wise,
and my thoughts are filled with insight.
4 I listen carefully to many proverbs
and solve riddles with inspiration from a harp.

5 Why should I fear when trouble comes,
when enemies surround me?
6 They trust in their wealth
and boast of great riches.
7 Yet they cannot redeem themselves from death*
by paying a ransom to God.
8 Redemption does not come so easily,
for no one can ever pay enough
9 to live forever
and never see the grave.

10 Those who are wise must finally die,
just like the foolish and senseless,
leaving all their wealth behind.
11 The grave is their eternal home,
where they will stay forever.
They may name their estates after themselves,
12 but their fame will not last.
They will die, just like animals.
13 This is the fate of fools,
though they are remembered as being wise.* *Interlude*

14 Like sheep, they are led to the grave,*
where death will be their shepherd.
In the morning the godly will rule over them.
Their bodies will rot in the grave,
far from their grand estates.
15 But as for me, God will redeem my life.
He will snatch me from the power of the grave. *Interlude*

16 So don't be dismayed when the wicked grow rich
and their homes become ever more splendid.
17 For when they die, they take nothing with them.
Their wealth will not follow them into the grave.
18 In this life they consider themselves fortunate
and are applauded for their success.
19 But they will die like all before them
and never again see the light of day.
20 People who boast of their wealth don't understand;
they will die, just like animals.

49:7 Or *no one can redeem the life of another.* **49:13** The meaning of the Hebrew is uncertain.
49:14 Hebrew *Sheol;* also in 49:14b, 15.

NOTES

49:1 ***people.*** The word *'ammim* [TH5971A, ZH6639] occurs in the introductory call to worship in Ps 47. Here, as there, all the nations are in view.

49:2 ***High and low.*** These terms translate what could be seen as synonyms in the Hebrew (*bene 'adam* [TH120, ZH132] and *bene-'ish* [TH376, ZH408]). But some element of contrast between the two groups is in view in light of the following colon. The NLT probably captures this contrast (see note on 4:2) but in reverse order. The line is chiastic: low + high / rich + poor.

49:4 ***solve.*** "Solve" is the sense of the word according to HALOT 3.987, but "expound" would make better sense in context, since the following verses expound on what those who trust in their wealth are like, and since there is, it seems, a riddle contained in the refrain (see note at 49:20).

49:5 *enemies.* The word *'awon 'aqebay* [TH5771/6119 or 6120, ZH6411/6811 or 6812] (sin of my heels) makes no sense. The NLT may be following BDB, which lists an *'aqeb* II (overreacher), but this would be the only occurrence of this word in the Hebrew Bible. Or the NLT may presume an emendation of the second word to *'oqebay* [TH6117, ZH6810] (my betrayers); see BHS, Dahood 1965:297, and HALOT 2.873. The point is the same in both cases: The "times when trouble comes" are the times "when enemies surround me."

49:7 *Yet.* The NLT presumes an emendation from *'akh* [TH251, ZH278] (brother) to the contrastive particle, *'ak* [TH389, ZH421]. Support for this emendation is found in some Hebrew mss and in 49:15a, which begins with *'ak* and also speaks of redemption. The MT could stand, but "A brother cannot redeem a man" is not the expected idiom; one would expect "A brother cannot redeem a brother" or "A man cannot redeem a man" (Craigie 1983:357).

redeem themselves. The NLT presumes a repointing of the vowels, resulting in a change from the active Qal to the reflexive Niphal.

49:11 *The grave.* The NLT presumes an emendation from *qirbam* [TH7130, ZH7931] (their inward parts) to *qibram* [TH6913, ZH7700] (their grave). This emendation finds support in the LXX, Syriac, and Vulgate.

49:13 *fools.* Lit., "[falsely] self-confident" (HALOT 2.489).

though they are remembered as being wise. This is an attempt to render an obscure Hebrew colon, which could be woodenly translated, "After them in their mouth they are pleased."

49:18 *consider themselves fortunate.* This is a case of an estimative Piel (Waltke and O'Connor 1990:§24.4g). With the estimative Piel the poet tells us what some people think to be true about themselves rather than what they are doing to themselves.

49:20 *People who boast of their wealth don't understand.* There is a riddle of sorts embedded in this line. Oral tradition traces the discovery of this riddle back to Patrick Skehan. The words *'adam biqar welo' yabin* could be translated, "A man with wealth but no understanding," and the line would finish, "is like the animals that perish." An alternative division of the consonants and a repointing of the final word would produce the following: *'adam biqar welo' y bin,* which could be translated, "A man with wealth but no Yodh in between." If we get the hint and remove the Yodh from in between the Beth and Qoph of *biqar* [TH871.2/3366, ZH928/3702] (with wealth), the result is *bqr,* which could be pointed *baqar* [TH1241, ZH1330], a word meaning "animal" that is a synonym of *behemah* [TH929, ZH989] in the second half of the line! "A man with wealth but no Yodh in between is like the animals that perish!"

COMMENTARY

Psalm 49 is a wisdom poem about how to live in the light of an inevitable death. Psalm 49 teaches us where to place our hope for life, given the reality of death. Our hope is not to be in wealth, whether that is the wealth we have or the wealth we wish we had. Our hope is to be in God. Wealth cannot redeem us from the power of death. Only God can.

Psalm 49 falls into three strophes: an introductory call to listen to the teaching (49:1-4), a warning that wealth cannot redeem from death (49:5-12), and a promise that God will redeem from death (49:13-20).

An Introductory Call to Listen (49:1-4). In keeping with the universal scope of the previous psalms and of Wisdom Literature in general, the introductory address has a distinctively universal scope (Craigie 1983:358). The instruction given in the poem applies to everyone regardless of national origin, and in the ancient context, this meant regardless of religion. This instruction applies to "everyone in the world" (49:1). It applies to those of low status and high status, to the rich as well as to the poor. No one is excluded. The rich and the poor are the particular focus in the introduction, because the poem addresses the question of the role that wealth may or may not play in saving people from death.

The poet provides his credentials, so to speak, in 49:3-4. His words can be relied upon as wise, for they come from insightful thoughts. Having paid careful attention to many proverbs himself, the poet is in a position to set forth his wisdom—teaching for the benefit of others.

Wealth Cannot Redeem (49:5-12). This instruction is not a detached discourse but arises out of the stuff of life. There is a temptation for the poor to fear when oppressed by enemies who are wealthy, especially when that oppression puts the poor in danger of death. It would be easy for the poor to think that they would be safe if only they too were wealthy. This is, after all, what the wealthy think. Well, perhaps not all the wealthy. The poet is speaking of the wealthy who "trust in their wealth and boast of great riches" (49:6): the wicked wealthy, those who think that their wealth will redeem them from death.

But they are wrong. They cannot redeem themselves by their wealth. All the wealth in the world is not enough to redeem a single soul. This principle is true across the board. It applies to the wise and to the foolish. The wise and the foolish will both die eventually (see Eccl 9:1-3), and no amount of wealth will stop that day from coming. In fact, on the day of death all leave behind whatever wealth they have (49:10; see Eccl 5:15). "You can't take it with you," as we say. The grave is destiny of all. Even if people have acquired numerous estates, they will end up dwelling in the grave forever.[1]

A refrain marks the end of the strophe and underscores the main point: Riches do not guarantee freedom from death. When it comes to death, humans are no different from animals. All die. Thus the wealthy ought not to trust in their wealth to redeem them. And the poor, especially when oppressed by the wealthy, ought not to think that the wealthy are somehow better off with regard to the prospect of death. Death is the great leveler, and wealth cannot redeem from death. But what wealth cannot do, God will do.

God Will Redeem (49:13-20). This strophe repeats themes from the previous strophe and adds a few additional thoughts, but it has a different central thrust. This strophe addresses those who are self-confident fools, those who are among those who trust their wealth in the previous strophe. Not earthly estates, but the grave will be their permanent dwelling. And whatever wealth they have amassed will remain behind when they depart this life.

In spite of the fact that they viewed themselves as fortunate in this life, as did others, death will show their true state of affairs. There will come a time of great reversal, a morning when a new day will dawn (see 30:5), when those whom they have oppressed will gain the upper hand (see Luke 16:19-31).

The central thrust of this strophe, however, stands in sharp contrast to that of the previous strophe. Whereas previously we were warned that wealth cannot redeem from death, here we are promised that God will redeem from death. While it may be the case that the poet had in view a deliverance from death in this life (see Ps 16), he may have been thinking of a deliverance from death in the life to come; certainly God is able to pay a "ransom beyond human means" (Eaton 1967:135-136). The application of this truth is the same as that found at the beginning of the previous strophe: There is no need to be dismayed when the wicked grow rich, for in the end they will lose their wealth and its concomitant power over the poor.

The refrain closes the psalm. Riches do not guarantee freedom from death. When it comes to death, humans are no different from animals. All die. But God interjects a radical difference: He redeems from death, so our trust and confidence can be placed squarely on him. Our trust and confidence will never be disappointed, because the Father redeemed the Son from death—not by keeping him from it, but by raising him after it. What the Father did for the Son he will do for all who trust in the Son (1 Cor 15:20).

ENDNOTES

1. "Forever" in the OT does not always (or even often) mean unbounded time or eternal timelessness. "It can be a time in one's life (Ps 77:5 [6]), a life span (Exod 21:6), or the furthest conceivable time (15:18)" (NIDOTTE 3.346). The "furthest conceivable time" is open to an unending future. A text like 90:2 probably has boundless time in view (NIDOTTE 2.350). Psalm 49 seems to approach this meaning as well, since it envisions escaping death.

◆ H. Psalm 50

A psalm of Asaph.

1 The LORD, the Mighty One, is God,
and he has spoken;
he has summoned all humanity
from where the sun rises to where
it sets.
2 From Mount Zion, the perfection of
beauty,
God shines in glorious radiance.
3 Our God approaches,
and he is not silent.
Fire devours everything in his way,
and a great storm rages around him.
4 He calls on the heavens above and
earth below
to witness the judgment of his
people.
5 "Bring my faithful people to me—
those who made a covenant with
me by giving sacrifices."
6 Then let the heavens proclaim his
justice,
for God himself will be the
judge. *Interlude*

7 "O my people, listen as I speak.
Here are my charges against you,
O Israel:
I am God, your God!
8 I have no complaint about your
sacrifices
or the burnt offerings you
constantly offer.
9 But I do not need the bulls from your
barns
or the goats from your pens.
10 For all the animals of the forest are
mine,
and I own the cattle on a thousand
hills.
11 I know every bird on the mountains,
and all the animals of the field are
mine.
12 If I were hungry, I would not tell you,

for all the world is mine and
everything in it.
13 Do I eat the meat of bulls?
Do I drink the blood of goats?
14 Make thankfulness your sacrifice
to God,
and keep the vows you made to
the Most High.
15 Then call on me when you are in
trouble,
and I will rescue you,
and you will give me glory."

16 But God says to the wicked:
"Why bother reciting my decrees
and pretending to obey my
covenant?
17 For you refuse my discipline
and treat my words like trash.
18 When you see thieves, you approve
of them,
and you spend your time with
adulterers.
19 Your mouth is filled with wickedness,
and your tongue is full of lies.
20 You sit around and slander your
brother—
your own mother's son.
21 While you did all this, I remained
silent,
and you thought I didn't care.
But now I will rebuke you,
listing all my charges against you.
22 Repent, all of you who forget me,
or I will tear you apart,
and no one will help you.
23 But giving thanks is a sacrifice that
truly honors me.
If you keep to my path,
I will reveal to you the salvation
of God."

NOTES

50:TITLE ***Asaph.*** Asaph was a Levite who assisted Heman in directing the music at the Tabernacle and the Temple (1 Chr 6:39-43; 15:17; 2 Chr 5:12). We are not certain as to why Ps 50 is separated from the other psalms of Asaph (73–83), but Ps 50 does fit into the context of the surrounding psalms.

50:1 ***The LORD, the Mighty One, is God.*** This translation conflates the words in the text, which could be translated "God, God, the LORD." This initial piling up of words for God has the rhetorical effect of underscoring the solemn nature of the event about to take place.

all humanity. The word *'erets* [TH776, ZH824] (earth) can be used in reference to earth's inhabitants (DCH 1.392).

50:3 ***he is not silent.*** For a time God was silent, but the time for him to speak has arrived. The storm in view is not a rainstorm with its accompanying thunder and lightning but an east-wind storm that is often associated in the OT with divine judgment.

Fire devours . . . a great storm rages. This language is never used in the context of a rainstorm but is typical of east-wind storms (e.g., Ezek 19:12; see Fitzgerald 1983:252-257); the term "great storm" is likewise not used of rainstorms but is typical of east-wind storms (e.g., Isa 40:24; see Fitzgerald 1983:195-198).

50:4 ***heavens above and earth below to witness.*** For heaven and earth as witnesses, see Deut 32:1.

50:5 ***made a covenant.*** It seems best to understand the participle here as referring to the imminent future: "about to make a covenant" (Craigie 1983:365; Joüon and Muraoka 1991:§121e; Waltke and O'Connor 1990:§37.6.f). Psalm 50 was probably used as part of a covenant-renewal ceremony.

50:6 ***the judge.*** At the heart of the word *shopet* [TH8199A, ZH9149] is the idea of one restoring things to right order (NIDOTTE 4.214; TLOT 3.1393). In this context he is restoring his relationship with his people to right order.

50:16 ***pretending to obey my covenant.*** Lit., "take up my covenant on your mouth." It was possible for some to say all the right things during the covenant-renewal ceremony while remaining unwilling to live in keeping with the covenant regulations.

50:18 ***you approve of them.*** The word *ratsah* [TH7521, ZH8354] means "take pleasure in." HALOT 3.1281 renders it "become friends with" here and in Job 34:9.

50:23 ***keep to my path.*** The Hebrew text is terse and difficult: *sam derek* [TH7760/1870, ZH8492/2006] (he who sets a way). Kraus (1988) may be correct in suggesting an emendation to *tam derek* [TH8535 or 8537/1870, ZH9447 or 9448/2006] ("perfect of way" or "he who lives with integrity"; see Job 4:6 and Prov 13:6).

COMMENTARY

The universal scope of Psalms 47–49 continues with the summons to all humanity from east to west in 50:1. But Psalm 50 has a sharp focus on the covenant community, which is called to renew its relationship with the Lord (50:1-6) by returning to grateful worship (50:7-15) and true obedience (50:16-23).

A Call to Renewed Relationship (50:1-6). God calls all humanity from east to west to witness a most solemn event: the renewal of his covenant relationship with his people. Perhaps humanity is called with a view toward becoming part of the covenant community, as in 47:1, 9. The first thing they witness is the theophanic presence of God, emanating from Zion, the city of the great king (48:2). This presence is not one of blessing, however; it is one of judgment, as the presence is manifest in a hot east-wind storm that could turn the arable land into a desert (e.g., Hos 13:15). The east wind that shattered enemy ships (48:7) now threatens to destroy the covenant community. In anticipation of the judgment scene God calls the heavens and earth as witnesses. The heavens and earth are given the task of summoning his covenant people to appear before him and of declaring his justice as the divine judge.

The threat of divine judgment presumes that something is out of order in the covenant relationship. The people have the name "faithful," but perhaps they are his people in name only. Are they truly the "faithful people" of God? The purpose of the summons is to restore order to the covenant relationship. Two areas are addressed in the rest of the psalm.

A Call to Grateful Worship (50:7-15). Formalism is an ever-present danger in the worship of God. It does not matter if the style of worship is traditional or contemporary. The danger of going through the external motions without the proper inner disposition is always present.

Here God has no objection to the form of worship on the one hand, while on the other he wants no more of it. Apparently, God's people had begun to think like their pagan neighbors that sacrifice met some need in God. The true and living God does not need the flesh of bulls and the blood of goats for food and drink. Besides, even if he did, he would not need humans to supply such needs, because he owns all the livestock in the world.

What God really wants in worship is our gratitude. The purest form of worship without gratitude evokes divine judgment. Gratitude comes from the attitude of dependence. So flowing out of grateful worship is a willingness to depend on God in times of trouble. Experiencing his deliverance, in turn, results in giving him glory. Worship at its heart is giving glory to God because we are grateful that we can depend on him for all that we need in life. The threat of judgment is intended to turn us from formalism to grateful worship.

A Call to True Obedience (50:16-23). Right along with formalism comes the danger of hypocrisy. The "wicked" are not pagans living outside the covenant community. Rather, the wicked are those who say all the right things during the covenant-renewal ceremony but who live in contradiction to their profession of faith. In spite of their pious profession, they treat God's laws like trash. They recite the commandments: "Do not commit adultery. Do not steal. Do not testify falsely against your neighbor." But then they live as adulterers, thieves, and slanderers.

Hypocrites can also make the potentially fatal mistake of misinterpreting God's patience. They may think of his patience as indifference, but that is a mistake. He will not remain silent forever; he will eventually break that silence and bring his discipline on his people. That judgment may be just around the corner, but it has not yet arrived, and God's patience continues to grant time for repentance (Rom 2:4).

The heart of the covenant is relationship, our relationship with God. Through Psalm 50, God calls us to renew our relationship with him from time to time, for example, as we celebrate the Lord's Supper. We are prone to fall into formalism in our worship and hypocrisy in our day-to-day living. God loves us too much to let us go that direction. He will discipline us to keep us in a vital relationship with him. But he calls us to an easier way than his discipline. He calls us to ongoing repentance from formalism and hypocrisy.

He says to us, "I am God, your God!" (50:7). Knowing who he is and all that he has done for us provides us with all the motivation we need to render to him our grateful worship and true obedience. Alluding to Psalm 50, the author of Hebrews tells us that with Jesus' help we can offer sacrifices that are very pleasing to God (Heb 13:15-16). These sacrifices consist in the praise that proclaims the glory of his name and the obedience of doing good, especially to those in need. Jesus can give us this help because "with his blood" he "ratified an eternal covenant" that has secured our salvation. "All glory to him forever and ever! Amen" (Heb 13:20-21).

◆ I. Psalm 51

For the choir director: A psalm of David, regarding the time Nathan the prophet came to him after David had committed adultery with Bathsheba.

1 Have mercy on me, O God,
because of your unfailing love.
Because of your great compassion,
blot out the stain of my sins.
2 Wash me clean from my guilt.
Purify me from my sin.
3 For I recognize my rebellion;
it haunts me day and night.
4 Against you, and you alone, have I sinned;
I have done what is evil in your sight.
You will be proved right in what you say,
and your judgment against me is just.*
5 For I was born a sinner—
yes, from the moment my mother conceived me.
6 But you desire honesty from the womb,*
teaching me wisdom even there.

[7] Purify me from my sins,* and I will
be clean;
wash me, and I will be whiter than
snow.
[8] Oh, give me back my joy again;
you have broken me—
now let me rejoice.
[9] Don't keep looking at my sins.
Remove the stain of my guilt.
[10] Create in me a clean heart, O God.
Renew a loyal spirit within me.
[11] Do not banish me from your presence,
and don't take your Holy Spirit*
from me.

[12] Restore to me the joy of your salvation,
and make me willing to obey you.
[13] Then I will teach your ways to rebels,
and they will return to you.
[14] Forgive me for shedding blood, O God
who saves;
then I will joyfully sing of your
forgiveness.
[15] Unseal my lips, O Lord,
that my mouth may praise you.

[16] You do not desire a sacrifice, or I
would offer one.
You do not want a burnt offering.
[17] The sacrifice you desire is a broken
spirit.
You will not reject a broken and
repentant heart, O God.⌋
[18] Look with favor on Zion and help her;
rebuild the walls of Jerusalem.
[19] Then you will be pleased with
sacrifices offered in the right
spirit—
with burnt offerings and whole
burnt offerings.
Then bulls will again be sacrificed
on your altar.

51:4 Greek version reads *and you will win your case in court.* Compare Rom 3:4. 51:6 Or *from the heart;* Hebrew reads *in the inward parts.* 51:7 Hebrew *Purify me with the hyssop branch.* 51:11 Or *your spirit of holiness.*

NOTES

51:1 *sins.* The word *pesha'* [TH6588, ZH7322] means "rebellion" and is used again in 51:3a [5a].

51:2 *Wash me.* The Hebrew has the consonants *hrbh* before the verb translated "wash." The Kethiv (Hiphil infinitive absolute ***harbeh*** [TH7235/7235C, ZH8049/2221]) seems preferable. The use would be adverbial (HALOT 1.255), as is often the case with this form (Tate 1990:5), and the sense would be something like "thoroughly." HALOT 3.1177 accepts the Qere (Hiphil imperative from *rabah*) and likewise glosses with "thoroughly."

guilt. The word *'awon* [TH5571, ZH6411] means "sin" in the sense of perversity, then the "guilt" that results from the sin, and finally the "punishment" that results from the guilt (TLOT 2.862-866). It is used again in 51:5 [7] and 51:9 [11].

sin. The word *khatta'th* [TH2403A, ZH2633] (and *khet'* [TH2399, ZH2628] in 51:5 [7] and 51:9 [11]) is the primary word for "sin" and is used again in 51:3 [5]. The verb from this root is used in 51:4 [6]. The literal sense is "a missing of the mark" (see the verb in Judg 20:16), which was readily transferred to a figurative missing of the mark (TLOT 1.407).

51:4 *against me.* There are no Hebrew words underlying the English "against me," but this is certainly the sense. God is not simply right in what he says in general but right when he says that David is guilty of sin.

51:6 *from the womb.* The word *tukhoth* [TH2910, ZH3219] is difficult, occurring only here and perhaps in Job 38:36. It may mean "entrails" or "darkness" (DCH 3.362; HALOT 2.373). Given the parallel with *sathum* [TH5640, ZH6258] ("secret," referring to one's "inmost being"), the reference seems to be to one's inner being (see Tate 1990:6 for a concise discussion of the interpretive possibilities).

51:9 *Remove.* This is the same verb that is translated "blot out" (*makhah* [TH4229, ZH4681]) in 51:1 [3], and the repetition forms a frame around the first stanza of the poem (51:1-9).

51:13 ***I will teach.*** The form of the verb is a cohortative that expresses firm resolve (Joüon and Muraoka 1991:§114c; Waltke and O'Connor 1990:§34.5.1a).

51:14 ***shedding blood.*** While *damim* [TH1818, ZH1947] can refer to bloodshed (DCH 2.443-444), and this would fit the context of David's having arranged the death of Uriah, the reference here may be to guilt in a more general and comprehensive sense (see Isa 4:4; Ezek 18:13; Hos 12:14 [15]; Mays 1994:200).

COMMENTARY

Psalm 51 grips our hearts as it exposes our need that results from our moral failures in life. Our moral failures are not simply a matter of what we do. They are a matter of what we do because of who we are. Our need is for something outside of ourselves to make a radical difference within ourselves. Our need is for God—but not for just any god. Our need is for the God who will speak in truth about our desperate condition and who will act in love for our salvation.

Our need is twofold: We need reconciliation (51:1-9), and we need transformation (51:10-19). We need justification, and we need sanctification. To experience these, we need repentance, and the way of repentance is set forth clearly and eloquently in Psalm 51.

Reconciliation (51:1-9). The first stanza focuses on reconciliation. Three strophes present a balanced prayer for this reconciliation: a plea for forgiveness (51:1-2), a confession of sin (51:3-6), and a plea for forgiveness (51:7-9). Together these strophes show the way to reconciliation through these themes: Depend on God's love, confess your sin, and ask for forgiveness.

Depend on God's love. Our moral failures will keep us from ever approaching God unless we are fully persuaded that he loves us. It is significant that the psalm does not begin with "my sins" but with "have mercy." In fact, the opening line piles up the language of love before ever mentioning sin: "Have mercy . . . because of your unfailing love. Because of your great compassion." How we view God determines how we respond to him. God is just, to be sure, but he is love. Because he is love, we dare to draw near to a just God. As James said, "God will be merciful when he judges you" (Jas 2:13).

David was fully aware of his sin. He had committed adultery with Bathsheba and had her husband, Uriah, moved up to the front lines, where he was sure to be killed. David's sins plagued his conscience day and night. What troubled him most deeply was that his sin was against God: "I have sinned against the LORD" (2 Sam 12:13). This is not to say that he had not sinned against Bathsheba, Uriah, and the whole nation for that matter. Sin always affects other people. The point is that ultimately and most importantly, sin is always against God, for it is God's will that is violated when we sin. So David knew that when God spoke in judgment against him, "You are that man!" (2 Sam 12:7), God was right and just.

Ask for forgiveness. David's plea for forgiveness is as intensely thorough as his confession of sin. Seven times he asks for forgiveness in one way or another. The stanza is framed by the pleas to have sin blotted out and removed (51:2, 7). Twice David asks to have his sins washed away (51:2, 7). He also asks God to purify him from his sin (51:2, 7) and pleads for God to quit taking notice of his sin (51:9).

- There is a difference between saying, "I'm sorry," and saying, "Please forgive me." David shows us here that asking for forgiveness is the path to reconciliation. This is true when relationships are broken between people, as well as when they are broken between people and God.

David knew that his problem ran deeper than a particular sin or even set of sins. "For I was born a sinner—yes, from the moment my mother conceived me," David acknowledged (51:5). His problem was "a whole life conditioned by sin from its beginning," and so his confession was a way of saying not just that he had sinned but that he was in his existence a sinner (Mays 1994:201). David needed more than reconciliation, as foundational as that may be. He also needed transformation at the very core of his being. Transformation comes from depending on God's love for forgiveness, which comes through confession.

Transformation (51:10-19). The second stanza focuses on transformation. Three strophes show how this transformation moves from the self (51:10-12) to other sinners (51:13-15) and finally to the whole community (51:16-19).

We are perpetually confronted with the temptation to blame others or our circumstances for our troubles. So we frequently pray that God would change other people and change our circumstances. David resists this temptation here. He prays, "Create in me a clean heart, O God" (51:10). "Change me," says David, "because I am the problem" (51:10; see Mays 1994:202).

The verb translated "create" is the same verb used in Genesis 1:1 (*bara'* [TH1254, ZH1343]). In the Old Testament this verb is used exclusively for divine activity. David is asking God to do for him something that David cannot do for himself. Only God can make the internal changes that David needs. It is David's responsibility to plead with God for these changes, but only God has the ability to effect the change. "Create" here does not mean to make something out of nothing. "Create" here means to transform something that already exists, to make it into something new (Isa 41:20; 43:1, 7, 15; 45:7, 8; 65:17-18; Mays 1994:202). So the creation of the clean heart is explained in terms of a renewing of the spirit.

This renewing of David's spirit will be the result of the presence of God's Holy Spirit, so David prays that God not remove the Holy Spirit from him. David may have had in mind the removal of what we might call the Spirit of office, who equipped David for carrying out his responsibilities as king,[1] or what we might call the Spirit of fellowship, who would be grieved and distanced by sin (Isa 59:2). The presence of the Spirit would not only effect a renewal but would also effect a willingness to obey. This would be coupled with a restoration of the joy that was already anticipated in 51:8: "Oh, give me back my joy again . . . let me rejoice."

Transformation of self is never an end in itself. Transformation of self leads to transformation of others. When we change, things around us change. David resolves to pass this transformation on to others. He uses words for "rebels" in 51:13 that are from the same roots as the vocabulary for sin in the first stanza (*pasha'* [TH6586, ZH7321], cf. *pesha'* [TH6588, ZH7322], and *khatta'* [TH2400, ZH2629], cf. *khatta'th* [TH2403A, ZH2633]). He was not therefore speaking of these "rebels" with disdain. Rather, he spoke as one sinner to others. His desire is not to "teach them a thing or two." Instead, he wants to teach them God's way of reconciliation and transformation that they too might return to God and live according to his ways.

David will teach them as he joyfully sings of God's great forgiveness and as he sings God's praise. This praise would no doubt recount his distress, his plea for reconciliation, and God's forgiveness, according to the typical pattern of the psalms of thanksgiving.

The instruction of others would no doubt have taken place in the Temple and in the context of sacrifices. But sacrifices don't please God, and he won't accept them, said David. In the context of 50:7-15, this clearly means that God does not want the sacrifices of formalism. As Psalm 50 teaches that God wants sacrifices from a grateful heart, Psalm 51 teaches that God wants sacrifices from a broken and repentant heart. Isaiah preached this same message, saying that God curses those who do not have humble and contrite hearts. He will not accept their sacrifices. But he blesses those whose hearts are broken, with the clear implication that he will accept their sacrifices (Isa 66:1-4). To have a renewed heart created in us, we must first have a broken heart, a heart that is humble and contrite before the magnitude of our sin and the even greater magnanimity of God's love.

The transformation of self and others culminates in the transformation of the entire community. Zion, the impregnable city of the great king (Ps 48) and the place from which "God shines in glorious radiance" (50:2), is here in need of divine favor and transformation. In the context of David's life, the reference could be to the completion of the walls that were yet unfinished until the reign of Solomon (1 Kgs 3:1; so Delitzsch 1982:142). But in the context of the final form of the Psalter in the postexilic era, the reference would be to the rebuilding of the city in the days of Nehemiah. In that context, the transformation of the city and the transformation of the community through repentance go hand in hand.[2] Just as individual sin has destructive consequences on others and the entire community, so individual reconciliation and transformation are envisioned as bringing blessing to the same.

The question arises, "How can God be just and forgiving at the same time?" The answer lies in the sacrifices referred to in the psalm. The sacrifice was a substitute for the sinner and bore the just punishment of God, so that the sinner might be reconciled and transformed. The apostle Paul understood this when he quoted part of 51:4 in his argument for the universality of human sinfulness (Rom 3:4). Universal sinfulness is the prelude to Paul's teaching on justification by faith in the sacrifice of Jesus Christ as our substitute (Rom 3:21-25). Because God punished Christ in our place, he is entirely just to forgive us our sins (Rom 3:26). This is the theological background of the second half of Romans, where Paul develops his teaching on our transformation. Because of all that God has done for us through his mercy, grace, and love for us in Christ, we give our whole lives to God as living sacrifices that he will be pleased with and that he will transform according to his will (Rom 12:1-2).

ENDNOTES

1. The Spirit of office was taken from King Saul in 1 Sam 16:14.
2. See my outline of the book of Ezra–Nehemiah in *The New Geneva Study Bible* (Nashville: Thomas Nelson, 1995).

◆ J. Psalm 52

For the choir director: A psalm of David, regarding the time Doeg the Edomite said to Saul, "David has gone to see Ahimelech."*

1 Why do you boast about your crimes,
great warrior?
Don't you realize God's justice
continues forever?
2 All day long you plot destruction.
Your tongue cuts like a sharp razor;
you're an expert at telling lies.
3 You love evil more than good
and lies more than truth. *Interlude*

4 You love to destroy others with your
words,
you liar!
5 But God will strike you down once and
for all.
He will pull you from your home
and uproot you from the land of
the living. *Interlude*

6 The righteous will see it and be
amazed.
They will laugh and say,
7 "Look what happens to mighty warriors
who do not trust in God.
They trust their wealth instead
and grow more and more bold in
their wickedness."

8 But I am like an olive tree, thriving in
the house of God.
I will always trust in God's unfailing
love.
9 I will praise you forever, O God,
for what you have done.
I will trust in your good name
in the presence of your faithful
people.

52:TITLE Hebrew *maskil*. This may be a literary or musical term.

NOTES

52:TITLE The incident referred to is recorded in 1 Sam 21:1-9 and 22:9-19. Doeg told Saul that Ahimelech, the high priest at Nob, had supplied David with provisions including food and Goliath's sword. At Saul's command, Doeg then massacred the priests at Nob and their families.

52:1 ***warrior.*** The reference is probably to Doeg the Edomite.

52:5 ***uproot you.*** There is a play on this idea in 52:8, where the psalmist is like an olive tree, which is thriving and not uprooted.

52:7 ***do not trust in God.*** Or, "do not make God their refuge." Trust is at the heart of the idea of making God one's refuge (see Introduction).

grow more and more bold in their wickedness. This translates the Heb. *ya'oz behawwatho* as the Qal imperfect as of the verb *'azaz* [TH5810, ZH6451] (grow bold). But in context, it is better understood to mean "take refuge in their destructive actions" (as from the verb *'uz* [TH5756, ZH6395], "take refuge"; HALOT 2.797). Doeg did not take refuge in God, but took refuge in the power of destruction.

COMMENTARY

Psalm 52, like Psalm 49, is an instructional poem (Gerstenberger 1988:216) that forces us to examine our hearts to find out the source of our security in life (McCann 1996:890). The opening line sets before us two alternatives: We can find our security in ourselves or in the unfailing love of God. The rest of the psalm unpacks these two alternatives in two strophes: security in self (52:1-5) or security in God (52:6-9).

Security in Self (52:1-5). Psalm 52:1 provides a synopsis of the whole psalm. Those who boast about their "crimes" are those who trust in their own power. "Boasting in" and "trusting in" are not identical concepts, but they are closely related. It is easy for us to trust in that which we can boast in, as 49:6 shows: "They trust in their wealth and boast of great riches." Finding security in our wealth is a theme in Psalm 49 that is picked up in this psalm as well (52:7), but Psalm 52 focuses on finding security in our own power, the power of a warrior bringing harm to others. The alternative is to find our security in the unfailing love of God that we can experience at any time during the day.

The weapon of destruction used by this "warrior" is the razor-sharp tongue of one skilled in deceit. The "evil" that is loved more than the "good" is explained in the following colon as lies that are opposed to truth. The lies in view are malicious, as their purpose is to bring harm to others.

While Doeg may have spoken the truth in a formal sense, Saul concluded from his words that Ahimelech had conspired with David against Saul. Such was certainly not the case. Doeg's words had the effect of deceiving Saul and resulted in the heinous "crime" of 85 priests and all their families being massacred. Though we have no record of this in Scripture, it is easy to imagine Doeg boasting in his power over others.

Ironically, such security in self is utterly false, for the day will come when God will bring just judgment.

Security in God (52:6-9). The unfailing love that David had sought in 51:1 is here offered as a source of true security. David says of himself: "I will always trust in God's unfailing love" (52:8). Contrary to the false security in self, which will be short-lived, security in God endures not just throughout the day but forever. So while those who trust in self will be uprooted, those who trust in God's unfailing love are like firmly planted olive trees that live a long, long time in the presence of God.

Such benefits are not for David alone but also for the entire community. All the righteous will see the demise of those who trust in themselves, and they will be amazed—not in the sense of being surprised, but in the sense of standing in awe of the God who maintains justice in the world he has made. As God laughed at the demise of his foes (2:4), so those who trust in God will one day laugh at the demise of their foes. Theirs will be a laugh of derision: Here is what happens to those who find their security in themselves rather than in God.

Because David can trust in God's unfailing love forever, he vows to give thanks to God forever for all that God has done for him. This vow is made before David has seen the demise of those who trust in themselves, so he concludes with a confession of trust: "I will trust in your good name in the presence of your faithful people" (52:9).

Psalm 52 serves as a warning and an encouragement. It warns those who would trust in themselves of the false security their lives are based on. It encourages those who find their security in God that his love is unfailing. In the present it may appear that security in self succeeds, but the eyes of faith can see into the future, and what they see is the success held out in Psalm 1: They are like trees planted by streams, succeeding in all they do.

◆ K. Psalm 53

For the choir director: A meditation; a psalm of David.*

1 Only fools say in their hearts,
"There is no God."
They are corrupt, and their actions
are evil;
not one of them does good!

2 God looks down from heaven
on the entire human race;
he looks to see if anyone is truly wise,
if anyone seeks God.
3 But no, all have turned away;
all have become corrupt.*
No one does good,
not a single one!

4 Will those who do evil never
learn?
They eat up my people like bread
and wouldn't think of praying to
God.
5 Terror will grip them,
terror like they have never known
before.
God will scatter the bones of your
enemies.
You will put them to shame, for God
has rejected them.

6 Who will come from Mount Zion to
rescue Israel?
When God restores his people,
Jacob will shout with joy, and Israel
will rejoice.

53:TITLE Hebrew *According to mahalath; a maskil.* These may be literary or musical terms. **53:3** Greek version reads *have become useless.* Compare Rom 3:12.

COMMENTARY

If you are familiar with hymnals from different ecclesiastical communities, you are aware of the phenomenon of slightly different versions of the exact same hymn. Psalm 53 is a slightly different version of Psalm 14.

The primary difference occurs at 14:5-6 // 53:5. Whereas Psalm 14 at this point focuses on the Lord protecting his people, Psalm 53 focuses on the Lord judging the foes, a focus that coincides with the context of Psalm 52 (McCann 1996:893). See the commentary on Psalm 14 for more details.

◆ L. Psalm 54

For the choir director: A psalm of David, regarding the time the Ziphites came and said to Saul, "We know where David is hiding." To be accompanied by stringed instruments.*

1 Come with great power, O God,
and rescue me!
Defend me with your
might.
2 Listen to my prayer, O God.
Pay attention to my plea.
3 For strangers are attacking me;
violent people are trying to
kill me.
They care nothing for God. *Interlude*

4 But God is my helper.
The Lord keeps me alive!
5 May the evil plans of my enemies be
turned against them.
Do as you promised and put an end
to them.

6 I will sacrifice a voluntary offering
to you;
I will praise your name, O LORD,
for it is good.
7 For you have rescued me from my
troubles
and helped me to triumph
over my enemies.

54:TITLE Hebrew *maskil.* This may be a literary or musical term.

NOTES

54:TITLE The event in view is recorded in 1 Sam 23:13-29. In 1 Sam 23:15, Saul is trying to kill David, and this same language is used in 54:3.

54:1 ***Come with great power.*** This renders the word *beshimka* [TH8034, ZH9005] (by your name), which is picked up in 54:6. The "name" is the power of Yahweh present and active on earth (Kraus 1988:516) and is explained in the following colon by the word *geburah* [TH1369, ZH1476] (might).

Defend. The word *din* [TH1777, ZH1906] is typically a judicial term, which, if used literally here, would indicate that the troubles the psalmist is facing are false accusations. On the other hand, *din* is also used in nonjudicial contexts (e.g., 110:6 and Gen 49:16-17; see Tate 1990:46).

54:3 ***strangers.*** "Strangers" is an accurate translation of the MT's *zarim* [TH2114B, ZH2424], and the word *zarim* is used for violent (ruthless) men in Isa 25:2-5 (Dahood 1965:2.24). But it is better to read *zedim* [TH2086A, ZH2294] (insolent people), following numerous mss and the almost exact parallel in 86:14. The word *zarim* occurs only one other time in the Psalter (109:11), whereas the *zedim* are more frequent opponents of the psalmist (19:13[14]; 86:14; 119:21, 51, 69, 78, 85, 122).

54:4 ***The Lord keeps me alive!*** Lit., "The Lord is the sustainer of my soul." The preposition Beth is the Beth of essence indicating the predicate (Joüon and Muraoka 1991:§133c and Waltke and O'Connor 1990:§11.2.5e). A wooden translation would be "The Lord in the sustainer of my soul," but Hebrew at times uses the preposition Beth ("in") where English uses the verb "is."

54:6 ***O Lord.*** The preposition Beth is the Beth of essence indicating the predicate (Joüon and Muraoka 1991:§133c and Waltke and O'Connor 1990:§11.2.5e).

54:7 ***For you have.*** The grammatical subject of the verb is "your name" from the previous colon. The NLT apparently interprets the underlying perfect tense as a rhetorical perfect for an action that is so certain to take place in the future that it can be spoken of as already accomplished in the past (Joüon and Muraoka 1991:§112h and Waltke and O'Connor 1990:§30.5.1e), and this is probably correct. A less likely possibility is to take the *ki* [TH3588, ZH3954] to mark a temporal clause and to interpret the perfect as a future perfect, "When your name will have."

COMMENTARY

Psalm 54 is a prayer with praise for the powerful presence of God to sustain and deliver the psalmist in the face of violent opposition.

Prayer in Dependence on God's Powerful Presence (54:1-3). The psalm opens with a prayer for God to rescue the psalmist by God's "name." God's name is not simply an identifier; his name is his identity (Mays 1994:206). The invocation of the "name" is the invocation of the divine presence. The second colon of the opening line explains that one key characteristic of the "name" is "might." The name is the powerful presence of the God that can rescue and defend no matter how stiff the opposition.

Saul was trying to kill David (1 Sam 23:15). Insolent and violent people were attacking the psalmist. This was because they cared nothing for God. They were among the fools who said in their hearts, "There is no God" (53:1). Since they lived as if God was not a person to be contended with, they were free in their own minds to perpetrate their violence.

Affirmation of Faith (54:4). In the face of such opposition, David was confident, knowing that God was present as his helper (see 46:1). Deliverance through God's powerful name still lay in the future for David, but at the present time God's power was available to sustain David. He prayed that the trouble others were causing him would recoil on their own heads. People do reap what they sow, but not in a purely mechanistic way. People reap what they sow because God's power is present to put an end to them. Yet when God puts an end to the violent, it is typically through the use of mechanisms that operate in the universe he has made and governs.

Prayer with Praise for God's Powerful Presence (54:5-7). Confident that God will not only sustain in the present but rescue from trouble in the future, David vows to offer to God a voluntary offering as an expression of his thanksgiving to God for the goodness of God's name. If God's name were only powerful, we would live in abject fear of him. But God's name is also good, so we know that the power of the name will always be for us and not against us. We will triumph through the power of the divine presence at work in our lives.

"The incredible greatness of God's power for us who believe him" says the apostle Paul, is "the same mighty power that raised Christ from the dead" (Eph 1:19-20). Whereas David experienced the power of the name in keeping him from dying, Jesus experienced that power in a far more radical and life-giving way when he was raised from the dead. We now can invoke the powerful name of God to sustain us in times of trouble and to eventually deliver us from those troubles, as we wait for the ultimate deliverance in our resurrection from the dead.

◆ M. Psalm 55

For the choir director: A psalm of David, to be accompanied by stringed instruments.*

1 Listen to my prayer, O God.
Do not ignore my cry for help!
2 Please listen and answer me,
for I am overwhelmed by my troubles.
3 My enemies shout at me,
making loud and wicked threats.
They bring trouble on me
and angrily hunt me down.

4 My heart pounds in my chest.
The terror of death assaults me.
5 Fear and trembling overwhelm me,
and I can't stop shaking.
6 Oh, that I had wings like a dove;
then I would fly away and rest!
7 I would fly far away
to the quiet of the wilderness.
Interlude

8 How quickly I would escape—
far from this wild storm of hatred.

9 Confuse them, Lord, and frustrate their plans,
for I see violence and conflict in the city.
10 Its walls are patrolled day and night against invaders,
but the real danger is wickedness within the city.
11 Everything is falling apart;
threats and cheating are rampant in the streets.

12 It is not an enemy who taunts me—
I could bear that.
It is not my foes who so arrogantly insult me—
I could have hidden from them.

[13] Instead, it is you—my equal,
my companion and close friend.
[14] What good fellowship we once enjoyed
as we walked together to the house of God.

[15] Let death stalk my enemies;
let the grave* swallow them alive,
for evil makes its home within them.

[16] But I will call on God,
and the LORD will rescue me.
[17] Morning, noon, and night
I cry out in my distress,
and the LORD hears my voice.
[18] He ransoms me and keeps me safe
from the battle waged against me,
though many still oppose me.
[19] God, who has ruled forever,
will hear me and humble them.
Interlude
For my enemies refuse to change their ways;
they do not fear God.

[20] As for my companion, he betrayed his friends;
he broke his promises.
[21] His words are as smooth as butter,
but in his heart is war.
His words are as soothing as lotion,
but underneath are daggers!

[22] Give your burdens to the LORD,
and he will take care of you.
He will not permit the godly to slip and fall.

[23] But you, O God, will send the wicked
down to the pit of destruction.
Murderers and liars will die young,
but I am trusting you to save me.

55:TITLE Hebrew *maskil.* This may be a literary or musical term. 55:15 Hebrew *let Sheol.*

NOTES

55:2 ***for I am overwhelmed by my troubles.*** This translates two difficult verbs in the Hebrew. The Hiphil imperfect *'arid* is from *rud* [TH7300, ZH8113], the Qal of which means "to roam about." For the Hiphil, BDB (923) provides, "shew restlessness (?)"; HALOT (3.1194) says "text uncertain." See Tate 1990:51 for a summary of options. The Hiphil cohortative *'ahimah* is from *hum* [TH1949, ZH2101], and it apparently means "to be disquieted" (DCH 2.504; BDB 223).

55:3 ***making loud and wicked threats.*** The word *'aqah* [TH6125, ZH6821] is obscure and may mean "screech," as a parallel term to "shout," or it may mean "pressure" (HALOT 2.873).

They bring trouble on me. The Hebrew is difficult, and a wooden translation would be "they cause trouble to shake on me."

hunt me down. The word *satam* [TH7852, ZH8475] means "to be at enmity with" (HALOT 3.1316).

55:8 ***far from this wild storm of hatred.*** There is no word for "hatred" in the Hebrew text, which could be translated "far from this tempestuous wind and storm."

55:11 ***Everything is falling apart.*** The word *hawwah* [TH1942A, ZH2095] occurs in 52:2 [4], where it is translated "destruction."

55:14 ***as we walked together.*** The NLT leaves the problematic *beragesh* [TH871.2/7285, ZH928/8094] (in unrest) untranslated. This word occurs nowhere else in the Hebrew Bible, and the sense here may be something like "crowd" or "throng" (Tate 1990:53). The shift in meaning may have been from "unrest" to "tumultuous crowd" of any kind.

COMMENTARY

Sometimes life can be pretty chaotic. Psalm 55 reflects that chaos. The chaos of life is reflected in the content of the psalm and in its structure. The psalm is full of difficult expressions, and there are relatively abrupt shifts between the seven strophes, contributing to a psalm that describes the life of a person overwhelmed by trouble.

The Cry for Help (55:1-5). Four different verbs are used in the first two lines to call on God for help: "Listen. . . . Do not ignore. . . . Please listen . . . answer." The psalmist is desperate. David is under great pressure because of the trouble angry foes were causing. David can feel the anguish deep within his heart and is terrified to death. Were we able to see him, we would see a man who was visibly shaken by overwhelming troubles.

The Urge to Run Away (55:6-8). Have you ever been in such difficult circumstances that you just felt like running away? That is exactly how David felt. Picture a bird quickly taking to flight when danger is present. This is a picture of David's heart: not the courage of a lion or the strength of a bear, but the timidity of a startled bird. He thought that the best solution to his trouble was to get as far away from the troublemakers as possible. But he stayed to face the foe head-on.

The Reign of Violence (55:9-11). The city, presumably Jerusalem, is full of violence, strife, wickedness, destruction, oppression, and deceit. It takes little mental effort for a modern reader to grasp the contemporary relevance of this ancient poem. David's response was to pray against the perpetrators of destruction. Our calling is to pray for them. In this age of gospel grace we pray and work not for judgment against "the city" but for its redemption.

The Betrayal by a Friend (55:12-14). It's one thing to be attacked by those whom you know are "enemies." That may be painful, but it is understandable. It's another thing altogether when a friend betrays you by becoming an "enemy." To be betrayed by a friend can be an incomprehensible experience. David knew what it was like to have an intimate ally become the enemy; after all, his once-trusted advisor Ahithophel joined Absalom in the coup against David (2 Sam 15:31). Betrayal to one degree or another by close friends is not an uncommon experience in life, and it is a theme that has been encountered already in the Psalter (31:11; 35:11-16; 38:11; 41:9; see also 88:8, 18).

The Prayer for Justice (55:15). David prayed not for personal vengeance but for justice on those who live evil lives. While we pray for them, we do so knowing that the day of just judgment will come on all who have not trusted in God for reconciliation and transformation (see Ps 51).

The Call of Confidence (55:16-19). Though life, at times, can have a discouraging face, there is always reason for hope. In the middle of it all, God is still king. He is still in control. Though we may not be able to see clear evidence of his reign, we are confident that he is Lord, and this confidence comes to expression in prayer. Sometimes we must pray "morning, noon, and night" for long periods of time. But we do so confident that the Lord is listening and will eventually rescue us from those who do not fear him (see 54:3 and 53:1).

The Betrayal by a Friend Revisited (55:20-21). Betrayal often comes in the form of duplicity: promises given but not kept and one thing said to your face while caustic remarks are made behind your back. What do you do when friends join the enemies who attack you?

The Ultimate Recourse (55:22-23). When life's load weighs you down, you can always unburden yourself on the Lord. The promise here is not that he will deliver you immediately but that he will sustain you until the time of deliverance arrives. He will never permit the righteous to fall in an ultimate sense. "The godly may trip seven times, but they will get up again" (Prov 24:16). Not so the wicked. Those who do not fear the Lord will fall down into the pit of destruction.

Sometimes life can be pretty chaotic: overwhelmed by trouble, tempted to run away, surrounded by violence, betrayed by friends. In those times we say with David, "But I am trusting you to save me" (55:23). We say this with great confidence because we are speaking to "God, who has ruled forever" (55:19).

◆ N. Psalm 56

For the choir director: A psalm of David, regarding the time the Philistines seized him in Gath. To be sung to the tune "Dove on Distant Oaks."*

1 O God, have mercy on me,
for people are hounding me.
My foes attack me all day long.
2 I am constantly hounded by those who slander me,
and many are boldly attacking me.
3 But when I am afraid,
I will put my trust in you.
4 I praise God for what he has promised.
I trust in God, so why should I be afraid?
What can mere mortals do to me?

5 They are always twisting what I say;
they spend their days plotting to harm me.
6 They come together to spy on me—
watching my every step, eager to kill me.
7 Don't let them get away with their wickedness;
in your anger, O God, bring them down.
8 You keep track of all my sorrows.*
You have collected all my tears in your bottle.
You have recorded each one in your book.

9 My enemies will retreat when I call to you for help.
This I know: God is on my side!
10 I praise God for what he has promised;
yes, I praise the LORD for what he has promised.
11 I trust in God, so why should I be afraid?
What can mere mortals do to me?

12 I will fulfill my vows to you, O God,
and will offer a sacrifice of thanks for your help.
13 For you have rescued me from death;
you have kept my feet from slipping.
So now I can walk in your presence, O God,
in your life-giving light.

56:TITLE Hebrew *miktam.* This may be a literary or musical term. 56:8 Or *my wanderings.*

NOTES

56:TITLE The event in view is recorded in 1 Sam 21:10-15. "Oaks" presumes reading *'elim* as a defectively spelled plural of *'ayil* [TH352A, ZH381] instead of reading the MT's *'elem* [TH482, ZH521] (silence).

56:1 ***people . . . foes.*** Both terms are singular in the Hebrew. There is a shift to the plural in the next verse. It seems that there is a single troublemaker who has acquired the help of others. The individual could very well be Saul, and the "others" could be his forces, as well as the Philistines. The fact that David sang this song while in Philistia does not require that the foes in view are first and foremost the Philistines.

56:2 ***slander.*** For the use of this word in the Psalter, see note at 5:8 [9].

56:4 ***I praise God for what he has promised.*** This verse is difficult syntactically. It seems the most natural translation would be, "In God—I praise his word—in God I trust" (see the rendering of 56:10-11 in Kraus 1988:525). The presence of a disjunctive accent on the first occurrence of *be'lohim* and a conjunctive accent on *'ahallel* would seem to favor this interpretation. This entire verse is a suspended subject that is picked up in the next colon.

why should I be afraid? The rhetorical question of the NLT expects a negative answer: There is no reason to be afraid. The Hebrew word is a negative indicative rather than an interrogative and expresses a resolve not to fear: "I will not be afraid" (see commentary).

56:5 ***always.*** Lit., "all day long," as in 56:1, 2 (NLT, "constantly"). The threefold repetition underscores the continual nature of the oppression.

twisting. The word *'atsab* is difficult here, as it usually means something relating to "hurt" in the various patterns. Zorell (1963:619) glosses the Piel here with "twist." KBL (725) takes it from *'atsab* [TH6087, ZH6771] and glosses it with "intertwine," but the third edition (HALOT 2.864) takes it from *atsab* II [TH6087A, ZH6772] (hurt another's feelings) and says the text is damaged.

56:7 ***Don't let them get away with their wickedness.*** Lit., "concerning evil save them," which makes no sense in light of the following colon. Given the meaning of the second colon, the first colon must have something to do with judgment on the foes. The NLT captures this general idea. An emendation of the verb from *pallet* [TH6403, ZH7117] (save) to *palas* II [TH6424A, ZH7143] ("examine"; HALOT 3.935) is one solution: "Examine them concerning their sin, and then in your anger, throw them down to the ground." See Tate (1990:67) for a survey of other proposed solutions.

56:8 ***You keep track. . . . You have collected.*** The verb translated "collected" is an imperative. In the context of the imperatives in the previous verse and the imperative "collect," the perfect verb translated "you keep track" is best taken as a precative perfect, "Keep track" (Joüon and Muraoka 1991:§112k and Waltke and O'Connor 1990:§30.5.c).

56:10 ***God . . . LORD.*** See note on 56:4.

what he has promised. Lit., "word." There is no pronoun suffix in the word. Either the suffix is to be understood from the parallel in 56:4 [5] (Calvin 1979:356), or the suffix is to be added by way of emendation (Kraus 1988:525).

56:11 ***why should I be afraid?*** See note on 56:4.

56:13 ***For you have rescued me.*** This same perfect verb was used in an almost identical clause and in the same final position in 54:7 [9], where it was interpreted as a rhetorical perfect for an action that is so certain to take place in the future that it can be spoken of as already accomplished in the past (Joüon and Muraoka 1991:§112h and Waltke and O'Connor 1990:§30.5.1e). The same sense fits here, as David has not yet experienced the rescue he prays for.

COMMENTARY

Faith and fear are opposites (Mays 1994:208). Yet, since we do not trust God perfectly, we at times experience faith and fear together. Like faith and fear, lamentation and confidence are also at times experienced together. Psalm 56 could be read as a lament or as a psalm of confidence. In actuality, it is a lament, as the opening line shows, prayed in a spirit of great confidence. There is clear movement in the poem as lamentation and confidence alternate until confidence prevails.

Have Mercy (56:1-2). In Hebrew, "Have mercy" are the first words heard in this psalm, just as in Psalm 51. No sooner are those words out of the psalmist's mouth than he is marshaling reasons as to why God should show him mercy. Some individual was hounding him and attacking him all day long. The oppression was relentless. But the hounding was not just by one individual. This individual had apparently drawn in a multiplicity of slanderers who were hounding David constantly. As "many" had attacked David in other situations (see 3:1-2), so now "many" were after him, and he was in need of great mercy from God.

I Will Not Fear (56:3-4). We at times long for the confidence David exhibited when he concluded this strophe with the question, "What can mere mortals do to me?" While it is true that people really can harm us in many ways—they can hurt us physically, abuse us emotionally, ruin our reputations—they can do no ultimate harm. Since God loves us and since nothing can separate us from his love, we are always perfectly safe: "Yes, and the Lord will deliver me from every evil attack and will bring me safely into his heavenly Kingdom" (2 Tim 4:18). Though we trust that this is true, we still can feel afraid when the attack is taking place. "While he allows that he felt fear, he declares his fixed resolution to persist in a confident expectation of the divine favour" (Calvin 1979:348). How do we move from feeling afraid to making the confident resolution: "I will not be afraid"?

There is a chiastic movement in this strophe (McCann 1996:902):

from feeling afraid
  to trust
    to praising God's Word
  to trust
to resolving not to be afraid.

The movement starts with acknowledging that we feel afraid at times. "I am afraid." That is where David started and where we must start if we want to replace fear with confidence. Yes, we fear. But we also put our trust in God at the same time. Here trusting God takes the concrete form of praising God's word, all of his word in general but his promises in particular. Promises like: "When God restores his people, Jacob will shout with joy, and Israel will rejoice" (53:6), "You have rescued me from my troubles and helped me to triumph over my enemies" (54:7), and "Give your burdens to the LORD, and he will take care of you" (55:22). Trusting in the promises of God results in our being able to move from "I am afraid" to "Why should I be afraid? What can mere mortals do to me?"

Eager to Kill (56:5-6). In this strophe David returns to describing his trouble. His foes always twisted his words. Their attack went on all day long, without ceasing. They plotted to harm him and watched him carefully for just the right opportunity to do him in.

My Enemies Will Retreat (56:7–9a). The initial request, "Have mercy on me," is now amplified. With regard to his enemies, David asked for God to examine them and then bring them down. With regard to himself, he prayed that God would fully consider his trouble by keeping track of his sorrows and collecting his tears in a bottle. If God would do this, then for certain he would bring about the retreat of David's foes. Whereas in strophe 2 (56:3-4) David moved to a position of confidence by saying how he felt, here he moves to confidence by asking for what he wants; the two steps go together.

I Will Not Fear (56:9b–11). This strophe is a virtual repetition of strophe 2 (56:3-4). The key difference lies in the beginning of the two strophes. David opened the first in fear, but he opened this one in confidence. "This I know: God is on my side!" He also doubled his praise of God's promises (56:10). As the psalm progresses, there is clear movement from fear to confidence and from lamentation to praise.

A Sacrifice of Thanks for Your Help (56:12–13). David was so confident that God would help him that he vowed to offer God a sacrifice of thanksgiving for the help he was certain he would receive. He was absolutely confident that God would eventually rescue him so that he would once again experience the blessed presence of God, his life-giving light.

This life-giving light is the Lord Jesus Christ (John 8:12). He experienced more severe opposition than we ever will. He trusted the promises of his Father. He was rescued from death, not by being kept from dying but by triumphing over death through his resurrection. He did all of this for us, that through faith in him we might appropriate Psalm 56 as our own, that we might move in our own troubles from fear to confidence and from lamentation to praise.

◆ O. Psalm 57

For the choir director: A psalm of David, regarding the time he fled from Saul and went into the cave. To be sung to the tune "Do Not Destroy!"*

1 Have mercy on me, O God, have mercy!
I look to you for protection.
I will hide beneath the shadow of your wings
until the danger passes by.
2 I cry out to God Most High,*
to God who will fulfill his purpose for me.
3 He will send help from heaven to rescue me,
disgracing those who hound me.
Interlude
My God will send forth his unfailing love and faithfulness.

4 I am surrounded by fierce lions
who greedily devour human prey—
whose teeth pierce like spears and arrows,
and whose tongues cut like swords.

5 Be exalted, O God, above the highest heavens!
May your glory shine over all the earth.

6 My enemies have set a trap for me.
I am weary from distress.
They have dug a deep pit in my path,
but they themselves have fallen into it. *Interlude*

7 My heart is confident in you, O God;
my heart is confident.

No wonder I can sing your praises!
8 Wake up, my heart!
Wake up, O lyre and harp!
I will wake the dawn with my song.
9 I will thank you, Lord, among all the people.
I will sing your praises among the nations.
10 For your unfailing love is as high as the heavens.
Your faithfulness reaches to the clouds.
11 Be exalted, O God, above the highest heavens.
May your glory shine over all the earth.

57:TITLE Hebrew *miktam.* This may be a literary or musical term. 57:2 Hebrew *Elohim-Elyon.*

NOTES

57:TITLE The event in view is either that recorded in 1 Samuel 22 or 24.

57:1 ***look to you for protection . . . I will hide.*** The verse uses the verb *khasah* [TH2620, ZH2879] twice. This verb is the main word for the motif of the Lord as refuge (see Introduction).

the danger. The word *hawwah* [TH1942A, ZH2095] has been used in 52:2 [4], 7 [9] and 55:11 [12] for violent destruction brought about by the wicked (see also 5:9 [10] and 38:12 [13]). For the use of a plural subject with a singular verb in poetry in particular, see Joüon and Muraoka 1991:§150j.

57:2 ***fulfill his purpose for me.*** The NLT agrees here with other English versions (e.g., NIV and RSV); Zorell (1963) glosses the verb *gamar* [TH1584, ZH1698] here with "bring to a good end" (see also BDB 170 and Tate 1990:74). Dahood (1965:2.51) understands the verb here and in 138:8 to mean "avenge"; he has been followed by HALOT 1.197 and DCH 2.365. Either sense is possible in context (see NIDOTTE 1.874-875 for a discussion of all uses of this word).

57:3 ***those who hound me.*** The word *sha'ap* [TH7602, ZH8634] means "to hound" and is used in 56:1 and 2 [2 and 3]. Perhaps it is best to take "those who hound me" as the subject of the verb "revile" in light of the verbal attacks referred to in 57:4 [5].

57:4 ***I am surrounded by.*** Lit., "I will lie down in the middle of." The verb is a cohortative that here expresses firm resolve (see Joüon and Muraoka 1991:§114c). While acknowledging the present dangers, the psalmist here expresses confidence more than he laments his circumstances.

57:6 ***have fallen.*** The enemies have not yet fallen into their own trap. This is an example of the rhetorical perfect: "They will certainly fall" (Joüon and Muraoka 1991:§112h; Waltke and O'Connor 1990:§30.5.1e). As in 57:3 [4], here the psalmist expresses confidence in the face of opposition.

57:7 ***My heart is confident.*** The words underlying the English translation is actually repeated twice in this verse for rhetorical effect.

57:8 ***my heart.*** Lit., "my glory." Some scholars understand the word *kabod* [TH3519, ZH3883] (glory) as a rough synonym of *nepesh* [TH5315, ZH5883] (soul) here and in several other psalms (7:5; 16:9; 30:12). See the notes at these other psalms for these examples; I argue that they do not seem convincing. Here *kabod* probably refers to the psalmist's personal honor, which he anticipates being restored through the Lord's intervention on his behalf.

57:9 ***among the nations.*** The NLT presumes an emendation from *bal-'ummim* [TH1077/523, ZH1153/569] (not peoples) to *balle'ummim* [TH871.2/1886.1/3816, ZH928/2021/4211] (among the peoples); see the notes on 108:3 [4]; 149:7; see also 44:14 [15].

COMMENTARY

Confidence in the face of adversity is the theme of this psalm, as it is of the previous psalm. Like Psalm 56, Psalm 57 is a lament in which the note of confidence dominates. While acknowledging the reality of the adversity he faced, David here expressed profound assurance that God would intervene on his behalf.

A refrain in 57:5 and 57:11 divides the psalm into two roughly equal stanzas. This refrain provides the ultimate perspective from which David experienced confidence in the face of adversity. The manifestation of the glory of God was David's chief concern. The poem can be further subdivided into four strophes, which are chiastically arranged: trust in God's unfailing love and faithfulness (57:1-3), confidence in the face of opposition (57:4-5), confidence in the face of opposition (57:6), and praise for God's unfailing love and faithfulness (57:7-11).

Trust in God's Unfailing Love and Faithfulness (57:1-3). "Have mercy on me" opens this psalm, just as this plea opened the previous psalm; here, however, the plea for mercy is made twice. The reason offered to support the plea is quite different in Psalm 57. Here the reason is trust, not opposition, as in the previous psalm. As a hiker would seek refuge from a violent storm by hiding in a cave, so David sought refuge from the violent storm of Saul's pursuit by taking refuge in God. By saying "until the danger passes by," David expressed faith that the storm would in fact pass over in due time. When we are in the middle of a stormy situation, we are tempted to think it will never end, but the eyes of faith penetrate to the future when all will be tranquil.

David had prayed for mercy based on God's unfailing love in 51:1. Here he prays for mercy and expresses his confidence that God will send his unfailing love (57:3).

Confidence in the Face of Opposition (57:4-6). Having confidence does not mean we pretend that the harsh realities of life don't exist. David was keenly aware that he faced foes as ferocious as ravenous lions that would devour him in a moment if they had the opportunity. Acknowledging the harsh realities of life does not mean we lack confidence. David resolved to lie down right in the middle of his adversaries. David was not resigning himself to defeat. He was affirming his confidence in the unfailing love and faithfulness of his God. Since he was certain that God would send forth his unfailing love and faithfulness, he knew he could lie down in the middle of these ravenous beasts and be perfectly safe. This text reminds us of Daniel in the lions' den. In the early morning the king ran out to see if Daniel's God was able to rescue him from the lions. Daniel said, "My God sent his angel to shut the lions' mouths so that they would not hurt me" (Dan 6:22). For Daniel, God sent his unfailing love and faithfulness in the form of an angel. For David, they came in the form of an escape route. We can always be confident in the face of opposition, knowing that God will send his unfailing love and faithfulness in one form or another. We can have this confidence because at just the right time God sent his unfailing love and faithfulness in the form of his Son and our Savior, the Lord Jesus Christ.

Confidence does not mean that we are untouched by the harsh realities of life. David said, "I am weary from distress." We feel pain. We feel afraid (56:3). We feel like giving up. We acknowledge how we feel. But then we feel confident, trusting that God's justice is a real operative force in the world. Our foes will reap what they have sown. Confidence wins out over pain, fear, and exhaustion.

Praise for God's Unfailing Love and Faithfulness (57:7-11). Confidence in God's unfailing love and faithfulness results in praise for these things in this final strophe. The three uses of words for waking up remind us of Psalm 3:5, where David lay down and slept and then woke up in the morning without fear of the thousands who surrounded him in opposition. Here David rouses his marred honor, his musical instrument, and the dawn itself to praise God. This praise was not to take place in private but "among all the people" and "among the nations." The universal audience for the praise of God was owing to the universal scope of the unfailing love and faithfulness of God. God's love is as high as the heavens, and his faithfulness reaches to the clouds. No matter what our circumstances may be, God's unfailing love and faithfulness are ever present. We may not see them, but they are there. We may not be experiencing them, but they are there. Being certain that God will "send" them, we praise God in the confident expectation of their manifestation in some concrete way in our lives. "The praise of God resounds, although the deciding turn of events has not yet taken place" (Kraus 1988:532).

Yes, opposition is at times all too painfully real. Yes, we can be confident that God will send us help as he sends us his unfailing love and faithfulness in some tangible way. But the ultimate reason for God to send his unfailing love is not our salvation. Our salvation is a means to an end. The end of it all is repeated twice in the psalm so that we will be overwhelmed by the ultimate reality: "Be exalted, O God, above the highest heavens. May your glory shine over all the earth" (57:5, 11).

◆ P. Psalm 58

For the choir director: A psalm of David, to be sung to the tune "Do Not Destroy!"*

1 Justice—do you rulers* know the
meaning of the word?
Do you judge the people fairly?
2 No! You plot injustice in your hearts.
You spread violence throughout the
land.
3 These wicked people are born sinners;
even from birth they have lied and
gone their own way.
4 They spit venom like deadly snakes;
they are like cobras that refuse to
listen,
5 ignoring the tunes of the snake
charmers,
no matter how skillfully they play.

6 Break off their fangs, O God!
Smash the jaws of these lions,
O LORD!
7 May they disappear like water into
thirsty ground.
Make their weapons useless in their
hands.*
8 May they be like snails that dissolve
into slime,
like a stillborn child who will never
see the sun.
9 God will sweep them away, both
young and old,
faster than a pot heats over burning
thorns.

10 The godly will rejoice when they see
injustice avenged.
They will wash their feet in the
blood of the wicked.
11 Then at last everyone will say,
"There truly is a reward for those
who live for God;
surely there is a God who
judges justly here on
earth."

58:TITLE Hebrew *miktam*. This may be a literary or musical term. **58:1** Or *you gods*. **58:7** Or *Let them be trodden down and wither like grass*. The meaning of the Hebrew is uncertain.

NOTES

58:1 ***rulers.*** The word *'elem* [TH482, ZH521] means "silence" (DCH 1.294). "Rulers" presumes an emendation to a form of *'ayil* [TH352, ZH380] ("leaders"; DCH 1.211) or to *'elim* [TH410A, ZH446], which could mean "gods," used sarcastically for "rulers" or "mighty men."

58:2 ***You spread violence throughout the land.*** Lit., "Your hands make a path for violence."

58:3 ***These wicked people are born sinners.*** Lit., "These wicked people have turned aside from the womb." The vocalization of the verb *zoru* (turned aside) is problematic. It is better to read either *zaru* (Qal perfect) or *nazoru* (Niphal perfect, presuming the loss of a Nun through haplography), taking the verb from *zur* II [TH2114, ZH2319] (HALOT 1.267).

58:7 ***Make their weapons useless in their hands.*** The Hebrew text is uncertain.

58:9 ***God will sweep them away.*** This verse is obscure. That the wicked will be swept away is clear.

COMMENTARY

Does it pay to live for God? Many of us have asked ourselves this question at different times in our lives. We ask this question in particular when life just does not seem to be fair. There is an even deeper question, however: Is there justice? If there is no justice, then it does not pay to live for God. But if there is justice, then it pays. Psalm 58 answers these two related questions.

Psalm 58 is comprised of two stanzas, each of which contains two strophes. The first stanza (58:1-5) addresses the problem of injustice in this world. The second stanza (58:6-11) resolves the issue.

The Reality of Injustice (58:1-5). The truth is that injustice is a reality in this world. Leaders often make unjust laws. Judges often issue unjust decisions. Crooked deals are made in political chambers and courtrooms alike. The hands of leaders are too often filled with violence, not justice. The sad truth is that this is the case not only in the civil sphere but also in the church. The church is not beyond the influence of unjust politics or self-serving injustice. Injustice is reality.

The word "violence" from the first strophe becomes the theme of the second strophe. Injustice is likened to the deadly venom of a viperous snake. And not only is this snake poisonous, but it is uncontrollable as well. Picture yourself in the presence of an uncontrollable venomous viper and you have a picture of the danger of injustice.

Injustice, like all sin, is not a superficial problem of a few wrong decisions here and there. Injustice, like all sin, is systemic in nature. It is the fruit of fallen human nature. Injustice is rooted in the human heart when that heart is still in the womb (see 51:5). It only takes the right conditions for the seeds of injustice in our own hearts to produce that hideous fruit. So while we are grieved at injustice in the world, we are not surprised.

A Prayer for Justice (58:6-11). With language as graphic as any in the Psalter, David prays for justice: first and foremost, justice for the unjust, and secondarily, justice for all. It is for poetic justice that David prays: "Break off their fangs." With broken fangs the venomous snakes would present no threat at all. The danger would be gone. Shifting the metaphor, he prays that the jawbones of ravenous lions should be smashed, so that they too would be rendered harmless. Shifting the metaphor once more, he prays that the unjust would be removed from the scene like water that is immediately absorbed by thirsty ground.

While we do not pray *against* the unjust but *for* them (Matt 5:43-48), we know that they will be held accountable. There will be justice meted out one day. This is the theme of the final strophe.

Injustice will be avenged one day, not by us as humans but by God himself, who says, "I will take revenge; I will pay them back" (Deut 32:35; cf. Rom 12:19). We will rejoice when that day comes. We will wash our feet in the blood of the unjust, i.e., we will see their utter defeat (68:23; Mays 1994:212). On that day we will experience in fullness the truth that it does pay to live for God because God is the just judge of all the earth.

This day of ultimate judgment stills lies in the future (Rev 20:11-15). Until this day comes, the unjust can repent and find mercy and grace to experience the forgiveness of their sin. The delay of God's justice demonstrates his kindness, tolerance, and patience, which are intended to lead the unjust to repentance.

As those who have repented and experienced the love of God in Christ, we now live to see justice established in this world to the degree that this is possible. We begin by rooting injustice out of our own hearts, homes, and churches, so that we will be fair and compassionate in all of our dealings, even as our Father in heaven is fair and compassionate.

◆ Q. Psalm 59

For the choir director: A psalm of David, regarding the time Saul sent soldiers to watch David's house in order to kill him. To be sung to the tune "Do Not Destroy!"*

1 Rescue me from my enemies, O God.
Protect me from those who have
come to destroy me.
2 Rescue me from these criminals;
save me from these murderers.
3 They have set an ambush for me.
Fierce enemies are out there
waiting, LORD,
though I have not sinned or
offended them.
4 I have done nothing wrong,
yet they prepare to attack me.
Wake up! See what is happening
and help me!
5 O LORD God of Heaven's Armies, the
God of Israel,
wake up and punish those hostile
nations.
Show no mercy to wicked traitors.
Interlude

6 They come out at night,
snarling like vicious dogs
as they prowl the streets.
7 Listen to the filth that comes from
their mouths;
their words cut like swords.
"After all, who can hear us?" they
sneer.
8 But LORD, you laugh at them.
You scoff at all the hostile
nations.
9 You are my strength; I wait for you
to rescue me,
for you, O God, are my fortress.
10 In his unfailing love, my God will
stand with me.
He will let me look down in triumph
on all my enemies.
11 Don't kill them, for my people soon
forget such lessons;

stagger them with your power, and
bring them to their knees,
O Lord our shield.
12 Because of the sinful things they say,
because of the evil that is on their
lips,
let them be captured by their pride,
their curses, and their lies.
13 Destroy them in your anger!
Wipe them out completely!
Then the whole world will know
that God reigns in Israel.* *Interlude*

14 My enemies come out at night,
snarling like vicious dogs
as they prowl the streets.
15 They scavenge for food
but go to sleep unsatisfied.*

16 But as for me, I will sing about your
power.
Each morning I will sing with joy
about your unfailing love.
For you have been my refuge,
a place of safety when I am in
distress.
17 O my Strength, to you I sing praises,
for you, O God, are my refuge,
the God who shows me unfailing
love.

59:TITLE Hebrew *miktam*. This may be a literary or musical term. 59:13 Hebrew *in Jacob*. See note on 44:4. 59:15 Or *and growl if they don't get enough*.

NOTES

59:TITLE The event in view is recorded in 1 Sam 19:11-18.

59:3 ***They have set.*** The NLT leaves *ki* [TH3588, ZH3954] (for) untranslated. Psalm 59:3-4a provides the reason as to why David makes the requests recorded in 59:1-2.

59:5 ***nations.*** Here and in 59:8 the word *goyim* [TH1471, ZH1580] is best taken to refer to David's foes within the people of Israel rather than external foes. His own people were acting like the nations that stand in opposition to the Lord and his anointed one in Ps 2.

59:6 ***as they prowl the streets.*** Lit., "they surround the city."

59:9 ***You are my strength.*** MT has "his strength." "My strength" follows the text in some mss, the LXX, and 59:17 [18]. It is better taken as a vocative, as in 59:17 [18], "O my Strength."

I wait for you to rescue me. According to BDB (1036) the verb *shamar* [TH8104, ZH9068] with the preposition *'el* [TH8104, ZH448] means "watch over" either in a positive sense (1 Sam 26:15) or in a hostile sense (2 Sam 11:16). "I will watch over you [God]" makes no sense. Emending the Shin to a Zayin would result in *'eleyka 'azammerah* [TH2167, ZH2376] (to you I sing praise), which is exactly what the matching colon says in 59:17 [18] (see BDB 1037). Psalm 59:9 and 17 are then a refrain.

59:10 ***his unfailing love.*** The Qere reads *'elohe khasdi* [TH2617/430, ZH2876/466], as in 59:17 ("the God who shows me unfailing love") and is probably correct: "The God who shows me unfailing love will come and help me."

59:14 ***as they prowl the streets.*** Lit., "they surround the city."

59:15 ***but go to sleep unsatisfied.*** The MT is better translated, "If they are not satisfied, they *stay around all night*" as from *lin* [TH3885A, ZH4328] (Kraus 1988:541; Tate 1990:92). If the second verb is emended to *wayyallinu* (from *lun* [TH3885, ZH4296]), the sense would be "they grumble [growl]"; see the footnote in the NLT.

59:17 ***the God who shows me unfailing love.*** This expression (*'elohe khasdi* [TH430/2617, ZH466/2876]) seems to hang at the end by itself. It occurs in 59:10 [11] right after the refrain of 59:9 [10], just as it occurs here at the end of the refrain. It is possible that the rest of the line in 59:10 [11] has fallen out of the text here in 59:17 [18] and should be inserted as the conclusion of the refrain.

COMMENTARY

False accusations cut to the quick of the soul like a sharp sword cuts to the bone. Many in Saul's court no doubt leveled false accusations against David and thereby fueled the fire of Saul's fearful rage against David. This rage grew to the point that Saul sent soldiers to kill David in his own house (see 1 Sam 19). Psalm 59 is a prayer to be rescued from these murderous enemies.

Psalm 59 is quite symmetrical, being comprised of two matching stanzas. The first stanza (59:1-10) is comprised of three strophes: petition with reasons (59:1-5), the enemy as snarling dogs (59:6-7), and statement of assurance (59:8-10). The second stanza follows the same sequence: petition with reasons (59:11-13), the enemy as snarling dogs (59:14-15), and statement of assurance (59:16-17). A refrain marks the end of each stanza and provides focus for the psalm: "O my Strength, to you I sing praises, for you, O God, are my refuge" (59:9, 17).

Rescue Me Because I Have Not Sinned (59:1-5). David's enemies surrounded him (59:7 and 59:14) without realizing that they themselves were surrounded (McCann 1996). The description of their setting an ambush for David (59:3-4a) is surrounded by David's pleas for God to intervene on his behalf (59:1-2 and 59:4b-5). Also, in the Hebrew text the enemies are surrounded by the pleas in 59:1-2 (McCann 1996:912): "Rescue me from my enemies. . . . Protect me from those who have come to destroy me." "Rescue me from these criminals; save me from these murderers." Appearances can be deceiving, as those who appeared to have the upper hand here did not.

David pleaded his case as one who was innocent. He used all three of the major words for sin in his protestation of innocence here, just as he used all three in his confession of sin in 51:1-2. This piling up of terms has the rhetorical effect of underscoring the vehemence of his protest. Obviously, David did not think that he was entirely sinless but only that in this situation he had done nothing to deserve the treatment he was receiving. His prayer was simple: Rescue me because I have not sinned.

The Enemy as Snarling Dogs (59:6-7). The enemy is here likened to wild and snarling dogs. Perhaps the picture is that just as wild dogs foam at the mouth, so the mouths of David's enemies poured out filth. Their words cut like a sword even though David knew that their accusations were false. The fact that we are at times innocent of the accusations brought against us does not mean that we are impervious to the pain those accusations cause.

To You I Sing Praise (59:8-10). "But LORD." What confidence those two words express! The language here evokes Psalm 2 and reminds us that the Lord reigns even over all the hostile forces arrayed against us. So puny is the threat that he laughs. As the Lord laughed, David resolved to sing praise to the God who was his refuge and strength. David was confident that God would show him unfailing love and that in the end he would come out victorious.

Destroy Them Because (59:11-13) In verses 1-5 the psalmist asked to be rescued from his enemies. Here he asks to have his enemies destroyed. The petition comes in three stages: Don't kill them (immediately), let them be captured, and then destroy them entirely. The reason for this staged destruction is threefold: that God's people might learn from the experience, that the nations might reap what they have sown, and that God's sovereignty might be published throughout the world.

The Enemy as Snarling Dogs (59:14-15). The enemy is once more likened to wild and snarling dogs. But here the point is that they are relentless. If they get no satisfaction, they continue to scavenge for food. Saul was relentless in his pursuit of David. There were times when his anger seemed to be assuaged, but those were brief lapses. The rage returned, and the pursuit continued. Sometimes it seems that nothing will satisfy those who oppose us.

To You I Sing Praise (59:16-17). "But as for me" answers to "But LORD" in 59:8. At the center of this strophe is the rock-solid truth that the Lord was David's refuge and place of safety. So in spite of the viciousness of the attacks against him, David could resolve to sing praise to God. He was hopeful that the morning would bring God's unfailing love and his deliverance from distress (see 3:5 and 5:3).

The truth of Psalm 2—all who take refuge in the Lord will be blessed—was a truth that the anointed king himself needed to rely on. It is a truth that we too can rely on, especially when we are falsely accused and attacked. God is our strength in the day of distress, so we can sing his praise with confidence that he will rescue us from every evil attack (2 Tim 4:18).

◆ R. Psalm 60

For the choir director: A psalm of David useful for teaching, regarding the time David fought Aram-naharaim and Aram-zobah, and Joab returned and killed 12,000 Edomites in the Valley of Salt. To be sung to the tune "Lily of the Testimony."*

1 You have rejected us, O God, and
broken our defenses.
You have been angry with us; now
restore us to your favor.
2 You have shaken our land and split
it open.
Seal the cracks, for the land
trembles.
3 You have been very hard on us,
making us drink wine that sent
us reeling.
4 But you have raised a banner for those
who fear you—
a rallying point in the face of
attack. *Interlude*

5 Now rescue your beloved people.
Answer and save us by your
power.
6 God has promised this by his
holiness*:
"I will divide up Shechem with joy.
I will measure out the valley of
Succoth.
7 Gilead is mine,
and Manasseh, too.
Ephraim, my helmet, will produce my
warriors,
and Judah, my scepter, will produce
my kings.
8 But Moab, my washbasin, will become
my servant,
and I will wipe my feet on Edom
and shout in triumph over
Philistia."

9 Who will bring me into the fortified
city?
Who will bring me victory over
Edom?
10 Have you rejected us, O God?
Will you no longer march with our
armies?
11 Oh, please help us against our
enemies,
for all human help is useless.
12 With God's help we will do mighty
things,
for he will trample down
our foes.

60:TITLE Hebrew *miktam*. This may be a literary or musical term. 60:6 Or *in his sanctuary*.

NOTES

60:TITLE The events in view are recorded in 2 Sam 8 and 2 Sam 10:13-19.

60:4 *you have raised.* In the context of the rejection of 60:1-3, 10, the perfect tense for past time is somewhat problematic. BHS and Kraus (1989:2) suggest emending the perfect to an imperative to fit the context. A better suggestion is to take the perfect as a precative in the context of the imperatives of 60:5 [7] (Joüon and Muraoka 1991:§113K; Waltke and O'Connor 1990:§30.5.4c): "Raise up."

60:5-12 These verses concur, with minor variations, with 108:6-13 [7-14].

60:6 *I will divide . . . with joy.* There are two verbs in the Hebrew here, both of which are cohortatives that express the firm resolve of God (Joüon and Muraoka 1991:§114c) in keeping with the promissory nature of the strophe (see commentary).

60:7 *Ephraim, my helmet, will produce my warriors, and Judah, my scepter, will produce my kings.* Lit., "Ephraim the stronghold of my head; Judah my scepter." While it is possible that *ma'oz ro'shi* [TH4581/7218, ZH5057/8031] means "helmet," DCH 5.386 takes this phrase to mean "my chief stronghold." HALOT 2.610 likewise lists this text under the meaning "stronghold." Heb. *mekhoqqeq* is the Polel participle of *khaqaq* [TH2710A, ZH2980], which means "commander" and then by extension "commander's scepter" (see DCH 3.304 and HALOT 1.347). The precise significance of this imagery is not easy to ascertain, but the general point is clear: In contrast to the humiliation of Moab, Edom, and Philistia stands the exaltation/dominion of Ephraim, which represents the northern tribes, and Judah, which represents the southern tribes (see Clifford 2002:284 and VanGemeren 1991:416).

60:8 *I will wipe my feet on Edom.* Lit., "I will throw my sandal over Edom." The idiom may refer to dominating someone or taking possession of something (see Kraus 1989:4; Tate 1990:102). The point would be the same in either case: The Lord will exercise his authority over Edom.

over Philistia. This translation presumes an emendation from *'alay* [TH5921/2967.1, ZH6584/3276] (over me) to *'ale* [TH5921, ZH6584] (over); see 108:9 [10] and Kraus 1989:2.

COMMENTARY

Have you ever faced a situation in which the person who held the solution was at the same time the problem? Perhaps you needed a favor from someone whom you had recently offended. This was the situation that David and the people of God found themselves in, according to Psalm 60. Human help was useless. Only divine aid would do. But God was seemingly against his people, not for them. What did David do? What can you do?

State the Problem and Ask for What You Want (60:1-5). The problem was that God was fighting against and not for his people because he was angry at them. He was "rejecting them" in the concrete sense that he was not victoriously leading them into battle (see 44:9 and 60:10). So serious was the problem that David described it by painting a cataclysmic picture of a cosmic earthquake that threatened to destroy the earth (see the commentary on 46:1-3). God's people were not drinking from his "river of delights" (36:8) but from the cup of divine displeasure.[1]

David asked God to reverse the situation he was facing. He prayed that God would restore or return the people to his favor. He asked that God would undo the fractures in the land. He asked that God would raise up a rallying point for the troops. He asked that God would save them. David made these requests not just for anybody but for those who, on the one hand, lived for the honor of God and who, on the other hand, were the objects of God's love. So when we pray, we pray as those who know that nothing can separate us from God's love and who therefore live to honor him regardless of our circumstances.

Remind Yourself of God's Promise (60:6–8). God's promise was twofold. First, the land of Israel was his special possession. It was the "fortress" from which God would go forth to conquer the nations, wielding the scepter of his power as he went. Second, the nations would become his possession through his triumph over them. The promise was that God owned all, would possess all, and would rule over all. The promise was that David and his sons would receive the nations as their inheritance and the ends of the earth as their possession (2:8). At the time envisioned in Psalm 60, there was not much tangible evidence that the promise would come true, but there was the promise. And the promise was God's promise, which no doubt brought courage to the hearts of God's people at that time.

The Lord Jesus Christ has told us that he has all authority in heaven and on earth, and so we should go and conquer the nations with the gospel of peace, being assured that he will be with us to the very end. At times when we look at our circumstances, they seem to deny the promise. But we have the promise, and it is Christ's promise. So we go forth with courage.

Raise Your Questions and Trust God for the Outcome (60:9–12). It was perhaps the king who asked, "Who will bring me victory over Edom?" The answer was that human resources alone were insufficient; only God could grant the victory needed. But would God? Was his "rejection" permanent? Would he never again march out with Israel's armies? There was no answer in the circumstances of the day. The answer lay in the promise alone.

The promise was believed by the people of that day. The evidence is twofold. First, the statement of 60:1, "You have rejected," has become a question, "Have you rejected?" Hearing the promise produced faith, though it was ever so feeble at first. Second, feeble faith blossomed into full confidence in the final line: "With God's help we will do mighty things, for he will trample down our foes." Faith came by listening to God's message, and what was true then is still true today (Rom 10:17).

There are times when the only thing we can cling to is the promise of God. But it is God's promise, and so we believe it. We believe it because he has given it. We believe it because he has demonstrated it in the Lord Jesus Christ. "For all of God's promises have been fulfilled in Christ" (2 Cor 1:20). Circumstances may give us the message that God has rejected us and is angry with us. Circumstances may give us the message that God is against us and not for us. But God's promise sends us a message to the contrary: Despite all of the adverse circumstances of life "overwhelming victory is ours through Christ, who loved us" (Rom 8:37). Armed with the promise of God, we say with David, "With God's help we will do mighty things."

ENDNOTES

1. See Isa 51:17, 21 for the only other uses of the word translated "reeling."

◆ S. Psalm 61

For the choir director: A psalm of David, to be accompanied by stringed instruments.

1 O God, listen to my cry!
Hear my prayer!
2 From the ends of the earth,
I cry to you for help
when my heart is overwhelmed.
Lead me to the towering rock of safety,
3 for you are my safe refuge,
a fortress where my enemies cannot reach me.
4 Let me live forever in your sanctuary,
safe beneath the shelter of your wings! *Interlude*

5 For you have heard my vows, O God.
You have given me an inheritance
reserved for those who fear your name.
6 Add many years to the life of the king!
May his years span the generations!
7 May he reign under God's protection forever.
May your unfailing love and faithfulness watch over him.
8 Then I will sing praises to your name forever
as I fulfill my vows each day.

NOTES

61:TITLE ***stringed instruments.*** The NLT presumes an emendation from the singular to the plural, for which there is evidence in Hebrew mss, LXX, and other ancient versions (see Kraus 1989:7).

61:2 It seems better to read this verse as a bicolon, with "lead me . . ." beginning the second colon. This follows the Masoretic punctuation. See note on 61:3.

Lead me to the towering rock. In the context of prayer, an imperfect verb is often equivalent to an imperative (Joüon and Muraoka 1991:§113m). The verb translated "lead" is the same verb translated "bring me victory" in 60:9 [11], and the word translated "rock" (*tsur* [TH6697, ZH7446]) sounds like the word translated "fortified city" (*matsor* [TH4692A, ZH5190]) in 60:9 [11]. In Ps 60 David wants to be led in victory to the fortress of Edom, whereas in Ps 61 he wants to be led to the rock/fortress, which is the presence of God himself.

61:3 ***for you are.*** It seems best to take this clause to go with what follows, not with what precedes, providing the reason for the vow made in 61:4. (See note at 61:4.)

61:4 ***Let me live.*** It is possible that the cohortative here expresses resolve (Joüon and Muraoka 1991:§114c): "I will live." This verse is then a vow that concludes the first strophe. The "vows" that God has heard (61:5 [6]) are the vows made in 61:4 [5]. Note that the second strophe also ends with a vow that is articulated with a cohortative, "I will sing . . . forever" (61:8 [9]).

61:6 ***Add.*** In the context of prayer an imperfect verb is often equivalent to an imperative (Joüon and Muraoka 1991:§113m).

61:7 ***under God's protection.*** Lit., "before/in the presence of God." The next colon specifies that his presence will be a protecting presence.

61:8 ***name . . . vows.*** God's name and David's vows are mentioned in 61:5 and thus form an *inclusio* around the second strophe.

as I fulfill. This infinitive is epexegetical or explanatory, "by fulfilling" (Waltke and O'Connor 1990:§36.2.3e). Praise was one aspect of fulfilling the vows.

COMMENTARY

There are times in life when we feel overwhelmed, exhausted, and spent. The situation David faced in the previous psalm must have been one of those times in his life. When we are overwhelmed, no matter what the reasons, the truth confronts us that human help is useless (60:11), but divine aid would enable us to do mighty things (60:12). This dependence on divine aid comes to expression in prayer. The prayer of Psalm 61 is comprised of two strophes (61:1-4, 5-8), each of which contains petitions and ends with vows.

A Prayer for Help (61:1-4). When his heart was overwhelmed by the troubles of life, David turned to God in prayer: "O God, listen to my cry! Hear my prayer!" He prayed "from the ends of the earth." The "ends of the earth" may indicate that David was geographically separated from the special presence of God in the sanctuary at Jerusalem, as, for example, when he was on a military campaign like the one that lies behind the previous psalm. Even if this is the case, the "ends of the earth" would also have referred to an existential separation from the divine presence like that clearly articulated in the previous psalm. When we feel overwhelmed by the troubles of this life, we too can feel this existential separation from God. "A sense of far-awayness from the divine presence, an at-the-end-of the earth experience, seems to be endemic to the spiritual life from time to time" (Tate 1990:116).

The truth is that even in those times God is only a prayer away. In prayer we bridge the apparent gap between ourselves and our God. In prayer we come to God and ask God to lead us to himself. He is "the towering rock of safety," the "safe refuge," the "fortress" in which we are safe from the onslaughts of life. Since he has shown himself to be such a God in the past, we resolve to live in his presence and under his protective wings in our tumultuous present.

A Prayer for the King (61:5-8). Knowing that God had heard the vows he had just made and having been persuaded that God would answer the requests of the first strophe, David was encouraged to make some specific requests for himself, which are the focus of the second strophe.

David's first request was for a long life. This long life entailed the "prosperity of the reigning monarch as well as the preservation of his dynasty," and the reference to "generations" brings into view "the well-being of his family for generations to come" (VanGemeren 1991:420). The prayer has in view the prosperous reign of David and his sons, reaching ultimately to David's greater Son, the Lord Jesus Christ.

David then prayed that he might reign in the presence of God, thus picking up the theme of the first strophe. He was, after all, the Lord's anointed, reigning as the Lord's vice-regent on the earth. Reigning in the presence of God entailed being guarded by God's unfailing love and faithfulness. David was, of course, the representative of the people when he prayed, so this prayer was a prayer for prosperity to be experienced by the king and people alike.

So too, this is a prayer for us as we are represented before God the Father by King Jesus. This is a prayer we offer for our prosperity and our reign as royal children of God (see Ps 8) and for our protection by the unfailing love and faithfulness of God in times when we are overwhelmed by life.

As David concluded the first strophe with a vow to live in the protective presence of God, so he closed the second strophe with a vow to praise God day after day. Since it is the divine presence and divine protection and divine blessing that enable us to be more than conquerors in the overwhelming circumstances of our lives, it is the divine name that we resolve to praise throughout our lives.

◆ T. Psalm 62

For Jeduthun, the choir director: A psalm of David.

1 I wait quietly before God,
for my victory comes from him.
2 He alone is my rock and my salvation,
my fortress where I will never be shaken.

3 So many enemies against one man—
all of them trying to kill me.
To them I'm just a broken-down wall
or a tottering fence.
4 They plan to topple me from my high position.
They delight in telling lies about me.
They praise me to my face
but curse me in their hearts. *Interlude*

5 Let all that I am wait quietly before God,
for my hope is in him.
6 He alone is my rock and my salvation,
my fortress where I will not be shaken.
7 My victory and honor come from God alone.
He is my refuge, a rock where no enemy can reach me.
8 O my people, trust in him at all times.
Pour out your heart to him,
for God is our refuge. *Interlude*

9 Common people are as worthless as a puff of wind,
and the powerful are not what they appear to be.
If you weigh them on the scales,
together they are lighter than a breath of air.

10 Don't make your living by extortion
or put your hope in stealing.
And if your wealth increases,
don't make it the center of your life.

11 God has spoken plainly,
and I have heard it many times:
Power, O God, belongs to you;
12 unfailing love, O Lord, is yours.
Surely you repay all people
according to what they have done.

NOTES

62:TITLE *For Jeduthun.* This presumes an emendation from *'al* [TH5921, ZH6584] (concerning) to *le* [TH3807.1, ZH4200] (for), for which there is support in a few mss and 39:TITLE [1], but see 77:TITLE [1] with *'al.*

62:2 *I will never be shaken.* The word *rabbah* [TH7227, ZH8041] (NLT, "never") functions adverbially here, and the sense is probably something like "I will not be shaken severely" rather than "I will not be shaken forever" (Tate 1990:118).

62:3 *against.* The verb *huth* [TH2050A, ZH2109] occurs only here. HALOT (1.243) suggests the meaning "attack"; DCH (2.507) suggests "threaten"; BDB (223) suggests "shout at." Rather than following one of these conjectures specifically, the NLT generalizes from the context and uses "against" to capture the sense rather than translating the verb directly.

all of them trying to kill me. The NLT presumes an emendation from the Pual (a passive verb form) to the Piel (an active form), for which there is support in several mss and later printed editions.

62:4 *They praise me to my face.* Lit., "They bless to his mouth [i.e., face]." The text is probably better understood as "they bless with their mouths," presuming an emendation to the third-person masc. pl., for which there is evidence in two Hebrew mss and the LXX. The NLT captures the contrast between the external action and the internal attitude.

62:5 *I . . . wait quietly.* The verb here is an imperative in the MT. An emendation to the noun *dumiyyah* [TH1747, ZH1875] would harmonize this verse with 62:1, but the last word in each line is different, so it seems best to leave the text as is.

62:7 ***He is my refuge.*** The NLT's pronoun "he" is, lit., "in God." The Beth on *'elohim* [TH430, ZH466] is the Beth of essence, which marks the predicate (Joüon and Muraoka 1991:§133c and Waltke and O'Connor 1990:§11.2.5e).

62:10 ***Don't make your living by extortion or put your hope in stealing.*** The first colon is best translated, "Don't trust in extortion." The second colon is best translated, "Don't vainly trust in robbery" (see HALOT 1.237).

COMMENTARY

Where does the ultimate source of your well-being lie? In what or in whom do you place your trust to get you out of hard times or keep you safe when all is well? From where do you derive your own sense of dignity? What provides you with a profound sense of security in life? For many, the answer to these questions lies in money and power. Psalm 62 provides a different answer.

The heart of the answer is found at the center of the poem (62:7): "My victory and honor come from God alone. He is my refuge, a rock where no enemy can reach me." This central line is preceded and followed by two eight-line stanzas (62:1-6, 8-12; see McCann 1996:922 for the structure). The first stanza expresses quiet confidence in God in the face of adversaries. The second encourages confidence in God, not in wealth or power.

Quiet Confidence in the Face of Adversity (62:1-6). "I wait quietly before God," said David. To wait quietly is one thing when all is well, but David waited quietly though there was a storm all around him. David was surrounded by enemies bent on his demise. These enemies were not foreigners but those who had access to David. They blessed David with their words, but all the while they were cursing him in their hearts. They took pleasure in lying about him as part of the plan to topple him from his position.

Surrounding the turmoil described in 62:3-4 are two nearly identical strophes of quietness (62:1-2 and 62:5-6). These strophes show us how David could be quiet in the middle of a storm. It was in the presence of God that David found quietness. He believed that God would deliver him from trouble. God was his source of protection and security. The presence of God provided inner serenity in spite of external turmoil.

While the two strophes are nearly identical, there are three differences. First, "hope" replaces "victory" at the end of the opening line of the second strophe. Second, an imperative replaces an indicative in the second strophe. These two changes indicate that the storm had not yet passed. Third, the adverb "severely" is missing in the second strophe, indicating that David had grown in confidence through the process of prayer (see note on 62:2). Whereas he began by being confident that he would not be severely shaken, he came to the place of being confident that he would not be shaken at all. Quieting his heart before God had changed David.

From this psalm we learn the importance of taking the time to be quiet before God when there is turmoil in our lives. Our temptation is to move into high gear to stay ahead of the storm. While there is a time and place for action, our activity is often a form of self-reliance. So our external pace is as hectic as our internal space. Quieting our souls before God and centering on him as the source of our well-being will produce the state of heart and mind needed to take action when appropriate.

Life in God Alone (62:7). Deliverance from difficulties, our sense of dignity and self-worth, and our security in life come from God alone. Idolatry is not so much a matter of external images of deity as it is a matter of the heart (Ezek 14:1-8). Idolatry is depending in an ultimate way on anything or anyone other than God. David affirmed that God was the source of his life in the most profound sense.

The idol of misplaced trust is often hard to detect. We think we are trusting God to supply our needs until we are faced with the possibility of losing our job. The anxiety we then experience indicates the presence of a hidden idol, misplaced trust in our job as the source of our security. We think we are depending on God's approval for our sense of personal well-being, until we come under severe criticism by others. The pain we then feel indicates the presence of an idol, misplaced dependence on the opinion of others as the source of our sense of self-worth. Such painful experiences are in reality a true blessing, as they give us the opportunity to rid our lives of idols and to grow in dependence on God alone for life.

Trust in God, Not in Wealth or Power (62:8-12). Wealth and power are two particularly insidious idols. So David instructed those around him not to trust in extortion or robbery, both of which are an exertion of power over others to increase one's wealth. He also instructed them not to make wealth the center of their lives should their wealth increase for any reason (see Paul's teaching in 1 Tim 6:17-19). Instead, they should put their trust in God at all times—when times are good as well as when times are not. David taught that when times are tough, one way we put our trust in God is by pouring out our hearts to him. We can honestly tell God all that we are thinking and feeling. We can be completely vulnerable in his presence, because he is our refuge, our place of safety, protection, and security.

Faith comes from listening to God's word (Rom 10:17), so David reminded himself and others that God has spoken. Two key characteristics God possesses are power and love. We can replace our dependence on our own power over others with a dependence on God's power. And God's power is never abusive, for his power is exercised in keeping with his unfailing love. So when we from time to time get caught up in the turmoil of life, we can quiet our souls before God, trusting that his power is at work in us to accomplish his loving purposes for us.

◆ U. Psalm 63

A psalm of David, regarding a time when David was in the wilderness of Judah.

[1]O God, you are my God;
I earnestly search for you.
My soul thirsts for you;
my whole body longs for you
in this parched and weary land
where there is no water.
[2]I have seen you in your sanctuary
and gazed upon your power and glory.
[3]Your unfailing love is better than life itself;
how I praise you!
[4]I will praise you as long as I live,
lifting up my hands to you in prayer.

[5]You satisfy me more than the richest
feast.
I will praise you with songs
of joy.
[6]I lie awake thinking of you,
meditating on you through the
night.
[7]Because you are my helper,
I sing for joy in the shadow of
your wings.
[8]I cling to you;
your strong right hand holds me
securely.
[9]But those plotting to destroy me will
come to ruin.
They will go down into the depths
of the earth.
[10]They will die by the sword
and become the food of jackals.
[11]But the king will rejoice in God.
All who trust in him will praise him,
while liars will be silenced.

NOTES

63:2 *your power and glory.* See 62:11 [12] for God's "power." The word for "glory" here is also used in 62:7 [8], where God is said to be David's "honor."

63:3 *Your unfailing love.* See 62:12 [13] for God's "unfailing love."

63:5 *I will praise you.* Lit., "my mouth" (*pi* [TH6310/2967.1, ZH7023/3276]) "will praise you." David's mouth praising God contrasts with his opponents' mouths being silenced in 63:11 (see note) and those same mouths uttering hypocritical blessings in 62:4 (see note).

63:10 *They will die by the sword.* The Hiphil of *nagar* [TH5064, ZH5599] means "pour out" but is used metaphorically with "on the edge of the sword" to mean "hand over" (HALOT 2.670). The verb form here is best translated, "*They* will hand *him* over" to the sword, but this makes no sense in context, which requires, "*One* will hand *them* over" to the sword. Perhaps a scribal error reversed these two elements.

63:11 *liars.* Lit., "mouth of those who speak a lie" (see note on 63:5).

COMMENTARY

David's experience of finding himself "in the wilderness" was not unique to him. Israel had spent 40 years in the wilderness before him, and Jesus spent 40 days in the wilderness after him. As Christians we too find ourselves from time to time "in the wilderness" for a variety of reasons. Israel was there because of her sin. David was there because of opposition from people. Perhaps we are there for one of these reasons or for another. It may be the loss of a loved one through death, a broken relationship, a prolonged or serious illness, or the loss of a job. The wilderness is a place where we experience isolation—separation from family, friends, the worshiping community, and seemingly even God himself. The wilderness is a place where we experience desolation—joylessness, disconsolation, sorrow, confusion, loneliness, barrenness, and lifelessness.

In the wilderness we find ourselves on a search. A search for answers, for security, for meaning, for significance. Yes, on the surface we may be searching for these or similar things. But in our souls we are on a search that only God himself can satisfy by his own presence. Psalm 63 was given to guide us in that search and to lead us to an experience of deep satisfaction.

The Search. The search is a personal search. "O God," began David. We are searching for God, the true and living God. We are searching neither for a theological concept nor for an impersonal power. We are searching for a person. As persons we are searching for the personal God, the God whom we know we correspond to in some way. He created us in his image, to be like him, to know him intimately. In our hearts we all know what Augustine knew: Our souls are restless until they find rest in the true and living God.

He is "my God," continued David. He is certainly not "ours" in that we own him, yet there is a sense in which we long to "possess" him as well as be possessed by him, to know him in the depths of our being as well as be known by him, to love him with our whole being as well as be loved by him, to be united to him.

The search is also intense. David said, "I earnestly search for you." This search is not a casual one, not one we are indifferent or hesitant about. It is consuming. It is likened to a search for water by a thirsty person trekking through a "parched and weary land where there is no water" (63:1). The search is so intense that our whole being is caught up in it. Body and soul together strain to find and be found. So occupied are we in this search that we cannot sleep. We find ourselves lying awake and searching throughout the entire night. Our soul is following hard after God, even as he is holding us securely by his right hand.

The Satisfaction. Ultimately satisfaction arises from the divine presence. It is an understatement to say that the satisfaction experienced in finding God in the wilderness far exceeds the satisfaction of the most lavish banquet this life could spread before us. In finding God we experience his power and glory. David had experienced this power and glory in the past, and the wilderness intensified his desire to know, once again, the presence of God in power and glory. Stripped of all external comforts, in the wilderness David's priorities were reset: God's unfailing love was all that really mattered, being more precious than life itself. The soul finds no greater satisfaction in life than that which it tastes as it drinks deeply of the love of God. In finding God we experience his help. God had been David's help many times in the past. In the wilderness David longed once again to experience God in the tangible form of help.

This satisfaction results in joyful praise. When David first uttered these words in the wilderness, he was not experiencing God's power, glory, unfailing love, and help—at least not in the form of being delivered from the wilderness. He was still there in that dry and weary land. Yet he was full of praise. So sweet was his anticipation of this power, glory, love, and help that he could already offer to God great heartfelt praise. "How I praise you!" "I will praise you with songs of joy." "I sing for joy in the shadow of your wings." "The king will rejoice in God." This praise was a token of that which he would render to God after his soul's desires had been fully satisfied. These desires would be satisfied, and the praise of his mouth would be heard most clearly when the mouths of his opponents were shut.

Through this psalm the Holy Spirit teaches us to search for our God all the more earnestly when we find ourselves in the wilderness of life. We can believe that his power and glory and love and help are there even when we cannot see evidence of them. Our souls can cling to him even when we see no evidence that his strong right hand is holding us securely. For though at times there may be no evidence in our experience, there is always evidence in the experience of our Lord Jesus. It was not during his temptation in the desert that he experienced the depths of the wilderness. It was on the cross. For on the cross he experienced isolation and desolation beyond human comprehension that we might know the indescribable satisfaction that awaits us at the end of our search for God's presence in our lives—his power, glory, love, and help.

◆ V. Psalm 64

For the choir director: A psalm of David.

1 O God, listen to my complaint.
Protect my life from my enemies' threats.
2 Hide me from the plots of this evil mob,
from this gang of wrongdoers.
3 They sharpen their tongues like swords
and aim their bitter words like arrows.
4 They shoot from ambush at the innocent,
attacking suddenly and fearlessly.
5 They encourage each other to do evil
and plan how to set their traps in secret.
"Who will ever notice?" they ask.
6 As they plot their crimes, they say,
"We have devised the perfect plan!"
Yes, the human heart and mind are cunning.

7 But God himself will shoot them with his arrows,
suddenly striking them down.
8 Their own tongues will ruin them,
and all who see them will shake their heads in scorn.
9 Then everyone will be afraid;
they will proclaim the mighty acts of God
and realize all the amazing things he does.
10 The godly will rejoice in the LORD
and find shelter in him.
And those who do what is right
will praise him.

NOTES

64:1 *Protect my life from my enemies' threats.* The words *pakhad 'oyeb* [TH6343/341, ZH7065/367] most naturally refer to David's "fear of the enemy" (HALOT 3.922). (This would be an objective genitive; see Waltke and O'Connor 1990:§9.5.2b.) David asked God to protect him from such dread rather than from the enemies themselves. Similarly, in 34:4 [5] David gave thanks for having been delivered from all his fears. Yet it is possible that the phrase is a metonym for "the threats that are the occasion of my dread of the enemy" (Tate 1990:131; see NIDOTTE 3.598).

64:7 *shoot . . . suddenly.* In 64:3-4 David's foes were shooting arrows and attacking suddenly. In 64:7 they are reaping what they have sown, as God suddenly shoots his arrows at them.

64:8-10. Most of the verbs in these verses are Waw-relative imperfects. Translating these verbs as future tenses is quite difficult, if not impossible to defend, but all major translations render them in the future (NLT, NIV, RSV, NRSV). This decision is probably owing to the belief that Ps 64 is a lament and that the deliverance needed has not yet been experienced. Perhaps these forms can be interpreted after the fashion of the rhetorical perfect, expressing assurance that the actions in view will so certainly take place that they can be spoken of as already having taken place; but there is little if any evidence for this interpretation. It seems more natural to say that 64:8-10 records the deliverance requested in 64:1-2 (see Kraus 1988:2.24).

64:10 ***those who do what is right.*** Lit., "the upright of heart." The use of "heart" here forms a contrast with the cunning heart in 64:6.

will rejoice . . . will praise. These same words occur in 63:11 [12]. The similar endings of these consecutive psalms link the two together.

COMMENTARY

By this point in the Psalter we have read lament after lament, and one more lament seems wearying to the soul. But life is just like that at times. One difficulty follows on the heels of another. Another trouble arises as soon as one abates. Just when order is emerging, chaos caves in on you. The Psalter brings the realities of life to expression.

Prayer for Relief (64:1-2). Like David we at times struggle not only with opposition from without but also with problems from within. As in other psalms, David here prayed for protection from his enemies who were plotting against him and scheming to do evil. But in addition to this external threat, David struggled within himself. The inner quietness that characterized him in Psalm 62 is not found in this opening strophe. David was plagued by a sense of dread. He dreaded what others might do to him. We too, at times, are engaged in an external battle and a war within. David freely brought both to God in prayer. Acknowledging both, he sought relief from both.

Description of Distress (64:3-6). David went on to describe the external distress he was experiencing. As in previous psalms, the weapons his foes wielded were not swords but destructive words. We have all heard that "sticks and stones may break my bones but words will never hurt me." And if we have stopped to think about that rhyme, we have realized just how false it is. We have all experienced the destructive power of words. We know how long it takes for the soul to mend when it has been pierced by lies, gossip, and slander. We know the dread felt when others are devising "the perfect plan" against us. Our all-knowing God knows what is going on before we pray, yet he invites us to describe to him the nature of the distress we are experiencing. He desires our honest communication in prayer. And through this communion we experience deliverance.

Description of Deliverance (64:7-9). God had his own arsenal of arrows that he himself shot at those who had shot arrows at David. David's foes reaped what they had sown. The words/tongues that they had intended for David's harm ricocheted and pierced their own hearts because of how they had used their own tongues. All who remained in the end stood in awe of God and his amazing, just ways.

Promise of Rejoicing (64:10). As joy and praise filled the mouths of those who trusted in the Lord in 63:11, so Psalm 64 ends with those who trust in the Lord by finding shelter in him rejoicing and praising the God who delivers his people from distress. The silencing of the liars promised in 63:11 has been accomplished by the end of Psalm 64.

Thus, in Psalm 64 we find great encouragement in times of distress to look to the Lord to protect us from the dread we experience within and the foes we face without.

W. Psalm 65

For the choir director: A song. A psalm of David.

1 What mighty praise, O God,
belongs to you in Zion.
We will fulfill our vows to you,
2 for you answer our prayers.
All of us must come to you.
3 Though we are overwhelmed by
our sins,
you forgive them all.
4 What joy for those you choose to
bring near,
those who live in your holy courts.
What festivities await us
inside your holy Temple.

5 You faithfully answer our prayers
with awesome deeds,
O God our savior.
You are the hope of everyone
on earth,
even those who sail on distant seas.
6 You formed the mountains by your
power
and armed yourself with mighty
strength.
7 You quieted the raging oceans
with their pounding waves
and silenced the shouting of the
nations.
8 Those who live at the ends of the
earth
stand in awe of your wonders.
From where the sun rises to where
it sets,
you inspire shouts of joy.

9 You take care of the earth and
water it,
making it rich and fertile.
The river of God has plenty of water;
it provides a bountiful harvest of
grain,
for you have ordered it so.
10 You drench the plowed ground with
rain,
melting the clods and leveling the
ridges.
You soften the earth with showers
and bless its abundant crops.
11 You crown the year with a bountiful
harvest;
even the hard pathways overflow
with abundance.
12 The grasslands of the wilderness
become a lush pasture,
and the hillsides blossom with joy.
13 The meadows are clothed with flocks
of sheep,
and the valleys are carpeted with
grain.
They all shout and sing for joy!

NOTES

65:1 ***belongs.*** The word *dumiyyah* [TH1747, ZH1875] means "silence," so the text is best translated "silence is praise to you." Though possible, this does not make very good sense. Revocalizing the text to *domiya* (Qal participle from *damah* I [TH1819, ZH1948]) results in "praise is fitting for you" (see DCH 2.447) or the NLT's "belongs to you." The LXX's *prepei* [TG4241A, ZG4560] (is fitting) provides support for this emendation.

65:2 ***for you answer our prayers.*** Lit., "O hearer of prayer" (see commentary).

65:3 ***Though we are overwhelmed by our sins, you forgive them all.*** The Heb. *dibre 'awonoth gaberu menni* is somewhat problematic. It is better to emend *menni* [TH4480/5204.1, ZH4946/5761] (from me) to *mennu* [TH4480/5105.1, ZH4946/5646] (from us) in keeping with the context and numerous Hebrew mss.

65:4 ***What festivities await us.*** The sense of the word *nisbe'ah* [TH7646, ZH8425] is "satisfaction," and the cohortative form makes this a request, not a statement. The satisfaction will be found in *tub betheka* [TH2898/1004, ZH3206/1074] (the goodness of your house), which probably refers to the good food eaten in the context of the sacrifices offered in payment of the vow mentioned in 65:1 (see 22:25-26 [26-27] and Futato 1984:154).

65:9 ***water it.*** Lit., "caused it to overflow." The picture is that of God sending so much rain that the land is overflowing with water.

The river of God. The word *peleg* [TH6388, ZH7104] is probably a metaphorical reference to the "channel" in the sky by which the rains come to water the earth (Futato 1984:175). See Job 38:25 for a similar picture, where God created a channel (*palag* [TH6385, ZH7103]) for the torrents of rain.

65:10 ***drench . . . leveling.*** The verbs are interpreted as infinitives absolute used for imperfects (Joüon and Muraoka 1991:§123w and Waltke and O'Connor 1990:§35.5.2a).

abundant crops. The word *tsemakh* [TH6780, ZH7542] refers to newly sprouting vegetation (HALOT 3.1034).

65:11 ***bountiful harvest.*** Lit., "good" (*tobah* [TH2896D, ZH3208]). Here the reference is probably to rain rather than "a bountiful harvest" (see the following note and the use of *tob* [TH2896, ZH3202] in 85:12).

the hard pathways overflow with abundance. The verb *ra'ap* [TH7491, ZH8319] (and the related *'arap* [TH7491, ZH6903]) typically refers to precipitation falling from the sky (see Deut 32:2; 33:28; Job 36:28; Prov 3:20), so the "pathways" would seem to refer to "tracks" in the sky on which the rains descend (Futato 1984:183). The tracks would be those of the Lord's rain-cloud chariot (see 104:3). The sense of the text is that the tracks overflow with (the rains that produce an) abundance (of crops).

COMMENTARY

Praise for answered prayer is the theme of Psalm 65. The psalm begins with the declaration that it is appropriate to praise the Lord in Zion. Praise is appropriate, especially as part of the fulfilling of vows. Such vows would have been made during the distressing situation recorded in Psalm 64, as well as on other occasions. At the beginning of 65:2 God is called the "hearer of prayer" (see note). Psalm 65 will focus on three kinds of prayers God heard and hears.

Praise for Restoration to the Divine Presence (65:1-4). Psalm 65:2 envisions all people coming to the Lord. In the context of subsequent references to "everyone on earth" (65:5) and "those who live at the ends of the earth" (65:8), all people would include the nations as well as Israel. Psalm 65:3 tells us why all people are coming to the Lord: Their hearts are filled with sin, and the Lord can forgive that sin in an ultimate way. The result of this forgiveness is twofold: (1) the joy of being restored to the divine presence (by being brought near to God in the Temple courts), and (2) the satisfaction that comes from experiencing all the good things that accompany life in the presence of God.

A sense of joy and satisfaction is what all people long for. Psalm 65 envisions a day when people from "the ends of the earth" come to God for forgiveness and experience joy and satisfaction in God's presence. We who have been restored to the divine presence through Jesus Christ know the appropriateness of praising the God who hears prayer.

Praise for Awesome Deeds (65:5-8). God hears and answers prayers not only by forgiving sin and restoring people to his presence but also by performing "awesome deeds" (65:5). The "awesome deeds" refer in the first place to God's originally creating the earth, his forming the mountains, and his removing the waters that would have rendered the earth uninhabitable.[1] These deeds, however, can hardly be construed as answers to human prayer. So, what did David have in mind when he said that God answers our prayers by forming mountains and quieting raging seas?

The fact that these verbs are participles in the Hebrew text leads to the suggestion that the reference is not only to the Lord's initial deeds—what we would call creation—but also to his ongoing deeds, what we would call providence. God has shown himself to be one who characteristically maintains order in the creation for the well-being of his people. This order is historical as well as cosmic, including the keeping of threatening nations at bay as well as the keeping of threatening seas at bay.

Chaos in a variety of forms continually threatens to overwhelm us in this life. So we pray for God to maintain order in our lives. As in the previous strophe, the "we" is identified as "everyone on earth" (65:5) and "those who live at the ends of the earth" (65:8). All people are putting their hope in the God who answers prayer with "awesome deeds," they are standing in awe of his wonders, and they are shouting for joy. They know the appropriateness of praising the God who hears prayer.

Praise for Abundant Provisions (65:9–13). God's maintaining of the cosmic order in general comes to sharp focus in this final strophe. For agriculturally based Israel, where there was no major irrigation system (see Deut 11:10-12), the heart of the cosmic order was the onset of the rainy season in the fall, resulting in lush vegetation in the spring. Psalm 65:9-10 describes the coming of the fall rains that soften the hard soil, allowing for plowing and planting, and that provide sufficient water for abundant new crops and other vegetation to sprout. Psalm 65:11-13 takes us through the winter and into the spring, when a bountiful harvest is just around the corner and when the flocks in the fields have all the vegetation they need. All of this, too, comes in answer to the prayers of God's people. As we pray for all that is necessary that we might have our daily bread, we pray in confidence, knowing that our God is a God who hears prayer.

He hears the prayers of all who come to him for forgiveness and restores them to the joy and satisfaction of his presence. That joy and satisfaction is experienced as God hears our prayers and performs awesome deeds—as he maintains order in our lives and provides abundantly for us in this life. So it is highly appropriate for us and for all to praise the God who hears prayer.

ENDNOTES

1. See commentary on Pss 74 and 104.

◆ X. Psalm 66

For the choir director: A song. A psalm.

1 Shout joyful praises to God, all the
earth!
2 Sing about the glory of his name!
Tell the world how glorious he is.
3 Say to God, "How awesome are
your deeds!
Your enemies cringe before your
mighty power.

[4] Everything on earth will worship you;
they will sing your praises,
shouting your name in glorious
songs." *Interlude*

[5] Come and see what our God has done,
what awesome miracles he performs
for people!
[6] He made a dry path through the Red
Sea,*
and his people went across on foot.
There we rejoiced in him.
[7] For by his great power he rules
forever.
He watches every movement of the
nations;
let no rebel rise in defiance.
Interlude

[8] Let the whole world bless our God
and loudly sing his praises.
[9] Our lives are in his hands,
and he keeps our feet from
stumbling.
[10] You have tested us, O God;
you have purified us like silver.
[11] You captured us in your net
and laid the burden of slavery
on our backs.
[12] Then you put a leader over us.*
We went through fire and flood,
but you brought us to a place of
great abundance.

[13] Now I come to your Temple with burnt
offerings
to fulfill the vows I made to you—
[14] yes, the sacred vows that I made
when I was in deep trouble.
[15] That is why I am sacrificing burnt
offerings to you—
the best of my rams as a pleasing
aroma,
and a sacrifice of bulls and male
goats. *Interlude*

[16] Come and listen, all you who fear God,
and I will tell you what he did
for me.
[17] For I cried out to him for help,
praising him as I spoke.
[18] If I had not confessed the sin in my
heart,
the Lord would not have listened.
[19] But God did listen!
He paid attention to my prayer.
[20] Praise God, who did not ignore my
prayer
or withdraw his unfailing love
from me.

66:6 Hebrew *the sea.* **66:12** Or *You made people ride over our heads.*

NOTES

66:2 *Tell the world how glorious he is.* The Heb. *simu kabod tehillatho* [TH7760/3519/8416, ZH8492/3883/9335] (give glory his praise) is difficult. The expression *simu kabod* means "give glory," but we would expect there also to be an indirect object marked by the prepositional Lamedh (see Josh 7:19; Isa 42:12), so some suggest adding *lo* [TH3807.1/2050.2, ZH4200/2257] (to him) and revocalizing *kabod* (glory) as *kebod* (glory of), resulting in "Give to him his glorious praise" (see Kraus 1989:34). Tate (1990:145) takes *kabod* as an adverb, citing Dan 11:39,[1] and renders the text, "Set forth gloriously his praise." It is possible to render the text, "Give glory as his praise" (so Delitzsch 1982:234). Though a precise understanding escapes us, the general sense is clear enough: God is to be praised in connection with his glory.

66:5 *for people.* Lit., "for the sons of man," a typical reference to humanity (DCH 2.206). This global reference fits into the context of the previous verse (all the earth) and the previous psalm (see 65:5, 8 [6, 9]).

66:6 *There we rejoiced in him.* The word *sham* [TH8033, ZH9004] (there) refers to the crossing of the sea mentioned in the two previous cola. The word *nismekhah* [TH8055, ZH8523] is an example of a "pseudo-cohortative" used for past time reference (so Waltke and O'Connor 1990:§34.5.3b). The sense of the colon is, "There we rejoiced in him." The people using the psalm were "there," not historically but liturgically, as they celebrated the Exodus in worship (Weiser 1962:470).

66:7 ***let no rebel rise in defiance.*** The verb *rum* [TH7311, ZH8123] with the preposition Lamedh means "to exalt oneself" (HALOT 3.1203). The sense is, "Let rebels not exalt themselves."

66:11 ***laid the burden of slavery on our backs.*** Lit., "put affliction in our hips."

66:20 ***Praise.*** The word *baruk* [TH1288A, ZH1385] (blessed be) echoes the opening of the third strophe of the second stanza ("bless," 66:8).

COMMENTARY

Psalm 66 is a fitting sequel to Psalm 65, as they share significant themes. In both psalms, God is praised (65:1; 66:2, 8) in the Temple (65:4; 66:13) for his "awesome" deeds (65:5; 66:3, 5) and as the one who listens to prayer (65:2; 66:18-20). Both have the fulfilling of vows in view (65:1; 66:13). And both psalms share a universal scope with all the earth being called upon to worship God (65:5; 66:1, 4) in awe (65:8; 66:16). But whereas Psalm 65 focuses on God's deeds in creation, Psalm 66 focuses on God's deeds in redemption.

Community Praise (66:1-12). The first stanza is comprised of three strophes, each of which begins with an imperative: "Shout" (66:1-4), "Come" (66:5-7), and "Bless" (66:8-12). In this stanza the focus is on the community at worship.

"All the earth" (66:1) and "everything on earth" (66:4) mark the boundaries of the first strophe and show that the community summoned to praise God is a global community, a perspective in keeping with that of the previous psalm. All the earth is portrayed as praising the "name" of God (66:2, 4). The name or character of God is known through his awesome deeds that manifest his mighty power, resulting in his enemies cringing before him. This "cringing" is a step toward the enemies joining the worshiping community, as the following two strophes will make clear (see also Pss 46 and 47).

The second strophe invites all to observe the awesome deed that God has done. That deed is the deliverance of Israel from Egyptian oppression through the Red Sea. What is amazing in this psalm is that this greatest of redemptive deeds in the Old Testament was done not simply for the benefit of Israel but for all humanity (see note on "people" on 66:5). Just as God chose Abraham and blessed him so that all the families of the earth might be blessed through him (Gen 12:1-3; see also Ps 67:1-2), so the Exodus was one more step in the outworking of God's redemptive plan for the world. As Terence Fretheim has said:

> *While the liberation of Israel is the focus of God's activity, it is not the ultimate purpose. The deliverance of Israel is ultimately for the sake of all creation (see [Exod] 9:16). The issue for God is finally not that God's name be made known in Israel but that it be declared to the entire earth (1991:13).*

The deliverance through the Red Sea was a specific manifestation of God's general sovereign ruling over the nations, which served as a warning not to rebel against him and an invitation to bless him, as the next strophe brings out.

The final strophe in the first stanza, like the first strophe, calls upon "the whole world" to sing the praises of God in light of his redeeming work (66:8). In this strophe, as in the previous one, the description is that of God's work in the lives of his people narrowly conceived, but the implications are for all. "Our lives are in his hands," says the psalmist, "and he keeps our feet from stumbling" (66:9).[2] This is not to say that the terrain is always smooth and easy. At times being in God's hands means we are tested and purified like silver in a crucible, experiencing deep affliction and misery in the process. But it is just like God to bring us through trials of fire and flood to a place of great abundance. This is why we bless him and sing aloud his praises.

While our experience of God's redeeming work is a corporate experience, it is also an individual experience. The individual perspective is taken up in the second stanza.

Individual Thanksgiving (66:13-20). First-person verbs mark a shift from community praise in the first stanza to individual thanksgiving in the second stanza: "I come," "I made," "I was in deep trouble," etc. "The second [stanza] shows a member of the community fully participating in and appropriating the communal deliverance as his very own" (Brueggemann 1984:138).

In the first strophe (66:13-15), the psalmist comes to the Temple to fulfill the vows made during the time of distress recorded in 66:8-12. The psalmist must have been a person of means, as indicated by the sizable offerings that included rams, bulls, and goats. We can presume that many, including the poor, would have enjoyed feasting on this occasion (see 22:25-26). These other worshipers are addressed directly in the second strophe.

The beginning note of the second strophe (66:16-19) in this stanza echoes the beginning note of the second strophe in the first stanza, as both invite people to "come." Here the invitation is to come and listen rather than come and see. Worshipers are invited to come and listen to the psalmist's personal testimony about what God did for him.

When in distress, the psalmist called out to God. Though in distress, the psalmist found reason enough to praise God. While it is easy to praise God after he has delivered us, it is incumbent upon us to praise him in the middle of our trials (see Rom 5:3-5 and Jas 1:2-4). Since sin separates us from God (Isa 59:2), confession of sin is a prerequisite to having our prayers answered. Such was the psalmist's experience, and such must be ours as well.

Having called out to God and having confessed sin, the psalmist received an answer. God listened and paid attention to his prayer. In what precise way we are not told, but we are encouraged nonetheless to follow the pattern set forth and to trust that God will listen to our prayers and deliver us from our trials, just as he did the psalmist.

A final blessing pronounced over God brings the psalm to a fitting conclusion. God is praised for not ignoring the psalmist's prayer and for not withdrawing his unfailing love in time of need. During times of trial and tribulation we are tempted to think that God has utterly forsaken us, but the testimony of this believer gives evidence to the contrary. God does not withdraw his unfailing love from us but in due time makes that love evident as we experience his delivering power.

ENDNOTES

1. See the "accusative of manner" in Waltke and O'Connor 1990:§10.2.2e.
2. For the use of the motif of not stumbling up to this point in the Psalter, see 10:6; 15:5; 16:8; 17:5; 21:7; 62:2, 6.

◆ Y. Psalm 67

For the choir director: A song. A psalm, to be accompanied by stringed instruments.

[1] May God be merciful and bless us.
  May his face smile with favor on us. *Interlude*

[2] May your ways be known throughout
   the earth,
  your saving power among people
   everywhere.
[3] May the nations praise you, O God.
  Yes, may all the nations praise you.
[4] Let the whole world sing for joy,
  because you govern the nations
   with justice
  and guide the people of the whole
   world. *Interlude*

[5] May the nations praise you, O God.
  Yes, may all the nations
   praise you.
[6] Then the earth will yield its
   harvests,
  and God, our God, will richly
   bless us.
[7] Yes, God will bless us,
  and people all over the world
   will fear him.

NOTES

67:2 ***May your ways be known.*** The Hebrew text has an infinitive construct here, so this clause is dependent on the previous verse and expresses purpose: "that your ways may be known" (see commentary).

67:4 ***guide the people of the whole world.*** The verb *nakhah* [TH5148, ZH5697] is used for God's "leading" of his people in and after the Exodus (e.g., 77:20 [21]; 78:14, 53; Exod 13:21; 15:13; see NIDOTTE 3.76). Here, however, he is "leading" the whole world.

67:6 ***will yield.*** The verb is in the perfect tense. The NLT is probably correct in interpreting the verb as a rhetorical perfect for action so certain to take place in the future that it can be spoken of as already accomplished in the past (Joüon and Muraoka 1991:§112h; Waltke and O'Connor 1990:§30.5.1e). However, the imperfect verbs in these last two verses may be jussives used to express a prayer, and if this is the case, the perfect would be a precative (Joüon and Muraoka 1991:§112k; Waltke and O'Connor 1990:§30.5.4c-d).

COMMENTARY

As believers, we often pray that God would bless us in a wide variety of ways. It is far too easy, however, for these blessings to become an end in and of themselves. We pray to be blessed that we might be blessed. Psalm 67 challenges us not to give up the pursuit of blessing, but to pursue blessings all the more earnestly with God's own intended outcome.

Psalm 67 is chiastically arranged: 67:1-2 is a prayer for blessing that results in the nations experiencing God's salvation, 67:3-5 is a prayer for the nations to glorify and enjoy God, and 67:6-7 returns to the theme of blessing that results in the nations experiencing God's salvation.

May God Bless Us for the Sake of the Nations (67:1-2). Psalm 67 begins with a prayer that echoes the Aaronic benediction (Num 6:22-27), a prayer that God would be merciful to and would bless his people. More will be said in the final strophe about the nature of the blessing desired, but here we learn that at the heart of this blessing is the presence of God. This is clear from the fact that the blessing of 67:1a is amplified in terms of the shining face of God in 67:1b. The shining face of God is metaphorical language for God's favorable presence among his people. This favorable presence is itself further explained by the phrase "your saving power" in 67:2b. So the blessing desired is nothing short of the experience of salvation in its fullness.

What is amazing in this psalm is that the saving blessing is sought, not as an end in and of itself, but as a means to a yet greater end: the salvation of people throughout the earth. "The blessing of the church is for the salvation of the nations" (Mays 1994:225). The psalmist prays that God would bless his people so that his saving ways might become known to people everywhere. Here we are reminded of the truth that God chose Abraham and blessed him so that "all the families on earth" might be blessed through him (Gen 12:1-3; see also Gal 3:8-9). In Psalm 66, God's saving actions in the Exodus are portrayed as having been done ultimately for the benefit of the whole human race (see 66:5-7). Psalm 67 expounds this same theme with a prayer for blessing on "us" so that blessing might come to "them."

If praying to be blessed is good, then it is even better to pray to be blessed that others might also be blessed. "The community of God here learns how to break away from all narrowness in the reception of salvation" (Kraus 1989:42).

May God Be Glorified and Enjoyed by the Nations (67:3-5). At the heart of the psalm is the psalmist's deep desire that the nations fully enjoy the saving benefits of the God of Israel. They will enjoy God governing them with justice, i.e., putting everything in right order that is not currently in right order in their world. They will also enjoy God leading them as he led Israel through the wilderness (see note on 67:4). Whereas in Psalm 66, the nations experience the benefits of the crossing of the Red Sea, here they experience the benefits of being led through the wilderness and into the Promised Land.

But the joy of the nations is surrounded by the grateful praise of God by the nations (67:3, 5). The psalmist prays for blessing on God's people so that the nations might become God's people, so that God might be praised throughout the whole earth.

Glorifying God and enjoying him go hand in hand. Experiencing his salvation brings great joy and results in giving him great glory.

God Will Bless Us for the Sake of the Nations (67:6-7). This final strophe repeats the vocabulary of "bless" from the first strophe. Here, however, the psalmist does not pray for blessing but expresses confidence that blessing is soon to be experienced. Blessing, moreover, comes in the concrete form of an abundant harvest. "Blessing" is thus not to be understood in ethereal or exclusively otherworldly terms. The blessing to be experienced is tangible and very much this-worldly.

This final strophe also shares the logic of the first strophe. The rich blessing enjoyed by God's people will be observed by people from all over the world. These people will, in turn, become part of that people who live in reverent worship of the true and living God.

Through this psalm God encourages us as his people to pursue the experience of his blessings in this life. These blessings include everything from the fruit of the Holy Spirit to material prosperity. This is good. In addition, God encourages us to seek these blessings so that others might see the truly abundant life that we have and desire that kind of life for themselves. God cannot use us to create in others a desire to have what we ourselves do not have. May we be blessed that others might be blessed through us.

Ultimately, though, we want to be blessed and be a blessing that we might experience great joy in God and give great glory to him. This is the heart of Psalm 67 and the heart of the true believer, for this is the heart of God. We see God's heart in his sending of the Lord Jesus Christ so that Jews and Gentiles might be blessed through faith in him (Gal 3:8-9).

◆ Z. Psalm 68

For the choir director: A song. A psalm of David.

1 Rise up, O God, and scatter your enemies.
Let those who hate God run for their lives.
2 Blow them away like smoke.
Melt them like wax in a fire.
Let the wicked perish in the presence of God.
3 But let the godly rejoice.
Let them be glad in God's presence.
Let them be filled with joy.
4 Sing praises to God and to his name!
Sing loud praises to him who rides the clouds.
His name is the LORD—
rejoice in his presence!

5 Father to the fatherless, defender of widows—
this is God, whose dwelling is holy.
6 God places the lonely in families;
he sets the prisoners free and gives them joy.
But he makes the rebellious live in a sun-scorched land.

7 O God, when you led your people out from Egypt,
when you marched through the dry wasteland, *Interlude*
8 the earth trembled, and the heavens poured down rain
before you, the God of Sinai,
before God, the God of Israel.
9 You sent abundant rain, O God,
to refresh the weary land.
10 There your people finally settled,
and with a bountiful harvest, O God,
you provided for your needy people.

11 The Lord gives the word,
and a great army* brings the good news.
12 Enemy kings and their armies flee,
while the women of Israel divide the plunder.
13 Even those who lived among the sheepfolds found treasures—
doves with wings of silver
and feathers of gold.
14 The Almighty scattered the enemy kings
like a blowing snowstorm on Mount Zalmon.

15 The mountains of Bashan are majestic,
with many peaks stretching high into the sky.
16 Why do you look with envy, O rugged mountains,
at Mount Zion, where God has chosen to live,
where the LORD himself will live forever?

17 Surrounded by unnumbered thousands of chariots,

the Lord came from Mount Sinai
into his sanctuary.
18 When you ascended to the heights,
you led a crowd of captives.
You received gifts from the people,
even from those who rebelled
against you.
Now the LORD God will live among
us there.
19 Praise the Lord; praise God our savior!
For each day he carries us in his
arms. *Interlude*
20 Our God is a God who saves!
The Sovereign LORD rescues us from
death.

21 But God will smash the heads of his
enemies,
crushing the skulls of those who
love their guilty ways.
22 The Lord says, "I will bring my enemies
down from Bashan;
I will bring them up from the depths
of the sea.
23 You, my people, will wash your feet in
their blood,
and even your dogs will get their
share!"

24 Your procession has come into view,
O God—
the procession of my God and King
as he goes into the sanctuary.
25 Singers are in front, musicians behind;
between them are young women
playing tambourines.
26 Praise God, all you people of Israel;
praise the LORD, the source of
Israel's life.
27 Look, the little tribe of Benjamin leads
the way.
Then comes a great throng of rulers
from Judah
and all the rulers of Zebulun and
Naphtali.

28 Summon your might, O God.
Display your power, O God, as you
have in the past.
29 The kings of the earth are bringing
tribute
to your Temple in Jerusalem.
30 Rebuke these enemy nations—
these wild animals lurking in the
reeds,
this herd of bulls among the weaker
calves.
Make them bring bars of silver in
humble tribute.
Scatter the nations that delight
in war.
31 Let Egypt come with gifts of precious
metals*;
let Ethiopia* bow in submission to
God.
32 Sing to God, you kingdoms of the
earth.
Sing praises to the Lord. *Interlude*
33 Sing to the one who rides across the
ancient heavens,
his mighty voice thundering from
the sky.
34 Tell everyone about God's power.
His majesty shines down on
Israel;
his strength is mighty in the
heavens.
35 God is awesome in his sanctuary.
The God of Israel gives power and
strength to his people.

Praise be to God!

68:11 Or *a host of women.* **68:31a** Or *of rich cloth.* **68:31b** Hebrew *Cush.*

NOTES

68:6 ***gives them joy.*** The word *kosharoth* [TH3574, ZH3938] apparently means "prosperity" (HALOT 2.467; DCH 4.378). The sense seems to be that "he leads [righteous] prisoners out into prosperity," in contrast to leading the rebels (of the following colon) into adversity.

68:13 ***Even those who lived . . .*** This verse is quite difficult, but the NLT seems to capture the general sense.

68:15 ***stretching high into the sky.*** The word *gabnunnim* [TH1386, ZH1493] means "rugged" as it is translated in the following verse.

68:19 ***carries us in his arms.*** The word *'amas* [TH6006, ZH6673] means "to bear a burden" (HALOT 2.846). The picture is that of God carrying our burdens for us rather than carrying us directly.

COMMENTARY

Psalm 68 has the reputation of being the most difficult psalm in the Psalter.[1] The psalm contains 15 words that occur only once in the Hebrew Bible (McCann 1996:944). Numerous relationships between words are obscure. Some of the poetic lines are perplexing. And the sense relations between the strophes are not always clear. In spite of all these interpretive problems, however, the main message of the poem is discernible, and key aspects of that message are evident.

Psalm 68 celebrates the reign of God. This celebration was not individual and private but corporate and public, as 68:24-27 makes clear. A grand liturgical procession is taking place, and at the center of the procession is God, the reigning king. With singers in the front and musicians in the rear, God is being escorted to his throne in his royal sanctuary. Celebration of God's reign explains why a thread of praise runs through the entire psalm: "Sing praises to God and to his name!" (68:4), "Praise the Lord; praise God our savior!" (68:19), "Praise God, all you people of Israel" (68:26), "Sing to God, you kingdoms of the earth" (68:32), "Praise be to God!" (68:35).

The reign of God is rooted in the character of God. The characteristic of God that occupies center stage in this celebration is his power: "Summon your might. . . . Display your power" (68:28), "his mighty voice thundering from the sky" (68:33), "Tell everyone about God's power . . . his strength is mighty in the heavens" (68:34), "The God of Israel gives power and strength to his people" (68:35).

God's power has been displayed in the past in a series of historical events through which his reign was established. The initial event was the exodus from Egypt, followed by the march through the wilderness. This procession through the wilderness culminated in the conquest of the Promised Land (68:10-14) and the enthronement of God in his royal sanctuary (68:17-18). Psalm 68 was perhaps used during a liturgical reenactment of this establishment of God's reign, the original procession being replicated in the liturgical procession (cf. 68:17 and 68:24).

The reign of God was not only established in the past, but it has implications for subsequent generations. Also running through the psalm is the thread of God blasting his enemies and blessing his people: "Rise up, O God, and scatter your enemies. . . . But let the godly rejoice" (68:1, 3), God "sets the [righteous] prisoners free and gives them joy. But he makes the rebellious live in a sun-scorched land" (68:6).

This dual theme provides support for the proposal of numerous scholars that Psalm 68 was originally used in the context of the autumnal Festival of Shelters. This feast was celebrated at the transition between the dry season and the rainy season, the transition between the end of one agricultural year's harvest and the beginning of another's plowing and planting. This meteorological context would explain the references to the Lord as "him who rides the clouds" (68:4) and "the one who rides across the ancient heavens" (68:33). The former expression is clearly a polemic against Baal, who was called in Ugaritic *rkb 'rpt* (Rider of the Clouds) in his role as provider of rain and the resultant fertility and prosperity.[2] It was not Baal, however, but the God of Israel who sent abundant rain to refresh the weary Promised Land so that his people might enjoy a bountiful harvest (68:9-10). During the Festival of Shelters, prayers would have been offered for the coming of the rains that were absolutely crucial for life in the land, and prayers would have been offered for the elimination of all hostile forces that could threaten prosperity in any way.

So Psalm 68 is eschatological in the sense that it calls us, as it called the original users of the psalm, to celebrate the reign of God in the face of evidence to the contrary. Yes, God reigns. Yes, the enemies have already been scattered. And yes, there are enemies that have not yet been scattered. As we live in this tension between what is already our experience of God's reign and what is not yet our experience, we need at least one thing: strength—the strength of God. And it is this strength displayed for us in the psalm that is also and finally promised to us in the psalm: "The God of Israel gives power and strength to his people" (68:35). He gives us power to face all the kinds of opposition we encounter in life. He gives us power to produce an "abundant harvest" in life. He gives us power to praise him as the source of our life. He gives us power to pray for our enemies that all of the "kingdoms of the earth" might one day join in the singing of the praises of the God who reigns (see Pss 65–67).

If the ancient people of God could live with this strength, how much more can we. For the ascension of the king to his throne in ancient times, whether in history or liturgy, was only a foreshadowing of the ultimate enthronement of the divine king in the person of the Lord Jesus Christ. Paul applies 68:18 to Christ in Ephesians 4:8, and then goes on to explain that this ascension of Christ was to the end "that he might fill the entire universe with himself" (Eph 4:10). Paul understood the main message of Psalm 68 and proclaimed that this message is embodied in the Lord Jesus Christ. The enthroned Christ gives us all that we need, that through us "he might fill the entire universe with himself" as all the "kingdoms of the earth" bring their tribute to the king who reigns.

ENDNOTES

1. "Psalm 68 is generally known as the most difficult of the psalms to interpret" (McCann 1996:944). "The difficulties of interpreting Psalm 68 are almost legendary" (Tate 1990:170). "There is hardly another song in the Psalter which in its corrupt text and its lack of coherence precipitates such serious problems for the interpreter as Psalm 68" (Kraus 1989:47).
2. For brief discussions see VanGemeren 1991:445 and Tate 1990:163, 176.

◆ AA. Psalm 69

For the choir director: A psalm of David, to be sung to the tune "Lilies."

1 Save me, O God,
for the floodwaters are up to
my neck.
2 Deeper and deeper I sink into
the mire;
I can't find a foothold.
I am in deep water,
and the floods overwhelm me.
3 I am exhausted from crying for help;
my throat is parched.

My eyes are swollen with weeping,
waiting for my God to help me.
4 Those who hate me without cause
outnumber the hairs on my head.
Many enemies try to destroy me
with lies,
demanding that I give back what
I didn't steal.

5 O God, you know how foolish I am;
my sins cannot be hidden from you.
6 Don't let those who trust in you be
ashamed because of me,
O Sovereign LORD of Heaven's
Armies.
Don't let me cause them to be
humiliated,
O God of Israel.
7 For I endure insults for your sake;
humiliation is written all over my
face.
8 Even my own brothers pretend they
don't know me;
they treat me like a stranger.

9 Passion for your house has consumed
me,
and the insults of those who insult
you have fallen on me.
10 When I weep and fast,
they scoff at me.
11 When I dress in burlap to show sorrow,
they make fun of me.
12 I am the favorite topic of town gossip,
and all the drunks sing about me.

13 But I keep praying to you, LORD,
hoping this time you will show me
favor.
In your unfailing love, O God,
answer my prayer with your sure
salvation.
14 Rescue me from the mud;
don't let me sink any deeper!
Save me from those who hate me,
and pull me from these deep waters.
15 Don't let the floods overwhelm me,
or the deep waters swallow me,
or the pit of death devour me.

16 Answer my prayers, O LORD,
for your unfailing love is wonderful.
Take care of me,
for your mercy is so plentiful.
17 Don't hide from your servant;
answer me quickly, for I am in
deep trouble!
18 Come and redeem me;
free me from my enemies.

19 You know of my shame, scorn, and
disgrace.
You see all that my enemies are
doing.
20 Their insults have broken my heart,
and I am in despair.
If only one person would show
some pity;
if only one would turn and
comfort me.
21 But instead, they give me poison*
for food;
they offer me sour wine for my
thirst.

22 Let the bountiful table set before
them become a snare
and their prosperity become a trap.*
23 Let their eyes go blind so they
cannot see,
and make their bodies shake
continually.*
24 Pour out your fury on them;
consume them with your burning
anger.
25 Let their homes become desolate
and their tents be deserted.
26 To the one you have punished, they
add insult to injury;
they add to the pain of those you
have hurt.
27 Pile their sins up high,
and don't let them go free.
28 Erase their names from the Book
of Life;
don't let them be counted among
the righteous.

29 I am suffering and in pain.
Rescue me, O God, by your saving
power.

30 Then I will praise God's name with
singing,

and I will honor him with
thanksgiving.
31 For this will please the LORD more than
sacrificing cattle,
more than presenting a bull with its
horns and hooves.
32 The humble will see their God at work
and be glad.
Let all who seek God's help be
encouraged.
33 For the LORD hears the cries of the
needy;
he does not despise his imprisoned
people.

34 Praise him, O heaven and earth,
the seas and all that move in them.
35 For God will save Jerusalem*
and rebuild the towns of Judah.
His people will live there
and settle in their own land.
36 The descendants of those who obey
him will inherit the land,
and those who love him will live
there in safety.

69:21 Or *gall.* **69:22** Greek version reads *Let their bountiful table set before them become a snare, / a trap that makes them think all is well. / Let their blessings cause them to stumble, / and let them get what they deserve.* Compare Rom 11:9. **69:23** Greek version reads *and let their backs be bent forever.* Compare Rom 11:10. **69:35** Hebrew *Zion.*

NOTES

69:6 *be ashamed . . . be humiliated.* The word *bosh* [TH954, ZH1017] is a synonym of the verb in the next colon (*kalam* [TH3637, ZH4007]), which also means "ashamed" or "disgraced."

69:20 *I am in despair.* The word *wa'anushah* is difficult. It appears to be a Waw-relative imperfect from the root *nush* [TH5136, ZH5683], which occurs only here and may mean "be sick" (see Zorell 1963:506; BDB 633).

69:26 *add to.* The word *'el . . . yesapperu* [TH413/5608, ZH448/6218] means "proclaim" (see note at 2:7). The general sense of *sipper 'el* is probably something like "talk about" rather than "add to." Since they would "talk about the pain of those you have hurt" in a negative way, "scoff" may be the particular sense in context.

69:32 *will see.* The verb is a rhetorical perfect for action that is so certain to take place in the future that it can be spoken of as already accomplished in the past (Joüon and Muraoka 1991:§112h; Waltke and O'Connor 1990:§30.5.1e).

COMMENTARY

Psalm 69 is the remarkable cry of a soul that has been in deep distress for a long time. The nature of the distress is not clear, though it is clear that the distress entails severe personal disgrace that has the potential of bringing disgrace on the larger community. At the same time, Psalm 69 is the remarkable cry of a soul that trusts in God to bring salvation for the benefit of the psalmist and the larger community and for the praise of God's own name.

The Floods Overwhelm Me (69:1-4). The plea of the psalmist is simple: "Save me, O God." The reason is deep: "The floodwaters are up to my neck." The intensity of the distress is communicated through the piling up of related images: "Deeper and deeper I sink into the mire. . . . I am in deep water . . . the floods overwhelm me." The protracted nature of the distress is equally clear: "I am exhausted from crying for help. . . . My eyes are swollen with weeping, waiting for my God to help me." The complexity of the distress arises from the presence of enemies who gratuitously add insult to injury through their vicious attacks on the psalmist. In these verses the cries of our own souls come to expression when we experience deep distress, the pain of which is compounded by misguided people, seeking our destruction rather than our restoration.

God Knows My Humiliation (69:5-12). In such overwhelming situations, we can take refuge in the truth that God knows what is going on in our lives. From this strophe, it is clear that God knows several things. First, God knows our sin. Sin may have been at the source of the psalmist's distress, though there is no confession or request for forgiveness. Even if sin was involved, this gave the opponents no just ground for their ill treatment of the psalmist. Sin, moreover, need never inhibit us from coming to God for deliverance from distress, for with God repentence always brings forgiveness.

Second, God knows our pain. We do not know if the psalmist was in physical pain, but his emotional pain is written all over the text, just as his humiliation was written all over his face. The shame and disgrace referred to may have been rooted in some inappropriate action on the part of the psalmist, but it was certainly exacerbated by the mistreatment he experienced at the hands of his foes, with the result that he became the target of public ridicule. Even his own family ostracized him, leaving him mistreated, misunderstood, and isolated, pains known by God.

Third, God knows our hearts. Even in such deep distress, the psalmist had a heart remarkably devoted to God. He was enduring the shame for God's sake. Heartfelt passion for God burned within. He was willing to bear the insults of those who were actually insulting God himself. While this was truly David's experience, it was ultimately the experience of the Lord Jesus Christ, who burned with passion for the house of God (see John 2:17, where John quotes Ps 69:9) and who bore the insults of those who insulted God (Rom 15:3). As it was Christ's experience, we should not be surprised if at times it is our experience as well.

The fact that God knows is the ground of petitions in this strophe. Here the psalmist prays that those who trust in God not be drawn into the humiliation he has been experiencing. The fact that God knows is also the ground of the petitions offered in the following strophe.

Don't Let the Floods Overwhelm Me (69:13-18). In spite of the depths of distress and the length of the trial, the psalmist kept right on praying, hoping that God would at any moment show favor by ending the ordeal. The psalmist could keep on looking for an answer to his prayers because he knew that God is characterized by wonderfully unfailing love and mercy. The petitions match the description of distress in 69:1-2, reinvoking the images of mud, sinking, deep waters, and overwhelming floods. Now, however, distress is not described, but deliverance from distress is desperately sought. This matching of language in description and petition teaches us the value of being honest in our prayers to God. Honestly telling God just how miserable our situation is facilitates our being specific as to just what we desire him to do for us.

God Knows My Humiliation (69:19-28). The psalmist, still feeling the pain of his problem, again takes recourse to the truth that God knows the depths of his inner turmoil. Here he lays bare another portrait of his heart. This time it is not a heart that is burning with passion for the house of God but one that is broken and in despair. The isolation he feels is acute, as he cannot find anyone to bring him comfort and consolation. On the contrary, when he expects food, he gets poison. When he expects a cup of cold water, he gets bitter vinegar. The only comfort he can lay hold of is his own knowledge that God knows.

The fact that God knows provides the grounds for a stinging imprecation against those who are mistreating him. As they have fed him poison and vinegar, so may their table bring about their own ruin. As his eyes have been swollen with weeping, so may their eyes no longer see. As he has been ostracized by his own family, so may their homes be desolate.[1] May they experience the full fury of God's wrath even to the point of having their names removed from the Book of Life. It is a powerful experience to walk in the shoes of this psalmist and an even more powerful experience to live out the New Testament teaching on praying for those who cause such deep problems and pain (Matt 5:44), extending grace in place of justice (Rom 12:12-18), and trusting that in the end mercy will triumph over judgment (Jas 2:13). Jesus demonstrated for us the New Testament perspective when he said, "Father, forgive them, for they don't know what they are doing" (Luke 23:34).

Rescue Me for Your Praise (69:29–36). The psalm concludes with a final acknowledgment of personal pain and a plea to be rescued. Salvation will result not only in benefit to the psalmist, but also in praise to God. This praise will arise from the psalmist himself as he vows to sing and give thanks to God, no doubt in the public arena of the Temple. As he was disgraced publicly, so he will praise God publicly. As God has been insulted by the opposition, so God will be praised by the opposed. Others, too, will see and join in the praise. These are the ones who trust in God (69:6), concerning whom the psalmist already expressed concern. Instead of being drawn into disgrace, they will be drawn into the chorus of joyful praise.

This praise will also be cosmic in scope, for the heavens, earth, and seas will join the chorus. This cosmic chorus will be appropriate, given the nationwide experience of salvation. As David had prayed in the beginning for personal salvation, so here he is confident that salvation will come to the whole of Jerusalem and in fact spread throughout out the land.

ENDNOTES

1. See Acts 1:20, which cites Ps 69:25, for an application to Judas Iscariot, who betrayed Jesus.

◆ BB. Psalm 70

For the choir director: A psalm of David, asking God to remember him.

[1] Please, God, rescue me!
Come quickly, LORD, and help me.
[2] May those who try to kill me
be humiliated and put to shame.
May those who take delight in my trouble
be turned back in disgrace.
[3] Let them be horrified by their shame,
for they said, "Aha! We've got him now!"
[4] But may all who search for you
be filled with joy and gladness in you.
May those who love your salvation

repeatedly shout, "God is great!"
5 But as for me, I am poor and
needy;
please hurry to my aid, O God.
You are my helper and my savior;
O LORD, do not delay.

NOTES

70:1 ***rescue.*** This same word (*natsal* [TH5337, ZH5911]) is used twice in 69:14 [15], where it is translated "rescue" and "pull me [out]."

70:2 ***be humiliated.*** This same word (*bosh* [TH954, ZH1017]) is used in 69:6 [7], where it is translated "be ashamed."

disgrace. This same word (*kalam* [TH3637, ZH4007]) is used in 69:6 [7], where it is translated "be humiliated."

70:3 ***shame.*** This same noun (*bosheth* [TH1322, ZH1425]) is used in 69:19 [20], where it is translated "scorn."

70:4 ***gladness.*** This same verb (*samakh* [TH8055, ZH8523]) is used in 69:32 [33] ("be glad").

those who love your salvation. This is the same group as "those who love him" in 69:36 [37]. "Your salvation" (*yeshu'atheka* [TH3444, ZH3802]) is referred to in 69:29 [30], where it is translated "your saving power."

shout. This verb (*'amar* [TH559, ZH606]) is used in 70:3 [4] for the destructive speech of the enemy, whereas it is used here for the God-honoring speech of the faithful.

God is great. The Piel of this verb (*gadal* [TH1431, ZH1540]) is used with God as the object in 69:30 [31], where it is translated "honor."

70:5 ***I am poor.*** This is the same expression (*wa'ani 'ani* [TH589/6041, ZH638/6714]) that is used in 69:29 [30], where it is translated "I am suffering."

needy. The "needy" are those whose cries the Lord hears in 69:33 [34].

hurry. This same verb (*khush* [TH2363, ZH2590]) is translated "Come quickly" in 70:1 [2].

helper. This word is from the same root (*'azar* [TH5826, ZH6468]) as the word translated "help me" (*'ezrathi* [TH5833, ZH6476]) in 70:1 [2]). Several mss have *'ezrathi* here in 70:5 [6], as does 40:17 [18]. (Psalm 40:13-17 [14-18] is a parallel text to Ps 70.)

COMMENTARY

Psalm 70 is a virtual duplicate of 40:13-17. It is debated as to which is the original version, but the literary integrity of Psalm 70 tips the scale in favor of it being the original (Mays 1994:233). A chiastic structure is evident in Psalm 70. The first and last strophes (70:1 and 70:5) form an *inclusio,* as they share a focus on the psalmist ("rescue me" and "I am poor and needy") and ask the Lord[1] to act quickly as the psalmist's help. The central two strophes (70:2-3 and 70:4) are prayers, one relating to those who "search for" the psalmist's harm and the other relating to those who "search for" the Lord.

Psalm 70 is highly integrated into its current literary context. Some have argued that Psalm 70 is part of Psalm 71 (see commentary on Ps 71), and Psalm 70 is clearly a sequel to Psalm 69. Psalms 69 and 70 share several key terms (see notes).

Come Quickly, Lord (70:1). The drawn-out distress of Psalm 69 has seemingly reached a crisis point. The rescue sought for in 69:14 is now sought for quickly. There are times in our lives when we need God not simply to intervene but to intervene quickly. Psalm 70 is a prayer for just such an occasion, as is clear from the opening and closing lines: "Come quickly" and "do not delay."

May Those Who Seek Me Be Humiliated (70:2-3). In 69:6 and 19, David experienced humiliation, shame, and disgrace at the hands of others. Here he prays that they would reap what they have sown by being humiliated, put to shame, and turned back in disgrace for having sought to destroy him.

May Those Who Seek You Be Joyful (70:4). By way of contrast, David prays that those who search for God might experience gladness just as he prayed for those who search for God in 69:6-7 to be glad (69:32). He also prays that they would join him in celebrating the greatness of God, as they experience his salvation (see note on 70:4).

Do Not Delay, Lord (70:5). At the close of Psalm 70 David finds himself in the same situation as he was in 69:29, "I am poor and in pain/needy." So he pleads with God, as in the first strophe, to hurry to be his helper without delay.

In closing, it should be noted that the similarity between 70:3 and Mark 15:29 has led the church to use Psalm 70 in commemoration of Jesus' sufferings on the cross. God the Father did delay in rescuing his Son during the crisis of the cross, but only for a short while. Since Jesus' prayer to be rescued was heard on the Day of Resurrection, we can be confident that ours will be also. From this psalm we also learn that it is appropriate to ask God to act quickly on our behalf when circumstances call for it. We may become distressed that our prayer may go unanswered for a time, but in those times the only course of action is to continue in prayer, as the psalmist did (see Ps 71).

ENDNOTES

1. The only two occurrences of the divine name in Ps 70 are in the first and last lines.

◆ CC. Psalm 71

1 O LORD, I have come to you for
protection;
don't let me be disgraced.
2 Save me and rescue me,
for you do what is right.
Turn your ear to listen to me,
and set me free.
3 Be my rock of safety
where I can always hide.
Give the order to save me,
for you are my rock and my
fortress.
4 My God, rescue me from the power
of the wicked,
from the clutches of cruel
oppressors.
5 O Lord, you alone are my hope.
I've trusted you, O LORD, from
childhood.
6 Yes, you have been with me from
birth;
from my mother's womb you have
cared for me.
No wonder I am always praising
you!

7 My life is an example to many,
because you have been my strength
and protection.
8 That is why I can never stop praising
you;
I declare your glory all day long.
9 And now, in my old age, don't set
me aside.

Don't abandon me when my
strength is failing.
10 For my enemies are whispering
against me.
They are plotting together to kill
me.
11 They say, "God has abandoned him.
Let's go and get him,
for no one will help him now."

12 O God, don't stay away.
My God, please hurry to help me.
13 Bring disgrace and destruction on
my accusers.
Humiliate and shame those who
want to harm me.
14 But I will keep on hoping for your
help;
I will praise you more and more.
15 I will tell everyone about your
righteousness.
All day long I will proclaim your
saving power,
though I am not skilled with words.*
16 I will praise your mighty deeds,
O Sovereign LORD.
I will tell everyone that you alone
are just.

17 O God, you have taught me from my
earliest childhood,
and I constantly tell others about
the wonderful things you do.
18 Now that I am old and gray,
do not abandon me, O God.
Let me proclaim your power to this
new generation,
your mighty miracles to all who
come after me.

19 Your righteousness, O God, reaches
to the highest heavens.
You have done such wonderful
things.
Who can compare with you, O God?
20 You have allowed me to suffer much
hardship,
but you will restore me to life
again
and lift me up from the depths of
the earth.
21 You will restore me to even greater
honor
and comfort me once again.

22 Then I will praise you with music on
the harp,
because you are faithful to your
promises, O my God.
I will sing praises to you with a lyre,
O Holy One of Israel.
23 I will shout for joy and sing your
praises,
for you have ransomed me.
24 I will tell about your righteous deeds
all day long,
for everyone who tried to hurt me
has been shamed and humiliated.

71:15 Or *though I cannot count it.*

NOTES

71:1 ***disgraced.*** The theme of "disgrace/shame" (*bosh* [TH954, ZH1017]) occurs in 71:13, 24, as it does in 70:2 [3].

71:2 ***rescue me.*** This same verb (Hiphil of *natsal* [TH5337, ZH5911]) occurs in 71:11, where the adversaries say there is no one to rescue the psalmist.

right. The word *tsidqatheka* [TH6662, ZH7404] (your righteousness) also occurs in 71:15, 16, 19, and 24, and is a major theme in the psalm (see commentary).

71:4 ***cruel.*** The word *me'awwel* [TH5765, ZH6401] is better translated "unjust" (HALOT 2.797).

71:6 ***you have been with me from birth.*** Lit., "I have leaned on you since birth." The picture is that of total dependence.

cared for me. The word *gozi* [TH1491, ZH1602] (my severer) is obscure. The context seems to require something like "care" or "sustain." See Tate 1990:209 for a discussion of proposed emendations, none of which are satisfying.

71:7 ***my strength and protection.*** The word *makhasi-'oz* [TH4268/5797, ZH4726/6437] is an example of the relatively rare interposition of a pronoun suffix within a construct state (Joüon and Muraoka 1991:§129a n. 4). The sense is "my strong protection."

71:8 ***all day long.*** The phrase *kol-hayyom* [TH3605/3117, ZH3972/3427] (all day long) also occurs in 71:15, 24.

71:12 ***hurry to help me.*** This same Hebrew phrase is translated "Come quickly . . . and help me" in 70:1 [2].

71:24 ***tell.*** The word *hagah* [TH1897, ZH2047] means "meditate" (see 1:2).

COMMENTARY

The apostle Paul once said, "Our hearts ache, but we always have joy" (2 Cor 6:10). Sorrow and joy are at times the simultaneous experience of the believer. Psalm 71 is a psalm of such sorrow and joy. As indicated by the opening line, Psalm 71 is a lament, but it "is a kind of confident, even jubilant, lament" (Tate 1990:211). Even as the psalmist pleads for deliverance, he expresses great praise for what God has done and great hope for what God will do. Three themes dominate this psalm: the plea that God not abandon the psalmist, faith in God's righteousness, and hopeful praise.

Except for Psalm 43, Psalm 71 is the only psalm in Book 2 that has no title. The psalm is written from the viewpoint of one who has attained a maturity that only comes through years of walking with God. Given the close connection of Psalm 71 with 70 (a psalm of David), and given the Solomonic authorship of Psalm 72, it is possible to read Psalm 71 as a psalm written by David in his later years.

Don't Abandon Me. Abandonment can be a terrifying experience. What does a son who has been abandoned by his father feel? How painful is it for an elderly mother to be abandoned by her children—left alone in a nursing home? The psalmist, now old and gray, pleads that he not be abandoned. But his concern is that he not be abandoned by God: "Don't set me aside. . . . Don't abandon me" (71:9), "Don't stay away" (71:12), "Do not abandon me, O God" (71:18). The feeling that God might perhaps abandon him arose quite naturally from the antagonism the psalmist had experienced at the hands of his adversaries, who said, "God has abandoned him. Let's go and get him, for no one will help him now" (71:11).

Here abandonment would have been experienced in the form of disgrace in the eyes of the community. So the opening plea is that God not let the psalmist be disgraced but that God be his refuge, "my rock of safety, where I can always hide" (71:3). Rather than abandonment, the psalmist sought God as his source of safety from enemy attack. The characteristic of God in which the psalmist sought refuge was God's righteousness.

I Trust in Your Righteousness. The righteousness of God is referred to five times in this psalm. The psalmist pleads for deliverance based on God's righteousness (v. 2). He pledges to tell others about God's righteousness (vv. 15-16). He proclaims that God's righteousness reaches to the highest heavens (v. 19). And he promises to meditate on God's righteousness all day long (v. 24). Righteousness here refers to God's action in putting things in right order that are not currently in right order (Tate 1990:208). The precise nature of his distress eludes us, as is often the case in the psalms. But we know that he was experiencing some degree of disgrace with the prospect of more disgrace coming in the future. Such disgrace was unjust. It was not right. He did not deserve to be shamed. So he trusted that God would put things right and that he would not be shamed. On the contrary, he prayed that those who sought his shame might themselves be shamed and disgraced; this prayer occurs at the midpoint and in the final line, as well as in the previous psalm (70:2).

Trust in God's righteousness was not a new experience for the psalmist, however. The psalmist had been trusting in God since childhood—no, even further back: from the womb (71:5-6, 17)! Years of trust enabled the psalmist to experience at this time in his life "a serenity often denied to the young" (Tate 1990:211), a serenity of faith that explains why this lament contains such a sustained note of hope and praise.

You Are My Hope and Praise. Years of life's experiences had taught the psalmist to hope in God alone. A deep pattern of hoping in God had developed within the psalmist, so now in his later years continual hoping in God came rather naturally to him. The twin of such hope was praise: "But I will keep on hoping for your help; I will praise you more and more" (71:14). God was not only the psalmist's hope, but he was also his praise. In fact, because God was the source of such hope the psalmist could not stop praising God, not even in the middle of a time of unjust adversity.

The nature of praise comes out rather clearly in this psalm. In 71:14 the psalmist says he will praise God, and the next several verses contain examples of that praise. Praise is proclaiming who God is and what he has done (Barker 1995:218 and Miller 1986:70). So the psalmist is going to tell people about God's righteousness and saving power, about how much God has done for him, and the nature of God's mighty deeds, that God alone is just and good, and that he is characterized by power and the working of mighty miracles. Who God is and what he has done are incomparable!

There are times when God allows us "to suffer much hardship." The Hebrew text is quite emphatic at this point, as it could be woodenly translated, "You have caused me to see hard times—many and troublesome." Yet such times can be filled with hope: "You will restore me to life again and lift me up from the depths of the earth" (71:20). This hope is ultimately grounded in the experience of our Lord Jesus Christ, who experienced ultimate hardship when he bore our sins and God's just wrath on the cross, and who experienced ultimate restoration when God raised him from the dead. Through faith in him, we can be confident during hard times that God "will restore [us] to even greater honor and comfort [us] once again" (71:21). So times of hardship can also be times of praise—praise joyfully sung to the music of harp and lyre—because God is faithful.

◆ DD. Psalm 72

A psalm of Solomon.

[1]Give your love of justice to the king,
O God,
and righteousness to the king's son.
[2]Help him judge your people in the
right way;
let the poor always be treated fairly.
[3]May the mountains yield prosperity
for all,
and may the hills be fruitful.
[4]Help him to defend the poor,

to rescue the children of the needy,
and to crush their oppressors.
5 May they fear you* as long as the sun shines,
as long as the moon remains in the sky.
Yes, forever!

6 May the king's rule be refreshing like spring rain on freshly cut grass,
like the showers that water the earth.
7 May all the godly flourish during his reign.
May there be abundant prosperity until the moon is no more.
8 May he reign from sea to sea,
and from the Euphrates River* to the ends of the earth.
9 Desert nomads will bow before him;
his enemies will fall before him in the dust.
10 The western kings of Tarshish and other distant lands
will bring him tribute.
The eastern kings of Sheba and Seba
will bring him gifts.
11 All kings will bow before him,
and all nations will serve him.

12 He will rescue the poor when they cry to him;
he will help the oppressed, who have no one to defend them.
13 He feels pity for the weak and the needy,
and he will rescue them.
14 He will redeem them from oppression and violence,
for their lives are precious to him.

15 Long live the king!
May the gold of Sheba be given to him.
May the people always pray for him
and bless him all day long.
16 May there be abundant grain throughout the land,
flourishing even on the hilltops.
May the fruit trees flourish like the trees of Lebanon,
and may the people thrive like grass in a field.
17 May the king's name endure forever;
may it continue as long as the sun shines.
May all nations be blessed through him
and bring him praise.

18 Praise the LORD God, the God of Israel,
who alone does such wonderful things.
19 Praise his glorious name forever!
Let the whole earth be filled with his glory.
Amen and amen!

20 (This ends the prayers of David son of Jesse.)

72:5 Greek version reads *May they endure.* **72:8** Hebrew *the river.*

NOTES

72:3 ***prosperity.*** The word *shalom* [TH7965, ZH8934] also occurs in 72:7 and 73:3.

for all. Lit., "for the people."

72:5 ***sun . . . moon.*** For the sun and moon in an image of longevity, see 89:36-37.

72:7 ***prosperity.*** The word is *shalom* [TH7965, ZH8934] as in 72:3.

72:19 ***Praise. . . . Amen and amen!*** Each boundary between the books of the Psalter is marked with a similar call to praise and a double "amen" (see 41:13 and 89:52).

72:20 ***This ends the prayers of David son of Jesse.*** Given this note, we might not expect to read any other psalms of David after Ps 72, but see Ps 101, 103, etc. How can we explain the psalms of David after Ps 72? Individual psalms were collected in the book of Psalms over a long period of time. Though the details are not clear, we do know that psalms were gathered into collections that were themselves later incorporated into larger collections. Psalm 72 obviously brought one of these earlier collections to a close, and the editorial note in 72:20 was kept with the psalm when this collection was brought together with other psalms.

COMMENTARY

Psalm 72 is a prayer for the king that brings Book 2 of the Psalter to a close. It is a prayer written for and probably by Solomon to be used at his coronation. It would, no doubt, have been used for the coronation of other Davidic kings, as well as on other royal occasions.

Among other functions, Psalm 72 shows that the covenant made with David has been effectively transferred to Solomon. This is accomplished by the imagery that Psalm 72 shares with Psalms 1 and 2. Whereas David would have been the original joyous person (in view in Ps 1) and also the anointed king (in Ps 2), Solomon is now that person and king in Psalm 72. The horticultural prosperity of Psalm 72 immediately evokes the picture of the tree planted along the riverbank that bears fruit without fail (Ps 1). The submission of the kings of the nations to God's king in Psalm 72 immediately brings to mind the promise in Psalm 2 that God's anointed would inherit the nations whose kings would serve him. Solomon is the new David.

Psalm 72 is comprised of five strophes (72:1-7, 8-11, 12-14, 15-17, 18-19) and a postscript (72:20). This prayer focuses on four aspects of the king's reign.

Prayer for a Just and Righteous Reign. Justice and righteousness are the foundation of godly governing. We know this to be true because justice and righteousness are the foundation of God's own reign (89:14; 97:2). So the foundational request for the Davidic king is that his reign be just and righteous. Such justice and righteousness were not inherent characteristics of the Davidic kings, as is shown by the history of the kings, and so the prayer is that God, who is in himself just and righteous, would grant these characteristics to David's descendants.

The primary way in which the king's justice and righteousness were to be manifest was in his concern for the poor, the needy, the oppressed, the defenseless, and the weak (72:2, 4, 12, 13, 14; see also 41:1). This concern was not to be motivated by a heartless desire to conform to a law but by great compassion: The true king was to feel deeply for the weak (72:13), whose lives were precious to him (72:14). In so doing he would be like God (see, for example, 68:5 and Isa 41:17).

Prayer for a Prosperous Reign. The just and righteous reign of a king would result in *shalom* [TH7965, ZH8934] (72:3, 7). This *shalom* is complete well-being for the whole cosmos. In the agriculturally based world of the Old Testament, cosmic well-being comes to expression in terms of mountains and hills producing abundant crops of grain, fields being covered with grass for the flocks, and fruit trees flourishing (72:3, 16). Since rain is that without which such bounty was impossible in Israel, the just and righteous reign of the king is likened to the rain that waters the earth (72:6). This rain and the resultant *shalom* would be enjoyed by the people (72:3). The people in view are first of all Israel. But then the peoples of the nations come immediately into view, since the prayer is for a worldwide reign.

Prayer for a Worldwide Reign. An ancient way of saying "worldwide" is found in 72:8: "May he reign from sea to sea [from the Persian Gulf in the east to the Mediterranean in the west] and from the Euphrates River [in the north] to the ends of the earth [in the south]." The worldwide scope of this reign is further elaborated in 72:9-10 by reference to the desert nomads (in the east) and those living on the islands (in the west). The mention of distant peoples of Sheba and Seba[1] adds specific color to the description of the worldwide reign of the just and righteous king (72:10). The climax is reached in 72:11, where we are told that "all nations" will serve this king! Yes, the promise made to Abraham, that all the families of the earth would be blessed through him (Gen 12:3), will be fulfilled through the Davidic king (72:17).

Prayer for a Long Reign. Given the worldwide prosperity that results from the just and righteous reign of the king, it is no wonder that the prayer includes the request for a long reign: "Long live the king!" (72:15). Since the people are instructed to call upon God on behalf of the king, it is clear that for the king to reign in justice and righteousness he will need divine blessing.

Prayer for a Dependent Reign. That the human king was dependent on the divine king is clear in several ways, two of which have already been seen: (1) The prayer starts with a request that God give justice and righteousness to the king, and (2) the people are to pray to God for the king. A third consideration is that the whole psalm itself is a prayer to God for the king. Why pray to God for the king? Because the king is totally dependent on God. A fourth factor is that the psalm ends in doxology that is directed to God. Praise is appropriately directed to the human king (72:15, 17), but the ultimate praise is directed to the ultimate source of the king's just and righteous reign, "the LORD God, the God of Israel, who alone does such wonderful things" (72:18). His glory will fill the whole earth (72:19)!

This prayer paints a glorious picture of what the ideal king would look like. But even Solomon in all his glory fell far short of the ideal. This psalm would have been read in the postexilic community as a prayer for the coming of the anointed king, the Messiah. The psalm drove the people to look into the future, when the justice and righteousness of God would be embodied in a human king. But only a king who was fully divine as well as fully human could live up to the ideal. Jesus came as this king. Jesus was filled with the justice and righteousness of God. Jesus treated the poor fairly, rescued the children of the needy, and had pity on the weak; they were all precious to him (Matt 11:4-6). Jesus came to bring *shalom* (Luke 2:14; John 14:27). These blessings for the nations did not come, however, with "swords loud clashing" but with "deeds of love and kindness."

This psalm prompts us to look forward to the day when King Jesus will come again. On that day "the mountains [will] yield prosperity for all, and . . . the hills [will] be fruitful. . . . The king's rule [will] be refreshing like spring rain . . . like the showers that water the earth. . . . He [will] reign from sea to sea. . . . All nations will serve him. . . . All nations [will] be blessed through him and bring him praise." Until that day, we pray that God would give us his justice and righteousness, and that we might do the will of God in bringing blessing to those who are in need and cannot do for themselves what God can do for them through us.

ENDNOTES

1. Sheba is an area in the south Arabian peninsula (see Isa 60:6; Jer 6:20; Ezek 27:22-25), and Seba may refer to a proximate locale (see Gen 10:7; Isa 43:3; 45:14; Joel 3:8).

◆ III. Book Three: Psalms 73–89

A. Psalm 73

A psalm of Asaph.

1 Truly God is good to Israel,
to those whose hearts are pure.
2 But as for me, I almost lost my footing.
My feet were slipping, and I was almost gone.
3 For I envied the proud
when I saw them prosper despite their wickedness.
4 They seem to live such painless lives;
their bodies are so healthy and strong.
5 They don't have troubles like other people;
they're not plagued with problems like everyone else.
6 They wear pride like a jeweled necklace
and clothe themselves with cruelty.
7 These fat cats have everything
their hearts could ever wish for!
8 They scoff and speak only evil;
in their pride they seek to crush others.
9 They boast against the very heavens,
and their words strut throughout the earth.
10 And so the people are dismayed and confused,
drinking in all their words.
11 "What does God know?" they ask.
"Does the Most High even know what's happening?"
12 Look at these wicked people—
enjoying a life of ease while their riches multiply.

13 Did I keep my heart pure for nothing?
Did I keep myself innocent for no reason?
14 I get nothing but trouble all day long;
every morning brings me pain.
15 If I had really spoken this way to others,
I would have been a traitor to your people.
16 So I tried to understand why the wicked prosper.
But what a difficult task it is!
17 Then I went into your sanctuary, O God,
and I finally understood the destiny of the wicked.
18 Truly, you put them on a slippery path
and send them sliding over the cliff to destruction.
19 In an instant they are destroyed,
completely swept away by terrors.
20 When you arise, O Lord,
you will laugh at their silly ideas
as a person laughs at dreams in the morning.

21 Then I realized that my heart was bitter,
and I was all torn up inside.
22 I was so foolish and ignorant—
I must have seemed like a senseless animal to you.
23 Yet I still belong to you;
you hold my right hand.
24 You guide me with your counsel,
leading me to a glorious destiny.
• 25 Whom have I in heaven but you?
I desire you more than anything on earth.
26 My health may fail, and my spirit may grow weak,
but God remains the strength of my heart;
he is mine forever.

[27] Those who desert him will perish,
for you destroy those who
abandon you.
[28] But as for me, how good it is to be
near God!
I have made the Sovereign LORD
my shelter,
and I will tell everyone about
the wonderful things
you do.

NOTES

73:TITLE ***Asaph.*** Asaph was a Levite, having descended from Gershon, who served as a music director in the Temple (see 1 Chr 6:39; 15:17; 2 Chr 5:12). Psalms 73–83 are "of Asaph."

73:3 ***prosper.*** The word is *shalom* [TH7965, ZH8934], which is also used in 72:3, 7.

73:7 ***These fat cats.*** This verse is extremely difficult. The first colon could be woodenly translated, "Their eye goes out from fat." This is perhaps an ancient idiom or metaphor, the specific meaning of which escapes us. The second colon could be woodenly translated, "Imaginations of the heart cross over." The specific meaning of this colon is equally obscure.

73:13 ***Did I keep my heart pure for nothing?*** By using an interrogative to translate the Hebrew indicative, the NLT weakens somewhat the sense of the Hebrew. The Hebrew starts with the same emphatic particle (*'ak* [TH389, ZH421]) that 73:1 begins with, which is there translated "Truly." In 73:13 the psalmist is making an emphatic statement about what he thought at one grievous stage in his turmoil: "Truly I kept my heart pure for nothing." By the end of the psalm the psalmist has retreated from this perspective on the situation.

73:14 ***trouble.*** The word here translated "trouble" occurs in 73:5, where it is translated "plagued with problems."

73:17 ***sanctuary.*** The word is plural, but a plural used in reference to a singular sanctuary has already been encountered in 43:3 and 46:4 [5].

73:18 ***Truly.*** This is the third use of the emphatic particle *'ak* [TH389, ZH421] (see note at 73:13).

73:21 ***bitter . . . torn up.*** The first colon contains the word *lebab* [TH3824, ZH4222] (heart), while the second contains the word *kilyoth* [TH3629, ZH4000] (kidneys). In other texts, this pair probably indicates a contrast between "thoughts" (*lebab*) and "emotions" (*kilyoth*); see notes at 7:9 and 16:7. "Bitter thoughts" and "pained feelings" could be the sense here.

73:22-23 ***to you.*** The word *'immak* [TH5973/3509.2, ZH6640/3870] could be translated "with you" and occurs two more times in 73:23 and 73:25 (see commentary).

73:25 ***you more than anything.*** This renders the word *'immeka* [TH5973/3509.2, ZH6640/3870]; see previous note.

COMMENTARY

Just the other day, one of my sons asked me why some people have it so easy in life. He asked me this because 73:14 is an apt description of our family's life and his in particular over the past several years: "I get nothing but trouble all day long; every morning brings me pain." We know the agony of saying, "My feet were slipping, and I was almost gone" (73:2).

There are times when life's experiences stretch our faith within microns of breaking. Such a crisis of faith comes to expression in Psalm 73. McCann (1996:968) sets forth accurately the structure of the psalm, based on the threefold use of *'ak* [TH389,

ZH421]) (truly) in 73:1, 13, and 18. Psalm 73:1-12 is an opening stanza that expresses the crisis of faith. The turning point in the crisis is recorded in the middle stanza of 73:13-17, and the resolution of the crisis is found in the final stanza of 73:18-28.

The Reason for the Crisis (73:1-12). The reason for the crisis comes to expression in two strophes: a short strophe that describes the psalmist's plight (73:1-3) and a long strophe that describes the wicked's prosperity (73:4-12).

The psalmist's plight begins with a great affirmation of faith: "Truly God is good to Israel, to those whose hearts are pure." But faith gave way to grave doubt at some point in his experience: "But as for me, I almost lost my footing. My feet were slipping, and I was almost gone." What was the occasion of such a deep crisis of faith? Psalm 73:3 supplies the answer: "For I envied the proud when I saw them prosper despite their wickedness."

But why would the prosperity (*shalom* [TH7965, ZH8934]) of the wicked be the occasion of such deep doubts? Because *shalom* should be the fruit of justice and righteousness, as we have just been taught in 72:1-20, not the result of wickedness! And at a more foundational level in the theology of the Psalter, prosperity was guaranteed to the righteous in 1:3b (with different vocabulary), while being categorically denied to the wicked in that very same psalm (1:4a)![1]

The prosperity of the wicked is detailed for us in 73:4-12. First, they are healthy. They know no pain and their bodies are healthy and strong. Second, they are trouble free. The day-to-day problems that plague most people are unknown to them. Third, they are wealthy. They make money hand over fist, and they wear the finest jewels and clothing. And all of this despite their wickedness! Their wickedness in general is arrogance. This arrogance manifests itself specifically in their cruel treatment of others and in their speech: "They scoff and speak only evil" (73:8), "Their words strut throughout the earth" (73:9), and they even "boast against the very heavens" (73:9), saying with disdain, "What does God know?" and "Does the Most High even know what's happening?" (73:11). In spite of such wickedness, they enjoy "a life of ease" (73:12). This is simply not the way things are supposed to be.

The Turning Point in the Crisis (73:13-17). A change begins with the psalmist's brutal honesty about what he thought and how he felt during the crisis: "Truly it has been for nothing that I kept my heart pure. . . . All I get is trouble all day long" (for rendering, see notes on 73:13-14). Sometimes the doubts of a believer run so deep that we think our faith is in vain. The Bible says that God is good to those who have pure hearts—and we are among the pure in heart, but where is the goodness of God? Sometimes it seems to be just a theological category with no concrete manifestation in our experience. The psalms grant us the permission to bring such brutally honest thoughts in prayer to God. As for the psalmist, so for us—honest articulation of the depths of the crisis can be the turning point in the crisis.

But the psalmist did not remain in this condition. He refused to "talk on in this way" (NRSV), so as not to betray his faith and his community of faith (73:15). Rather, he resolved to find a resolution to the crisis, difficult as that may have been. The resolution came when the psalmist came into the presence of God in the sanctuary and brought the future into the equation.

The Resolution of the Crisis (73:18-28). As the crisis was described in two strophes, one short and one long, so the resolution is described in two strophes, one short and one long. Now, however, the description is reversed: the plight of the wicked (73:18-20) and the prosperity of the righteous (73:21-28).

The plight of the wicked is briefly described in terms of being on a slippery path and being suddenly swept away. While there is an appearance of stability, it is just that—an appearance. In reality, the wicked are in a desperately perilous situation. Their prosperity will prove to be short-lived[2] and as insubstantial as a dream that vanishes upon awakening.

The description of the prosperity of the righteous begins with a confession of just how bitterly painful the crisis had been (73:21) and just how foolish the psalmist had been. Hindsight is always 20/20. In the middle of the crisis, however, our vision is often blurred. The psalmist said that during the crisis he had the sense of an animal "to you" (73:22), i.e., in the sight of God. The marvel of God's unconditional love is that while the psalmist was like an animal, he nonetheless "belong[ed] to you" (73:23)—that is, his hand was in the powerful and loving hand of God himself.

With new clarity brought about by thinking beyond the present, the psalmist became confident that God would lead him to a glorious future, one that stood in sharp contrast with that of the wicked. That future was not yet his experience. His circumstances had not yet changed. His health may have been failing and his life force[3] diminishing, but God was there to give him inner strength. So God himself became the psalmist's supreme desire in heaven and on earth. Though not yet experiencing the glorious future, the psalmist did already experience the ultimate good from which all future goodness would flow, the presence of God: "But as for me, how good it is to be near God!" (73:28). God is good to his people (73:1), so our supreme good is to be near him, whether we are in the green meadows or the dark valley of death (Ps 23).

The psalmist's hope of a "glorious destiny" was no doubt a hope for this life. We, too, must have this hope in the middle of crisis—hope that we will experience a glorious future in this life. Yet we know that this life is characterized to one degree or another by suffering—suffering, however, that does not compare to the glory that will be ours in the resurrection (Rom 8:18). At times, we groan in this life (Rom 8:23), but we groan with our eyes fixed on a future that is guaranteed to be glorious by the resurrection of Jesus Christ from the dead. And like the psalmist, only to a much greater degree, we already experience the ultimate good, for we have the Holy Spirit within us as a foretaste of that future glory (Rom 8:23). So as we groan, we make the "Sovereign LORD [our] shelter" and "tell everyone about the wonderful things" God does (73:28).

ENDNOTES

1. Psalm 37 raises this same problem in a number of verses (see 37:1, 7, 35).
2. Psalm 37 resolves the problem of the prosperity of the wicked along these same lines (see 37:2, 9, 10).
3. For the Hebrew word *leb* [TH3820, ZH4213] (heart) as the vital force of life, see HALOT 2.514.

◆ B. Psalm 74

A psalm of Asaph.*

1 O God, why have you rejected us
so long?
Why is your anger so intense
against the sheep of your own
pasture?
2 Remember that we are the people you
chose long ago,
the tribe you redeemed as your own
special possession!
And remember Jerusalem,* your
home here on earth.
3 Walk through the awful ruins of
the city;
see how the enemy has destroyed
your sanctuary.

4 There your enemies shouted their
victorious battle cries;
there they set up their battle
standards.
5 They swung their axes
like woodcutters in a forest.
6 With axes and picks,
they smashed the carved
paneling.
7 They burned your sanctuary to the
ground.
They defiled the place that bears
your name.
8 Then they thought, "Let's destroy
everything!"
So they burned down all the places
where God was worshiped.

9 We no longer see your miraculous
signs.
All the prophets are gone,
and no one can tell us when it will
end.
10 How long, O God, will you allow our
enemies to insult you?
Will you let them dishonor your
name forever?
11 Why do you hold back your strong
right hand?
Unleash your powerful fist and
destroy them.

12 You, O God, are my king from ages
past,
bringing salvation to the earth.
13 You split the sea by your strength
and smashed the heads of the sea
monsters.
14 You crushed the heads of Leviathan*
and let the desert animals
eat him.
15 You caused the springs and streams
to gush forth,
and you dried up rivers that never
run dry.
16 Both day and night belong to you;
you made the starlight* and
the sun.
17 You set the boundaries of the earth,
and you made both summer and
winter.

18 See how these enemies insult you,
LORD.
A foolish nation has dishonored
your name.
19 Don't let these wild beasts destroy
your turtledoves.
Don't forget your suffering people
forever.

20 Remember your covenant promises,
for the land is full of darkness and
violence!
21 Don't let the downtrodden be
humiliated again.
Instead, let the poor and needy
praise your name.

22 Arise, O God, and defend your cause.
Remember how these fools insult
you all day long.
23 Don't overlook what your enemies
have said
or their growing uproar.

74:TITLE Hebrew *maskil.* This may be a literary or musical term. **74:2** Hebrew *Mount Zion.* **74:14** The identification of Leviathan is disputed, ranging from an earthly creature to a mythical sea monster in ancient literature. **74:16** Or *moon;* Hebrew reads *light.*

NOTES

74:2 ***chose.*** The word *qanah* [TH7069/7069B, ZH7864/7865] means "create" and/or "acquire" here (HALOT 3.1112; see Exod 15:16; Isa 11:11), and the following colon specifies that the creation and acquisition took place by means of redemption.

74:5 ***They swung their axes like woodcutters in a forest.*** The NLT presumes two emendations: (1) *yiwwada'* [TH3045, ZH3359] (let it be known) to *yigde'u* [TH1438, ZH1548] (they chopped) and (2) *mebi'* [TH935, ZH995] (one who brings up) to *mabo'* [TH3996, ZH4427] (entrance). "Woodcutters" renders a word for "axes." The line is difficult in the details, but the general sense is clear enough.

74:18 ***See.*** The word *zekor* [TH2142, ZH2349] was used in 74:2, where it was translated "remember." This second use marks the beginning of the third strophe, which returns us to the mood of the first strophe.

74:20 ***Remember.*** The verb is a different verb than that used in 74:2, 18 and is not a key term in the structure of the psalm.

COMMENTARY

There are times in life when present circumstances offer us no evidence that God is present in—let alone in control of—our situation. Psalm 74 was written for just such a time. Psalm 74 leads us to live eschatologically, to live believing that God reigns "amid circumstances that seem to deny" that reign (McCann 1996:974). In this regard Psalm 74 is a companion psalm to Psalm 73, as both address the problem of the apparent success of the wicked.[1] But whereas Psalm 73 is from the perspective of the individual, Psalm 74 is from the perspective of the community (McCann 1996:972).

Psalm 74 addresses the problem in three strophes. The first (74:1-11) is dominated by the agonizing "why?" The second (74:12-17) affirms that God is king in spite of present evidence to the contrary. And the third (74:18-23) is dominated by petitions that God remember and not forget his people.

Why? (74:1-11). This first strophe is bracketed by the painful "why?" (74:1, 11). The occasion of the "why?" is spelled out in 74:3-8. The city (Jerusalem) lay in ruins. Worse than that, the sanctuary had been destroyed. Enemy troops had gone through the sanctuary, desecrating the Holy Place and smashing everything in sight. As if this were not enough, they then burned the sanctuary to the ground, shouting their victorious battle cries all the while. To add insult to injury, they went throughout the land, destroying every place they could find where God was worshiped. The wicked were thoroughly successful in their campaign against God and his people.

As painful as all that must have been, deeper pain welled up from another source. Why was the holy God doing nothing about this sacrilege? His right hand was certainly powerful enough to eradicate the enemy troops, so why was he holding back? Why this prolonged rejection of his people? After all, they were his people, the sheep of his own pasture. He had acquired them as his special possession by redeeming them from oppression in Egypt. And Jerusalem was the place he himself had chosen as his dwelling place. The prophetic word had always been that the Lord was mighty to save, but now no word was being heard, and there was no evidence that God was at hand to save in this situation. If not for the sake of his special possession, would God not at least act for the honor of his own name?

Though as Christians we have never had this same experience, many of us have had similar experiences—similar in that our lives have been in "awful ruins," and we have been painfully perplexed as to why God was doing nothing about it. What is the best response in such a situation? The first response we are taught here is to bring the painful "why?" to expression. The question is there deep in our hearts. Our pain is as intense as God's anger. We know it. God invites us to express it in prayer. The second response is found in the second strophe.

God Is King (74:12-17). In the face of the perplexity and pain the psalmist cried out, "You, O God, are my king from ages past, bringing salvation to the earth." With no evidence of God's salvation in the present, the psalmist grounded his faith in God's salvation in the distant past. He then described this salvation in mythopoetic imagery (74:13-14)—that is, he took images from the mythology of surrounding cultures and used these images metaphorically to communicate theological truth about the true and living God. The splitting of the sea (*yam* [TH3220, ZH3542]), the sea monsters' heads, and the crushing of the heads of Leviathan allude to the mythological defeat of Yam by Baal (a Canaanite deity) and perhaps to the defeat of Tiamat by Marduk (a Babylonian deity). The confession of faith here, however, is that it is the Lord God of Israel, not Baal or Marduk, who is the true king from ages past (*qedem* [TH6924, ZH7710]; 74:12).

God's kingship is also seen in the order he established at the time of creation. He provided ground water, while at the same time separating the sea from the dry land (74:15; see 104:6-12). He established the order of day and night and the order of the seasons as well. All of this was the work of the Creator-King, as Psalm 93 will declare.

Given that the ancient time (*qedem* [TH6924, ZH7710]) when God acquired his people involved his work of redemption at the crossing of the Red Sea and his work of creation, it is better to interpret the mythopoetic language of 74:12-14 in reference to both creation and the redemption at the Red Sea rather than to one or the other. Both in creation and in redemption God has shown himself to be the cosmic king, who establishes his reign in keeping with his sovereign will. This truth provided the foundation upon which the psalmist built (in the final strophe) his pleas for God to act.

Remember (74:18-23). This final strophe begins with the plea that God "remember" (see note on 74:18). This plea calls to mind the first plea of the psalm: "Remember that we are the people you chose long ago" (74:2). The plea is that God would act in the present in keeping with his actions in the past, that he would show himself in the present to be the king who brings salvation to his people. What God is asked to remember in particular is the dishonor that has been brought on his own name (74:18, 22) by means of the destruction of his sanctuary and the defeat of his people. The enemies that had been victorious over God's people would have concluded that their god had likewise been victorious over the God of Israel. So the psalmist pleaded with God to act for the honor of God's own name.

But the psalmist also pleaded for God to act for the sake of his suffering people.

God's people were afflicted, their land was filled with darkness and violence, and they were disgraced. In spite of the sin that had provoked God's anger, they were still his people. So the psalmist pleaded for God to remember his covenant promises, like those made to Abraham, Isaac, and Jacob, and to arise to defend his own cause, which would entail defending his special possession.

When our circumstances seem to deny that God is king over the world he has made, Psalm 74 encourages us to articulate the agony of our confusion and the ecstasy of our faith. When there is no evidence in the present for God's reign in our lives, we too can look back to what God did in ages past. To what he did in establishing the marvelous order in creation. To what he did in accomplishing our redemption through the life, death, and resurrection of the Lord Jesus Christ. When our faith reaches back to God's work of creation and redemption, it finds a sure anchor for the soul. That anchor is the heart of the message of the Psalter and the heart of the Christian faith: "You, O God, are my king from ages past" (74:12). This anchor keeps us safe and secure in the storms of life.

ENDNOTES

1. McCann (1996:972) has pointed out numerous lexical links that tie the two psalms together: "sanctuary" (73:17; 74:3), "cruelty/violence" (73:6; 74:20), "right hand" (73:23; 74:11), "destruction/ruins" (73:18; 74:3). In addition are the repetitions of "God" (*'el* [TH410A, ZH446]; 73:11, 17; 74:8) and "not knowing" (73:22; 74:9).

◆ C. Psalm 75

For the choir director: A psalm of Asaph. A song to be sung to the tune "Do Not Destroy!"

[1] We thank you, O God!
We give thanks because you are near.
People everywhere tell of your wonderful deeds.

[2] God says, "At the time I have planned,
I will bring justice against the wicked.
[3] When the earth quakes and its people live in turmoil,
I am the one who keeps its foundations firm. *Interlude*

[4] "I warned the proud, 'Stop your boasting!'
I told the wicked, 'Don't raise your fists!
[5] Don't raise your fists in defiance at the heavens
or speak with such arrogance.' "
[6] For no one on earth—from east or west,
or even from the wilderness—
should raise a defiant fist.*
[7] It is God alone who judges;
he decides who will rise and who will fall.
[8] For the LORD holds a cup in his hand
that is full of foaming wine mixed with spices.
He pours out the wine in judgment,
and all the wicked must drink it,
draining it to the dregs.

[9] But as for me, I will always proclaim what God has done;
I will sing praises to the God of Jacob.
[10] For God says, "I will break the strength of the wicked,
but I will increase the power of the godly."

75:6 Hebrew *should lift.*

NOTES

75:1 ***you are near.*** Lit., "your name is near"; see 76:1 for the greatness of God's name.

75:4 ***Don't raise your fists!*** Lit., "Don't raise a horn." The horn was primarily a symbol of power (132:17; 1 Sam 2:10). People raising their own horn was a figure for autonomous and defiant self-assertion; here it is defiance against the rule of God, who is enthroned in heaven.

75:8 ***all the wicked.*** Lit., "all the wicked of the earth." The psalm has a noticeably eschatological orientation.

75:10 ***For God says, "I will break . . ."*** "For God says" is supplied by the NLT. While God as the speaker is possible, as in 75:2-5, it seems more likely that the psalmist is the speaker, as in the previous verse. For similar sentiments expressed by a psalmist in the last line of another psalm see 101:8. See also 118:10-11, where the psalmist vows to "destroy," literally, "cut off" (*mul* [TH4135A, ZH4577]) the enemy.

strength . . . power. Both of these words translate the word for "horn" (see note on 75:4).

COMMENTARY

As indicated by the opening line, Psalm 75 is a psalm of thanksgiving. But whereas psalms of thanksgiving typically thank God for deliverance from some trouble in the past, Psalm 75 gives thanks for what God will do at some point in the future—that is, he will judge the wicked and bless the righteous (75:10). The psalm can be divided into four strophes (VanGemeren 1991:490): communal thanksgiving (75:1), a divine oracle (75:2-5), a prophetic oracle (75:6-8), and individual thanksgiving (75:9-10).

Communal Thanksgiving (75:1). Psalm 75 begins with the community as a whole giving thanks to God. They give thanks in particular for the nearness of God. This nearness was not just a theological concept, however. God's nearness was manifest in concrete ways, referred to as "your wonderful deeds." These "deeds" probably refer both to God's works of creation and providence (Job 9:10; 37:5) in light of the reference to the earth and its foundations in 75:3 and to his works of redemption, whether of the nation (Exod 3:20) or the individual (9:1 [2]; see NIDOTTE 3.616). One such deed is divine judgment, the topic of the second strophe.

Divine Oracle (75:2-5). The psalms usually contain human words addressed to God, so it is striking when God becomes the speaker in a psalm, as is the case here.[1] In this divine oracle, God gives a promise and a warning. The promise is that he will eventually bring judgment (75:2-3). This judgment will be against the wicked (though, as we will see, it has implications for the righteous as well) and will come about at God's appointed time. That time is no doubt in this lifetime, but the reference to "all the wicked" of the earth in 75:8 provides an eschatological perspective and leads to the conclusion that the final day of judgment is in view (Mays 1994:249). In the meantime, there may be a tremendous amount of turmoil from time to time and from place to place, but God promises to maintain sufficient cosmic order that chaos will never reign supreme. No matter how chaotic our lives may become, we can rest assured that God is still in control and will never let us be completely overwhelmed. So we can say with the apostle Paul, "We are pressed on every side by troubles, but we are not crushed. We are perplexed, but not driven to despair. We are hunted down, but never abandoned by God. We get knocked down, but we are not destroyed" (2 Cor 4:8-9).

The warning is that people ought not to live in arrogant defiance of God's rule (75:4-5). The implicit message is that such defiant rebels will experience the judgment of God at the time that he has planned. This divine oracle is supported by the prophetic oracle that follows in the third strophe.

Prophetic Oracle (75:6-8). The prophetic oracle begins with an affirmation of divine sovereignty (75:6-7). No human being has the ultimate power to raise another human being up or make that person fall. Only God has such sovereign power (see 1 Sam 2:6). This sovereign power explains why he and he alone can judge in an ultimate sense.

Following this affirmation is a threat of divine judgment. Typical of the prophets (e.g., Isa 51:17-20; Jer 49:12-13), the psalmist uses the image of the cup of foaming wine as a figure for divine wrath. On the final day of judgment, this cup will be drunk to its very dregs by those who have remained rebellious against God's rule (Rev 14:10; 16:19; 18:6).

The good news of the gospel is, however, that Jesus has drunk the cup of wrath in our place that we might not have to drink it (Mark 14:36; John 18:11). Though he had done nothing to merit judgment, he bore judgment as he bore our sins in his body on the cross. As a result, he now offers the cup of the new covenant, his blood poured out, that we might be forgiven and be blessed. Praise for such blessing is the topic of the final strophe.

Individual Thanksgiving (75:9-10). Whereas the psalm begins with the community proclaiming God's mighty miracles, it ends with the individual vowing to proclaim what God has done. As in Psalm 66, so too here, the individuality of the believer and the believer's participation in the community are validated. While God works on behalf of his community, the individual is responsible for appropriating the benefits of that work and for praising God for it. God is, after all, the God of the individual and the "God of Israel" at the same time.

In the final line, the psalmist vows to do his part to see that the strength (lit., "horn") of the wicked be cut off. Believers will in some sense participate in the final judgment (1 Cor 6:3). But it is our present task to warn those who live in arrogant defiance of God's rule to desist, and to invite them to trust in the Christ who has drunk the cup of divine wrath in the place of sinners. Then they too will experience the increase of power spoken of in the final colon.

This increase of power or lifting up of the horn refers to the bestowal of power, joy, health, and prestige (DBI 400). Such a raising up of our horn is possible because God made a promise to raise up a horn for his people by sending the Messiah (132:17), a promise he fulfilled in the Lord Jesus Christ (Luke 1:69).

ENDNOTE

1. See also 32:8-9 and Ps 50 for other examples of such divine speech.

D. Psalm 76

For the choir director: A psalm of Asaph. A song to be accompanied by stringed instruments.

1 God is honored in Judah;
his name is great in Israel.
2 Jerusalem* is where he lives;
Mount Zion is his home.
3 There he has broken the fiery arrows
of the enemy,
the shields and swords and weapons
of war. *Interlude*

4 You are glorious and more majestic
than the everlasting mountains.*
5 Our boldest enemies have been
plundered.
They lie before us in the sleep
of death.
No warrior could lift a hand
against us.
6 At the blast of your breath, O God
of Jacob,
their horses and chariots lay
still.

7 No wonder you are greatly feared!
Who can stand before you when
your anger explodes?
8 From heaven you sentenced your
enemies;
the earth trembled and stood silent
before you.
9 You stand up to judge those who do
evil, O God,
and to rescue the oppressed of the
earth. *Interlude*

10 Human defiance only enhances your
glory,
for you use it as a weapon.*
11 Make vows to the LORD your God, and
keep them.
Let everyone bring tribute to the
Awesome One.
12 For he breaks the pride of princes,
and the kings of the earth fear him.

76:2 Hebrew *Salem*, another name for Jerusalem. **76:4** As in Greek version; Hebrew reads *than mountains filled with beasts of prey.* **76:10** The meaning of the Hebrew is uncertain.

NOTES

76:1 *his name is great.* Whereas 75:1 celebrated the nearness of God's name (see note), this psalm celebrates the greatness of that name, and thus links the two psalms.

76:4 *You are glorious.* The word *na'or* means "be lighted up," and while it is possible to understand it as a reference to God's glory, this would be the only place where such a use is found. By simply rearranging the order of the letters from *na'or* [TH215, ZH239] to *nora'* [TH3372, ZH3707] the meaning shifts from "glorious" to "feared" (see note at 76:7). If the first *'attah* [TH859, ZH911] is deleted in 76:7 (see note), then 76:4 and 76:7 would both start new strophes on the same note: "You are feared."

everlasting mountains. As indicated by the footnote, the NLT follows the LXX here. The MT would be translated "mountains of prey," the sense of which is not clear. The NIV's "more majestic than mountains rich with game" is possible.

76:6 *God of Jacob.* This title for God was used in 75:9 and thus links the two psalms.

76:7 *you are greatly feared!* The Hebrew text has the pronoun *'attah* [TH859, ZH911] both before and after the word *nora'* [TH3372, ZH3707], which is unusual syntax. The first *'attah* is not represented in the LXX and should perhaps be deleted. If the emendation from *na'or* [TH215, ZH239] (be lighted) to *nora'* [TH3372, ZH3707] (feared) in 76:4 is not accepted, this is the first of four uses of the root *yare'* (fear). In 76:8 [9] the earth "trembles/fears" in response to God's sentence; in 76:11 [12], God is the "Awesome/Fear-Inspiring One"; and in 76:12 [13], God is "feared" by the kings of the earth. This motif supports the psalm's celebration of the greatness and majesty of God.

76:9 *to judge.* The root *shapat* [TH8199, ZH9149] (judge) is also used in 75:2, 7 [3, 8]. In Ps 75 the promise is that God will judge. That promise is fulfilled in Ps 76.

to rescue. God's judgment on the wicked is his way of rescuing the righteous.

76:10 ***enhances your glory.*** This same verb (Hiphil of *yadah* [TH3034A, ZH3344]) is used twice in 75:1, where it is translated "thank." In Ps 75 the righteous "thank" God, and in Ps 76 human opposition "thanks" God. Everything ultimately works for the glory of God.

COMMENTARY

Psalm 75 ended on the note that the strength of the wicked would be cut off and the power of the godly would be increased at some point in the future. Psalm 76 follows with a celebration of that judgment and rescue. While human agency is in view in 75:10, divine agency is the focus of Psalm 76. In light of the opening verses, Psalm 76 is often categorized as a psalm of Zion, but as Mays (1994:250) has said, "The psalm is more about the resident of Zion than about Zion itself." The focus of the four strophes bears this out: God is known among his people (76:1-3), God is majestic in battle (76:4-6), God is awesome in judgment (76:7-10), and God is awesome among the nations (76:11-12).

God Is Known among His People (76:1-3). God is known among his people, not only in the tribe of Judah but throughout the 12 tribes of Israel (Kraus 1989:109). These 12 tribes found in Zion (Jerusalem) the center of their hope, for in Jerusalem they found their God. Jerusalem was God's "home"—the place where his special presence was located (see Pss 45–48). Jerusalem was the headquarters from which God went forth to vanquish his and Israel's foes. These victories won for his "name" a great reputation among his people, a reputation as the victorious divine warrior. These victories are amplified in the second strophe.

God Is Majestic in Battle (76:4-6). The immensity of the mountains allowed them to serve as a figure for God's character. Here God's majesty in battle is compared to the "everlasting mountains." God is majestic in battle only because he is victorious. In fact, he has shown himself to be victorious over the "boldest enemies," who "lie before us in the sleep of death" and whose weaponry lies as silent as their corpses.

God Is Awesome in Judgment (76:7-10). The rebuke by the divine warrior was at the same time an expression of the anger of the divine judge, as warrior and judge are roles of the divine king (Longman 1995:44). God judges from his throne in heaven, and his judgment is cosmic in scope, resulting in the earth trembling in silence before his tribunal. The purpose of this judgment is salvific. In judging the wicked, God's purpose is "to rescue the oppressed of the earth." The oppressed who are rescued give thanks to God for his salvation, and thus human opposition to God and his people ultimately serves to enhance the glory of God.

God Is Awesome among the Nations (76:11-12). The thanksgiving offered to God would have been a key aspect of the fulfilling of the vows made to him by the oppressed at the time of their trouble. Along with thanksgiving, tribute would have been brought to God as the victorious king. Tribute would have been brought by the defeated princes and kings who now, along with God's people, stand in awe of him.

Psalm 76 begins with God being well-known among his people and ends with him being well-known among the nations. The path to this spreading fame encompasses opposition to this fame by human forces. Not only will such opposition never stop the spread of God's fame, such opposition ultimately ends up facilitating that spread.

From this we learn that everything we experience in life produces a benefit. That benefit is not always evident in the middle of the battle, but by faith we know that God is at work in it all for our good and his glory (Rom 8:28). At the moment of the crucifixion of the Lord Jesus Christ, who could have imagined the cosmic good that was being accomplished and the eternal glory that God was gaining? What was true of Christ's life and death is also true of ours. With hindsight we will see the good and the glory of the past. So with the foresight of faith, we live out the present and fearlessly face the future.

◆ E. Psalm 77

For Jeduthun, the choir director: A psalm of Asaph.

1 I cry out to God; yes, I shout.
Oh, that God would listen to me!
2 When I was in deep trouble,
I searched for the Lord.
All night long I prayed, with hands
lifted toward heaven,
but my soul was not comforted.
3 I think of God, and I moan,
overwhelmed with longing for
his help. *Interlude*

4 You don't let me sleep.
I am too distressed even to pray!
5 I think of the good old days,
long since ended,
6 when my nights were filled with joyful
songs.
I search my soul and ponder the
difference now.
7 Has the Lord rejected me forever?
Will he never again be kind to me?
8 Is his unfailing love gone forever?
Have his promises permanently
failed?
9 Has God forgotten to be gracious?
Has he slammed the door on his
compassion? *Interlude*

10 And I said, "This is my fate;
the Most High has turned his hand
against me."
11 But then I recall all you have done,
O LORD;
I remember your wonderful deeds
of long ago.
12 They are constantly in my thoughts.
I cannot stop thinking about your
mighty works.
13 O God, your ways are holy.
Is there any god as mighty as you?
14 You are the God of great wonders!
You demonstrate your awesome
power among the nations.
15 By your strong arm, you redeemed
your people,
the descendants of Jacob and
Joseph. *Interlude*

16 When the Red Sea* saw you, O God,
its waters looked and trembled!
The sea quaked to its very depths.
17 The clouds poured down rain;
the thunder rumbled in the sky.
Your arrows of lightning flashed.
18 Your thunder roared from the
whirlwind;
the lightning lit up the world!
The earth trembled and shook.
19 Your road led through the sea,
your pathway through the mighty
waters—
a pathway no one knew was there!
20 You led your people along that road
like a flock of sheep,
with Moses and Aaron as their
shepherds.

77:16 Hebrew *the waters.*

NOTES

77:1-10. The verb tenses in this first half of the psalm are quite difficult (Tate 1990:271). It is possible to read them as in the present tense (so NLT), resulting in the psalm being interpreted as a lament (Kraus 1989:114). It is also possible to read them in reference to the past (so KJV and NIV), resulting in the psalm being interpreted as a song of thanksgiving. On the whole, commentators read 77:1-10 as a lament (see commentary).

77:1 *I cry out to God.* The Heb. *qoli 'el-'elohim* [TH6963/430, ZH7754/466] (my voice to God) is repeated in the second colon of this line, though it is not translated in the NLT. The repetition underscores the intensity of the psalmist's search for God.

77:2 *All night long I prayed.* The Heb. *lo' tapug* [TH3808/6313, ZH4202/7028] means "did not grow weary"; the picture is that of hands outstretched to God in prayer over a protracted period of time in relentless pleading.

but my soul was not comforted. Lit., "my soul refused to be comforted."

77:11-12 Three verbs are used in these two verses to emphasize the degree of mental activity the psalmist engaged in while pondering God's actions in the past: *zakar* [TH2142, ZH2349] ("remember"; 2 times), *hagah* [TH1897, ZH2047] (meditate), and *siakh* [TH7878, ZH8488] (muse).

77:11 *long ago.* Here the word *miqqedem* [TH6924, ZH7710] refers to the distant past, when God saved Israel at the Red Sea; *miqqedem* also recalls 77:5, where it refers to the more recent past of the psalmist's own experiencing of God's blessings.

77:18 *Your thunder roared from the whirlwind.* "Your thunder roared" translates the phrase *qol ra'amka* [TH6963, ZH7754] (lit, "voice of your roar"). The word *galgal* [TH1534, ZH1649] may mean "whirlwind" (DCH 2.347) but typically means "wheel" and refers at times to chariot wheels (Ezek 26:10). The expression *qol . . . galgal* (noise of . . . wheels) occurs in Ezek 26:10 in reference to the sound made by chariot wheels. The sense of *qol ra'amka baggalgal* seems to be "your thunderous roar was in your chariot wheels," and the picture is that of the Lord as Divine Warrior fighting from his chariot.

COMMENTARY

Ambiguity characterizes this difficult psalm. It is unclear whether the first half of the psalm (77:1-10) expresses lamentation or thanksgiving. It is equally unclear whether the second half (77:11-20) entails doubt or confidence. There is a benefit in this ambiguity, which we will consider after we have looked at the main thoughts in the poem.

Asking Anguishing Questions (77:1–10). This first stanza begins with a strophe that describes a relentless searching (77:1-3). Twice in the opening line the psalmist says he cried out to God (see note on 77:1), hoping that God would listen. The occasion was some sort of deep trouble, the precise nature of which we are not told. But this deep trouble provoked a relentless searching for God, a searching that went on even at night. The intensity of the search is shown by the fact that the psalmist's hands were stretched out to God in prayer throughout the night without weariness causing them to drop. The psalmist was like a dog with a bone: Nothing but divine intervention would bring the search to an end. The very thought of God did not bring comfort but only resulted in greater groaning. Believing in a God who is not evidently at work in a time of deep trouble just adds insult to injury until we are virtually overwhelmed with longing for God to act on our behalf.

Times of deep trouble may also be times of painful remembering (77:4-6). During sleepless nights, the psalmist was "too distressed even to pray!" Part of the reason for such distress was the radical contrast between the way things were in the present and the way they had been in the past. As in 42:4 ("My heart is breaking as I remember how it used to be"), so here, remembering the good old days in contrast to present troubles only deepened the pain.

The culmination of the relentless searching and the painful remembering was brutal questioning (77:7-10).

Has the Lord rejected me forever?
  Will he never again be kind to me?
Is his unfailing love gone forever?
  Have his promises permanently failed?
Has God forgotten to be gracious?
  Has he slammed the door on his compassion?

These are the questions of a soul driven to brutal honesty by a desperate situation. Here the Holy Spirit instructs us that such questions are not off-limits in prayer; rather, God invites us to engage in such brutal questioning before his face in prayer. The strophe and stanza are brought to a close with the seemingly hopeless declaration:

And I said, "This is my fate;
  the Most High has turned his hand against me."

Remembering Remarkable Deeds (77:11-20). The style, if not the mood, changes in this second stanza, as indicated by the shift from third- to second-person address. This shift in style has the effect of bringing God's presence into the psalmist's situation (Mays 1994:252). Whereas in the previous stanza the psalmist had recalled his own recent past, here he recalls the distant past and God's actions therein.

The psalmist begins by recalling God's wonderful deeds "of long ago" (77:11). It will not be until the third strophe that we find out what deeds are in view. Here the psalmist simply tells us that he remembered, meditated, and mused on what God had done in days long past. This recalling was as relentless as the searching of the first strophe.

Greater specificity is provided in the second strophe, which tells us of the psalmist's recalling God's holy ways (77:13-15). The holiness of God is his separateness from all else in his creation and thus evokes the rhetorical question as to whether there is any god comparable to the God of Israel. The implied answer is, "Of course not." And this answer is bolstered by the following references to God's "great wonders" and the "awesome power" he has demonstrated among the nations with their competing gods. The precise nature of God's wonderful deeds and holy ways is finally revealed in the last line of the strophe: They were deeds of redemption. When and how this redemption was accomplished is the subject of the closing strophe.

The stanza and psalm come to a close with the psalmist recalling God's saving presence (77:16-20). Here we find out that the "wonderful deeds of long ago" refer in particular to the deliverance at the Red Sea. This text pictures the Lord coming as the Divine Warrior mounted on his chariot to deliver his people at the Red Sea. He came wielding the weapons of rain, thunder, and lightning, causing the land to tremble and the sea to convulse. With his chariot at the vanguard, the Lord made a way where there was no way, a way through the mighty waters of the Red Sea, so that his people could follow him to safety, as they followed the lead of Moses and Aaron, the human shepherds appointed by the divine shepherd.

Because of its inherent ambiguity, this psalm can be read in three ways. First, it can be read as a psalm of thanksgiving for deliverance experienced—experienced in the recent past and rooted in the saving events of the distant past. Second, it can be read as a lament expressing deep hope rooted in the distant past. In this case the second stanza entails hope that God will work in the psalmist's present circumstances just as he worked in the distant past. Third, it can be read as a lament with very little if any hope, in accord with the pattern of Psalm 88. In this case, the second stanza does not recall the distant past as a basis for hope in the present but fosters deep pain as a second example of the deep contrast between the way God used to work and the way he is not working in the psalmist's present circumstances.

None of these readings can be ruled out, and thus the ambiguity, which seems to make the meaning of the text evasive, actually broadens the use of the text. In fact, it is quite easy to envision this psalm being read first in the third sense; then, as God's word produces faith, in the second sense; and finally in the first sense, after God has shown that he does not reject his people forever, that his unfailing love is never gone forever, that his promises never fail, that he has not forgotten to be kind, and that he will never ultimately slam the door on his compassion.

There are times of deep trouble in our lives when even what God has done in the person and work of the Lord Jesus Christ seems far removed and irrelevant to our present troubles. Yet, even when reflecting on what Christ has done in the redemptive history of the past creates greater moaning, it can mysteriously create new faith (Rom 10:17), for God's word always accomplishes his purposes (Isa 55:10-11). So by faith we look forward to the future when we will sing with thanksgiving in our hearts for deliverance experienced when the Holy Spirit brought to us the saving benefits of the person and work of the Lord Jesus Christ.

◆ F. Psalm 78

A psalm of Asaph.*

1 O my people, listen to my instructions.
Open your ears to what I am saying,
2 for I will speak to you in a parable.
I will teach you hidden lessons from our past—
3 stories we have heard and known,
stories our ancestors handed down to us.
4 We will not hide these truths from our children;
we will tell the next generation
about the glorious deeds of the LORD,
about his power and his mighty wonders.
5 For he issued his laws to Jacob;
he gave his instructions to Israel.
He commanded our ancestors
to teach them to their children,
6 so the next generation might know them—
even the children not yet born—
and they in turn will teach their own children.
7 So each generation should set its hope anew on God,

not forgetting his glorious miracles
and obeying his commands.
8 Then they will not be like their ancestors—
stubborn, rebellious, and unfaithful,
refusing to give their hearts to God.

9 The warriors of Ephraim, though
armed with bows,
turned their backs and fled on the
day of battle.
10 They did not keep God's covenant
and refused to live by his
instructions.
11 They forgot what he had done—
the great wonders he had shown
them,
12 the miracles he did for their ancestors
on the plain of Zoan in the land of
Egypt.
13 For he divided the sea and led them
through,
making the water stand up like
walls!
14 In the daytime he led them by a cloud,
and all night by a pillar of fire.
15 He split open the rocks in the
wilderness
to give them water, as from
a gushing spring.
16 He made streams pour from the rock,
making the waters flow down like
a river!

17 Yet they kept on sinning against him,
rebelling against the Most High in
the desert.
18 They stubbornly tested God in their
hearts,
demanding the foods they craved.
19 They even spoke against God himself,
saying,
"God can't give us food in the
wilderness.
20 Yes, he can strike a rock so water
gushes out,
but he can't give his people bread
and meat."
21 When the LORD heard them, he was
furious.
The fire of his wrath burned against
Jacob.
Yes, his anger rose against Israel,
22 for they did not believe God
or trust him to care for them.
23 But he commanded the skies to open;
he opened the doors of heaven.
24 He rained down manna for them to eat;
he gave them bread from heaven.
25 They ate the food of angels!
God gave them all they could hold.
26 He released the east wind in the
heavens
and guided the south wind by his
mighty power.
27 He rained down meat as thick as dust—
birds as plentiful as the sand on the
seashore!
28 He caused the birds to fall within their
camp
and all around their tents.
29 The people ate their fill.
He gave them what they craved.
30 But before they satisfied their craving,
while the meat was yet in their
mouths,
31 the anger of God rose against them,
and he killed their strongest men.
He struck down the finest of Israel's
young men.

32 But in spite of this, the people kept
sinning.
Despite his wonders, they refused
to trust him.
33 So he ended their lives in failure,
their years in terror.
34 When God began killing them,
they finally sought him.
They repented and took God
seriously.
35 Then they remembered that God was
their rock,
that God Most High* was their
redeemer.
36 But all they gave him was lip service;
they lied to him with their tongues.
37 Their hearts were not loyal to him.
They did not keep his covenant.
38 Yet he was merciful and forgave their
sins
and did not destroy them all.

Many times he held back his anger
and did not unleash his fury!
39 For he remembered that they were merely mortal,
gone like a breath of wind that never returns.

40 Oh, how often they rebelled against him in the wilderness
and grieved his heart in that dry wasteland.
41 Again and again they tested God's patience
and provoked the Holy One of Israel.
42 They did not remember his power
and how he rescued them from their enemies.
43 They did not remember his miraculous signs in Egypt,
his wonders on the plain of Zoan.
44 For he turned their rivers into blood,
so no one could drink from the streams.
45 He sent vast swarms of flies to consume them
and hordes of frogs to ruin them.
46 He gave their crops to caterpillars;
their harvest was consumed by locusts.
47 He destroyed their grapevines with hail
and shattered their sycamore-figs with sleet.
48 He abandoned their cattle to the hail,
their livestock to bolts of lightning.
49 He loosed on them his fierce anger—
all his fury, rage, and hostility.
He dispatched against them
a band of destroying angels.
50 He turned his anger against them;
he did not spare the Egyptians' lives
but ravaged them with the plague.
51 He killed the oldest son in each Egyptian family,
the flower of youth throughout the land of Egypt.*
52 But he led his own people like a flock of sheep,
guiding them safely through the wilderness.
53 He kept them safe so they were not afraid;
but the sea covered their enemies.
54 He brought them to the border of his holy land,
to this land of hills he had won for them.
55 He drove out the nations before them;
he gave them their inheritance by lot.
He settled the tribes of Israel into their homes.

56 But they kept testing and rebelling against God Most High.
They did not obey his laws.
57 They turned back and were as faithless as their parents.
They were as undependable as a crooked bow.
58 They angered God by building shrines to other gods;
they made him jealous with their idols.
59 When God heard them, he was very angry,
and he completely rejected Israel.
60 Then he abandoned his dwelling at Shiloh,
the Tabernacle where he had lived among the people.
61 He allowed the Ark of his might to be captured;
he surrendered his glory into enemy hands.
62 He gave his people over to be butchered by the sword,
because he was so angry with his own people—his special possession.
63 Their young men were killed by fire;
their young women died before singing their wedding songs.
64 Their priests were slaughtered,
and their widows could not mourn their deaths.

65 Then the Lord rose up as though waking from sleep,
like a warrior aroused from a drunken stupor.

[66] He routed his enemies
and sent them to eternal shame.
[67] But he rejected Joseph's descendants;
he did not choose the tribe of
Ephraim.
[68] He chose instead the tribe of Judah,
and Mount Zion, which he loved.
[69] There he built his sanctuary as high
as the heavens,
as solid and enduring as the earth.
[70] He chose his servant David,
calling him from the sheep pens.
[71] He took David from tending the ewes
and lambs
and made him the shepherd of
Jacob's descendants—
God's own people, Israel.
[72] He cared for them with a true
heart
and led them with skillful hands.

78:TITLE Hebrew *maskil.* This may be a literary or musical term. **78:35** Hebrew *El-Elyon.* **78:51** Hebrew *in the tents of Ham.*

NOTES

78:54 ***holy land . . . land of hills.*** The word *qodsho* [TH6944, ZH7731] and *har* [TH2022, ZH2215] mean "his holiness" and "mountain" respectively. The NLT interprets them as references to the land and mountains in general, but the references are in all likelihood to the holy mountain of Jerusalem in particular. For previous references in the Psalter to this "holy mountain" see 2:6; 3:4; 15:1; 43:3; 48:1; see also 78:68-69.

78:63 ***died before singing their wedding songs.*** The Hebrew text simply says, "they were not praised." The NLT may be correct in its interpretation of what this means (see HALOT 1.249).

COMMENTARY

Psalm 78 is the first of what have customarily been called historical psalms (see also 105, 106, and 136). As a historical psalm, Psalm 78 is clearly and intentionally "history with a lesson." Notice how Psalm 78 begins: "O my people, listen to my instructions." The express purpose of the recitation of the history contained in this psalm is to pass on instruction to the community. Notice also how Psalm 105 ends: "All this happened so they would follow his decrees and obey his instructions." The historical events themselves are said to have had an instructional purpose, and by implication the record of those events was likewise instructional.

What does Psalm 78 teach? The Westminster Shorter Catechism asks, "What do the Scriptures primarily teach?" The answer: "The Scriptures primarily teach what man is to believe concerning God and what duty God requires of man." Psalm 78 primarily teaches us about God's justice and mercy and about our response of faith and obedience. We are taught these lessons not only by the content but also by the structure of the psalm.

It seems best to understand the structure as a slight modification of that proposed by McCann 1996:990, which is itself a slight modification of that proposed by Clifford 1981. Psalm 78:1-8 should probably be read as the introduction that states the purpose of the psalm. The recital of Israel's history from Egypt to David is broken into two parts, both of which follow the same basic pattern:

The first recital (78:9-39):
- God's people rebelled (78:9-11)
- God was merciful (78:12-16; Egypt and field of Zoan)

God's people rebelled against the "Most High" (78:17-20)
God heard and was angry (78:21-33)
God provided forgiveness (78:34-39)
The second recital (78:40-72):
God's people rebelled (78:40-42)
God was merciful (78:43-55; Egypt and field of Zoan)
God's people rebelled against the "Most High" (78:56-58)
God heard and was angry (78:59-64)
God chose Zion and David (78:65-72)

This pattern underscores God's justice and mercy. The psalm also teaches us how to respond to who God is, but it teaches us by way of negative example: "Then they will not be like their ancestors—stubborn, rebellious, and unfaithful, refusing to give their hearts to God" (78:8). When we contrast 78:5 and 78:8, it is clear that the ancestors told their children the right things but then failed to do the right things themselves. Thus while "knowledge does not guarantee faithfulness," "knowing the story is the foundation for faith and hope and life" (McCann 1996:990, 993).

The introduction (78:1-8) indicates that the purpose of the recitation of Israel's history is to teach. The goal of the instruction is not the brute memorization of historical data but growth in faith and obedience. This instruction was never intended solely for the original audience but was envisioned as being passed on to each subsequent generation. The idea of passing on this instruction did not originate with human beings but with God himself. The instruction is given by means of a "parable." This is not to say that the events contained in the psalm are not historical, but, as McCann (1996:990) has pointed out, they are recited so that future generations could "compare"[1] themselves with the ancestors so as not to fail as they had.

Who God Is. According to Psalm 78, God is a God of justice. The fourth section of each recital says that God heard and was then angry (78:21 and 78:59). What God heard is recorded in the third section of each recital (78:17-20 and 78:56-58). God heard how his people had rebelled against him as the "Most High" (78:17 and 78:56). God's justice is not arbitrary in any way but is in fact his commensurate response to the sin of his people. While God's justice comes to expression in this psalm, justice is not the final or ultimate word. Mercy is.

God's mercy is highlighted in the structure of this psalm in two ways. It is the first characteristic we are told about in each recital. Each recital begins on a negative note, a brief recording of the people's sin (78:9-11 and 78:40-42). The second section of each recital contains a confession of God's mercy (78:12-16 and 78:43-55). Each of these sections focus on God's mercy in "Egypt" and the "plain of Zoan."[2] The first (78:12-16) has a further focus on God's dividing of the Red Sea and his provisions in the wilderness, while the second (78:43-55) has a further focus on the 10 plagues, and then refers to the crossing of the sea, the provisions in the wilderness, and the conquest of the Promised Land. All of this mercy had been forgotten by the ancestors (78:11, 42), and this forgetting resulted in rebellion against God.

God's mercy is also the last characteristic we are told about in each recital and the poem as a whole. In the final section of the first recital (78:34-39), the psalmist tells us that God "was merciful and forgave their sins" (78:38) for "he remembered that they were merely mortal" (78:39). In the final section of the second recital (78:65-72) the psalmist tells us that God did not completely reject his people but chose Zion and David. Zion (Jerusalem) was chosen as the place where God's sanctuary would be located, where God would dwell among his people, and where sacrifice would be offered and sin atoned for. David was chosen to care for God's people as a shepherd cares for the ewes and the lambs in the flock. By the time this psalm was being used in the exilic and postexilic community of God's people, this reference to David would have been interpreted messianically, since there was no longer a Davidic king reigning over God's people (McCann 1996:990).

"The last word is the triumph of grace" (Mays 1994:258). The purpose of the recitals was not negative but positive: that present and future generations would not forget, but would remember God's merciful miracles and would respond appropriately (78:7).

What Our Response Is. The response called for in this ancient psalm is the same response set forth in the old hymn, "Trust and Obey." Psalm 78:7 encapsulates this response: "So each generation should set its hope anew on God, not forgetting his glorious miracles and obeying his commands." The emphasis in the two recitals is on the failure of the ancestors to obey (78:10, 17, 32, 37, 40, 56, 57, 58). But explicit mention is also made of their failure to believe: "for they did not believe God or trust him to care for them" (78:22) and "they refused to trust him" (78:32). Their lack of obedience was simply the natural outworking of their lack of faith. This is the same description of the ancestors as that recorded in the book of Hebrews: "To whom was God speaking. . . . Wasn't it the people who disobeyed him? So we see that because of their unbelief they were not able to enter his rest" (Heb 3:18-19).

The apostle Paul saw this same pattern still operating in his own day (Rom 11:20, 30), and it still operates in ours. Thus, Psalm 78 is highly applicable to us. It calls us to remember all of God's mercy to us, especially his saving presence with us and his saving reign over us through his messianic shepherd, the Lord Jesus Christ. Because of God's great mercy to us in Jesus Christ we respond with lives of faith and obedience. "This is truly the way to worship him" (Rom 12:1).

ENDNOTES

1. A parable is basically a comparison, e.g., "The Kingdom of God is like . . ." (Mark 4:26).
2. Zoan is the Hebrew name for the Egyptian city of Tanis.

◆ G. Psalm 79

A psalm of Asaph.

1 O God, pagan nations have conquered
your land,
your special possession.
They have defiled your holy Temple
and made Jerusalem a heap of ruins.
2 They have left the bodies of your
servants
as food for the birds of heaven.
The flesh of your godly ones
has become food for the wild
animals.
3 Blood has flowed like water all around
Jerusalem;
no one is left to bury the dead.

4 We are mocked by our neighbors,
an object of scorn and derision to
those around us.

5 O LORD, how long will you be angry
with us? Forever?
How long will your jealousy burn
like fire?
6 Pour out your wrath on the nations
that refuse to acknowledge you—
on kingdoms that do not call upon
your name.
7 For they have devoured your people
Israel,*
making the land a desolate
wilderness.
8 Do not hold us guilty for the sins of
our ancestors!
Let your compassion quickly meet
our needs,
for we are on the brink of despair.

9 Help us, O God of our salvation!
Help us for the glory of your name.
Save us and forgive our sins
for the honor of your name.
10 Why should pagan nations be allowed
to scoff,
asking, "Where is their God?"
Show us your vengeance against the
nations,
for they have spilled the blood of
your servants.
11 Listen to the moaning of the
prisoners.
Demonstrate your great power by
saving those condemned to die.

12 O Lord, pay back our neighbors seven
times
for the scorn they have hurled at
you.

13 Then we your people, the sheep of
your pasture,
will thank you forever and ever,
praising your greatness from
generation to generation.

79:7 Hebrew *devoured Jacob.* See note on 44:4.

NOTES

79:3 ***Blood has flowed.*** Lit., "They have poured out blood." The verb translated "poured out" is *shapak* [TH8210, ZH9161], and this verb is repeated in 79:6, where the psalmist calls on God to "pour out" his wrath on the nations who "pour out" the blood of his people.

79:4 ***mocked.*** The word *kherpah* [TH2781, ZH3075] is repeated in 79:12, where it is translated "scorn." In 79:12 God is the object of the scorn of the "neighbors," whereas in 79:4 Israel is the object of the neighbor's mockery. To mock Israel is to mock God.

79:9 ***forgive.*** The word *kapar* [TH3722, ZH4105] means "atone."

79:11 ***saving.*** The Hiphil of *yathar* [TH3498, ZH3855] means "leave over," "be left over," "give prosperity," and "have priority" (HALOT 2.452). None of these meanings makes good sense in this context. Kraus (1989:133) and Tate (1990:298) retain the MT and gloss the word with "preserve," but there is no clear justification for this gloss. Perhaps it is better to emend the text to the Hiphil of *nathar* [TH5425B, ZH6002], which is used in the context of releasing prisoners (see 105:20 and Isa 58:6). There is support for this emendation in Syriac.

COMMENTARY

A national disaster has occurred, and Psalm 79 articulates the agony of that disaster. The problem is described in 79:1-5, followed by a series of petitions in response to the problem (79:6-12). The psalm ends with a promise of eternal praise to God by his people (79:13).

The Problem (79:1-5). The Temple was defiled, and Jerusalem was a heap of ruins. Corpses have not received a proper burial and are exposed to the ravages of scavengers. All of this was the work of the nations that had invaded the land. The historical situation that best fits this description is the destruction of Jerusalem in 587 BC at the hands of the Babylonians. In 79:1-3 the problem is with "them," the nations that have caused such devastation in the lives of God's people. But the problem is also with "us." The text says, "We are mocked . . . an object of scorn and derision" (79:4). The community reels in the experience of disgrace.

Ultimately, however, the problem lies with God. He could end the problem immediately simply by turning away his jealous anger. In the situation at hand, the problem caused by the nations for the people found its ultimate source in God.[1]

The Petitions (79:6-12). The petitions fall into three categories. The first petition is that God "pour out" his wrath on the nations (79:6) as an expression of his poetic justice on those who "pour out" the blood of God's people (see note at 79:3). Vengeance on those who have spilled the blood of God's servants, even sevenfold vengeance on those who have scorned God by mocking his people, is the outworking of the biblical principle that one reaps what one sows. This is the way God has designed his world to work.

The second petition is for forgiveness. The devastation described in 79:1-3 is owing to the anger of God, which is his response to the sins of his people. So twice the people plead with God for forgiveness: "Do not hold us guilty for the sins of our ancestors!" (79:8) and "forgive our sins" (79:9). The atrocities committed by the nations, wrong though they were, do not mitigate the sins committed by God's people. Atonement is what is called for, and atonement is what is requested by contrite Israel dependent on the compassion of God.

The third petition is for help. "Help us" is the cry of 79:9. The help needed is "salvation" (79:9), salvation from the devastation of 79:1-3 and salvation for those moaning like prisoners who long to be set free from the bondage of death that entangles them (79:11).

These petitions have the glory of God as their ultimate motivation. "Help us for the glory of your name . . . forgive our sins for the honor of your name" cries the community. By removing scorn from his people, God would thereby remove scorn from his own name. This desire for the glory of God's name leads to the final verse of the psalm, a promise to praise God eternally when he will have answered the prayers of his people.

The Praise (79:13). In spite of their former sins, the community says to God, we are still "your people, the sheep of your pasture." As such they vow to "thank you forever and ever" praising his "greatness from generation to generation."

When we sin and reap what we have sown, we find in Psalm 79 clear instruction for experiencing restoration. We humble ourselves under the discipline of God, confessing our sins to him, lamenting the consequences we are reaping, and pleading for forgiveness and deliverance from our distress. And we can be certain that God will hear and answer our prayers, because Jesus has already experienced ultimate devastation in our place and has been raised to life that we might be restored.

ENDNOTES

1. See also Ps 13 for the threefold nature of the problem in a psalm of lament: the enemy, the self, and God.

◆ H. Psalm 80

For the choir director: A psalm of Asaph, to be sung to the tune "Lilies of the Covenant."

1 Please listen, O Shepherd of Israel,
you who lead Joseph's descendants
like a flock.
O God, enthroned above the cherubim,
display your radiant glory
2 to Ephraim, Benjamin, and
Manasseh.
Show us your mighty power.
Come to rescue us!

3 Turn us again to yourself, O God.
Make your face shine down upon us.
Only then will we be saved.
4 O LORD God of Heaven's Armies,
how long will you be angry with our
prayers?
5 You have fed us with sorrow
and made us drink tears by the
bucketful.
6 You have made us the scorn* of
neighboring nations.
Our enemies treat us as a joke.

7 Turn us again to yourself, O God of
Heaven's Armies.
Make your face shine down upon us.
Only then will we be saved.
8 You brought us from Egypt like a
grapevine;
you drove away the pagan nations
and transplanted us into your
land.
9 You cleared the ground for us,
and we took root and filled the land.
10 Our shade covered the mountains;
our branches covered the mighty
cedars.
11 We spread our branches west to the
Mediterranean Sea;
our shoots spread east to the
Euphrates River.*
12 But now, why have you broken down
our walls
so that all who pass by may steal
our fruit?
13 The wild boar from the forest
devours it,
and the wild animals feed on it.

14 Come back, we beg you, O God of
Heaven's Armies.
Look down from heaven and see
our plight.
Take care of this grapevine
15 that you yourself have planted,
this son you have raised for yourself.
16 For we are chopped up and burned by
our enemies.
May they perish at the sight of your
frown.
17 Strengthen the man you love,
the son of your choice.
18 Then we will never abandon you again.
Revive us so we can call on your
name once more.

19 Turn us again to yourself, O LORD God
of Heaven's Armies.
Make your face shine down upon us.
Only then will we be saved.

80:6 As in Syriac version; Hebrew reads *the strife.* **80:11** Hebrew *west to the sea, . . . east to the river.*

NOTES

80:TITLE *Lilies of the Covenant.* In the Hebrew text the words translated "lilies" and "covenant" are separated by a major disjunctive accent (specifically, *'athnach*), and the first word is not in the construct state, so the two words are not to be read together according to the ancient tradition. These two words occur, however, in a construct relationship in the title to Ps 60. Thus, the emendation presumed by the NLT may be warranted.

80:2 *Show us.* The word *'orerah* [TH5782, ZH6424] means "awaken." The picture is that of God's power being aroused from sleep so as to be employed for the benefit of his people (see 44:23 [24]).

80:6 *scorn.* The word *madon* [TH4066, ZH4506] means "strife" (HALOT 2.548). "Scorn" presumes an emendation to *manod* [TH4493, ZH4506] (HALOT 2.600; see 44:13-14 [14-15]).

COMMENTARY

The theme of Psalm 80 is found in the refrain: "Turn us again to yourself, O LORD God of Heaven's Armies. Make your face shine down upon us. Only then will we be saved." Psalm 80 is a prayer for restoration to God's favor that will result in deliverance from distress. The threefold refrain grows in intensity as the vocative grows from "O God" (80:3) to "O God of Heaven's Armies" (80:7) to "O LORD God of Heaven's Armies" (80:19).

At the heart of this refrain is the image of God's face shining on the community. God's face being turned away or hidden from someone is an image of the absence of God and his blessing (13:1; 27:9; 30:7; 44:24; 69:17; 88:14; 102:2; 104:29; 143:7).[1] By way of contrast, God's face shining on someone is an image of his presence in blessing (4:6-8; 31:16; 44:3; 67:1; 119:135).[2] This image evokes the Aaronic benediction: "May the LORD smile [lit., make his face shine] on you and be gracious to you" (Num 6:25). The plea for God's face to shine is made in a time of trouble, when his blessings are absent. Thus "the psalm in its continued use belongs to the repertoire of the afflicted people of God on their way through the troubles of history" (Mays 1994:264).

Two other images play key roles in this psalm: God as shepherd (80:1-3 and 80:4-7) and God as vinedresser (80:8-14a, 14b-19). The four strophes are chiastically arranged:

Pleading for the shepherd's favor (80:1-3)
  Lamenting the shepherd's anger (80:4-7)
  Lamenting the vinedresser's neglect (80:8-14a)
Pleading for the vinedresser's favor (80:14b-19)

Pleading for the Shepherd's Favor (80:1-3). The psalmist begins by addressing God as the "Shepherd of Israel" and "you who lead Joseph's descendants like a flock." This image of the shepherd and his flock continues the imagery found in 77:20; 78:70-72; 79:13 (McCann 1996:998). But the address is quite extraordinary. "Please listen" implies that the shepherd is inattentive to the concerns of the sheep; "Display your radiant glory" implies that the shepherd's glorious presence is absent; "Show us [lit., awaken] your mighty power" implies that the shepherd is asleep. To the community it appears as if God is inattentive, absent, and asleep (McCann 1996:999).

Yet the community is still the community of faith. They call upon God as their shepherd-king (Mays 1994:262). In spite of appearances, they believe God to be the one "enthroned above the cherubim." The cherubim stood on the top of the Ark of the Covenant, the footstool of God's throne on earth (DBI 43). Addressing God as the one "enthroned above the cherubim" is an affirmation of faith in his reign in spite of evidence to the contrary. In faith the community here pleads for God's favor to be experienced.

Lamenting the Shepherd's Anger (80:4-7). The shepherd image continues in the language of God providing food and drink. But in the community's present circumstances God is feeding them sorrow and giving them buckets full of tears to drink—and this in sharp contrast to God's provision of life-giving food and water in the wilderness (Tate 1990:314). And as in 79:4, so too here, the community is the object of scorn to the "neighbors."

Here we learn the important lesson that faith does not preclude the honest lamenting of our deepest troubles. Faith, rather, gives us boldness to bring our distress to expression in the very presence of the one who "fed us with sorrow and made us drink tears by the bucketful." God invites such honest dialogue, knowing that it is part of the path to restoration.

Lamenting the Vinedresser's Neglect (80:8–14a). The lamenting continues in this strophe, though the image changes. Here the image shifts to that of the vinedresser. The vinedresser brought a vine out of Egypt with the intention of transplanting it in the Promised Land. Much preparation would be necessary before the vine could be replanted in the new vineyard. In reality, the pagan nations would have to be removed from the land, and this removal is expressed in the metaphorical language of the ground being cleared. The vinedresser did everything necessary to have a fruitful vine. And fruitful it was: It "took root and filled the land," spreading from the Mediterranean to the Euphrates.

"But now, why have you broken down our walls?" (80:12). What a painful question. What a stark contrast. What an honest lament about God's apparent lack of care for his vineyard in the present. "Why have you broken down our walls so that all who pass by may steal our fruit?" asks the community of faith. Deep perplexity rises to the surface with this question. The next strophe contains an implicit confession of sin (80:18), but in this psalm not even the sin of the community can explain God's treatment of his flock and vineyard and thus remove the perplexity. But "Why?" is not the final word of the psalm. Lamenting gives way to pleading once again for favor.

Pleading for the Vinedresser's Favor (80:14b–19). "Take care of this grapevine that *you yourself* have planted" (italics mine). The image of Israel as a vine then shifts to the more personal image of Israel as a "son," a son that God has raised for himself. The appeal here is the ultimate appeal to God's own purposes. God purposed to take the vine from Egypt and to successfully transplant it in the Promised Land. God did everything necessary to ensure its success. Will God now fail to complete the work that he himself began? The son of God's choice must have the strength of God himself to be a faithful son in the present and future, presenting all of his life to God as his response to God's restorative favor. So the psalm ends with the third occurrence of the refrain: "Turn us again to yourself, O LORD God of Heaven's Armies. Make your face shine down upon us. Only then will we be saved."

Israel never was that faithful son in the full sense. That is why Jesus had to come. He is the truly faithful son. He said, "I am the true grapevine, and my Father is the gardener" (John 15:1). Jesus then went on to say, "Yes, I am the vine; you are the branches. Those who remain in me, and I in them, will produce much fruit. For apart from me you can do nothing" (John 15:5). United to Jesus Christ by faith, we are the son-vine-flock of God, having in Jesus all that is necessary to produce much fruit in our own lives and in the lives of many around us (DBT 630).

So this psalm encourages us to know who we are in Christ and to plead for God's favor in times of trouble, believing that "God, who began the good work within you, will continue his work until it is finally finished on the day when Christ Jesus returns" (Phil 1:6).

ENDNOTES

1. All of these verses contain the Hebrew word *paneh* [TH6440, ZH7156] (face).
2. All of these verses contain the Hebrew word *paneh* (face) and a verb that could be translated "shine."

◆ I. Psalm 81

*For the choir director: A psalm of Asaph, to be accompanied by a stringed instrument.**

1 Sing praises to God, our strength.
Sing to the God of Jacob.
2 Sing! Beat the tambourine.
Play the sweet lyre and the harp.
3 Blow the ram's horn at new moon,
and again at full moon to call a festival!
4 For this is required by the decrees of Israel;
it is a regulation of the God of Jacob.
5 He made it a law for Israel*
when he attacked Egypt to set us free.

I heard an unknown voice say,
6 "Now I will take the load from your shoulders;
I will free your hands from their heavy tasks.
7 You cried to me in trouble, and I saved you;
I answered out of the thundercloud
and tested your faith when there was no water at Meribah.
Interlude

8 "Listen to me, O my people, while I give you stern warnings.
O Israel, if you would only listen to me!
9 You must never have a foreign god;
you must not bow down before a false god.
10 For it was I, the LORD your God,
who rescued you from the land of Egypt.
Open your mouth wide, and I will fill it with good things.

11 "But no, my people wouldn't listen.
Israel did not want me around.
12 So I let them follow their own stubborn desires,
living according to their own ideas.
13 Oh, that my people would listen to me!
Oh, that Israel would follow me, walking in my paths!
14 How quickly I would then subdue their enemies!
How soon my hands would be upon their foes!
15 Those who hate the LORD would cringe before him;
they would be doomed forever.
16 But I would feed you with the finest wheat.
I would satisfy you with wild honey from the rock."

81:TITLE Hebrew *according to the gittith.* **81:5** Hebrew *for Joseph.*

NOTES

81:3 *at full moon.* The word *keseh* [TH3677A, ZH4057] is apparently an alternative form of *kese'* [TH3677, ZH4057] ("full moon"; HALOT 2.487).

81:5 *Egypt.* Lit., "land of Egypt," as in 81:10.

I heard an unknown voice. There are two possible interpretations of this colon: the NLT, like the NRSV and most contemporary commentators, understands the colon as introducing the following section, whereas other translations (e.g., NIV) understand the reference to be the foreign language of Egypt in connection with the previous two cola.

81:6 ***I will take the load.*** It seems better to take the perfect tense as a reference to the past (I relieved) in keeping with the past-time references in the following verses.

81:16 ***I would feed you.*** The NLT may be correct in presuming an emendation from the problematic third-person (he) Waw-relative imperfect to the first-person (I) imperfect with the simple Waw, which would provide agreement with the following colon, but Hebrew poetic conventions did not require absolute agreement in these matters as we might.

COMMENTARY

Praise (81:1-5a) and preaching (81:5b-16) are juxtaposed in this psalm. The two strophes are, however, integrated into a larger whole, as indicated by the repetitions of *'erets mitsrayim* [TH776/4714A, ZH824/5213] (land of Egypt) in 81:5, 10 [6, 11] and *yisra'el* [TH3478, ZH3776] (Israel) in 81:4, 8, 11, 13 [5, 9, 12, 14]. There is integration, however, on a deeper level. The preaching takes place in the context of praise, which is one aspect of the appropriate response to the preaching.

Psalm 81:5b-16 is remarkable preaching by God himself. In this sermon God reveals something of his heart for his people. And the psalm as a whole reveals something of what our response to God's heart is to be.

God Responds to Our Cries (81:6-7). There are times when the burdens of life weigh heavily on our shoulders, times when our hands are put to burdensome tasks. Such was the lot of Israel in Egypt. But when the Israelites cried out to God in their trouble, God was responsive. He answered and saved his people, relieving them of their burdens and heavy tasks. God's heart is not cold toward us as his people. He is responsive to the cries that arise from us in times of trouble.

God Warns Us of Danger (81:8-9). There are mortal dangers that we face in life, dangers not only to our bodies but to our souls. The chief danger is that of turning to false gods. Israel was chiefly tempted to turn to Baal, the god of the Canaanites, who was thought to be the provider of the rain without which life would have been impossible in the Promised Land. Though the temptation to bow down to objects made of wood or stone is not one that most of God's people face today, we are tempted to set up idols in our hearts (see Ezek 14:1-8)—that is, we are tempted to look to someone or something other than the Lord as the ultimate source of our well-being in life. Such idolatry does not lead to life but to death. And God has always loved his people too much to let them wander down that path of destruction. From his heart of love, God warns us of the dangers of idolatry.

God Promises Us Abundance (81:10). The Israelites were not to turn to false gods, for it was the Lord, the true and living God, who rescued them from their bondage to the Egyptians. Likewise, we are not to turn to false gods, because it is the true and living God who, through the life and death and resurrection of the Lord Jesus Christ, has rescued us from the bondage of sin and the miseries that accompany that sin. And God's heart is so magnanimous that his rescue comes with a promise of great abundance: "Open your mouth wide, and I will fill it with good things."

God Lets Us Suffer Consequences (81:11-15). At times, in spite of God's magnanimous heart, our heart is stubbornly set in its own way. We do not listen to God's instructions that are intended to give us life. At such times, we are like stubborn

Israel at Meribah (see Exod 17 and Num 20). We do not trust God or obey him. So he lets us follow our own stubborn hearts and live according to our own desires, even when the consequences are trouble. God lets us suffer the consequences of our stubbornness—being oppressed by enemies and foes of various kinds. This is, in a sense, contrary to his own heart. Though he lets us go our own way, his heart longs for us to choose a different path: "Oh, that my people would listen to me! Oh, that Israel would follow me, walking in my paths!" God's heart longs for us to follow him and to experience the blessings that flow from that faithfulness.

God Longs to Bless (81:16). God would rather bless us abundantly than have us experience the negative consequences of stubborn hearts. So the psalm ends with a deep expression of God's heart that is full of blessing for us: "But I would feed you with the finest wheat. I would satisfy you with wild honey from the rock." "God wills abundance, not just manna in the wilderness, but 'the finest of wheat' . . . and not just water from the rock . . . but honey" (McCann 1996:1004). He truly longs to bless us richly. So great is his heart toward us, God longs to bless us more than we long to be blessed by him.

In response to this revelation of God's heart, we are to listen to him. The verb "listen" occurs five times in this psalm (see 81:5, 8 [twice], 11, 13) and is a key theme. God longs for us to listen to him, because he knows that when we listen we live—we live the abundant life that he has created for us.

As we listen to God's voice, following him and walking in his paths, we live. And as we live as a result of God's abundant blessings, we respond with worship (81:1-5a). Psalm 81 is ultimately not a sermon but a song of praise that arises from our hearts in response to the most bountiful heart of God. Since God's blessings are abundant, our worship is exuberant. We worship with song, with tambourine, with lyre and harp, and with trumpets sounding. We worship God because he has taught us that worship is the appropriate response to his heart. We worship him because we listen to him whose heart is bountiful toward us.

◆ J. Psalm 82

A psalm of Asaph.

1 God presides over heaven's court;
he pronounces judgment on the heavenly beings:
2 "How long will you hand down unjust decisions
by favoring the wicked? *Interlude*

3 "Give justice to the poor and the orphan;
uphold the rights of the oppressed and the destitute.
4 Rescue the poor and helpless;
deliver them from the grasp of evil people.
5 But these oppressors know nothing;
they are so ignorant!
They wander about in darkness,
while the whole world is shaken to the core.
6 I say, 'You are gods;
you are all children of the Most High.
7 But you will die like mere mortals
and fall like every other ruler.' "

8 Rise up, O God, and judge the earth,
for all the nations belong to you.

NOTES

82:1 *presides.* Lit., "stands" (see commentary).

heaven's court. The word *'adath-'el* [TH5712/410A, ZH6337/446] (assembly of God) may refer, as indicated by the NLT, to a heavenly assembly. In light of the reference to God pronouncing judgment in 82:1b, this must be a judicial assembly. A heavenly assembly of the gods is referred to in the almost identical Ugaritic phrase *'dt ilm* ("assembly of the gods"; HALOT 2.790). (The difference in the Ugaritic phrase is that the second noun is plural, "gods.") There are heavenly assemblies referred to in the OT (89:5-8; 1 Kgs 22:19-23; Job 1:6-12; 2:1-6), but those assembled before God are angelic beings rather than the divine beings of Ugaritic mythology.

judgment on. Lit., "judgment among/in the midst of."

heavenly beings. The word *'elohim* [TH430, ZH466] typically refers to the true and living God (Exod 20:2) or other gods (Exod 20:3) but is probably used several times for human judges (see Exod 21:6; 22:8, 9, NIV). This same word is used in 82:6, where it refers to the same group as in 82:1 and is translated "gods." Three interpretations are possible. First, the reference is to the so-called gods of the surrounding nations and is used as part of a polemic against the dominion of wickedness in this world (VanGemeren 1991:534). Second, the reference is to angelic beings (Briggs 1906:2.215). (Concerning this interpretation Calvin [1979:330] says, "To apply it to angels is a fancy too strained to admit of serious consideration.") Third, the reference is to human judges (Calvin 1979:330; Delitzsch 1982:402). The last option is the most likely in view of the deaths of these "gods" in 82:7 and the lack of biblical support for the idea that angelic beings were commissioned to judge, uphold the rights of, rescue, or deliver poor and oppressed human beings. The third interpretation also fits with the use of this text by Jesus in John 10:34-36. However, one problem with this interpretation is that the court where God is judging "in the midst of the gods" may be in heaven, whereas human judges would have been on the earth and not assembled in the heavenly court. This problem may be resolved either in light of the interface between what takes place in heaven and on earth (see 1 Kgs 22:19-23; Job 1:6-12; 2:1-6) or—and this is more likely—by understanding the "assembly of God" in 82:1 to be located on earth after the analogy of the *'adath yhwh* [TH5712/3068, ZH6337/3378] ("assembly of the LORD"; see Num 27:17; 31:16; Josh 22:16)—keeping in mind that the word "heaven's" in the NLT is an interpretative addition to the Hebrew text.

82:5 *the whole world is shaken to the core.* For the idea of the earth being shaken (*mot* [TH4131, ZH4572]), see 46:1-3. The phrase "to the core" renders the word *mosede* [TH4144, ZH4587] (foundations of).

COMMENTARY

In Psalm 81 God speaks to the entire community. In Psalm 82 he speaks to the judges of that community. Those judges have not judged rightly, so they themselves are being judged by God. As in Psalm 81, so too here, people suffer the consequences of their own actions. The psalm seems to be chiastically arranged (Tate 1990:334):

God judges the judges (82:1)
  The indictment of the judges (82:2)
    The responsibility of the judges (82:3-4)
      The result of the failure of the judges (82:5)
    The status of the judges (82:6)
  The sentence of the judges (82:7)
God judges the earth (82:8)

This structure focuses our attention on the result of human failure (the center) and the need for divine intervention (the outer frame).

God Judges the Judges (82:1). The psalm opens abruptly with a declaration that God is standing in the court. It was probably the case that in the ancient Near East judges sat during the arguments of a trial but then stood to pronounce the sentence (Tate 1990:335). Accordingly, the picture here would be that of God standing and rendering his verdict against the accused. Psalm 82:2-7 thus records God's own summary of the whole trial.

The Indictment of the Judges (82:2). The judges are accused of rendering unjust decisions. In particular, they are accused of showing favoritism toward the wicked. Such favoritism is contrary to the just character of God, who never shows favoritism, especially to the detriment of the defenseless (Deut 10:17-18). The "wicked" are probably the wealthy and the powerful who, with help from the injustice of the judges, have oppressed the poor and the helpless (see 82:3-5) with impunity.

The Responsibility of the Judges (82:3-4). The verbs in this strophe are all imperatives. These imperatives do not express what the judges ought to do in the future but are a rhetorical way of articulating what they ought to have done in the past. These judges ought to have brought justice in general, and justice to the defenseless in particular, because in so doing they would have been judging according to the pattern of God himself (see 9:7-9, 18; 10:17-18; 146:7-9). These verses then lay out the judges' responsibilities, which they failed to execute.

The Result of the Failure of the Judges (82:5). Injustice shakes society at its very foundation. As God's own reign is founded on justice (97:2), so is human society. Pervasive injustice will inevitably result in the collapse of society.

The Status of the Judges (82:6). Since God is *the* judge, human judges functioning as his agents of justice are said to be "gods" themselves. Calvin (1979:330) says, "The name *gods* is to be understood as *judges,* on whom God has impressed special marks of his glory." Similarly, in Exodus 4:16, Moses will be "god" to Aaron, who will then speak to Pharaoh on behalf of Moses. This special status brings with it the responsibilities spelled out in the corresponding strophe (82:3-4).

The Sentence of the Judges (82:7). The judges are guilty of the indictment recorded in the corresponding strophe (82:2), so this sentence is pronounced against them: "But you will die like mere mortals and fall like every other ruler."

God Judges the Earth (82:8). To rectify the problem of injustice at the hands of human judges it will be necessary for the divine judge to rise up and execute justice. And by judging the "heavenly beings" (82:1), God will judge the "earth" (82:8). By judging the heavenly beings, God will be putting the affairs of the earth back into proper order. The world will not be shaken to its core; rather, its foundations will be held firmly in place. All the nations belong to God. They are ultimately under his dominion. His rule and justice will finally prevail.

◆ K. Psalm 83

A song. A psalm of Asaph.

1 O God, do not be silent!
Do not be deaf.
Do not be quiet, O God.
2 Don't you hear the uproar of your
enemies?
Don't you see that your arrogant
enemies are rising up?
3 They devise crafty schemes against
your people;
they conspire against your precious
ones.
4 "Come," they say, "let us wipe out
Israel as a nation.
We will destroy the very memory
of its existence."
5 Yes, this was their unanimous
decision.
They signed a treaty as allies
against you—
6 these Edomites and Ishmaelites;
Moabites and Hagrites;
7 Gebalites, Ammonites, and
Amalekites;
and people from Philistia and Tyre.
8 Assyria has joined them, too,
and is allied with the descendants
of Lot. *Interlude*

9 Do to them as you did to the
Midianites
and as you did to Sisera and Jabin
at the Kishon River.
10 They were destroyed at Endor,
and their decaying corpses fertilized
the soil.
11 Let their mighty nobles die as Oreb
and Zeeb did.
Let all their princes die like Zebah
and Zalmunna,
12 for they said, "Let us seize for our
own use
these pasturelands of God!"
13 O my God, scatter them like
tumbleweed,
like chaff before the wind!
14 As a fire burns a forest
and as a flame sets mountains
ablaze,
15 chase them with your fierce storm;
terrify them with your tempest.
16 Utterly disgrace them
until they submit to your name,
O LORD.
17 Let them be ashamed and terrified
forever.
Let them die in disgrace.
18 Then they will learn that you alone
are called the LORD,
that you alone are the Most High,
supreme over all the earth.

NOTES

83:1 ***O God, do not be silent . . . deaf . . . quiet.*** The Hebrew text contains three synonymous negative imperatives. The force of the verse could be captured by sheer repetition in English: "O God, don't be silent, don't be silent, don't be silent."

83:2 ***Don't you hear . . . ?*** The Hebrew text contains a statement rather than a question. The statement begins with "for," which provides the reason for the petition in 83:1, as is typically the case in laments.

83:10 ***their decaying corpses fertilized the soil.*** Lit., "they became dung on the ground." This expression is regularly used of decaying corpses (2 Kgs 9:37; Jer 8:2; 9:22; 16:4; 25:33), but "fertilized" is not graphic enough. The text may not be as polite as English usage requires.

83:16 ***until they submit to your name.*** The verb (Piel of *baqash* [TH1245, ZH1335]) means "seek" and is an indirect volitive used to express purpose (Joüon and Muraoka 1991:§116d), so the sense is "so that they may seek your name."

83:18 ***Then they will learn that you alone are called the* L**ORD**.** The word that lies behind the English "you are called" is *simka* [TH8034/3509.2, ZH9005/3870] (your name), the exact expression used in 83:16. These two uses of "your name" are significant for our understanding of the psalm (see commentary).

COMMENTARY

Psalm 82 brings us face-to-face with two harsh realities of different sorts. First, there are times in our lives when God seems to be sitting idly by in harsh silence, while our very existence is threatened with extinction. Second, there are psalms, like Psalm 83, that call down God's judgment on people with a harsh tone that seems inconsistent with his love (see Deut 10:18-19 and Matt 5:43-45). Reflecting on this psalm will provide us insight for living with these realities. Two strophes make up this community lament: a prayer for God's action (83:1-8) and a prayer for God's vengeance (83:9-18).

Prayer for God's Action (83:1-8). The psalm begins with a petition, the threefold nature of which emphasizes the desperation of those who pray: "O God, don't be silent, don't be silent, don't be silent." We may know the truth that "he who watches over Israel never slumbers or sleeps" (121:4), but there are times when the dire nature of our circumstances seems to belie that truth. Such was the case in the circumstances of God's people that lie behind this psalm. These circumstances, and thus the reason for the petition in 83:1, are detailed for us in 83:2-8.

The reason for the petition begins with the contrast between the tumult of the enemies of God and the apparent silence of God himself. Perhaps the uproar of the enemy will pull God out of his silent inactivity. The enemies of God demonstrate their arrogant animosity toward him by plotting the extinction of his people. There may never have been an occasion when the nations listed here actually allied themselves against Israel. Rather, the text may be expressing in stereotypical and hyperbolic language the desperation of the community of faith when facing extinction from hostile, foreign powers (see Tate 1990:345). This lack of historical specificity has made it easier for later generations of believers to appropriate this psalm when in their own dire straits. God teaches us through this psalm that prayer is the appropriate approach to a God who seems to be sitting idly by as we suffer.

Prayer for God's Vengeance (83:9-18). The nature of the vengeance prayed for is expressed primarily in figurative language. The figures begin with a series of similes from Israel's past history. The defeat of the Midianites and their leaders (Oreb, Zeeb, Zebah, and Zalmunna) at the hand of Gideon (Judg 6–8) is referred to, as is the defeat of Sisera and Jabin at the hands of Deborah and Jael (Judg 4–5). The prayer is that God would treat the present enemies as he had treated the enemies in the past.

Next follows a series of similes from the realm of nature's destructive side. "Scatter them like tumbleweed" conjures up the picture of rolling thistles and dried stubble mixed with dust and driven by the wind (Tate 1990:348). "Like chaff before the wind" is a common picture of judgment, taken from the practice of threshing grain in the wind.[1] The image of chaff driven by the wind is frequently associated with the image of a consuming fire,[2] as is the case here.

The literal nature of the vengeance is found in the language of shame, disgrace, terror, and destruction. The prayer for vengeance is hyperbolic, since the nations perish so that they may know something of who God is. The hyperbolic nature of the prayer is supported by the express purpose of the prayer. This purpose is twofold in keeping with the twofold use of "your name." The first reason given for the vengeance is that the enemy might "submit to your name" (see note on 83:16). The second reason is that the enemy might "learn that you alone are called the LORD" and that they might know that the Lord alone is "the Most High, supreme over all the earth." As Psalm 82 ended with the affirmation of God's sovereign possession of the nations, so Psalm 83 ends with the prayer that the nations, even the enemy nations experiencing the vengeance of God, might seek him and know him as Lord of all.

Thus, in this psalm even the vengeance of God is taken up into his saving purposes for the world. It is God's will that in the end "at the name of Jesus every knee should bow, in heaven and on earth and under the earth, and every tongue confess that Jesus Christ is Lord, to the glory of God the Father" (Phil 2:10-11).

ENDNOTES

1. See 1:4; 35:5; 83:13; Job 13:25; 21:18; Isa 17:13; 29:5; 41:2; Dan 2:35; Hos 13:3; Zeph 2:2; Matt 3:12; Luke 3:17.
2. See Exod 15:7; Isa 33:11; Mal 4:1; Matt 3:12; Luke 3:17.

◆ L. Psalm 84

*For the choir director: A psalm of the descendants of Korah, to be accompanied by a stringed instrument.**

1 How lovely is your dwelling place,
O LORD of Heaven's Armies.
2 I long, yes, I faint with longing
to enter the courts of the LORD.
With my whole being, body and soul,
I will shout joyfully to the living God.
3 Even the sparrow finds a home,
and the swallow builds her nest and raises her young
at a place near your altar,
O LORD of Heaven's Armies, my King and my God!
4 What joy for those who can live in your house,
always singing your praises.
Interlude

5 What joy for those whose strength comes from the LORD,
who have set their minds on a pilgrimage to Jerusalem.
6 When they walk through the Valley of Weeping,*
it will become a place of refreshing springs.
The autumn rains will clothe it with blessings.
7 They will continue to grow stronger,
and each of them will appear before God in Jerusalem.*

8 O LORD God of Heaven's Armies, hear my prayer.
Listen, O God of Jacob. *Interlude*

9 O God, look with favor upon the king, our shield!
Show favor to the one you have anointed.

10 A single day in your courts
is better than a thousand anywhere else!
I would rather be a gatekeeper in the house of my God
than live the good life in the homes of the wicked.

[11] For the LORD God is our sun and
our shield.
He gives us grace and glory.
The LORD will withhold no good thing
from those who do what is right.
[12] O LORD of Heaven's Armies,
what joy for those who trust
in you.

84:TITLE Hebrew *according to the gittith.* **84:6** Or *Valley of Poplars;* Hebrew reads *valley of Baca.* **84:7** Hebrew *Zion.*

NOTES

84:1 *your dwelling place.* The word is plural but the reference is to the singular dwelling of God in Jerusalem (see 84:4, 7, 10 [5, 8, 11]); the plural of intensity is also used in reference to God's dwelling in 43:3, 46:4 [5], and 132:7.

84:6 *springs . . . rains.* McCann (1996:1014) says, "The mention of springs and rain may imply a connection with the pilgrimage Festival of Tabernacles, which is associated elsewhere with rain (Zech 14:16-19)." The Festival of Tabernacles (or Shelters) was celebrated in the fall in connection with the onset of the rainy season, and the likely reference to the fall rains in the following psalm (85:12) supports McCann's suggestion.

COMMENTARY

There is a restlessness, a longing, in our hearts as human beings, a restlessness that can only be satisfied by the presence of God. Psalm 84 brings this longing to expression. Psalm 84 is a lovely psalm about the lovely dwelling place of God. The longing for the dwelling of God that comes to expression in this psalm is reminiscent of Psalms 42–43, but Psalm 84 does not contain the discouraging tone of Psalms 42–43. In Psalms 42–43 the psalmist painfully laments being separated from God's dwelling, whereas here the psalmist joyfully anticipates entering God's dwelling at the culmination of a pilgrimage. But if the truth be known, the longing is for a presence more than a place. The place is longed for because of the presence that is there, the presence of God.

The Loveliness of God. The loveliness of the dwelling is a reflection of the loveliness of the God who dwells there (Mays 1994:274). Four times he is called "LORD of Heaven's Armies" (84:1, 3, 8, 12), a title that speaks of God's transcendent sovereignty over all he has made. He is "the living God" (84:2), the one who is himself alive and the source of all other life. He is "my King and my God" (84:3), not just the transcendent God but the God whose presence is personal and immanent. As "sun" and "shield" (84:11; see note), God is the source of all light (physical and spiritual) and all protection.

The Blessings from God. God's loveliness is also seen in the bounty of the blessings he bestows. There are times when the pilgrim must "walk through the Valley of Weeping," but in the mystery of his loveliness, God transforms such a valley into "a place of refreshing springs" (84:6). In his lovely bounty God "gives . . . grace and glory" to his children; he does not withhold a single good thing from them (84:11). So his children are three times declared to be "happy" (*'ashre* [TH835A, ZH897]; 84:4, 5, 12 [5, 6, 13])—that is, they experience total well-being (see note at 1:1). This happiness is the gift of God's grace granted to those (1) who live in his presence (84:4), (2) who are not ultimately self-reliant but who find in God the source of their strength (84:5), and (3) who live a life of faith in God (84:12). Such people are never static but experience continued growth throughout life's pilgrimage to the deeper presence of God.

The Longing for God. God's loveliness and blessings explain the psalmist's deep longing for God. As I write, the swallows have returned to my neighborhood and are busily building their homes in the eaves of neighborhood houses. But neither their nests nor our houses are ultimately "home." The divine presence is home—home for the swallows (84:3) and home for us in an even deeper sense. Our longing for the divine presence is so intense that we would give up a thousand days elsewhere for just one day at home. We would rather have the humblest station in God's presence than the most exalted station apart from that presence. We are willing to endure much pain for the privilege of his presence.

The Prayer to God. Psalm 84:8-9 is a prayer for the king to experience the favor and mercy of God, for as the king is blessed by God, so will the people be blessed. This is seen in the fact that the king and God are both said to be "shield" (84:9, 11). It is typically the case that God's protection, and for that matter, all of his blessings, comes through human agency. And the principle human agent during the monarchy was the king, the Lord's anointed, the representative of the people. The ultimate anointed and royal human representative is at the same time God himself—the Lord Jesus Christ. He is the presence of God. He is the strength of God in whom we trust and in whom we experience the loveliness and blessings of God.

The Praise of God. The loveliness of God, the blessings from God, the longing for God, and the prayer to God find their culmination in the praise of God: "With my whole being, body and soul, I will shout joyfully to the living God" (84:2). And the happy ones who live in God's presence are "always singing [God's] praises" (84:4). "How lovely is your dwelling place, O LORD of Heaven's Armies" (84:1).

◆ M. Psalm 85

For the choir director: A psalm of the descendants of Korah.

**1 LORD, you poured out blessings on
your land!
You restored the fortunes of Israel.*
2 You forgave the guilt of your people—
yes, you covered all their sins.
Interlude
3 You held back your fury.
You kept back your blazing anger.**

**4 Now restore us again, O God of our
salvation.
Put aside your anger against us
once more.
5 Will you be angry with us always?
Will you prolong your wrath to all
generations?
6 Won't you revive us again,
so your people can rejoice in you?
7 Show us your unfailing love, O LORD,
and grant us your salvation.**

**8 I listen carefully to what God the LORD
is saying,
for he speaks peace to his faithful
people.
But let them not return to their
foolish ways.
9 Surely his salvation is near to those
who fear him,
so our land will be filled with his
glory.**

[10] Unfailing love and truth have met
together.
Righteousness and peace have
kissed!
[11] Truth springs up from the earth,
and righteousness smiles down from
heaven.
[12] Yes, the LORD pours down his
blessings.
Our land will yield its bountiful
harvest.
[13] Righteousness goes as a herald before
him,
preparing the way for his steps.

85:1 Hebrew *of Jacob*. See note on 44:4.

NOTES

85:1 ***poured out blessings.*** The word *ratsah* [TH7521, ZH8354] means "favored," but this favoring is not a bare disposition within God; it is that, plus a concrete manifestation of that favorable disposition in time and space. The NLT captures the concrete outworking of God's favorable disposition (see 85:12).

restored the fortunes of. The NLT correctly translates the idiom *shub shebuth* [TH7725/7622, ZH8740/8654], which occurs a number of times in the MT (e.g., 14:7; 53:6 [7]; 126:4; Deut 30:3; Job 42:10; Jer 29:14; Amos 9:14). Traditionally this idiom has been understood to have a narrow meaning of "restoration from captivity" (see KJV and NASB). While the phrase may refer in some contexts to a return from captivity, such a return would only be one instance of a "restoration of fortunes" (NIDOTTE 4.58).

85:3 ***You kept back your blazing anger.*** This is often translated "You turned from your hot anger" (NRSV, ESV), but the Hiphil of *shub* [TH7725, ZH8740] (turn, cause to return) is transitive, and the Mem translated as the preposition "from" may have originally been attached to the verb as an enclitic (Tate 1990:365). The enclitic Mem is an archaic grammatical particle of uncertain function but is usually associated with the genitive function of nouns. For a full discussion see Waltke and O'Connor 1990:§9.8. The result in English is a rendering like that of the NLT.

85:4 ***Now restore us again.*** The word *shubenu* [TH7725, ZH8740] is problematic—since this Qal form of *shub* is generally intransitive, it cannot take "us" as an object. One proposed solution assumes a dative nuance (e.g., "turn to/for our benefit") for the object suffixed pronoun (see Dahood 1968:287). The NLT presents another solution (Kraus 1989:173), which understands the Qal as transitive and equivalent to the Hiphil of the same verb, *hashibenu* ("turn us"; 80:3 [4]); compare the Qal of *male'* [TH4390, ZH4848] which means both "be full" (intransitive) and "fill" (transitive), though "fill" is usually expressed with the Piel.

85:8 ***I listen carefully.*** The cohortative is here used to express resolution (Joüon and Muraoka 1991:§114c).

for. The word *ki* [TH3588, ZH3954] is here emphatic and introduces what God has to say (Tate 1990:365) rather than a reason for listening carefully.

peace. The word *shalom* [TH7965, ZH8934] refers to total well-being. In this context *shalom* has a twofold focus: (1) restoration of fellowship with God in keeping with 85:1-7 and (2) agricultural prosperity in keeping with 85:10-13. For other texts where *shalom* refers to agricultural prosperity see 72:3, 7 and 147:14.

85:9 ***his glory.*** As God's favor is not abstract but concrete in 85:1, so too his glory is concrete: His glory filling the land will be experienced when the land yields bountiful crops (85:12).

85:11 ***smiles down.*** Lit., "looks down."

85:12 ***his blessings.*** This is a rendering of the word *tob* [TH2896, ZH3202] (good), which in context would refer first and foremost to the fall rains that get the agricultural year going and that set the stage for the bountiful crops of 85:12. For this same use of "good" see 65:11 [12].

Our land will yield its bountiful harvest. For this language and image see 67:6.

85:13 ***the way for his steps.*** The text envisions God as coming to his people. First and foremost in this context, his coming will be experienced when the fall rains come (see Ps 29).

COMMENTARY

There are times in our spiritual lives when its seems as if we have gone one step forward and two steps backward. Such was the situation that gave rise to Psalm 85. The psalm recalls a past occasion when God's people experienced his restorative grace (85:1-3), but in their present circumstances they stand in need of that grace once again (85:4-7). The promise of restoration is given along with a word of exhortation, to the end that God's people not return to the foolish ways that had evidently brought them into the troublesome situation in which they find themselves (85:8-9). The concrete form of restoration they are looking for is the coming of the rains that result in a bountiful harvest (85:10-13).

The logic and language of this psalm is remarkably similar to Psalm 126, and the situation envisioned in both psalms parallels that of the postexilic community as recorded in Haggai 1: The sin of the people yielded drought and a poor harvest. It is, however, not hard to imagine this situation as having existed any number of times throughout Israel's history.

Prayer for Restoration (85:1-7). The prayer for restoration in the present begins with a recollection of restoration in the past. The psalmist recalls a time when God "restored the fortunes of" his people (85:1). This language presumes that God's people were in need of some kind of restoration, which they then experienced. The needed restoration centered on the return to a right relationship with God through the forgiveness of sins. These sins had resulted in God's anger with his people. Accordingly, the restoration involved a withdrawal of that anger.

"Now restore us again. . . . Put aside your anger" (85:4) indicates that the community had fallen back into old sinful ways. Thus they were once again experiencing God's anger and standing in need of restoration. Grief must have characterized the community, so they pleaded for revival and the restoration of joy that could only come from experiencing salvation (see 51:12). This plea for salvation was rooted in God's unfailing love.

As often as we slide backward and reap the consequences of our sins, we can still come to God for complete restoration, not on the basis of our inherent goodness, but because God is characterized by unfailing love for us as his people.

Promise of Restoration (85:8-9). A representative of the people (the "I" of 85:8) resolved to listen carefully to hear what God would say in response to the prayer of the previous verses. God's response was one of grace. He promised "peace" to his people, peace rooted in a restored relationship with himself through forgiveness and peace experienced in restoration from the negative consequences of sin. This promise of peace was given, along with an exhortation to remain faithful in the future by honoring God with a life of wisdom.

As we come to God for restoration, we do so with great hope that is rooted in the promise of God himself, and we come with great humility that is committed to the transformation of our lives. Wise living would honor God and would result in the land being filled with his glory. The nature of this glory-filled land comes to expression in the final strophe.

Picture of Restoration (85:10–13). Much of the language in this marvelous picture of restoration is to be read literally and metaphorically at the same time. The language of unfailing love, truth, righteousness, and peace is to be understood literally in reference to personal characteristics of God, his people, and their relationship. The restoration takes place because the Lord pours down blessings: his unfailing love, his truth, his righteousness, his peace. The restoration takes place as God's people now live in unfailing love for God and for others, in truth, in righteousness, and in peace.

At the same time this language paints a picture of the land being restored to right order with abundant rain resulting in abundant crops. Truth springing up from the earth and righteousness looking down from heaven are metaphors for the crops that spring up from the land after the rains fall down from the sky. The blessing that God pours down is the rain, without which a bountiful harvest would have been impossible, as is clear from the literal reference to bountiful crops.

While restoration from drought and famine may not be the restoration we stand in need of, this psalm gives us great encouragement to come boldly to God for his restorative grace when we stand in need. He promises to restore us to himself through the forgiveness of our sins, and he promises to restore us to total peace and well-being. Our confidence is even greater than the psalmist's, for we know that our representative, the Lord Jesus, has experienced in his resurrection from the dead the ultimate restoration that guarantees our own.

◆ N. Psalm 86

A prayer of David.

1 Bend down, O LORD, and hear my
prayer;
answer me, for I need your help.
2 Protect me, for I am devoted to you.
Save me, for I serve you and
trust you.
You are my God.
3 Be merciful to me, O Lord,
for I am calling on you constantly.
4 Give me happiness, O Lord,
for I give myself to you.
5 O Lord, you are so good, so ready to
forgive,
so full of unfailing love for all who
ask for your help.
6 Listen closely to my prayer, O LORD;
hear my urgent cry.
7 I will call to you whenever
I'm in trouble,
and you will answer me.

8 No pagan god is like you, O Lord.
None can do what you do!
9 All the nations you made
will come and bow before you, Lord;
they will praise your holy name.
10 For you are great and perform
wonderful deeds.
You alone are God.

11 Teach me your ways, O LORD,
that I may live according to your
truth!
Grant me purity of heart,
so that I may honor you.

[12] **With all my heart I will praise you,**
O Lord my God.
I will give glory to your name forever,
[13] **for your love for me is very great.**
You have rescued me from the
depths of death.*

[14] **O God, insolent people rise up**
against me;
a violent gang is trying to kill me.
You mean nothing to them.
[15] **But you, O Lord,**
are a God of compassion and mercy,
slow to get angry
and filled with unfailing love and
faithfulness.
[16] **Look down and have mercy on me.**
Give your strength to your servant;
save me, the son of your servant.
[17] **Send me a sign of your favor.**
Then those who hate me will be put
to shame,
for you, O LORD, help and comfort me.

86:13 Hebrew *of Sheol.*

NOTES

86:2 ***I serve you.*** Lit., "I am your servant." "Your servant" also occurs in 86:4, 16.

86:4 ***me.*** Lit., "your servant."

86:9 ***they will praise.*** The word *wikabbedu* [TH3513, ZH3877] means "they will give glory to your name." This same verb is used in 86:12, where the psalmist says, "I will give glory to your name."

86:11 ***purity of heart.*** The Hebrew text does not contain the Piel of *taher* [TH2891, ZH3197] or *khata'* [TH2398, ZH2627], either of which could be translated "purify" (see 51:2 [4] for the former and 51:7 [9] for the latter). The text uses the Piel of *yakhad* [TH3161, ZH3479], which means "unite"; "unite my heart" means "give me an undivided heart" (DCH 4.195; see also HALOT 2.405).

honor you. Lit., "fear your name." Heb. *shemeka* [TH8034/3509.2, ZH9005/3870] (your name) occurs three times in 86:8-13. For an "undivided heart" (*lebab shalem* [TH3824/8003, ZH4222/8969]) coupled with the fear of God, as in Ps 86, see 2 Chr 19:9.

86:13 ***You have rescued me.*** It is probably better to interpret *wehitsalta* [TH5337, ZH5911] as a Waw-relative perfect with a future reference, since 86:1-7 and 86:14-17 indicate that the psalmist has not yet been rescued. The statement is accordingly an affirmation of faith.

86:16 ***son of your servant.*** Lit., *ben-'amatheka* [TH1121/519, ZH1201/563] (son of your maidservant).

COMMENTARY

Psalm 86 is a prayer for help in a time of trouble. While much of the language of this psalm can be found in other psalms, the way in which the language has been shaped makes this psalm unique. The poem is chiastic (Tate 1990:378).

Save your servant (86:1-4)
  God is full of unfailing love (86:5-6)
    Trouble strikes (86:7)
      They will glorify God's name (86:8-10)
        Teach me to honor your name (86:11)
      I will glorify God's name (86:12-13)
    People rise up against me (86:14)
  God is full of unfailing love (86:15)
Save your servant (86:16-17)

This structure gives us key insights into responding to our own times of trouble.

Save Your Servant (86:1-4, 16-17). Save! When we experience trouble—physical, psychological, financial, interpersonal—we are to ask God to deliver us. Psalm 86 is fundamentally a prayer of salvation. This salvation is not from our sins, nor is it sought in the life to come. This salvation is from trouble that we are presently experiencing, and it is sought for in this life. There were people who were trying to kill David (86:14). The salvation that David sought was the preservation of his life. While there may be no one trying to kill us, our troubles are just as concrete as David's were, and so the salvation that we seek is equally as tangible (see the commentary on Ps 85).

When we call on God to save, we do so in the context of a relationship. We are his servants, and he is our Lord. Three times David refers to himself as "servant" (86:2, 4, 16) and once as "son of your maidservant" (86:16) which indicates that he was "born to it," that being a servant is at the core of his identity (Mays 1994:279). Seven times David refers to God as "Lord" (*'adonay* [TH113/136, ZH123/151]).[1] In all seven occurrences David speaks of God as "*my* Lord."[2] In the ancient world, the lord was responsible to provide protection for his servant. Servants depended on their lord for help and strength in times of trouble. It is this relationship that provides the context for the prayer for salvation. Often when we think of God as "Lord," we think of him as "boss," the one who tells us what to do. Here we learn that our "Lord" is our protector, not only because of the nature of the relationship, but also because of the nature of our Lord.

God Is Full of Unfailing Love (86:5-6, 15). David twice confesses that God is "full of unfailing love." God is not at all like the lords of this world (Matt 20:25). Our Lord is no cruel tyrant, no hard-hearted master who "lords it over us." He is full of unfailing love! He is merciful and gracious. He is good and always ready to forgive. He does not get angry quickly. He helps and comforts his servants. Knowing a Lord like this, we come to him humbly and honestly for salvation in our times of trouble. And we come knowing that our salvation will result in God's glory.

Glorify God's Name (86:8-10, 12-13). David resolves to glorify God's name, because he knows that God's unfailing love for him is very great. And since God's unfailing love is very great, David knows that God will eventually rescue him from his deepest troubles.

Not only does David resolve to glorify God's name, he also envisions "all the nations" coming to glorify God's name.[3] Nowhere among the gods of the nations is there a god like the true and living God. In fact, he alone is God. Since God is creator of all the nations, he will be glorified by all the nations, as they come to bow before him as their Lord (see 46:10). His redemption will be as broad as his creation, so that in the end "at the name of Jesus every knee should bow, in heaven and on earth and under the earth, and every tongue confess that Jesus Christ is Lord, to the glory of God the Father" (Phil 2:10-11).

Teach Me to Honor Your Name (86:11). Since the glory of God's name is the goal of creation and redemption, David prays (at the very center of this psalm): "Teach me your ways, O LORD, that I may live according to your truth! Grant me purity of heart, so that I may honor you" (86:11). David's hope for the glory of God's name in the future impacts how David wants to live in the present (see 1 John 3:2-3). We respond to trouble not only by seeking salvation from our Lord but also by resolving to honor God with our lives, even while we are in trouble.

Our circumstances may change, but God's truth never does. Living according to his truth is always the best path. At times our hearts are divided. We are double minded. We have divided loyalties. We are not perfectly devoted to God in our hearts. But even then he is full of unfailing love and will teach us and grant us the single-minded devotion we seek, that we, along with the nations, may honor his name with our lips and with our lives.

ENDNOTES

1. See 86:3, 4, 5, 8, 9, 12, 15, which all have the divine name "Lord" (*'adonay* [TH113/136, ZH123/151]), as opposed to "LORD," which is the translation of the divine name *yhwh* [TH3068, ZH3378].
2. See "my King and my God" in 84:3.
3. See this theme in other psalms like 46–49.

◆ O. Psalm 87

A song. A psalm of the descendants of Korah.

[1]On the holy mountain
stands the city founded by the LORD.
[2]He loves the city of Jerusalem
more than any other city in Israel.*
[3]O city of God,
what glorious things are said
of you! ***Interlude***

[4]I will count Egypt* and Babylon among
those who know me—
also Philistia and Tyre, and even
distant Ethiopia.*
They have all become citizens of
Jerusalem!
[5]Regarding Jerusalem* it will
be said,
"Everyone enjoys the rights of
citizenship there."
And the Most High will personally
bless this city.
[6]When the LORD registers the nations,
he will say,
"They have all become citizens
of Jerusalem." ***Interlude***

[7]The people will play flutes* and sing,
"The source of my life springs from
Jerusalem!"

87:2 Hebrew *He loves the gates of Zion more than all the dwellings of Jacob.* See note on 44:4. **87:4a** Hebrew *Rahab,* the name of a mythical sea monster that represents chaos in ancient literature. The name is used here as a poetic name for Egypt. **87:4b** Hebrew *Cush.* **87:5** Hebrew *Zion.* **87:7** Or *will dance.*

NOTES

87:3 ***of you.*** The word *bak* [TH871.2/3509.2, ZH928/3870] is repeated in 87:7, where it is translated "from Jerusalem." This repetition is a key to the structure of the psalm (see commentary).

87:4 ***They have all become citizens.*** The Hebrew text is more rhetorically powerful than the NLT suggests. While it is true that the nations have become citizens of Jerusalem, the language here and in 87:5 and 87:6 is that of being born (*yullad*) in Jerusalem. The nations are pictured as belonging in Jerusalem just as much as those who are citizens by birth. Also, the word *yullad-sham* [TH3205/8033, ZH3528/9004] (born there) is repeated in 87:6 and supplies a second key to the structure of the poem (see commentary).

87:5 *citizenship.* The word *yullad-bah* [TH3205/871.2/1886.3, ZH3528/928/2023] (born in it) connects this verse with the uses of *yullad* in 87:4 and 87:6 and the uses of the preposition *be* in 87:2 and 87:7. This verse is the center of a concentrically formed strophe (see commentary).

COMMENTARY

"All the nations you made will come and bow before you, Lord; they will praise your holy name" (86:9). Psalm 87 expands this theme with a touching beauty that portrays Jerusalem as the mother and birthplace of all the nations. This psalm affirms two fundamental truths (Mays 1994:280-281): Jerusalem is the city of God (87:1-2), and the city of God is the spiritual home of all the nations (87:3-7). The second strophe (87:3-7) is chiastically arranged (Smith 1988:357-358).

In you (87:3)
  Born there (87:4)
    Born in her (87:5)
  Born there (87:6)
In you (87:7)

This structure supports the theme of Jerusalem as central in God's plan for the nations.

Jerusalem, City of God (87:1-2). Like Psalms 46, 48, 76, and 84, Psalm 87 celebrates the truth that Jerusalem is the city where the special presence of God dwelt. This city, situated on the holy mountain (see 2:6; 3:4 [5]; 15:1; 43:3; 48:1 [2]), is the "city of God" because of God's choice (78:68; 132:13)—a choice based not on "the worth of the place, but the free love of God" (Calvin 1979:398; see 78:68). God loves the city as the place where he has chosen to grant the gift of salvation and all the joys that accompany that salvation (132:13-16). As the following strophe declares, this salvation is for all the nations of the world.

Jerusalem, Home of the Nations (87:3-7). "Glorious things" have already been said of Jerusalem in previous psalms. For example:

A river brings joy to the city of our God,
  the sacred home of the Most High.
God dwells in that city; it cannot be destroyed.
  From the very break of day, God will protect it. (46:4-5)

How great is the LORD,
  how deserving of praise,
in the city of our God,
  which sits on his holy mountain!
It is high and magnificent;
  the whole earth rejoices to see it!
Mount Zion, the holy mountain,
  is the city of the great King! (48:1-2)

The glorious thing said of Jerusalem in Psalm 87 is that Jerusalem is the spiritual home not just of Israel but of all of the nations of the world. Former enemy nations like Egypt, Babylon, and Philistia are no longer enemies. They are citizens in the commonwealth of Israel. And they are not merely naturalized citizens; they are family. The nations are recorded in the registry of God as his very own children, having been "born" in his city. The name used for God in 87:5, "the Most High" (*'elyon* [TH5945B, ZH6610]), is most appropriate in this context of God's universal, saving reign over the nations of the earth.

The celebration comes to a close and a climax, as the nations are heard singing the song of God's salvation found in Jerusalem, "The source of my life springs from Jerusalem!"

Psalm 87 is rooted in the theology of the covenant made with Abraham: "All the families on earth will be blessed through you" (Gen 12:3). The apostle Paul develops this theme in the book of Galatians, where he says, "All who put their faith in Christ share the same blessing Abraham received because of his faith" (Gal 3:9). This "all" includes all the nations, for now "there is no longer Jew or Gentile" (Gal 3:28). All who have faith in the Lord Jesus Christ are "children of God" and familial heirs of the promises of God (Gal 3:26, 29). People from all the nations can thus say of the heavenly Jerusalem, "She is our mother" (Gal 4:26) and "The source of my life springs from Jerusalem!" (87:7).

Psalm 87 thus invites us to celebrate the heavenly Jerusalem, the presence of God himself, as the source of our very lives, and it calls us to invite "the nations," even our "enemies," to join in this celebration by placing their faith in the Lord Jesus Christ. Psalm 87 also invites us to live now in the light of the future when "at the name of Jesus every knee should bow, in heaven and on earth and under the earth, and every tongue confess that Jesus Christ is Lord, to the glory of God the Father" (Phil 2:10-11).

◆ P. Psalm 88

For the choir director: A psalm of the descendants of Korah. A song to be sung to the tune "The Suffering of Affliction." A psalm of Heman the Ezrahite.*

1 O LORD, God of my salvation,
I cry out to you by day.
I come to you at night.
2 Now hear my prayer;
listen to my cry.
3 For my life is full of troubles,
and death* draws near.
4 I am as good as dead,
like a strong man with no strength left.
5 They have left me among the dead,
and I lie like a corpse in a grave.
I am forgotten,
cut off from your care.
6 You have thrown me into the lowest pit,
into the darkest depths.
7 Your anger weighs me down;
with wave after wave you have engulfed me. ***Interlude***

8 You have driven my friends away
by making me repulsive to them.
I am in a trap with no way of escape.
9 My eyes are blinded by my tears.
Each day I beg for your help, O LORD;
I lift my hands to you for mercy.
10 Are your wonderful deeds of any use to the dead?
Do the dead rise up and praise you? ***Interlude***

11 Can those in the grave declare your unfailing love?
Can they proclaim your faithfulness in the place of destruction?*

12 Can the darkness speak of your
wonderful deeds?
Can anyone in the land of
forgetfulness talk about your
righteousness?
13 O LORD, I cry out to you.
I will keep on pleading day by day.
14 O LORD, why do you reject me?
Why do you turn your face from me?
15 I have been sick and close to death
since my youth.
I stand helpless and desperate
before your terrors.
16 Your fierce anger has overwhelmed
me.
Your terrors have paralyzed me.
17 They swirl around me like floodwaters
all day long.
They have engulfed me completely.
18 You have taken away my companions
and loved ones.
Darkness is my closest friend.

88:TITLE Hebrew *maskil.* This may be a literary or musical term. 88:3 Hebrew *Sheol.* 88:11 Hebrew *in Abaddon?*

COMMENTARY

"Darkness is my closest friend." These are the final words in this darkest of all laments. These have been my words. Psalm 88 brings to expression like no other psalm the depths of despair experienced by the believer. Unlike other laments, this psalm contains no affirmation of faith, no expression of confidence, no praise, not even a vow to praise in the future. It has been said that in the Psalms one can find words to express any and all of our dark emotions. Psalm 88 contains God-given words for believers to use while groping through in the darkest night of the soul.

The Psalmist's Trouble. The psalmist's trouble began in the body. Physical illness always holds the potential of bringing on the darkness of despair, especially when that illness is prolonged. The psalmist says, "I have been sick and close to death since my youth" (88:15). When days become weeks that become months that become years, a door is opened for the darkness to enter. And the psalmist's illness was not only prolonged, it was also grave. In fact, the psalmist was virtually in the grave. Death was drawing near, and the psalmist was "like a corpse in a grave" in the eyes of the community (88:5). He loathed the prospect of literally descending into the grave, "the place of destruction" and "darkness," "the land of forgetfulness" (88:11-12). He felt "helpless and desperate" (88:15).

Trouble in the body was thus the occasion for trouble in the soul. Trouble in the soul often has three dimensions: trouble in relation to others, to God, and to ourselves (see commentary on Ps 13). Such is the case in Psalm 88. It is often difficult enough to be ill for a long time. But insult is added to injury when illness is coupled with abandonment. When we first become ill, friends are usually there to comfort and help. But for a variety of reasons, friends can fall away as time goes on. The psalmist's companions had abandoned him, and, even worse, they had begun to loathe him. The psalmist felt his friends had "left [him] among the dead" and "forgotten" about him (88:5).

But even more painful was the feeling of being rejected by an angry God. Notice the emphasis on God's actions against the psalmist: "You have thrown me into the lowest pit" (88:6), "Your anger weighs me down; with wave after wave you have engulfed me" (88:7), "You have driven my friends away by making me repulsive to them" (88:8), "O LORD, why do you reject me? Why do you turn your face from me?" (88:14), "You have taken away my companions and loved ones" (88:18). Feelings of being rejected by God can easily be generated by prolonged and grave illness (not to mention other serious trouble). The questions of 88:14—"O LORD, why do you reject me? Why do you turn your face from me?"—are questions that lie deep within the soul, questions that must come to expression as part of the healing process, questions that God in Psalm 88 grants believers the freedom to raise. And since God grants us the freedom to raise these brutally honest questions, we can grant ourselves the freedom to raise them and to allow others to raise them without fear of condemnation.

The illness itself, with the added burden of feelings of abandonment and rejection, produced within the psalmist himself feelings of despair. Words for "darkness" occur three times in this psalm. The psalmist had been thrown down "into the darkest depths" (88:6) and loathed the prospect of entering the "darkness" of death (88:12). He had searched everywhere for light. He had looked to his friends. He had looked to his God: "Each day I beg for your help, O LORD; I lift my hands to you for mercy" (88:9). But he found no light. He found only "darkness" (88:18).

The Psalmist's Recourse. Luther spoke of being in the "state in which Hope despairs, and yet Despair hopes at the same time" (quoted in Perowne 1966:1.180). Though imperceptible to the natural eye, there is a faint glimmer of hope in this psalm, evident in the fact that the psalmist has recourse to prayer. He says, "Now hear my prayer; listen to my cry" (88:2). Prayer, even despairing prayer, is an expression of hope. Though in utter darkness, faith sees an invisible ray of hope's light. So from the darkest depths the psalmist cries, "O LORD . . . I will keep on pleading day by day" (88:13). Someone once said there is no failure until one decides to quit. Lost in the darkness, faith says, "I will not quit; I will keep on pleading."

How do we as New Testament believers use this psalm with integrity? Do we let the darkness of this psalm hang like a pall, or do we let the resurrection of the Lord Jesus Christ—and the hope of our own—shatter the darkness? I believe there is a tendency in our own struggles and our attempts to support others in theirs, a tendency to move too quickly to hope in the life to come as a panacea for struggles in this life. Moving too quickly to hope in the life to come can mean that we never bring the darkness of our despair to expression and might actually hinder the healing process. It also can mean that we are not doing justice to the full value of this life that comes to expression in hope for salvation in this life, a hope that is regularly displayed in the book of Psalms.

Psalm 88 can be most useful in those times when "Hope despairs, and yet Despair hopes at the same time." Psalm 88 is a vehicle for expressing before the face of God and in our own hearing the pain of our bodies and the darkness of our souls. And it allows us to express a profound hope for wellness—in body and soul—in this life, even as we wait for absolute wellness in the life to come.

Psalm 88 invites us to honestly embrace the dark night of the soul, and at the same time it opens a window for a ray of hope to penetrate that darkness, so that we will not quit but will keep on pleading, until "the Sun of Righteousness will rise with healing in his wings" (Mal 4:2).

◆ Q. Psalm 89

A psalm of Ethan the Ezrahite.*

1 I will sing of the LORD's unfailing love forever!
Young and old will hear of your faithfulness.
2 Your unfailing love will last forever.
Your faithfulness is as enduring as the heavens.

3 The LORD said, "I have made a covenant with David, my chosen servant.
I have sworn this oath to him:
4 'I will establish your descendants as kings forever;
they will sit on your throne from now until eternity.' " *Interlude*
5 All heaven will praise your great wonders, LORD;
myriads of angels will praise you for your faithfulness.
6 For who in all of heaven can compare with the LORD?
What mightiest angel is anything like the LORD?
7 The highest angelic powers stand in awe of God.
He is far more awesome than all who surround his throne.
8 O LORD God of Heaven's Armies!
Where is there anyone as mighty as you, O LORD?
You are entirely faithful.

9 You rule the oceans.
You subdue their storm-tossed waves.
10 You crushed the great sea monster.*
You scattered your enemies with your mighty arm.
11 The heavens are yours, and the earth is yours;
everything in the world is yours—you created it all.
12 You created north and south.
Mount Tabor and Mount Hermon praise your name.
13 Powerful is your arm!
Strong is your hand!
Your right hand is lifted high in glorious strength.
14 Righteousness and justice are the foundation of your throne.
Unfailing love and truth walk before you as attendants.
15 Happy are those who hear the joyful call to worship,
for they will walk in the light of your presence, LORD.
16 They rejoice all day long in your wonderful reputation.
They exult in your righteousness.
17 You are their glorious strength.
It pleases you to make us strong.
18 Yes, our protection comes from the LORD,
and he, the Holy One of Israel, has given us our king.

19 Long ago you spoke in a vision to your faithful people.
You said, "I have raised up a warrior.
I have selected him from the common people to be king.
20 I have found my servant David.
I have anointed him with my holy oil.
21 I will steady him with my hand;
with my powerful arm I will make him strong.
22 His enemies will not defeat him,
nor will the wicked overpower him.
23 I will beat down his adversaries before him
and destroy those who hate him.
24 My faithfulness and unfailing love will be with him,
and by my authority he will grow in power.
25 I will extend his rule over the sea,
his dominion over the rivers.
26 And he will call out to me, 'You are my Father,
my God, and the Rock of my salvation.'
27 I will make him my firstborn son,

the mightiest king on earth.
28 I will love him and be kind to him
forever;
my covenant with him will never end.
29 I will preserve an heir for him;
his throne will be as endless as the
days of heaven.
30 But if his descendants forsake my
instructions
and fail to obey my regulations,
31 if they do not obey my decrees
and fail to keep my commands,
32 then I will punish their sin with
the rod,
and their disobedience with beating.
33 But I will never stop loving him
nor fail to keep my promise to him.
34 No, I will not break my covenant;
I will not take back a single word
I said.
35 I have sworn an oath to David,
and in my holiness I cannot lie:
36 His dynasty will go on forever;
his kingdom will endure as the sun.
37 It will be as eternal as the moon,
my faithful witness in the sky!"
Interlude

38 But now you have rejected him and
cast him off.
You are angry with your anointed
king.
39 You have renounced your covenant
with him;
you have thrown his crown in the
dust.
40 You have broken down the walls
protecting him
and ruined every fort defending him.
41 Everyone who comes along has
robbed him,
and he has become a joke to his
neighbors.
42 You have strengthened his enemies
and made them all rejoice.
43 You have made his sword useless
and refused to help him in battle.
44 You have ended his splendor
and overturned his throne.
45 You have made him old before his
time
and publicly disgraced him.
Interlude

46 O LORD, how long will this go on?
Will you hide yourself forever?
How long will your anger burn like
fire?
47 Remember how short my life is,
how empty and futile this human
existence!
48 No one can live forever; all will die.
No one can escape the power of the
grave.* *Interlude*

49 Lord, where is your unfailing love?
You promised it to David with
a faithful pledge.
50 Consider, Lord, how your servants are
disgraced!
I carry in my heart the insults of
so many people.
51 Your enemies have mocked me,
O LORD;
they mock your anointed king
wherever he goes.

52 Praise the LORD forever!
Amen and amen!

89:TITLE Hebrew *maskil*. This may be a literary or musical term. **89:10** Hebrew *Rahab*, the name of a mythical sea monster that represents chaos in ancient literature. **89:48** Hebrew *of Sheol*.

NOTES

89:TITLE *Ethan the Ezrahite.* The reference to the "Ezrahite" clearly connects this psalm with Ps 88, which mentions Heman the Ezrahite in its title; both psalms express deep distress. Ethan the Ezrahite is referred to in 1 Kgs 4:31, as a man of inestimable wisdom in the days of Solomon. The original context of Ps 89 may have been the sack of Jerusalem by Shishak, pharaoh of Egypt, during the reign of Rehoboam (see 1 Kgs 14:25-28; 2 Chr 12:1-12; Delitzsch 1982:33-34).[1] In the literary context of the final form of the Psalter, however, the psalm is to be read in the light of the sack of Jerusalem by the Babylonians in 587 BC.

89:1 ***unfailing love.*** The word *khesed* [TH2617, ZH2876] is used seven times in this psalm (89:1 [2], 2 [3], 14 [15], 24 [25], 28 [29], 33 [34], 49 [50]). The final use is in the plural as is this first use.

faithfulness. The word is *'emunah* [TH530, ZH575], and it, too, is used seven times (89:1 [2], 2 [3], 5 [6], 8 [9], 24 [25], 33 [34], 49 [50]). God's unfailing love and his faithfulness are key motifs in this psalm (see McCann 1996:1036).

89:18 ***our protection.*** Lit., "Our shield" (*maginnenu* [TH4043, ZH4482]). It is true that the Lord is our shield/protection (3:3), but here it seems that the shield is the protection afforded by the Davidic king mentioned in the following colon. For "shield" as a metaphor for a ruler, see note on 47:9.

89:52 ***Praise. . . . Amen and amen!*** Each boundary between the books of the Psalter is marked with a similar call to praise and a double "amen" (see 41:13 and 72:19).

COMMENTARY

The contrast between heights of praise (89:1-37) and depths of lamentation (89:38-51) has led some scholars to conclude that Psalm 89 is a composite of originally unrelated materials. The contrast between praise and lamentation is striking, but not nearly as problematic as the contrast between the psalmist's theology in the first part and his experience in the second. God had unequivocally promised that the Davidic covenant would endure forever, but all the evidence pointed to the fact that God had renounced that covenant. "Theological crisis" is too cerebral a phrase to capture the anguish experienced when the unfailing love of God seems to have failed and when the faithfulness of God seems to have evaporated into unreliability.

Can we depend on God's unfailing love and faithfulness? This is the question that torments our souls when our experience seems to contradict our theology, when our lives show no evidence that God's promises are reliable. This was the question raised by numerous events in the history of Israel but most poignantly by the Exile. "Lord, where is your unfailing love?"

The reliability of God's unfailing love and faithfulness, each referred to seven times in Psalm 89 (see notes), is the existential question that drives this final psalm in Book 3. The Psalter opened with the inauguration of the Davidic covenant, Book 1 ended with the confirmation of that covenant, and Book 2 ended with the transfer of the covenant to Solomon. But at the end of Book 3 the covenant with David seems to have been terminated. The crisis this caused was more profound than the question, "Has the covenant with David been abrogated?" The crisis struck at the very heart of faith. "Is God reliable? Does he keep his word?"

Confidence in God's Unfailing Love and Faithfulness (89:1-37). Psalm 89 opens on a remarkably high note of praise to God for his unfailing love and faithfulness: "I will sing of the LORD's unfailing love forever! Young and old will hear of your faithfulness" (89:1). This praise is followed by an equally remarkable note of confidence: "Your unfailing love will last forever. Your faithfulness is as enduring as the heavens" (89:2).

Not only the psalmist, but also "myriads of angels" will praise God for his faithfulness. These myriads, mighty though they may be, do not compare with the Lord:

None are as mighty as he whose very character is faithfulness. This faithfulness has been displayed in a number of ways.

God has been faithful in the exercise of his power (89:9-13). This power was displayed at the time of creation when God subdued the waters that would have prohibited life (see 104:6-9). God's crushing "the great sea monster" (Rahab) alludes to ancient mythology to affirm that it was the Lord God of Israel and no other god who brought initial order to the world in which humans now live.[2] This order is seen in the heavens and the earth, in the north and the south, on Mount Tabor and Mount Hermon. This order was brought about and is currently maintained by God's powerful arm and hand as well as his unfailing love. It is no wonder that those who hear the joyful call to worship and walk in the light of the Lord's presence are "happy"—i.e., they experience total well-being.[3]

A second way in which God's unfailing love and faithfulness have been exercised is the giving of a king to his people (89:18). Psalm 89:3-4 and 19-37 rehearse the salient feature of the covenant made with David (see 2 Sam 7). At the very heart of this covenant is God's promise that God's "faithfulness and unfailing love" will be with David (89:24). This promise entailed another, that David's dynasty would never come to an end (89:33-36). The sun and moon shine day after day and night after night as faithful witnesses to God's pledge to be faithful to his covenant made with David. It is after this high note of confidence in the faithfulness and unfailing love of God that the psalm takes a radical turn, a turn from confidence to doubt.

Doubts about God's Unfailing Love and Faithfulness (89:38-51). The depths of the doubts are signaled by the words "But now" (89:38). All the evidence from life's experiences indicated that God had in fact rejected the Davidic dynasty and renounced the covenant. The Davidic crown had been trampled in the dust. Jerusalem, the Davidic capital, lay in ruins. The enemies, who were supposed to never defeat David (89:22), were rejoicing in having the upper hand in battle after battle (89:42-43). David's throne had been completely overturned (89:44).

Thus the agonizing cry, "O LORD, how long will this go on? Will you hide yourself forever? How long will your anger burn like fire?" (89:46). And even more painful is the question, "Lord, where is your unfailing love?" (89:49). All of your promises, all that you have purportedly done in the past, all this talk of power and praise—what good is it in the real world in which I live? Does what I believe make any difference in my world, or is it all just pious platitudes that serve to numb the pain?

Perhaps no other psalm articulates with more pathos the agony of soul that is felt when life's experiences call into question the unfailing love and faithfulness that are "God's very character." Perhaps no other psalm can bring as much balm to the soul as does this one. That balm is brought in part by the freedom this psalm grants to be brutally honest with ourselves and with God in admitting the deep doubts we have at times, doubts that God is faithful, that God is love. When faith and experience conflict, pretending that all is well will not do. Denial lacks integrity and indicates shallow spirituality. Honest wrestling is the path to growth and to God.

It may not comfort some to be confronted with the fact that the question raised in 89:49 finds no explicit answer in the psalm itself. True, the psalm's first and last words are words of praise, but the tension between faith and experience is left ringing in our ears with the question, "Lord, where is your unfailing love?" The psalmist had to wait for an answer—and in his own historical experience he never got the answer. We, too, often must wait. But while we wait, with doubts arising from our own experience, we also wait with confidence, because we have seen the answer to the psalmist's question in the person of the Lord Jesus Christ, the son of David (Matt 1:1) and the King of Israel (Mark 15:26-32).

ENDNOTES

1. Note that the king is the speaker in 89:50-51, and a preexilic date is thus seemingly presumed, though these words could have been spoken by Jehoiachin or Zedekiah (see 2 Kgs 24:8-25:30).
2. The reference to "the great sea monster" may also allude to the defeat of Egypt at the crossing of the Red Sea; see 87:4 and Isa 30:7, which refer to Egypt with the name Rahab.
3. For "happy" (*'ashre* [TH835A, ZH897]), see note on 1:1.

◆ IV. Book Four: Psalms 90–106

A. Psalm 90

A prayer of Moses, the man of God.

1 Lord, through all the generations
you have been our home!
2 Before the mountains were born,
before you gave birth to the earth
and the world,
from beginning to end, you are God.

3 You turn people back to dust, saying,
"Return to dust, you mortals!"
4 For you, a thousand years are as
a passing day,
as brief as a few night hours.
5 You sweep people away like dreams
that disappear.
They are like grass that springs up
in the morning.
6 In the morning it blooms and
flourishes,
but by evening it is dry and withered.
7 We wither beneath your anger;
we are overwhelmed by your fury.
8 You spread out our sins before you—
our secret sins—and you see
them all.
9 We live our lives beneath your wrath,
ending our years with a groan.

10 Seventy years are given to us!
Some even live to eighty.
But even the best years are filled with
pain and trouble;
soon they disappear, and we fly
away.
11 Who can comprehend the power of
your anger?
Your wrath is as awesome as the
fear you deserve.
12 Teach us to realize the brevity of life,
so that we may grow in wisdom.

13 O LORD, come back to us!
How long will you delay?
Take pity on your servants!
14 Satisfy us each morning with your
unfailing love,
so we may sing for joy to the end
of our lives.
15 Give us gladness in proportion to our
former misery!
Replace the evil years with good.
16 Let us, your servants, see you work
again;
let our children see your glory.
17 And may the Lord our God show us
his approval
and make our efforts successful.
Yes, make our efforts successful!

NOTES

90:TITLE ***Moses.*** He is referred to only eight times in the book of Psalms, and seven of the occurrences are in Book 4 (77:20 [21]; 90:TITLE [1]; 99:6; 103:7; 105:26; 106:16, 23, 32). This piling up of references to Moses in Book 4 together with the framing effect of one occurrence of "Moses" in the title of the opening psalm and three occurrences in the closing Ps 106 demonstrates a Mosaic orientation in Book 4 (Wilson 1993:76). Book 4, in some ways, as indicated by the title to the opening psalm, takes us back to truths that predate the monarchy and therefore transcend its ups and downs.

90:1 ***Lord.*** "Lord" (*'adonay* [TH136, ZH151]) occurs only here and in the final verse. God is "the Lord of all, the ruler over all the world" (Kraus 1989:215).

home. The word *ma'on* [TH4583A, ZH5061] is part of the semantic field of "refuge" (see Introduction). In the following psalm (Ps 91:9), *ma'on* is used as a parallel term for "refuge" (*makhseh* [TH4268, ZH4726]; see also 71:3). So the Lord being our "home" is another way of saying he is our "refuge."

90:2 ***born . . . gave birth.*** The Hebrew text uses verbs for birth (*yalad* [TH3205, ZH3528] and *khil* [TH2342A, ZH2655]) as metaphors for God's creative work. For a related picture, see Job 38:8.

90:3 ***You turn.*** The verb is a short imperfect form (*tasheb* [TH7725, ZH8740]), which is typically used as a jussive and sometimes as a past tense. Sometimes the jussive vocalization is difficult to explain and may be owing to defective spelling (Joüon and Muraoka 1991:§114*l*).

you mortals! Heb., *bene-'adam* [TH1121/120, ZH1201/132] (human beings), which gives the central strophe a universal scope.

90:13 ***come back.*** This is the same verb (*shub* [TH7725, ZH8740]) that is used in 90:3, where God turns people back to dust.

COMMENTARY

"Lord, where is your unfailing love?" is the agonizing question that ends Book 3 (89:49). Does the absence of the Davidic king mean the absence of God's unfailing love? Does the conflict between faith and experience in our lives mean that God's unfailing love has failed? (See commentary on Ps 89.) How do we live in the absence of God's anointed king? How do we live with the tensions produced by the apparent failure of God's promises in our lives? Book 4 provides the heart of the answer to these questions.

Book 4 begins with the only psalm attributed to Moses and contains seven of the eight references to Moses in the Psalter as a whole. What is the point of this preoccupation with Moses at this juncture in the Psalter? The point seems to be that God's unfailing love had been upon Israel long before there was a covenant with David. Though in the postexilic era there was no Davidic king to take refuge in (see 2:12), the Lord was still Israel's dwelling place (90:1; 91:1) and would continue to be the refuge in whom his people could trust (91:2).

Psalm 90 is a prayer comprised of three strophes. The prayer opens with an affirmation of faith in the Lord as the eternal refuge of his people (90:1-2). The middle strophe laments the pain and trouble of the human condition (90:3-11). The prayer concludes with a series of requests, at the heart of which is "Satisfy us each morning with your unfailing love" (90:14).

The Lord Is Our Dwelling Place (90:1-2). This opening strophe is chiastically arranged:

You
  All generations
    Before the mountains
    Before the earth
  Without beginning or end
You

"The literary structure makes a theological point. The divine 'You' is all-encompassing of time and space. Human life and the life of the world find their origin and destiny in God" (McCann 1996:1041).

When all sources of security in life have been stripped away (as was the case during the Exile, when the Temple and Davidic monarchy had been annihilated), we are able to see clearly the true source of security: "Lord, through all the generations you have been our home!" Before there was a Temple, before there was a Davidic king on the throne, before Moses, before the mountains were created, before God made the earth, the Lord was there. He who is without beginning or end has always been God, and as God he has always been the source of human security. It often takes the bottom falling out of life for us to return to this rock-solid truth: The Lord is our dwelling place.

Life Can Be Full of Pain and Trouble (90:3-11). This second strophe describes the way life may be for people in general. That the human race as a whole is in view is clear from the references to the *bene-'adam* [TH1121/120, ZH1201/132] (human beings) and returning to dust (90:3). "Return to dust" alludes to God's curse on the race in Genesis 3:19, which is also mentioned in Ecclesiastes 3:20 and 12:7. Just as there are common blessings that God bestows on all (Matt 5:45), there is also a common curse on the whole of the creation: "All creation was subjected to God's curse" (Rom 8:20). Psalm 90 is describing what life may be like under this common curse that is God's response to our sin as a race. It is this common "anger," "fury," and "wrath" of God to which the psalmist refers.

People may live 70 or 80 years, but it is often the case that "even the best years are filled with pain and trouble" (90:10). The nature of this pain and trouble is not specified, but the laments found in the previous 89 psalms and the events of our own lives give abundant testimony to the kinds of pain and trouble that are envisioned here.

The inevitable outcome of this life of trouble is death. God sweeps "people away like dreams that disappear" (90:5). As God said after we sinned as a race, "By the sweat of your brow will you have food to eat until you return to the ground from which you were made. For you were made from dust, and to dust you will return" (Gen 3:19). Death seems to be the final, grim word.

But even though we groan, we groan "as in the pains of childbirth" (Rom 8:22), which means we groan with hope (Rom 8:23). While the apostle Paul focuses our attention on our ultimate hope, the resurrection (Rom 8:23), Moses focuses our attention on the hope that we have for this life.

The Lord Can Replace Pain with Prosperity (90:12-17). Psalm 90:3-11 is misunderstood if it is read in such a way as to lead to the conclusion that this present life can be nothing but "pain and trouble" that culminates in death. The central strophe is using a broad brush, as is clear from the fact that many people do not live to see their 70th birthday, and many others, including Moses himself, live well beyond 80 years. That the second strophe is not consigning the race to nothing but pain and trouble is belied by the thanksgiving psalms that have preceded this psalm and by the final strophe of Psalm 90. For why would Moses pray as he does in these verses if our only hope for this life is "pain and trouble"? The hope held out in the final strophe is that the Lord can replace pain with prosperity in this present life.

The mood changes in these final verses, which are marked by a series of volitives (imperatives and jussives). The first is "Teach us." Relief from the common curse will take wise living on our part. And since wise living is not natural to us after the fall of the race, instruction is required, and God is the only one who holds the key to wise living (Job 28). So our hope is directed toward God. He must "come back to us" and take pity on us. The wages of our sin is death, but life is the gift of God's grace (Rom 6:23).

The pain and trouble of this life can be ever so frustrating, but God is able to replace our frustrations with satisfaction. Thus we are taught to pray, "Satisfy us each morning with your unfailing love" (90:14). Satisfaction is a real hope for this life, because of God's unfailing love. "His anger lasts only a moment, but his favor lasts a lifetime! Weeping may last through the night, but joy comes with the morning" (30:5). The satisfaction hoped for is not a passing satisfaction either: "Satisfy us . . . so we may sing for joy to the end of our lives."

Moses teaches us to pray that we will be blessed to the extent to which we have suffered. God can replace our misery with gladness, the years of trouble with years of good. And we can pray that in this life, as David elsewhere testifies, "You have turned my mourning into joyful dancing. You have taken away my clothes of mourning and clothed me with joy" (30:11).

In place of God's anger, we can experience his "work again" (90:16). And our hope for our children is that rather than experiencing God's wrath, they will experience the glory of God's work in their lives. But God's replacing pain and trouble with success requires his favor, so this is the final request, "May the Lord our God show us his approval." This approval is not just a favorable disposition on God's part. This approval is experienced as God gives us success in our lives in place of the failures we have encountered. And to make this final point with more force, the request is repeated: "Make our efforts successful. Yes, make our efforts successful!"

While it is true that "if our hope in Christ is only for this life, we are more to be pitied than anyone in the world" (1 Cor 15:19), it is also true that "everyone who has given up house or wife or brothers or parents or children, for the sake of the Kingdom of God, will be repaid many times over in this life, and will have eternal life in the world to come" (Luke 18:29-30; see also 1 Tim 4:8). Our hope for this life and for the life to come is rooted in the person and work of the Lord Jesus Christ (Isa 53:3-5), who fills our hearts through the Holy Spirit, in whom we now experience a foretaste of the life to come (Rom 8:23).

B. Psalm 91

[1]Those who live in the shelter of the
Most High
will find rest in the shadow of the
Almighty.
[2]This I declare about the LORD:
He alone is my refuge, my place
of safety;
he is my God, and I trust him.
[3]For he will rescue you from every trap
and protect you from deadly
disease.
[4]He will cover you with his feathers.
He will shelter you with his wings.
His faithful promises are your armor
and protection.
[5]Do not be afraid of the terrors of the
night,
nor the arrow that flies in the day.
[6]Do not dread the disease that stalks
in darkness,
nor the disaster that strikes at
midday.
[7]Though a thousand fall at your side,
though ten thousand are dying
around you,
these evils will not touch you.
[8]Just open your eyes,
and see how the wicked are
punished.

[9]If you make the LORD your refuge,
if you make the Most High your
shelter,
[10] no evil will conquer you;
no plague will come near your
home.
[11] For he will order his angels
to protect you wherever you go.
[12] They will hold you up with their hands
so you won't even hurt your foot
on a stone.
[13] You will trample upon lions and
cobras;
you will crush fierce lions and
serpents under your feet!

[14] The LORD says, "I will rescue those
who love me.
I will protect those who trust in my
name.
[15] When they call on me, I will answer;
I will be with them in trouble.
I will rescue and honor them.
[16] I will reward them with a long life
and give them my salvation."

NOTES

91:1 *shelter . . . shadow.* Both of these words (*sather* [TH5643, ZH6260] and *tsel* [TH6738, ZH7498]) are part of the semantic field of "refuge" (see Introduction).

91:2 *This I declare.* The NLT faithfully represents the MT. The LXX presumes a third-person verb here and supports an emendation from *'omar* [TH559, ZH606] (I will say) to *yo'mar* (he will say). This emendation would eliminate the difficult shift from third-person address (91:1) to first-person address (91:2).

91:3 *he will rescue you.* Psalm 91:3-13 is a consistent second-person address (see note at 91:9). Rather than the more impersonal third-person address *about* someone, the psalmist chooses the more personal second-person address *to* someone.

91:4 *He will cover you.* The verb is a short imperfect form (*yasek* [TH5526, ZH6114]), which is typically used as a jussive and sometimes as a past tense. Sometimes, however, the jussive vocalization is difficult to explain and may be owing to defective spelling (Joüon and Muraoka 1991:§114*l*).

protection. The word *sokherah* [TH5507, ZH6089] occurs only here and apparently refers to a literal wall (HALOT 3.750). The word would then be a metonym for protection, as indicated in the NLT.

91:9 *your refuge.* The Hebrew word reads "my refuge." The sudden shift to the first person in this colon alone in 91:3-13 is difficult. The NLT is probably correct in presuming the emendation from *makhsi* [TH4268/2967.1, ZH4726/3276] (my refuge) to *makhseka* [TH4268/3509.2, ZH4726/3870] (your refuge).

shelter. The word *ma'on* [TH4583A, ZH5061] is used here, as in 90:1, as a synonym for "refuge" (see note at 90:1).

91:10 *conquer.* This rare verb (*'anah* II [TH579, ZH628]) means "happen/befall" (DCH 1.333; HALOT 1.70). No evil befalling you is a more radical promise than no evil conquering you.

91:16 *I will reward them.* This verb is from the same root (*saba'* [TH7646, ZH8425]) as the verb used in 90:14 in the request, "Satisfy us each morning."

COMMENTARY

The dangers—both real and imagined—of living in this world can be the source of debilitating fears and anxieties. Psalm 91 has provided God's people "through all the generations" (90:1) with an antidote to these fears and anxieties. The "faithful promises" (91:4) of this psalm have the therapeutic effect of "anchoring the soul in the midst of anxieties" (Mays 1994:297).

The metaphor of God as refuge is a dominant theme in the Psalter, second in my estimation only to that of God as king (see Introduction). As a psalm of refuge, Psalm 91 is tied to the preceding psalm ("Lord . . . you have been our home!"; 90:1) and to the following ("They will declare . . . He is my rock!"; 92:15) and to Psalm 94 ("But the LORD is my fortress; my God is the mighty rock where I hide"; 94:22). These refuge psalms are tied to the kingship Psalms 93, 95–99, not only by their juxtaposition but also by the interlocking mechanism found in the (dis)placement of Psalm 93 before Psalm 94 (Wilson 1993:75-76). This group of refuge and kingship psalms provides the heart of the answer to the question raised in 89:49 ("Lord, where is your unfailing love?"), as well as the dominant theological affirmation of the Psalter as a whole: The Lord is king; blessed are all who take refuge in him.

Psalm 91 is comprised of three strophes. In the first the psalmist affirms in third-person address that God is our refuge (91:1-2). Then follows a second-person description of how the Lord is our refuge (91:3-13). The psalm concludes with God himself confirming in first-person speech that he is, in fact, our refuge (91:14-16).

The Affirmation of God as Refuge (91:1-2). It is appropriate that the affirmation of God as refuge uses the appellations "Most High" (*'elyon* [TH5945B, ZH6610]) and "Almighty" (*shadday* [TH7706, ZH8724]). Both appellations speak of God's kingship. "Most High" is associated with the Lord's kingship in 47:2—"For the LORD Most High is awesome. He is the great King of all the earth." This psalm celebrates the exercise of God's power in the subduing of the enemy. "Almighty" is used only one other time in the Psalter (68:14) in a psalm that calls upon the Lord as king (68:24) to use his power (68:28) to vanquish the enemy.

Since the Most High and the Almighty are our shelter, we can be confident that we will find rest as we trust in him, though the dangers of life threaten. Thus the psalmist tells us that we can truly know the Lord as our "refuge" and "place of safety" and can, therefore, say with confidence, "I trust him."

The Description of God as Refuge (91:3-13). There is perhaps no more expansive portrait of God's providential protecting of his children than that painted in these verses. God protects his children from every form of trouble: from the hunter's trap and fatal plague and from unexpected attack and disaster, such that no evil or plague will even come near, not even the stubbing of a toe on a rock. And this protection is operative all the time: during the night and the day—even in the brightest part of the day and the darkest part of the night. And this protection has an offensive element to it, because it ensures great victories over fierce lions and poisonous vipers. Even though a thousand—no, ten thousand others—are dying on all sides, God's children will only see but not be touched by this trouble.

The Confirmation of God as Refuge (91:14-16). In this final strophe, God speaks directly in the first person to confirm the truth that he is our refuge. He promises to rescue and protect those who love and trust him. He promises to answer them when they call on him for help in times of trouble. In 90:14 the psalmist prayed that God would "Satisfy us each morning with [his] unfailing love." Here God answers that request with a promise, "I will reward them with a long life and give them my salvation" (91:16).

The question at this point is, how are we to use this psalm? How are we to understand these promises of protection?

Perhaps we are to understand this text literally. If we make God our refuge, then our lives will be trouble-free. This is the obvious reading of the text. The problem with this reading is that it does not seem to square with the testimony of other Scripture texts or the testimony of the lives of God's children. For example, it does happen that good and righteous people die young (Eccl 7:15) and experience tremendous adversity (Job 1–2). Some suffer for doing good (1 Pet 2:20) and are even persecuted because of their righteousness (Matt 5:10). And in this very psalm the psalmist envisions God being with his children when they are in trouble (91:15). Then there is the theological question: How well do I have to trust God to experience the fulfillment of these promises? Do I have to trust him perfectly? If so, what good are the promises? For who among us can so trust God?

Perhaps we are to understand this text hyperbolically. The first element of the promise, the "trap," is not to be taken literally; the hunter's trap (91:3) is a metonym for the schemes that our human enemies formulate against us. God's wings and feathers (91:4) are not literal but zoomorphic. God's promises (91:4) are not literal armor but symbolic of protection. The shift from one thousand to ten thousand (91:7) gives every appearance of being a figurative numerical device.[1] Given the context of all this nonliteral language and the use of hyperbole in the Bible (Fouts 1997; Gibson 1998:14-16), it is quite reasonable to interpret these promises as hyperbole used for rhetorical effect. But if the promises are hyperbole, one might ask, "What good are they?" To what extent will God actually protect us from trouble in this life. What reality lies behind the hyperbole?

Perhaps we are to understand this text eschatologically. In 2 Timothy 4:17-18 Paul, using language similar to that of Psalm 91, says, "But the Lord stood with me and gave me strength so that I might preach the Good News in its entirety for all the Gentiles to hear. And he rescued me from certain death [lit., from the lion's mouth]. Yes, and the Lord will deliver me from every evil attack and will bring me safely into his heavenly Kingdom." Here, being delivered from the lion's mouth and every evil attack does not mean a trouble-free life, for Paul was writing from a prison cell from which he did not expect deliverance but death (2 Tim 4:6). The protection Paul was confident he would experience seems to have been from everything that would have prevented him from entering into God's heavenly Kingdom in the life to come. Psalm 91 could be read similarly. But are the promises of God good only for the life to come and not at all for this life? Paul himself did not think so: "Physical training is good, but training for godliness is much better, promising benefits in this life and in the life to come" (1 Tim 4:8).

Perhaps we are not forced to choose among the literal, hyperbolic, and eschatological interpretations. Perhaps each provides a window on the truth. The promises do contain a hyperbolic element. But does not the hyperbole function to produce faith in these promises in the concrete circumstances of this life? Certainly, the purpose of the text is to instill within us faith in God as the ultimate source of our protection from the dangers of this life (see Ps 90), even as we wait for the perfection of the life to come, when we will be categorically free from all danger.

We are to use Psalm 91 to facilitate our trust in God and not to tempt his providence. Satan misused this psalm when he tempted Jesus to jump off the pinnacle of the Temple, saying, "If you are the Son of God, jump off! For the Scriptures say, 'He will order his angels to protect you. And they will hold you up with their hands so you won't even hurt your foot on a stone'" (Matt 4:6). Jesus responded by saying, "The Scriptures also say, 'You must not test the LORD your God'" (Matt 4:7). In other words, the promises of Psalm 91 must be used in keeping with other teachings in the Scriptures in general and the teaching on not testing God in particular. Irresponsible living can find no shelter in the words of Psalm 91. But people who trust in a sovereign God and who do their best to live responsibly before him will most assuredly "find rest in the shadow of the Almighty."

ENDNOTES

1. See, for example, the numerical sayings in Prov 30:15, 18, 21, 29; Amos 1:3 mg, 6, 9, 11, 13; 2:1 mg, 4, 6.

◆ C. Psalm 92

A psalm. A song to be sung on the Sabbath Day.

1 It is good to give thanks to the LORD,
to sing praises to the Most High.
2 It is good to proclaim your unfailing
love in the morning,
your faithfulness in the evening,
3 accompanied by the ten-stringed harp
and the melody of the lyre.

4 You thrill me, LORD, with all you have
done for me!
I sing for joy because of what you
have done.
5 O LORD, what great works you do!
And how deep are your thoughts.
6 Only a simpleton would not know,
and only a fool would not
understand this:
7 Though the wicked sprout like
weeds
and evildoers flourish,
they will be destroyed forever.
8 But you, O LORD, will be exalted
forever.

[9] Your enemies, LORD, will surely perish;
all evildoers will be scattered.
[10] But you have made me as strong as
a wild ox.
You have anointed me with the
finest oil.
[11] My eyes have seen the downfall of
my enemies;
my ears have heard the defeat of
my wicked opponents.
[12] But the godly will flourish like palm
trees
and grow strong like the cedars
of Lebanon.
[13] For they are transplanted to the LORD's
own house.
They flourish in the courts of our
God.
[14] Even in old age they will still produce
fruit;
they will remain vital and green.
[15] They will declare, "The LORD is just!
He is my rock!
There is no evil in him!"

NOTES

92:1 ***Most High.*** See commentary on 91:1-2.

92:2 ***unfailing love . . . faithfulness.*** These two characteristics of God were called into question in Ps 89. Having encountered the Lord as refuge in Pss 90 and 91, the psalmist now praises God's unfailing love and faithfulness.

92:4 ***You thrill me.*** The NLT leaves the particle *ki* [TH3588, ZH3954] (for) untranslated. Psalm 92:4 provides the explicit reason why the affirmations of the previous verses are true.

92:7 ***weeds.*** The word *'eseb* [TH6212, ZH6912] is typically translated "grass," but "weeds" does a nice job of capturing the contrast between the flourishing of the wicked "like weeds" and the flourishing of the righteous "like palm trees" and "like the cedars of Lebanon" (92:12).

92:8 ***But you, O LORD, will be exalted forever.*** This sole monocolon stands at the midpoint of the psalm in a number of ways: (1) It is the middle verse, (2) there are 52 words preceding and following, and (3) the divine name occurs three times before and three times after, making the occurrence in this line the middle of seven. (This sevenfold use of the divine name could be related to the use of the psalm "on the Sabbath," which was the seventh day.)

92:11 ***my enemies.*** The MT reads *shuray* [TH7788-7791, ZH8803], and *shur* is commonly used for "wall." Zorell 1963:831 lists a *shur* III for Ps 92:11, which he translates *hostes mei* (my enemies) but then suggests an emendation to *shoreray* [TH8324, ZH8806] (my enemies), since this would be the only attestation of *shur* III. Gesenius 1949:812 lists a *shur* I, meaning "a lier in wait, an enemy" but cites only Ps 92:11 as an instance. It seems that the NLT presumes the emendation to *shoreray*, which is an easier route to "my enemies" than the proposal of a unique *shur*, especially given the use of *shoreray* (my enemies) elsewhere in the Psalms (see 5:8 [9]; 27:11; 54:5 [7]; 56:2 [3]; 59:10 [11]).

92:13 ***transplanted.*** The verb *shathal* [TH8362, ZH9278] occurs only one other time in the Psalter, and the image is quite similar: "They are like trees planted [*shathul*] along the riverbank, bearing fruit each season" (1:3).

92:15 ***declare.*** The Hebrew has the same verb form translated "proclaim" in 92:2 [3] (*lehaggid* [TH5046, ZH5583]). These two verbs form an *inclusio* around the psalm.

COMMENTARY

Sometimes we cannot figure out what God is doing in our lives. Such was the case in 88:14, where the psalmist cried out, "LORD, why do you reject me?" We, too, experience the reality expressed by God through the prophet Isaiah, "My thoughts are nothing like your thoughts. . . . And my ways are far beyond anything you could imagine. For just as the heavens are higher than the earth, so my ways are higher than your ways and my thoughts higher than your thoughts" (Isa 55:8-9). According to 92:5, God's ways are not just high, but also deep. The psalmist has here come to understand truly, though not comprehensively, something of God's thoughts and ways. This is in contrast to the doubts that characterize Psalm 88. The keynote of Psalm 92 is praise.

The structure of the psalm focuses our attention on the exaltation of the Lord (92:8). This central verse is preceded by seven lines containing 52 words, which praise the Lord (92:1-4) and affirm the ephemeral nature of the prosperity of evildoers (92:5-7). The central verse is then followed by seven lines containing 52 words, which affirm the demise of evildoers (92:9-11) and the prosperity of the godly, who praise the Lord (92:12-15).

The Lord Is Exalted Forever (92:8). The central affirmation of Psalm 92 is found in the central verse (92:8): "But you, O LORD, will be exalted forever." God is sovereignly situated in heaven from where he rules over the affairs on the earth. Even in the darkness of Psalms 88, 89, and 90:3-11, the Lord is in control, though his ways are difficult to comprehend (92:5).

Evildoers Will Not Flourish (92:5-7 and 92:9-11). One thing that is most difficult to understand in dark days is the apparent prosperity of evildoers. To every appearance they "sprout like weeds" and "flourish" (92:7). Yet, their "flourishing" is like that of "weeds" or "grass." Psalm 90:5-6 has just presented the image of grass springing up in the morning and withering away that very same day. Psalm 103:15-16 has this same image of grass sprouting only to wither away quickly.[1] The psalmist's choice of "weeds" to describe the prosperity of evildoers communicates two ideas: (1) There is prosperity, but (2) it is short-lived (at least in God's time frame).

This is one thing about God's ways that evildoers do not understand: They mistake their "flourishing" for a permanent condition, while in reality it is a prelude to eternal destruction (92:6-7). There is no doubt about this: "Your enemies, LORD, will surely perish; all evildoers will be scattered" (92:9). Thus the psalmist can say, "My eyes have seen the downfall of my enemies; my ears have heard the defeat of my wicked opponents" (92:11). This theme brings us back to the beginning of the Psalter, where we were told that the wicked will not succeed but "are like worthless chaff, scattered by the wind" (1:4).

As 92:5-7 and 92:9-11 surround 92:8, so we make the affirmation that the Lord reigns, though we are at times surrounded by evil (McCann 1996:1051). Since the Lord reigns, his people will ultimately flourish.

The Godly Will Flourish (92:1-4 and 92:12-15). In contrast to evildoers who "flourish" like "weeds," the godly will "flourish like palm trees and grow strong like the cedars of Lebanon" (92:12). In contrast to the evildoers who sprout but wither that very same day, the godly will remain vital and green and will still produce fruit even in old age (92:14).

This is so because the godly are connected to the Lord, who is exalted in heaven. They are connected to him because they have been transplanted into the Lord's house (92:13). They live in his presence and under his beneficent authority. They live with delight in his instruction for living (1:2) and with confidence in his character. They know the Lord to be just, and so they know they must ultimately prosper, because they have taken refuge (see 2:12) in him who can do no wrong: "He is my rock! There is no evil in him!" They also know the Lord to be full of unfailing love and faithfulness and that he has already done great things, both in his work of creation and his work of redemption. This is why the psalm begins on the high note of praise, "It is good to give thanks to the LORD, to sing praises to the Most High."

The structure of the psalm teaches us how to live with the apparent prosperity of the wicked, whether we are walking through dark days or have just been brought into the light. At the heart of our response is proclamation, and at the heart of our proclamation is, "But you, O LORD, will be exalted forever" (92:8). And surrounding this proclamation are two other proclamations: that God is characterized by unfailing love and faithfulness (92:2) and that he is a place of safety for us (92:15). In this way the psalm produces faith within us, faith that we will flourish as we take refuge in the Most High.

ENDNOTES

1. This is a frequent image in the Old Testament. For other examples, see 37:2; 102:4 [5], 11 [12]; 129:6; Isa 40:6-8. The Hebrew words for "grass" vary, but the picture is the same (see NIDOTTE 3.546).

D. Psalm 93

1 The LORD is king! He is robed in
majesty.
Indeed, the LORD is robed in majesty
and armed with strength.
The world stands firm
and cannot be shaken.

2 Your throne, O LORD, has stood from
time immemorial.
You yourself are from the
everlasting past.
3 The floods have risen up, O LORD.
The floods have roared like thunder;
the floods have lifted their
pounding waves.
4 But mightier than the violent raging
of the seas,
mightier than the breakers on the
shore—
the LORD above is mightier than
these!
5 Your royal laws cannot be changed.
Your reign, O LORD, is holy forever
and ever.

NOTES

93:1 ***The LORD is king!*** For a brief discussion of this key phrase and a defense of the translation "The Lord has become king!" see the note on 47:8.

majesty. The word *ge'uth* [TH1348, ZH1455] is used only two other times in the Psalter, one in relation to the arrogance of the ungodly (17:10) and the other in relation to the raging of the seas (89:9 [10]). In 93:1 the word refers to the illustriousness of the Lord (HALOT 1.169), who rules over the raging waters (and the raging of the ungodly).

93:3 ***floods have risen up . . . have roared . . . have lifted.*** The first two verbs are in the perfect tense and are best translated in the past tense. The third verb is an imperfect. If the shift to the imperfect is more than stylistic variation, the nuance is repeated lifting in the past (Joüon and Muraoka 1991:§113e) for dramatic effect.

93:4 ***above.*** The word *marom* [TH4791, ZH5294] has just been used in a similar way (92:8 [9]) in reference to God's being exalted.

93:5 ***Your reign, O LORD, is holy forever and ever.*** The Hebrew text is quite difficult. The text seems to say, "Holiness is appropriate to your house, O LORD, forever." The reference is to the Temple in Jerusalem (see commentary).

COMMENTARY

Psalm 93 is the first of a group of psalms (Pss 93, 95–99) that celebrate the kingship of the Lord. These psalms form the heart of the book of Psalms with their affirmation that the Lord reigns over the world that he has made (see Introduction). Psalm 93 opens with the acclamation that the Lord has become king; just when and how will be told in the following verses.

As an ancient monarch would have been robed in splendid regalia, so the Lord as king is robed in "majesty." This majesty is the dignity, the illustriousness, the glorious reputation he has earned through the deeds that will soon be rehearsed. As an ancient monarch would have been armed with helmet, breastplate, sword, and greaves, so the Lord is armed with "strength." Psalm 68, which also celebrates God's kingship, calls upon people to praise God for both his majesty and his power in the context of his vanquishing the hostile forces of the nations.

But it is not the hostile nations that are primarily in view in Psalm 93. The hostile forces are the "floods" and the "violent raging of the seas." In "time immemorial" (93:2) when the Lord formed the dry land (Gen 1:9-10) by rebuking the seas (104:7), the Lord demonstrated that he is mightier than these forces. When the world was established, the Lord's throne was established. Though from one perspective, God has been king from eternity, from a historical perspective, God became king and established his throne at the time of creation, when he "quieted the raging oceans" (65:7; see also 74:12-17) to make habitable dry land.

The Lord has also demonstrated that he is mightier than the raging nations when he dried up the waters of the Red Sea so that his people might be delivered from oppression to the peace of the Promised Land. Psalm 65:7 makes this connection between the seas of creation and the Red Sea explicit: "You quieted the raging oceans with their pounding waves and silenced the shouting of the nations." This connection is only implicit in Psalm 93 but finds support in the final line.

Just as God's victory over the seas at the time of creation was followed by the establishment of his throne, from where he rules over the world, so his victory over the Egyptians at the Red Sea was followed by the establishment of his house in Jerusalem, from where he ruled over his people Israel. He ruled over Israel in particular through the "royal laws" that he issued on Mount Sinai. Living according to God's royal decrees is living in the holiness that is appropriate for those who live under his reign.

Psalm 93 inspires us to live with confidence. Our God is Lord of creation and Lord of the nations. No hostile forces we encounter in our lives can ultimately withstand our king, who is "armed with strength." His greatest demonstration of this power was when he raised Jesus Christ from the dead (Eph 1:19-20). He grants this same strength to us who believe (29:11; 68:35; Eph 1:19) that we might conquer all the hostile forces we face in our lives. Psalm 93 also inspires us to live in holiness. God's royal power is at work in us that we might conquer the sin that remains within us and live lives of holiness to the glory of our king (Rom 6:5-14).

We live with confidence and holiness, knowing that the Lord is now reigning (1 Cor 15:25) and that the day is coming when he will begin to reign in an ultimate and consummate way (Rev 11:17).

◆ E. Psalm 94

1 O LORD, the God of vengeance,
O God of vengeance, let your glorious justice shine forth!
2 Arise, O judge of the earth.
Give the proud what they deserve.
3 How long, O LORD?
How long will the wicked be allowed to gloat?
4 How long will they speak with arrogance?
How long will these evil people boast?
5 They crush your people, LORD,
hurting those you claim as your own.
6 They kill widows and foreigners
and murder orphans.
7 "The LORD isn't looking," they say,
"and besides, the God of Israel* doesn't care."

8 Think again, you fools!
When will you finally catch on?
9 Is he deaf—the one who made your ears?
Is he blind—the one who formed your eyes?
10 He punishes the nations—won't he also punish you?
He knows everything—doesn't he also know what you are doing?
11 The LORD knows people's thoughts;
he knows they are worthless!

12 Joyful are those you discipline, LORD,
those you teach with your instructions.
13 You give them relief from troubled times
until a pit is dug to capture the wicked.
14 The LORD will not reject his people;
he will not abandon his special possession.
15 Judgment will again be founded on justice,
and those with virtuous hearts will pursue it.

16 Who will protect me from the wicked?
Who will stand up for me against evildoers?
17 Unless the LORD had helped me,
I would soon have settled in the silence of the grave.
18 I cried out, "I am slipping!"
but your unfailing love, O LORD, supported me.
19 When doubts filled my mind,
your comfort gave me renewed hope and cheer.

• 20 Can unjust leaders claim that God is on their side—
leaders whose decrees permit injustice?
21 They gang up against the righteous
and condemn the innocent to death. ABORTION
22 But the LORD is my fortress;
my God is the mighty rock where I hide.
23 God will turn the sins of evil people back on them.
He will destroy them for their sins.
The LORD our God will destroy them.

94:7 Hebrew *of Jacob.* See note on 44:4.

NOTES

94:5 ***those you claim as your own.*** The word *nakhalah* [TH5159, ZH5709] (inheritance) is paired again with God's "people" in 94:14, where it is translated "special possession."

94:10 ***punishes . . . punish.*** Two different words are used. The first word (*yasar* [TH3256, ZH3579]) means "discipline, warn, instruct" (HALOT 2.418; DCH 3.238). Here the participle is parallel to the participle in the following colon, which is best translated "teaches," so "instruct" is the best choice for *yasar* in this context. The second word (Hiphil of *yakakh* [TH3198, ZH3519]) means "rebuke."

He knows everything. Lit., "He teaches humanity," which implies that he knows all.

94:19 ***doubts.*** The word *sar'appim* [TH8312, ZH8595] occurring only here and in 139:23, apparently means "disturbing thoughts" (HALOT 3.1358), and is related to the synonymous *se'ippim* [TH5587A, ZH8546] (Job 4:13; 20:2).

COMMENTARY

How do we best respond to those who hurt us deeply by their sinful words and deeds? The desire to take revenge may dominate our thinking, or it may be just under the surface. God knows this, which is why he said through the apostle Paul, "Dear friends, never take revenge. Leave that to the righteous anger of God. For the Scriptures say, 'I will take revenge; I will pay them back,' says the LORD" (Rom 12:19). But how do we "leave that to God," when we have in fact been wronged or when oppression and injustice are staring us in the face? Psalm 94 provides us with five key aspects of the answer to these questions.

Vengeance Belongs to God (94:1-7). A proper response begins with acknowledging that vengeance belongs to God. This implies acknowledging that we have truly been wronged and hurt in a given situation. The psalmist acknowledges that evildoers "crush your people, LORD, hurting those you claim as your own" (94:5). They "kill" and "murder" those who have no human defenders: widows, foreigners, and orphans. When wronged, we may be tempted to think that the best response is just to say, "That's okay," but down deep inside we know that it is not okay. Injustice is never okay. Or we may be tempted to think that a quick "I forgive" is the best course of action, but such forgiveness may in fact be a form of denial that we hurt.

Responding in a godly way begins with acknowledging the wrong and acknowledging that vengeance belongs to God. He is the "judge of the earth," whom we call upon to take action (94:2) in regard to the "evil people." Such people have not only wronged us, but they also boast and gloat, thinking they will get away scot-free. The temptation for us to avenge ourselves grows if we begin to think as they do. The temptation loses some of its grip when we realize that God knows what is going on. So we can "leave that to God."

God Knows What Is Happening (94:8-11). It is foolish to think that God neither knows nor cares about what goes on in his creation. As we have been created in the image of God, our ears and eyes tell us that God is neither deaf nor blind. As the infinite Creator, he hears all and sees all. "He knows everything" (94:10), even "people's thoughts" (94:11). We often do not know enough to take the appropriate action when wronged. But God knows with precision the best course of action to take in each situation. Knowing that God knows frees us to give the "evildoers" over to God for him to deal with them. He will teach them and even rebuke them in the most appropriate way. So we can "leave that to God."

Happiness Is Available (94:12-15). It is striking that right in the middle of this psalm of vengeance there is a "beatitude," a declaration of supreme blessedness. The Hebrew word *'ashre* [TH835A, ZH897], translated "joyful" in English, is translated *makarios* in the Septuagint, and this Greek *makarios* [TG3107, ZG3421] is used in the Beatitudes (Matt 5:1-12). Even in situations where we have been wronged and hurt, we can experience "beatitude," because God is there to discipline us—that is, to disciple us by teaching us from his word. When we know his ways and walk in them, we experience true "happiness" (see Ps 1). We can learn deep lessons about God, others, and ourselves when we experience injustice in this life.

While God is there to teach us, he is also there to give us "relief from troubled times" (94:13). While we are in the middle of such times, we may feel that God has abandoned us, but the truth is, "The LORD will not reject his people; he will not abandon his special possession" (94:14). He will bring justice in his own time and in his own way. That "judgment will again be founded on justice" implies both that the wrongdoers will receive their just deserts and that we will have a reward, so we ourselves can "pursue" a just path in this life (94:15).

Protection from the Wicked (94:16-19). When wronged and hurt, we often feel defenseless. "Who will protect me? Who will stand up for me?" These are the cries of our souls. Sometimes we look around and find no human support, and if the Lord were not there, it would have been all over for us. But the truth is, the Lord's unfailing love is there to support us (94:18). And even though our minds are deeply agitated with all sorts of disturbing thoughts, God has a way of coming to comfort us and bring us joy in the middle of sorrow. So we can "leave that to God."

People Reap What They Sow (94:20-23). The end of the psalm in certain ways brings us back to the beginning. We read here another acknowledgment of the wrongs that have been committed against us (94:21) and the arrogance of the evildoers (94:20). We also read the assurance that God is just: "God will turn the sins of evil people back on them" (94:23). People will reap what they sow (Hos 8:7; 10:12; 2 Cor 9:6; Gal 6:7-9). So we can "leave that to God."

While Psalm 94 provides five key aspects on how best to respond when we are wronged, there is, it seems, a difference between our response as New Testament believers and that of the ancient psalmist. In the same sermon that Jesus taught the Beatitudes he also said, "But I say, love your enemies! Pray for those who persecute you!" (Matt 5:44). He wants us to pray *for* them, for in so doing we are like our Father in heaven (Matt 5:45), who in this era between the two comings of Christ, is being kind, tolerant, and patient—giving people time to turn from their sin and to avoid his judgment (Rom 2:4). Since our hope and prayer is that those who have wronged us may "learn their lesson" and experience the "unfailing love" of God, we can "leave that to God."

F. Psalm 95

1 Come, let us sing to the LORD!
Let us shout joyfully to the Rock of our salvation.
2 Let us come to him with thanksgiving.
Let us sing psalms of praise to him.
3 For the LORD is a great God,
a great King above all gods.
4 He holds in his hands the depths of the earth
and the mightiest mountains.
5 The sea belongs to him, for he made it.
His hands formed the dry land, too.

6 Come, let us worship and bow down.
Let us kneel before the LORD our maker,
7 for he is our God.
We are the people he watches over,
the flock under his care.
If only you would listen to his voice today!
8 The LORD says, "Don't harden your hearts as Israel did at Meribah,
as they did at Massah in the wilderness.
9 For there your ancestors tested and tried my patience,
even though they saw everything I did.
10 For forty years I was angry with them,
and I said,
'They are a people whose hearts turn away from me.
They refuse to do what I tell them.'
11 So in my anger I took an oath:
'They will never enter my place of rest.' "

NOTES

95:2 ***Let us sing.*** The verb (Hiphil of *rua'* [TH7321, ZH8131]) is used in 95:1, where it is translated "Let us shout joyfully."

95:4 ***He holds in his hands.*** The Hebrew phrase *beyado* [TH3027, ZH3338] (in his hand) means "in his power" (DCH 4.90).

95:6 ***our maker.*** The participle translated "maker" comes from the same root (*'asah* [TH6213A, ZH6913]) as the verb translated "made" in 95:5. "Maker" refers here not to God's act of creation as in Genesis 1, but to his act of redemption whereby he "created" a people for himself (Enns 1993:258-261). The language of creation is used in a variety of texts as a reference to God's creating Israel through the act of redeeming Israel, first from Egypt, then later from Babylon (74:1-2; Exod 15:16; Isa 43:14-17; 54:5; Hos 8:13-14).

COMMENTARY

Christians have often been called to worship with the words of 95:1-7a. Rarely have the words of 95:7b-11 been included in these invitations to worship God. The words of this latter section seem harsh and inappropriate for a summons to worship. Scholars also have noted the change in mood from the first stanza to the second, some even arguing that Psalm 95 is comprised of two originally separate compositions, a hymn of praise (95:1-7a) and a Levitical or prophetic sermon (95:7b-11). There is, however, a demonstrable connection between the two halves (Enns 1993), as we will see.

Psalm 95 reveals two foundational truths to us about God: He is the great God, and he is our God. The psalm also calls for two appropriate responses to this revelation: worship and submission.

The Revelation of God. Psalm 95 teaches us that "the LORD is a great God, a great King above all gods" (95:3). Polytheism, the belief in the existence of many gods, surrounded Israel on every side. At times, as is the case here, the language of polytheism is used in the Bible to teach us something about the true God. Psalm 95:3 does not intend to affirm the existence of gods other than the Lord (see 96:4-5); rather, the intention is to affirm the ultimate supremacy of the God of Israel over the whole world: He is the supreme king. This point is made with a vertical image: God exerts power over the whole earth from its lowest depths to its highest peaks. Then a horizontal image is employed to underscore the affirmation: He owns the sea and the dry land. That God owns and controls the world is proven by the corollary truth that he created the world (see 24:1-2). As sole creator of the world, God is transcendently sovereign over the world.

Yet we must not think that such a transcendent God is too high above his creation to be involved with it. Psalm 95 also teaches us that this transcendent God "is our God," and we are the people under his care (95:6-7). Just as the world belongs to God because he created it, we are his people because he is "our maker." He was Israel's maker in the sense that through the Exodus he created Israel to be his people, the sheep under his care. (Thus, 74:1-2 similarly joins the images of God as Israel's shepherd, creator, and redeemer.) The transcendent king of the world is at the same time our maker, our redeemer, and our shepherd who intimately watches over our lives and cares for us.

Our Response to God. Having taught us two related truths about God, Psalm 95 also teaches two correlative responses to this revelation. The response set forth in the first stanza is worship. This first stanza (95:1-7) is comprised of two strophes with the same structure. Each contains a call to worship followed by a reason for heeding the call. We have already examined the reasons: "For the LORD is a great God" and "for he is our God." The first call seems to envision a procession, when it says, "Let us come to him." Those who make their way into the presence of God do so with exuberant worship appropriate to the great king. There is singing, joyful shouting, expressions of thanksgiving, and psalms of praise. The second call has in view prostration, as it uses the language of bowing and kneeling. The exuberance of the first stanza is thus balanced by the acts of homage in the second. To bow and kneel before the great king is to acknowledge his lordship over the lives of his worshipers.

Submission to the king's lordship breaks the bounds of worship and penetrates all of life. Thus, the response sought after in the second stanza of Psalm 95 is a life of submission. Motivation for such submission is provided by means of the negative example of Israel's disobedience at Meribah/Massah, where Israel argued with Moses and tested the Lord (see Exod 17 and Num 20). When the Israelites came to Rephidim and found no water, they grumbled and complained, as it seemed to them that the Lord was not providing adequately for their needs. There they "tested the LORD by saying, 'Is the LORD here with us or not?'" (Exod 17:7). The first stanza of Psalm 95 has just celebrated the watchful care of the Lord for his people, so the warning not to be like the wilderness generation, which doubted the Lord's care, is particularly appropriate.

As God's children there are times when we, too, doubt his care to some degree. In those times we must be on our guard so that our hearts do not become calloused, resulting in our turning away from the Lord. The reality of this danger for Christians today is confirmed by the use of Psalm 95 in Hebrews 3–4. There we are told that "we are God's house, if we keep our courage and remain confident in our hope in Christ" (Heb 3:6) and we are then warned in Hebrews 3:8-11 to listen to God, using the words of 95:7-11. In Hebrews 3:15 we are told never to forget the warning of Psalm 95, and this warning is repeated for a third time in Hebrews 4:7.

The reality of the danger and the severity of the warning are not intended, however, to instill doubt but to produce faith. This faith is produced in at least two ways. First, we are to be committed to one another in the body of Christ. We are told to "warn each other every day, while it is still 'today,' so that none of you will be deceived by sin and hardened against God" (Heb 3:13). As we care for each other in this way, we experience God's care for us as the sheep of his pasture. Second, we are to "remain confident in our hope in Christ," who was the faithful Son (Heb 3:6). When he was in the wilderness, Jesus refused to let his hunger turn him from utter dependence on his Father's provision, he refused to put his Father's care to the test, and he refused to worship anyone but his Father alone (Matt 4:1-11). His faithfulness is our redemption, as we trust that in giving us his Son it is utterly unthinkable that our Shepherd-King will now fail to give us anything we need for this life or the life to come.

So we, like the first singers of Psalm 95, are called to know that the Lord is a great God and that he is our God. We likewise are invited to worship him with shouts of joy and lives of submission.

◆ G. Psalm 96

1 Sing a new song to the LORD!
Let the whole earth sing to the LORD!
2 Sing to the LORD; praise his name.
Each day proclaim the good news that he saves.
3 Publish his glorious deeds among the nations.
Tell everyone about the amazing things he does.
4 Great is the LORD! He is most worthy of praise!
He is to be feared above all gods.
5 The gods of other nations are mere idols,
but the LORD made the heavens!
6 Honor and majesty surround him;
strength and beauty fill his sanctuary.
7 O nations of the world, recognize the LORD;
recognize that the LORD is glorious and strong.
8 Give to the LORD the glory he deserves!
Bring your offering and come into his courts.
9 Worship the LORD in all his holy splendor.
Let all the earth tremble before him.
10 Tell all the nations, "The LORD reigns!"
The world stands firm and cannot be shaken.
He will judge all peoples fairly.
11 Let the heavens be glad, and the earth rejoice!
Let the sea and everything in it shout his praise!
12 Let the fields and their crops burst out with joy!
Let the trees of the forest rustle with praise
13 before the LORD, for he is coming!
He is coming to judge the earth.
He will judge the world with justice,
and the nations with his truth.

NOTES

96:1 *new song.* The "new song" is typically a song of salvation sung to the Creator-King in the context of military victory (33:3; 40:3; 96:1; 98:1; 144:9; 149:1; Isa 42:10; Longman and Reid 1995:45).

the whole earth. The word *'erets* [TH776, ZH824] (earth) is here being used figuratively. In the context of 96:1-10, *'erets* is a metonym for the inhabitants of the earth (see BDB 76), the "nations of the world" (96:7). In 96:11 *'erets* is personified (NIDOTTE 1.520), along with other aspects of creation. This personification is at least anticipated in the use of *'erets* in 96:1. "The whole earth" thus has in view the physical world and its inhabitants.

96:2 *proclaim.* The word *basar* [TH1319, ZH1413] means "bring news," which is generally good news in a military context (TWOT 1.135; NIDOTTE 1.775).

96:3 *his glorious deeds.* The NLT has captured well the sense of the word *kabod* [TH3519, ZH3883] (glory), which refers here not to an abstract quality of God but to the glorious things he has done in time and space, as is clear from the surrounding terms, *yeshu'ah* [TH3444, ZH3802] (salvation) and *nipla'oth* [TH6318A, ZH7098] (amazing deeds).

96:4 *Great is the LORD!* This statement links Ps 96 back to Ps 95, which says, "The LORD is a great God" (95:3). The NLT leaves the particle *ki* [TH3588, ZH3954] (for) untranslated. This particle, typical in hymns, marks the beginning of the reasons as to why the call to worship is to be heeded.

96:5 *idols.* When used in reference to non-Israelite gods, the word *'elilim* [TH457, ZH496] is used to indicate that such gods are ineffective nonentities or mere idols (HALOT 1.56). Thus, the affirmation that the Lord is "to be feared above all gods" (96:4) is not a tacit affirmation of polytheism but a denial of it (see 95:3 and 115:4).

96:6 *Honor and majesty.* For this pair used as referring to royal garments, see note on 21:5.

strength. In 93:1 "strength" (*'oz* [TH5797, ZH6437]) was part of God's royal regalia.

96:7-9 *recognize.* The Hebrew imperative *habu* [TH3051, ZH2035] is used three times here: twice in 96:7 and once at the beginning of 96:8, where it is translated "give." The language of 96:7-9 has been carried over from 29:1-2. The addressees here, however, are the human families of the world, not the angelic hosts of Ps 29. In keeping with the cultic activity of the earthly Temple of Ps 96, offerings are to be brought by the human worshipers.

96:9 *Let all the earth tremble.* Given the immediate context of human worshipers in 96:7-10, the word *'erets* [TH776, ZH824] here would seem to have human inhabitants of the earth in view. And given the frequency of the image of the physical world trembling at the presence of God,[1] the physical earth would also seem to be in view.

96:10 *cannot be shaken.* For this image of the earth as unshakable from the time of creation onward, see 93:1 and 104:5.

COMMENTARY

Good news! The true God and king of the universe is coming to put everything in right order! "Let the whole earth sing to the LORD."

Liturgy, history, and eschatology meet in Psalm 96. This psalm was no doubt used in the worship of God at the sanctuary in Jerusalem, as is clear from the reference to bringing offerings into the sanctuary courts and the association of Psalm 96 with a liturgical procession of the Ark of the Covenant (1 Chr 16). Psalm 96 would thus have been used to celebrate in worship the present reign of the Lord. Yet, this reign was not an atemporal truth. It was rooted in God's acts of salvation in history. Psalm

96 would have been sung as a new song of victory to the Lord, the Divine Warrior, as he returned from battle in triumph (Longman and Reid 1995:45).[2] Perhaps the return from the Babylonian captivity is the original victory in view (Delitzsch 1982:90), but the historical ambiguity of the psalm makes it appropriate for the celebration of any "victory" (Longman 1984:272). While the Lord was envisioned as "coming" (96:13) into the city as a recently triumphant king, the cosmic scope of the psalm and its call to the nations and the whole created realm to reaffirm the Lord's kingship give the psalm a decidedly eschatological cast (Kraus 1989:252).

Sing to the Lord (96:1-6). All the inhabitants of the earth are summoned to sing the new song that celebrates the salvation accomplished by the God of Israel (96:1-2). Like a group of messengers announcing the good news of a king's recent victory in battle, the inhabitants of the earth are to announce the good news of the victory of Israel's divine king. The Lord's saving deeds are to be announced by the nations and throughout the nations (96:3), for these saving deeds are of great significance for the nations.

This significance is first and foremost spiritual in nature. As Israel was warned not to turn away from God (95:10), so the nations are called to turn from their gods to the God of Israel, whose saving work is a demonstration of his greatness and his supremacy. He alone is to be revered by the nations, because he alone is worthy of such homage. The gods of the nations are not worthy, for they are nonentities. They are mere idols, not winners of great military victories on behalf of their peoples. They are mere idols, not creators of the heavens. The Lord God of Israel is the God who has truly acted in time and space—first to create the world, then to save it. He is the only true God, so all who live under the heavens are summoned to worship him. And the worship of God is no dull service, for he is surrounded by majesty and strength and beauty, and his reign is the reign of a good and beneficent king.

Sing to the Lord, the King (96:7-10). The nations of the world are called upon to recognize the Lord as their king, to recognize that he is the truly glorious and strong deity, to recognize that he is the deity who deserves to be glorified, to recognize that he is the one to whom we are to present our sacrifices (cf. Rom 12:1-2), to recognize that he is the one who reigns over the nations, to recognize that he is the one who maintains the stability that enables life to continue in this world (cf. Acts 14:16-17), and to recognize that he "will judge all peoples fairly."

Most people in the West do not have to cross a single border to announce this good news to the nations, for the nations—people from every kind of religious background—now live in our own countries. We can announce the good news of our good king like the psalmist and like the apostle Paul in Acts 17:

> *He is the God who made the world and everything in it . . . he is Lord of heaven and earth. . . . He himself gives life and breath to everything, and he satisfies every need. . . . He created all the nations throughout the whole earth. . . . His purpose was for the nations to seek after God and perhaps feel their way toward him and find him—though he is not far from any one of us. For in him we live and move and exist. . . . And since this is true, we shouldn't think of God as an idol designed by craftsmen from gold or silver or stone. God overlooked people's ignorance about these things in*

earlier times, but now he commands everyone everywhere to repent of their sins and turn to him. For he has set a day for judging the world with justice by the man he has appointed, and he proved to everyone who this is by raising him from the dead. (Acts 17:24-31)

This good news is of great significance not only for the nations but also for the creation itself, as the final strophe makes clear.

Sing to the Lord, the Judge (96:11–13). One function of the Divine Warrior was that of judging (Miller 1973:170-175). Here the prospect of the Lord coming to judge does not generate fear but joy. And joy not just for humans but also for the whole of creation. The heavens, earth, sea, fields, crops, trees—all are exuberant in praise because the Lord is coming to judge. The picture we are to have in our minds at this point is not so much that of a judge rendering decisions from a bench as it is that of the Creator putting everything in his creation back into "right order."

Restoration of a disturbed order is the idea communicated here by the Hebrew word *shapat* [TH8199, ZH9149] ("judge"; see TLOT 3.1393). As a result of human sin the created order has been disrupted (Gen 3:17-19; Rom 8:20). The creation is now eagerly anticipating the day when it will be liberated from "death and decay" (Rom 8:21). This very liberation is in view in Psalm 96: the liberation of human beings from death and decay and the concomitant liberation of the whole created order. Everything will be put into right order when the Lord comes in eschatological judgment, for God's ultimate act of salvation in the first coming of the Lord Jesus Christ was an act that has reconciled everything to God, everything in heaven and on earth (Eph 1:10; Col 1:20).

That the Lord is king is good news. Good news for the nations. Good news for the creation. Good news that the whole earth can sing about. Good news that we can proclaim each day.

ENDNOTES

1. Here the Hebrew root is *khil* [TH2342A, ZH2655], which is also used in 29:8; 77:16 [17]; 97:4; 114:7.Other roots used for this same image are *ragaz* [TH7264, ZH8074] (18:7 [8]; 77:18 [19]), *ra'ash* [TH7493, ZH8321] (60:2 [4]; 68:8 [9]) and *nut* [TH5120, ZH5667] (99:1).
2. Longman 1984 convincingly argues that Ps 98, along with analogous psalms like Ps 96, is a victory hymn of the Divine Warrior.

◆ H. Psalm 97

[1] The LORD is king!
Let the earth rejoice!
Let the farthest coastlands be glad.
[2] Dark clouds surround him.
Righteousness and justice are the foundation of his throne.
[3] Fire spreads ahead of him
and burns up all his foes.
[4] His lightning flashes out across the world.
The earth sees and trembles.
[5] The mountains melt like wax before the LORD,
before the Lord of all the earth.
[6] The heavens proclaim his righteousness;

every nation sees his glory.
7 Those who worship idols are disgraced—
all who brag about their worthless gods—
for every god must bow to him.
8 Jerusalem* has heard and rejoiced,
and all the towns of Judah are glad
because of your justice, O LORD!
9 For you, O LORD, are supreme over all the earth;
you are exalted far above all gods.
10 You who love the LORD, hate evil!
He protects the lives of his godly people
and rescues them from the power of the wicked.
11 Light shines on the godly,
and joy on those whose hearts are right.
12 May all who are godly rejoice in the LORD
and praise his holy name!

97:8 Hebrew *Zion.*

NOTES

97:1 *The LORD is king!* For a brief discussion of this key phrase and a defense of the translation "The Lord has become king!" see the note on 47:8.

97:7 *idols.* See note on 96:5.

must bow. The NLT aptly captures the sense of the imperative, here used to express an emphatic future (Joüon and Muraoka 1991:§115p).

97:12 *May all who are godly rejoice . . . and praise.* The verbs here are imperatives, corresponding to the imperative in 97:10, "hate evil." These three imperatives surround 97:10-12 and show the focus of this section.

COMMENTARY

Joy should characterize the lives of God's children, not just in heaven but now on earth, says Psalm 97. But how can this be when "the power of the wicked" seems to be dominant everywhere and "evil" is rampant (97:10)? By living in the truth that "The LORD is king!"

Psalm 97, like Psalms 47, 93, 95, 96, 98, and 99, reaffirms the fundamental truth that God reigns over—is in control of—the world that he has made. Psalm 97:1-6 paints a picture of the king when he appears in his world. The following strophe (97:7-9) describes how various human beings react to the Lord's appearance. And 97:10-12 spells out for those who love God several implications of God's appearance and reign.

Appearance of the King (97:1-6). The divine king appears in this psalm in his role as Divine Warrior (Mays 1994:311). Storm imagery is typical for the appearance of the Divine Warrior, and here the image is that of a hot east-wind storm (Fitzgerald 1983:129-130). The "dark clouds" (97:2) are generated by the swirling dust of the east wind. The "fire" that "burns" (97:3) and "the mountains [that] melt like wax before the LORD" (97:5) are hyperbolic references to the great heat of such storms. The lightning, too, while more characteristic of rainstorms, is associated with east-wind storms (Dalman 1928:1.107).

This appearing is not that of a malevolent despot, however, but that of a king whose reign is founded on righteousness and justice. He appears in order to establish right order (see commentary on 96:11-13) throughout the world. This right order requires the removal of all who stand opposed to that order (97:3; see 104:35), so the earth "trembles" (97:4), as "the heavens proclaim his righteousness" and "every nation sees his glory" (97:6).

Reactions among People (97:7-9). It is impossible to have no reaction to this glorious appearance of "the Lord of all the earth" (97:5, 9). Two reactions are recorded in this second strophe. The first is that of those who have not lived in dependence on God but who have put all their hopes in ineffective idols, whether the more crude idols made of wood and stone or the more sophisticated idols like wealth and power. Disgrace is written all over the faces of those who have not placed their trust in the true and living God, for to him every knee will bow (Phil 2:9-10), even those of rival gods.

The second reaction is that of Jerusalem and Judah, here used as figures for those who "love the LORD" (97:10), who are "godly" (97:11-12). Upon hearing that the Lord has come to put everything back into right order ("justice"; 97:8b), those who love the Lord are filled with joy and gladness (97:8a). While disgrace is a reality in this psalm, joy and gladness are the dominant notes (97:1, 8, 11, 12). The appearing of the one who is "supreme over all the earth" and "exalted far above all gods" (97:9) is good news (see Ps 96) for those who trust him.

Implications for the Righteous (97:10-12). This good news brings with it implications for daily life. Three imperatives bring out these implications. The first is "hate evil" (97:10). Evil is that which is contrary to the right order established by the Lord. Evil is that which is out of accord with his ways. Evil is not to be chosen as a way of life nor as a way in any aspect of life. Evil is to be rejected, even when it seems that those who have chosen the evil path have the upper hand in life.

Hating evil may bring some fear along with it, for those who reject evil may at times face the prospect of abuse in one form or another at the hands of those with more power. But faith that the Lord "protects the lives of his godly people and rescues them from the power of the wicked" drives away fear. "When I am afraid, I will put my trust in you. . . . I trust in God, so why should I be afraid? What can mere mortals do to me?" (56:3-4).

The second imperative is "rejoice" (97:12a). Not just "rejoice," however, but "rejoice in the LORD," for the Lord is king and has come to put everything in right order. Psalm 97, like Psalm 96, looks back to an appearing of the Lord at some point in history, but it also looks forward to an appearing at some point in the future: The psalm is eschatological (McCann 1996:1070). As Christians, we can choose to be happy because we can look back and know that God has appeared in the Lord Jesus Christ to put everything in right order. And even though we do not yet see everything in right order (Heb 2:8), we know that the Lord Jesus reigns now and will reign until the very last foe, death itself, is subdued underneath his feet (1 Cor 15:25-26). This will happen when he appears again at the end of history as we now know it. Since the Lord reigns now, we can be happy now, even as we await the fullness of his reign and our happiness in the future.

Since our happiness ultimately depends on the reign of the Lord, the third and final imperative is "praise his holy name" (97:12b). Here God's holiness does not mean he is inaccessible or unapproachable; rather, it means that he is willing to come and establish his righteousness and justice on earth as it is in heaven (McCann 1996:1070). The establishment of his right order is our hope of happiness, so his holy name is the object of our praise now and forevermore.

◆ I. Psalm 98

A psalm.

[1] Sing a new song to the LORD,
for he has done wonderful deeds.
His right hand has won a mighty
victory;
his holy arm has shown his saving
power!
[2] The LORD has announced his
victory
and has revealed his righteousness
to every nation!
[3] He has remembered his promise to
love and be faithful to Israel.
The ends of the earth have seen the
victory of our God.

[4] Shout to the LORD, all the earth;
break out in praise and sing
for joy!
[5] Sing your praise to the LORD with
the harp,
with the harp and melodious
song,
[6] with trumpets and the sound of the
ram's horn.
Make a joyful symphony before the
LORD, the King!

[7] Let the sea and everything in it shout
his praise!
Let the earth and all living things
join in.
[8] Let the rivers clap their hands
in glee!
Let the hills sing out their songs
of joy
[9] before the LORD.
For the LORD is coming to judge
the earth.
He will judge the world with justice,
and the nations with fairness.

NOTES

98:1 ***new song.*** The "new song" is typically a song of salvation sung to the Creator/King in the context of military victory (33:3; 40:3; 96:1; 98:1; 144:9; 149:1; Isa 42:10; Longman and Reid 1995:45).

wonderful deeds. See 96:3, where this same word *nipla'oth* [TH6318A, ZH7098] is translated "amazing things."

98:3 ***The ends of the earth have seen.*** Compare 97:4, 6.

98:6 ***Make a joyful symphony.*** The Hebrew imperative (*hari'u* [TH7321, ZH8131]) is the same as in 98:4, where it is translated "shout." The two occurrences envelop the strophe and articulate the basic idea.

98:7 ***shout his praise!*** This renders the word *yir'am* [TH7481, ZH8306], which means "roar" and evokes the sound of the roaring waves that crash unendingly on the shore.

98:8 ***Let the rivers clap their hands.*** Two verbs are used for clapping in the OT: *makha'* [TH4222, ZH4673] (98:8) and *taqa'* [TH8628, ZH9546]. Both are associated with victory. Victors clap for joy at the defeat of their enemies (47:1 [2]; Ezek 25:6; Nah 3:19). So when the rivers clap their hands, they do so to celebrate the Divine Warrior's victory announced in 98:1-3 (see Keel 1997:335). (In Isa 55:12 trees clap their hands as the desert is turned into an oasis for the people of God.)

COMMENTARY

As I write this section, there is on my desk a request for aid for Turkey. An earthquake there has displaced some 60,000 people and taken the lives of perhaps up to 40,000 others. I recently received news that a former student of mine has been killed in an automobile accident. He had spent much time and energy in advancing his education so that he might train many others for ministry in his homeland, Nigeria. And just like that, his life on earth ended. It is in this kind of world that we are called to sing Psalm 98 with its central affirmation that the Lord is king: king over his people (98:1-3), king over the nations (98:4-6), and king over the creation (98:7-9).

There are times when we sing this psalm with sight, having just experienced God's wonderful saving power in our lives, as was the case with Israel when this psalm was originally composed. There are other times when we must sing by faith in the face of much evidence to belie the truth that there is a good God in control of this world, as did the Israelites when they sang this psalm in the middle of the harsh realities of postexilic life (see Haggai and Ezra—Nehemiah). In whatever circumstances we sing Psalm 98, we sing the heart of the book of Psalms and the heart of the Christian faith: The Lord is king. Psalm 98 calls us to celebrate the ever-expanding reign of our God.

Celebrate His Reign over His People (98:1-3). "He has done wonderful deeds" (98:1). The Lord had done wonderful things for the nation of Israel. The precise referent behind the "mighty victory" (98:1) that the Lord had won is not specified. The exodus from Egypt in Israel's distant past may be in view, and so too the return from Babylon in the more recent past. This historical ambiguity, rather than being a liability, was actually an asset as it made the psalm usable in any circumstance in which Israel experienced God's "mighty victory" (Longman 1995:272). In the same way, it makes it ever usable for us.

The Lord's saving acts on behalf of Israel were evidence of his love for and faithfulness to that one nation (98:3). Out of all the nations of the earth, Israel was his special people. But his intention was never to confine his saving benefits to that one nation. He intended that his "victory" be revealed to "every nation" (98:2) and that his salvation be seen by the "ends of the earth."[1] Thus the exodus from Egypt was itself for the benefit of Israel and for the benefit of the whole human race (66:5-6; see note on 66:5). This expanded horizon is picked up in the second strophe.

Celebrate His Reign over the Nations (98:4-6). This central strophe is bounded by the invitation to "shout." Psalm 98:4 tells us who is to shout: "all the earth." Psalm 98:6 tells us where the shouting is to take place: "before the LORD, the King." Not just Israel, but "all the earth" is now assembled in the presence of the king of the nations, and "all the earth" is shouting for joy at the "mighty victory" of the Lord. Human voices are breaking out in praise all over the earth, accompanied by stringed and wind instruments that form a symphony of praise to the victorious king. But not even an earth full of human music is sufficient for celebrating the "mighty victory" of the king, for this victory is ultimately cosmic in scope.

Celebrate His Reign over the Earth (98:7-9). "The LORD is coming to judge the earth" (98:9). So "the sea and everything in it," "the earth and all living things," "the rivers," and "the hills" are shouting out their joyful praise. Whereas the nations were singing "before the LORD" in the previous scene (98:6), now all the components of the earth are singing out their songs of joy "before the LORD" (98:9). The whole cosmos is singing in anticipation of the Lord's "coming to judge the earth," for this coming is to set everything in the whole cosmos back into right order (see commentary on 96:11-13).

Even though Israel had experienced the "mighty victory" of God in the past, not everything was yet in "right order" in the present—not in Israel, not in the nations, not in the cosmos. So Psalm 96 lifted God's people's eyes to the full experience of his "mighty victory" at some point in the future, when he would come to set everything in his creation right.

And he did come to do just that in the person of the Lord Jesus Christ, who lived and died and was raised that everything in the created realm might be reconciled to the Creator and brought together under one authority—the authority of the King of kings (Eph 1:10; Col 1:20; Rev 19:16). We who have come to faith in Christ celebrate his reign over us. And we know that this reign is not to be contained within the walls of the church, but the king who has all authority has commissioned us to make disciples of "all the nations" (Matt 28:19). And we do so in a world where everything is not yet in right order—in a world of violent earthquakes and tragic automobile accidents—but where everything will one day be in right order "for the LORD is coming to judge the earth." So with great joy we join our voices with the nations and the whole cosmic order to celebrate the heart of our hope: The Lord is king!

ENDNOTES

1. The Exodus was intended to reveal God's sovereignty to the Egyptians (see Exod 7:5; 14:4, 18).

◆ J. Psalm 99

1 The LORD is king!
Let the nations tremble!
He sits on his throne between the cherubim.
Let the whole earth quake!
2 The LORD sits in majesty in Jerusalem,*
exalted above all the nations.
3 Let them praise your great and awesome name.
Your name is holy!
4 Mighty King, lover of justice,
you have established fairness.
You have acted with justice
and righteousness throughout Israel.*
5 Exalt the LORD our God!
Bow low before his feet, for he is holy!

6 Moses and Aaron were among his priests;
Samuel also called on his name.
They cried to the LORD for help,
and he answered them.
7 He spoke to Israel from the pillar of cloud,
and they followed the laws and decrees he gave them.

[8]O LORD our God, you answered them.
You were a forgiving God to them,
but you punished them when they
went wrong.

[9]Exalt the LORD our God,
and worship at his holy mountain
in Jerusalem,
for the LORD our God is holy!

99:2 Hebrew *Zion.* 99:4 Hebrew *Jacob.* See note on 44:4.

NOTES

99:3 ***praise.*** The Hiphil of *yadah* [TH3034A, ZH3344] is at times rendered "praise" in the NLT and at other times "thank" (e.g., 7:17 [18]; 9:1 [2]; 28:7; 30:12 [13]; 35:18). Here the sense is probably "thank" in the context of the previous psalms, where the nations are pictured as experiencing the saving benefits of the Lord's salvation (96:1-10; 97:1; 98:1-3).

99:4 ***Mighty King, lover of justice.*** This colon is quite difficult. The Hebrew seems to say, "The strength of the king loves justice" (NASB), but "strength" as the subject of "love" is odd. For a concise discussion of interpretive options see Tate 1990:526-527. Howard (1997:85-86) may be correct in interpreting *'oz* [TH5797, ZH6437] as "Strong One," resulting in "The Strong One is king! He loves justice."

99:6 ***They cried to the LORD for help.*** Here the word *qara'* [TH7121, ZH7924] probably refers not to a general cry for help, but to intercession for mercy needed in the wake of sin. See Exod 32:7-14 and 1 Sam 7:5-11, where Moses and Samuel intercede in this way for Israel (McCann 1996:1075).

99:8 ***a forgiving God . . . but you punished them.*** Perhaps Numbers 14 is in view, where the Lord forgave his people (Num 14:20) but nevertheless punished them in the wilderness (Num 14:21-23). The participle *noqem* [TH5358, ZH5933] (punishing) should probably be understood to be parallel to the previous participle *nose'* [TH5375, ZH5951] (forgiving) and therefore governed by *'el* [TH410A, ZH446] (God). (For another text that collocates *'el* and *noqem,* see Nah 1:2.) The Lord was both a forgiving God and a punishing God (Brueggemann 1984:149).

COMMENTARY

Psalm 99 is the last in a series of psalms (93–99) that celebrate the Lord's kingship. "The LORD is king!" is thus the governing affirmation of this psalm. The refrain (99:5, 9) shows us that exalting the king is the specific purpose of this psalm. And the threefold repetition of *qadosh* [TH6918, ZH7705] ("holy"; 99:3, 5, 9) shows us that holiness is the focus of the exaltation.

Exalt the Holy King Who Reigns (99:1-5). As in other psalms of this genre (see Pss 47, 96, 98), the Lord's reign is not just over Israel but over all the nations (99:1-3). While that reign emanated from his throne situated between the cherubim in Jerusalem, it was to extend to all the nations of the earth. The Lord is no mere local deity. He is "exalted above all the nations" (99:2), so all the nations are to praise his great and awesome name. They are to give thanks for the great and awesome things the Lord has done for them. They are also to join in the confession that the Lord's name is "holy." The Lord's holiness evokes a deep sense of awe. Thus the nations tremble, and the earth quakes at the reality of his holy reign.

The Lord reigns over all the nations with justice. The one who reigns is the "Strong One" (see note on 99:4). His power, however, is never abusive, never used in a tyrannical or oppressive manner. Such an abuse of power is impossible for a king who is a "lover of justice." Because he loves to see everything done right, he acts with justice, fairness, and righteousness "throughout Israel." So Israel, along with the nations, is to exalt the Lord as the king who reigns, bowing at his feet and confessing that he is holy. The Lord's holiness is the justice, fairness, and righteousness that characterize how the Lord interacts with people in the world.

Exalt the Holy King Who Responds (99:6-9). The twofold repetition of the Lord's answering prayer (99:6, 8) shows that his holiness does not mean detachment or uninvolvement. Moses, Aaron, and Samuel are held up as illustrations of the way the Lord responds to his people. These three men were known as great intercessors whose prayers were answered by God. God had spoken to each of them, and their lives were generally characterized by obedience to God's principles. They were not, however, sinless (e.g., Num 12:1-15; 20:1-13). But they found the Lord to be "a forgiving God" (99:8).

Though he forgave, he also "punished." While forgiving and punishing may seem to be mutually exclusive, they were not and are not. God's own self-testimony includes the following:

> *Yahweh! The LORD! The God of compassion and mercy! I am slow to anger and filled with unfailing love and faithfulness. I lavish unfailing love to a thousand generations. I forgive iniquity, rebellion, and sin. But I do not excuse the guilty.* (Exod 34:6-7)

In Numbers 14:18, Moses used these words while interceding for the Israelites who had sinned in the wilderness. God both forgave them (Num 14:20) and made them experience negative consequences for their failure to live by faith in him (Num 14:21-23). Sin often has negative consequences that the Lord metes out.

While it is true that "He forgives *all* my sins" (103:3), it is not true that he punishes us for *all* our sins: "He does *not* punish us for *all* our sins; he does not deal harshly with us, as we deserve" (103:10; my italics). God's mercy wins out over his judgment (Jas 2:13). Moreover, even when he lets us experience trouble in the wake of our sin, this too is a token of his great love for us, "For the LORD disciplines those he loves, and he punishes each one he accepts as his child" (Heb 12:6). So both his "forgiving" and his "punishing" are expressions of his love.

It is because he is "our God" (99:9) that he responds to us when we call on him. And so we respond by exalting him in worship and following his principles in our day-to-day living.

◆ K. Psalm 100

A psalm of thanksgiving.

1 Shout with joy to the LORD, all the earth!
2 Worship the LORD with gladness.
Come before him, singing with joy.
3 Acknowledge that the LORD is God!
He made us, and we are his.*
We are his people, the sheep of his pasture.
4 Enter his gates with thanksgiving;
go into his courts with praise.
Give thanks to him and praise his name.
5 For the LORD is good.
His unfailing love continues forever,
and his faithfulness continues to each generation.

100:3 As in an alternate reading in the Masoretic Text; the other alternate and some ancient versions read *and not we ourselves.*

NOTES

100:2 *Worship the* LORD *with gladness.* The masc. pl. Qal imperative of *'abad* [TH5647, ZH6268] occurs only one other time in the Psalter (i.e., 2:10-11), where the "rulers of the earth" are exhorted to "worship/serve the LORD with reverent fear."

100:3 *Acknowledge.* This imperative is fourth of seven in the poem, marking it out as the central imperative. While the word *yada'* [TH3045, ZH3359] sometimes means "acknowledge," the clear examples of this sense are in the context of acknowledging sin (51:3 [5]; Isa 59:12; Jer 3:13; 14:20; DCH 4.99). When followed by the particle *ki* [TH3588, ZH3954] (that), *yada'* regularly means "know/realize/be aware" (DCH 4.100). "Know" is conceptually different from the other six liturgical imperatives, further marking it out as the central imperative (McCann 1996:1078).

and we are his. Some Hebrew mss read *welo' 'anakhnu* [TH3808/587, ZH4202/636], so the KJV and NASB have "and not we ourselves." The NLT (so too the NIV) follows other word texts and the Qere that read *welo 'anakhnu* [TH3807.1/2050.2/587, ZH4200/2257/636]; this reading is supported by some ancient versions as well. There are 14 other passages where *lo* [TH3807.1/2050.2, ZH4200/2257] is to be read for *lo'* [TH3808, ZH4202]; the Masorah indicates 17, but 2 are doubtful (see Delitzsch 1982:105). See Howard 1997:92-94 for a full discussion of the issue.

his people. The word *'ammo* [TH5971A, ZH6639] is the central word of the poem, having 20 words before and after it. That we are "his people" is the heart of the psalm (Howard 1997:96).

100:4 *Enter.* The Hebrew text has the same word (*bo'u* [TH935, ZH995]) as is translated "come" in 100:2. These two occurrences surround 100:3, which contains the central affirmation of the psalm (Howard 1997:96).

COMMENTARY

"The crescendo of praise that has been building since Psalm 93 reaches a climax in Psalm 100" (Howard 1997:180). Psalm 100 brings to a conclusion the central celebration of the Lord's kingship, a kingship that makes him "Lord of all the earth" (97:5) and "supreme over all the earth" (97:9). His glorious deeds have been published "among the nations," (96:3) and his righteousness has been revealed "to every nation" (98:2). So it is fitting that Psalm 100 addresses "all the earth" with its invitation (100:1-4) and motivation (100:5) to worship the Lord.

The Invitation to Worship (100:1-4). There are seven imperatives in these verses. "Acknowledge that the LORD is God" (100:3) is the central imperative. It is central in that it is preceded and followed by three imperatives and surrounded by the imperative "come" (100:2b, 4a). It also stands somewhat apart from the other imperatives. Knowing is different from the liturgical actions envisioned in the other six imperatives. Knowing is foundational to doing. At the foundation of worship is knowing the central truth about the one we worship. Simply put, "the LORD is God!" But there were and are many gods calling for worship. Who is this God? He is the one who "made us," perhaps in the sense that he created us, but especially in the sense that he saved us.[1] And the biblical logic is that since he made us, we belong to him (see 24:1-2). Yet how do we belong to him? One word in the Hebrew gives the answer: *'ammo* [TH5971A, ZH6639]—"his people." Not his enemies. "His people." And not just any kind of people. We are "the sheep of his pasture" (100:3), "the people he watches over" (95:7). We are the people he loves and cares for, as a shepherd loves and cares for his sheep. In knowing him, we know ourselves, for to know that he is the God who made us is to know that we are the people he loves. This knowledge is the spring from which all the actions of worship flow.

Surrounding this knowledge of who God is and who we are is the dual invitation to enter his presence with songs of thanksgiving (100:2b, 4a). We have responded to the call to "serve the LORD with reverent fear" (2:11), and we have submitted to "God's royal son" (2:12), so we do not enter with servile fear but to "serve/worship the LORD with gladness" (100:2). And in this spirit of gladness we shout for joy, give thanks to him, and bless his name.

The Motivation for Worship (100:5). What is implicit about the character of God in 100:3 becomes explicit in 100:5: "The LORD is good." The king who is "robed in majesty and armed with strength" (93:1) is good. "The God of vengeance" (94:1) is good. The "great King above all gods" (95:3) is good. The God who "will judge all peoples fairly" (96:10) is good. The God before whom "every god must bow" (97:7) is good. The God who "has revealed his righteousness to every nation" (98:2) is good. The God who "punished them when they went wrong" (99:8) is good. The God who "made us" to be his people (100:3) is good. This is why we shout for joy, worship with gladness, come before him with songs of joy, give him thanks, and bless his name.

And we are secure in this goodness, because "his unfailing love continues forever, and his faithfulness continues to each generation." He is our God forever. We are his people forever. We are the sheep he cares for forever. So we worship him forever. When we think about the kind of God our God is, is it too much to ask that we worship and serve him with the whole of our lives (Rom 12:1)? We belong to him, a God who is good and loving and faithful. We should honor him with the whole of our lives.

ENDNOTES

1. See the discussion of 95:6-7 and McCann 1996:1078.

◆ L. Psalm 101

A psalm of David.

1 I will sing of your love and justice,
LORD.
I will praise you with songs.
2 I will be careful to live a blameless life—
when will you come to help me?
I will lead a life of integrity
in my own home.
3 I will refuse to look at
anything vile and vulgar.
I hate all who deal crookedly;
I will have nothing to do with them.
4 I will reject perverse ideas
and stay away from every evil.
5 I will not tolerate people who slander
their neighbors.
I will not endure conceit and
pride.
6 I will search for faithful people
to be my companions.
Only those who are above reproach
will be allowed to serve me.
7 I will not allow deceivers to serve in
my house,
and liars will not stay in my
presence.
8 My daily task will be to ferret out the
wicked
and free the city of the LORD from
their grip.

NOTES

101:1 ***your love and justice.*** The word *khesed* [TH2617, ZH2876] (love) refers to God's covenant loyalty, and *mishpat* [TH4941, ZH5477] (justice) here probably has the sense "law" (HALOT 2.652), given the context that focuses on obedience. The Hebrew text lacks the pronoun "your." Based on the following colon, "your" may be implied, but based on the content of the psalm as a whole, David is also celebrating in song God's love and law as they come to expression in his own life and the lives of those around him.

101:2 ***I will be careful to live a blameless life.*** The verb is a cohortative used to express firm resolution (Joüon and Muraoka 1991:§114c).

COMMENTARY

Our conduct flows out of our character, and our character is shaped by our ultimate commitments (Mays 1994:322). Psalm 101 challenges us at the level of commitment. It challenges us to commit to being people of godly character in ourselves and in our relations with others.

Being a person of godly character begins with inner resolve. David resolved to lead a blameless life. To be blameless means to keep one's self from sin (18:23). While no one is absolutely sinless (Eccl 7:20), the Bible nonetheless speaks of people as being blameless (15:2; Gen 6:9; Job 1:1; Prov 2:21), as living in harmony with God and his ways. Commitment to having a blameless character was David's firm resolution and is the beginning of our own development of godly character.

Commitment to having a godly character has the first opportunity to show up in our homes. David said, "I will lead a life of integrity in my own home" (101:2). The word translated "integrity" is related to the word translated "blameless" in the previous sentence. Home is where character is shaped and tested. So David's commitment to godly character came to expression first in relation to those in his own household. Sometimes we can do the right things in public, but those actions may rise from sources other than the deep wells of character within. Our actions in the home are often a true reflection of our character. Thus, commitment to godly character in the home is a foundation stone.

The commitment to character does not stay at home but reaches out in our relations with others. There is a proverb that says, "Walk with the wise and become wise; associate with fools and get in trouble" (Prov 13:20). This does not mean that we should have no association at all with "fools," for if it did, we would not be able to live in this world (1 Cor 5:10). It does mean that we live with an awareness that close associations will affect us. In keeping with this, David resolved not to have close associations with crooked people, slanderers, the arrogant, and deceivers—to mention a few. Conversely, he was committed to drawing to himself godly associates who themselves were "above reproach" (101:6). The Hebrew word here echoes that of 101:2, where David resolved to live a blameless life of integrity. In other words, David resolved to have close associations with those who shared his commitment to godly character. Such associations will have a mutually sharpening effect (Prov 27:17). Thus, we will find it necessary to limit some associations and increase others in light of our commitment to godly character.

This commitment cannot be kept in our own strength. This is why in the middle of his opening resolution David interjected the question: "When will you come to help me?" David longed to be godly, and he knew that God's presence in his life was the key to that godliness, so he prayed for God to come to him. In a similar way, another psalmist resolved to obey God and pleaded for God to stick with him in the process (119:8). God is always present with us in terms of his general presence, but we must seek after that special presence that enables us to keep our spiritual commitments.

Since the ability to keep the commitment to godly character comes from God's presence in our lives, David began this psalm by celebrating God's love and law in song. Psalm 101 is a celebration of the Lord's covenant commitment to his people—a commitment that empowers us to be committed to a life of integrity before God and in relation to others.

◆ M. Psalm 102

A prayer of one overwhelmed with trouble, pouring out problems before the LORD.

1 LORD, hear my prayer!
Listen to my plea!
2 Don't turn away from me
in my time of distress.
Bend down to listen,
and answer me quickly when I call
to you.
3 For my days disappear like smoke,
and my bones burn like red-hot
coals.
4 My heart is sick, withered
like grass,
and I have lost my appetite.
5 Because of my groaning,
I am reduced to skin and bones.
6 I am like an owl in the desert,
like a little owl in a far-off
wilderness.
7 I lie awake,
lonely as a solitary bird on
the roof.
8 My enemies taunt me day after day.
They mock and curse me.
9 I eat ashes for food.
My tears run down into my drink
10 because of your anger and wrath.
For you have picked me up and
thrown me out.
11 My life passes as swiftly as the
evening shadows.
I am withering away like grass.
12 But you, O LORD, will sit on your
throne forever.
Your fame will endure to every
generation.
13 You will arise and have mercy on
Jerusalem*—
and now is the time to pity her,
now is the time you promised to
help.
14 For your people love every stone in her
walls
and cherish even the dust in her
streets.
15 Then the nations will tremble before
the LORD.
The kings of the earth will tremble
before his glory.
16 For the LORD will rebuild Jerusalem.
He will appear in his glory.
17 He will listen to the prayers of the
destitute.
He will not reject their pleas.
18 Let this be recorded for future
generations,
so that a people not yet born will
praise the LORD.
19 Tell them the LORD looked down
from his heavenly sanctuary.
He looked down to earth from heaven
20 to hear the groans of the prisoners,
to release those condemned to die.
21 And so the LORD's fame will be
celebrated in Zion,
his praises in Jerusalem,
22 when multitudes gather together

and kingdoms come to worship
the LORD.

23 He broke my strength in midlife,
cutting short my days.
24 But I cried to him, "O my God, who
lives forever,
don't take my life while I am so
young!
25 Long ago you laid the foundation of
the earth
and made the heavens with your
hands.
26 They will perish, but you remain
forever;
they will wear out like old
clothing.
You will change them like a garment
and discard them.
27 But you are always the same;
you will live forever.
28 The children of your people
will live in security.
Their children's children
will thrive in your presence."

102:13 Hebrew *Zion;* also in 102:16.

NOTES

102:TITLE *overwhelmed.* The word *'atap* [TH5848A, ZH6494] here means to be weak or to be without strength (HALOT 2.814). It is also used in 61:2 [3], where the psalmist feels weak in the face of overwhelming circumstances.

102:2 *time . . . when.* The word translated "time" and "when" is the phrase *beyom* [TH871.2/3117, ZH928/3427] (in [the] day). The psalmist's "days" are referred to in 102:3, 11, 23, 24 [4, 12, 24, 25]; see commentary.

102:11 *My life.* Lit., "My days"; see note at 102:2.

102:22 *multitudes.* The word *'ammim* [TH5971A, ZH6639] (nations) recalls the use of *'am* (people) in 102:18 [19].

102:24 *I cried.* The verb is an imperfect, which is more naturally taken here as a present tense. The psalmist is in the process of praying rather than recounting a past prayer.

who lives forever. Lit., "whose years are from generation to generation." The Lord's "years" are also referred to in 102:27 [28] and are contrasted in the psalm with the psalmist's "days"; see commentary.

while I am so young! Lit., "in the middle of my days"; see note at 102:2.

COMMENTARY

Sometimes the troubles of this life can feel overwhelming. We feel weak and unable to stand under the load. Such was the case for the author of Psalm 102, as the title indicates: "A prayer of one overwhelmed with trouble." The title also indicates the best way of working through those feelings of being overwhelmed—it comes by "pouring out [our] problems before the Lord." Honest prayer is a key to moving from being overwhelmed to being an overcomer in life.

Pour Out Your Problems before the Lord (102:1-11). When the load of life's troubles gets so heavy that we feel we have no strength to go on, there is a path to renewed strength and confident living. That path begins by calling on the Lord to intervene (102:1-2), coupled with honestly pouring out our problems before him (102:3-11). There will be days of distress; in those days, we call on the Lord to intervene. "LORD, hear. . . . Listen. . . . Don't turn away. . . . Bend down to listen, and answer me quickly" (102:1-2). Days of distress are days when we cry out to God to respond quickly to deliver us from the distress.

Metaphorical and literal language are combined in a powerful outpouring of problems in 102:3-11. The language is that of illness: "My bones burn like red-hot coals. . . . I have lost my appetite. . . . I am reduced to skin and bones" (102:3-5). Death seems to be imminent, as the psalmist's days "disappear like smoke" (102:3) and his days pass "as swiftly as the evening shadows" (102:11). Added to illness is isolation. The psalmist likens himself to a lonely owl sitting far off, isolated from community in a desolate place. In the middle of sleepless nights, he is like a lonely bird on a rooftop. Then there is the animosity directed toward him by the "enemies" who have disdain for him and not compassion. Most painful, however, are the feelings of abandonment by God: "You have picked me up and thrown me out" (102:10). The psalmist was sick in heart as well as in body. And he let nothing go unspoken in prayer. From his example, the Holy Spirit teaches us to pour out our problems before the Lord with complete candor.

Days of deep distress are often days when we feel the fleeting nature of our human existence on this planet. The repetition of the word "days" in 102:3 and 102:11 and the related metaphors of smoke and fleeting shadows envelop this section and bring to expression feelings of meaningless transience.[1] In the darkness of this sense of transience is a ray of light that eventually dispels the darkness, inasmuch as human transience provides the backdrop for a grand display of divine eternality.

Put Your Focus on the Lord (102:12-22). "But you, O LORD," sounds a note of contrast and, therefore, of hope. There is someone who is not subject to the fleeting nature of human existence—someone who is characterized by "forever," who will "endure to every generation" (102:12). And this one does not just exist forever. He will rule forever. Above and in all the troubles of this life is the Lord, who reigns as king of the creation he has made. Focusing on his eternal reign is our turning point in the move from being overwhelmed to being overcomers in life. Contrary to appearances and our perspective skewed by trouble, life is not ultimately a fleeting experience of chaotic activity, because there is a divine king who reigns.

And this king is no harsh tyrant, for he is not only characterized by eternality but also by showing "mercy" and "pity" to his people (102:13). The scope has broadened in 102:12-22 from the individual to the community. Restoration of the community is the hope of the individual who prays, "The LORD will rebuild Jerusalem" (102:16) and "will listen to the prayers of the destitute" (102:17). Ultimately the one and the many are interconnected,[2] so that the salvation of the one is not possible apart from the salvation of the many, and the restoration of the many is the restoration of the one. Love for the community of the many is beautifully expressed in 102:14: "For your people love every stone in her walls and cherish even the dust in her streets." And the community bursts the bounds of Jerusalem narrowly conceived, as the "nations" and the "kings of the earth" come into view in 102:15.

In the context of 102:15, the "people not yet born" in 102:18 is probably a nation created from the nations of the earth. As God once "looked down" from heaven to see the misery of captive Israel (Exod 2:25; 14:24), so he once again has "looked down . . . to hear the groans of the prisoners, to release those condemned to die" (102:19-20). The immediate referent may be the community of exiles in Babylon (McCann 1996:1087). Yet it seems that the referent is more inclusive, embracing the "nation yet to be created," which seems to be the "multitudes/nations" at the close of this section (102:22), which gather together to worship the true God. Thus, God is not now looking down from heaven on the whole human race to see if any are righteous (14:2; 53:2) but to deliver the nations from their groans and condemnation.

Pray Confidently to the Lord (102:23-28). The individual does not get lost in the community. The final section opens with a return to the cry of the one. While the truth of who God is and what he is doing is a turning point from being overwhelmed to being an overcomer, the pain of the problems may yet remain. The short "days" of the psalmist are back in view in 102:23, as his thoughts come back to his true "midlife" crisis. So he renews his prayer to God, who is characterized not by fleeting "days" but by "years" that go on from generation to generation, who is "always the same," and who lives forever (102:27).

In this closing section, the psalmist looks back not to the Exodus but to God's initial act of creation: his founding the earth and establishing the heavens. As ancient and therefore seemingly permanent as the heavens and the earth may appear, they will perish and be discarded like old clothes, says the psalmist. This is said not to denigrate the creation but to provide a counterpoint for the magnification of the Lord, who will "remain forever" (102:26). Since God will remain forever, the psalmist and future generations "will live in security" and "thrive" in the divine presence. It is on this great note of confidence that the psalm comes to an end.

Even in the overwhelming troubles of life, we are overcomers, because there is an eternal and merciful divine king ruling the cosmos. Despite overwhelming troubles, "overwhelming victory is ours" (Rom 8:37) because God not only looked down from heaven, but he also came down in the person of the Lord Jesus Christ so that nothing can ever separate us from his love (Rom 8:35).

ENDNOTES

1. See also the meditations on the transience of human existence in Pss 39 and 90.
2. See Ps 103, which also moves from the individual (103:3-5) to the community (103:6-10).

◆ N. Psalm 103

A psalm of David.

[1] Let all that I am praise the LORD;
with my whole heart, I will praise his holy name.
[2] Let all that I am praise the LORD;
may I never forget the good things he does for me.
[3] He forgives all my sins
and heals all my diseases.
[4] He redeems me from death
and crowns me with love and tender mercies.
[5] He fills my life with good things.
My youth is renewed like the eagle's!

[6] The LORD gives righteousness
and justice to all who are treated unfairly.
[7] He revealed his character to Moses
and his deeds to the people of Israel.
[8] The LORD is compassionate and merciful,

slow to get angry and filled with
unfailing love.
9 He will not constantly accuse us,
nor remain angry forever.
10 He does not punish us for all our sins;
he does not deal harshly with us,
as we deserve.
11 For his unfailing love toward those
who fear him
is as great as the height of the
heavens above the earth.
12 He has removed our sins as far
from us
as the east is from the west.
13 The LORD is like a father to his
children,
tender and compassionate to those
who fear him.
14 For he knows how weak we are;
he remembers we are only dust.
15 Our days on earth are like grass;
like wildflowers, we bloom and die.
16 The wind blows, and we are gone—
as though we had never been here.
17 But the love of the LORD remains
forever
with those who fear him.
His salvation extends to the children's
children
18 of those who are faithful to his
covenant,
of those who obey his
commandments!

19 The LORD has made the heavens his
throne;
from there he rules over everything.

20 Praise the LORD, you angels,
you mighty ones who carry out his
plans,
listening for each of his commands.
21 Yes, praise the LORD, you armies
of angels
who serve him and do his will!
22 Praise the LORD, everything he has
created,
everything in all his kingdom.

Let all that I am praise the LORD.

NOTES

103:5 ***life.*** The word *'adi* [TH5716, ZH6344] ("jewelry"; cf. Isa 49:18) is problematic in context (see, e.g., NIV, "desires"; NASB, "years": and NKJV, "mouth"). NLT's "life" presumes a simple emendation to *'od* [TH5750/2967.1, ZH6388/3276] (duration), which is likewise used with a pronominal suffix in 104:33 in parallel with *khayyay* [TH2416/2967.1, ZH2644/3276] (my life); see Allen 1983:18.

103:22 ***Let all that I am.*** The Hebrew text has the exact same wording as is found in 103:1 and 103:2. The repetition of language brings the psalm back to the starting point and provides closure to the whole.

COMMENTARY

Psalm 103 is the first of four songs of praise that form the conclusion to Book 4. It is appropriate for the book that celebrates the kingship of the Lord to come to a close on such a high note of praise. Two invitations to praise the Lord (103:1-2 and 103:20-22) surround the central section of the poem (103:3-19), which contains the praise called for in the introduction and conclusion. The central section shares with Psalm 102 the alternating perspectives of the individual (103:3-5) and the community (103:6-19). The good things the Lord does for the individual are celebrated in the context of the good things God does for the community as a whole.

Individual Invitation to Praise the Lord (103:1-2). Twice the psalmist exhorts himself to praise the Lord. This praise is to be wholehearted praise, owing to the holy character of the God who is praised. Specific aspects of God's holy character will come to expression in the central section of the poem. And God's holy character is revealed in particular through "the good things he does," which are enumerated in 103:3-19.

Praise for the Lord's Benefits (103:3-19). This section is a detailing of the good things God has done—the benefits people receive from him. Who are these benefits for? And what are the benefits God grants?

The benefits are for "those who fear him." This is stated three times in 103:11, 13, and 17. "Those who fear him" are those "who follow his ways," in the language of 128:1. They are "those who are faithful to his covenant" and "those who obey his commandments," according to 103:18. While this faithfulness and obedience must be real, it cannot be perfect, for if perfection is required, no one would receive the benefits. As the proverb says, "Who can say . . . I am pure and free from sin?" (Prov 20:9). That sinlessness is not meant is also abundantly clear from the first and chief benefit enumerated: "He forgives" (103:3).

He Forgives Our Sins. We do not always obey God's commandments. God does not get angry at us very quickly, and even if he does, he does not remain angry very long. If the Lord did hold on to his anger over our sins, who could ever survive (130:3)? No one could, for our sins are a burden that would crush us. They can trouble us in body, mind, and spirit. But they need not, because God forgives. He forgives comprehensively: "He forgives all my sins." We can bring any and all sin to the Lord, knowing that he will forgive them all. He forgives thoroughly: "He has removed our sins as far from us as the east is from the west" (103:12). He does not forgive partially, leaving us with some guilt to carry. His forgiveness is a complete removal of sin. He forgives because of his character: "The LORD is compassionate and merciful" (103:8) and "The LORD is . . . tender and compassionate" (103:13). It is just like God to forgive! It is in perfect keeping with the "unfailing love" that fills his heart. He forgives in response to our frailty: "For he knows how weak we are; he remembers we are only dust" (103:14). Just as God was merciful to Paul because Paul acted "in ignorance and unbelief" (1 Tim 1:13), so he is merciful to us. We are like grass—here today and gone tomorrow—but the Lord's great love "remains forever" (103:17).[1]

His unfailing love "is as great as the height of the heavens above the earth" (103:11). His unfailing love is seen in his willingness to sacrifice his Son for our sins (John 15:13) and to raise him up for our forgiveness (Rom 4:25). As we believe in a God of such love, mercy, and grace, we have no hesitation in coming to him just as we are with all of our sins, for we know how freely he forgives.

He Heals Our Diseases. The benefit of healing[2] follows the benefit of forgiveness. We have seen that there are times when sickness is the result of sin (see Pss 32 and 38). The corollary is that healing can come in the wake of forgiveness. This is why James says,

> *Such a prayer offered in faith will heal the sick, and the Lord will make you well. And if you have committed any sins, you will be forgiven. Confess your sins to each other and pray for each other so that you may be healed. The earnest prayer of a righteous person has great power and produces wonderful results.* (Jas 5:15-16)

Since sickness can lead to death, God not only heals but also redeems his people from death. So bountiful is God in his "love and tender mercies" that his healing is followed by his filling of our lives with good things and blessing us with the youthful vigor necessary to enjoy them (see 1 Tim 6:17).

Universal Invitation to Praise the Lord (103:20-22). The theme of Book 4 and the theme of the book of Psalms is "The LORD is king!" (93:1; 95:3; 96:10; 97:1; 98:6; 99:1; 102:12). His throne is in heaven. This does not mean that God is unknowable and unreachable. It *does* mean that God is above all of life and is not subject to its vicissitudes. Since he is above all, he can and does rule over all (see Ps 93). As the one who rules over all, he can forgive all and heal all.

Since his throne is in heaven, the angelic inhabitants of heaven are invited to join in the praise of God. Interestingly, these angelic beings are repeatedly described as living in conformity to God's ways. They "carry out his plans, listening for each of his commands" and "serve him and do his will" (103:20-21). In so doing, they provide us with an exemplary response to the loving and merciful character of God. Since he rules over everything, "everything he has created, everything in all his kingdom" (103:22) is invited to join in his praise. Vast and innumerable though this praising choir may be, individual people in all their humanness are not insignificant. Each person's praise counts: "Let all that I am praise the LORD."

ENDNOTES

1. See Ps 102 for more on the contrast between human transience and divine eternality.
2. See Brown 1995 for a full discussion of God as healer.

◆ O. Psalm 104

1 Let all that I am praise the LORD.

O LORD my God, how great you are!
You are robed with honor and majesty.
2 You are dressed in a robe of light.
You stretch out the starry curtain of the heavens;
3 you lay out the rafters of your home in the rain clouds.
You make the clouds your chariot;
you ride upon the wings of the wind.
4 The winds are your messengers;
flames of fire are your servants.*

5 You placed the world on its foundation
so it would never be moved.
6 You clothed the earth with floods of water,
water that covered even the mountains.
7 At your command, the water fled;
at the sound of your thunder, it hurried away.
8 Mountains rose and valleys sank
to the levels you decreed.
9 Then you set a firm boundary for the seas,
so they would never again cover the earth.

10 You make springs pour water into the ravines,
so streams gush down from the mountains.
11 They provide water for all the animals,
and the wild donkeys quench their thirst.
12 The birds nest beside the streams

and sing among the branches of the
trees.
13 You send rain on the mountains from
your heavenly home,
and you fill the earth with the fruit
of your labor.
14 You cause grass to grow for the
livestock
and plants for people to use.
You allow them to produce food from
the earth—
15 wine to make them glad,
olive oil to soothe their skin,
and bread to give them strength.
16 The trees of the LORD are well cared for—
the cedars of Lebanon that he
planted.
17 There the birds make their nests,
and the storks make their homes
in the cypresses.
18 High in the mountains live the wild
goats,
and the rocks form a refuge for
the hyraxes.*

19 You made the moon to mark the
seasons,
and the sun knows when to set.
20 You send the darkness, and it becomes
night,
when all the forest animals prowl
about.
21 Then the young lions roar for their
prey,
stalking the food provided by God.
22 At dawn they slink back
into their dens to rest.
23 Then people go off to their work,
where they labor until evening.

24 O LORD, what a variety of things you
have made!
In wisdom you have made them all.
The earth is full of your creatures.
25 Here is the ocean, vast and wide,
teeming with life of every kind,
both large and small.
26 See the ships sailing along,
and Leviathan,* which you made
to play in the sea.

27 They all depend on you
to give them food as they need it.
28 When you supply it, they gather it.
You open your hand to feed them,
and they are richly satisfied.
29 But if you turn away from them, they
panic.
When you take away their breath,
they die and turn again to dust.
30 When you give them your breath,* life
is created,
and you renew the face of the
earth.

31 May the glory of the LORD continue
forever!
The LORD takes pleasure in all he
has made!
32 The earth trembles at his glance;
the mountains smoke at his touch.

•33 I will sing to the LORD as long as
I live.
I will praise my God to my last
breath!
34 May all my thoughts be pleasing
to him,
for I rejoice in the LORD.
35 Let all sinners vanish from the face
of the earth;
let the wicked disappear forever.

Let all that I am praise the LORD.

Praise the LORD!

104:4 Greek version reads *He sends his angels like the winds, / his servants like flames of fire.* Compare Heb 1:7. **104:18** Or *coneys,* or *rock badgers.* **104:26** The identification of Leviathan is disputed, ranging from an earthly creature to a mythical sea monster in ancient literature. **104:30** Or *When you send your Spirit.*

NOTES

104:1 ***robed with honor and majesty.*** This language describes the Lord as clothed in the regalia of a king. The pair *hod wehadar* [TH2556/1926, ZH2806/2077] is used in 21:5 [6] for the human king and in 96:6 for the divine king. The word *hod* is used by itself in reference to royalty in 1 Chr 29:25 and Zech 6:13, as is *hadar* in 145:12 and Dan 11:20. For another portrait of the Lord clothed in royal regalia, see 93:1, where he is robed in majesty and strength.

104:3 ***rafters.*** The "beams" in view here are more likely foundation beams needed to secure God's palace on the celestial ocean. See 24:2, where God secured the earth on the foundation laid on the terrestrial ocean.

rain clouds. The word *mayim* [TH4325, ZH4784] (waters) probably refers here not to rain clouds but to the "waters of the heavens" of Gen 1:7. These waters are above the expanse (Gen 1:6), which contains the stars (Gen 1:17). These are the "vapors [lit., waters] high above the clouds" (148:4). The language is a metaphorical reference to the cosmic waters of the celestial ocean from which come the rains (see Seely 1991, 1992, 1997).

the clouds your chariot . . . you ride. The word *'abim* [TH5645, ZH6265] refers to rain clouds (NIDOTTE 3.332-334). For other texts where the Lord is portrayed as riding on the clouds or skies or winds, see 18:9 [10]; 68:4 [5], 33 [34]; Deut 33:26; Isa 19:1.

104:4 ***winds . . . flames of fire.*** This may be a reference to the hot, crop-consuming winds that blow from the desert east of Israel, in contrast to the winds of 104:3 that blow from the sea to the west of Israel and bring the life-giving rains (Futato 1984:16-17). The merism (figure of speech that uses two poles or extremes to communicate a totality) formed by the contrasting winds would emphasize the Lord's omnipotence: Since the Lord is lord of the east wind and lord of the west wind, he is Lord of all.

104:7 ***your command.*** For similar texts that use the language of cosmic battle for God's creative activity, see 74:13-14 and 106:9; see also Luke 8:22-25 and DBI 929, 931-932.

104:14 ***food.*** The word *lekhem* [TH3899, ZH4312] here refers not to food in general but to grain in particular, as it does in Isa 28:28; 30:23; 36:17 (DCH 4.535). Together with the wine and oil that are mentioned in the next verse, a triad is formed (grain, wine, and oil) that follows the harvest sequence (Futato 1984:42-45); see Deut 11:14; Joel 2:24.

104:15 ***bread.*** The word *lekhem* [TH3899, ZH4312] here refers to food in general and summarizes the preceding grain, wine, and oil.

104:30 ***your breath.*** The word *ruakh* [TH7307, ZH8120] here refers in the first place to the west winds of 104:3 that bring the life-renewing rains to the earth.

104:32 ***smoke.*** This could be a reference to the scorching east winds, forming a contrast with the west winds of 104:30 (Futato 1984:104-113).

104:35 ***Let all that I am praise the LORD.*** The Hebrew text has the exact same wording as is found in 104:1a. The repetition of language brings the psalm back to the starting point and provides closure to the whole; see 103:1-2, 22.

COMMENTARY

Psalm 104 is the quintessential creation psalm. Other psalms confess that God is the Creator (see 93:1; 95:3-5; 96:5; 102:25; 103:19), and some even have extended meditations on God's creative work (see 8:3-8; 19:1-6; 74:12-17). But none match the grandeur of Psalm 104.[1]

Psalm 104 is a creation *hymn.* The psalmist's reflections on God's work of creation result in worship. Psalm 104 begins and ends with "Praise the LORD." The psalm opens with praise for the majesty of the royal Creator (104:1-2a). Then follow two stanzas that praise the Lord for the stability of the universe he has made (104:2b-9) and for his abundant supply in the world (104:10-30). The psalm concludes with praise and prayers for the Creator's glory (104:31-35).

Psalm 104 is clearly paired up with Psalm 103 by the repeated self-exhortation that opens and closes each psalm: It could be translated "Praise the LORD, I tell myself," an exhortation that occurs nowhere else in the Bible. "Together the pair praise the LORD as the savior who forgives and creator who provides" (Mays 1994:331). And like Psalm 103, Psalm 104 sees its theme as an expression of the Lord's kingship, as the first stanza of Psalm 104 makes clear.

Praise for the Majesty of the Creator-King (104:1-2a). Praise for the Creator begins by praising him as a Creator-King, regaled in royal majesty. Most of the psalms mentioned above connect God's creative work with his kingship (93:1; 95:3-5; 96:5; 103:19). God's description as "great" (*gadol* [TH1419, ZH1524]) is frequently associated with his royal reign (see 47:2 [3]; 48:1 [2]; 76:1 [2]; 95:3; 96:4; 99:2; see also 74:12-17). The portrait of God being "robed with honor and majesty" is likewise a royal image (see note on 104:1). That God is "dressed in a robe of light" is an unparalleled expression in the Bible.[2] In context, the picture must be one of God in the radiant splendor of his royal majesty. It is the divine king who created and sustains the world in which we live. Since we know him to be "compassionate and merciful . . . filled with unfailing love . . . tender and compassionate" (103:8, 13), we expect his creation to reflect his character. And it does, as the following two stanzas draw out.

Praise for the Stability of the Universe (104:2b-9). We have already learned in summary fashion that the Creator-King has established a world that cannot be shaken (see 93:1). This truth is now painted in greater detail in this stanza of Psalm 104.

Ancient Near Eastern myths expressed in a variety of forms how the world was brought about when one god won kingship over all competing gods. Elements of these myths lie behind the portrait in 104:2b-9 (see Mays 1994:332-333), which in the context of Psalms 93–100 affirms that the God of Israel is the true Creator-King of the universe (see 95:3-5; 96:4-5).

The universe is portrayed as existing in an upper and a lower layer: the heavens (104:2b-4) and the earth (104:5-9).[3] The creation of the upper layer of the universe is described in terms of God building his royal palace in the heavens (see 103:19) by stretching out the heavens like a tent curtain and by laying the foundations on the celestial ocean (104:2b-3a). From this palace God rode forth as the Divine Warrior on his chariot made up of the clouds, surrounded by his heavenly entourage (104:3b-4), the west and east winds. He is the undisputed master of these elements of his creation.

Next God created the lower layer. Though not stated explicitly, the earth is pictured as founded on waters in such a way that it is not subject to the churning of those waters (see 24:1-2): It can never be moved. Like God's heavenly palace founded on the celestial waters, the earth was founded on the terrestrial waters. Neither the celestial nor the terrestrial waters pose any threat to the king or the stability of the world he has made. As is stated in Genesis 1:9, the terrestrial waters originally covered the entire earth (104:6), a situation that stood in opposition to God's design for a world inhabited by plants, animals, and people. So the Lord rebuked the hostile waters (see 106:9; Matt 8:26; Mark 4:39), sending and confining them to the seas (104:7, 9), and thus allowing the dry land to appear (104:8). The resultant stable universe in general and the waters under the control of the Lord in particular are an affirmation of the reign of the Creator-King over his creation (Mays 1994:333).

Praise for the Supply of the Universe (104:10-30). If all water were completely confined to the seas, life on earth would be impossible. So the Creator-King provided life-giving waters in the form of ground water and rain water. These beneficial sources of water provide life for wild animals, domesticated animals, agricultural plants, wild plants, and people.

The Lord also provided for the changing of time. The moon marks the months, and the sun marks the days. Night is the time ordained for the wild animals to prowl for food, while the daylight hours have been set aside for human labor. These regularities in the creation are testimonies to the reign of the Creator-King.

The psalmist seems to be awestruck at this point, and an exclamation of praise rolls from his lips: "O LORD, what a variety of things you have made!" (104:24). This vast variety is a testimony to the wisdom of the Creator-King. His wisdom is seen not only on the dry land, where the Israelite poet was at home, but also on the sea. So there is a passing reference to the vastness of the ocean with its teeming life. One life-form is Leviathan, which in the myths of the ancient Near East was a hostile force that contended with the would-be-victorious god; but in Psalm 104 Leviathan is pictured as a frolicking creature that delights its Creator.

Food, one of the basics of life, is now brought into sharp relief. An author could describe in scientific detail the various food chains in this world and their interconnections. We could read descriptions of the hunting habits of the lion and the feeding ways of fish. But what the psalmist provides is a theological picture of the total dependence of all of life on the Creator's personal provision. God is pictured as extending his hand to personally feed each of his creatures. The king whose throne is in heaven (103:19) is intimately involved in the day-to-day care of his creation. There is a cycle that includes death (104:29) and new life (104:30), and this cycle, too, results from the Creator-King's governance of his created realm.

Prayer and Praise for the Glory of the Creator (104:31-35). To reflect on the king's creation is to reflect on the king's glory, for the creation is the visible manifestation of his glory (see 19:1-4). So enthralled is the poet with the king's creation glory that he wants this state of affairs to last forever. So he prays, "May the glory of the LORD continue forever!" The psalmist prays for God's glorious creation to endure, so that the Lord can take pleasure in the creation and others can rejoice in the Creator. Since sin can diminish the gloriousness of creation, the psalmist also prays for the removal of all who would threaten the glory so evident in the creation (104:35).

The final word, however, is "praise." The psalmist's will is to "praise my God." The transcendent Creator-King is the immanent "my God" (104:1, 33), who personally made me and personally takes care of me. So, "I will sing to the LORD as long as I live. I will praise my God to my last breath!" (104:33).

How fitting it is, then, that at the end of this glorious psalm about God's glorious creation is the first occurrence in the book of Psalms of that heartfelt cry of the soul, "Hallelujah!"[4]

ENDNOTES

1. Psalm 148 is a magnificent hymn that calls on all creation to praise God, but it does not really describe God's creative work.
2. The closest text to this one is 1 Tim 6:16, which says, "He lives in light so brilliant that no human can approach him." See also Rev 12:1 with its picture of a woman clothed with the sun.
3. The universe is also pictured as two-layered in Ps 148, where the upper layer is described in 148:1-6, and the lower in 148:7-14. A three-layered universe is pictured in texts like Exod 4:20—heaven, earth, water under the earth.
4. "Hallelujah" is rendered in the NLT as "Praise the LORD!"

◆ P. Psalm 105

1 Give thanks to the LORD and proclaim his greatness.
Let the whole world know what he has done.
2 Sing to him; yes, sing his praises.
Tell everyone about his wonderful deeds.
3 Exult in his holy name;
rejoice, you who worship the LORD.
4 Search for the LORD and for his strength;
continually seek him.
5 Remember the wonders he has performed,
his miracles, and the rulings he has given,
6 you children of his servant Abraham,
you descendants of Jacob, his chosen ones.

7 He is the LORD our God.
His justice is seen throughout the land.
8 He always stands by his covenant—
the commitment he made to a thousand generations.
9 This is the covenant he made with Abraham
and the oath he swore to Isaac.
10 He confirmed it to Jacob as a decree,
and to the people of Israel as a never-ending covenant:
11 "I will give you the land of Canaan
as your special possession."

12 He said this when they were few in number,
a tiny group of strangers in Canaan.
13 They wandered from nation to nation,
from one kingdom to another.
14 Yet he did not let anyone oppress them.
He warned kings on their behalf:
15 "Do not touch my chosen people,
and do not hurt my prophets."

16 He called for a famine on the land of Canaan,
cutting off its food supply.
17 Then he sent someone to Egypt ahead of them—
Joseph, who was sold as a slave.
18 They bruised his feet with fetters
and placed his neck in an iron collar.
19 Until the time came to fulfill his dreams,*
the LORD tested Joseph's character.
20 Then Pharaoh sent for him and set him free;
the ruler of the nation opened his prison door.
21 Joseph was put in charge of all the king's household;
he became ruler over all the king's possessions.
22 He could instruct the king's aides as he pleased
and teach the king's advisers.

23 Then Israel arrived in Egypt;
Jacob lived as a foreigner in the land of Ham.
24 And the LORD multiplied the people of Israel

until they became too mighty for
their enemies.
25 Then he turned the Egyptians against
the Israelites,
and they plotted against the LORD's
servants.

26 But the LORD sent his servant Moses,
along with Aaron, whom he had
chosen.
27 They performed miraculous signs
among the Egyptians,
and wonders in the land of Ham.
28 The LORD blanketed Egypt in
darkness,
for they had defied his commands
to let his people go.
29 He turned their water into blood,
poisoning all the fish.
30 Then frogs overran the land
and even invaded the king's
bedrooms.
31 When the LORD spoke, flies descended
on the Egyptians,
and gnats swarmed across Egypt.
32 He sent them hail instead of rain,
and lightning flashed over the land.
33 He ruined their grapevines and fig
trees
and shattered all the trees.
34 He spoke, and hordes of locusts came—
young locusts beyond number.
35 They ate up everything green in the
land,
destroying all the crops in their
fields.
36 Then he killed the oldest son in each
Egyptian home,
the pride and joy of each family.

37 The LORD brought his people out
of Egypt, loaded with silver
and gold;
and not one among the tribes of
Israel even stumbled.
38 Egypt was glad when they were gone,
for they feared them greatly.
39 The LORD spread a cloud above them
as a covering
and gave them a great fire to light
the darkness.
40 They asked for meat, and he sent
them quail;
he satisfied their hunger with
manna—bread from heaven.
41 He split open a rock, and water
gushed out
to form a river through the dry
wasteland.
42 For he remembered his sacred promise
to his servant Abraham.
43 So he brought his people out of Egypt
with joy,
his chosen ones with rejoicing.
44 He gave his people the lands of pagan
nations,
and they harvested crops that
others had planted.
45 All this happened so they would
follow his decrees
and obey his instructions.

Praise the LORD!

105:19 Hebrew *his word.*

NOTES

105:1 ***his greatness.*** The word *'alilah* [TH5949, ZH6613] means "deeds" or "actions" (HALOT 2.833) and is used elsewhere for God's deeds that result in salvation (see Isa 12:4).

105:44 ***they harvested.*** The word *yarash* [TH3423, ZH3769] means "take possession of" and is similar in meaning to *nakhalah* [TH5159, ZH5709] (special possession) in 105:11. One can "take possession of" various things like vineyards (1 Kgs 21:15, 16, 18), olive orchards (Neh 9:25), and fields (Obad 1:19), and perhaps this is why the NLT glosses with "harvested." But in Ps 105:44 Israel is taking possession of the *'amal* of the peoples, a word that means "acquisitions" (HALOT 2.845), which would include the agricultural produce, regardless of who did the harvesting, and also things like cities and houses and wells (for the concept, see Deut 6:10-12).

COMMENTARY

Psalm 105, an exhilarating poem, is a recitation of history (like Pss 78, 106, and 136) from the time of Abraham to the conquest of Canaan in the days of Joshua. An exhilarating recitation of history? Yes! How so? This simple recitation of history moves the soul as it magnifies the saving miracles of God and then shows us the simple response he calls for in our lives.

The poem is a hymn that divides into two uneven stanzas. Psalm 105:1-6 is the invitation to sing God's praise, and 105:7-45 constitutes the praise we are to render.

Magnify God's Miracles (105:7–45). The opening verses (105:1-6) refer to "what [God] has done," "his wonderful deeds," "the wonders he has performed," and "his miracles." These are spelled out for us in 105:7-44.

First, God promised his people the land of Canaan (105:7-11). All of God's miracles recorded in this psalm are rooted in the covenant that the Lord made with Abraham, Isaac, and Jacob. While that covenant had numerous promises attached to it, the promise highlighted here is, "I will give you the land of Canaan as your special possession" (105:11). The rest of the psalm is a record of the circuitous route the Lord led his people on in the process of fulfilling this promise.

Second, God protected Israel's ancestors in the land of Canaan (105:12-16). As a small group of foreign nomads, the ancestors could have been subject to the oppression of the city-states between which they wandered. But God would have none of that. He protected his chosen people and let no one bring them any harm. But then the time came for God to bring the fulfillment of his promise to the next level. To do so he brought a severe famine on the land of Canaan, such that his people would eventually have to leave the land they had been promised they would possess. A most unusual turn of events!

Third, God provided for his people in Egypt (105:17-22). Before the ancestors ever arrived in Egypt, God was at work to provide for them. Through the malice of his brothers, Joseph was sold as a slave to caravanners heading for Egypt. Little did they or he know what God was doing through them. The early days in Egypt were hard for Joseph. He may have had no clue that his character was being tested or that his life in its fine details was a key cog in a divine plan for the salvation not only of his family but also of the nations. All he knew for sure was that his feet were bruised and his neck ached as he sat chained in prison. But God eventually reversed Joseph's fortunes in Egypt. He was not only set free from prison but was given a greater authority than anyone in Egypt except the pharaoh himself. God moved Joseph from the prison to the palace to provide for his people.

Fourth, God delivered his people from Egypt (105:23-38). Once foreigners in Canaan, the ancestors were now foreigners in Egypt. Under the blessing of Joseph and God, they multiplied and became mighty—too mighty. God's ways are not our ways, and he does not always use the same ways. Whereas he did not allow anyone to oppress the ancestors while they wandered in Canaan, God turned the hearts of the Egyptians so that they oppressed his people when they became too mighty for their Egyptian hosts. Like the famine in Canaan and the hardships of Joseph, the oppression in Egypt was another step in the circuitous route of God's fulfilling his promise to Abraham, Isaac, and Jacob. And as the Lord had sent Joseph, so the Lord sent Moses to deliver Israel from the oppression of the Egyptians. This deliverance could have been accomplished in a single event, but God chose to use a series of miraculous events that culminated in the death of the firstborn son of each Egyptian family. Through this series of miracles, God "brought his people out of Egypt, loaded with silver and gold" (105:37). And their oppressors were glad they were gone! It is just like God to give his people gladness in proportion to their former misery (90:15)!

Fifth, God provided for his people in the wilderness en route to the Promised Land (105:39-42). He provided them guidance by means of the cloud and the fire. He provided them food and water, as well. All this, we are reminded, was because God remembered his covenant promise to Abraham. God had not forgotten. To the contrary, he had been at work in marvelous and miraculous ways to fulfill his promise.

Finally, God fulfilled his promise and gave the land of Canaan to his people (105:43-44). God had promised, "I will give (*nathan* [TH5414, ZH5989]) you the land" (105:11), and he kept that promise: "He gave (*nathan*) his people the lands" (105:44). God had promised them Canaan as a "special possession" (105:11), and he kept that promise: "They harvested crops that others had planted" (105:44).

Psalm 105:7-44 does not speak of the sins of Joseph's brothers or the rebellion of Israel in the wilderness or any other sins. They mention but do not develop the role humans played in the events recorded. These verses are a pure recounting of "what [God] has done," "his wonderful deeds," "the wonders he has performed," and "his miracles." Why? What is the psalmist's purpose in magnifying the miracles of God?

Respond to God's Miracles (105:1-6, 45). Psalm 105:45 tells us explicitly why all this happened and implicitly why all this was recorded: so that God's people might live in keeping with his instructions for life. His promise, his protection, his provisions, his deliverance, his fulfillment—all his miracles—were to motivate the present generation to love him and keep his commands. Miracles motivate us to obey. "By focusing exclusively on God's activity . . . Psalm 105 articulates the priority of grace . . . exodus precedes Sinai; deliverance precedes demand; grace comes first" (McCann 1996:1106). In terms of our motivation, Christ's cross precedes his commands.

The obedience called for in the last verse of the psalm is an obedience joined to the gratitude of the first verse. Worship characterized by grateful praise is the only reasonable response to the marvelous display of God's miracles in the history of redemption (see Rom 12:1-2). While these miracles may have had the salvation of Israel in focus, they always had the salvation of the nations in view (see 66:5-6 and 67:1-2). Just as the promise to Abraham was a means to the end that the nations might be blessed (Gen 12:3), the grateful worship of Psalm 105 is worship with a mission: "Let the whole world know what he has done. . . . Tell everyone about his wonderful deeds" (105:1-2).

◆ Q. Psalm 106

1 Praise the LORD!

Give thanks to the LORD, for he is good!
His faithful love endures forever.
2 Who can list the glorious miracles of the LORD?
Who can ever praise him enough?
3 There is joy for those who deal justly with others
and always do what is right.

4 Remember me, LORD, when you show favor to your people;
come near and rescue me.
5 Let me share in the prosperity of your chosen ones.
Let me rejoice in the joy of your people;
let me praise you with those who are your heritage.

6 Like our ancestors, we have sinned.
We have done wrong! We have acted wickedly!
7 Our ancestors in Egypt
were not impressed by the LORD's miraculous deeds.
They soon forgot his many acts of kindness to them.
Instead, they rebelled against him at the Red Sea.*
8 Even so, he saved them—
to defend the honor of his name
and to demonstrate his mighty power.
9 He commanded the Red Sea* to dry up.
He led Israel across the sea as if it were a desert.
10 So he rescued them from their enemies
and redeemed them from their foes.
11 Then the water returned and covered their enemies;
not one of them survived.
12 Then his people believed his promises.
Then they sang his praise.

13 Yet how quickly they forgot what he had done!
They wouldn't wait for his counsel!
14 In the wilderness their desires ran wild,
testing God's patience in that dry wasteland.
15 So he gave them what they asked for,
but he sent a plague along with it.
16 The people in the camp were jealous of Moses
and envious of Aaron, the LORD's holy priest.
17 Because of this, the earth opened up;
it swallowed Dathan
and buried Abiram and the other rebels.
18 Fire fell upon their followers;
a flame consumed the wicked.

19 The people made a calf at Mount Sinai*;
they bowed before an image made of gold.
20 They traded their glorious God
for a statue of a grass-eating bull.
21 They forgot God, their savior,
who had done such great things in Egypt—
22 such wonderful things in the land of Ham,
such awesome deeds at the Red Sea.
23 So he declared he would destroy them.
But Moses, his chosen one, stepped between the LORD and the people.
He begged him to turn from his anger and not destroy them.

24 The people refused to enter the pleasant land,
for they wouldn't believe his promise to care for them.
25 Instead, they grumbled in their tents
and refused to obey the LORD.
26 Therefore, he solemnly swore
that he would kill them in the wilderness,
27 that he would scatter their descendants among the nations,
exiling them to distant lands.

28 Then our ancestors joined in the
worship of Baal at Peor;
they even ate sacrifices offered to
the dead!
29 They angered the LORD with all these
things,
so a plague broke out among them.
30 But Phinehas had the courage to
intervene,
and the plague was stopped.
31 So he has been regarded as a
righteous man
ever since that time.

32 At Meribah, too, they angered the
LORD,
causing Moses serious trouble.
33 They made Moses angry,*
and he spoke foolishly.

34 Israel failed to destroy the nations
in the land,
as the LORD had commanded them.
35 Instead, they mingled among the
pagans
and adopted their evil customs.
36 They worshiped their idols,
which led to their downfall.
37 They even sacrificed their sons
and their daughters to the
demons.
38 They shed innocent blood,
the blood of their sons and
daughters.
By sacrificing them to the idols of
Canaan,
they polluted the land with murder.
39 They defiled themselves by their evil
deeds,
and their love of idols was adultery
in the LORD's sight.

40 That is why the LORD's anger burned
against his people,
and he abhorred his own special
possession.
41 He handed them over to pagan
nations,
and they were ruled by those who
hated them.
42 Their enemies crushed them
and brought them under their cruel
power.
43 Again and again he rescued them,
but they chose to rebel against
him,
and they were finally destroyed
by their sin.
44 Even so, he pitied them in their distress
and listened to their cries.
45 He remembered his covenant with
them
and relented because of his
unfailing love.
46 He even caused their captors
to treat them with kindness.

47 Save us, O LORD our God!
Gather us back from among the
nations,
so we can thank your holy name
and rejoice and praise you.

48 Praise the LORD, the God of Israel,
who lives from everlasting to
everlasting!
Let all the people say, "Amen!"

Praise the LORD!

106:7 Hebrew *at the sea, the sea of reeds.* **106:9** Hebrew *sea of reeds;* also in 106:22. **106:19** Hebrew *at Horeb,* another name for Sinai. **106:33** Hebrew *They embittered his spirit.*

NOTES

106:8 ***demonstrate.*** The Hiphil of the word *yada'* [TH3045, ZH3359] is better translated here as "make known." God's deliverance of his people at the Red Sea was for the purpose of making his saving power known to the nations (see 66:5-7; 98:2).

106:9 ***commanded.*** The word *ga'ar* [TH1605, ZH1721] means "rebuke." The waters of the Red Sea stood in opposition to the Lord's plan for his people, so he rebuked them, and the dry path appeared. See 104:7 for the use of this same verb for God's work of dividing the sea from the dry land at the time of creation.

COMMENTARY

Psalms 105 and 106 both magnify the grace of God, but in differing ways. Psalm 105 is a pure recounting of the saving grace of God with no reference to Israel's sin. Psalm 106 is a recounting of Israel's sin for the purpose of magnifying the saving grace of God. Psalm 105 culminates in motivation to obedience (105:45); Psalm 106 culminates in a petition for deliverance (106:47). Both psalms share the same focus, seen in the opening call, "Give thanks to the LORD."

Romans 5:20 captures the heart of Psalm 106: "As people sinned more and more, God's wonderful grace became more abundant." Human sin is the backdrop against which the "wonderful grace" of God shines brightly. This is true in our lives. This is true in Psalm 106. Most of Psalm 106 is occupied with a confession of sin (106:6-46). Within these verses are repeated references to God's saving grace. The truth that God saved a sinful people in the past provides the theological basis for calling on God to save a people who have sinned in the present. Because of God's saving grace, the whole psalm is wrapped in the language of thanksgiving and praise.

Our Confession of Sin. "Like our ancestors, we have sinned," says the psalmist (106:6). The psalmist in all probability does not have two sets of sins in view, those of the ancestors and those of the present generation. Rather, the sins of the distant past and the more recent past are seen as parts of a whole history characterized by disobedience to the Lord's instructions, the consequences of which are being experienced by the present generation (see also Neh 9). The sins of the community have resulted in the community's being exiled from the Promised Land (106:47).

Numerous examples of community sin are recorded in Psalm 106. They include the rebellion of Dathan and Abiram (106:16-18; Num 16:1-40), the making of the golden calf (106:19-20; Exod 32:1-8), the failure to enter the land (106:24-25; Num 14), the worship of Baal of Peor (106:28; Num 25), the rebellion at Meribah (106:32; Exod 17), and the failure to drive the Canaanites out of the land and the resultant idolatry (106:34-39; Judg 1–2). This is not a record of minor transgressions but of major violations of Israel's covenant responsibilities.

Why? What lay at the root of rebellion? Two foundational failures. First, forgetting. Second, not trusting. Three times we are told that Israel "forgot" (106:7, 13, 21). They forgot God's many acts of kindness. They forgot all that he had done for them in the past. They forgot, in particular, his saving grace that had brought them out of Egypt. They forgot, not in the sense that they had no memory of these things, but in the sense that the memory of what God had done did not produce within them the response of obedience. God's saving miracles and the record of those miracles were intended to produce grateful obedience (106:45), but they did not. Why not? Because they did not combine their memory of what God had done with faith (see Heb 4:2). "They wouldn't believe his promise to care for them" (106:24). They would believe for a time (106:12), but that faith seemed to dwindle very quickly (106:13), and the old pattern of disobedience reemerged.

In light of the amazing record of God's saving miracles recorded in Psalm 105, the record of Israel's sin in Psalm 106 is incredible. Yet what comes through ever so brightly in this dismal history of sin and rebellion is the saving grace of God. "They rebelled. . . . Even so, he saved them" (106:7-8). "Again and again he rescued them, but they chose to rebel against him. . . . Even so, he pitied them" (106:43-44). Why? "He remembered his covenant" (106:45). The covenant in view is the covenant with their ancestors, with Abraham, Isaac, and Jacob (105:8-11, 42). What kept God faithful to his covenant promises? "His unfailing love" (106:45). The record of human sin is dwarfed by the record of divine love that saves those who "have sinned," "done wrong," and acted wickedly" (106:6).

Our Call for Salvation. While the record of repeated sin could lead to despair, the record of God's saving grace leads to hope—hope that God will save in the present as he has in the past. "Save us, O LORD our God!" (106:47). Because of his love and in spite of our sin, he is still "our God" upon whom we can call for salvation. The "he saved them" of the past (106:8) leads to the "save us" of the present (106:47).

We can call on him for the salvation of the community (106:47). This verse envisions Israel in exile in Babylon. The salvation they needed was to be gathered back from among the nations. As such, the salvation of the individual finds its place in the context of the salvation of the community. "Remember me, LORD, when you show favor to your people" (106:4). God's favor is not simply a disposition within God, though it is that. God's favor is experienced in the tangible prosperity and joy for which the psalmist hopes (106:5). The psalmist longs to experience God's favor in the concrete realities of life here and now. The hope of the individual and the community is that God will once again demonstrate his love as he has so often done in the past.

Our Celebration of Grace. This psalm, which exposes so much sin, starts with the words, "Praise the LORD! Give thanks to the LORD, for he is good!" And it ends on a similar note: "Save us . . . so we can thank your holy name and rejoice and praise you." Thus the confession of sin is ultimately a sacrifice of praise to the God of saving grace, whose "faithful love endures forever" (106:1). And his saving grace comes to us through a mediator. On one occasion that mediator was Moses who "stepped between the LORD and the people" (106:23). On another occasion, it was Phinehas who "had the courage to intervene" (106:30). But Moses and Phinehas were only precursors of the true mediator, "for there is only one God and one Mediator who can reconcile God and humanity—the man Christ Jesus" (1 Tim 2:5). And we have all benefited from the rich blessings Jesus brought to us—"one gracious blessing after another" (John 1:16). These gracious blessings stir our hearts to obey him—from hearts full of gratitude and praise (106:1, 47). On this note Book 4 comes to a close:

Praise the LORD, the God of Israel,
  who lives from everlasting to everlasting!
Let all the people say, "Amen!"

  Praise the LORD!

◆ V. Book Five: Psalms 107–150

A. Psalm 107

1 Give thanks to the LORD, for he is good!
His faithful love endures forever.
2 Has the LORD redeemed you? Then speak out!
Tell others he has redeemed you from your enemies.
3 For he has gathered the exiles from many lands,
from east and west,
from north and south.

4 Some wandered in the wilderness,
lost and homeless.
5 Hungry and thirsty,
they nearly died.
6 "LORD, help!" they cried in their trouble,
and he rescued them from their distress.
7 He led them straight to safety,
to a city where they could live.
8 Let them praise the LORD for his great love
and for the wonderful things he has done for them.
9 For he satisfies the thirsty
and fills the hungry with good things.

10 Some sat in darkness and deepest gloom,
imprisoned in iron chains of misery.
11 They rebelled against the words of God,
scorning the counsel of the Most High.
12 That is why he broke them with hard labor;
they fell, and no one was there to help them.
13 "LORD, help!" they cried in their trouble,
and he saved them from their distress.
14 He led them from the darkness and deepest gloom;
he snapped their chains.
15 Let them praise the LORD for his great love
and for the wonderful things he has done for them.
16 For he broke down their prison gates of bronze;
he cut apart their bars of iron.

17 Some were fools; they rebelled
and suffered for their sins.
18 They couldn't stand the thought of food,
and they were knocking on death's door.
19 "LORD, help!" they cried in their trouble,
and he saved them from their distress.
20 He sent out his word and healed them,
snatching them from the door of death.
21 Let them praise the LORD for his great love
and for the wonderful things he has done for them.
22 Let them offer sacrifices of thanksgiving
and sing joyfully about his glorious acts.

23 Some went off to sea in ships,
plying the trade routes of the world.
24 They, too, observed the LORD's power in action,
his impressive works on the deepest seas.
25 He spoke, and the winds rose,
stirring up the waves.
26 Their ships were tossed to the heavens
and plunged again to the depths;
the sailors cringed in terror.
27 They reeled and staggered like drunkards
and were at their wits' end.
28 "LORD, help!" they cried in their trouble,

and he saved them from their
distress.
29 He calmed the storm to a whisper
and stilled the waves.
30 What a blessing was that stillness
as he brought them safely into
harbor!
31 Let them praise the LORD for his great
love
and for the wonderful things he has
done for them.
32 Let them exalt him publicly before
the congregation
and before the leaders of the
nation.

33 He changes rivers into deserts,
and springs of water into dry, thirsty
land.
34 He turns the fruitful land into salty
wastelands,
because of the wickedness of those
who live there.
35 But he also turns deserts into pools of
water,
the dry land into springs of water.
36 He brings the hungry to settle there
and to build their cities.
37 They sow their fields, plant their
vineyards,
and harvest their bumper crops.
38 How he blesses them!
They raise large families there,
and their herds of livestock
increase.

39 When they decrease in number and
become impoverished
through oppression, trouble, and
sorrow,
40 the LORD pours contempt on their
princes,
causing them to wander in trackless
wastelands.
41 But he rescues the poor from trouble
and increases their families like
flocks of sheep.
42 The godly will see these things and
be glad,
while the wicked are struck silent.
43 Those who are wise will take all this to
heart;
they will see in our history the
faithful love of the LORD.

NOTES

107:2 ***enemies.*** The word *tsar* II [TH6862A, ZH7640] means "enemy." The word *tsar* I [TH6862, ZH7639] means "trouble" and occurs in 107:6, 13, 19, 28. Between these two possible meanings, the NLT's choice of "enemy" is probably correct in this context (HALOT 3.1052), and a play on the "troubles" enumerated in the rest of the psalm is clear.

107:3 ***south.*** The word *yam* [TH3220, ZH3542] means "sea," and since the Mediterranean is to the west of Israel, *yam* can mean "west" (DCH 4.226), but not "south." An emendation to *yamin* [TH3225, ZH3545] (south) provides the fourth point on the compass.

107:4 ***lost and homeless.*** The same Hebrew expression, *'ir moshab* [TH5892/4186, ZH6551/4632], occurs in 107:7, where it is translated "a city where they could live." The repetition underscores the particularity with which the Lord met the need of his people. See also the repetition of "darkness and deepest gloom" in 107:10, 14, and "waves" (*se'arah* [TH5591A, ZH6194]) in 107:25, 29.

107:8 ***Let them praise.*** The word translated "praise" here and in 107:15, 21, 31 is the same verb that is translated "give thanks" in 107:1.

107:25 ***the winds rose.*** The expression *ruakh se'arah* [TH7307/5591A, ZH8120/6194] refers to gale-force winds (HALOT 2.762), the kind that terrified the seasoned sailors in the story of Jonah (see *sa'ar-gadol* [TH5591/1419, ZH6193/1524] in Jonah 1:4). The word *se'arah* [TH5591A, ZH6194] occurs again in 107:29, where it is translated "storm" (see note at 107:4).

COMMENTARY

Psalm 107 is a grand invitation to give thanks to the Lord for his unfailing love demonstrated in the wonderful deeds he has consistently done for his people. The psalm opens with an invitation to "give thanks" (*hodu,* Hiphil imperative of *yadah*) for God's unfailing love (*khesed*) in 107:1-3. Four examples of his love are then provided in 107:4-32, and each example contains another invitation to "give thanks" (*yadah* [TH3034A, ZH3344]) to the Lord for his unfailing love (*khesed* [TH2617, ZH2876]; 107:8, 15, 21, 31; see note on 107:8). Psalm 107:33-42 is a hymn of thanksgiving and is followed by a concluding exhortation to lay hold of the unfailing love of God, embedded in the history of Israel and in the psalm.[1]

Invitation to Give Thanks for God's Unfailing Love (107:1-3). Like Psalms 105 and 106, Psalm 107 opens with an invitation to give thanks to the Lord for his goodness and unfailing love. The unfailing love (*khesed* [TH2617, ZH2876]) of God is the dominant theme of this psalm. God's unfailing love forms an *inclusio* around the entire poem (107:1 and 107:43) and is repeated in the refrain of 107:8, 15, 21, 31. The counter theme is expressed in 107:2: trouble (McCann 1996:1117; see note on 107:2). Repeated instances of trouble in the history of Israel provided the occasion for repeated displays of God's unfailing love in the past. Whatever our trouble may be in the present, Psalm 107 bolsters our faith that God's unfailing love will be there for us as it has always been there for God's people in the past.

Illustrations of God's Unfailing Love (107:4-32). Four illustrations of God's unfailing love are spelled out in 107:4-9, 10-16, 17-22, and 23-32. The two inner illustrations contain explicit references to Israel's rebellion against God's instruction (see 107:11, 17); the two outer illustrations do not. All four follow the same pattern: (1) God's people experience trouble; (2) they cry out to God in their trouble; (3) they are rescued; and (4) they are invited to give thanks for God's unfailing love demonstrated in their deliverance. These illustrations teach us several lessons.

First, we may experience trouble in a variety of forms. Some were homeless and hungry, lost in the wilderness of life (107:4-5). Some were oppressed and depressed because of their rebellion (107:10-12). Some were sick to the point of death because of their rebellion (107:17-18). Some were at their wits' end, overwhelmed by the storms of life (107:23-27). Trouble comes in a variety of shapes and sizes.

Second, we can cry out to God when we are in trouble. "LORD, help!" is our cry (107:6, 13, 19, 28). This is neither a long prayer nor a sophisticated prayer, but it can be an effective prayer. There are times when the distress we experience is so deep that "Lord, help!" is the only prayer we can muster, like the two blind men who could only shout "Son of David, have mercy on us!" (Matt 9:27; 20:30-31). But when this prayer comes from a sincere heart and a simple faith, God moves into action.

Third, we can count on God's unfailing love in concrete ways that correspond to our trouble. "He rescued them from their distress" (107:6, 13, 19, 28). Though the refrain repeats the same language, God's unfailing love comes to us in a variety of ways that correspond to our need. Some were homeless and hungry (107:4-5), and the Lord gave them a home and food (107:7, 9). Some were in the darkness of despair (107:10), and the Lord led them out of that darkness (107:14). Some were sick (107:17-18), and the Lord healed them (107:20). Some were caught in the storm (107:25-27), and the Lord brought them to a safe harbor (107:29-30). God's unfailing love is not simply a disposition within God. It is that and it is more: It is his wonderful deeds (107:8, 15, 21, 31) that he performs in the here and now of our lives to meet our deepest needs. God does not just say he loves us; he shows it in his actions (cf. 1 John 3:18).

Fourth, we can respond by giving thanks for God's unfailing love. "Let them praise the LORD for his great love" (107:8, 15, 21, 31) is the invitation we are given in response to God's unfailing love demonstrated in our deliverance. This thanksgiving is to be as specific as God's deliverance: "For he . . . fills the hungry with good things . . . he broke down their prison gates" (107:9, 16).

Celebration of God's Unfailing Love (107:33-42). Psalm 107:33-42 is a hymnic example of thanksgiving to God. It confesses that from one perspective the trouble we experience comes from God's hand. The desert experience of 107:4-5 is the result of God's changing rivers into deserts and springs into dry land in response to our sin (107:33-34). Rather than being a discouraging picture of God, this is actually an encouraging one, for he who turns rivers into deserts can also turn deserts into pools of water and dry land into flowing springs. Because God is in a sense at the source of the trouble, he is also at the source of the solution. And that source is an abundant source. He provides the homeless with cities and the hungry with fields that produce bountiful harvests. They have large families and great wealth as a result of God's blessing. Though troubles may come, the Lord rescues them, resulting in great joy.

Exhortation to Take to Heart God's Unfailing Love (107:43). Wisdom requires reflection. Those who are wise take the time to reflect on life's experiences. Reflecting on the experiences recorded in Psalm 107 could lead one to be discouraged by the repeated sin of God's people and repeated misery that followed in sin's wake. But that is not the direction this psalmist would have us go. Reflection on life's experiences provides us an opportunity to see in our lives the unfailing love of the Lord. Our sin and its misery is but the backdrop against which God's love shines in all its brilliance. While it is foolish to say we have no sin (1 John 1:8), it is equally foolish to get stuck focusing on that sin. Wisdom is the skill of seeing God's unfailing love in all the twists and turns of our lives. Wisdom gives thanks to the Lord because he is so good and because his unfailing love endures forever.

ENDNOTES

1. On the structure of the poem see McCann 1996:1117 and VanGemeren 1991:681.

◆ B. Psalm 108

A song. A psalm of David.

[1]My heart is confident in you,
O God;
no wonder I can sing your praises
with all my heart!
[2]Wake up, lyre and harp!
I will wake the dawn with my song.
[3]I will thank you, LORD, among all
the people.
I will sing your praises among
the nations.
[4]For your unfailing love is higher
than the heavens.

Your faithfulness reaches to the
clouds.
5 Be exalted, O God, above the highest
heavens.
May your glory shine over all the
earth.

6 Now rescue your beloved people.
Answer and save us by your power.
7 God has promised this by his holiness*:
"I will divide up Shechem with joy.
I will measure out the valley of
Succoth.
8 Gilead is mine,
and Manasseh, too.
Ephraim, my helmet, will produce my
warriors,
and Judah, my scepter, will produce
my kings.
9 But Moab, my washbasin, will become
my servant,
and I will wipe my feet on Edom
and shout in triumph over Philistia."

10 Who will bring me into the fortified
city?
Who will bring me victory over
Edom?
11 Have you rejected us, O God?
Will you no longer march with
our armies?
12 Oh, please help us against our
enemies,
for all human help is useless.
13 With God's help we will do mighty
things,
for he will trample down our foes.

108:7 Or *in his sanctuary.*

NOTES

108:3 ***among the nations.*** The NLT presumes an emendation from *bal-'ummim* [TH1077/523, ZH1153/569] (not peoples) to *balle'ummim* [TH871.2/3816, ZH928/4211] (among the peoples); see the notes on 57:9 [10]; 149:7; see also 44:14 [15].

108:8 ***Ephraim, my helmet, will produce my warriors, and Judah, my scepter, will produce my kings.*** Lit., "Ephraim the stronghold of my head; Judah my scepter." While it is possible that *ma'oz ro'shi* [TH4581/7218, ZH5057/8031] means "helmet," DCH 5.386 takes this phrase to mean "my chief stronghold." HALOT 2.610 likewise lists this text under the meaning "stronghold." Heb. *mekhoqqeq* is the Polel participle of *khaqaq* [TH2710A, ZH2980], which means "commander" and then by extension "commander's scepter" (see DCH 3.304 and HALOT 1.347). The precise significance of this imagery is not easy to ascertain for certain, but the general point is clear: In contrast to the humiliation of Moab, Edom, and Philistia stands the exaltation/dominion of Ephraim, which represents the northern tribes, and Judah, which represents the southern tribes (see Clifford 2002:284 and VanGemeren 1991:416).

108:11 ***Have you rejected us, O God?*** The Hebrew text contains a negative adverb, and this verse seems to answer the question of the previous verse with another rhetorical question: "Is it not you, O God? You who have rejected us and no longer march with our armies?" (See NIV and NKJV.)

COMMENTARY

Each portion of God's word was written at a particular time and place for a particular reason. But the applicability of God's word goes beyond that first situation. God's word speaks again and again in new situations. Psalm 108 is testimony to this truth.

Psalm 108 is a combination of material from Psalms 57 and 60. Psalm 108:1-5 [2-6] is taken from 57:7-11 [8-12], while verses 6-13 [7-14] come from 60:5-12

[7-14]. Some scholars, (e.g., Kraus 1989:333), see no rhyme or reason to the combination, especially given the odd order of praise followed by lament. While not frequent, this order has already been encountered in Psalm 40. And just as the first part of Psalm 40 answered to Psalm 39, so the first part of Psalm 108 answers to Psalm 107 (McCann 1996:1121). As the second part of Psalm 40 echoes the explicit need expressed in the previous Psalm 39, so the second part of Psalm 108 echoes the implicit need expressed in the previous psalm.

Thanksgiving to God for His Unfailing Love (108:1-5). Psalm 107 repeatedly *calls on* those rescued from trouble to give thanks (*yadah* [TH3034A, ZH3344]) to the Lord for the demonstration of his unfailing love (*khesed* [TH2617, ZH2876]; 107:1, 8, 15, 21, 31). Psalm 108 answers that call by giving thanks (*yadah;* 108:3 [4]) for God's unfailing love (*khesed;* 108:4 [5]; see McCann 1996:1121). In keeping with the call to give thanks in public (107:32), the psalmist gives thanks "among all the people" and "among the nations" (108:3). In the wake of being rescued by God's unfailing love, the psalmist awakens his instruments that he might awaken the new day with songs of praise to the God whose unfailing love transcends the heavens. Petition joins praise as the first part of the psalm ends with the prayer that God's glory shine throughout the world.

Dependence on God for His Divine Aid (108:6-13). Being rescued once does not mean being rescued once and for all. Having been lifted from the pit of despair and having praised God's unfailing love in public (40:1-10), David found himself once again surrounded by troubles "too many to count" (40:11-17). So having thanked God in public for his unfailing love (108:1-5), David once again stood in need of God's saving aid (108:6-13). And though genuinely perplexed by God's apparent disfavor, David remained confident that with God's help he would be able to do mighty things.

David and his army will do the mighty things—gain victory over Edom in particular (108:10)—and they will do them because God's strong arm will be at work in them and through them. Here the Holy Spirit teaches us that it is incumbent upon us to do our utmost in all of life's situations and at the same time to depend entirely on God, not our human resources (108:12). Confidence in God is the beginning and the ending of this psalm: "My heart is confident in you, O God. . . . With God's help we will do mighty things" (108:1, 13).

◆ C. Psalm 109

For the choir director: A psalm of David.

1 O God, whom I praise,
don't stand silent and aloof
2 while the wicked slander me
and tell lies about me.
3 They surround me with hateful words
and fight against me for no reason.
4 I love them, but they try to destroy me
with accusations
even as I am praying
for them!
5 They repay evil for good,
and hatred for my love.
6 They say,* "Get an evil person to
turn against him.
Send an accuser to bring him
to trial.

7 When his case comes up for judgment,
let him be pronounced guilty.
Count his prayers as sins.
8 Let his years be few;
let someone else take his position.
9 May his children become fatherless,
and his wife a widow.
10 May his children wander as beggars
and be driven from their ruined
homes.
11 May creditors seize his entire estate,
and strangers take all he has earned.
12 Let no one be kind to him;
let no one pity his fatherless
children.
13 May all his offspring die.
May his family name be blotted out
in a single generation.
14 May the LORD never forget the sins of
his fathers;
may his mother's sins never be
erased from the record.
15 May the LORD always remember these
sins,
and may his name disappear from
human memory.
16 For he refused all kindness to others;
he persecuted the poor and needy,
and he hounded the brokenhearted
to death.
17 He loved to curse others;
now you curse him.
He never blessed others;
now don't you bless him.
18 Cursing is as natural to him as his
clothing,
or the water he drinks,
or the rich food he eats.
19 Now may his curses return and cling
to him like clothing;
may they be tied around him like
a belt."
20 May those curses become the LORD's
punishment
for my accusers who speak evil of me.
21 But deal well with me, O Sovereign
LORD,
for the sake of your own reputation!
Rescue me
because you are so faithful and good.
22 For I am poor and needy,
and my heart is full of pain.
23 I am fading like a shadow at dusk;
I am brushed off like a locust.
24 My knees are weak from fasting,
and I am skin and bones.
25 I am a joke to people everywhere;
when they see me, they shake their
heads in scorn.

26 Help me, O LORD my God!
Save me because of your unfailing
love.
27 Let them see that this is your doing,
that you yourself have done it, LORD.
28 Then let them curse me if they like,
but you will bless me!
When they attack me, they will be
disgraced!
But I, your servant, will go right
on rejoicing!
29 May my accusers be clothed with
disgrace;
may their humiliation cover them
like a cloak.
30 But I will give repeated thanks to
the LORD,
praising him to everyone.
31 For he stands beside the needy,
ready to save them from those who
condemn them.

109:6 Hebrew lacks *They say.*

NOTES

109:4 ***try to destroy me.*** This verb (*satan* [TH7853, ZH8476]) is quite rare, occurring only in 38:20 [21] and 109:4 as a finite verb and in 71:13 and 109:20, 29 as a participle (translated "accusers"; cf. the infinitive in Zech 3:1). The sense seems to be "to be hostile toward" (see HALOT 3.1316), and this hostility here comes to expression in verbal accusations (NIDOTTE 3.1231). The related noun (*satan* [TH7854, ZH8477]) occurs in 109:6, where it is likewise translated "accuser."

COMMENTARY

"Psalm 109 contains the most vehement of the imprecations in the Psalter" (Mays 1994:348). For 15 verses (109:6-20) the psalmist calls curse after curse on his enemies to the point of praying for the annihilation of the enemy's entire family (109:13). Can we who have been taught by Jesus to love and pray for our enemies (Matt 5:44) make any use of such a psalm?

This psalm expresses how we truly feel at times. Psalm 109 is the lament of someone who has been falsely accused. What David had been accused of we are not told, but we know that the accusations are slanderous, false, and hateful (109:2-3). David's accusers had no justifiable reason to be attacking him. To the contrary, their hatred was in response to David's love (109:4-5). David had the freedom to express how poor and needy he felt himself to be, and how pained and passing his life seemed to be at this juncture (109:22-25). As with all the laments, the Holy Spirit here teaches us to bring to expression how we feel about ourselves in the difficult circumstances of life.

Psalm 109 also expresses how we may feel about others when they are the source of deep pain in our lives. Perhaps our pain has never been as severe as David's, so perhaps our words have never been as vehement. Perhaps we have never uttered words like, "May his children become fatherless, and his wife a widow. . . . May all his offspring die. May his family name be blotted out in a single generation" (109:9, 13). Perhaps we have. We may, at least, have had similar thoughts that we suppressed as best we could. Perhaps the expression of these thoughts and feelings in prayer brought sufficient relief such that David felt no need to take vengeance into his own hands but could leave that with God (McCann 1996:1127).

"I will take revenge; I will pay them back" (Deut 32:35) was the Lord's instruction to his people in the Old Testament, and it is still his instruction to us in the New Testament (Rom 12:19; Heb 10:30). In this psalm, as harsh as it may be, David follows that instruction. This prayer was David's way of saying that he would not take matters into his own hands but would trust the Lord to deal with his enemies in a just way. They who had accused him would themselves be accused. They who had cursed others would themselves be cursed. They who had condemned others would themselves be condemned. Since God is just, we can leave the execution of that justice to him.

Still, the psalmist was praying against those who persecuted him. The theocracy, God's reign in Israel from the time of Moses to the time of Christ, was a shadow of future events (Heb 10:1). One of those events is the final judgment of God. The destruction of the Canaanites in the days of Joshua was a shadow of the final judgment and not, therefore, normative for how we are to deal with our neighbors who do not believe in Jesus. The imprecations against the wicked in the book of Psalms were also shadows of the final judgment—appropriate for the era of the theocracy, but not for this present age. The gospel era is one of kindness, tolerance, and patience—intended to bring people to repentance and faith (Rom 2:4). This is the day of salvation (2 Cor 6:2). And this is why Jesus taught us to love our enemies and to pray *for* them, not against them. This is why Paul taught us to pray that God would bless our enemies (Rom 12:14; 1 Cor 4:12). Like the psalmist we leave vengeance to God, but unlike the psalmist we pray that God would bless those who bring pain into our lives.

Ultimately, the psalmist expressed great confidence in God. In the final analysis, Psalm 109 is a prayer for help: "O God . . . don't stand silent and aloof. . . . Help me, O LORD my God! Save me because of your unfailing love" (109:1, 26). The psalmist is so confident that the Lord will help that he can say, "Let them curse me if they like, but you will bless me!" (109:28). Though his enemies persecuted the poor and needy, David was certain that God "stands beside the needy, ready to save them" (109:31). While others surrounded David with slanderous, false, and hateful words (109:2-3), David surrounded his situation with words of praise and thanksgiving, because he knew that God is love and that God's love will triumph in the end.

◆ D. Psalm 110

A psalm of David.

1 The LORD said to my Lord,
"Sit in the place of honor at my right hand
until I humble your enemies,
making them a footstool under your feet."

2 The LORD will extend your powerful kingdom from Jerusalem*;
you will rule over your enemies.
3 When you go to war,
your people will serve you willingly.
You are arrayed in holy garments,
and your strength will be renewed each day like the morning dew.

4 The LORD has taken an oath and will not break his vow:
"You are a priest forever in the order of Melchizedek."

5 The Lord stands at your right hand to protect you.
He will strike down many kings when his anger erupts.
6 He will punish the nations
and fill their lands with corpses;
he will shatter heads over the whole earth.
7 But he himself will be refreshed from brooks along the way.
He will be victorious.

110:2 Hebrew *Zion.*

NOTES

110:1 ***footstool under your feet.*** This metaphor pictures a footstool made out of vanquished enemies. For pictures of Egyptian thrones with vanquished enemies as footstools, see Keel 1997:254-255. This metaphor is probably related to the ancient practice of the victorious king placing his foot on the neck of the vanquished foe (see Josh 10:24).

110:2 ***you will rule.*** The verb form is an imperative in the Hebrew, which is here used to express a promise that will certainly be fulfilled in the future (Joüon and Muraoka 1991:§114p; Waltke and O'Connor 1990:§34.4c).

110:4 ***Melchizedek.*** Melchizedek was a king-priest who ruled over Jerusalem (Gen 14:18). David also was a king-priest who ruled over Jerusalem with particular responsibility for the proper worship of God. In its original setting the psalm referred to David and his descendants. Since one of those descendants is Jesus, the psalm takes on richer meaning in light of his coming. The author of Hebrews thus sees in Jesus both the royal son of Psalm 2 and the "priest forever in the order of Melchizedek" of Psalm 110.

COMMENTARY

No one wants to suffer defeat in any of life's battles or challenges. We all want to be victorious. In fact, "victorious" is the last word in Psalm 110, and victorious is the final word pronounced over our lives.

Psalm 110 is a promise of victory. This psalm falls into two natural halves (110:1-3 and 110:4-7). In each half a declaration delivered by the Lord in the first person (110:1 and 110:4) is followed by a promise about the Lord in the third person (110:2-3 and 110:5-7). Promise fills Psalm 110 from beginning to end, and the promise can be summarized in one word: victory.

The victory is first and foremost a divine victory. It is at the very same time a human victory, for the divine victory is accomplished through human agency. Psalm 110 picks up the key motif of the Psalter that was first articulated in Psalm 2: The Lord reigns over the nations through his anointed (messianic) king. Psalm 89 and the lack of a Davidic king in the exilic and postexilic eras seemed to call into question the fulfillment of the promise contained in Psalm 2. Psalms 93–99 reaffirmed the reality of the Lord's reign in spite of seeming evidence to the contrary. Psalm 110 echoes that reaffirmation and goes on to reassert the certainty of the promise of Davidic dominion over all the earth (see also Ps 132).

The Promise of the Lord's Victory. The Lord as the Divine Warrior who goes before his people to fight for them is a common theme in the Old Testament (e.g., 24:8; Judg 4:14; 1 Sam 17:47; 2 Chr 20:15; Isa 42:13; see Longman and Reid 1995). This theme permeates Psalm 110: "until I humble your enemies" (110:1), "The LORD will extend your powerful kingdom" (110:2), "He will strike down many kings" (110:5), "He will punish . . . he will shatter" (110:6), "He will be victorious" (110:7). The battle is not ultimately ours, but the Lord's (1 Sam 17:47). So, too, the victory is not ultimately ours, but the Lord's.

The Lord reigns over the whole earth (Pss 93–99), and that reign will be realized throughout the whole earth: "He will shatter heads over the whole earth" (110:6). The "kings of the earth" who once raged against the Lord (2:2) will, in the end, be subdued by the Lord. In Psalm 110 the Lord promises that he will be victorious.

The Promise of the Messiah's Victory. As in Psalm 2, so in Psalm 110, the Lord's victory entails the Messiah's victory. The enemies will be subdued under the Messiah's feet. The Messiah's dominion will extend outward from Jerusalem, and he will rule. His potentially waning vigor on the day of battle will be renewed. So while the victory is ultimately the Lord's, it is at the same time the Messiah's victory. The Messiah's victory can be traced both to the Lord's agency and to the willing service of the Messiah's human troops. Divine sovereignty is the arena in which human responsibility is played out.

Psalm 110 is the most frequently quoted psalm in the New Testament because Jesus is the Messiah anticipated in this psalm. Jesus quoted David's words in 110:1 when discussing the identity of the Messiah (Matt 22:44). And Peter identified Jesus as the Messiah spoken of in Psalm 110 (Acts 2:34; see also Heb 1:13). As Jesus became in a special sense the messianic son on the day of his resurrection (see commentary on Ps 2), so his messianic reign began when he was raised from the dead. In Peter's words, "God has made this Jesus, whom you crucified, to be both Lord and Messiah" (Acts 2:36). Having been crucified, Jesus was made Lord and Messiah through his resurrection. And since that time God has been in the process of extending the Messiah's dominion through the spreading of the gospel throughout the whole earth.

We are his people who now serve him willingly. The Messiah who now has all authority in heaven and on the earth has given us our marching orders: "Therefore, go and make disciples of all the nations, baptizing them in the name of the Father and the Son and the Holy Spirit. Teach these new disciples to obey all the commands I have given you" (Matt 28:19-20). And our victory in this, our primary calling as the church, is certain, for the Messiah has given us this promise: "And be sure of this: I am with you always, even to the end of the age" (Matt 28:20).

All of life is the "day of battle" when we serve the Messiah's cause with willing spirits. With our words and deeds, in our attitudes and actions, we participate in the victory that belongs to the Lord and Messiah, Jesus.

◆ E. Psalm 111*

1 Praise the LORD!

I will thank the LORD with all
my heart
as I meet with his godly people.
2 How amazing are the deeds of the
LORD!
All who delight in him should
ponder them.
3 Everything he does reveals his glory
and majesty.
His righteousness never fails.
4 He causes us to remember his
wonderful works.
How gracious and merciful is our
LORD!
5 He gives food to those who fear him;
he always remembers his covenant.
6 He has shown his great power to his
people
by giving them the lands of
other nations.
7 All he does is just and good,
and all his commandments are
trustworthy.
8 They are forever true,
to be obeyed faithfully and with
integrity.
9 He has paid a full ransom for his
people.
He has guaranteed his covenant
with them forever.
What a holy, awe-inspiring name
he has!
10 Fear of the LORD is the foundation
of true wisdom.
All who obey his commandments
will grow in wisdom.

Praise him forever!

111 This psalm is a Hebrew acrostic poem; after the introductory note of praise, each line begins with a successive letter of the Hebrew alphabet.

NOTES

111:2 *ponder.* The word *darash* [TH1875, ZH2011] here means "seek with interest, be intent on, study, interpret" (DCH 2.474; see also HALOT 1.233, "worthy to be studied").

111:3 *glory and majesty.* The words *hod wehadar,* as a pair, refer to royal splendor (see note on 104:1).

111:9 *awe-inspiring.* The word *nora'* comes from the same root (*yare'* [TH3372, ZH3707]) as the noun translated "fear" in 111:10 (*yir'ah* [TH3374, ZH3711]).

COMMENTARY

Psalms 111 and 112 are twin psalms. Both begin with "Praise the LORD!" (*halelu yah* [TH1984A/3050, ZH2146/3363]). Both are alphabetic acrostics with each colon starting with the subsequent letter in the Hebrew alphabet. Both focus on the fear of the Lord, and they have key vocabulary in common (see commentary on Ps 112). The primary difference is that Psalm 111 focuses on God and Psalm 112 focuses on God's people.

God Is to Be Thanked. The first words after the opening *halelu yah* are "I will thank the LORD." Psalm 111 is a psalm of thanksgiving and praise to the Lord for his "deeds" (111:2), for "everything he does" (111:3), for his "wonderful works" (111:4), and for "all he does" (111:7). These mighty works of the Lord are worthy to be pondered by those who delight in them (111:2). As delightful meditation on God's instruction is the source of true happiness (Ps 1), so too delightful study of God's works is the source of great rewards (111:10). The "works" of the Lord are diverse in this psalm, and the diversity is unified in one word: covenant. Covenant is relationship: "I will always be your God and the God of your descendants after you" (Gen 17:7). Covenant is that which God established (111:9) and that which God remembers (111:5).

God Established the Covenant through Redemption. Foundational to the works of God is the character of God. He is glorious and majestic, the sovereign who reigns over his people. And he is no tyrannical sovereign, for he is characterized by a righteousness that never fails and by grace and mercy that bless his people (111:4).

His character is demonstrated in his works. God's "wonderful works" (111:4) are a reference to God's mighty acts of delivering his people from bondage in Egypt (Exod 3:20; 34:10; see Mays 1994:356). His provision of food recalls his provision of manna in the wilderness (see Exod 16; cf. Num 11). His granting Israel the "lands of other nations" (111:6) refers to the conquest of Canaan in the days of Joshua. Here we have a concise recounting of the central events in God's redemption of his people set forth as the motivation for the old covenant community to praise God. The analogous motivation for the new covenant community is our deliverance from sin and its misery through Jesus' incarnation, perfect obedience, substitutionary atonement, resurrection, and ascension to the Father's right hand, from where he has poured out his Spirit into our hearts.

God Administered the Covenant through Commandments. God "guaranteed his covenant" (111:9): His covenant came with commandments given on Mount Sinai. All that God does is just and good, says the psalmist, and his giving his people commandments is, accordingly, just and good (111:7). God's commandments are trustworthy instruction in the just and good way to live in God's world. They are reliable guides to be followed from the heart. We obey with grateful hearts the God who in his grace and mercy has provided a full ransom for us. In Jesus Christ, God has done everything necessary to be merciful to people in keeping with his justice. Jesus lived a life of perfect conformity to God's commandments in our place, and with his death he paid the just penalty for our sins so that God can both be just and forgive those who have violated his will but believe in Jesus (Rom 3:26).

Our obedience is a response to what God has done. This is seen in that our obedience (111:7-9) follows God's works of salvation (111:2-6). Our obedience is also a response to God's character. He is holy in his essence, so it is fitting for us to be holy as we live in relation with him and each other. Our reverence for our holy God is the very foundation of living the wise kind of life that will bring great reward in this life and the life to come.

God Is to Be Praised. As this psalm opened with words of praise and thanksgiving (111:1), so it closes with words of praise (111:10b). Praise the Lord for who he is: glorious and majestic, gracious and merciful, just and good. Praise the Lord for what he has done: He has provided the "full ransom" and the instruction needed to live a life of purpose and significance. "Praise him forever!"

◆ F. Psalm 112*

1 Praise the LORD!

How joyful are those who fear
the LORD
and delight in obeying his
commands.
2 Their children will be successful
everywhere;
an entire generation of godly people
will be blessed.
3 They themselves will be wealthy,
and their good deeds will last
forever.
4 Light shines in the darkness for the
godly.
They are generous, compassionate,
and righteous.
5 Good comes to those who lend money
generously
and conduct their business fairly.
6 Such people will not be overcome
by evil.
Those who are righteous will be
long remembered.
7 They do not fear bad news;
they confidently trust the LORD to
care for them.
8 They are confident and fearless
and can face their foes
triumphantly.
9 They share freely and give generously
to those in need.
Their good deeds will be
remembered forever.
They will have influence and honor.
10 The wicked will see this and be
infuriated.
They will grind their teeth in anger;
they will slink away, their hopes
thwarted.

112 This psalm is a Hebrew acrostic poem; after the introductory note of praise, each line begins with a successive letter of the Hebrew alphabet.

NOTES

112:2 ***successful.*** The Hebrew text has *gibbor* [TH1368A, ZH1475] (warrior), which the NLT takes as a metaphor for "success" (cf. HALOT 1.172, "metaph. influential, respected").

godly. This same word (*yesharim* [TH3477A, ZH3838]) occurs in 111:1b.

112:3 ***their good deeds will last forever.*** This same expression is repeated in 112:9 and occurs in 111:3, where it is used of God and translated "His righteousness never fails" (see commentary).

112:4 ***They are generous, compassionate, and righteous.*** These adjectives are singular in Hebrew, whereas the presumed antecedent, "the godly," is plural. The first two adjectives also occur in 111:4, followed by the divine name as the subject: "Gracious and merciful is our LORD." It would seem, therefore, that the third adjective in 111:4 is the subject[1] with the first two being predicates: "The one who is righteous is gracious and merciful" (see commentary).

112:8 ***They are confident.*** The Hebrew text contains the word "heart," as does 111:1.

112:9 ***They will have influence and honor.*** Lit., "Their horn will be lifted high." To "lift up the horn" is a figure for "bestowing power, joy, health, and prestige" (DBI 400; see 75:10; 89:17, 24; 92:10; 132:17; 148:14).

112:10 ***thwarted.*** This final word (*to'bed* [TH6, ZH6]) is also the final word in Ps 1. In both texts, the path or hopes of the wicked are destroyed, in contrast to the righteous, who prosper.

COMMENTARY

Happiness is the longing of the human heart. Who does not want to be truly and profoundly happy? This quest for happiness is validated by Psalm 112, which begins with the words, "How joyful are those who . . ." This same word for "joyful" or "happiness" (*'ashre* [TH835A, ZH897]), in fact, opens the whole book of Psalms, in 1:1. This same expression opens 32:1, 41:1, 119:1-2, and 128:1, and occurs in 13 other psalms as well.[2] While not providing an exhaustive understanding of the Hebrew word *'ashre,* Psalm 112 does teach us much about biblical happiness, as it answers two fundamental questions for us: (1) What does complete happiness include? and (2) Who can be completely happy?

What Does Complete Happiness Include? In the language of the psalm, happiness and prosperity go hand in hand, as the happiness of 1:1 is largely defined by the prosperity of 1:3b. Psalm 112 fills this out by describing happiness in four areas of life.

Familial prosperity. "Their children will be successful" (112:2). To see one's children succeeding in life is a source of great happiness. As the proverb says, "A wise child brings joy to a father" (Prov 10:1). Psalm 128 similarly paints a picture of a happy man seated at a table surrounded by prospering children.

Financial prosperity. "They themselves will be wealthy" (112:3a). While we are not to love money (1 Tim 6:10), we are to enjoy the measure of wealth we have in this life as the gift of God (Eccl 5:19; 1 Tim 6:17).

Emotional prosperity. "They are confident and fearless" (112:8). Happy people may have significant foes to face in this life, and bad news may be just around the corner, but truly happy people are not the slaves of their emotions; their emotions are rather their servants that lead them to God (see Allender and Longman 1994).

Spiritual prosperity. "Their good deeds will last forever" (112:3b, 9b). The truly happy person is the person who has a relationship with God through faith (84:4-5, 12), a relationship that is rooted in the forgiveness of sins (32:1). "The wicked" may seem to be happy, but their happiness is short-lived (Ps 73). Their hopes for happiness will be thwarted (112:10), for true familial, financial, and emotional prosperity is at home with spiritual prosperity. This leads to the next question.

Who Can Be Completely Happy? In brief, the answer is "those who fear the LORD" (112:1a). Psalm 111 ended on the note that the fear of the Lord is the foundation of true wisdom. This theme is amplified in the whole of Psalm 112. *Happy people follow God's instructions.* In Psalm 1 the happy person delights in the Lord's instruction.

Here in Psalm 112 the happy person is the one who fears the Lord, and this means they "delight in obeying his commands" (112:1b). Since God's commandments are a revelation of his character (see 111:7), delighting in God's commands means delighting in being like God.

Happy People Are like God. The repetition of key words and phrases in Psalms 111 and 112 beautifully portray the happy person of Psalm 112 as one whose character is like that of God in Psalm 111. Both are gracious and merciful (111:4; 112:4). Both have a righteousness that never fails (111:3; 112:3, 9). Both act with justice for all (111:7; 112:5). Both give generously (111:5-6; 112:9). And both are remembered on into the future (111:4; 112:6). Happy people are like God.

Happy People Worship God. As Psalm 111 opened with "Praise the LORD," so does Psalm 112. While our happiness does depend on our fearing the Lord, delighting in his commands, and being like him, this is all a matter of his saving grace, as Psalm 111 has just made clear. Divine grace is the ultimate source of human happiness (Eccl 5:19-20), so truly happy people hear the call to praise God and respond with grateful hearts: "Happy are those who hear the joyful call to worship, for they will walk in the light of your presence, LORD" (89:15).

ENDNOTES

1. Note that a few mss do not have the conjunction on this third adjective. If the conjunction is original, it can be taken as emphatic. See Pope 1953, Wernberg-Möller 1958, and HALOT 1.258, and see Job 4:6b for emphatic Waw on the subject of a nominal sentence.
2. See 2:12; 33:12; 34:8 [9]; 40:4 [5]; 65:4 [5]; 84:4, 5, 12 [5, 6, 13]; 89:15 [16]; 94:12; 106:3; 127:5; 137:9; 144:15; 146:5.

◆ G. Psalm 113

1 Praise the LORD!

Yes, give praise, O servants of the
LORD.
Praise the name of the LORD!
2 Blessed be the name of the LORD
now and forever.
3 Everywhere—from east to west—
praise the name of the LORD.
4 For the LORD is high above the nations;
his glory is higher than the heavens.

5 Who can be compared with the LORD
our God,
who is enthroned on high?
6 He stoops to look down
on heaven and on earth.
7 He lifts the poor from the dust
and the needy from the garbage
dump.
8 He sets them among princes,
even the princes of his own
people!
9 He gives the childless woman
a family,
making her a happy mother.

Praise the LORD!

NOTES

113:5-6 The main point of these two lines is clear enough: The God of Israel is incomparable (113:5a). His incomparability is seen in his transcendent enthronement in heaven (113:5b). Verse 6 also affirms the Lord's incomparability, but in which of two ways? One way is to take the line as a second affirmation of the Lord's transcendence. The straightforward reading of the line, adopted by most major translations, is that the Lord is so highly exalted that he has to stoop down to look on the heavens, let alone the earth. A second reading is to isolate 113:6a ("He stoops down to look") and understand it as an affirmation of the Lord's immanence. Some have accomplished this by transposing 113:6b ("on heaven and on earth") after 113:5a and then reading 113:5b and 113:6a as a line (e.g., "He is enthroned on high, he stoops down to look"; Kraus 1989:367). Others have accomplished the same thing by taking 113:5b and 113:6a as a parenthetical remark placed in the middle of the natural sense unit of 113:5a and 113:6b (e.g., "Who is like Yahweh our God—enthroned so high, looking down so low—in heaven or on earth,"Allen 1983:99). This latter reading is preferable to the others. Psalm 113:5a and 6b do seem to be the key statement of the Lord's incomparability, especially when compared to texts like Deut 3:24, "Is there any god in heaven or on earth who can perform such great and mighty deeds as you do?" and 1 Kgs 8:23, "O LORD, God of Israel, there is no God like you in all of heaven above or on the earth below." Psalm 113:5b and 6a support the main proposition by means of contrast: God is incomparable in heaven and on earth in that while he reigns on high, he at the same time condescends to care for the needy. "He is exalted and yet he cares. Or, better, the Lord is exalted, therefore, he is able to deliver" (VanGemeren 1991:714).

COMMENTARY

With its opening "Praise the LORD!" (*halelu yah* [TH1984A/3050, ZH2146/3363]) Psalm 113 continues the theme of praise in Psalms 111 and 112, both of which begin with "Praise the LORD!" What are the elements of "praise"? Psalm 113:1-3 provides a concise, though not exhaustive, theology of praise (Mays 1994:361). Psalm 113:4-9 praises the Lord for his incomparable greatness and thereby provides us instruction on why we are to heed the call of 113:1-3 to praise the Lord.

The Lord Is to Be Praised (113:1-3). The Lord is to be praised by his servants. He is the Lord who has created us and redeemed us. We are his people, who find our identity and our purpose for living by having a relationship with him. Serving him is our satisfaction and significance. We are to praise the Lord's "name." His name is his nature (Exod 34:5-7). To praise his name is to praise all of the qualities that characterize the Lord (NIDOTTE 4.148). As 113:4-9 demonstrates, the incomparable character of the Lord makes him worthy to be praised throughout all time (113:2) and throughout all space (113:3).

The Incomparable Lord Is to Be Praised (113:4-9). These verses demonstrate why the Lord is to be praised. They do not offer an exhaustive set of reasons but focus on one—the Lord's incomparability: "Who can be compared with the LORD our God?" (113:5a). This rhetorical question demands a negative answer: no one! And this answer is all-inclusive, for the Lord's incomparability extends to both heaven and earth.

One expected dimension of the Lord's incomparability is his transcendent exaltation. That the Lord is "high (*ram* [TH7311, ZH8123]) above the nations" (113:4) is an affirmation of his transcendent reign as king, as is clear from 99:1-2, "The LORD is king . . . exalted [*ram*] above all the nations." Thus, in Psalm 113 it is as the exalted king that the transcendent Lord "is enthroned on high" (113:5). So exalted is he, in fact, that "his glory is higher than the heavens" (113:4). That which transcends us—the heavens—is itself transcended by the glorious Lord.

A second and unexpected dimension of the Lord's incomparability is his immanent compassion. The one "who is enthroned on high" is no aloof deity; he is at the same time the one who "stoops to look" (113:6). He is filled with compassion for those who live on the earth. He is filled with compassion for those who have been humbled by life's circumstances. Two classes of humbled people are mentioned: the poor and the barren. Both have been brought low in a world that values wealth and children (see Ps 112:2-3). Both are the objects of the exalted Lord's caring gaze. Both experience the reversal that results from an outpouring of the Lord's compassion. Because the Lord is enthroned (*yashab* [TH3427, ZH3782]; 113:5) on high, he is able to lift the poor from their desperate straits and to seat (*yashab;* 113:8) them with wealthy princes. Because the Lord is seated (*yashab*) on high, he is able to, literally, "seat [*yashab*] the barren woman in a home" (113:9), making her a happy mother of children. Hannah experienced this reversal (1 Sam 1–2), as did, in another sense, Mary (Luke 1:46-55).

With the birth of Mary's son, "the exalted one has chosen to be humbled, and the humbled are thus exalted" (McCann 1996:1139). Jesus came to reverse the misery brought into the world by our sin. He came "to make his blessings flow far as the curse is found." He did so by taking the position of a servant and humbling himself to the point of death on the cross, for which God has exalted him (Phil 2:6-11). And in exalting him, God has exalted us in him (Col 3:1-4).

◆ H. Psalm 114

1 When the Israelites escaped from Egypt—
when the family of Jacob left that foreign land—
2 the land of Judah became God's sanctuary,
and Israel became his kingdom.

3 The Red Sea* saw them coming and hurried out of their way!
The water of the Jordan River turned away.
4 The mountains skipped like rams,
the hills like lambs!
5 What's wrong, Red Sea, that made you hurry out of their way?
What happened, Jordan River, that you turned away?
6 Why, mountains, did you skip like rams?
Why, hills, like lambs?

7 Tremble, O earth, at the presence of the Lord,
at the presence of the God of Jacob.
8 He turned the rock into a pool of water;
yes, a spring of water flowed from solid rock.

114:3 Hebrew *the sea;* also in 114:5.

NOTES

114:1 ***foreign land.*** The Hebrew text has "foreign people"; the first colon refers to the land, the second to the people.

114:3 ***saw them coming.*** The Hebrew text simply says "saw" and does not tell us what was seen. Psalm 114:7 answers the question as to what was seen.

COMMENTARY

Stories evoke responses. Psalm 114 tells a story in brief form in 114:1-2. One response to this story is then recorded in 114:3-4, along with the question as to why this particular response was drawn out (114:5-6). The rationale for this response is given in 114:7-8, but the rationale comes in the form of an imperative. The imperative indicates that the response of some in the past is to be the response of all in the present.

A Story (114:1-2). The descendants of Abraham were for a time slaves in the foreign land of Egypt. They eventually escaped from that oppressive situation and made their way to the land of Canaan, where they took up residence. But the real story is that in this process Judah became the place where God's special presence became manifest. And since God is king, Israel became his kingdom. But there is more to the story.

A Response (114:3-6). Two bodies of water hindered Israel in leaving Egypt and in entering the land of the presence: the Red Sea and the Jordan River. Both the Red Sea and the Jordan River saw something when Israel stood on their banks. What they saw we are not told, but that they saw something awesome is clear from their response. The waters of the Red Sea and the Jordan River moved to make a path for the Israelites on their pilgrimage to the land of the Presence. In addition, the mountains (of Sinai?) skipped like rams and the surrounding hills like young lambs. Why? What did they see? A horde of wandering slaves?

A Rationale (114:7-8). How they saw it we are not told, but implicitly we are told what the waters and the mountains saw. They saw the presence of the Lord God of Israel. Perhaps the Sea saw the Cloud of the Presence (Exod 14:19-20). Perhaps the River saw the Ark of the Presence (Josh 3:14-16). They saw the Presence, and they fled trembling. The divine presence was known to make mountains skip (29:6) and the earth tremble (97:4). And so the earth—the land and its inhabitants—are called upon to tremble at the Presence.

The psalm concludes with the reminder that the Presence is beneficent: God provides water in the wasteland. This note brings us back to Psalm 2, where the leaders of the nations, and thus those whom they lead, are called upon to serve the Lord and to rejoice with trembling (2:11). To this call is added the promise that great joy will be experienced by all who find protection in the Lord God of Israel (2:12).

This story was only a dress rehearsal. The Presence came in the person of Jesus Christ (John 1:14). With his coming, the Kingdom has come (Matt 12:28), and he is still found to be a beneficent king for all who find protection in him (Matt 9:35).

◆ I. Psalm 115

1 Not to us, O LORD, not to us,
but to your name goes all the glory
for your unfailing love and
faithfulness.
2 Why let the nations say,
"Where is their God?"
3 Our God is in the heavens,
and he does as he wishes.
4 Their idols are merely things of silver
and gold,
shaped by human hands.
5 They have mouths but cannot speak,
and eyes but cannot see.
6 They have ears but cannot hear,

and noses but cannot smell.
7 They have hands but cannot feel,
and feet but cannot walk,
and throats but cannot make
a sound.
8 And those who make idols are just
like them,
as are all who trust in them.

9 O Israel, trust the LORD!
He is your helper and your shield.
10 O priests, descendants of Aaron, trust
the LORD!
He is your helper and your shield.
11 All you who fear the LORD, trust the
LORD!
He is your helper and your shield.

12 The LORD remembers us and will
bless us.
He will bless the people of Israel
and bless the priests, the
descendants of Aaron.
13 He will bless those who fear
the LORD,
both great and lowly.

14 May the LORD richly bless
both you and your children.
15 May you be blessed by the LORD,
who made heaven and earth.
16 The heavens belong to the LORD,
but he has given the earth to all
humanity.
17 The dead cannot sing praises to the
LORD,
for they have gone into the silence
of the grave.
18 But we can praise the LORD
both now and forever!

Praise the LORD!

NOTES

115:10 ***priests, descendants of Aaron.*** The word *beth 'aharon* [TH1004/175, ZH1074/195] means "family of Aaron," and appears again in 115:12. In both verses "priests" is an addition, explaining the priestly office of the "family of Aaron" for the modern reader.

COMMENTARY

Trusting is essential to living successfully. There must be trust in our families, in our churches, in our companies if we are going to enjoy the prosperous life held out to us in Psalm 1. Trusting other people is part of the fabric of life. Yet 118:8-9 is soon going to tell us not to trust human beings. What is going on? Texts like Psalm 118 are addressing the question of where we should place our ultimate trust. That is the issue raised in Psalm 115. We live in a world much like that of the person who wrote Psalm 115. There are forces in the world that would both undermine our faith in the true God and then substitute idols for him. Psalm 115 is a psalm of praise to "the LORD, who made heaven and earth," a psalm that bolsters our faith as we confess three things about trusting the Lord.

Trusting the Lord Excludes Idols (115:2-11). There are voices that say to us in a variety of ways, "Where is your God?" Israel, for example, would have heard these voices in the postexilic community, when the once glorious and independent state of Israel was reduced to the status of a small province in the Persian Empire. If the God of Israel is the true God, as Israel's faith affirmed, why were the Israelites in such dire straits? Perhaps we hear these same voices when, for example, healing does not come or the prodigal child does not return or the job has just been lost, though we have prayed and prayed. The seeming impotence of our God makes us ripe to be tempted to substitute another god for him.

There is an antidote to this temptation. The antidote, oddly enough, is to trust.

Trusting is being certain that something is the case even when we cannot see any evidence that it is the case (Heb 11:1). This is why the apostle Paul says "we live by believing and not by seeing" (2 Cor 5:7). Trusting means we affirm two correlative truths.

First, the God of the Bible is sovereign, meaning he possesses supreme power. This is the truth affirmed in the statement, "Our God is in the heavens, and he does as he wishes" (115:3). He is in heaven, not limited as those on earth are limited. He does as he wishes, or as Daniel 4:35 says, "He does as he pleases among the angels of heaven and among the people of the earth. No one can stop him or say to him, 'What do you mean by doing these things?'" No one can challenge his right to act as he wishes, and no one can challenge his power to so act, either.

Second, the idols of the nations are powerless in contrast to the sovereign God. They are "merely things of silver and gold" (115:4) with no inherent power. In contrast to the Lord "who made heaven and earth" (115:15) they have been made by human hands. They appear to have all the organs to exercise personal power, but they are powerless to speak, to see, to hear. "The polemic, moreover, believes that the gods represented by the images are as impotent and unreal as their copies" (Mays 1994:367). Peter once said, "Lord, to whom would we go? You have the words that give eternal life" (John 6:68). There are no substitutes for the true and living God.

When we substitute something or someone for the true and living God as the object of our ultimate trust, we become as powerless as the god we have fashioned. "If human work sets the boundaries for the reach of trust, then those who trust are limited to possibilities of their own making and the power of their own potential" (Mays 1994:367). When we trust the unlimited God, then unlimited possibilities, power, and blessing are available for us.

Trusting the Lord Brings Blessings (115:12-15). Four times in 115:12-13 we are told that the Lord will bless. He will bless "us," "Israel," "the descendants of Aaron," and "those who fear the LORD." The repetition of these three categories of God's people serves to underscore the connection between trusting and being blessed. Those who trust (115:9-11) are those who are blessed (115:12-13). And they are not just blessed but "richly" blessed (115:14) by "the LORD, who made heaven and earth" (115:15). He who created the vast resources of the universe will remember those who trust him, "both great and lowly . . . you and your children," and he will pour out blessings on them.

Trusting the Lord Yields Praise (115:1, 16-18). The one we ultimately trust is the one we ultimately praise. Since we ultimately trust the Lord, he is the object of our worship: "Not to us, O LORD, not to us, but to your name goes all the glory for your unfailing love and faithfulness" (115:1). The impotent idols are not the object of our trust, so they are not the objects of praise. Psalm 135:15-18 has a shortened version of the polemic against idols, and that polemic is followed not by an exhortation to trust the Lord but by an exhortation to praise the Lord.

At the very beginning of Psalm 115 we are reminded that the fount of all blessing is the unfailing love of God. It is because of his love that we trust him. It is because of his love that our trust results in blessing. It is because of his love that he gets all the glory while we live. "The earth" (115:16) is the sphere God has given to us. "The earth" is the sphere of our existence in this life. "The earth" is where we live for the glory and praise of God before we die and enter the silence of the grave. There is a life of praise after death, but that life does not come into view here (see 88:10-12). The perspective of the psalmist is from this life before death. It is now that we trust, now that we are blessed, and now that we praise him whom we trust—but not just now, "both now and forever! Praise the LORD!" (115:18).

◆ J. Psalm 116

1 I love the LORD because he hears
my voice
and my prayer for mercy.
2 Because he bends down to listen,
I will pray as long as I have breath!
3 Death wrapped its ropes around me;
the terrors of the grave* overtook me.
I saw only trouble and sorrow.
4 Then I called on the name of
the LORD:
"Please, LORD, save me!"
5 How kind the LORD is! How good he is!
So merciful, this God of ours!
6 The LORD protects those of childlike
faith;
I was facing death, and he
saved me.
7 Let my soul be at rest again,
for the LORD has been good to me.
8 He has saved me from death,
my eyes from tears,
my feet from stumbling.
9 And so I walk in the LORD's presence
as I live here on earth!
10 I believed in you, so I said,
"I am deeply troubled, LORD."
11 In my anxiety I cried out to you,
"These people are all liars!"
12 What can I offer the LORD
for all he has done for me?
13 I will lift up the cup of salvation
and praise the LORD's name for
saving me.
14 I will keep my promises to the LORD
in the presence of all his people.

15 The LORD cares deeply
when his loved ones die.
16 O LORD, I am your servant;
yes, I am your servant, born into
your household;
you have freed me from my chains.
17 I will offer you a sacrifice of
thanksgiving
and call on the name of the LORD.
18 I will fulfill my vows to the LORD
in the presence of all his people—
19 in the house of the LORD
in the heart of Jerusalem.

Praise the LORD!

116:3 Hebrew *of Sheol.*

NOTES

116:2 ***as long as I have breath!*** Lit., "and in my days." The "and" is another example of the emphatic Waw; see endnote 1 for Ps 112.

116:15 ***The LORD cares deeply when his loved ones die.*** Lit., "Precious in the LORD's eyes is the death of his loved ones." In the context, the psalmist did not die but was delivered from death. So the sense seems to be not that their death is special but that they are so precious that he keeps them from dying (Kraus 1989:388-389). This interpretation is confirmed by 72:14, which says, "He will redeem them from oppression and violence, for their lives are precious to him." The last clause is quite similar to 116:15 and could be literally translated "for their blood [death] is precious in his eyes." Here their "blood" (death) being "precious" to God clearly means he keeps them from dying.

COMMENTARY

Psalm 116 is arguably the most personal of all the songs of thanksgiving. There seems to be a level of intimacy between the psalmist and God that is unparalleled in other similar psalms. This psalm brings to expression the thoughts and feelings of a person who was in the deepest of trouble—facing death—and who experienced what it means to be precious in God's sight, precious enough to be restored to health (116:3-11). In this psalm tender thoughts and feelings flow from the heart of the psalmist to the Lord in response to the Lord's goodness to the psalmist (116:1-2, 12-19).

The Lord's Goodness to Us (116:3-11). Giving thanks to the Lord at times includes recounting the troubles we have experienced in the past. Sometimes those troubles are deep and dark, as they were for the composer of Psalm 116: "Death wrapped its ropes around me; the terrors of the grave overtook me. I saw only trouble and sorrow" (116:3). Not only was there the physical problem of the life-threatening situation the psalmist faced, but there was also the mental anguish that came along with it (116:10-11). The psalmist recounts it all. This recounting was not a private affair; it took place in public (116:18-19). Public worship provides a great setting for giving thanks to God, including the recounting of our troubles.

Thanksgiving moves on, however, from recounting the trouble we were in to also recounting how we pleaded with the Lord for deliverance: "Then I called on the name of the LORD: 'Please, LORD, save me!'" (116:4). When we plead with the Lord for deliverance, we can be completely honest with him about how we feel and what we think about our circumstances. The psalmist said, "I am deeply troubled" (116:10) and "These people are all liars" (116:11). Candid and frank honesty in prayer is a priceless gift that the Psalter gives to us (see commentary on Ps 13).

The thanksgiving reaches its climax as the psalmist recounts how God is the deliverer. "He saved me" (116:6), "He has saved me from death" (116:8), says the psalmist. The Lord at the same time delivered the psalmist from the mental anguish: "He has saved . . . my eyes from tears" (116:8). Thanksgiving not only recounts *that* God has saved but also *why* God has saved: "How good he is! So merciful . . . the LORD has been good to me" (116:5, 7). God is good, and he is merciful. His goodness and mercy are more than dispositions within him. They come to expression in concrete forms of salvation in our lives. In the psalmist's case, God's goodness and mercy brought him back from the edge of death. We, too, can expect to experience the goodness and mercy of the Lord in specific deliverance from specific trouble.

The First Response Is Love (116:1-2, 12-19). When we have been delivered from deep waters, a question naturally arises from our hearts: "What can I offer the LORD for all he has done for me?" (116:12). The Lord's deliverance elicits a response from the one delivered. This response can come in a variety of forms. Two are drawn out in this psalm. The first is love (116:1-2). Psalm 116:1 is one of only two times in the Bible where someone says, "I love the LORD," the only other one being another psalm of thanksgiving (18:1). Love naturally flows from the heart of someone whose every groan the Lord has pitied. Love naturally flows from the heart of someone who has experienced being "precious in the sight of the Lord" (116:15, NIV), so precious that the Lord bent down and listened to the groaning prayers (116:2) of someone with childlike faith (116:6)—he listened and delivered. Though we may have sensed great distance between ourselves and the Lord while in distress (e.g., 10:1), after being delivered, we are drawn closer and closer to him. We love him because he loved us enough to save us from our distress.

The Second Response Is Praise (116:12-19). "I will . . . praise the LORD's name for saving me" (116:13b). It is good and right to promise the Lord that if he will deliver us, we will repay him publicly with praise. Such vows were routinely made by the ancients when in distress. The song of thanksgiving was part of fulfilling just such a vow (116:14, 18). Public praise and thanksgiving flow from the lips of the one whom the Lord has delivered. In the old covenant the song of thanksgiving would have been accompanied by a sacrifice of thanksgiving (116:17), which would have been shared with the poor (22:25-26). In the new covenant we thank God by offering ourselves as living sacrifices (Rom 12:1). Such sacrifices include doing God's will in general (Rom 12:2), and they involve, like their Old Testament counterpart, sharing with those who are in need (Heb 13:16). A life of loving praise is not too much to ask of those who have been touched by the goodness and mercy of the Lord (Rom 12:12).

◆ K. Psalm 117

1 Praise the LORD, all you nations.
Praise him, all you people of
the earth.
2 For he loves us with unfailing love;
the LORD's faithfulness
endures forever.

Praise the LORD!

COMMENTARY

Psalm 117 is the smallest of all the psalms, but its theme is one of the grandest: the worldwide worship of the true and living God. The structure is simple. Psalm 117:1 is a call to praise, and verse 2 provides the reason for or the content of that praise.

The message is simple, as well. Not just Israel or the house of Aaron but all the nations are invited in this psalm to praise the Lord. Many other psalms have already brought to expression this invitation to the nations (e.g., Pss 2, 46–49, 65–67, 93–100, 102, 105). The conciseness of Psalm 117, however, brings this invitation into the limelight with a simple brilliance matched by no other psalm. The book of Psalms looks forward to the day when "a vast crowd, too great to count, from every nation and tribe and people and language" will stand "in front of the throne and before the Lamb" to worship God (Rev 7:9). Why will they worship? They will worship because they will have been loved with an unfailing love (117:2), not just because they have been created by God.

God's love for the nations is one of the grandest themes in the ancient book of Psalms. God's love for the nations is one of the grandest themes Christians have to sing in the modern world. His love is unfailing. His faithfulness is unending. His will is that he be praised among all the peoples of the earth. "Praise the LORD!"

◆ L. Psalm 118

1 Give thanks to the LORD, for he is good!
His faithful love endures forever.

2 Let all Israel repeat:
"His faithful love endures forever."
3 Let Aaron's descendants, the priests,
repeat:
"His faithful love endures forever."
4 Let all who fear the LORD repeat:
"His faithful love endures forever."

5 In my distress I prayed to the LORD,
and the LORD answered me and set
me free.
6 The LORD is for me, so I will have no
fear.
What can mere people do to me?
7 Yes, the LORD is for me; he will help me.
I will look in triumph at those who
hate me.
8 It is better to take refuge in the LORD
than to trust in people.
9 It is better to take refuge in the LORD
than to trust in princes.

10 Though hostile nations surrounded me,
I destroyed them all with the
authority of the LORD.
11 Yes, they surrounded and attacked me,
but I destroyed them all with the
authority of the LORD.
12 They swarmed around me like bees;
they blazed against me like a
crackling fire.
But I destroyed them all with the
authority of the LORD.
13 My enemies did their best to kill me,
but the LORD rescued me.
14 The LORD is my strength and my song;
he has given me victory.
15 Songs of joy and victory are sung in
the camp of the godly.
The strong right arm of the LORD
has done glorious things!
16 The strong right arm of the LORD is
raised in triumph.
The strong right arm of the LORD
has done glorious things!
17 I will not die; instead, I will live
to tell what the LORD has done.
18 The LORD has punished me severely,
but he did not let me die.

19 Open for me the gates where the
righteous enter,
and I will go in and thank the LORD.
20 These gates lead to the presence of
the LORD,
and the godly enter there.
21 I thank you for answering my prayer
and giving me victory!

22 The stone that the builders rejected
has now become the cornerstone.
23 This is the LORD's doing,
and it is wonderful to see.
24 This is the day the LORD has made.
We will rejoice and be glad in it.
25 Please, LORD, please save us.
Please, LORD, please give us success.
26 Bless the one who comes in the name
of the LORD.
We bless you from the house of the
LORD.
27 The LORD is God, shining upon us.
Take the sacrifice and bind it with
cords on the altar.
28 You are my God, and I will praise you!
You are my God, and I will exalt
you!

29 Give thanks to the LORD, for he is
good!
His faithful love endures forever.

NOTES

118:5 *answered me and set me free.* Lit., "answered me in the open space." This is an example of breviloquence (Kraus 1989:393). The sense is "answered me and brought me into the open space." The "open space" (*merkhab* [TH4800, ZH5303]) contrasts with the "distress/narrow straits" (*metsar* [TH4712, ZH5210]) of the previous colon. Psalm 31:8 [9] uses *merkhab* in a similar way: "You have not handed me over to my enemies but have set me in a safe place [*merkhab*]." For the same idea with different vocabulary, see 66:12.

118:12 ***they blazed against me like a crackling fire.*** The line is difficult. The sense seems to be "they attacked like a fire attacks thorns" (see DCH 2.457).

COMMENTARY

The call to "Give thanks to the LORD" has already been heard (106:1; 107:1), will be heard again (136:1), and is the surrounding summons of Psalm 118 (118:1, 29). Psalm 118 is a marvelous song of thanksgiving. The focus of the thanksgiving is on God's goodness and enduring love (see 118:2-4). Inside the *inclusio* of 118:1, 29 are two strophes. The first strophe (118:5-18) testifies to how the psalmist experienced the goodness and enduring love of God in being delivered from distressing circumstances. The second (118:19-28) invites us into the drama of thanksgiving liturgy. Five key concepts permeate this wonderful psalm.

Thanksgiving. Thanksgiving is the dominant note in Psalm 118. The psalm opens with a strophe (118:1-4) that is an extended call to give thanks to the Lord for his goodness and unfailing love. As in 115:9-11, the whole community is called upon to give thanks to the Lord under the rubrics of "Israel," "Aaron's descendants," and "all who fear the LORD." While Psalm 118 is an individual psalm of thanksgiving, the salvation of the individual has implications for the whole community, and thus the whole congregation is invited to join in the celebration of praise.

Simply put, the psalmist was in deep distress; he prayed to the Lord; the Lord rescued him; and now he gives thanks for his salvation. It seems that the individual psalmist was the king, who was granted military victory over foreign armies. These opposing nations surrounded the king and his armies like a swarm of angry bees (118:10-12), but the king emerged victorious. Perhaps this psalm was sung as the victorious army approached the city gates or when the king as the representative approached the gates of the Temple to thank the Lord for answered prayer experienced on the battlefield (118:19-21) and to offer the thanksgiving sacrifice on the altar.

The opponents had apparently despised the king as worthless, but contrary to their expectation, he now stood as the preeminent one, exalted in the eyes of all. As the exalted one, he exalts and praises his God, the source of his salvation (118:28).

Divine Sovereignty. It is God who has absolute power and authority in the world. The reason the psalmist gives thanks to God is that God exercised his sovereign power on behalf of the psalmist. This divine sovereignty is referred to in a number of ways in the psalms. Three times the psalmist tells us that "the strong right arm of the LORD" is the ultimate reason for his victory in battle (118:15-16). His victory was through the Lord's strength and because of the Lord's help. The day of victory was a day orchestrated by the Lord. The psalmist's exaltation was the Lord's doing. And three times the psalmist tells us his foes were defeated "with the authority [name] of the LORD" (118:10-12). This last reference is reminiscent of David, when he said that Goliath came against him with "sword, spear, and javelin" but that David came with a far more powerful arsenal, as he came "in the name of the LORD" (1 Sam 17:45). So when we face opponents as the psalmist did, we know that they do not have absolute power over us, because our God is the sovereign one in the world.

Human Responsibility. There is a corresponding truth to the divine sovereignty of God, and that is the truth of human responsibility or agency. At the same time that the psalmist attributes victory to the "authority [name] of the LORD," he says three times, "I destroyed them all" (118:10-12). Moreover, the fact that the Lord helped him presumes that he was doing something, that he was acting. While the sovereignty of God gets higher profile in this psalm, it does not overshadow or exclude the correlative truth of our responsibility for our own actions in this world.

Confidence in God. That God is sovereign and that we must act are two truths that dovetail with a third truth: When we act, our confidence is ultimately in God. "It is better to take refuge in the LORD than to trust in people" (118:8), whether those people are others or ourselves. "It is better to take refuge in the LORD than to trust in princes" (118:9): Even powerful and influential people are not to take the place of God as the ultimate object of our trust.

When we act and when we face opposition, we can have great confidence because God is absolute in power and authority. We can say, "The LORD is for me, so I will have no fear. What can mere people do to me? Yes, the LORD is for me. . . . I will look in triumph at those who hate me" (118:6-7). We can sing, "The LORD is my strength and my song. . . . I will not die; instead, I will live to tell what the LORD has done" (118:14, 17).

Pleading with God. Having been delivered from his foes in the recent past did not mean that there would never be foes to face again in the future. In fact, while giving thanks for deliverance from distress, the psalmist saw new foes on the horizon. But having experienced God's sovereign power in the past, he had (and we have) confidence in the present if new foes arise. "Please, LORD, please save us. Please, LORD, please give us success" (118:25) was the psalmist's plea, even as he gave thanks for deliverance. And this was a confident plea. The psalmist was confident that in the near future he would "look in triumph" on his foes, as he had in the past (118:7).

It seems that his confidence in the Lord was a confidence that someone was coming "with the authority [name] of the LORD." This someone would be the person through whom divine power would be exerted to accomplish the salvation and secure the success of the community (118:26). Ultimately, this one came in the person of the Lord Jesus Christ.

In Jesus' day, there was an expectation of one to come: "Are you the Messiah we've been expecting, or should we keep looking for someone else?" was the question put to Jesus by John the Baptist's disciples (Matt 11:3). At his triumphal entry Jesus came in fulfillment of this hope: "Praise God for the Son of David! Blessings on the one who comes in the name of the LORD! Praise God in highest heaven!" (Matt 21:9). Though he came to Jerusalem in triumph, that triumph would be won through being rejected and suffering on the cross. Jesus said to them, "Didn't you ever read this in the Scriptures? 'The stone that the builders rejected has now become the cornerstone. This is the LORD's doing, and it is wonderful to see'" (Matt 21:42, citing Ps 118:22-23). Finally, looking forward to a time to come after his suffering, Jesus gave this eschatological promise: "For I tell you this, you will never see me again until you say, 'Blessings on the one who comes in the name of the LORD!'" (Matt 23:39, citing Ps 118:26).

We are not in the same position as the psalmist was, for the Son of David has come and has established his reign. But like the psalmist, we, too, look for Jesus to come to deliver us from our foes and the distressing situations in this life, even as we await his coming at the end of the age. About this final coming John said, "I heard a loud shout from the throne, saying, 'Look, God's home is now among his people! He will live with them, and they will be his people. God himself will be with them. He will wipe every tear from their eyes, and there will be no more death or sorrow or crying or pain. All these things are gone forever'" (Rev 21:3-4). And Jesus' last canonical words are, "Yes, I am coming soon!" (Rev 22:20), to which we respond, "Amen! Come, Lord Jesus!" (Rev 22:20).

◆ M. Psalm 119*

Aleph

1 Joyful are people of integrity,
who follow the instructions of the LORD.
2 Joyful are those who obey his laws
and search for him with all their hearts.
3 They do not compromise with evil,
and they walk only in his paths.
4 You have charged us
to keep your commandments carefully.
5 Oh, that my actions would consistently
reflect your decrees!
6 Then I will not be ashamed
when I compare my life with your commands.
7 As I learn your righteous regulations,
I will thank you by living as I should!
8 I will obey your decrees.
Please don't give up on me!

Beth

9 How can a young person stay pure?
By obeying your word.
10 I have tried hard to find you—
don't let me wander from your commands.
11 I have hidden your word in my heart,
that I might not sin against you.
12 I praise you, O LORD;
teach me your decrees.
13 I have recited aloud
all the regulations you have given us.
14 I have rejoiced in your laws
as much as in riches.
15 I will study your commandments
and reflect on your ways.
16 I will delight in your decrees
and not forget your word.

Gimel

17 Be good to your servant,
that I may live and obey your word.
18 Open my eyes to see
the wonderful truths in your instructions.
19 I am only a foreigner in the land.
Don't hide your commands from me!
20 I am always overwhelmed
with a desire for your regulations.
21 You rebuke the arrogant;
those who wander from your commands are cursed.
22 Don't let them scorn and insult me,
for I have obeyed your laws.
23 Even princes sit and speak against me,
but I will meditate on your decrees.
24 Your laws please me;
they give me wise advice.

Daleth

25 I lie in the dust;
revive me by your word.
26 I told you my plans, and you answered.
Now teach me your decrees.
27 Help me understand the meaning of your commandments,
and I will meditate on your wonderful deeds.
28 I weep with sorrow;

encourage me by your word.
29 Keep me from lying to myself;
give me the privilege of knowing your instructions.
30 I have chosen to be faithful;
I have determined to live by your regulations.
31 I cling to your laws.
LORD, don't let me be put to shame!
32 I will pursue your commands,
for you expand my understanding.

He

33 Teach me your decrees, O LORD;
I will keep them to the end.
34 Give me understanding and I will obey your instructions;
I will put them into practice with all my heart.
35 Make me walk along the path of your commands,
for that is where my happiness is found.
36 Give me an eagerness for your laws
rather than a love for money!
37 Turn my eyes from worthless things,
and give me life through your word.*
38 Reassure me of your promise,
made to those who fear you.
39 Help me abandon my shameful ways;
for your regulations are good.
40 I long to obey your commandments!
Renew my life with your goodness.

Waw

41 LORD, give me your unfailing love,
the salvation that you promised me.
42 Then I can answer those who taunt me,
for I trust in your word.
43 Do not snatch your word of truth from me,
for your regulations are my only hope.
44 I will keep on obeying your instructions
forever and ever.
45 I will walk in freedom,
for I have devoted myself to your commandments.
46 I will speak to kings about your laws,
and I will not be ashamed.
47 How I delight in your commands!
How I love them!
48 I honor and love your commands.
I meditate on your decrees.

Zayin

49 Remember your promise to me;
it is my only hope.
50 Your promise revives me;
it comforts me in all my troubles.
51 The proud hold me in utter contempt,
but I do not turn away from your instructions.
52 I meditate on your age-old regulations;
O LORD, they comfort me.
53 I become furious with the wicked,
because they reject your instructions.
54 Your decrees have been the theme of my songs
wherever I have lived.
55 I reflect at night on who you are, O LORD;
therefore, I obey your instructions.
56 This is how I spend my life:
obeying your commandments.

Heth

57 LORD, you are mine!
I promise to obey your words!
58 With all my heart I want your blessings.
Be merciful as you promised.
59 I pondered the direction of my life,
and I turned to follow your laws.
60 I will hurry, without delay,
to obey your commands.
61 Evil people try to drag me into sin,
but I am firmly anchored to your instructions.
62 I rise at midnight to thank you
for your just regulations.
63 I am a friend to anyone who fears you—
anyone who obeys your commandments.
64 O LORD, your unfailing love fills the earth;
teach me your decrees.

Teth

65 You have done many good things for
me, LORD,
just as you promised.
66 I believe in your commands;
now teach me good judgment and
knowledge.
67 I used to wander off until you
disciplined me;
but now I closely follow your word.
68 You are good and do only good;
teach me your decrees.
69 Arrogant people smear me with lies,
but in truth I obey your
commandments with all my heart.
70 Their hearts are dull and stupid,
but I delight in your instructions.
71 My suffering was good for me,
for it taught me to pay attention
to your decrees.
72 Your instructions are more valuable
to me
than millions in gold and silver.

Yodh

73 You made me; you created me.
Now give me the sense to follow
your commands.
74 May all who fear you find in me a
cause for joy,
for I have put my hope in your
word.
75 I know, O LORD, that your regulations
are fair;
you disciplined me because
I needed it.
76 Now let your unfailing love
comfort me,
just as you promised me, your
servant.
77 Surround me with your tender mercies
so I may live,
for your instructions are my delight.
78 Bring disgrace upon the arrogant
people who lied about me;
meanwhile, I will concentrate on
your commandments.
79 Let me be united with all who
fear you,
with those who know your laws.
80 May I be blameless in keeping your
decrees;
then I will never be ashamed.

Kaph

81 I am worn out waiting for your
rescue,
but I have put my hope in your
word.
82 My eyes are straining to see your
promises come true.
When will you comfort me?
83 I am shriveled like a wineskin in
the smoke,
but I have not forgotten to obey
your decrees.
84 How long must I wait?
When will you punish those who
persecute me?
85 These arrogant people who hate your
instructions
have dug deep pits to trap me.
86 All your commands are trustworthy.
Protect me from those who hunt me
down without cause.
87 They almost finished me off,
but I refused to abandon your
commandments.
88 In your unfailing love, spare my life;
then I can continue to obey your
laws.

Lamedh

89 Your eternal word, O LORD,
stands firm in heaven.
90 Your faithfulness extends to every
generation,
as enduring as the earth you
created.
91 Your regulations remain true to this
day,
for everything serves your plans.
92 If your instructions hadn't sustained
me with joy,
I would have died in my misery.
93 I will never forget your
commandments,
for by them you give me life.
94 I am yours; rescue me!
For I have worked hard at obeying
your commandments.

95 Though the wicked hide along the way
to kill me,
I will quietly keep my mind on your
laws.
96 Even perfection has its limits,
but your commands have no limit.

Mem

97 Oh, how I love your instructions!
I think about them all day long.
98 Your commands make me wiser than
my enemies,
for they are my constant guide.
99 Yes, I have more insight than my
teachers,
for I am always thinking of your laws.
100 I am even wiser than my elders,
for I have kept your commandments.
101 I have refused to walk on any evil path,
so that I may remain obedient to
your word.
102 I haven't turned away from your
regulations,
for you have taught me well.
103 How sweet your words taste to me;
they are sweeter than honey.
104 Your commandments give me
understanding;
no wonder I hate every false way
of life.

Nun

105 Your word is a lamp to guide my feet
and a light for my path.
106 I've promised it once, and I'll promise
it again:
I will obey your righteous
regulations.
107 I have suffered much, O LORD;
restore my life again as you
promised.
108 LORD, accept my offering of praise,
and teach me your regulations.
109 My life constantly hangs in the
balance,
but I will not stop obeying your
instructions.
110 The wicked have set their traps for me,
but I will not turn from your
commandments.
111 Your laws are my treasure;
they are my heart's delight.
112 I am determined to keep your decrees
to the very end.

Samekh

113 I hate those with divided loyalties,
but I love your instructions.
114 You are my refuge and my shield;
your word is my source of hope.
115 Get out of my life, you evil-minded
people,
for I intend to obey the commands
of my God.
116 LORD, sustain me as you promised, that
I may live!
Do not let my hope be crushed.
117 Sustain me, and I will be rescued;
then I will meditate continually on
your decrees.
118 But you have rejected all who stray
from your decrees.
They are only fooling themselves.
119 You skim off the wicked of the earth
like scum;
no wonder I love to obey your laws!
120 I tremble in fear of you;
I stand in awe of your regulations.

Ayin

121 Don't leave me to the mercy of my
enemies,
for I have done what is just and
right.
122 Please guarantee a blessing for me.
Don't let the arrogant oppress me!
123 My eyes strain to see your rescue,
to see the truth of your promise
fulfilled.
124 I am your servant; deal with me in
unfailing love,
and teach me your decrees.
125 Give discernment to me, your
servant;
then I will understand your laws.
126 LORD, it is time for you to act,
for these evil people have violated
your instructions.
127 Truly, I love your commands
more than gold, even the finest gold.
128 Each of your commandments is right.
That is why I hate every false way.

Pe

129 Your laws are wonderful.
No wonder I obey them!
130 The teaching of your word gives light,
so even the simple can understand.
131 I pant with expectation,
longing for your commands.
132 Come and show me your mercy,
as you do for all who love your name.
133 Guide my steps by your word,
so I will not be overcome by evil.
134 Ransom me from the oppression of evil people;
then I can obey your commandments.
135 Look upon me with love;
teach me your decrees.
136 Rivers of tears gush from my eyes
because people disobey your instructions.

Tsadhe

137 O LORD, you are righteous,
and your regulations are fair.
138 Your laws are perfect
and completely trustworthy.
139 I am overwhelmed with indignation,
for my enemies have disregarded your words.
140 Your promises have been thoroughly tested;
that is why I love them so much.
141 I am insignificant and despised,
but I don't forget your commandments.
142 Your justice is eternal,
and your instructions are perfectly true.
143 As pressure and stress bear down on me,
I find joy in your commands.
144 Your laws are always right;
help me to understand them so I may live.

Qoph

145 I pray with all my heart; answer me, LORD!
I will obey your decrees.
146 I cry out to you; rescue me,
that I may obey your laws.
147 I rise early, before the sun is up;
I cry out for help and put my hope in your words.
148 I stay awake through the night,
thinking about your promise.
149 In your faithful love, O LORD, hear my cry;
let me be revived by following your regulations.
150 Lawless people are coming to attack me;
they live far from your instructions.
151 But you are near, O LORD,
and all your commands are true.
152 I have known from my earliest days
that your laws will last forever.

Resh

153 Look upon my suffering and rescue me,
for I have not forgotten your instructions.
154 Argue my case; take my side!
Protect my life as you promised.
155 The wicked are far from rescue,
for they do not bother with your decrees.
156 LORD, how great is your mercy;
let me be revived by following your regulations.
157 Many persecute and trouble me,
yet I have not swerved from your laws.
158 Seeing these traitors makes me sick at heart,
because they care nothing for your word.
159 See how I love your commandments, LORD.
Give back my life because of your unfailing love.
160 The very essence of your words is truth;
all your just regulations will stand forever.

Shin

161 Powerful people harass me without cause,
but my heart trembles only at your word.
162 I rejoice in your word

like one who discovers a great
treasure.
163 I hate and abhor all falsehood,
but I love your instructions.
164 I will praise you seven times a day
because all your regulations are just.
165 Those who love your instructions have
great peace
and do not stumble.
166 I long for your rescue, LORD,
so I have obeyed your commands.
167 I have obeyed your laws,
for I love them very much.
168 Yes, I obey your commandments and
laws
because you know everything I do.

Taw

169 O LORD, listen to my cry;
give me the discerning mind you
promised.
170 Listen to my prayer;
rescue me as you promised.
171 Let praise flow from my lips,
for you have taught me your
decrees.
172 Let my tongue sing about your word,
for all your commands are right.
173 Give me a helping hand,
for I have chosen to follow your
commandments.
174 O LORD, I have longed for your rescue,
and your instructions are my
delight.
175 Let me live so I can praise you,
and may your regulations help me.
176 I have wandered away like a lost
sheep;
come and find me,
for I have not forgotten your
commands.

119 This psalm is a Hebrew acrostic poem; there are twenty-two stanzas, one for each successive letter of the Hebrew alphabet. Each of the eight verses within each stanza begins with the Hebrew letter named in its heading. **119:37** Some manuscripts read *in your ways.*

COMMENTARY

"Oh, how I love your instructions! I think about them all day long" (119:97). Perhaps this verse captures better than any other the heart of the longest psalm in the Psalter. Psalm 119 is a masterful celebration of the *torah* [TH8451, ZH9368] of the Lord (119:1). This poem is composed of 22 strophes, one for each letter of the Hebrew alphabet. Each strophe is made up of eight lines, and each line of a given strophe starts with the same letter of the alphabet; so, for example, the first eight lines all start with the letter Aleph. This alphabetic acrostic form serves to underscore the completeness of the celebration of the Lord's *torah,* the perfection of that *torah* (see 119:96), and its comprehensive wisdom that is applicable to all of life (see 119:98-100).

While *torah* has customarily been translated "law," it is preferable to translate it as "instruction" or "teaching" in this context, as in 1:1 (see note on 1:1 and Mays 1994:382), 78:1, and Proverbs 1:8. The related verb (the Hiphil of *yarah* [TH3384E, ZH3723]), which means "teach," is used in 119:33 and 119:102. Seven other synonyms are used, yielding a total of eight words used for the Lord's instruction; this eight matches the eight lines per strophe (Allen 1983:139) and further underscores the message of the poem. The eight words in order of frequency are *torah* [TH8451, ZH9368] ("instruction"; 25 times), *dabar* [TH1697, ZH1821] ("word"; 24 times), *mishpatim* [TH4941, ZH5477] ("laws"; 23 times), *'eduth* [TH5715, ZH6343] ("statute"; 23 times), *mitswah* [TH4687, ZH5184] ("commandment"; 22 times), *khoq* [TH2706, ZH2976] ("prescription, rule"; 21 times), *piqqudim* [TH6490, ZH7218] ("instructions, procedures"; 21 times), and *'imrah* [TH565, ZH614] ("promise"; 19 times).

The word *torah* is the lead term, as indicated by its use in 119:1 and the fact that it is the most frequent term (Allen 1983:139), and it highlights God's instruction as the theme of the song. Rather than examine the psalm strophe by strophe, we will ponder five things that Psalm 119 teaches us about the Lord's instruction.

Our Attitude toward the Lord's Instruction. Love is the first word. We love the Lord's instruction very much (119:167). In fact, we love it more than "the finest gold" (119:127). Our love means we honor that instruction (119:48). We not only love to study it (119:97), we also love to put it into practice (119:127-129).[1] Coupled with our love for the Lord's instruction is our delight in it: "How I delight in your commands! How I love them!" (119:47). We delight in the Lord's instruction as we would delight in finding a great treasure (119:111). This delight is joined with our longing to experience more of God's salvation (119:174) and thus serves as a basis for our appealing to the Lord for his mercy in our lives. Our love and delight in the Lord's instruction shows that our relation to this instruction is not just a matter of external conformity to principles but a desire that comes from deep within our hearts. We search for God with all our hearts (119:2), hide his instruction within our hearts (119:11), and desire to put his instructions into practice with our hearts (119:34). "Of 'legalistic piety' there is not a trace" in this psalm (Kraus 1989:420). Rather, in Psalm 119 we read of a relationship wherein we desire from our hearts to live in keeping with the instructions of our God.[2]

Our Desire for the Lord's Instruction. Repeatedly the psalmist uses an imperative verb form to ask God for instruction. We desire that the Lord teach us both so we can better understand his instruction (119:26-27) and so we can better put those instructions into practice (119:33). Good judgment for living well in God's world is one key thing we want to learn from the Lord (119:66). We want to learn from the Lord, because of his character: He is good (119:68), and he is love (119:64, 124, 135), so we can be confident that all he teaches us will be for our good and that we might love even as he loves. Our desire to be taught by the Lord is one way we show him that we are grateful for his goodness and love (119:108).

Our Resolve to Live in Keeping with the Lord's Instruction. Committing ourselves to live in keeping with the Lord's instruction is our choice. It is a choice that the psalmist made (119:113, 173). That this choice is coupled with a firm resolve is seen in 119:30: "I have chosen to be faithful; I have determined to live by your regulations." The psalmist wholeheartedly searches for and devotes himself to God's word (119:2, 10, 45, 94). The psalmist also frequently uses the cohortative to express this resolve,[3] as in the expressions, "I will study your commandments and reflect on your ways" (119:15), "I will meditate on your wonderful deeds" (119:27), "I will obey your decrees" (119:145).[4] This resolve is no fair-weather commitment but is strong even in the face of hardship and opposition. Throughout the psalm we read words like: "Even princes sit and speak against me, but I will meditate on your decrees" (119:23); "The proud hold me in utter contempt, but I do not turn away from your instructions" (119:51); "Evil people try to drag me into sin, but I am firmly anchored to your instructions" (119:61); "Though the wicked hide along the way to kill me, I will quietly keep my mind on your laws" (119:95); "Many persecute and trouble me, yet I have not swerved from your laws" (119:157).[5] This resolve results in great benefits.

Our Benefits from the Lord's Instruction. Following the Lord's instructions results in great benefits to us. One benefit is peace: "Those who love your instructions have great peace and do not stumble" (119:165). Another is comfort: "Your promise revives me; it comforts me in all my troubles" (119:50; see also 119:52, 76). Another is freedom: "I will walk in freedom, for I have devoted myself to your commandments" (119:45). Along with the mention of these benefits are the frequent references to the tremendous, life-renewing power of God's word, e.g., "I lie in the dust; revive me by your word" (119:25) and "I have suffered much, O LORD; restore my life again as you promised" (119:107).[6] And then there is the hope that fills our hearts through the medium of God's instruction: "Do not snatch your word of truth from me, for your regulations are my only hope" (119:43) and "I rise early, before the sun is up; I cry out for help and put my hope in your words" (119:147).[7] The psalmist says, "Your instructions are more valuable to me than millions in gold and silver" (119:72). One of the reasons this is so is because of all the benefits God's instruction brings into our lives. Another is because our Lord's instruction reveals his heart.

Our Lord's Heart in His Instruction. When we look into the heart of God, we see his unfailing love. All of his instruction to us is a revelation of his love for us. Because the earth is full of his unfailing love, we want him to teach us his principles for living well on this earth (119:64). We want the Lord to deal with us according to his unfailing love, including teaching us his principles (119:124). We anticipate experiencing his salvation based on the unfailing love he has for us (119:41, 149, 159), and we resolve to respond to his love by living in keeping with the principles he has taught us (119:88). Ultimately, it is because of our Lord's heart revealed in his instructions that we say, "Oh, how I love your instructions! I think about them all day long" (119:97).

ENDNOTES

1. See also 119:113, 119, 140, 159, 163, 165.
2. See also 119:2, 7, 10, 11, 32, 34, 36, 58, 69, 70, 80, 111, 112, 145, 161.
3. Waltke and O'Connor 1990:§34.5.1a.
4. See also 119:17, 18, 34, 44, 73, 88, 115, 117, 134, 146.
5. See also 119:69, 81, 83, 87, 115, 134, 141, 143, 161, 174.
6. See also 119:37, 40, 88, 93, 149, 154, 156, 159.
7. See also 119:49, 74, 81, 114.

◆ N. Psalm 120

A song for pilgrims ascending to Jerusalem.

1 I took my troubles to the LORD;
I cried out to him, and he answered my prayer.
2 Rescue me, O LORD, from liars
and from all deceitful people.
3 O deceptive tongue, what will God do to you?
How will he increase your punishment?
4 You will be pierced with sharp arrows
and burned with glowing coals.
5 How I suffer in far-off Meshech.
It pains me to live in distant Kedar.
6 I am tired of living
among people who hate peace.
7 I search for peace;
but when I speak of peace, they want war!

NOTES

120:TITLE ***A song for pilgrims ascending to Jerusalem.*** Psalms 120–134 are a collection of psalms known as the "Psalms of Ascent," based on the title of each one, "Song of the Ascents." The purpose of this collection seems to have been to encourage God's people to make pilgrimage to Jerusalem (Crow 1996). Jerusalem (Zion) was the city God chose for his own dwelling place (132:13). Owing to God's presence there, Jerusalem (Zion) was a safe place for the Israelites to journey to (125:1). But Jerusalem (Zion) was more than a safe place; it was the place from which God dispensed his blessings on his people (128:5; 133:3; 134:3). To journey to Jerusalem was to journey to the presence of God to receive the blessings needed for life (133:3).

120:2 ***liars . . . deceitful people.*** The Hebrew text has singulars here. While there was probably a group of adversaries, they were probably led by one instigator.

120:4 ***glowing coals.*** Lit., "coals of a broom bush." The broom tree, because of the hardness of its stem, was used for making charcoal (Kraus 1989:424; VanGemeren 1991:770).

120:5 ***Meshech . . . Kedar.*** Meshech refers to a people who lived in the mountains to the southeast of the Black Sea (HALOT 2.646). Kedar refers to a nomadic people who lived between Egypt and Edom (HALOT 3.1072). Because of the geographical distance, it is likely that these references are metaphorical for hostile barbarians (Allen 1983:146).

COMMENTARY

There are times in this life when we long for peace, but those around us seem bent on bringing strife into our lives. Such was the situation for the composer of Psalm 120. The position of this psalm at the beginning of the pilgrim psalms shows us that the longing for peace goes hand in hand with the longing for the saving presence of God. In and through the presence of God, we will experience peace, and strife will end.

Giving Thanks for Answered Prayer (120:1). At times in the Psalms "answered prayer" is equivalent to being delivered from trouble. So in 34:4 [5] the psalmist says, "I prayed to the LORD, and he answered me. He freed me from all my fears." (The word translated "freed" is the same word translated "rescue" in 120:2.) God answered by freeing the psalmist. At other times, however, the "answered prayer" is an assurance of a deliverance yet to be experienced. An example of this kind of "answered prayer" is found in Psalm 3. In 3:4 [5] the psalmist testifies, saying, "I cried out to the LORD, and he answered me from his holy mountain," using the same verbs for "cried out" and "answered" as in 120:1. Yet the surrounding verses make clear that the psalmist had not yet been delivered. Such seems to be the case in Psalm 120. In 120:1 the psalmist gives thanks for answered prayer that came in the form of a great assurance that deliverance would eventually come. So for this deliverance the psalmist prayed in the following verse.

Praying for Complete Deliverance (120:2). Certain that deliverance was coming, the psalmist simply prayed, "Rescue me." He needed to be rescued from an adversary who was using lies and deceit as weapons against the psalmist. We do not know what the precise nature of the lies were. But this mode of attack was frequent in the ancient world (e.g., 3:7; 4:2; 5:6, 9) and is still too common today. The Holy Spirit teaches us through the example of the psalmist to depend on God for deliverance in these circumstances and not to take matters into our own hands.

Warning about Reaping What One Sows (120:3-4). A question is raised in 120:3: "O deceptive tongue, what will God do to you? How will he increase your punishment?" The answer is given in 120:4: "You will be pierced with sharp arrows and burned with glowing coals." Destructive words are elsewhere compared to arrows (57:4; 64:3) and fire (Prov 16:27; see Jas 3:6), so the point is that the deceitful adversary will reap what he has sown (see 7:15; 9:15; 35:8). The psalmist understood what Paul would later articulate when he said in Galatians 6:7, "Don't be misled—you cannot mock the justice of God. You will always harvest what you plant." So, too, we can be assured that those who would harm us with lies will end up only harming themselves.

Longing for Peace (120:5-7). In the time between the assurance of being delivered and the deliverance itself, there is a longing for peace, which comes to expression at the end of the psalm. The psalmist bemoans the protracted adversity he has experienced. He feels as if he has been through a war. His adversary and opponents, though counted among the people of God, have been acting like the hostile barbarians of distant lands, hating by their actions the peace of God's presence. It is as if the psalmist could endure the strife no longer. Every overture he made for peace was thrown back in his face with increased animosity. Yet, through it all, he maintained his commitment: "I search for peace."

This peace will be a recurring theme in the Psalms of Ascent. This first Psalm of Ascent could well have served as a prayer upon embarking on the journey to Jerusalem. As pilgrims heading for the fullness of God's presence, we long for the fullness of peace with great assurance that God will establish it in our lives. This assurance is strengthened by the experience of peace through the Holy Spirit, whose fruit is peace and in whom we now have the firstfruits of the full harvest of peace.

◆ O. Psalm 121

A song for pilgrims ascending to Jerusalem.

1 I look up to the mountains—
does my help come from
there?
2 My help comes from the LORD,
who made heaven and earth!

3 He will not let you stumble;
the one who watches over you will
not slumber.
4 Indeed, he who watches over Israel
never slumbers or sleeps.

5 The LORD himself watches over you!
The LORD stands beside you as your
protective shade.
6 The sun will not harm you by day,
nor the moon at night.

7 The LORD keeps you from all harm
and watches over your life.
8 The LORD keeps watch over you as you
come and go,
both now and forever.

NOTES

121:1 ***does my help come from there?*** This translation presumes that the poet viewed the mountains as a potential source of aid, perhaps as the dwelling place of the gods. The sense of the word *me'ayin* [TH4480/370, ZH4946/402], however, is "from where?" (DCH 1.220;

HALOT 1.42), so the question is broader: "Where does my help come from?" The mountains are better understood as a potential place of danger than a potential source of help (see commentary).

121:3 *watches.* The word *shamar* [TH8104, ZH9068] is the key word of this psalm, occurring 6 times. It is translated with the English "watches" in 121:3, 4, 5, with "keeps" and "watches" in 121:7, and with "keeps watch" in 121:8.

COMMENTARY

Life is a journey. Along the way we face difficulties. These difficulties can either be stumbling blocks or stepping-stones. How can we turn potential stumbling blocks into stepping-stones? Psalm 121 guides us into an aspect of the answer.

Psalm 121 would have served pilgrims well as they journeyed to Jerusalem for one of the major festivals at the Temple, where they would enjoy the special presence of God. The chain of mountains running north to south down the center of Israel would have posed numerous threats to the travelers. The trek itself would have been arduous enough, and then there were dangers from the likes of wild animals and robbers. Casting a glance at the mountains raised the natural question, "Where will I look to find the help necessary for a successful journey?" Alternative answers may have been contemplated, but the text gives an immediate answer as if to say, "There are no real alternatives; there is only one source of help." That source is the LORD. And who is the LORD? None other than the one who created the heavens and the earth. Since he is the creator of all, he is the controller of all. Since he is the creator and controller of all, he is the creator and controller of the mountains. Therefore, he is all the help necessary to navigate the mountains successfully.

What was true back then is still true today. In the Lord we have absolutely all the help we need to navigate the mountains of life as we journey to our ultimate destination, the perfect presence of God in heaven. We know that he has all the wisdom we need and all the power we need. Above all else, we know that his wisdom and power are ours, as his watchful eye is on us each step of the way.

Six times the psalm affirms that the Lord watches over us along life's journey. As the one who watches over us, he is the one who protects us. He protects us all the time. Even when we are sleeping, his watchful eye, which never tires or sleeps, is upon us. He watches over us night and day to protect us from all harm. The Lord does not protect us from a distance but takes his protective stand right beside us (121:5). While the ancient Israelites would have needed shade from the scorching sun (121:5-6), we need protection from the hostile forces operative all around us in this life. The promise of the psalm is that the Lord will keep us from all evil as we look to him as the ultimate source of our help. In all of our comings and goings, the Lord keeps watch over us, not only in the present but also on into the distant future (121:8).

By trusting that the Lord is watching over us every step of the way and every moment of the day, we can turn potential stumbling blocks into stepping-stones. As we walk by faith in him, the mountains of life are not barriers to his presence but places where we experience his watchful care until we arrive in the new Jerusalem, where we will enjoy him forever.

◆ P. Psalm 122

A song for pilgrims ascending to Jerusalem. A psalm of David.

[1] I was glad when they said to me,
"Let us go to the house of the LORD."
[2] And now here we are,
standing inside your gates,
O Jerusalem.
[3] Jerusalem is a well-built city;
its seamless walls cannot be breached.
[4] All the tribes of Israel—the LORD's people—
make their pilgrimage here.
They come to give thanks to the name of the LORD,
as the law requires of Israel.
[5] Here stand the thrones where judgment is given,
the thrones of the dynasty of David.
[6] Pray for peace in Jerusalem.
May all who love this city prosper.
[7] O Jerusalem, may there be peace within your walls
and prosperity in your palaces.
[8] For the sake of my family and friends,
I will say,
"May you have peace."
[9] For the sake of the house of the LORD our God,
I will seek what is best for you,
O Jerusalem.

NOTES

122:5 *dynasty of David.* "Dynasty" in Hebrew is the word *beth* [TH1004, ZH1074] (house of), which is also used in 122:1, 9 in the phrase "house of the LORD" (see commentary).

122:9 *what is best.* The sense of the word *tob* [TH2896, ZH3202] (good) is probably "prosperity" here in the context of *shalah/shalwah* [TH7951/7962, ZH8922/8932] ("prosper/prosperity"; 122:6, 7) and *shalom* [TH7965, ZH8934] ("peace"; 122:6, 7, 8); see 21:3 [4] and 25:13, where *tob* is translated "prosperity"; see also *tobah* [TH2896D, ZH3208] in 106:5 and *tub* [TH2898, ZH3206] in 128:5.

COMMENTARY

The rabbis referred to Jerusalem as the "navel of the universe" (see Williams 1989:407), and it is amazing that after so many years this ancient city still plays such a key role in modern life. Sacred to Jews, Christians, and Muslims, Jerusalem is still the destination of pilgrims from around the world as it was the destination of Israelites in ancient days. The psalm begins with joy at the pilgrim's arrival in Jerusalem (122:1-2) and then celebrates the significance of the city (122:3-5) before concluding with a prayer for peace and prosperity for the city and for all who love it (122:6-9).

Rejoicing in Jerusalem (122:1-2). The psalmist rejoiced "in" Jerusalem in two senses. First, he rejoiced in Jerusalem geographically. Having been living away from Jerusalem (Ps 120) and having endured the arduous journey to Jerusalem (Ps 121), the psalmist was glad to finally be in Jerusalem. Great joy filled the hearts of the pilgrims when their feet felt the ground within the city gates. The journey was over; they had arrived. Second, the psalmist rejoiced in Jerusalem spiritually. The primary significance of the city was that it was the location of "the house of the LORD." References to "the house of the LORD" (122:1, 9) envelop the psalm and draw our attention to the quintessential significance of the city and the psalm: the experience of the presence of God (see 84:6-7). In Jerusalem stood "the house of the LORD," and to arrive at the house of the Lord was to arrive at the destiny for which we were created: the presence of God.

Today, we need not make a pilgrimage to Jerusalem, or to any other city for that matter, in order to experience the presence of God (John 4:21), because the house of the Lord has come to us in the person of the Lord Jesus Christ (John 1:14). And as we believe in him, we are the house where the Lord dwells by his Spirit (1 Cor 3:16; 6:19; Eph 2:21-22). We, like the psalmist, can rejoice daily in the presence of God, especially since one of the fruits of his Spirit is joy (Gal 5:22).

Exulting over Jerusalem (122:3-5). Like other psalms about Zion (Jerusalem), Psalm 122 celebrates the splendor of the city of God. Three dimensions of this splendor are celebrated in this psalm. One dimension is that Jerusalem was a place of safety. Jerusalem was a "well-built city" that provided security from outside hostile forces. With its fortified walls and palaces (122:7) and its many towers and strong citadels (48:12-13), Jerusalem was a symbol of security. We have already been taught that true security came not from the city but from the presence of God within the city (see commentary on Ps 48). So we can experience the security symbolized by the city apart from the city when the presence of the Spirit fills our lives.

The second dimension of the city's splendor is that Jerusalem was a place of praise. The reason for making the pilgrimage was "to give thanks to the name of the LORD." At the Festival of Tabernacles, for example, the ancient Israelites would have given thanks for the blessings of the past year, blessings like freedom from military oppression and bountiful harvests. Since the Lord was the ultimate source of all blessings, gratitude was expressed to him by the worshiping community. We should be grateful for all the blessings the Lord showers down on us in this life.

The third dimension of the city's splendor is that Jerusalem was a place of justice. There was a second "house" in Jerusalem, "the house of David." In this house was a throne where the king sat to administer justice. Among other functions, the monarchy was to provide justice for the people of God. God's people rightly expected to receive justice at the hands of the human king. The human king was, however, an administrator of the divine king's justice. The divine king was the one people were to ultimately look to for justice, yet in the normal course of events the divine king dispensed his justice through the human king. The structure of the poem underscores this teaching, as the one reference to the house of David in 122:5 is surrounded by the two references to "the house of the LORD" in 122:1 and 9. The position of the reference to the house of David shows us that the exercise of justice by the human king was central, as it derived from the justice of God (McCann 1996:1183). Human administration is righteous when it is in keeping with divine justice. While we may look to humans for justice in this life, we place our ultimate hope for justice in God.

Praying for Jerusalem (122:6-9). Peace and prosperity are the longings of the human heart. They are not automatic in this life, as the Psalms of Ascent have already shown us. While the psalmist was committed to peace, many others seemed to thrive on strife (120:6-7). Having arrived at Jerusalem and the houses of God and David, the pilgrims hoped and prayed for peace. This peace certainly includes the absence of the hostility and strife experienced among the scoundrels of Meshech and the people of Kedar (120:5), but there is much more to it than that. Peace would result from the exercise of justice, which would not only bring an end to social turmoil but would also bring about prosperity on all levels (see 72:1-7 and

NIDOTTE 4.132). Thus, coupled with the prayer for peace is a prayer for prosperity. The word for prosperity itself carries the idea of being undisturbed by trouble and therefore prosperous in all ways (NIDOTTE 4.117-118). So it is good and right for us to pray for and expect peace and prosperity as we live out our lives in the presence of God (see 1 Tim 2:1-2).

The psalmist not only prays "for" peace and prosperity, he also prays "for the sake of" others. These prayers for peace and prosperity are neither individualistic nor self-centered. They are offered for the sake of family and friends and the entire house of God. In keeping with this, Paul has urged us to "pray for all people. Ask God to help them; intercede on their behalf, and give thanks for them. Pray this way for kings and all who are in authority so that we can live peaceful and quiet lives marked by godliness and dignity" (1 Tim 2:1-2).

In keeping with this psalm, let us rejoice in the presence of God and exult in that presence as a place of safety, praise, and justice. And let us pray for peace and prosperity to flow into our lives from the presence of God.

◆ Q. Psalm 123

A song for pilgrims ascending to Jerusalem.

[1] I lift my eyes to you,
O God, enthroned in heaven.
[2] We keep looking to the LORD our God
for his mercy,
just as servants keep their eyes on
their master,
as a slave girl watches her mistress
for the slightest signal.
[3] Have mercy on us, LORD, have
mercy,
for we have had our fill of
contempt.
[4] We have had more than our fill of the
scoffing of the proud
and the contempt of the
arrogant.

NOTES

123:4 *scoffing of the proud.* The NLT presumes an emendation by adding a Lamedh in the Hebrew phrase, changing the MT from "the scoffing, the proud" to "the scoffing *of* the proud." This emendation (see Kraus 1989:436) makes sense out of a difficult text and brings this phrase into conformity with the syntax of the following phrase, "the contempt of the arrogant."

COMMENTARY

The simple words "have mercy" have often been the cry of the soul on the lips of God's ancient people (4:1; 6:2; 9:13; 25:16; 27:7; 30:10; 31:9; 41:4, 10; 51:1; 56:1; 57:1; 86:3, 16; 119:29, 58, 132; 123:3). Whether two blind men (Matt 9:27), a gentile mother (Matt 15:22), or a troubled father (Matt 17:15), many people have come to God for help with the brief words, "Have mercy." Perhaps you have known dark days, when "have mercy" was the only prayer you could utter. These words form the heart of the prayer offered in Psalm 123, which in its brevity teaches us the simplicity and profundity of heartfelt prayer for divine aid.

Our Posture (123:1-2). When we come to God in time of need, a certain posture is appropriate. Psalm 123 commends this posture. It is the posture, however, of our souls, not our bodies, that is in view. We come humbly before our sovereign God. As the one "enthroned in heaven," God rules over all that he has made (see 2:4), and he is absolute in power over the affairs of this world. So we come humbly before him, lifting our eyes up to him who is above us. We look to him as a humble servant looks to his master or as a humble slave girl looks to her mistress. Because he is absolute in power, we come before him humbly, but we also come confidently before our merciful God. If we knew him only to be absolute in power, terror could keep us from approaching him. But we also know him to be merciful, and his love for us drives away all such terror (1 John 4:18). We come, confident that our merciful God (111:4; 116:5; 145:8) will not turn us away. Our confidence is likewise rooted in the sovereignty of God, for since he is absolute in power, he has the power to help us in time of need.

Our Plea (123:3-4). Our plea can be, and at times must be, quite simply a plea for mercy: "Have mercy on us, LORD, have mercy." The repetition of the plea underscores the desperation of the situation (see 57:1 [2]). Two blind men were so desperate that they could only cry out, "Son of David, have mercy on us!" (Matt 9:27). There was the cry of desperation from a mother for her demon-possessed daughter, "Have mercy on me, O Lord, Son of David!" (Matt 15:22). And how many desperate fathers have pleaded, "Lord, have mercy on my son" (Matt 17:15)? A variety of circumstances have given rise to this plea, as the previous citations make clear. In Psalm 123 it is a plea because of contempt. Having been the object of the contempt and mockery and scoffing of boastful adversaries, the community pleads for mercy and bolsters that prayer with the admission that they have simply had enough and can take no more. Degraded and dehumanized humans plead to the Divine for deliverance.

These people who pray in Psalm 123 have something in common on a deep level with the blind men, with the mother of the demon-possessed daughter, and with the father of the seizure-afflicted son. They all long to be restored to the fullness of God's intention for human beings created in his image. They bring this longing humbly and confidently to the God who is absolute in power and full of mercy. They come humbly and confidently to the God who is powerful enough and merciful enough to make the blind see, to make the demon-possessed free, and to make those afflicted with seizures whole. To such a God we lift our eyes humbly and confidently in times of desperate need with the simple, profound words, "Have mercy."

◆ R. Psalm 124

A song for pilgrims ascending to Jerusalem. A psalm of David.

1 What if the LORD had not been on
our side?
Let all Israel repeat:
2 What if the LORD had not been on
our side
when people attacked us?
3 They would have swallowed us alive
in their burning anger.
4 The waters would have engulfed us;
a torrent would have
overwhelmed us.
5 Yes, the raging waters of their fury

would have overwhelmed our
very lives.
6 Praise the LORD,
who did not let their teeth tear
us apart!
7 We escaped like a bird from a hunter's
trap.
The trap is broken, and we are free!
8 Our help is from the LORD,
who made heaven and earth.

NOTES

124:1 ***on our side.*** Lit., "for us" (so too in 124:2; see Rom 8:31).

124:4-5 ***The waters . . . us . . . the raging waters . . . our very lives.*** The two references to "the waters" (*hammayim* [TH4325, ZH4784]) are found in the first and last cola in the Hebrew text. The two inner cola use *napshenu* [TH5315/5105.1, ZH5883/5646] (translated "us" and "our very lives"). In the poetic structure, the threatening waters thus surround the people of God, just as their enemies had done (see McCann 1996:1190).

124:7 ***We escaped . . . we are free.*** The word *napshenu* [TH5315/5105.1, ZH5883/5646] ("our soul," here translated "we") speaks of one who was surrounded by raging waters in 124:4-5 but is now free. This freedom is the dominant note of these lines, as the verb *malat* [TH4422, ZH4880] occurs in the first colon ("We escaped") and last colon ("we are free") of this two-line verse.

COMMENTARY

What would it be like to go up against overwhelming hostile forces with no one at all to help, to face an unconquerable enemy all alone? What would it be like to live without the help of God? These questions, which we do not often ask ourselves, are not only raised in this psalm (124:1-5), but they are also answered. And the answers, though not pleasant, are quite beneficial. Such reflection resulted in praise to God for his help in the psalm (124:6-8), and it will do the same in our lives (see Williams 1989:415-418).

Reflecting on What Could Have Happened (124:1-5). What would happen if we faced hostile adversaries far more powerful than us and the Lord were not on our side? "They would have swallowed us alive"—a terrifying experience just like when the earth swallowed Korah, Dathan, Abiram, their families, and all their followers alive (Num 16:31-32). It would have been like being swept away by a rushing torrent of floodwaters that leave nothing but devastation in their wake.

Blessing the Lord for What Did Happen (124:6-8). The first strophe contains sobering images. These images could be depressing were they not contrary to fact. The fact is, however, that the Lord *was* on the side of the ancient singers, and he is on our side as well. He has proven that he is on our side by not sparing his Son and giving him up for us all (Rom 8:32). Thus, no one can now ultimately stand against us (Rom 8:31), and we can join the chorus that blesses God, the source of our help.

What really happened is portrayed with two more vivid images. Though we were totally vulnerable, like the small prey of a ferocious animal, the Lord did not permit our enemies to tear us apart. Though we were hopelessly trapped, like a snared bird in a hunter's trap, the Lord broke the trap, and we escaped. We escaped!

We escaped because the Lord is on our side, so we bless the Lord. We bless the Lord by acknowledging publicly ("Let all Israel repeat") that "our help is from the

LORD" (124:8). We believed that the Lord who made the heavens and the earth was our help (121:2), and we then experienced the help of the Maker of heaven and earth (124:8), so we bless the Lord. The one who created the universe is the very one who is on our side. Truly, "If God is for us, who can ever be against us?" (Rom 8:31).

◆ S. Psalm 125

A song for pilgrims ascending to Jerusalem.

1 Those who trust in the LORD are as
secure as Mount Zion;
they will not be defeated but will
endure forever.
2 Just as the mountains surround
Jerusalem,
so the LORD surrounds his people,
both now and forever.
3 The wicked will not rule the land of
the godly,
for then the godly might be
tempted to do wrong.
4 O LORD, do good to those who
are good,
whose hearts are in tune with you.
5 But banish those who turn to crooked
ways, O LORD.
Take them away with those who
do evil.

May Israel have peace!

NOTES

125:3 *The wicked will not rule.* The particle *ki* [TH3588, ZH3954] at the beginning of the Hebrew line is left untranslated in the NLT. The sense here is "surely."

COMMENTARY

As the first word in the Hebrew text (*habbotekhim* [TH1886.1/982, ZH2021/1053]) indicates, Psalm 125 is about "those who trust" in the Lord. Those who trust in the Lord are referred to in a wide variety of ways in this short poem. They are "his people" (125:2b), "the godly" (125:3), "those who are good" (125:4a), those "whose hearts are in tune" with God (125:4b), and "Israel" (125:5b). Those who trust in the Lord are also contrasted with "the wicked" (125:3a), "those who turn to crooked ways" (125:5a), and "those who do evil" (125:5b). The poem opens with an affirmation about those who trust (125:1-3) and closes with a prayer for those who trust (125:4-5).

An Affirmation about Those Who Trust (125:1-3). The basic affirmation about those who trust in the Lord is expressed in a simile, literally, "They are like Mount Zion." The NLT rightly interprets this figure with the words "as secure as." "Mount Zion" evoked a sense of security for the ancient Israelites much like the "Rock of Gibraltar" communicates security to modern people. As we trust in the Lord, we, too, can be as secure as the Rock of Gibraltar.

Ultimately, what made Mount Zion so secure was not the fortifications around the city but the presence of God within the city (46:5). By way of extension, the security of those who trust in the Lord is the presence of the Lord himself in their lives. This becomes explicit in the second image. Those who trust in the Lord are like Jerusalem in a second sense. Just as Jerusalem is surrounded by mountains, so, too, those who trust in the Lord are surrounded by the divine presence. Again, the picture is one of security. As the mountains surrounding Jerusalem were an aspect of the city's natural defenses, so the Lord was the defense of his people. In 34:7, it was the angel of the Lord who surrounded God's people to deliver them from hostile forces arrayed against them. While the Lord may use external means to protect and deliver us, this psalm teaches us to put our trust in the Lord himself and not the means he uses. It is his presence in our lives that is always the key factor.

One thing the Lord protects us from is doing wrong, and one way the Lord protects us from doing wrong is by not permitting evil to so dominate our situation that the temptation to do wrong is too strong for us. We do not know for certain whether the "wicked" were foreign oppressors or troublemakers from within the community of God's people. What we do know is that the Lord, not the wicked, ultimately rules our lives. Though for a time sin may hold sway in our world, the Lord will not let this situation endure permanently, nor will it ever be the case that yielding to sin is inevitable. God will always make a way of escape (1 Cor 10:13).

This affirmation about the security of those who trust in the Lord gives us great confidence to pray to the end that we might experience this security in this life.

A Prayer for Those Who Trust (125:4-5). In the first part of the prayer (125:4-5a), the psalmist simply asks God to see to it that people reap what they have sown. He prays that the Lord would "do good" to those who are "good." Now Psalms 14:1 and 53:1 have taught us that "not one of them does good!" So how can the psalmist refer to "those who are good"? This psalmist is not alone, for David has said that people repaid him evil for the "good" that he did (35:12), and another psalmist invites us to "do good" (37:3). This later invitation is significant, because it is coupled with the invitation to "trust" the Lord: "Trust in the LORD and do good." So, too, in Psalm 125, "those who are good" (125:4) are "those who trust in the LORD" (125:1). Doing good in this context is not a substitute for relating to God by faith; rather, it is the expression of genuine faith in the Lord. Those who do good have hearts that are in tune with God, which implies that their lives are in tune with his will. This is not to say that they are perfect, but that they are living genuine lives of faith and obedience. The prayer is that the Lord would reward those who are genuinely good through faith in the Lord by granting that they experience good in this life.

Conversely, the psalmist prays that those who turn from the Lord to crooked paths would reap what they have sown and be carried away with those who do evil. The reason for this is that their presence disturbs the peace (*shalom* [TH7965, ZH8934]) of the believers. Those who trust in the Lord are those who are for peace, but not all are for peace (120:7). The removal of those opposed to peace is part of the path to peace (see commentary on 104:31-35). As in 122:6, so too here, the psalmist prays for peace in the full sense of the term: the absence of strife and injustice and the presence of tranquility and prosperity. When the rule of evil is broken and the rule of God is manifest, there is righteousness and joy and peace through the Holy Spirit's presence (Rom 14:17). This peace of the Spirit's presence is ours because the Lord Jesus has done everything necessary to accomplish this peace by killing enmity through his death on the cross (Eph 2:14-15). Because he is the Prince of Peace (Isa 9:6), we can pray that the Israel of God (Gal 6:16) would "have peace" (125:5b) now and forevermore.

◆ T. Psalm 126

A song for pilgrims ascending to Jerusalem.

[1]When the LORD brought back his exiles
to Jerusalem,*
it was like a dream!
[2]We were filled with laughter,
and we sang for joy.
And the other nations said,
"What amazing things the LORD
has done for them."
[3]Yes, the LORD has done amazing
things for us!
What joy!

[4]Restore our fortunes,
LORD,
as streams renew the
desert.
[5]Those who plant in tears
will harvest with shouts
of joy.
[6]They weep as they go to plant
their seed,
but they sing as they return
with the harvest.

126:1 Hebrew *Zion.*

NOTES

126:1 ***brought back his exiles to Jerusalem.*** Lit., "restored the fortunes of Zion." The expression is a general one that can be applied to numerous situations (NIDOTTE 4.19; Kraus 1989:449-450; for the validity of the rendering "fortunes," see Allen 1983:170), the return from the Babylonian exile being one of them. The language of restored fortunes marks the beginning of both strophes in this psalm (see 126:4).

it was like a dream! Lit., "we were (*hayinu* [TH1961, ZH2118]) like dreamers" (see note on 126:3).

126:3 ***What joy!*** Lit., "We were (*hayinu* [TH1961, ZH2118]) glad." The repetition of "we were" (see previous note on 126:1) serves as an *inclusio* for the first strophe and underscores the theme of elation.

126:6 ***to plant their seed . . . with the harvest.*** Lit., "carrying the bag of seed . . . carrying their sheaves." The repetition of the participle "carrying" serves to underscore the reversal of circumstances: then carrying seed with tears, but now carrying sheaves with joy.

COMMENTARY

Perhaps we can all look back to days that were like a dream come true, days that were filled with joy and laughter because of a marvelous reversal of circumstances. Tears and grief were replaced with gladness and joy when the Lord intervened to bring restoration, whether that restoration was of a broken relationship, a sick body, or a tormented mind. Psalm 126:1-3 remembers with joy this restoration experience. The joy of those past days may not, however, characterize our present situation because of some new adversity we are experiencing. Prayer for restoration may now be the cry of our heart, as is the case in 126:4-6. The Holy Spirit teaches us through Psalm 126 how to overcome present adversity by remembering the past and praying for the future.

Remembering Restoration. "When the LORD restored" is the theme of 126:1-3. This restoration was no small matter, as can be seen from the people's response. They were elated. It was like a dream come true. Laughter filled their mouths, and joy filled their songs. The restoration in view was probably that of the return from the Babylonian captivity, given that this restoration was known about in nations outside of Israel. And this restoration was not just *known* about on the international scene; it was *celebrated* there, as well. People in other nations marveled at what the God of Israel had done in restoring his people. "What amazing things the LORD has done for them" was what the nations said in amazement. Whereas in other psalms the nations join the chorus sung by Israel (e.g., Ps 47), here Israel chimes in to agree with the joyful song of the nations: "Yes, the LORD has done amazing things for us! What joy!" (126:3).

When facing adversity in the present, it does the soul good to learn from the past. By remembering the ecstasy we tasted when the Lord restored us in the past, we experience renewal to live in the present, with hope and courage and confidence that the God who restored us from adversity back then will do so again.

Praying for Restoration. The prayer in the present is quite simple and echoes the remembrance of the past: "Restore our fortunes, LORD." "Do for us now what you did for us back then" is what we find ourselves praying at times. This simple prayer is then amplified with an agrarian image. The image begins with the onset of the rainy season as the first winter rains fall. These rains convert the waterless wadis into rushing rivers that renew the parched land and make plowing and planting possible (see commentary on 65:9-10). Planting with tears could be because of the potential for failure that confronted the farmer. Too much rain after planting could wash the seed away. Too little rain could mean the death of the newly sprouted seed.

This language may best be interpreted literally. Soon after the return from captivity, the people of God faced numerous adverse circumstances in the land. Among those adversities were poor harvests because of drought due to the people's misplaced priorities (see Hag 1:7-11). Psalm 126 fits this situation quite well. However, the agrarian imagery could have been figurative for some other set of circumstances, and we may certainly use this prayer regardless of the nature of the adversity we may be facing.

No matter what kind of setback we may have experienced, we can pray with confidence to the Lord to "restore our fortunes." As in the days of Haggai, we may need to realign ourselves with God's priorities as we pray. As we do, we pray with hope and confidence that the God who restored our fortunes in the past will do so again in the present. We pray with hope and confidence because the ultimate restoration of fortunes has already taken place in the resurrection of Jesus Christ from the dead. He who was rich became poor for our sake and was restored to his exalted status that we might experience the restorative power of God now and forevermore (2 Cor 8:9). When we experience that restoration of fortunes, we return to Psalm 126:1-3 to celebrate with great joy the amazing things that God has done for us. It is "like a dream" come true! "What joy!"

◆ U. Psalm 127

A song for pilgrims ascending to Jerusalem. A psalm of Solomon.

1 Unless the LORD builds a house,
the work of the builders is wasted.
Unless the LORD protects a city,
guarding it with sentries will do no good.

2 It is useless for you to work so hard
from early morning until late at night,
anxiously working for food to eat;
for God gives rest to his loved ones.

[3]Children are a gift from the LORD;
they are a reward from him.
[4]Children born to a young man
are like arrows in a warrior's
hands.

[5]How joyful is the man whose quiver
is full of them!
He will not be put to shame when
he confronts his accusers at the
city gates.

NOTES

127:1 ***will do no good.*** This translates the word *shaw'* [TH7723, ZH8736], which is translated "wasted" in 127:1a and "useless" in 127:2a. This threefold repetition underscores the focus of these verses: the uselessness of human self-sufficiency.

127:3 ***gift.*** Lit., "inheritance" (see commentary).

they. The Hebrew text here contains a metaphorical picture of children as "the fruit of the womb."

127:5 ***whose quiver is full of them!*** The NLT, like other English translations (e.g., NIV and NASB) use the passive voice here, despite the active voice in the word (Piel with a direct object—"who fills his quiver with them"). Perhaps the passive voice is motivated by the desire to honor the context, which certainly emphasizes divine activity. But while divine activity is paramount, human activity is not irrelevant. Similar to the passive rendering is Allen's understanding (1983:177) of the subject of the Piel to be the Lord, based on 127:3. While this interpretation is possible, the intervening material in 127:4 makes it unlikely. The natural reading of the text is to take the man as the subject (see Calvin 1979:110, Kraus 1989:452, and the syntactically analogous 1:1; 40:4 [5]).

He will not be . . . when he confronts. The verbs in the Hebrew are plural, and while they may refer to blessed fathers, generalized from the one father in the previous line, it seems more natural to understand the subject as the sons who are defending their father (see commentary).

COMMENTARY

What does it take to succeed? We frequently ask ourselves or are asked this very question by others. What does it take to succeed in the ordinary affairs of life such as building a house, maintaining safety in our communities, and earning a living? While we often turn to human endeavors to answer this question—and rightly so, because the validity of human activity is pervasively affirmed in the Scriptures—Psalm 127 provides another and essential perspective: Divine involvement in our routine affairs is what makes these activities successful.

Psalm 127 makes this positive point in two strophes. The first (127:1-2) is cast in negative terms, while the second (127:3-5) makes the point from a positive perspective.

The Uselessness of Human Self-sufficiency (127:1-2). "Useless," repeated three times in these two verses, is the key term of this strophe. In the first two lines, "useless" is the first word in the second colon. Then in the third line, "useless" is brought forward to be the first word in the first colon so as to rivet our attention on this concept. This strophe raises a number of questions. In what way is God involved in the building of one house and not in the building of another? In what sense is human activity useless without divine involvement? How do we understand the interface between divine and human activity? How does God want us to live in light of this teaching?

In some sense God is at work in all human activity. "For in him we live and move and exist" (Acts 17:28). "He makes everything work out according to his plan" (Eph 1:11). "The LORD has made everything for his own purposes, even the wicked for a day of disaster" (Prov 16:4). Yet the psalmist presumes that there is some sense in which God is not involved in some human activity. There are times when we can say, "God was not in that," at least in some sense.

"Useless" here seems to mean "not producing the desired result." Why do people build houses? Why do people strive to build safe communities? Why do people toil to earn a living? The answer appears to be found in the *shalom* [TH7965, ZH8934] that is a running motif in the Psalms of Ascent (120:6, 7; 122:6, 7, 8; 125:5; 128:6). People want "peace" in the full sense of the term, the absence of harm and the presence of tranquility with prosperity (see 122:6). When people strive for this good end without faith in God and in ways contrary to his principles, God is not "in it," and they do not experience the *shalom* they are looking for. When people work with total dependence on self and without faith in God, their activities are "useless"—they do not produce the desired result. The desired result is *shalom,* but the actual experience is the opposite. This is pictured for us in 127:2, which portrays people having to rise before dawn and work into the wee hours of the night only to sit down and eat with an anxious heart—hardly the *shalom* they are seeking to attain.

The alternative is to be vigorously engaged in all of life's activities out of faith in God and in keeping with his principles. Then our hard work will be accompanied not by anxiety but by a sleeplike tranquility. We can do our very best, leaving the outcome in God's hands and experiencing sleep at night as one part of the *shalom* we experience throughout the day. God's will is this: "Whatever you do, do well" (Eccl 9:10; see 1 Cor 10:31) and "My righteous ones will live by faith" (Heb 10:38).

The Fruitfulness of Divine Agency (127:3-5). The theme shifts in this strophe from uselessness to fruitfulness, and the key term here is "children." The word for "children" occurs in 127:3a and 127:4a. In addition, children are referred to by means of a pronoun in 127:5a and figuratively in 127:3b as, literally, "the fruit of the womb." By focusing on children, the poet is portraying for us the fruitfulness in all of life that is ours when God is at work in our lives as we trust him and live out his principles. Children are a central aspect of the *shalom* [TH7965, ZH8934] we long for, as 128:6 will make clear: "May you live to enjoy your grandchildren. May Israel have peace [*shalom*]!"

Children are a reminder that we must live by faith in God's work in our lives, even as we work to build a home. On the one hand, children are an inheritance (see note on 127:3). An inheritance is a gift granted by the Lord, not a wage paid out to a worker. On the other hand, children are a reward (NIDOTTE 3.1245), the fruit of a woman's womb and the result of a man's activity in filling his quiver with them. Thus, the complementary perspectives on human and divine activity from the first strophe are reiterated in this second strophe.

The point of all this is that children contribute to and are a key component of the *shalom* we long for. Children (in the Old Testament culture, sons in particular) are likened to arrows in a warrior's quiver. These arrows would have been used to defend against the aggression of the enemy and thereby to establish safety within the city. So, too, the man who fills his quiver with children is pictured as having more than adequate defense, should he, for example, find himself embroiled in some legal dispute with personal enemies in the city gates, the place where legal matters would have been adjudicated. God would have established *shalom* through the agency of vigorous children.

Of course, the teaching of this psalm pertains to matters of the spirit as well as matters of the body. Thus Paul teaches us, "Work hard to show the results of your salvation, obeying God with deep reverence and fear. For God is working in you, giving you the desire and the power to do what pleases him" (Phil 2:12-13). The central teaching of this psalm, applicable to both body and spirit, is that when we turn away from self-sufficiency and replace it with a faith in God that lives out his principles, our activities are not useless but are fruitful—they produce the desired result of *shalom*. They are fruitful because God is at work in them and through them.

◆ V. Psalm 128

A song for pilgrims ascending to Jerusalem.

1 How joyful are those who fear
the LORD—
all who follow his ways!
2 You will enjoy the fruit of your labor.
How joyful and prosperous you
will be!
3 Your wife will be like a fruitful
grapevine,
flourishing within your home.
Your children will be like vigorous
young olive trees
as they sit around your table.
4 That is the LORD's blessing
for those who fear him.

5 May the LORD continually bless
you from Zion.
May you see Jerusalem prosper
as long as you live.
6 May you live to enjoy your
grandchildren.
May Israel have peace!

NOTES

128:1 ***How joyful.*** For a discussion on the word *'ashre* [TH835A, ZH897], see note on 1:1.

128:2 ***You will enjoy the fruit of your labor.*** Lit., "You will eat the produce of your hands." The verb "eat" recalls 127:2, where those who do not live in keeping with God's principles eat with anxiety-ridden hearts.

128:4 ***blessing.*** When God is the subject and humans are the object of the Heb. *barak* [TH1288A, ZH1385] in the Piel, the sense is that God "furnishes them with the power of fertility and growth, and he grants them life, happiness, and success" (TLOT 1.273). Here the Pual means that those who fear the Lord are thus empowered with life by the Lord.

128:5 ***May you see.*** For the imperative used as a wish form, see Waltke and O'Connor 1990:§34.4b. This same use of the imperative is found in 128:6, "May you live to enjoy."

128:6 ***peace.*** The word is *shalom* [TH7965, ZH8934].

COMMENTARY

Psalm 128 is a companion to Psalm 127. Psalm 128 amplifies Psalm 127, as it begins where Psalm 127 leaves off: "How joyful" (127:5; 128:1). The focus on family and work ties the two together. However, Psalm 128 does not contain any of the negative perspective found in Psalm 127. Instead, it brings in the "fear of the LORD" as the key to experiencing the blessed life pictured for us in 128:1-4 and prayed for in 128:5-6.

A Picture of the Blessed Life (128:1-4). Like Psalm 1, Psalm 128 begins with *'ashre* [TH835A, ZH897], a word that speaks of well-being in every area of life (see commentary on Ps 112). The Hebrew word *'ashre* opens the first colon of 128:1 and the last colon of 128:2, focusing our attention on well-being or blessedness as the key theme of this psalm.

Psalm 128 teaches us again what 112:1 has already taught us—a life of blessedness is experienced by those who fear the Lord. Psalm 128 makes this point emphatically as the expression "who fear the LORD" is found in the opening and closing cola of the first strophe (128:1a and 128:4b). The fear of the Lord includes a number of aspects, and the aspect in view here is found in 128:1b: To fear the Lord is to follow his ways. To fear the Lord is to live in keeping with the principles he has revealed to us. Living in accord with God's principles brings great benefit into our lives. As Mays (1994:404) has said, "Well doing and doing well are interdependent." This is not to bring a legalism or perfectionism into our walk with God, for part of living in keeping with his principles is to acknowledge our failures and receive God's forgiveness freely offered to us based on the perfect obedience of Jesus Christ (1 John 1:6-10).

While doing well in all areas of life is included in the meaning of *'ashre* [TH835A, ZH897], two areas of life are singled out in this psalm: work and family. Psalm 127:2 paints the picture of the futility of working hard from sunup into the wee hours of the night, only to eat food with an anxious heart. By way of contrast, 128:2 paints a picture of experiencing joy and satisfaction in work in terms of "eating the fruit of your labor."[1] This language is probably rooted in the literal experience of ancient farmers eating the produce from the fields that their hands worked, but the language can be stretched to include all joy and satisfaction experienced in all of life's work.

As in Psalm 127, so in Psalm 128, pride of place goes to well-being in the family. Fertility and health are experienced by those who follow the ways of the Lord. Not barrenness, but fertility characterizes the home of those who fear the Lord. As the man had a quiver full of children in the previous psalm, here his wife is likened to a vine laden with grapes. In both images an abundance of children correlates with an abundance of divine blessing. The agricultural image continues as these children are likened to olive trees planted all around the dinner table. The picture of the table picks up the opening image of eating the produce of one's hands. A husband and father, a wife and mother, a plethora of children enjoying a good meal around a common table—this was the quintessential picture of prosperity in the ancient world.

The first strophe closes with the declaration that the previous picture of the well-being (*'ashre* [TH835A, ZH897]) that characterizes those who fear the Lord is at the same time a description of how those who fear the Lord are "blessed" (*barak* [TH1288A, ZH1385]). The word *barak* is a rough synonym of *'ashre* (TLOT 1.273); the latter focuses on the resultant state of well-being, while the former focuses on the divine empowerment that brings about that well-being. Fearing the Lord by following his ways is the path to experiencing the empowerment that results in blessedness.

A Prayer for the Blessed Life (128:5-6). The response to this description of well-being in work and family is prayer. Since the Lord empowers, the Lord is petitioned. "May the LORD continually bless [*barak*] you from Zion" is the basic petition (128:5). Zion was the location of the divine presence, and the divine presence is the source of all blessing (see also 134:3).

Zion (Jerusalem) is not only the source of blessing but also the larger sphere of blessing. The second petition is, therefore, for the prosperity of Jerusalem. As Jerusalem prospered, so too would all who lived in Jerusalem. So the prayer is that Jerusalem would prosper as long as the psalmist lived. We do not live in Jerusalem, and the divine presence is no longer specially present there (see John 4:21). Jesus Christ is the divine presence (John 1:1, 18). All blessings are ours in him (Eph 1:3; Mays 1994:403). All the riches necessary to meet our every need are available in Christ (Phil 4:19).

The next petition returns to the sphere of the family. Living to see and enjoy grandchildren was one of the chief blessings in the ancient world (see Job 42:16-17). Then we return to a final petition for *shalom* on all Israel. *Shalom* [TH7965, ZH8934] is a synonym for both *'ashre* [TH835A, ZH897] and *barak* [TH1288A, ZH1385] (blessed). *Shalom* is not only peace in the sense of the absence of strife, but it is also "well-being, success, good fortune" (TLOT 3.1339). The hope and prayer of the ancient was for well-being for the individual, the family, the city, and the nation. In keeping with the eschatological thrust of the Psalms and the scope of the new covenant (Matt 28:19), we expand this prayer even further to include all the nations of the earth. Our prayer is that, through the messianic king, all nations will be blessed (72:17).

ENDNOTES

1. For "eating" as a figure for joy and satisfaction, see Eccl 2:24; 3:13; 5:18-20.

◆ W. Psalm 129

A song for pilgrims ascending to Jerusalem.

1 From my earliest youth my enemies
have persecuted me.
Let all Israel repeat this:
2 From my earliest youth my enemies
have persecuted me,
but they have never defeated me.
3 My back is covered with cuts,
as if a farmer had plowed long
furrows.
4 But the LORD is good;
he has cut me free from the ropes
of the ungodly.
5 May all who hate Jerusalem*
be turned back in shameful defeat.
6 May they be as useless as grass on a
rooftop,
turning yellow when only half grown,
7 ignored by the harvester,
despised by the binder.
8 And may those who pass by
refuse to give them this
blessing:
"The LORD bless you;
we bless you in the LORD's name."

129:5 Hebrew *Zion*.

NOTES

129:1 ***earliest.*** The NLT takes the adverb *rabbath* [TH7227A, ZH8041] as modifying "youth." Word order and parallel uses (65:9 [10]; 123:4) would argue for taking the adverb here and in the following verse as modifying the verb: "From my youth my enemies have *severely* persecuted me" (see HALOT 3.1172, "in rich measure").

129:4 ***good.*** The word *tsaddiq* [TH6662, ZH7404] means "righteous" and is the opposite of the word *resha'im* [TH7563, ZH8401] (the ungodly) in the following colon.

COMMENTARY

Though the tone and mood of Psalm 129 are quite different from that of the previous psalm, Psalm 129 does provide a kind of sequel to Psalm 128. The agricultural imagery from Psalm 128 is continued in Psalm 129, as is the passion for the well-being of Zion (Jerusalem). Both psalms likewise use the word "bless" (*barak* [TH1288A, ZH1385]) as a key term. The key differences are (1) rather than describing the well-being of those who fear the Lord (128:1-4), Psalm 129 begins by celebrating victory over the enemies of Israel in 129:1-4; and (2) rather than praying for "blessing" (*barak;* 128:5-6), Psalm 129 prays for the withholding of "blessing" (*barak*) in 129:5-8.

A Celebration of Deliverance (129:1-4). Though written in first person, 129:1-4 is the testimony of Israel as a whole. This is clear from 129:1b, where Israel is invited to use the words provided by the psalmist (Mays 1994:404).

For a long time ("from my earliest youth") and with great intensity (*rabbath* [TH7227A, ZH8041]), an unnamed adversary had persecuted Israel. Both the length of time and the intensity of the persecution are underscored by the repetition of the same language in 129:1a and 129:2a. The pain and agony of the persecution are graphically portrayed by the image of a farmer cutting a deep and long furrow on the back of the psalmist. But the final and determinative cut was not made by the enemy. It was rather made by the Lord, when the Lord cut the cords that had bound the tortured psalmist. In spite of the length and intensity of the torment, Israel came out victorious. The enemy was not able to finish Israel off once and for all because the Lord showed himself to be a righteous savior. It is this righteous salvation that the delivered community celebrates.

The Holy Spirit here teaches us neither to forget nor to take for granted but to celebrate the deliverance that the Lord has granted us in our own experiences in life, especially that greatest of all deliverances, the deliverance from sin (see 130:3-4).

A Prayer for No Blessing (129:5-8). Whereas the psalmist of Psalm 128 prayed for blessing in the form of agricultural and familial success (see 128:2, 5-6), the psalmist of Psalm 129 prays that "all who hate Jerusalem" would experience no such blessing. The "shameful defeat" (129:5) prayed for would come in the form of a failed harvest (129:5-7). The enemy is pictured as grass on a rooftop, which withers as soon as it sprouts because of the intense sun and lack of moisture. This grass is described as being so useless that the reaper does not bother to take it in hand, nor does the one who binds the grain bother to gather it in the fold of his garment. Since the harvest is pictured as such a complete failure, it is impossible to think that a passerby would invoke the blessing of the Lord on such farmers. The prayer is that there be no concrete evidence of divine blessing in the lives of the enemy.

Jesus has taught us to pray *for* those who persecute us, not against them (Matt 5:44). In the same way, the apostle Paul has taught us to bless those who persecute us (Rom 12:14). The blessing we desire for ourselves (128:5-6) we should desire for all others, even our opponents in this life. The difference in perspective between the two testaments can best be attributed to differing redemptive-historical contexts. Ancient Israel was a theocracy that anticipated the eternal order with its judgment and separation of the righteous and the wicked. The gospel age is a time of salvation, during which God exercises his patience that is intended to lead people to repentance (Rom 2:4; 2 Pet 3:9). Our attitudes and actions toward our enemies are, therefore, quite different from those of ancient Israelites.

◆ X. Psalm 130

A song for pilgrims ascending to Jerusalem.

1 From the depths of despair, O LORD,
I call for your help.
2 Hear my cry, O Lord.
Pay attention to my prayer.

3 LORD, if you kept a record of our sins,
who, O Lord, could ever survive?
4 But you offer forgiveness,
that we might learn to fear you.

5 I am counting on the LORD;
yes, I am counting on him.
I have put my hope in his word.
6 I long for the Lord
more than sentries long for the dawn,
yes, more than sentries long for the dawn.

7 O Israel, hope in the LORD;
for with the LORD there is unfailing love.
His redemption overflows.
8 He himself will redeem Israel
from every kind of sin.

NOTES

130:5 *I am counting on.* The word *qawah* [TH6960, ZH7747] means "to wait for," "to hope" (HALOT 3.1082) and is a synonym of *yakhal* [TH3176, ZH3498] ("wait," "hope"; HALOT 2.407) used at the end of this verse ("I have put my hope in") and in 130:7.

COMMENTARY

What Martin Luther said about Psalm 13 applies equally to Psalm 130, which likewise articulates the "state in which Hope despairs, and yet Despair hopes at the same time" (quoted in Perowne 1966:1.180). In the beginning the psalmist is crying out from the depths of despair, but in the end he is encouraging others to hope in the Lord (130:7), even as he himself is hoping in the Lord and his word (130:5-6). The nature of the psalmist's distress is not at all clear, though personal sin is at least part of the cause (130:3). Since sin is part of the cause, forgiveness is part of the solution (130:4, 8). But deliverance from the depths requires deliverance from sin's misery as well as its guilt, so the hope of the psalm is hope for redemption (130:7).

Psalm 130 can be divided into four strophes, each comprised of two poetic lines. The first focuses on the cry for help (130:1-2), the second on the prayer for forgiveness (130:3-4), the third on the hope for divine intervention (130:5-6), and the final on the encouragement of others (130:7-8).

Crying for Help (130:1-2). "The word 'depths' . . . names the chaotic forces that confront human life with destruction, devastation, and death, and that are regularly symbolized by water" (McCann 1996:1205). It is as if the psalmist was about to drown in the deep waters of personal distress (see 69:1-2, 14). But like Jonah (Jonah 2:2), the psalmist did not give up and die but cried out (*qara'* [TH7121, ZH7924]) to God from that watery abyss of despair. He pleaded with God to hear his cry for help and to answer his prayer. When there seems to be no hope in our circumstances, as was the case with Abraham (see Rom 4:18), God is there. We can cry out to him from our own depths and believe him for what we cannot see at the moment.

Asking for Forgiveness (130:3-4). If the prerequisite for our hoping in God to deliver us is our own moral perfection, then we truly have no hope. If God were to hold us personally accountable for our sins with strict justice, then who could ever survive? The truth is that God does not punish us for all our sins, nor does he deal with us as we deserve (103:10), for he is "a God of forgiveness, gracious and merciful, slow to become angry, and rich in unfailing love" (Neh 9:17). His forgiveness has, as one of its goals, the restoration of our relationship with him, "that we might learn to fear [him]" (130:4b). To fear the Lord, as we have seen in 128:1, involves our walking in his ways. God does not forgive so that we will continue on the wrong path. He forgives so that we might turn from the path of destruction and walk the path of life out of gratitude for his grace.

Waiting for the Lord (130:5-6). While deliverance from sin's guilt comes immediately, deliverance from sin's consequences may take time. So we, like the psalmist, find ourselves having to wait. Psalm 130:5 draws out the language of waiting, even as our waiting is at times drawn out: "I am counting [waiting] on the Lord; yes, I am counting [waiting] . . . I have put my hope in his word." Then in 130:6 a drawn-out picture is added to intensify the nature of the waiting: "I long [wait] . . . more than sentries long [wait] . . . yes, more than sentries long [wait] for the dawn." But this waiting is the waiting of hope, as the verbs employed could just as easily be translated with the word "hope." While still in the depths, we hope in the Lord and in particular in his word of promise. We find that word of promise in the final strophe.

Encouraging Others (130:7-8). The psalmist must have encouraged his own soul even as he turned to give a word of promise to those around him and more so to all the people of God. The word of promise is the foundation of hope. That word of promise is a word about who God is and what God does. The Lord is characterized by "unfailing love." Nothing, absolutely nothing, can ever separate us from that love that is ours through faith in Christ Jesus (see Rom 8:38-39). This unfailing love is the fountain from which "his redemption overflows." So we can have confidence that God will free us "from all our iniquities" (130:8, lit.). The word translated "iniquities" can refer to (1) sin, (2) the guilt that comes from sin, or (3) the punishment and misery that comes from the guilt of sin (HALOT 2.800). Perhaps the word is used here and elsewhere to refer to this whole complex of ideas: sin and guilt and misery. The word "all" (NLT, "every") fits with the idea, and the Bible clearly teaches elsewhere that God saves people from the guilt of sin and from its misery. Could an overflowing supply of salvation arising from the unfailing love of God do less? Never.

◆ Y. Psalm 131

A song for pilgrims ascending to Jerusalem. A psalm of David.

1 **LORD, my heart is not proud;**
my eyes are not haughty.
I don't concern myself with matters too great
or too awesome for me to grasp.
2 **Instead, I have calmed and quieted myself,**
like a weaned child who no longer cries for its mother's milk.
Yes, like a weaned child is my soul within me.

3 **O Israel, put your hope in the LORD—**
now and always.

NOTES

131:1 ***I don't concern myself.*** Lit., "I do not walk about in" (see commentary).

COMMENTARY

We live in a noisy world. External noises bombard our ears daily—the noise of jets and freeways and lawn mowers and sirens. Then there are all the internal noises of deadlines and commitments and activities. At a deeper level still is the noise of anxiety and fear and uncertainty and guilt. The problem is not one of finding a time and place to be alone. The problem is how to find quietness for the soul in the middle of all of life's noises (Gire 1996:27). Inner quietness in the middle of a noisy world is possible, and Psalm 131 shows the way.

Two Requirements. Psalm 131 sets forth two requirements for experiencing inner quietness. The first requirement is, odd as it may seem, effort. Quietness takes effort. Now, quietness certainly is a gift of God's grace. "Whatever is good and perfect comes down to us from God our Father, who created all the lights in the heavens" (Jas 1:17). This gift is ours through faith in the Lord Jesus, who has accomplished everything necessary for us to live with still and quiet souls. Yet quietness is our responsibility, a result of our effort. Note that the psalmist said, "I have calmed and quieted myself." The Hebrew here is emphatic, being in the form of an oath, and stresses the need for our taking intentional steps to experience inner quietness and peace. The psalmist does not tell us what he did to quiet his soul, but there are concrete steps to take when the noise level begins to rise. The first step is simply to acknowledge the noise by saying something like "I feel afraid" or "I feel worried," whatever the case may be. A second step is to recall Scripture. Is the noise fear? Bring to mind 56:3b-4. Is the noise worry? Bring to mind Matthew 6:25-31. Having Scripture stored up in our hearts is of great benefit to quieting our souls in the middle of daily activities. A third step is to ask God for what you want and then to trust him to give you what you need (Matt 6:32-34). These steps can be taken at any time—while in a meeting or on the highway, while at the park with the children, or at an interview for a job.

The second requirement is humility. Humility is the opposite of arrogance, and arrogance and quietness cannot occupy the same space. Note how inner quietness is first of all a matter of the heart: "My heart is not proud" (131:1). A heart that is arrogant is usually a heart that feels insecure, insignificant, or out of control. Such a heart looks through the eyes ("my eyes are not haughty") to find ways to satisfy the deep longings for security, significance, and control. The result is often a frantic running around (lit., "I have not walked about"), faster and faster, doing more to have more, to be more. Arrogance increases the noise level within. Humility and quietness, by contrast, are roommates. They are the fruit of three truths. We are absolutely secure in the love that God has for us in Christ Jesus (Rom 8:38-39). All of our activities in the Lord are significant because of the resurrection (1 Cor 15:58). We can take charge of our lives because God is in control of all things for our good (Rom 8:28-32). As we focus our hearts on God—his love, purpose, and power—inner quietness is ours.

Two Results. The first result of our effort and humility is quietness within. The picture the psalmist paints is that of a weaned child on its mother's lap. Anyone who has been around a hungry nursing baby knows that when that baby is near the mother's breast, the picture is anything but one of quietness. By way of contrast, a weaned child can be near the breast with no grasping and no agitation—still, quiet, and tranquil. This is a picture of what our lives can be like, regardless of what is going on in the world around us. Though there may be noise all around, there can be quietness within for the humble of heart.

The second result is ministry to others. As soon as David has quieted his own soul, he begins to minister to others: "O Israel, put your hope in the LORD" (131:3). Inner quietness is not a retreat into self-centeredness, but it is an inner-centeredness from which we reach out to others. We, like David, want others to experience what we have experienced. By definition, one who hopes in the Lord is one who is humble, so one who hopes in the Lord is one who has inner quietness. Hoping in the Lord is turning away from self-sufficient, frantic living and turning to a quiet dependence on God (see Ps 127). Hoping in the Lord is a quiet dependence on the God who is characterized by "unfailing love" (130:7) and who gives overflowing redemption (130:8).

Noise and quietness are not mutually exclusive. We may not be able to control the noise level in the world around us, but we can control the noise level within. God has made a way for us to quiet our souls like a weaned child on its mother's lap. By hoping in him, we can experience quietness in a noisy world.

◆ Z. Psalm 132

A song for pilgrims ascending to Jerusalem.

1 LORD, remember David
and all that he suffered.
2 He made a solemn promise to the LORD.
He vowed to the Mighty One of Israel,*
3 "I will not go home;
I will not let myself rest.
4 I will not let my eyes sleep
nor close my eyelids in slumber
5 until I find a place to build a house for the LORD,
a sanctuary for the Mighty One of Israel."
6 We heard that the Ark was in Ephrathah;
then we found it in the distant countryside of Jaar.
7 Let us go to the sanctuary of the LORD;
let us worship at the footstool of his throne.
8 Arise, O LORD, and enter your resting place,

along with the Ark, the symbol of
your power.
9 May your priests be clothed in
godliness;
may your loyal servants sing for joy.
10 For the sake of your servant David,
do not reject the king you have
anointed.
11 The LORD swore an oath to David
with a promise he will never take
back:
"I will place one of your descendants
on your throne.
12 If your descendants obey the terms of
my covenant
and the laws that I teach them,
then your royal line
will continue forever and ever."
13 For the LORD has chosen Jerusalem*;
he has desired it for his home.
14 "This is my resting place forever,"
he said.
"I will live here, for this is the home
I desired.
15 I will bless this city and make it
prosperous;
I will satisfy its poor with food.
16 I will clothe its priests with
godliness;
its faithful servants will sing
for joy.
17 Here I will increase the power of David;
my anointed one will be a light for
my people.
18 I will clothe his enemies with shame,
but he will be a glorious king."

132:2 Hebrew *of Jacob;* also in 132:5. See note on 44:4. **132:13** Hebrew *Zion.*

NOTES

132:11 *swore.* This same verb is translated "made a solemn promise" in 132:2. The repetition serves to mark the beginnings of the two strophes of the poem, one focusing on David's oath to the Lord and the other on the Lord's oath to David.

132:17 *increase the power of.* The image in the Hebrew is that of "causing a horn to grow." The horn was a symbol of power.

my anointed one will be a light for my people. The Hebrew text is figurative: "I will prepare a lamp for my anointed one." In light of the previous colon, the "anointed one" is David. "Preparing a lamp" is a metaphorical reference to providing a son to sit on the throne of David. This metaphor is used in 1 Kgs 11:36; 15:4; 2 Kgs 8:19.

COMMENTARY

Sometimes our hearts are filled with mixed emotions. This was also the case with ancient pilgrims when they made their way to Jerusalem after returning from captivity in Babylon. The Babylonians had destroyed the two key institutions in the life of Israel: the Temple and the monarchy. Early on in the postexilic community the Temple was rebuilt, and this was a cause of great joy (see Ezra 6:15-16). It was also a time of joy for pilgrims as they journeyed to Jerusalem and saw the rebuilt Temple. But the monarchy was never reestablished. There was no Davidic king reigning over Israel, and this in spite of the promise that David would always have a son reigning on the throne (see, e.g., 89:35-37). So pilgrimage to Jerusalem probably also brought up feelings of sadness and confusion. Psalm 132 provided those pilgrims words to express the longings of their heart for the coming of the son of David to reign over them.

While Jerusalem plays a major role in this psalm, center stage is held by the dynasty of David. The first half of the psalm is a prayer for the restoration of the dynasty (132:1-10). The second half provides God's answer to that prayer with a reaffirmation of the promise to David (132:11-18).

A Prayer for David's Dynasty (132:1-10). Two related petitions surround this first strophe: "LORD, remember David" (132:1) and "do not reject the king" (132:10). Psalm 132:1-10 is thus a prayer for the continuance of the Davidic dynasty. This prayer no doubt had profound meaning for those living in the aftermath of the Exile and return, when there was no Davidic king reigning in Jerusalem. That God had promised David a perpetual dynasty was clear. How that promise was working out in history was not so clear (see 89:49). We, likewise, at times understand God's promises all too well but are perplexed when we don't see those promises coming to reality in our lives. By faith we keep on praying as we continue our journey.

The majority of the strophe serves to motivate the Lord to answer the petitions. The first reason given is "all that [David] suffered." In a similar way, the psalmist in 89:50 asks God to "remember" (NLT, "consider") the disgrace of the community. The reference in Psalm 132 is probably to all of the hardships David experienced after his anointing and before his coronation, when he was the object of Saul's jealous rage. These hard times were, however, part of the path David had to walk in preparation for his establishment of God's dwelling in Jerusalem. That is the subject of 132:2-9.

David swore an oath to the effect that nothing would stop him from providing God a dwelling place (132:2-5). Psalm 132:6-18 recalls a major accomplishment of David in this regard—his bringing the Ark of the Covenant up from Kiriath-jearim to Jerusalem. That David suffered much but finally succeeded in securing Jerusalem and bringing the Ark there was to motivate the Lord to keep the promise he had made to David. Similarly, Nehemiah sought to motivate the Lord to act on his behalf, based on what Nehemiah had done for the Lord (Neh 13:14, 22, 31). As Nehemiah 13:22 makes clear, such motivation is not contradictory to God's acting in mercy and grace but is complementary to it: "Remember this good deed also, O my God! Have compassion on me according to your great and unfailing love." While we are always aware of our need for God's mercy and grace, we can also ask him to act on our behalf, based on our service to him.

A Promise to David's Dynasty (132:11-18). A reaffirmation of God's promise comes to the pilgrims in response to their prayer. Just as David had sworn an oath (*nishba'* [TH7650, ZH8678]; 132:2) to the Lord, the Lord swore an oath (*nishba'*; 132:11) to David. The Lord swore never to *take back* (*shub* [TH7725, ZH8740]; 132:11) his promise, and in short, that promise is that the Lord will not *reject* (*shub*; 132:10b) the Davidic dynasty. As in Psalm 89, so too here, individual sons may not participate in the promise owing to their own personal failures, but the promise to the dynasty stands firm: The Lord will increase the power of David and will maintain a lamp (keep a son) on the throne (132:17).

The reason the Lord gives for keeping his promise directly correlates with the reason the pilgrims used to motivate him to keep the promise: Jerusalem. Here, however, it is not David's responsibilities with respect to Jerusalem, but it is God's own choice of Jerusalem (132:13-14). The dovetailing of human responsibility (132:1-10) and divine sovereignty (132:11-18) is a hallmark of the Bible's own presentation of these two concepts. Because the Lord desired and chose Jerusalem as his dwelling place, he himself will see to it that Jerusalem prospers (132:15;

see 128:5). Part of that prosperity will involve the increased power of the Davidic dynasty, which necessitates the glorious maintenance of that dynasty.

The postexilic community continued to sing this psalm by faith until the promise came to fulfillment in the Lord Jesus Christ. Zechariah no doubt had 132:17 in mind when he said in reference to Jesus, God "has sent us a mighty Savior from the royal line of his servant David" (Luke 1:69). A wooden translation of Luke 1:69 would be "raised up a horn of salvation," which echoes 132:17. Jesus is the promised Son of David. God's promise may have been delayed from a human point of view, but the promise came true. Since Jesus has come, we can be confident that all of God's promises to us will likewise come true, because all of God's promises are absolutely certain in Christ (2 Cor 1:20). When our hearts are filled with mixed emotions, especially because of the apparent gap between what God has promised and what we are experiencing, we pray in faith and we journey by faith in the certain promise of God.

◆ AA. Psalm 133

A song for pilgrims ascending to Jerusalem. A psalm of David.

**1 How wonderful and pleasant it is
when brothers live together in harmony!
2 For harmony is as precious as the anointing oil
that was poured over Aaron's head,
that ran down his beard
and onto the border of his robe.
3 Harmony is as refreshing as the dew from Mount Hermon
that falls on the mountains of Zion.
And there the LORD has pronounced his blessing,
even life everlasting.**

NOTES

133:1 ***wonderful.*** The word *tob* [TH2896, ZH3202] (good for the intended purpose) is the same word used throughout Gen 1 (see commentary).

133:2 ***precious.*** The word translated "precious" is *tob* [TH2896, ZH3202], which occurs in 133:1, where it is translated "wonderful." This repetition underscores the link between the affirmation in 133:1 and the image in 133:2.

133:2-3 ***poured . . . ran . . . falls.*** These three English words all translate the same word, *yored* [TH3381, ZH3718] (descend). The repetition seems to dramatize the descent of the Lord's blessing on those who live in unity.

133:3 ***has pronounced.*** The word is *tsiwwah* [TH6680, ZH7422] (command). When used with "blessing," the sense is "send" (see Lev 25:21; Deut 28:8; HALOT 3.1011). The perfect tense is here used to express a general truth (Joüon and Muraoka 1991:§112d; Waltke and O'Connor 1990:§30.4b).

COMMENTARY

Harmony in the home is a deep longing of the human heart. The harmony of the first home ended when sin entered the world, and the relationship of the first two brothers ended in murder. Strife has sought to displace harmony in the home ever since, but strife was not God's original intention. Psalm 133 celebrates God's original design of a harmonious home by praising harmony (133:1), painting two pictures of harmony (133:2-3a), and promising a blessing for harmony in the home (133:3b).

Praise of Harmony (133:1). Harmony in the home is praised as "good" and "pleasant." Just as all of God's original works of creation were said to be "good" (Gen 1:1–2:3), so harmony in the home is "good" (NLT, "wonderful"). Harmony is God's design for the home. "Good" here means that the home functions according to God's intended purpose when harmony reigns (see NIDOTTE 2.353). Harmony also makes the home a pleasant place for family members and for others who enter the home. A home that is "good" and "pleasant" is a godly home, for God himself is "good" and "pleasant" (135:3). Festive occasions, as when the ancient Israelites made pilgrimage to Jerusalem or when we celebrate holidays, are quintessential times for experiencing the goodness and pleasantness of a harmonious home. To describe this harmony the psalmist paints two pictures for us.

Pictures of Harmony (133:2–3a). First of all, harmony is like the oil used to anoint Aaron. The anointing oil was a fragrant mixture of olive oil and spices (Exod 30:22-28). The simile was probably intended to evoke the fragrance of the oil. It was no doubt a pleasant fragrance and therefore appropriate as a comparison for the pleasantness of harmony in the home.

The second picture is that of the copious dew of Mount Hermon. Dew from Mount Hermon does not literally fall on Mount Zion. The picture is that of a superabundance of dew on Mount Zion. In ancient Israel dew played a significant role in agriculture (NIDOTTE 2.363), as it refreshed the dry ground and the plants. Harmony is likewise a source of refreshment for all who enter the harmonious home.

Both the oil and the dew have a characteristic in common that is also part of the image in addition to their fragrant and refreshing qualities: Both are said to descend. The verb *yarad* [TH3381, ZH3718] (descend) is used three times in these two images ("poured . . . ran . . . falls"). It seems that the poet also wants us to picture harmony as coming down from above (see Jas 1:17). It is a gift of God's grace. Harmony is "good" and "pleasant," because it comes from the God who is himself "good" and "pleasant" (see note on 135:3). We have to do everything we can to live in harmony with others (Rom 12:18), and we must trust God to grant the gift of harmony through our efforts.

Promise for Harmony (133:3b). God not only grants harmony as a gift as we do our part to live at peace with others, but he also goes on to bless us when we live in harmony. "Blessing" (*barak* [TH1288A, ZH1385]) is a theme in previous Psalms of Ascent (128:4, 5; 129:8; 132:15) and will be in the final Psalm of Ascent (134:3). In this psalm we are taught that blessing descends like oil and dew where people are living in harmony. This underscores the importance of doing our utmost to live at peace with others (Rom 12:18). The blessing that descends on harmonious living is nothing short of life in all of its fullness.

As believers, we are one body, indwelt by one Spirit, having one Lord and one Father, so we work to keep ourselves united in the Holy Spirit (Eph 4:3-6). Christ's purpose was and is to create one new person from many believers (Eph 2:15), so we live in harmony with his purpose when we live in harmony with others. As we do so, we receive the blessing of life from his gracious hand.

◆ BB. Psalm 134

A song for pilgrims ascending to Jerusalem.

[1] **Oh, praise the LORD, all you**
servants of the LORD,
you who serve at night
in the house of the
LORD.

[2] **Lift up holy hands in prayer,**
and praise the LORD.

[3] **May the LORD, who made**
heaven and earth,
bless you from Jerusalem.*

134:3 Hebrew *Zion*.

NOTES

134:1 ***all you servants of the* LORD.** In the context of the pilgrim psalms (Pss 120–134), the "servants of the LORD" are probably lay worshipers rather than priests or Levites. This same phrase is used in a general call to worship in 113:1, and the word "servant" is used in 135:14 for all of God's people (Mays 1994:414).

134:2 ***Lift up holy hands in prayer.*** A wooden translation of the phrase would be, "Lift up your hands holiness." "Holiness" is an adverbial accusative, requiring some kind of qualification in English. The NLT's interpretation is possible, but it is better to understand the accusative as "direction toward" (Allen 1983:216). The situation in view is probably that of worshipers in the Temple courtyard (see 135:2) being instructed by a priest to raise their hands in worship toward the Temple proper (see 28:2 for an analogous situation).

COMMENTARY

"Blessing" is the concluding theme of the Psalms of Ascent, as the verb "bless" (*barak* [TH1288A, ZH1385]) occurs once in each verse. The verb "bless" has been used five times up to this point in these psalms (124:6; 128:4, 5; 129:8; 132:15), and the noun "blessing" has been used two times (129:8; 133:3). So Psalm 134 serves as a fitting conclusion to the Psalms of Ascent. "Bless" has been used for human praise of deity (124:6) and for divine empowerment of humans (128:4, 5; 132:15; 133:3). "Bless" is used in both directions in this psalm, which focuses on "mutuality of blessing" (McCann 1996:1217): our blessing God (134:1-2) and God blessing us (134:3).

Bless the Lord (134:1-2). "Bless the Lord" (lit.) forms an *inclusio* around these two verses, as it opens 134:1 and closes 134:2, and this *inclusio* centers our thoughts on the main idea. To bless the Lord is to praise him as the ultimate source of all blessing. To bless the Lord is to attribute to him all empowerment that makes life possible. To bless the Lord is to confess our ultimate dependence upon him for all that we are, do, and have in this life. It is thus appropriate that those who bless the Lord are called "servants of the LORD," for servants depend on their master for all of life (see 123:2). Lifting hands to the Lord is at times a gesture of petition (28:2) and at times a gesture of praise (63:4). In 134:2 it is a gesture of praise, and in either case lifting hands to the Lord is an indicator of our dependence on him. As the ancient Israelites were summoned to bless the Lord at the conclusion of the pilgrimage, we are reminded that we live in him and that all blessing comes from him, so we bless him at all times and in all places.

May the Lord Bless You (134:3). As the pilgrims departed Jerusalem, they departed with words of blessing ringing in their ears: the summons to bless the Lord and the prayer for the Lord to bless them. This is a prayer that the Lord would "share with his devoted followers from his own resources of omnipotence so that abundant life may be theirs" (Allen 1983:218). The blessing is said to come from Zion (Jerusalem), the location of the special presence of God in ancient times. We now look not to any special geographical location but to the person of the Lord Jesus Christ, who is the presence of God incarnate. But since Jesus is in heaven, we look to his Spirit, who dwells within us as the source of abundant life (see commentary at Ps 128). As we look to God for blessing, we do so with confidence, for the God to whom we look is able to bless. We know that he is able to bless because he has demonstrated his power in making heaven and earth. Since he has the power to create and sustain the universe, he has the power to empower us for life. Since he empowers us, we have all that we need for abundant life now and forever.

Psalm 134 concludes the Psalms of Ascent by teaching us that there exists a circle of blessing. By blessing the Lord, we open ourselves to receive his power, which comes "flooding into our own lives" (Allen 1983:218). And as that power floods into our lives, we heed the call to bless the Lord. And the circle of blessing continues to repeat itself again and again and again.

◆ CC. Psalm 135

1 Praise the LORD!

Praise the name of the LORD!
Praise him, you who serve the LORD,
2 you who serve in the house of the LORD,
in the courts of the house of our God.

3 Praise the LORD, for the LORD is good;
celebrate his lovely name with music.
4 For the LORD has chosen Jacob for himself,
Israel for his own special treasure.

5 I know the greatness of the LORD—
that our Lord is greater than any other god.
6 The LORD does whatever pleases him
throughout all heaven and earth,
and on the seas and in their depths.
7 He causes the clouds to rise over the whole earth.
He sends the lightning with the rain
and releases the wind from his storehouses.
8 He destroyed the firstborn in each Egyptian home,
both people and animals.
9 He performed miraculous signs and wonders in Egypt
against Pharaoh and all his people.
10 He struck down great nations
and slaughtered mighty kings—
11 Sihon king of the Amorites,
Og king of Bashan,
and all the kings of Canaan.
12 He gave their land as an inheritance,
a special possession to his people Israel.

13 Your name, O LORD, endures forever;
your fame, O LORD, is known to every generation.
14 For the LORD will give justice to his people
and have compassion on his servants.

15 The idols of the nations are merely
things of silver and gold,

shaped by human hands.
16 They have mouths but cannot speak,
and eyes but cannot see.
17 They have ears but cannot hear,
and noses but cannot smell.
18 And those who make idols are just like them,
as are all who trust in them.

19 O Israel, praise the LORD!
O priests—descendants of Aaron—praise the LORD!
20 O Levites, praise the LORD!
All you who fear the LORD, praise the LORD!
21 The LORD be praised from Zion,
for he lives here in Jerusalem.

Praise the LORD!

NOTES

135:3 ***lovely.*** This word (*na'im* [TH5273, ZH5833]) is translated "pleasant" in 133:1, where it is similarly paired with "wonderful/good."

135:5 ***I know.*** The expression is emphatic in the Hebrew in that the personal pronoun is added in front of the verb ("I *myself* know"; Waltke and O'Connor 1990:§16.3.2e).

135:8 ***He destroyed.*** The same verb (*nakah* [TH5221, ZH5782]) is used in 135:10, where it is translated "struck down."

135:19-21 ***praise . . . be praised.*** The first four occurrences of "praise" and the words "be praised" all translate the same verb (*barak* [TH1288A, ZH1385]), translated "bless" in Ps 134:3 and "praise" in 134:1-2. This repetition links the two psalms.

COMMENTARY

Psalm 135 answers the call to praise the Lord that was issued in Psalm 134. The threefold call to "praise" or "bless" (*barak* [TH1288A, ZH1385]) the Lord in Psalm 134 is answered with a fourfold call to "praise" (*barak*) the Lord in 135:19-20. And those called to bless the Lord in both psalms are the "servants of the LORD" who "serve in the house of the LORD" (134:1; 135:1-2). Psalm 135:1-3 constitutes the opening call to praise the Lord; Psalm 135:4-18 constitutes the praise proper. Psalm 135:4-6 seems to provided a synopsis of the praise: the Lord's relationship with his people (135:4) and his supremacy over the gods of the nations (135:5) as manifestations of his sovereign power (135:6). Psalm 135:7-18 expands on this synopsis with praise of the Lord's acts on behalf of his people (135:7-14) and recognition of the impotence of idols (135:15-18). A closing call to bless the Lord brings the psalm to its conclusion (135:19-21).

Call to Praise (135:1-3). "Praise the LORD" (*halelu yah* [TH1984A/3050, ZH2146/3363]) is an exclamation characteristic of Book 5 (Pss 107–150).[1] With this exclamation, the praise of Psalms 111–116 is resumed. The worshipers are assembled in the Temple courts, where they will praise the Lord because he is "good" and "pleasant." In the literary context the implication is that worshipers praise the Lord because they have experienced his goodness and pleasantness in their own living together in harmony (see 133:1).

Praise of the Sovereign Lord (135:4-18). The worshipers praise the Lord because of his relationship with his people (135:4, 7-14). This relationship began with the Lord's choice of Israel to be his "special treasure." The implications of being his special treasure are spelled out in 135:7-14. In the context of the following psalm (see 136:4-9, 25), which is a sequel to this psalm, 135:7 refers to God's provision of the rain that resulted in abundant harvests (see Pss 65 and 104 and Deut 11:13-15). This verse may also allude to the Lord as the Divine Warrior who goes to battle on behalf of his people (Mays 1994:417; see Longman and Reid 1995:31-47)—especially in light of the following verses. With "miraculous signs and wonders" (135:9) the Lord destroyed (135:8) the Egyptians to redeem his special treasure from slavery. He then "struck down . . . mighty kings . . . all the kings of Canaan" (135:10-11) in order to give his special treasure the land of Canaan as their own "special possession" (135:12). All of these actions proceed from the great compassion of the Lord.

The worshipers also praise the Lord because of his supremacy over idols (135:5, 15-18).[2] The psalmist says with certainty, "I know" (135:5a). What he knows is that the God of Israel is greater than all the gods of the nations (135:5b). That the Lord could deliver Israel from the Egyptians and then give them the land of Canaan is proof positive that the Lord is supreme over the gods of Egypt and Canaan. The gods of the nations have never done any such thing and can do no such thing, because they are impotent (135:15-17). Their impotence is contrasted with the Lord's omnipotence in that while the Lord "does" (*'asah* [TH6213, ZH6913]; 135:6) whatever he wants to do, the idols have been made (*'asah;* 135:18) by human hands. This section of praise has within it an implicit call to trust the Lord, as it warns that those who trust the gods of the nations will become as impotent as they are (135:18; see Ps 115).

God's relationship with his people and his supremacy over idols is because of his sovereign power (135:6). To say that the Lord is sovereign is simply to say that he is absolute in power as he reigns over the affairs of heaven and earth. This same confession has already been made in 115:3, and a similar confession is found in Daniel 4:35. The Lord has the right to do whatever he wants, he has the power to do whatever he wants, and he in fact does whatever he wants in heaven and on earth. One thing he wanted to do and did was to create a special treasure for himself by taking one nation out of the other nations to be his own. In so doing, he demonstrated his supremacy over the gods of those nations and thereby testified to his sovereign power over all. The choice of this one nation was for the ultimate purpose of blessing the nations in the fullness of time (47:9; Gen 12:3; Matt 28:18-20).

Call to Praise (135:19-21). The fourfold call to praise in 135:19-20 is chiastically arranged, as the laity are called in the outside cola, and the priests and Levites are called in the inner two cola. All Israel without exception is summoned to bless the Lord for the exercise of his sovereign power on their behalf. The Lord is then blessed from Zion. Zion is thus the location from which blessing flows to God's people (128:5) and the location where the Lord himself is blessed (135:21).

The God who once lived in Jerusalem has now taken up residence in our hearts. He has chosen us to be his special people (Eph 1:3-6) and summons us to place our ultimate trust in him rather than in the impotent idols we might choose to set up in our hearts (see Ezek 14:1-8). As we trust in him, we experience more and more of the redemptive benefits that are ours in Christ (Eph 1:7-12)—to the end that we might give him all the praise and glory (Eph 1:3, 6, 12).

ENDNOTES

1. The exclamation occurs only three times outside of Book 5, and all of these occurrences are at the very end of Book 4 (104:35; 105:45; 106:1, 48). The other occurrences in Book 5 are found in 111:1; 112:1; 113:1, 9; 115:18; 116:19; 117:2; 146:1, 10; 147:1, 20; 148:1, 14; 149:1, 9; 150:1, 6.
2. See Ps 115, from which this material has probably been taken.

◆ DD. Psalm 136

1 Give thanks to the LORD, for he is good!
His faithful love endures forever.
2 Give thanks to the God of gods.
His faithful love endures forever.
3 Give thanks to the Lord of lords.
His faithful love endures forever.

4 Give thanks to him who alone does
mighty miracles.
His faithful love endures forever.
5 Give thanks to him who made the
heavens so skillfully.
His faithful love endures forever.
6 Give thanks to him who placed the
earth among the waters.
His faithful love endures forever.
7 Give thanks to him who made the
heavenly lights—
His faithful love endures forever.
8 the sun to rule the day,
His faithful love endures forever.
9 and the moon and stars to rule the
night.
His faithful love endures forever.

10 Give thanks to him who killed the
firstborn of Egypt.
His faithful love endures forever.
11 He brought Israel out of Egypt.
His faithful love endures forever.
12 He acted with a strong hand and
powerful arm.
His faithful love endures forever.
13 Give thanks to him who parted the
Red Sea.*
His faithful love endures forever.
14 He led Israel safely through,
His faithful love endures forever.
15 but he hurled Pharaoh and his army
into the Red Sea.
His faithful love endures forever.
16 Give thanks to him who led his people
through the wilderness.
His faithful love endures forever.

17 Give thanks to him who struck down
mighty kings.
His faithful love endures forever.
18 He killed powerful kings—
His faithful love endures forever.
19 Sihon king of the Amorites,
His faithful love endures forever.
20 and Og king of Bashan.
His faithful love endures forever.
21 God gave the land of these kings as an
inheritance—
His faithful love endures forever.
22 a special possession to his servant
Israel.
His faithful love endures forever.

23 He remembered us in our
weakness.
His faithful love endures forever.
24 He saved us from our enemies.
His faithful love endures forever.
25 He gives food to every living
thing.
His faithful love endures forever.
26 Give thanks to the God of heaven.
His faithful love endures forever.

136:13 Hebrew *sea of reeds;* also in 136:15.

NOTES

136:4 *Give thanks.* While "Give thanks" occurs in the English text of the NLT in 136:4-25, the word *hodu* [TH3034A, ZH3344] (give thanks) occurs only at the beginning of 136:1-3, 26. Psalm 136:1-3 and verse 26 thus form an *inclusio* around the psalm.

136:10 *who killed*. This translates the Hiphil of *nakah* [TH5221, ZH5782], which is translated "struck down" in 136:17. This same verb was used in 135:8, 10, also referring to God's actions against the Egyptians and other foreign kings.

COMMENTARY

Two key concepts occupy center stage in Psalm 136: gratitude and God's faithful love. Psalm 136 is a psalm that expresses gratitude to God for the abundant manifestations of his unfailing love. As such, it is a sequel to Psalm 135, for both psalms praise/give thanks to God because he is "good" (135:3; 136:1). Psalm 136 can, in fact, be read as an expansion of Psalm 135 (McCann 1996:1223), as Psalm 136 expands on the themes of creation (135:7; 136:4-9), the Exodus (135:8-9; 136:10-15), and the granting of Canaan to Israel (135:10-12; 136:17-22). Psalm 136 does not, however, simply expand on these themes. By means of the refrain, Psalm 136 focuses our attention on the underlying source of all of God's mighty works: his faithful love that endures forever.

Gratitude for God's Faithful Love in Creation (136:4-9). Gratitude goes to God because only he does "mighty miracles" (136:4). In the context of the previous psalm this means that the Lord alone—not the impotent gods of the nations (135:15-17)—does "mighty miracles." These "mighty miracles" encompass all of the works that will be recited in 136:5-25. The first mighty miracle is God's work of creation. God created the heavens with the heavenly lights to rule the day and night and established the earth on the waters (see commentary on 24:1-2). We are told of God's creative miracles so that we will give thanks in general and give thanks for his "faithful love" in particular. God's creative work was motivated by his faithful love (see also 36:5-7; 145:13, 17). It is most important for us to see that the Creator is the God of love and that the creation bears witness to this love (Futato 2000:65-84). Our understanding of who God is plays a determinative role in our understanding of ourselves. As Creator, God acted in love. As creatures made in his image, we are called to act in love. We declare our gratitude by giving thanks to God. We demonstrate our gratitude by loving as God loves.

Gratitude for God's Faithful Love in the History of Redemption (136:10-22). The poet seems to set forth God's past miracles in redemptive history in two movements (Exodus and conquest), marked by the repetition of "killed/struck down" (*nakah* [TH5221, ZH5782]) in 136:10 and 136:17. God's mighty miracles, which were demonstrations of his faithful love, can be viewed from two different perspectives, one negative and one positive. From a negative perspective, as difficult as it may be to fathom, God demonstrated his faithful love by striking down the Egyptians and other foreign kings. From a positive perspective, he demonstrated his faithful love by bringing his people out of Egypt and granting them the Promised Land as their inheritance. The latter required the former, because the Egyptians and the other nations chose to oppose God and what he was doing in redemptive history (see Ps 2). Delivering Israel through the Red Sea entailed the death of the Egyptians (136:11-15). Bringing Israel into the Promised Land entailed the death of those who opposed this action (136:17-22). God certainly takes no delight in the death of those who oppose him; he would rather have them submit to him and live (Ezek 33:11). But death is the inevitable outcome of standing in opposition to God's redemptive work in the world. It was God's intention to bring Israel out of Egypt and to bring them into the Promised Land as part of the preparation for the coming of his Son to be the Savior of the world. Those who stood in opposition to God's plan were struck down as a result of their rebellion (see Ps 2). It was God's love for his people and ultimately for the world (John 3:16) that motivated his actions in the history of redemption.

Gratitude for God's Faithful Love in Present Salvation (136:23-24). To see evidence of God's faithful love, the community that originally used Psalm 136 could not only look back to God's past acts of salvation in the history of redemption, but they could also look to mighty miracles God had done in their own lives. We do not know for sure what is referred to by "our weakness" (136:23), nor can we identify "our enemies" (136:24). Perhaps Israel's return from Babylonian captivity is in view. What we do know is that God's unfailing love is not just demonstrated in the distant past: It is seen in our own experience. For God's faithful love "endures forever." As he saved in the past, he saves in the present. His love is not diminished by time. What he has done in the past and in our own lives bears witness to what he will do in the future as well, for he "is the same yesterday, today, and forever" (Heb 13:8).

Gratitude for God's Faithful Love and Providential Care (136:25). Corresponding to God's mighty miracles in creation is his work of providence, referred to in terms of his provision of food for "every living thing." God's providential care for his creation is motivated by his love for the creation he has made (see 36:5-7; 145:13, 17). God's provision of sunshine and rain and the food that grows as a result is a demonstration of his faithful love. And this love is extended to all, even to those who oppose God and his ways in the world (Matt 5:44-45). As his children, we are called to love as he loves, even to the point of loving those who stand in opposition to us.

Gratitude for the Faithful Love of the God of Heaven (136:1-3, 26). Gratitude for God's faithful love is to characterize our lives. That love was first seen in God's creative work. It was then seen in the history of redemption. It has also been seen in our own lives. It is seen in God's care for the entire creation he has made. This love endures forever, because it is the love of "the God of gods" (136:2), "the Lord of lords" (136:3), and "the God of heaven" (136:26). All of these titles point to God's supremacy—his supremacy over the gods of the nations (see 135:15-18), his supremacy over the kings of the nations (see Ps 2), and his supremacy over the whole of his creation. How marvelous to know and to live in the light of the truth that this supremacy is not that of a despot but of the God who is characterized by "faithful love" that "endures forever."

◆ EE. Psalm 137

1 Beside the rivers of Babylon, we sat
and wept
as we thought of Jerusalem.*
2 We put away our harps,
hanging them on the branches
of poplar trees.
3 For our captors demanded a song
from us.
Our tormentors insisted on a joyful
hymn:
"Sing us one of those songs
of Jerusalem!"

[4]But how can we sing the songs of
the LORD
while in a pagan land?
[5]If I forget you, O Jerusalem,
let my right hand forget how to
play the harp.
[6]May my tongue stick to the roof of
my mouth
if I fail to remember you,
if I don't make Jerusalem my
greatest joy.
[7]O LORD, remember what the
Edomites did
on the day the armies of Babylon
captured Jerusalem.
"Destroy it!" they yelled.
"Level it to the ground!"
[8]O Babylon, you will be
destroyed.
Happy is the one who pays
you back
for what you have done to us.
[9]Happy is the one who takes your
babies
and smashes them against
the rocks!

137:1 Hebrew *Zion;* also in 137:3.

NOTES

137:1 ***thought of.*** The word is *zakar* [TH2142, ZH2349] (remember) and is used again in 137:6 and 137:7. The threefold repetition of "remember" focuses our attention on the central theme of the psalm: remembering the devastation of the past.

COMMENTARY

When we look into the past, we see times when the devastation was so great that we would just like to forget about it and go on. Such a desire to forget may be understandable, but it is really a form of denial. Remembering is part of the path to healing. Psalm 137 gives us insight into how to remember past devastation.

Israel had such an experience when Jerusalem was destroyed by the Babylonians and the people were taken into captivity. Psalm 137 remembers this devastation and was probably written shortly after the return from captivity, when the memory of exile in Babylon and the destruction of Jerusalem was still a fresh wound. The poem is divided into three strophes, each containing the key word "remember." In the first strophe (137:1-4) the community remembers with tears the destruction of Jerusalem. The resolve to remember and not to forget is the point of the second strophe (137:5-6). The final strophe (137:7-9) calls upon God to remember what the Edomites and Babylonians did and to pay them back in kind.

Remembering with Tears (137:1-4). While they were exiles in the land of Babylon, the Israelites would have gathered from time to time at outdoor locations. These were times of corporate mourning. As God's people remembered the once glorious city of Jerusalem now lying in ruins, they wept. Salt was poured into their fresh wounds as their captors taunted them to sing the joyful songs that had once characterized their lives. In the current circumstances, that was impossible. Their pain was so great that they could not play harp or lyre. The hurt was so deep they could not sing; they could only weep.

Whether as individuals or families or churches, we too have known those times when we could not sing a note, but could only weep in the face of devastation. Remembering can do that. Remembering has the power to evoke grief that is perhaps buried deep in the soul. Remembering can confront us with pain we might like to forget. Remembering brings the hurt to expression—not to harm, but to help us experience relief by working through the pain. When the pain is so great that we cannot sing, our Father invites us into his presence to remember with tears.

Remembering with Resolve (137:5-6). As the ancient community remembered the devastation, the people resolved not to forget but to remember always. Their resolve was extraordinarily firm, as they used the ancient form of a self-maledictory oath (see NIDOTTE 3.32-33). No doubt, they remembered the devastation, but I think the resolve went beyond that. The resolve was also to remember the joys they once had. The resolve was to re-create that joy out of the dust of devastation. It appears that this is what is meant by the third colon in 137:6, which seems to amplify what it means to "remember." To "remember" in this context is amplified in terms of "mak[ing] Jerusalem my greatest joy" (137:6). This is the expression of devotion to God and the place where his special presence was manifested in ancient times. This is the expression of commitment to rebuild. Rebuilding would require learning from past mistakes so that they would not be repeated. Without remembering, the past would inevitably repeat itself. Rebuilding would also require remembering the beauty of the past that it might be re-created in the present. That was the task of the recently returned exiles (see Ezra 3).

The energy used in remembering the devastation can be turned to remembering the joy. Learning from the past can lead to rebuilding in the present. Tears can lead to joy when we remember with resolve.

Remembering with Anger (137:7-9). Deep hurt is often overlaid with anger. The deeper the hurt, the more vehement the anger. The ancient Israelites were enraged at the atrocities committed against them. There were the atrocities committed by the Babylonians, including their slaughter of Israel's children (see Lam 2:21-22). And there were the atrocities committed by the Edomites, who first of all stood by and did nothing to defend Israel, and who then joined in the destruction itself (see Obad 1:11-14). Psalm 137:7-9 articulates anger at these atrocities with a vehemence that is unparalleled in the book of Psalms. Before judging this anger we must admit that it is deeply honest, as deeply honest as the tears that were shed. We must admit that we have had similar thoughts and feelings, as well, if we have ever been deeply hurt. It will benefit no one to deny these feelings or to attempt to suppress them. When such feelings are within, our Father invites us into his presence to remember with anger. And as we do, perhaps we will learn something about the anger of God (Allender and Longman 1994:68-72).

What then can we do with such anger?[1] For our own well-being and that of others, having remembered with anger, we must let go of the anger and leave it with God. People will reap what they have sown (Prov 22:8; 26:27; Hos 8:7; 2 Cor 9:6). But it is not for us to take vengeance on those who have hurt us; we can leave that with God (Rom 12:19). We bless rather than curse (Rom 12:14), and we pray *for* those who have hurt us rather than *against* them (Matt 5:44-45), because Jesus has come to bring salvation, and the Father is exercising patience that leads people to repentance (Rom 2:4; 2 Pet 3:9). The Lord Jesus has borne the full fury of God so that those who trust in him will never taste that fury but will enjoy God's favor.

The following psalm hints at this, as all the kings of the earth are singing the Lord's praises (138:4-5) rather than taunting the Lord's people to sing (137:3).

Remembering past devastation can be painful, but as we work through the pain, remembering can be productive. By remembering with tears, resolve, and anger, we can produce beauty in the present that bodes well for the future.

ENDNOTES

1. A more detailed answer to this question can be found in Allender and Longman 1994:72-77.

◆ FF. Psalm 138

A psalm of David.

[1]I give you thanks, O LORD, with all
my heart;
I will sing your praises before
the gods.
[2]I bow before your holy Temple as
I worship.
I praise your name for your
unfailing love and faithfulness;
for your promises are backed
by all the honor of your name.
[3]As soon as I pray, you answer me;
you encourage me by giving me
strength.

[4]Every king in all the earth will thank
you, LORD,
for all of them will hear your words.
[5]Yes, they will sing about the LORD's
ways,
for the glory of the LORD is very
great.
[6]Though the LORD is great, he cares
for the humble,
but he keeps his distance from
the proud.

[7]Though I am surrounded by troubles,
you will protect me from the anger
of my enemies.
You reach out your hand,
and the power of your right hand
saves me.
[8]The LORD will work out his plans for
my life—
for your faithful love, O LORD,
endures forever.
Don't abandon me, for you
made me.

NOTES

138:2 ***for your promises are backed by all the honor of your name.*** The NLT reflects one attempt to make sense out of a difficult text. A more literal translation would be, "because you have exalted your word above the entirety of your name" (see NKJV). But this translation is problematic because the clause itself provides the reason for praising God's "name." "I will give thanks to your name . . . because you have exalted your word above your name" makes little sense. An emendation seems warranted, and the emendation that makes the best sense is to read *kol* as an absolute instead of as a construct form—that is, to read *kol-* (with *qamets khatuf* and *maqqeph*) [TH3605, ZH3972] (all of) as *kol* (with *holem;* "all"). The result would be "all" as a substantival, "I will give thanks to your name . . . because you have exalted your name above *all else.*" "Your word [promises]" (*'imrah* [TH565, ZH614]) may have been added after the text was corrupted, or it may have been originally conjoined to "your name" with a conjunction that was later dropped; the sense would then be "because you have exalted your name and your word above all else." "Your word" as an addition to "your name" makes sense in context, where the kings are going to give thanks when they hear the Lord's "words" (*'imrah;* 138:4). The NLT succeeds in capturing the general idea, i.e., the supreme position of God's name and word.

138:3 ***As soon as I pray, you answer.*** Since this is a song of thanksgiving, it is natural to read the perfect tense followed by the Waw-relative imperfect as referring to the past. The psalmist here gives thanks for answered prayer in a specific situation.

138:5 ***they will sing.*** The verb translated "sing" (*shir* [TH7891, ZH8876]) is the same verb used in 137:3, where the Babylonians taunt the Israelites to "sing" the songs of Jerusalem. Psalm 138 envisions the day when the nations will have ceased their rebellion and have become the people of God (see 47:9).

138:7 ***Though.*** "Though" may lead the reader of English to think that the psalmist is in some current trouble. "If" interprets the trouble as potential and future.

138:8 ***faithful love.*** The same word (*khesed* [TH2617, ZH2876]) is used in 138:2, where it is translated "unfailing love."

COMMENTARY

Thanksgiving is the theme of Psalm 138, as indicated by the threefold repetition of the Hiphil of *yadah* [TH3034A, ZH3344] ("give thanks/praise"; 138:1, 2, 4). The psalm opens with personal and individual thanksgiving for answered prayer (138:1-3). This thanksgiving is then globalized to include "every king in all the earth" (138:4-6). The thanksgiving results in a great confidence that as God has saved in the past, so he will save in the future if troubles again arise (138:7-8).

Thanksgiving for Answered Prayer (138:1-3). At some point in the recent past, the psalmist was in trouble and prayed for help. God answered that prayer by giving the psalmist the strength he needed to persevere through the trouble and come out victorious on the other side. God sometimes delivers us from trouble and at other times grants the endurance we need to make it through the trouble. No matter which way he answers our prayers, he is worthy of our thanksgiving.

And the thanks we give should be wholehearted, because we understand that when God answers our prayers he does so because of his unfailing love for us and his faithfulness to us. The ancient worshiper is pictured in the outer court, bowing toward the Holy Place, as was the case in 135:2. That he sings the praise of God "before the gods" (138:1b) does not indicate a belief in the existence of other gods but is a rhetorical profession of his sole allegiance to the Lord God of Israel as the only true God (see 96:4-5). Since the gods of the nations are idols, the next strophe envisions the kings of those nations as joining in the worship of the God of Israel.

Thanksgiving by the Kings of the Earth (138:4-6). In the previous psalm, the foreigners were taunting God's people to "sing" (*shir* [TH7891, ZH8876]) the songs of Jerusalem (137:3), but now the kings of all the earth have changed their tune. They are now joining God's people to give thanks to the Lord and to "sing" (*shir*) his praises (138:4-5). What has happened to bring about this change of heart? The kings have heard God's word. We are not told in this psalm what this word is, but we know that it is a word of blessing for all who will take refuge in the Lord God of Israel (see 2:12). This theme of the nations joining God's people to sing God's praises has already been encountered (see Pss 46–49, 65–67, 87, 93–100, 102, 105, 117) and will be met again (Pss 148, 150). This is a marvelous testimony to God's love for the nations—even in their opposition to him, his ways, and his people. His word of promise will triumph in the end; the nations will give thanks to him, "for the glory of the LORD is very great" (138:5).

The greatness of the Lord's glory does not distance him from the humble. He does distance himself from the proud and from those who refuse to take refuge in him (see 2:12), but he cares for the humble. They know it, and they, too, give him thanks.

Thanksgiving Resulting in Confidence (138:7-8). Pausing to give thanks and envisioning the nations eventually joining in that thanksgiving generated confidence within the psalmist. As the Lord had given the psalmist the strength to persevere through trouble in the past, the psalmist expresses confidence that if trouble arises in the future, the Lord will preserve him and save him from it. In fact, he is confident that the Lord will work out his plan for the psalmist's life, because the Lord's unfailing love will always be there (see the refrain in Ps 136). This does not mean that we walk into the future presumptuously. Rather, we walk into the future confidently, with a prayerful dependence on our Creator, who will love us to the end.

◆ GG. Psalm 139

For the choir director: A psalm of David.

**1 O LORD, you have examined my heart
and know everything about me.
2 You know when I sit down or stand up.
You know my thoughts even when
I'm far away.
3 You see me when I travel
and when I rest at home.
You know everything I do.
4 You know what I am going to say
even before I say it, LORD.
5 You go before me and follow me.
You place your hand of blessing
on my head.
6 Such knowledge is too wonderful
for me,
too great for me to understand!**

**7 I can never escape from your Spirit!
I can never get away from your
presence!
8 If I go up to heaven, you are there;
if I go down to the grave,* you are
there.
9 If I ride the wings of the morning,
if I dwell by the farthest oceans,
10 even there your hand will guide me,
and your strength will support me.
11 I could ask the darkness to hide me
and the light around me to become
night—
12 but even in darkness I cannot hide
from you.
To you the night shines as bright
as day.
Darkness and light are the same
to you.**

**13 You made all the delicate, inner parts
of my body
and knit me together in my
mother's womb.
14 Thank you for making me so
wonderfully complex!
Your workmanship is
marvelous—how well I know it.
15 You watched me as I was being
formed in utter seclusion,
as I was woven together in the dark
of the womb.
16 You saw me before I was born.
Every day of my life was recorded
in your book.**

Every moment was laid out
before a single day had passed.

17 How precious are your thoughts about
me,* O God.
They cannot be numbered!
18 I can't even count them;
they outnumber the grains of sand!
And when I wake up,
you are still with me!

19 O God, if only you would destroy the
wicked!
Get out of my life, you murderers!
20 They blaspheme you;
your enemies misuse your name.

21 O LORD, shouldn't I hate those who
hate you?
Shouldn't I despise those who
oppose you?
22 Yes, I hate them with total hatred,
for your enemies are my enemies.

23 Search me, O God, and know my
heart;
test me and know my anxious
thoughts.
24 Point out anything in me that offends
you,
and lead me along the path of
everlasting life.

139:8 Hebrew *to Sheol.* **139:17** Or *How precious to me are your thoughts.*

NOTES

139:3 ***You see me when I travel and when I rest at home.*** Lit., "You have measured my traveling and my stretching out [to rest]." This is a merism (a figure of speech that uses two poles or extremes to communicate a totality) for the thoroughness of God's knowledge.

139:4 ***You know what I am going to say even before I say it.*** The second colon could be translated "You know all of it." The use of the word "all" underscores the thorough nature of the Lord's knowledge of us.

139:7 ***I can never escape.*** In the Hebrew this is a rhetorical question, lit., "Where will I go?"

139:9 ***the farthest oceans.*** Lit., "the end of the sea." The previous colon refers to the "east" under the figure of "the wings of the morning," i.e., where the sun rises. So, too, this colon refers to the west in terms of "the end of the sea," i.e., the farthest edge of the Mediterranean.

139:23 ***Search.*** This same verb in the Hebrew (*khaqar* [TH2713, ZH2983]) is used in 139:1, where it is translated "examined." The two occurrences form an *inclusio* around the poem and focus our attention on the intimate nature of our relationship with God.

139:24 ***lead.*** This same verb in Hebrew (*nakhah* [TH5148, ZH5697]) is used in 139:10, where it is translated "guide."

COMMENTARY

To have an intimate relationship with someone is a deep longing of the human heart, perhaps the deepest. To know and be known and loved is the soul's passion. Such a relationship is the heartbeat of Psalm 139. The Hebrew verb for "know" (*yada'* [TH3045, ZH3359]) is used six times in this psalm (139:1, 2, 4, 14, 23a, 23b) as well as the cognate noun *da'ath* [TH1847, ZH1981] once (139:6). In verses 1, 2, and 4 the word speaks of God's knowledge of us, 139:14 speaks of our knowledge of God, and the final two occurrences of the word in 139:23 ask God to know us ever more deeply. All that the human heart longs for is found in our relationship with God.

Psalm 139 is comprised of two stanzas. In the first stanza (139:1-18) the psalmist reflects on who God is in terms of God's knowledge (139:1-6), presence (139:7-12), and care (139:13-18). This reflection is not abstract and theoretical but highly personal. It is not God's omniscience in general that has captured the heart of the psalmist; it is God's personal knowledge of "me." It is not God's omnipresence in the abstract that is in view; it is God's all-surrounding presence of "me." It is not God's care of creation in general but his personal care of "me" that is the motivation for thanksgiving. Reflecting on God in relation to "me" leads naturally into the second stanza (139:19-24), where the psalmist responds with two key components for intimate relationship: loyalty (139:19-22) and humility (139:23-24).

Reflecting on God (139:1-6). God's personal knowledge of me is the theme of these opening verses. "LORD, you . . . know everything about me" (139:1). "You know when I sit down or stand up" (139:2). "You know what I am going to say" (139:4). "Such knowledge [of me] is too wonderful" (139:6). It is not God's knowledge alone but the thorough nature of that knowledge that is incomprehensibly astounding to me as I reflect on it. He knows when I sit and stand, a merism for every situation I am in. He knows "my thoughts even when I'm far away" (139:2b), and he knows "what I am going to say even before I say it" (139:4). He knows when I am traveling and when I am stopping for a rest (another merism).

While being known is perhaps our deepest longing, it is also one of our deepest fears. After their initial sin, Adam and Eve hid from God because they were afraid. They were afraid that to be known as they were, sins and all, would mean being rejected. Thus arose the internal conflict between the desire to be known and the desire to avoid rejection. Such fear of rejection does not come into view in these opening verses of Psalm 139. This must be because of what linguists call nonspecified shared information. There must be some knowledge about the relationship that God and a person share that is not spelled out in this text. Psalm 130, along with many other psalms, has already specified what this knowledge is. It is true that if God knows me as a guilty sinner, then I cannot hope to have a relationship with him (130:3). But both God and I know that he forgives (130:4). I know and God knows that his unfailing love for me endures forever (Pss 136; 138:8). I can be known without fear because God is love and forgives all my sins. I know clearly what the psalmist knew dimly: that I am secure in the love of God because the Lord Jesus has lived a perfect life in my place, died on the cross to pay the penalty for my sins, and was raised for my justification. Through faith in the Lord Jesus Christ, I can experience the intimate relationship my heart longs for. I can know and be known and loved.

The relational nature of God's knowledge in 139:1-6 is expressed in 139:5, where God is in front of me as well as behind me—and his hand of blessing is on top of me. His knowledge encompasses my whole life. This truth leads directly to the reflection in the next strophe with its focus on the pervasive presence of God.

God's Presence around Me Is Pervasive (139:7-12). The question is raised in 139:7 (see note) as to whether or not I can ever be outside of the presence of God. Psalm 139:8-12 answers the question with a resounding no! Psalm 139:8 contains a merism on the vertical axis: Neither an ascent to heaven nor a descent into the grave will take me from God's presence. A merism on the horizontal axis is found in 139:9-10: Neither a journey to the farthest east nor to the farthest west will remove me from the guiding and supportive presence of God. These merisms have covered the extremes of both axes to portray the inescapable presence of God. Two other extremes, darkness and light, come into view in 139:11-12. Perhaps if there were no light and I were totally engulfed in darkness, I could be hidden from the presence of God. But no, such is not the case. For God's presence is not confined to the light. In fact, his presence transcends the categories of darkness and light. There is nowhere I can be where I am not in God's presence.

As with God's knowledge, so with his presence. His presence could strike fear into my heart, as it did in the hearts of Adam and Eve after they sinned. But it does not, for in Christ I know his presence to be that of a shepherd who guides and supports me wherever I am. I find great peace and comfort knowing that the whole of my life is enveloped by the presence of the God who is always for me. That he is for me is the focus of the third part of this reflection.

God's Care for Me Is Precious (139:13-18). When I think of a newborn baby, I think of the word "precious." God's thorough knowledge of me and his pervasive, guiding, and supportive presence with me entails his precious care for me. This knowledge, presence, and care did not begin when I became an adult, nor an adolescent, nor even a newborn baby. God's knowledge of me, presence with me, and care for me began before I was even born (139:16a).

Though I was hidden from human view in my mother's womb, I was not hidden from the gaze of God. His eye was on me, and I was in his thoughts from my very beginning. When I was in the utter seclusion of the womb, God was watching over the process of my formation. As I stop to reflect honestly on myself, I know very well that I am the wonderfully complex and marvelous workmanship of the God who cares about the fine details of my life. He cares about the minute details of my body, for he formed my inner parts and wove them together—like one weaves a fine tapestry—when I was in my mother's womb. He cares about the fine details of my daily living, for each day and every moment of my yet-to-be-experienced life was laid out by the precious and thoughtful plan of God (139:16-17a; see 138:8). The precious thoughts God had about me in the process of forming me outnumber the grains of sand on the seashore (139:18). They can no more be counted than they can be comprehended. Though I may fall asleep reflecting on my relationship with God, when I wake up, I find that his guiding and supportive presence is still with me, along with his thorough knowledge of me and his precious care for me.

What kind of response is called for by my reflections on God's knowledge, presence, and care? The two strophes of the second stanza answer this question.

Responding to God (139:19-24). In the first place, I am called to be *loyal* (139:19-22). An intimate relationship cannot exist in the absence of loyalty, and loyalty is what comes to expression in this strophe. The Lord hates what is "evil" (*resha'* [TH7562, ZH8400]; 45:7 [8]) and hates those who love violence, as in 11:5 (*rasha'* [TH7563A, ZH8401]; see also 5:4). So out of loyalty to the Lord the psalmist hates the wicked (*rasha'* [TH7563A, ZH8401]), who hate the Lord. The Lord's enemies are the psalmist's enemies. In the gospel era, the Christian's loyalty may not come to expression in the same way that the ancient psalmist's did (see commentary on 137:7-9), but my loyalty to the Lord will come to expression in a variety of ways, some of which are at least analogous to the loyalty the psalmist expresses here. I am called to love my enemies as an expression of my loyalty to my Father, who loves them (Matt

5:43-45), and at the same time I am also called to "hate what is wrong" and to "hold tightly to what is good" (Rom 12:9). This is not always easy, and it is at times quite costly, but such loyalty is an aspect of my intimate relationship with God. I am called to this kind of loyalty not out of arrogance, but out of humility.

Second, I am called to be *humble* (139:23-24). Humility, like loyalty, can be expressed in many ways. Here it appears in the form of teachability. Arrogance and teachability cannot occupy the same space, for arrogance says, "I know it all already." Humility and teachability go hand in glove, for humility says, "I have much more to learn." Knowing that the Lord has already (lit.) "searched" me (139:1), I want the Lord to "search" me more deeply (139:23). Though the Lord already knows everything about me (139:1) and even knows my thoughts (139:2), I want the Lord to "know my heart" (139:23a) and to know my thoughts even more (139:23b). This means that I want the intimacy of relationship to deepen even more, and this takes humility. I am humble, open to learning anything about myself that is out of accord with who God is and what his will is for my life. I want the Lord to know me so that I can know myself better. I want the Lord to know me, so that he can "lead me along the path of everlasting life" (139:24) and that path is walked in a humble and loyal relationship with the God who knows me (139:1-6), who is always present with me (139:7-12), and who cares for me (139:13-18)—all because of his love for me in the Lord Jesus Christ.

◆ HH. Psalm 140

For the choir director: A psalm of David.

1 O LORD, rescue me from evil people.
Protect me from those who are violent,
2 those who plot evil in their hearts
and stir up trouble all day long.
3 Their tongues sting like a snake;
the venom of a viper drips from their lips. *Interlude*

4 O LORD, keep me out of the hands of the wicked.
Protect me from those who are violent,
for they are plotting against me.
5 The proud have set a trap to catch me;
they have stretched out a net;
they have placed traps all along the way. *Interlude*

6 I said to the LORD, "You are my God!"
Listen, O LORD, to my cries for mercy!
7 O Sovereign LORD, the strong one who rescued me,
you protected me on the day of battle.
8 LORD, do not let evil people have their way.
Do not let their evil schemes succeed,
or they will become proud. *Interlude*

9 Let my enemies be destroyed
by the very evil they have planned for me.
10 Let burning coals fall down on their heads.
Let them be thrown into the fire
or into watery pits from which they can't escape.
11 Don't let liars prosper here in our land.
Cause great disasters to fall on the violent.

12 But I know the LORD will help those they persecute;
he will give justice to the poor.
13 Surely righteous people are praising your name;
the godly will live in your presence.

NOTES

140:2 *stir up*. The NLT, along with most major versions, presumes an emendation from *yaguru* ("they attack," from *gur* II [TH1481A, ZH1592]) to *yegaru* ("they stir up," from *garah* [TH1624, ZH1741]); see Allen 1983:265, HALOT 1.202, and DCH 2.374.

COMMENTARY

Psalm 140 is the first in a series of laments (Pss 140–143). These laments remind us of the beginning of the book of Psalms, where the emphasis is on lamentation (see, e.g., Pss 3–7, 10–13). But these laments lead to the great blessings of 144:12-15 and the great praise of Psalms 145–150. Thus, Psalms 140–150 mirror the structure of the Psalter as a whole, which moves from lamentation to praise (see Introduction, pp. 4-5), and the direction of our pilgrimage as God's people (Futato 1999). Knowing that blessing and praise are ours (Pss 144–150) empowers us to enter these psalms with the joyful expectation of a positive outcome in the Psalter and in our lives.

There have been a variety of attempts to outline the structure of Psalm 140 (see McCann 1996:1239). The simplest approach is to follow the shifts in content and to divide the psalm into three strophes. The first (140:1-5) is a prayer for deliverance. The second (140:6-11) is a corresponding prayer for the enemy to be destroyed. The third (140:12-13) is an affirmation of a positive outcome for God's people.

Rescue Me from the Violent (140:1-5). Those from whom the psalmist wants to be rescued are evil. Their evil comes in the form of violence. Their evil violence is calculated from cold hearts. They seem to thrive on bringing trouble into the lives of others, for they continually stir up trouble. Their violence is first and foremost verbal, as they seek to poison others with the venomous words they spew out. Their violent words then translate into violent actions, signified by the prayer to be kept out of their "hands," with which they constantly set traps for the psalmist. As violence and arrogance often go hand in hand, these violent people act with great pride, but their violent pride will be their downfall (Prov 16:18).

May They Reap What They Have Sown (140:6-11). The Lord is sovereign; he is absolute in power. He is a strong savior, so the psalmist prays that in his mercy the Lord will not let the violent triumph. He prays for them to reap what they have sown. He prays that their violence will be their own undoing. He prays that the Lord will bring them down. He knows that the Lord often works in such a way that the traps people set for others end up entrapping themselves (35:8; Prov 26:27).

I Am Confident (140:12-13). Petitions give way to confidence in the final strophe, as indicated by the opening words, "But I know," and the emphatic word "Surely." The psalmist is confident that the Lord will set things right for the afflicted. Thus, the godly, even when abused, can choose to praise the name of God, for not even violence done against them can separate them from the loving presence of the God in whom they live (Rom 8:38-39).

Jesus endured terrible things at the hands of sinful people (Heb 12:3). He was empowered to endure by the joy set before him (Heb 12:2). We can do the same by keeping our faith in him. Keeping our faith focused on the blessings he has for us (144:12-15) and the praise we have for him (Pss 145–150) empowers us to live in the present even in the face of violent attacks against us. In spite of violent opposition to us, "Overwhelming victory is ours through Christ, who loved us" (Rom 8:37).

◆ II. Psalm 141

A psalm of David.

1 O LORD, I am calling to you. Please hurry!
Listen when I cry to you for help!
2 Accept my prayer as incense offered to you,
and my upraised hands as an evening offering.

3 Take control of what I say, O LORD,
and guard my lips.
4 Don't let me drift toward evil
or take part in acts of wickedness.
Don't let me share in the delicacies
of those who do wrong.

5 Let the godly strike me!
It will be a kindness!
If they correct me, it is soothing medicine.
Don't let me refuse it.
But I pray constantly
against the wicked and their deeds.
6 When their leaders are thrown down from a cliff,
the wicked will listen to my words and find them true.
7 Like rocks brought up by a plow,
the bones of the wicked will lie scattered without burial.*
8 I look to you for help, O Sovereign LORD.
You are my refuge; don't let them kill me.
9 Keep me from the traps they have set for me,
from the snares of those who do wrong.
10 Let the wicked fall into their own nets,
but let me escape.

141:7 Hebrew *scattered at the mouth of Sheol.*

NOTES

141:1 ***when I cry.*** The word (*qara'* [TH7121, ZH7924]) is the same one used at the beginning of the verse, where it is translated "I am calling."

141:4 ***Don't let me share.*** The Waw on the front of *bal* [TH1077, ZH1153] (don't) is emphatic (see Pope 1953 and Wernberg-Möller 1958).

141:7 ***the bones of the wicked.*** The NLT presumes an emendation from *'atsamenu* [TH6106/5105.1, ZH6795/5646] (our bones) to *'atsmehem* [TH6106/1992.1, ZH6795/2157] (their bones). This emendation is supported by the context and the LXX.

COMMENTARY

Psalm 141 is the second in a series of four laments (Pss 140–143) that lead to blessings (144:12-15) and praise (Pss 145–150) at the end of the book of Psalms (see commentary on 140).

I Am Praying (141:1-2). The repetition of the verb "call" at the beginning and end of 141:1 sets the tone for Psalm 141. It is a prayer for help, and the help is needed immediately, as indicated by the plea, "Please hurry!" In every other occurrence of this imperative in the book of Psalms (22:19 [20]; 38:22 [23]; 40:13 [14]; 70:1, 5

[2, 6]; 71:12), "hurry" (*khushah* [TH2363, ZH2590]) is used in conjunction with a word for "help" (*'ezrah* and *'ezer* [TH5833/5828, ZH6476/6469]; 70:5 [6]). The psalmist is in a desperate situation with no time to lose. Upraised hands are a symbol of the psalmist's plea to God, which he wishes to have accepted even as incense and the evening sacrifice were accepted by God.

I Am Praying for Deliverance from Temptation (141:3-5a). The psalmist begins by praying for himself. He prays for deliverance from sin in his own life. As the tongues of others have been used in destructive ways (140:3), the psalmist prays for his own tongue to be kept from such evil. When read in the context of the previous psalm, this prayer can be understood as a prayer that the psalmist not repay evil for evil. He also prays that he be kept from other evil practices that characterize those who oppose him and God's ways. If he finds himself straying, his prayer is that godly people would be there to restore him to the right path (see Gal 6:1).

I Am Praying for the Downfall of the Wicked (141:5b-7). The psalmist not only prays for himself; he also prays against the wicked. The Hebrew of these verses is quite difficult. They are a prayer for the downfall of the wicked with an intriguing request that the wicked come to see the error of their ways and the rightness of the psalmist's words. This same movement from prayer against the wicked to promise that they will hear a good word has just been encountered in Psalm 137 (imprecation) and 138:4 ("Every king in all the earth will thank you, LORD, for all of them will hear your words.").

I Am Praying for Deliverance from the Wicked (141:8-10). In the meantime, the psalmist needs to be delivered from the traps others have set for him. He knows that his God is ultimately in control as the "Sovereign Lord"; so he seeks refuge in the Lord (see "Theological Concerns" in the Introduction). His prayer is that his opponents reap what they have sown and that he escape.

Though the troubles of this life may, at times, seem endless to us, as evidenced by this series of laments so near the end of the book of Psalms, we find here the courage to overcome these troubles in light of the blessings (144:12-15) and praise (Pss 145–150) that are ours in Christ Jesus our "Sovereign Lord" (see commentary on Ps 140).

◆ JJ. Psalm 142

A psalm of David, regarding his experience in the cave. A prayer.*

1 I cry out to the LORD;
  I plead for the LORD's mercy.
2 I pour out my complaints before him
  and tell him all my troubles.
3 When I am overwhelmed,
  you alone know the way I should turn.
Wherever I go,
  my enemies have set traps for me.
4 I look for someone to come and help me,
  but no one gives me a passing thought!
No one will help me;
  no one cares a bit what happens to me.
5 Then I pray to you, O LORD.
  I say, "You are my place of refuge.
  You are all I really want in life.
6 Hear my cry,
  for I am very low.

Rescue me from my persecutors,
for they are too strong for me.
7 Bring me out of prison
so I can thank you.
The godly will crowd around me,
for you are good to me."

142:TITLE Hebrew *maskil*. This may be a literary or musical term.

NOTES

142:4 *I look.* The Hebrew text actually contains two imperatives, "look" and "see," which are addressed to God.

No one will help me. Lit., "A place to flee has perished from me." The "place to flee" (*manos* [TH4498, ZH4960]) is part of the semantic domain for the concept of "refuge" (see "Theological Concerns" in the Introduction). The idea here is that David felt as if he had no place to escape for safety.

142:5 *I pray.* The verb translated "pray" (*za'aq* [TH2199, ZH2410]) is the same verb translated "cry out" in 142:1. The repetition marks the beginning of the two strophes in the psalm.

142:7 *you are good to me.* Given the future orientation of the previous verb ("will crowd around me"), the imperfect of *gamal* [TH1580, ZH1694] is better understood as a reference to the Lord's future actions ("for you will deal generously with me").

COMMENTARY

Pursued by Saul again and again, David, a fugitive, probably felt too tired to keep running, but he had no choice. Exhaustion and discouragement can characterize the lives of those enduring severe adversity. Physical weakness, emotional fatigue, and spiritual depletion often plague those afflicted by other troubles. Psalm 142 brings all of these feelings to expression, along with an underlying confidence in God's ability to deliver.

This psalm can be divided into two strophes, each beginning with a reference to the psalmist crying out (*za'aq* [TH2199, ZH2410]) to God (142:1 and 142:5). The focus of the first strophe (142:1-4) is on the adverse circumstances the psalmist faces, while the focus of the second (142:5-7) is on the requests he makes to God (note the imperatives, "Hear," "Rescue," "Bring me out"). But these boundaries are not rigid, as is clear from the request in 142:4 ("look"; see note on 142:4) and the descriptions of adversity in 142:6-7.

Adverse Circumstances. In this psalm David brings to expression the deep emotional response that accompanied the adversity he was experiencing. He clearly felt overwhelmed (142:3). The concept of being overwhelmed is translated "I am losing all hope" in 143:4. The verb is used in the context of being weakened to the point of death in 107:5. Adversity, especially protracted adversity, can produce in the human soul this profound sense of being overwhelmed. David felt "very low" because he believed his adversaries were "too strong" for him (142:6). Utterly overwhelmed by his circumstances, he expressed his feelings in prayer.

David also felt trapped. Feeling that there is nowhere to turn for help and no way of escape can be terrifying. David said, "Wherever I go, my enemies have set traps for me" (142:3). He felt as if there was no place to which he could retreat for safety. He likened his situation to that of being locked up in prison with no way of escape

(142:7). Feeling trapped in adverse circumstances only deepens the adversity, as it can paralyze the one who feels this way.

Finally, David felt abandoned. To feel overwhelmed and trapped is bad enough, but it is even worse when one feels all alone in the darkness. When David looked to others for help, no one was there: "I look for someone to come and help me, but no one gives me a passing thought!" (142:4). He concluded that no one cared a bit about what happened to him. It can be devastating to go through hard times and find that friends and even family are not there to support you. Through David, the Holy Spirit teaches us where to turn when feeling overwhelmed, trapped, and abandoned.

Honest Prayer. David held nothing back in his prayers to God. He poured out his complaints and honestly told God all about his troubles, not because God needed to be informed, but because David needed to be honest as part of the path to victory. Pouring out his complaints and reciting in prayer all of his troubles would have also served to motivate God to move into action on David's behalf. Thus, along with telling God exactly how he felt and what he thought, David asked God specifically for what he wanted. "Hear my cry" (142:6a); "Rescue me" (142:6b); "Bring me out of prison" (142:7). David wanted to experience deliverance in the real world from the very real trouble he was experiencing. While he may have wanted grace to endure the troubles, he prayed for deliverance from them. By this example, the Holy Spirit teaches us to pray and not to give up—to expect God to work on our behalf. And he teaches us to pray with great confidence.

Confident Hope. While there may have been no place in sight to which David could flee for safety, by faith he knew that God was his "place of refuge" (142:5). David was confident that God would show up in his life in some way as the safe haven from the storm. He lived in the hope that eventually the righteous would once again be crowding around him—when the generosity of God would be lavished on him. This hope was every bit as real as the feelings of being overwhelmed, trapped, and abandoned. This hope came to expression in his prayer even when there was no basis for it in his current circumstances. "Faith enabled him to rise higher, and to conclude, contrary to the judgment of the flesh, that his welfare was secure in the hand of God" (Calvin 1979:182, writing on Ps 13).

Clear Purpose. In all of this David never lost his sense of purpose in life. That purpose is shown in one key colon in this poem: "so I can thank you" (142:7). While David longed for deliverance for his own benefit, he also longed to be able to give thanks publicly for all that God had done for him (see 66:16). He longed to tell others of the goodness of God, experienced in being delivered from the adverse circumstances he was in. In this longing, he anticipated the Lord Jesus Christ, who now praises God in the great assembly for the grand deliverance he experienced in being raised from the dead (Heb 2:12). His resurrection is the fountain of hope for our deliverance from the adversity we experience in this life. So we, like David, live with the purpose of giving thanks to God for his kind generosity to us in the Lord Jesus Christ.

◆ KK. Psalm 143

A psalm of David.

1 Hear my prayer, O LORD;
listen to my plea!
Answer me because you are faithful
and righteous.
2 Don't put your servant on trial,
for no one is innocent before you.
3 My enemy has chased me.
He has knocked me to the ground
and forces me to live in darkness
like those in the grave.
4 I am losing all hope;
I am paralyzed with fear.
5 I remember the days of old.
I ponder all your great works
and think about what you have
done.
6 I lift my hands to you in prayer.
I thirst for you as parched land
thirsts for rain. *Interlude*

7 Come quickly, LORD, and answer me,
for my depression deepens.
Don't turn away from me,
or I will die.
8 Let me hear of your unfailing love
each morning,
for I am trusting you.
Show me where to walk,
for I give myself to you.
9 Rescue me from my enemies, LORD;
I run to you to hide me.
10 Teach me to do your will,
for you are my God.
May your gracious Spirit lead me
forward
on a firm footing.
11 For the glory of your name, O LORD,
preserve my life.
Because of your faithfulness, bring
me out of this distress.
12 In your unfailing love, silence all
my enemies
and destroy all my foes,
for I am your servant.

NOTES

143:1 *plea.* This "plea" is in particular a "plea for grace" (*takhanun* [TH8469, ZH9384]; BDB 337).

143:2 *no one is innocent before you.* According to the Hebrew, the sense is, "No one who is alive is righteous enough to be declared innocent in your presence." This is why the psalmist asks not to be judged: He, like all others, would not be found to be in the right.

COMMENTARY

Psalm 143 is the last in a final series of laments (Pss 140–143) before the transitional Psalm 144 that leads to the doxological conclusion to the entire book (Pss 145–150). This psalm naturally falls into two stanzas. The repetition of "answer me" in 143:1 and 143:7 marks the beginning of the two successive stanzas.[1] Both stanzas open with introductory strophes containing pleas to be heard (143:1-2 and 143:7). The first stanza has two more strophes that focus on the psalmist's complaint (143:3-4 and 143:5-6). The second stanza also has two more strophes that focus on the psalmist's requests for deliverance (143:8-10a and 143:10b-12).[2]

Answer Me (143:1-6). This first stanza is basically a plea for God to answer prayer. The plea is first of all a plea for grace (143:1-2). Unlike some laments, which call on God to answer because the psalmist is innocent of wrong in some particular situation (cf. Ps 7), this plea is made in spite of the reality of sin. No specific sin is confessed, however. The sin in view is that which characterizes "everyone alive." The psalmist is aware that no one can stand before God and expect to be declared righteous, based on his or her own performance in living in keeping with God's law (see, e.g., 14:1-3 and 130:3). No one can plead for God to act on the basis of an absolute human righteousness. When approaching God from this ultimate perspective, everyone must plead for God to act based on his grace.

The psalmist also pleads for God to act because he is overwhelmed by adversaries (143:3-4), as in the previous psalm. "I am losing all hope" translates the same expression rendered in 142:3 with "I am overwhelmed." The psalmist feels overwhelmed and hopeless, having been "chased," "knocked . . . to the ground," and forced "to live in darkness."

David was desperate (143:5-6). As a thirsty land desperately reaches up to heaven for rain, so David desperately reached his hands up to God for grace. Reflecting on God's acts of salvation in the past only served to heighten David's desperation for God to act in the present to deliver David from his adversaries.

Answer Me (143:7-12). The second stanza is, like the first, a plea for God to answer prayer and for him to answer quickly. The sense of desperation felt in the previous strophe is carried over into the second stanza by the word "quickly." This sense of urgency is more emphatic in the Hebrew text, where the word translated "quickly" is actually an imperative, "Hurry!" (which is the very first word of the stanza). As in Psalm 142, so too here, the psalmist wants deliverance in real time and space.

Answer in Real Time (143:8-10a). We do not know who the adversaries were or the exact nature of their persecution of David, but we do know that in David's mind he could not wait a month or even a week for deliverance. Whatever the circumstances, David needed to experience God's unfailing love in concrete ways the very next morning. He expected this unfailing love to come in the form of guidance, deliverance, and being taught more about how to live in keeping with the divine will for his life. He was praying to God in faith and running to God for protection, because God was his God.

Answer in Real Space (143:10b-12). The "firm footing" of which David speaks is literally "level ground." He was not looking for an otherworldly experience; he was looking for salvation in the real world in which he lived. He wanted freedom from his enemies, which entailed their demise. He pleaded with God at the end as he had at the beginning; he came to God as God's humble "servant" (143:2 and 143:12). As God's servant, David longed for the personal ministry of God's Spirit in his life. As his sense of purpose came to expression in 142:7, so too here David's ultimate goal in seeking deliverance was the glory of God's name (143:11a).

From this psalm we learn that we are secure in God, even if at times we feel overwhelmed and desperate in the face of great adversity. We have the God-given freedom to be honest with the Lord and to plead with him to act quickly to bring concrete solutions to our all-too-real problems. We can root our appeal in our plight, but ultimately we ground our appeal in the grace of our God who, for his own glory, is characterized by a love for us that can never fail.

ENDNOTES

1. Note also the repetition of the negative adverb *'al-* [TH408, ZH440] (NLT, "don't") in 143:2 and 143:7.
2. These two strophes are distinguished in Hebrew by the shift from the imperative in 143:8-10a to the injunctive imperfect (Joüon and Muraoka 1991:§113m; Waltke and O'Connor 1990:§31.5b) in 143:10b-12.

◆ LL. Psalm 144

A psalm of David.

1 Praise the LORD, who is my rock.
He trains my hands for war
and gives my fingers skill for battle.
2 He is my loving ally and my fortress,
my tower of safety, my rescuer.
He is my shield, and I take refuge
in him.
He makes the nations* submit
to me.

3 O LORD, what are human beings that
you should notice them,
mere mortals that you should think
about them?
4 For they are like a breath of air;
their days are like a passing
shadow.

5 Open the heavens, LORD, and come
down.
Touch the mountains so they billow
smoke.
6 Hurl your lightning bolts and scatter
your enemies!
Shoot your arrows and confuse
them!
7 Reach down from heaven and rescue
me;
rescue me from deep waters,
from the power of my enemies.
8 Their mouths are full of lies;
they swear to tell the truth, but
they lie instead.

9 I will sing a new song to you, O God!
I will sing your praises with a
ten-stringed harp.
10 For you grant victory to kings!
You rescued your servant David
from the fatal sword.
11 Save me!
Rescue me from the power of
my enemies.
Their mouths are full of lies;
they swear to tell the truth, but
they lie instead.

12 May our sons flourish in their youth
like well-nurtured plants.
May our daughters be like graceful
pillars,
carved to beautify a palace.
13 May our barns be filled
with crops of every kind.
May the flocks in our fields multiply
by the thousands,
even tens of thousands,
14 and may our oxen be loaded down
with produce.
May there be no enemy breaking
through our walls,
no going into captivity,
no cries of alarm in our town
squares.
15 Yes, joyful are those who live like this!
Joyful indeed are those whose God
is the LORD.

144:2 Some manuscripts read *my people.*

NOTES

144:12 ***May our sons flourish in their youth.*** Psalm 144:12 is introduced with the word *'asher* [TH834, ZH889]. This word is probably used here as a conjunction that introduces the anticipated results (see HALOT 1.99; DCH 1.432) of God answering the petitions of 144:3-11. The sense would then be, "so that our sons may flourish in their youth."

COMMENTARY

Psalm 144 marks a transition from the final group of laments (Pss 140–143) to the doxological conclusion of the book of Psalms (Pss 145–150). The central strophe (144:3-11) is like the previous laments in that it contains petitions for deliverance from trouble. And the notes of praise from the first strophe (144:1-2) and of blessing from the last strophe (144:12-15) pave the way to the concluding doxologies.

Praise (144:1-2). Psalm 144:1-2 is reminiscent of 18:1-2. Whereas in Psalm 18, David expressed his "love" (*rakham* [TH7355, ZH8163]) for the Lord, here he expresses "praise" (*barak* [TH1288A, ZH1385]). God is praised as David's "refuge," his ultimate source of protection in the battles of life. Quite a few of the words from the "refuge" semantic domain are piled up in 144:1-2: "rock," "fortress," "tower of safety," and "shield." And the primary verb "take refuge" (*khasah* [TH2620, ZH2879]) is also used.

At the beginning of the book of Psalms (1:1 and 2:12), the Lord had promised that David would experience "blessedness" if he chose to "take refuge" in the Lord. Here at the beginning of Psalm 144, David praises the Lord who has, in fact, been his refuge and strength through all of the battles he has fought and who was faithful to his promise to give David the nations as his inheritance. This psalm likewise gives us great encouragement to believe God's promise to us. He is always there as our refuge. There is always a place of safety for us, even in the middle of the battles of life.

Petition (144:3-11). The praise of 144:1-2 provided David with great confidence, as he once again found himself facing a host of human foes and needing the Lord to show up in his life as his refuge and strength (144:3-11). David begins this strophe with a brief reflection on humanity (144:3-4), which is quite similar to that found in 8:4. The question is the same: "What are human beings?" But the response is different (see McCann 1996:1255). Whereas in Psalm 8 the question is answered in terms of humanity as created in the image of God with dominion over the earth, here the question is answered in terms of human transience (see Pss 39 and 90). It is not humanity in its glory that occupies David's mind at this point but humanity in its weakness. It is from the position of acknowledging his weakness that David moves on to petition the Lord to show up in his life as a mighty Savior.

David wants God to manifest himself in the real time and real space of David's life (see commentary on Ps 143). In particular, he wants the Lord to show up as the Divine Warrior, armed with lightning bolts for arrows, for the purpose of scattering the enemies. The Lord has done so many times in the past and is called upon to do the same in the present. Remembering what God has done in the past serves to bolster our faith in what he will do in the present (see 143:5). As has so frequently been the case in the book of Psalms (see 4:2; 5:9; 7:14), the weapon of the foe is deceitful speech (144:8, 11) wielded against David to bring about his downfall.

Psalm 144:9 is probably a vow to sing a new song once David has experienced God's salvation (see Allen 1983:289). The consequences of the salvation are then spelled out in the final strophe.

Prosperity (144:12-15). The final verses paint a picture of prosperity (*'ashre* [TH835A, ZH897]; 144:15) that is similar to that found in Psalm 112. The effect of this picture is to teach that God's salvation has practical and tangible consequences in this life (as well as in the life to come). As in Psalm 112, so too here, prosperity is well-being in the family: sons and daughters full of beauty and grace. Also as in Psalm 112, economic prosperity is second on the list: fields producing bumper crops and flocks increasing exponentially. A dimension of prosperity touched on here and not in Psalm 112 is social well-being: freedom from external threat and internal violence. Well-being in family, finances, and society is at the heart of the prosperity held forth in the book of Psalms.

Psalm 144 ends with a beatitude that places the divine stamp of approval on such a state of prosperity and reminds us that such prosperity is rooted in serving the Lord as our God. This beatitude echoes the beginning of the Psalms: "What joy for all who take refuge in him!" (2:12). David took refuge in the Lord and then expected to experience the prosperity of God's salvation as the consequence. Through David's example, the Holy Spirit invites us to do the same.

◆ MM. Psalm 145*

A psalm of praise of David.

1 I will exalt you, my God and King,
and praise your name forever
and ever.
2 I will praise you every day;
yes, I will praise you forever.
3 Great is the LORD! He is most worthy
of praise!
No one can measure his
greatness.

4 Let each generation tell its children
of your mighty acts;
let them proclaim your power.
5 I will meditate* on your majestic,
glorious splendor
and your wonderful miracles.
6 Your awe-inspiring deeds will be on
every tongue;
I will proclaim your greatness.
7 Everyone will share the story of your
wonderful goodness;
they will sing with joy about your
righteousness.

8 The LORD is merciful and
compassionate,
slow to get angry and filled with
unfailing love.
9 The LORD is good to everyone.
He showers compassion on all
his creation.
10 All of your works will thank you,
LORD,
and your faithful followers will
praise you.
11 They will speak of the glory of your
kingdom;
they will give examples of your
power.
12 They will tell about your mighty
deeds
and about the majesty and glory
of your reign.
13 For your kingdom is an everlasting
kingdom.
You rule throughout all generations.

The LORD always keeps his promises;
he is gracious in all he does.*
14 The LORD helps the fallen
and lifts those bent beneath their
loads.
15 The eyes of all look to you in hope;
you give them their food as they
need it.
16 When you open your hand,
you satisfy the hunger and thirst
of every living thing.
17 The LORD is righteous in everything
he does;
he is filled with kindness.

[18] The LORD is close to all who call
on him,
yes, to all who call on him in truth.
[19] He grants the desires of those who
fear him;
he hears their cries for help and
rescues them.
[20] The LORD protects all those who
love him,
but he destroys the wicked.

[21] I will praise the LORD,
and may everyone on earth bless
his holy name
forever and ever.

145 This psalm is a Hebrew acrostic poem; each verse (including 13b) begins with a successive letter of the Hebrew alphabet. **145:5** Some manuscripts read *They will speak*. **145:13** The last two lines of 145:13 are not found in many of the ancient manuscripts.

NOTES

145:8 *filled with unfailing love.* The word translated "filled" is from the root *gdl* [TH1419, ZH1524]; a wooden translation would be "great of unfailing love." This same word is used in 145:3a, "Great is the LORD," and a related noun is used in 145:3b, "No one can measure his greatness." Greatness has previously been used in association with the Lord's kingship (see 47:2; 48:1; 95:3; 96:4; 99:2).

145:12 *They will tell about your mighty deeds.* The NLT leaves untranslated who is being told about God's mighty deeds—namely, "the sons of man" (i.e., "all humanity"). Compare the universal scope of 145:15-16, 21.

145:13 *The LORD always keeps his promises; he is gracious in all he does.* This poetic line is missing in the Leningrad Codex and is supplied in the NLT (see mg) from one Hebrew manuscript and the LXX and Syriac.

145:14 *The fallen . . . those bent beneath their loads.* The NLT leaves the word for "all" (*kol* [TH3605, ZH3972]) untranslated twice in this verse ("all the fallen . . . all those bent"). The word *kol* occurs 17 times in the psalm and is obviously a key term (see commentary).

145:17 *filled with kindness.* The NLT leaves the word for "all" (*kol* [TH3605, ZH3972]) untranslated here; the line could be translated "kind in all he does" (see previous note).

145:20 *the wicked.* The NLT leaves the word for "all" (*kol* [TH3605, ZH3972]) untranslated here; the line could be translated "all the wicked" (see note on 145:14).

COMMENTARY

With Psalm 145 we encounter the beginning of the climax of the book of Psalms. The beginning of this climax is signaled by the use of *tehillah* [TH8416, ZH9335] (psalm of praise) in the title to this psalm (*tehillah* is used in no other title). The odd masculine plural of this feminine noun was seemingly created just for use in the title to the entire book ("Book of Praises"). As indicated by the title of the whole book and by the content of Psalms 145–150, the whole book has been driving toward praise as its final destination. We are now at the gate of that destination.

Psalm 145 is an alphabetic acrostic with one line per letter of the Hebrew alphabet. Two kinds of lines characterize this psalm. One kind expresses the psalmist's intention to praise the Lord or asserts that others will praise the Lord. The other kind is praise proper, where the psalmist recounts who God is or what God has done. The focus of praise is on the Lord who reigns as king forever (145:1, 13); the psalm draws out key aspects of what that reign is like throughout the whole creation he has made.

The Intention to Praise. In the opening two verses, David expresses his own intention to praise God. His intention or resolve to praise the Lord is indicated grammatically by the use of the cohortative in these two verses and in 145:5 (see van der Merwe, Naudé, and Kroeze 1999:§19.4.3; Joüon and Muraoka 1991:§114c; and Waltke and O'Connor 1990:§34.5.1a). The psalmist is the explicit subject of the verbs for "praise" in 145:1-2, 5-6, and 21. David, however, also envisions praise coming not only from himself but also from others. These others include God's "faithful followers" (145:10), but the choir for praising the God who is "most worthy of praise" (145:3) must be comprised ultimately of "everyone on earth" (145:21). But even a choir composed of everyone on earth is not sufficient. Nothing less than "all of [God's] works" (145:10) will do for the praise of the king of the universe. This grand choir will praise God now and "forever and ever" (145:1, 21) and "forever" (145:2).

The Giving of Praise. The psalmist begins by affirming the greatness of God. This greatness is seen in God's "awe-inspiring deeds" (145:6) and the fullness of his unfailing love (see note on 145:8). While we can see evidence of God's greatness, that greatness is immeasurable. One amazing truth is that this God whose greatness transcends our finite minds is at the same time "close to all who call on him" (145:18). His greatness does not make him unapproachable. Rather, because he is so great, we can approach him with confidence. This is true, however, only because of who God is. He is good. In fact, he is "good to everyone" (145:9), and the story of his "wonderful goodness" is for everyone (145:7). And God's goodness comes to expression in his being "merciful and compassionate, slow to get angry, and filled with unfailing love" (145:8). In his love he shows particular concern for the downtrodden, and he rescues all who cry out to him, fulfilling the deepest desires of their heart. More than that, he provides for the needs of "every living thing" (145:15-16), and all of his actions are characterized by righteousness and love.

Psalm 145 has a distinctively universal orientation, which stands in bold relief when the text is read in Hebrew. The Hebrew word for "all" (*kol* [TH3605, ZH3972]) is used 17 times in this psalm. Since not all of these occurrences are translated with "all" in English, some of the rhetorical power of the psalm is lost in translation. The Lord is faithful in *all* he says and is kind in *all* does (145:13, 17). He is good to *all* people and has compassion on *all* his creation (145:9). He helps *all* the fallen and *all* those bowed down under heavy loads (145:14). He satisfies the desires of *all* living creatures (145:15-16). He is close to *all* who call on him sincerely (145:18), protects *all* who love him (145:20a), but destroys *all* who do not call on him or love him (145:20b). So *all* human beings will bless him (145:21), and *all* of his works will thank him (145:10). David leads the way in blessing the Lord *all* the days of his life (145:2). This use of "all" anticipates the final verse of the book of Psalms: "Let everything [*all*] that breathes sing praises to the LORD!" (150:6).

David resolved to praise the Lord and affirmed that everyone on earth will do the same (145:21). Psalms 146–150 are then provided as examples of the praise that appropriately fills our hearts and mouths.

NN. Psalm 146

[1] Praise the LORD!

Let all that I am praise the LORD.
[2] I will praise the LORD as long as
I live.
I will sing praises to my God with
my dying breath.

[3] Don't put your confidence in powerful
people;
there is no help for you there.
[4] When they breathe their last, they
return to the earth,
and all their plans die with them.
[5] But joyful are those who have the God
of Israel* as their helper,
whose hope is in the LORD their God.
[6] He made heaven and earth,
the sea, and everything in them.
He keeps every promise forever.
[7] He gives justice to the oppressed
and food to the hungry.
The LORD frees the prisoners.
[8] The LORD opens the eyes of the
blind.
The LORD lifts up those who are
weighed down.
The LORD loves the godly.
[9] The LORD protects the foreigners
among us.
He cares for the orphans and
widows,
but he frustrates the plans of
the wicked.

[10] The LORD will reign forever.
He will be your God, O Jerusalem,*
throughout the generations.

Praise the LORD!

146:5 Hebrew *of Jacob.* See note on 44:4. **146:10** Hebrew *Zion.*

NOTES

146:3 ***there is no help for you there.*** This colon contains the phrase *ben-'adam* [TH1121/120, ZH1201/132] (mere mortals). The sense is, "Do not trust in powerful people; they are mere mortals in whom no help can be found." When read in the context of 146:5 and 146:10, the point is that our confidence is to be in God, not in human beings, even if they are powerful. This same point has already been made with nearly the same vocabulary in 118:8-9.

146:5 ***joyful are those.*** For the Heb. *'ashre* [TH835A, ZH897] (blessed) as denoting well-being in every area of life, see Pss 1; 112; 144:12-15.

146:8 ***The LORD lifts up those who are weighed down.*** See 145:14.

COMMENTARY

Psalm 146 is the first of the five final Hallelujah psalms that bring the book of Psalms to its conclusion. Each of these psalms begins and ends with the exclamation "Hallelujah!" or "Praise the LORD!" The praise of God is the destiny of the Psalms, and it is our destiny as well. The path to that destiny is the way of faith. So the first psalm in this grand doxology calls us to praise the Lord (146:1-2) and to trust him as well (146:3-10). As we will see, praise and faith always go together (Westermann 1981:155, 160-161), for faith in God as our ultimate help and hope produces praise for him in our lives.

Praise the Lord (146:1-2). After the initial exclamation of praise, a self-invitation to praise the Lord follows: "Let all that I am praise the LORD." Such an invitation to praise is also found with different vocabulary in 103:1 and 104:1. This invitation is followed by an expression of firm resolve to accept the invitation. "I *will* praise" and "I *will* sing" are not future tenses in Hebrew but are cohortatives, forms used for the expression of firm resolution to action (see van der Merwe, Naudé, and Kroeze 1999:§19.4.3; Joüon and Muraoka 1991:§114c; Waltke and O'Connor 1990:§34.5.1a). And the psalmist does not simply resolve to praise the Lord at some point in the future but rather throughout the entirety of life: "as long as I live" and "with my dying breath." The reason for this commitment to a life of praise is that the Lord is absolutely trustworthy, and this is the subject of the next strophe.

Trust the Lord (146:3-10). The exhortation to trust the Lord is introduced by a warning against placing faith in human beings, even if those human beings are "powerful people." It is tempting to place faith in people, because we can see them and touch them. They are tangibly present with us and can seemingly provide immediate help in concrete ways. Yet we must never place our ultimate faith in them, because even powerful people are still "mere mortals" (see note on 146:3). The most powerful people in the world will one day stop breathing and "return to the earth." At that very moment any help they might be giving us will disappear. In the words of 118:8-9:

> It is better to take refuge in the LORD
> than to trust in people.
> It is better to take refuge in the LORD
> than to trust in princes.

So our psalmist says of humans, "There is no help (*teshu'ah* [TH8668, ZH9591]) for you there."

By way of contrast, the psalmist pronounces that those who trust the Lord are blessed (see 1:1). To trust the Lord is to depend on him to be your helper. To trust the Lord is to place your hope in him for help. This is not to say that human help is of no value at all. First Samuel 11:9-13 makes this clear. Saul promised that there would be "help/rescue" (*teshu'ah*) for the people the very next day. First Samuel 11:13 makes it clear that in Saul's mind the Lord was the one who granted the "help/rescue" (*teshu'ah*). But the way in which the Lord provided the help was through Saul's military prowess. Saul divided the army into three detachments and launched a surprise attack that roundly defeated the foe. To trust the Lord and not humans is to depend on him as the help behind the help (see commentary on 127:1-2).

In 146:6-10 the psalmist spells out three reasons why we can place our trust in the Lord. First, he is the Creator (146:6). In contrast to mere mortals, who have been created from and return to the earth (146:4; Gen 2:7), the Lord is the Creator not only of the earth but also of the seas and even the heavens. A God who has the wisdom and power to create the universe certainly has the wisdom and power necessary for us to experience well-being in every area of our lives. This God, moreover, is a God of abundance, as is clear from the fact that he created "everything in them," i.e., in the earth, the heavens, and the seas. A God of wisdom and power and bounty is a God to whom we can entrust our lives.

Second, he is the Redeemer (146:6b-9). It is conceivable that one could imagine a malevolent creator, but the creator of the universe who is revealed to us in the Bible is a good God. His word can be trusted, and he is a God of great compassion.

No word for "compassion" is found in these verses, but compassion exudes from them; God is described as giving justice to the oppressed and food to the hungry, freeing the prisoners and giving sight to the blind, lifting the burdens of those bent beneath life's load, and protecting the foreigners and caring for orphans and widows. He loves those who live in keeping with his will, while those who do not love him ultimately experience frustration. God's compassion is not just a disposition within him; it is a disposition that motivates him to act in real time and space for real people with real needs. A God of such realistic compassion for people in need is a God to whom we can entrust our lives.

Third, he is the king forever (146:10). In contrast to mere mortals, whose power lasts a moment in the span of history, God sits as the king who "will reign forever." The psalmist reminds us that the king is "your God." He is the God with whom we have an intimate relationship and the God who at the same time is the absolute ruler over all space and throughout all time. He is a God to whom we can most certainly entrust every detail of our lives, now and forever.

As we trust our Creator, Redeemer, and King, we experience him as our God who gives wisdom, power, and compassion—our God who meets our every need. With the psalmist, our response is to resolve to live a life of praise, exclaiming, "Praise the LORD!"

◆ OO. Psalm 147

1 Praise the LORD!

How good to sing praises to
our God!
How delightful and how fitting!
2 The LORD is rebuilding Jerusalem
and bringing the exiles back to
Israel.
3 He heals the brokenhearted
and bandages their wounds.
4 He counts the stars
and calls them all by name.
5 How great is our Lord! His power
is absolute!
His understanding is beyond
comprehension!
6 The LORD supports the humble,
but he brings the wicked down
into the dust.

7 Sing out your thanks to the LORD;
sing praises to our God with a harp.
8 He covers the heavens with clouds,
provides rain for the earth,
and makes the grass grow in
mountain pastures.
9 He gives food to the wild animals
and feeds the young ravens when
they cry.
10 He takes no pleasure in the strength
of a horse
or in human might.
11 No, the LORD's delight is in those who
fear him,
those who put their hope in his
unfailing love.

12 Glorify the LORD, O Jerusalem!
Praise your God, O Zion!
13 For he has strengthened the bars
of your gates
and blessed your children within
your walls.
14 He sends peace across your nation
and satisfies your hunger with the
finest wheat.
15 He sends his orders to the world—
how swiftly his word flies!
16 He sends the snow like white wool;
he scatters frost upon the ground
like ashes.
17 He hurls the hail like stones.*

Who can stand against his freezing
cold?
[18] Then, at his command, it all melts.
He sends his winds, and the ice
thaws.
[19] He has revealed his words to Jacob,
his decrees and regulations to Israel.
[20] He has not done this for any other
nation;
they do not know his regulations.

Praise the LORD!

147:17 Hebrew *like bread crumbs.*

NOTES

147:6 ***supports.*** The Polel of *'ud* [TH5749, ZH6386] is used only here and in 146:9, where it is translated "cares for" (see commentary).

147:9 ***and feeds the young ravens when they cry.*** This is not an independent clause in the Hebrew but is a second indirect object for the verb "gives food to." The Lord feeds not only the wild animals in general but also the young ravens that cry out to him.

147:10-11 ***pleasure . . . delight.*** Both are translations of the same Hebrew verb, which is the last word in verse 10 and the first word in verse 11. Repeating the verb in both lines draws out the contrast in 147:10-11 more clearly.

COMMENTARY

Psalm 147 is the second psalm in the concluding five-psalm doxology, and this psalm sets forth the praise of God in three strophes (147:1-6, 7-11, 12-20), each of which is marked at the beginning with "praise" (147:1, 7, 12). Two major themes occur in these strophes (God as Creator and Redeemer), but each strophe plays its own variation on these themes. As do the other psalms in this five-psalm doxology, Psalm 147 begins and ends with the exclamation "Hallelujah!" or "Praise the LORD!"

Praise the Lord (147:1–6). The call to praise is issued in this opening strophe not with the expected imperatives but with exclamations: "How good! How delightful! How fitting!" Implicit in these exclamations is the idea that since praise is so good and delightful and appropriate, praise is something that we would certainly want as a regular part of our lives. This strophe guides us into three dimensions of praising God.

We can praise God for his work of restoration (147:2-3). This psalm has the return from Exile in view and the rebuilding of Jerusalem, as is clear from 147:2. Psalm 147:3 is reminiscent of 146:7-8 with its portrayal of the Lord as one who restores broken hearts and broken bodies. In this world things get broken—relationships, bodies, hearts. God is to be praised because he shows up in our lives where we are broken. He shows up to restore us to the well-being that he created us to live in. He showed up in Jesus, who casts out demons and heals to fulfill "the word of the Lord through the prophet Isaiah, who said, 'He took our sicknesses and removed our diseases'" (Matt 8:17). Because of God's work of restoration, we exclaim, "Hallelujah!"

We can also praise God for his work of creation (147:4-5). God knows his creation intimately. We know there are billions of stars. He knows their exact number! We have named many stars. He has named each and every one! What a testimony to his intimate and pervasive knowledge! What a testimony to his power! "How great is our Lord! His power is absolute! His understanding is beyond comprehension!" (147:5). If he knows the impersonal stars by name, how much more does he know those created in his personal image by name. Our names have been recorded in the Lamb's Book of Life (Rev 21:27). God's knowledge of and power over his creation in general and our lives in particular evoke from deep within us the exclamation "Hallelujah!"

Finally, we can praise God for his support (147:6). In 146:9 God both supports (see note on 147:6) the defenseless and frustrates the wicked. In a similar vein, according to 147:6, God both supports the afflicted and humbles the wicked. The idea seems to be that the Lord supports those who live in keeping with his ways by eliminating those who would disrupt their well-being. Because of his compassionate support, we exclaim, "Hallelujah!"

Praise the Lord (147:7-11). This second call to praise the Lord comes in the form of imperatives, as one would expect. The second imperative comes from the same root (*zamar* [TH2167, ZH2376]) as "to sing praises" in 147:1. Two elements are added to this second summons, however: thanksgiving and the use of instruments. Instruments will be mentioned in Psalm 149 and will play a major role in Psalm 150. This strophe guides us into two further dimensions of the praise of God.

We can praise God for his provision (147:8-9). The psalm unfolds a beautiful picture of God's provision colon by colon. First, God provides clouds. From the clouds he provides rain. Through the rain God provides vegetation. With the vegetation God provides food for the wild animals in general and for the young ravens in particular. As human beings we praise the Lord for his provision of all that is necessary for our fellow creatures to eat and thus to thrive in God's world. But we also know that his provision for the animals is a witness to the truth that he also provides us with all that is necessary for our life. In fact, if he provides for the animals, he will certainly provide for us (Matt 6:25-34). Because of God's abundant provision, our hearts are not full of anxiety, but our mouths are filled with the exclamation "Hallelujah!"

We can also praise God for how he delights in us (147:10-11). How marvelous to think that the creator of the universe not only knows us by name but also delights in us! He certainly delights in everything that is good in us, including things like the physical strength he has given us and we have developed. Psalm 147:10 does not intend to say that God has absolutely no delight in our physical strength or beauty or our mental powers, etc. When read with the following line, the point is that God takes no delight in our substituting things like physical strength for our faith in him. As we live in keeping with his ways and depend upon his unfailing love, God truly delights in us—in everything about us. His unfailing love for us and his delight in us call forth the exclamation "Hallelujah!"

Praise the Lord (147:12-20). Two more imperatives from two more roots (*shabakh* [TH7623, ZH8655] and *halal* [TH1984A, ZH2146]) introduce this final strophe of praise. The imperatives in 147:7 are plural, so the point has already been made in Hebrew that praise is to come from a group of people. In 147:12 it becomes explicit that the chorus of praise is to be corporate in nature. All the inhabitants of Jerusalem (Zion) are called upon to praise the Lord. Our individual praise is pleasing to God, and it is important for us to join our voices in the corporate praise of our Creator and Redeemer. This final strophe guides us into three additional dimensions of the praise of God.

We can praise God for his bounty (147:13-14). Whereas in 147:2 God restored the broken-down city, here he blesses it with bounty. He fortifies the city and fills it with a new generation of his children. His bounty brings peace/*shalom*/well-being [TH7965, ZH8934] in all areas of life that spills out of the city and floods the entire nation. He not only feeds the animals, but he feeds us with the finest of foods that satisfy both body and soul. Because our God is a generous God who pours out his bounty on us, we exclaim, "Hallelujah!"

We can also praise God for his governance by his word (147:15-18). God not only created all things by his word (33:6), he also governs all things by that same powerful word (Heb 1:3). Snow and frost and hail and freezing and thawing are not simply natural processes; they are the direct result of God's speaking to his creation. Just as his word governs the elements, so his word governs our lives. We can rest securely in the knowledge that our lives are governed by the word of our God, who is full of unfailing love for us. Because of his good governance of the universe and our lives, we exclaim, "Hallelujah!"

Finally, we can praise God because of his guidance by his word (147:19-20). Not only does his providential word govern our lives from behind the scene, but his revealed word gives us all the guidance we need to please him and prosper in his world. The principles revealed in the Scriptures are a lamp for our feet and a light for our path (119:105). As we meditate on them and live them out, we experience success and well-being in every area of life (Ps 1). While in the old covenant era this revelation was given to Israel alone (147:20; see also Rom 3:1-2), it was God's intention that Israel would be the channel through which this revelation would go to the nations. This truth is already sketched out in the book of Psalms (see commentary on Ps 49) and is painted in full color in the New Testament (see Matt 28:18-20). Because of God's guidance provided to us through his word, we exclaim, "Hallelujah!"

◆ PP. Psalm 148

1 Praise the LORD!

Praise the LORD from the heavens!
Praise him from the skies!
2 Praise him, all his angels!
Praise him, all the armies of heaven!
3 Praise him, sun and moon!
Praise him, all you twinkling stars!
4 Praise him, skies above!
Praise him, vapors high above the clouds!
5 Let every created thing give praise to the LORD,
for he issued his command, and they came into being.
6 He set them in place forever and ever.
His decree will never be revoked.

7 Praise the LORD from the earth,
you creatures of the ocean depths,
8 fire and hail, snow and clouds,*
wind and weather that obey him,
9 mountains and all hills,
fruit trees and all cedars,
10 wild animals and all livestock,
small scurrying animals and birds,
11 kings of the earth and all people,
rulers and judges of the earth,
12 young men and young women,
old men and children.

13 Let them all praise the name of the LORD.
For his name is very great;
his glory towers over the earth and heaven!
14 He has made his people strong,
honoring his faithful ones—
the people of Israel who are close to him.

Praise the LORD!

148:8 Or *mist*, or *smoke*.

NOTES

148:4 ***vapors high above the clouds!*** Lit., "the waters which are above the heavens." The reference is to the waters in Gen 1:6-7 that are above the expanse (NLT, "space"), as opposed to the waters below the expanse that comprise the seas (see Seely 1991).

148:6 ***His decree will never be revoked.*** The NLT does a good job of rendering the Hebrew text at this point. It seems, however, that the text is to be emended slightly (so too Kraus 1989:561). The verb is singular, and the NLT takes the singular noun translated "decree" as the subject. It seems better to emend the verb to the plural to understand the created elements in the previous verses as the subject, and to take "decree" (*khoq* [TH2706, ZH2976]) as the implied object. The sense is: "He set in place laws (for the creation), and the created elements cannot break (*'abar* [TH5674, ZH6296]) those laws." This is the same idea communicated with the same vocabulary in Jer 5:22 with regard to the seashore: "I, the LORD, define the ocean's sandy shoreline as an everlasting boundary [*khoq*] that the waters cannot cross [*'abar*]." Here there is double entendre. The word translated "boundary" is the same word translated "decree" in Ps 148. The word translated "cross" is the same verb used in Ps 148. By setting a "law" in place, God established the "boundary" or seashore, and the waters can neither "break" that law nor "cross" that shoreline. This same idea is communicated in 104:9: "You set a firm boundary for the seas, so they would never again cover the earth." For the use of this vocabulary in relation to human longevity, see Job 14:5. The general idea is that the creation runs according to laws that God set in place at the time of creation (see 147:15-18).

148:8 ***fire.*** In this context the word *'esh* [TH784, ZH836] probably refers to lightning, as is the case in other texts like Exod 9:23: "So Moses lifted his staff toward the sky, and the LORD sent thunder and hail, and lightning [fire] flashed toward the earth" (see NIDOTTE 1.534).

COMMENTARY

Psalm 148 is a call to the whole universe to praise the Lord. The majority of the lines call on various aspects of creation to praise the Lord, with only three and a half lines providing praise proper. Two stanzas make up this psalm. The first stanza (148:1-6) summons the created elements in the heavens to praise the Lord, while the second stanza (148:7-14) is a parallel call to the elements of the earth. The opening of the second strophe of each stanza (148:5 and 148:13) is marked by the jussive ("Let . . . praise") in the first colon, which is followed by a reason clause ("for") in the second colon. And the second verse in each of the second strophes (148:6 and 148:14) begins with a Waw-relative imperfect, a verb form that occurs only in these two places in the entire psalm. The highly structured nature of these two stanzas underscores the idea of a highly structured universe that exists at God's command and for his praise.

Praise the Lord from the Heavens (148:1-6). Three dimensions of the heavens are singled out in this stanza. First, the angelic inhabitants of the heavens are called upon to praise the Lord. There have been similar calls to the angels in Psalms 29 and 103:20-21. Then the sun, moon, and stars are issued the call to worship; and finally the call goes out to the waters that are above the heavens. The effect is to summon all of the created elements in the heavens to praise the Lord.

The reason they are to heed the call is twofold. First, God called them into being by his word. This is the point made implicitly in Genesis 1 by the eightfold repetition of "and God said" at the beginning of each creative event. This same point is made explicitly in 33:6: "The LORD merely spoke, and the heavens were created. He breathed the word, and all the stars were born." Second, God sustains their existence by his word. This point was just made in 147:15-18. Since they owe their very existence to God, the praise of his name characterizes their existence.

Praise the Lord from the Earth (148:7-14). The first element of the earth to be summoned to praise the Lord is the sea with its creatures. The call then goes to the lightning, hail, snow, and wind. We would associate these with "heaven," but the ancient Israelites viewed them as part of the "earth" in a bipartite universe. In this scheme everything beneath the "expanse" of Genesis 1 is the earth, probably because these elements all come in contact with the earth and thus were experienced on the earth. The first point of contact on the earth for elements like hail and snow would be the tops of the mountains and hills, so they are the next elements to be mentioned. Then come the trees on the hills, followed by the animals, reptiles, and birds. Finally human beings are summoned to praise the Lord from the top down, from kings to children. We are summoned along with all our fellow creatures. We stand with the rest of the creation as finite creatures, existing for the praise of our Creator. Yet we stand at the climax of the list, as in Genesis 1, as God's unique image bearers.

As in the first stanza, two reasons are given to motivate a positive response to the call to worship. One is the transcendent nature of God's glory. The whole creation is glorious, especially the human race (see Pss 8; 149:4-5). But this glory is derivative. We are filled with the glory of one whose glory transcends earth and heaven (148:13; see 8:1). All of the glory possessed by the finite creation redounds to the glory of the infinite Creator. The second reason draws our attention to redemption. The Lord has empowered his people for abundant life and bestowed great honor on us (see 149:4-5) as those who have an intimate relationship with him. Because of who Jesus is and what he has done, we can have a special closeness to the creator of heaven and earth (Heb 7:19; 10:22).

As we approach the end of the book of Psalms, we hear the crescendo of praise growing louder and louder. We see the choir growing larger and larger. We see our own place in the chorus. We sense the heart of our reason of being: We exist to live an abundant life in the presence of the God who is worthy to be praised by us and by the whole of the universe he has made both now and forevermore.

◆ QQ. Psalm 149

1 Praise the LORD!

Sing to the LORD a new song.
Sing his praises in the assembly of the faithful.

2 O Israel, rejoice in your Maker.
O people of Jerusalem,* exult in your King.
3 Praise his name with dancing, accompanied by tambourine and harp.
4 For the LORD delights in his people;
he crowns the humble with victory.
5 Let the faithful rejoice that he honors them.
Let them sing for joy as they lie on their beds.

6 Let the praises of God be in their mouths,
and a sharp sword in their hands—
7 to execute vengeance on the nations
and punishment on the peoples,

[8] to bind their kings with shackles
and their leaders with iron chains,
[9] to execute the judgment written
against them.
This is the glorious privilege of his
faithful ones.

Praise the LORD!

149:2 Hebrew *Zion.*

NOTES

149:4 *crowns.* The Piel of *pa'ar* [TH6286, ZH6995] is better rendered with English "glorifies" (HALOT 3.908). God elsewhere glorifies (*pa'ar*) the Temple (Ezra 7:27; Isa 60:7, 13), Zion (Isa 60:9), and his people (Isa 55:5).

149:5 *he honors.* The word *kabod* [TH3519, ZH3883] could be translated "glory," and this would tie 149:4 and 149:5 more tightly together.

149:7 *on the peoples.* The NLT presumes an emendation from *bal-'ummim* [TH1077/523, ZH1153/569] (not peoples) to *balle'ummim* [TH871.2/1886.1/3816, ZH928/2021/4211] (on the peoples). This emendation has been necessary numerous times in the Psalms (see 44:14 [15]; 57:9 [10]; 108:3 [4]).

COMMENTARY

In this fourth psalm of the fivefold doxological conclusion to the book of Psalms, we have a celebration of the Lord's kingship. God's people are called to exult in their king (149:2). The reign of God entails the glorification of those who live in keeping with his principles (149:4-5) and the judgment of those who do not (149:6-9). This twofold entailment is reminiscent of the second psalm in the Psalter. Psalm 2 promises well-being to those who take refuge in the Lord and destruction for those who do not.

Psalm 149:1-4 focuses on the community at worship, while 149:6-9 has the judgment of the nations in view. This leaves 149:5 as the turning point between the two sections (Ceresko 1986:185). Psalm 149:5 contains the second of the three references to "the faithful" (*khasidim* [TH2623A, ZH2883]) in the psalm (McCann 1996:1275). The first is at the end of the first line (149:1b), and the third is at the end of the last line (149:9b). The second is in the first colon of the middle of the nine lines of the poem (149:5a). This threefold repetition leads to the conclusion that the reign of God is being viewed in relation to and from the perspective of the "faithful." In this psalm we see the faithful at worship (149:1-4), in glory (149:5), and at work (149:6-9).

The Faithful at Worship (149:1-4). The opening call, "Sing to the LORD a new song," has already been encountered in this exact form in 96:1 and 98:1. Both of these earlier psalms celebrate the kingship of God (see 96:10 and 98:6), so we should not be at all surprised to find the people of Jerusalem being called to exult in the "King" in 149:2. Before the Lord is called "King" in this psalm, he is called "Maker." The title "Maker" probably refers to the Lord as the one who formed his people through the Exodus and the wilderness experience (so McCann 1996:1275, and see note on 95:6). But in context an echo of God as Creator is not at all hard to hear (see 146:6, which also uses the word *'oseh* [TH6213A, ZH6913]; see also 147:4, 8-9, and 148).

Whereas in Psalm 2 the rulers of the nations were assembled to rebel against the divine king and his human messiah, here the faithful are assembled to praise and worship the king. Their worship is joyful and exuberant, as is clear from the references to the dancing and instruments that are a part of the worship (149:3). This exuberance will grow exponentially in the final psalm (see 150:3-5).

The reason for the worship is stated in 149:4: "The LORD delights in his people." We have already met this beautiful truth in the fivefold doxology in 147:10-11, where the Lord does not delight in those who depend on their own abilities and resources as the basis of their relationship with him, but in those who honor him by trusting him and living in keeping with his principles. This same point is made in 149:4, when the second colon amplifies the first by referring to the "humble" as those who experience God's salvation. The Lord delights in the humble, and his delight comes in the concrete form of salvation. Salvation is the glorification of the humble (see note on 149:4). Salvation is a recrowning of human beings with the glory and honor with which they were originally created. At creation we were originally crowned with glory and honor (see 8:5). "Salvation" from the narrowest to the broadest sense is a restoration to original glory, a glory we have all fallen short of (Rom 3:23). We celebrate the reign of God, because God's reign means our salvation, our restoration to glory (see Rom 8:28-30).

The Faithful in Glory (149:5). As the hinge verse, 149:5 looks back to the previous section, especially the final note on the glorification of God's people in 149:4b. With 149:4b still ringing in our ears, the "glory" referred to in 149:5a (see note) is almost certainly the glory of human beings. To be sure, this glory is derived from the glory of God (see commentary on Ps 8), but it is still a glory that is predicated of human beings. God's people here are exulting because the reign of God has resulted in their being transformed into the glorious image of their Creator and Redeemer (see Col 3:10). As the hinge verse, 149:5 looks forward to the following section, especially the final note on the "glory" of the "faithful." Their glory is experienced through doing the work that God called them to do.

The Faithful at Work (149:6-9). Worship and work are related. Verse 6a refers back to the community at worship, while 149:6b pictures them at work, establishing the reign of God.

These verses clearly presuppose the existence of the theocracy, when the people of God and the nation of Israel were one and the same. During the theocracy, an Israelite would be one of God's people, and the "nations" would be the "enemy." From the days of Joshua, Israel was charged with the military conquest of the nations living within the Promised Land (see, e.g., Deut 7:2). This vanquishing of the foe is in view in Psalm 2, where the human king would break the enemy with an "iron" rod, similar to how the people of God were to bind the foes with "iron" chains in 149:8. The establishing of the Kingdom of God through military victory was "the glorious privilege of his faithful ones" (149:9).

We, however, do not live in a theocracy, as did ancient Israel. The church has not been invested with the power of the sword to do its work (see Matt 26:52). We have been given a sword, but the sword we wield is "the sword of the Spirit, which is the word of God" (Eph 6:17; so Calvin 1979:316). We, like Israel, have as our work the establishing of the Kingdom of God on earth, but we use the sword of the Spirit to deliver the nations from sin and its misery and to bring them into the Kingdom of God's Son, a kingdom of light and freedom and forgiveness (Col 1:11-14). This is our glory: bringing others into a relationship with the Spirit of God through the work of Jesus Christ, whereby they, like us, are transformed from one level of glory to another (2 Cor 3:18).

God has created and redeemed us for glory, and he has called us to bring others into the experience of that glory. Human glory is now the result of the reign of God being established in our lives, and human glory has as its result the glory of God filling the earth more and more. The note that surrounds the psalm and the note that surrounds our lives is the glory of God: "Praise the LORD!" (149:1, 9).

◆ RR. Psalm 150

1 Praise the LORD!

Praise God in his sanctuary;
praise him in his mighty heaven!
2 Praise him for his mighty works;
praise his unequaled greatness!
3 Praise him with a blast of the ram's horn;
praise him with the lyre and harp!
4 Praise him with the tambourine and dancing;
praise him with strings and flutes!
5 Praise him with a clash of cymbals;
praise him with loud clanging cymbals.
6 Let everything that breathes sing praises to the LORD!

Praise the LORD!

COMMENTARY

"Praise" is the dominant note when we come to the final psalm in the book of Psalms. It is because of the momentum toward praise that characterizes the overall shape of the book of Psalms that the ancients called the Psalter "The Book of Praises" (see Introduction). Like the four preceding psalms, Psalm 150 begins and ends with "Hallelujah!" or "Praise the LORD!" Unlike the preceding psalms, and all other psalms for that matter, Psalm 150 is one extended invitation to praise the Lord. Thirteen times in six verses we are commanded to praise the Lord. Within the body of the psalm, every colon begins with the imperative "praise" except the final colon, where the poet switches to a jussive: "Let everything . . . praise." This shift signals the close of the psalm and sets us up to hear with clarity and conviction the final call to praise.

Given the repetition of the command to praise in each colon, Psalm 150 reads as a psalm comprised of a single strophe. Yet there is a movement of thought in the psalm from universal praise (150:1) to focused praise (150:2) to exuberant praise (150:3-5) and finally back to universal praise (150:6).

Universal Praise (150:1). The call to praise first goes out to the inhabitants of the heavens, i.e., the angels and the sun, moon, and stars (see 148:1-3), so that the heavenly sanctuary, where God's might is so clearly evident, might be filled with those who praise the Lord. Such calls to praise the Lord have occurred elsewhere in the Psalms (see 29:1-2; 103:20-21). Since there is no explicit call to human beings in the psalm, and yet worship in the earthly sanctuary is clearly in view in 150:3-5, there is an implicit call in 150:1 for earthly worshipers to follow the lead of the heavenly worshipers (see commentary on Ps 29). The total effect is to summon the whole universe to praise the Lord, with the accent here on the heavenly realm.

Focused Praise (150:2). The praise of God is focused on his "mighty works" and his "greatness." God's deeds are called *geburoth* [TH1369, ZH1476] (mighty works) six times in the book of Psalms. The reality of these mighty works gives rise to the praise of God for them (71:16; 145:4, 12; 150:2). They are works of salvation (20:6), which are innumerable (106:2). The focus of praise is on the mighty acts the Lord as king has carried out in saving his people and bringing them into glory (see 149:4 and commentary).

Those mighty acts came to their fullness in the Lord Jesus Christ, who lived a perfect life of righteousness in our place, died to pay the penalty for our sins, and was raised from the dead so that we might have abundant life now and forever. The Spirit of God continues to work in our lives, bringing this salvation more and more into reality in our daily experiences. As we continue to experience the greatness of our king through his mighty works of salvation on our behalf, we join the heavenly worshipers in praising him for his "mighty works" and his "unequaled greatness."

Exuberant Praise (150:3-5). Because of how great God is and how mighty his works on our behalf are, only exuberant praise will do. In ancient worship, a multitude of instruments were used: a variety of wind instruments, stringed instruments, and percussion. The percussion was loud, and the worshipers no doubt danced with all their might (see 2 Sam 6:14). Exuberance in worship will be manifested outwardly in different ways in different cultures and subcultures, but the external differences will come from the same internal fountain—hearts that are overflowing with praise to the Lord for the great things he has done.

That the message of praise is often musical in form is no accident. While no exhaustive answer is available to the question as to why God has chosen to use music, it seems that God has chosen to imbed the message of praise in music for a number of reasons (see Frame 1986). Music makes the message memorable. All of God's key acts are accompanied by music: Creation (Job 38:7), the Exodus (Exod 15), the Incarnation (Luke 1:46-55), and the final redemption (Rev 5:9). Music is also powerful. God does not simply want us to comprehend the message; he wants us to be moved by it, moved in every aspect of our being, and music has a unique power to move the human spirit. God wants to move us, so he communicates in a way that touches the mind and the body and emotions and the spirit. Music does that. The praise of God is to be exuberant, and music is a channel for that exuberance to come to expression.

Universal Praise (150:6). The last line in the poem calls upon "everything that breathes" to praise the Lord. The emphasis here is probably on living creatures on the earth and human beings in particular, but the angelic hosts of heaven cannot be excluded. In other hymns of praise, the call to worship has gone out to individuals (103:1), to the priests (135:19), to the people of Israel (68:26), to all the nations of the earth (117:1), to the angelic hosts (29:1-2), and to the whole created realm (Ps 148). It seems best to take "everything that breathes" ultimately to be synecdoche for the entire cosmos. God has created us, and ultimately all things, for his praise and glory (Isa 43:7). We arrive at our divine destiny when we arrive where the Psalms end—the praise of God. But the end of the book of Psalms is only a beginning for us. It is the beginning of an eternal life of praise to our Creator and Redeemer, who sent his Son that we might have abundant life now and forever. "Praise the LORD!"

BIBLIOGRAPHY

Abrams, M. H.

1985 *A Glossary of Literary Terms.* 5th ed. Fort Worth: Holt, Reinhart & Winston.

Allen, Leslie C.

1983 *Psalms 101–150.* Word Biblical Commentary 21. Waco: Word.

Allender, Dan B., and Tremper Longman III

1994 *Cry of the Soul: How Our Emotions Reveal Our Deepest Questions about God.* Colorado Springs: NavPress.

Alter, Robert

1985 *The Art of Biblical Poetry.* New York: Basic Books.

1992 *The World of Biblical Literature.* New York: Basic Books.

Anderson, A. A.

1972 *The Book of Psalms.* 3 vols. Greenwood, SC: Attic.

Anderson, George W.

1973 Characteristics of Hebrew Poetry. Pp. 1523-1529 in *The New Oxford Annotated Bible.* Editors, Herbert G. May and Bruce M. Metzger. New York: Oxford.

Auffret, Pierre

1982 *La Sagesse a Bati sa Maison. Etudes structures littéraires dans l'Ancien Testament et spécialmement dans les Psaumes.* Fribourg: Vandenhoeck & Ruprecht.

Barker, Kenneth L.

1995 Praise. Pp. 219-234 in *Cracking Old Testament Codes: A Guide to Interpreting the Literary Genres of the Old Testament.* Editors, D. Brent Sandy and Ronald L. Giese. Nashville: Broadman & Holman.

Barré, Michael L.

1995 Hearts, Beds, and Repentance in Psalm 4,5 and Hosea 7,14. *Biblica* 76:53-62.

Beckwith, Roger

1985 *The Old Testament Canon of the New Testament Church and Its Background in Early Judaism.* London: SPCK.

Beekman, John, and John Callow

1974 *Translating the Word of God.* Grand Rapids: Zondervan.

Bennett, Robert A.

1975 Wisdom Motifs in Psalm 14–53—Nabal and 'Esah. *Bulletin of the American School of Oriental Research* 220:15-21.

Berlin, Adele

1985 *The Dynamics of Biblical Hebrew Parallelism.* Bloomington: Indiana University.

Berlin, Adele, and L. Knorina

2008 *The Dynamics of Biblical Parallelism.* Rev. ed. Grand Rapids: Eerdmans.

Berry, Donald K.

1995 *An Introduction to Wisdom and Poetry of the Old Testament.* Nashville: Broadman & Holman.

Botha, P. J.

1991 The Junction of the Two Ways: The Structure and Theology of Psalm 1. *Old Testament Essays* 4:381-396.

1994 Psalm 24: Unity and Diversity. *Old Testament Essays* 7:360-369.

Brachter, Robert G., and William D. Reyburn

1991 *A Translator's Handbook on the Book of Psalms.* New York: United Bible Societies.

Braude, William G., translator

1959 *The Midrash on Psalms.* New Haven: Yale University Press.

Brennan, J. P.

1980 Psalms 1–8: Some Hidden Harmonies. *Biblical Theology Bulletin* 10:25-29.

Brettler, Marc

1993 Images of YHWH the Warrior in Psalms. *Semeia* 61:135-165.

Briggs, C. A.
1906 *A Critical and Exegetical Commentary on the Book of Psalms.* Greenwood, SC: Attic.

Brockelmann, Carl
1965 *Hebräische Syntax.* Neukirchen: Verlag der Buchhandlung des Erziehungsvereins.

Brown, Michael L.
1995 *Israel's Divine Healer.* Grand Rapids: Zondervan.

Brueggemann, Walter
1984 *The Message of the Psalms.* Minneapolis: Augsburg.

Bullinger, E. W.
1968 *Figures of Speech in the Bible, Explained and Illustrated.* Grand Rapids: Baker.

Burger, J. A.
1995 Psalm 1 and Wisdom. *Old Testament Essays* 8:327-339.

Bushell, Michael
1980 *The Songs of Zion.* Pittsburgh: Crown & Covenant.

Caird, George B.
1980 *The Language and Imagery of the Bible.* Philadelphia: Westminster.

Calvin, John
1972 *Institutes of the Christian Religion.* Translator, Henry Beveredge. Grand Rapids: Eerdmans.
1979 *Commentary on the Book of Psalms.* Translator, James Anderson. Grand Rapids: Baker.

Ceresko, Anthony B.
1985 The ABCs of Wisdom in Psalm XXXIV. *Vetus Testamentum* 35:99-104.
1986 Psalm 149: Poetry, Themes (Exodus and Conquest), and Social Function. *Biblica* 67:177-194.
1990 The Sage in the Psalms. Pp. 217-230 in *The Sage in Ancient Israel and the Ancient Near East.* Editors, John G. Gammie and Leo G. Perdue. Winona Lake, IN: Eisenbrauns.

Childs, Brevard S.
1971 Psalm Titles and Midrashic Exegesis. *Journal of Semitic Studies* 16:137-150.
1979 *Introduction to the Old Testament as Scripture.* Philadelphia: Fortress.

Clifford, Richard J.
1972 *The Cosmic Mountain in Canaan and the Old Testament.* Cambridge, MA: Harvard University Press.
1981 In Zion and David a New Beginning: An Interpretation of Psalm 78. Pp. 121-142 in *Traditions in Transformation.* Editors, Baruch Halpern and Jon D. Levenson. Winona Lake, IN: Eisenbrauns.
2002 *Psalms 1-72.* Nashville, TN: Abingdon Press.

Clines, David J. A.
1969 Psalms Research Since 1955: II: The Literary Genres. *Tyndale Bulletin* 20:105-125.
1974 The Tree of Knowledge and the Law of Yahweh (Psalm XIX). *Vetus Testamentum* 24:8-14.

Coetzee, J. H.
1992 A Survey of Research on the Psalms of Lamentation. *Old Testament Essays* 5:151-174.

Cohen, Chaim
1996 The Meaning of *Tslmwt* "Darkness": A Study in Philological Method. Pp. 287-309 in *Texts, Temples, and Traditions: A Tribute to Menahem Haran.* Editors, Michael V. Fox et al. Winona Lake, IN: Eisenbrauns.

Cohen, Herbert
1996 Hinds in Psalm 29. *Jewish Biblical Quarterly* 24:258-259.

Cohen, Samuel I.
1995 Psalm 47: Numerical and Geometrical Devices Used to Emphasize the Author's Message. *Jewish Biblical Quarterly* 23:258-264.

Collins, Terence
1971 The Physiology of Tears in the Old Testament. *Catholic Biblical Quarterly* 33:18-38, 185-197.

Craigie, Peter C.
1983 *Psalms 1-50.* Word Biblical Commentary 19. Waco: Word.

Creach, Jerome F. D.
1996 *Yahweh as Refuge and the Editing of the Hebrew Psalter.* Journal for the Study of the Old Testament Supplement 217. Sheffield: Sheffield Academic.

Crenshaw, James L.

1986 *Old Testament Story and Faith: A Literary and Theological Interpretation.* Peabody, MA: Hendrickson.

Cross, Frank Moore

1950 Notes on a Canaanite Psalm. *Bulletin of the American School of Oriental Research* 117:19-21.

1966 The Divine Warrior in Israel's Early Cult. Pp. 11-30 in *Biblical Motifs: Origins and Transformations.* Editor, Alexander Altmann. Cambridge, MA: Harvard University Press.

Crow, Loren D.

1996 *The Songs of Ascent (Psalms 120–134): Their Place in Israelite History and Religion.* Society of Biblical Literature Dissertation Series 148. Atlanta: Scholars Press.

Dahood, Mitchell

1965 *Psalms 1–50.* Anchor Bible Commentary 16. Garden City, NY: Doubleday.

1968 *Psalms 51–100.* Anchor Bible Commentary 17. Garden City, NY: Doubleday.

1970 *Psalms 101–150.* Anchor Bible Commentary 17A. Garden City, NY: Doubleday.

Dalman, Gustave

1928–1942 *Arbeit und Sitte in Palästina.* 7 vols. Gütersloh: Evangelischer Verlag.

Davis, Ellen F.

1992 Exploding the Limits: Form and Function in Psalm 22. *Journal for the Study of the Old Testament* 53:93-105.

Day, John

1995 *Psalms.* Old Testament Guides. Sheffield: Sheffield Academic.

Delitzsch, Franz

1982 *Biblical Commentary on the Book of Psalms.* Grand Rapids: Eerdmans. (Orig. pub. 1871.)

Dillard, Raymond B., and Tremper Longman III.

2006 *An Introduction to the Old Testament.* Grand Rapids: Zondervan.

Dobbs-Allsopp, F. W.

1995 The Syntagma of *bat* Followed by a Geographical Name in the Hebrew Bible: A Reconsideration of Its Meaning. *Catholic Biblical Quarterly* 57:451-470.

Donald, Trevot

1963 The Semantic Field of "Folly" in Proverbs, Job, Psalms, and Ecclesiastes. *Vetus Testamentum* 13:285-292.

Driver, G. R.

1967 Hebrew Homonyms. Pp. 50-64 in *Hebräische Wortforschung: Festschrift zum 80. Geburtstag von Walter Baumgartner.* Leiden: Brill.

Eaton, John

1967 *Psalms.* London: SCM Press.

1986 *Kingship and the Psalms.* Sheffield: Journal for the Study of the Old Testament Press.

1995 *Psalms of the Way and the Kingdom.* Journal for the Study of the Old Testament Supplement 119. Sheffield: Sheffield Academic.

Emerton, John A.

1996 Are There Examples of Enclitic *Mem* in the Hebrew Bible? Pp. 321-338 in *Texts, Temples and Traditions: A Tribute to Menahem Haran.* Editors, Michael V. Fox et al. Winona Lake, IN: Eisenbrauns.

Enns, Peter E.

1993 Creation and Re-creation: Psalm 95 and Its Interpretation in Hebrews 3:1–4:13. *Westminster Theological Journal* 55:255-280.

Estes, Daniel J.

1997 *Hear, My Son: Teaching and Learning in Proverbs 1–9.* Grand Rapids: Eerdmans.

Fishbane, M.

1979 Psalm 19. Creation, Torah, and Hope. Pp. 84-90 in *Text and Texture: Close Readings of Selected Biblical Texts.* New York: Schocken.

Fisher, Walter R.

1980 Genre: Concepts and Applications in Rhetorical Criticism. *Western Journal of Speech Communication* 44:290.

Fitzgerald, Aloysius

1983 Lord of the East Wind. Diss., Pontifical Biblical Institute.

Fokkelman, J. P.

2001 *Reading Biblical Poetry: An Introductory Guide.* Louisville: Westminster John Knox.

Fouts, David M.

1997 A Defense of the Hyperbolic Interpretation of Large Numbers in the Old Testament. *Journal of the Evangelical Theological Society* 40:377-389.

Frame, John M.

1986 Music in Worship. *New Horizons* 7:1-2.

Freedman, David Noel

1976 The Twenty-Third Psalm. Pp. 139-166 in *Michigan Oriental Studies in Honor of George C. Cameron.* Editor, L. I. Orlin. Ann Arbor: University of Michigan.

1987 Another Look at Biblical Hebrew Poetry. Pp. 11-28 in *Directions in Biblical Hebrew Poetry.* Editor, Elaine R. Follis. Sheffield: Journal for the Study of the Old Testament Press.

Fretheim, Terence

1991 *Exodus.* Louisville: John Knox.

Frye, Northrop

1971 *Anatomy of Criticism: Four Essays.* Princeton: Princeton University Press.

Futato, Mark D.

1984 A Meteorological Analysis of Psalms 104, 65, and 29. Ph.D. diss., The Catholic University of America.

1999 Suffering as the Path to Glory: The Book of Psalms Speaks Today. *Modern Reformation* 8:24-27.

2000 *Creation: A Witness to the Wonder of God.* Phillipsburg, NJ: Presbyterian & Reformed.

2002 *Transformed by Praise: The Purpose and Message of the Psalms.* Phillipsburg, NJ: Presbyterian & Reformed.

2004 *Joy Comes in the Morning: Psalms for All Seasons.* Phillipsburg, NJ: Presbyterian & Reformed.

2007 *Interpreting the Psalms: An Exegetical Handbook.* Grand Rapids: Kregel.

Gaebelein, Paul W., Jr.

1990 Psalm 34 and Other Biblical Acrostics: Evidence from the Aleppo Codex. *Maarav* 5-6:127-143.

Gerstenberger, Erhard S.

1988 *Psalms Part 1: With an Introduction to Cultic Poetry.* Grand Rapids: Eerdmans.

Gesenius, H. F. W.

1949 *Gesenius' Hebrew and Chaldee Lexicon to the Old Testament Scriptures.* Grand Rapids: Eerdmans.

Gibson, J. C. L.

1998 *Language and Imagery in the Old Testament.* Peabody, MA: Hendrickson.

Giese, Ronald L., Jr.

1995 Literary Forms of the Old Testament. Pp. 5-28 in *Cracking Old Testament Codes: A Guide to Interpreting the Literary Genres of the Old Testament.* Editors, D. Brent Sandy and Ronald L. Giese. Nashville: Broadman & Holman.

Gire, Ken

1996 *Windows of the Soul: Experiencing God in a New Way.* Grand Rapids: Zondervan.

Gitay, Y.

1996 Psalm 1 and the Rhetoric of Religious Argumentation. Pp. 232-240 in *Literary Structure and Rhetorical Strategies in the Hebrew Bible.* Editors, L. J. De Regt et al. Assen, the Netherlands: Van Gorcum.

Glass, Jonathan T.

1987 Some Observations on Psalm 19. Pp. 147-160 in *The Listening Heart: Essays in Wisdom and the Psalms in Honor of Roland E. Murphy, O. Carm.* Editors, Kenneth G. Hogland et al. Sheffield: Journal for the Study of the Old Testament Press.

Goldingay, John

1978 Repetition and Variation in the Psalms. *Jewish Quarterly Review* 68:146-151.

2007 *Psalms 42-89.* Grand Rapids: Baker Academic.

Grol, Harm W. M. van

1996 Psalm 27:1-6: A Literary Stylistic Analysis. Pp. 23-38 in *Give Ear to My Words: Psalms and Other Poetry in and Around the Hebrew Bible: Essays in Honour of Professor N. A. Van Uchelen*. Editor, Janet Dyk. Kampen: Kok Pharos.

Hackett, Jo Ann, and John Huehnergard

1984 On Breaking Teeth. *Harvard Theological Review* 77:259-275.

Harrison, R. K.

1969 *Introduction to the Old Testament.* Grand Rapids: Eerdmans.

1986 Why Hebrew Sheol Was Translated "Grave." Pp. 58-71 in *The NIV: The Making of a Contemporary Translation*. Editor, Kenneth L. Barker. Grand Rapids: Zondervan.

Holladay, William H.

1993 *The Psalms through Three Thousand Years: Prayerbook of a Cloud of Witnesses.* Minneapolis: Fortress.

Hossfeld, F. L., and E. Zenger

1993 Wer darf hinaufziehn zum Berg JHWHs? Zur Redactionsgeschichte und Theologie der Psalmengruppe 15-24. Pp. 166-182 in *Biblicalische Theologie und gesellschaftlicher Wandel. Für Norbert Lofink SJ.* Editors, G. Brualik et al. Freiburg: Herder.

Howard, David M., Jr.

1993 Editorial Activity in the Psalter: A State-of-the-Field Survey. Pp. 52-70 in *The Shape and Shaping of the Psalter.* Editor, J. Clinton McCann. Sheffield: Journal for the Study of the Old Testament Press.

1997 *The Structure of Psalms 93–100.* Winona Lake, IN: Eisenbrauns.

Hummel, Horace D.

1957 Enclitic Mem in Early Northwest Semitic, Especially Hebrew. *Journal of Biblical Literature* 76:85-107.

Irvine, Stuart A.

1995 A Note on Psalm 14:4. *Journal of Biblical Literature* 114:463-466.

Janzen, J. Gerald

1995 The Root Shkl and the Soul Bereaved in Psalm 35. *Journal for the Study of the Old Testament* 65:55-69.

Joüon, Paul, and T. Muraoka

1991 *A Grammar of Biblical Hebrew.* Rome: Pontifical Biblical Institute.

Keel, Othmar

1997 *The Symbolism of the Biblical World: Ancient Near Eastern Iconography and the Book of Psalms.* Winona Lake, IN: Eisenbrauns.

Kelly, Page H., Daniel S. Mynatt, and Timothy G. Crawford

1998 *The Masorah of Biblia Hebraica Stuttgartensia: Introduction and Annotated Glossary.* Grand Rapids: Eerdmans.

Kidner, Derek

1964 *Proverbs.* Tyndale Old Testament Commentary 15. Downers Grove, IL: InterVarsity.

1973a *Psalms 1–72.* Tyndale Old Testament Commentary 14a. Downers Grove, IL: InterVarsity.

1973b *Psalms 73–150.* Tyndale Old Testament Commentary 14b. Downers Grove, IL: InterVarsity.

Kirkpatrick, A. F.

1902 *The Book of Psalms.* Cambridge: Cambridge University Press.

Kline, Meredith G.

1972 *The Structure of Biblical Authority.* 2nd ed. Grand Rapids: Eerdmans.

Köhler, Ludwig

1957 *Old Testament Theology.* Philadelphia: Westminster.

Kraus, Hans-Joachim

1979 *Theology of the Psalms.* Minneapolis: Augsburg.

1988 *Psalms 1–59: A Commentary.* Minneapolis: Augsburg.

1989 *Psalms 60–150: A Commentary.* Minneapolis: Augsburg.

Kselman, John S.

1987 A Note on Psalm 4,5. *Biblica* 68:103-105.

Kugel, James L.

1981 *The Idea of Biblical Hebrew Poetry: Parallelism and Its History.* New Haven: Yale University Press.

Kuntz, J. Kenneth

1983 Psalm 18: A Rhetorical-Critical Analysis. *Journal for the Study of the Old Testament* 26:3-31.

Leeman, Saul

1996 The Atbash-Acrostic. *Jewish Biblical Quarterly* 24:43-45.

Léon-Dufour, Xavier

1973 *Dictionary of Biblical Theology.* 2nd ed. Gaithersburg, MD: The Word Among Us.

Levenson, Jon D.

1985 *Sinai and Zion: An Entry Into the Jewish Bible.* Minneapolis: Winston.

Lewis, C. S.

1958 *Reflections on the Psalms.* San Diego: Harcourt Brace Jovanovich.

Longman, Tremper, III

1984 Psalm 98: A Divine Warrior Victory Psalm. *Theological Journal of the Evangelical Theological Society* 27:267-84.

1985 Form Criticism, Recent Developments in Genre Theory, and the Evangelical. *Westminster Theological Journal* 47:46-67.

1988 *How to Read the Psalms.* Downers Grove, IL: InterVarsity.

1993 Biblical Poetry. Pp. 80-91 in *A Complete Literary Guide to the Bible.* Editors, Leland Ryken and Tremper Longman III. Grand Rapids: Zondervan.

1995 Lament. Pp. 197-216 in *Cracking Old Testament Codes: A Guide to Interpreting the Literary Genres of the Old Testament.* Editors, D. Brent Sandy and Ronald L. Giese. Nashville: Broadman & Holman.

Longman, Tremper, III, and Daniel G. Reid

1995 *God Is a Warrior: Studies in Old Testament Biblical Theology.* Grand Rapids: Zondervan.

Luther, Martin

1960 *Word and Sacrament.* Luther's Works 35. Philadelphia: Fortress.

Mays, James L.

1980 Psalm 13. *Interpretation* 34:279-283.

1987 The Place of Torah-Psalms in the Psalter. *Journal of Biblical Literature* 106:3-12.

1989 *Psalms.* Louisville: John Knox.

1993a The Language of the Reign of God. *Interpretation* 47:117-126.

1993b The Question of Context in Psalms Interpretation. Pp. 14-20 in *The Shape and Shaping of the Psalter.* Editor, J. Clinton McCann. Sheffield: Journal for the Study of the Old Testament Press.

1994 The Centre of the Psalms. Pp. 231-246 in *Language, Theology, and the Bible: Essays in Honour of James Barr.* Editors, Samuel E. Balentine and John Barton. Oxford: Clarendon.

McCann, J. Clinton

1992 The Psalms as Instruction. *Interpretation* 46:117-128.

1993a Books I-III and the Editorial Purpose of the Hebrew Psalter. Pp. 93-107 in *The Shape and Shaping of the Psalter.* Editor, J. Clinton McCann. Sheffield: Journal for the Study of the Old Testament Press.

1993b *A Theological Introduction to the Book of Psalms: The Psalms as Torah.* Nashville: Abingdon.

1996 *The Book of Psalms.* The New Interpreter's Bible 4. Nashville: Abingdon.

Merwe, Christo H. J. van der, Jackie A. Naudé, and Jan H. Kroeze

1999 *A Biblical Hebrew Reference Grammar.* Sheffield: Sheffield Academic.

Milgrom, J.

1967-1968 The Cultic Significance of Shegaga and Its Influence in Psalms and Job. *Jewish Quarterly Review,* n.s., 58:115-125.

Miller, Patrick D., Jr.

1973 *The Divine Warrior in Early Israel.* Cambridge, MA: Harvard University Press.

1986 *Interpreting the Psalms.* Philadelphia: Fortress.

1993 The Beginning of the Psalter. Pp. 83-92 in *The Shape and Shaping of the Psalter.* Editor, J. Clinton McCann. Sheffield: Journal for the Study of the Old Testament Press.

1994a Kingship, Torah Obedience, and Prayer: The Theology of Psalms 15-24. Pp. 127-142 in *Neue Wege der Psalmenforshung: für Walter Beyerlin.* Editors, Klause Seybold and Eric Zenger. Freiburg: Herder.

1994b The Theological Significance of Biblical Poetry. Pp. 213-230 in *Language, Theology, and the Bible: Essays in Honour of James Barr.* Editors, Samuel E. Balentine and John Barton. Oxford: Clarendon.

Milne, Pamela
1974–1975 Psalm 23: Echoes of the Exodus. *Studies in Religion* 4:237-247.

Mosca, Paul
1985 Psalm 26: Poetic Structure and the Form-Critical Task. *Catholic Biblical Quarterly* 47:212-237.

Mowinckel, Sigmund
1962 *The Psalms in Israel's Worship.* 2 vols. Nashville: Abingdon.

Muraoka, Takamitsu
1985 *Emphatic Words and Structures in Biblical Hebrew.* Jerusalem: Magnes.

Murphy, Roland E.
1959 A New Classification of Literary Forms in the Psalms. *Catholic Biblical Quarterly* 21:83-87.

1963 A Consideration of the Classification "Wisdom Psalms." *Vetus Testamentum Supplement* 9:157-167.

Nowell, Irene
1996 Psalm Therapy. *The Bible Today* 34:9-14.

Pardee, Dennis
1978 *YPH* "Witness" in Hebrew and Ugaritic. *Vetus Testamentum* 28:204-213.

Perowne, J. J. Stuart
1966 *The Book of Psalms.* Grand Rapids: Zondervan.

Petersen, David L., and Kent Harold Richards
1992 *Interpreting Hebrew Poetry.* Minneapolis: Fortress.

Pope, Marvin H.
1953 "Pleonastic" Waw before Nouns in Ugaritic and Hebrew. *Journal of the American Oriental Society* 73:95-98.

Power, E.
1928 The Shepherd's Two Rods in Modern Palestine and Some Passages of the Old Testament. *Biblica* 9:434-442.

Prinsloo, G. T. M.
1995a Hope against Hope—A Theological Reflection on Psalm 22. *Old Testament Essays* 8:61-85.

1995b Polarity as Dominant Textual Strategy in Psalm 8. *Old Testament Essays* 8:370-387.

Rendtorff, Rolf
1986 *The Old Testament: An Introduction.* Philadelphia: Fortress.

Roberts, J. J. M.
1973 The Davidic Origin of the Zion Tradition. *Journal of Biblical Literature* 92:329-344.

Ryken, Leland
1984 *How to Read the Bible as Literature.* Grand Rapids: Zondervan.

Sandy, D. Brent, and Ronald L. Giese, editors
1995 *Cracking Old Testament Codes: A Guide to Interpreting the Literary Genres of the Old Testament.* Nashville: Broadman & Holman.

Sawyer, J. F. A.
1970 An Analysis of the Context and Meaning of the Psalm Headings. *Glasgow Oriental Society Transactions* 22:26-38.

Schokel, L. A.
1988 *Manual of Hebrew Poetics.* Roma: Editrice pontificio Istituto biblico.

Schroeder, Christoph
1996 "A Love Song": Psalm 45 in the Light of Ancient Near Eastern Marriage Texts. *Catholic Biblical Quarterly* 58:417-432.

Seely, Paul H.
1991 The Firmament and the Water Above. Part I: The Meaning of *raqia'* in Gen 1:6-8. *Westminster Theological Journal* 53:227-240.

1992 The Firmament and the Water Above. Part II: The Meaning of "The Water Above the Firmament" in Gen 1:6-8. *Westminster Theological Journal* 54:31-46.

1997 The Geographical Meaning of "Earth" and "Seas" in Genesis 1:10. *Westminster Theological Journal* 59:231-256.

Smick, Elmer B.
1982 Mythopoetic Language in the Psalms. *Westminster Theological Journal* 44:88-98.

Smith, Mark S.
1988 The Structure of Psalm LXXXVII. *Vetus Testamentum* 38:357-358.

Tappy, Ron
1995 Psalm 23: Symbolism and Structure. *Catholic Biblical Quarterly* 57:255-280.

Tate, Marvin E.
1990 *Psalms 51–100.* Word Biblical Commentary 20. Dallas: Word.

Terrien, Samuel
1993 Wisdom in the Psalter. Pp. 51-72 in *In Search of Wisdom: Essays in Memory of John G. Gammie.* Editors, Leo G. Perdue et al. Louisville: Westminster/John Knox.

Thomas, D. Winton
1953 A Consideration of Some Unusual Ways of Expressing the Superlative in Hebrew. *Vetus Testamentum.* 3:209-224.

Thompson, J. A.
1980 *The Book of Jeremiah.* Grand Rapids: Eerdmans.

Vall, Gregory
1997 Psalm 22:17b: "The Old Guess." *Journal of Biblical Literature* 116:45-56.

Vang, Carsten
1995 Ps 2,11-12—A New Look at an Old Crux Interpretum. *Journal for the Study of the Old Testament* 9:162-185.

VanGemeren, Willem
1984 Sheol. Pp. 1011-1012 in *Evangelical Dictionary of Theology.* Editor, W. A. Elwell. Grand Rapids: Baker.

1991 Psalms. Pp. 1-880 in *Psalms—Song of Songs.* Expositor's Bible Commentary 5. Grand Rapids: Zondervan.

Vos, Geerhardus
1972 Eschatology of the Psalter. Pp. 323-365 in *Pauline Eschatology.* Editor, Geerhardus Vos. Grand Rapids: Eerdmans.

Waltke, Bruce K.
1981 A Canonical Process Approach to the Psalms. Pp. 3-18 in *Tradition and Testament: Essays in Honor of Charles Lee Feinberg.* Editors, John S. Feinberg and Paul D. Feinberg. Chicago: Moody.

1991 Superscripts, Postscripts, or Both. *Journal of Biblical Literature* 110:583-596.

Waltke, Bruce K., and M. O'Connor
1990 *An Introduction to Biblical Hebrew Syntax.* Winona Lake, IN: Eisenbrauns.

Watson, Wilfred G. E.
2005 *Classical Hebrew Poetry: A Guide to Its Techniques.* Journal for the Study of the Old Testament Supplement 26. Sheffield: Journal for the Study of the Old Testament Press.

Weiser, Artur
1962 *The Psalms.* Philadelphia: Westminster.

Wernberg-Möller, P.
1958 "Pleonastic" Waw in Classical Hebrew. *Journal of Semitic Studies* 3:321-326.

Westermann, Claus
1980 *The Psalms: Structure, Content, and Message.* Minneapolis: Augsburg.

1981 *Praise and Lament in the Psalms.* Atlanta: John Knox.

1989 *The Living Psalms.* Grand Rapids: Eerdmans.

Wharton, James A.
1993 Psalm 47. *Interpretation* 47:163-165.

Whitelam, Keith W.
1992 King and Kingship. *Anchor Bible Dictionary* 4.40-48. Garden City, NY: Doubleday.

Williams, Donald M.
1989 *Psalms 73–150.* The Communicator's Commentary 14. Dallas: Word.

Williamson, H. G. M.
1985 *Ezra, Nehemiah.* Word Biblical Commentary 16. Waco: Word.

Wilson, Gerald H.
1985 *The Editing of the Hebrew Psalter.* Chico, CA: Scholars Press.

1992 The Shape of the Book of Psalms. *Interpretation* 46:129-142.

1993 Shaping the Psalter: A Consideration of Editorial Linkage in the Book of Psalms. Pp. 72-82 in *The Shape and Shaping of the Psalter.* Editor, J. Clinton McCann. Sheffield: Journal for the Study of the Old Testament Press.

Wolff, Hans Walter
1974 *Anthropology of the Old Testament.* Philadelphia: Fortress.

Woodward, Branson L., Jr., and Michael E. Travers
1995 Literary Forms and Interpretation. Pp. 29-44 in *Cracking Old Testament Codes: A Guide to Interpreting the Literary Genres of the Old Testament.* Editors, D. Brent Sandy and Ronald L. Giese. Nashville: Broadman & Holman.

Young, Edward J.
1949 *An Introduction to the Old Testament.* Grand Rapids: Eerdmans.

Zenger, Erich
1994 New Approaches to the Study of the Psalms. *Proceedings of the Irish Biblical Association* 17:37-54.

Zorell, F.
1963 *Lexicon Hebraicum Veteris Testamenti.* Rome: Pontifical Biblical Institute.
1968 *Lexicon Hebraicum at Aramaicum Veteris Testamenti.* Rome: Pontifical Biblical Institute.

The Book of
Proverbs

GEORGE M. SCHWAB

INTRODUCTION TO
Proverbs

PEOPLE DO NOT LIKE TO THINK OF THEMSELVES AS FOOLS. No doubt you, the reader, already feel wise in choosing to advance in your understanding of the book of Proverbs. After all, no fool would seek out God's wisdom! You may consider yourself particularly savvy before even opening the pages of this book. This is why it is important that before continuing to read, you stop and hold up true wisdom as a mirror, seeing how you fare when critiqued by Proverbs. True wisdom does not consist in mere abstractions but is eminently practical. How do you fare when you measure yourself by the ideals in Proverbs?

Do you listen thoroughly before you respond to people (18:13)? Do you know when to keep your mouth shut (10:19)?
Do you show moderation in food and drink (20:1; 23:20-21)? Are you drawn in by illicit pleasures (ch 5)?
Do you lose your temper under pressure (12:16; 14:29)?
Do you readily take advice? Do you receive criticism with a humble attitude (13:10)? Do you seek honors for yourself (25:27)?
Do you know how to work diligently (14:23)? Are your two primary counselors Pastor Pillow and Deacon Sheets (26:14)?
Do you plan ahead and save some of your money (21:20)? Or is money an all-consuming thought for you (23:4)?
Are you considerate of your friends and their schedules (25:17)?
Are you responding with concern for the poor (21:13)?

This short self-evaluation is a reminder that every person behaves foolishly in some areas of life and needs to grow in wisdom. Reading and applying the book of Proverbs can help that growth. Enter the school of Wisdom and expect to grow in the very areas of life in which you judge yourself lacking.

AUTHORS AND DATES OF WRITING

The book of Proverbs is the work of several authors spanning many years. The primary author of Proverbs is undoubtedly Solomon. Unless everything the Bible records concerning Solomon is dismissed and he is treated as a virtual fiction, he towers over the wisdom enterprise of the Old Testament and must be acknowledged as constitutive. Many cognate wisdom materials predate Solomon and reveal that Wisdom Literature was extant long before his reign. For example, the Egyptian *Instruction of Amenemope* seems to share particular affinity with the Sayings of the

Wise (22:17ff). Between the Exodus and the chaos near the end of Judah's monarchy, Solomon was the only king the Bible records as cultivating friendly relations with Egypt (e.g., 1 Kgs 3:1). The Bible ascribes the authorship of many such writings to Solomon (1 Kgs 4:32), as does Proverbs (1:1; 10:1; 25:1). Although one cannot *prove* his authorship to critics distrustful of this witness, it is patently obvious that Solomon *could have* produced something like it. Brueggemann (1990:130-131) considers it "sociologically probable" that Solomon patronized the wisdom effort—since under his administration "everything seemed to work. The creation functioned, as did the social system"—a condition conducive to producing material like Proverbs, which commends a predictable world.

Citing no fewer than 30 instructional texts from Mesopotamia and Egypt, Kitchen (1977:85) is able to characterize Proverbs 1–24 as straddling the second and first millennia BC. Earlier texts often include prologues appealing to sons to hearken. Although the content of Proverbs's Prologue (chs 1–9) seems early, its length is more typical of first-millennium texts; on the other hand, these texts are more autobiographical and do not include extended appeals to listen. "In terms of date, such a transitional role would undoubtedly fit best at the end of the 2nd millennium BC and into the early 1st millennium BC—exactly the period when Solomon reigned." To claim that the Prologue is postexilic seems as anachronistic as claiming the same for the Sayings of the Wise!

Steinmann has extensively compared the vocabulary, conceptualizations, and modes of expression of the first nine chapters with the rest of the book, and his statistics indicate that one author produced chapters 1–9, 10:1–22:16, and 25–29, "exactly as the book itself indicates" (2000:674). He also observes that the Sayings of the Wise are similar to these, as is the poem of 31:10-31, which might also be Solomonic. The acrostic poem about the Woman of Virtue (31:10-31) references trading ships and merchants (Canaanites, 31:24), which seems to Crook most comfortable in the Solomonic era and not later (1954:137-138). Lyons also argues on economic grounds for the poem's early date (1987:238, contra Yoder 2003:429).

Proverbs's first recension might have featured a version of chapters 1–9, adopting the convention of many ancient instructional works to begin with a prologue. This was followed by an anthology of proverbs that crystallized into what we presently know as 10:1–22:16. Then a piece of Yahwetized Egyptian wisdom akin to *Amenemope* was appended—the Sayings of the Wise (22:17–24:22). Perhaps the book closed with the Woman of Virtue, an acrostic poem, as an epilogue (31:10-31), balancing the image of Lady Wisdom in the Prologue. Of course, this early edition was only a sample of all the literature Solomon produced.

About 250 years later, Hezekiah's court assembled and included other smaller Solomonic compositions (approximately 25:1–29:27) after the Sayings but before the Woman of Virtue acrostic poem, leaving her as the climax of the work. According to Steinmann (2000), these enjoy a high probability of having been cut from the same cloth as the earlier chapters.

Four units of text seem to have been late in their final placement: the oracle of Agur (30:1-14), the poem of threes and fours (30:15-33), the oracle of Lemuel (31:1-9), and the appendix to the 30 sayings (24:23-34). Their locations were finally standardized in the Hebrew text, apparently after their translation into Greek. (See the overview to the Epilogue, 30:1–31:31, for more details concerning this stage in Proverbs's growth).

Editorial activity probably continued. For example, Wolters (1985:580) posits a Greek wordplay in 31:27, which would indicate editing as late as the Hellenistic era. A number of Aramaic terms appear, which may be vestiges of the Persian period (see note on 22:21). The Septuagint includes proverbs absent in the Masoretic Text, indicative of creative subediting. Scribes likely polished Proverbs well into the Hellenistic era, culminating a tradition that began long before Solomon assumed the ancient task of inscripturating his great wisdom.

Sources for Proverbs. The Bible depicts Israel's faith in Yahweh (which scholars of the ancient Near East refer to as Yahwism) as unique in its monotheism and self-consciously distinct from the surrounding religions. However, Egyptian wisdom in particular predates Proverbs and yet exhibits distinctive similarities to it. This makes it apparent that the authors of Proverbs incorporated existing material into the biblical text—material that originated outside Israel's worship of Yahweh.

The adoption of alien elements into the biblical text was not mechanical but living and organic. Israel's faith controlled the recycling process without compromising the character of that faith. This is analogous to an organism's consumption of food—the food becomes part of it. Without food it would starve, yet the food does not change the creature's unique biological structure (or else it would die). The stuff of culture was reorganized in accordance with the spiritual dynamics of Yahwism.

Craigie identified modes of incorporating non-Israelite material into biblical wisdom texts. The first is "direct borrowing," the second is "adaptation of foreign materials" (called "Yahwization"), and the third is "creativity in the use of the resources of oral poetry" (Craigie 1971:28-30). Bryce submits a similar scheme. The first is the "adaptive" stage, where a proverb's Egyptian origin can be discerned; the second is the "assimilative" stage, where Egyptian materials have become "semitized." Thirdly, the "integrative" stage is where foreign material is fully dissolved into an Israelite text (Bryce 1979:58-114).

In creating a statue, a sculptor imposes an aesthetic quality on marble that was not present before the sculpting. It becomes a work of art according to aesthetic principles that transcend the marble itself—even though there is no part of the work not composed of marble and the marble itself is unchanged as marble. Canaanite, Babylonian, and Egyptian materials, having been molded into something new, should not be understood on the basis of its raw form, but according to the higher order that was imposed on the lower. (Even "direct borrowing" realigns the borrowed material through fresh context, changing its meaning. A raw piece of marble intentionally attached to a sculpture serves an artistic purpose.) A transcendent framework controlled the incorporation of cultural artifacts into what became the inspired canon. Egyptian wisdom has been recycled according to the principle of Yahwism, altering its original message and creating new expressions of Israelite faith.

A student of Scripture must presuppose this spiritual dynamic when comparing cognate texts with Proverbs. When comparing Proverbs and the Egyptian *Instruction of Amenemope,* for example, one really compares the whole Israelite culture (of which Proverbs is a part) with the whole Egyptian culture (*Book of the Dead* and all). This comparison clarifies how Israelite tradition demanded that Yahweh explicitly be named as the beginning and end of *khokmah* [TH2451, ZH2683] (wisdom). Something like the *Instruction of Amenemope* was the model for Proverbs's Sayings of the Wise (see the overview of the anthology 22:17-24:34)—and yet it was modified to be Yahweh-centric (see note on 22:19).

But in what culture and belief system did Amenemope ruminate? Egyptian literature speaks of the *ma'ath,* "truth, justice, and order" that holds together creation (Purdue 1994:37). But the religion of Egypt also included a well-developed doctrine of the afterlife. Any theory of Proverbs's dependency upon Egypt by definition acknowledges that this wisdom tradition developed in the shadow of the pyramids (monuments to their belief in the hereafter). Apparently, wisdom material has never existed in any context in which an afterlife was not acknowledged. Thus, the modern exegete should not exclude this viewpoint from the biblical Proverbs (see 12:28; 15:24).

Nonetheless, some have posited an early form of *khokmah* that exhibits no religious context, no faith in the divine to guarantee order, and no doctrine of eternal life. This theorized "wisdom" simply spoke to pragmatic matters of life. McKane, for example, divides his treatment of proverbs into three categories: Class A, which are "old wisdom" proverbs designed to promote the individual's success; Class B, which are community-minded; and Class C, which "are identified by the presence of God-language . . . expressive of a moralism which derives from Yahwistic piety" (1970:11). McKane understands Class C as a later "reinterpretation" of Class A. Thus, his commentary is difficult to read, since he perpetually deconstructs the integral text of Proverbs according to his assumptions. It is as if he wrests proverbs out of both ancient Egyptian and Israelite religious contexts and transposes them into the modern world where "secularity" has meaning! "To ascribe a primitively 'secular' character to the origins of any phase of human life in ancient times . . . is to go against all that we really know of ancient man" (Skehan 1971:23). The extant book of Proverbs clearly is religious and knows of no wisdom apart from trusting Yahweh.

Some of the Egyptian Wisdom Literature claims to be written for training officials' sons as courtiers (R. Williams 1990:19-20). It would not be surprising, then, for portions of Proverbs to have arisen within the Israelite court. Modern exegetes should not eschew this provenance for at least some parts of the book, especially given its claims of royal patronage (1:1; 10:1; 25:1; 31:1).

AUDIENCE

As the book of Proverbs grew over time, the intended audience also changed. It is possible that some of the smaller units were written as part of an educational program to train young sons to serve in government and to be able to successfully navigate and converse in the royal court. Literacy was largely the privilege of the elite; outside of religious and political circles, few would have been privy to the original book of Proverbs.

In time, the wisdom perspective became more and more popular in religious communities throughout Israel. This was especially the case in the Second Temple period, when many more wisdom books were written and disseminated throughout the Jewish communities of faith. The seminal viewpoint of Proverbs had by this time worked its way into the hearts and minds of all the people and had become fully democratized. Every citizen could embrace Wisdom, love her, and commit to fully walk her path—including rich and poor, man and woman, slave and free. No doubt Proverbs by Jesus' time was as widely read and cherished as the Psalter or Isaiah or any other book sacred to the Jews.

CANONICITY AND TEXTUAL HISTORY

The Hebrew Bible can be divided into three large sections: the Law, the Prophets, and the Writings. The Writings include the wisdom books such as Proverbs, Ecclesiastes, Job, and the Song of Songs. Other books in this collection are the Psalms, Lamentations, some historical works, and Daniel. In the Septuagint and English versions, the poetical books are in the center of the Old Testament, with the prophetic books at the end. The Hebrew Bible, however, ends with the Writings.

In the order of the Hebrew Bible, the book of Proverbs, which ends with the exemplary woman of Proverbs 31, neatly gives way to a historical example of just this sort of woman as recorded in the book of Ruth (2:11; 3:11). This in turn gives way to the Song of Songs, which explores in full measure the wise choice of the sage in selecting the woman of great worth as his lifelong partner in making a satisfying life.

The Masoretic Text. Between the fall of ancient Rome and the rise of the early Middle Ages (roughly AD 500–800), Christian Europe experienced its "dark ages." But Jewish scholarship flourished, and great advances were made by the Masoretes—scholars who preserved, stabilized, enhanced, and transmitted the Hebrew text.

In the early stages of the written Hebrew language, vowels were not written. The vowels were learned through orally reciting the text. (This is why the correct pronunciation of God's name YHWH has been lost—because the Jews stopped speaking it for fear of violating the commandment not to misuse God's name—see Exod 20:7 and Deut 5:11.) The Masoretes added vowels in the form of dots (points) above, below, and within the consonants. (Some consonants, such as Waw and Yodh, are also sometimes used as vowels.) These points indicate how the word is *vocalized*—how to pronounce it when reading. When a scholar suggests changing these, it is called *repointing* (e.g., see note on 27:25).

The vast majority of Hebrew words are built on a three-consonant root. Consider the English word "song." This word has three consonants that define its basic meaning, "s_ng." Supplying a vowel (such as "a," "i," "o," or "u") produces a noun or verb associated with the basic meaning of the root, that is, a musical performance with words. Depending how the Masoretes added vowels, a group of Hebrew consonants becomes a noun (as with English "song") or verb ("sing") and so on. The many words that can be built on the same root are called *cognates*. For example, the note on 3:13 refers to several cognates from the same root (see also note on 29:5). Sometimes translations differ in their identification of a word's root and thus its meaning. In 26:10, for example, the NLT and KJV greatly differ due to identifying different roots for the same word (see note).

The Masoretes also divided the verses in Proverbs in halves, indicating the primary structure of each verse. In this commentary, a slash is used to represent this division (e.g., "The fear of Yahweh is discipline for wisdom / And before glory comes humility"; see note on 15:33). In addition, the Masoretes made marginal notes in the text, suggesting alternative readings where they believed the text had suffered a copyist's error or had been damaged in some way. "What is written" (the suspicious original) is called the *Kethiv;* "what to read" (their suggested alternative) is called the *Qere.* It is normal practice for scholars to follow Qere. Many Kethiv-Qere issues are not noted in this commentary; Qere is simply followed (compare note on 16:19).

The result of the Masoretes' work is called the Masoretic Text (MT). The best representative complete copy of their work extant today is Codex Leningradensis, which dates to about AD 1000.

The Ancient Versions. The Old Testament had been translated in antiquity into many different languages. Each of these versions witness to the original Hebrew text from which it was made, called its *Vorlage.* The Jewish Targum is an Aramaic translation; the Vulgate was a widely used Latin translation. There are also the Peshitta (Syriac translation), and, most importantly, the Old Greek translation, sometimes called the Septuagint (abbreviated as LXX, from the Roman numeral for "seventy"—the traditional number of Greek translators).

When struggling with a difficult Hebrew text, often scholars will employ the Septuagint to suggest a different *Vorlage* that resolves the difficulty. Unfortunately, it is likely that the Greek translator struggled with the same difficult verse as his modern-day counterpart! As such, the usefulness of the Septuagint in shedding light on particularly troublesome verses is almost negligible. Of course, easily understood and sensible verses have no need of "correction." Thus, the Septuagint is most useful for only mildly difficult verses. Even here, the Septuagint is often of marginal value, since it is, after all, only a translation, and the translator had his own style and agenda. For example, the Septuagint often seeks to facilitate the text, to make it flow better, sometimes by *interpolating,* i.e., adding explanatory material (a word here, a phrase there; see notes on 2:6; 12:12; 13:15; 19:29). The Septuagint exhibits a different macrostructure from the Masoretic Text, seemingly translated from a *Vorlage* predating the final form of Proverbs's various parts. (See the commentary on the Epilogue, 30:1–31:31.)

Biblia Hebraica Stuttgartensia. The critical text of the thousand-year-old Codex Leningradensis is published as *Biblia Hebraica Stuttgartensia* (BHS); it continues the Masoretes' work in suggesting alternative readings to suspicious texts, called *conjectural emendations.* No two ancient manuscripts are identical. Errors of transmission plagued every ancient text. For example, when two instances of the same letter were juxtaposed, sometimes a scribe accidentally skipped one, and it was not transmitted to subsequent copies. This is called *haplography* (see note on 16:22). Or, perhaps a sleepy scribe might unintentionally write the same word(s) more than once (*dittography*)—see notes on 10:10 and 16:16. In such cases, BHS suggests ways to "restore" the text to its precorrupted state.

Suspect texts put scholars between a rock and a hard place. On the one hand, if it is in fact a misprint, then the text is damaged and any attempt to read it in a straightforward manner will result in a meaning unintended by its author. On the other hand, if the text is baffling yet perfectly preserved, and the commentator mistakes it for an error and "corrects" it, the result will be an artificial verse of the scholar's own imagination—and *not* the biblical text! For example, Driver (1951:191-192) emends three out of four words of 28:2, generating a completely different verse (cf. notes on 21:4; 22:5, 10). Waltke and Garrett spin out nuance and meaning from a word in 28:6 that may be a simple pointing error (see note).

Let us also look at 26:23. The Hebrew reads "burning lips," which NLT rejects in favor of the emendation "smooth lips" (see note). If it is in fact an error, then to assign a meaning of "a kiss of warm friendship or love" is to spin out implications on a misspelled typo (Whybray 1994a:378). But Waltke (2005:362) emends the text to "smooth"—then proceeds to make commentary on his own invented proverb, which is *not* before him on the page of his Hebrew text! Only one of these two readings is correct, but there is no unequivocal way to decide which. Errors of transmission or damage due to mishap have done irreversible harm to the text's clarity, much to the dismay of the community of faith. But scholars of the church such as Whybray or Waltke, continuing the work of the Masoretes, must decide such matters.

A number of criteria are at issue in making these decisions. First, the unchanged proverb should be confusing to read, but not nonsensical. If the verse were unintelligible, no emendation would be valid, since any proposal would be reflective of the scholar's imagination, not the Hebrew text (see note on 19:7). The smaller the proposed change, the more persuasive it is. A word found only once in the Hebrew Bible (called a *hapax legomenon*) is often emendation bait, since it may be simply a misspelling of a more common word. (But sometimes these must be left untranslated; see note on 29:21.) In addition, words of similar spelling—even cognates from other languages (Aramaic, Arabic, etc.)—when substituted for the suspicious one may yield very good sense. It is also helpful if the versions (like LXX) provide an alternative reading that confirms the conjecture. Some well-understood mechanism of error (e.g., haplography, dittography) should be suggested to explain how the error arose.

In the end, the scholar's judgment is a matter of taste and discretion; textual criticism is an art, not a science. There is no mechanical or automatic way to identify an error and how to correct it. In this commentary, the predilection is to give Masoretic Text the benefit of the doubt in the absence of compelling data to the contrary.

LITERARY STYLE

Poetics.

Parallelism. The distinguishing feature of Hebrew poetry is its parallelism. Virtually every verse in Proverbs is a pair of lines (cola), the second line usually relating to the first and carrying its thought further (Kugel 1981:52). There are various ways the two cola may relate to each other.

Each colon states its case in either a positive or a negative sense. For example, speaking of the wickedness of fools and their comeuppance is negative; applauding the wise or righteous is positive. A verse with a negative and positive line—a "parallelism of opposites" (Longman 2002:41)—is called *antithetic* (see note on 12:12). Examples of this are as follows: "A wise child brings joy to a father; / a foolish child brings grief to a mother" (10:1); "Lazy people are soon poor; / hard workers get rich" (10:4); "The godly care for their animals, / but the wicked are always cruel" (12:10).

Synonymous proverbs emphatically reword in the second line what the first line asserts: "The way of the godly leads to life; / that path does not lead to death" (12:28); "Evil people will bow before good people; / the wicked will bow at the gates of the godly" (14:19). *Comparative* proverbs complete the thought of the first line in the second: "There is a path before each person that seems right, / but it ends in death" (14:12); "The poor are despised even by their neighbors, / while the rich have many 'friends'" (14:20); "The LORD is watching everywhere, / keeping his eye on both the evil and the good" (15:3). *Emblematic* proverbs set a symbol parallel with its referent, as with each verse of 27:17-22: "As iron sharpens iron, / so a friend sharpens a friend" (27:17); "As a face is reflected in water, / so the heart reflects the real person" (27:19); "Lazy people irritate their employers, / like vinegar to the teeth or smoke in the eyes" (10:26). *Consequential* proverbs set two lines in logical sequence: "When the wicked die, their hopes die with them, / for they rely on their own feeble strength" (11:7); "A king detests wrongdoing, / for his rule is built on justice" (16:12). *Focusing* proverbs move from the general case in the first line to the specific in the second: "Punishment is made for mockers, / and the backs of fools are made to be beaten" (19:29).

Pithiness, imagery, wordplay. Hebrew poetry strives to say much with few words; it is crisp, brief, terse (Longman 1987:121; for examples, see 25:18; 29:17). Thus, it characteristically lacks particles and helpful modifiers, often leaving to the reader the job of supplying missing words. Proverbs may express a word in the first line, which is "gapped" or "elided" in the second line, or vice versa. This is called *elision* or *ellipsis* (see 10:23; 11:10)—yet another way the proverb remains pithy (Longman 1987:122). For example, 14:14 reads in Hebrew, "The faithless of heart will be sated with his ways / And a good man from his own." The second line is meant to be read with the first line supplying necessary verbiage: "A good man [will be sated] from his own [ways]."

Another attribute of biblical poetry is its use of imagery and figures of speech. For example, Proverbs presents the image of the two paths to signify two life directions and two lifestyles. Throughout Proverbs many images are utilized that forcefully convey its overarching themes, such as the image of Lady Wisdom (ch 8).

Various figures of speech are also employed in the book of Proverbs. *Merism* is the juxtaposition of two opposites to convey the whole, such as "day and night" or "heaven and earth." Another example is, "The rich and poor have this in common: / The LORD made them both" (22:2)—i.e., he made everyone. *Synecdoche* replaces a broader term with a narrower or vice versa (such as "bread" for "food"). In 30:4, "breath" (NLT, "wind") might be a synecdoche for "life" (see note). *Metaphor* (see 30:5; note on 14:14) compares two things to suggest a common trait: "Wisdom is a tree of life" (3:18); "He is a shield" (30:5). Metaphor is another device that makes proverbs terse; a simple comparison conveys much with few words. If "God is a shield" were restated in nonmetaphorical speech, how many words would be required to unpack all that the metaphor implies? *Simile* is like a metaphor, but uses "like" or "as." Examples of this in Proverbs are as follows: "Poverty will pounce on you like a bandit" (6:11); "A quarrelsome wife is as annoying as constant dripping" (19:13); "They have teeth like swords" (30:14). *Allegory* is an extended metaphor, such as in 27:23-27, which treats shepherds and flocks, but allegorically addresses kings and kingdoms (see also 5:15-23).

Other poetic devices are employed in Proverbs. Take note of the use of *paronomasia* (punning and wordplay). This takes similar- or identical-sounding words and juxtaposes them to ornament the maxim and to add amusement, and perhaps to help in memorization. (For examples, see 6:27; 13:20; 26:10, 18; 31:27.) A single word may also have two meanings (double entendre). Sometimes when two senses are possible, both are meant to be considered (13:7; 17:17; 19:22).

"What is the effect of a proverb as we ponder it? Most emphatically, a good proverb is not designed to put an end to thought on a subject but instead to stimulate further thought and application. The proverb is a catalyst to reflection" (Ryken and Longman 1993:277). Ryken's salient point should be kept in mind when struggling with difficult verses. For example, what is the meaning of 22:6, "Direct your children onto the right path, / and when they are older, they will not leave it"? The ramifications of that proverb alone require another whole book. This commentary is meant to help stimulate thought, not to give the definitive answers to the meanings of every proverb.

Literary Structuring of the Proverbs. Various identifiable devices are implemented in Proverbs to help organize and group units of text. One noted above is the *acrostic* poem. The Woman of Virtue (31:10-31) is comprised of 22 verses, each beginning with a successive Hebrew letter. This identifies the poem as a unit of text. Other units in Proverbs, though not alphabetic acrostics, seem modeled upon the form and also should be approached as units (e.g., 2:1-22; 27:1-22).

Another way to bind together verses into units is the device of the *chiasmus* or *chiasm*. The word derives from the Greek letter chi (X), because it compares the first element of a unit with the last, and the second to the second-to-last, forming a conceptual "X." For example, consider "The Sabbath is made for man, not man for the Sabbath." This may be analyzed as follows:

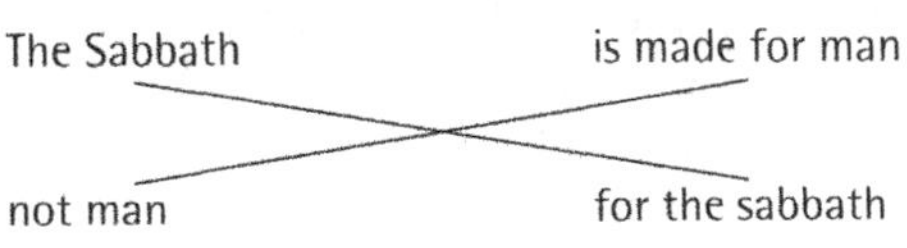

One may diagram the sentence as A B B′ A′. More complex chiasms include many other elements. Such a complex chiasm no longer looks like an X. In these cases, the chiasm is better represented in this manner:

A. the fool and folly (*'ewil* [TH191A, ZH211]) 12:15-16
  B. concealing (*kasah* [TH3680, ZH4059]) by the prudent (*'arum* [TH6175, ZH6874]) 12:16
    C. the truth (*'emunah* [TH530, ZH575]) 12:17
      D. the righteous (*tsedeq* [TH6664, ZH7406]) and the witness of falsehoods (*sheqer* [TH8267, ZH9214]) 12:17
        E. tongue of the wise brings healing 12:18
        E′. lips of truth are established forever 12:19
      D′. the righteous (*tsaddiq* [TH6662, ZH7404]) and Yahweh's detesting of falsehoods (*sheqer*) 12:21-22
    C′. Yahweh's delight in truth (*'emunah*) 12:22
  B′. the prudent (*'arum*) conceals (*kasah*) 12:23
A′. the fool and folly (*'iwweleth* [TH200, ZH222]) 12:23

Often, such an arrangement is designed to highlight its central material; the center verse of a unit enjoys pride of place even when not chiastic (for examples, see notes on 11:19 and 12:4).

The book also binds verses together into larger blocks of text by utilizing key words. For example, 16:1-9 employs the divine name Yahweh eight times; 16:10-15 repeatedly uses the word "king." These verses are not together accidentally, but are obviously grouped according to these key words. Many such key words are used throughout the book, which is sometimes obscured in English translation. For example, 15:29-32 uses the root *shm'* [TH8085, ZH9048] four times in four verses, glossed as "hears," "news," and "listen" in the NLT. Sometimes key words bind a unit tightly; sometimes they are merely suggestive.

Inclusion is a method of creating a unit's boundary by beginning and ending with a similar word or phrase. For example, the Hebrew of 1:2 reads *lada'ath khokmah umusar* [TH1847/2451/4148, ZH1981/2683/4592] (lit., "for knowledge, wisdom, and discipline")—three words precisely duplicated in 1:7, delineating 1:2-7 as a unit. Another example is found in 3:13-18, where the first word (*'ashre* [TH835A, ZH897]) and last word (*'ashar* [TH833A, ZH887]) come from the root *'shr,* "joyful, happy," enclosing the unit of text.

Sometimes a word occurs in two successive verses not to bind them together but to form a seam between them. This may be illustrated from prose. Ruth 1:19 in Hebrew uses "came to Bethlehem" twice, the first to end a paragraph, the second to begin a new one. Proverbs 5:15-19 ends with *shagah* [TH7686, ZH8706] (go astray), forming a seam with 5:20-23, which is also bounded by *shagah.* Sometimes two successive units will begin (or end) with the same word or phrase (a "head-head" or "tail-tail" pattern). For example, 8:5-11 and 8:12-16 both begin with "good judgment." Another instrument is the bridge (also called the *janus*), a verse or unit that relates both to what precedes and follows (e.g., 22:16).

Of course, material bounded by inclusion or similar devices ideally will treat a common theme. If a hypothetical inclusion is inferred but the enclosed proverbs fail to cohere, perhaps it is not an inclusion at all. This criterion cannot be pressed too far, however, since obvious chiasms also are comprised of multifarious verses (29:3-15).

Thematic arrangement is also used in Proverbs, and this is the method easiest to observe in English translation. In fact, most of the materials outside 10:1–22:16 and 25:1–29:27 are grouped by theme, sometimes in an almost prose-like fashion. For example, 1:8-19 treats the gang; 1:20-33, Lady Wisdom (as do chs 8 and 9). There are extended warnings against the loose woman that comprise whole chapters (5, 7), with chapter 7 essentially recounting a story with a moral.

The obvious weakness of this quest to identify poetic units is that it can be arbitrary, and often the results reveal the ingenuity of the critic rather than elucidating the text. No two analysts discover the same units of text. An inclusion for one may be a head-head pattern to another or may simply be judged accidental. It is also possible to examine the same text in different ways and discover contradictory chiasms, each with its own center! In addition, the text seems somewhat sloppier than the modern ideal of a hierarchical outline, and thus sometimes the scholar is tempted to seek justification for why the proposed analysis does not quite fit. For example, Bryce discovers an inclusion bounding 25:2-27 as a unit (1972:151), and 26:1-12 is also an obvious unit due to the key word "fool." But what is to be done with 25:28, which is left floating in between? In this commentary, it is attached to the stanza 25:23-28, extending Bryce's poem by one verse, and although a lucid reason is given, the sensibilities of the commentator (who dislikes leaving a verse without context) play a role.

"In the final analysis, the number of discourses or where the divisions are made have no impact on our understanding of their content" (Longman 2002:23). The specific identification of the book's overall structure is less important than the general idea of interpreting the proverbs in light of others in near proximity. My basic approach is to read any proverb in the context of whatever unit of text in which it occurs, to see them almost as parts of an ongoing narrative—in a word, to read them epexegetically, each interpreted by the others. I have asked, why is this axiom placed here and not somewhere else? Is the reader intended to see connections with the surrounding material? In any event, every commentator must break the book down into manageable portions, even if they are simply the traditional chapters. The sections proposed in this commentary, subjective though they might be, should at least offer some advantage over a chapter-by-chapter approach.

MAJOR THEMES

Wisdom and Creation. Wisdom Literature draws upon unchanging aspects of life rather than the advances of sacred history—mostly arguing from creation, not redemption. Yahweh's answer to Job cites nature as evidence of his competence (Job 38–39). Ecclesiastes focuses on the events of life that are "under the sun" (Eccl 1:14). In both cases, other perspectives were readily available (e.g., Yahweh is trustworthy because he delivered Israel from slavery), but wisdom presents another avenue to God—an avenue exemplified in creation (3:19-20; 8:22-31). Creation eloquently points away from itself to the wisdom of the Creator. The prudent think of God when they comprehend God's providential care of the universe.

It is common for commentators to interpret this focus on nature to imply that wisdom is available apart from a covenanted relationship with Yahweh. In a volume entitled *Wisdom in Israel*, von Rad devotes a chapter to "The Self-Revelation of Creation" (1972:144), where he argues that wisdom is intrinsic to the cosmos and to know wisdom is to understand this order—in part through natural science (1972:288). The sage's "task was to understand the true character of reality and to live in harmony with that discovery" (Crenshaw 1981:63). Estes remarks:

> *When Yahweh created the universe he embedded within it elements of causality and predictability. Through observation humans can discern the ways in which Yahweh has structured the world, and teach those patterns to others. The universe is not arbitrary, for Yahweh has constructed it with recognizable design. Neither is the world amoral, for Yahweh's order is intimately related to his righteous character.* (1997:29)

In this view, the image of Lady Wisdom represents this discoverable orderliness placed within culture and nature. God's voice stands "behind her, more distant, but still audible" (Purdue 1994:78).

While it is true that God's craftsmanship can be intuited everywhere, wisdom is not gained through observation! There is a difference between observing nature to find *illustrations* of wisdom and observing nature to *discover* what wise behavior is in the first place. Take the example of the ant, often used to sell the idea that the sage gains insight from nature (6:6-8):

> *Take a lesson from the ants, you lazybones. / Learn from their ways and become wise!*
> *Though they have no prince / or governor or ruler to make them work,*
> *they labor hard all summer, / gathering food for the winter.*

"By going to the ant, observing it, and considering the implications of what it does, the learner can gain wisdom" (Estes 1997:90). But does the sage really observe the ant to see how humans should live? Ants' successful survival strategy also includes these behaviors: inhuman bloodthirstiness toward those of different color; a callous refusal to share abundance with other insects; and the monstrous enslavement of aphids. Why then does the sage tout them as models to follow? Because in one—and only one—respect they exemplify wisdom. People who resemble the ant in this single activity are wise. Thus, one is not really modeling one's behavior on observation. One decides what is and is not wise before coming to the anthill for illustrations. Should we overthrow our governments because the locust has no king (30:27)? We do not work in summer to ward from winter because ants do; we do not march in rank because locusts do. We come already knowing these actions are wise; we intuit the Creator's wisdom for us reflected even in insects. When we read, "Whether a tree falls north or south, it stays where it falls" (Eccl 11:3), we do not infer wisdom in the tree—yet it (and other inanimate objects) may serve to illustrate principles for life.

It is *Yahweh's* wisdom that is omnipresent; every fact of life, all reality, does testify eloquently to *him*. Creation reflects the Creator's character. His creativity and great skill are seen in the intricacies of all things. The reliable patterns of experience that sages observe declare the glory of God, their guarantor; human wisdom is the ability to connect these patterns with the fear of Yahweh—not to live autonomously from him. "The LORD tears down the house of the proud, / but he protects the property of widows" (15:25). No principle embedded in creation automatically ensures the widow's well-being and avenges her. "No human wisdom or understanding or plan / can stand against the LORD. The horse is prepared for the day of battle, / but the victory belongs to the LORD" (21:30-31). It is the all-wise God with whom the sage reckons and about whom he speaks confidently.

Solomon did not become wise by studying nature. First, he asked Yahweh for wisdom. Having been granted this prudent request, Solomon then was able to speak of nature and justice and every matter of wisdom. The goal of this enterprise was to know God; so perceiving the patterns of life was a step along the way, not the ultimate goal. An atheist who understands the workings of the cosmos or masters political norms so as to live harmoniously with his fellows is *not* wise in the fullest, proverbial sense of the word. The goal of life is knowledge of Yahweh (1:7)—thus any so-called "knowledge" that fails to lift the student to contemplate God is misleading and not really knowledge at all but a misrepresentation of reality. Yes, Ezekiel calls pagan navigators and craftsmen, literally, "wise" (Ezek 27:8-9), but only in a limited sense; they were *not* wise to worship idols. The book of Daniel labels the Chaldeans "wise men," but they did not know Yahweh, so they could not help their king (Dan 2, 4–5). Ants are called very wise for knowing the seasons—understanding how the world works—yet they do not possess that acumen offered in Proverbs which consists in fearing Yahweh. Locusts are masterful in cooperating with their comrades, but they do not call on the name of the Lord. One may label them, with the atheistic scientist, "unusually wise"—but comprehensive sagacity eludes them.

Thus the book of Proverbs should be regarded as God's Word just as much as the writings of Moses or Isaiah. The heavy-handed "thus says the LORD" is absent from Proverbs, and there is not an appeal to his mighty acts, yet Wisdom is herself divine, present from the beginning of creation, and revealed here in the book of Proverbs. She offers abundant life—and damnation to any who neglect her (Murphy 1966:10-11).

The Theology of Wisdom. Virtually every book of the Bible exhibits a wisdom aspect, easily identifiable through its employment of wisdom terminology, such as *khokmah* [TH2451, ZH2683] (wisdom), *binah* [TH998, ZH1069] (understanding), *sakal* [TH7919, ZH8505] (be wise), *da'ath* [TH1847, ZH1981] (knowledge), *musar* [TH4148, ZH4592] ("discipline" or "instruction"), and *'armah* [TH6195, ZH6893] (prudence). There is a dimension of knowledge and learning ever-present in the Bible's call for foolish and sinful humanity to turn to God. He invites us: "Come now, let us reason together," (Isa 1:18, ESV); "Learn from me," says Jesus (Matt 11:29, ESV). But Yahweh's school, wherein one learns to be wise, is primarily taught here in the book of Proverbs. Enter this course of study and become wise.

The words "wisdom" or "wise" are often a gloss of the Hebrew *khokmah* [TH2451, ZH2683] or its cognates. But what is *khokmah*? Solomon's wisdom is described in 1 Kings 4:29-34.

God gave Solomon very great wisdom and understanding, and knowledge as vast as the sands of the seashore. In fact, his wisdom exceeded that of all the wise men of the East and the wise men of Egypt. He was wiser than anyone else, including Ethan the Ezrahite and the sons of Mahol—Heman, Calcol, and Darda. His fame spread throughout all the surrounding nations. He composed some 3,000 proverbs and wrote 1,005 songs. He could speak with authority about all kinds of plants, from the great cedar of Lebanon to the tiny hyssop that grows from cracks in a wall. He could also speak about animals, birds, small creatures, and fish. And kings from every nation sent their ambassadors to listen to the wisdom of Solomon.

After chapters describing Solomon's Temple, palace, wealth, and achievements, the Queen of Sheba exclaims, "Praise the LORD your God, who delights in you and has placed you on the throne of Israel. Because of the LORD's eternal love for Israel, he has made you king so you can rule with justice and righteousness" (1 Kgs 10:9). Solomon's wisdom was seen in his ability to understand the things that today are normally associated with education; it is as if he had degrees in zoology, botany, architecture, art, music, literature, and political science!

But is it through study that one becomes wise? Consider Proverbs's own exemplars of extraordinary wisdom, noted in 30:24-28.

There are four things on earth that are small but unusually wise:
Ants—they aren't strong, but they store up food all summer.
Hyraxes—they aren't powerful, but they make their homes among the rocks.
Locusts—they have no king, but they march in formation.
Lizards—they are easy to catch, but they are found even in kings' palaces.

Ants know nothing of botany and have never composed a sonnet—yet they are called "unusually wise" in Solomon's Proverbs. What do they have in common with Solomon? Perhaps a text like Exodus 35:25 can shed some light on the question: "All the women who were *skilled* (from *khakam* [TH2450, ZH2682], the adjectival cognate of *khokmah* [TH2451, ZH2683]) in sewing and spinning. . ." See also Ezekiel 27:8, "Your helmsmen were *skilled* men from Tyre." Wisdom here means skill, ability, competency. Ants, hyraxes, and locusts are all adept at what they do. Weavers, oarsmen—any person or creature with a proficiency at something—possesses some measure of *khokmah*. In Solomon's case, this faculty was developed beyond other humans in many spheres.

Solomon's greatest examples of wisdom are seen in his exercise of government. In a dream, he asked of Yahweh, "Give me an understanding heart so that I can govern your people well and know the difference between right and wrong. For who by himself is able to govern this great people of yours?" (1 Kgs 3:9). First Kings then gives one shining example of his awesome depth of mind in making profound "Solomonic" judicial decisions (1 Kgs 3:16-28). Lady Wisdom identifies herself this way: "Because of me, kings reign, and rulers make just decrees. Rulers lead with my help, and nobles make righteous judgments" (8:15-16).

But good government is not the highest skill one can master. Wisdom in its ultimate sense is described in Deuteronomy 4:5-8.

Look, I now teach you these decrees and regulations just as the LORD my God commanded me, so that you may obey them in the land you are about to enter and occupy.

> *Obey them completely, and you will display your wisdom and intelligence among the surrounding nations. When they hear all these decrees, they will exclaim, "How wise and prudent are the people of this great nation!" For what great nation has a god as near to them as the* LORD *our God is near to us whenever we call on him? And what great nation has decrees and regulations as righteous and fair as this body of instructions that I am giving you today?*

Wisdom is chiefly the skill of living a righteous life before Yahweh. A sage knows how to please the living God. This is why Proverbs asserts that knowledge and wisdom begin with revering him (1:7; 9:10).

But this wisdom is particularly focused on handling matters that do not change over time—even as the Lord moves history from one redemptive epoch to another. The Israelites were slaves in Egypt until Yahweh delivered them with a mighty hand. Much changed with that deliverance, but much did not. In the Promised Land they still had to get up in the morning and prepare meals, do chores, raise their children, and so on. Biblical wisdom focuses on those things that have changed little over the course of redemptive history—despite the substantial changes God has wrought.

Thus, the wisdom books in the Bible reveal an alternative way of approaching God; they do not draw upon redemption for their genius, their kerygma, or their message. One will find very few references in Proverbs, Job, and Ecclesiastes to things that are very important elsewhere, such as the law of Moses, the covenant, David and the monarchy, the cultic purity laws (including Temple worship and animal sacrifice), the Exodus tradition, the anti-idolatry polemic, the Exile and restoration, the special status of Israel, and so on. These things all have changed radically since Christ has come (the food laws are abrogated, history has climaxed, and prophecy has been fulfilled), but matters of wisdom have not.

Proverbs in Relationship to the Rest of Scripture. Wisdom material tends to bracket out other modes of relating to God so as to clearly present its distinctive approach. This makes it seem more international in character and focuses on creation over redemption. However, this does not necessarily imply that Proverbs is hermetically sealed off from the other faith traditions of Israel or that sages did not embrace them. Proverbs is, among other things, a historical document, a product of the religious culture from which it cannot be divorced. It is one of a collection of diverse ancient writings and ought to be read in company with them.

For example, there are occasional uses of cultic language such as prayer, almsgiving, and blood sacrifices in Proverbs (3:9-11; 7:14; 14:9; 15:8, 26, 29; 16:6; 17:1; 21:3, 27; 22:6; 28:9-10; 29:4). In these cases, wisdom is found in one's attitude and integrity. Proverbs does not tell us what to pray or how to offer sacrifices, but it reminds us that God judges the inner motives of the worshiper. In this, Proverbs is in lockstep with the prophets (1 Sam 15:22; Isa 1:11-17; 58:6; Hos 6:6).

Proverbs also draws upon other biblical motifs, revealing the sage's comfort with them. The phrase "tree of life" is found in Proverbs a number of times—uniquely in the Old Testament outside of Genesis. It first appears in 3:18 in the context of creation themes, perhaps even with an implicit reference to Adam. Patriarchal history may lie behind 30:23. Leviticus 25 covers the same ground as 28:8. It should not be out-of-bounds to seek connections within the Canon for meaning—although that meaning is often transformed into a wisdom context. For example, terminology at home in Mosaic legislation ("commandment," "law") is employed to designate the lessons of wisdom (4:2-4; 6:20; 7:2; 13:14; 28:4-10; 29:18), as is language of prophecy and oracle (16:10; 29:18; 30:1; 31:1).

If there is a New Testament book of wisdom, it is James. Jesus Christ is mentioned infrequently by James, and his redeeming work on the cross is not referenced at all. James presents Jesus not as the suffering Savior who was crucified and rose again, but as the upholder of order in the church, the Judge before whom one gives account (Jas 2:1, 7; 5:9). James explicitly commends wisdom (Jas 1:5; 3:13-17) and treats timeless topics such as the tongue (Jas 1:26; 3:1-12), strong emotion (Jas 1:19-20; 4:1-3), and the rich and poor (Jas 1:9-11; 2:1-9; 5:1-5).

If the fear of the Lord is the beginning of wisdom according to Proverbs, we begin to gain wisdom today by becoming a disciple of Christ and entering his school (Matt 11:29). Jesus is the new Solomon, speaking wise words to Israel, especially in his parables (Matt 13). The parable (Gk., *parabolē* [TG3850, ZG4130]) was Jesus' characteristic manner of teaching in the synoptic Gospels, and *parabolē* is often used by the Septuagint to translate Hebrew *mashal* [TH4912, ZH5442] (proverb). After speaking to them in parables, the people marveled, "Where does he get this wisdom?" (Matt 13:54).

Paul takes biblical wisdom in a different direction. To Paul, the greatest example of God's wisdom on display for all to see is not in the creation, but in the mind-boggling way God has construed the salvation of the world: "God has united you with Christ Jesus. For our benefit God made him to be wisdom itself" (1 Cor 1:30). Jesus is wisdom incarnate, the one whom we believe over against the world's fine-sounding philosophies.

> *I want them to be encouraged and knit together by strong ties of love. I want them to have complete confidence that they understand God's mysterious plan, which is Christ himself. In him lie hidden all the treasures of wisdom and knowledge. I am telling you this so no one will deceive you with well-crafted arguments. (Col 2:2-4)*

Christ is God's wisdom on display: He lived among his people speaking words of wisdom, he calls upon all to listen, and he makes them wise. In him, creation and redemption are united as displays of God's magnificent profundity in ordaining how all things work together for our good.

Jesus himself is the paradigmatic wise man. This sage par excellence has become Lord and Christ; his people are called to walk in his ways, in the ways of wisdom. Thus, the book of Proverbs continues to be normative for Christians today, informing our ethics and mores. Jesus has not transformed the meaning of proverbs as radically as he has other portions of Scripture. But in the light of the gospel, Christians may discern more clearly than Solomon how it is that the proverbs speak truth—for we know that the world itself has an end, that Jesus will return, and all wrongs will be righted then—and the veracity of the proverbs, which we can uphold only through faith, will then be clearly seen as unmitigated truth.

The law was given by Moses, who offended God and so was forbidden to enter the Promised Land. The law is weak and cannot make us righteous. We must first become justified in Christ; then we may incorporate its righteous principles into our life. Solomon of the profligate harem gave his name to the Song of Songs, which cannot teach you how to love. You must first experience the love of God in Christ—then you will be free to love as God intends. And the book of Proverbs is also weak and cannot make you wise. "Solomon himself is . . . the wise king who fell into idolatry and became foolish. But the good news is that one 'greater than Solomon' (Matthew 12:42) has come. Once a person has experienced God's grace through Christ and has been given a new heart, he or she can begin to desire and to live a truly wise life" (Schwab 1995:6). The beginning of wisdom is to first come to Jesus. Then the proverbs will teach you how to wisely follow in ever-increasing measure.

OUTLINE

The hierarchical organization for Proverbs is given in the outline below. In this commentary, the major divisions of the book are called anthologies—large collections of smaller compositions or poems. (I call a unit a "composition" if it is rather eclectic and large, a "poem" if it is smaller or exhibits a tight thematic unity.) Compositions are composed of sections or segments (sections are complex, segments are simple and undivided). Sections are made from stanzas or strophes (a stanza is simple, a strophe is complex), and strophes are subdivided into parts. Thus the hierarchy of the nomenclature is as follows:

- Anthology (of poems and/or compositions)
  - Poem
  - Composition (of sections and/or segments)
    - Segment
    - Section (of stanzas and/or strophes)
      - Stanza
      - Strophe
        - Part

Proverbs can be parsed into five anthologies: the Prologue, Proverbs of Solomon, Thirty Sayings of the Wise, Hezekiah's Proverbs of Solomon, and the Epilogue. This fivefold division of Solomon's *torah* [TH8451, ZH9368] (1:8) mirrors the fivefold division of the books of Moses's *torah* and the five books of Psalms (Pss 1–41, 42–72, 73–89, 90–106, and 107–150).

- I. The Prologue (1:1–9:18)
  - A. Title (1:1)
  - B. Opening (1:2-7)
  - C. Father's Warning about the Gang (1:8-19)
  - D. Wisdom's Call; Who Listens? (1:20-33)
  - E. Two Paths (2:1-22)
  - F. Wisdom, Yahweh, and Life (3:1–4:27)
    1. Father's admonition to trust Yahweh (3:1-35)
    2. Father's admonition to get wisdom (4:1-9)
    3. Life versus stumbling (4:10-27)

- G. Wisdom and Pleasure (5:1–7:27)
  1. Advice about sex (5:1-23)
  2. Father's warnings (6:1-19)
  3. Warnings against immorality (6:20–7:27)
- H. Wisdom, Yahweh, and Life (8:1-36)
- I. Wisdom's Banquet; Who Listens? (9:1-18)

II. Proverbs of Solomon (10:1–22:16)
- A. The Righteous and the Wicked (10:1–11:31)
  1. Preface to Solomon's Proverbs (10:1-5)
  2. Proverbs about concealing and speaking (10:6-32)
  3. Wisdom in the community (11:1-31)
- B. Speech and Deeds (12:1-28)
- C. The Way of Wisdom and the Way of Death (13:1–14:27)
  1. Desiring and craving (13:1-25)
  2. Building the house (14:1-11)
  3. Death and how to escape it (14:12-27)
- D. The Wisdom of Yahweh and the King (14:28–16:15)
  1. The wisdom of Yahweh (14:28–16:9)
  2. The wisdom of the king (16:10–15)
- E. The Way of Wisdom and the Way of Death (16:16–19:12)
  1. The path of wisdom (16:16–17:6)
  2. The path of the fool (17:7–18:7)
  3. The strength of wisdom (18:8–19:12)
- F. Speaking and Doing before Yahweh (19:13–21:1)
- G. The Wicked and the Righteous (21:2–22:16)

III. "Thirty" Sayings of the Wise (22:17–24:34)
- A. Preface (22:17-21)
- B. The Thirty Sayings (22:22–24:22)
- C. Appendix to the Thirty Sayings (24:23-34)

IV. Hezekiah's Proverbs of Solomon (25:1–29:27)
- A. Title (25:1)
- B. Discovering Glory (25:2-28)
- C. Doing What Is Fitting (26:1-16)
- D. Damaging Speech (26:17-28)
- E. Domestic Life (27:1-22)
- F. Wisdom for Leaders (27:23–29:27)

V. Epilogue to Proverbs (30:1–31:31)
- A. The Oracle of Agur (30:1-14)
- B. Poem of Threes and Fours (30:15-33)
- C. The Words of King Lemuel (31:1-9)
- D. The Heroine (31:10-31)

COMMENTARY ON

Proverbs

◆ I. The Prologue (1:1–9:18)
A. Title (1:1)

These are the proverbs of Solomon, David's son, king of Israel.

NOTES

1:1 *Solomon.* The consonants of Solomon's name (*shelomoh* [TH8010, ZH8976]) have numerical values that add up to 375 (*sh* = 300, *l* = 30, *m* = 40, *h* = 5; also equal to $5^3 \times 3$), which is the number of verses in the first anthology of Solomon's proverbs (10:1–22:16). This correspondence is likely the product of later work in the book. This feature shows an order that transcends the individual proverbs themselves.

COMMENTARY

The title names the historical author, a typical practice for late-second and early-first-millennium Wisdom Literature (Kitchen 1977:95). Steinmann finds in his study of Proverbs's vocabulary, thought, and modes of expression that chapters 1–9, 10:1–22:16, and 25–29 were all authored by the same person. There is no reason to suppose that the Prologue was not part of the whole book from the beginning (Steinmann 2000:659-674).

The first nine chapters of Proverbs constitute its Prologue. This initial anthology of compositions is where the theological foundation is laid and the issues are framed for the remainder of the book—the "proverbs of Solomon" that begin in 10:1. It is here that the book unequivocally establishes its Yahweh-centric orientation. Wisdom is a matter of reverencing God and learning how to live a righteous life before him. The book is first of all instruction material for young people to help guard them from beguiling influences and point them in the right direction for life. What is at issue in this material is the soul, the life, the ultimate destiny of a person. Abundant and eternal life comes by a relationship with Yahweh in the context of a community of faith. By this criterion, Proverbs is of course also profitable and beneficial for every teachable soul to read and internalize. Hear, all you who are weary and burdened; take up the discipline of wisdom and learn from it, and you shall find wisdom for your souls (3:1-2).

The Prologue is composed of eight major compositions or poems (plus a one-verse title), as shown:

Title (1:1)
Opening (1:2-7)
Father's warning about the gang (1:8-19)
Wisdom's call; who listens? (1:20-33)
Two paths (2:1-22)
Wisdom, Yahweh, and life (3:1–4:27)
Wisdom and pleasure (5:1–7:27)
Wisdom, Yahweh, and life (8:1-36)
Wisdom's banquet; who listens? (9:1-18)

"Wisdom speaks for herself at the beginning (1:20-33) and at the end (8:1-36; 9:1-6; also 9:11-12?). In between, the sage formulates his own teaching, subordinate to that of Wisdom" (Skehan 1971:1). The Opening promises to every tractable person a disciplined mind, which will be able to distinguish right from wrong in various circumstances. The next section portrays one potentially attractive threat to a juvenile: peer pressure. Another evil voice is the loose woman, whose sales pitch veils her fatal reward. Opposite her is the wisdom of God, personified as a woman, that is transmitted by the wise parents and calls the inexperienced to be savvy and to fear Yahweh. Two paths are set before a young person—with two destinations. Some voices call to one, the parents call to the other. The way of wisdom is guarded by Yahweh and leads to life. Contrary to this is the seduction of the loose woman, perhaps the greatest peril the young man will face.

After describing all the wiles of the loose woman, Lady Wisdom is given voice, sets her banquet, and invites all interested in learning to dine. Then the meal begins in the rest of the book.

◆ B. Opening (1:2-7)

2 Their purpose is to teach people
wisdom and discipline,
to help them understand the
insights of the wise.
3 Their purpose is to teach people
to live disciplined and successful
lives,
to help them do what is right, just,
and fair.
4 These proverbs will give insight to the
simple,
knowledge and discernment to the
young.
5 Let the wise listen to these proverbs
and become even wiser.
Let those with understanding
receive guidance
6 by exploring the meaning in these
proverbs and parables,
the words of the wise and their
riddles.

7 Fear of the LORD is the foundation of
true knowledge,
but fools despise wisdom and
discipline.

NOTES

1:2 ***Their purpose is to teach people wisdom and discipline, to help them understand the insights of the wise.*** Lit., "For knowledge, wisdom, and discipline / To understand sayings of those with understanding."

1:3 ***disciplined.*** *Musar* [TH4148, ZH4592], as in 1:2.

1:4 ***insight to the simple, knowledge and discernment to the young.*** The "simpletons" or the "naive" are closely linked with the "youth." The term for simple, *petha'yim* [TH6612, ZH7343], is similar to the Hebrew word for "open"—their minds are open, empty, unfurnished rooms needing to be filled with knowledge; they are open-minded, that is, open to anything, easily influenced, impressionable. Youths have not yet made a commitment to a path in life. Proverbs promises that their needs will be met if they will only read. See Waltke's discussion on *petha'yim* (2004:111).

1:5-6 The Opening claims another benefit. The meaning of proverbs (*mashal* [TH4912, ZH5442]), the enigmatic and counter-intuitive lessons of the sage, will become perspicuous—the "light will go on" and the reader will "get it."

Jesus spoke in parables, and his disciples did not understand. Later and privately he explained them. In a similar way, read Proverbs and you will experience the "Aha!" of comprehending what those wiser than you have counseled but until now have not understood. Read and be guided onto the path of wisdom. Ideas and locutions with elusive signification will become clear. But it is not only youths and simpletons who benefit by reading: The person of understanding who is already wise will grow in learning and counsel by heeding Proverbs (Cascante Gómez 1998:408).

1:5 ***Let the wise listen.*** Note the imperative mood; this is a command.

COMMENTARY

The opening to the book of Proverbs quickly sets the tone for the book and frames the issues. Proverbs 1:2 begins with the words *da'ath khokmah umusar* [TH1847/2451/4148, ZH1981/2683/4592] (knowledge, wisdom, and discipline), which are repeated in 1:7—an inclusion that bounds 1:2-7 as a unit and serves as the book's opening. All who desire to learn wisdom are invited to enter into the world of Proverbs and learn. Those who do not are already condemned as fools. The Opening clearly identifies wisdom with a religious life, a life that acknowledges God.

Note the rich wisdom vocabulary. No fewer than eight verbs and at least sixteen nouns are employed to communicate that "these proverbs were written for you to become wise" (Tepox 2001:216-222). This lavish use of language invites the reader to enter and partake of the rich meal prepared therein.

Knowledge is introduced here as anything but an abstract philosophy. This is akin to James 3:13-18:

> *If you are wise and understand God's ways, prove it by living an honorable life, doing good works with the humility that comes from wisdom. But if you are bitterly jealous and there is selfish ambition in your heart, don't cover up the truth with boasting and lying. For jealousy and selfishness are not God's kind of wisdom. Such things are earthly, unspiritual, and demonic. For wherever there is jealousy and selfish ambition, there you will find disorder and evil of every kind. But the wisdom from above is first of all pure. It is also peace loving, gentle at all times, and willing to yield to others. It is full of mercy and good deeds. It shows no favoritism and is always sincere. And those who are peacemakers will plant seeds of peace and reap a harvest of righteousness.*

The book of Proverbs is not for those who desire a philosophical explanation of the world. It is for those who want to live an upright life in the community. Wise instruction is immediately connected with the skill of living in community. Wisdom is the art of justice, of playing fair, of doing right. Knowledgeable people are those who behave appropriately in society.

In the book of Proverbs, there are three kinds of people: those who love wisdom, those who are uncommitted, and those who despise wisdom. The nomenclature of the first category includes the wise (*khakam* [TH2450A, ZH2682]), the understanding (*nabon*, Niphal participle of *bin* [TH995B, ZH1067]), the faithful (*khasid* [TH2623A, ZH2883]), the good (*tobim* [TH2896, ZH3202]; cf. 2:20), the righteous (*tsaddiq* [TH6662, ZH7404]), the upright (*yesharim* [TH3477A, ZH3838]), and the blameless (*tamim* [TH8549, ZH9459]).

The uncommitted, who are not clearly on one path or another, to whom appeals are needed, include the child (*beni* [TH1121/2967.1, ZH1201/3276]; lit., "my son"), the youth (*na'ar* [TH5288, ZH5853]), and the naive (*petha'yim* [TH6612, ZH7343]; see note on 1:4). "Only *petha'yim* believe everything they're told! / The prudent carefully consider their steps" (14:15). "If you punish a mocker, the *petha'yim* become wise; / if you instruct the wise, they will be all the wiser" (21:11). "The instructions of the LORD are perfect, reviving the soul. The decrees of the LORD are trustworthy, making wise the *petha'yim*" (Ps 19:7). The *petha'yim* need good teaching most of all. As the *petha'yim* learn prudence and knowledge, they cease to be empty and open and are filled with wisdom. Children and youth (*na'ar*) require discipline. "Don't fail to discipline your children. They won't die if you spank them. Physical discipline may well save them from death" (23:13-14). Good teaching and imposed discipline fill up the simple with wisdom and provoke the youth to choose it.

Those who hate instruction include the fool (*'ewil* [TH191A, ZH211]), sinner (*khatta'im* [TH2400, ZH2629]), fool (*kesil* [TH3684, ZH4067]), scoffer (*lets* [TH3887A, ZH4370]), evil (*ra'* [TH7451A, ZH8273]), alien (*nokri* [TH5237A, ZH5799]), wicked (*rasha'* [TH7563A, ZH8401]), treacherous (*bogedim* [TH898, ZH953]), stranger (*zarah* [TH2214C, ZH2424]), sluggard (*'atsel* [TH6102A, ZH6789]), adulteress (*zonah* [TH2181B, ZH2390]), and transgressor (*pesha'* [TH6588, ZH7322]). "No harm comes to the godly, but the *resha'im* have their fill of trouble" (12:21). "*'Ewil* think their own way is right, but the wise listen to others" (12:15).

Lovers of wisdom heed instruction and grow ever wiser, haters of discipline reject the good and perish, and the undecided could go either way. Haters of wisdom do not listen to good counsel, and Proverbs has nothing to say to them.

Having listed the benefits of reading and the classes of people whom Proverbs serves, two great alternatives for human life are spelled out (1:7). On the one hand, the beginning of knowledge is to fear Yahweh. On the other hand, fools despise the essence of what Proverbs offers. This choice is before the reader: Will you revere Yahweh, or will you scorn knowledge? To be wise is to conduct oneself equitably in society and reverently before God; fools care nothing for this and thus are contemptible. The gauntlet is thrown down; the line is drawn in the sand—what kind of a person will you be? If a fool, then stop reading Proverbs—and this commentary—and go live your short life of folly. If a wise person, then read on and benefit.

◆ C. Father's Warning about the Gang (1:8-19)

8 My child,* listen when your father
corrects you.
Don't neglect your mother's
instruction.
9 What you learn from them will crown
you with grace
and be a chain of honor around
your neck.

10 My child, if sinners entice you,
turn your back on them!
11 They may say, "Come and join us.
Let's hide and kill someone!
Just for fun, let's ambush the
innocent!
12 Let's swallow them alive, like the
grave*;
let's swallow them whole, like those
who go down to the pit of death.
13 Think of the great things we'll get!
We'll fill our houses with all the
stuff we take.
14 Come, throw in your lot with us;
we'll all share the loot."

15 My child, don't go along with them!
Stay far away from their paths.
16 They rush to commit evil deeds.
They hurry to commit murder.
17 If a bird sees a trap being set,
it knows to stay away.
18 But these people set an ambush
for themselves;
they are trying to get themselves
killed.
19 Such is the fate of all who are greedy
for money;
it robs them of life.

1:8 Hebrew *My son;* also in 1:10, 15. 1:12 Hebrew *like Sheol.*

NOTES

1:8 ***listen.*** The appeal to listen (1:8-9) precedes the description of the gang's solicitation.

instruction. Heb., *torah* [TH8451, ZH9368] (law). The only "law" in Proverbs is the parents' heartfelt and impassioned entreaty to heed wisdom. Proverbs's *torah* (like Moses's) has five major divisions (see "Outline" in the Introduction).

1:9 ***crown you with grace.*** Egyptians wore pendants of the goddess Ma'at about the neck, symbolizing "eternal life" (Waltke 2004:188). Perhaps this is a parallel with wisdom's benefits.

1:10 ***My child.*** Precisely, "my son" throughout.

entice you. Lit., "attempt to persuade" (Clines and Gunn 1978:23).

1:11 ***Just for fun.*** Lit., "Without cause." This is the same term as Job 1:9, lit., "Does Job serve God *for nothing?*" and Job 2:3, "You urged me to harm him *without cause.*"

1:14 ***we'll all share the loot.*** Lit., "There shall be one purse to all of us." The solidarity and unity of the gang is highlighted.

1:15-16 ***Stay far away. . . . They rush.*** The Hebrew uses "feet" in each of these two phrases as a synecdoche for life direction.

1:17 ***bird.*** Lit., "possessor of wing." This is parallel to 1:19; the "possessor" of violent gain is ensnared and robbed of life.

being set. Lit., "being scattered." Driver reads *mezorah* [TH2219, ZH2430] (scattered) as *mezurah* [TH2115, ZH2318] (pressed) with the versions (cf. Obad 1:7). The verb would then refer to the action of springing a trap: "In vain is the net drawn tight" (1951:173-174). The bird will escape if the net is not yet drawn tight. However, the action of "spreading" a net is similar to that of "scattering" seed, consistent with *mezorah* as in the MT.

COMMENTARY

After the Opening's verses, the first example of wisdom's challenge is a warning against the seductive gang. The first wise voice is the father who pleads with his son to stand firm. This is followed by a description of the gang, which speaks of blood no less than three times. Wisdom avoids violence and does not exploit the helpless.

The first voice heard in the book (besides the parents') belongs to the gang. The gang offers camaraderie. They share one purse and have a common lot; they act as a brotherhood. In addition, they promise riches; precious wealth, spoil from their victims, belongs to the fraternity. There is a third seduction—the thrill of possessing and wielding the power of life and death. They lie in wait for murder; they identify themselves with the power of the grave and the pit. They are hell's agents, grim reapers who swallow the innocent alive—death incarnate. This excitement and pleasure beguiles and enlivens the band and calls to the youth to join.

The wise parents also appeal to the youth, claiming that the gang cannot deliver on its promises. As birds are ensnared by the invisible net, so the gangsters cannot see the trap they have set for themselves. They lie in wait for their own blood. In the end, the grave swallows them, and the pit takes them.

In Proverbs, consideration of a thing's end is wisdom. To see where a path leads is to discriminate whether it is fit for travel. Consider the end of the gang and be wise. For all its promises, it ultimately cannot deliver anything but death. The voice of peer pressure requires the antidote of parental instruction. In opposition to the gang, true wisdom is a garland of grace and a chain of honor around the neck. Choose this!

◆ D. Wisdom's Call; Who Listens? (1:20-33)

20 Wisdom shouts in the streets.
She cries out in the public square.
21 She calls to the crowds along the main street,
to those gathered in front of the city gate:
22 "How long, you simpletons,
will you insist on being simpleminded?
How long will you mockers relish your mocking?
How long will you fools hate knowledge?
23 Come and listen to my counsel.
I'll share my heart with you
and make you wise.

24 "I called you so often, but you wouldn't come.
I reached out to you, but you paid no attention.
25 You ignored my advice
and rejected the correction I offered.
26 So I will laugh when you are in trouble!
I will mock you when disaster overtakes you—
27 when calamity overtakes you like a storm,
when disaster engulfs you like a cyclone,
and anguish and distress overwhelm you.

28 "When they cry for help, I will not answer.
Though they anxiously search for me, they will not find me.
29 For they hated knowledge
and chose not to fear the LORD.
30 They rejected my advice
and paid no attention when I corrected them.

31 Therefore, they must eat the bitter
fruit of living their own way,
choking on their own schemes.
32 For simpletons turn away from me—
to death.
Fools are destroyed by their own
complacency.
33 But all who listen to me will live in
peace,
untroubled by fear of harm."

NOTES

1:20 *Wisdom.* Heb., *khokmoth* [TH2454, ZH2684], a plural form rather than the singular form (*khokmah* [TH2451, ZH2683]) used of Wisdom in 8:1. It is a feminine plural parsed as a singular. This is similar to the plural *'elohim* [TH430, ZH466] for God or the masculine singular *behemoth* [TH929, ZH989] (Job 40:15). She, Wisdom, is a larger-than-life single entity, omnipresent and inescapable—the matrix of life.

shouts . . . cries out. Wisdom is personified as a woman. Here, her evangelistic message is portrayed as impossible to ignore: She cries aloud, gives her voice, calls, and speaks. She delivers her loud appeal in the most public places—the heights, the city square, and the gates (1:21). To avoid Wisdom one must shut one's eyes and stop one's ears and commit oneself to folly.

1:22 *insist on being simpleminded.* Lit., "love simplicity?"

mockers . . . fools. The mocker or scoffer (*lets* [TH3887A, ZH4370]) and the fool (*kesil* [TH3684, ZH4067]) are committed to a self-destructive path. They are part of the anti-wisdom complex, the company of those who despise the teachings found in the book of Proverbs. "Anyone who rebukes a *lets* will get an insult in return. Anyone who corrects the wicked will get hurt. So don't bother correcting *lets;* they will only hate you. But correct the wise, and they will love you" (9:7-8). See 26:1-12 for verses that pertain to the *kesil.*

1:23 *I'll share my heart with you.* Lit., "I will pour out my Spirit upon you." *Ruakh* [TH7307, ZH8120] (spirit) could be glossed "wrath" (cf. Judg 8:3). Emerton suggests *ruakh* connotes "utterance" (1968:612).

1:24 *I called you so often.* Each segment begins with a reference to calling. Wisdom calls upon the city to listen in the first two (1:20, 24); in the third, fools call to her after it is too late to save them (1:28). She urgently pleads with mockers and fools to listen, but they refuse.

1:25 *advice.* Waltke argues that "prophet, priest, and sage all speak with divine authority" (1987:65-78)—this is "advice" necessary to your soul.

1:26 *I will laugh.* She laughs at the folly of fools who bring about their own easily avoidable calamity. Laughter in the face of future events also characterizes the woman of virtue (31:25).

1:27 *overwhelm you.* Folly results in devastation like a tsunami. Wisdom has sent out the storm warning; the sirens have blared, but to no avail. Fools ignored her. Now the wave has swept over them, and any drowning cries for help go unanswered, since nothing can be done.

1:28 *When they cry.* The first word in Hebrew, *'az* [TH227, ZH255], is a time marker that often starts a new section. For the third time, the verb *qara'* [TH7121, ZH7924] (to call) is employed (see 1:20, 24). Finally, fools call upon Wisdom, but she has gone.

1:29 *to fear the LORD.* For the second time in ch 1, the benchmark for wisdom—the fear of Yahweh—is advised. To choose not to revere Yahweh is to hate knowledge. The wisdom of Proverbs is anything but secular; true wisdom is found in one's religious attitude toward the true and living God.

1:30 ***corrected.*** Three times Wisdom mentions counsel and correction (1:23, 25, 30). Fools and mockers do not wish to change; they hate to be rebuked. Thus the very thing that could have saved them they reject—and this has a humorous side. It is like a man sitting on the branch of a tree and sawing it off, not realizing he will fall. The branch is Wisdom's reproof, and the fall is final. On the way down, the fool cries, "Help!"—but it is too late because the branch is sawed off!

1:32 ***simpletons . . . Fools.*** The words *petha'yim* [TH6612, ZH7343] and *kesil* [TH3684, ZH4067] are again mentioned in the summation (see 1:22). The *petha'yim* have remained wayward, and the *kesil* have continued in self-delusion with a false sense of security.

COMMENTARY

Having been entreated by the voice of the gang, the reader now hears the call of Wisdom in three segments. "She calls to the crowds" (1:21), saying, "I called you so often, but you wouldn't come" (1:24). Finally, fools in distress call for help, but Wisdom will not answer them. The time to heed her call is today—to avoid the calamity of folly tomorrow.

Wisdom is here personified in the image of a woman. The commentary on chapter 8 discusses this at greater length. At this point, she is not yet associated with the wisdom of Yahweh, nor with creation. However, she is related to the community and the city; with an in-your-face approach, she makes known the path of knowledge. The text suddenly gives her voice after the wise father summarizes the fate of the gangster, and her warnings are immediately followed by the father's further admonition to listen: "My child, listen to what I say. . . . Tune your ears to wisdom" (2:1-2). Wisdom seems to be the personification of the parents' admonitions and warnings. She is the antidote to the gang. Everywhere the child turns there is seduction to folly, but also echoes of lessons learned at home. (See commentary on 3:13-20.)

Wisdom is not esoteric and cryptic, hidden knowledge known only to the initiated. Rather, wisdom is everywhere! Children are raised with it. It shouts from the highest place in the city; it guards the gate; it is unavoidable. The father's words are at one with reality and the facts of life, which are encountered every day. To not listen, then, is an active choice. The fool *chooses* folly. The mocker is engaged in misinterpreting every fact encountered from the moment he wakes until he returns to sleep at night.

The reason for this is that the simpleton *loves* being simple, the mocker *relishes* mocking, and the fool *hates* knowledge (1:22). Elsewhere Wisdom claims, "All who hate me love death" (8:36). The primary motive of a human being is love; people pursue their hearts' desires. Those in the anti-wisdom complex have hearts that love folly, love naiveté, and, ultimately, love death. The wise love wisdom (4:6).

Every person's defining moment is religious; it is whether or not they revere the Lord. Proverbs envisions a dynamic and vital relationship between the sage and the God of Israel. Wisdom ultimately is a gift from God, so learning a set of truisms does not automatically make one wise. Wisdom is learning the precepts of societal living before the face of the living God. Fools choose to reject this and thus lose any hope of acquiring a realistic understanding of the world.

◆ E. Two Paths (2:1-22)

1 My child,* listen to what I say,
and treasure my commands.
2 Tune your ears to wisdom,
and concentrate on understanding.
3 Cry out for insight,
and ask for understanding.
4 Search for them as you would for
silver;
seek them like hidden treasures.
5 Then you will understand what it
means to fear the LORD,
and you will gain knowledge of God.
6 For the LORD grants wisdom!
From his mouth come knowledge
and understanding.
7 He grants a treasure of common sense
to the honest.
He is a shield to those who walk
with integrity.
8 He guards the paths of the just
and protects those who are faithful
to him.

9 Then you will understand what is
right, just, and fair,
and you will find the right way
to go.
10 For wisdom will enter your heart,
and knowledge will fill you with joy.
11 Wise choices will watch over you.
Understanding will keep you safe.
12 Wisdom will save you from evil people,
from those whose words are twisted.
13 These men turn from the right way
to walk down dark paths.
14 They take pleasure in doing wrong,
and they enjoy the twisted ways
of evil.
15 Their actions are crooked,
and their ways are wrong.

16 Wisdom will save you from the
immoral woman,
from the seductive words of the
promiscuous woman.
17 She has abandoned her husband
and ignores the covenant she made
before God.
18 Entering her house leads to death;
it is the road to the grave.*
19 The man who visits her is doomed.
He will never reach the paths of life.

20 Follow the steps of good men instead,
and stay on the paths of the
righteous.
21 For only the godly will live in the land,
and those with integrity will remain
in it.
22 But the wicked will be removed from
the land,
and the treacherous will be
uprooted.

2:1 Hebrew *My son.* 2:18 Hebrew *to the spirits of the dead.*

NOTES

2:1 ***My child, listen to what I say.*** Lit., "My son, if you receive my words." This introduces a new section. Proverbs 2:1 and 2:3-4 each begin with the particle *'im* [TH518, ZH561], often glossed "if." *If* you take my words . . . *if* you call to understanding . . . *if* you seek it. Proverbs 2:5, 9 each begin with *'az* [TH227, ZH255] (then). *If* the child heeds the call of wisdom, *then* the specified results follow. Proverbs 2:1-4 sets up the condition, 2:5-9 the benefits.

commands. As *torah* [TH8451, ZH9368] was the mother's instruction in 1:8, so here "commandment" (*mitswah* [TH4687, ZH5184], as in "bar mitzvah" or "son of the law") is the father's earnest appeal. Language that elsewhere in Scripture refers to the Mosaic law here invokes parental guidance. This is part and parcel of Wisdom Literature—not the heavy-handed thunder from Sinai, but the reasoned persuasion of trusted parents is what protects the child.

2:2 ***concentrate.*** Precisely, "incline (*tatteh* [TH5186, ZH5742]) your heart."

2:3 *Cry out for insight.* Lit., "If for insight you cry out." The youth is expected to "cry out" and to "give voice" for wisdom—reflecting the actions of Wisdom herself (1:20-21).

2:4 *Search for them as you would for silver.* Lit., "If you seek her as silver."

2:5 *Then . . . fear the* LORD. If the exhortation of 2:1-4 is heeded, then (*'az* [TH227, ZH255]) benefits follow—the first and most important being to understand how to venerate Yahweh and know God. The chief skill in life is to know how to live righteously before the Lord.

2:6 *For the* LORD *grants wisdom!* Wisdom is a gift from Yahweh. He speaks knowledge and understanding. Again, wisdom is not chiefly knowledge of the world; it is knowledge of and from God.

From his mouth. The LXX reads "from his presence," apparently reflecting *mppnyw;* this diverges from the consonantal Hebrew text (*mppyw*) by one letter.

2:7 *common sense.* See note on 3:21.

He is a shield. Yahweh is a shield to guard the paths of the just (2:8).

2:8 *those who are faithful to him.* Reading Qere, "He guards the path of his faithful ones" (from *khasid* [TH2623A, ZH2883]). The "path" is cited twice in the verse (*'orakh* [TH734, ZH784], "path"; *derek* [TH1870, ZH2006], "way"). The *khasid* (as in "Hasidic Jew") is one who shows *khesed* [TH2617, ZH2876], covenant fidelity (see Waltke 2004:100).

2:9 *Then.* The second "then" clause follows the preceding "if" statements.

fair. Lit., "equitable," Heb., *umesharim* [TH4339, ZH4797]. The LXX reads as a verb: "*directing* all your paths aright."

the right way. A third term in two verses is employed for life direction: *ma'gal* [TH4570A, ZH5047], meaning "course, track." In the remainder of ch 2, these words average about one per verse. The orientation of one's life is the crucial question.

2:12 *Wisdom will save you from evil people.* Lit., "To save you from the path of evil."

twisted. Lit., "perversities," Heb., *tahpukoth* [TH8419, ZH9337], also in 2:14; found 10 times in the OT, once outside Proverbs: "They are a twisted generation, children without integrity" (Deut 32:20). There, Yahweh is disgusted because they worship idols. A man with a heart of *tahpukoth* plots evil and stirs up trouble (6:14; 16:28). This pervert is a whisperer, one who through his mouth seeks only to destroy. God hates this (8:13), and in the end the deviant will be silenced (10:31). The path of evil is to heed the man of twisted words.

2:13 *turn from.* Lit., "abandon," Heb., *'azab* [TH5800, ZH6440].

2:14 *evil.* Heb., *ra'* [TH7451A, ZH8273], used twice in 2:14 ("Delighting to do evil / Rejoicing in the perversities of evil") and found also in 2:12. Like the English word "evil," it has a broad semantic range. In this context it refers to the destructive character of those who abandon the straight for the perverse.

2:15 *actions.* Lit., "paths." The NLT emphasizes the point that a literal "path" is not in view, but rather "actions," "evil people," and so on. The path is an image for life direction and associated behaviors and attitudes.

2:16 *immoral.* Heb., *zarah,* from *zur* [TH2114C, ZH2424], meaning "be estranged, be foreign." The woman's principle characteristic is that she has made herself a stranger to the community. Waltke calls her the "unchaste wife," "an outsider" who "remains at heart a prostitute" (2004:120).

seductive words. The last few verses warned against the twisted words of the evil man; now the smooth words of the loose woman call to the youth. LXX clarifies her symbolic value by translating this verse as "To make you far from the straight way, and estranged from right judgment." "Whereas the MT . . . speaks of a certain kind of (apparently literal) woman, the LXX speaks of the dangers of evil counsel" (Giese 1993:290-291).

2:17 *abandoned her husband.* The Hebrew verb is *'azab* [TH5800, ZH6440], also in 2:13. There, people abandon the upright path; here, she abandons "the partner of her youth." For a discussion of the youth (*ne'urim* [TH5271, ZH5830]; see also *na'ar* [TH5288, ZH5853]), see commentary on 1:2-7. The youth is warned of women who forsake the covenants made in their youth.

covenant. This word is found only here in Proverbs. The term in this context has no significance beyond the marriage vow. The covenant is similar in this respect to the reference to "land" (see note on 2:21 and Garrett 1993:76). In the same way, *torah* [TH8451, ZH9368] and *mitswah* [TH4687, ZH5184] do not signify the Mosaic law but the admonitions of the parents.

before God. To abandon one's spouse is to abandon God. It is God who is ignored by the one who forsakes marital vows.

2:18 *death . . . grave.* The immoral woman is associated with death, using language reminiscent of the gang (1:12). Like the gang, she is an agent of hell. The verse is lit., "For her house bows down to death, / her tracks to the shades." The *repa'im* [TH7496, ZH8327] (shades) are spirits of the dead (Job 26:5; Ps 88:10 [11]; Isa 14:9). We should perhaps emend *shakhah* [TH7743, ZH8755] (sinks down) to *shukhah* [TH7745, ZH8757] (pit), yielding, "Her house is a pit extending to death." This restores gender agreement with "her house," *bethah* [TH1004/1886.3, ZH1074/2023] (Whybray 1994a:56).

2:19 *The man who visits her.* Lit., "all who go in to her." This is a euphemism for coitus; her vagina is a gateway to damnation and death. Her seductive power is fatal.

paths of life. Wisdom is not a matter of self-actualization or self-improvement. It is not about enhancing one's portfolio or learning healthy habits or pragmatic ways to get more of what you want out of life. Rather, wisdom is about *life and death.* If the boy does not take to heart and incorporate within himself the lessons of the father, he will *lose his life!* This is why the father is so persistent and impassioned in his insistence that he is listened to (and that the law of the mother is heeded); this is why Wisdom shouts publicly to all, demanding that the simple give up their ways. *Salvation* is the work of Wisdom.

2:20 *instead.* Lit., "therefore." In Hebrew this is the first word, which denotes the beginning of the conclusion. Note the dual mention of the path.

2:21 *land.* It would be inconsistent with wisdom material and the message of Proverbs to see in the word "land" an implied reference to the history of Israel. "Land" here signifies "community" with overtones of peace, wealth, and long life (see also 28:19).

2:22 *removed.* Lit., "cut off." They are, in fact, removed from the "land" into the realm of the shade and the grave (2:18).

COMMENTARY

Chapter 2 begins with "my child" and clearly outlines the two paths in life that are set before the youth. Proverbs 2:1-11 promises wisdom, understanding, and knowledge—gifts from Yahweh. The first two stanzas of 2:12-19 begin with the phrase "To save you." These delineate from what, or from whom, the youth needs saving. The poem concludes with an adjuration to walk the good path (2:20-22).

To heed Wisdom is to learn to fear Yahweh, and Yahweh gives this wisdom to those who fear him. It is not a body of truths or principles or the cosmic/social order that constitutes Wisdom, as if Wisdom is a demiurge standing between people and God; it is with Yahweh that the sage has to reckon. Wisdom is direct knowledge of God, not indirect knowledge mediated by the natural order. Knowledge of the world flows from this primary knowledge. The book of Proverbs is about learning to revere Yahweh. To learn wisdom, then, is to please God.

The Benefits of Wisdom (2:1-11). *If* you receive and treasure the commands and words of the parent; *if* you are attentive to wisdom and incline yourself to understanding; *if* you cry out for discernment; *if* you seek it like silver or search for it like treasure: *then* you will know Yahweh and will find God; *then* Yahweh will speak wisdom, knowledge, and understanding to you; *then* God will be a shield to you and will guard your blameless paths; *then* you will discern how to live rightly in society and what is good; *then* wisdom and knowledge will be internalized in you, and you will have joy and be guarded in whatever you do. "If you need wisdom, ask our generous God, and he will give it to you. He will not rebuke you for asking" (Jas 1:5).

The promise to sons and daughters is that Yahweh will guard the steps of all who internalize wisdom. "Wisdom means not only knowing but also *wanting* to do what is right and to avoid sin. This desire will protect you from the tragic consequences of immorality" (Fox 1994:243). Rich vocabulary is again employed to convey the major theme—a person needs to be *guarded.* God is a shield; in 2:8 he guards you (*natsar* [TH5341, ZH5915]) and keeps you (*shamar* [TH8104, ZH9068]); in 2:11 discretion keeps you (*shamar*), and understanding watches over you (*natsar*). What God does, wisdom does—guards you, watches over you, and keeps you. But guards you from what? Why is the function of vigilance and protection so important? What is so dangerous that the path must be defended? From what must the minor be saved? These are the subjects of the next section.

To Save You (2:12-22). Proverbs 2:12-15 and 2:16-19 each begin with the phrase "To save you from." As noted above, various terms are used for the "path," "way," or "course." At issue is life direction. What will define your life? To what end is your personality and whole existence trending? Are you equipped to resist the temptation to redefine what is "good" for you? The only thing that can save you is to be prepared in advance. Orient yourself toward God. Commit to live blamelessly before Yahweh. Heed the words of wisdom, or else you will lose your shield.

The second chapter of Proverbs introduces the reader to the image of the two paths. For the uncommitted youth, two directions are possible. One, the "path of wisdom," leads to prosperity, honor, health, and life. The "path of folly" leads to poverty and loss, shame and disgrace, disease and death. Note that there is no middle ground, no moderate path between the two. One cannot have a little folly mixed in with a life of wisdom and expect the rewards of wisdom. This is so because of the overarching paradigm of life direction. One's life is either given to wisdom, or it is not. If it is given to wisdom, foolish ways will be eschewed.

Along the way, the youth is subject to multifarious voices that call out for a hearing, trying to turn the uncommitted to their way of life. So far in Proverbs, the reader has been introduced to the voice of the wise parents, the call of the gang, the enticements of the loose woman, and the preaching of Wisdom. The gang and the loose woman offer tangible goods and services: pleasures, powers, and attractive rewards. All that the parents have to offer are words. "When the end of the matter is not yet in sight . . . the only thing he has to counterbalance the appeal of folly is faith that the path of wisdom is better. In other words, the content of the counselor's instruction is all that the counselee has to protect him from death" (Schwab 1995:8). Parental cajoling, instruction, and imposed discipline are all there is to save the youth's soul. Faith is required—faith that father and mother know better and have the child's best interest at heart.

Along with the image of the two paths, chapter 2 also features the image of two women. The first woman is not an actual human being, but a symbol for the wise counsel of the parents that is encountered and echoed in all of life. This wisdom that begins at home shouts at passersby to turn and be saved. The other woman is a human being, the loose woman who illustrates the kinds of temptations to the path of folly that menace the youth. She and the gang lead only to death; the other woman offers life. This feminine imagery is developed in later chapters.

Chapters 1–2 provide the reader's first impressions of the book. To know Yahweh is to walk the right path. Yahweh presents through the parents a wisdom that is reflected in the entire world for the discerning to recognize; folly speaks through the gang and the loose woman to turn the youth awry. Many temptations jeopardize the life of the child; heeding Wisdom is a matter of life and death. This defines the theological framework within which the proverbs of Solomon in subsequent chapters should be understood. Christianity is *the* Way (Acts 9:2; 19:9, 23; 22:4; 24:14, 22) of life.

Chapter 2 has 22 verses, the same number as letters in the Hebrew alphabet (cf. 31:10-31). Waltke calls chapter 2 an acrostic poem (2004:216-217) and discovers that the sections of his divisions begin with the first and middle letters of the alphabet in sequence (Aleph, Lamedh). The second word of the final stanza (2:20) follows a logical particle and begins with Taw, the final Hebrew letter. Thus there are formal correspondences between chapter 2 and 31:10-31. When Proverbs draws to a close, the issues raised in chapter 2 are resolved with the youth, now no longer a youth but an adult, committed to Wisdom, making an abode in her house. Love for Wisdom has been chosen, love of death rejected.

◆ F. Wisdom, Yahweh, and Life (3:1–4:27)

1. Father's admonition to trust Yahweh (3:1-35)

1 My child,* never forget the things
I have taught you.
Store my commands in your heart.
2 If you do this, you will live many years,
and your life will be satisfying.
3 Never let loyalty and kindness leave
you!
Tie them around your neck as
a reminder.
Write them deep within your heart.
4 Then you will find favor with both
God and people,
and you will earn a good
reputation.

5 Trust in the LORD with all your heart;
do not depend on your own
understanding.

6 Seek his will in all you do,
and he will show you which path to take.

7 Don't be impressed with your own wisdom.
Instead, fear the LORD and turn away from evil.
8 Then you will have healing for your body
and strength for your bones.

9 Honor the LORD with your wealth
and with the best part of everything you produce.
10 Then he will fill your barns with grain,
and your vats will overflow with good wine.

11 My child, don't reject the LORD's discipline,
and don't be upset when he corrects you.
12 For the LORD corrects those he loves,
just as a father corrects a child in whom he delights.*

13 Joyful is the person who finds wisdom,
the one who gains understanding.
14 For wisdom is more profitable than silver,
and her wages are better than gold.
15 Wisdom is more precious than rubies;
nothing you desire can compare with her.
16 She offers you long life in her right hand,
and riches and honor in her left.
17 She will guide you down delightful paths;
all her ways are satisfying.
18 Wisdom is a tree of life to those who embrace her;
happy are those who hold her tightly.

19 By wisdom the LORD founded the earth;
by understanding he created the heavens.
20 By his knowledge the deep fountains of the earth burst forth,
and the dew settles beneath the night sky.

21 My child, don't lose sight of common sense and discernment.
Hang on to them,
22 for they will refresh your soul.
They are like jewels on a necklace.
23 They keep you safe on your way,
and your feet will not stumble.
24 You can go to bed without fear;
you will lie down and sleep soundly.
25 You need not be afraid of sudden disaster
or the destruction that comes upon the wicked,
26 for the LORD is your security.
He will keep your foot from being caught in a trap.

27 Do not withhold good from those who deserve it
when it's in your power to help them.
28 If you can help your neighbor now, don't say,
"Come back tomorrow, and then I'll help you."

29 Don't plot harm against your neighbor,
for those who live nearby trust you.
30 Don't pick a fight without reason,
when no one has done you harm.

31 Don't envy violent people
or copy their ways.
32 Such wicked people are detestable to the LORD,
but he offers his friendship to the godly.

33 The LORD curses the house of the wicked,
but he blesses the home of the upright.

34 The LORD mocks the mockers
but is gracious to the humble.*

35 The wise inherit honor,
but fools are put to shame!

3:1 Hebrew *My son;* also in 3:11, 21. **3:12** Greek version reads *And he punishes those he accepts as his children.* Compare Heb 12:6. **3:34** Greek version reads *The LORD opposes the proud / but favors the humble.* Compare Jas 4:6; 1 Pet 5:5.

NOTES

3:1 ***the things I have taught you . . . my commands.*** Again, *torah* [TH8451, ZH9368] and *mitswah* [TH4687, ZH5184] do not denote the law of Moses given at Sinai and constitutive of a special covenant with Israel. Rather, *torah* and *mitswah* signify the father's wise tutelage of the minor.

in your heart. The human heart is one theme in 3:1-4 and is mentioned in the first verse of the following section (3:5).

3:2 ***you will live many years.*** Precisely, "for length of days and years of life . . . will be added to you." Is this promise merely for this life, or does it have in view a life beyond the grave? Although the language here apparently anticipates nothing beyond the ripe old age of the sage who will finally die, Proverbs as a whole anticipates a grander fate for the wise. Waltke (2004:104) notes that the phrase here, "length of days and years of life," is used in Isa 53:10 to anticipate the Suffering Servant's life after being made an offering for sin—it prophesies Christ's resurrection. Might not 3:2 also project a dimension beyond natural death? See notes on 12:28 and 15:24.

3:3 ***Never let loyalty and kindness leave you.*** That is, "faithfulness" (*khesed* [TH2617, ZH2876]) and "truth" (*'emeth* [TH571, ZH622]). These are often paired in Proverbs, denoting unwavering, unfailing, constant faithfulness to Yahweh. "Leave you" is from *'azab* [TH5800, ZH6440], the same word as in 2:13 and 2:17, where evil men "turn from the right way" and the promiscuous woman abandons her husband. Do not leave *khesed* and *'emeth* as she left her beloved.

Tie them around your neck. Overland (2000:424-440) suggests that the use of *qashar* [TH7194, ZH8003] (bind) as a metaphor is derived from Deut 6:8, "Tie them [the commands] to your hands and wear them on your forehead." The only occurrences of the word in a figurative sense are in Proverbs and Deuteronomy. He also argues that *khesed* connotes covenantal love, the kind of loyalty demanded in Deut 6:5.

Write them deep within your heart. This line appears superfluous and is absent from the LXX (but present in other ancient versions); perhaps it is an interpolation from 6:21 and 7:3. In any case, discussion of the heart introduces this stanza and the next and is appropriate to the immediate theme of the internalization of wisdom. Overland (2000:428) argues that the pairing of *qashar* (bind) with *kathab* [TH3789, ZH4180] (write) derives from Deut 6:8-9.

3:4 ***with both God and people.*** Lit., "in the eyes of God and man." In Proverbs, the important question is in whose eyes a thing is viewed. See notes on 3:7 and 17:8.

3:5 ***Trust in the LORD with all your heart.*** Proverbs 3:5-12 uses the divine name five times in eight verses. Again the theme of the human heart is at issue; think Yahweh's thoughts after him and pursue his agenda rather than your own. Overland (2000:428-429) argues that the unique reference in Proverbs here to the "whole heart" suggests a well-known exemplar behind it, such as Deut 6:5 (see notes on 3:3).

3:6 ***Seek his will.*** Lit., "know him," that is, experience him, acknowledge him. Johnson (2002:278-284) suggests that the implied antecedent is "trust, security, confidence."

3:7 ***Don't be impressed with your own wisdom.*** For the second time in this section, the child is warned against trusting in the self, lit., being "wise in your own eyes." This is set off against the fear of Yahweh. To reverence God is to *not* have faith in yourself and your own grasp of the situation.

3:8 ***for your body.*** Heb., *leshorreka* [TH8270, ZH9219], traditionally translated "for your navel." The LXX reads "for your body," which could imply the Hebrew form *lish'ereka*

[TH7607, ZH8638]. The word *shor* [TH8270, ZH9219] is found elsewhere only in Ezek 16:4 and possibly also Song 7:2 [3] and Job 40:16. In Ezek 16:4 it means "umbilical cord"; in Job 40:16, perhaps "loins"; in Song 7:2, it is probably "vagina." The Arabic *sirr* can mean "coitus." If translated "navel," it serves as a synecdoche for the whole biological life of the person, thus NLT glosses "body" (with LXX). But if rendered "loins," it additionally refers to one's sex life, the power to engender, which leads naturally to the next lengthy section on sex and wisdom.

and strength for your bones. "Strength" is lit., "drink" or "refreshment." In parallel with "healing" this might mean "medicine." The Hebrew word for "bones" (*'etsem* [TH6106, ZH6795]) is found five times in Proverbs (3:8; 12:4; 14:30; 15:30; 16:24). Psychological distress and pleasure are both experienced "in the bones." The word depicts the condition of body and mind, the status of the whole person; this is similar to the contemporary colloquialism, "He felt it deep in his bones."

3:9 ***the best part.*** Lit., "firstfruits." This is a rare reference in Proverbs to a cultic act—that of offering a sacrifice to Yahweh. Although Proverbs is Wisdom Literature and does not argue from redemptive themes, it should not be read as separate from the religious life and rich faith of Israel.

3:10 ***he will fill your barns.*** This is a straightforward promise of wealth and prosperity to the one who participates in the right worship of Yahweh.

3:11 ***the LORD's discipline.*** The discipline of Yahweh requires honoring him through the prescribed rituals of worship. Again, the fear of Yahweh is the beginning of wisdom.

3:12 ***just as a father corrects a child.*** The stanza is bound as a unit by the preponderance of the divine name. It climaxes in this verse with the revelation that Yahweh adopts the one who honors him by accepting his discipline and reproof and revering him with the firstfruits of labor. God becomes the father who delights over his child. God's love is seen in his reproof, for the Lord is committed to the youth's blessed life.

3:13 ***Joyful.*** Heb. *'ashre* [TH835A, ZH897] is an introductory word of blessing, the first word in the verse. The last word of 3:18 is the cognate participle *me'ushar* [TH833A, ZH887]. See Gen 30:13: "And Leah named him Asher (*'asher* [TH836, ZH888]), for she said, 'What joy (*'asher* [TH833A, ZH887]) is mine! Now the other women will celebrate (*'ashar*) with me.'" Maidens praise (*'ashar*) the girl in Song 6:9; the wise woman's children bless (*'ashar*) her in Prov 31:28. In the condition of *'ashre* blessedness, the person or nation has "arrived." Leah entered this state of perfection after having birthed Asher.

the person . . . the one. Heb. *'adam* [TH120, ZH132], here used for humanity in general, can also be glossed as a personal name, "Adam." It is unusual for the word to be used twice in a single verse of Proverbs (the only other occurrence is in 27:19, lit., "The heart of a man reflects the man"). Whybray calls the repetition here "surprising" (1994a:66). This dual occurrence draws the reader to notice the word and might convey unusual significance; perhaps it is a double entendre for humanity in general with an echo of the Garden of Eden. (See note on 3:18.)

3:15 ***rubies.*** Heb. *peninim* [TH6443, ZH7165] is found also in 8:11, 20:15, and 31:10, probably with the meaning "ruby corals."

3:16 ***long life.*** Lit., "length of days." The benefits of finding wisdom are beginning to accumulate; the next verse promises *shalom* [TH7965, ZH8934], and 3:18 illustrates the full measure of "long life" in the image of the tree of life, which elsewhere signifies immortality.

3:17 ***satisfying.*** Heb. *shalom* [TH7965, ZH8934] connotes satisfaction, peace, and well-being. The Christ is the Prince of *shalom* (Isa 9:6).

3:18 ***tree of life.*** McKinlay (1999:73-84) identifies the tree of life with Wisdom herself. The fruit of the righteous is the fruit of the tree of life (11:30). A dream fulfilled is a tree of life (13:12). Gentle words are a tree of life (15:4). Outside of Proverbs the phrase only occurs in Genesis 2–3, where any who eat of it live forever (Gen 3:22). Proverbs 3:18 is followed by a brief recollection of Genesis. There is a motif of eternal life associated with the acquisition of wisdom—in some manner, to lay hold of wisdom is to enter a state of blessedness analogous to what Adam would have experienced had he eaten of the tree of life. Perhaps this is why the section begins by citing the name of Adam twice: "Joyful is *'adam* [TH120, ZH132] who finds wisdom, / *'adam* who gains understanding" (3:13). The wise man or woman is such an Adam partaking of the fruit of life. "In the wider canonical perspective . . . the tree of life speaks of immortality" (Estes 1997:58).

3:19 ***earth . . . heavens.*** The same words found in Gen 1:1.

wisdom . . . understanding. The same words (*khokmah* [TH2451, ZH2683] and *tebunah* [TH8394, ZH9312]) are utilized in 3:13 referring to humanity's/Adam's blessedness. For the first time, Wisdom is identified as involved in the creation of heaven and earth. Yahweh, who made the world with wisdom and placed in it the tree of life for Adam, also makes this wisdom available to all humanity.

3:20 ***deep fountains.*** This is the same word as in Gen 1:2, "deep waters," another reference to the Creation in Genesis.

3:21 ***common sense.*** This is a wisdom term found twice outside Proverbs and Job, denoting ability to perform effectively (Job 5:12, "succeed"; Isa 28:29; Mic 6:9).

3:22 ***refresh.*** Lit., "give life to" (*khayyim* [TH2416, ZH2644]) as in "tree of life" (*'ets-khayyim* [TH6086, ZH6770]; 3:18).

necklace. From *gargeroth* [TH1621, ZH1738], meaning "neck." With the prefix *le* [TH3807.1, ZH4200], the Hebrew phonemes *r, g,* and *l* are heard that comprise the Hebrew *regel* [TH7272, ZH8079] (foot). This leads into the following four verses, bound by the repeated word "foot." These verses follow this pattern:

A Then . . . your foot will not stumble (3:23)
  B When you lie down, you will not fear (3:24)
  B' You will not fear (3:25)
A' For Yahweh will guard your foot (3:26)

3:23 ***on your way.*** The sage is securely oriented—his feet (life direction) do not misstep.

3:24 ***bed.*** Waking and sleeping, the wise are secure, i.e., all the time, in every circumstance (see 6:22).

3:25 ***afraid of sudden disaster.*** Lit., "do not fear a sudden fear."

3:26 ***the Lord is your security.*** The stanza ends again with Yahweh, who guarantees all these benefits promised to the wise and discerning. It is not a clever understanding of the world order that watches over the wise; it is Yahweh who keeps the foot—the life direction—from slipping. Therefore, the faithful need not fear.

3:27 ***Do not.*** Each verse of this stanza begins with the negative particle *'al* [TH408, ZH440], "do not" or "is not." This device binds these verses together as a unit.

those who deserve it. Lit., "those who possess it." Do not withhold tangible good from those who possess internal goodness. One with ethical good has a claim on good things; the fool and sluggard have no such claim.

3:28 ***If you can help your neighbor now.*** Precisely, "When you have it with you." The last word, "with you," is also the last word of the next verse, a device that helps tie the two verses together. Garrett suggests that those who deserve good (3:27) may be "laborers who have earned their pay" (1993:84). The LXX adds, "For you do not know what tomorrow will birth." Fox (1984:63-69) argues from Egyptian wisdom that LXX has behind it a Hebrew original.

3:30 ***harm.*** This verse ends with "harm," the word used in 3:29, which helps to tie the two verses together. Here, however, the topic is broader than "your neighbor"; a general word for humanity is used (*'adam* [TH120, ZH132]).

3:31 ***violent people.*** Lit., "the man of violence" (*khamas* [TH2555, ZH2805]). The climax of the stanza comes with the admonition not to envy the violent one. To do the things against which the stanza counsels is to walk the path of violence. A youth might envy the power that the violent man seems to wield, and so one may consider *khamas* to be yet another voice that tempts the youth to a path of destruction.

3:32 ***Such.*** The verse begins with *ki* [TH3588, ZH3954], which in this case functions to continue the thought from the previous verse. Proverbs 3:31 is tied to the prior stanza by the device of the initial *'al* [TH408, ZH440] (not), which 3:27-31 shares. Waltke calls 3:31 a "janus" which serves to tie the stanzas together; it is the "emphatic center line" between two units (2004:269). This stanza could just as well be defined as 3:31-35.

detestable. Lit., "an abomination," *to'ebah* [TH8441, ZH9359]. In the Mosaic law, an abomination is to bring together that which natural order and religious duty would keep separate, e.g., with regard to sexual relations (Lev 18:22-30; 20:13), idols (Deut 7:25-26), consuming animals (Deut 14:3), or dishonest scales (Deut 25:16). This last definition is echoed in Proverbs (11:1; 20:23). Yahweh rightly judges and abhors the perpetrators of harm. The path of wisdom is the skill of living a righteous life before the Lord.

3:33 ***curses . . . blesses.*** Although Wisdom Literature does not argue from redemptive history, neither is it hermetically sealed off from the traditions of Israel. The motif of Yahweh issuing curses and blessings draws upon a knowledge of the covenant in Deut 28. Those who abominate their ways are cursed by Yahweh; he blesses the godly and upright. There are two paths: one of cursing, one of blessing.

3:34 ***gracious to the humble.*** James 4:6 quotes this verse, exhorting Christians to resist the devil and draw close to God. He does this in the context of a discussion on what may be described as two paths: friendship with the world or friendship with God (Jas 4:1-10). The struggle is an inner one, a matter of the heart. First Peter 5:5 also cites the verse to illustrate how the church should function as a community of faith. Like James, in close proximity he also warns of the devil (1 Pet 5:8-9). Beware of the devil, who would tempt you from the right path.

3:35 ***inherit.*** This renders the word *yinkhalu* [TH5157, ZH5706]. Driver (1951:177) questions how the wise can *inherit* honor and so emends to *nekhelu* [TH2470C, ZH—], yielding, "the wise are *adorned with* honor." Perhaps the use of "inheritance" language, like so much else in ch 3, echoes sacred history. As the Israelites were to inherit the land, so the wise inherit wisdom, appropriated by trust in Yahweh (3:32-33).

honor. Lit., "glory." The prime example of this is the glory of Solomon the wise (1 Kgs 3:10-14).

COMMENTARY

The themes introduced in the preceding two chapters are developed more fully in this chapter. Again the father admonishes the child to get wisdom, that is, to trust Yahweh. He promises more benefits absolutely, and warns against more dire consequences. The psychology of the heart is developed as the repository and center of a person's wisdom. One notably absent image in this composition is that of the woman, either positive or negative. This is reserved for the next composition. Chapter 3 comprises the father's heartfelt urging for the undeveloped child to learn wisdom. Various dimensions of meaning are supplied to flesh out how this takes place and what it entails. In chapter 4, the father at length exhorts the youth to choose the right path, and again targets the heart as the religious axis. All this is necessary to prepare the youth for the major temptation he will soon face—sex.

Chapter 3 begins with the father's enjoining the child to listen; he reveals that it is Yahweh who truly adopts the child in wisdom. With wisdom comes manifold promises, not the least of which is a long and happy life. Wisdom is identified with Yahweh's creative activity. The universe itself was fashioned with the same wisdom that the child is urged to acquire. After focusing his attention on various snares along the way, the father again returns to his major thesis: Yahweh and wisdom are one.

The First Stanza (3:1-4). The section opens with the father again urging the morally unformed youth to internalize the lessons of childhood, to commit to *khesed* [TH2617, ZH2876] and *'emeth* [TH571, ZH622], to write the instructions of prudence and virtue on the heart. He gives an unqualified promise: Life and favor with God and the community will follow. The next stanza unequivocally nails down the foundational principle of wisdom: The true Father of a person is Yahweh; the earthly parents' *torah* [TH8451, ZH9368] and *mitswah* [TH4687, ZH5184] are the words of God. It is in response to the parents' words that the juvenile must decide between wisdom and folly.

Proverbs 3:1-35 is the first of three sections in the composition consisting of chapters 3–4. Its six stanzas treat the heart, wisdom's overarching value, Yahweh as the true subject of wisdom, and how this impacts the behavior of the wise in community.

The Second Stanza (3:5-12). The first stanza (3:1-4) begins the section with the urgent parental entreaty to dedicate oneself to *khesed* [TH2617, ZH2876] and *'emeth* [TH571, ZH622], to internalize the lessons taught by the father—and by God. This thought is continued in the second stanza (3:5-12), where the promise of being adopted as Yahweh's child is offered. It is as if the text dares the reader to reread the phrase "my child" no longer as an appeal from the mouth of the parents, but rather from the mouth of Yahweh. Hebrews 12:5-6 admonishes Christians to take this seriously, embrace the Father's discipline, and walk the path of the Suffering Servant while awaiting the assured benedictions.

Trust Yahweh. Know him. Fear him. Honor him with the firstfruits. Do not lean on your own understanding. Do not be wise in your own eyes. Turn from evil. Do not reject his discipline. Do not loathe his reproof. Do this, and he *guarantees* that he will make your paths smooth, keep your body vigorous and strong, fill your barns and vats to overflowing, and love you and adopt you as his own child.

The wisdom offered in the book is for those who desire to know their God, who honor him with gifts and offerings, and who want to know the straight way. God adopts such people and assumes the task of their instruction—which is not always pleasant (hence the admonition not to shun it). The climactic verses of the stanza are quoted in Hebrews 12:5-6. Hebrews 12:1-13 argues that the Christian life is one of struggle against sin. In this struggle, Christians are called to remember Jesus on the cross—enduring shame and hostility from evil people. Christ suffered what is proper for those on the path of folly to suffer. His innocent blood was shed by a "gang" (see 1:11-12). As Christians follow Jesus, their willingness to bear pain for the sake of ultimate honor also inspires them to submit willingly to painful discipline. Christians are called to trust him and not their own understanding, to embrace his reproof and discipline and thus experience the love of the Father.

Thus, the unqualified guarantee of health and wealth is given in the context of the overall program of learning wisdom—so difficulties and setbacks (the correction of the Lord) can be expected. The ultimate example of this is Christ on the cross, who "learned obedience from the things he suffered" (Heb 5:8). Christians also enjoy the blessedness of God's favor, understanding that the blessings of health and wealth serve the higher goal of knowing God. The long life that is promised uses the language of the resurrected Christ in Isaiah 53:10, and the ultimate fulfillment of the promises of Proverbs may be regarded along the lines of that enjoyed by the Suffering Servant—after the travail of his soul.

Overland (2000:435-440) persuasively argues that 3:1-12 reflects Deuteronomy 6:4-9,

> *Listen, O Israel! The LORD is our God, the LORD alone. And you must love the LORD your God with all your heart, all your soul, and all your strength. And you must commit yourselves wholeheartedly to these commands that I am giving you today. Repeat them again and again to your children. Talk about them when you are at home and when you are on the road, when you are going to bed and when you are getting up. Tie them to your hands and wear them on your forehead as reminders. Write them on the doorposts of your house and on your gates.*

Proverbs employs this material to convey the overriding importance of being wise before Yahweh. The covenant called Israel to love Yahweh with a whole heart; the wise trust him with a whole heart. Moses says to bind commands on one's hands and forehead; the prudent tie loyalty and kindness to the neck and heart. Deuteronomy calls Israel to love Yahweh with their "strength" (*me'od* [TH3966A, ZH4394], perhaps connoting material wealth); the sage honors God from the vats and barns. The devout attitude toward Yahweh adjured in Deuteronomy is made to serve the kerygma of the sage. To love wisdom is to love Yahweh; the instructions of the wise are not secondary revelation but encounters with the living God.

The Third, Fourth, and Fifth Stanzas (3:13-31). The third stanza of this section (3:13-20) is actually a strophe consisting of two parts, 3:13-18 and 3:19-20. The former is bounded by an inclusion of "joyful, happy" (*'ashar* [TH833A, ZH887]). The first verse of this part and the next contain "wisdom" (*khokmah* [TH2451, ZH2683]). The creative wisdom of Yahweh and its surpassing value are at issue in both parts. Drawing on creation language and themes, the writer presents Wisdom as incomparably beneficial to whoever finds her. She is compared with precious jewels that people value and pursue. But those cannot offer what she offers—long life and blessedness.

The third stanza (3:13-20) as a whole again promotes the surpassing worth of gaining understanding and wisdom—the wisdom of God by which he created the heavens and the earth. This wisdom is omnipresent; to reject it, one must hate all creation. For the first time in Proverbs, Wisdom is revealed as constitutive in Yahweh's work of creation. The same "wisdom" and "understanding" with which Yahweh founded the heavens and earth is available to every person who heeds her call. This sheds new light on why Wisdom was inescapable to the youth in 1:20-33. All of creation reflects the infinite sagacity of the Creator. This limitless sapience obtrudes on humanity, exacting a response of love or hatred from every person. The fool walks a path against the grain of existence itself; the parents' wise counsel is in harmony with reality. "[Lady Wisdom] is, then, the revelation of God, not merely the self-revelation of creation. She is the divine summons issued in and through creation, sounding through the vast realm of the created world and heard on the level of human experience" (Murphy 1985:9-10).

The fourth stanza (3:21-26) addresses a person's inclination in life with the image of the foot. Yahweh will ensure that your "foot" will not stumble; therefore, waking or sleeping, you need not fear. This inclination of mind has ramifications in the social sphere. The fifth stanza (3:27-31) contrasts the path of doing good to your neighbor with the path of doing violence. This spells out what it means to be wise and what it takes to acquire the life promised in the earlier stanzas of the section. One should treat the innocent neighbor, in Jesus' words, as one would like to be treated (Matt 7:12). He said this is the essence of the law and the prophets—and it is also the essence of Proverbs.

The Sixth Stanza (3:32-35). The final stanza of this section returns explicitly to Yahweh as the one with whom all people must reckon. Yahweh mocks the mockers and shames the fool, but he gives grace and honor to the wise. The third stanza uses images and motifs from the Garden of Eden and challenges the reader to partake of the fruit of the tree of life—and so become a child of God. The final stanza uses language that echoes the glory of Solomon, who inherited the kingdom, and again challenges the reader to avoid what Yahweh hates (such as Solomon's idolatry, 2 Kgs 23:13) and comport oneself as a just and upright member of the community. In all this, life and glory and freedom from fear will accompany the wise in whatever they do and wherever they go.

In chapter 3, sacred history is not simply ignored. Motifs and images such as *torah* [TH8451, ZH9368] and *mitswah* [TH4687, ZH5184], creation and the tree of life, covenantal blessings and curses, the ritual offering of firstfruits, references to the Shema, and language of abomination and glory are transformed and made to serve the kerygma of the sage. To possess wisdom is to fulfill the Old Testament ideals of Yahwism: The fear of the Lord is the beginning of wisdom.

◆ 2. Father's admonition to get wisdom (4:1-9)

1 My children,* listen when your father
corrects you.
Pay attention and learn good
judgment,
2 for I am giving you good guidance.
Don't turn away from my
instructions.
3 For I, too, was once my father's son,

tenderly loved as my mother's
only child.

4 My father taught me,
"Take my words to heart.
Follow my commands, and you
will live.
5 Get wisdom; develop good judgment.
Don't forget my words or turn away
from them.
6 Don't turn your back on wisdom, for
she will protect you.
Love her, and she will guard you.
7 Getting wisdom is the wisest thing
you can do!
And whatever else you do, develop
good judgment.
8 If you prize wisdom, she will make
you great.
Embrace her, and she will honor
you.
9 She will place a lovely wreath on your
head;
she will present you with a beautiful
crown."

4:1 Hebrew *My sons.*

NOTES

4:1 ***My children, listen.*** This is repeated in 4:10, where it begins the next segment. The first word in Hebrew is emphatic: "Listen!"

4:2 ***instructions.*** Heb., *torah* [TH8451, ZH9368].

4:4 ***commands, and you will live.*** Heb., *mitswah* [TH4687, ZH5184] (commandment). The issue is one of life and death; to listen is to gain life.

4:5 ***Get wisdom.*** Lit., "Acquire wisdom." The verb *qanah* [TH7069, ZH7864] is found five times in 4:5-7. Lit., "Get wisdom, get understanding. . . . Get wisdom, and in your getting get understanding." This is an urgent plea.

4:6 ***Love her.*** Simpletons love simplicity (see note on 1:22). Yahweh loves those he corrects as a child (3:12). If such a son or daughter loves wisdom and does not forsake her, she will be there when needed.

4:7 ***Getting wisdom is the wisest thing you can do.*** Lit., "The beginning of wisdom is this: 'Get wisdom!'" The verse is omitted in the LXX. Much of this section is modified in LXX, perhaps indicating a somewhat different *Vorlage.*

4:8 ***prize wisdom.*** Lit., "prize her." "Wisdom" is supplied by the NLT. "Prize" is from the Pilpel stem of *salal* [TH5549, ZH6147], a unique form in the OT (see 15:19 for the more typical Qal form).

COMMENTARY

In this section the father identifies himself with the situation of the child—in the past he, too, was enjoined to listen by his own parents. The father was teachable when he was instructed, and now he speaks as one who knows whereof he speaks. This is not a theoretical argument. The parent's lecture has behind it the force of history, the compelling logic of experience: "Don't turn away from (*'azab* [TH5800, ZH6440]) my instructions. . . . Don't turn your back on (*'azab*) wisdom" (4:2, 6). Wisdom—my words—she will guard you and protect you, *as she did me.* She will make you great like me (4:8). She will crown you with honor like me (4:8-9). I, your father, am a living illustration of the truth of what I say—so *listen!*

The beginning of wisdom is to get wisdom (4:7). This language echoes 1:7, which says, literally, "The beginning of knowledge is the fear of Yahweh," but instead of pointing to God, it points back to wisdom as its own source. In addition, the authority for the instruction is the father's experience, not an appeal to Yahweh. McKane considers that this section is "free from Yahwistic reinterpretation and, in this respect, contrasts strongly" with prior material in Proverbs (1970:302-303). He sees here a very different perspective from the religious and Yahweh-centered motivations seen earlier. However, at the sage's disposal was a rich arsenal of pedagogical tools. Appealing to Yahweh, which of course also connects the wisdom of the parent with the wisdom on display in creation, is but one technique. Other methods are employed, and here uniquely the father speaks of his own childhood. This does not imply that Yahweh is out of mind here; contra McKane, there is no radically different approach to wisdom. Other examples of variety in persuasive methodology are preemptive warnings, vivid role models, descriptive riches, and appeals to the community (Schwab 1995). Heeding one's father and mother, awareness of the mores and politics of the community, using one's own mind, and noting the wise ordering of things are all harmonious and mutually reinforcing avenues to learn the skill of living a righteous life before Yahweh. There is no godless path to wisdom.

◆ 3. Life versus stumbling (4:10-27)

10 My child,* listen to me and do as I say,
and you will have a long, good life.
11 I will teach you wisdom's ways
and lead you in straight paths.
12 When you walk, you won't be held back;
when you run, you won't stumble.
13 Take hold of my instructions; don't let them go.
Guard them, for they are the key to life.

14 Don't do as the wicked do,
and don't follow the path of evildoers.
15 Don't even think about it; don't go that way.
Turn away and keep moving.
16 For evil people can't sleep until they've done their evil deed for the day.
They can't rest until they've caused someone to stumble.
17 They eat the food of wickedness
and drink the wine of violence!

18 The way of the righteous is like the first gleam of dawn,
which shines ever brighter until the full light of day.
19 But the way of the wicked is like total darkness.
They have no idea what they are stumbling over.

20 My child, pay attention to what I say.
Listen carefully to my words.
21 Don't lose sight of them.
Let them penetrate deep into your heart,
22 for they bring life to those who find them,
and healing to their whole body.

23 Guard your heart above all else,
for it determines the course of your life.

24 Avoid all perverse talk;
stay away from corrupt speech.

25 Look straight ahead,
and fix your eyes on what lies before you.
26 Mark out a straight path for your feet;
stay on the safe path.
27 Don't get sidetracked;
keep your feet from following evil.

4:10 Hebrew *My son;* also in 4:20.

NOTES

4:10 ***long, good life.*** See note on 3:2 and commentary on 12:28. The life envisioned is equated with the tree of life in 3:18.

4:12 ***stumble.*** Note the image of the path. To stumble is to fail to make wise choices and decisions.

4:13 ***Take hold.*** Heb., *khazaq* [TH2388, ZH2616], used in 7:13 for the behavior of the loose woman toward the simpleton ("She threw her arms around him") and in Deut 22:25 for rape. Here, the teen is urged to aggressively seize *musar* [TH4148, ZH4592] (discipline, instruction) and never let go.

they are the key to life. Lit., "she is your life."

4:14 ***the path of evildoers.*** The subject switches to the alternate path before the youth.

4:15 ***Don't even think . . . don't go . . . Turn away . . . keep moving.*** Note the rich vocabulary engaged to punctuate the thought; four of the five words in this sentence are second-person verbs (counting *'al-ta'abar-bo* as one word). Repetition is necessary to reach the imperiled juvenile.

4:16 ***stumble.*** From *kashal* [TH3782, ZH4173], also in 4:19 (the last word of the strophe). The wicked subsist in causing to stumble.

4:19 ***stumbling.*** The wicked, who cannot sleep without causing others to stumble, themselves stumble in their path because they cannot see where they are going. This is reminiscent of the gang (1:8-19), who lie in wait for their own blood. They cause themselves to stumble.

4:20 ***My child.*** The third and last strophe of this section begins again with an appeal to the parents' offspring to pay attention.

Listen carefully. Lit., "Incline your ear."

4:21 ***Don't lose sight of them. Let them penetrate deep into your heart.*** Lit., "Do not let them depart from your eyes. / Keep them in the midst of your heart." The "eyes" are the outlook, the perspective, the presuppositions one embraces to explain the world. The parent beseeches the immature one to have a mental attitude informed by these words of wisdom. Wisdom begins with the ear and then affects the sight.

4:22 ***life . . . healing.*** Internalized wisdom enlivens the whole person. See commentary on the stanza 3:5-12.

4:23 ***Guard your heart.*** The heart (*leb* [TH3820, ZH4213]) is the target for the wise counsel of Proverbs, found 97 times in the book with various significations: It signifies reason in 41% of its occurrences, emotions in 22%, trust in 20%, volition in 14%, and behavior in 3%. Fools die for lack of a heart (10:21). He who follows vain persons is devoid of a heart (11:12; 12:11). This certainly means devoid of a wise or understanding heart. The heart can be perverse (12:8), heavy (12:25), sick (13:12), merry (15:13), proud (16:5), wise (16:21), or hard (28:14). The heart is the source of life (4:23). One must open one's heart to understanding (2:2), wisdom (2:10), and counsel (3:1; 4:4). It can also be open to evil counsel (7:25). Planning and intellectual activity are functions of the heart (6:18; 16:1); the term is used for both volitional activity (2:2; 4:4, 23) and behavior (6:32; 12:23; 27:23). "Heart" is a word that Proverbs uses to describe the entire internal life of a person. It is an internal reflection of the person (19:8; 20:5; 27:19; Schwab 1995:8-9). The most used meaning is the rational faculties of a person, glossed as "mind" (12:8; 16:23), "concentrate" (2:2), and so on. It is the religious center of a person, which orients the mind, will, and emotions—hence the source of life. What the heart loves is at issue. Does it love folly or wisdom? Yahweh or evil? "The heart of man is the proper target for counsel; through it his life is comprehended (17:16; 18:2; 19:3)" (Schwab 1995:9).

4:24 ***perverse talk.*** The heart is the wellspring of one's speech (Matt 12:34). What is spoken reveals the heart. A guarded heart naturally leads to reforming the mouth.

4:25 ***Look straight ahead . . . fix your eyes.*** As in 4:21, internalized wisdom controls one's outlook on life. Here the student is reminded to look down the narrow path and not deviate by gawking at evil.

4:26 ***your feet.*** One's life direction follows one's faith commitments.

COMMENTARY

This section can be divided into three stanzas. The initial and final verses of the first stanza (4:10-13) end with *khayyim* [TH2416, ZH2644] (life). Walk without stumbling and live! "Stumble" (4:12, from *kashal* [TH3782, ZH4173]) is found twice in the next stanza (4:14-19). The third stanza (4:20-27) begins "My child" (as does the first stanza) and treats the heart and its relation to the path of life. In the first stanza, the father promises that his words will be the key of life to the youth (4:13). Wisdom's path will vitalize and extend the youth's life. Having yet again emphasized the overriding importance of listening to his words, in the next stanza he characterizes the contrary way as eating and drinking violence and death, walking in darkness, and stumbling in ignorance of what lies ahead.

The discussion of life path and wisdom is clarified in the last stanza. Here is specified the process of how wisdom enters into a person and influences inner change, resulting in external and visible reform. Wisdom initially enters the awareness of the parents' intellectually unformed progeny through the ear (4:20). Moral and ethical instruction is heard. It works its way down (through much repetition!) into the heart, which is the wellspring of life, the control center of all other faculties (4:21). Having integrated the many lessons of childhood, one's whole being is enlightened and invigorated (4:22). The religious kernel of a youth must be diligently guarded from folly (4:23). Having been thus transformed, the speech is affected. In other words, having *received* wise counsel, one begins to *offer* wise counsel to others (4:24). The verse states this negatively: One ceases to utter deception. The wise have learned to look straight ahead, to view the world through the lens of wisdom and not folly (4:25). Thus, understanding circumstance and situation, one puts this into practice, actually doing the deeds consistent with wise counsel (4:26), careful not to turn aside to the right or left (4:27).

This is the procedure by which a person is converted. "Faith comes from hearing" (Rom 10:17). Paul argues that the word of God must first be preached, then believed in the heart, simultaneously changing what a person confesses with the mouth (Rom 10:9). This, in turn, results in a changed way of living (Rom 12:1-2). In Proverbs, this process is necessary to prepare the juvenile for adult temptations soon to come. To this subject the book now turns.

◆ G. Wisdom and Pleasure (5:1–7:27)

1. Advice about sex (5:1–23)

1 My son, pay attention to my
wisdom;
listen carefully to my wise counsel.
2 Then you will show discernment,
and your lips will express what
you've learned.
3 For the lips of an immoral woman are
as sweet as honey,

and her mouth is smoother
than oil.
4 But in the end she is as bitter as
poison,
as dangerous as a double-edged
sword.
5 Her feet go down to death;
her steps lead straight to the grave.*
6 For she cares nothing about the path
to life.
She staggers down a crooked trail
and doesn't realize it.

7 So now, my sons, listen to me.
Never stray from what I am about
to say:
8 Stay away from her!
Don't go near the door of her
house!
9 If you do, you will lose your honor
and will lose to merciless people
all you have achieved.
10 Strangers will consume your wealth,
and someone else will enjoy the
fruit of your labor.
11 In the end you will groan in anguish
when disease consumes your body.
12 You will say, "How I hated discipline!
If only I had not ignored all the
warnings!
13 Oh, why didn't I listen to my teachers?
Why didn't I pay attention to my
instructors?
14 I have come to the brink of utter ruin,
and now I must face public
disgrace."

15 Drink water from your own well—
share your love only with
your wife.*
16 Why spill the water of your springs
in the streets,
having sex with just anyone?*
17 You should reserve it for yourselves.
Never share it with strangers.

18 Let your wife be a fountain of blessing
for you.
Rejoice in the wife of your
youth.
19 She is a loving deer, a graceful doe.
Let her breasts satisfy you always.
May you always be captivated by
her love.
20 Why be captivated, my son, by an
immoral woman,
or fondle the breasts of a
promiscuous woman?
21 For the LORD sees clearly what a man
does,
examining every path he takes.
22 An evil man is held captive by his
own sins;
they are ropes that catch and
hold him.
23 He will die for lack of self-control;
he will be lost because of his great
foolishness.

5:5 Hebrew *to Sheol.* 5:15 Hebrew *Drink water from your own cistern, / flowing water from your own well.* 5:16 Hebrew *Why spill your springs in the streets, / your streams in the city squares?*

NOTES

5:1 ***listen carefully.*** Precisely, "Incline your ear," an idiom repeated in the mournful cry of 5:13: "Why didn't I pay attention [incline my ear]?"

5:2 ***what you've learned.*** Lit., "knowledge," the very thing the loose woman does not have; she "doesn't realize" (5:6).

5:3 ***lips.*** Heb., *sapah* [TH8193, ZH8557]. Her lips are contrasted with the wise lips of 5:2. Note the sensual description of her lips: honey and oil. Keep in mind that her lips are a symbol for her speech—contrasted with the parents' words of wisdom. Dahood compares 5:3 to 10:31-32 and 15:7: "In summary, the wise man warns his pupil that his lips must overflow with knowledge if he is successfully to avoid the wiles of the harlot, whose lips are honey that drips" (1973:65-66).

5:4 ***in the end.*** The end of a matter is an important wisdom argument.

double-edged sword. Lit., "sword of mouths." This phrase is perhaps, in the context of her lips, a double entendre for both "edge" and "speech." Berman argues for just this sort of wordplay in various contexts (Judg 3:16-19; Ps 149:6; Heb 4:12; Rev 1:16; 2:12), a "metaphor for the potency of speech" (2002:292). See also 5:3, "mouth, palate."

5:5 ***lead straight to.*** Lit., "grasp," from *tamak* [TH8551, ZH9461], which is also the last word of 5:22, "hold him." Waltke reads "Her steps lay hold of the grave" (2004:302); KJV translates "her steps take hold on hell." See also 4:4, "Let your heart hold fast my words" (RSV). What one takes hold of—words of wisdom or the grave—reveals one's end. She seizes the grave; one who heeds her will be seized by unbreakable bondage (5:22).

5:7 ***So now, my sons.*** This stanza begins again with the appeal to listen to parental instruction, the antidote to the loose woman's oily words.

5:8 ***the door of her house.*** This is a possible double entendre; perhaps her "opening" is her vagina. See note on 2:19. Observe also multiple uses of the verbal form in the highly erotic Song 5:2-6.

5:9 ***your honor.*** Heb., *hod* [TH1935, ZH2086], used only here in Proverbs. In Num 27:20, Moses gave some of his *hod* (authority) to Joshua. In 1 Chr 29:25, *hod* is royal splendor; in Hab 3:3, God's "brilliant splendor" fills the heavens. Whatever in the young man reflected kingly glory or was lofty and commanded respect would be cruelly lost (see Kline 1986:67).

5:10 ***someone else.*** Lit., "into the house of an alien." Turn into the tempting house of the loose woman (5:8) and a stranger's house will become the repository of your spent labors.

5:11 ***In the end.*** The final result, where a path leads, is a powerful argument employed by the parent.

your body. She is the anti-wisdom, the photographic negative to promises of health and vitality to the wise (3:8); with the loose woman, one's flesh and body are wearied and one's wealth is doomed.

5:12 ***hated.*** What one loves and hates defines the person. Fools hate discipline.

5:13 ***teachers.*** Used only here in Proverbs, this form from *moreh* [TH4175B, ZH4621] is perhaps a wordplay with *marah* [TH4751, ZH5257] (bitter) from 5:4.

pay attention. This echoes the language of 5:1, "incline [the] ear."

5:14 ***public disgrace.*** What is at issue is the future status of the man in the community. He is envisioned as a slave to others who fill their houses with the fruit of his labor. His reputation is bankrupt, with bodily and fiscal ramifications.

5:15 ***share your love only with your wife.*** NLT mg notes the Hebrew: "flowing water from your own well." The wife is not explicitly mentioned until the end of 5:18.

5:16 ***having sex with just anyone?*** NLT mg notes the Hebrew: "your streams in the city squares?" "The adulteress is presented as one who encroaches upon the wife's territory. She taps into a closed hydraulic system and tries to make it spring a leak. Everything that she offers is properly enjoyed within legitimate marriage" (Schwab 2002:164).

5:18 ***fountain.*** Cf. Song 4:12.

5:19 ***loving . . . love.*** The verse repeats "love" (*'ahab* [TH158, ZH172] and *'ahabah* [TH160, ZH173], cf. the verb *'ahab* [TH157, ZH170]), with the sense of the nuptial embrace. The wife is called a deer and a doe, language reminiscent of Song 2:7, 4:5, and 7:3. Her breasts satisfy (*rawah* [TH7301, ZH8115]), satiate, saturate her husband. NLT in 7:18 translates *rawah* as "drink our fill" of love.

be captivated. Zalcman notes that the verb *shagah* [TH7686, ZH8706] always has a negative connotation (except here) and suggests repointing to *sagah* [TH7685, ZH8436], meaning "increase, thrive" (2003:433-434).

5:20 *my son.* Again the appeal to the immature begins a unit.

5:21 *the* L*ORD*. It is not with the cosmic order or an unfeeling "Wisdom" that a person has to reckon; it is before Yahweh that one makes decisions. God upholds a moral universe and personally guarantees that consequences follow.

examining. The last three verses contain three ironic reversals. The first is in the use of the verb *palas* [TH6424A, ZH7143] (examines, weighs). This term is found in 5:6 to describe the loose woman and how she "cares nothing about the path to life." People do not evaluate their ways—but Yahweh does. In the end, they will be surprised that the things to which they gave no thought were the most important.

5:22 *catch and hold him.* The second reversal: The one who seizes is seized. In 5:5 the loose woman's steps "seized" hell (see note). Now, the man who flirts with her is "seized" by his own sin and cannot escape the terrible bondage his folly failed to warn him about. Unexpectedly, a man who thinks he is "free" to sin discovers too late that such freedom is a chimera and is in reality thralldom. "Everyone who sins is a slave of sin" (John 8:34).

5:23 *he will be lost.* The third and final reversal: The man who is "captivated" (*shagah* [TH7686, ZH8706]) by the loose woman (5:20) is lost (*shagah*). Be lost in your wife's love (5:19), not with the loose woman (5:20), lest you be lost (5:23) in your folly and die.

COMMENTARY

The next lengthy composition of Proverbs spans chapters 5–7 and treats the subject of sex (and other ensnaring pitfalls of life) in three sections. The first section (5:1-23) compares wedded bliss to the temptations of extramarital excursions. The second section (6:1-19) appropriately includes in this discussion the subjects of indebtedness and sloth—two conditions of entrapment that initially offer some pleasure or benefit. Finally, the third section (6:20–7:27) returns to the subject of sex, vividly portraying the temptress and her end.

The first section (5:1-23) can be divided into four stanzas. The first (5:1-6) introduces the main themes of the section, beginning (once again!) with the call to listen. The second (5:7-14) repeats the call to listen and ends with the haunting cry of the young man who failed to listen (5:13), using language from 5:1: "Oh, why didn't I listen to my teachers?" The third stanza (5:15-19), with the figure of delicious water, impresses the young man to enjoy his own wife and no other—avoiding the public streams available to all. This stanza ends with *shagah* [TH7686, ZH8706] (captivated), which creates a seam with the next stanza that is bound with the inclusion of *shagah* (5:20, "captivated"; 5:23, "be lost") and reminds the reader that Yahweh is concerned with how one pursues sex.

The young man faced with adult temptations only has the wise counsel of the parents for protection. The loose woman's words are smooth and sweet, and to the inexperienced they seem preferable to father and mother's pedantic and repetitious moralizing. Nevertheless, the sage can powerfully argue from reality—citing what the seductions will inevitably do to the boy. She is death incarnate. Her life is unconsidered and unexamined. She is an agent of hell.

The parents can see the truth and argue from faith in a consequence-laden world that there is no *life* to be found with her. She is antilife; concourse with her will bring the unsuspecting man to disease, poverty, shame, and death. The life of an individual is bound up with community status—which the one who spurns reproof will lose. Rather than be a public leader with glory and honor, that one will become a laughingstock. The man's tortured lament (as envisioned by the parents) is so frightening that the reader cannot but be haunted by it. Wise parents know how to argue persuasively!

Oh, why didn't I listen to my teachers?
  Why didn't I pay attention to my instructors?
I have come to the brink of utter ruin,
  and now I must face public disgrace. (5:13-14)

Immediately after hearing of this evil fortune to the one who enters her house, the counselee is advised in an allegory to "drink" from his own private water source and not pursue public fountains of pleasure. Chisholm (2000:397-409) reads the imagery of water as a symbol for the wife as a never-ending headspring of sexual enjoyment. She is a well, not a mere cistern that holds runoff water, which represents the sexual pleasure to which the husband has access. Following this, the image of springs overflowing in the streets and city squares refers to the wife's sexual desirability—if she so desired, she could satisfy them all (like the loose woman)—but she reserves herself for him alone. The loose woman offers nothing that the wife cannot superabundantly provide. However, Kruger suggests that the streets and open places (5:16; see NLT mg) are the stomping grounds of the loose woman, as opposed to the wife with but one husband (5:15). "Entanglements with her will finally lead to a situation where the young man's dearly-earned wealth and heritage will pass into the hands of someone outside the family circle" (Kruger 1987:68). Kaiser agrees that 5:16 concerns the loose woman with unrestrained extramarital interests (2000:106-116). Waltke identifies the public streams as "any female source of sexual satisfaction" (2004:319).

"The antidote to the seductive power of the sexually aggressive trollop is to be content with one's own wife. The wife . . . is the 'blessed' water from whom the man is encouraged to drink (Prov 5:15-18)" (Schwab 2002:163). With this in mind, clearly it is *not* only wise words of parental instruction that help keep the boy on the straight and narrow—the wife's breasts and enticing streams of pleasure do also, with which the loose woman must compete.

Finally, an unexpected denouement is elaborated. Unbeknownst to the loose woman, who does not care about (weigh) her path (5:6), Yahweh all along is weighing the path of all people (5:21; see note). Those who seize upon death and folly, thinking themselves free, are themselves seized and ensnared by their own sin (5:22), like the gang that lies in wait for their own blood (1:18). In the end, to be captivated by the loose woman results in being captured in great folly—such a one will lose his life in death.

The discussion of sexual temptation pauses at this point, and other behaviors are treated in the next section, after which sex returns to the forefront.

2. Father's warnings (6:1-19)

1 My child,* if you have put up security
for a friend's debt
or agreed to guarantee the debt of
a stranger—
2 if you have trapped yourself by your
agreement
and are caught by what you said—
3 follow my advice and save yourself,
for you have placed yourself at your
friend's mercy.
Now swallow your pride;
go and beg to have your name
erased.
4 Don't put it off; do it now!
Don't rest until you do.
5 Save yourself like a gazelle escaping
from a hunter,
like a bird fleeing from a net.

6 Take a lesson from the ants, you
lazybones.
Learn from their ways and become
wise!
7 Though they have no prince
or governor or ruler to make them
work,
8 they labor hard all summer,
gathering food for the winter.
9 But you, lazybones, how long will you
sleep?
When will you wake up?
10 A little extra sleep, a little more
slumber,
a little folding of the hands to rest—
11 then poverty will pounce on you like
a bandit;
scarcity will attack you like an
armed robber.

12 What are worthless and wicked people
like?
They are constant liars,
13 signaling their deceit with a wink of
the eye,
a nudge of the foot, or the wiggle
of fingers.
14 Their perverted hearts plot evil,
and they constantly stir up trouble.
15 But they will be destroyed suddenly,
broken in an instant beyond all
hope of healing.

16 There are six things the LORD hates—
no, seven things he detests:
17 haughty eyes,
a lying tongue,
hands that kill the innocent,
18 a heart that plots evil,
feet that race to do wrong,
19 a false witness who pours out lies,
a person who sows discord in a
family.

6:1 Hebrew *My son.*

NOTES

6:1 ***My child.*** Heb., "my son." In warnings against the loose woman, NLT glosses "my son" (e.g., 5:1, 7). Here, however, sex is not at issue, and gender-inclusive language can again be employed without confusion.

guarantee the debt. Lit., "clapped for a stranger your palms (hands)." See also 11:15; 17:18; 22:26.

6:2 ***caught.*** From *lakad* [TH3920, ZH4334], the same word as in 5:22 to describe how sin ensnares the wicked. There are a number of correspondences between indebtedness and sexual entanglements here. For example, the "mouth" is what causes all the problems of debt—lit., "You have been captured by the words of your mouth" (6:2), just as the loose woman's words entice (5:3). The wicked also have a false mouth (6:12). The "stranger" (6:1, from *zar* [TH2214B, ZH2424]) parallels the dangerous "strange woman" (5:3, from *zar*). In addition there is the motif of "lying down" (6:9), elsewhere a euphemism for sex (e.g., 2 Sam 11:4); and the reference to the "gazelle" (6:5)—an epithet for the sexually charged wife (5:19; Song 4:5).

6:3 *your friend's mercy.* Lit., "You have come into the hand (palm) of your friend." If you have clapped your "palms" in a pledge (see note on 6:1), you put yourself into the "palm" of another.

beg to have your name erased. Lit., "rage against your friend." "Rage against" comes from *rahab* [TH7292, ZH8104]. As a noun, this is glossed as Rahab [TH7293, ZH8105], the mythological monster (Job 26:12; Isa 51:9). It can indicate strong sexual arousal (Song 6:5, where the girl's eyes "overpower" the boy). The sense in 6:3 is to passionately and aggressively attack the problem until it is resolved. Liability is no circumstance for laxity or passivity—rage like Leviathan! Part of this counsel is to "swallow your pride" and do whatever it takes to get out of this kind of financial obligation.

6:4 *Don't put it off; do it now! Don't rest until you do.* Lit., "Do not give sleep to your eyes, / Nor slumber to your eyelids." When in debt, rest and relaxation are roads to poverty. This observation naturally leads into the next part of the strophe, which compares the sluggard to the tireless ant.

6:5 *gazelle . . . bird.* These images of entrapment are drawn from trapping and hunting. In the Masoretic Text, both animals are said to escape "from the hand," reinforcing the image of being in the hand (power) of one's neighbor from 6:3. The NLT emends the first *miyyad* [TH4480/3027, ZH4946/3338] (from the hand) to *mitsayyad* [TH4480/6719, ZH4946/7475] (hunter). Comparing the liable person to trapped animals leads naturally into the next part, an excursus that confronts the sluggard with the figure of the ant.

6:6 *Take a lesson from the ants, you lazybones.* Lit., "Go to the ant!" The imperative "Go!" (*halak* [TH1980, ZH2143]) is also found in 6:3, lit., "Go! Humble yourself!" Action is required. "Lazybones" or "sluggard" (*'atsel* [TH6102A, ZH6789]) occurs again in 6:9, an inclusion that binds the part into a recognizable unit. See 26:13-16, which revisits the theme of the sluggard. The reference to the "ways" (or paths) of the ant is typical of Wisdom Literature; 30:24-25 calls the ant "unusually wise."

6:7 *no prince . . . to make them work.* They are self-motivated. Are you listening, lazybones?

6:8 *they labor . . . gathering.* When there is work to be done, do it! The LXX uniquely adds a short paragraph here lauding the virtues of the bee, introducing an association between wisdom and strength (see Giese 1992:404-411).

6:9 *how long will you sleep?* The *'atsel* [TH6102A, ZH6789] is again mentioned, ending the excursus. Sleep as a topic is resumed, picking up where 6:1-5 left off.

6:10 *a little.* Three times the word "little" is used; three times synonyms for inactivity are employed. A little bit of rest will lead to the consequences of 6:11.

6:11 Lit., "Like one walking, your poverty will come in / And your need like a man with a shield." "One walking" and "man" form a seam with the following verse, which uses the same words. The personification of poverty and want as violent individuals leads naturally into the next stanza, which introduces this very kind of villain Yahweh hates. Foolishly pledging one's property for another, and being passive about it, will savage one as surely as the worthless one (*beliya'al* [TH1100, ZH1175]) of 6:12-19.

6:12 *worthless.* Heb., *beliya'al* [TH1100, ZH1175]. *Beliya'al* is a "fatal disease" (Ps 41:8); humans who are a disease on society are also *beliya'al*. They falsely accuse and murder the innocent (1 Kgs 21:10-13; NLT, "scoundrels") and abuse what is holy (1 Sam 2:12). Here the extended description emphasizes the many avenues by which the *beliya'al* seeks to disrupt and destroy civilization. Waltke calls the *beliya'al* the "insurrectionist" (2004:341). Note that their primary characteristic is the "false mouth" (NLT, "constant liars"). The voice of the mischief maker is part of the cacophony of folly (9:13-15).

6:13 ***wiggle.*** From *yarah* I [TH3384, ZH3721]. It might also mean "direct" with a gesture (from *yarah* III [TH3384E, ZH3723]); "he teacheth with his fingers" (KJV).

6:14 ***Their perverted hearts plot evil.*** For "perverted," see note on 2:12. "Plot" translates *kharash* [TH2790, ZH3086], often glossed "engrave, plow." In their hearts they inscribe evil. The phrase is seen again in 6:18 in the catalogue of behaviors Yahweh detests.

6:15 ***But . . . suddenly.*** "Suddenly" is repeated twice, emphasizing the surprising reversal in store for the *beliya'al.* What guarantees the downfall of the troublemaker? No impersonal cosmic or social order secures this end; it is secured by Yahweh's active participation in the affairs of wisdom, made explicit in the next part.

6:16 ***six . . . seven.*** The rhetorical device of listing a number of elements in a category, then one more for good measure, is found elsewhere in Proverbs (30:15, 18, 21, 29), the Bible (Amos 1:3–2:6), and comparative extrabiblical materials. "There are two things which are good / and a third which is pleasing to Šamaš" (Lindenburger 1983:65); "For seven years let Baal fail, for eight the rider on the clouds" (Gibson 1977:115).

the LORD . . . detests. Again, it is Yahweh to whom the wicked must give account. He abominates abominable behavior; to understand this is the essence of wisdom. See note on 3:32. What one loves and hates defines a person; Yahweh hates antisocial malefactors.

6:17 ***hands that kill the innocent.*** Lit., "hands that pour out innocent blood."

6:19 ***discord in a family.*** Lit., "strife between brothers."

COMMENTARY

In this section, the composition pauses from its main thesis (sex) and digresses into other conditions that could entrap an unsuspecting fellow as surely as misguided infatuation. In the first strophe, the condition of indebtedness is described as one being captured; it uses language from the description of how sin ensnares the wicked in 5:22. An allegory—reminiscent of an allegory earlier in the composition (5:15-19)—presents anesthetic sloth lulling a person into inaction until a personified Poverty overpowers him. Sloth is a subtopic under the rubric of debt; it is the enemy of self-sufficiency. Yahweh is revealed in the second strophe as the one before whom a person lives. God abominates the *beliya'al* man who is haughty and whose life consists in doing evil, like the gang introduced in chapter 1.

Wise parents counsel their offspring to warn not only against entanglements due to the sex drive, but also against the threat of bondage in any disadvantageous condition. Thus, the poem here focuses on debt, sloth, and the antisocial troublemaker. Each of these shares a characteristic with harmful sex: Something good is exchanged for supposed freedom and power. In the case of the hooligan, the gain is not explicitly stated but may be inferred from 1:10-19 (see commentary). After these topics are explored, warnings about sex resume.

For whatever reason, a young adult may get into debt. Perhaps the eyes were agog at some item for purchase, and a contract was drawn up to pay later for some pleasure today. In this respect debt is similar to sex with the loose woman—one must pay tomorrow for today's enjoyment. The parent frames this as bondage, using language that had described the entanglements of sin (5:22) and urges the debtor, "Save yourself." This is no time for dignity or self-respect; "swallow your pride; go and beg" (6:3) until, through much effort, you painfully extricate yourself from the dire predicament.

The writer praises hard work analogous to that of the ants. If people are self-motivated and take advantage of opportunities, they are much less likely to seek debilitating loans. Sleep and inactivity bring poverty. Idleness is its own pleasure and also has this feature in common with harmful sex: Enjoy it now, but pay later. A little flirtation with lounging about, and the antilife forces of poverty will savage you.

Although matters of financing and work ethic seem to be quite secular, the section reminds the reader that it is an issue to Yahweh all along, particularly in the case of the worthless (*beliya'al*) individual (see note on 6:12). God ensures that the principles of sound wisdom operate and are reliable. This is why the parents can offer such grand promises, certain of their trustworthiness. It is the Creator who rewards wisdom and folly, a God who is known by name and through other traditions of Israel.

It is not as if the sage happened by an anthill and observed the ants' industry, then concluded through extrapolation into the human sphere that people ought to go and do likewise. Rather, the sage with God-given wisdom already knew that sloth is harmful and enterprise is advantageous, and he then used the ant as an excellent illustration of the point. Jesus used lilies to illustrate a different lesson (Luke 12:27-28)—although they do *not* make their clothing, Solomon the sage was not as gloriously panoplied (J. Jones 1995:175-177). Nature provides ample illustrations for lessons drawn from divinely endowed sapience.

The seven items Yahweh hates (lit., "abominations to his soul," 6:16), are tied to the language of the *beliya'al* man from the previous part of the strophe. God hates haughty eyes; the *beliya'al* winks the eye. God hates a lying tongue and one who "pours out lies" (6:19); the *beliya'al* is a constant liar. God hates hands that shed innocent blood; the *beliya'al* wiggles the fingers. God hates a heart that plots evil; the *beliya'al* has such a heart. God hates feet swift to harm; the *beliya'al* nudges the foot. Finally, God hates, literally, "one who sends strife," (NLT, "a person who sows discord") and the *beliya'al* sends out strife (6:14). It is Yahweh who ensures that such a person suddenly perishes (6:15).

◆ 3. Warnings against immorality (6:20–7:27)

20 My son, obey your father's commands,
and don't neglect your mother's instruction.
21 Keep their words always in your heart.
Tie them around your neck.
22 When you walk, their counsel will lead you.
When you sleep, they will protect you.
When you wake up, they will advise you.
23 For their command is a lamp
and their instruction a light;
their corrective discipline
is the way to life.
24 It will keep you from the immoral woman,
from the smooth tongue of a promiscuous woman.
25 Don't lust for her beauty.
Don't let her coy glances seduce you.

26 For a prostitute will bring you to
poverty,*
but sleeping with another man's
wife will cost you your life.
27 Can a man scoop a flame into his lap
and not have his clothes catch on
fire?
28 Can he walk on hot coals
and not blister his feet?
29 So it is with the man who sleeps with
another man's wife.
He who embraces her will not go
unpunished.

30 Excuses might be found for a thief
who steals because he is starving.
31 But if he is caught, he must pay back
seven times what he stole,
even if he has to sell everything in
his house.
32 But the man who commits adultery
is an utter fool,
for he destroys himself.
33 He will be wounded and disgraced.
His shame will never be erased.
34 For the woman's jealous husband will
be furious,
and he will show no mercy when he
takes revenge.
35 He will accept no compensation,
nor be satisfied with a payoff of
any size.

CHAPTER 7

1 Follow my advice, my son;
always treasure my commands.
2 Obey my commands and live!
Guard my instructions as you guard
your own eyes.*
3 Tie them on your fingers as a
reminder.
Write them deep within your heart.

4 Love wisdom like a sister;
make insight a beloved member
of your family.
5 Let them protect you from an affair
with an immoral woman,
from listening to the flattery of
a promiscuous woman.

6 While I was at the window of my
house,
looking through the curtain,
7 I saw some naive young men,
and one in particular who lacked
common sense.
8 He was crossing the street near the
house of an immoral woman,
strolling down the path by her
house.
9 It was at twilight, in the evening,
as deep darkness fell.
10 The woman approached him,
seductively dressed and sly of heart.
11 She was the brash, rebellious type,
never content to stay at home.
12 She is often in the streets and markets,
soliciting at every corner.
13 She threw her arms around him and
kissed him,
and with a brazen look she said,
14 "I've just made my peace offerings
and fulfilled my vows.
15 You're the one I was looking for!
I came out to find you, and here
you are!
16 My bed is spread with beautiful
blankets,
with colored sheets of Egyptian
linen.
17 I've perfumed my bed
with myrrh, aloes, and cinnamon.
18 Come, let's drink our fill of love until
morning.
Let's enjoy each other's caresses,
19 for my husband is not home.
He's away on a long trip.
20 He has taken a wallet full of money
with him
and won't return until later this
month.*"

21 So she seduced him with her pretty
speech
and enticed him with her flattery.
22 He followed her at once,
like an ox going to the slaughter.
He was like a stag caught in a trap,
23 awaiting the arrow that would
pierce its heart.

He was like a bird flying into a snare,
little knowing it would cost him
his life.

24 So listen to me, my sons,
and pay attention to my words.
25 Don't let your hearts stray away
toward her.
Don't wander down her wayward
path.
26 For she has been the ruin of many;
many men have been her victims.
27 Her house is the road to the grave.*
Her bedroom is the den of
death.

6:26 Hebrew *to a loaf of bread.* **7:2** Hebrew *as the pupil of your eye.* **7:20** Hebrew *until the moon is full.* **7:27** Hebrew *to Sheol.*

NOTES

6:20 *commands . . . instruction.* Heb., *mitswah* [TH4687, ZH5184] and *torah* [TH8451, ZH9368]; see notes on 2:1 and 3:1. Both words occur again in 6:23, forming an inclusion that binds 6:20-23 into a readily discernable unit. In addition, the imperative "Obey!" (*netsor* [TH5341, ZH5915]) sounds similar to "lamp" (*ner* [TH5216A, ZH5944]) of 6:23, perhaps another verbal link.

6:21 *Keep . . . in your heart. Tie . . . neck.* See note on 3:3. There the object of *qashar* [TH7194, ZH8003] (tie, bind) was the neck, but here it is the heart. Miller suggests with reference to Egyptian parallels that ornaments worn around the neck, and here the "bound teachings," are intended to ward the wearer from harm (1970:129-130). See Deut 6:7-8 and 11:18-20. Whybray calls this verse a "*convergence* of wisdom and Deuteronomic teaching" (1994a:103).

6:22-23 *their . . . they.* In the Hebrew, plural pronouns are not used; rather, the subject is feminine singular. A modified NLT translation would read,

When you walk, her counsel will lead you.
When you sleep, she will protect you.
When you wake up, she will advise you.
For her command is a lamp
and her instruction a light;
her corrective discipline is the way to life. (6:22-23)

The NLT correctly identifies "her" with the parents' wise guidance and so glosses with plurals. However, the trade-off is that the association between this and the image of Lady Wisdom is lost in translation. She *is* the parents' words of wisdom. This has important ramifications in ch 8, where the figure of Lady Wisdom is developed. The power of female allurement is counterbalanced with the personified feminine appeal of Wisdom.

6:22 *they will advise you.* Lit., "She will muse with you," from *siakh* [TH7878K, ZH8488], used only here in Proverbs. This can be glossed "meditate" or "muse" (Ps 119:15, 23). Here, she aids the man to think in a way that befits wisdom; he thinks her thoughts after her.

6:23 *the way to life.* The section introduces the well-lit path of life found in reproof and discipline—the only protection against the wiles of the loose woman. The inverse to this is the way of death, warned against in the closing stanza (7:24-27), framing the section with the issue of life and death.

6:24 *immoral woman.* Lit., "woman of evil," the first of five occurrences in the strophe. Note that her chief sex organ is her "tongue"; her speech defines the temptation.

6:25 *beauty . . . coy glances.* Both her words and her physical appearance are enticing. The eroticism of a woman's glance is also seen in Song 6:5.

seduce you. Lit., "catch you."

6:26 ***a prostitute will bring you to poverty.*** Lit., "the price of a prostitute unto a piece of bread" (see NLT mg). The second colon reads, "The wife of a man hunts the precious soul." Garrett suggests, "Although the price of a prostitute may be as much as a loaf of bread/ [another] man's wife hunts the precious life" (1993:100). "Soul" (*nepesh* [TH5315, ZH5883]) often connotes a person's appetites, so Scott translates, "A prostitute's price is a loaf of bread / But a married woman hunts with keener appetite" (1965:61).

6:27 ***Can a man scoop a flame.*** Hebrew syntax creates a wordplay by juxtaposing "man" (*'ish* [TH376, ZH408]) and "fire" (*'esh* [TH784, ZH836]); see 2 Kgs 1:12 for the same wordplay. Fire is a destructive force that must be handled with extreme care. Sex is like this—if misused it will scorch and ruin.

6:28 ***feet.*** In the Hebrew Bible "feet" is used as a euphemism for genitalia. The NLT glosses the idiom in Deut 28:57, "what comes out from between her feet," as "afterbirth." The "water of the feet" (Isa 36:12) is "urine"; "foot hair" (Isa 7:20; see NLT mg) is "pubic hair"; and in Song 5:3, the girl did not want to soil her "feet." The double entendre presents the image of a man walking on hot coals—*and* of a man putting his loins in harm's way.

6:29 ***embraces her.*** Lit., "touches her" (*naga'* [TH5060, ZH5595]), used in Proverbs only here, where it means to "touch" in a sexual way. In 6:33, the closing verse of the next part, the related noun *nega'* [TH5061, ZH5596] (wounds) is used. Leviticus 15:19-27 prohibits touching (*naga'*) a menstruating woman. LXX translates *naga'* with *haptomai* [TG680, ZG721], the same word Paul uses in 1 Cor 7:1, "It is good for a man not to *touch* a woman" (NLT mg).

6:30 ***because he is starving.*** Lit., "to fill his soul." *Nepesh* [TH5315, ZH5883] (soul) often means "appetite"; see note on 6:26.

6:31 ***if he is caught.*** Lit., "when he is found," from *matsa'* [TH4672, ZH5162]. The word is also found in 6:33, which contrasts the thief with the adulterer. When the thief is "found," he will pay, but that is not as bad as what the adulterer will "find"—reproach that will not be blotted out.

seven times. This is not a reference to the law of Moses (cf. Lev 6:1-5; Num 5:6-7); the number seven indicates complete satisfaction made to the victim and the community. See note on 6:16. If the thief repays "sevenfold," what will the adulterer pay?

everything in his house. Identically phrased in Song 8:7, lit., "all the wealth of his house." There, the man is "utterly scorned," using the same verb (*buz* [TH936, ZH996]) as in 6:30 (lit., "One does not *despise* a thief"; cf. 1:7, "Fools *despise* wisdom and discipline"). The preceding verse, Song 8:6, speaks of love as a fire. In the same way, a man who takes fire into his lap will be scorched, will find dishonor, and, unlike the thief who steals out of hunger, will be despised. The same result befalls the man in Song 8:6-7, who sacrifices his fortune for the flame of love. Both passages portray burning love as dangerous and self-destructive. "Wisdom brings *hon* [TH1952, ZH2104] ("wealth"; Prov. 8:18). But Love (i.e., sexual attraction) brings anti-*hon*" (Schwab 2002:57).

6:32 ***utter fool . . . destroys himself.*** "Utter fool" is more precisely glossed as "lacking heart" (*leb* [TH3820, ZH4213]). "Adultery with a married woman is so lethal a business that he who perpetrates it is mentally deficient" (McKane 1970:330). See note on 4:23. "Destroys himself" is lit., "ruins his soul" (*nepesh* [TH5315, ZH5883]). See note on 6:26.

6:33 ***wounded.*** This comes from the root *ng'*, found in Proverbs elsewhere only in 6:29, and as there, it closes a part of this strophe. To "touch" (*naga'* [TH5060, ZH5595]) results in "wounds" (*nega'* [TH5061, ZH5596]). The noun usually has the sense of "plague," particularly a disease of the skin (Lev 13). It also describes the wounds of the stricken Suffering Servant (Isa 53:8).

6:34 ***the woman's jealous husband will be furious.*** Lit., "Jealousy is the rage (*khamath* [TH2534, ZH2779]) of a man," another echo of Song 8:6-7, where jealousy is used as a virtual synonym for fiery and dangerous love. Here, jealousy is the result of illicit sex, and like the fire of Song 8:6-7, it will not be quenched. This is the mechanism by which the life of the adulterer is put in hazard. The woman's husband will, as an agent of vengeance, bring down on the offender every conceivable retribution. Driver emends *khamath* to *takhem* [TH2552, ZH2801], yielding, "Jealousy inflames a man" (1951:177).

when he takes revenge. Lit., "on the day of vengeance." Peels points out that "vengeance" (*naqam* [TH5359, ZH5934]) usually connotes action taken by proper authorities, not private revenge. Adultery is compared with thievery (6:30-33); both make the offender liable:

> If he thinks that he could stop the deceived husband from making the case public with the help of . . . [compensation or payoffs] he is greatly mistaken. . . . In the case of theft a material settlement can be one of the options, yet in the case of adultery it is out of the question. . . . The adulterer is not able to escape the yom naqam [day of revenge]. The law will certainly take its course. (Peels 1994:270-274)

7:1 ***my son.*** Again the section turns to a new stanza, where the sage implores the son to heed his words.

7:2 ***commands . . . instructions.*** Again the words *torah* [TH8451, ZH9368] and *mitswah* [TH4687, ZH5184] are employed with the promise of life (see note on 2:1).

your own eyes. Lit., "pupil of your eyes"—determinative of the boy's outlook and viewpoint (see note on 4:21). "Pupil" is singular, "eyes" are dual. Driver and the Vulgate solve this discrepancy by changing "eyes" to the singular (1951:178); LXX changes "pupil" to the plural! Biblical poetry does not always necessitate numerical concord.

7:3 ***Tie them . . . Write them.*** See notes on 3:3. See also Jer 31:33.

7:4 ***Love wisdom like a sister.*** Cf. Song 4:9-10; 5:1 (see NLT mg). A passionate embrace is envisioned.

beloved member of your family. Heb., *moda'* [TH4129, ZH4530], elsewhere used in the Bible only in Ruth 2:1. Ruth 2:1 and a related noun (*moda'ath* [TH4130, ZH4531]) in Ruth 3:2 both describe Boaz. Naomi sent Ruth in 3:1-4 to approach Boaz the *moda'ath* in private, undress his feet, and lie down next to him. The word is consonantally identical with *madda'* [TH4093, ZH4529] (knowledge), a synonym of the word translated "insight" in 7:4 (*binah* [TH998, ZH1069]). Thus, a double entendre is employed, where the youth is encouraged to call "insight" his "relation." The youth is to be intimately familiar with wisdom in order to guard against the woman introduced in the next verse.

7:5 ***immoral woman.*** Lit., "strange, foreign" woman (see note on 2:16). Her words counter the wise parents'. Grossberg calls her the "social outsider" who is "deviant" (1994:20).

7:6 ***at the window . . . looking.*** O'Connell has identified seven instances in the Bible of the "looking down from a window" scene that involves a woman and something death-like (1991:235-239). Here the father sees from his window the loose woman leading the youth to death. Rahab the harlot let the spies out of her window (Josh 2:15). Michal did the same for David (1 Sam 19:12). She later "looked down" from a window and despised him, so she died childless (2 Sam 6:16, 23). Jezebel was defenestrated (2 Kgs 9:30-33). See also Tob 3:10-15, where a woman who has been widowed seven times prays by a window. Burns argues (with LXX) that since this is a type-scene, the text envisions a woman looking down from the window (1995:22)—the scene beginning with the woman spotting the boy and making her way down the stairs and out to meet him. However, the Hebrew is first-person sg. and in its present context denotes the wise father. See Gen 26:8 for a similar variation of the type-scene.

7:7 *naive young men.* Three terms are used for these young men: the naive or simpletons (*petha'yim* [TH6612, ZH7343]), "sons," and "youth" (*na'ar* [TH5288, ZH5853]). See commentary on the poem 1:1-7. A very adult temptation accosts the "son" of another family—not fortunate enough to have a wise father to warn of this trap!

7:8 *street . . . path.* Note the imagery of the path (*derek* [TH1870, ZH2006]).

7:9 *deep darkness.* No fewer than four Hebrew words are utilized for the darkness of the hour. The dark path is also mentioned in 4:19. This is the opposite to the light of the wise way (6:23). "Deep darkness" is lit., "in the pupil (*be'ishon* [TH871.2/380, ZH928/413]) of the night"; "pupil" is also found in 7:2. Although there may be a play on words (one's "pupil" will be light, or one will be lost to the "pupil" of darkness), it should perhaps be emended to *'eshun* [TH380A, ZH854] (see 20:20), meaning "in the time" of the night.

7:10 *sly of heart.* "Sly" comes from *natsar* [TH5341, ZH5915], which has the force "keep, guard." She "guards" her heart in the sense that her purposes are secret. The boy does not know with whom he is dealing. Whybray suggests it implies that her activities are hidden from her husband (1994a:114).

7:11 *brash.* From *hamah* [TH1993, ZH2159], usually found with the sense "growls, roars." The verb is used of female sexual orgasm in Song 5:4 (her "bowels *roiled* upon him"; Schwab 2002:67). Thus there may be a sexual connotation to the brashness here.

rebellious. From *sarar* [TH5637, ZH6253], used in Hos 4:16 in a sexually charged sense; it is perhaps etymologically related to *shor* [TH8270, ZH9219] ("navel, loins"; see note on 3:8).

never content to stay at home. Lit., "Her feet do not settle in her house." The feet are a symbol of her life direction (see 3:23); her life is not oriented to her domestic obligations. However, "feet" is also a double entendre for her pubic region (see note on 6:28); her sex life is not gratified at home. LXX reads, "She is excited and profligate." Reading an initial predicate participle and a pleonastic Waw before a second modifying participle, one may loosely translate, "She growls with lust. / Her vulva is not satisfied at home."

7:12 *She is often in the streets and markets.* Lit., "Now (*pa'am* [TH6471, ZH7193]) outside, now (*pa'am*) in the streets." The language echoes 1:20, the provenance of Wisdom. Just as wisdom is everywhere discerned, temptations to folly are ubiquitous. *Pa'am* has the basic meaning "feet," continuing the image of 7:11. Her so-called feet (see Song 7:1) are everywhere lying in wait (23:28).

soliciting. From the Heb. *'arab* [TH693, ZH741], this same verb in 1:11 has the sense "lie in wait" to kill the innocent.

7:13 *a brazen look.* Precisely, "She hardens her face" (also in 21:29), meaning "to put up a strong front while lying" (Garrett 1990:682).

7:14 *peace offerings . . . vows.* Some commentators (e.g., McKane 1970:335) argue that she is fulfilling a vow made to Aphrodite. Garrett is persuasive in reading her "brazen look" (7:13) as a barefaced ploy: "her claim of prostituting herself for the sake of a vow (to Yahweh) is simply a maneuver meant to ease the conscience of the foolish young man. She is, after all, a devout woman" (1990:682). Her particular background is not at issue in the text. She is purposely an "open-ended character who defies specific interpretation" (S. Jones 2003:67). The point is not to second-guess the loose woman's religion; her self-disclosure is designed only to seduce.

7:16 *beautiful blankets . . . colored sheets . . . linen.* O'Connell suggests the materials here, particularly "linen," have a double meaning; both bedsheets and grave cloths were made of linen. The fool is "oblivious to her intention to prepare him for burial" (O'Connell 1991:238).

7:17 ***myrrh, aloes, and cinnamon.*** These sultry fragrances are found in the girl's delectable "garden" (Song 4:14). O'Connell discovers "mortuary aspects of the seductress's bed chamber" in the spices (1991:238); "her couch is his coffin" (S. Jones 2003:70).

7:18 ***drink our fill.*** Heb., *rawah* [TH7301, ZH8115] (see note on 5:19). Grossberg equates the language of imbibing love to Song 5:1 (1994:9), contra my opinion (Schwab 2002:98-105). Grossberg also notes that contrary to Song of Songs, in Prov 7 the loose woman does all of the talking and pursuing; the boy is quite passive (1994:12).

7:19 ***my husband.*** Lit., "the man." This somewhat cold reference "may suggest contempt or strangement on the part of the wife" (Whybray 1994a:116).

7:21 ***she seduced him with her pretty speech.*** "She seduced him" is from *natah* [TH5186, ZH5742] (incline) as in 2:2; 4:20; 5:1. "Pretty speech" is from *leqakh* [TH3948, ZH4375], ordinarily glossed with the sense of "learning." "Let the wise listen . . . and become even *wiser*" (1:5); "For I am giving you good *guidance*" (4:2). The text uses wisdom language to describe the persuasion of the loose woman (cf. 2:18, where her house "inclineth" to death). She is the pseudo-parent, speaking counterfeit wisdom, which is ultimately antilife.

flattery. Lit., "lips," indicating both her speech and her kisses. S. Jones argues this also refers to her pudenda (2003:70).

7:22 ***like a stag caught in a trap.*** Lit., "as [one in] fetters to punishment [goes] a fool" (*'ewil*). NLT emends *'ewil* [TH191A, ZH211] to *'ayyal* [TH354, ZH385] (stag). The LXX reads "dog"; Vulgate, "lamb."

7:23 ***like a bird flying into a snare.*** This image was used for the gang in 1:17. The loose woman is a trap, and the fool loses his life following her. Burns notes that in the text the boy's death seems to immediately follow the sex act: "*La petite mort* of orgasm leads inevitably to extinction" (1995:29). He associates the linkage between sex and death here with related myths such as Baal's or Dumuzi's death. However, a didactic purpose may be seen in that the "trap" is elusive and unknown to the ignorant; death will arrive when not expected (cf. 6:15; see note on 6:34).

cost him his life. "Life" (or "soul") translates *nepesh* [TH5315, ZH5883] (see 6:26). Boorer compares the strange woman with the figures of Leviathan and Behemoth in Job as sources of death and chaos (1996:187-204).

7:24 ***my sons.*** Again the appeal to a son begins a new stanza.

7:27 ***road to the grave.*** Her path is the road to death. She is a pied piper leading numerous fools to the abode of the damned (see 2:18).

den of death. S. Jones suggests that "den" (*kheder* [TH2315, ZH2540]) metaphorically refers to her genitals (2003:70). He cites Newsom: "Her vagina is the gate of Sheol. Her womb, death itself" (1989:156).

COMMENTARY

The composition Wisdom and Pleasure, which encompasses chapters 5–7, climaxes in its third and final section with a vivid depiction of the loose woman and what will happen if you walk her path (6:20–7:27). This section's five stanzas alternate back and forth between the father's urging his son to listen and graphic descriptions of the great power of female allurement. The section begins with the father saying, "Obey your father! Don't neglect your mother!" The next stanza describes the loose woman and what will happen to the man who touches her. This is followed again by the father directly addressing his son to be familiar with Wisdom instead of the loose woman. The fourth stanza is the most detailed description of sexual temptation in the Bible, the father proactively dramatizing the loose woman's appeal. The theme of sex has come to full expression here. Finally, the last stanza concludes that the issue is one of life and death.

The wise parent again seeks to save the boy's life, using every pedagogical technique available. He obviously cares deeply for the youth's life, repeating and repeating the urgent message before it is too late. Other sons were not so warned and thus are ill equipped for the persuasive powers of the death-dealing adulteress (7:7). Knowing this, the parent never tires of issuing warnings to the young adult. Wise parents constantly pepper their children with truisms, platitudes, rules, warnings, sentiments, value judgments, and recommendations. These create in the child the ability to discriminate between good and evil and to evaluate what is best when the time comes (Schwab 1995:16).

The parents' words are called laws and commandments, language elsewhere connoting the law of Moses. For a young person, the guidance of parents *is* what is known of God. Parents should be regarded in their moral judgments as the mouthpiece of God. Of course, this assumes wise parents; it also assumes that the youth will choose the path of wisdom. Like the law is to the psalmist (Ps 119:105), the parents' strictures, prohibitions, and admonishments are a bright lamp to light the way. The gravity of this becomes clear when one remembers that the loose woman and the evildoer walk in darkness (4:19; 7:9). The commandments of the parents are put in the mouth of a woman: "Her counsel will lead you . . . she will advise you" (see note on 6:22). This woman, introduced as personified Wisdom and encountered again in chapter 8, seeks to persuade the boy to love her rather than the immoral woman.

Burning with lust for a married woman is like holding red-hot coals in one's shirt; third-degree burns will result (6:27-28). The Song of Songs also compares love to fire and warns against it. Love is portrayed as a fire that cannot be doused. In human experience, most fires can be adequately extinguished with water. Only a conflagration would be able to cross rivers. It does not seem to matter what the "many waters" and "rivers" symbolically portray—the message is clear: Love, as a fire, will not yield to any other power. It is beyond the power of any forces in human experience to quench it (Schwab 2002:63-64).

Once a curtain in a house catches fire, it is difficult to put it out. Once a fire has a foothold, the whole domicile is in hazard. Do not play with fire! This is the figure the wise parent uses to reveal the folly of adultery. Rather than be attracted to the loose woman, the boy should make love to wisdom, embracing her and adoring her first. This will ward him from other loves (7:4-5).

The memorable climax of the section is the graphic description of a seduction. Hayes calls this "imagined speech" (1974:256). The father is preemptively dramatizing what it will be like on the streets for the boy. The loose woman brings out her full arsenal. First, she hunts him (7:12) in the darkness of night (7:7-9). She is dressed to kill. She haunts the same locale that Wisdom does—folly is as omnipresent in our society as wisdom. Growling with lust and psychologically unable to stay home (7:11), the nymphomaniac waylays him (7:13), lies to him to ease his conscience (7:14), makes him feel special and unique (7:15), and bombards his senses with the apparel and allure of sex (7:16-17). With her perfume, incense, linen sheets, and fine bed, she entices him. The Song of Songs also describes a sexually frenzied woman who searches in the streets for her lover (Song 5:2-8). Unlike the girl of the Song, the dangerous adulteress leaves her covenanted husband (2:17) and his house to seek satisfaction with many lovers (7:26). "Come, let's drink our fill of love until morning" (7:18). This language echoes the vocabulary of the wife's sexual pleasures (5:19). She trespasses on the bride's turf; she offers to the man what is only proper for the espoused to provide. She creates the illusion that the deed is safe (7:19-20). With her beguiling coquetry she works against wisdom, turning him to a different "teaching" (see note on 7:21). He follows her into her bed and partakes of all the pleasures she promised.

At this point, modern television and media might fade out, and leave one with the impression that a wonderful thing has happened. But the envisioned scenario, so aptly rendered by the experienced father, is not quite finished. He continues:

He followed her at once,
 like an ox going to the slaughter.
He was like a stag caught in a trap,
 awaiting the arrow that would pierce its heart.
He was like a bird flying into a snare,
 little knowing it would cost him his life. (7:22-23)

An invisible trap is there. Youths cannot perceive it. All a youth possesses to save his soul is faith in the words of the parents. They have told him where this behavior leads, but he cannot perceive it. What will the father's son do? Will he turn and be caught, like the boy in the imagined scenario, or will he shun her? This is the tension of the introductory chapters of the book. Which path will he choose? Just in case the young man has missed it, the father makes the point one more time: Her vagina is a door to Sheol (2:19; 7:27; see notes). She is an agent of hell; she is Death incarnate, and her slain are legion.

Murphy comments on the preponderance of warnings about sex in chapters 1–9.

> *When one considers the general tone of the first nine chapters of Proverbs, the extraordinary emphasis given to sexual conduct is striking, even oppressive. . . . The emphasis seems out of all proportion to the importance of sexual conduct. In the various collections of sayings which constitute the book, the only other references to this topic are the advice of Lemuel's mother in 31:3 (which is very general) and the description of the wicked woman as a "deep pit" in 22:14 and 23:27. This fact is in striking contrast to the attention given to sexual conduct in chaps. 1–9. (1988:600)*

He observes that more material is devoted to the loose woman than to any other subject, including Wisdom herself. He posits an association between Wisdom and Eros; the youth is called to fall in love with her (Wisdom) as he might his own wife. "Sexual fidelity is also a symbol of one's attachment to Lady Wisdom . . . Unless Lady Wisdom is pursued as the beloved, all the advice of the sage is in vain" (Murphy 1988:603). In other words, the loose woman has a symbolic value: She represents the path of folly as well as phony philosophies of life that are self-destructive, offer false hope, and are inimical to the worship of Yahweh.

Traditional sagacity renders a wise life as that which is able to control the venereal appetite. In fact, the blessed life of a sage with a virtuous woman is the culmination of a life of wisdom (ch 31). A sage can successfully embrace a wife in love and find blessing and honor (Schwab 2001:83-84). The watershed moment in the life of a sage is how he handles temptations of various sorts, especially in the arena of sex. The prudent are able to discern the truth of the matter and see clearly that death awaits whoever chases the loose woman. One who cannot do this and make choices accordingly is a fool.

◆ H. Wisdom, Yahweh, and Life (8:1-36)

1 Listen as Wisdom calls out!
Hear as understanding raises her voice!
2 On the hilltop along the road,
she takes her stand at the crossroads.
3 By the gates at the entrance to the town,
on the road leading in, she cries aloud,
4 "I call to you, to all of you!
I raise my voice to all people.
5 You simple people, use good judgment.
You foolish people, show some understanding.
6 Listen to me! For I have important things to tell you.
Everything I say is right,
7 for I speak the truth
and detest every kind of deception.
8 My advice is wholesome.
There is nothing devious or crooked in it.
9 My words are plain to anyone with understanding,
clear to those with knowledge.
10 Choose my instruction rather than silver,
and knowledge rather than pure gold.
11 For wisdom is far more valuable than rubies.
Nothing you desire can compare with it.

12 "I, Wisdom, live together with good judgment.
I know where to discover knowledge and discernment.
13 All who fear the LORD will hate evil.
Therefore, I hate pride and arrogance,
corruption and perverse speech.
14 Common sense and success belong to me.
Insight and strength are mine.
15 Because of me, kings reign,
and rulers make just decrees.
16 Rulers lead with my help,
and nobles make righteous judgments.*

17 "I love all who love me.
Those who search will surely find me.
18 I have riches and honor,
as well as enduring wealth and justice.
19 My gifts are better than gold, even the purest gold,
my wages better than sterling silver!
20 I walk in righteousness,
in paths of justice.
21 Those who love me inherit wealth.
I will fill their treasuries.

22 "The LORD formed me from the beginning,
before he created anything else.
23 I was appointed in ages past,
at the very first, before the earth began.
24 I was born before the oceans were created,

before the springs bubbled forth
their waters.
25 Before the mountains were formed,
before the hills, I was born—
26 before he had made the earth and
fields
and the first handfuls of soil.
27 I was there when he established the
heavens,
when he drew the horizon on the
oceans.
28 I was there when he set the clouds
above,
when he established springs deep
in the earth.
29 I was there when he set the limits
of the seas,
so they would not spread beyond
their boundaries.
And when he marked off the earth's
foundations,
30 I was the architect at his side.
I was his constant delight,
rejoicing always in his presence.
31 And how happy I was with the world
he created;
how I rejoiced with the human
family!

32 "And so, my children,* listen to me,
for all who follow my ways are
joyful.
33 Listen to my instruction and be wise.
Don't ignore it.
34 Joyful are those who listen to me,
watching for me daily at my gates,
waiting for me outside my home!
35 For whoever finds me finds life
and receives favor from the LORD.
36 But those who miss me injure
themselves.
All who hate me love death."

8:16 Some Hebrew manuscripts and Greek version read *and nobles are judges over the earth.* **8:32** Hebrew *my sons.*

NOTES

8:1 ***Wisdom calls out.*** In Hebrew, the verse begins with a question: "Does not Wisdom call?" She is called by different names: "wisdom" and "understanding." She "live[s] together" (8:12) with "good judgment," "knowledge," and "discernment." Together with 8:14 ("common sense," "success," "strength") and 8:20 ("righteousness," "justice"), it is not hard to determine who she is: the representation and personification of all wisdom virtues.

8:2-3 ***the hilltop . . . the gates.*** The city gates "designate the heart of commerce, judicial activity, and social exchange, and here the 'heights' would suggest the top of the city wall . . . in contrast to the 'stranger' who operates under cover of darkness . . . to bring her captive youth into her house. It is also in contrast to the setting of the wisdom teacher . . . who assumes a private one-to-one relationship to the youth" (Murphy 1998:49). Her call is quite public, meant to be heard by all.

8:4 ***I call to you, to all of you!*** Lit., "To you, males, I call!" In keeping with the context of the preceding material, perhaps she intends to target those susceptible to the wiles of the loose woman.

8:5 ***You simple people . . . foolish people.*** The *petha'yim* [TH6612, ZH7343] (simple) are targeted by Wisdom. Interestingly, so is the *kesil* [TH3684, ZH4067] (fool), who by definition will not listen (1:7). Perhaps it is for the benefit of the *petha'yim* that the *kesil* are called. See commentary on 1:2-7. Cf. 21:11a: "If you punish a mocker, the *petha'yim* become wise."

use . . . show. The word *habinu* [TH995, ZH1067] (get understanding) is repeated in both cola. The LXX glosses the second with *entithēmi* [TG1783.1, ZG1951], "imbibe, instill, impart." If emended to *hakinu* [TH3559, ZH3922], it yields the rendering "and the fool should internalize sense (heart)!"

8:6 *important things.* Lit., "nobles" (*negidim* [TH5057, ZH5592]). Emended to *negadim* [TH5048A, ZH5584], it yields "right things."

8:7 *detest every kind of deception.* Lit., "abomination to my lips is wickedness." The LXX inserts "before me" after "abomination," realigning the structure of the verse: "are abominable before me false [wicked] lips." (See 12:22 and note on 3:32.)

8:8-9 Her counsel is the opposite of that of the loose woman; this is obvious to the sage.

8:11 *wisdom . . . it.* The stanza closes with an editorial comment that speaks of wisdom in the third person and is not formally part of her speech. Here wisdom is again compared to "rubies." See note on 3:15.

8:12 *I, Wisdom.* The new stanza begins with Lady Wisdom again speaking in the first person.

8:13 *All who fear the LORD will hate evil.* This first line has been considered a late addition, although it is found in all versions. However, the chiastic patterning in Hebrew ("hate . . . evil . . . evil . . . hate") evinces a formal unity to the verse as is. The reference to hating here serves as counterpoint to the next stanza, which treats love and loving. The line serves as a reminder that wisdom is not autonomous from Yahweh—the subject of the section's last stanza. Thus, the line is *not* "totally unrelated to the context" (Whybray 1994a:124). Wisdom identifies herself in terms of those who worship God.

8:14 See note on 8:1. The figure of Lady Wisdom encompasses all wisdom virtues.

8:15 Solomon asked for wisdom particularly in matters of state (1 Kgs 3:9).

8:16 *make righteous judgments.* Lit., "judges of righteousness" (*tsedeq* [TH6664, ZH7406]), the last word being identical to the last word of 8:15. LXX and an inner-MT variant read "judges of the earth" (*'arets* [TH776, ZH824]; see RSV).

8:17 *I love.* Like the previous stanza, this begins with an emphatic "I" (8:12). The Hebrew reads, "I ones-loving-me I love." This echoes 8:13: "Ones-fearing Yahweh hate evil . . . I hate." Both stanzas begin with verses ending with the verb *matsa'* [TH4672, ZH5162]: "I find," "find me."

8:18 *enduring wealth and justice.* Hurowitz argues from Akkadian cognates that "enduring wealth" is best understood as "negotiable wealth," i.e., cash, traveling money (2000:252-254). "Justice" (*tsedaqah* [TH6666, ZH7407]) is here paired with "wealth." Contra RSV and some commentators, Proverbs never denotes "prosperity" with *tsedaqah;* in 8:20 *tsedaqah* parallels "justice" (*mishpat* [TH4941, ZH5477]).

8:21 *inherit wealth.* The word *yesh* [TH3426A, ZH3780] (here rendered "wealth") indicates "existence" and is often glossed "there is . . ." (14:12; 16:25; 18:24). Nowhere else in biblical Hebrew is it used as a noun (although it is in later Hebrew). The immediately following exposition of Yahweh's work of creation might expand the sense of *yesh* beyond mere property or riches to something more substantial—blessedness, eternity, glory. In 3:35 the wise "inherit honor"—the only other place in chs 1–9 where an inheritance is mentioned, again in close proximity to treatment of God's creation (3:19-20). Hurowitz suggests on the basis of Akkadian cognates that "wealth" should be glossed "treasures" (2000:252-257).

8:22 *The LORD formed me.* "Formed" comes from *qanah* [TH7069, ZH7864], which in Proverbs always has the sense "acquire, get, purchase." Elsewhere it can mean acquire in the sense of "give birth to" (as in the etymology of Cain in Gen 4:1; see also 8:24-25). It can also mean "to possess," as in, lit., "possessor of heaven and earth" (Gen 14:19). This is the preferable sense used here: "Yahweh possessed me from the beginning" (Harding 1986:276). Often in Proverbs, humans are called to "get/acquire [*qanah*] wisdom" (e.g., 4:5, 7; 16:16)—imitating the God who also had acquired this wisdom from eternity (see note on 4:5). Perhaps this is why *qanah* is used here, contra Vawter, who argues Yahweh "discovers" preexistent wisdom (1980:205-216). Wisdom is, of course, *not* preexistent, having been "brought forth" (see 8:24 and note). *Qanah* is not "form, create." "The core of the problem is Why did the LXX translators choose *ktizein* [TG2936, ZG3231] ("to create")? . . . In the end . . . no explanation suffices except that it was tendentious: the translator held some theory of interpretation of this passage" (Irwin 1986:133-142). This poor choice has created many false impressions about the origin and nature of Lady Wisdom.

from the beginning. Precisely, "his first way." The book urges humans to walk wisdom's path, the path that Yahweh made first priority for himself. Sages walk as God walks. God's first path is the path of wisdom, and thus for humans to walk the path of wisdom is to follow in God's own footsteps.

8:23 ***I was appointed.*** Lit., "I was established."

before the earth began. This is the first of four times "earth" is cited in 8:23-31, one of a number of terms that bind the stanza as a unit.

8:24 ***I was born.*** Lit., "I was brought forth." Again in 8:25, Wisdom says she was "brought forth" before the oldest features of the earth took shape. "Oceans" or "deep" is found in 8:24-28 three times; the only other reference in Proverbs is in 3:20. Yee claims that Wisdom being "born" is an origin comparable to that of human beings. "Woman Wisdom not only personifies God's own wisdom but also the human wisdom tradition itself. Divine and human wisdom find their unity in the personification of Woman Wisdom" (Yee 1992:85-96).

8:25 ***before.*** Heb., *lipne* [TH3807.1/6440, ZH4200/7156], from *paneh* (face), found three times in 8:25-30. There are many such verbal links throughout this stanza, including the repeated *qedem* [TH6924, ZH7710] in 8:22-23 (also translated "before"), found in Proverbs only there, and "I was born," repeated in 8:24-25.

8:26-29 With wisdom God created every aspect of creation.

8:30 ***I was the architect at his side.*** "Architect" assumes an emendation to *'amman* [TH542, ZH588] (craftsman), which is found only at Song 7:2 in the Hebrew Bible. The unemended text of 8:30 has the hapax legomenon *'amon* [TH525, ZH570] (a Qal infinitive absolute of the common verb *'aman* [TH539, ZH586]), lit., "faithfully." Wisdom is *not* portrayed as a craftsman or architect elsewhere in the passage, and this emendation introduces a new thought into the text. Wisdom is not the cosmic order; she is an aspect of the Creator, always present with him in his work of creation. *'Amon* (cf. *'amen* [TH543, ZH589]) with the sense "Amen, faithful" might be seen in Rev 3:14, "This is the message from the one who is the Amen—the faithful and true witness, the beginning of God's new creation" (Scott 1960:213-223). See also Fox (1996:699-702), who argues that *'amon* means "growing up" as a child who delights in the new creation. This also introduces a new thought. For a development of this basic idea, see Hurowitz 1999:391-400.

8:30-31 ***delight . . . rejoicing . . . happy . . . rejoiced.*** According to Yee (1982:61), these verses have a chiastic pattern:

A. I was his constant delight (*sha'ashu'im* [TH8191, ZH9141])
  B. rejoicing always (*mesakheqeth* [TH7832, ZH8471])
  B.' how happy I was (*mesakheqeth*)
A.' how I rejoiced (*sha'ashu'im*).

8:31 ***human family.*** This repetition closes the section begun in 8:4 (NLT, "all people").

8:32 ***And so . . . listen.*** The final segment of this section draws the moral of the story: Embrace her! Love her! Heed her! Three times in three verses (vv. 32-34) "listen" is repeated.

for all who follow my ways are joyful. This is the first nine chapters in a nutshell. Those who possess Wisdom also possess joy.

8:33 ***my instruction.*** This "instruction" is about to commence in ch 10.

8:34 ***daily.*** Lit., "day by day"; the same phrase describes Wisdom beside God in the Creation (8:30)—again, this is the image of God, who "day by day" is attended by his wisdom. Unlike God, however, who possessed her from eternity, the sage must diligently seek her, watch for her by the gates, and guard her house.

8:35 ***favor from the LORD.*** To have wisdom is to have life from God.

8:36 ***love death.*** This recalls the stanza 8:17-21, which claims that Wisdom loves those who find her (8:17), and those who love her "inherit wealth" (8:21). Fools, however, hate her and love death. See commentary on 1:20-33. Again, life (8:35) and death are at issue here.

COMMENTARY

The next composition of the Prologue is the poem of chapter 8. The previous composition developed the theme of alluring sex (with other temptations) and how this endangers an inexperienced man. The section climaxed with a graphic description of the loose woman, portraying her powers of seduction in a very realistic fashion. Now, it is Wisdom's turn to speak. Immediately after the father speaks to the plural "sons" (7:24-27), Wisdom herself has her say.

The poem may be divided in two: The first, longer section (8:1-31) is her appeal; the second, shorter segment (8:32-36), beginning "And so, my children . . ." draws out the moral of the story. The first section may be divided into five stanzas. In the first stanza (8:1-4), Wisdom initiates her call to all who will listen. In the second stanza (8:5-11), Wisdom exclaims that her gifts are far more valuable than rubies. In the third stanza (8:12-16), Wisdom herself speaks of what she knows; specifically, Wisdom knows where to "discover" knowledge. The fourth stanza (8:17-21) is bound by the inclusion "love" and discusses whom she loves and who loves her. Finally, the fifth stanza (8:22-31) highlights the fact that the universe displayed Yahweh's wisdom from its genesis. The transition between the last two stanzas is abrupt; the Septuagint adds a verse between 8:21 and 8:22, tying wisdom's present advice to events of the deep past.

The wisdom and knowledge explored so incisively in the book of Proverbs treats human society and matters of equity, justice, and consideration of one's neighbor. It addresses pitfalls such as adultery, sloth, greed, anger, and violence—and how the thoughtful and disciplined hearts of the wise can navigate in such a world with success. However, the wellspring of sagacity and the upholder of a consequence-laden world is none other than Yahweh, the God who revealed himself to Israel in various ways. Acknowledgment of one's dependence upon this God is the first step down the path of wisdom. Knowledge, prudence, and discretion in human affairs begin and end with a life lived before the face of the living God. This God enforces the principles of wisdom for humanity, knows all, and displays his limitless power and skill—in the counsel of wise parents, in the proverbs of Solomon, and in the manner in which the cosmos was created. They are observable to all with eyes to see. By wisdom, kings render judgments beyond the ken of ordinary citizens. And God, whose purposes are unfathomable, rules the earth in wisdom. The Lord's sovereign and creative wisdom is personified in the figure of Lady Wisdom, who connects the content of the book of Proverbs with the fashion of the universe itself. The passage is unique in the Bible, and in ancient Near Eastern literature, despite some striking similarities (Whybray 1965:504-514).

The First and Second Stanzas (8:1-11). In the first stanza (8:1-4) Lady Wisdom calls out in the public places, boldly evangelizing the city. Good sense, prudence, and knowledge are difficult to ignore. After all, to deny them one must renounce all of reality. Her counsel should be sought before silver and gold; her price excels precious treasures. The wisdom displayed through one's experiences calls one to do right. Wisdom's opposite is called "devious," "crooked" (8:8)—abominable to possessors of true knowledge and understanding. The second stanza (8:5-11) emphasizes the upright, beneficial, and wholesome advice she offers. It ends by comparing Wisdom with rubies. Part of Wisdom's call here is to use "good judgment"—a term repeated in the beginning of the third stanza (8:12-16).

The Third Stanza (8:12-16). The stanza that mentions the fear of Yahweh also connects wisdom with the ability of rulers to judge and administrate. Wisdom is not realpolitik, a pragmatic approach unrelated to ethical or religious considerations, a clever skill to manage government. Wisdom to rule is firstly a posture of dependence on God the Creator, and those with this attitude rule wisely. How could one rule who does not hate evil and reverence God? Perjury and lies are inimical to social order—one in a position of authority must eschew such things.

The Fourth Stanza (8:17-21). The poem greatly emphasizes the overriding value and worth of truth and knowledge. Wisdom compares favorably with silver, gold, and rubies. Yet she promises riches to those who love her (8:18-19). This paradox is resolved in recognizing that in Proverbs wealth is a good thing, but a greedy man who pursues it above all else will find only folly and, ultimately, poverty. In the words of Agur, "Give me neither poverty nor riches! . . . For if I grow rich, I may deny you and say, 'Who is the Lord?' And if I am too poor, I may steal and thus insult God's holy name" (30:8-9). Wealth by itself is a spiritual trap. "Human desire is never satisfied" (27:20); the rich man is subject to self-delusion (18:11; 28:11); he is prone to antisocial behavior (18:23; 22:16; 28:6). However, if one pursues wisdom instead of riches, one will acquire both. This is exemplified in what happened to Solomon.

> *The Lord was pleased that Solomon had asked for wisdom. So God replied, "Because you have asked for wisdom in governing my people with justice and have not asked for a long life or wealth or the death of your enemies—I will give you what you asked for! I will give you a wise and understanding heart such as no one else has had or ever will have! And I will also give you what you did not ask for—riches and fame! No other king in all the world will be compared to you for the rest of your life! And if you follow me and obey my decrees and my commands as your father, David, did, I will give you a long life." (1 Kgs 3:10-14)*

The Fifth Stanza (8:22-31). Yahweh possessed Wisdom without measure before the universe was created, which he fashioned with understanding and great skill; the cosmos itself reveals the infinite sagacity of its Creator. True wisdom recognizes this. False claims to wisdom reject it, as Paul argues in Romans 1:

> *But God shows his anger from heaven against all sinful, wicked people who suppress the truth by their wickedness. They know the truth about God because he has made it obvious to them. For ever since the world was created, people have seen the earth and sky. Through everything God made, they can clearly see his invisible qualities—his eternal power and divine nature. So they have no excuse for not knowing God. Yes, they knew God, but they wouldn't worship him as God or even give him thanks. And they began to think up foolish ideas of what God was like. As a result, their minds became dark and confused. Claiming to be wise, they instead became utter fools. And instead of worshiping the glorious, ever-living God, they worshiped idols made to look like mere people and birds and animals and reptiles.* (Rom 1:18-23)

The point of 8:22-31 is *not* to foster speculation on the identity of Lady Wisdom, but to highlight that the wisdom espoused in the book has the same origin as the wisdom discerned in creation. Fools reject wise counsel, and those who refuse to glorify the God of creation become fools also (Rom 1:22). There is a sense in which all people everywhere "know" God—that he is there and that they owe him allegiance. But fools willfully and culpably suppress this knowledge and worship whatever their darkened hearts conceive (Rom 1:21-23), exchanging the truth about God for falsehoods (Rom 1:25). After laying this foundation in Romans, Paul demonstrates that this rejection of God is far-reaching; when he gave people a clearer revelation (the law), they continued to sin against him (Rom 2–3).

There is a common theme in this: God's character, put on display in creation, is united to his verbal revelation in the Bible. This can be seen in Psalm 19, which first speaks of the heavens "proclaiming" and "speaking" of God (Ps 19:1-6), then seamlessly transitions to the law making one wise (Ps 19:7-14). "Both Wisdom and the Law act as revelatory extensions of Yahweh's character, informing believers how to live as a covenant people" (D. Williams 1994:275-279).

The rich metaphor of Lady Wisdom has three loci of meaning. First, she is the divine wisdom, possessed by the Creator from eternity. Second, she can be

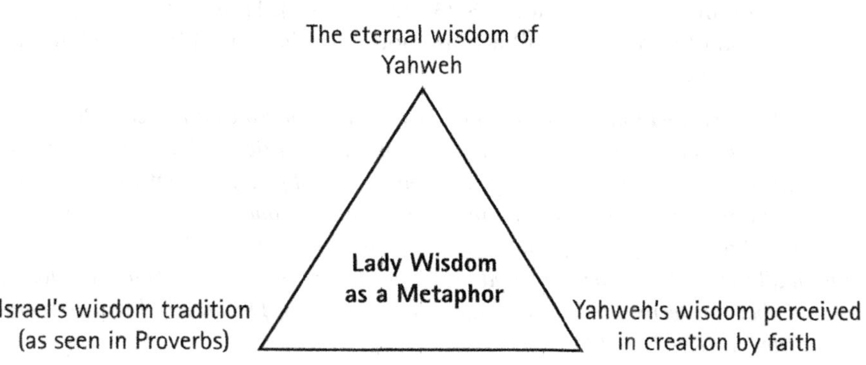

intuited through observing how God governs and orders all things in the creation. Finally, she represents the wisdom tradition of Israel, as expressed in the book of Proverbs.

Lady Wisdom is not a "hypostasis," a somewhat independent being from Yahweh (i.e., a different "Person" like the Father, Son, Spirit are different Persons). She is a symbol of God's wisdom, a wisdom that in the fullness of time did indeed conceive and bring forth Christ. "This wisdom the poet here personifies; he does not speak of the personal Logos, but the further progress of the revelation points to her actual personification in the Logos" (Delitzsch 1874:183). In Jesus the wisdom tradition (which draws on creation themes) catches up to redemption. The creation that had been the ultimate expression of God's wisdom is now shown to be penultimate, the ultimate being the wise manner in which God has saved his people from sin and death through Jesus Christ. "Christ is the power of God and the wisdom of God" (1 Cor 1:24). "In him lie hidden all the treasures of wisdom and knowledge" (Col 2:3). Fools not only reject the message of the heavens and earth; they also reject the gospel of Jesus. In Proverbs, this is foreshadowed by the specter of individuals who disdain the tutelage of Lady Wisdom—who hate her and thereby love death (8:36).

The Christian impulse to see in the figure of Lady Wisdom a preincarnate Christ has been a pitfall throughout the history of the church. Since she claims to have been "acquired"—which the Septuagint translates as "created" (see note on 8:22)—Christ then seems to be a secondary being without fully divine status. One hermeneutical technique, used by Athanasius, was to argue that "creation" means "incarnation" in this context (Kannengiesser 1999:6-77). Some sects, such as the Jehovah's Witnesses, incorrectly use Proverbs 8:22 to argue that Jesus was created by God and therefore is not equal to the eternal God (see Harding 1986).

The mistake of reading Lady Wisdom as a hypostasis and not a personification has caused some of her attributes to be confused with Jesus' person in a way not envisioned before the twentieth century. Some commentators in modern times see the presentation of Lady Wisdom as providing a way to rewrite Christology. It is as if they lift Lady Wisdom out of her wisdom context and insert her into the Gospels as part of Jesus' history. Thus, some today affirm "Jesus-Sophia, wisdom incarnate in the person of Jesus of Nazareth" (Alnor 1999), as though she were one and the same as the Logos of John 1:1, 14. But the *logos* [TG3056, ZG3364] of John 1 (who was with God, was God, and became flesh) and the figure of Wisdom (*sophia* [TG4678, ZG5053]) are completely different entities. The interpreter must keep clear the distinction between a poetic figure and a historical man! In this light, Jobes says, "Jesus Christ should not be renamed Sophia-Jesus because he is *not* merely an idea in the history of religions recently made passé by feminist ideology; according to the witness of the New Testament, he is Lord of history to whom all social movements must someday give an account" (2000:226-250).

Who is Lady Wisdom? She is a poetic personification of life and favor from Yahweh. Love her and find divine favor; hate her and die a fool's death. She invites all humanity (8:34) into her home, where their instruction will begin. Jesus also invited all to come to him for instruction, in Matthew 11:28-30.

Then Jesus said, "Come to me, all of you who are weary and carry heavy burdens, and I will give you rest. Take my yoke upon you. Let me teach you, because I am humble and gentle at heart, and you will find rest for your souls. For my yoke is easy to bear, and the burden I give you is light."

Wisdom in the next poem again issues her salvific call. She prepares her table and invites all who hear to enter and dine with her. The meal will soon begin!

◆ I. Wisdom's Banquet; Who Listens? (9:1-18)

1 Wisdom has built her house;
she has carved its seven columns.
2 She has prepared a great banquet,
mixed the wines, and set the table.
3 She has sent her servants to invite
everyone to come.
She calls out from the heights
overlooking the city.
4 "Come in with me," she urges the
simple.
To those who lack good judgment,
she says,
5 "Come, eat my food,
and drink the wine I have mixed.
6 Leave your simple ways behind, and
begin to live;
learn to use good judgment."

7 Anyone who rebukes a mocker will
get an insult in return.
Anyone who corrects the wicked
will get hurt.
8 So don't bother correcting mockers;
they will only hate you.
But correct the wise,
and they will love you.
9 Instruct the wise,
and they will be even wiser.
Teach the righteous,
and they will learn even more.

10 Fear of the LORD is the foundation
of wisdom.
Knowledge of the Holy One results
in good judgment.

11 Wisdom will multiply your days
and add years to your life.
12 If you become wise, you will be the
one to benefit.
If you scorn wisdom, you will be
the one to suffer.
13 The woman named Folly is brash.
She is ignorant and doesn't
know it.
14 She sits in her doorway
on the heights overlooking the city.
15 She calls out to men going by
who are minding their own
business.
16 "Come in with me," she urges the
simple.
To those who lack good judgment,
she says,
17 "Stolen water is refreshing;
food eaten in secret tastes the
best!"
18 But little do they know that the dead
are there.
Her guests are in the depths of
the grave.*

9:18 Hebrew *in Sheol.*

NOTES

9:1 *Wisdom.* Unlike the Hebrew of 8:1, the word here is plural (see note on 1:20).

carved its seven columns. "Carved" is Heb., *khatsebah* [TH2672, ZH2933] (hewn out). Perhaps this should read *hitsibah* [TH5324, ZH5893] (erect, set up), as implied by LXX. Ahlström suggests it refers to cut foundations of stone, rendering emendation unnecessary (1979:74-76). Skehan suggests that the seven "columns" of Wisdom's house are the seven poems he sees between the frame of chs 1 and 8–9 (1971:9); his structure is not followed in this commentary.

9:2 ***set the table.*** The verb *'arak* [TH6186, ZH6885] (set in order, put in array) highlights the careful arrangement of wisdom material found in the book. Proverbs are not haphazard or random but are organized, set in place: a voluptuous culinary event.

9:4 ***lack good judgment.*** Lit., "lack heart" (see note on 4:23). Wisdom calls to undeserving souls—come in and learn.

9:5 ***eat . . . drink.*** The image of Lady Wisdom is now augmented with another—the image of a meal. She has skillfully readied it, made all the arrangements; now the needy must simply enter her house and partake.

9:6 ***Leave your simple ways.*** Lit., "leave simpletons," that is, forsake the company of other simpletons.

9:7 ***mocker.*** Lit., "scoffer," found three times in this segment (9:7, 8, 12). The contrast between this character and the wise could not be greater.

hurt. Lit., "his blemish." To reprove the wicked is to blemish oneself. This is as Jesus said: "Don't waste what is holy on people who are unholy. Don't throw your pearls to pigs! They will trample the pearls, then turn and attack you" (Matt 7:6).

9:8 ***hate . . . love.*** One's heart is revealed in what one hates and loves (see commentary on 1:20-33). The wise *love* correction. Proverbs asks the reader, Do you love correction? Or do you hate being reproved?

9:9 ***Instruct the wise, and they will be even wiser.*** The Prologue of chs 1–9 has come full circle to 1:5.

9:10 ***Fear of the LORD is the foundation of wisdom.*** This recalls 1:7, which continues by contrasting the *'ewil* [TH191A, ZH211], who despise wisdom. Perhaps this is intended to form an inclusion with it (Estes 1997:35).

Holy One. This is plural in Hebrew but parallel to Yahweh (see 30:3).

9:11 ***Wisdom.*** This is not in the Hebrew text; rather, it reads, "For by me your days will be multiplied." This is the only place in this segment where Wisdom speaks in the first person. Instead of "by me," Peshitta and Targum gloss "by her." The LXX reads "for in this way." The NLT clarifies any ambiguity by inserting "Wisdom." The extant Hebrew looks like Lady Wisdom speaking, but the segment's overall impression reads like the parents' words—the two are merging into a single voice.

9:13 ***The woman named Folly.*** The antithesis of Lady Wisdom, the "woman of folly" (*kesiluth* [TH3687, ZH4070]) is plural, like "Wisdom" in 9:1 (see note on 1:20; see 26:1-12 for verses that address the *kesil* [TH3684, ZH4067], "fool").

brash. This is the participle of *hamah* [TH1993, ZH2159] (see note on 7:11). She moans with passion so as to seduce with stolen "water." Her description begins with libidinous overtones.

doesn't know it. She is characterized by ignorance. The LXX reads, "knows not modesty/ shame."

9:14 ***on the heights overlooking the city.*** Lit., "on a throne at the heights of the city." "The pretentious imposter presents herself as an empress who rules a city, and the gullible bow to her authority" (Waltke 2004:444).

9:15 ***men . . . who are minding their own business.*** Lit., "those making their paths straight." She specifically targets citizenry who are living the life of wisdom, who are faithful and upright.

9:16 This verse is virtually identical with 9:4. Both women appeal to simpletons who have not yet chosen a path.

9:17 *Stolen water . . . food eaten in secret.* See commentary on the section 5:1-23. She offers the thrill of illicit sex. Having rejected Wisdom's well-prepared repast, the simple who enter Folly's abode enjoy her secret pleasures—alternative "food" to the dish of knowledge. "Seductive advertising has to compensate for lack of preparation" (McKinlay 1999:79). "Instead of offering meat and wine, Folly offers only water and bread" (Stallman 2000:123).
9:18 *the dead.* Lit., "the shades" (see note on 2:18).

COMMENTARY

This poem consists of three segments, the first describing Wisdom's banquet (9:1-6) and the last her antithesis, personified Folly (9:13-18). The central segment (9:7-12) is a montage of what seems to be the words of the father. His voice combines with Lady Wisdom's, and the two speak as one by the time the Prologue of chapters 1–9 concludes.

Both Wisdom and Folly cry out, with virtually identical wording in Hebrew: "'Come in with me,' she urges the simple. / To those who lack good judgment, she says . . ." (9:4, 16). Proverbs 9:7, the start of the middle segment, is also worded to sound like these verses. Byargeon calls this intentional "paronomasia"; in tandem with other literary devices, this suggests the middle segment functions as a purposeful center, a "theological summary" of chapters 1–9 (1997:367-375). As such, it is also a summation of the whole book of Proverbs, for the Prologue is where its foundation is laid.

Wisdom calls to the naive, urging them to listen and learn. This wisdom is not found by studying nature, gathering polls, or being familiar with the latest research. It begins with an attitude of dependency before God. Mockers have no interest in him and injure themselves. Do not try to instruct them, says Wisdom, for the attempt will be a blemish on you—you should have known better.

Wisdom has set her table. The drinks are mixed. The servants stand ready. And the meal is about to be served—it will begin in 10:1 with the proverbs of Solomon. (In this way, "the editor's intent seems to point the reader to the proverb collection in chapters 10–30 for the specific elements of Wisdom's way"—Camp 1987a:104.) Before the meal begins, however, one last discordant voice is warned against. Proverbs pauses before Solomon's carefully prepared and ordered supper is brought out—it pauses for the reader to consider, "Have I counted the cost of discipleship? Am I willing to forgo folly and enter into the holy estate of wisdom (beginning with knowledge of the Holy One)?"

Beware! With the inauguration of Solomon's wisdom, expressed proverbially in the subsequent chapters, there are always foolish counterparts, negative pseudowisdom that draws the unsuspecting away from Yahweh and to self-destruction. Anti-proverbs abound: "No good deed goes unpunished"; "Only the good die young"; "Eat, drink, and be merry, for tomorrow we die"; "Nice guys finish last"; and, of course, "Murphy's Law" (which downplays God's trustworthy governance of the world), "Anything that can go wrong will go wrong." "Stolen water is refreshing; food eaten in secret tastes the best!" (9:17). "I will get even for this wrong" (20:22). "The lazy person claims, 'There's a lion out there! If I go outside, I might be killed!'" (22:13). Beware of false wisdom!

All is now ready. The theological foundation has been laid. The warnings have been issued. The siren has sounded for the coming tsunami (1:27). The table is prepared. The proverbs are carefully arranged. Go on now and imbibe "The proverbs of Solomon" (10:1) if you would be wise.

II. Proverbs of Solomon (10:1–22:16)

The anthology of 10:1–22:16 can be parsed into seven compositions, as follows:

A. The righteous and the wicked (10:1–11:31)
B. Speech and deeds (12:1-28)
C. The way of wisdom and the way of death (13:1–14:27)
D. The wisdom of Yahweh and the king (14:28–16:15)
E. The way of wisdom and the way of death (16:16–19:12)
F. Speaking and doing before Yahweh (19:13–21:1)
G. The wicked and the righteous (21:2–22:16)

At various points, there are clusters of verses that reiterate the main thesis—wisdom is a life lived before Yahweh; wisdom is religious (10:22-30; 15:2-11; 15:29–16:11; 19:13-23; 20:22–21:1; 21:30–22:5). Fifty-five times the divine name is invoked in this anthology—averaging about once every seven verses.

A. The Righteous and the Wicked (10:1–11:31)

1. Preface to Solomon's Proverbs (10:1-5)

The proverbs of Solomon:

A wise child* brings joy to a father;
a foolish child brings grief to a mother.

2 Tainted wealth has no lasting value,
but right living can save your life.

3 The LORD will not let the godly go hungry,
but he refuses to satisfy the craving of the wicked.

4 Lazy people are soon poor;
hard workers get rich.

5 A wise youth harvests in the summer,
but one who sleeps during harvest is a disgrace.

10:1 Hebrew *son;* also in 10:1b.

NOTES

10:1 *The proverbs of Solomon.* This is the title to the whole anthology (10:1–22:16). Here formally begins the "proverbs," a collection of parallel binary verses each more or less self-standing, although enriched by others in their immediate context. The Prologue is over—the main course is now served. The title's brevity implies previous introductory material (Kitchen 1977:98). See note on 1:1.

A wise child. Lit., "a wise son." The very first proverb in this section is linked with the Prologue, again couched in terminology of parents appealing to offspring. What entails a wise child is spelled out in the subsequent verses.

10:3 *The LORD.* Yahweh is at the center of the preface, underscoring the fact that wisdom is anything but secular.

refuses to satisfy the craving of the wicked. Lit., "The craving of the wicked is expelled" (*hadap* [TH1920, ZH2074]). In Num 35:20, 22 *hadap* is used for murder and manslaughter; in Deut 6:19 it describes the driving out of the Canaanites—a violent rejection and driving away. Righteousness saves from death; wickedness alienates one from God, resulting in death.

10:4 ***Lazy . . . hard workers.*** This helps to define the wise and foolish son. Without 10:3 this might give the false impression that one's own efforts alone can save one from poverty. Diligence characterizes the wise and righteous, sloth the wicked fool. Both have their reward. Waltke translates, "A poor person is made with a slack palm" (2004:448).

10:5 ***wise youth . . . one who sleeps.*** In the Hebrew, the word "son" is found twice, recalling 10:1 and closing the section.

COMMENTARY

Overview of Proverbs 10–11. Antithetical proverbs that contrast the righteous and the wicked dominate the content of chapters 10–11. The word "righteous" (*tsaddiq* [TH6662, ZH7404], often rendered "godly" in NLT) occurs 66 times in Proverbs, about one-third of these in chapters 10–11. The word "wicked" (*rasha'* [TH7563A, ZH8401]) has a comparable frequency and ratio. The first lesson of the Proverbs of Solomon anthology is that the wicked and righteous must be clearly distinguished. Contrasting them highlights the glory of the righteous and the aberration of the wicked.

Proverbs 10–11 consists of five sections. The first prefaces Solomon's proverbs and is bound by a contrast of wise and foolish youths centered on a reminder that Yahweh is the guarantor of the consequence-laden world (10:1, 5). The second section consists of two stanzas: The former is bound by the inclusion, "the words of the wicked conceal violent intentions" (10:6, 11), and the latter bound by an inclusion about "concealing" or "covering" love (10:12) or hate (10:18). The third section begins and ends with a discussion about the lips of the wise and the righteous (10:19-32). The fourth section (11:1-28) treats wisdom and folly in the community. Finally, the fifth (11:29-31) concludes the composition.

Preface to Solomon's Proverbs (10:1-5). The preface to the proverbs of Solomon connects with the Prologue of the first nine chapters: The address is to the youth, in relation to the parents, who must choose to live a life of righteousness or wickedness before Yahweh. Sloth is especially at issue here; the wise do not shun work. Heim argues that the preface to Solomon's proverbs (10:1-5) is a coherent discourse, each verse co-referential in meaning and form, bound by the four instances of "son."

> *The wise son who delights the father (v. 1) is the competent son who works in summer (v. 5), so becoming rich through his diligent hand (v. 4). He does not need wicked tricks in order to make a living, so his righteousness saves him from death in a (financial?) crisis (v. 2) because YHWH will fulfill his expectations (v. 3). The foolish son who is his mother's sorrow (v. 1) is the disgraceful son who sleeps during harvest time (v. 5), becomes poor because of his laziness (v. 4), and has to use tricks to gain wealth (v. 2). So the Lord will reject his desires (v. 3). (1993:203)*

The creative Wisdom of God has issued the invitation to you, the reader, to enter her house and be well fed (9:1-6). If you read on, then you have made your choice to enjoy her cuisine. Let it permeate your soul and become part of you. Jesus said to

Martha, "Mary has chosen the good portion" (Luke 10:42, RSV), the good morsel, the choicest part of the meal—sitting at Jesus' feet to imbibe his wisdom. Similarly, one who digests the proverbs of Solomon will grow ever wiser and be adopted by God himself, becoming a son who follows the way of wisdom.

◆ 2. Proverbs about concealing and speaking (10:6-32)

6 The godly are showered with blessings;
the words of the wicked conceal
violent intentions.

7 We have happy memories of the godly,
but the name of a wicked person
rots away.

8 The wise are glad to be instructed,
but babbling fools fall flat on their
faces.

9 People with integrity walk safely,
but those who follow crooked paths
will slip and fall.

10 People who wink at wrong cause
trouble,
but a bold reproof promotes peace.*

11 The words of the godly are a
life-giving fountain;
the words of the wicked conceal
violent intentions.

12 Hatred stirs up quarrels,
but love makes up for all offenses.

13 Wise words come from the lips of
people with understanding,
but those lacking sense will be
beaten with a rod.

14 Wise people treasure knowledge,
but the babbling of a fool invites
disaster.

15 The wealth of the rich is their fortress;
the poverty of the poor is their
destruction.

16 The earnings of the godly enhance
their lives,
but evil people squander their
money on sin.

17 People who accept discipline are on
the pathway to life,
but those who ignore correction
will go astray.

18 Hiding hatred makes you a liar;
slandering others makes you a fool.

19 Too much talk leads to sin.
Be sensible and keep your mouth
shut.

20 The words of the godly are like
sterling silver;
the heart of a fool is worthless.

21 The words of the godly encourage
many,
but fools are destroyed by their lack
of common sense.

22 The blessing of the LORD makes
a person rich,
and he adds no sorrow with it.

23 Doing wrong is fun for a fool,
but living wisely brings pleasure
to the sensible.

24 The fears of the wicked will be
fulfilled;
the hopes of the godly will be
granted.

25 When the storms of life come, the
wicked are whirled away,
but the godly have a lasting
foundation.

26 Lazy people irritate their employers,
like vinegar to the teeth or smoke
in the eyes.

27 Fear of the LORD lengthens one's life,
but the years of the wicked are cut
short.

28 The hopes of the godly result in
happiness,

but the expectations of the wicked
come to nothing.

29 The way of the LORD is a stronghold
to those with integrity,
but it destroys the wicked.

30 The godly will never be disturbed,
but the wicked will be removed
from the land.

31 The mouth of the godly person gives
wise advice,
but the tongue that deceives will
be cut off.

32 The lips of the godly speak helpful
words,
but the mouth of the wicked speaks
perverse words.

10:10 As in Greek version; Hebrew reads *but babbling fools fall flat on their faces.*

NOTES

10:6 ***the words of the wicked conceal violent intentions.*** The wicked are characterized as having a mouth that "conceals" or "hides" violence.

10:8 ***to be instructed.*** Heb., *mitswoth* [TH4687, ZH5184] (commandments); see 2:1.

babbling fools fall flat on their faces. Lit., "Foolish lips are thrust down." "Thrust down" (from *labat* [TH3832, ZH4231]) also appears in 10:10. It only occurs elsewhere in Hos 4:14, "You will be *destroyed.*"

10:9 ***will slip and fall.*** Hebrew reads (with LXX), "will be made known" (*yiwwadea'*, the Niphal of *yada'* [TH3045, ZH3359], "to know"). The NLT follows an emendation to *yeroa'* (Niphal of *ra'a'* [TH7489, ZH8317]), yielding, lit., "suffer harm," as in 11:15. Note the imagery of the two paths.

10:10 ***a bold reproof promotes peace.*** This follows LXX (so NLT mg); Hebrew reads identically with 10:8, "Babbling fools fall flat on their faces." This is either dittography or poetic repetition. If intentional, the stanza forms a chiasm with 10:9 in the center—the contrast between the blameless and twisted paths.

10:11 ***the words of the wicked conceal violent intentions.*** This closes the inclusion from 10:6, a "self-contained group of proverbs" (Whybray 1994a:158).

10:12 ***love makes up for.*** The verb (*kasah* [TH3680, ZH4059], "conceal") is the same as in 10:6, 11; here, love "covers" offenses, contrasted with hatred that "stirs up quarrels." Hatred is used with *kasah* in 10:18, closing the stanza.

10:13 ***lips of people with understanding.*** These contrast with the "foolish lips" of 10:8 and perhaps 10:10 (see note).

those lacking sense will be beaten with a rod. Lit., "a rod for the back of one lacking heart." The "rod for the back" is a synecdoche of the species, one instance representing all forms of imposed discipline. The envisioned methods of correction would not exclude the verse's specific example.

10:14 ***treasure.*** Not in the sense of "value, cherish." Wise people *store up* knowledge.

10:15 ***the rich.*** The rich trust in their riches rather than Yahweh (18:10-11). This attitude of autonomy from God leads to unjust practices and oppression of the poor (18:23). See commentary on 8:17-21.

10:16 ***enhance their lives.*** Lit., "The wages of the righteous surely is life."

sin. Thomas (1964:295-296) argues that "sin" is not the antithesis of "life," suggesting the sense "penury." Waltke, however, has no problem pitting "life" and "sin" as opposite poles, calling *lekhatta'th* [TH2403A, ZH2633] a "metonymy for the death that clings to sin" (2004:464).

10:17 ***to life.*** This is identical with 10:16, "enhance their lives" (*lekhayyim* [TH2416, ZH2644]). The two verses are parallel:

The earnings of the godly *lekhayyim*
The revenue of the wicked is surely sin.
The path *lekhayyim* is keeping discipline
One who ignores reproof goes astray.

10:18 ***Hiding hatred.*** The stanza concludes with the issue of "hiding" or "covering," closing the inclusion from 10:12. There, one "covers" all offenses with love; here, one "covers" one's hatred with "lips of deceit." The theme of speech continues in the next section. "Hiding" is a masculine participle, while "hatred" and "lips" are feminine. The NLT inserts a second-person pronoun as subject: "makes *you* a liar." Garrett, following the LXX, emends the verse to "He who forgives hatred has righteous lips / but he who spreads defamation is a fool" (1993:120).

10:19 ***mouth.*** Lit., "lips," forming a seam with the previous section and repeating these sections' key word representing speech.

10:20 ***worthless.*** Precisely, "small."

10:21 ***encourage.*** Lit., "pasture."

are destroyed. Lit., "will die." The reference to death leads naturally into the next stanza, which treats the eternal foundation for life Yahweh gives freely to the wise.

10:22 ***The blessing of the*** **L*ORD*.** This verse deviates from the antithetic parallelism characteristic of Solomon's proverbs up to this point. The next deviation is 10:26 (immediately before Yahweh is mentioned again), which divides the strophe into two parts. In the first part, all of the antithetic proverbs make a negative statement in the first colon and a positive in the second. After 10:26 this reverses.

he adds no sorrow with it. "Sorrow," from *etseb* [TH6089A, ZH6776], can also mean "labor" (5:10) or "work" (14:23). Thus, alternatively, "One's labor cannot add to it." Both parts of the strophe begin with Yahweh "adding" blessedness.

10:25 ***lasting foundation.*** Heb., "foundation of eternity" (*'olam* [TH5769, ZH6409]). Wisdom claims she was possessed by Yahweh from *'olam* (8:23). "The scenario anticipates the eschatological age to come when the wicked are removed from the earth and only the righteous remain" (Waltke 2004:475).

10:26 ***Lazy people.*** As with 10:22, this emblematic proverb is not antithetic, but unlike 10:22, it consists of two negative cola rather than two positive cola. This creates a seam breaking the strophe into two parts, each part ending with a reference to *'olam* [TH5769, ZH6409] (10:25, 30), a rare word in Proverbs (six times). See 6:6-9 for treatment of the sluggard. "What smoke, vinegar, and a lazy employee all have in common is that they are irritants which are unpleasant to experience and difficult to endure" (McKane 1970:417).

10:27 ***lengthens one's life.*** This part begins by claiming that reverencing Yahweh "adds days"; it ends (in 10:30) claiming that the godly are unshaken to eternity (*'olam* [TH5769, ZH6409]). The establishment of the godly and the malefactor's eradication are both permanent.

10:29 ***The way of the*** **L*ORD*.** Note the image of the path.

to those with integrity. Lit., "to integrity," an anthimeria (substitution of one part of speech for another) for "to those with integrity."

10:30 ***The godly will never be disturbed.*** Lit., "The godly, until eternity (*'olam* [TH5769, ZH6409]), will not be shaken."

10:31-32 This small couplet concludes the section, again treating the "mouth" and "lips" of the righteous (NLT, "godly").

10:31 ***gives wise advice.*** Lit., "bears fruit wisdom." The speech of the godly is fruitful and profitable; the "tongue" of the wicked has no future and will be silenced.

10:32 ***perverse words.*** Both verses of this stanza mention "perversities" (*tahpukoth* [TH8419, ZH9337]), which NLT renders "that deceives" in 10:31.

COMMENTARY

The second section of chapter 10 consists of two stanzas (10:6-11, 12-18). The first might be a chiasm as follows:

A. Concealing violence (10:6)
  B. Babbling fools fall flat on their faces (10:8)
    C. Imagery of two paths (10:9)
  B'. Babbling fools fall flat on their faces (10:10)
A'. Concealing violence (10:11)

As the righteous and the wicked are contrasted, the impression that builds in the mind of the reader is that of two categories, two manners of living: One manner cuts corners, cheats, flouts Yahweh and the community and does harm to it; the other is characterized by hard work, playing fair, and reverence to God. These two categories loom ever larger and become ever clearer as moral and ethical patterns of thinking are gradually formed in the mind of the reader. The words of the wicked conceal violence against the community. Their words *seem* appropriate and even beneficial, but they are deceptive. In the end, they will be found out. People remember the righteous fondly, and in the end their wise words will be recognized as such. But the reputation of the wicked will rot like a corpse, for their concealed violence will inevitably be realized (10:7). "Remember, the sins of some people are obvious, leading them to certain judgment. But there are others whose sins will not be revealed until later. In the same way, the good deeds of some people are obvious. And the good deeds done in secret will someday come to light" (1 Tim 5:24-25).

The spoken word is especially at issue in this section. Note the expressions: "words of the wicked" (10:6), "babbling fools" (10:8), "words of the godly" (10:11, 20, 21), "wise words" (10:13), "babbling of a fool" (10:14), "liar" (10:18), "too much talk" (10:19), and so on. One person covers all offenses with love; another conceals hatred with lies. One's conceptualization of reality is shaped by words.

The book of Proverbs does not consist of mere platitudes; its words have power to save souls from the realm of death into the realm of life (2:10-12). Wise counsel has the power to affect an anxious heart (12:25). The tongue of the wise rescues potential victims (12:6) and heals people (12:18). Reckless words pierce like swords (12:18). A gentle word can break a bone (25:15). The counselor has the power to influence others (17:22). Therefore, counsel must be very carefully given. Fools apply proverbs with no skill and so do damage (26:7, 9). A counselor must be skilled at their use and recognize the potential for harm if counsel is offered with anything but the highest degree of precision and care. Note that this principle balances what was said above: The call of Wisdom must be heard, but the words used must be very carefully applied (Schwab 1995:11).

The next section consists of three stanzas (10:19-32). The first and last begin with "mouth" and terminate with the phrase, "the words/lips of the godly" (10:19-21,

31-32). The longer middle stanza (10:22-30) mentions Yahweh three times, particularly promising an eternal foundation and permanent life to the wise. The promise to the righteous is that Yahweh will guarantee an eternal foundation (10:25) and eternal stability (10:30). The wicked, however, suffer permanent and irreversible termination (10:25, 30). Each category of person has a set of expectations, hopes, and desires that are forward-looking, envisioning a future condition. Yahweh promises that the future will satisfy the deep yearnings of the righteous, but the wicked will be sorely disappointed (10:24, 28). Thus time will reveal whose conception of reality—whose speech—was properly and profitably shaped. The lips of the wise have a future; the lips of the wicked do not. The wicked utter perversities and will be cut off; the godly speak knowledge that will bear fruit unto life.

◆ 3. Wisdom in the community (11:1-31)

1 The LORD detests the use of dishonest scales,
but he delights in accurate weights.

2 Pride leads to disgrace,
but with humility comes wisdom.

3 Honesty guides good people;
dishonesty destroys treacherous people.

4 Riches won't help on the day of judgment,
but right living can save you from death.

5 The godly are directed by honesty;
the wicked fall beneath their load of sin.

6 The godliness of good people rescues them;
the ambition of treacherous people traps them.

7 When the wicked die, their hopes die with them,
for they rely on their own feeble strength.

8 The godly are rescued from trouble,
and it falls on the wicked instead.

9 With their words, the godless destroy their friends,
but knowledge will rescue the righteous.

10 The whole city celebrates when the godly succeed;
they shout for joy when the wicked die.

11 Upright citizens are good for a city and make it prosper,
but the talk of the wicked tears it apart.

12 It is foolish to belittle one's neighbor;
a sensible person keeps quiet.

13 A gossip goes around telling secrets,
but those who are trustworthy can keep a confidence.

14 Without wise leadership, a nation falls;
there is safety in having many advisers.

15 There's danger in putting up security for a stranger's debt;
it's safer not to guarantee another person's debt.

16 A gracious woman gains respect,
but ruthless men gain only wealth.

17 Your kindness will reward you,
but your cruelty will destroy you.

18 Evil people get rich for the moment,
but the reward of the godly will last.

19 Godly people find life;
evil people find death.

20 The LORD detests people with crooked hearts,

but he delights in those with
integrity.

21 Evil people will surely be punished,
but the children of the godly will
go free.

22 A beautiful woman who lacks
discretion
is like a gold ring in a pig's snout.

23 The godly can look forward to
a reward,
while the wicked can expect only
judgment.

24 Give freely and become more wealthy;
be stingy and lose everything.

25 The generous will prosper;
those who refresh others will
themselves be refreshed.

26 People curse those who hoard their
grain,
but they bless the one who sells
in time of need.

27 If you search for good, you will find
favor;
but if you search for evil, it will
find you!

28 Trust in your money and down you go!
But the godly flourish like leaves in
spring.

29 Those who bring trouble on their
families inherit the wind.
The fool will be a servant to the
wise.

30 The seeds of good deeds become
a tree of life;
a wise person wins friends.*

31 If the righteous are rewarded here on
earth,
what will happen to wicked
sinners?*

11:30 Or *and those who win souls are wise.* 11:31 Greek version reads *If the righteous are barely saved, / what will happen to godless sinners?* Compare 1 Pet 4:18.

NOTES

11:1 *scales . . . weights.* Scales and weights were the standards of monetary valuation, the mechanics of a just and equitable economic system. God enforces the system of fair exchange on which the financial health of society depends. Yahweh hates those who manipulate and pervert the necessary underpinnings of civilization for their own advantage.

11:2 *Pride . . . humility.* As Yahweh delights in an honest marketplace (11:1), so an honest self-knowledge of one's place in society is consistent with the community's well-being. This is wisdom contrary to self-promotion, which leads only to public disgrace.

11:4 *day of judgment . . . can save.* The phrase "day of judgment" (or "day of wrath") is found also in Ezek 7:19 and in the parallel Zeph 1:18. Proverbs sets the phrase parallel to "death"—the day of judgment comes to every person at their death, gold and silver notwithstanding. But righteousness saves (see note on 12:28).

11:5 *beneath their load of sin.* In the Hebrew this is a single word, *berish'atho* [TH7564, ZH8402] (in his wickedness), perhaps a pun with *berishto* [TH7568, ZH8407], meaning "in his net" (Kselman 2002:546).

11:6 *rescues.* Lit., "saves." Again, righteousness saves from death (11:4), falling (11:5), and entrapment (11:6).

ambition. From *hawwah* [TH1942/A, ZH2094/2095], which can mean "desire, greed, ambition," "disaster, destruction," and "word." Kselman suggests the term is deliberately chosen for its several meanings (2002:545); their "ambition" traps them, they are trapped unto "destruction," and they are trapped by their "words."

11:7 *When the wicked die, their hopes die with them.* Lit., "In the dying of a wicked man hope perishes." Waltke renders, "When a human being dies, hope perishes" (2004:481).

This complimentary parallel proverb closes the stanza with another mention of death. LXX reads, "The dying of the just man does not destroy hope."

for they rely on their own feeble strength. Lit., "the hope of the powerful perishes." LXX reads, "But the pride of the ungodly perishes," glossing *'onim* [TH202, ZH226] with "ungodly" rather than "powerful." The NLT glosses *'abadah* [TH6, ZH6] adjectivally (feeble), although this is also the verb in the first line (their hopes *die*).

11:8 ***rescued.*** From *khalats* [TH2502, ZH2740], occurring only here and in 11:9 in Proverbs. Thematically, the verse relates to the previous stanza, but verbal ties with 11:9 also bind it to 11:9-14, which are grouped with the device of an initial Hebrew letter Beth. The verse is echoed in 11:15 (closing the stanza), which contrasts the security of the sensible with the distress of the inattentive (the final word beginning with Beth).

11:9 ***rescue.*** What rescues the godly from trouble (11:8) is knowledge (11:9). In 11:9-11, both halves of each verse begin with Beth.

11:11 ***city.*** Note verbal correspondences between this verse and 11:10.

talk. Lit., "mouth," which recalls 11:9 ("words").

11:12 ***neighbor.*** For the second time in this stanza the neighbor is the target of the morally malformed individual's evil words (11:9). The sensible person "keeps quiet."

11:13 ***keep a confidence.*** Lit., "covers a matter," parallel to "keeps quiet" in 11:12. This verse has no initial Beth—thus there is a pause before the heightened rhetoric of 11:14.

11:14 ***a nation falls.*** The stanza has treated the neighbor (11:9, 12) and the city (11:10-11) in chiastic fashion. These principles are now applied on a national scale. It is not enough to be free of wicked talk and gossip; a people cannot stand without wise counsel. Countries require godly advice and wise voices. Nations as whole entities also walk paths of wisdom or folly.

11:15 ***it's safer not to guarantee another person's debt.*** The stanza ends contrasting the avoidable suffering of the debtor with the security of those repulsed by gratuitous risk.

11:16 ***A gracious woman gains respect.*** Lit., "gains (*tamak* [TH8551, ZH9461]) glory." This woman is contrasted with the tasteless woman of 11:22, an inclusion circumscribing the stanza. See notes on 31:19-20, where the woman of virtue supports (*tamak*) the district. The LXX reads, "A gracious wife brings to her husband glory."

ruthless men. Driver suggests a positive sense to *'aritsim* [TH6184, ZH6883], i.e., "vigorous" (1951:180); see Ps 37:35. Perhaps this should be emended to *kharutsim* [TH2742E, ZH3026] (diligent), yielding, "The diligent gain wealth." As such, the stanza begins with a synonymous verse on the virtues of diligence and finding a good wife. It ends with a non-antithetic proverb treating the antithesis of this woman (11:22).

11:18 ***for the moment . . . will last.*** The contrast in Hebrew is a pun between the "deceptive (*sheqer* [TH8267, ZH9214]) wage" and the "true reward (*seker* [TH7938, ZH8512])."

11:19 ***Godly people.*** Hebrew reads, "Surely righteousness (tends) to life." The NLT (with LXX) follows the emended reading *ben* [TH1121, ZH1201] instead of *ken* [TH3651, ZH4026] (surely), yielding "son of righteousness."

life . . . death. The centerpiece of the stanza is the ultimate contrast between life and death. The rewards of godliness include the gracious wife, true wages, and life; the wicked incur deceptive wages, self-harm, and death. Garrett argues that both death and life are permanent, hence implying *eternal* life (1993:126).

11:20 ***The Lord.*** Immediately after discriminating between life and death, Yahweh is revealed as the one who is actively engaged, hating or enjoying people's inner motives ("crooked hearts") and actions ("those with integrity," lit., "ones blameless of path").

11:22 ***beautiful woman who lacks discretion.*** The woman who "turns aside" from "taste, discretion" has a beauty as deceptive and facile as the lying wage of 11:18. The two women who frame the stanza recall the Prologue, where the one represents wise virtues in which Yahweh delights and which lead to life; the other represents the baneful existence of those soon to perish. How disappointing the woman without discretion must be! Her pursuers are surely deceived.

11:23 ***The godly can look forward to a reward.*** Precisely, "The desire of the godly is only good." They desire what is beneficial.

the wicked can expect only judgment. Lit., "The expectation of the wicked is wrath." See note on 11:4 for "wrath." Unlike the godly who desire only good, the wicked are malevolent. The harm they wish for others will find them (see 11:25, 27).

11:25 ***refresh . . . refreshed.*** Refreshment or saturation (from *rawah* [TH7301, ZH8115]) is a euphemism for sexual fulfillment in 5:19 and 7:18. One who refreshes will be refreshed; one's actions rebound back on oneself. BHS suggests (with Syriac) emending the verbs to the root *'arar* [TH779, ZH826]: "He who curses will be cursed," an antithetical proverb that dovetails with the subject in 11:26. This ignores the "agricultural metaphors" that these verses also share (Waltke 2004:505).

11:27 ***good.*** Again, a person's character influences their circumstances: seek evil, find evil; seek good, find good.

11:28 ***Trust in your money.*** This stanza tacitly, but not explicitly, points to God. One who "trusts" in money marginalizes Yahweh (3:5; 28:26; 29:25).

down you go. Lit., "he will fall." Cf. Jer 17:5-6, "Cursed are those who put their trust in . . . human strength."

the godly flourish like leaves. This closes the inclusion from 11:23 and ends the stanza. The conceptualization of the godly as a budding tree is an image recalled in 11:30. Cf. Jer 17:7-8, "Blessed are those who trust in the LORD. . . . They are like trees. . . . Their leaves stay green, and they never stop producing fruit."

11:29 ***servant.*** Lit., "slave." This is the first of three consecutive non-antithetic proverbs.

11:30 ***The seeds of good deeds become a tree of life.*** Lit., "The fruit of the righteous is a tree of life." The fruit of the godly is the fruit of the tree of life. See flora imagery in 11:28.

wins friends. See NLT mg, "and those who *win souls* are wise"; lit., "gets/takes souls." The LXX seems to have read *khamas* [TH2555, ZH2805] (violent, lawless) instead of *khakam* [TH2450, ZH2682] (wise) and understood "gets/takes souls" as killing, thus rendering, "The soul of the lawless is untimely cut off." "Taking" a soul elsewhere always connotes killing (Bratcher 1983:337). But Delitzsch glosses "winneth souls" (1874:249). Snell reads "get" in the intellectual sense ("I get what you mean") and translates, "One who comprehends souls is wise" (1983:364). Irwin argues that the first half of the verse images the wise as a fruitful tree and renders, "The wise gathers lives" as one would pick fruit, saving souls from death (1984:98).

11:31 ***what will happen.*** The verse argues from consequences observed on this earth to recompense beyond what is presently known.

COMMENTARY

The contrast between the righteous and the wicked continues in the four stanzas of this section. The first stanza (11:1-7) begins by acknowledging Yahweh as the upholder of ethical dealings, before whom one should be humble. The stanza ends with a consequentially parallel proverb (11:7), deviating from the antithetic pattern.

The second stanza (11:8-15) is framed by two verses highlighting the security of the righteous and the tenuous state of the wicked; between these the verses are grouped with the device of an initial Beth. The third stanza (11:16-22) is bound by the inclusion "woman"; the fourth (11:23-28) with the inclusion "good" and "godly." The composition concludes with a final segment of three non-antithetic verses (11:29-31).

This section teaches that the wicked pervert the community by dishonestly meting out goods and services (11:1) and by wrongly appraising their own status. Yahweh detests this behavior and brings death upon such people. This death is described in language used by the prophets for the eschatological judgment of the whole earth. This judgment falls on every person eventually in their own death. Just as gold and silver will not save from Yahweh's wrath in the future (Ezek 7:19; Zeph 1:18), so it will not deliver from death. But right living brings deliverance. The hopes and expectations of godly people do not disappoint, but the wicked have no future (11:7).

Speech is crucial to the well-being of the community. The godless ruins his neighbor with his mouth, and the wicked tears apart the town (11:9, 11). Gossip destroys privacy and ruins reputations. The upright hold their tongue and will not broadcast other people's personal information (11:12-13). But it is not enough for a land to merely keep silent; many wise and able advisers are needed for good government. Ethical speech is wise speech; a nation's rulers can lead the nation down a path of wisdom or folly.

The image of the woman of virtue, which ends the book, and the image of two women and two paths, are briefly echoed in 11:16-22. Two women embody two manners of living—beneficial or detrimental to the community. These frame the stanza that sets Yahweh as the one who is intimately involved in every person's life. Not only the behavior visible to all, but also the inner motivations of the heart are open to him and evoke a positive or negative reaction from him. This relationship with God is assumed when the stanza makes its bold promises of life and death.

There is a principle guaranteed in the world that what one gives one will get; our behavior and attitudes bounce back on us. This is the theme of 11:23-28. The righteous desire what is good and find it. They give freely, and they grow wealthier. The generous prosper. But wrath will find the wicked who are at enmity with their neighbor. To tightly withhold your goods from those in need leads to poverty and curses. Look for evil and you will find it.

The composition concludes by heightening the issues: The wise become the tree of life, saving souls. The wicked inherit wind and have their just deserts stored up for a future display of God's judgment. On earth we see the principle of moral consequences at work in that even the righteous suffer for their misdeeds, but we do not yet see the terrible consequence, the final death that awaits the fool who persists in his folly (11:31). The final verse reads, "If the righteous are rewarded here on earth, / what will happen to wicked sinners?" The verse is cited in 1 Peter 4:18 as a normative rule for Christian living, which also points to a future when all God's promises will be fulfilled. This shows how a verse may take on new meaning when employed by Christians in the light of Christ's death, resurrection, and second coming. The New Testament incorporates the proverb into the history of redemption and infuses it with import and significance. To paraphrase 1 Peter 4:17–5:1, "God wisely captured in a nutshell the whole experience of suffering Christians. We suffer now (according to the proverb), experiencing Judgment Day in advance. But another Day is coming (according to the proverb) when the tables will be turned—the wicked will be judged and the righteous vindicated. In that hope, keep striving to live faithfully before God."

◆ B. Speech and Deeds (12:1-28)

1 To learn, you must love discipline;
it is stupid to hate correction.

2 The LORD approves of those who are good,
but he condemns those who plan wickedness.

3 Wickedness never brings stability,
but the godly have deep roots.

4 A worthy wife is a crown for her husband,
but a disgraceful woman is like cancer in his bones.

5 The plans of the godly are just;
the advice of the wicked is treacherous.

6 The words of the wicked are like a murderous ambush,
but the words of the godly save lives.

7 The wicked die and disappear,
but the family of the godly stands firm.

8 A sensible person wins admiration,
but a warped mind is despised.

9 Better to be an ordinary person with a servant
than to be self-important but have no food.

10 The godly care for their animals,
but the wicked are always cruel.

11 A hard worker has plenty of food,
but a person who chases fantasies has no sense.

12 Thieves are jealous of each other's loot,
but the godly are well rooted and bear their own fruit.

13 The wicked are trapped by their own words,
but the godly escape such trouble.

14 Wise words bring many benefits,
and hard work brings rewards.

15 Fools think their own way is right,
but the wise listen to others.

16 A fool is quick-tempered,
but a wise person stays calm when insulted.

17 An honest witness tells the truth;
a false witness tells lies.

18 Some people make cutting remarks,
but the words of the wise bring healing.

19 Truthful words stand the test of time,
but lies are soon exposed.

20 Deceit fills hearts that are plotting evil;
joy fills hearts that are planning peace!

21 No harm comes to the godly,
but the wicked have their fill of trouble.

22 The LORD detests lying lips,
but he delights in those who tell the truth.

23 The wise don't make a show of their knowledge,
but fools broadcast their foolishness.

24 Work hard and become a leader;
be lazy and become a slave.

25 Worry weighs a person down;
an encouraging word cheers
a person up.

26 The godly give good advice to
their friends;*
the wicked lead them astray.

27 Lazy people don't even cook the game
they catch,
but the diligent make use of
everything they find.

28 The way of the godly leads to life;
that path does not lead to death.

12:26 Or *The godly are cautious in friendship;* or *The godly are freed from evil.* The meaning of the Hebrew is uncertain.

NOTES

12:1 *love discipline.* Language from the Prologue (chs 1–9) is invoked to begin a new composition. It particularly commends the knowledge and discipline found here in Solomon's book.

stupid. Lit., "brutish" (cf. 30:2).

12:2 *The LORD . . . condemns.* The composition begins by placing Yahweh front and center to all its predications. The "wicked" is a key word in this segment (four times) and continues throughout the composition. The first use of the root word, however, is a verb attributed to Yahweh! He "condemns" (*rasha'* [TH7561, ZH8399]) the "man of devices." Perhaps God's condemnation is paradigmatic: The wicked are people God condemns—this is what it means to be wicked. Yahweh establishes the several categories of life; people choose in which to live.

12:3 *Wickedness never brings stability.* Lit., "will not be established the man of wickedness." This can be read epexegetically with 12:2, "The one Yahweh condemns will not be established."

12:4 *A worthy wife.* Lit., the "wife of virtue," identically phrased in 31:10. She is the center of the segment, again recalling the Prologue of chs 1–9. She is the pinnacle of the sage's blessedness.

bones. See note on 3:8.

12:6 *murderous ambush.* Themes from the first chapters (cf. 1:8-19) are again in view—an appropriate beginning to a new composition.

12:7 *stands firm.* The extent of this promise is seen most clearly in 12:28, the concluding verse of the composition.

12:8 *A sensible person wins admiration.* Lit., "According to the mouth of his insight one will be praised."

warped mind. Lit., "one bent of heart." "Bent" is from *'awah* [TH5753, ZH6390], found only here in Proverbs. Saul used the word in cursing his son: "You son of a *perverse* and rebellious woman!" (1 Sam 20:30, NIV).

12:9 *Better to be.* This is the first of 12 "better-than" proverbs in the book. Each begins with *tob* [TH2896, ZH3202] (it is good, it is better) and describes two less-than-perfect conditions. The sage weighs their relative worth and declares one preferable—although neither is entirely satisfactory. The presence of the *tob*-proverb underscores awareness of the compromising and imperfect nature of the human situation; the wise are realists. Solomon's bold promises are not naive but recognize that sometimes one must choose the lesser of two adverse circumstances. Verses similar to the *tob*-proverb compare two positives, e.g., wisdom is better than rubies and gold (8:11, 19), patience is better than power (16:32). Five of the better-than proverbs treat the debilitating condition of a bad marriage and an upset house. Living with the wrong woman limits one's enjoyment of the benefits of a wise life (17:1; 21:19; 25:24).

an ordinary person with a servant. "Ordinary person" comes from the Niphal participle of *qalah* [TH7034, ZH7829], found only here in Proverbs; elsewhere it is glossed as "lightly esteemed" (1 Sam 18:23, KJV). To *qalah* one's parents (Hiphil stem) is to "dishonor" them (Deut 27:16). The ordinary citizen is assumed to have a servant; Proverbs was written for a moderately wealthy audience. The opposite of having a servant is to starve! (See commentary on 8:1-36.) Some translations (e.g., RSV) gratuitously emend to make reflexive: "Better is a man who works for himself."

self-important. Heb., *mimmithkabbed,* the Hithpael participle of *kabed* [TH3513, ZH3877], thus, "than one glorifying oneself." Better to be thought lowly while doing well than be thought highly of while poor. Perception is *not* reality; image does *not* trump substance.

12:10 *cruel.* "To their animals" is implied from the first line. Lit., "The compassion of the wicked is cruel."

12:12 *loot.* Heb., *metsod* [TH4685, ZH5178], glossed as "trap" in Eccl 7:26 and as "bulwarks" in Eccl 9:14 (KJV). Whatever the wicked covet is contrasted with the root of the godly. The proverbs of the prior segment were all antithetic, the positive preceding the negative line. This segment reverses that order, ending in a double positive.

the godly are well rooted and bear their own fruit. Lit., "The root of the righteous gives" (*yitten* [TH5414, ZH5989]). Waltke (2004:516) emends the verb (with LXX) to *yitan* [TH3495.1, ZH3851], "endures" (see Isa 33:16).

12:13 Connected with 12:12 by its fourth word, *ra'* [TH7451A, ZH8273] (wicked), and with 12:14 by "words" (lit., "lips" and "mouth"). In 12:13, trouble departs; in 12:14 good returns.

12:14 *bring many benefits.* Lit., "will be sated with good," the same word as in the last verse of the previous segment: "One who works the land will be *sated* with bread" (12:11). The godly are full, satisfied with good things.

brings rewards. Lit., "will return to him" (reading Kethiv). MT's Qere reading is in the Hiphil: "will cause to return." Waltke suggests this implies Yahweh as agent (2004:517).

12:15 *think their own way is right.* Lit., they "think [their] way is upright in their eyes." See note on 3:7. The "way" forms an inclusion with 12:26, 28.

the wise listen to others. Lit., "The one who hears counsel is wise." The person who heeds the book of Proverbs is wise.

12:17 *tells.* "The verb 'tells' is literally 'breathes'; truth is to be something as natural as breathing" (Murphy 1998:91).

12:19 *stand the test of time.* Lit., "will be established forever." This is a blessedness that never ends (see note on 12:28).

12:20 *planning peace.* Lit., "counselors of peace."

12:22 *The LORD detests lying lips.* See note on 3:32.

12:23 *foolishness.* This line ends with "folly" (*'iwweleth* [TH200, ZH222]) to recall the second word of 12:15 and the first word of 12:16 in Hebrew (*'ewil* [TH191A, ZH211]).

12:24 *Work hard and become a leader.* Lit., "The hand of the diligent will rule." "Diligent" is found also in 12:27.

12:25 *encouraging word.* Here is an example of speech bringing healing (see 12:18).

12:26 *give good advice to their friends.* Lit., "The righteous espies his neighbor." Emerton (1964:192-193) suggests emending *yather mere'ehu* [TH8446/7453, ZH9365/8276] to *yuttar mera'ah* [TH5425/7451B, ZH6000/8288] (evil), yielding "delivered from harm" (cf. NLT's second marginal reading).

12:27 ***the diligent make use of everything they find.*** Lit., "The diligent [cook] the precious riches of the land" (reading the last word as *'adam* [TH121A, ZH135]; cf. HALOT 1.14). "Cook" is implied from the first line. Two proverbs on the subject of laziness frame the stanza (12:24, 27). Driver unnecessarily reverses the order of "riches" and "diligent" and reads *'adam* [TH120, ZH132] as "man," its more frequent meaning, yielding the rendering "the wealth of the diligent man is much" (1951:180).

12:28 ***that path does not lead to death.*** The composition ends with a synonymous proverb. The phrase "not-death" (*'al-maweth* [TH408/4194, ZH440/4638]) is only found here in the Bible. Three words are used for "path" in this verse: "In the way of righteousness is life / And the path of a pathway is not-death." This verse reveals *la trajectoire extraordinaire,* the ultimate way, the Journey of journeys. On the basis of Ugaritic cognates, Dahood translates the phrase *'al-maweth* as "immortality," e.g., the immortality Anat offered to give to Aqhat—the "unending blissful existence with the gods reserved at least for some mortals" (1960:180). The life offered by Yahweh is stated clearly—elsewhere promised in more ambiguous language (3:2, "you will live many years"; 4:10, "a long, good life"; 11:4, "right living can save you from death"; 12:7, "stands firm"; 12:19, "stand the test of time"). What is promised to the wise is nothing less than eternal life with Yahweh. Some scholars question the MT of 12:28b. Where MT has *nethibah* [TH5410A, ZH5986] (path), LXX glosses "bearing malice" leading "to death," creating an antithetic proverb. But the oral tradition preserved in MT unequivocally records "not-death," and synonymous proverbs correlate with textual seams. The next composition similarly concludes in 14:27, "Fear of the LORD is a life-giving fountain; it offers escape from the snares of death."

COMMENTARY

Chapter 12 can be divided into four segments. Proverbs 12:1-7 begins with a reminder that people should be receptive to wisdom, and it calls the reader to love wisdom virtues. This is analogous to how the previous composition began (10:1-5). One is also reminded that true knowledge consists in a posture of dependency and respect toward Yahweh. The "wicked" are named as often in this segment as in the rest of the composition. Interestingly, the first use of the root word for the wicked (*rasha'* [TH7561, ZH8399]) is a verb referring to Yahweh as the definer of what constitutes the "wicked." The second segment (12:8-11) opens and closes on the theme of the "heart," describing those without sense. The third segment (12:12-14) is three verses bound by common words and the theme of speech, terminating in a non-antithetic proverb. The next section (12:15-28) is parsed into two stanzas plus a concluding verse and is bound by the inclusion of the "way." The first stanza (12:15-23) has many internal key words, including an inclusion of the "fool" and "folly" (12:15, 16, 23). The second stanza (12:24-27) is bounded by the inclusion "diligence." Finally, 12:28 concludes the composition with the startling and unequivocal promise of everlasting life.

The Wise and the Foolish (12:1-14). This composition begins with many connections to the Prologue of chapters 1–9, calling the reader to listen to the wise counsel of this book. The heart of this appeal is the wife of virtue, the crown of her husband. She is contrasted with the foolish woman, who shames him and reduces him to misery. These portray two lives: The just enjoy favor from God and will not be shaken; the "condemned" lie in wait for blood but are overthrown.

The wicked have twisted minds and are senseless, pursuing vanities and wasting time, while the diligent work hard and acquire food and possessions. Perhaps the wicked look good in the eyes of their neighbors for a while, but pretended status and feigned compassion cannot replace works consistent with wisdom: attending to the land and speaking words of insight. It is better to have substance without image than the reverse.

The wicked are ensnared and trapped by their own desires and schemes, but the godly escape such pitfalls and are sated with all that life has to offer. Why then would one choose evil? Proverbs's answer is that such a one has no sense. The fool and the wicked are liars. The two paths can be conceptualized as two modes of speech: truth-telling or lying. Of course, the big Truth, the first Counsel that is commended is the book of Proverbs itself. Those who love wisdom speak wisdom and counsel knowledge. They hold back retorts, they report truth, and their words heal. Delighting Yahweh, their pronouncements of right and wrong are sure and certain—forever. But the fool has no self-restraint, deluding himself that he is upright. Nothing he says is true, for truth does not characterize him; he *is* a falsehood. Yahweh detests such falsehood and ensures that perversion of rightly established order does not stand. A tree is known by its fruits, which is as Jesus said:

> *A tree is identified by its fruit. If a tree is good, its fruit will be good. If a tree is bad, its fruit will be bad. You brood of snakes! How could evil men like you speak what is good and right? For whatever is in your heart determines what you say. A good person produces good things from the treasury of a good heart, and an evil person produces evil things from the treasury of an evil heart. And I tell you this, you must give an account on judgment day for every idle word you speak. The words you say will either acquit you or condemn you.* (Matt 12:33-37)

The Path of Life and the Path of Folly (12:15-28). The section begins with the call to heed Solomon's counsel—contrasting the fool's self-delusion of uprightness. The first stanza is glued together with many key words, some of which are arranged in the following pattern.

A. the fool and folly (*'ewil* [TH191A, ZH211]) 12:15-16
- B. concealing (*kasah* [TH3680, ZH4059]) by the prudent (*'arum* [TH6175, ZH6874]) 12:16
  - C. the truth (*'emunah* [TH530, ZH575]) 12:17
    - D. the righteous (*tsedeq* [TH6664, ZH7406]) and the witness of falsehoods (*sheqer* [TH8267, ZH9214]) 12:17
      - E. the tongue of the wise brings healing 12:18
      - E'. lips of truth are established forever 12:19
    - D'. the righteous (*tsaddiq* [TH6662, ZH7404]) and Yahweh's detesting of falsehoods (*sheqer*) 12:21-22
  - C'. Yahweh's delight in truth (*'emunah*) 12:22
- B'. the prudent (*'arum*) conceals (*kasah*) 12:23

A'. the fool and folly (*'iwweleth* [TH200, ZH222]) 12:23

There are other puns, wordplays, and verbal connections as well, including "counsel" (*'etsah/ya'ats* [TH6098/3289, ZH6783/3619], 12:15, 20); the "witness" (*'ed* [TH5707, ZH6332],

12:17), "forever" (*la'ad* [TH5703, ZH6329], 12:19), and "until" (*we'ad* [TH5704, ZH6330], 12:19); "evil" (*ra'* [TH7451A, ZH8273], 12:20) and "trouble" (12:21); and "heart" (*leb* [TH3820, ZH4213], 12:20, 23). The word "falsehood" appears again in the center, at the end of the middle verse (12:19). This is a tightly interwoven stanza centered on the promise of the everlasting establishment of truth-tellers. Yahweh is revealed as the one before whom every person speaks falsehoods or truth (12:22).

The next stanza is bound by the inclusion of "diligent" (*kharuts* [TH2742F, ZH3026]) in 12:24 and 12:27. It ends with *'adam* [TH121A, ZH135] ("land"; see note on 12:27) in the final line, a wordplay with the *'adam* [TH120, ZH132] (man) concluding the previous stanza (12:23). Finally, the section ends with the inclusion of the "way" (12:15, 26, 28)—climaxing with the promise of everlasting life.

One line of argumentation in chapters 1–9 is the end, the terminus of a life course. (See commentary on the poems 1:8-19 and 2:1-22.) At the end of the fool's life, he laments: "Oh, why didn't I listen to my teachers? Why didn't I pay attention to my instructors? I have come to the brink of utter ruin, and now I must face public disgrace" (5:13-14). But what is the end of the wise? The Teacher of Ecclesiastes, dissatisfied with traditional sagacity (Eccl 8:17), questions its predications of an afterlife (Eccl 3:21). Apparently just such an assertion was part and parcel of the teachings with which he wrestled. To the Teacher in Ecclesiastes, the final end of a person is the grave—but not so to the sage of Proverbs! Proverbs, unlike the Teacher, *guarantees* blessedness to the righteous.

For example, how is it possible that it is "Better to be poor and honest / than to be dishonest and rich" (28:6)? Elsewhere, the blameless man is promised security (10:9) and refuge (10:29). Presumably refuge and security still belong to the righteous man despite his poverty. Innocent blood is shed in 1:11, yet the passage concludes that the murderers are the ones who truly die (1:19). The life hereafter must include those elements of justice that are promised but aborted in the case of untimely death. The deep structure behind the proverbs of Solomon must have a partially developed idea of immortality in order to make these bald promises and "better than" statements. "The way of the godly leads to life; that path does not lead to death" (12:28). Perhaps every promise made to the righteous is constitutive of the life eternal: They will not go hungry (10:3), their desires will be granted (10:24), they are rescued from trouble (11:8), their house stands firm (12:7), and they are rewarded with prosperity (13:21) (Schwab 1995:16).

The book of Proverbs is sapiential literature and has its own inner logic, but it should not be read in isolation from the streams of tradition that constituted the faith of ancient Israel. The book self-consciously wants the reader to make connections with these traditions outside its own genre. For example, in a small number of instances the cult (i.e., the system of prescribed worship rituals) is explicitly referenced, showing awareness and approval of Israel's worship forms, including the sacrificial system, prayers, and almsgiving. However, *where* to worship, *how* to make sacrifice, *what* to offer, *when* to do so, and *before whom* (i.e., priests) are not specified. What is at issue is the inner heart attitude of the worshiper. "The LORD is more pleased when we do what is right and just / than when we offer him sacrifices" (21:3). In a similar way, Proverbs insists that all wisdom starts with the fear of

Yahweh, but it does not depict for the reader what fearing Yahweh looks like. What does it mean to fear Yahweh? This is a point of contact with Israel's other religious constructs, which are left more or less unspecified and undefined in Proverbs.

In a similar way, the book of Proverbs envisions the sage enjoying the benefits of wisdom beyond what transpires in the here-and-now. Consider the first example of the path of wisdom presented to the reader in 1:8-19. A man walks the blameless path but is unjustly and violently killed. But Proverbs does not see this as an aberrant violation of the principles of wisdom. Quite the contrary! In this scenario, it is the *criminals* who are robbed of life (1:18-19). The path of wisdom promises a garland of eternal life (see note on 1:9), and the path of folly promises certain death, despite the counterexamples that the real world seems to present. Without defining the shape of immortality, the sage recognizes that wisdom exceeds the happenstances of this world. "In the way of righteousness there is life; / along that path is immortality" (12:28, NIV).

Christians understand this proverbial hope in an afterlife in light of the whole Bible. To the Christian, newness of life—wherein all the promises made to the righteous in Proverbs are known to be true in the absolute, unmitigated, unequivocal sense—is seen in the resurrection of Christ. He is the blameless man whom the wicked waylaid and killed; yet it is he who now possesses abundant life, and he promises this life to all who are his. But the antisocial reprobates who care nothing for the righteous path will perish. (See also commentary on 13:1–14:27.)

◆ C. The Way of Wisdom and the Way of Death (13:1–14:27)

1. Desiring and craving (13:1-25)

1 A wise child accepts a parent's
discipline;*
a mocker refuses to listen to
correction.

2 Wise words will win you a good meal,
but treacherous people have an
appetite for violence.

3 Those who control their tongue will
have a long life;
opening your mouth can ruin
everything.

4 Lazy people want much but get little,
but those who work hard will
prosper.

5 The godly hate lies;
the wicked cause shame and
disgrace.

6 Godliness guards the path of the
blameless,
but the evil are misled by sin.

7 Some who are poor pretend to be rich;
others who are rich pretend to be
poor.

8 The rich can pay a ransom for their
lives,
but the poor won't even get
threatened.

9 The life of the godly is full of light
and joy,
but the light of the wicked will be
snuffed out.

10 Pride leads to conflict;
those who take advice are wise.

11 Wealth from get-rich-quick schemes
quickly disappears;
wealth from hard work grows over
time.

12 Hope deferred makes the heart sick,
but a dream fulfilled is a tree
of life.

13 People who despise advice are asking
for trouble;
those who respect a command will
succeed.

14 The instruction of the wise is like
a life-giving fountain;
those who accept it avoid the snares
of death.

15 A person with good sense is respected;
a treacherous person is headed for
destruction.*

16 Wise people think before they act;
fools don't—and even brag about
their foolishness.

17 An unreliable messenger stumbles
into trouble,
but a reliable messenger brings
healing.

18 If you ignore criticism, you will end
in poverty and disgrace;
if you accept correction, you will
be honored.

19 It is pleasant to see dreams come
true,
but fools refuse to turn from evil
to attain them.

20 Walk with the wise and become
wise;
associate with fools and get in
trouble.

21 Trouble chases sinners,
while blessings reward the
righteous.

22 Good people leave an inheritance
to their grandchildren,
but the sinner's wealth passes
to the godly.

23 A poor person's farm may produce
much food,
but injustice sweeps it all away.

24 Those who spare the rod of discipline
hate their children.
Those who love their children care
enough to discipline them.

25 The godly eat to their hearts'
content,
but the belly of the wicked goes
hungry.

13:1 Hebrew *A wise son accepts his father's discipline.* 13:15 As in Greek version; Hebrew reads *the way of the treacherous is lasting.*

NOTES

13:1 ***A wise child accepts a parent's discipline.*** The composition begins by recalling the Prologue, where the sage admonishes the child to listen to wise counsel. This is how the previous two compositions opened (10:1; 12:1).

refuses to listen to correction. Lit., "will not hear a rebuke." This is identical in Hebrew to 13:8b, where it is translated "won't even get threatened."

13:2 ***Wise words will win you a good meal.*** Lit., "From the fruit of the mouth of a man he eats goodness." To "eat" is to "enjoy" the good. Emerton suggests, "He may eat good" (1984:95), i.e., the possibility exists.

appetite. Heb., *nepesh* [TH5315, ZH5883], often glossed "soul," here signifies the craving of the treacherous for violence.

13:3 ***Those who control their tongue will have a long life.*** Lit., "One who guards his mouth keeps his soul" (*nepesh* [TH5315, ZH5883]).

13:4 ***Lazy people want much but get little.*** Lit., "The soul [*nepesh*] of the sluggard craves but gets nothing."

those who work hard will prosper. Lit., "The *nepesh* of the diligent will be made fat."

13:5 ***hate lies.*** Lit., "hates a false thing."

cause shame and disgrace. The MT reads, "causes to stink and displays shame." The NLT reads *yab'ish* [TH887, ZH944] as *yabish* (from *bosh* [TH954, ZH1017], "cause shame").

13:7 ***pretend to be poor.*** The usual antithetical form suggests the second line is positive. Garrett proposes that the one appearing to be poor may be rich "on a more fundamental level" (1993:136). However, it is also possible that both conditions are negative, since both misrepresent the truth: "Both are instances of unbalanced and immoderate behavior" (McKane 1970:458). The wise may ponder both hypotheses.

13:8 ***The rich can pay a ransom for their lives.*** Since the rich can buy their way out of trouble, they need not hear rebuke (implied from the second line; see note on 13:1).

but the poor won't even get threatened. The Hebrew is identical with 13:1b, closing the inclusion from 13:1. Contra NLT, *ge'arah* [TH1606, ZH1722] never means "threaten," but always incrimination; the line should be read as in 13:1b. It is difficult to censure both rich and poor, since there is little leverage with either group. The line should read, "*Neither* do the poor heed rebuke." Thus the stanza ends with a synonymous proverb with rich and poor forming a merism representing all who feel that wise counsel does not apply to them (see 14:20; 30:9).

13:9 ***The life of the godly is full of light and joy.*** Lit., "The light of the godly *rejoices*" (*yismakh* [TH8055, ZH8523]). Driver suggests from a Ugaritic cognate the alternate semantic value "shines brightly" (1951:180).

snuffed out. Note that the light of the righteous does *not* get snuffed out. This is expanded in the closing verse of the stanza (13:14).

13:11 ***Wealth from get-rich-quick schemes.*** The MT reads "wealth of *hebel* [TH1892, ZH2039]," the favorite word of the Teacher in Ecclesiastes: "*hebel habalim* . . . all is *hebel*" (Eccl 1:2). *Hebel* in Proverbs means a puff of air, something impermanent (a "vanishing mist," 21:6). Beauty is *hebel* ("does not last," 31:30). Ways in which *hebel* wealth might be obtained include "tyranny, injustice, extortion, lies, and windfalls, at the expense of others" (Waltke 2004:561). The NLT needlessly follows the emendation (with LXX) of *mebohal* [TH926, ZH987] (hastily gotten).

13:12 ***deferred.*** Waltke suggests the deferment might be permanent, i.e., one's hope shall *never* be realized (2004:563).

tree of life. The life tree is experienced by those whose desires are fulfilled—and the way to secure this is explained in the following verse: "Respect [the] command" of wisdom and of God.

13:13 ***advice . . . command.*** The advice (lit., "word") and the "command" (*mitswah* [TH4687, ZH5184]) elsewhere signify the wise instruction of the parents (2:1; 3:1; 4:4; 6:20) in conjunction with *torah* [TH8451, ZH9368]—which appears in the following verse, concluding the stanza.

13:14 ***instruction of the wise.*** The stanza concludes with a synonymous proverb promising life and escape from death to those heeding wisdom's *torah*.

13:15 ***destruction.*** This follows the LXX (see NLT mg).

13:16 ***fools.*** Heb., *kesil* [TH3684, ZH4067], also in 13:19-20.

brag about their foolishness. Lit., "spreads out folly."

13:18 ***criticism.*** Lit., "discipline, instruction."

13:19 ***refuse.*** Lit., "detest."

13:20 ***become wise.*** Both this and the prior stanza end with explicit reference to wisdom (13:14).

associate . . . trouble. Note the pun in Hebrew: "associate" from *ra'ah* [TH7462C, ZH8287], "get in trouble" from *ra'a'* [TH7489, ZH8317].

13:21 ***the righteous.*** Heb., *tsaddiq* [TH6662, ZH7404], found three times in this stanza, is the mirror image of *kesil* [TH3684, ZH4067] in the previous stanza. Proverbs 13:20-21 is the seam between treatment of the *kesil* and the *tsaddiq*.

A. 13:16 *kesil*
  B. 13:17-18 (two skipped verses)
    C. 13:19 *kesil*
      D. 13:20 *kesil*
      D'. 13:21 *tsaddiq*
    C'. 13:22 *tsaddiq*
  B'. 13:23-24 (two skipped verses)
A'. 13:25 *tsaddiq*

13:22 ***Good people.*** Note the wordplay; the last word of 13:21 in Hebrew (NLT, "blessings") is identical with the first of 13:22, *tob* [TH2896, ZH3202].

13:24 ***spare the rod.*** See note on 10:13.

hate . . . love. People are categorized by what they love and hate. See commentary on 1:20-33.

care enough to discipline them. Lit., "seeks him with discipline." Wise parents who love their children actively pursue them with the rod. Those who refrain hate them, caring nothing for their future or character.

13:25 ***eat to their hearts' content.*** Lit., "eat to the satisfaction of their *nepesh* [TH5315, ZH5883]"—closing the inclusion from 13:2-8 and ending the section.

COMMENTARY

This composition opens with a reminder that the mark of the wise is tractability; the sage as parent admonishes the child again to listen. The first lengthy section (13:1-25) is built of four stanzas and bounded by an inclusion of eating and appetite. The first stanza repeats the key word *nepesh* [TH5315, ZH5883] (appetite) five times and is bounded with the inclusion "will not hear correction" (see notes on 13:1, 8). Proverbs 13:9-14 treats the theme of heeding advice. The *kesil* [TH3684, ZH4067] (fool) appears in the next stanza (13:15-20) three times, and the last stanza (13:21-25) covers the godly person.

The condition of one's "life," "soul," and/or "appetite" (*nepesh* [TH5315, ZH5883]) is a natural topic in the treatise of wisdom. Treacherous people hunger and thirst for violence (13:2). One's life is protected from danger by appropriate speech—while life is ruined by the opposite (13:3). Both diligent and slothful people have a *nepesh*—the one satisfied and fattened with goodness, the other goes empty. One is all image; the other is substance (13:7). When in trouble, in need of ransom or atonement, both the availability of great resources and the destitution of any resources put a person in spiritual hazard. Such people cannot be compelled to listen to wise counsel, which is the very thing that defines a mocker (13:1, 8). The safe path, the wise course, is to heed counsel, but this takes humility and is not compatible with arrogance and pride (13:10).

As noted in the Introduction, if there is a New Testament book of wisdom, it is

James. The book of James explicitly treats timeless topics such as how to speak, how to handle passions, and how to handle living in a world with disparity between social classes. James describes two kinds of "wisdom"—one is true, from God above, which is the sort of wisdom espoused in the book of Proverbs. The other is the false "wisdom" of fools, which is really an anti-wisdom. He sharply contrasts them in James 3:13-18:

> *If you are wise and understand God's ways, prove it by living an honorable life, doing good works with the humility that comes from wisdom. But if you are bitterly jealous and there is selfish ambition in your heart, don't cover up the truth with boasting and lying. For jealousy and selfishness are not God's kind of wisdom. Such things are earthly, unspiritual, and demonic. For wherever there is jealousy and selfish ambition, there you will find disorder and evil of every kind. But the wisdom from above is first of all pure. It is also peace loving, gentle at all times, and willing to yield to others. It is full of mercy and good deeds. It shows no favoritism and is always sincere. And those who are peacemakers will plant seeds of peace and reap a harvest of righteousness.*

True wisdom is to be teachable. It is (in the words of Proverbs) to heed wisdom's *mitswah* [TH4687, ZH5184] and *torah* [TH8451, ZH9368]. Those who do so are promised the longings of their hearts: a tree of life and a fountain of life. But riches can distract from that purpose (13:11). Beware of *hebel* wealth! (See note on 13:11.) Embrace diligence and patience, and your *nepesh* [TH5315, ZH5883] will be satisfied. The fool distributes folly and hates to turn away from evil—like the one who withholds the rod from his child. The wise person, who pursues the child with discipline, is the one who leaves an inheritance lasting for generations (13:22).

◆ 2. Building the house (14:1-11)

[1] A wise woman builds her home,
but a foolish woman tears it down
with her own hands.

[2] Those who follow the right path fear
the LORD;
those who take the wrong path
despise him.

[3] A fool's proud talk becomes a rod that
beats him,
but the words of the wise keep
them safe.

[4] Without oxen a stable stays clean,
but you need a strong ox for a large
harvest.

[5] An honest witness does not lie;
a false witness breathes lies.

[6] A mocker seeks wisdom and never
finds it,
but knowledge comes easily to
those with understanding.

[7] Stay away from fools,
for you won't find knowledge
on their lips.

[8] The prudent understand where they
are going,
but fools deceive themselves.

[9] Fools make fun of guilt,
but the godly acknowledge it and
seek reconciliation.

[10] Each heart knows its own bitterness,
and no one else can fully share
its joy.

[11] The house of the wicked will be
destroyed,
but the tent of the godly will
flourish.

NOTES

14:1 ***A wise woman builds her home . . . a foolish woman tears it down.*** The first composition of this anthology (chs 10–11) also included a middle section treating two women (11:16-22); see also 12:4. The present segment is bounded by houses of two women (14:1) and dwellings of the wicked and upright (14:11). As Yahweh employed Lady Wisdom to build the cosmos (8:30), so wise women everywhere build their own families. Of course, she and her evil counterpart represent a manner of living as well (14:11).

14:2 ***fear the LORD . . . despise him.*** The two women are reflected in two attitudes toward Yahweh.

14:4 ***a stable stays clean.*** Some commentators unnecessarily emend *'ebus* [TH18, ZH17] (manger) to *'epes* [TH657A, ZH700] (not) and read *bar* [TH1250, ZH1339] as "grain" instead of "empty" [TH1249, ZH1338], yielding the rendering "Where there are no oxen, there is no grain" (RSV). In both readings, however, the point is that it is important to maintain the tools of the trade to prosper. The first line suggests the reasoning of the short-sighted fool or sluggard; the second line highlights the industry of the right-minded individual. The proverb asks: Which are you?

14:5 ***honest witness . . . false witness.*** Again the proverb asks: Which are you? Categories of life are being defined for the reader, and a response is unavoidable—you are either one or the other. Illusions of middle ground vanish in the face of the sage's keen insight into human nature. "Since you have heard about Jesus . . . throw off your old sinful nature and your former way of life. . . . Put on your new nature. . . . Stop telling lies. Let us tell our neighbors the truth" (Eph 4:21-25).

14:7 ***Stay away from fools.*** This is similar to the adage "Bad company corrupts good character" (1 Cor 15:33). This proverb may be the center of a chiasm, as shown here:

A. Scoffer uselessly seeks wisdom / knowledge readily available to the discerning (14:6)
  B. Stay away from fools! Knowledge is not found with them (14:7)
A'. The prudent has wisdom / the fool has folly (14:8)

This triplet is framed with verses that treat the falsehood of the lying fools and the truthfulness of the upright (14:5, 9). This in turn is circumscribed by two proverbs that treat the private or domestic life of an individual (14:4, 10). Finally, the segment is bounded by the inclusion of one's domicile (14:1, 11). If 14:1-3 is grouped as developing a common theme (perhaps an inclusion of "wisdom" may be discerned there), the segment becomes a rough chiasm with 14:7 in the center.

14:9 ***Fools make fun of guilt, but the godly acknowledge it and seek reconciliation.*** "Guilt" may be implied in the second line without interpolating a pronominal suffix. NLT supplies the implied verb "seek," and glosses *ratson* [TH7522, ZH8356] as "reconciliation." Alternatively, perhaps the imagery here is drawn from the rituals of sacrificial worship: *'asham* [TH817, ZH871] = "guilt offering" (its normal usage) and *ratson* = God's acceptance of it (cf. Lev 22:20; Jer 6:20). Wisdom material is not hermetically sealed off from the other traditions of Israel (see 15:8).

14:10 ***Each heart knows.*** The inner life of an individual is private and unknown to others (14:13). See 20:5.

14:11 ***The house of the wicked . . . the tent of the godly.*** The theme of two residences returns from 14:1, identifying two categories of people. The "house" or "tent" symbolizes a manner of life; one flourishes and one is destined for extermination. The curse on the wicked will reach them within the refuge of their houses, and the godly will be blessed and established despite their transient homes.

COMMENTARY

The first section of this chapter begins with the wise woman's domicile and ends by contrasting the homes of the wicked and the righteous (14:1, 11). There are two manners of living as well as two patterns of thinking and behavior that the wise discern. One is the "abode" that is eternally established, built up by the wise wife who fears Yahweh and prospers with well-kept implements of productivity, truth-telling, and good discernment. The other "abode" is fated to extinction, torn down by foolish wives who despise God and damaging themselves through evil words. Their careers have failed due to neglect, lying, and inappropriate behavior (14:1, 2, 4, 5, 6-9, 11).

Proverbs 14:10 reads, "Each heart knows its own bitterness, and no one else can fully share its joy." Solomon was aware of people with a heavy heart (25:20). They are not forgotten. Neither are those with a bitter heart (14:10) or an aching heart (14:13), those with family strife (17:1), the crushed in spirit (17:22), depressed people (18:14), the alcoholic (23:29-35), the slothful, and the angry (22:24). When he arranged his proverbs, Solomon had these kinds of people in mind (Schwab 1995:8).

The inner pain or joy of a person, although invisible, is within the purview of sapience. The wise can plumb even the depths of the human heart and draw out what is needed to offer healing counsel. "The purpose in a man's mind is like deep water, but a man of understanding will draw it out" (20:5, RSV). The counsel offered in the book not only teaches categories of right and wrong, justice and equity, and fair and truthful dealings with one's neighbor in society. It also comforts those who suffer deep hurts and grief, a private burden unknown to all but the wise.

◆ 3. Death and how to escape it (14:12-27)

12 There is a path before each person
that seems right,
but it ends in death.

13 Laughter can conceal a heavy
heart,
but when the laughter ends, the
grief remains.

14 Backsliders get what they deserve;
good people receive their reward.

15 Only simpletons believe everything
they're told!
The prudent carefully consider their
steps.

16 The wise are cautious* and avoid
danger;
fools plunge ahead with reckless
confidence.

17 Short-tempered people do foolish
things,
and schemers are hated.

18 Simpletons are clothed with
foolishness,*
but the prudent are crowned with
knowledge.

19 Evil people will bow before good
people;
the wicked will bow at the gates
of the godly.

20 The poor are despised even by their
neighbors,
while the rich have many "friends."

21 It is a sin to belittle one's neighbor;
blessed are those who help
the poor.

22 If you plan to do evil, you will be lost;
if you plan to do good, you will
receive unfailing love and
faithfulness.

23 Work brings profit,
but mere talk leads to poverty!

[24] Wealth is a crown for the wise;
the effort of fools yields only
foolishness.

[25] A truthful witness saves lives,
but a false witness is a
traitor.

[26] Those who fear the LORD are secure;
he will be a refuge for their children.

[27] Fear of the LORD is a life-giving
fountain;
it offers escape from the snares
of death.

14:16 Hebrew *The wise fear.* **14:18** Or *inherit foolishness.*

NOTES

14:12 *it ends in death.* The section begins with the ominous deadly path that deceptively appears upright. This is followed with another non-antithetical double negative (comparative) proverb also highlighting deceptive appearances. The section ends with two double positives, climaxing with the way to avoid death—fearing Yahweh (14:26-27). This proverb (14:12) is used again at the beginning of another stanza (16:25).

14:13 *but when the laughter ends, the grief remains.* Lit., "and the end of joy may be grief."

14:14 *Backsliders get what they deserve.* Lit., "The faithless of heart will be sated with his ways."

good people receive their reward. Lit., "and a good man from his own." Supplying the elided "sated with his ways" from the first line yields, "A good man [will be sated] from his own [ways]." The "way" of a person satiates them—backsliders are filled with whatever they deserve. The good are satisfied with goodness. This is a mixed metaphor of the "path" and the "meal."

14:15 *believe.* The verb *'aman* [TH539, ZH586] here denotes a naive trust, an unwarranted gullibility. Thus the savvy do not "believe" deceitful words (26:25).

their steps. Again the image of the path is used, albeit with an alternative Hebrew word used only here in Proverbs, *'ashur* [TH838, ZH892]. Cf. 14:21, which ends with *'ashre* [TH835A, ZH897] (blessed).

14:16 *cautious.* See NLT mg, "The wise fear." The wise fear Yahweh (14:26-27) and turn aside from the path that seems right but ends in death (14:12). The fool, however, rages on in blind confidence and plunges into danger (evil).

14:17 *foolish things.* Heb., *'iwweleth* [TH200, ZH222], used twice in the beginning of the stanza (14:17-18) and twice in the end (14:24; see note).

14:18 *are clothed with.* Cf. NLT mg, "inherit," which is preferable in my view. NLT perhaps follows the emendation in BHS from *nakhalu* [TH5157, ZH5706] (to inherit) to *khali* [TH2481, ZH2717] ("ornament"; cf. 25:12). This sets "clothed with foolishness" in parallel with "crowned with knowledge" (Driver 1951:181). Emendations based solely upon restoring expected parallelism are precarious, and the idea "to inherit" may be preferable here (see note on 3:35). The stanza closes with the wise again "crowned" with no parallel apparel apart from another conjecture (14:24).

14:19 *will bow . . . will bow.* The Hebrew does not repeat the verb; it is elided in the second line. This synonymous proverb is the heart of the stanza, promising the subjugation of the evil and wicked to the judgments of the good and righteous. This thought is continued in the next doubly negative (comparative) proverb.

14:20 *the rich have many "friends."* Precisely, "Those who love the rich are many." Waltke calls this verse "a necessary corrective" to 14:19 (2004:598). "Indeed, the reinterpreting intent of v. 21 is plain" (Scherer 1997:67). Although the wicked will bow before the righteous, the rich have the ability to counterfeit this end; like chameleons they masquerade as upright—and people are attracted to them. In the same way, the godly poor may appear like the wicked, shunned by the community. But the natural order of things will be asserted (14:27). Proverbs 14:19-20 continues to be explicated in 14:21-24.

14:21 ***the poor.*** This proverb is an expansion of 14:19-20. The one who despises the afflicted will bow before those who favor them (in 14:20 the "neighbor" hates the needy; in 14:21 the neighbor *is* the needy).

14:22 ***plan.*** Heb. *kharash* [TH2790, ZH3086] is often glossed as "engrave" or "plow." Those who inscribe evil upon their hearts will bow before those inscribing good (14:19).

unfailing love and faithfulness. Heb., *khesed we'emeth* [TH2617/571, ZH2876/622], "faithfulness and truth" (see note on 3:3).

14:23 ***profit . . . poverty.*** This nuances 14:20—often the prosperous are righteous and the poor are indolent.

14:24 ***Wealth is a crown for the wise.*** The stanza is drawing to a close, recapitulating themes from 14:18, where "the prudent are crowned with knowledge." Here, building upon 14:23 and 14:19-20, wealth is an unqualified good when enjoyed by the wise.

the effort of fools yields only foolishness. Like the prior stanza, this one ends with the fool—lit., "The folly of fools is folly." BHS unnecessarily suggests *liwyath* [TH3880, ZH4292] (wreaths) for *'iwweleth* [TH200, ZH222] (folly), yielding, "Folly is the garland of fools" (RSV).

14:25 ***saves lives.*** The topic of saving souls is here resumed as the antidote to the way that seems upright but leads to death, which began the section (14:12). The composition ends with the ultimate response to this—only with Yahweh is there life.

14:26 ***Those who fear the LORD are secure.*** Those fearing Yahweh are genuinely "secure" (*mibtakh* [TH4009, ZH4440], from root *batakh* [TH982, ZH1053]), as opposed to the fool with reckless confidence (also from *batakh*) in himself (14:16).

for their children. Lit., "for their sons." Here the sons, as it were, inherit a refuge (see 3:35).

14:27 ***escape from the snares of death.*** See note on 12:28. This comparative proverb closes the composition with its ultimate perspective: The fear of Yahweh leads to immortality.

COMMENTARY

The second part of chapter 14 is circumscribed by references to death—what leads to it and how to escape it. This section is composed of three stanzas. The first (14:12-16) is united by the key words "path," "heart," and "person" and ends by treating the fool. The second stanza (14:17-24) is delimited with the inclusion *'iwweleth* [TH200, ZH222] and also ends by treating the fool. The third stanza of three lines (14:25-27) repeats the motif of fearing Yahweh.

The way of life is elusive to some, and deceptive alternatives lure the unwary to their deaths. The fatal direction *seems* promising; the simple believe whatever they hear, and a faithless heart is sated with its choices. Laughter and joy are even deceptive, concealing pain and sorrow. The wise understand this, but the naive cannot discern past appearances. The prudent and disciplined are careful in their life decisions, keenly seeing past any façade to the truth.

Eventually the natural order of things is asserted, and the quick-tempered man, the hated schemer, simpletons, and devisers of evil will inevitably submit to the judgments and censure of the prudent, who are crowned with knowledge, show compassion to the poor, and value honest work. Although the presence or absence of riches may create the illusion that the wicked prosper, the ultimate truth of human existence (14:19) always shows in the end. Jesus noted the same truth in his discussion with his disciples that the presence or absence of riches in this world can create a false impression to people whose minds can only comprehend the here and now. But in the future, when the Kingdom of God is visibly manifest, things will be quite different. The great will be small then, and those who seem insignificant now will inherit the earth.

> *Then Jesus said to his disciples, "I tell you the truth, it is very hard for a rich person to enter the Kingdom of Heaven. I'll say it again—it is easier for a camel to go through the eye of a needle than for a rich person to enter the Kingdom of God!" The disciples were astounded. "Then who in the world can be saved?" they asked. Jesus looked at them intently and said, "Humanly speaking, it is impossible. But with God everything is possible." Then Peter said to him, "We've given up everything to follow you. What will we get?" Jesus replied, "I assure you that when the world is made new and the Son of Man sits upon his glorious throne, you who have been my followers will also sit on twelve thrones, judging the twelve tribes of Israel. And everyone who has given up houses or brothers or sisters or father or mother or children or property, for my sake, will receive a hundred times as much in return and will inherit eternal life. But many who are the greatest now will be least important then, and those who seem least important now will be the greatest then." (Matt 19:23-30)*

Jesus spoke of the time when the "world [will be] made new" (Matt 19:28), using the word *palingenesia* [TG3824, ZG4098], translated "regeneration" (RSV) or "new birth" (NLT) in Titus 3:5. Those who have suffered for their faith will participate in the regeneration of the world, the renewal of all things. Then the proverbs that promise all good things will be experienced as unequivocal promises. Those who walked the path of wisdom will arrive at their destination and receive eternal life.

The development of wisdom in Israel seems to have always been predicated upon the belief in an afterlife. This can be demonstrated in three contexts of sapiential material.

First, very ancient wisdom material, such as the *Instruction of Amenemope,* bears striking resemblance to the Hebrew book of Proverbs. The Egyptian interest in the afterlife is patent. It is in the context of such an aspiration that the pyramids were built—and it is in this culture that sages ruminated, producing works cognate with Solomon's Proverbs. (Solomon is compared with Egyptian sages in 1 Kgs 4:30.) The hereafter was not just a tangential aspect of their religion; it was an important motivator, a dynamic feature of the Egyptian civilization that lasted through the Old Kingdom all the way up until the Christianization of Egypt. It is within this mindset that the ancient sages produced their instruction material.

Another fertile source of wisdom material dates to the Second Temple period, between the writing of the Old Testament and the New Testament. Apparently, interest was invigorated in wisdom at this time, and works such as Sirach (Ecclesiasticus) and the Wisdom of Solomon were produced. It is patent that in this period in Israel there was a well-developed belief in the afterlife.

Finally, a third locus of interest is the book of Proverbs itself. Proverbs yields a number of verses in key places that highlight the perspective of eternity (3:2; 12:28; 14:27). Although for the most part Proverbs treats how to live in the present world and does not counsel being so heavenly minded that you are no earthly good, it does hold out for the wise a hope that lies beyond the theater of this life.

The fear of Yahweh is the beginning of wisdom. This discipline yields immortality and guarantees honor and glory to one whose business is to save souls from death; eternal security is found with him (14:25-27). The composition ends on this note. (See also the commentary on 12:1-28.)

◆ D. The Wisdom of Yahweh and the King (14:28–16:15)

1. The wisdom of Yahweh (14:28–16:9)

28 A growing population is a king's glory;
a prince without subjects has nothing.

29 People with understanding control their anger;
a hot temper shows great foolishness.

30 A peaceful heart leads to a healthy body;
jealousy is like cancer in the bones.

31 Those who oppress the poor insult their Maker,
but helping the poor honors him.

32 The wicked are crushed by disaster,
but the godly have a refuge when they die.

33 Wisdom is enshrined in an understanding heart;
wisdom is not* found among fools.

34 Godliness makes a nation great,
but sin is a disgrace to any people.

35 A king rejoices in wise servants
but is angry with those who disgrace him.

CHAPTER **15**

1 A gentle answer deflects anger,
but harsh words make tempers flare.

2 The tongue of the wise makes knowledge appealing,
but the mouth of a fool belches out foolishness.

3 The LORD is watching everywhere,
keeping his eye on both the evil and the good.

4 Gentle words are a tree of life;
a deceitful tongue crushes the spirit.

5 Only a fool despises a parent's* discipline;
whoever learns from correction is wise.

6 There is treasure in the house of the godly,
but the earnings of the wicked bring trouble.

7 The lips of the wise give good advice;
the heart of a fool has none to give.

8 The LORD detests the sacrifice of the wicked,
but he delights in the prayers of the upright.

9 The LORD detests the way of the wicked,
but he loves those who pursue godliness.

10 Whoever abandons the right path will be severely disciplined;
whoever hates correction will die.

11 Even Death and Destruction* hold no secrets from the LORD.

How much more does he know the
human heart!

12 Mockers hate to be corrected,
so they stay away from the wise.

13 A glad heart makes a happy face;
a broken heart crushes the spirit.

14 A wise person is hungry for
knowledge,
while the fool feeds on trash.

15 For the despondent, every day brings
trouble;
for the happy heart, life is a
continual feast.

16 Better to have little, with fear for the
LORD,
than to have great treasure and
inner turmoil.

17 A bowl of vegetables with someone
you love
is better than steak with someone
you hate.

18 A hot-tempered person starts fights;
a cool-tempered person stops
them.

19 A lazy person's way is blocked with
briers,
but the path of the upright is an
open highway.

20 Sensible children bring joy to their
father;
foolish children despise their
mother.

21 Foolishness brings joy to those with
no sense;
a sensible person stays on the right
path.

22 Plans go wrong for lack of advice;
many advisers bring success.

23 Everyone enjoys a fitting reply;
it is wonderful to say the right thing
at the right time!

24 The path of life leads upward for the
wise;
they leave the grave* behind.

25 The LORD tears down the house of
the proud,
but he protects the property of
widows.

26 The LORD detests evil plans,
but he delights in pure words.

27 Greed brings grief to the whole family,
but those who hate bribes will live.

28 The heart of the godly thinks carefully
before speaking;
the mouth of the wicked overflows
with evil words.

29 The LORD is far from the wicked,
but he hears the prayers of the
righteous.

30 A cheerful look brings joy to the
heart;
good news makes for good health.

31 If you listen to constructive criticism,
you will be at home among
the wise.

32 If you reject discipline, you only harm
yourself;
but if you listen to correction, you
grow in understanding.

33 Fear of the LORD teaches wisdom;
humility precedes honor.

CHAPTER 16

1 We can make our own plans,
but the LORD gives the right answer.

2 People may be pure in their own eyes,
but the LORD examines their
motives.

3 Commit your actions to the LORD,
and your plans will succeed.

4 The LORD has made everything for his
own purposes,
even the wicked for a day of
disaster.

5 The LORD detests the proud;
they will surely be punished.

6 Unfailing love and faithfulness make
atonement for sin.

By fearing the LORD, people avoid
evil.

[7]When people's lives please the LORD,
even their enemies are at peace
with them.

[8]Better to have little, with godliness,
than to be rich and dishonest.

[9]We can make our plans,
but the LORD determines our
steps.

14:33 As in Greek and Syriac versions; Hebrew lacks *not.* **15:5** Hebrew *father's.* **15:11** Hebrew *Sheol and Abaddon.* **15:24** Hebrew *Sheol.*

NOTES

14:28 ***has nothing.*** Lit., "is the destruction of [a prince]." The measure of a king is his subjects.

14:29 ***a hot temper shows great foolishness.*** Curb your emotions—particularly when in the king's presence!

14:30 ***jealousy is like cancer in the bones.*** Perhaps this maxim is especially applicable while serving in the highly political atmosphere of the royal court.

bones. See note on 3:8.

14:31 ***their Maker.*** The king and Yahweh are both powerful figures before whom one must behave with restraint and consideration, since it is dangerous to insult either. God takes it personally when the poor are mistreated; the wise king does not tolerate abuse of his subjects. Honoring the poor glorifies God.

14:32 ***are crushed.*** Niphal of *dakhah* [TH1760, ZH1890]; see note on 26:28.

the godly have a refuge when they die. This is another verse promising that the rewards of righteousness do not terminate in death. The RSV (with LXX) emends this to "finds refuge through his integrity." But "Proverbs consistently encourages faith in the LORD . . . never faith in one's own piety" (Waltke 2004:583). Read together with 14:31, this verse indicates that when people glorify God by favoring the needy, they need not fear death.

14:33 ***wisdom is not found among fools.*** The Hebrew reads, "In the midst of fools [wisdom] is made known." See mg note in NLT, which supplies "not" based on the ancient versions. But if MT preserves the original reading, the line states that "within" (*qereb* [TH7130, ZH7931]) the fool wisdom is "made manifest" (Niphal of *yada'* [TH3045, ZH3359]); there is no better illustration of sound counsel than observing its opposite.

14:34 ***a nation . . . any people.*** Issues on a national scale are in view.

disgrace. Heb., *khesed* I [TH2617A, ZH2875], found elsewhere only in Lev 20:17, not to be confused with its common homonym *khesed* II [TH2617A, ZH2876] (see 2:8). See note on 19:22.

14:35 ***A king rejoices in wise servants.*** The king is like God, powerful to accomplish his will and able to judge and reward his servants. Fear the king and serve him well!

15:1 ***deflects anger.*** Illustrations abound, such as Abigail's gracious words before the murderously angry David (1 Sam 25) or Daniel's before Nebuchadnezzar (Dan 2:12-14, 27-45).

harsh words. Whybray glosses this as "a word which causes pain" (1994a:225).

15:2 ***makes knowledge appealing.*** Lit., "commends (*tetib* [TH3190, ZH3512]) knowledge."

belches out foolishness. "Belches out" comes from *naba'* [TH5042, ZH5580], found four times in Proverbs. It is found also in the concluding verse of the part 15:25-28, where NLT renders it as "overflows."

15:3 ***The LORD is watching everywhere.*** This comparative proverb is found at a seam, where Yahweh is introduced as the one before whom all people live. This is echoed again when the part draws to a close (15:11).

15:4 ***tree of life.*** See notes on 11:30. A wise word that heals the brokenhearted in some small way restores what was lost when humanity ate the forbidden fruit and "whets the appetite to restore Paradise" (Waltke 2004:615).

15:5 ***parent's discipline.*** Precisely, "the discipline of his father." The image of the wise parent advising offspring on the paths of life is reminiscent of the Prologue of chs 1–9. There, Yahweh is revealed as the one who adopts the wise as his "sons," and with him they enjoy the fruit of the tree of life (3:12, 18). Here, Yahweh observes the good who embody the healing properties of the tree of life (Rev 22:2) and the evil who despise the father's discipline (15:3-5). God-centered rhetoric characterizes this part of the strophe.

15:7 ***give good advice.*** Lit., "scatter knowledge." The wise disseminate wisdom; they educate others. BHS unnecessarily suggests emending (with the Greek OT of Symmachus) to *yitseru* [TH5341, ZH5915], hence, "guard knowledge." The word is used several ways in Proverbs—the lips of the wise "scatter" knowledge (15:7), and the wise with power "scatter" the wicked (20:26).

15:8 ***The LORD detests.*** The sacrifice of the wicked is an "abomination" to Yahweh. As in 15:1-3, this material is reminiscent of ch 3. Here, worship rituals and prayer are at issue (see 3:9). Sacrifices offered by unworthy pseudo-worshipers repel God; the prayers of the upright delight him. "Bring no more vain offerings; incense is an abomination to me" (Isa 1:13, RSV). The subject of Yahweh's hatred of the wicked continues in the next verse.

15:9 ***the way of the wicked.*** This might include religious duties or acts of (insincere) worship, which are loathed by God (15:8).

15:10 ***the right path.*** As in 15:9, the image of the path describes a person.

whoever hates correction will die. This is the first of three non-antithetical proverbs that form a seam between two parts of this strophe. Death is the end of those who hate reproof, the opposite of the tree of life (which is equated with healing words, 15:4).

15:11 ***Death and Destruction.*** Continuing the thought of 15:10, Yahweh understands the mystery of death—an eternal reality awaiting those who hate correction.

How much more does he know the human heart! Lit., "the hearts of the sons of Adam." Again this part echoes ch 3, where "Adam" and all people are metaphorically offered the tree of life, found in words of wisdom (3:13, 18; see also 15:3). Yahweh's omniscience frames this part of the strophe.

15:12 ***Mockers hate to be corrected.*** Lit., "A mocker does not love one who reproves him." The verse has verbal affinity not with 15:10 ("whoever hates") but with 15:9 ("he loves"). The verse asks the reader, "Do you love those who correct you?"

15:13 ***A glad heart.*** Lit., "a heart of joy." The theme of joy is resumed in the next part. The next verse also treats the condition of the heart.

makes . . . happy. From *yatab* [TH3190, ZH3512], the verbal form of one of the key words in this part, *tob* [TH2896, ZH3202], meaning "good" or "better than."

broken heart. Lit., "aching" heart, elsewhere only in 10:10, which NLT translates "trouble." The part of the strophe that treats what is "good" opens with a reminder of a soul's bitterness attending one who suffers and grieves; the wise know how to approach such people (see commentary on 14:1-11).

15:14 ***A wise person.*** The Hebrew begins with *leb* [TH3820, ZH4213] (heart), as does 15:13, thus linking the two verses. A heart seeking knowledge has a personality foundation unavailable to those imbibing folly.

while the fool feeds on trash. This follows Qere, "but the mouth of," rather than Kethiv, "but the face of." "Feeds" comes from *ra'ah* [TH7473, ZH8286], which with humans as subject usually means "tending" a herd or flock (when not used metaphorically); with animals as the subject it means "graze." The object is not "trash" but "folly." While the wise seek knowledge, fools "graze upon" folly like unthinking cattle. Alternatively, fools "pasture" their students with folly.

15:15 ***despondent.*** Precisely, "afflicted." Usually *'ani* [TH6041, ZH6714] denotes the "poor" or "destitute." But see the note on 3:34 (where *'ani* is glossed "humble") and 16:19, where the "poor" are literally the "low of spirit." The aphorism treats two alternative outlooks on life—one impoverished and one glad.

continual feast. This continues the "meal" image from 15:14, seen again in 15:17. The proverb contrasts the outlook of the "afflicted" heart with the perspective of the *tob* [TH2896, ZH3202] (good) heart. How one sees the world is at issue.

15:16 ***Better to have little.*** In this verse the fear of Yahweh—with little else—is preferable to everything else the world has to offer. This paradigmatic proverb sets the stage for the next. See note on 12:9.

15:17 ***is better than.*** The Hebrew begins as in 15:16, with *tob* [TH2896, ZH3202] (better). There are some intangibles in this world that turn the usual hierarchy of valuation on its head; "love" cannot be bought, and yet it is worth more than the fattened calf. The wise who fear Yahweh cultivate this kind of home; thus, their rewards in part are experienced in this world. The *tob* heart with its positive outlook (15:15) illustrates this. See note on 12:9.

15:19 ***open highway.*** Heb., *salal* [TH5549A, ZH6148] (cast up, raise up), elsewhere in Proverbs only in 4:8: "*prize* wisdom." Here it is a passive participle denoting a raised causeway. The sluggard sees nothing but impediments; the upright have clear and unhindered resolve for achieving their goals.

15:20 ***Sensible children . . . foolish children.*** Lit., "a wise son . . . a foolish man." This verse recalls the opening verses in major compositions elsewhere, such as 10:1 and 13:1, and harkens back to the Prologue. This part is a miniature version of the book of Proverbs, completing the strophe's motif of the youth's responsibility to heed the parent (15:5). The theme of "joy" also opened the previous part in 15:13.

15:21 ***joy.*** This is the same word for "joy" in 15:20, there indicating the joy of the father with a wise son. Here it denotes the unsuitable joy toward folly felt by the one "lacking heart/sense." What brings joy defines a person—degenerates find joy in immoral stupidities.

15:22 ***many advisers bring success.*** The wise seek the counsel of many. This helps to establish (*qum* [TH6965, ZH7756]) their plans.

15:23 ***Everyone enjoys a fitting reply.*** Lit., "Joy to a man with an answer of his mouth." True joy is found in a timely word—especially from many counselors (15:22).

15:24 ***The path of life.*** This consequential proverb follows a synonymous one, found at a seam between two strophes. Here, the promised life is "upward" and set opposite to *sheol* [TH7585, ZH8619] (which LXX renders as *hadēs* [TG86, ZG87]). It is a straightforward guarantee of a life hereafter (see note on 12:28). "Salvation from the grave is more than being spared an untimely death, for otherwise the path of life is swallowed up in death, an unthinkable thought in Proverbs" (Waltke 2004:634). Whybray cites Dan 12:2-3 for clarification on the sort of doctrine this verse "may appear to suggest" (1994a:234): "Many of those whose bodies lie dead and buried will rise up, some to everlasting life and some to shame and everlasting disgrace. Those who are wise will shine as bright as the sky, and those who lead many to righteousness will shine like the stars forever."

15:25 ***The Lord tears down the house of the proud.*** God actively destroys the house (*beth* [TH1004, ZH1074]) of those who are not humble before him. It is not some sort of "cosmic order" that ensures this—it is Yahweh who acts against those who are proud. Although one may perceive secondary causes as instruments of this downfall, he is a personal God who causes whatever comes to pass against those who boast in their own strength.

15:26 ***The Lord detests evil plans.*** When Yahweh hates something, its destruction is inevitable (see the previous verse).

pure words. Of the 96 times *tahor* [TH2889, ZH3196] occurs in the OT, 69 are in the Pentateuch; and sometimes "pure" and "abomination" are found in close proximity (Lev 20:13 and 25; Deut 12:22 and 31; 23:11 and 18; Ezek 22:11 and 26; 44:13 and 23), always in a cultic or ritual sense. Here, ceremonial imagery is appropriated into wisdom language—one is clean not through ritual but through pure speech. "It's not what goes into your mouth that defiles you; you are defiled by the words that come out of your mouth" (Matt 15:11).

15:27 ***Greed.*** Lit., "One who covets covetousness." Such a one brings grief to his "house"—presumably the house Yahweh eventually destroys (15:25).

will live. Life is the opposite of bringing trouble upon one's house. See note on 17:8 for the "bribe."

15:28 ***overflows.*** From *naba'* [TH5042, ZH5580], used four times in Proverbs, including the concluding verse of the section 14:28–15:2 (see note on 15:2).

15:29 ***he hears the prayers of the righteous.*** This part is united by the theme of hearing (from *shama'* [TH8085, ZH9048]) and begins with Yahweh setting the pattern—although inaccessible to the wicked, he listens attentively to the righteous.

15:30 ***A cheerful look.*** Precisely, "the light of the eyes." "Light" is equated with life in 4:18; 6:23; 13:9 (Waltke 1996:92), perhaps a symbol for the outlook of the wise resulting in edifying counsel. See note on 4:22.

good news . . . good health. "News" is from the same root as "hears" in 15:29. Good news has emotional and physical effects. "Makes for good health" is lit., "makes fat the bone." See note on 3:8 for "bone."

15:31 ***listen to constructive criticism.*** Lit., "the ear hearing reproof of life." Criticism that brings life is at issue—the wise understand this. See notes on the stanza 4:20-26.

15:32 ***listen to correction.*** To reject discipline (*musar* [TH4148, ZH4592], also in 15:33) is to forfeit one's life; but to hear reproof (*tokakhath* [TH8433A, ZH9350]) is to acquire a "heart." This is the opposite of lacking a heart (15:21).

15:33 ***Fear of the Lord.*** The part opened with Yahweh listening to the prayers of the righteous; here it ends with wisdom in fearing Yahweh. The verse literally reads, "The fear of Yahweh is discipline for wisdom / And before glory comes humility."

16:1 ***We can make our own plans.*** Lit., "To a man (*'adam* [TH120, ZH132]) are the plans of the heart." This opens an inclusion that closes in 16:9: "The heart of *adam* devises his way." People "design what they will say and do, but the Lord decrees what will endure and form part of his eternal purposes" (Waltke 2005:9).

but the Lord gives the right answer. Lit., "but from Yahweh is the tongue's answer." This also is echoed in 16:9. In Jesus' words, "Don't worry about how to respond or what to say. God will give you the right words at the right time. For it is not you who will be speaking—it will be the Spirit of your Father speaking through you" (Matt 10:19-20).

16:2 ***in their own eyes.*** The important consideration is *who* weighs a matter.

the* LORD *examines their motives. Lit., "Yahweh weighs spirits." God evaluates our spirit—our motives, our inner self—to see if we are truly innocent. His judgment may be different from what seems true "in our own eyes." God rules over our spirit.

16:3 *Commit your actions to the* LORD*, and your plans will succeed.* Precisely, "Roll away to Yahweh your deeds / and let be established your plans." Since God rules over your plans, give them to him and in this way cooperate with his unknown and sovereign will.

16:4 *even the wicked.* All things and everyone fit into Yahweh's grand "purposes" (lit., "answer," see 16:1), including the reprobates, who are destined for ruin. Delitzsch argues against *prædestinatio al malum* here, asserting that "the wicked also has his place in God's order of the world" (1874:337). Although the language is typically uncompromising, it should be read coordinately with the next verse and roughly paraphrased, "Yahweh made everyone—even those who are wicked—and he will answer them on the day of judgment." This verse has pride of place in that it is the exact middle of this anthology, the Proverbs of Solomon. God's unfathomable purposes are of central importance.

16:5 *the proud.* Lit., "every proud heart." "Every" or "all" is one of the key words in this part, here for the third time. Yahweh rules over *every* path (16:2, lit.), *everything* (16:4), and *every* heart. There is nothing outside God's dominion. This verse elaborates on the teaching from 16:4 about the role of the wicked.

16:6 *atonement for sin.* See note on 2:1. In the Mosaic law iniquity was atoned by the blood of animals. But here the inner conformity to the purposes and character of God covers sin. The sage again appropriates cultic language to argue for a parallel approach to God—the way of wisdom.

16:7 *are at peace.* Hiphil of *shalam* [TH7999A, ZH8971], "[Yahweh] causes to sue for peace."

16:8 *and dishonest.* Lit., "and without justice." "Justice" is found twice in the next segment (16:10-11), helping to tie the two units together. This proverb is embedded in a part that otherwise uniformly employs the name "Yahweh." Reading epexegetically (with regard to its immediate context), the verse should also exhibit a divine orientation. Because of the truths specified about God here, the maxim confidently asserts that it is better for a season to be righteous with little than to have great riches reserved for the day of disaster. See notes on 12:9 and 15:16.

16:9 *We can make our plans.* Lit., "the heart of *adam* devises his way," closing the inclusion from 16:1. God rules over every human step.

COMMENTARY

This section focuses on the wisdom of Yahweh and of the king, who is presented as being an expression of God. The Hebrew word *melek* [TH4428, ZH4889] (king) occurs 32 times in Proverbs, seven in this composition (14:28–16:15). Proverbs 14:28 is the first time it is found in the "Proverbs of Solomon" anthology (although it is used once in 1:1 and again, incidentally, in 8:15); the composition is framed with the use of the word "king" (14:28, 35; 16:10-15), where dealing with royalty becomes an important topic. Instead of the usual opening verse(s) recalling the father nurturing his son, this composition introduces the wise king who nurtures his populace.

In the middle of this section, 15:29-33 has an increasing frequency of non-antithetical proverbs climaxing in the section treating the king (16:10-15), in which only 2 of 12 lines are negative. Proverbs 16:16 begins a new composition no longer characterized by antithetical proverbs. In the anthology up to 15:33, out of 184 verses, only 28 are clearly non-antithetic. In the next 15 verses (completing the composition), only 6 are antithetic. The anthology is transitioning away from using proverbs that contrast opposites as a method of highlighting wisdom and folly.

Waltke (1996:88) argues that 15:30–16:15 is a unit and parses it into three parts: 15:30-33, 16:1-9, and 16:10-15. These are obvious units, formed respectively by the key words "hearing," "Yahweh," and "king." Contra Waltke, 16:10-15 can also be seen as closing the inclusion from 14:28-35 (itself bound by the repetition of "king")—a unit that introduces the king in this anthology.

According to the criteria above, 15:33 should be included with the second part, since it does not have "hearing" and does have "Yahweh." However, 15:33 closes the "Yahweh" inclusion from 15:29 and continues the thought of "discipline" (*musar* [TH4148, ZH4592]) from 15:32. In addition, 16:1-9 is bound by the inclusion *'adam* [TH120, ZH132]. Thus, 15:33 is a bridge proverb, smoothly transitioning between the strophe's first and second parts. As 15:33 includes the key word "Yahweh" from the next part, "Yahweh" also spills over into the third part in 16:11.

Wisdom before the King (14:28–15:2). When in the presence of royalty, it is especially crucial to know one's place and curb one's impulses. It is also essential to be skillful in handling issues concerning the nation, particularly in one's responsibility toward the disadvantaged and vulnerable in the kingdom. Although royal proverbs do not necessarily imply an original use as educational material for imperial service, such a setting does bring a particular clarity to the importance of wisdom virtues.

The king is introduced as a proper and significant topic in matters of wisdom. Imagine the self-possessed courtier serving at the royal court and the careful manner in which he must weigh his words before speaking. He must restrain himself from emotionalism, advocate for the poor and for justice, present himself as a skillful speaker before his lord, and manage political positioning of his rivals and peers. These same skills ought to define the conduct of the prudent in *any* situation, royal or common. Personality traits that comprise a successful court adviser also make a successful neighbor and a prosperous citizen with a life pleasing to one's Maker.

Yahweh and Wisdom (15:3–16:9). This section is enclosed by two concentrated units of Yahweh proverbs, the first being the initial part of the first strophe, and the last being the second strophe. This totals 16 Yahweh verses in a section of 40 verses, exactly 40 percent. The first strophe (15:3-24) treats Yahweh as Father of the sage. The strophe is 22 verses long, the number of letters in the Hebrew alphabet. Yahweh is also the subject of the next strophe (15:25–16:9), which contains 12 Yahweh proverbs in 18 verses.

When the wicked participate in religious activities, they are hypocritical and unaware that Yahweh absolutely detests being associated with them. God expressed this through his prophets. Isaiah declares,

> "What makes you think I want all your sacrifices?"
> says the LORD.
> "I am sick of your burnt offerings of rams
> and the fat of fattened cattle.
> I get no pleasure from the blood
> of bulls and lambs and goats.

When you come to worship me,
  who asked you to parade through my courts with all your ceremony?
Stop bringing me your meaningless gifts;
  the incense of your offerings disgusts me!
As for your celebrations of the new moon and the Sabbath
  and your special days for fasting—
they are all sinful and false.
  I want no more of your pious meetings.
I hate your new moon celebrations and your annual festivals.
  They are a burden to me. I cannot stand them!
When you lift up your hands in prayer, I will not look.
  Though you offer many prayers, I will not listen,
  for your hands are covered with the blood of innocent victims.
Wash yourselves and be clean!
  Get your sins out of my sight.
  Give up your evil ways.
Learn to do good.
  Seek justice.
Help the oppressed.
  Defend the cause of orphans.
  Fight for the rights of widows." (Isa 1:11-17)

God is intensely interested in our inner integrity, in the unblemished character of his sons and daughters (15:8-9). He is omnipresent and omniscient—ever watching and weighing the deeds of the righteous and the wicked (15:3). There are no secrets from him (15:11). He is the wise Father (15:5), who loves his own children (15:9), delights in their prayers (15:8), and ensures that their houses are filled with good things (15:6).

The children of God are known by their response to him—which is governed in turn by their inner heart attitude. The wise learn from his correction (15:5), and their lips imitate God's in supplying life-giving counsel (15:4, 7). Those who care nothing for Yahweh or his counsel are the wicked. They crush tender personalities (15:4), they are full of trouble (15:6), and they are hypocritical in their religion (15:8). God detests them.

When Jesus encountered the self-righteous hypocrites of his day, his reaction mirrored 15:8. He hated them as counterfeit worshipers fit only for Sheol. "What sorrow awaits you teachers of religious law and you Pharisees. Hypocrites! For you cross land and sea to make one convert, and then you turn that person into twice the child of hell you yourselves are!" (Matt 23:15). Perhaps Jesus had Proverbs in mind when he said, "Therefore also the Wisdom of God said, 'I will send them prophets and apostles, some of whom they will kill and persecute.' . . . Nothing is covered up that will not be revealed, or hidden that will not be known" (Luke 11:49; 12:2, RSV). In other words, as Sheol and Abaddon lie open before God, so the hearts of all people will be exposed, including every secret deed, which reveals the falsehood of their sacrifices and prayers. Some Christians died for worshiping in an unworthy manner (1 Cor 11:27-30), and Paul spoke of the future when wicked people "will act religious, but they will reject the power that could make them godly. Stay away from people like that!" (2 Tim 3:5). Truly, the fear of the Lord is the beginning of wisdom.

Mockers *hate* correction; they *do not love* rebuke (15:10, 12); the prudent *hear* and take it to heart (15:5). Proverbs asks the reader, "How do you deal with criticism? Are you quick to offer excuses and to defend yourself? Or do you cherish and embrace it?" The wise value rebuke; fools can't stand it and perish.

There are different hearts that people live with—the joyful and the burdened, the discerning and the cheerful (15:13-15). For some, life is a continual feast, a never-ending party, a celebration of the goodness of living as a gift from God; for others the days are bad, and they live with a crushed spirit. One's outlook on life determines the difference (15:15, 30). In Jesus' words, "Your eye is a lamp that provides light for your body. When your eye is good, your whole body is filled with light. But when your eye is bad, your whole body is filled with darkness. And if the light you think you have is actually darkness, how deep that darkness is!" (Matt 6:22-23).

Jesus also says to rejoice and be glad when persecuted, for great is your reward in heaven (Matt 5:12)! That which brings joy to a person defines the person. A wise son gladdens a father (15:20), a word fitly spoken brings joy (15:23), and a glad heart is cheering (15:13). But those who find joy in asinine irreverences lack spiritual reality (15:21). Those who rejoice in the good, however, are assured their lives will not terminate in hades (15:24). God, who casts down the house of the proud (15:25) and is far from the wicked (15:29), hears the prayers of his saints and gives honor to those who are humble (15:33). Such discipline from God, which some despise (15:32), constitutes the essence of wisdom leading to eternal life.

Part and parcel of wisdom is to recognize that it is the personal God, the Father, before whom everyone lives and breathes and has their being (Dan 5:23). This divine dimension to human existence and experience compels all thoughtful individuals to bow before their Maker. Wisdom ultimately is found in this posture of dependence and accountability. The Father rules the apt tongue, although a person expresses the thoughts of his or her own heart (16:1, 9). He appraises our worth and quality, although we may have quite a different self-image (16:2). All people are encompassed by his sovereign mastery. Even wicked sinners serve a purpose—to put on display God's justice and wrath (16:4). This is what Paul teaches in Romans 9:

> *So you see, God chooses to show mercy to some, and he chooses to harden the hearts of others so they refuse to listen. . . . When a potter makes jars out of clay, doesn't he have a right to use the same lump of clay to make one jar for decoration and another to throw garbage into? In the same way, even though God has the right to show his anger and his power, he is very patient with those on whom his anger falls, who are destined for destruction. He does this to make the riches of his glory shine even brighter on those to whom he shows mercy, who were prepared in advance for glory. And we are among those whom he selected, both from the Jews and from the Gentiles. (Rom 9:18, 21-24)*

The wise understand this—and conform their lives accordingly by "rolling" their own actions and plans into the waiting arms of the Father, who will anchor them in eternity and guarantee that they will prosper according to his will (16:3). But the wicked he abhors. This is why it is better to suffer the lack of good things now, being confident in the loving care of God, than to experience anything this world has to offer (16:8). Yahweh will, in the end, right all wrongs and reveal his plan; the wicked are destined for destruction and the righteous for glory (15:33). "Humanity participates with God in creating history, but God establishes only what is pure and purges away the dross" (Waltke 2005:12).

◆ 2. The wisdom of the king (16:10-15)

10 The king speaks with divine wisdom;
he must never judge unfairly.

11 The LORD demands accurate scales and balances;
he sets the standards for fairness.

12 A king detests wrongdoing,
for his rule is built on justice.

13 The king is pleased with words from righteous lips;
he loves those who speak honestly.

14 The anger of the king is a deadly threat;
the wise will try to appease it.

15 When the king smiles, there is life;
his favor refreshes like a spring rain.

NOTES

16:10 ***The king speaks with divine wisdom.*** Lit., "divination (*qesem* [TH7081, ZH7877]) is upon the lips of the king." *Qesem* (only here in Proverbs) was taboo in Israel (Deut 18:10; 1 Sam 15:23; 2 Kgs 17:17; Ezek 13:6). However, here it is uniquely positive. The king stands above ordinary citizenry; his knowledge has a divine dimension, and his profundity images God. This equation between Yahweh and his king continues throughout the segment.

16:11 ***The LORD demands accurate scales.*** Lit., "just (*mishpat* [TH4941, ZH5477]) balances"; this Hebrew word is linked to 16:10 (NLT, "judge") and points to 16:8 (NLT, "dishonest" is lit., "no *mishpat*"), the only verse in the previous part that is missing the key word "Yahweh." On the other hand, 16:11 has the key word "Yahweh" instead of "king"! This device reiterates the link between God and his king. (Also, 16:8 is the second-to-last verse in its part, and 16:11 is the second-from-first in its segment.) The "great income" of 16:8 is parallel to the fair dealings God requires.

he sets the standards for fairness. Lit., "The stones of the bag are his doing." "Doing" (*ma'aseh* [TH4639, ZH5126]) is found in 16:3, where one is adjured to "roll away" (as a stone; see 26:27) one's plans to Yahweh. See note on 11:1.

16:12 ***A king detests wrongdoing.*** "Detests" is from *to'abath* [TH8441, ZH9359] (abomination), previously used 11 times in Proverbs. Except for highlighting the perversity of fools in 13:19, *to'abath* always describes Yahweh's attitude of revulsion toward depravity (e.g., 3:32; 8:7; 15:8-9; 16:5). Here, what is abominable to the king is also important for the discerning to understand. See note on 3:32. Delitzsch, writing in the days of very fallible kings, interpreted alternatively that the verse is a warning to kings—those who commit wickedness are an abomination (1874:342).

his rule is built on justice. Lit., "In righteousness is established (*kun* [TH3559, ZH3922]) the throne." Psalm 89:14 speaks of Yahweh similarly: "Righteousness and justice are the foundation (*makon* [TH4349, ZH4806]) of your throne." The king's throne is like God's—built on justice—and in this respect also the king is like God.

16:13 ***The king is pleased.*** "Pleased" (*ratson* [TH7522, ZH8356]) usually refers to Yahweh's attitude, often contrasted with its opposite—what he finds detestable (*to'ebah* [TH8441, ZH9359]); see 11:1, 20; 12:22; 15:8. Reading 16:12-13 together, the king again images God; he is pleased with righteous lips and abominates wickedness.

16:14 ***The anger of the king is a deadly threat.*** Precisely, "The wrath of the king is like messengers of death." In Ugaritic myth, the great gods such as Baal or Mot (Death) had messengers. Here the king is like Death incarnate to whomever his wrath is directed (see McKane 1970:488).

the wise will try to appease it. Lit, "The wise man will cover it." "Cover" (*kapar* [TH3722, ZH4105]) appears elsewhere in Proverbs only in 16:6, glossed "atonement" for sin before Yahweh. As the wise atone for offenses before God, so the king's wrath must be "covered."

16:15 ***When the king smiles, there is life.*** Lit., "In the light of the face of the king is life." This is antithetical to the previous verse treating his wrath. The second line continues the thought: "His favor refreshes like a spring rain." Equating light and cloud with an imminent presence (the "face") draws upon divine imagery (Pss 18:8-15; 68:1-10; 104:1-4). The king has the power of life and death—fear him as you do God!

COMMENTARY

Every verse in this segment except 16:11 has the key word *melek* [TH4428, ZH4889] (king), ending the composition on a climactic note. It is not only God with whom one has to reckon but also the wise and powerful king. The prudent understand the connection between ultimate and derivative authority and respect both.

Commentators struggle to reconcile this segment with reality. No king is infallible or above corruption. Yet the assertions made here concerning the attitude of the wise toward the living king should not be mitigated due to the jaded reality-checks of history and experience. Wisdom is not learned through observation! It is best to allow Proverbs to have its say and meditate upon its implications, perhaps with David, Solomon, and Hezekiah as food for thought. A proverb invites further discussion on a matter; "The proverb is a catalyst to reflection" (Ryken and Longman 1993:277). For example, it should come as no surprise that only in the King of kings are these verses fully realized.

But God is not the only personage with the power of life and death. The king is like God, and while in the king's presence one must behave as one would before Yahweh. The king's frown is like divine messengers of death; his smile gives life (16:14-15). In fact, his face is as light and cloud, reminding one of God, who comes in cloud and great glory. "But even as he spoke, a bright cloud overshadowed them, and a voice from the cloud said, 'This is my dearly loved Son, who brings me great joy. Listen to him.' The disciples were terrified and fell face down on the ground" (Matt 17:5-6). The king of Israel is God's adopted son (2 Sam 7:14); to be in his presence is like being in the presence of the God who gives life or death. The distinction between the king and God is sometimes blurred in the Old Testament. Psalm 45 has to delineate which "god" is being mentioned (Ps 45:7), because the king is assigned divine prerogatives (Ps 45:6, 17). Hebrews 1:8-9 cites this in reference to Christ, arguing his deity over even the angels (messengers; see note on 16:14).

In Jesus the equation of God and king finds unequivocal expression—he quite literally will judge the earth and assign each to his place, either to eternal damnation or everlasting blessedness. "In him was life, and the life was the light of men" (John 1:4, RSV). Those who bow before this king—the Son of God—are wise (Ps 2:10-12).

The counsel of Proverbs is designed to shape and mold the character of those who embrace and love wisdom. It is intended to change them internally in the here-and-now, creating a personality pleasing to Yahweh, who loves and adopts such people, guarding their steps, until the body dies and (according to conventional wisdom) the spirit returns to God, who gave it (Eccl 3:21). "Fear of the LORD is a life-giving fountain; it offers escape from the snares of death" (14:27).

◆ E. The Way of Wisdom and the Way of Death (16:16–19:12)

1. The path of wisdom (16:16–17:6)

16 How much better to get wisdom
than gold,
and good judgment than silver!

17 The path of the virtuous leads away
from evil;
whoever follows that path is safe.

18 Pride goes before destruction,
and haughtiness before a fall.

19 Better to live humbly with the poor
than to share plunder with the
proud.

20 Those who listen to instruction will
prosper;
those who trust the LORD will be
joyful.

21 The wise are known for their
understanding,
and pleasant words are persuasive.

22 Discretion is a life-giving fountain to
those who possess it,
but discipline is wasted on fools.

23 From a wise mind comes wise speech;
the words of the wise are
persuasive.

24 Kind words are like honey—
sweet to the soul and healthy for
the body.

25 There is a path before each person
that seems right,
but it ends in death.

26 It is good for workers to have an
appetite;
an empty stomach drives them on.

27 Scoundrels create trouble;
their words are a destructive blaze.

28 A troublemaker plants seeds of strife;
gossip separates the best of
friends.

29 Violent people mislead their
companions,
leading them down a harmful path.

30 With narrowed eyes, people plot evil;
with a smirk, they plan their
mischief.

31 Gray hair is a crown of glory;
it is gained by living a godly life.

32 Better to be patient than powerful;
better to have self-control than
to conquer a city.

33 We may throw the dice,*
but the LORD determines how they
fall.

CHAPTER 17

1 Better a dry crust eaten in peace
than a house filled with
feasting—and conflict.

2 A wise servant will rule over the
master's disgraceful son
and will share the inheritance of
the master's children.

[3]Fire tests the purity of silver and gold,
but the LORD tests the heart.

[4]Wrongdoers eagerly listen to gossip;
liars pay close attention to slander.

[5]Those who mock the poor insult their
Maker;
those who rejoice at the misfortune
of others will be punished.

[6]Grandchildren are the crowning glory
of the aged;
parents* are the pride of their
children.

16:33 Hebrew *We may cast lots.* 17:6 Hebrew *fathers.*

NOTES

16:16 *How much better to get wisdom than gold . . . silver.* The language of the Hebrew is unexpected, reading "To acquire wisdom—how much better than gold!" BHS suggests deleting *mah* [TH4100, ZH4537] (how much), noting the ancient versions and possible dittography in the word chain *khokmah mah* [TH2451, ZH2683]. However, at the opening verse of a new composition, the reader may expect an appeal designed to grab the attention (which may also explain the unusual form of the initial word); this recalls language from 3:14; 8:10, 19, which compare wisdom and knowledge to silver and gold. "Get" or "acquire" is the word used of Yahweh's possession of wisdom from eternity (8:22). Wisdom has surpassing value and should be cherished and pursued.

16:17 *The path of the virtuous.* The image of the path begins the new composition (16:16–19:12). The first and last words in the verse are both glossed "path" but are different in Hebrew, the latter being the common word *derek* [TH1870, ZH2006] and the former, used only here in Proverbs, being *mesillah* [TH4546, ZH5019], often rendered "highway."

whoever follows that path is safe. Lit., "He who keeps his soul is he who watches his path." The metaphor of the path is mixed with that of standing guard. "Life is conceived dynamically; it is a journey along a road and to lose one's way is to lose one's life" (McKane 1970:501). This proverb is the exact center of the book of Proverbs by the reckoning of the Masoretes.

16:18 *haughtiness.* Precisely, "haughtiness of spirit." The use of *ruakh* [TH7307, ZH8120] (spirit) ties this verse with the next.

16:19 *humbly.* Lit., "low of spirit." The words "pride" and "proud" (*ga'on/ge'eh* [TH1347/1343, ZH1454/1450]) also bind 16:18-19 as a pair (see note on 12:9).

with the poor. NLT follows Kethiv; reading with Qere yields, "Better to be low of spirit with the *downtrodden.*"

16:20 *Those who listen to instruction will prosper.* Lit., "He who gives attention to the word finds good." The word of God is in view, as expressed in the book of Proverbs (8:22-36; 22:17-19; 30:5-6).

trust the LORD. The composition reminds the reader in its first stanza that trusting Yahweh is the necessary prerequisite to the blessed life.

16:21 *The wise are known for their understanding.* Lit., "The wise in heart will be called discerning."

and pleasant words are persuasive. Lit., "and sweetness of lips increase learning." This sweetness is associated with honey in 16:24.

16:22 *to those who possess it.* Lit., "its possessor" (*be'alayw* [TH1167/2050.2, ZH1251/2257]); the MT is somewhat difficult, not signifying precisely to whom discretion is a benefit. Perhaps the preposition *le* [TH3807.1, ZH4200] (to) was lost by haplography from the final letter of the preceding word, *sekel* [TH7922, ZH8507]—that is, failing to see two identical letters side by side, a scribe simply wrote one of them.

discipline is wasted on fools. Lit., "discipline of fools is folly." It is foolish to try to instruct such. Alternatively, what fools regard as discipline is in reality more folly. Both interpretations merit cerebration.

16:23 ***From a wise mind comes wise speech.*** Lit., "The heart of the wise teaches his mouth." The first line has verbal connections with the first lines of the previous two verses. The sage's apt skill in speech grows and becomes ever finer and more gracious. This is not an accident, for the prudent purposefully train themselves to express their wisdom with clarity and persuasion.

the words of the wise are persuasive. Lit., "to his lips he increases learning." See 16:21 for an almost identical wording, binding these verses together.

16:24 ***Kind words are like honey.*** Lit., "A honeycomb of honey are words of beauty."

sweet. Related to the word in 16:21 (NLT, "pleasant"), binding this verse to the stanza.

body. Lit., "bones." See note on 3:8.

16:25 ***There is a path.*** Note the image of the path. This verse is identical with 14:12 (see note there). This path, unlike that of 16:17, only *seems* upright. It is actually the path of death. The first comment in this stanza on the various conditions of people regards our capacity for self-deception. This is one reason why one must trust in Yahweh to be secure.

16:26 ***an empty stomach drives them on.*** Between noting the camouflaged path of death and the individuals who walk it, the stanza pauses to highlight a simple alternative—working for a living! Those who busy themselves toiling at evil and driven by greed are on the path addressed here; far better to be a laborer driven by necessity than trying to weasel shortcuts.

16:27 ***Scoundrels create trouble.*** Lit., "The man of *beliya'al* digs evil." "Digs" (from *karah* [TH3738, ZH4125]) appears elsewhere only in 26:27, where it is rendered as "He who digs a pit will fall into it" (RSV). The evil man symbolically digs a malicious pit to harm others; the next line continues the thought with the image of arson.

16:28 ***A troublemaker plants seeds of strife.*** Lit., "The man of perversities spreads strife." See notes on 26:20.

16:29 ***Violent people.*** Lit., "The man of violence." Proverbs 16:27-29 begins each verse with *'ish* [TH376, ZH408] (man), an obvious structuring device designed to make these proverbs be read not independently but as a group.

harmful path. The idea of the path draws the stanza near to a close, echoing its opening: One's companions unsuspectingly walk a bad way—leading to no good, even death (16:25).

16:30 ***evil.*** Lit., "perversities," as in 16:28.

with a smirk, they plan their mischief. Lit., "He pinches his lips completing evil," recalling 16:27 in its use of "evil" and "lips": "An ungodly man diggeth up evil: and in his lips there is as a burning fire" (KJV). "Completing evil" (from *kalah* [TH3615, ZH3983]) indicates mischief had reached its full measure, finishing in evil. This contrasts with the path of righteousness in the next verse.

16:31 ***it is gained by living a godly life.*** Lit., "in the path of righteousness it is found." By invoking the "path," this verse serves as a bridge with the preceding section. There, the path of death stretches beneath the feet of those self-deluded scoundrels who rationalize malice as they stride to complete their own destruction. In contrast to this is the life-preserving righteous path. The crown jewels of those on this path are the gray hairs on their heads—their long life. This resplendent diadem reveals the superiority of wisdom over gold (16:16), since gold and silver cannot add one day to your life (see Matt 6:24-27). The experience of long years is but the foretaste of the endless stretch of time that is the path of life (12:28)—see note on 17:6.

16:32 ***Better to be patient than powerful.*** Precisely, "Better to be long of anger than a mighty man." "Long of anger" means "slow to anger." Yahweh's sovereignty in this segment is sandwiched between two "better-than" proverbs, hinting that these point beyond themselves to a blessedness Yahweh guarantees past the second-best options of this life. See commentary on 12:1-28 and note on 12:9.

better to have self-control. Lit., "[Better is] he who rules his spirit" (*ruakh* [TH7307, ZH8120]). The word "better" is carried over from the first line. This apothegm compacts two "better-than" statements into a single verse. It is good for people to have the ability to rule over their own emotions and spirit. This is in the sphere of human competency; this is their domain. God's domain is treated next.

16:33 ***the LORD determines how they fall.*** Lit., "from Yahweh is its every judgment." Everything that transpires—outside the realm of one's own spirit (*ruakh* [TH7307, ZH8120])—is in God's competent control (21:30-31). We should concentrate on governing our own passions and trust him with the rest.

17:1 ***a house filled with feasting—and conflict.*** Precisely, "a house full of the sacrifices of strife." "Sacrifices" (from *zebakh* [TH2077, ZH2285]) is almost always found in a cultic context. Perhaps the only exception is Ps 51:17, "The sacrifice you desire is a broken spirit." The sacrifices God requires are those people characterized by being "long of anger" (see note on 16:32), having an appropriate spirit before him. A fitting attitude is a better sacrifice than a ram or goat offered with an unsuitable one; to rule the spirit is the sacrifice Yahweh wants. Familial strife undermines the gray head and threatens an inglorious end (Gen 42:38; 44:29-31). See note on 12:9.

17:2 ***disgraceful son.*** The wise servant is in a higher social position, in the end, than the shameful but privileged son. This status includes sharing the inheritance with his "brothers," becoming in effect an adopted son through wisdom. "Inheritance" points to the future perpetuation of the family beyond the physical life of the gray-headed father.

17:3 ***the LORD tests the heart.*** Silver and gold may be inherited, but the true inheritance is wisdom herself (3:35), enjoyed by Yahweh's adopted children (3:12). The heart is tested the way bullions are smelted and purified. The wise in heart are preferred and exalted before the privileged son (17:2). Perhaps the "fire" of testing is the Lord's discipline that his adoptive sons and daughters are warned not to abhor (3:11).

17:4 ***eagerly listen to gossip.*** Liars and evildoers listen to anything and everything except the wisdom of God.

17:5 ***their Maker.*** The segment's penultimate maxim points to the Creator, who identifies with the poor and takes their mistreatment personally.

17:6 ***the crowning glory of the aged.*** The segment closes by explicitly mentioning the crown of the aged—a dimension of life that stretches beyond death into the far future, symbolic of the spiritual reality of immortality.

parents are the pride of their children. Lit., "The splendor of sons are their fathers." The word "splendor" (*tip'ereth* [TH8597, ZH9514]), seen as modifying the crown in 16:31, is used to describe Aaron's resplendent robes (Exod 28:2, 40), which image the glory of God in original creation (Kline 1986:43). See commentary.

COMMENTARY

This composition begins at the physical center of the book of Proverbs, which the Masorah indicates as 16:17 but in most English versions is 16:18: "The path of the virtuous leads away from evil / whoever follows that path is safe." This is Proverbs in a nutshell. This portion can be divided into two parts. The first part (16:16-30) discusses such topics as the path of life, wisdom, people, and speech—a fitting beginning to a new movement. The next segment (16:31–17:6), enclosed by the image of the crown, treats what is splendid relating to parents and children.

The composition begins with references to the overarching value of wisdom (the path of life, the blessing that comes from trusting Yahweh) beyond material wealth (16:16-17). Key to the whole wisdom enterprise is a humble spirit. Pride is so inimical to the path of wisdom that it is better to be poor—even oppressed—than haughty (16:18-19). This can be said with certainty because Yahweh guarantees the outcome of a person's life.

The wise in heart speak pleasant words, bringing healing to the body and sweetening the soul like honey; they are a veritable fountain of life. This is not an accident, for the wise actively seek to improve their expression and conceptualization so as to live better and to help others discover the path of life (16:20-24).

In the next section (16:25-30), we see different sorts of people: the *beliya'al,* the perverse, the violent. These have at least one characteristic in common—each is self-deceived (16:25). All of them are sure and certain of their own path, of their own rightness and legitimacy; but all are walking the path leading to death (16:25). The human capacity for delusional thinking is one reason why God must be trusted before one's own wisdom. In the words of Jeremiah 17:9-10, "The human heart is the most deceitful of all things, and desperately wicked. Who really knows how bad it is? But I, the LORD, search all hearts and examine secret motives. I give all people their due rewards, according to what their actions deserve."

One must therefore attend to ruling one's own attitudes, passions, and spirit (16:32). This is a more important conquest than taking a city or skill at warfare. A patient person with a broken spirit (Ps 51:17) is the kind of person who can approach God. Religious sacrifices and cultic offerings made by unworthy people in an environment of foolish pride and conflict are poor substitutes (see note on 17:1). Samuel condemned Saul with these words:

> *What is more pleasing to the LORD: your burnt offerings and sacrifices or your obedience to his voice? Listen! Obedience is better than sacrifice, and submission is better than offering the fat of rams. Rebellion is as sinful as witchcraft, and stubbornness as bad as worshiping idols. So because you have rejected the command of the LORD, he has rejected you as king. (1 Sam 15:22-23)*

Over all else, God is absolutely sovereign, even in rendering decisions by casting lots (16:33). Therefore, tend to your personality, your outlook on life, and ensure it is one of trust and obedience; then trust God your Father with the rest. This results in a crown of glory—experienced now as a long life untarnished by diminished powers and unbowed by debilitating diseases of old age. McKane (1970:501) remarks on how old age is treated as a sign of glory, not decrepitation:

It is remarkable that old age is viewed so exclusively in its aspect of fulfillment—it is a crown of glory—and that nothing of the sadness and despair of old age is allowed to emerge, the failing of strength and the withering away of powers. The estimate reflects life in a society where the status of greybeards was assured, where "knowledge" was a conservative concept, where wisdom was correlated with a long experience of life and the elders had weight in counsel and power in affairs.

The unsullied and glorious life of senior citizens spoken of here—including those of extreme old age—is a *symbolic* crown pointing beyond themselves to a perfect life with God (16:31). A further symbol of this perpetual blessedness that stretches beyond the grave is another crown of the aged—their children and grandchildren, stretching from generation to generation (17:6).

A worthy wife is also such a symbolic crown (12:4), as is wealth (14:24), but wisdom is one's true crown (4:9), leading to immortality (12:28). The "glory" (*tip'ereth* [TH8597, ZH9514]) of sons are their fathers (17:6). Children reflect the glory of their Maker by making themselves a part of an ongoing family history of wisdom, as in chapter 4,

My children, listen when your father corrects you.
  Pay attention and learn good judgment,
for I am giving you good guidance.
  Don't turn away from my instructions.
For I, too, was once my father's son,
  tenderly loved as my mother's only child.

My father taught me,
"Take my words to heart.
  Follow my commands, and you will live.
Get wisdom; develop good judgment.
  Don't forget my words or turn away from them." (4:1-5)

The glory of a person is in how they join the path of wisdom that stretches back in time to Creation and in how in their own time they propagate the tradition to generations to come. This is a death-transcending dimension that includes the life hereafter promised to the wise. Jesus, who shared the divine glory with his Father from eternity (John 17:5) and who in John's vision is the personification of glory (Rev 1:12-16), now enjoys in full measure all of the promises made to the wise. This glory is accessible to all who embrace a life of wisdom, not shunning the discipline of God, but submitting to him as Father (3:11-12).

◆ 2. The path of the fool (17:7–18:7)

7 Eloquent words are not fitting for a fool;
even less are lies fitting for a ruler.

8 A bribe is like a lucky charm;
whoever gives one will prosper!

9 Love prospers when a fault is forgiven,
but dwelling on it separates close friends.

10 A single rebuke does more for a person of understanding

than a hundred lashes on the back
of a fool.

11 Evil people are eager for rebellion,
but they will be severely punished.

12 It is safer to meet a bear robbed of her
cubs
than to confront a fool caught in
foolishness.

13 If you repay good with evil,
evil will never leave your house.

14 Starting a quarrel is like opening a
floodgate,
so stop before a dispute breaks out.

15 Acquitting the guilty and condemning
the innocent—
both are detestable to the LORD.

16 It is senseless to pay tuition to
educate a fool,
since he has no heart for learning.

17 A friend is always loyal,
and a brother is born to help in time
of need.

18 It's poor judgment to guarantee
another person's debt
or put up security for a friend.

19 Anyone who loves to quarrel loves sin;
anyone who trusts in high walls
invites disaster.

20 The crooked heart will not prosper;
the lying tongue tumbles into
trouble.

21 It is painful to be the parent of a fool;
there is no joy for the father of
a rebel.

22 A cheerful heart is good medicine,
but a broken spirit saps a person's
strength.

23 The wicked take secret bribes
to pervert the course of justice.

24 Sensible people keep their eyes glued
on wisdom,
but a fool's eyes wander to the ends
of the earth.

25 Foolish children* bring grief to their
father
and bitterness to the one who gave
them birth.

26 It is wrong to punish the godly for
being good
or to flog leaders for being honest.

27 A truly wise person uses few words;
a person with understanding is
even-tempered.

28 Even fools are thought wise when they
keep silent;
with their mouths shut, they seem
intelligent.

CHAPTER 18

1 Unfriendly people care only about
themselves;
they lash out at common sense.

2 Fools have no interest in
understanding;
they only want to air their own
opinions.

3 Doing wrong leads to disgrace,
and scandalous behavior brings
contempt.

4 Wise words are like deep waters;
wisdom flows from the wise like a
bubbling brook.

5 It is not right to acquit the guilty
or deny justice to the innocent.

6 Fools' words get them into constant
quarrels;
they are asking for a beating.

7 The mouths of fools are their ruin;
they trap themselves with their lips.

17:25 Hebrew *A foolish son.*

NOTES

17:7 ***not fitting.*** "Fitting" comes from Heb. *na'weh* [TH5000, ZH5534], also glossed "beautiful" (Song 1:5) and "lovely" (Song 2:14). Here, it denotes an appropriate concurrence of elements. The wise know the fittingness of things. This aspect of sagacity also begins the section 26:1-12, where the *un*suitable behavior of fools is treated.

fool. The "lip of excellence" is inapplicable to a fool (*nabal* [TH5036A, ZH5572], used elsewhere in Proverbs at 17:21 and 30:22). The *nabal* says in his heart that there is no God (Ps 14:1; see also 1 Sam 25:25). Similarly, the "lip of falsehood" is incongruous for rulers.

17:8 ***A bribe is like a lucky charm.*** Lit., "A stone of favor is a bribe in the eyes of its owner." The bribe altogether fails in 6:35. The important consideration is in whose eyes the bribe magically performs. The suborner is deceived as surely as those walking the fatal path that seems right (16:25). "People may be pure *in their own eyes,* but the LORD examines their motives" (16:2, my italics). What is pleasing in the eyes of Yahweh is fitting and right; what is evil "in his eyes" (Hebrew of 24:18) is *not* favored (see note on 17:23).

17:9 ***Love prospers when a fault is forgiven.*** Lit., "He who covers a fault (*pesha'* [TH6588, ZH7322]) seeks love" (*'ahabah* [TH160, ZH173], from *'ahab* [TH157, ZH170]). This is mirrored in the stanza's closing proverb, 17:19, lit., "He who loves (*'ahab*) transgression (*pesha'*) loves strife; / He who raises his door seeks destruction." The contrast is between "covering" an offense and "loving" it, between "seeking" love and "seeking" disaster.

17:11 ***are eager for.*** Lit., "seeks" (*baqash* [TH1245, ZH1335]), connecting with 17:9 and 17:19.

17:12 ***It is safer to meet.*** Lit., "For a man to meet." Loewenstamm (1987:222) emends *be'ish* [TH871.2/376, ZH928/408] (for a man) to *beye'ushah* [TH2976, ZH3286], yielding "To meet a bereaved bear *in her desperation.*" However, if the preposition *be* [TH871.2, ZH928] marks the object of the infinitive (as it does with *'akhaz* [TH270, ZH296] in Job 38:13; Eccl 2:3), the line makes sense as it is: "[Better for] a bereaved bear to meet a man than . . ." (cf. Waltke and O'Connor 1990:594). This verse highlights the violent irrationality of fools—they are dangerous, and it is best to keep one's distance.

17:13 ***evil.*** The use of "evil" ties this verse together with 17:11.

17:14 ***stop before a dispute breaks out.*** Lit., "So—before breaks-out the dispute, forsake!" Driver gratuitously conjectures from an Arabic cognate *natush,* "before the dispute breaks out and dashes [you] to the ground" (1951:182).

17:15 ***detestable to the LORD.*** Yahweh hates perpetrators of injustice. The judicious comments found here have a divine dimension to them; it is foolish to forget this and imagine wisdom is possible apart from the fear of the Lord (see next verse).

17:16 ***It is senseless to pay tuition to educate a fool.*** Precisely, "Why is there money in the hand of a fool to acquire wisdom?" The fool has no capacity for knowledge.

17:17 ***a brother is born to help in time of need.*** The Hebrew is more ambiguous: "a brother is born (*yalad* [TH3205, ZH3528]) for adversity." The NLT reads as a synonymous proverb, but it could also be antithetic, highlighting familial strife. In both occurrences of *yalad* in the next stanza (17:21, 25), the offspring is a fool who torments the family. The reader is left to ponder both permutations.

17:18 ***It's poor judgment.*** Lit., "a person lacking heart." As in 17:16, money is tied to lack of heart (i.e., sense)—in such hands lucre serves no good purpose.

17:19 ***anyone who trusts in high walls invites disaster.*** Lit., "He who raises his door seeks destruction." This proverb is antithetical to 17:9.

17:20 ***will not prosper.*** Lit., "will not find good."

17:21 ***the parent of a fool.*** There is no incrimination of the parent here. It is the fool who torments his family; blame lies at the feet of the one lacking sense.

17:22 *a broken spirit saps a person's strength.* Lit., "A crushed spirit makes dry the bone" (*gerem* [TH1634, ZH1752]). See note on 3:8, which treats the synonym *'etsem* [TH6106, ZH6795].

17:23 *The wicked take secret bribes to pervert the course of justice.* This aphorism enjoys pride of place, being placed at the center of the stanza's chiastic structure. Here the wicked utilize the "lucky charm" of 17:8. Montgomery finds that no use of the bribe (*shokhad* [TH7810, ZH8816]) in the OT is positive: "It is condemned because it perverts justice and shows partiality, is akin to robbery, is used by the rich to further the exploitation of the poor, and puts those who practice it under God's judgment" (2000:137); contra Whybray, who claims that here and in 17:8 "opposite views are expressed about the morality of giving and taking bribes" (1994a:261). See note on 17:8.

17:24 *Sensible people keep their eyes glued on wisdom.* Lit., "Wisdom is in the presence of the understanding man." A fool goes everywhere and anywhere except to the one with true wisdom.

17:25 *Foolish children.* See note on 17:21.

17:26 *It is wrong to punish the godly.* The stanza ends with an axiom that dovetails with 17:23 (its center), highlighting the perversion of justice, perhaps the catalyst being a bribe.

17:27 *A truly wise person uses few words.* Precisely, "He who withholds words knows knowledge."

even-tempered. Kethiv reads, "cold of spirit"; Qere, "valued of spirit."

17:28 *when they keep silent.* This follows the thought of the previous verse.

intelligent. From the same root as "understanding" in 17:27. Whybray points out that the fool "is incapable of keeping quiet" (1994a:263)!

18:1 *Unfriendly people care only about themselves.* Lit., "He who separates himself seeks his own desire." The second line logically follows the first—self-absorbed people are disconnected from the community and inappropriately "break out" against what others see as obvious facts of life. The recluse is hopelessly out of touch and cannot respond considerately. BHS unnecessarily emends *letha'awah* [TH3807.1/8378, ZH4200/9294] (to desire) to *letho'anah* [TH3807.1/8385, ZH4200/9301] (pretext).

18:2 *understanding.* This is a verbal link with 17:27. The fool cannot be silent—neither can he speak perceptively.

18:4 *Wise words are like deep waters.* Lit., "Deep waters are the words of the mouth of a man."

wisdom flows from the wise like a bubbling brook. Lit., "a bubbling brook, a fountain of wisdom."

18:5 *to acquit the guilty.* Lit., "to lift the face of the wicked."

18:6 *Fools' words . . . they are asking for a beating.* Precisely, "The lips of a fool . . . and his mouth calls for beatings" (see next note).

18:7 *The mouths of fools . . . with their lips.* Lit., "The mouth of a fool . . . and his lips." Clearly 18:6-7 are linked, and they end the section with two verbally similar proverbs underscoring the fool's foul mouth.

COMMENTARY

The fool is mentioned nine times in twenty-nine proverbs, averaging about once every three verses. "Fool" is a key word in this section, although a looser and less definitive device than those seen elsewhere (e.g., 26:1-12). The section may be parsed into three stanzas (each with three "fool" proverbs) following an opening couplet (17:7-8): the first stanza bound by the triple inclusion of "love," "seeking," and "transgression" (17:9-19); the next a complex pattern bound with "not good" and the verb "begetting/ bearing" (17:20-26); and finally, a concluding stanza treating speech (17:27–18:7). The penultimate section (17:20-26) has an interesting chiastic structure:

A. not finding good (*tob*) (17:20)
  B[1]. the parents of a fool (17:21)
    B[2]. 17:22 linked with 17:21 by "joy/cheerful"
      C. bribes pervert justice (17:23)
    B[1]. 17:24 linked with 17:25 by "fool"
  B[2]. the parents of a fool (17:25)
A. what is not (*lo'* [TH3808, ZH4202]) good (*tob* [TH2896, ZH3202]) (17:26)

The first section begins with a comment about what is not fitting for a fool (17:7). Knowing what is fitting and appropriate on different occasions is part and parcel of wisdom. A bribe is not fitting any more than lies are for a ruler or eloquent words for a fool (17:7-8). If one is trusting in a bribe, one is practicing folly even though the bribe might seem to bring success for a while. Montgomery explains how the bribe, even though it worked, is condemned by God:

> *As far as the giver of the bribe is concerned, he has been successful; his actions have achieved their purpose. He imagines that he has acted cleverly, that he is prosperous; but in reality, he is only wise in his own eyes. This is surely not true wisdom. On the contrary, the careful reader will immediately pick up on the implicit condemnation. . . . In context, the reader is meant to understand the futility of the actions of the self-deluded who imagine that everything can be bought. (2000:139)*

Unfortunately, the fool cannot learn this or any feature of sagacity, though the lesson is driven in a hundred times (17:10). He has no capacity for wisdom (17:16). He torments his parents (17:21, 25). He goes everywhere and anywhere—his "eyes wander to the ends of the earth"—but he does not seek the wise (17:24). Although even a fool might be considered wise if he refrained from speaking, he cannot do so and at every opportunity continues to gush out his foul and antisocial opinions (17:28–18:7).

◆ 3. The strength of wisdom (18:8–19:12)

8 Rumors are dainty morsels
  that sink deep into one's heart.

9 A lazy person is as bad as
  someone who destroys things.

10 The name of the LORD is a strong
    fortress;
  the godly run to him and
    are safe.

11 The rich think of their wealth as
    a strong defense;
  they imagine it to be a high wall
    of safety.

12 Haughtiness goes before destruction;
  humility precedes honor.

13 Spouting off before listening to the
    facts
  is both shameful and foolish.

14 The human spirit can endure a sick
    body,
  but who can bear a crushed spirit?

[15] Intelligent people are always ready
to learn.
Their ears are open for knowledge.

[16] Giving a gift can open doors;
it gives access to important people!

[17] The first to speak in court sounds right—
until the cross-examination begins.

[18] Flipping a coin* can end arguments;
it settles disputes between powerful
opponents.

[19] An offended friend is harder to win
back than a fortified city.
Arguments separate friends like
a gate locked with bars.

[20] Wise words satisfy like a good meal;
the right words bring satisfaction.

[21] The tongue can bring death or life;
those who love to talk will reap the
consequences.

[22] The man who finds a wife finds
a treasure,
and he receives favor from the LORD.

[23] The poor plead for mercy;
the rich answer with insults.

[24] There are "friends" who destroy each
other,
but a real friend sticks closer than
a brother.

CHAPTER 19

[1] Better to be poor and honest
than to be dishonest and a fool.

[2] Enthusiasm without knowledge is
no good;
haste makes mistakes.

[3] People ruin their lives by their own
foolishness
and then are angry at the LORD.

[4] Wealth makes many "friends";
poverty drives them all away.

[5] A false witness will not go
unpunished,
nor will a liar escape.

[6] Many seek favors from a ruler;
everyone is the friend of a person
who gives gifts!

[7] The relatives of the poor despise them;
how much more will their friends
avoid them!
Though the poor plead with them,
their friends are gone.

[8] To acquire wisdom is to love oneself;
people who cherish understanding
will prosper.

[9] A false witness will not go unpunished,
and a liar will be destroyed.

[10] It isn't right for a fool to live in luxury
or for a slave to rule over princes!

[11] Sensible people control their temper;
they earn respect by overlooking
wrongs.

[12] The king's anger is like a lion's roar,
but his favor is like dew on the
grass.

18:18 Hebrew *Casting lots.*

NOTES

18:8 ***Rumors.*** Lit., "The words of a gossip" (*nirgan* [TH5372, ZH8087], from *ragan* [TH7279, ZH8087]). Mutterers ruin friendships (16:28) and stoke the fires of quarrel (26:20). This verse is repeated verbatim in 26:22—a poem on the topic of "malefic words" (see notes on 26:20).

one's heart. Lit., "the chambers of the belly." Like delicious morsels, gossip and innuendo are eagerly ravened. Compare with 18:20, where one's stomach is made full by what one says.

18:9 ***is as bad as.*** Precisely, "is brother to." The "brother" is again at issue in the last proverb of both this stanza (18:19) and the next (18:24).

18:10 ***The name of the LORD.*** The word "name" (*shem* [TH8034, ZH9005]) occurs seven times in Proverbs, but this is the only occurrence where it is explicitly tied with "Yahweh." Twice it is used in a negative statement about the wicked (10:7; 21:24) and once about a good reputation (22:1)—interestingly, again compared with wealth. It refers to God in 30:4 as a question—What is his name and what is the name of his son? Finally, it is again set over against riches (30:8-9), which if enjoyed too much could cause even the sage to "insult God's holy name."

strong fortress. Lit., "tower of strength."

are safe. From *sagab* [TH7682, ZH8435], which means "set aloft, be on high." The name of Yahweh is a strong tower to which the righteous flee for safety. This is contrasted in the next verse.

18:11 ***strong defense.*** Lit., "city of strength." The strong city is again in view in 18:19.

they imagine it to be a high wall of safety. See 10:15, which shares the same first line.

18:12 ***Haughtiness goes before destruction; humility precedes honor.*** Lit., "Before a downfall, a man's heart is exalted / but before glory humility." The word "exalted" is connected thematically with the "high" wall of 18:11. Note the two ways of self-exaltation and self-depreciation. A self-deprecating tax collector and a self-exalting Pharisee stood before God in Jesus' parable, and only one left justified (Luke 18:10-14).

18:13 ***Spouting off before listening to the facts.*** Lit., "One who returns a word before he hears." A counselor is "genuinely intent to listen to the situation before speaking" (Schwab 1995:16). The prudent know how to listen; fools simply talk. Knowing when to speak is as important as knowing what to say. This relates to 18:12, where glory is promised to those who refrain from exalting their own hearts.

18:14 ***crushed spirit.*** The "crushed spirit" is another "counseling" issue—counselors must know how to listen (18:13) and not simply spout off trite, canned, and facile solutions. See commentary on the composition 13:1–14:27.

18:15 ***learn . . . knowledge.*** Both come from the same word in Hebrew: "The heart of the discerning acquires *knowledge.* / The ear of the wise seeks *knowledge.*" Counselors should not approach crushed spirits (18:14) with answers at the ready—they should seek knowledge, acquire understanding, listen (18:13), and humble their hearts (18:12) before speaking words of comfort (18:13).

18:16 ***Giving a gift can open doors.*** Lit., "A man's gift (*mattan* [TH4976, ZH5508]) makes room for him." See note on 17:8. Montgomery calls the gift here a "transactional bribe" designed to "facilitate a process that is deemed both just and within the law" (2000:140). He distinguishes this from "variance bribes" calculated to pervert justice. This view is contra Waltke, who says, "These transactional gifts secure preferential treatment and . . . adversely affect the administration of justice and the best interests of the community. They inherently favor the rich over the poor and subvert the trust that should accompany public office" (2005:82). Bribes are akin to false weights or displacing boundary markers—all tamper with the cornerstones of civilization for one's own advantage. And yet it is worth pondering why the bribe is couched in such positive-sounding terms. Perhaps the reader is meant to struggle here. Gifts are so appealing!

18:17 ***until the cross-examination begins.*** Lit., "comes in his neighbor and searches him." This is the first of three proverbs treating disputes—again highlighting the difficulty of discerning the spoken word. One must listen before speaking, restrain oneself, seek knowledge, and hear both sides of the story before deciding a case; one must also beware the bribe.

18:18 ***arguments.*** Heb., *midyanim* [TH4079/4066, ZH4517/4506], found again in the next verse and used a total of 10 times in the OT, all in Proverbs. Usually it refers to the contentious and obstinate wife (19:13; 21:9, 19; 25:24; 27:15); once to the alcoholic (23:29).

18:19 ***An offended friend is harder to win back than a fortified city.*** Lit., "An offended brother is a strong city"—recalling the strong city from 18:11. "Harder to win back than" is an interpolation. The text may not envision winning back the brother; see 17:17 and 18:24. The "strong" city ends the stanza with one of the key words of the section.

Arguments separate friends like a gate locked with bars. Precisely, "and arguments like a bar of a castle." "Separate friends" is an interpolation. Like castle gates, arguments are strong and difficult to breach.

18:20 ***Wise words satisfy like a good meal.*** Lit., "From the fruit of the mouth of a man his belly will be satisfied." This opens like the previous stanza (18:8), where words entered the belly's chambers. Here, true satisfaction comes by knowing when and how and what to speak.

18:21 ***The tongue can bring death or life.*** Lit., "Death and life are in the hand of the tongue." At issue in the fruit of a person's mouth (18:20) is life and death—not mere advancement or self-promotion. When the stakes are this high, the reader might expect Yahweh to be acknowledged, and so he is in the following verse.

those who love to talk will reap the consequences. Lit., "Her lovers will eat her fruit." The "fruit" links with 18:20, which denotes speech that satisfies the belly. Camp identifies "Lady Tongue" as a metaphor analogous to Lady Wisdom. "Woman Language offers two fruits, death and life, and those who become her lovers can expect to taste of both" (1987b:52)—depending on whether the speech a person loves is perverted or true. The image transitions in the next verse to a flesh-and-blood woman—the beneficent wife who embodies the life in the hand of Lady Language.

18:22 ***favor from the LORD.*** The center of this stanza, between the delimited inclusion of the "man" (*'ish* [TH376, ZH408]) of 18:20 and 24, is the good woman *'ishah* [TH802, ZH851], the high point of Yahweh's blessings. Those eating the fruit of wisdom will reap the benefit of a life beatified with the auspicious wife.

18:23 ***the rich answer with insults.*** Lit., "The rich answer with hard things" (*'az* [TH5794, ZH6434]). This stanza mirrors the previous one, beginning with words that penetrate into the belly, discussion of the spiritually vacuous rich, and ending with comments on the brother and adverse situation (in the next verse). See note on 10:15. The rich trust in their wealth as a strong (*'oz* [TH5797, ZH6437]) city—and, in this verse, they become like what they trust, speaking *'azzoth* to the disadvantaged.

18:24 ***There are "friends" who destroy each other.*** Precisely, "A man of friends can be broken in pieces."

but a real friend sticks closer than a brother. Lit., "There is one who loves that clings more than a brother" (cf. 18:19).

19:1 ***fool.*** BHS needlessly emends *kesil* [TH3684, ZH4067] (fool) to *'ashir* [TH6223A, ZH6938] (rich) for better parallelism.

19:2 ***is no good.*** A verbal link with 19:1 is formed through the use of *tob* [TH2896, ZH3202]; the verse also begins with the connecting particle *gam* [TH1571, ZH1685] (also), another indicator of their association.

makes mistakes. Lit., "sins." As the English proverb puts it, "Fools rush in where angels fear to tread."

19:3 ***People ruin their lives by their own foolishness.*** Lit., "A man's folly perverts his way." The path of a person is at issue (see 19:2).

and then are angry at the LORD. "Angry" from *za'ap* [TH2196, ZH2406] (vex, rage), a rare root found twice in Proverbs—here and to close the inclusion in 19:12. There, it is the king who is angry. These two linked verses proverbially associate Yahweh and the king, creating a boundary for the segment.

19:4 ***poverty drives them all away.*** Lit., "a poor man is separated from his friends." "Friends" (*rea'* [TH7453, ZH8276]) appears in both cola. This thesis resumes in 19:6-7.

19:5 ***will not go unpunished.*** Lit., "will not be clean, be free." He will not be found innocent (see 6:29). This line is repeated exactly in 19:9.

nor will a liar escape. Except for these last two words (*lo' yimmalet* [TH3808/4422, ZH4202/4880]), the verse is repeated exactly in 19:9. There, the final word is *yo'bed* [TH6, ZH6] (will be destroyed).

19:6 ***the friend.*** This resumes the thought from the first line of 19:4, "Wealth makes many 'friends';" its second line is reflected in the next verse.

19:7 ***The relatives of the poor despise them.*** Lit., "All the brothers of the needy hate him."

their friends. This is the fourth use of *rea'* [TH7453, ZH8276] in this segment, here the cognate form *merea'* [TH4828, ZH5335]. One theme here is phony friends, which NLT puts in quotes (19:4). Because one's associates are unreliable, true security is found only in wisdom and knowledge, the subject of the following verse. This is the second of three lines that form a tricolon. The following is a very wooden gloss of the verse that preserves the Hebrew word order. Where one Hebrew word is glossed by multiple English words, the English words are joined by hyphens:

	All	the-brothers-of-the-needy	hate-him	
How	much-more	his-friends	are distant	from-him
He-pursues		with-words	to-him-are-they	

are gone. Qere reads, "to him are they," presumably referring to "his words" (a phrase that is set parallel to his friends and brothers). Qere would imply that his words are his only possession left. Kethiv reads, "are not they," meaning the friends are gone. Garrett considers the third line "unintelligible" and says that it "ought to be left untranslated" (1993:171).

19:8 ***To acquire wisdom is to love oneself.*** Precisely, "He who gets a heart loves his soul."

will prosper. Lit., "will find good." In 19:7, the needy "pursues with words" to no avail. But one who pursues knowledge will find all that is good.

19:9 ***will be destroyed.*** This is almost identical with 19:5 (see note).

19:10 ***It isn't right.*** Lit., "it is not fitting" (see note on 17:7).

19:11 ***control their temper.*** Lit., "prolongs his anger"—that is, his anger rises slowly. Waltke alternatively renders "relaxes his face" (2005:89). The motif of anger has resumed from the beginning of the segment (19:3).

they earn respect by overlooking wrongs. Lit., "and splendor is to pass over an offense." See note on 17:6 concerning *tip'ereth* [TH8597, ZH9514]. There is wisdom in not allowing an insult to inflame one's ire. Mastering this virtue is glorious.

19:12 ***The king's anger.*** See note on 19:3. The segment ends with the closing of the inclusion. This maxim captures the opposite truth from 19:11—it is not fitting for anger to always be restrained; justice sometimes demands it (16:14).

his favor is like dew on the grass. The previous composition also ended with a reference to the king and life-giving precipitation (16:15).

COMMENTARY

The first section (18:8–19:2) of this portion is loosely glued together with the key word "strength" and is composed of several stanzas bound with inclusions. The first two begin by noting words that penetrate deep into a person (18:8, 20), and both end with a comment on the brother in negative circumstances (18:19, 24). The second is also framed with "love" (18:21-24). The section ends with a final verse couplet treating what is good (19:1-2). Words having the root *'z* (used in words meaning "rich" or "strength"; on biliteral roots, see GKC §30g) are found four times in this section, near the beginning and the end and once in the middle (18:19), highlighting what is strong and fortified. The strength of the rich is their wealth (18:11); thus, they presume to be "strong" or "harsh" with the weak (18:23). Yahweh alone is the truly reliable fortress (18:10). When the righteous call on the divine name of Yahweh, it is like fleeing to an impregnable tower. The rich trust instead in their riches, which they imagine to be a strong city with fortified walls. This is a delusion—one of the many paths that seem right but end in death (18:10-11).

Words spoken in a fitting manner satisfy (18:20). These words are characterized by a careful search for knowledge (18:15), obtained by listening rather than speaking (18:13) and by hearing both sides (18:17), perhaps gaining insight to comfort the crushed spirit (18:14). There are those who foolishly speak out of turn, seeking to exalt themselves (18:12). This attitude can separate even brothers (18:19). The path of life a person walks, when characterized by folly, is perverted and ruined. Rushing ahead with willful abandon, they sin (19:2; see note). Experiencing ruination does not lead to an examination of their offensive ways and turning from thoughtless misconduct. Instead, they irrationally blame and rage against God (19:3). This rage will fall back on the fool when the king, God's appointed executioner of righteousness, becomes disgusted with such behavior (19:12).

It is worthy to note that there are a number of references in the final segment (19:3-12) to government and law. There are the powerfully rich (19:4, 6), subject to bribes. Perjurers are at issue during trials (19:5, 9). The "ruler" (19:6) and "prince" (19:10) are addressed, as is the king (19:12). Leadership requires truth and a sense of equity and fairness. The uneducated and untrained slave and the ethically malformed fool are unsuited for positions of power over others. Proverbs acknowledges the wise slave favored by kings and destined to rule (14:35; 17:2). But there are those whose servitude is a result of their own folly; these are monsters, often causing social upheaval (11:29; 30:22).

◆ F. Speaking and Doing before Yahweh (19:13–21:1)

[13] A foolish child* is a calamity to
a father;
a quarrelsome wife is as annoying
as constant dripping.

[14] Fathers can give their sons an
inheritance of houses and wealth,
but only the LORD can give an
understanding wife.

[15] Lazy people sleep soundly,
but idleness leaves them hungry.

[16] Keep the commandments and keep
your life;

despising them leads to
death.

17 If you help the poor, you are lending
to the LORD—
and he will repay you!

18 Discipline your children while there
is hope.
Otherwise you will ruin their lives.

19 Hot-tempered people must pay the
penalty.
If you rescue them once, you will
have to do it again.

20 Get all the advice and instruction
you can,
so you will be wise the rest of your
life.

21 You can make many plans,
but the LORD's purpose will prevail.

22 Loyalty makes a person attractive.
It is better to be poor than dishonest.

23 Fear of the LORD leads to life,
bringing security and protection
from harm.

24 Lazy people take food in their hand
but don't even lift it to their mouth.

25 If you punish a mocker, the
simpleminded will learn a lesson;
if you correct the wise, they will be
all the wiser.

26 Children who mistreat their father or
chase away their mother
are an embarrassment and a public
disgrace.

27 If you stop listening to instruction,
my child,
you will turn your back on
knowledge.

28 A corrupt witness makes a mockery
of justice;
the mouth of the wicked gulps
down evil.

29 Punishment is made for mockers,
and the backs of fools are made
to be beaten.

CHAPTER 20

1 Wine produces mockers; alcohol leads
to brawls.
Those led astray by drink cannot
be wise.

2 The king's fury is like a lion's roar;
to rouse his anger is to risk your
life.

3 Avoiding a fight is a mark of honor;
only fools insist on quarreling.

4 Those too lazy to plow in the right
season
will have no food at the harvest.

5 Though good advice lies deep within
the heart,
a person with understanding will
draw it out.

6 Many will say they are loyal friends,
but who can find one who is truly
reliable?

7 The godly walk with integrity;
blessed are their children who
follow them.

8 When a king sits in judgment, he
weighs all the evidence,
distinguishing the bad from the
good.

9 Who can say, "I have cleansed my
heart;
I am pure and free from sin"?

10 False weights and unequal
measures*—
the LORD detests double standards
of every kind.

11 Even children are known by the way
they act,
whether their conduct is pure, and
whether it is right.

12 Ears to hear and eyes to see—
both are gifts from the LORD.

13 If you love sleep, you will end in
poverty.
Keep your eyes open, and there
will be plenty to eat!

[14] The buyer haggles over the price,
saying, "It's worthless,"
then brags about getting a bargain!

[15] Wise words are more valuable
than much gold and many rubies.

[16] Get security from someone who
guarantees a stranger's debt.
Get a deposit if he does it for
foreigners.*

[17] Stolen bread tastes sweet,
but it turns to gravel in the mouth.

[18] Plans succeed through good counsel;
don't go to war without wise advice.

[19] A gossip goes around telling secrets,
so don't hang around with chatterers.

[20] If you insult your father or mother,
your light will be snuffed out in
total darkness.

[21] An inheritance obtained too early
in life
is not a blessing in the end.

[22] Don't say, "I will get even for this
wrong."
Wait for the LORD to handle the
matter.

[23] The LORD detests double standards;
he is not pleased by dishonest
scales.

[24] The LORD directs our steps,
so why try to understand everything
along the way?

[25] Don't trap yourself by making a rash
promise to God
and only later counting the cost.

[26] A wise king scatters the wicked like
wheat,
then runs his threshing wheel over
them.

[27] The LORD's light penetrates the human
spirit,*
exposing every hidden motive.

[28] Unfailing love and faithfulness protect
the king;
his throne is made secure through
love.

[29] The glory of the young is their
strength;
the gray hair of experience is the
splendor of the old.

[30] Physical punishment cleanses away
evil;*
such discipline purifies the heart.

CHAPTER 21

[1] The king's heart is like a stream of
water directed by the LORD;
he guides it wherever he pleases.

19:13 Hebrew *son;* also in 19:27. **20:10** Hebrew *A stone and a stone, an ephah and an ephah.* **20:16** An alternate reading in the Masoretic Text is *for a promiscuous woman.* **20:27** Or *The human spirit is the LORD's light.* **20:30** The meaning of the Hebrew is uncertain.

NOTES

19:13 ***A foolish child is a calamity to a father.*** The composition opens with a couplet covering the complex relationships between the father, son, wife, and God. Here, the scion who is a fool brings mischief upon his sire. This tragedy is matched only by the second line—the drip, drip, drip of the quarrelsome wife. The wretched man's condition in both untenable circumstances is offset by the next verse.

19:14 ***only the LORD can give an understanding wife.*** The father in this pair of verses is above reproach, the source of blessedness, but he is subject to fools (19:13).

19:15 ***Lazy people sleep soundly.*** Lit., "Laziness (*'atslah* [TH6103, ZH6790]) causes one to fall into a deep sleep." Sloth beguiles a person into inactivity—surely a deathlike condition. Even though *'atslah* is a hapax legomenon, a number of cognates ensure its meaning (19:24; 31:27; Eccl 10:18).

idleness leaves them hungry. Precisely, "The appetite (*nepesh* [TH5315, ZH5883]) of the idle will be hungry." There are two properties of sloth: It hypnotizes and it emaciates. It is an addictive evil that destroys the indulger.

19:16 ***Keep the commandments and keep your life.*** The last phrase, "and keep your *nepesh* [TH5315, ZH5883]," ties this proverb with the preceding. "Commandments" (*mitswah* [TH4687, ZH5184]) is used elsewhere in Proverbs for the instruction of the wise parents (2:1; 3:1; 4:4).

despising them leads to death. Lit., "One despising his ways will die" (following the Qere). Note the image of the path, yet another link to the Prologue along with *mitswah,* the father-son relationship, and the role of women in matters of wisdom (see also 19:18). BHS reads *derakayw* [TH1870/2050.2, ZH2006/2257] (his ways) as *dabar* [TH1697, ZH1821] (word), hence RSV, "he who despises the word." McKane quips, "the emendation . . . removes the difficulty . . . without dealing faithfully with it," and suggests that "his ways" refers to Yahweh (1970:523).

19:17 ***lending to the LORD.*** Charity has a divine dimension. God takes it personally and rewards the philanthropist: "What is *given* to them (who are unable to repay) is regarded as *lent* to him so that repayment . . . will surely be made" (Whybray 1994a:282).

19:18 ***Otherwise you will ruin their lives.*** Lit., "And to his death do not raise your *nepesh* [TH5315, ZH5883]." Delitzsch understood this (citing LXX) to denote "unrestrained abuse," not to "put the child to death in the case of guilt" (1875:30). This makes little sense. The NLT correctly has the second line continuing the thought of the first; it is the *neglect* of discipline that constitutes passionately desiring (lit., "raising the soul to") the child's demise.

19:19 ***Hot-tempered people must pay the penalty.*** Lit., "A man of great wrath bears the penalty." Do not enable such a person, for their only hope for change is to face the consequences.

19:20 ***Get all the advice and instruction you can.*** Precisely, "Hear counsel and receive discipline!"

the rest of your life. Lit., "in your end" (see commentary on 1:8-19). Waltke glosses, "in your final destiny" (2005:92).

19:21 ***the LORD's purpose will prevail.*** Lit., "But the counsel of Yahweh—it will stand." In 19:20, much counsel (*'etsah* [TH6098, ZH6783]) is counseled—but only God's counsel will establish whatever plans result. What is this counsel? The book of Proverbs, beginning with the fear of the Lord. See 12:15 and 15:22.

19:22 ***Loyalty makes a person attractive.*** Lit., "The desire of a man is loyalty" (*khesed* II [TH2617, ZH2876]). Although the poor are generally avoided (19:7), a man of integrity may find support (see commentary on 22:6). But if *khesed* I [TH2617A, ZH2875] is read here (see note on 14:34), then translate (contra LXX), "The avarice of a man is his disgrace." Sages may ponder the verity of both plausible readings (1:6).

19:23 ***Fear of the LORD leads to life.*** The section ends with this climactic note—to fear Yahweh is to find life. His counsel is what ultimately stands (see commentary on 12:1-28).

19:24 ***Lazy people.*** The first part of this verse is the same as 26:15a (see note). An absurd proverb illustrates the sloth's ridiculousness. It takes *some* effort to lift a fork to one's mouth—ultimately, the indolent are loath to do even that. No wonder idleness brings starvation (19:15)!

19:25 ***If you punish a mocker.*** Lit., "Strike a mocker." The punishment is corporeal.

the simpleminded will learn a lesson. See note on 1:4 for *petha'yim* [TH6612, ZH7343]. The mocker cannot learn, but when publicly flogged, an observant half-wit may have an eye-opening experience and wise up!

19:26 ***Children who mistreat.*** The Hebrew uses stronger language: "He who assaults the father causes the mother to flee." Using Arabic cognates, Driver suggests the semiotic values, "He who silences his father" (usurping his authority) "vexes his mother" (1955:373). Evil offspring are a distinct possibility in any family, and to "mistreat the parents is the quintessential act of the mocker" (Garrett 1993:173). This naturally prompts the corrective of the following verse.

19:27 ***If you stop listening to instruction, my child.*** Read emphatically, "Cease, my son, to listen to instruction, and . . ." There is urgency in the appeal for the child to heed the words of life. The stanza pauses to call upon the simple to wake up and pay attention. Evil offspring are mockers—to which the segment now returns.

19:28 ***A corrupt witness makes a mockery of justice.*** Lit., "A *beliya'al* [TH1100, ZH1175] witness mocks justice." See notes on 6:12-15 for the *beliya'al* man who derides everything good. This is what evil offspring who scorn instruction become. Hopefully youths will observe such consequences and learn to be better (19:25).

the mouth of the wicked gulps down evil. "Gulps down" comes from *bala'* I [TH1104, ZH1180] (see 1:12). Since the mouth usually signifies speech, BHS conjectures *yabbia'* [TH5042, ZH5580], as in 15:28, "The mouth of the wicked overflows with evil words." Since this is without external support, it seems preferable to follow the MT's multivalent figure of the mouth.

19:29 ***Punishment is made for mockers.*** Lit., "judgments (*shepatim* [TH8201, ZH9150]) are established for mockers." They are why laws are on the books. Beatings are intended for the backs of fools. It is to society's benefit that such are made objects of public disgrace and retribution. The MT presents a focusing proverb that moves from the general to the specific case, and the use of *shepatim* ties it with *mishpat* [TH4941, ZH5477] of 19:28, "A *beliya'al* witness scorns justice." This justice exists—says 19:29—to punish mockers such as these. But LXX glosses *shepatim* as *mastiges* [TG3148, ZG3465] (whips), perhaps reading *shebatim* [TH7626, ZH8657], as in 26:3, "a rod [*shebet*] for the back of fools." Although a different *Vorlage* may have existed, the MT seems preferable.

20:1 ***Wine produces mockers; alcohol leads to brawls.*** The segment ends with a final shot at mockery, which arises under the influence of drink. See commentary on the oracle 31:1-9. One "led astray" (*shagah* [TH7686, ZH8706]) by inebriation is not wise. See notes on 5:19, 23, where love leads astray (*shagah*). One must be wise in the enjoyment of either pleasure. The sage knows how to control the venereal appetite—and how to handle his liquor.

20:2 ***The king's fury is like a lion's roar.*** Compare with 19:12 (the boundary of a composition). The king again appears in 20:8.

to rouse his anger is to risk your life. Lit., "The one angering him sins against his soul." The issue of "sin" resumes in 20:9, which together with the "king" closes an inclusion, demarcating the segment.

20:3 ***a mark of honor.*** The Hebrew employs *'ish* [TH376, ZH408], "the glory of a man." The word is found again twice in 20:5 and twice in 20:6.

20:4 ***will have no food at the harvest.*** See notes on 19:15 and 19:24 treating the sluggard. Here, the Hebrew reads "so he asks during harvest and has nothing." The idler does finally get out of bed and offer to plow—long after the work is finished and harvest has come! Laggards procrastinate to privation.

20:5 ***Though good advice lies deep within the heart.*** Lit., "Like deep waters is the counsel of a man's heart." One who understands how to draw out the subterranean thoughts of another possesses an important and advantageous therapeutic skill (see commentary on

13:1–14:27). Waltke interprets "deep waters" as the hidden purposes of the schemer, which the wise king is competent to bring to light (2005:131).

20:6 ***Many . . . one.*** As in the previous maxim, two "men" are at issue: One "claims his own loyalty (*khesed* [TH2617, ZH2876])" and the other is the elusive "man of faithfulness." Many make claims about themselves; very few are credible.

20:7 ***blessed are their children who follow them.*** Precisely, "Blessed are his sons after him." This man does "walk in integrity"—the counterpoint to 20:6.

20:8 ***weighs all the evidence, distinguishing the bad from the good.*** The actual idiom here reads, "scattering in his eyes all evil." An agricultural image is employed of "scattering, sifting, winnowing." This recalls 20:4, which speaks of plowing and harvesting. The king (20:2) dissipates those who anger him by their evil and sin (see notes on 15:7; 20:26).

20:9 ***Who can say.*** Along with 20:7, this verse also interprets 20:6 (which ends with, lit., "Who can find?"). Who can say "I have cleansed my heart"—the heart of deep waters (20:5) that the skilled can draw out? Who can say "I am pure and free from sin"—the self-destructive sin of 20:2 (see note)? The segment ends by returning to its opening themes of the king and sin. The following section also ends with the themes of the king and the heart—Yahweh is revealed as the heart's master, not only able to draw out its intentions but also to direct it wherever he will (21:1).

20:10 ***False weights and unequal measures.*** See NLT mg, "a stone and a stone, an ephah and an ephah." "Indeed both of them" (*gam-shenehem* [TH8147, ZH9109]) are an abomination to Yahweh—see note on 11:1.

20:11 ***Even children.*** Proverbs characterizes youths as simple and uncommitted to the path of life, needing discipline. Yet even youths can be impressive beyond their peers by good behavior. How much more the adult! Waltke alternatively renders "the way they act" as "evil deeds" and "are known" as "dissembles," yielding a proverb treating dishonest youths with a rhetorical question, "Is he pure?"—the answer being "No!" (2005:120).

20:12 ***both are gifts from the LORD.*** "Indeed both of them" (*gam-shenehem* [TH8147, ZH9109]) are from Yahweh (see 20:10). Both are gifts, so use them honorably and with consideration. Be attuned to truth and see the world as God would have you see it. The "eyes" link into the next triplet.

20:13 ***Keep your eyes open.*** This is one way to utilize the gift of Yahweh (20:12); wakefulness and industry sate one with food.

20:14 ***The buyer haggles over the price.*** Lit., "'It is bad! It is bad!' says the buyer." This is an everyday observation exposing the casual duplicity of humanity.

20:15 ***Wise words.*** Lit., "lips of knowledge." True riches are not found in haggling over a purchase or even in hard work, but in wisdom and knowledge.

20:16 ***foreigners.*** NLT correctly follows Kethiv, footnoting Qere, "promiscuous woman."

20:17 ***sweet.*** From *'areb* [TH6156, ZH6853], which shares a root with *'arab* I [TH6148, ZH6842], meaning "take in pledge," tying this proverb with 20:16 and 20:19. Falsehood leads to ultimate dissatisfaction.

20:18 ***don't go to war without wise advice.*** Lit., "and with counsels make war!"—a metaphor "of the struggle to succeed or survive in daily life" (Whybray 1994a:297).

20:19 ***hang around.*** The Hithpael of *'arab* II [TH6148A, ZH6843], sharing the same root consonants with the verb of 20:16 and with *'areb* [TH6148, ZH6842] of 20:17. The shared consonantal base is used as a principle for grouping the verses.

chatterers. The Hebrew uses the verb *pathah* [TH6601, ZH7331] (be simple, be deceived) with "lips," thus "one of silly lips," or "chatterer."

20:20 ***in total darkness.*** This follows the Kethiv, "pupil (middle) of the night" (*'ishon* [TH380, ZH413]; see 7:2, 9). Qere uses the hapax legomenon *be'eshun* [TH380A, ZH854], meaning "*in the time of* the night."

20:21 ***An inheritance obtained too early in life.*** Kethiv reads, "an inheritance *greedily* [obtained]" (root *bakhal* [TH973A, ZH1042], elsewhere only in Zech 11:8), contra Qere, "an inheritance *hastily* [obtained]" (root *bahal* [TH926, ZH987]).

is not a blessing in the end. Lit., "at its end will not be blessed." The word "blessed" closes the antithetical chiasm from "he who curses" in 20:20. "At its end" in 20:7 also refers to an inheritance. Perhaps the manner in which one curses his parents is by prematurely demanding one's promised property. This situation is described in Jesus' parable of the Prodigal Son (Luke 15:11-16). The honorable older brother in the end inherited all that was the father's (Luke 15:31), presumably leaving the younger with no further heritage.

20:22 ***Wait for the LORD to handle the matter.*** Every verb is volitional here: "Do not say! . . . "I will repay! . . . Wait!" At the end of the verse in Hebrew, the sage expresses his wish for Yahweh's handling of the matter, lit., "and may he save you!"

20:23 ***The LORD detests double standards.*** Lit., "An abomination to Yahweh is a stone and a stone," closing the inclusion from 20:10. Equity and justice are his province; mercantile practices are performed before the living God, who promises to save the injured from cheating businessmen.

20:24 ***The LORD directs our steps.*** This continues the motif of Yahweh proverbs from the previous strophe—lit., "From Yahweh are the steps of a man." The second line reads, "How then shall *'adam* [TH120, ZH132] understand his way?" The answer to the rhetorical question is, of course, to trust Yahweh with one's life.

20:25 ***Don't trap yourself by making a rash promise to God.*** Lit., "It is a snare for *'adam* [TH120, ZH132] to rashly [say], 'It is holy!'" The LXX glosses this as "to consecrate his own [property]." The reference to the deity is implied; the NLT makes this explicit. One should trust Yahweh (20:24), but you dare not invoke his name rashly.

20:26 ***A wise king scatters the wicked.*** Verses treating Yahweh and the king intertwine in this last part—ultimately uniting the whole composition in 21:1. Here, the king winnows the wicked like chaff, recalling the image from 20:8.

runs his threshing wheel over them. "Threshing" is an interpolation; the Hebrew simply says "wheel." Delitzsch says, "It is only meant that a wise king . . . separates the godless, and immediately visits them with merited punishment, as he who works with the winnowing shovel gives chaff to the wind" (1875:57).

20:27 ***The LORD's light penetrates the human spirit.*** Precisely, "The breath of *'adam* [TH120, ZH132] [is] the lamp (*ner* [TH5216A, ZH5944]) of Yahweh." Loewenstamm (following M. Seidel) repoints *ner* to *nar,* the participial form of *nir* [TH5214, ZH5774] ("to plow"; Hos 10:12), producing "Yahweh plows a person's spirit" (1987:223). This continues the agricultural imagery from 20:26 and again associates the king with Yahweh. Of course, it is simpler to carry over the verb ("penetrates, searches") from the second line, leaving the MT intact.

exposing every hidden motive. Lit., "searching (*khopes* [TH2664, ZH2924]) all the chambers of the belly." *Khopes* may be glossed "dig" to balance the reading "plow" (suggested for *ner* above), meaning that God excavates what is hidden in the heart (Loewenstamm 1987:223).

20:28 ***Unfailing love . . . love.*** In both cases *khesed* [TH2617, ZH2876] is used, sometimes translated "loyalty" in NLT.

20:29 ***of experience.*** This is an interpolation, absent in Hebrew (see note and commentary on 16:31).

20:30 ***purifies the heart.*** "Purifies" is carried over from the first line (NLT, "cleanses"). "The heart" glosses the idiom, "chambers of the belly" (see 20:27).

21:1 ***The king's heart.*** Yahweh in 20:27 is revealed as the one who exposes what is underneath the surface of a person's thoughts. Here, the heart of the highest authority in the land is metaphorically a channel of water that God turns and directs. This is the third composition to conclude with a reference to the king and life-giving waters (see also 16:10-15 and 19:3-12).

COMMENTARY

This composition can be parsed into four sections. The first (19:13-23) features the key word "Yahweh," found four times in 11 verses. The second (19:24–20:1) addresses the "mocker," also appearing four times. The third deals with different kinds of people (20:2-9), repeating the word *'ish* [TH376, ZH408] (five times) and opening and closing with the king. Finally, the last section (20:10–21:1) can be divided into two stanzas, the first bound with the inclusion "stone and stone" (20:10-23; see notes), and the second returning to Yahweh (20:24–21:1). The use of Yahweh in this stanza intertwines with the key word "king," and this composition is the third in a row which ends by comparing the king with life-giving water (21:1; see note).

The section opens by reminding the reader of the familial setting of timeless wisdom. What is in view is the training up of children into a life of maturity and moral acumen (19:13-14). The highest blessedness a person can experience is a wise wife—a gift from God, not to be taken for granted, because the lack of this gift is readily apparent in the world and eminently observable in other men's households. We are told to teach children to seek from God a worthy spouse, the very embodiment of the path of life. Yahweh controls whether a man has a beneficent or a maleficent wife. The father can supply some good things, but only God can supply the wise woman. Parents should teach their sons to look for her and how to recognize her. Of course, the book of Proverbs may be appropriated by both sexes, and women today, who along with men take great risk when marrying, must ultimately look to the Lord for a compatible spouse. One must also trust God to bless with judicious children. This composition points to Yahweh as the source of all meaningful blessedness—unmistakably proving that the wisdom found here is spiritual.

The first section then warns that if parents neglect to discipline their children, the parents in effect desire their deaths. Chasten them while there is hope, while there is an expectation of change (19:18)! For example, a hot-tempered person must be made to face the consequences of his actions. To rescue children from their problems again and again will only evacuate any possible benefit of the punishment; the hothead will learn nothing and repeat his offense again (19:19). Do not spare the rod!

A sensible person will not shun the advice of other people and will actively seek it (19:20). However, what actually happens in life is according to the counsel of Yahweh, who desires to lead people in the path of wisdom (19:21). This "counsel" should be viewed as the overarching Counsel against which all other counselors' proposals must be weighed. The fear of Yahweh is the beginning of wise advice, the starting place for the making of plans and decisions. This is where life is to be found—life that is on the opposite pole from the death that awaits those without discipline and instruction (19:16, 18). Children who ignore and despise discipline are mockers, scoffing at everything of value and worth and fit only to be flogged and punished (19:29). The instrument of this punishment is the government, the king. He sifts the evil (20:8), and those who arouse his ire sin against themselves (20:2).

Not all are fools and sinners. There are godly people who have honesty and integrity (20:6-9). These enjoy blessedness beyond their years—literally, "after them," which signifies a dimension of timelessness for the righteous "walking to and fro" (20:7; *halak* [TH1980, ZH2143] in the Hithpael) with integrity. What is pure and right and blameless, and what is evil and unclean and faithless, is hidden deep in the heart. But one of skill—especially the king—can measure the worth of another and reveal it, drawing out one's purposes and clandestine thoughts.

Jesus was born to reveal the thoughts of the hearts of many (Luke 2:35). He "knew the thoughts" of his critics and declared that they were evil and soon to face judgment, for God's Kingdom had come (Matt 12:25-37). Jesus is the king who scatters the wicked and understands every hidden thought (Matt 9:4). Who can say, "I am pure and free of sin?" Only this king, who blamelessly walked the earth, leaving eternal blessings to all who follow him (20:7).

The final section (20:24–21:1) is a strophe displaying a series of complex, interlocking verses. The word *'adam* [TH120, ZH132] is found in 20:24, 25, and 27. The "king" (*melek* [TH4428, ZH4889]) occurs in 20:26, 28; 21:1, which together demarcate a smaller unit). "Yahweh" also appears three times (20:24, 27; 21:1). Two verses end with the phrase "chambers of the belly" (20:27, 30; see notes). This shows that many proverbs are not in proximity at random but are purposely grouped by verbal and thematic similitude.

This section begins by telling us that people cannot understand even their own lives and why they do what they do (20:24), let alone understand the Almighty. But God enlightens the inner motivations and hidden thoughts of every person (20:27). According to God's perspective, loyalty and righteousness establish earthly power (20:28), and aged people rival the powers of youth with their wits and knowledge of God (20:29). When the government punishes an evildoer, the punishment may have rehabilitative value (20:30)—but this ultimately comes from Yahweh, who turns the thoughts and desires even of kings in the direction he wills (21:1). This does not leave monarchs innocent of wrongdoing, however, because the crowned head is still responsible for his own choices. Although God overrides and ultimately stands behind the course of history, he does not do this in a way that compromises human culpability. It is the rare king who willingly and cooperatively participates in all God's stated will. Jesus was self-consciously aware of this, as is evident in his claim: "When you have lifted up the Son of Man on the cross, then you will understand that I AM he. I do nothing on my own but say only what the Father taught me. And the one who sent me is with me—he has not deserted me. For I always do what pleases him" (John 8:28-29). Jesus has always done what pleases God his Father, who taught him everything needful for a wise and godly life. He is our preeminent example.

◆ G. The Wicked and the Righteous (21:2–22:16)

2 People may be right in their
own eyes,
but the LORD examines their heart.

3 The LORD is more pleased when we do
what is right and just
than when we offer him sacrifices.

4 Haughty eyes, a proud heart,
and evil actions are all sin.

5 Good planning and hard work lead to
prosperity,
but hasty shortcuts lead to poverty.

6 Wealth created by a lying tongue
is a vanishing mist and a deadly
trap.*

7 The violence of the wicked sweeps
them away,
because they refuse to do what
is just.

8 The guilty walk a crooked path;
the innocent travel a straight road.

9 It's better to live alone in the corner
of an attic
than with a quarrelsome wife in
a lovely home.

10 Evil people desire evil;
their neighbors get no mercy from
them.

11 If you punish a mocker, the
simpleminded become wise;
if you instruct the wise, they will
be all the wiser.

12 The Righteous One* knows what is
going on in the homes of the
wicked;
he will bring disaster on them.

13 Those who shut their ears to the cries
of the poor
will be ignored in their own time
of need.

14 A secret gift calms anger;
a bribe under the table pacifies fury.

15 Justice is a joy to the godly,
but it terrifies evildoers.

16 The person who strays from common
sense
will end up in the company of the
dead.

17 Those who love pleasure become
poor;
those who love wine and luxury
will never be rich.

18 The wicked are punished in place of
the godly,
and traitors in place of the honest.

19 It's better to live alone in the desert
than with a quarrelsome,
complaining wife.

20 The wise have wealth and luxury,
but fools spend whatever they get.

21 Whoever pursues righteousness and
unfailing love
will find life, righteousness, and
honor.

22 The wise conquer the city of the
strong
and level the fortress in which
they trust.

23 Watch your tongue and keep your
mouth shut,
and you will stay out of trouble.

24 Mockers are proud and haughty;
they act with boundless arrogance.

25 Despite their desires, the lazy will come to ruin,
for their hands refuse to work.

26 Some people are always greedy for more,
but the godly love to give!

27 The sacrifice of an evil person is detestable,
especially when it is offered with wrong motives.

28 A false witness will be cut off,
but a credible witness will be allowed to speak.

29 The wicked bluff their way through,
but the virtuous think before they act.

30 No human wisdom or understanding or plan
can stand against the LORD.

31 The horse is prepared for the day of battle,
but the victory belongs to the LORD.

CHAPTER 22

1 Choose a good reputation over great riches;
being held in high esteem is better than silver or gold.

2 The rich and poor have this in common:
The LORD made them both.

3 A prudent person foresees danger and takes precautions.
The simpleton goes blindly on and suffers the consequences.

4 True humility and fear of the LORD
lead to riches, honor, and long life.

5 Corrupt people walk a thorny, treacherous road;
whoever values life will avoid it.

6 Direct your children onto the right path,
and when they are older, they will not leave it.

7 Just as the rich rule the poor,
so the borrower is servant to the lender.

8 Those who plant injustice will harvest disaster,
and their reign of terror will come to an end.*

9 Blessed are those who are generous,
because they feed the poor.

10 Throw out the mocker, and fighting goes, too.
Quarrels and insults will disappear.

11 Whoever loves a pure heart and gracious speech
will have the king as a friend.

12 The LORD preserves those with knowledge,
but he ruins the plans of the treacherous.

13 The lazy person claims, "There's a lion out there!
If I go outside, I might be killed!"

14 The mouth of an immoral woman is a dangerous trap;
those who make the LORD angry will fall into it.

15 A youngster's heart is filled with foolishness,
but physical discipline will drive it far away.

16 A person who gets ahead by oppressing the poor
or by showering gifts on the rich will end in poverty.

21:6 As in Greek version; Hebrew reads *mist for those who seek death.* **21:12** Or *The righteous man.* **22:8** The Greek version includes an additional proverb: *God blesses a man who gives cheerfully, / but his worthless deeds will come to an end.* Compare 2 Cor 9:7.

NOTES

21:2 *People may be right in their own eyes.* The theme of the eyes continues in 21:4 and 10.

the LORD examines their heart. See note on 16:2. Here, Yahweh "weighs" hearts. This verse creates a seam with 21:1, picking up on the theme of Yahweh and the heart. This is similar to how the final verse of the anthology (22:16) anticipates the first of the wise sayings (22:22).

21:3 *sacrifices.* A number of proverbs deal with cultic practices (3:9; 15:8; 17:1). See commentary on the compositions 14:28–16:15 and 16:16–19:12. The final composition of this anthology opens here by highlighting God's preference for wise living over the outward performance of cultic duties. One may be upright in one's own eyes—by being very religious—but Yahweh weighs the heart to see if there is righteousness and justice there.

21:4 *Haughty eyes.* This recalls the potentially self-deluded eyes of 21:2.

evil actions are all sin. Some Hebrew mss read, "The *lamp* (*ner* [TH5216A, ZH5944]) of the wicked is sin"; others (including the Leningrad Codex) read *nir* [TH5215, ZH5776] (fallow ground), yielding, "the *untilled earth* of the wicked is sin." The LXX reads "lamp." Driver hypothesized an Arabic cognate meaning "branding iron" and glossed, "The mark of the wicked is sin" (1951:185). The NLT renders it "evil actions." "The *'or* of the wicked" is a phrase found in 13:9 (where it is compared with, lit., the "light of the righteous") and in 24:20; in both cases, the *ner* (light or lamp) is destined to be put out, meaning their lives and hopes will fail. However, in 6:23 the "light" signifies guidance and direction, and that is the sense here, developing the imagery of the "eyes" from the first line. What guides the wicked, what "lights" their way, is sin—their haughty eyes and prideful hearts. The Lord who examines hearts sees this sin, despite the hypocritical sacrifices offenders may offer. "Wicked" is a key word here, found five times in nine verses (21:4-12).

21:6 *a vanishing mist and a deadly trap.* NLT follows the LXX (see NLT mg). The MT reads "a fleeting vapor for those seeking death." Both texts agree that treasures gained through deception are fleeting and deadly.

21:8 *The guilty.* A hapax legomenon. Perhaps we should repoint the single lemma *wazar* [TH2054, ZH2261] into two words, *wezar* [TH2050.1/2214B, ZH2256/2424] (see Exod 29:33), yielding, "[There is] a man crooked in his way, even a stranger."

walk . . . travel. These verbs, not in the Hebrew text, were supplied by the translators.

straight road. "Road" is carried over from the first line. Lit., "but the innocent—his conduct is straight." "Conduct," the final word, shares the same root with "created," the first word of 21:6 in Hebrew.

21:9 *It's better to live alone.* See note on 12:9. The point is made again with more extreme language in 21:19, closing an inclusion that bounds the stanza.

21:10 *their neighbors get no mercy from them.* Lit., "does not find favor in his eyes his neighbor," meaning either "his neighbor favors him not" or NLT's choice, "he favors not his neighbor." The latter is probably correct.

21:11 *the simpleminded become wise.* See notes on 19:25, a similar verse.

if you instruct the wise, they will be all the wiser. Lit., "and in instructing (Hiphil infinitive of *sakal* [TH7919, ZH8505]) the wise he will get knowledge."

21:12 *The Righteous One.* The Hebrew begins with a Hiphil participle of *sakal* [TH7919, ZH8505] (see note on 21:11), meaning, "one considering, prospering," followed by the modifier "righteous." The NLT (via capitalization) presents this as a title for God—a unique usage in the OT. This "righteous one" overthrows the wicked in the second line—a function usually reserved for God. Although this reading may be correct, the verse can also be seen in the light of 21:10-11. In 21:10, the wicked crave evil (*ra'* [TH7451A, ZH8273], from the root *ra'a'* I [TH7489, ZH8317]) and are hostile to the "neighbor" (*rea'* [TH7453, ZH8276], from the root *ra'ah* II [TH7462C, ZH8287]); in 21:11 punishing such people is eye-opening to the simple, and the wise are "instructed" (*sakal*); in 21:12 "the righteous man" (see NLT mg) knows (*sakal*) the situation and takes legal punitive action against the miscreant, bringing "ruin" (*ra'*). See note on 6:34, where just such a case is contemplated; see also 21:22.

21:13 ***Those who shut their ears to the cries of the poor.*** Antisocial behavior is also treated in 21:10.

21:14 ***secret gift . . . bribe.*** See notes on 17:8 and 17:23. Yet another antisocial behavior is treated here. The secretive nature of the payment reveals its underhanded character; it is used to desensitize a person's legitimate grievance.

21:15 ***Justice is a joy to the godly.*** This is the counterpoint to 21:14. Evildoers, fearing justice, attempt to undermine the court.

21:16 ***will end up in the company of the dead.*** Lit., "in the assembly of the shades (*repa'im* [TH7496, ZH8327]) will rest" (see note on 2:18). The issue at hand is ever a matter of life and death. Wandering from wisdom leads one to the abode of the damned.

21:17 ***Those who love . . . those who love.*** A person is characterized by what he or she loves (see commentaries on the poems 1:1-7 and 1:20-33). "Pleasure" (*simkhah* [TH8057, ZH8525]) ties the verse with 21:15, there glossed "joy."

luxury. Lit., "oil," as in 21:20.

21:18 ***The wicked . . . the godly.*** See note on 21:12, where the wicked and the righteous are also juxtaposed.

21:19 ***It's better to live alone.*** See 21:9, which expresses the same thought. These twin proverbs are an inclusion creating a boundary for the stanza. See note on 12:9.

21:20 ***luxury.*** Lit., "oil," as in 21:17. Lovers of oil and wine are poor (21:17), but lovers of wisdom have homes bursting with all these things and more.

21:21 ***life, righteousness, and honor.*** Not only do the wise enjoy material prosperity, but spiritual virtues bless them, including honor (or "glory"); see note on 3:35. The "righteous" finding "righteousness" seems tautologous; BHS (with LXX) suggests omitting "righteousness" due to supposed dittography from the first line. However, see 21:24, where similar repetition is employed; see also 21:26.

21:22 ***The wise conquer the city of the strong.*** Lit., "A wise man scales the city of the mighty." The wise not only enjoy material and spiritual blessedness, they also wield influence—none can withstand their justified purposes. The taking of a city here is probably metaphorical (see note on 20:18; see also 21:12).

21:23 ***Watch . . . you will stay out.*** The Hebrew uses the same verb in both cola: "*He who guards* his mouth and his tongue / *guards* from troubles his soul."

21:24 ***Mockers are proud and haughty.*** Lit., "The proud and haughty—Mocker is his name."

they act with boundless arrogance. Lit., "one acting 'in excess of pride'" (Driver 1951:185). "Acting" ties this verse to the next. Note the patterned use of *zed* [TH2086, ZH2294] ("proud," the first word) and *zadon* [TH2087, ZH2295] ("pride," the last word).

21:25 ***Despite their desires, the lazy will come to ruin.*** Lit., "The desire of the sluggard puts him to death." What is at issue is a matter of life and death.

to work. This is the same verb as in 21:24, translated as "act"—a verbal link between the two verses.

21:26 ***Some people are always greedy for more.*** Lit., "All day he desires desire"—perhaps referring to the desire (same word) of the sluggard in 21:25.

21:27 ***The sacrifice of an evil person.*** The composition began with a reference to sacrifices out of step with an inner life of obedience and integrity (21:3; see note there).

21:28 ***a credible witness will be allowed to speak.*** Lit., "A man who listens will speak forever." Emerton intriguingly argues, "A lying witness is likely to give himself away as he talks. . . . Anyone who listens carefully . . . may be able to catch him out." Thus the "listening man" is not a witness but a lawyer or judge; "forever" is used superlatively; and the final verb is *dabar* I [TH1696A, ZH1818] (destroy), yielding the rendering, "A lying witness will perish, and he who listens will subdue (or, destroy) [him] completely" (1988:167). Whybray argues that a judge's decision "has binding force for the future" (1994a:316).

21:29 ***bluff their way through.*** The idiom is "hardens his face" (see note on 7:13). They "put up a strong front while lying" (Garrett 1990:682).

think before they act. Lit., "discern his way," reading Qere both times.

21:30 ***can stand against the LORD.*** "Can stand" is an interpolation. This is the first of four Yahweh proverbs grouped into six verses (21:30–22:4). The segment begins by asserting the failure of human wisdom when placed before God—his overriding counsel and profundity trump all mortal self-confidence. The next verse continues this thought.

21:31 ***victory belongs to the LORD.*** Lit., "With Yahweh is salvation." As in the previous verse, the sage recognizes that Yahweh cannot be fathomed and that all one's preparations for war—just as all one's lofty thoughts—cannot determine with certainty the outcome of events. The universe is not managed by an impersonal force called "wisdom" but by a named God known to the wise.

22:1 ***a good reputation.*** Lit., "a name" (cf. note on 21:24). The LXX includes the modifier "good," which correctly expresses the idea of the Hebrew (so NLT).

22:2 ***The LORD made them both.*** Lit., "Yahweh made them all." The social divide pales in comparison to their shared status of being creatures of God. Both are then accountable to him—see notes on 13:8. The ancient versions glossed as in the NLT: "both of them."

22:3 ***takes precautions.*** Lit., "hides himself" (see 27:12).

22:4 ***fear of the LORD.*** This verse closes the segment with an unqualified promise of riches and honor and life to those who humbly respect their Lord—the one who has made both rich and poor (22:2).

22:5 ***thorny.*** Thorns (so glossed by LXX, from *tsen* [TH6791, ZH7553]; elsewhere only in Job 5:5) indicate an unkempt pathway. Driver needlessly suggests an alternative meaning, "basket" (i.e., "trap"), from Aramaic and Arabic cognates (1951:186).

whoever values life will avoid it. Lit., "one guarding his soul stays far (*rakhaq* [TH7368, ZH8178]) from them." The verb *rakhaq* is rare in Proverbs (seven times) and recurs in 22:15 to close the inclusion. The image of the path continues in the next verse.

22:6 ***Direct your children.*** "Direct" is from *khanak* [TH2596, ZH2852], a rare word found elsewhere only in Deut 20:5, 1 Kgs 8:63, and 2 Chr 7:5, always in the sense of *dedicating* a structure to God. If one's own home was not *consecrated,* one was not prepared for holy war. See also the cognate nouns *khanukkah* [TA/ZA10273, S2598], from Aramaic, and Heb., *khanukkah* [TH2598, ZH2853], used for the "dedication" of cultic objects (Num 7:10-11; Neh 12:27; Dan 3:2-3). Here, religious language is employed to highlight the needed level of devotion. Every parent mimics Solomon the wise, who dedicated the Temple, by similarly committing their child to the path of wisdom. This involves long-term moral and religious education, not lacking in physical discipline (22:15). Hildebrandt also sees here the initiation of a cadet into manhood and adult responsibilities (1988:10).

onto the right path. Lit., "in accordance with his way." Delitzsch argues that this denotes the child's nature: "The education of the youth . . . ought to regulate itself according to . . . the degree of development [to] which the mental and bodily life of the youth has arrived" (1875:86-87; cf. Garrett 1993:188). But the image of the path does not predicate human nature but rather a lifestyle and system of valuation that are both learned and chosen—"the way he ought to go" (McKane 1970:564), "according to the standard and status of what would be demanded of the *na'ar* [TH5288, ZH5853] in that culture" (Hildebrandt 1988:18). This verse should be seen in the light of the first nine chapters of Proverbs. The "path" (*derek* [TH1870, ZH2006]) with the third-person pronominal suffix is found 18 times in Proverbs, culminating in its final usage here. In every case it signifies life direction and moral character. See the way of the oppressor (3:31), of the ant (6:6), of the loose woman (7:25), of Wisdom (3:17), and of God (8:22). Here, youths committed by wise parents to the good path (not the thorny one of 22:5) are set for life. The themes of 22:5-6 resume in 22:15.

22:7 ***the borrower is servant to the lender.*** Themes from the Prologue of the first nine chapters are being revisited; first the image of the path and the importance of instructing the youth (22:5-6) and now the condition of debt is at issue (see 6:1-5).

22:8 ***their reign of terror.*** This is a credible gloss of "the rod of his wrath." At the end of this verse, the LXX includes an additional proverb: "God blesses a man who gives cheerfully, but his worthless deeds will come to an end" (see NLT mg). Paul cites this line in 2 Cor 9:7.

22:9 ***Blessed are those who are generous.*** Lit., "He who has a good eye will be blessed."

because they feed the poor. Lit., "For he gives from his bread to the poor." The blessed one takes from his own bread to give to those with none.

22:10 ***insults.*** Lit., "shame, disgrace," as in 3:35; 6:33; 11:2. The mocker causes nothing good; eliminate him and the community is better off. Driver extensively emends the second line to read per the ancient versions, "and, if he sits in the court-house, he dishonors it" (1951:186). Although the LXX probably followed another *Vorlage,* such emendation is speculative. The MT makes sense and so is preferred.

22:11 ***will have the king as a friend.*** The one of pure heart and gracious lips (the opposite of a mocker) is appreciated by the king who drives away mockers. The LXX reads, "The Lord loves holy hearts, and acceptable to him is everyone unblemished; with lips the king shepherds"—making this verse into a Yahweh proverb.

22:12 ***The LORD preserves those with knowledge.*** Lit., "The eyes of Yahweh watch over knowledge." Immediately after mentioning the king, a Yahweh proverb follows.

plans. Lit., "words."

22:13 ***The lazy person claims.*** The words of the idler are *not* guarded by Yahweh; lacking knowledge, he generates excuses to remain inactive, thus broadcasting his lack of confidence in God and recapitulating 6:6-9.

22:14 ***The mouth of an immoral woman.*** "Mouth" usually denotes speech in Proverbs, but perhaps here it is also a double entendre for her vulva (see notes on 5:8; 7:27; and especially 30:20). This imagery recalls the Prologue.

dangerous trap. Lit., "deep pit" (see also 23:27).

those who make the LORD angry. Yahweh curses sinners who will make a great and unrecoverable fall into her, which will cost them their lives (9:18).

22:15 ***A youngster's heart is filled with foolishness.*** Lit., "Folly is being bound in the heart of a youth." The section returns to the subject of the youth, closing the inclusion. It is significant that the youth is treated immediately after the loose woman is addressed—reminiscent of 7:6-23. It is precisely because the youth is inwardly foolish that he or she must be dedicated to the discipline of the right path. (See this proverb's antecedent in 22:5-6.)

physical discipline will drive it far away. Lit., "The rod of discipline will drive it far" (see note on 22:8). "Will drive it far" closes the inclusion from 22:5, where one guarding his/her life stays far from the path of thorns and snares.

22:16 ***the poor.*** This verse stands outside the previous section, which was bounded by the double inclusion of "being far" and the youth. The "poor" (*dal* [TH1800, ZH1924]) anticipates its dual occurrence in 22:22; the verse is a bridge that introduces a topic to be resumed after the next anthology's introductory material (22:17-21).

COMMENTARY

After an introductory couplet affirms that wisdom comes from Yahweh (21:2-3), the final composition of the anthology recaps the gulf between the wicked and the wise (21:4-29). The anthology draws near to an end by focusing on Yahweh (21:30–22:4). The differences between folly and wisdom are addressed in 22:5-15. The final verse (22:16) serves as a bridge to the next anthology.

The first seven verses of this section (22:2-8) display an intricate pattern, as illustrated in this diagram:

21:2	every	path of a man		upright	in his eyes	but weighs	hearts	Yahweh
21:3	to do	righteous-ness	and justice	is pleasing	to Yahweh	more than sacrifice		
21:4	haughti-ness	of eyes	and pride	of heart	the lamp of	the wicked	is sin	
21:5	schemes	diligent	surely	to profit	but all	ones hastening	surely	to poverty
21:6	making of	treasures	by tongue	falsehood	vapor	fleeting	ones seeking	death
21:7	violence of	wicked	drags away	for	they refuse	to do	justice	
21:8	being crooked	path of a man		guilty	but the innocent	straight	his conduct	

There are many such verbal connections here, evincing a tightly knit text. This interlocking verbiage is typical for the book of Proverbs. Note the juxtaposition of "poverty" and "death" or "Yahweh" and "sacrifice." The more one meditates upon the passage, the more connections one finds.

Overall, this section of Proverbs (21:2–22:16) teaches that a godly life has an inner and an outer component, with the inner driving the outer. Those who inwardly fear Yahweh and shun evil express love and devotion by outwardly performing prescribed religious duties (i.e., the ones God revealed through Moses). These cultic acts do not earn favor with God, however. At times people might forget this and continue the rites even while their hearts contemplate evil. In this manner, a person can become self-deluded, imagining himself or herself to be right with God and forgetting that the Lord weighs hearts, looking for justice and righteousness (21:2-3). This last composition of the anthology begins with a reminder that wisdom is not so much an outer performance of one's duties before God and society, but an inner attitude pleasing to him. With this fact kept in mind, one may continue to read about how to express love for God outwardly.

One way to live in the world before Yahweh is to reject the antisocial lifestyle and attitudes of the wicked—and to protect the innocent from them (21:11). The wicked will ultimately bring about their own demise (21:4-7, 16-18), but in the meantime they live aggressively and uncharitably in the community. The imagery for a society under these conditions is living in a house with a spouse who saps your strength and oppresses your mind. How much better to see justice done and the wicked thrown down than to allow evildoers free rein for their destructive impulses.

Those who pursue wisdom rather than money or social advancement will enjoy every good thing—materially, spiritually, and politically (21:20-22). No device of the foolhardy or wicked can withstand the onslaught of the righteous when their cause is just. Contrast this with slothful people who have strongly felt desires but will not work, tacitly committing suicide (21:25-26).

Much can be said about Yahweh in connection with these themes. No plan or device of even the wise will stand against the sovereignty of the Almighty (21:30-31). God rules over the whole world; he made both the rich and poor, who together are responsible to him and held accountable for how they conduct themselves in their respective stations in life (22:2). Those who are prudent "hide" from danger, while simpleminded fools plunge ahead, full of misguided self-confidence. Consequently, they will suffer (22:3). But the rewards to all who fear God and live humbly before him are all good things, including glory and life (22:4).

Following this, the writer tells parents to "direct your children onto the right path, and when they are older, they will not leave it" (22:6). This bold promise guarantees that the youth will remain on the path the wise parents have set. Here is an example of a proverb that is absolutely true—but is qualified and interpreted by other proverbs. Left on its own, this maxim would blame the parents if the youth chooses a foolish lifestyle. But consider 17:21, which alternatively suggests a rebellious child is an evil fortune and does not indict the guardians for any neglect. Compare also 19:7 and 19:22; the first observes how people are revolted by the poor and the other observes how this is mitigated. Or compare 16:3 (a promise that plans are founded when committed to God) and 21:31 (a caution against presuming one's preparations will avail in battle). Each proverb requires the other for its full sense; they delimit and interpret one another. A single proverb does not speak the whole truth about a subject. Proverbs 22:6 is a promise from God, but it is not the *whole* truth on raising godly children. To correctly interpret any single proverb, one must be aware of what all of the other proverbs say about that subject. Therefore, one must know all of them to fully understand any one of them. Simply pulling a single proverb out of this wisdom environment and claiming it or living by it is insufficient. It is the whole book that makes one wise, not any one apothegm on its own. Thus the reader "rightly avoids absolutizing any given saying or group of sayings" (Murphy 1987:399-400). In the same way, 22:6 assumes a wise son and says nothing about the tragedy of the fool who shames good parents.

Young people, full of foolish notions and misguided ideas, are easily swayed by peer pressure and lack experience to anticipate the various sorts of pitfalls and temptations they will eventually encounter. The parent must deal with this injudiciousness so that a child can be properly socialized and prepared for the adult world. At times, harsh measures are required (22:15). Guiding a child in the path of wisdom is a matter of long-term, ceaseless application of correction and instruction. Hopefully, folly will be left far behind (one "stays far away," 22:5; folly is "driven far away," 22:15) as the youth chooses the path of wisdom and begins to exhibit the traits Yahweh expects, such as generosity (22:9) and purity (22:11). One who is spiritually malformed displays just the opposite: wickedness (22:8), mockery (22:10), and sloth (22:13). The one Yahweh protects from harm (22:12); the other he allows to become the loose woman's prey—and she drags his soul down to the pit (22:14).

◆ III. "Thirty" Sayings of the Wise (22:17–24:34)

The third anthology of compositions in the book of Proverbs, unlike the previous one (the "Proverbs of Solomon"), is not comprised of binary proverbs, each made of two parallel verses. Although verses are interwoven in the previous anthology and understandable in the larger context of stanzas or segments, they also are written such that, individually, each expresses a complete thought and stands on its own. In this respect, "proverbs" are unlike the Prologue of chapters 1–9, where a single thought is developed in an almost prose-like form (e.g., the loose woman in 7:6-23 or Lady Wisdom in ch 8). The Sayings of the Wise are like the Prologue in this respect. These 70 verses are technically not "proverbs" either and may be designated "sayings"—a general term that does not imply any sort of parallelism.

The proverbs of Solomon (10:1–22:16) usually speak in the third person. But in 22:17, the mode of writing shifts to the second person, which is another connection between the Sayings of the Wise and the first nine chapters. This shift is obscured somewhat in the NLT, because one method of rendering a text in gender-neutral language is to rewrite third-person proverbs (which in English are gender-specific) in the second person. For example, 19:21 in Hebrew reads, "Many schemes are in the heart of a man." The NLT translates this as, "You can make many plans." Thus, the NLT sacrifices one of the differences between the proverbial materials of 10:1–22:16 and the sayings of 22:17–24:34 for the sake of gender inclusiveness. Translators must make choices, and no translation can accomplish everything.

Another indication that 22:17–24:34 is a new movement is that it begins with its own preface—a fresh start directly appealing to readers to pay attention (see 22:17-21).

The "Thirty Sayings" (22:17–24:22) are followed by "Further Sayings" (24:23-34), which the Septuagint places after 30:14, seemingly indicating that at one time the position of the "Further Sayings" was fluid and subject to change. However, since it is just 12 verses, continues the form of "sayings," and seems to be an extension of the prior material, it is treated here as an appendix to the anthology of the "Thirty Sayings" (see commentary on 24:23-34).

◆ A. Preface (22:17–21)

17 Listen to the words of the wise;
apply your heart to my instruction.
18 For it is good to keep these sayings
in your heart
and always ready on your lips.
19 I am teaching you today—yes, you—
so you will trust in the LORD.
20 I have written thirty sayings* for you,
filled with advice and knowledge.
21 In this way, you may know the truth
and take an accurate report to those
who sent you.

22:20 Or *excellent sayings;* the meaning of the Hebrew is uncertain.

NOTES

22:17 ***Listen.*** Lit., "Incline your ear and listen"—both verbs are volitional. Note how the whole verse matches *Amenemope* (see commentary).

apply your heart. Lit., "set (*shith* [TH7896, ZH8883]) your heart." *Shith* is a rare word in Proverbs, appearing again with the word "heart" in closing the anthology at 24:32 (see note).

22:18 ***in your heart.*** Lit., "in your belly." Compare this to *Amenemope* (see commentary). The opening verses of these two documents are too parallel to be accidental; in other words, some literary kinship is apparent. See the next verse.

always ready. Precisely, "They may be established together." Waltke renders this as "fixed together" (2005:218).

22:19 ***I am teaching you today—yes, you.*** Rendsburg (2001:194) curiously emends *hayyom 'ap-'attah* [TH1886.1/3117, ZH2021/3427] (today—yes you) to *ymnm'pth,* yielding, "I have made known to you Amenemope."

trust in the LORD. At this point the text deviates from *Amenemope* (see commentary) as the sage clarifies that his goal is to lead his readers to trust in the God known to Israel as Yahweh—*not* to trust any Egyptian deity or worldview.

22:20 ***thirty sayings.*** "Sayings" is not in the Hebrew text. NLT has mildly emended the Kethiv *shilshom* [TH8032, ZH8997] (third day ago) to *sheloshim* [TH7970, ZH9001] (thirty). This innovation is driven by the discovery of the *Instruction of Amenemope,* which consists of 30 chapters. Formerly, interpreters either used the Qere reading ("adjutants," *shalishim* [TH7991B, ZH8957]) or the LXX's gloss, "threefold" (cf. *shelishi* [TH7992, ZH8958]). Origen, in his *First Principles,* argued from this verse the threefold sense of Scripture (literal, moral, and spiritual). Some scholars cannot identify 30 discernable sayings here (Whybray 1994b:96). Waltke notes that in *Amenemope* (see commentary) the introduction to the Thirty Sayings is itself one of the 30 (2005:22). See Emerton (2001b) for various ways of parsing the sayings.

22:21 ***In this way, you may know the truth.*** Lit., "To make you know correctly words of truth." "Correctly" (*qosht* [TH7189A, ZH7999]) is an Aramaic loan word used elsewhere only in Dan 2:47; 4:37 [34]. Cody argues from Aramaic usage a semiotic value as "apt, just" and translates, "To teach you probity fitting you to return reports which inspire confidence in the man who sends you" (1980:424). BHS suggests deleting the word "correctly," which the NLT does.

COMMENTARY

The passage following 22:17 is a new movement in the book; it begins with its own preface (22:17-21)—a fresh start directly appealing to readers to pay attention. Interestingly and perhaps significantly, this appeal has many similarities with the first two chapters of the ancient Egyptian *Instruction of Amenemope* (ANET 421-422), as illustrated below.

Amenemope	Proverbs 22:17-23
Give thy ears, hear what is said, Give thy heart to understand them. To put them in thy heart is worthwhile, (But) it is damaging to him who neglects them Let them rest in the casket of thy belly, That they may be a *key* in thy heart. . . .	Listen to the words of the wise; apply your heart to my instruction. For it is good to keep these sayings in your heart and always ready on your lips. I am teaching you today—yes, you— so you will trust in the LORD. I have written thirty sayings for you, filled with advice and knowledge. In this way, you may know the truth and take an accurate report to those who sent you.
Guard thyself against robbing the oppressed And against overbearing the disabled.	Don't rob the poor just because you can, or exploit the needy in court. For the LORD is their defender. He will ruin anyone who ruins them.

Much ink has been spilt over the last century by scholars seeking to explain the affinity between these two texts. The Egyptian *Instruction* probably predates Solomon by several centuries (Emerton 2001b:432). Although the Sayings of the Wise do not follow *Amenemope* closely enough to be directly dependent, there are enough verbal and thematic connections to postulate some kind of historical overlap. Solomon enjoyed close relations with Egypt, and one may imagine an Egyptian courtier in his court reproducing from memory a piece of profound literature that Solomon deemed worthy of inclusion—after being recast into a Yahwistic mold. Waltke argues from the comparison (shown above) that one distinctive mark of Israelite and Solomonic wisdom is the clear affirmation that trusting Yahweh is the goal of knowledge and the whole sapiential enterprise.

> *It is instructive to note that in the introduction to the "Thirty Sayings of the Wise," which bears such a strong resemblance to chapter one in the* Instruction of Amen-em-Ope, *the Israelite sage uniquely adds that his purpose is that his readers' "trust may be in the* LORD*" (Prov. 22:19, NIV). In that unique addition the essential theological relevance and distinctiveness of the biblical book stands out.* (1979:237)

This God-centered orientation distinguishes the wisdom of Proverbs. "Secular wisdom" is an oxymoron and rejected by any true sage as inadequate.

Nonetheless, it is worth noting that both this section of Proverbs and *Amenemope* speak of 30 sayings/30 chapters as providing the necessary teachings for people to attain wisdom. *Amenemope* chapter 30 (ANET 424) reads as follows:

> *See thou these thirty chapters:*
> *They entertain, they instruct;*
> *They are the foremost of all books;*
> *They make the ignorant to know.*
> *If they are read out before the ignorant,*
> *Then he will be cleansed by them.*
> *Fill thyself with them; put them in thy heart,*
> *And be a man who can interpret them,*
> *Who will interpret them as a teacher.*
> *As for the scribe experienced in his office,*
> *He will find himself worthy (to be) a courtier.*

◆ B. The Thirty Sayings (22:22–24:22)

22 Don't rob the poor just because you can,
or exploit the needy in court.
23 For the LORD is their defender.
He will ruin anyone who ruins them.

24 Don't befriend angry people
or associate with hot-tempered people,
25 or you will learn to be like them
and endanger your soul.

26 Don't agree to guarantee another person's debt
or put up security for someone else.
27 If you can't pay it,
even your bed will be snatched from under you.

28 Don't cheat your neighbor by moving the ancient boundary markers
set up by previous generations.

29 Do you see any truly competent workers?
They will serve kings
rather than working for ordinary people.

CHAPTER 23

1 While dining with a ruler,
pay attention to what is put before you.
2 If you are a big eater,
put a knife to your throat;
3 don't desire all the delicacies,
for he might be trying to trick you.

4 Don't wear yourself out trying to get rich.
Be wise enough to know when to quit.
5 In the blink of an eye wealth disappears,
for it will sprout wings
and fly away like an eagle.

6 Don't eat with people who are stingy;
don't desire their delicacies.
7 They are always thinking about how
much it costs.*
"Eat and drink," they say, but they
don't mean it.
8 You will throw up what little you've
eaten,
and your compliments will be wasted.

9 Don't waste your breath on fools,
for they will despise the wisest advice.

10 Don't cheat your neighbor by moving
the ancient boundary markers;
don't take the land of defenseless
orphans.
11 For their Redeemer* is strong;
he himself will bring their charges
against you.

12 Commit yourself to instruction;
listen carefully to words of
knowledge.

13 Don't fail to discipline your children.
They won't die if you spank them.
14 Physical discipline
may well save them from death.*

15 My child,* if your heart is wise,
my own heart will rejoice!
16 Everything in me will celebrate
when you speak what is right.

17 Don't envy sinners,
but always continue to fear the LORD.
18 You will be rewarded for this;
your hope will not be disappointed.

19 My child, listen and be wise:
Keep your heart on the right course.
20 Do not carouse with drunkards
or feast with gluttons,
21 for they are on their way to poverty,
and too much sleep clothes them
in rags.

22 Listen to your father, who gave you
life,
and don't despise your mother
when she is old.
23 Get the truth and never sell it;
also get wisdom, discipline, and
good judgment.
24 The father of godly children has cause
for joy.
What a pleasure to have children
who are wise.*
25 So give your father and mother joy!
May she who gave you birth be
happy.

26 O my son, give me your heart.
May your eyes take delight in
following my ways.
27 A prostitute is a dangerous trap;
a promiscuous woman is as
dangerous as falling into a
narrow well.
28 She hides and waits like a robber,
eager to make more men unfaithful.

29 Who has anguish? Who has sorrow?
Who is always fighting? Who is
always complaining?
Who has unnecessary bruises? Who
has bloodshot eyes?
30 It is the one who spends long hours
in the taverns,
trying out new drinks.
31 Don't gaze at the wine, seeing how
red it is,
how it sparkles in the cup, how
smoothly it goes down.
32 For in the end it bites like a poisonous
snake;
it stings like a viper.
33 You will see hallucinations,
and you will say crazy things.
34 You will stagger like a sailor tossed
at sea,
clinging to a swaying mast.
35 And you will say, "They hit me, but
I didn't feel it.
I didn't even know it when they
beat me up.
When will I wake up
so I can look for another drink?"

CHAPTER 24

1 Don't envy evil people
or desire their company.
2 For their hearts plot violence,
and their words always stir up
trouble.

3 A house is built by wisdom
and becomes strong through good sense.
4 Through knowledge its rooms are filled
with all sorts of precious riches and valuables.

5 The wise are mightier than the strong,*
and those with knowledge grow stronger and stronger.
6 So don't go to war without wise guidance;
victory depends on having many advisers.

7 Wisdom is too lofty for fools.
Among leaders at the city gate, they have nothing to say.

8 A person who plans evil
will get a reputation as a troublemaker.
9 The schemes of a fool are sinful;
everyone detests a mocker.

10 If you fail under pressure,
your strength is too small.

11 Rescue those who are unjustly sentenced to die;
save them as they stagger to their death.
12 Don't excuse yourself by saying, "Look, we didn't know."
For God understands all hearts, and he sees you.
He who guards your soul knows you knew.
He will repay all people as their actions deserve.

13 My child,* eat honey, for it is good,
and the honeycomb is sweet to the taste.
14 In the same way, wisdom is sweet to your soul.
If you find it, you will have a bright future,
and your hopes will not be cut short.

15 Don't wait in ambush at the home of the godly,
and don't raid the house where the godly live.
16 The godly may trip seven times, but they will get up again.
But one disaster is enough to overthrow the wicked.

17 Don't rejoice when your enemies fall;
don't be happy when they stumble.
18 For the LORD will be displeased with you
and will turn his anger away from them.

19 Don't fret because of evildoers;
don't envy the wicked.
20 For evil people have no future;
the light of the wicked will be snuffed out.

21 My child, fear the LORD and the king.
Don't associate with rebels,
22 for disaster will hit them suddenly.
Who knows what punishment will come
from the LORD and the king?

23:7 The meaning of the Hebrew is uncertain. **23:11** Or *redeemer.* **23:14** Hebrew *from Sheol.* **23:15** Hebrew *My son;* also in 23:19. **23:24** Hebrew *to have a wise son.* **24:5** As in Greek version; Hebrew reads *A wise man is strength.* **24:13** Hebrew *My son;* also in 24:21.

NOTES

22:22 ***Don't rob the poor just because you can.*** Lit., "Do not rob the poor man (*dal* [TH1800, ZH1924]) because he is poor (*dal*). The use of *dal* recalls its antecedent in the bridge proverb at the end of the previous section (22:16).

22:23 ***is their defender.*** There is a repetition here in Hebrew: "will contend their contention."

He will ruin . . . who ruins. Note the repetition of "ruin" that echoes the duplication of *dal* in 22:22. The clause literally reads, "and he will rob [the life] from those who rob them of life" (*nepesh* [TH5315, ZH5883]). "Squeezing out of life" is what Yahweh will do to those who are "squeezing . . . the poor by rapacious oppression" (Cody 1980:426).

22:24 ***Don't befriend angry people.*** Lit., "Do not associate yourself with a lord of anger."

or associate with. Lit., "do not come in."

22:25 ***or you will learn to be like them.*** Lit., "lest you learn his ways."

and endanger your soul. Lit., "and you are snatched in a snare for your soul." Thus sayings 2 (22:22-23) and 3 (22:24-25) both warn about hazards to your soul (see note on 22:23).

22:26 ***to guarantee another person's debt.*** A wooden rendering is "do not be among those who clap the palm."

put up security for someone else. Lit., "among those who take on a pledge of debts."

22:27 ***will be snatched.*** From *laqakh* [TH3947, ZH4374], linking sayings 3 (22:24-25) and 4 (22:26-27). In the Hebrew it is a rhetorical question: "Why should he take your bed from under you?"

22:28 ***Don't cheat your neighbor by moving the ancient boundary markers.*** The same statement appears in 23:10a.

set up by previous generations. Lit., "which your fathers made." This verse constitutes the fifth saying and is expanded in 23:10-11 (see notes and commentary) to complete a chiasm.

22:29 ***ordinary people.*** Lit., "dark men," with the sense "obscure." This is the sixth saying (see note on 23:9).

23:1 ***pay attention to what is put before you.*** Hebrew has an intensifying infinitive, "Discerningly discern!" It could also be rendered, "Pay attention to *who* is before you"—i.e., consider the status of the host.

23:2 ***big eater.*** Lit., "lord of appetite" (*nepesh* [TH5315, ZH5883]). The severe metaphor, "put a knife to your throat," vigorously makes the point.

23:3 ***don't desire all the delicacies.*** The phrase is repeated virtually verbatim in 23:6, where the basic theme of wariness in the face of a meal continues.

23:4 ***wear yourself out.*** From *yaga'* [TH3021, ZH3333], used only here in Proverbs.

Be wise enough to know when to quit. Precisely, "From your understanding, cease!" Alternatively, Waltke glosses, "Stop trusting in your own insight" (2005:226).

23:5 ***In the blink of an eye wealth disappears.*** The Hebrew is a rhetorical question, "Do your eyes fly upon it and it is not?" The motif of flight continues in the next line, "For [it] surely makes for itself wings, like an eagle that flies to heaven." "Weariness" (see 23:4), "eagles," and words meaning "wings" are also associated in Isa 40:31, "But those who trust in the LORD will find new strength. They will soar high on wings like eagles. They will run and not grow weary. They will walk and not faint."

23:6 ***Don't eat with people who are stingy.*** Lit., "Do not eat the bread of an evil eye." This saying resumes and expands the discussion of 23:1-3. The idiom "evil eye" occurs once more in the OT: lit., "A man hastening to be rich has an evil eye" (28:22).

23:7 ***They are always thinking about how much it costs.*** Lit., "For as he reckons in his soul thus he is." "Reckons" (*sha'ar* [TH8176, ZH9132]) is a hapax legomenon that LXX glosses as "hair" (from *se'ar* [TH8181, ZH8552]). If "hair" is original, repointing could yield, "Surely as a hair in your throat (*nepesh* [TH5315, ZH5883]) thus it is"—leading to the next verse. The Mishnaic Hebrew supplies the correct meaning, "reckon."

23:8 ***You will throw up what little you've eaten.*** Lit., "[as for] your morsel [that] you ate—you will vomit it up." "The meaning is that the guest will afterwards regret and be revolted by the whole incident" (Whybray 1994a:334). Perhaps the metaphor is a disgusting way of saying there is no such thing as a free lunch—the pound of flesh you enjoyed will be required of you.

23:9 ***Don't waste your breath on fools.*** Lit., "In the ears of a fool do not speak." "Speak" ties sayings 9 (23:6-8; NLT, "compliments") and 10 (23:9) together. Just as pleasant words are wasted on the "evil eye," so they are wasted on the fool. "Ears" balances nicely with "seeing" in 22:29, the corresponding element in the chiasm.

for they will despise the wisest advice. Lit., "for he will despise the wisdom of your words." "Your words" (*milleka* [TH4405/3509.2, ZH4863/3870]) is an unusual term, used only here in Proverbs. With the pronominal suffix, it appears similar to the word "kings" found in 22:29—perhaps an adornment of the chiasm.

23:10 ***Don't cheat . . . boundary markers.*** This is the same wording as 22:28a.

defenseless orphans. The boundaries of the defenseless were particularly vulnerable.

23:11 ***he himself will bring their charges against you.*** This saying expands on 22:28, adding the elements of the fatherless and the Redeemer, who upholds society's necessary structures. If God did not redeem civilization from unscrupulous opportunists, culture would inevitably erode and justice would fail (see note on 11:1). In addition to completing the chiasm, the phrase "For their Redeemer . . . will bring their charges" harkens back to 22:23, closing an inclusion of 10 sayings.

23:12 ***Commit yourself to instruction.*** Lit., "Let your heart enter in to discipline!" The second line reads, lit., "and your ears to the words of knowledge."

23:13 ***They won't die if you spank them.*** Lit., "If you smite him with the rod he will not die" (see note on 10:13).

23:14 ***Physical discipline.*** The language here recapitulates 23:13b, lit., "You with the rod must smite him." The "rod" signifies all manner of correction, not only corporeal (Heskett 2001:183). Contra Heskett, the actual mode of discipline exemplified in the saying should not be rejected.

save them from death. Lit., "His soul from Sheol you will deliver." The saying is about life and death; "discipline leads to life and indiscipline to the land of the dead" (McKane 1970:386).

23:15 ***My child, if your heart is wise.*** This sentiment is repeated in 23:19.

23:16 ***Everything in me.*** Lit., "My kidneys will exult." Powerful emotions are physically felt in the midriff area, as in the expression "butterflies in my stomach." "Kidneys" (used only here in Proverbs) is used for the bowels (Exod 29:13) and for intense emotion (Ps 73:21). The father's unspeakable elation makes his stomach leap to his throat.

23:17 ***Don't envy sinners.*** Lit., "Let not your heart be jealous of sinners!" The "heart" is at issue—either harboring wisdom (23:15) and keeping to the right path (23:19) or being jealous for the fleeting gains made by sinners. Envy is a repeated theme in the Thirty Sayings (see 24:1, 19).

always continue to fear the LORD. Lit., "in the fear of Yahweh all the day" (English must supply a verb). "Be jealous/zealous" can be carried over from the first line, yielding, "Be zealous in the fear of Yahweh always!" Remembering God and his promised blessings is the antidote for the temptation to envy the advances of sinners. This thought is developed in the next verse.

23:18 ***You will be rewarded for this; your hope will not be disappointed.*** Lit., "Surely there is a latter end, and your hope will not be cut off." There remains a final disposition both for the sinner and the upright. They will be extinguished, but your hope in Yahweh will not be "cut off." Keep the faith!

23:19 ***Keep your heart.*** Following the reading *'ashar* I [TH833, ZH886] (see 9:6) yields, "Let your heart *walk straight* upon the path!" Following the reading *'ashar* II [TH833A, ZH887] (see 31:28) yields, "May your heart *be blessed* on the path!" Sages may contemplate both truths.

23:20 ***Do not carouse with drunkards.*** Lit., "Do not be with imbibers of wine!" "Imbibers" is found in Proverbs only here and in the next verse.

23:21 ***and too much sleep clothes them in rags.*** Poverty and rags will attend profligacy. Since this end is paradigmatic of all sinners, why then would you envy them (23:17-18)?

23:22 ***your mother.*** The Hebrew sentence is arranged so that "mother" is the final word, and—except for the imperative "listen!"—"father" is the first word. Thus, the admonition is framed with wise parents.

23:23 ***Get.*** From *qanah* [TH7069, ZH7864], also glossed "buy," "possess," or "acquire" (see note on 8:22). The child is urged to imitate God by acquiring wisdom.

23:24 ***to have children who are wise.*** See NLT mg, "to have a wise son." Even this is not quite the literal Hebrew, which instead of "son" uses the participle (reading Qere) "one being born"—verbally corresponding with 23:22 ("he who begot you") and 23:25 ("she who gave you birth").

23:25 ***she who gave you birth.*** The mother is noted twice in this verse, presumably to balance the double reference to the father in 23:22.

23:26 ***take delight in following my ways.*** "Following" is an interpolation. The NLT follows Kethiv, "take delight in my ways." Qere (with LXX) has "guard my ways."

23:27 ***dangerous trap.*** Lit., "deep pit."

23:28 ***eager to make more men unfaithful.*** Lit., "Faithless ones among mankind she increases" (see note on 9:15).

23:29 ***bloodshot eyes.*** Lit., "redness of eyes." Probably the reference is not only to scleritis. "Suspicion of alcohol abuse should be heightened when there are outward signs such as facial erythema, puffiness of the face and eyelids, a coated tongue, bronchitis, insomnia, depression, headaches, or a history of physical trauma" (Jelinek 1998:69). "Redness" (*khakliluth* [TH2448, ZH2680]) is a hapax legomenon closely related to *khaklili* [TH2447, ZH2679] of Gen 49:12, "His eyes are *darker* than wine."

23:30 ***the one who spends long hours in the taverns.*** Lit., "those who linger over wine."

trying out new drinks. Lit., "those who go to search for mixed wine" (*mimsak* [TH4469, ZH4932]), elsewhere only in Isa 65:11.

23:31 ***how red it is, how it sparkles in the cup.*** Lit., "when it is red, when it gives its eye in the cup." "Eye" connects with 23:29, "redness of eyes." Wine is red with an "eye"; imbibers' eyes are red—they look alike! Driver (1951:187) perhaps misses the point when he dismisses the Hebrew text as "absurd" and emends *ra'ah* [TH7200, ZH8011] (gaze at) to *rawah* [TH7301, ZH8115] (drink deeply). How wine looks, and how the winebibber looks, are at issue. "If the alcoholic keeps away from the substance, then he or she will not fall back under its spell" (Jelinek 1998:70).

23:32 ***in the end.*** The same term as in 23:18 (see note). The result overshadows the initial titillating attraction. Consider the end and be wise.

bites . . . stings. Perhaps this is an allusion to a hangover. "Stings" (from *parash* [TH6567A, ZH7301]) conveys the idea of poison. The bite of venomous serpents is a metaphor for alcohol; death comes swiftly for alcoholics.

23:33 ***You will see hallucinations.*** Lit., "Your eyes will see strange things." Intoxication is like an altered mental state caused by snake venom.

you will say crazy things. Lit., "Your heart will utter perversities."

23:34 ***You will stagger like a sailor tossed at sea.*** Lit., "You will be like one who lies in the heart of the sea." Jelinek calls this "bed spins" (1998:71).

clinging to a swaying mast. Lit., "and like one who lies at the top of a mast." "A common phrase heard among alcoholics when they fall down is, 'Make the ground stop spinning so I can stand up'" (Jelinek 1998:71).

23:35 ***They hit me . . . they beat me.*** The closing verse mimics the repetitive opening line, "Who has anguish? Who has sorrow?"

24:4 ***Through knowledge.*** This parallels "by wisdom" in the previous verse; both begin with the preposition *be* [TH871.2, ZH928].

24:5 ***The wise are mightier than the strong.*** NLT follows the LXX (see NLT mg). The Hebrew reads, lit., "A wise man [rallies] in strength" ("rallies" is carried over from the second line). Waltke (2005:267) observes that these sayings are in alphabetic sequence (Aleph begins 24:1, Beth 24:3, and Gimel 24:5).

those with knowledge grow stronger and stronger. Lit., "and a man of knowledge rallies strength." "Knowledge" ties together 24:4-5; knowledge secures precious riches—and strength. Of course, the "man of wisdom" ties back to the "wisdom" that builds one's house (24:3).

24:7 ***Wisdom is too lofty for fools.*** "Wisdom" here is plural but treated as singular (see notes on 1:20-21, where Wisdom cries out at the gate for all to hear). With Driver (1951:188), NLT follows the reading *ramoth* [TH7311, ZH8123] (high) instead of *ra'moth* [TH7215, ZH8029] (coral).

24:8 ***will get a reputation as a troublemaker.*** Lit., "They will call him a lord of schemes."

24:9 ***The schemes of a fool are sinful.*** Lit., "Devising folly is sin." NLT understands the abstract "folly" as concrete "fool." "Folly" relates to 24:7, "fool."

24:10 ***If you fail under pressure, your strength is too small.*** Lit., "If you are slack in the day of adversity, your strength will be limited."

24:11 ***unjustly sentenced to die.*** Lit., "those being taken to death." Whybray takes this to indicate victims of foul play (1994a:347).

save them as they stagger to their death. Lit., "and [from] those tottering to the slaughter, do not withhold [your help]!" Alternatively, it could mean "and those tottering to the slaughter—hold them back!" Do not be slack on that day; for their sake your strength must not fail (24:10).

24:12 ***Don't excuse yourself by saying, "Look, we didn't know."*** No excuse is legitimate for allowing atrocities in your midst. Claiming the community was unaware or uninformed is rejected as an excuse.

For God understands all hearts, and he sees you. Lit., "Does not he who weighs hearts consider?" In the day of adversity, do not be slack. Do what you can. God holds the people responsible for complacency when they permit evildoers to destroy lives around them.

He will repay all people as their actions deserve. Lit., "He will render to mankind (*'adam* [TH120, ZH132]) according to his work."

24:15 ***the house where the godly live.*** Lit., "his resting place."

24:16 ***The godly may trip seven times, but they will get up again.*** Lit., "For the righteous may fall seven times and will rise." "Seven" denotes full and consummate completeness (6:31; 9:1).

24:19 ***don't envy the wicked.*** Cf. 23:17, which also juxtaposes envying sinners with fearing Yahweh.

24:20 ***have no future.*** Lit., "There is no latter end."

24:21 ***rebels.*** The Hebrew is a participle from *shanah* [TH8138, ZH9101], meaning "changing ones," as in KJV, "them that are given to change." Unstable people are no friends of God and have no inner grounding that would allow them to stand when times get difficult. The LXX (cf. RSV, NRSV) reads, "Do not disobey *either of them*"—see *shenehem* [TH8147/3963.1, ZH9109/4392] (two of them) of 24:22.

24:22 ***for disaster will hit them suddenly.*** Lit., "For suddenly their calamity will rise." "Will rise" echoes 24:16, where the righteous are promised to "rise again" after a complete and seemingly final demise.

Who knows what punishment will come from the LORD and the king? "The Lord and the king" is an interpolation. Lit., "And ruin [from] both of them, who knows?" "Knows" (*yada'* [TH3045, ZH3359]) is the last word of the verse, with similar spelling to the last word of 24:20, perhaps tying the verses together (see note on 23:9).

COMMENTARY

In counting the "Thirty Sayings," the introduction (22:20-21) should likely be considered the first saying. Twenty-nine sayings follow this. The first section (22:22–23:11) consists of 10 sayings grouped into two stanzas. The first stanza (22:22-27) of the first section includes sayings 2–4, each verbally linked to the next to form a sentence chain. The second stanza (22:29–23:11) of the first section includes sayings 5–11 and is organized in a chiastic pattern of seven elements as shown here:

- A. Boundaries—established by previous generations (22:28)
  - B. Skill before the king (22:29)
    - C. Caution with the ruler's delicacies (23:1-3)
      - D. Fleetingness of money—it is not the goal of life (23:4-5)
    - C'. Caution with the stingy man's delicacies (23:6-8)
  - B'. Fools (23:9, contrasting with 22:29)
- A'. Boundaries—established by God (23:10-11)

The second section is found in 23:12-21; it contains sayings 12–15. The third section is found in 23:22–24:22; it contains sayings 16–30.

Sayings 2–4. The second saying (22:22-23) pertains to the poor. This may be compared to *Amenemope* chapter 2 (ANET 422):

Guard thyself against robbing the oppressed
And against overbearing the disabled.
Stretch not forth thy hand against the approach of an old man.

The saying in Proverbs invokes Yahweh, the defender of the poor who will wring from the oppressor the life they have wrung from others.

The third saying (22:24-25) pertains to the angry man. This may be compared to *Amenemope* chapter 9 (ANET 423):

Do not associate to thyself the heated man,
Nor visit him for conversation.

How to handle strong passions is part and parcel of living a wise life before Yahweh. Emotions such as anger or sexual desire can be very destructive and lead one into folly. The wise are skilled at governing such feelings and will not be ruled by them. James (the New Testament "wisdom book") also treats the topic of passions:

> *What is causing the quarrels and fights among you? Don't they come from the evil desires at war within you? You want what you don't have, so you scheme and kill to get it. You are jealous of what others have, but you can't get it, so you fight and wage war to take it away from them. Yet you don't have what you want because you don't ask God for it. And even when you ask, you don't get it because your motives are all wrong—you want only what will give you pleasure. (Jas 4:1-3)*

The third of the Sayings of the Wise reminds the reader that a temper or an angry disposition leads only to folly.

The fourth saying (22:26-27) pertains to borrowing. There is no comparable material in *Amenemope.*

Sayings 5–11. The fifth saying pertains to boundaries (22:28). Compare this to Amenemope chapter 6 (ANET 422):

> *Do not carry off the landmark at the boundaries of the arable land,*
> *Nor disturb the position of the measuring-cord;*
> *Be not greedy after a cubit of land,*
> *Nor encroach upon the boundaries of a widow . . . .*
> *Guard against encroaching upon the boundaries of the fields,*
> *Lest a terror carry thee off.*
> *One satisfies god with the will of the Lord,*
> *Who determines the boundaries of the arable land. . . .*

The sixth saying (22:29) pertains to displaying skill before the king. This may be compared to *Amenemope* chapter 30 (ANET 424):

> *As for the scribe who is experienced in his office,*
> *He will find himself worthy (to be) a courtier.*

The opposite of gaining favor with God and man (22:29) is living as a fool (23:9). These two proverbs (sayings 6 and 10) constitute two sayings that contrast one another in the chiasm of the first poem. The first begins "Do you see?" and the second begins, literally, "In the ear . . ." The contrast is this: While the value and worth of the diligent worker cannot be overstated, the fool will not, cannot, and does not ever understand this—and will ever persist in his self-destructive and worthless ways.

The seventh saying (23:1-3) pertains to exercising caution regarding the ruler's delicacies. Compare this to *Amenemope* chapter 23 (ANET 424):

> *Do not eat bread before a noble,*
> *Nor lay on thy mouth at first.*
> *If thou art satisfied with false chewings,*
> *They are a pastime for thy spittle.*
> *Look at the cup which is before thee,*
> *And let it serve thy needs.*

This is the first saying of three that deal with how to handle wealth and the wealthy. In this case, a politically powerful man with an agenda is viewed as a threat—do not trust his overtures! If you are an undisciplined eater, prone to weakness in the area of food, beware, for this can be exploited. Satan used hunger to tempt Jesus (Matt 4:2-4), who replied that one's life does not consist in eating and drinking but in imbibing the word of God. An unscrupulous schemer may one day use food to tempt you. Will your god be your belly (Phil 3:19), or will you hold on to your senses and be wise? Consider food to be a test, a rite of passage in the eyes of the host.

The eighth saying (23:4-5) pertains to the fleetingness of money. This may be compared to *Amenemope* chapter 7 (ANET 422):

Cast not thy heart in pursuit of riches,
(For) there is no ignoring Fate and Fortune.
Place not thy heart upon externals,
(For) every man belongs to his (appointed) hour.

God did not mean for human beings to be worked to death; this is one reason he instituted the Sabbath. As quickly as your eye darts upon wealth, wealth darts away. Remember this when you dine in the house of the rich: Money is ephemeral and unreliable. Wisdom, however, has an eternal weight of value.

The ninth saying (23:6-8) pertains to exercising caution with a stingy man's delicacies. In Proverbs, the stingy person is actually wealthy, but he is tightfisted toward others. Compare this to *Amenemope* chapter 11 (ANET 423):

Be not greedy for the property of a poor man,
Nor hunger for his bread.
As for the property of a poor man, it (is) a blocking to the throat,
It makes a vomiting *to the gullet.*
If he has obtained *by false oaths,*
His heart is perverted to the belly.
The mouthful of bread (too) great thou swallowest and vomitest up,
And art emptied of thy good.

Saying 10 (23:9) concerns the fool. This may be compared to *Amenemope* chapter 21 (ANET 424).

Empty not thy belly to everybody,
Nor damage (thus) the regard for thee.
Spread not thy words to the common people,
Nor associate to thyself one (too) outgoing of heart.
Better is a man whose talk (remains) in his belly
Than he who speaks it out injuriously.

This parallels saying 6, which pertains to the stupid actions of the fool (see comments above on saying 6).

Saying 11 (23:10-11) pertains to boundaries. This may be compared to *Amenemope* chapter 6 (see quote above in saying 5). After this verse there is no further comparable material in *Amenemope* for the remainder of the Thirty Sayings.

Sayings 12–15. Saying 12 (23:12) is a call to attune oneself to learning once again, and it begins a poem of four sayings.

Saying 13 (23:13-14) provides instruction for the discipline of youth. The command to discipline one's children continues the thought from 23:12, where the reader is called to internalize discipline. (For a discussion of the youth, see commentary on 1:2-7.) If one's child internalizes discipline, he or she will *never* lose the path of life.

Saying 14 (23:15-19) repeats the adjuration for "my child" to "be wise" in "your heart." This long saying is enclosed with an inclusion (23:15, 19). The center of the saying (23:17) invokes the fear of Yahweh.

Saying 15 (23:20-21) marks the halfway point of the Thirty. It also anticipates the conclusion of the further sayings of the wise—an examination of the self-destructive sluggard who also indulges in "sleep" (24:33). In addition, it ties back to its antecedent on the subject of poverty (22:22-23), demarcating the first half of the Sayings.

Sayings 16–30. Saying 16 (23:22-25) is an appeal to the child to listen to the parents' counsel. This appeal is bounded by the inclusion "father . . . mother" and is tightly enmeshed with verbal repetition ("to beget/bear" in 23:22, 24, 25; "wise/wisdom" in 23:23, 24; "rejoice," from *gil* [TH1523, ZH1635], in 23:24, 25; "rejoice," from *samakh* [TH8056, ZH8524] in 23:24, 25; "father" again in 23:24)—an appropriate beginning to the second half of the Thirty, a poem of 14 sayings.

Saying 17 (23:26) is an appeal from the father to his son to follow his directions wholeheartedly.

Saying 18 (23:27-28) is an exhortation from the father to his son to stay away from the lures of prostitutes, which is a major theme in the early chapters of Proverbs.

Saying 19 (23:29-35) is an extended warning against alcoholism. The saying concludes with a sarcastic comment on the addictive quality of alcohol. The drunkard lives for the next drink regardless of the personal suffering entailed.

Saying 20 (24:1-2) warns people not to envy the wicked. Being zealous for the fear of Yahweh is contrary to being envious of sinners (23:17).

Saying 21 (24:3-4) extols wisdom. A house is built by wisdom (24:3). This theme is also found in 14:1, "A wise woman builds her home," and 9:1-2, where personified Wisdom built her house and filled it with a banquet. A person's family and legacy are established through a lifestyle lived scrupulously and intentionally before God and the community.

Saying 22 (24:5-6) extols the importance of exercising wisdom in important national matters, such as whether or not to wage war. The wisdom commended here is not a matter of one prudent man's unilateral insight. Wisdom is possessed by the community and by the court (see also note on 20:18). Any major decision in life should involve much counsel.

In Saying 23 (24:7), Wisdom calls for all to hear (cf. 9:1-3). But fools who have not entered her house have no wisdom to offer, and they should keep silent when judgment is rendered (lit., "does not open his mouth"). This thought closes the group of sayings treating wisdom.

Saying 24 (24:8-9) pertains to the foolishness of schemers. One way of illustrating virtue is to highlight its opposite. Those who practice sin, mockery, and evil do not heed Wisdom's words and will not enter her house.

Saying 25 (24:10-12) pertains to complacency. This admonishes people to rise to the occasion so as to be equal to the task at hand.

Saying 26 (24:13-14) says wisdom is like honey. The verse is not about honey, of course, but has resumed the theme of wisdom from saying 23. Those who have moral fiber need to stand firm during days of adversity. Their reward will be sweet blessings, the best of which is eternal life.

Saying 27 (24:15-16) begins with the statement, "Don't wait in ambush at the home of the godly" (24:15). Either the verse rhetorically addresses the wicked with a warning (which, of course, will not be heeded), or it means that one who does such things is wicked. The next verse (24:16) says, "The godly may trip seven times, but they will get up again." The sevenfold fall of the righteous may appear to be his demise, but the righteous, unlike the wicked, will rise again. In other words, the righteous are indestructible. This is why Daniel and his associates emerged unscathed from the fiery furnace and the lion's pit. Therefore, be strong on the day of adversity, and do what is right!

Saying 28 (24:17-18) warns people not to rejoice in the failings of others. Proverbs 24:17 links to the previous verse with the word "falling" in the first line and "stumbling" in the second. People are reassured that falling is not indicative of the final state of affairs. We should refrain from gloating when another stumbles, for God determines who falls and who rises again (24:18).

Saying 29 (24:19-20) proclaims the fate of the wicked. Their lamp will be snuffed out and forever darkened—unlike the fate of the righteous.

Saying 30 (24:21-22) speaks of fearing God and the king. God (and his terrestrial representative) determines the outcome of events. The Thirty Sayings end here by recalling the first saying (22:19), which is a summons to fear Yahweh.

The Significance of the Thirty Sayings. The Sayings of the Wise are not simply a reconstructed version of Egyptian instructional material; they are purposefully organized and selected to help the reader understand who God is (22:19), and in understanding him, gain newness of life not only today (23:17-18), but forever (24:16). One is admonished to set one's heart upon these principles of life so that transformation of character may take place.

How you treat the powerless and helpless is important to God. If you take advantage of them, God will cause what you have done to fall back upon you—and you will lose your very soul (22:22-23; see notes). Your soul is at hazard if you befriend an angry person and learn to be hotheaded yourself (22:24-25). How you handle your passions reveals your character.

The ancient boundary markers are analogous to the weights and measures of the marketplace. God stands behind the traditional parameters of commerce and property (22:28). He protects society from those who would cheat and steal. Instead of trying to work around civilization's superstructure of equity, simply apply yourself to working hard and well. If you do, you will gain status in the community, having favor with God and man (22:29). The helpless and defenseless are particularly vulnerable. Although in this world the vulnerable may not perceive any special recourse, they do have a very strong Advocate (23:11), who also has a stake in the ancient boundary markers, the weights and measures, equitable courts, and everything on which citizens depend and rely for life. The wise are always conscious of this fact; fools are not (Ps 14).

The one who tampers with money and property is analogous to the false host, whose overtures cannot be trusted, who pretends friendship and hospitality while plotting against you (23:1-3, 6-8). Manipulators and calculating profiteers will use your own appetites against you; they will seduce you with pleasures and delights, all the while seeking to take advantage. This contrasts the beneficent promises of God in Isaiah 55:1-2:

"Is anyone thirsty?
Come and drink—
even if you have no money!
Come, take your choice of wine or milk—
it's all free!
Why spend your money on food that does not give you strength?
Why pay for food that does you no good?
Listen to me, and you will eat what is good.
You will enjoy the finest food.

These promises come to their consummate fulfillment in Jesus Christ, who has given of himself freely on behalf of his people. Pursuing money (23:4), like going after delicacies, is unsatisfying (23:5). Money is fleeting. Wisdom is more valuable than gold or silver.

This wisdom requires a person's commitment, which essentially is a form of fearing Yahweh (23:17). Be reverent before God and remember that he brings all things to conclusion and works out his purposes; then you will be able to avoid the temptation to envy sinners, who by whatever perverted means advance themselves and seem prosperous (23:18). In the words of Psalm 37:1-11:

Don't worry about the wicked
or envy those who do wrong.
For like grass, they soon fade away.
Like spring flowers, they soon wither.

Trust in the LORD and do good.
Then you will live safely in the land and prosper.
Take delight in the LORD,
and he will give you your heart's desires.

Commit everything you do to the LORD.
Trust him, and he will help you.
He will make your innocence radiate like the dawn,
and the justice of your cause will shine like the noonday sun.

Be still in the presence of the LORD,
and wait patiently for him to act.
Don't worry about evil people who prosper
or fret about their wicked schemes.

Stop being angry!
  Turn from your rage!
Do not lose your temper—
  it only leads to harm.
For the wicked will be destroyed,
  but those who trust in the LORD will possess the land.

Soon the wicked will disappear.
  Though you look for them, they will be gone.
The lowly will possess the land
  and will live in peace and prosperity.

The drunkard and glutton are good examples of this; they while away their lives until they are left with rags and poverty (23:21). This is the end of sinners—now and forever. But if one attends to discipline, that person may be saved from the grave. It takes a great exercise of faith to say no to a pleasure. People whose "god is their appetite" have no awareness of being "citizens of heaven" (Phil 3:19-20). It also takes faith not to be jealous of sinners. Both situations require us to trust God with the future (23:18)—and trust that he will reward those who do so.

Some who live for pleasure have become ensnared by it. Alcohol is addictive. The alcoholic awakens in strange surroundings, full of bruises and unable to account for the physical trauma he or she suffered, but then begins anew the search for drink (23:35). Likewise, the whoremonger pursues pleasure to his own hurt (23:27). This is one reason why it is crucial for youths to heed their parents' admonitions (23:22-25).

The way to avoid temptations is to take the path of wisdom and knowledge. One must be able to "see through" and avoid snares that threaten life. Wisdom is the solid foundation on which to build (24:3). The wise are strong, successful, and able to render sound judgment (24:6-7). Because of their faith in God, they will always rise again even if they fall (24:16). People who are secure do not change their opinion with every new trend or fleeting consensus (see note on 24:21), but stand firm for what is right.

◆ C. Appendix to the Thirty Sayings (24:23-34)

23 Here are some further sayings of the wise:

It is wrong to show favoritism when
  passing judgment.
24 A judge who says to the wicked, "You
  are innocent,"
  will be cursed by many people and
  denounced by the nations.
25 But it will go well for those who
  convict the guilty;
  rich blessings will be showered on
  them.

26 An honest answer
  is like a kiss of friendship.

27 Do your planning and prepare your
  fields
  before building your house.

28 Don't testify against your neighbors
  without cause;
  don't lie about them.
29 And don't say, "Now I can pay them
  back for what they've done to me!
  I'll get even with them!"

[30] **I walked by the field of a lazy person,**
the vineyard of one with no common sense.
[31] **I saw that it was overgrown with nettles.**
It was covered with weeds,
and its walls were broken down.
[32] **Then, as I looked and thought about it,**
I learned this lesson:
[33] **A little extra sleep, a little more slumber,**
a little folding of the hands to rest—
[34] **then poverty will pounce on you like a bandit;**
scarcity will attack you like an armed robber.

NOTES

24:23 ***Here are some further sayings of the wise.*** See commentary for an explanation of this opening statement.

It is wrong. The Hebrew text ends the verse with "is not good." This ties in with the last word of 24:25, which is "good" (see note).

to show favoritism. Lit., "to regard face." This saying treats partiality in judgment; one should condemn the wicked and exonerate the righteous.

24:24 ***cursed by many people.*** The world will curse a judge who shows partiality. Such a one is simply not up to the task of rendering a verdict.

24:25 ***for those who convict the guilty.*** Lit., "for those reproving."

rich blessings will be showered on them. Lit., "upon them will come blessings of good."

24:26 ***An honest answer.*** Lit., "One who returns right words." Just as the people bless the magistrate who reproves the wicked, a truthful answer is a breath of fresh air, like a kiss of friendship.

like a kiss of friendship. Cohen argues that the verb *nashaq* [TH5401, ZH5975] (kiss) has the meaning "to seal up, to bind," and translates, "He that gives forthright judgment will silence all hostile lips" (1982:422). What drives his analysis is his inability to discover a "satisfactory meaning in this context." However, it is normal for proverbial material to supply startling and unexpected concrete images in comparison with a moral judgment. Wisdom is "sweet" like honey (24:13); the sluggard is like vinegar (10:26). A "forthright judgment" is like a friend's kiss—*and* it silences hostile lips. If Cohen's analysis is correct, then the saying puns two meanings, and the wise may cogitate both insights.

24:27 ***before building your house.*** See 24:3-4, where "a house is built by wisdom" and adorned by knowledge. Here, the manner in which such wisdom is employed is seen in one's careful planning and foresight. The well-prepared field contrasts the sluggard's, which is so vividly portrayed in 24:30-34.

24:28 ***Don't testify against your neighbors without cause.*** The courtroom setting has returned, recalling the second saying.

24:29 ***I'll get even with them!*** Lit., "I will return to the man according to his work." This verse recalls 24:12, where God, lit., "will return to a man according to his work"—the work of complacently standing back and letting the innocent suffer. Although you are called to take action to save the innocent, do not take vengeance against the perpetrator, for in doing so you will be putting yourself in the place of God. This exemplifies how proverbs or sayings must be viewed in the context of the book (cf. 17:21 and 22:6; 19:7 and 19:22).

24:30 ***with no common sense.*** Lit., "a man lacking heart." The sluggard has no intelligence, no regard for his own life or its necessary maintenance. He is the paradigm of any form of folly—graphically illustrating what is true invisibly for any other foolish permutation. The disintegration and wreck of his life is plainly visible (24:31).

24:32 ***Then, as I looked and thought about it.*** Lit., "And I saw, I set my heart, I saw" (see 22:17).

24:33 This verse has the same wording as 6:10.

24:34 ***poverty.*** The Hebrew expression is *resheka* [TH7389/3509.2, ZH8203/3870] (your poverty); cf. 6:11, which has *re'sheka* (your poverty). Except for the difference of spelling in this word, the two verses are identical.

COMMENTARY

The statement "Here are some further sayings of the wise" (24:23a) demarcates the following material as a separate unit. In Hebrew this is two words, *gam-'elleh lakhakamim* [TH428, ZH465] ("also these belong to wise ones"). This is meant to be read in the light of 22:17, "the words of wise," perhaps identifying 24:23-34 as an addendum to what precedes. Luc argues against 24:23a being a title: "Why should this second collection . . . need a separate title when it is placed as a continuation of a collection that already contains a title with 'the words of the wise'?" (2000:253). He argues that all other titles contain the words "proverbs of" or "words of" (as in 25:1). Thus, these 12 verses may be regarded as a supplement to the words of the wise.

One of the messages of this section is that a wise person is one who makes plans. Before choosing a lifestyle ("before building your house"), we should make all necessary preparations to ensure our plans will come to fruition (24:27). Jesus calls us to build our lives on him.

> *A large crowd was following Jesus. He turned around and said to them, "If you want to be my disciple, you must hate everyone else by comparison—your father and mother, wife and children, brothers and sisters—yes, even your own life. Otherwise, you cannot be my disciple. And if you do not carry your own cross and follow me, you cannot be my disciple.*
>
> *"But don't begin until you count the cost. For who would begin construction of a building without first calculating the cost to see if there is enough money to finish it? Otherwise, you might complete only the foundation before running out of money, and then everyone would laugh at you. They would say, 'There's the person who started that building and couldn't afford to finish it!'*
>
> *"Or what king would go to war against another king without first sitting down with his counselors to discuss whether his army of 10,000 could defeat the 20,000 soldiers marching against him? And if he can't, he will send a delegation to discuss terms of peace while the enemy is still far away. So you cannot become my disciple without giving up everything you own." (Luke 14:25-33)*

The opposite of this diligent cost-counting and high commitment is the easy road, pursuing shortcuts and catering to bodily cravings—such as the natural inclination toward inactivity. The Sayings of the Wise concludes with the example of just this sort of person, detailing how his field is overgrown with weeds and his wall is broken down.

The field of the sluggard is a metaphor for any life devoid of discipline and instruction. Every fool's life is in disarray, although this may not be visible to all who know him. But one addicted to sloth loves sleep and does not tend his property. One may paraphrase 24:33-34 as "A little folly, a little neglect of God's word, a little cheating, a little sin, and judgment will fall upon you suddenly; you will not escape the consequences." The way of escape is to heed the exhortation of God's word: "'Awake, O sleeper, rise up from the dead, and Christ will give you light.' So be careful how you live. Don't live like fools, but like those who are wise. Make the most of every opportunity in these evil days. Don't act thoughtlessly, but understand what the Lord wants you to do" (Eph 5:14-17).

◆ IV. Hezekiah's Proverbs of Solomon (25:1–29:27)

Van Leeuwen treats chapter 25 as a unit with an overarching theme, namely, "The king and mankind are engaged in a search for wisdom . . . as it encompasses and pertains to the social order" (1988:74-75). More precisely, people search for what is glorious or honorable. Proverbs 26:1-16 employs the key words "fool" and "sluggard" in the sense that they don't know what is fitting or proper in various situations. "Things that are in themselves good are misapplied where they are not fitting . . . the idea of fittingness is the poem's central concern" (Van Leeuwen 1988:100). The next poem (26:17-28) explores the spoken word. "In sum, this proverb poem presents the Negative actavants [*sic*] . . . who cause strife and hurt by verbal violence and deception" (Van Leeuwen 1988:122). Proverbs 27:1-22 focuses on domestic life. The remaining material (27:23–29:27), though loosely organized, generally pertains to rulers and kings. The major divisions in this commentary of chapters 25–27 are informed by Van Leeuwen's analysis.

◆ A. Title (25:1)

These are more proverbs of Solomon, collected by the advisers of King Hezekiah of Judah.

NOTES

25:1 ***more proverbs.*** There are 138 verses in this section (25:2–29:27). The consonants of Hezekiah's name (*kh* = 8, *z* = 7, *q* = 100, *y* = 10, *h* = 5) numerically total 130, being 100 more than the Thirty Sayings (22:22–24:22). Perhaps some can be grouped to count as one unit (25:6-7, 9-10, 21-22; 26:18-19, 24-25; 27:15-16, 23-24, 26-27), totaling 130.

COMMENTARY

The written traditions of Israel present Hezekiah as an enthusiastic worshiper of Yahweh. In 2 Chronicles, Hezekiah is a second Solomon, having sway over the 12 tribes (not just Judah) and opening the doors of the Temple and dedicating it just as Solomon had done (2 Chr 29–30). Carasik (1994:291-295) identifies a number of associations between Solomon and Hezekiah, such as the proverbial key word *sakal* [TH7919, ZH8505] (be successful, be wise) applied to Hezekiah in 2 Kings 18:7, his adept use of a proverb (2 Kgs 19:3), and the use of root *btkh* [TH982, ZH1053] to characterize both Solomon's era (1 Kgs 4:25 [5:5], "safety") and Hezekiah's (e.g.,

2 Kgs 18:5, he "trusted" in Yahweh). Thus, Hezekiah's reputation as a sage can be perceived in literary connections independent of this title.

B. Discovering Glory (25:2-28)

2 It is God's privilege to conceal things
and the king's privilege to discover them.

3 No one can comprehend the height of heaven, the depth of the earth,
or all that goes on in the king's mind!

4 Remove the impurities from silver,
and the sterling will be ready for the silversmith.
5 Remove the wicked from the king's court,
and his reign will be made secure by justice.

6 Don't demand an audience with the king
or push for a place among the great.
7 It's better to wait for an invitation to the head table
than to be sent away in public disgrace.

Just because you've seen something,
8 don't be in a hurry to go to court.
For what will you do in the end
if your neighbor deals you a shameful defeat?

9 When arguing with your neighbor,
don't betray another person's secret.
10 Others may accuse you of gossip,
and you will never regain your good reputation.

11 Timely advice is lovely,
like golden apples in a silver basket.

12 To one who listens, valid criticism
is like a gold earring or other gold jewelry.

13 Trustworthy messengers refresh like snow in summer.
They revive the spirit of their employer.

14 A person who promises a gift but doesn't give it
is like clouds and wind that bring no rain.

15 Patience can persuade a prince,
and soft speech can break bones.

16 Do you like honey?
Don't eat too much, or it will make you sick!

17 Don't visit your neighbors too often,
or you will wear out your welcome.

18 Telling lies about others
is as harmful as hitting them with an ax,
wounding them with a sword,
or shooting them with a sharp arrow.

19 Putting confidence in an unreliable person in times of trouble
is like chewing with a broken tooth or walking on a lame foot.

20 Singing cheerful songs to a person with a heavy heart
is like taking someone's coat in cold weather
or pouring vinegar in a wound.*

21 If your enemies are hungry, give them food to eat.
If they are thirsty, give them water to drink.
22 You will heap burning coals of shame on their heads,
and the LORD will reward you.

23 As surely as a north wind brings rain,
so a gossiping tongue causes anger!

24 It's better to live alone in the corner of an attic
than with a quarrelsome wife in a lovely home.

[25] Good news from far away
is like cold water to the thirsty.

[26] If the godly give in to the wicked,
it's like polluting a fountain or
muddying a spring.

[27] It's not good to eat too much honey,
and it's not good to seek honors
for yourself.

[28] A person without self-control
is like a city with broken-down walls.

25:20 As in Greek version; Hebrew reads *pouring vinegar on soda.*

NOTES

25:2 ***privilege . . . privilege.*** Lit., "glory" or "honor." God has the glory of concealing a *dabar* [TH1697, ZH1821]—a "word" or "thing" or "matter." The king's "glory" is in discovery, searching out what is hidden. "The God of Prov 25:2 can conceal and thus, by implication, reveal. His hidden wisdom comprises not only his acts of creation but also his plans and judgments in history" (Van Leeuwen 1988:75). This proverb sets the tone for the chapter, which is about humanity seeking for the divinely sanctioned good. Where this good seems counterintuitive, Yahweh is invoked by name as motivation for the sage to seek the highest way rather than natural inclinations (25:21-22). This composition is also irreducibly religious.

25:3 ***No one can comprehend.*** The final word in Hebrew, "searchable," connects with the king's calling to "discover" in 25:2. The king's mind is like the heavens and earth—unfathomable and inscrutable. By wisdom kings render judgments beyond the ken of ordinary citizens.

25:4 ***the sterling will be ready for the silversmith.*** Lit., "will come out for the silversmith a vessel." The process of casting the vessel is not mentioned, as Aaron claimed, "I threw it [the gold] in the fire and there came out (*yatsa'* [TH3318, ZH3655]) his calf (Exod 32:24)" (Van Leeuwen 1986b:113).

25:5 ***Remove.*** This is the same word as in 25:4, "Remove the impurities." The wicked are the dross; once they are removed, the throne will be established in righteousness. This is one path to glory recognized by thoughtful kings (see notes on 16:12).

25:6 ***Don't demand an audience with the king.*** Lit., "Do not honor yourself before the king." And the second line reads, "nor stand in the place of great men."

25:7 ***It's better to wait for an invitation to the head table.*** Lit., "For it is better to say to you, 'Come up here!'" Here is another path to glory (see 25:27).

than to be sent away in public disgrace. Lit., "than for you to be lowered before the prince."

Just because you've seen something. Lit., "that which your eyes have seen." The NLT interprets this as beginning the thought of the following verse.

25:8 ***don't . . . go.*** NLT follows MT; other translations repoint *tetse'* [TH3318, ZH3655] to *totse'* (Hiphil), yielding, "do not cause to go" or "bring" (see RSV).

what will you do. This uses second-person direct address. This is not a proverb, but a saying, which continues in the next verse.

25:10 ***you will never regain your good reputation.*** Lit., "your infamy will not turn away [i.e., not cease]." (The last word in Hebrew is *shub* [TH7725, ZH8740]; see 25:13.) Here is a path away from glory.

25:11 ***Timely advice is lovely.*** Lit., "a word spoken upon its ____." The blank space represents *'open* [TH655, ZH698], a hapax legomenon, perhaps with the same sense as *'opan* [TH212, ZH236], meaning "wheels" (McKane 1970:584). The context indicates a meaning "in its time," "in its situation," "fitly."

25:12 ***To one who listens, valid criticism.*** Lit., "A wise reprover to a listening ear."

25:13 ***They revive the spirit of their employer.*** Lit., "And the soul (*nepesh* [TH5315, ZH5883]) of his lords will return." The verse ends with the verb *shub* [TH7725, ZH8740] as in 25:10.

25:14 ***A person who promises a gift but doesn't give it.*** Lit., "A man who boasts of his gifts falsely."

25:15 ***Patience can persuade a prince.*** Heb., *qatsin* [TH7101, ZH7903], a different term than "prince" in 25:7 (*nadib* [TH5081A, ZH5618]); see note on 25:7.

soft speech can break bones. The power in the reasoned content of a wise courtier's delivery cannot be withstood. The skeleton of one's opponent—the framework of his argument—will gloriously crack under tempered scrutiny.

25:16 ***Do you like honey?*** Lit., "If you find honey." The maxim is not about honey but about overstaying one's welcome in a neighbor's house (25:17).

Don't eat too much, or it will make you sick! Lit., "Eat your sufficiency, lest you are satiated (*saba'* [TH7646, ZH8425]) with it and you vomit it." "Here honey is a liminal symbol for boundaries which must not be transgressed" (Van Leeuwen 1986a:107-108). Cross the line and ingloriously disgorge.

25:17 ***Don't visit your neighbors too often.*** Lit., "Make rare your foot in the house of your neighbor"—if you would find glory.

or you will wear out your welcome. Lit., "Lest he become satiated (*saba'* [TH7646, ZH8425]) with you and will hate you." Verses 16-17 are bound together with the phrase "lest you/he are/become satiated," guiding the reader to associate them.

25:18 ***Telling lies about others.*** Precisely, "A man who bears false witness against his neighbor." As in 25:17, this verse pertains to one's treatment of one's neighbor.

ax . . . sword . . . sharp arrow. In the Hebrew text, these words begin the verse. NLT interpolates, "is as harmful as hitting them with an . . . wounding them with a . . . shooting them with a . . ." Biblical poetry is characterized by pithiness, saying much with few words (Longman 1987:121). The proverb is nine words in Hebrew; NLT uses 25 words to translate it!

25:19 ***chewing with a broken tooth.*** Lit., "breaking a tooth."

walking on a lame foot. Lit., "a foot made wavering."

25:20 ***Singing cheerful songs to a person with a heavy heart.*** Sages know not only what to say, but when and how to say it. The heavy heart requires a special approach. "A wise counselor is not quick to speak (10:18; 17:28). He is genuinely intent to listen to the situation before speaking (18:13). A counselor does not wear out his welcome (25:16-17), sing songs to a heavy heart (25:20), or speak in haste (29:20)" (Schwab 1995:16).

pouring vinegar in a wound. Cf. NLT mg. The MT reads, "vinegar on soda" (*nether* [TH5427, ZH6003]), a word found elsewhere only in Jer 2:22 to describe a component of soap.

25:21 ***enemies.*** NLT glosses with a plural subject, while in Hebrew it is singular, lit., "if *one hating you* is hungry." In 25:17, the hater is an overused host; here, your hospitality can overcome his distaste for you. Treatment of an antagonized associate opens and closes the stanza. Meinhold (1992:247) compares this maxim to David sparing Saul in the cave (1 Sam 24:18-20).

25:22 ***You will heap burning coals of shame on their heads.*** Lit., "For you are snatching up coals upon his head." Perhaps this was originally an Egyptian "repentance ritual," whereby the contrite man literally carried coals on his head in a clay dish as his penance, such as described in Kio 2000:423-424. Thus, the proverb seeks to provoke the vexed neighbor to reconsider his stance. See also Isa 6:1-8, "an instance of a connection between burning coals and repentance and cleansing" (Kio 2000:423-424). It takes faith to treat a disagreeable person well, trusting Yahweh to reward such merciful acts with reconciliation. It is God, not an observed order of boundaries in society, who is invoked here. Paul cites this verse as a way of overcoming evil with good (Rom 12:20-21).

25:23 ***north wind.*** In Hebrew, *ruakh* [TH7307, ZH8120] (wind) is the first word; it is also the last word of 25:28, either defining the stanza or occurring accidentally (Whybray 1994a:368). Vattioni (1965) argues that the language derives from the proverbs of Ahiqar.

a gossiping tongue causes anger. Lit., "and a tongue of secrecy [gives birth to] an angry face"; "gives birth to" (NLT, "brings") is carried over from the first line.

25:24 ***lovely home.*** Lit., "a house in common." This "better-than" proverb employs the stanza's key word, *tob* [TH2896, ZH3202] (good). The wife is associated with the gossip of 25:23 and the fountain and well of 25:26. (See also notes on 12:9; 27:15.)

25:25 The verse begins in Hebrew with "cold water." This refreshing drink contrasts with the next verse, which begins with "muddied spring."

25:26 ***polluting a fountain or muddying a spring.*** The "fountain" (*ma'yan* [TH4599, ZH5078]) and "well/spring" (*maqor* [TH4726, ZH5227]) are found in 5:16-18 to describe the desirable wife. Here, the untenable circumstance of the righteous "tottering" before the wicked (cf. 25:5) is like living with a repugnant woman—to which a man prefers the corner of a roof (25:24).

25:27 ***to eat too much honey.*** This closes the section's inclusion, begun in 25:16 (Bryce 1972:154). Overeating honey was there compared with overstaying a welcome, here with ugly, self-serving behavior.

it's not good to seek honors for yourself. Alternatively, Van Leeuwen suggests, "to seek difficult things is (no) glory" (1986a:112)—an axiom about not transgressing one's limits. Bryce proposes the opposite: "to search out difficult things is glorious" (1972:150).

25:28 ***A person without self-control.*** Lit., "A man who has no limit/hindrance over his spirit." The Hebrew word *ruakh* [TH7307, ZH8120] closes the inclusion begun in 25:23. The reader may protest against overlapping inclusions; if this seems an insurmountable problem, the proverb may be viewed as standing more or less isolated between two great units. Waltke attaches it to the following poem as the first of seven "perverted types of humanity" (2005:337).

COMMENTARY

Bryce identifies the presence of "seeking" and "glory" (NLT, "privilege," "honors") in 25:2-3 and in 25:27 as that which bounds the entire composition. He calls this composition a "wisdom-book" akin to the Egyptian *Instruction of Sehetepibre* (Bryce 1972:151).

God the Creator gloriously hides mysteries in the world for humanity to discover. Solomon's glory (1 Kgs 3:13) was displayed in discerning the hidden truth at court when two parties gave mutually exclusive accounts of the facts (1 Kgs 3:16-28). Kings also fathom the secret purposes of rivals or stratagems at war. Every citizen finds glory in appropriately approaching one's neighbors or superiors or in finding the correct and propitious design of a word in its time. Wise people carefully learn what is suitable and glorious for them. Oswald Chambers associates 25:2 with Deut 29:29, which says, "The LORD our God has secrets known to no one. We are not accountable for them, but we and our children are accountable forever for all that he has revealed to us, so that we may obey all the terms of these instructions." Chambers argues that God hides the lessons of obedience in temptations (meant to be overcome), difficulties, hardships, and disappointments (1985:29). It is partially through experiencing these that we learn and grow in faithfulness and maturity.

Proverbs 25:6-7 speaks of how one should behave in the presence of the king. "It's better to wait for an invitation to the head table than to be sent away in public disgrace" (25:7). Jesus gave the same advice in Luke 14:7-11:

> *When Jesus noticed that all who had come to the dinner were trying to sit in the seats of honor near the head of the table, he gave them this advice: "When you are invited to a wedding feast, don't sit in the seat of honor. What if someone who is more distinguished than you has also been invited? The host will come and say, 'Give this person your seat.' Then you will be embarrassed, and you will have to take whatever seat is left at the foot of the table!*
>
> *"Instead, take the lowest place at the foot of the table. Then when your host sees you, he will come and say, 'Friend, we have a better place for you!' Then you will be honored in front of all the other guests. For those who exalt themselves will be humbled, and those who humble themselves will be exalted."*

Jesus used this principle as a paradigm for the Kingdom of God and who was great in it—and the rewards for the humble in the resurrection (Luke 14:12-24). Reading the proverb in the light of the New Testament can expand its meaning to include the eschaton and the final ushering in of the Kingdom—complete with eternal rewards. Jesus is the king whose mind is unfathomable, and it is before this king that one should not boast but patiently serve, awaiting the benediction, "Well done, my good and faithful servant" (Matt 25:21).

This humble attitude should govern our behavior here and now toward our neighbor. It is easy to lose our good reputation (25:10) if we leak out some private matter to advance ourselves in court (25:9). Do not quickly file a lawsuit (25:8)! Along these lines, it is also important to watch what we say and how we say it. We should be received as gracious speakers of truth (25:11-14). "Let your conversation be gracious and attractive so that you will have the right response for everyone" (Col 4:6). This composition also tells us not to overstay our welcome in another's house (25:16). Furthermore, if we have offended our neighbor, we should treat him well, meet his needs, and work hard to be a good neighbor. With God's blessing we can win him back (25:21-22).

Proverbs calls the wise to assuage the hunger and thirst of their enemies. We should be able to treat our critics with kindness and mercy. This attitude is the opposite of promoting oneself and seeking one's own honor (25:27). Our attitude should be that of Jesus, who, though he was God, humbled himself as God's servant and became obedient to die on the cross for our redemption. As a result of Jesus' humbling himself, God the Father exalted him greatly, giving him the name that is above every other name in heaven or on earth (Phil 2:6-11). If Jesus did not seek his own glory, should we? It is on this note that the composition draws to a close: Seeking one's own glory is sickening to others—especially to the king and to God (25:6-7, 27). We should humbly serve others, waiting for God to exalt us.

C. Doing What Is Fitting (26:1-16)

1 Honor is no more associated with fools
than snow with summer or rain with
harvest.

2 Like a fluttering sparrow or a darting
swallow,
an undeserved curse will not land
on its intended victim.

3 Guide a horse with a whip, a donkey
with a bridle,
and a fool with a rod to his back!

4 Don't answer the foolish arguments
of fools,
or you will become as foolish as
they are.

5 Be sure to answer the foolish
arguments of fools,
or they will become wise in their
own estimation.

6 Trusting a fool to convey a message
is like cutting off one's feet or
drinking poison!

7 A proverb in the mouth of a fool
is as useless as a paralyzed leg.

8 Honoring a fool
is as foolish as tying a stone to a
slingshot.

9 A proverb in the mouth of a fool
is like a thorny branch brandished
by a drunk.

10 An employer who hires a fool or
a bystander
is like an archer who shoots at
random.

11 As a dog returns to its vomit,
so a fool repeats his foolishness.

12 There is more hope for fools
than for people who think they
are wise.

13 The lazy person claims, "There's a lion
on the road!
Yes, I'm sure there's a lion out
there!"

14 As a door swings back and forth on
its hinges,
so the lazy person turns over
in bed.

15 Lazy people take food in their hand
but don't even lift it to their
mouth.

16 Lazy people consider themselves
smarter
than seven wise counselors.

NOTES

26:1 ***Honor is no more associated with fools.*** "Honor" or "glory" (*kabod* [TH3519, ZH3883]) connects with the previous composition (25:27). As it is not honorable to seek one's own honor, so it is not "fitting" to give honor to a fool. See note on 17:7 for "fitting" (from *na'weh* [TH5000, ZH5534]). This poem explores what is and is not suitable, appropriate, or fitting—beginning with an introductory proverb citing meteorology.

26:2 ***an undeserved curse.*** Lit., "a curse without cause." This proverb uniquely lacks the section's key word "fool." Van Leeuwen thematically connects this with the previous verse: "In 26:1b something positive is (mis-)applied to someone negative. . . . In 2b, the relation is reversed. Something bad is misapplied to someone good" (1988:92). He observes that the topic of the stanza is not the fool per se, but the "various [improper] relations" highlighted, which are also seen in the undeserved curse (1988:90). "Honor" (26:1) denotes "heaviness, weightiness," and the "curse" here denotes "flightiness, lightness"—another contrast of the two verses (Waltke 1998:45).

26:3 ***Guide.*** Hebrew lacks the verb and simply brings together elements that belong with one another: whip and horse, bridle and ass, rod and the fool's back (cf. Isa 1:2-3).

26:4 ***Don't answer the foolish arguments of fools.*** Lit., "Do not answer a fool according to his folly." The injunction is to not come down to the level of the fool by engaging in his twisted argumentation.

or you will become as foolish as they are. Lit., "lest you also will be compared with him." You will be no better than he if you dignify his words with a response. As such, Jesus would not speak a word to Herod (Luke 23:9).

26:5 ***Be sure to answer the foolish arguments of fools.*** Lit., "Answer a fool according to his folly." The injunction is to not allow the fool's twisted argumentation to stand unchallenged.

or they will become wise in their own estimation. Lit., "lest he will be wise in his own eyes"—the worst form of folly (26:12). A fool should not be permitted to win the argument; this would tacitly give him honor (26:1). Jesus stopped the mouths of his opponents (Luke 20:40).

26:6 ***drinking poison.*** Lit., "drinking violence." Entrusting an irresponsible person with even small tasks is ruinous.

26:7 ***useless as a paralyzed leg.*** Lit., "lame legs dangle." Whybray considers "dangle" to be an anomalous form of *dalal* [TH1809A, ZH1938], (brought low). "Legs" are from *shoq* [TH7785, ZH8797], the thigh or knee. The sense is clear: A proverb used by someone ignorant of its proper application has no traction.

26:8 ***tying a stone to a slingshot.*** Lit., "as binding a stone in a sling." "Sling" is a hapax legomenon (*margemah* [TH4773, ZH5275]) derived from *ragam* [TH7275, ZH8083], "stone to death." "It is a nonsense and an absurdity to tie a stone in a sling, for a stone is put in a sling so that it may be ejected" (McKane 1970:598). A fool will only clunk himself on the head.

26:9 The fool has no understanding of the appropriate situation wherein a proverb is effective. In 26:7 this results in its ineffective use. Here, pretended wisdom does harm, like a drunk flailing with "a thorny branch"—randomly riving nearby unfortunates.

26:10 ***An employer who hires a fool or a bystander.*** Snell (1991:352) commends the emendation (with Targum) of *shoker* [TH5674, ZH6296] (hires) to *shikkor* [TH7910A, ZH8893], linking with the preceding verse by yielding "one hiring a fool or a vagabond drunk." The two verses are already linked by paronomasia (Waltke 1998:47). The "bystander" is, lit., "one passing through"—a vagrant with no stake in the community's welfare.

an archer who shoots at random. Lit., "[like] an archer (*rab* III [TH7228, ZH8043]) piercing (from *khalal* II [TH2490A, ZH2726]) all." KJV reads, "The great (*rab* I [TH7227, ZH8041]) God that formed all things both rewardeth the fool, and rewardeth transgressors."

26:11 ***As a dog returns to its vomit.*** The noun "vomit" always results from drink in OT, thus associating the verse with 26:9 (Van Leeuwen 1988:97). Second Peter 2:21-22 quotes this aphorism as part of a tirade against false teachers who corrupt the church, never repenting of their evil: "It would be better if they had never known the way to righteousness than to know it and then reject the command they were given to live a holy life."

26:12 ***There is more hope for fools.*** Up to this point, the worst possible condition envisaged is being a fool. But now, surprisingly, an even worse situation is suggested. There is more "hope" for the rehabilitation of the fool than for "people who think they are wise." This is the punch line of the section: The fool is not, after all, the ultimate in spiritual depravity. To save the fool from this state, one is adjured to testify against his folly (26:5).

26:13 ***The lazy person claims.*** The "sluggard" (*'atsel* [TH6102A, ZH6789]) is the key word of this segment. This is the last of three units pertaining to him (6:6-11; 24:30-34).

26:14 ***hinges.*** This is the only example in the OT of *tsir* I [TH6735, ZH7494] (see HALOT). The characteristic motion of the layabout is tossing and turning upon his mattress.

26:15 ***take food in their hand.*** Lit., "hides his hand in the dish." 26:15a is identical to 19:24a (see note).

but don't even lift it to their mouth. The shirker lacks the energy to follow through on what he begins, absurdly illustrated here.

26:16 ***Lazy people consider themselves smarter.*** Lit., "The sluggard is wiser in his own eyes." This directly ties in with the climax of the previous section, where the fool has more hope than a self-opinionated, vainly egotistical pseudo-sage. The sluggard is such a one!

than seven wise counselors. Lit., "than seven men who return (*shub* [TH7725, ZH8740]) discretion (*ta'am* [TH2940, ZH3248])." In Hebrew, the first word of 26:15 is similar to the last in 26:16, associating the proverbs; both also employ *shub*. Heb. *ta'am* signifies a cultured savoring of upright deportment, an intuition of what is right and good. The woman of virtue has this (31:18); her opposite does not (11:22). In relation to food, the term also means "palate" (Exod 16:31). Here, it serves as a pun—the slothful lacking energy to "taste" his food thinks he is better than seven sages with "taste" (Van Leeuwen 1988:109)!

COMMENTARY

This section tells people how to behave appropriately in different situations and thereby avoid behaving like a fool. One important exhortation is "Don't answer the foolish arguments of fools, or you will become as foolish as they are" (26:4). Should you answer a fool according to his folly? Of course not! The Bible says not to. If you attempt such a thing, you will be dragged down to their level and be no different from them. The next verse says, "Be sure to answer the foolish arguments of fools, or they will become wise in their own estimation" (26:5). Should you answer a fool according to his folly? Of course! The Bible says to. If you hold back, the fool will only become emboldened and pursue folly even further. "[I]t is by inescapable acts of interpretation that a man defines himself as wise or foolish. Humanity, which has no lack of fools, forces a person to judge and act wisely over against the fool—or to be counted one with him" (Van Leeuwen 1988:105). Jesus responded to his critics by answering all of their questions, until they were afraid to ask him any more (see Luke 20).

Should you answer a fool according to his folly? Yes and no. The Bible both prohibits it and commands it—a seeming contradiction. The conundrum is resolved in the recognition that each proverb has its own application, its own situation to which it speaks. Not every proverb is always applicable all the time. Individual proverbs, when placed side by side, seem to contradict. In actuality, each proverb lies dormant until a need invokes it. This is one of the strengths of the genre: a proverb may lay out of sight like a land mine, until one's path leads into a situation where it speaks. Then it explodes with formative and revealing power to aid the learned in their choices (Schwab 1995:16).

Proverbs require the sage to be sensitive to the situation, to know the times, and to understand the person with whom he or she speaks. At times, it is fitting and appropriate to answer the fool. Other times, it would be unsuitable and improper. "Wisdom, to a very large extent, is a matter of interpreting people, events, situations, actions in relation to norms for existence" (Van Leeuwen 1988:100). Fools do not possess such talent; when they try to utilize a word of wisdom they fail miserably, with either no effect at all (26:7) or with harmful consequence (26:9). These are people who sing songs to a heavy heart (25:20), who speak before listening (18:13). "It is unfitting, downright dangerous, for the sake of everyone to honor a fool by educating him with proverbs and entrusting him with responsible service, but fitting to punish and rebuke him" (Waltke 1998:50).

It takes wisdom to know how and when to apply wisdom; therefore, before one can gain wisdom from the book of Proverbs, one must already be wise! Proverbs assumes that the reader is wise already and is able to intuitively understand under what circumstances the various proverbs apply. In a dream, God offered to grant Solomon whatever he asked for. Solomon asked God for wisdom (1 Kgs 3:5-12). This was a very wise thing to request. In asking for it, Solomon demonstrated that he already had it! In a similar way, by imbibing the book of Proverbs, the reader demonstrates that he or she already possesses a measure of wisdom. Add to this God-given sagacity the observations and admonitions of Proverbs, and you shall grow in learning.

The wise know the appropriateness of things; they understand their circumstances. The opposite of this is to think you are wise—like the fool or the sluggard, who is self-deluded and unaware of what is expected or required in life (26:12, 16). The damage these people do with their language is treated next.

◆ D. Damaging Speech (26:17-28)

17 Interfering in someone else's argument
is as foolish as yanking a dog's ears.

18 Just as damaging
as a madman shooting a deadly weapon
19 is someone who lies to a friend
and then says, "I was only joking."

20 Fire goes out without wood,
and quarrels disappear when gossip stops.

21 A quarrelsome person starts fights
as easily as hot embers light charcoal or fire lights wood.

22 Rumors are dainty morsels
that sink deep into one's heart.

23 Smooth* words may hide a wicked heart,
just as a pretty glaze covers a clay pot.

24 People may cover their hatred with pleasant words,
but they're deceiving you.
25 They pretend to be kind, but don't believe them.
Their hearts are full of many evils.*
26 While their hatred may be concealed by trickery,
their wrongdoing will be exposed in public.

27 If you set a trap for others,
you will get caught in it yourself.
If you roll a boulder down on others,
it will crush you instead.

28 A lying tongue hates its victims,
and flattering words cause ruin.

26:23 As in Greek version; Hebrew reads *Burning*. **26:25** Hebrew *seven evils.*

NOTES

26:17 ***Interfering in someone else's argument.*** Lit., "One passing by (*'abar* I [TH5674, ZH6296]) gets infuriated (*'abar* II [TH5674A, ZH6297], see 24:21) with a dispute not his own."

dog's ears. The term for "dog" is found elsewhere in Proverbs only in 26:11. These proverbs are not arranged haphazardly but grouped verbally and thematically; it is no surprise that certain words are found in close proximity.

26:18 ***shooting a deadly weapon.*** Precisely, "who throws firebrands, arrows, and death." There is a possible pun here: "Throw" or "shoot" is from *yarah* I [TH3384, ZH3721], but *yarah* III [TH3384E, ZH3723] means "teach" (e.g., 4:11); see note on 6:13 for this lexicographical ambiguity. Here, one "shoots" a deadly weapon by "teaching" (speaking) dissimulations (26:19).

26:19 ***lies.*** To deceive (*ramah* II [TH7411A, ZH8228]) one's neighbor in this way is like a madman disseminating death and destruction. Contention and disharmony are caused by an evil tongue, a theme continued throughout this poem. But the word "lie" may be part of another pun (see preceding note), since the same form (*ramah* I [TH7411, ZH8227]) can mean "shoot." Hence, Waltke (2005:341) suggests a conceptual wordplay between *ramah* in this verse and *yarah* in 26:18, strengthening the force of the simile.

26:20 ***Fire goes out without wood.*** This continues the motif of the firebrand from the previous stanza. The gossiper puts fuel on the fire of upset and strife.

and quarrels disappear when gossip stops. "Gossip" (*nirgan* [TH5372, ZH8087], Niphal of *ragan* [TH7279, ZH8087]) is found four times in Proverbs (16:28; 18:8; 26:20, 22). The term describes the Israelites' complaining or grumbling against Yahweh (Deut 1:27; Ps 106:25). Perhaps gossip (telling tales, breaking confidences) is not at issue here, but muttering and grouching so as to sour others.

26:21 Lit., "Coals to hot embers and wood to fire and a contentious man to kindle a dispute." This verse has "wood," "fire," and "contention" in common with the preceding, highlighting again the firelike quality of "gossip."

26:22 This verse is identical to 18:8 (see note).

26:23 ***Smooth words may hide a wicked heart, just as a pretty glaze covers a clay pot.*** MT reads, "Silver-slag (*kesep sigim* [TH3701/5509, ZH4084/6092]) is overlaid upon a potsherd, burning (*doleqim* [TH1814, ZH1944]) lips overlay an evil heart." The NLT (cf. NIV, RSV, ESV) follows Driver's (1951:191) suggestion (based on Ugaritic *spsg*) to read *kesapsig* [TH3509.1/5509, ZH3869/6213], "like glaze," rather than "silver dross/slag." For *doleqim*, the NLT reads with the LXX (cf. RSV) *khalaqim* [TH2505, ZH2744] (smooth). If the reading with *khalaqim* is accepted, it would begin the next segment and in fact form an inclusion with 26:28 (*khalaq* [TH2509, ZH2747]), but even so, neither of these changes is actually necessary.

In the MT as it stands, *doleqim* climaxes the motif of speech and fire with "incendiary" lips—which throughout 26:17-23 have set the town ablaze. In a complex image, they appear to be beautiful (like silver leaf), but only have a thin veneer camouflaging an evil heart (the ugly potsherd). In this verse, the idea of "burning lips" may also be intended to apply to the deceptive "lips" in 26:24—both extending the conflagration motif and suggesting a deceitful "kiss of warm friendship or love" (Whybray 1994a:378) that conceals hatred.

26:24 ***their hatred.*** Three times in this segment hatred is at issue (26:24, 26, 28). In each case it is hidden behind guile and flattery, continuing the theme of 26:23.

26:25 ***They pretend to be kind.*** Lit., "For when he speaks graciously."

Their hearts are full of many evils. Lit., "For seven abominations are in his heart" (cf. NLT mg).

26:26 ***their hatred.*** Some cover up their hatred, but in the assembly it is inevitable that their true attitudes will come to light—"Society will see through the postures of the malicious person and will be armed against his malice" (McKane 1970:604-605).

26:27 ***If you set a trap for others, you will get caught in it yourself.*** NLT captures the sense of the Hebrew; lit., "One who digs a pit will fall into it."

26:28 ***flattering words cause ruin.*** "Flattering" (*khalaq* [TH2509, ZH2747]) closes a possible inclusion begun in 26:23 (see note). "Ruin" (*midkheh* [TH4072, ZH4510]) is a hapax legomenon from the root *dakhah* [TH1760, ZH1890], meaning "be cast down, thrust down" (see note on 14:32).

COMMENTARY

Another concern of the sage pertains to the manner in which people can control the tongue and utilize it in the service of wisdom. God has endowed speech with the power to found and build up or to destroy and tear down. God demonstrated his creative power when he spoke the world into existence. He invested this power of the spoken word in his prophets, so that when they issued oracles of judgment they were determining the shape of things to come. Consider Jeremiah 1:10, where God called Jeremiah using these words:

> Today I appoint you to stand up
> against nations and kingdoms.
> Some you must uproot and tear down,
> destroy and overthrow.
> Others you must build up
> and plant.

In the book of Proverbs, the spoken word also has power. But it is not only on the lips of the wise that speech is powerful. Fools are also born with the innate power God has placed in human speech; unfortunately, they wield that power in a manner destructive to the community.

Proverbs 26:17-28 focuses on these malefic words and condemns them. Proverbs 26:17-19 comprises a stanza on "crazy speech" fit only for ignoramuses who interfere in matters that do not pertain to them (26:17) and pass off lies as something funny (26:18-19). Proverbs 26:20-22 focuses on the "gossip" or grumbler, who brings down the whole community into a cesspool of bitterness. The tongue can be dangerously evil. James says it well: "A tiny spark can set a great forest on fire. And the tongue is a flame of fire. It is a whole world of wickedness, corrupting your entire body. It can set your whole life on fire, for it is set on fire by hell itself" (Jas 3:5-6). James connects the fiery character of evil speech with hellfire.

Grumbling and murmuring have caused serious problems for God's people. Paul spoke of this in his letter to the Corinthian church:

> *And don't grumble as some of [the Israelites] did, and then were destroyed by the angel of death. These things happened to them as examples for us. They were written down to warn us who live at the end of the age. If you think you are standing strong, be careful not to fall. The temptations in your life are no different from what others experience. (1 Cor 10:10-13)*

Grumbling was among the Israelites' sins (Deut 1:27). They impugned God's character, accusing Yahweh of being motivated by hatred of them. This led to loss of confidence, fearfulness, and the inability to accomplish God's purposes

(Deut 1:28-33). Yahweh responded in anger by condemning that generation to wander (Deut 1:34-35).

Paul claims the record of Israel's wanderings was preserved for the benefit of Christians—who are tempted as they were. In the church, gossips and slanderers can enfeeble the faithful and undermine the work of building the Kingdom of God and growing the church. All of the ills that Proverbs warns about can befall the church if church leadership is not wise and able to discern evil speech. Quarrels, rumor-mongering, contentions, and disunity all have their source in the tongue, which is like a fire destructively setting the community of faith ablaze.

This section of Proverbs also speaks of those who conceal a malevolent attitude behind fine-sounding words (26:24-26). Fine-sounding religious speech should not deceive savvy Christians. Beware of the heart motivated by selfish ambition and jealousies!

◆ E. Domestic Life (27:1-22)

1 Don't brag about tomorrow,
since you don't know what the day will bring.

2 Let someone else praise you, not your own mouth—
a stranger, not your own lips.

3 A stone is heavy and sand is weighty,
but the resentment caused by a fool is even heavier.

4 Anger is cruel, and wrath is like a flood,
but jealousy is even more dangerous.

5 An open rebuke
is better than hidden love!

6 Wounds from a sincere friend
are better than many kisses from an enemy.

7 A person who is full refuses honey,
but even bitter food tastes sweet to the hungry.

8 A person who strays from home
is like a bird that strays from its nest.

9 The heartfelt counsel of a friend
is as sweet as perfume and incense.

10 Never abandon a friend—
either yours or your father's.
When disaster strikes, you won't have to ask your brother for assistance.
It's better to go to a neighbor than to a brother who lives far away.

11 Be wise, my child,* and make my heart glad.
Then I will be able to answer my critics.

12 A prudent person foresees danger and takes precautions.
The simpleton goes blindly on and suffers the consequences.

13 Get security from someone who guarantees a stranger's debt.
Get a deposit if he does it for foreigners.*

14 A loud and cheerful greeting early in the morning
will be taken as a curse!

15 A quarrelsome wife is as annoying
as constant dripping on a rainy day.

16 Stopping her complaints is like trying to stop the wind
or trying to hold something with greased hands.

17 As iron sharpens iron,
so a friend sharpens a friend.

18 As workers who tend a fig tree are allowed to eat the fruit,

so workers who protect their
employer's interests will be
rewarded.

19 As a face is reflected in water,
so the heart reflects the real person.

20 Just as Death and Destruction* are
never satisfied,
so human desire is never satisfied.

21 Fire tests the purity of silver
and gold,
but a person is tested by being
praised.*

22 You cannot separate fools from their
foolishness,
even though you grind them like
grain with mortar and pestle.

27:11 Hebrew *my son.* **27:13** As in Greek and Latin versions (see also 20:16); Hebrew reads *for a promiscuous woman.* **27:20** Hebrew *Sheol and Abaddon.* **27:21** Or *by flattery.*

NOTES

27:1 *Don't brag.* From *halal* [TH1984A, ZH2146], which also begins 27:2.

will bring. Lit., "will bear," "will give birth to."

27:2 *Let someone else praise you.* Lit., "Let a stranger (*zar* [TH2214B, ZH2424]) praise you." The word "stranger" in the NLT is a gloss of *nakri* [TH5237A, ZH5799]. Both appellations appear again in 27:13, indicating persons of unknown character. A sage must not praise himself (27:1); because of his good deeds, even distant people of cursory or tangential relation will iterate his good reputation.

27:3 *weighty.* Heb. *netal* [TH5192, ZH5748] is a hapax legomenon, perhaps related to *natal* [TH5190, ZH5747] (to bear, lift); here it is parallel with *kobed* [TH3514, ZH3880] (heavy).

but the resentment caused by a fool is even heavier. Lit., "but the vexation of a fool is heavier than both of them," referring either to the resentment caused by fools or to the vexation fools themselves inappropriately express, which weighs down on the people who have to deal with them.

27:4 *Anger . . . wrath.* These tie v. 4 with "vexation" (NLT, "resentment") in 27:3.

cruel. Heb. *'akzeriyuth* [TH395, ZH427] is a hapax legomenon related to the modifier *'akzari* [TH393/394, ZH425/426] (see 5:9; 11:17; 12:10; 17:11).

jealousy is even more dangerous. Precisely, "but who can stand before jealousy?" See notes on 6:34.

27:5 *rebuke.* Heb., *tokakhath* [TH8433A, ZH9350], found in Proverbs 16 times, connotes correction, "constructive criticism" meant for the restoration and well-being of its recipient. It is painful to hear, and one's first inclination may be to reject it (1:23-25, 30; 3:11; 5:12; 10:17; 12:1), but the wise appreciate it (15:5, 31-32). The sage who adores his son but keeps silent about these matters ("hidden love") may in the short term avoid confrontation, but in the long term he will lose him. See note on 12:9 regarding the better-than proverb.

27:6 *Wounds from a sincere friend are better.* Lit., "Faithful are the wounds of one who loves." As in the previous verse, true love is seen in wounding ("rebuking") when necessary; the "one who hates" only compliments.

many kisses. "Many" is from *'athar* [TH6280, ZH6984], which elsewhere means "entreat, supplicate." Although here it might mean "inordinate" (see Ezek 35:13), its ordinary usage suggests "soliciting kisses," "kisses to beseech"—a pseudo-friendly, but self-serving overture. The word "kisses" is found only here and in Song 1:2.

27:7 *A person who is full refuses honey.* Lit., "The sated appetite (*nepesh* [TH5315, ZH5883]) tramples a honeycomb." Cf. 25:16, which uses honey as a metaphor for the sweetness of neighborly concord. Perhaps a similar meaning is intended here; one with many associates scorns a new acquaintance; the lonely befriend even unsavory people. "This is a 'proverb' with an unlimited scope for interpretation, with a province as wide as the possibilities of our human situation" (McKane 1970:612).

27:8 ***from home.*** Precisely, "from his place." This verse repeats "stray" in each line, as 27:7 repeated *nepesh* [TH5315, ZH5883], forming a stylistic pairing. Home is where the heart is. The opposite to being a vital part of the community is to "wander." A person should be rooted and have a "support network." Perhaps "wander" (*nadad* [TH5074, ZH5610]; see also *nud* [TH5110, ZH5653]) is related to the hapax legomenon *nedeh* [TH5078, ZH5613] in Ezek 16:33, a sexually charged term; the "straying" may include chasing the "strange woman" alien to the community (27:13-16). The theme of near and far is resumed in 27:10.

27:9 ***The heartfelt counsel of a friend is as sweet as perfume and incense.*** Lit., "Oil and incense gladden the heart; / The counsel of the *nepesh* [TH5315, ZH5883] is sweetness to his friend." "Sweetness" echoes 27:7. There, to a hungry man even what is bitter seems sweet; here, a friend's "heartfelt counsel" is sweet and "gladdens the heart"—the very thing the father desires from his son (27:11). In the second line the LXX reads, "The soul is broken by calamities" (see RSV).

27:10 The stanza concludes with a verse treating distance in relation to neighborliness in time of need, divided as shown:

Your-neighbor	and-the-neighbor of-your-father	do-not-forsake
And-the-house	of-your-brother	do-not-enter in-the-day of-your calamity
Better a-neighbor nearby	than-a-brother	who-is-far

"Friend" in NLT is from *rea'* [TH7463, ZH8291] (as in 27:9, 14, 17); NLT's "neighbor" is from *shaken* [TH7934, ZH8907], used only here in Proverbs (although see the verbal form in 8:12, "I, Wisdom, *live together with*"). Whybray remarks, "The three lines appear to be completely independent of one another. . . . There is no point in trying to relate these points of view" (1994a:382). However, unity may be found in the perspective of distance. This could be paraphrased as, "Do not forsake your nearby neighbors and friends of the family in their distress. When you are in distress, do not leave town to seek your distant kin. Your nearby friends are in a better position to help." McKane offers this rendition: "Do not abuse your brother's solicitude for you, a solicitude which you can take for granted just because of the strength of family solidarity. Do not make it a practice of paying him a visit only when you have a hard-luck story to tell him" (1970:614).

27:11 ***Then I will be able to answer my critics.*** Lit., "that I may return a word to him who reproaches me." The conduct of one's offspring goes far in vindicating the manner of life one has lived.

27:12 This verse is virtually identical with 22:3. Here, the father exhorts the son to be prudent, to avoid evil. One such evil trap is treated next.

27:13 ***Get a deposit if he does it for foreigners.*** NLT follows the LXX (see NLT mg); MT has "for a strange woman bind him!" Waltke prefers the MT because it is the more difficult reading (2005:369); "Probably by her enticements and flatteries, she seduced some male to become indebted to her" (2005:382). See note on 20:16.

27:14 This is practical wisdom for those living in close quarters. Well-intentioned but thoughtless actions will embarrass you.

27:15 ***quarrelsome wife.*** Lit., "a wife of contentions" (see 21:9; 25:24).

rainy. *Sagrir* [TH5464, ZH6039] is a hapax legomenon in the OT but is found in later Hebrew. The father's warning against this baneful condition continues in the next verse. The verse concludes with *nishtawah* (are alike), *shawah* [TH7737, ZH8750] in the reflexive Nithpael stem.

27:16 ***Stopping her complaints is like trying to stop the wind.*** Precisely, "Those hiding [*tsapan*] her hide [*tsapan*] wind." In Proverbs, *tsapan* [TH6845, ZH7621] usually signifies "laying up, storing, treasuring" (2:1, 7; 7:1; 10:14). "Wind" often connotes strong emotion such as anger (16:18; 25:28). Thus, "to cherish her is to cherish wrath."

or trying to hold something with greased hands. Lit., "And [her] 'oil' encountered (*qara'* II [TH7122, ZH7925]) his vitality (right hand)"—reading *yiqra'* as a progressive non-perfective (see Waltke and O'Connor 1990:504). In Proverbs, *qara'* II always connotes sexual encounters with the "strange woman" or equivalent (7:10, 15; 9:18)—who was warned against earlier in the stanza as dangerous (27:13). One's "right hand" here is one's sexual potency (see Song 2:6; 8:3); "oil" (a luxury in 21:17, 20; 27:9) is a synecdoche for the whole complex of her allure (cf. 5:3). The husband married her since his vitality was not forewarned against her sexual power; thus, he is bound to her foul personality forever. To paraphrase 27:15-16, "A galling leak during a steady rain is like a bellicose wife, and if you marry her you marry her disposition—so beware of her advances!"

27:17 ***so a friend sharpens a friend.*** Lit., "so let a man sharpen the face of his neighbor." "Face" anticipates 27:19; "neighbor" recalls 27:9, 14. One man whets the "appearance, the deportment, the nature, and manner of the conduct . . . the habits and character" (Delitzsch 1875:213) of another. The verse is not about iron, of course, but the process of refining and improving one's thinking. This thought is resumed in 27:21 under the image of the crucible and furnace.

27:18 ***As workers who tend a fig tree.*** "Tending" comes from *natsar* [TH5341, ZH5915], a synonym of *shamar* [TH8104, ZH9068] ("protect"; see 2:8; 13:3). The rewards of enterprise and diligence are obvious; but if one expects "fruit" or "honor" from working hard to reform a fool, one will be disappointed (27:22).

27:19 ***As a face is reflected in water, so the heart reflects the real person.*** Lit., "As water the face [is] to the face, / Thus the heart of the man is to the man." The condition of one's heart is reflected in what one says and does. The wise can discern a neighbor's secret purposes this way (see 20:5). In addition, "It is through introspection, through self-examination in depth, that a man acquires self-knowledge" (McKane 1970:616).

27:20 ***Just as Death and Destruction are never satisfied, so human desire is never satisfied.*** Lit., "Sheol and Abaddon are not satisfied / And the eyes of the man are not satisfied." The desires, cravings, lusts, and hopes of people are as unquenchable as death and the grave.

27:21 ***Fire tests the purity of silver and gold.*** Lit., "A crucible for silver and a furnace for gold." The theme of refining a person in the context of social interactions recalls 27:17.

but a person is tested by being praised. Lit., "A man [is refined] by the mouth of his praise"—the sage is proven by the "praise" spoken about him, closing an inclusion from 27:1-2, where "strangers" praise the wise. "His praise" additionally signifies the people he praises. You are known by whom you tout and applaud. The Christian heralds Jesus.

27:22 ***grind them like grain with mortar and pestle.*** Pounding grain in a mortar with a pestle is an image representing the deeply ingrained hardheadedness of a fool's frame of mind. Even after much suffering, punishment, legal action, and consequences, the stubborn idiot simply will not learn.

COMMENTARY

Chapter 27 begins with a poem of 22 verses, the same number as letters in the Hebrew alphabet. Proverbs also concludes with an acrostic poem in 22 verses (31:10-31), each beginning with sequential Hebrew letters. Chapter 2 also has 22 verses and may be patterned on an alphabetic acrostic, evidenced by strategic placement of Hebrew letters such as Aleph in the beginning of stanzas and Taw as the first letter of the last stanza (after a particle; see commentary on the poem). Proverbs 27:1 and 22 both begin with Aleph (the first letter of a particle); in 27:22 the next word has an initial Taw. Although hardly uncommon, this is tantalizingly suggestive of purposeful arrangement. The middle verse (27:11) stands out due to the father's direct address—"Be wise, my child"—reminiscent of the beginning of chapter 2. The poem is delineated with an inclusion of the verb *halal* [TH1984A, ZH2146], found twice in 27:1-2, and the related hapax legomenon *mahalal* [TH4110, ZH4545] in 27:21.

Another point on structure: Proverbs 27:17 uses metallic imagery ("iron"), and the next proverb cites agriculture; this is duplicated in 27:21 ("silver . . . gold") and 27:22. Between these pairs are two proverbs sharing the word *'adam* [TH120, ZH132] and a stylistic repetition ("face . . . face" in 27:19 and "sated . . . sated" in 27:20). Thus, the organization of these six emblematic proverbs appears as follows:

- A^1. Iron and iron (27:17)
  - A^2. Tending the tree (27:18)
    - B. Face and face (27:19)
    - B. Sated and sated (27:20)
  - A^1. Silver and gold (27:21)
- A^2. Grinding the grain (27:22)

Life is sometimes paradoxical. It is unseemly and pretentious to boast about tomorrow or to sing your own praises. But if you quietly go about your business and do it well, others will recognize your worth and your reputation will spread far and wide beyond your own circle of acquaintances (27:1-2). Another counterintuitive phenomenon is to associate pain and defeat with one's friends and family, leaving acceptance and kisses to the enemy (27:5-6). Yet one with discernment prefers the uncomfortable "wounds" and rebukes of the wise to the deceptive and harmful assurances and overtures of flatterers. Those with your best interests at heart will be your biggest critics; those who seek to manipulate or use you will blandish you.

In the Bible, God exposes our nature. This is for our good so that we can change and grow into maturity. Other philosophies of life might tell you that you are fine as you are, but not biblical religion. The Bible's claims on us are radical and thoroughgoing—and this is what we need. Because God loves us, he speaks to us. Others who care nothing for our reformation and eternal salvation only adulate, lulling us into complacency about the state of our soul.

Another seeming contradiction is that those who are nearby, who are not invested in us, and who have no bond of blood to obligate them are at times better suited to help in time of need than family (27:10). Family is important, but so is neighborliness and friendship. Christians find their true kindred in the church. What we do reflects upon the family (27:11), and it is through the parents' admonitions—which at times may be painful—that a youth grows into maturity (27:12). One of the benefits of listening to parental warnings is avoiding pitfalls in life, particularly those presented by the strange woman (27:13).

No one truly knows us but God, because our heart is hidden. How well do you know yourself (27:19)? Can you afford to be brutally honest about all of the ways you are not the person you should be? Proverbs is a mirror to peer into—what do you look like? Are you wise? Consider 27:20. Is your appetite boundless? Are you satiable? Or do you continually lust for more? Do you earn enough money to be content? Paul says that contentment should be normal for a Christian; beyond that is an inordinate and harmful love for money (1 Tim 6:6-10). If your god is your stomach, you can hardly live as a citizen of heaven (Phil 3:19-20). Christians, who have been forgiven and need not imagine a phony righteousness of their own to stand before God, are constitutionally capable of being honest with themselves about how much they compromise their faith and chase after worldly goals or pleasures.

A person is often defined by his community, particularly by the praise he receives, and also by the praise he renders. Christians are called to witness to Christ and make him famous. Paul states this exhortation well: "Live wisely among those who are not believers, and make the most of every opportunity. Let your conversation be gracious and attractive so that you will have the right response for everyone" (Col 4:5-6).

◆ F. Wisdom for Leaders (27:23–29:27)

23 Know the state of your flocks,
and put your heart into caring for your herds,
24 for riches don't last forever,
and the crown might not be passed to the next generation.
25 After the hay is harvested and the new crop appears
and the mountain grasses are gathered in,
26 your sheep will provide wool for clothing,
and your goats will provide the price of a field.
27 And you will have enough goats' milk for yourself,
your family, and your servant girls.

CHAPTER 28

1 The wicked run away when no one is chasing them,
but the godly are as bold as lions.

2 When there is moral rot within a nation, its government topples easily.
But wise and knowledgeable leaders bring stability.

3 A poor person who oppresses the poor
is like a pounding rain that destroys the crops.

4 To reject the law is to praise the wicked;
to obey the law is to fight them.

5 Evil people don't understand justice,
but those who follow the LORD understand completely.

6 Better to be poor and honest
than to be dishonest and rich.

7 Young people who obey the law are wise;
those with wild friends bring shame to their parents.*

8 Income from charging high interest rates
will end up in the pocket of someone who is kind to the poor.

[9] God detests the prayers
of a person who ignores the law.

[10] Those who lead good people along an evil path
will fall into their own trap,
but the honest will inherit good things.

[11] Rich people may think they are wise,
but a poor person with discernment can see right through them.

[12] When the godly succeed, everyone is glad.
When the wicked take charge, people go into hiding.

[13] People who conceal their sins will not prosper,
but if they confess and turn from them, they will receive mercy.

[14] Blessed are those who fear to do wrong,*
but the stubborn are headed for serious trouble.

[15] A wicked ruler is as dangerous to the poor
as a roaring lion or an attacking bear.

[16] A ruler with no understanding will oppress his people,
but one who hates corruption will have a long life.

[17] A murderer's tormented conscience will drive him into the grave.
Don't protect him!

[18] The blameless will be rescued from harm,
but the crooked will be suddenly destroyed.

[19] A hard worker has plenty of food,
but a person who chases fantasies ends up in poverty.

[20] The trustworthy person will get a rich reward,
but a person who wants quick riches will get into trouble.

[21] Showing partiality is never good,
yet some will do wrong for a mere piece of bread.

[22] Greedy people try to get rich quick
but don't realize they're headed for poverty.

[23] In the end, people appreciate honest criticism
far more than flattery.

[24] Anyone who steals from his father and mother
and says, "What's wrong with that?"
is no better than a murderer.

[25] Greed causes fighting;
trusting the LORD leads to prosperity.

[26] Those who trust their own insight are foolish,
but anyone who walks in wisdom is safe.

[27] Whoever gives to the poor will lack nothing,
but those who close their eyes to poverty will be cursed.

[28] When the wicked take charge, people go into hiding.
When the wicked meet disaster, the godly flourish.

CHAPTER 29

[1] Whoever stubbornly refuses to accept criticism
will suddenly be destroyed beyond recovery.

[2] When the godly are in authority, the people rejoice.
But when the wicked are in power, they groan.

[3] The man who loves wisdom brings joy to his father,
but if he hangs around with prostitutes, his wealth is wasted.

[4] A just king gives stability to his nation,
but one who demands bribes destroys it.

[5]To flatter friends
is to lay a trap for their feet.

[6]Evil people are trapped by sin,
but the righteous escape, shouting
for joy.

[7]The godly care about the rights of
the poor;
the wicked don't care at all.

[8]Mockers can get a whole town
agitated,
but the wise will calm anger.

[9]If a wise person takes a fool to court,
there will be ranting and ridicule
but no satisfaction.

[10] The bloodthirsty hate blameless
people,
but the upright seek to help them.*

[11] Fools vent their anger,
but the wise quietly hold it back.

[12] If a ruler pays attention to liars,
all his advisers will be wicked.

[13] The poor and the oppressor have this
in common—
the LORD gives sight to the eyes of
both.

[14] If a king judges the poor fairly,
his throne will last forever.

[15] To discipline a child produces
wisdom,
but a mother is disgraced by an
undisciplined child.

[16] When the wicked are in authority, sin
flourishes,
but the godly will live to see their
downfall.

[17] Discipline your children, and they will
give you peace of mind
and will make your heart glad.

[18] When people do not accept divine
guidance, they run wild.
But whoever obeys the law
is joyful.

[19] Words alone will not discipline
a servant;
the words may be understood,
but they are not heeded.

[20] There is more hope for a fool
than for someone who speaks
without thinking.

[21] A servant pampered from childhood
will become a rebel.

[22] An angry person starts fights;
a hot-tempered person commits
all kinds of sin.

[23] Pride ends in humiliation,
while humility brings honor.

[24] If you assist a thief, you only hurt
yourself.
You are sworn to tell the truth, but
you dare not testify.

[25] Fearing people is a dangerous trap,
but trusting the LORD means safety.

[26] Many seek the ruler's favor,
but justice comes from the LORD.

[27] The righteous despise the unjust;
the wicked despise the godly.

28:7 Hebrew *their father.* **28:14** Or *those who fear the LORD;* Hebrew reads *those who fear.* **29:10** Or *The bloodthirsty hate blameless people, / and they seek to kill the upright;* Hebrew reads *The bloodthirsty hate blameless people; / as for the upright, they seek their life.*

NOTES

27:23 The doubly imperatival appeal to understand the needs of those under one's care opens the segment's urgent entreaty.

27:24 ***riches don't last forever, and the crown might not be passed to the next generation.*** This is a metaphor for the governance of a kingdom; the "sheep" are one's population. They require constant maintenance and care—or else they will be lost along with their king.

27:26 ***sheep . . . goats.*** Lit., "lambs" (*kebasim* [TH3532, ZH3897]) and goats (*'attudim* [TH6260, ZH6966]).

27:27 ***goats'.*** This is another Hebrew term, *'izzim* [TH5795, ZH6436]. In this segment five separate terms are used for flocks of sheep and goats. Rich vocabulary creatively conveys the essential idea that all the varied aspects and responsibilities under one's charge must be accommodated and preserved; "if monarchs provide well for their subjects, they will return the favor" (Malchow 1985:245).

28:1 ***the godly are as bold as lions.*** This verse is the first of six structural elements in the composition (see commentary) contrasting the righteous and the wicked. "Bold" is from *batakh* [TH982, ZH1053], often glossed "trust" (28:25-26). Although Yahweh is not explicitly mentioned in chs 26–27, the confidence that befits trusting him is implicit.

28:2 ***When there is moral rot within a nation, its government topples easily.*** Lit., "By transgression of the land its princes are many," i.e., many arise who would be king.

But wise and knowledgeable leaders bring stability. Precisely, "But with a man who understands knowledge thus it is prolonged." The LXX reads, "Through sins of ungodly men conflicts arise, but a cunning man will extinguish them."

28:3 ***A poor person who oppresses the poor.*** Lit., "A man (*geber* [TH1397, ZH1505]) who is poor (*rash* [TH7326A, ZH8133]) and one who oppresses the poor (*dallim* [TH1800, ZH1924])." BHS needlessly suggests emending *rash* to *ro'sh* [TH7218, ZH8031] (ruler) or (with LXX) to *rasha'* [TH7563A, ZH8401] (wicked). Rather than reading the entire phrase as the description of a single person, it seems that two persons are described: the poor man and his oppressor. The latter is the pounding "rain that washes away"—leaving nothing for the former (Waltke 2005:395). This observation develops 28:2 as an example of the need for good government.

28:4 ***to obey the law is to fight them.*** Lit., "Those guarding *torah* strive with them." Throughout Proverbs, *torah* [TH8451, ZH9368] signifies not the law of Moses, but the pedagogy of judicious parents (e.g., 1:8; 3:1; 4:2; 6:20); see 28:7, "A discerning son keeps *torah.*" In 28:9 *torah* is associated with prayer—Yahweh rejects those who despise their progenitors' guidance and who honor disreputable evildoers. Part and parcel of wisdom *torah* is knowing whom to revere. (See also note on 28:8.)

28:6 ***dishonest.*** Heb., *derakayim* (dual form), meaning "perverse of two ways." Dual *derek* [TH1870, ZH2006] is found again only in 28:18 in the OT. Waltke glosses it as "double-dealing ways" (2005:395). Garrett muses, "If this alludes to the doctrine of the two ways, the point is that the evil call the good way bad and the bad way good" (1993:223). The "path" appears again in 28:10. This is the final "better-than" proverb (see note on 12:9; cf. 19:1).

28:7 ***Young people who obey the law are wise.*** Lit., "One keeping instruction [*torah*] is a discerning son" (see notes on 28:8-9).

those with wild friends bring shame to their parents. Lit., "One associating with gluttons humiliates his father" (see notes on 23:20-21 and the commentary on 22:17–24:34). Note the equation of *torah* [TH8451, ZH9368] with the father-son relationship.

28:8 A literal translation of this verse would be, "One who increases his wealth by usury and interest, / For one favoring the poor he will gather it." "Usury" is used only here in Proverbs, as is "interest." "Interest" usually occurs with "usury" in OT. Observe that in a section featuring *torah,* one bit of legislation (from Lev 25:35-38) is cited. Here, Proverbs uniquely seems to invoke a Mosaic prohibition against mistreating the disadvantaged. Those who internalize *torah* understand this instinctively (28:5); those who do not are antisocial miscreants (28:3).

28:9 ***God.*** NLT supplies this subject, which is absent in Hebrew: lit., "One turning away his ear from hearing *torah,* / Even his prayer [is] an abomination." NLT renders *torah* [TH8451, ZH9368] as "law" here, although throughout Proverbs it denotes parental counsel. The beginning of this counsel is to fear Yahweh.

28:10 ***trap.*** Heb., *shekhuth* [TH7816, ZH8819], a hapax legomenon related to *shakhath* [TH7845, ZH8846] ("pit"; see 26:27).

the honest. Heb., *tamim* [TH8549, ZH9459], a word found 47 times in the Pentateuch (out of 91 times in the OT), often glossed "with no defects, without blemish" (e.g., Lev 23:12). Here, it means morally untainted (as in 2:21; 11:5, 20).

28:11 ***Rich people may think they are wise.*** Lit., "In his own eyes a rich man is a sage."

but a poor person with discernment can see right through them. Riches tempt the powerful to overestimate their intelligence and spiritual condition; from the vantage point of the subjugated such claims are examined and found wanting—thus confirming that the skill to discern great matters is enjoyed by all classes.

28:12 ***When the godly succeed, everyone is glad.*** Lit., "When the righteous triumph (*'alats* [TH5970, ZH6636]; see 11:10), great is the glory (*tip'ereth* [TH8597, ZH9514])." "Every occurrence of [*'alats*] . . . has a context of victory, a victory won or to be won by God, giving His people cause and liberty to 'rejoice'" (Millard 1975:88). See note on 17:6.

When the wicked take charge, people go into hiding. Lit., "And when the wicked arise, humankind (*'adam* [TH120, ZH132]) will be searched for." This verse is a structural element in the composition (Malchow 1985:239), delineating the end of one section and the start of another; see also 28:28.

28:13 ***they will receive mercy.*** In Hebrew this is a single word, from *rakham* [TH7355, ZH8163], related to *rakhamim* [TH7356, ZH8171] (mercies) of 12:10 and to *rekhem* [TH7358, ZH8167] (womb). It refers to feminine compassion, as of a mother for her child (1 Kgs 3:26).

28:14 ***Blessed are those who fear to do wrong.*** Lit., "Blessed is the man always dreading" (cf. NLT mg). An effective leader is one who confesses his sins (28:13) and accedes to God.

the stubborn are headed for serious trouble. Lit., "One hardening his heart will fall in to evil." The expression "to evil" (*ra'ah* [TH7451B, ZH8288]) uses the old accusative suffix, signifying direction. Autonomy from God leads to ruin.

28:16 ***A ruler with no understanding will oppress his people.*** Lit., "A leader who lacks sense [perpetrates] many oppressions," reading pleonastic Waw before *rab* [TH7227, ZH8041] (many) and supplying an implied verb. Alternatively, this could be emended to *yareb* [TH7235, ZH8049], creating the needed verb: "*multiplies* extortions" (Waltke 2005:396).

28:17 ***A murderer's tormented conscience will drive him into the grave.*** Precisely, "A man being oppressed with life-blood will flee unto a pit." "Oppressed" (Qal passive participle) ties this verse to 28:16. "The murderer will be a fugitive until he dies, and however hard he may endeavor to run away from death, he is being borne irresistibly toward the place where life will be swallowed up in death" (McKane 1970:626).

28:18 The verse could be rendered, "One walking blamelessly will be delivered, / But one perverse of two ways will fall once" (*be'ekhath* [TH259, ZH285]). BHS emends (with Syriac) to *beshakhath* [TH7845, ZH8846] (in a pit)—see 28:10. In fact, the "blameless," the "way," and a "fall" are also found in 28:10—thus sequential stanzas (skipping two intermediate verses) both end with lexically similar proverbs. See note on 28:6 for the expression "two ways."

28:19 ***A hard worker has plenty of food.*** Lit., "One serving his land is sated (*yisba'* [TH7646, ZH8425]) with food." (See note on 2:21 for "land"; cf. 12:11.)

ends up in poverty. Lit., "is sated (*yisba'* [TH7646, ZH8425]) with poverty." A play on words, since one cannot actually be "sated" with poverty.

28:20 ***get into trouble.*** Lit., "will not be guiltless" (*naqah* [TH5352, ZH5927]); see note on 19:5.

28:21 ***Showing partiality.*** Precisely, "regarding the face." Whybray observes the fittingness of placing this axiom between two others "condemning those who use unscrupulous means to acquire wealth, and [28:21] may be seen as an example of how this can be done" (1994a:395).

for a mere piece of bread. "Bread" is also employed in 28:19, connecting the verses; some are so prone to evil that they transgress for a morsel of bread.

28:22 ***Greedy people.*** Lit., "an evil-eyed man" (see note on 23:6). "Greed for money is just one expression of [his] misanthropy" (McKane 1970:627).

headed for poverty. Lit., "lack will come upon them."

28:24 ***no better than a murderer.*** Lit., "He is a companion to a man making ruin."

28:25 ***Greed causes fighting.*** Lit., "One broad of soul excites contention."

trusting the Lord leads to prosperity. Precisely, "One who trusts in Yahweh will be made fat." Near the end of the section, the issue of "trusting" or "confidence" (from *batakh* [TH982, ZH1053]) is resumed, recalling its antecedent in 28:1. Here, a Yahweh proverb is sandwiched between two others treating "the sin of selfishness or self-centeredness" (Whybray 1994a:396).

28:26 ***is safe.*** Lit., "will be delivered" or "will escape." "Trusting" Yahweh is juxtaposed with "trusting" in one's "own heart." To walk in wisdom is to trust God; to trust God is to distrust oneself and reject autonomy.

28:27 ***those who close their eyes to poverty will be cursed.*** Precisely, "one hiding his eyes, many curses." NLT carries over "poverty" from the first line.

28:28 ***When the wicked take charge, people go into hiding.*** Lit., "When the wicked arise, humanity hides itself" (see 28:12).

When the wicked meet disaster, the godly flourish. Lit., "and when they perish, the righteous become many." This verse is a structural element in the composition (Malchow 1985:239), delineating the end of one section and the start of another—after a comment of central importance (29:1).

29:1 ***will suddenly be destroyed beyond recovery.*** Cf. 6:15. This proverb is labeled "central" by Malchow because it "introduces a new topic, the necessity of heeding discipline" (1985:241).

29:2 Compare this maxim to 28:28, another structural element in the composition. The people rejoice when the righteous rule. This connects with the following verse, where one loving wisdom "brings joy" to his father.

29:3 ***prostitutes.*** The segment gets started with a warning about sex pitted against joy brought to the father; it ends with the shamed mother (29:15).

29:4 ***gives stability to his nation.*** Lit., "causes to stand a land" (Hiphil of *'amad* [TH5975, ZH6641]; cf. 12:7; 25:6; 27:4).

one who demands bribes destroys it. Lit., "a man of offerings throws it down." "Offerings" (*terumoth* [TH8641, ZH9556]) elsewhere always has a cultic referent (e.g., Exod 35:24; Lev 7:14; 2 Chr 31:10). Here, a king's "gift" uses terminology proper for the worship of God alone, highlighting his effrontery and impiety. Government should never seek to replace God. Compare this with the king of 29:14, whose throne is established forever.

29:5 ***To flatter friends.*** Lit., "a man (*geber* [TH1397, ZH1505]) who flatters (*khalaq* [TH2505, ZH2744]) his neighbor." *Geber* is found in Proverbs eight times, describing the man enraged by adultery (6:34) and the way of a man with a young woman (30:19). The word *khalaq* and its various cognates (*khalaq* [TH2509, ZH2747], *kheleq* [TH2506A, ZH2749], *khelqah* [TH2513, ZH2753]) occur 12 times, including references to the "flattery" of the loose woman (2:16; 5:3; 6:24; 7:5, 21).

lay a trap for their feet. Lit., "spreads (*parash* [TH6566, ZH7298]) a net for his feet." "Feet" (*pa'am* [TH6471, ZH7193]) is found elsewhere only in 7:12, where the loose woman seeks to ensnare. This verse seems to engage proverbial language of feminine seduction.

29:6 ***Evil people are trapped by sin.*** Precisely, "In transgression an evil man [finds a] snare"—perhaps the snare of flattery (29:5).

but the righteous escape, shouting for joy. Lit., "The righteous sings and rejoices." As in the first line, the verb must be supplied by the translator.

29:7 ***The godly care about the rights of the poor.*** Lit., "The righteous man (*tsaddiq* [TH6662, ZH7404]) knows the case (*din* [TH1779, ZH1907]) of the poor." *Tsaddiq* couples 29:6-7. *Din* is a function of rulers (20:8; 31:5, 8).

the wicked don't care at all. Lit., "The wicked do not understand knowledge." "To 'understand knowledge' is to know right from wrong, especially in the treatment of the poor, and to know Yahweh's ways" (Garrett 1993:229). This verse uses the key words "righteous" and "wicked" that distinguish the composition's structural elements, but here they are not plural and seem otherwise dissociated from the organizing scheme (see Malchow 1985:240).

29:8 ***Mockers can get a whole town agitated.*** "Men of mocking wheeze (*puakh* [TH6315, ZH7032]) against a city." The Hebrew word for "mocking" appears elsewhere in Proverbs only in 1:22.

29:9 ***If a wise person takes a fool to court.*** Lit., "A wise man disputes with a foolish man (*'ish 'ewil* [TH376/191A, ZH408/211])." The word "wise" unites 29:8-9.

there will be ranting and ridicule but no satisfaction. Lit., "he quakes and laughs but no rest." The irrepressible fool is pitted against the sensible sage again in 29:11.

29:10 ***The bloodthirsty hate blameless people.*** This first line reads, "Men (*'anshey* [TH376, ZH408]) blood (*dam* [TH1818, ZH1947]) hate (*sane'* [TH8130, ZH8533]) blameless (*tam* [TH8535, ZH9447])." The first and third words use the same letters, and the second and fourth "rhyme." This artifice adorns the center of the chiasm (see commentary).

but the upright seek to help them. See note in NLT, which gives the Hebrew, "as for the upright, they seek their life." "Upright" recurs in 29:27; "seek" in 29:26. Thus the chiasm's middle verse relates to the conclusion of the anthology. But RSV emends *wisharim* [TH3477A, ZH3838] (and the upright) to *uresha'im* [TH7563A, ZH8401] (wicked)—for how can the upright seek the life of the blameless? Waltke persuasively identifies the bloodthirsty as subject in the second line: "and as for the upright, they [the bloodthirsty] seek to kill each of them" (2005:400).

29:11 ***Fools vent their anger.*** Lit., "All his spirit a fool brings out," i.e., a fool always loses his temper. The corner of the chiasm has been turned, and themes are being revisited; here, the irrepressible fool is compared with the wise who restrains destructive passions (see 29:8-9).

29:12 ***wicked.*** This key word is again at issue, recalling 29:6-7.

29:13 ***The poor and the oppressor have this in common.*** Lit., "The poor (*rash* [TH7326A, ZH8133]) and the man of oppressions (*tekakim*) meet together (*pagash* [TH6298, ZH7008])."

Pagash and *rash* perhaps pun with *parash* [TH6566, ZH7298] (spread) and *resheth* [TH7568, ZH8407] (trap) of 29:5 (the corresponding verse in the chiasm). This is the only verse in the OT with *tekakim,* the plural form of *tok* [TH8496, ZH9412] (oppression).

the* Lord *gives sight to the eyes of both. Precisely, "The one who causes both of their eyes to shine is Yahweh." See the parallel 22:2, "The rich and poor have this in common: The Lord made them both," which is placed exactly 14 verses away from the last verse of the first anthology of Solomonic proverbs; 29:13 is 14 verses away from the conclusion of the second. "[T]he poor as well as the rich owe the light of life . . . to God" (Delitzsch 1875:249).

29:15 *To discipline a child produces wisdom.* Lit., "A rod and rebuke (*tokakhath* [TH8433A, ZH9350]) give wisdom." As *tokakhath* recalls 29:1, the segment closes by recalling the "central" proverb of the anthology.

but a mother is disgraced by an undisciplined child. Lit., "but a child (*na'ar* [TH5288, ZH5853]) let loose brings shame to his mother." For a discussion of the *na'ar,* see commentary on 1:2-7. "Let loose" is the Pual participle of *shalakh* [TH7971, ZH8938], connoting "allowed to go" or "left to himself." Waltke observes that this is the only place in Proverbs where "mother" occurs alone, "corroborating the interpretation that the breaking apart of the compound 'father' and 'mother' between these two proverbs [29:15 and 29:3] is deliberate" (2005:430). Thus "mother" here relates to "father" of 29:3, concluding the chiasm.

29:16 *When the wicked are in authority, sin flourishes.* Lit., "When the wicked increase, transgression increases." This verse is a structural element in the composition; cf. 28:28; 29:2.

but the godly will live to see their downfall. Emerton compares "to see" (*ra'ah* [TH7200, ZH8011]) with "gloated" (also *ra'ah*) in Obad 1:13, and concludes that the intended meaning is satisfaction the righteous enjoy from seeing justice done (2001a:196).

29:17 *they will give you peace of mind.* Lit., "he will give you rest."

will make your heart glad. Precisely, "let him give delicacies to your soul!" When the child is disciplined, everyone benefits.

29:18 *When people do not accept divine guidance, they run wild.* The Hebrew word *khazon* (divine guidance) is *always* a prophetic word (Isa 1:1), sometimes paired with revelatory dreams (Dan 1:17). Hence KJV, "Where there is no *vision,* the people perish," or RSV, "Where there is no *prophecy* the people cast off restraint," or NIV, "Where there is no *revelation.*" The next line sets this ecstatic utterance parallel to "keeping *torah.*" *Torah* [TH8451, ZH9368] = *khazon* [TH2377, ZH2606]; wisdom instructions *are* inspired oracles—see the oracle of Agur (30:1). Kings *divine* wisdom (see note on 16:10); Wisdom "prophesies" throughout the city (1:20; 8:4). Visionary language is engaged to assert that wisdom is inspired.

29:19 *the words may be understood, but they are not heeded.* Lit., "Although he understands, there is no response." The implication is that mere talk is ineffective and must be backed up with physical discipline. The servant must be motivated.

29:20 In Hebrew, this verse begins, lit., "Do you see someone who speaks. . . ?" The verb "see" is related to the noun translated "divine guidance" in 29:18. This proverb means that "whoever speaks before he has had leisure to think, and to weigh carefully the form of words which is most judicious and effective, is a fool of the worst kind" (McKane 1970:635-636).

29:21 *will become a rebel.* Lit., "in his latter end he will be a _____." The final word (*manon* [TH4497, ZH4959]) is an unexplained hapax legomenon. Thus the blank space has been filled in with a variety of wise-sounding options: RSV, "heir"; NIV, "grief"; NASB, KJV, "son"; NEB, "ungrateful."

29:22 *An angry person starts fights.* Lit., "A man of anger stirs up contention."

a hot-tempered person commits all kinds of sin. Lit., "a master of wrath [stirs up] great transgression." The verb is carried over from the first line.

29:23 ***Pride ends in humiliation.*** Precisely, "The pride of a man (*'adam* [TH120, ZH132]) makes him low (*tashpilennu* [TH8213, ZH9164])."

humility brings honor. Lit., "Lowliness (*shapal* [TH8217, ZH9166]) of spirit grasps glory" (see previous note).

29:24 ***If you assist a thief, you only hurt yourself.*** Lit., "One dividing a share with a thief hates his own soul." The accessory places himself both in physical and spiritual hazard (see 1:22; 8:36).

You are sworn to tell the truth, but you dare not testify. Lit., "He hears an oath (*'alah* [TH423, ZH460]) but does not report"—presumably to prevent self-incrimination. The usual meaning of *'alah* is "cursing," hence KJV, "He heareth cursing, and bewrayeth it not"—cowardly silence damns the accomplice.

29:25 ***Fearing people is a dangerous trap.*** Lit., "The tremblings of man give a snare." Isaac trembled violently upon discovering that Jacob stole the blessing (Gen 27:33). Fearing people leads both to moral weakness through intimidation and ungodly hero worship. Note that this stanza treats various permutations of fearing and trusting in people (see note on 11:28).

trusting the LORD means safety. Lit., "One trusting (*batakh* [TH982, ZH1053]) in Yahweh will be exalted." *Batakh* may close an inclusion begun in 28:1. Here, trusting God is set against inordinately revering or dreading people.

29:26 ***Many seek the ruler's favor.*** In 29:24, one example of "fearing" people is displayed; here, sycophants exhibit another, "seeking the face of a ruler." Set off against this is knowing Yahweh as the only true arbiter of justice.

justice comes from the LORD. Precisely, "From Yahweh is man's justice" (*mishpat-'ish* [TH4941, ZH5477])—the only verse in Proverbs ending with *'ish* [TH376, ZH408]. The stanza closes with two Yahweh proverbs highlighting how trusting in God and not people is the way of wisdom—this is Proverbs in a nutshell.

29:27 ***The righteous despise the unjust; the wicked despise the godly.*** Lit., "Abomination (*to'ebah* [TH8441, ZH9359]) to the righteous is an iniquitous man, / And an abomination (*to'ebah*) to the wicked is the upright way (*yeshar-darek* [TH3477A, ZH3838])." This structural element closes the composition and the anthology of Hezekiah's Solomonic proverbs. The last thought fittingly is *derek* [TH1870, ZH2006] (path)—one final reminder of the imagery of the two paths. Choose one and walk it!

COMMENTARY

Malchow (1985:238-243) argues from the content and structure of chapters 28–29 that this section is a manual for the purpose of training future rulers. The composition opens with an allegorical introduction (27:23-27). Themes such as law (or wisdom instruction) and justice for the poor predominate in 28:2-11. Proverbs 28:13-27 presents various cautionary observations to the future monarch, and 29:3-15 alerts the reader to various pitfalls a king will encounter. Chiasms and an alphabetizing stanza make up 29:17-26. These are "organized around six strategically placed and interrelated" verses—28:1, 12, 28; 29:2, 16, 27 (each of which speak of the righteous and the wicked)—with 29:1 being the "central" proverb, according to Malchow. The following commentary generally follows his observations.

Proverbs 27:23-27 serves as an introduction to the organized material in chapters

28–29. There are three levels of meaning in this introduction. First, it is a straightforward pastoral admonition for a leader to be savvy and diligent in keeping a flock. Second, its advice can be extended to any craft or career; the same principles apply to knowing one's tools and maintaining them. Third, this segment is an allegory about leaders. "The reference to the crown in v. 24 points to the poem's original provenance and suggests that the pastoral image is a metaphor for an ideal ruler" (Waltke 2005:390).

Proverbs 28:1 serves as a structural element to organize the following composition (28:2-11). This section consists of two stanzas followed by a concluding proverb. The key words "law" and "understanding" occur four and five times respectively. The first stanza (28:2-5) progresses from the ethical underpinning of society in general, through the problem of exploitation and inevitable conflict over wise precepts (*torah*), to the invocation of the Yahweh as guarantor of justice. The first and last word of the second stanza (28:6-10) is *tob* [TH2896, ZH3202] (better, good), which encloses a chiasm:

A. The good (*tob* [TH2896, ZH3202]), the path (*derek* [TH1870, ZH2006]) (28:6)
  B. The law (*torah* [TH8451, ZH9368]) (28:7)
    C. The poor (*dal* [TH1800, ZH1924]) (28:8)
  B.′ The law (*torah*) (28:9)
A.′ The good (*tob*), the path (*derek*) (28:10)

The final verse (28:11) also pertains to the poor (*dal*). Perhaps this section and the next (28:12-28) might be considered a unit, since 28:1 and 28:25-26 use *batakh* [TH982, ZH1053] (trust), a possible inclusion. *Batakh* also concludes the composition in 29:25—the first of two Yahweh proverbs ending its last stanza.

Proverbs 28:12–29:1 is a section best entitled "Humanity under Human Rule." It concerns not only rulers but also the governed. The wise must know how to live well as a citizen as much as how to administer the powers of state. The hard worker is commended along with the wise ruler (28:19). The next verse (28:20) focuses on the trustworthy person—one who is contrasted with a person hungry for wealth or power. The fugitive (28:16-17) is a typical example of a life lived guiltily before both God and the earthly ruler. No good flows from evil; no good follows sin. Greed, violence, corruption, and wickedness all pursue the perpetrator to the grave. The ruler is not responsible for the behavior of the governed; the governed are. The wise take this to heart and live accordingly.

The analysis of 29:2-15 begins with 29:3 (29:2 is used to organize the composition as a whole), where one's "wisdom" (*khokmah* [TH2451, ZH2683]) affects one's father. The word *khokmah* is seen again in 29:15, a proverb treating the shamed mother. The "just king" and "king judges" appear in 29:4 and 29:14. In 29:5, the word "trap" or "net" (*resheth* [TH7568, ZH8407]) is employed, verbally similar to the *rash* [TH7326A, ZH8133] (poor) of 29:13, and both verses employ body-part imagery. The composition's key words, "righteous" and "wicked," are found in 29:6-7 and again in 29:12. In the same way, 29:8 and 9 are paired by the adjective "wise," which appears once in 29:11. The remaining verse (29:10) uses *baqash* [TH1245, ZH1335] (seek) and *yashar* [TH3477A, ZH3838] (upright)—terms that draw the anthology to an end in 29:26-27. This creates a chiasm:

- A. Wisdom and the father's joy (29:3)
  - B. The just king (29:4)
    - C. The *resheth* and one's feet (29:5)
      - D. The wicked (29:6-7; paired through "righteous")
        - E. The wise and the unruly fool (29:8-9)
          - F. The "upright seek" (29:10)
        - E'. The wise and the unruly fool (29:11)
      - D'. The wicked (29:12)
    - C'. The *rash* and one's eyes (29:13)
  - B'. The judging king (29:14)
- A'. Wisdom and the mother's shame (29:15)

Another binding device is the key word *'ish* [TH376, ZH408] (man) found eight times between 29:3-13, usually beginning a verse.

The first and last verses of 29:16-27 are structural elements that serve to organize the whole composition. Between them are two chiasms that relate to each other, since the center of each one ends with a negative particle and the failure of an expected response, which thereby disrupts the process of instruction and truth. In both cases, physical discipline or violence is in view, either positively or negatively.

The first chiasm (29:17-21) sets "children" parallel to the "youth," (29:17, 21) and "vision" (*khazon* [TH2377, ZH2606]) parallel to "seeing" (*khazitha* [TH2372, ZH2600]) (29:18, 20). Other words glue together the stanza, such as "slave" (29:19, 21) and "words" (29:19-20). The second chiasm (29:22-26) begins and ends (uniquely in Proverbs) with the key word *'ish* [TH376, ZH408]. Also, *rab* [TH7227, ZH8041] appears toward the end of the first verse and at the beginning of the last verse. Between them, *'adam* [TH120, ZH132] is exceptionally employed in chapter 29, breaking the pattern of utilizing *'ish*.

- A. Discipline your children (29:17)
  - B. The vision (*khazon*) (29:18)
    - C. With -mere words, he *will not answer* (29:19)
  - B'. Seeing (*khazitha*) (29:20)
- A'. The pampered youth (29:21)
- A. Man (*'ish*) and many (*rab*) transgressions (29:22)
  - B. Pride of *'adam* (29:23)
    - C. With curses, one *will not report* (29:24)
  - B'. Tremblings of *'adam* (29:25)
- A'. Many (*rab*) seek, justice-of-man (*'ish*) (29:26)

As to the final stanza (29:22-27), Hurowitz notes that the two initial words begin with Aleph, the first letter of the Hebrew alphabet. The second line (29:22b) begins with Beth. The next verses follow in alphabetical order, though they do not include every letter of the alphabet: Gimel (first letter of 29:23), Daleth (last letter of 29:23), Heth (29:24, 25), and Resh (29:26; Hurowitz 2001:122). Both lines of 29:27 start with *to'abath* [TH8441, ZH9359]—which begins and ends with Taw, the last letter of the alphabet (Skehan 1971:23). Thus, Hezekiah's proverbs of Solomon crescendo with an alphabetizing stanza.

Wisdom for Leaders. Proverbs 28:5 tells us that those who seek Yahweh understand all. To seek after God is to know justice and keep his instructions. Such people grasp truth and then strive against those unable to apprehend the rudiments of justice. Thus, the composition begins, after the introductory material of 27:23-27, with a quick survey of some challenges faced by leaders—living ethically, taking care of the defenseless, and dealing with conflicts in relation to *torah* and faith (28:2-5). The great issues of life are also faced, of course, by every citizen who rules in his or her respective domain (27:23-27).

Every Christian has a sphere of responsibility, a metaphorical "flock" to shepherd. For many, the primary area of responsibility is the family and rearing of children. Knowing the state of our flock (27:23) means understanding the needs of our young ones and providing for them adequately. We need to "put our hearts" into caring and pasturing them. In the same way, pastors are charged to care for God's church. Jesus told Peter to "feed my lambs" (John 21:15). The word "pastor" means "shepherd," and ministers of the gospel are called to "know the state" of their people, tending and caring for them.

Those who seek after God understand these things, but evildoers do not (28:5). The *torah* of parents is, in the present era, the clear instruction of the gospel and Christian virtues and disciplines. Children who embrace this instruction can discern "all things"; they will be in constant conflict with those who praise—or idolize—representatives of the path of perversion (28:4-6). Many books of the New Testament clearly distinguish who is "in" and who is "out" of the Kingdom, the church. In short, they excoriate false teachers—heretics—as traitors to the gospel who are destined for damnation (see Matt 7:22-23; 24:11; John 10:1-16; Gal 1:8-9; 1 Tim 4:1-5; 2 Pet 2; 1 John 4:1-6). The Christian is called to discernment. Christians praise Jesus, heed his call, and so understand what is necessary to please God. False teachers and reprobates who reject Christ have no such understanding. According to the proverb, "to obey the law is to fight them" (28:4).

One example of how true knowledge is displayed is in one's treatment of the disadvantaged. Solomon condemns usury and charging interest (28:8). The economy of our civilization, however, is founded on charging interest on loans. This was not always the case. Israel's proscription against it was common in the ancient Near East, and in the medieval period Christians generally followed the biblical injunction. Today, should not alternatives to this method of advancement be made available to the truly poor (such as interest-free loans)? At the very least, the diaconal ministry of local churches should avoid charging interest when providing aid to a person in need. Remember that this service is analogous to other means of grace such as preaching or the Lord's Supper—which are freely offered.

The moral caliber of a politically powerful individual has far-reaching ramifications for the well-being of the population. The actions of ordinary citizens affect a few people: family, friends, neighbors, business partners. But a leader has been invested with the ability to affect the whole land. When government is administered incompetently and justice is not upheld, the hard-working citizens withdraw and suffer (28:12, 15-16, 28). But when a godly person receives responsibility, those affected will rejoice (28:16, 23, 28).

The ultimate example of good government is the manner in which Jesus Christ rules his church. He compared his administration with the exercise of political power in the world:

> *So Jesus called them together and said, "You know that the rulers in this world lord it over their people, and officials flaunt their authority over those under them. But among you it will be different. Whoever wants to be a leader among you must be your servant, and whoever wants to be first among you must be the slave of everyone else. For even the Son of Man came not to be served but to serve others and to give his life as a ransom for many." (Mark 10:42-45)*

Jesus' leadership model is one of service. When he—the King of kings, who today invisibly wields all real power and who someday will be recognized by every person on earth—returns to reward the righteous, his rewards will be in relation to how great a servant one was to those in need, who could not reciprocate (see Luke 14:12-14).

The counsel of the wise father and mother remains consistent throughout the book of Proverbs—here again there is a warning about the allure of sex (29:3). Wise rulers are aware of many pitfalls, such as flattery (as powerful in its own way as sex), agitators, and liars (29:5, 8, 12). Of course, it is also vitally important for every citizen to be aware of these traps. No one is immune to them, and it takes a savvy and discerning personality to identify such. It seems that one litmus test for wise dealing is in the treatment of the disadvantaged. The godly care about their rights, but wicked people exploit them (29:7). When presented with this test of your character, remember that God made both you and the poor person. Show them mercy (29:13-14).

Where there is no revelation, people are unbridled in the liberties they take with regard to themselves, the family, the community, and the living God (29:18). When life is not self-ordering or self-interpreting, people need to hear from God. They require a transcendent perspective that explains the world and their roles within it. The wise father and the servant's master image God by virtue of their authority to define how the underlings' lives should be ordered (29:17, 21). "Divine guidance" in 29:17-21 is of one piece with discipline imposed by powerful figures. The sage thrives in both conditions: He accepts discipline and counsel when in the lower place, and he offers it when in the higher. However, fools cannot do either. They cannot learn (29:19) and cannot teach. In fact, one who strives to teach in ignorance is actually compared to the fool and found lacking—such a one is a fool's fool (29:20)!

Proverbs 29:22-26 is a small chiasm that pertains to emotions. First, the angry man is highlighted (29:22). Such a one is unable to imitate God by displaying discipline in wisdom but only causes disruption. The next noncandidate for imaging God is the prideful person who seeks his own honor, and not God's (29:23). Again, people like this will neither heed nor give wise counsel. Next, 29:24 underscores the impotence of the coward who cannot speak the truth when it is needed and thus can accomplish no earthly good at all.

The second anthology of Solomon's proverbs climaxes with a unit treating the fear of human beings versus trusting Yahweh (29:25-27). Trembling before people is a snare (29:25). Jeremiah 17:5-10 likens fearing humans to being a shrub in the desert, alone, stunted, thirsty, and dried out. People are unreliable and will let you down. Putting them on a pedestal only leads to disappointment; harboring expectations leads to frustration. But trusting Yahweh, says Jeremiah, makes one like a powerful tree firmly rooted by streams of water—unbothered by heat or drought, fruitful, vibrant. It is easy to look to other people for what only God can supply, and this propensity of the human heart is so insidious that Jeremiah calls it "the most deceitful of all things" (Jer 17:9).

For fear of the people, a person keeps silent when obligated to speak (29:24). It is not the ruler who guarantees justice, but God (29:26). The fear of Yahweh is the beginning of the wise path, which the wicked hate. Do not fear them! Walk the upright way, being confident in God (29:27). It is on this climactic note that Solomon's second anthology of proverbs concludes. Hallelujah!

◆ V. Epilogue to Proverbs (30:1–31:31)

Proverbs's final two chapters include two superscriptions (30:1; 31:1) but at least four blocks of material: the Oracle of Agur (30:1-14), the poem of Threes and Fours (30:15-33), the Oracle of Lemuel (31:1-9), and the Woman of Virtue acrostic poem (31:10-31). Although separate, they show signs of having been edited as a unit, such as the possible use of chiasm (Steinmann 2001:62).

When the Septuagint was created, the four blocks of material were in existence, but their placement seems not to have been finalized. The Septuagint distributes the four blocks in a different order than the Masoretic Text, as shown in the stylized representation below.

<table>
<tr><th>OLD GREEK PROVERBS</th><th>MASORETIC TEXT</th></tr>
<tr><td>Prologue</td><td>Prologue</td></tr>
<tr><td>First Anthology of Proverbs</td><td>First Anthology of Proverbs</td></tr>
<tr><td>Sayings of the Wise</td><td>Sayings of the Wise</td></tr>
<tr><td>Oracle of Agur</td><td>Further Sayings</td></tr>
<tr><td>Further Sayings</td><td rowspan="3">Second Anthology of Proverbs</td></tr>
<tr><td>Three and Four</td></tr>
<tr><td>Oracle of Lemuel</td></tr>
<tr><td rowspan="3">Second Anthology of Proverbs</td><td>Oracle of Agur</td></tr>
<tr><td>Three and Four</td></tr>
<tr><td>Oracle of Lemuel</td></tr>
<tr><td>Woman of Virtue</td><td>Woman of Virtue</td></tr>
</table>

In the Septuagint, Agur's oracle logically follows the Sayings of the Wise and precedes the Further Sayings. Lemuel's oracle ends with an admonition to a king, which naturally leads to Hezekiah's anthology. The whole work climaxes with the Virtuous Woman, just as in the Masoretic Text. Since 30:1-33 (Agur and Threes and Fours) seems not to have been a unit historically, the halves are commented on separately but as parts of the same anthology.

The Masoretic Text of Proverbs groups the "oracles" at the end, immediately before the Woman of Virtue. There is a discernable logic to this as well. Consider 29:18, which holds together divine oracles and *torah* as both necessary and wise. The Prologue frames wise counsel in language of law (e.g., 6:21, "Keep their words always in your heart," echoes Deut 6:6-8, promoting Proverbs as equal partner with the law of Moses). The Epilogue, however, is cast as inspired oracles. Perhaps the book is arranged to frame its message with both "law" and ecstatic utterance. Lady Wisdom had cried out as a prophetess, publicly declaring the way of life (8:1–9:18); Proverbs 30–31 resumes this modality with oracles, both Agur's (asking about God's son) and Lemuel's mother's (given to her son). Thus, a prophetic motif also frames the book. Plöger suggests that chapters 30–31 serve as an appendix to Solomon's second collection, just as the Sayings of the Wise do for his first (1984:xiv).

McCreesh persuasively argues that the Woman of Virtue summarizes Proverbs. Both the wife in the Epilogue and Wisdom in the Prologue deserve praise, are compared to "jewels" (3:15; 8:11; 31:10), are trustworthy providers (4:6-9; 31:11), and laugh at the future (1:26; 31:25). McCreesh concludes, "In chapter 31 wisdom is a faithful wife and a skilled mistress of her household, finally settling down with her own" (1985:46). And the Woman of Virtue acrostic poem echoes the alphabetical poem in chapter 2.

Thus, the Epilogue thematically complements the Prologue. Oracles, various subjects (such as the danger of sex), and finally Lady Wisdom incarnated in the young man's wife frame the book and justify the placement of these blocks of poetry as in the Masoretic Text over against the Septuagint.

◆ A. The Oracle of Agur (30:1-14)

The sayings of Agur son of Jakeh contain this message.*

I am weary, O God;
I am weary and worn out, O God.*
2 I am too stupid to be human,
and I lack common sense.
3 I have not mastered human wisdom,
nor do I know the Holy One.

4 Who but God goes up to heaven and comes back down?
Who holds the wind in his fists?
Who wraps up the oceans in his cloak?
Who has created the whole wide world?
What is his name—and his son's name?
Tell me if you know!

5 Every word of God proves true.
He is a shield to all who come to him for protection.
6 Do not add to his words,
or he may rebuke you and expose you as a liar.

7 O God, I beg two favors from you;
let me have them before I die.

[8]First, help me never to tell a lie.
Second, give me neither poverty
nor riches!
Give me just enough to satisfy
my needs.
[9]For if I grow rich, I may deny you
and say, "Who is the LORD?"
And if I am too poor, I may steal
and thus insult God's holy name.

[10] Never slander a worker to the employer,
or the person will curse you, and
you will pay for it.

[11] Some people curse their father
and do not thank their mother.
[12] They are pure in their own eyes,
but they are filthy and unwashed.
[13] They look proudly around,
casting disdainful glances.
[14] They have teeth like swords
and fangs like knives.
They devour the poor from the
earth
and the needy from among
humanity.

30:1a Or *son of Jakeh from Massa;* or *son of Jakeh, an oracle.* **30:1b** The Hebrew can also be translated *The man declares this to Ithiel, / to Ithiel and to Ucal.*

NOTES

30:1 ***Agur.*** The name of the otherwise-unknown Agur means "I sojourn." To sojourn is to live as an immigrant or refugee in another country (see Ruth 1:1; 2 Kgs 8:2; Ps 105:23). Perhaps the name indicates a self-denunciating view of himself as an outsider to divine knowledge.

contain this message. Heb., *hammassa' ne'um geber* [TH4853A/5002/1397, ZH5363/5536/1505] (the oracle the man's utterance). Except here and 31:1, *hammassa'* never occurs superfluously in a title in the OT, leading some to read it as a place name, "Massa" (so NLT mg). *ne'um* also describes a prophet in an ecstatic state (2 Sam 23:1; Ps 36:1 [2]). Numbers 24:3 records Balaam's *mashal* [TH4912, ZH5442] (proverb), "the message [*ne'um*] of the man [*geber*] whose eyes see clearly"—followed by an inspired oracle. See notes on 31:1.

I am weary, O God; I am weary and worn out, O God. Or, "to Ithiel, to Ithiel and Ucal"; so KJV, NIV, et al. (see NLT mg), and earlier scholars (e.g., Lawson 1980:831; Wardlaw 1982:318). When we emend *le'ithi'el* [TH3807.1/384, ZH4200/417] (to Ithiel) to *la'ithi 'el* [TH3811/410A, ZH4206/446], this can be redivided into three different renderings: (1) "I have wearied myself, God" (Kidner 1964:178); (2) "I am not God / I am not God / that I should have power" (Torrey 1954:95); (3) "There is no God, there is no God" (Scott 1965:176). All these retain the dubious repeated word, which LXX reckons as an address. "Ucal" can likewise be understood as a verb (from *ykl* [TH3201, ZH3523]) rather than as a name, which here would mean "prevail" or "endure" (see 30:21). Maybe we should consider this compromise: "to Ithiel. I am weary, O God, but I endure" (cf. Waltke 2005:455). Ithiel is an otherwise unknown personage. (One might conjecture that he was Agur's own son?) The address "to Ithiel" is like the next chapter's oracle addressed by Lemuel's mother to Lemuel.

30:2 ***I am too stupid to be human, and I lack common sense.*** Lit., "Surely I am too brutish to be a man; / I do not have human understanding." Agur considers himself a brute, a subhuman (see 12:1), hyperbolically ignorant.

30:3 ***nor do I know the Holy One.*** The Hebrew is plural, "holy ones" (cf. note on 9:10). Agur has specified what he is so ignorant about—divine matters. Knowledge of God is wisdom; one unenlightened in this realm is bestial (30:2).

30:4 ***but God.*** NLT interpolates "but God," which is absent in Hebrew. Who ascends to heaven and descends? God ascends (Ps 68:18 [19]) and descends (Exod 19:11); Jacob dreamed of angels doing both, when God declared his name and promised Jacob seed and land to the four points of the compass (ends of the earth?) in Gen 28:12-15.

Who holds the wind in his fists? "Wind" translates Heb. *ruakh* [TH7307, ZH8120]. In Job 34:14-15 and Ps 104:29-30 it is said that God "gathers *ruakh*"—a formula indicating death, since *ruakh* ("breath," "spirit," "wind") is a synecdoche for "life." When God collects a creature's spirit, it dies. God is never said elsewhere in the OT to gather *ruakh* in the sense of "wind." Perhaps it means, "Who gathers breath in his hand, to dispense it to give life?" Either way, the thought is, "Who controls life? Who has all life in his hand?" The question may be readily answered: No one besides Yahweh.

Who wraps up the oceans in his cloak? Lit., "Who has bound the waters in a garment?" The waters are here life-giving streams, not salty; they are "in their garment"—a metaphor for the clouds (see Job 26:8). The waters that rain on the earth comprise and mediate life (like *ruakh* in the previous line). Perhaps "binding" the waters to clouds is a reference to drought (Job 12:15), thus, "Who has the power to dispense or withhold life on earth?"

Who has created the whole wide world? Precisely, "Who has established the ends of the earth?" "The ends of the earth" almost always indicates the universal rule of God, knowledge of Yahweh in all nations, and their rejection of idols (see Pss 2:8; 22:27; Isa 52:10; Jer 16:19; Mic 5:4; Zech 9:10). Note the prophetic references; after all, this is supposed to be an oracle! The four rhetorical questions form a chiasm:

A. God encompasses heaven and earth
  B. God controls life-breath
  B'. God controls life-water
A'. God establishes "the ends of the earth"

What is his name—and his son's name? Tell me if you know! The first answer comes in 30:9, where Agur supplies the name Yahweh. But who is his son? The son is ever-present in Proverbs, incessantly admonished by his mentor to heed wisdom. Those who follow wisdom become sons of wisdom (8:32) and adopted by Yahweh (3:11-12). Perhaps the son of Yahweh par excellence is the wise king (ideally Solomon), and in the NT, the son is Jesus. Alden finds many allusions to this verse in the NT, citing John 3:13; Acts 2:34; Rom 10:6; and Eph 4:9—all of which speak of the Son of God coming from heaven (1983:208).

30:5 ***Every word of God proves true.*** The word for "God" in Hebrew is *'eloah* [TH433, ZH468], only here in Proverbs but common in Job. His every word is "smelted, refined"—a metaphor for being error-free, wholly reliable, and true.

30:6 ***Do not add to his words.*** Do not contribute any of your own wisdom; do not presume to have knowledge to offer—this would be error, dross. "God's word is not to be compensated by human wisdom" (R. Moore 1994:97); cf. Deut 29:29.

expose you as a liar. The verb appears in the Niphal elsewhere only in Job 41:9 [1]. Agur's vocabulary has a number of connections with Job.

30:7 ***O God.*** The words are not in Hebrew.

before I die. This means "before it is too late" (as in Gen 27:4; 45:28). See Franklyn 1983:249.

30:8 ***give me neither poverty nor riches.*** This is a plea for the middle-class life, which avoids the temptations of both extremes.

30:9 ***For if I grow rich.*** Precisely, "lest I become sated"—and behave as the fool of 30:22.

Who is the Lord? The "God's . . . name" (NLT interjects "holy") is given as the answer. This echoes the questions of 30:4, "Who . . . goes up to heaven. . . . What is his name?"

30:10 ***or the person will curse you.*** The word "curse" links this verse with the next.

30:11 ***Some people curse their father and do not thank their mother.*** Each verse of 30:11-14 begins with *dor* [TH1755A, ZH1887] (generation), lit., "a generation [that] curses his father and does not bless his mother." The alternative to becoming a son or daughter of Yahweh is now explored.

30:12 ***They are pure in their own eyes.*** Lit., "A generation is pure in his eyes." "Eyes" links with the next verse.

30:13 ***They look proudly around, casting disdainful glances.*** Lit., "A generation—how lofty his eyes! And his eyelids are lifted up."

30:14 ***They.*** Lit., "A generation." God judged a faithless generation to wander for 40 years (Num 32:13); see also Deut 29:18-27; Luke 11:29-32.

COMMENTARY

The oracle of Agur is included in the Epilogue of Proverbs as another voice beside the more strident voices of the wise father or Lady Wisdom. The name "Agur" seems to mean "foreign"—he feels like an outsider to the human sapiential enterprise. Not only is he unable to fathom the mind of God, he cannot even understand human reason. He claims no innate knowledge, no common sense; he has nothing to confidently assert. He is weary but perseveres; although a failure as a sage, he knows where truth can be found—with God (30:5-6).

This outsider seems to counterbalance the rest of Proverbs, wherein Wisdom's path is clear, known, and walked without stumbling. Agur seems less certain of his ability to grasp sapiential principles, though he is keenly aware of his deep dependency on the Creator for life and direction. Job also called himself a stranger (using a term sharing a root with "Agur") in Job 19:15, "My servants and maids consider me a stranger. / I am like a foreigner to them." Job in his distress was an Agur.

There are a number of connections between the oracle of Agur and the book of Job. Throughout Proverbs the term translated "God" is always *'elohim* [TH430, ZH466]—except in Agur's oracle. Here, two alternative words are employed: *'eloah* [TH433, ZH468] (30:5) and *'el* [TH410A, ZH446] (30:1). Although very rare in Proverbs, the former is found in Job over 40 times, and the latter over 50 times—they are Job's favorite terms for God. Job's friends first label him "weary" (Job 4:2, 5), using the verb Agur chose in 30:1 (*la'ah* [TH3811, ZH4206]). Job describes himself near the end of his monologue (Job 31:23) as being unable to endure. But Agur says he can endure (see final note on 30:1). It is as if Agur put together Job's friends' first description with his last self-description—using Job's language for God—to produce the verse, "The man's utterance to Ithiel / I am weary, God, but I endure." Agur calls himself the "man" (*geber* [TH1397, ZH1505]) that God calls Job to be (Job 38:3). Proverbs 30:1 seems to identify Agur with Job's weariness of human counsel (and of suffering) and with the "strong man" that Job should have been, but to contrast Agur with Job's despair: While Job could *not* endure, Agur *does* endure. In the next verse, Agur emulates Yahweh's rhetorical questioning of Job in chapters 38–41 (perhaps labeling his poem an "oracle" recalls the mode of revelation Job experienced). Agur's confession of ignorance recalls Job 42:3: "I was talking about things I knew nothing about, things far too wonderful for me." Agur begins the oracle where Job ends, in a confession of absolute ignorance and poverty of wisdom. Job 41:9 [1] uses the Niphal stem of the verb *kazab* [TH3576, ZH3941]—found in this form elsewhere only in Agur's warning that God will "expose you as a liar" (30:6). In this verse, Agur is concerned that one avoid God's rebuke (*yakakh* [TH3198, ZH3519]). This word is quite common in Job, and it may be argued that "reproving" is Job's main theme. Job defends himself from it in Job 6:25 (see also Job 6:26; 13:6, 15; 19:5; 23:4, 7, etc.). Job used the word to define his desired dialogue between himself and God (Job 13:15). Eliphaz in his opening address (Job 5:17) declares, "But consider the joy of those corrected [*yakakh*] by God!"

Although Agur's words are treated as a different poem from the Poem of Threes and Fours, perhaps another reference to Job can be seen in 30:32, where it is said that if you are foolish in your pride and exalt yourself, you should "cover your mouth in shame"—the very response Job made to God (Job 40:4).

Agur's echoes of Job are taken from key passages, always the beginning or ending of discourses. These connections appear to be purposeful, not random coincidences. The one element in Agur's oracle that does not mirror Job is the reference to God's words. How may one avoid being proved a liar as Job was? How may one avoid God's rebuke? By taking refuge in God's words. In 30:1-9, it is as though Agur offers God's word as the answer to Job. God's words are the connecting link between the God of creation (who tames Leviathan) and the sage. Do not add to his words *as Job did,* and so prove to be a liar *as Job was.* And for the sage, these words are found in the book of Proverbs.

The poem of Agur provides a blueprint for a wise life. The first step is to renounce any pretense to independent or intrinsic wisdom. The next step is to remember and name the God of creation—the Father who calls you to listen to his words. A balanced and moderate life is best suited for wisdom, wisdom that comes from his word, not from observations of nature and society. If you will not be Yahweh's "son," then you will also despise your earthly parents, being part of a generation cut off from his graces, vividly described in 30:11-14 (see notes). These are the two paths of Agur.

It is notable that Agur, who offers an "oracle," agrees with the prophets that the plight of the poor is in part due to the oppression of the rich (30:14). Pleins suggests that Proverbs, while calling the wealthy to be sympathetic and charitable, has no interest in changing social structures that promote poverty (1987:65). Our "Great Society" in the United States has tried to alter these structures by transferring some of the wealth to the disadvantaged, yet many are still below the poverty line. Perhaps if today's citizens were to personally embrace the admonitions of Proverbs, this would significantly change.

◆ B. Poem of Threes and Fours (30:15-33)

15 The leech has two suckers
  that cry out, "More, more!"*

There are three things that are never
    satisfied—
  no, four that never say, "Enough!":
16 the grave,*
  the barren womb,
  the thirsty desert,
  the blazing fire.

17 The eye that mocks a father
  and despises a mother's
    instructions

will be plucked out by ravens of the
valley
and eaten by vultures.

18 There are three things that amaze me—
no, four things that I don't
understand:
19 how an eagle glides through the sky,
how a snake slithers on a rock,
how a ship navigates the ocean,
how a man loves a woman.

20 An adulterous woman consumes a
man,
then wipes her mouth and says,
"What's wrong with that?"

21 There are three things that make the
earth tremble—
no, four it cannot endure:
22 a slave who becomes a king,
an overbearing fool who prospers,
23 a bitter woman who finally gets a
husband,
a servant girl who supplants her
mistress.

24 There are four things on earth that are
small but unusually wise:
25 Ants—they aren't strong,
but they store up food all summer.
26 Hyraxes*—they aren't powerful,
but they make their homes among
the rocks.
27 Locusts—they have no king,
but they march in formation.
28 Lizards—they are easy to catch,
but they are found even in kings'
palaces.

29 There are three things that walk with
stately stride—
no, four that strut about:
30 the lion, king of animals, who won't
turn aside for anything,
31 the strutting rooster,
the male goat,
a king as he leads his army.

32 If you have been a fool by being proud
or plotting evil,
cover your mouth in shame.

33 As the beating of cream yields butter
and striking the nose causes
bleeding,
so stirring up anger causes quarrels.

30:15 Hebrew *two daughters who cry out, "Give, give!"* 30:16 Hebrew *Sheol.* 30:26 Or *Coneys,* or *Rock badgers.*

NOTES

30:15 ***The leech has two suckers that cry out, "More, more!"*** Lit., "To the leech are two daughters, 'Give! Give!'" (*hab* [TH3051, ZH2035]). "Leech" (*'aluqah* [TH5936, ZH6598]) is a hapax legomenon in the OT, but is found in later Hebrew. Although annelid worms employ two suckers, "it was probably not common knowledge that only the anterior one had a mouth" (North 1965:282). "Daughters," then, would be figurative of these two suckers. Alternatively, the idea may be that anything that "leeches" is a figurative daughter or offspring of a leech—four are subsequently listed. The five Hebrew words of this line are a proverb in their own right and introduce the following characterization of satiation (per LXX).

three things . . . four. The poetic device of opening with "three . . . four" here uniquely follows the number "two." "The leech has two daughters that suck! Suck! Behold three [of its daughters] are never sated, four never replete."

30:16 The ranks of the dead are ever swelling; the barren womb is never full of semen, but endlessly drinks up more; and the land ravenously sponges rain. Fire does not willingly abstain from available fuel. Waltke pairs them as follows: The grave "ever yearns to end life" while the womb "ever yearns to produce it"—and the land produces what fire destroys (2005:487-488).

30:17 ***eye.*** See note on 27:20, where the eye of man is another insatiable entity, as is Sheol.
mother's instructions. The reading in the LXX is "elderly mother."

ravens. Heb., *'orbe* [TH6158, ZH6854], which sounds like "four" (*'arba'* [TH702, ZH752]), making 30:17 a bridge between two "three and four" sayings.

eaten by vultures. Lit., "eaten by *sons* of the eagle"—balancing the leech's "daughter" (30:15). This verse is connected with the previous two through the motif of eating or consuming. "Eagle" is found three times in Proverbs, the last in 30:19, another link between 30:17 and the other "three and four" sayings.

30:18 *amaze me . . . I don't understand.* Lit., "too wonderful for me . . . I do not know." The next verses supply the numerals' referent, "there are three [ways]. . . four [ways]." The first stanza moved from two to four; this will move from three to five.

30:19 Lit., "The way (*derek* [TH1870, ZH2006]) of an eagle in heaven / the way of a serpent upon a rock / the way of a ship in the heart of the sea / and the way of a man with a young woman." Modes of propulsion are cause for wonder and awe—and a profound recognition of ignorance—in four observations. The fourth wonder is the manner in which a man moves himself forward with a young maiden. The maiden is analogous to the heavens, rock, and waters. Agur claims ignorance to the question of how a man navigates through the medium of love (Schwab 2002:160).

30:20 *adulterous woman.* Lit., "Thus is the *way* (*derek* [TH1870, ZH2006]) of an adulteress."

consumes a man, then wipes her mouth. NLT interpolates "man"; it should be rendered as "eats, then wipes her mouth." "The way of a man with a maid smoothly transitions to the discussion of the way of an adulteress. Immoral sexual activity is referenced under the image of eating. She wipes her 'mouth' and claims that she has done no wicked thing" (Schwab 2002:160). See 22:14 for the "mouth" of an adulteress—a possible euphemism for her vulva. "Eating" connects with 30:15-16. Crenshaw connects this with Gen 39:6-9, where Potiphar's "food" is metaphorically his wife (1990:20). See the Prologue for warnings about the loose woman, especially 9:17.

30:21 Each verse of this stanza (and the second line of 30:21) begins with *takhath* [TH8478A, ZH9393] (under). "*Under* three the earth quakes / And *under* four it cannot bear up." Four examples follow, climaxing with two kinds of unbearable women.

30:22 *a slave who becomes a king.* Heb. *ki* [TH3588, ZH3954] (NLT, "who") should be read in its temporal sense throughout the stanza, "an underling *when* he becomes king." Cf. 17:2, where the wise servant is better suited to rule than the foolish son. Here, the world cannot tolerate the confused regime such an ill-advised prospect brings.

an overbearing fool who prospers. Lit., "a fool when sated with food." Such a person hardly threatens the social order of the land, but he or she is impossible to live with at home. Another domestic example follows.

30:23 *a bitter woman who finally gets a husband.* Lit., "under a hated woman (Qal passive participle from *sane'* [TH8130, ZH8533]) when (*ki* [TH3588, ZH3954]) married." The word *sane'* indicates opposition or struggle (e.g., 2 Sam 19:4-6; Ps 35:19; Mal 1:3). It is glossed "unloved" in Gen 29:31, describing Leah, the paradigmatic lonely wife who contended with her sister for love and was constitutionally unable to refrain from conceptualizing her birthing success as warfare (Van Leeuwen 1986b:608-609). "Time after time, Leah would name her sons in accordance with her ambition for her husband's love. . . . Love is analyzed in a trajectory from the way of a man with a virgin, to the way of the dangerous adulteress, terminating in the traditional accounts of inner-familial strife" (Schwab 2002:161).

a servant girl who supplants her mistress. This is reminiscent of Hagar in Gen 16, another story highlighting domestic discord.

30:24 ***unusually wise.*** Lit., "surpassingly wise." What follows are examples of greatly skilled creatures, able to accomplish what pertains to life, implying that "human beings who acquire wisdom can overcome their natural disadvantages" (Whybray 1994a:419).

30:25 ***Ants—they aren't strong.*** Lit., "The ants are a people not strong." "People" links this with 30:26. "Ants" is found elsewhere in the OT only in 6:6-8.

30:26 ***Hyraxes—they aren't powerful.*** These could be badgers or coneys (see NLT mg)—small rodent-like animals with sharp teeth and padded feet. They are called, lit., "a people not mighty."

they make their homes among the rocks. Lit., "They set their house in the rock" (*sela'* [TH5553, ZH6152]).

30:27 ***Locusts—they have no king, but they march in formation.*** Lit., "King is not to the locust (*'arbeh* [TH697, ZH746]) / And they go forth dividing its all," meaning "all go out in ranks." "King" ends 30:28, linking the verses and introducing the subject of kings. "Locust" (like "raven" in 30:17) puns with "four" (*'arba'ah* [TH702, ZH752]).

30:28 ***Lizards.*** Heb., *semamith* [TH8079, ZH8532], a hapax legomenon probably intending "gecko."

30:29 ***stately.*** This is repeated in both cola—"stately step . . . stately walk." What follows is a list of creatures who rule in their own domain.

30:30 ***the lion, king of animals.*** The word "king" is a gloss of *gibbor* [TH1368, ZH1475]; it could be more precisely rendered, "mighty among the beasts."

30:31 ***the strutting rooster.*** The Hebrew word *zarzir* [TH2223, ZH2435] is a hapax legomenon. Perhaps it could also refer to a horse, greyhound, or starling. Perhaps this is a rooster "lifting its comb" (Haupt 1926:353).

a king as he leads his army. Lit., "a king (*'alqum* [TH510, ZH554]) with him." *'Alqum* is an unexplained hapax legomenon. Perhaps it should be divided as *'al-qum* [TH408/6965, ZH440/7756], meaning "no (up)rising" and rendered as "a king no one dares resist" (Waltke 2005:462). He is comically compared with a pathetically self-important goat. But the two verses also form a chiasm that principally compares kings with lions (A *lion,* B rooster, B' goat, A' *king*). Like the rest, he rules in his domain.

30:32 ***If you have been a fool.*** "Fool" (*nabal* [TH5034B, ZH5571]) recalls *nabal* [TH5036A, ZH5572] from 30:22, the folly exhibited in fools sated with food, slaves ruling, and domestic upset.

cover your mouth in shame. This is the same response of Job to God (Job 40:4).

30:33 ***beating . . . striking . . . stirring.*** These three words are identical in Hebrew (*mits* [TH4330, ZH4790]) and each is followed by an identical verb from *yatsa'* [TH3318, ZH3655] ("bring forth"; cf. NLT, "yields . . . causes . . . causes").

quarrels. Exalting yourself as a fool (the vice of the preceding verse) inevitably produces "quarrels" (*rib* [TH7379, ZH8190]). The *rib* can connote a lawsuit, necessitating arbitration from the government (18:17; 25:9).

COMMENTARY

The poetic device of listing "three . . . and four" conveys an orderliness to things, a quality of being countable, knowable, and designed. The Poem of Threes and Fours lampoons a bankrupt civilization and in doing so lodges a sober critique. The earth "cannot bear up" when society is overturned and thwarted. The poem shines the spotlight on various readily observable phenomena—aspects of ordinary life—with the ultimate goal of calling to attention (1) the order that God has established, (2) how humans meddle with this order, causing distress and crises, and (3) the way of wisdom in light of this.

First, the order that God has established is highlighted in two schemas: (1) principles built into the universe that hunger or consume without any internal restraint (30:15-16), and (2) that which transcends human understanding, especially the manner of propulsion through various media (which is a synecdoche for all wondrous things), particularly the mystery of sexual relations (30:18-19). These two examples of the nature of God's creation are punctuated with moral comments. The antisocial "eye" (which is never satisfied; 27:20) will be plucked by agents of consumption (30:17). The "eating" adulteress offers a detour from the mysterious medium of the maiden (30:20). There are any number of natural "paths"—including the proper sexual path—which are healthy and thus tacitly sanctioned by the Creator; but there is also the deviant sexual path that denies the conscience (30:20). McKane suggests that the barren womb is the focus of 30:15-16: "Insatiable death, the thirsty land and the greedy fire are all metaphors of her appetite for sexual intercourse, for the fierce urge to remove the reproach of her barrenness" (1970:656). Not only are fire and land never satiated, but some people are not, either—those who are never content with their lot in life. There is no amount of money or power that can satisfy, so all who live for such things are constrained to ever expend their energy on the acquisition of more. When Leah birthed her sons, she named them after her heartfelt wish— "Now my husband will love me. . . . Surely this time my husband will feel affection for me"—but of course he never did. Finally, she learned to be content in Yahweh (Gen 29:31-35).

Next, various social aberrations are noted that sour or ruin human life—particularly, when good things happen to individuals who cannot manage the sudden change of fortune and so ruin the community's serenity (30:21-23). People may react to particular blessings in such a way that turns it into a curse for others—resulting in a social earthquake (30:21). The response to these observations is to aspire to wisdom.

The animal world illustrates how to conduct oneself with prudence (30:24-28). This stanza is the longest in the poem, with each animal enjoying its own verse. Thus, more attention is given to the subject of lessons on display in creation than any other in the poem. Not only is the world full of that which consumes and that which is beyond knowing, it also presents numerous pictures useful to the wise.

The ants' prodigious wisdom is their infallible preparations during times of plenty for times of want (30:25). When humans such as Joseph propose the same, the world recognizes one "filled with the spirit of God," exceptionally "intelligent or wise" (Gen 41:38-39). The hyraxes (or rock badgers) wisely preserve their lives from attack by exploiting the natural defenses God provided for them (30:26; cf. Ps 104:18). A people who dwell in rocks (*sela'* [TH5553, ZH6152]) such as Esau (Edom), are wise (Obad 1:3, 6-8). Wise kings command humans, and victory testifies to sagacious leadership (16:32; 24:6-7). But locusts are successful in pursuing their goals without a ruler (30:27). If humans were as savvy as locusts, kings would be unnecessary (Daube 1985). The lizards can do what most people cannot—find their way into the homes of kings (30:28). If the king represents life enjoyed to its fullest degree, lizards enjoy royal privilege, skilled at entering the places where abundant life is found. "There are those who despite their weakness and vulnerability make such good use of the resources which they have that they attain to eminence of the first rank—to the circle of the court" (McKane 1970:662).

Part of being wise is to know one's place in the social order of things. Therefore, even when one perceives an overblown ruler strutting like a peacock, wisdom dictates that he deserves our respect—to trifle with him is like frivoling with a lion (30:29-31). Since there are both wise and foolish, powerful and weak, and two sexes, conduct yourself humbly and wisely, aware of what is fitting and accepting the reality of moral consequence (30:17, 32-33).

◆ C. The Words of King Lemuel (31:1-9)

The sayings of King Lemuel contain this message,* which his mother taught him.

2 O my son, O son of my womb,
O son of my vows,
3 do not waste your strength on women,
on those who ruin kings.

4 It is not for kings, O Lemuel, to guzzle wine.
Rulers should not crave alcohol.
5 For if they drink, they may forget the law
and not give justice to the oppressed.
6 Alcohol is for the dying,
and wine for those in bitter distress.
7 Let them drink to forget their poverty
and remember their troubles no more.

8 Speak up for those who cannot speak for themselves;
ensure justice for those being crushed.
9 Yes, speak up for the poor and helpless,
and see that they get justice.

31:1 Or *of Lemuel, king of Massa;* or *of King Lemuel, an oracle.*

NOTES

31:1 ***The sayings of King Lemuel contain this message.*** This can be rendered also as "The sayings of Lemuel, king of Massa" or "the sayings of King Lemuel, an oracle" (see NLT mg and commentary).

which his mother taught him. "Mother" complements the Prologue, where the father solely gives voice to the wise parents. She "disciplined" (*yasar* [TH3256, ZH3579]) the king (see 19:18; 29:17).

31:2 She thrice repeats "son" (*bar* [TH1248, ZH1337], a late biblical Hebrew form, identical with the Aramaic word) with increasing force, lit., "What, my son! And what, son of my womb! And what, son of my vows!" "Vows" implies that her counsel has behind it her legal status as queen mother. He is the fruit not only of her womb but also of her marriage covenant and royal position. Thus, he should listen!

31:3 ***on those who ruin kings.*** Lit., "your ways to the ruin of kings." The key word "king" (Aramaic, *melakin* [TA/ZA10421, S4430]) is found again here and twice more in the next verse. Descriptions of the alternative follow her warnings (31:10-31).

31:4 His mother's repetitious style reads, lit., "It is not for kings, Lemuel, it is not for kings to drink wine." Key words such as "drink," "wine," and "strong drink" appear here, opening the main topic of the oracle. Note the juxtaposition of alcohol with sex (31:3).

crave. Kethiv reads "or" and Qere reads "what." In fact, neither is suitable to the verse, and it is best emended to *'awweh* [TH185, ZH205], meaning "desire" (see 23:3, 6).

31:5 *not give justice to the oppressed.* Lit., "change judgment (*din* [TH1779, ZH1907]) for all the sons of affliction." Addiction to alcohol, it is feared, will lead to "forgetting what is decreed"—the king will become negligent, and the people will suffer. *Din* is another key word, here specifying the rationale for refusing alcohol.

31:6 *bitter distress.* Lit., "bitter of soul." The verse commands, "Give strong drink to those perishing!" As emphatically as Lemuel is told not to drink, he is unequivocally ordered to give it to unfortunates. Waltke considers this satire: "The sarcastic command aims to debunk intoxicants as useless" (2005:509). Even so, "There is no prohibitionist fervour in this directive and no absolute veto on wine" (McKane 1970:410). God blesses with wine (3:9-10).

31:7 Drinking much ameliorates the suffering of poverty and hard toil, but it does this by dulling the mind—is this the way of wisdom?

31:8 *Speak up.* Here and in 31:9, the verse begins with "Open your mouth!"—not to pour in drink, but to speak on behalf of the "dumb" (*'illem* [TH483A, ZH522]) and the "sons of *khalop.*" The word *khalop* [TH2475, ZH2710] is perhaps a unique form of *khalap* [TH2498, ZH2736] (pass on), thus, "passing away."

31:9 *speak up for the poor and helpless, and see that they get justice.* Lit., "Open your mouth! Judge [for] the righteous! Judge [for] the afflicted and needy!" Again, the king should open his mouth to judge, not to imbibe wine. Alcohol has some value, but is unsuitable for those in positions of responsibility.

COMMENTARY

Over a century ago Toy observed, "'Lemuel' might be regarded as 'king of Massa' if there were any good ground for supposing that there was such a country Massa, governed by a king and somehow associated with wisdom and learning; but of such a land nothing is known" (1899:539). Today that supposition still stands, despite the Arabic clan Massa, known in Toy's day (Gen 25:14). Lemuel, though his nationality is unidentified, is probably non-Israelite. The Septuagint translates "Lemuel" as "spoken by God." As in 30:1, the words of Lemuel are identified as a divinely sanctioned, authoritative oracle.

The oracle is a strong warning against kings' abusing alcohol. Lewis lists various kings who met their demise under the influence of alcohol, such as Ben-hadad (1 Kgs 20:16) and Belshazzar (Dan 5); Herod (Mark 6:21-25) was tricked into beheading John while under the influence of alcohol (1982:322). Proverbs universally condemns drunkenness as unwise, but in 31:6-7 its anesthetic quality seems to be commended. But the wise do not value benumbed senses.

Christians struggle with the issue of alcohol consumption and often conclude that any use of alcohol is unjustified. Often the argument rests not on scriptural grounds but on the great dangers of alcohol, such as those noted by Lewis (1982), who concludes his essay citing statistics and modern social ills traceable to alcohol. But sexual profligacy is at least as dangerous, yet no one today advocates its total abstinence for all Christians, though in the past many vowed lifelong celibacy (which is continued today in the Roman Catholic priesthood and religious orders). Other Christians claim Jesus as a model on the use or nonuse of alcohol. Not only did Jesus contribute the best wine in the house (John 2), and not only did he institute a sacrament requiring alcohol consumption (Luke 22:17-18), but his conduct throughout his ministry earned him the reputation of being a "drunkard" (Matt 11:19)! How many teetotaling Christians today follow his example?

Although the ancient world did not value abstinence from either wine or sex, both are axiomatically risky. Wisdom must be exercised in governing both of these sensual pleasures. Leaders and rulers must not become alcoholics or sex addicts, which would lead to their own demise and that of the people they govern.

◆ D. The Heroine (31:10-31)

10* Who can find a virtuous and capable wife?
She is more precious than rubies.
11 Her husband can trust her,
and she will greatly enrich his life.
12 She brings him good, not harm,
all the days of her life.

13 She finds wool and flax
and busily spins it.
14 She is like a merchant's ship,
bringing her food from afar.
15 She gets up before dawn to prepare breakfast for her household
and plan the day's work for her servant girls.

16 She goes to inspect a field and buys it;
with her earnings she plants a vineyard.
17 She is energetic and strong,
a hard worker.
18 She makes sure her dealings are profitable;
her lamp burns late into the night.

19 Her hands are busy spinning thread,
her fingers twisting fiber.
20 She extends a helping hand to the poor
and opens her arms to the needy.
21 She has no fear of winter for her household,
for everyone has warm* clothes.
22 She makes her own bedspreads.
She dresses in fine linen and purple gowns.
23 Her husband is well known at the city gates,
where he sits with the other civic leaders.
24 She makes belted linen garments
and sashes to sell to the merchants.

25 She is clothed with strength and dignity,
and she laughs without fear of the future.
26 When she speaks, her words are wise,
and she gives instructions with kindness.
27 She carefully watches everything in her household
and suffers nothing from laziness.

28 Her children stand and bless her.
Her husband praises her:
29 "There are many virtuous and capable women in the world,
but you surpass them all!"

30 Charm is deceptive, and beauty does not last;
but a woman who fears the LORD will be greatly praised.
31 Reward her for all she has done.
Let her deeds publicly declare her praise.

31:10 Verses 10-31 comprise a Hebrew acrostic poem; each verse begins with a successive letter of the Hebrew alphabet. 31:21 As in Greek and Latin versions; Hebrew reads *scarlet*.

NOTES

31:10 ***virtuous and capable.*** In Hebrew this is one word (*khayil* [TH2428, ZH2657]), elsewhere translated "wealth" or "strength" (13:22; 31:3). Gafney glosses it as "powerful"

(2000:26); Yoder, "substance" (2003:427); Gutstein, "valor" (1999:36)—a "manly" trait (LXX, *andreian;* cf. *anēr* [TG435, ZG467], "man"). See the book of Ruth for what such a woman is like (Ruth 3:11).

wife. This is the first word in Hebrew, beginning with Aleph, the first letter of the alphabet. The initial letter of each verse is in alphabetical order, forming an alphabetic acrostic for all 22 verses (see NLT mg). Waltke observes that Aleph also terminates the first line (2005:510). "Who can find" her?—the implication is that such a woman is valuable and rare (Yoder 2003:432), although this is mitigated somewhat in 31:29 (see note). For an English translation that retains the acrostic, see Riess 1997:142-143.

rubies. Lit., "corals." This word appears four times in Proverbs, used twice to describe the surpassing value of Lady Wisdom. "Wisdom is more precious than rubies; nothing you desire can compare with her" (3:15; 8:11; see notes). "The poet applies to the wife in chapter 31 what has been said of wisdom" (McCreesh 1985:42).

31:11 ***trust her.*** The verb *batakh* [TH982, ZH1053] begins the verse; note the initial Beth (second letter of the alphabet). The noun *betakh* [TH983, ZH1055] denotes the security enjoyed by all who heed Lady Wisdom in the final verse of her introductory poem (1:33).

she will greatly enrich his life. Lit., "*shalal* there is no lack." *Shalal* [TH7998, ZH8965] ordinarily denotes "plunder" (1:13; 16:19), thus KJV, "so that he shall have no need of spoil." Various alternative meanings have been proposed; Kassis argues that it comes from an Arabic cognate meaning "wealth" (2000:258). Lady Wisdom also enriches the sage (8:18-19). "Loot" is martial imagery—she is an Amazon, metaphorically victorious in battle, daily winning spoils of war.

31:12 ***She brings him good.*** Lit., "She rewards him (*gemalathhu* [TH1580, ZH1694]) with good (*tob* [TH2896, ZH3202])." Note the initial Gimel (third letter of the alphabet).

31:13 ***She finds.*** Heb., *dareshah* [TH1875, ZH2011]. Note the initial Daleth (fourth letter of the alphabet).

and busily spins it. Lit., "and works with delight (*khepets* [TH2656, ZH2914]) her palms." Similarly, Lady Wisdom in 8:11 is "better" (*tob* [TH2896, ZH3202]; see 31:12) . . . than anything you desire (*khepets*)," particularly "rubies."

31:14 ***She is.*** Heb., *hayethah* [TH1961, ZH2118]. Note initial He (fifth letter of the alphabet).

like a merchant's ship. McCreesh suggests she is compared to Solomon, "the only one in Israel's history to build a merchant fleet" (1985:43).

her food. She provides food for her family—even as Wisdom sets her table: "Come, eat my food" (9:5).

31:15 ***She gets up before dawn.*** Lit., "And she rises (*wattaqam* [TH6965, ZH7756]) while yet night." Note initial Waw (sixth letter of the alphabet). Sometimes in the Bible alphabetic poems are incomplete in some way (Pss 25 and 34 lack the Waw line, Ps 145 lacks the Nun line, Lam 2–4 reverse Ayin and Pe). Here, however, is a perfect acrostic—beautifying the flawless lady.

breakfast. Lit., "prey." This is "an incomplete metaphor for a lioness, which hunts its prey at night" (Waltke 2005:511). She is a figurative huntress.

plan the day's work for her servant girls. In Hebrew this is two words, "and-statutes [*khoq*] for-her-maidservants." The word *khoq* [TH2706, ZH2976] is found three times in Proverbs; Wisdom was beside God when he set a boundary (*khoq*) for the sea and marked off (*khaqaq* [TH2710, ZH2980]) the land (8:29). This wife apportions daily chores, imaging God's apportioning the universe with Wisdom.

31:16 ***She goes to inspect.*** Heb., *zamemah* [TH2161, ZH2372]. Note the initial Zayin (seventh letter of the alphabet).

buys it. From *laqakh* [TH3947, ZH4374], meaning "she takes it"; sometimes *laqakh* denotes violent acquisition (1:19), but it is usually benign.

with her earnings. Lit., "from the fruit of her palms." Wisdom's "fruit" is better than gold (8:19). This woman's fruit is a never-ending benefit. She plants a vineyard with it—complementing her food with wine (31:14; cf. 9:5).

31:17 ***She is energetic and strong, a hard worker.*** Lit., "She girds her loins (*khagrah* [TH2296, ZH2520], note the initial Heth, the eighth letter of the alphabet) with strength (*'oz* [TH5797, ZH6437]) / "She makes firm (*'amets* [TH553, ZH599]) her arms." This language echoes Yahweh making firm (*'amets*) the skies and strengthening (*'azaz* [TH5810, ZH6451]) springs (8:28)—accompanied by Lady Wisdom. Elsewhere in the OT, only men "gird their loins." This is "another example of this woman being described in a way usually reserved for men" (Szlos 2000:102). "Arms" are icons of her potency.

31:18 ***She makes sure.*** Lit., "She tastes" (*ta'amah* [TH2938, ZH3247]). Note the initial Teth (ninth letter of the alphabet).

her dealings are profitable. Heb., *ki tob sakhrah* [TH3588/2896/5504, ZH3954/3202/6087] (that good is her profit). *Sakhar* appears elsewhere in Proverbs only in 3:14 (twice), also following *ki tob:* "For better is her profit than the profit of silver," describing personified Wisdom.

31:19 ***Her hands.*** Heb., *yadeha* [TH3027, ZH3338]. Note the initial Yodh (10th letter of the alphabet).

are busy spinning thread, her fingers twisting fiber. Lit., "reach out in the *kishor* [TH3601, ZH3969], and her palms grasp the *pelek* [TH6418, ZH7134]." *Kishor* is a hapax legomenon, glossed "distaff" since Luther; this gloss is now supported with Sumerian and Aramaic cognates (Rendsburg 1997). *Pelek* elsewhere refers to a "district" (Neh 3:9, 12, 14-18), the only exception being an obscure phrase in 2 Sam 3:29, although "all the ancient versions agree that *pelek* means 'spindle'" and cognates may be found from many Semitic languages (Wolters 1994:96). However, Erika Moore, in an unpublished paper, suggests for *kishor* the semantic value "region," based on an Akkadian cognate (E. Moore:1994). This yields, "Her hands reach out to the region, and her palms support the district." Moore observes here a series of concentric circles: The woman cares for her husband, her servants, and the town. This is especially persuasive, considering its strong linkage with the next verse.

31:20 ***helping hand.*** The first word in Hebrew is *kappah* [TH3709, ZH4090] (her palm). Note the initial Kaph (11th letter of the alphabet). This and the previous verse can be examined as follows—note the chiastic paralleling (Brockmöller 2001:12):

Her-hands reach-out in-the-region	and-her-palms support (the)-district
Her-palm spreads-out to-the-afflicted	and-her-hands reach-out to-the-needy

"Her concern for those oppressed . . . is a direct parallel with the ethical behavior King Lemuel's mother demands of her son and in this way serves to unite the chapter" (Gafney 2000:27). Hers is a kingly responsibility.

31:21 ***She has no fear.*** Heb., *lo'-thira'* [TH3808/3372, ZH4202/3707]. Note the initial Lamedh (12th letter of the alphabet).

her household. Interestingly, it is her house, not her husband's. The feminine possessive pronoun is suffixed to "house" in Proverbs 12 times: seven in the Prologue referencing

Wisdom's or the loose woman's houses, four times in the Wife of Virtue acrostic, and once in 14:1 (see note).

warm clothes. This follows the Greek and Latin versions (see NLT mg); the Hebrew is *shani* I [TH8144, ZH9106] (scarlet). It could be repointed to *shenayim* [TH8147, ZH9109] (second), yielding, "doubly clothed"—i.e., clothed in multiple layers, which could lead to the idea of being "warm," the idea that the NLT has opted for.

31:22 *bedspreads.* This is the first word in Hebrew (*marbaddim* [TH4765, ZH5267]). Note the initial Mem (13th letter of the alphabet). This word occurs elsewhere in the OT only in the loose woman's boudoir (7:16). Wisdom and Folly are both actualized in flesh-and-blood women.

31:23 *is well known.* Heb., *noda'* [TH3045, ZH3359]; it begins this verse. Note the initial Nun (14th letter of the alphabet).

civic leaders. Lit., "elders of the land." "Land" (*'erets* [TH776, ZH824]) occurs four times in 8:22-31. There, Wisdom was faithfully beside Yahweh in creating the "earth." Here, the worthy wife supports her man who manages the land. Crook suggests that the husband is known for his fine apparel (1954:139).

31:24 *linen garments.* This is the first word in Hebrew (*sadin* [TH5466, ZH6041]). Note the initial Samekh (15th letter of the alphabet).

merchants. Lit., "Canaanites"—that is, Phoenicians, sea people.

31:25 *She is clothed with strength and dignity.* "Strength" is the first word in Hebrew (*'oz* [TH5797, ZH6437]). Note the initial Ayin (16th letter of the alphabet). This segment has spoken of literal clothing: fine linen, belts, warm, colorful. Here clothing becomes a metaphor for the invisible qualities of virtue, with which she is preeminently attired. She adorns her family in fine raiment but invests herself with forcefulness (see 31:17) and comportment.

she laughs without fear of the future. Lit., "She laughs at the latter day." "Laugh" occurs six times in Proverbs, three describing Lady Wisdom's laughter (1:26; 8:30-31). "The wife has the same posture [as Wisdom] with regard to what will come" (McCreesh 1985:42).

31:26 *When she speaks, her words are wise.* Lit., "She opens her mouth with wisdom." "Her mouth" (*piha* [TH6310, ZH7023]) is the first word in Hebrew; note initial Pe, the 17th letter of the alphabet.

she gives instructions with kindness. "Instructions" comes from *torah* [TH8451, ZH9368], "kindness" from *khesed* [TH2617, ZH2876] (see note on 2:8). See 1:8 and 6:20 for her *torah*. These words are "drawn from the common wisdom vocabulary" of Proverbs (McCreesh 1985:35).

31:27 *She carefully watches everything in her household.* Lit., "She watches over (*tsopiyah* [TH6822, ZH7595]) the ways of her house." Note the initial Tsadhe (the 18th letter of the alphabet). Wolters suggests that the unusual morphology of *tsapah* is used because *tsopiyah* transliterates and sounds like the Greek word for wisdom, *sophia* (1985:580). This wordplay suggests a double entendre, "*Sophia* (is) the ways of her house," again associating the wife with Lady Wisdom. This requires a late editorial date for the form of the verb, almost synchronous with its translation into Greek.

and suffers nothing from laziness. Lit., "the bread of idleness she does not eat"—yet another "wisdom theme" (McCreesh 1985:35). Contrast her with Folly, who offers men secret bread (9:17).

31:28 *stand.* Lit., "rise," the first word in Hebrew (*qamu* [TH6965, ZH7756]). Note the initial Qoph (the 19th letter of the alphabet).

bless her. "Bless" comes from *'ashar* II [TH833A, ZH887]. "Wisdom is a tree of life . . . happy ['ashar] are those who hold her tightly" (3:18). Here, those happy sons confer the same benediction on her. She is their tree of life. (See notes on 3:13; 23:19.)

31:29 *There are many virtuous and capable women in the world.* Lit., "Many (*rabboth* [TH7227, ZH8041]) daughters have done *khayil* [TH2428, ZH2657]," balancing "sons" of 31:28. This observation nuances the opening line, "A woman of *khayil*, who can find?" Apparently, such women are available, but to find one requires the eyes of a sage. Note the initial Resh (the 20th letter of the alphabet) in *rabboth.*

you surpass them all! This phrase denotes warring against hostile forces, as in Josh 8:3, "set out to attack" (Wolters 2001:10). Hausmann equates her surpassing value with Wisdom (1992:263).

31:30 *Charm is deceptive.* "Charm" or "gracefulness" comes from *khen* [TH2580, ZH2834]. Here, outward attractiveness can be deceiving and is contrasted with inner praiseworthiness. "Deceptive" is actually the first word in the Hebrew (*sheqer* [TH8267, ZH9214]); note the initial Shin (the 21st letter of the alphabet).

beauty does not last. "Beauty" is used elsewhere in Proverbs only in 6:25 in a warning against the loose woman (see note on 6:25). Farmer notes that here such beauty is called fleeting (*hebel* [TH1892, ZH2039]), the word glossed "vanity" or "meaningless" in Ecclesiastes (1991:145). (The Hebrew Bible places Ruth—the OT example of the woman of *khayil* [TH2428, ZH2657]—and Song of Songs between Proverbs and Ecclesiastes.) What is *not* "vain" or "impermanent" is embracing the first principle of wisdom—the fear of Yahweh (1:7). With this thought, the book of Proverbs has returned full circle to its opening.

31:31 *Reward her for all she has done.* The initial word in Hebrew is *tenu,* which is either from *nathan* [TH5414, ZH5989], meaning "Give!" or *tanah* [TH8567, ZH9480], meaning "rehearse" (Whybray 1994a:431). If the latter, it should be repointed to *tannu* and read, "Laud her for the fruit of her hands." Note the initial Taw, the 22nd and final letter of the alphabet.

Let her deeds publicly declare her praise. Lit., "Let her works praise her in the gates." The "gates" are where her husband conducts business (31:23) and where Lady Wisdom cries out for all to hear (1:21; 8:3). Wisdom cries at the gates of the city in the Prologue, and in the Epilogue, the wife's praises are heard there.

COMMENTARY

Proverbs 31:10-12 introduces the virtuous woman as an unending source of beneficence to her husband. "Palms" occurs four times in 31:13-20, highlighting her ceaseless efforts. Proverbs 31:21-25 focuses on her care for "clothing"—how she garbs her family and herself—featuring the husband. She is his reputation's matrix, clothing him with fame:

A. She clothes her family (31:21)
  B. What she makes (31:22)
    C. Her husband is known at the gate (31:23)
  B'. What she makes (31:24)
A'. She clothes herself (31:25)

The poem concludes by referencing her words and the praises she elicits from others (31:26-31). Her mouth speaks wisdom, and she does not eat idleness.

In the Septuagint version of Proverbs, the poem on the virtuous woman immediately follows chapter 29, and thereby strikes a stark contrast with the "man of iniquity" of 29:27 (Cook 1996:544). The Masoretic Text places this poem after Lemuel's warnings. All versions agree in concluding with her poem; thus, this marvelous woman is the crown of Proverbs. The question is why. How is lauding the wonderful wife a fitting conclusion to this book? Would the reader not expect instead a poem extolling Wisdom?

McCreesh notes that her works eclipse the husband's, who "is left with little or nothing to do! . . . The husband does not have the place of honor in the poem. It is with the wife that the poem concludes, voicing the praise given her" (1985:27-28). The worthy (*khayil* [TH2428, ZH2657]) wife contrasts the women of Lemuel's oracle, to whom kings should not give their *khayil* (31:3). "The book of *Proverbs* closes, consequently, with the same theme with which it began: a contrast between the women whose ways lead to death, and the woman Wisdom who promises life" (McCreesh 1985:40). McCreesh concludes that the poem treats none other than Lady Wisdom, "a faithful wife and skilled mistress of her household, finally settled down with her own"—the same Wisdom who was beside the Creator when the world was made (1985:46). Gutstein (1999:38) shares the same view:

> *One may wonder why the reference in Chapter 31 is to an exceptional woman and not an exceptional man. The answer . . . is that it is Woman who has been associated with wisdom throughout Proverbs. . . . The author meant the passage to be an allegory, a poem extolling the virtues, beauties and advantages not of a good woman but of Wisdom personified as female.*

One difficulty with this interpretation is that the poem seems to describe a flesh-and-blood woman. The Prologue's Folly has a very real woman as her exemplar—the temptress. Should not Wisdom also have a corporeal counterpart? Hawkins lists significant differences between Wisdom and the wife: Wisdom publicly preaches to attract followers and is *not* a wife and mother too preoccupied with daily business to seek devotees (1996:17)! Crook reads the poem as an "instruction for a marriageable maiden," which complements schools for training boys. "The Woman of Worth is an ideal; there never was any such person" (Crook 1954:139-140). Women should strive for this ideal, even though she is just that—a goal, not a reality. But Hawkins submits there is no evidence that such girls' schools existed (1996:13)—and as the conclusion to Proverbs, some wisdom significance is expected, even if she serves as a model for wives. Thus Wolters argues for "the Valiant Wife as the personification of Wisdom—not in an allegorical sense, but in the sense of an earthly embodiment of what it means to be wise" (1984:165). She is an example of what wisdom looks like; her virtue flows from fearing Yahweh (31:30)—wisdom's first principle. Wisdom is shown not to be abstractly philosophical but intensely practical—the fabric of everyday living.

The wise person knows how to avoid the temptress—and how to live happily, successfully, and long with the wife of his youth. The essence of a wise life, in fact, consists in this great skill. Pursuit of Wisdom entails pursuit of a good woman—and failure at finding one will often bring a man to take another kind of woman (Eccl 7:23-29). It is precisely at this point that Solomon's wisdom failed him and led to the ever-increasing folly of idolatry (Schwab 2001:81; see commentary on 6:20–7:27). Here, the wise person has entered Wisdom's house, taken his abode with her, and loved her—and so receives her love (see 8:17). This path of wisdom includes a chosen lifestyle of marital fidelity. The blessedness enjoyed by such a man substantially comes to him *through* his God-fearing wife—who personifies in her many tangible accomplishments what Wisdom looks like. She is an ideal, then, not only for wives, but in a sense for husbands as well, because to be wise is to be like her. And receiving the blessings of wisdom is like receiving the benefits of a virtuous spouse.

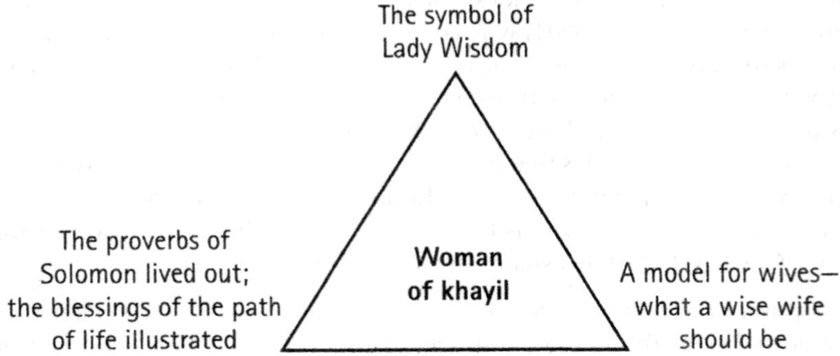

In the Prologue, Lady Wisdom represents divine wisdom, possessed by Yahweh from eternity; she is the matrix of the created order, intuited through observation; she is the wisdom tradition of Israel, her exemplar being the proverbs of Solomon. The book concludes with another complex figure, the Woman of *khayil* [TH2428, ZH2657], again with at least three loci of meaning.

First, her description resembles that of Lady Wisdom in the Prologue. She is a symbol of God's wisdom—as a man should regard divine wisdom, so he should regard her: beyond price, worthy of praise, the never-ending source of blessedness. This wisdom is not an abstract ideal, but something concrete and practical, the very fabric of daily life. She is God's highest gift to undeserving humanity. "Wisdom has built her house" (9:1)—that is, through Lady Wisdom the family is fed (by both parents), through Lady Wisdom they are clothed. The wisdom of Yahweh is the means by which they sustain their reputation, face the future, strike deals with traders, buy land, plant vineyards, spin wool, guide their servants, and so on. God supplies the skills of life.

Second, she is the "wife's example" (Kidner 1985:35), written so women may aspire to emulate her. She is contrasted with the loose woman (folly incarnate) through similar descriptive language. She is the temptress's antidote, a giver of blessedness and life rather than a stealer. Ruth is such a woman and is called so in Ruth 3:11. Consider her fidelity, her ceaseless work, her rising to the occasion. Proverbs 12:4 also speaks of the woman of *khayil* [TH2428, ZH2657] (see note): "A worthy wife is a crown for her husband, but a disgraceful woman is like cancer in his bones." She is "a portrait of a human being who exemplifies the meaning of wisdom as the art of life, the art of going about the business of living in this world in the right relation to one's tasks and fellow creatures" (Metlitzki 1986:26). Every woman may be guided by this lofty ideal. The "work of women" is "Wisdom's work" (Camp 1987a:104).

But what *is* the model for women presented here? Almost every verse underlines her self-assured confidence and vast capabilities in traditionally male language. Wolters argues that her description is a heroic hymn, perhaps patterned on the Song of Deborah (Judg 5) or the Song of the Sea (Exod 15), which both extol Yahweh as a warrior (2001:12). She is "valiant" (31:10), like a conqueror gaining plunder (31:11), a nocturnal predator making the kill (31:15), a "taker" of land (31:16), "girding her loins" with strength, with powerful arms (31:17), supporting the community like a king (31:9, 20), fearless (31:21, 25), astute in business dealings (31:18, 24), counseling wisdom (31:26), and publicly praised in the city (31:31). She provides materially for her household (31:11-14, 18, 21, 27) and earns fame for her man (31:23). This is the Proverbs 31 ideal, ladies. Go and do likewise.

Third, she illustrates the successful wisdom enterprise as enshrined in the book of Proverbs. The wise person knows how to identify and take a good woman as wife, and in doing so, clarifies his own pathway to one of life, honor, wealth, and happiness. It is through his wife that the amplest benefits of wisdom come—she is Wisdom's avatar. She is his crown, and she is the mark of wisdom, the visible sign of his insight.

The book of Proverbs begins by presenting two choices before the youth—the path of wisdom or the path of folly. These are personified in two women. One is Lady Wisdom, an attribute of God, present at creation, omnipresent, calling upon all to make a covenant with her, to love her, to enter her house, to marry her. She is the matrix of abundant life from Yahweh. Her opposite is Folly, who also calls out for all to hear; she is unavoidable. Folly is incarnated in the Prologue in a number of voices such as the gang, but especially in the loose woman—a very real, flesh-and-blood temptress. She is not merely a metaphor or allegory, even though she exemplifies the path to death. She embodies the call of Folly to the young man. He stands at the fork in the road, and both voices appeal to him to walk their paths. What will he do? Throughout the book, the appeal to take the right path is repeated (19:27; 23:15; 27:11; 31:2-3). But will he listen? What kind of life will he choose?

Although a good wife is commended in the Prologue and the father is given voice, there is no analogous picture painted there as counterweight to the loose woman, no flesh-and-blood, detailed illustration of what Wisdom looks like. The reader must wait for the very end of Proverbs to see the Virtuous Wife, the ultimate argument against the wiles of Folly and her agent, the loose woman. This young man, now older, has made his choice, and we see him settled in with Wisdom—living day by day blessed with his heroic and capable wife.

Significantly, the book of Revelation climaxes with a vision of two women. One, the Whore Babylon, seeks to seduce the world with all manner of pleasures (Rev 17). The other, the Bride of Christ, inherits all the promises of Proverbs: life with Yahweh, who has become her Father (Rev 21:2, 7, 9-11). The foretaste of this bliss, to which Proverbs points, is best experienced today in one's own marriage (Eph 5:22-33). Nonetheless, both married people and those who are single must wait, along with all the promises of the book, for the latter day when the true meaning of the path of life, to which Lady Wisdom calls, will be revealed. It is in this hope that Christians aspire to live a life of wisdom.

BIBLIOGRAPHY

Ahlström, Gösta W.
1979 The House of Wisdom. *Svensk Exegetisk Arsbok* 44:74–76.

Alden, Robert L.
1983 *Proverbs.* Grand Rapids: Baker.

Alnor, Jackie
1999 Invasion of the Sophia Women. *The Christian Sentinel.* http://www.cultlink.com/sentinel/sophia.htm.

Alter, Robert
1985 *The Art of Biblical Poetry.* New York: Basic Books.

Anbar, Moshe
1972 Proverbes 11:21, 16:5, *yd lyd* "Sur le Champ." *Biblica* 53:537–538.

Berman, Joshua
2002 The "sword of mouths" (Jud. iii 16; Ps. cxlix 6; Prov. v 4): A Metaphor and its Ancient Near Eastern Context. *Vetus Testamentum* 52:291–303.

Boorer, Suzanne
1996 A Matter of Life and Death: A Comparison of Proverbs 1–9 and Job. Pp. 187–204 in *Prophets and Paradigms.* Editors, Gene M. Tucker and Stephen Breck Reid. Sheffield: Sheffield Academic Press.

Bratcher, Robert G.
1983 A Translator's Note on Proverbs 11:30. *Bible Translator* 34.3:337–338.

Brockmöller, Katrin
2001 Chiasmus und Symmetrie: Zur Discussion um eine Sinnvolle Struktur in Spr 31,10–31. *Biblische Notizen* 110:12–18.

Brueggemann, Walter
1990 The Social Significance of Solomon as a Patron of Wisdom. Pp. 117–132 in *The Sage in Israel and the Ancient Near East.* Editors, John G. Gammie and Leo G. Perdue. Winona Lake, IN: Eisenbrauns.

Bryce, Glendon E.
1972 Another Wisdom-Book in Proverbs. *Journal of Biblical Literature* 91.2:145–157.

1979 A Legacy of Wisdom: The Egyptian Contribution to the Wisdom of Israel. Lewisburg, PA: Bucknell University Press.

Burns, John Barclay
1995 Proverbs 7,6–27: Vignettes from the Cycle of Astarte and Adonis. *Scandinavian Journal of the Old Testament* 9.1:20–36.

Byargeon, Rick W.
1997 The Structure and Significance of Prov 9:7–12. *Journal of the Evangelical Theological Society* 40:367–375.

Callaway, Phillip R.
1984 Deut 21:18–21: Proverbial Wisdom and Law. *Journal of Biblical Literature* 103.3:341–352.

Camp, Claudia V.
1987a Female Voice, Written Word: Women and Authority in Hebrew Scripture. Pp. 97–113 in *Embodied Love: Sensuality and Relationship as Feminist Values.* Editors, Paula Cooey, Sharon Farmer, and Mary Ellen Ross. San Francisco: Harper & Row.

1987b Woman Wisdom as Root Metaphor: A Theological Consideration. Pp. 45–76 in *The Listening Heart.* Editors, Kenneth G. Hoglund and Roland E. Murphy. Journal for the Study of the Old Testament Supplement Series 58. Sheffield: Sheffield Press.

1990 The Female Sage in the Biblical Wisdom Literature. Pp. 185–203 in *The Sage in Israel and the Ancient Near East.* Editors, John G. Gammie and Leo G. Perdue. Winona Lake, IN: Eisenbrauns.

Carasik, Michael
1994 Who Were the "Men of Hezekiah" (Proverbs xxv 1)? *Vetus Testamentum* 44.3:289–300.

Cascante Gómez, Fernando A.
1998 Proverbs 1:1–19. *Interpretation* 52.4:407–411.

Chambers, Oswald

1985 Where God Hides His Glory. *Christianity Today* 29.16:29.

Chisholm, Robert B.

2000 Drink Water from Your Own Cistern: A Literary Study of Proverbs 5:15-23. *Bibliotheca Sacra* 157:397-409.

Clifford, Richard

1975 Proverbs IX: A Suggested Ugaritic Parallel. *Vetus Testamentum* 25:298-306.

Clines, D. J. A., and D. M. Gunn

1978 "You Tried to Persuade Me" and "Violence! Outrage!" in Jeremiah XX 7-8. *Vetus Testamentum* 28:20-27.

Cody, Aelred

1980 Notes on Proverbs 22,21 and 22,23b. *Biblica* 61 no 3:418-426.

Cohen, Jeffrey M.

1982 An Unrecognized Connotation of *nsq peh* with Special Reference to Three Biblical Occurrences. *Vetus Testamentum* 32.4:416-424.

Cook, Johann

1996 Exodus 38 and Proverbs 31: A Case of Different Order of Verses and Chapters in the Septuagint. Pp. 537-549 in *Studies in the Book of Exodus*. Editor, Mark Vervenne. Leuven, Belgium: Leuven University Press.

Craigie, P.

1971 The Poetry of Ugarit and Israel. *Tyndale Bulletin* 22:3-31.

Crenshaw, James L.

1981 *Old Testament Wisdom*. Atlanta: John Knox.

1990 Impossible Questions, Sayings, and Tasks. *Semeia* 17:19-34.

Crook, Margaret B.

1954 The Marriageable Maiden of Proverbs 31:10-31. *Journal of Near Eastern Studies* 13:137-140.

Dahood, Mitchell

1960 Immortality in Proverbs 12:28. *Biblica* 41.2:176-181.

1973 Honey that Drips: Notes on Proverbs 5:2-3. *Biblica* 54.1:65-66.

1987 Love and Death at Ebla and their Biblical Reflections. Pp. 93-99 in *Love and Death in the Ancient Near East*. Editors, John Marks and Robert Good. Gilford, CT: Four Quarters.

Daube, David

1985 A Quartet of Beasties in the Book of Proverbs. *Journal of Theological Studies* 36.2:380-386.

Delitzsch, Franz

1874 *Proverbs of Solomon*, vol. 1. Translator, M. G. Easton. Edinburgh: T&T Clark.

1875 *Proverbs of Solomon*, vol. 2. Translator, M. G. Easton. Edinburgh: T&T Clark.

Driver, G. R.

1951 Problems in the Hebrew Text of Proverbs. *Biblica* 32:173-197.

1955 Proverbs 19:26. *Theologische Zeitschrift* 11:373-374.

Emerton, John A.

1964 Note on Proverbs 12:26. *Zeitschrift für die alttestamentliche Wissenschaft* 76.2:191-193.

1968 Note on the Hebrew Text of Proverbs 1:22-3. *Journal of Theological Studies* 19:609-614.

1984 The Meaning of Proverbs 13:2. *Journal of Theological Studies* 35:91-95.

1988 The Interpretation of Proverbs 21,28. *Zeitschrift für die alttestamentliche Wissenschaft* 100:161-170.

2001a Looking on One's Enemies. *Vetus Testamentum* 51.2:186-196.

2001b The Teaching of Amenemope and Proverbs xxii 17-xxiv 22: Further Reflections on a Long-Standing Problem. *Vetus Testamentum* 51.4:431-465.

Estes, Daniel J.

1997 *Hear, My Son*. Grand Rapids: Eerdmans.

Farmer, Kathleen A.

1991 *Who Knows What Is Good? A Commentary on the Books of Proverbs and Ecclesiastes*. International Theological Commentary. Grand Rapids: Eerdmans.

Fox, Michael V.
1984 LXX Proverbs 3:28 and Ancient Egyptian Wisdom. *Hebrew Annual Review* 8:63-69.

1994 The Pedagogy of Proverbs 2. *Journal of Biblical Literature* 113:233-243.

1996 'Amon Again. *Journal of Biblical Literature* 115:699-702.

Franklyn, Paul
1983 The Sayings of Agur in Proverbs 30: Piety or Skepticism? *Zeitschrift für die alttestamentliche Wissenschaft* 95.2:238-252.

Freedman, David Noel
1997 Proverbs 2 and 31: A Study in Structural Complementarity. Pp. 47-55 in *Tehillah le-Moshe*. Editors, Mordecai Cogan, Barry L. Eichler, and Jeffrey H. Tigay. Winona Lake, IN: Eisenbrauns.

Gafney, Wilda
2000 Who Can Find a Militant Feminist? A Marginal(ized) Reading of Proverbs 31:1-31. *AME Zion Quarterly Review* 112.2:25-31.

Garrett, Duane A.
1990 Votive Prostitution Again: A Comparison of Proverbs 7:13-14 and 21:28-29. *Journal of Biblical Literature* 109:681-682.

1993 *Proverbs, Ecclesiastes, Song of Songs.* New American Commentary 14. Nashville: Broadman & Holman.

Gibson, J. C. L.
1977 *Canaanite Myths and Legends.* Edinburgh: T&T Clark.

Giese, Ronald L., Jr.
1992 Strength through Wisdom and the Bee in LXX-Prov 6:8a-c. *Biblica* 73.3:404-411.

1993 Dualism in the LXX of Prov 2:17: A Case Study in the LXX as Revisionary Translation. *Journal of the Evangelical Theological Society* 36:289-295.

Greenfield, Jonas C.
1985 The Seven Pillars of Wisdom (Prov 9:1): A Mistranslation. *Jewish Quarterly Review* 76.1:13-20.

Grossberg, Daniel
1994 Two Kinds of Sexual Relationships in the Hebrew Bible. *Hebrew Studies* 35:1-25.

Gunneweg, Antonius
1992 Weisheit, Prophetie und Kanonformel: Erwägungen zu Proverbia 30,1-9. Pp. 253-260 in *Alttestamentlicher Glaube und biblische Theologie.* Stuttgart: Kohlhammer.

Gutstein, Naphtali
1999 Proverbs 31:10-31: The Woman of Valor as Allegory. *Jewish Bible Quarterly* 27:36-39.

Harding, William N.
1986 An Examination of Passages Cited by the Jehovah's Witnesses to Deny Jesus is God. Pp. 273-279 in *Interpretation and History.* Editors, R. L. Harris et al. Singapore: Christian Life Publishers.

Haupt, Paul
1926 Four Strutters. *Journal of Biblical Literature* 45:350-354.

Hausmann, Jutta
1992 Beobachtungen zu Spr 31,10-31. Pp. 261-266 in *Alttestamentlicher Glaube und biblische Theologie.* Stuttgart: Kohlhammer.

Hawkins, Tom R.
1996 The Wife of Noble Character in Proverbs 31:10-31. *Bibliotheca Sacra* 153:12-23.

Hayes, J. H.
1974 *Old Testament Form Criticism.* San Antonio: Trinity University Press.

Healy, J. F.
1989 Models of Behavior: Matt 6:26 (|| Luke 12:24) and Prov 6:6-8. *Journal of Biblical Literature* 108:497-498.

Heim, Knut
1993 Coreferentiality, Structure and Context in Proverbs 10:1-5. *Journal of Translation and Textlinguistics* 6.3:183-209.

Heskett, Randall J.
2001 Proverbs 23:13-14. *Interpretation* 55.2:181-184.

Hildebrandt, Ted
1988 Proverbs 22:6a: Train up a Child? *Grace Theological Journal* 9.1:3-19.

Hurowitz, Victor

1999 Nursling, Advisor, Architect? *khmwn* and the Role of Wisdom in Proverbs. *Biblica* 80.3:391-400.

2000 Two Terms for Wealth in Proverbs viii in Light of Akkadian. *Vetus Testamentum* 50.2:252-257.

2001 Proverbs 29.22-27: Another Unnoticed Alphabetic Acrostic. *Journal for the Study of the Old Testament* 92:121-125.

Irwin, William H.

1984 The Metaphor in Prov 11:30. *Biblica* 65:97-100.

1986 Where Shall Wisdom Be Found? *Journal of Biblical Literature* 48:133-142.

Jelinek, Erik

1998 Alcoholism and the Book of Proverbs: A Look at Alcoholism as Shown in Proverbs 23:29-35. *Journal of Ministry in Addiction & Recovery* 5.2:65-74.

Jobes, Karen

2000 Sophia Christology: The Way of Wisdom? Pp. 226-250 in *The Way of Wisdom*. Editors, J. I. Packer and Sven K. Soderlund. Grand Rapids: Zondervan.

Johnson, Timothy

2002 Implied Antecedents in Job xl 2b and Proverbs iii 6a. *Vetus Testamentum* 52.2:278-284.

Jones, John N.

1995 "Think of the Lilies" and Prov 6:6-11. *Harvard Theological Review* 88:175-177.

Jones, Scott C.

2003 Wisdom's Pedagogy: A Comparison of Proverbs vii and 4Q184. *Vetus Testamentum* 53.1:65-80.

Kaiser, Walter C.

2000 True Marital Love in Proverbs 5:15-23 and the Interpretation of Song of Songs. Pp. 106-116 in *The Way of Wisdom*. Editors, J. I. Packer and Sven K. Soderlund. Grand Rapids: Zondervan.

Kannengiesser, Charles

1999 Lady Wisdom's Final Call: The Patristic Recovery of Proverbs 8. Pp. 65-77 in *Nova Doctrina Vetusque*. Editors, Fredric W. Schlatter, Douglas Kries, and Catherine Brown Tkacz. New York: Peter Lang.

Kassis, Riad A.

2000 A Note on *SHALAL* (Prov xxxi 11b). *Vetus Testamentum* 50.2:258-259.

Kidner, Derek

1964 *Proverbs*. Tyndale Old Testament Commentary. Downers Grove, IL: InterVarsity.

1985 *The Wisdom of Proverbs, Job, and Ecclesiastes*. Downers Grove, IL: InterVarsity.

Kio, Stephen

2000 What Does "You Will Heap Burning Coals Upon His Head" Mean in Romans 12.20? *Bible Translator* 51.4:418-424.

Kitchen, K. A.

1977 Proverbs and Wisdom Books of the Ancient Near East. *Tyndale Bulletin* 28:69-114.

Kline, Meredith

1986 *Images of the Spirit*. Self-published.

Kruger, Paul

1987 Promiscuity or Marriage Fidelity: A Note on Prov 5:15-18. *Journal of Northwest Semitic Languages* 13:61-68.

Kselman, John S.

2002 Ambiguity and Wordplay in Proverbs xi. *Vetus Testamentum* 52.4:545-548.

Kugel, James L.

1981 *The Idea of Biblical Poetry*. London: Yale University Press.

Lawson, George

1980 *Exposition of Proverbs*. Grand Rapids: Kregel. (Orig. pub. 1829.)

Lewis, Jack P.

1982 Difficult Texts from the Psalms and Proverbs. Pp. 311-323 in *Difficult Texts of the Old Testament Explained*. Editor, Wendell Winkler. Hurst, TX: Winkler Publications.

Lichtheim, M.

1983 *Late Egyptian Wisdom Literature in the International Context*. Switzerland: Biblical Institute of Fribourg.

Lindenburger, J. M.
1983 *The Aramaic Proverbs of Ahiqar.* Baltimore: Johns Hopkins Press.

Loewenstamm, Samuel E.
1987 Remarks on Proverbs 17:12 and 20:27. *Vetus Testamentum* 37.2:221-224.

Longman, Tremper, III
1987 *Literary Approaches to Biblical Interpretation.* Grand Rapids: Zondervan.

2002 *How to Read Proverbs.* Downers Grove, IL: InterVarsity.

Luc, Alex
2000 The Titles and Structure of Proverbs. *Zeitschrift für die alttestamentliche Wissenschaft* 112.2:252-255.

Lyons, Ellen Louise
1987 A Note on Proverbs 31:10-31. Pp. 237-245 in *The Listening Heart.* Editors, Kenneth G. Hoglund and Roland E. Murphy. Journal for the Study of the Old Testament Supplement Series 58. Sheffield: Sheffield Press.

MacIntosh, Andrew Alexander
1970 Note on Proverbs 25:27. *Vetus Testamentum* 20.1:112-114.

Malchow, Bruce V.
1985 A Manual for Future Monarchs. *Catholic Biblical Quarterly* 47:238-245.

McCreesh, Thomas
1985 Wisdom as Wife: Proverbs 31:10-31. *Revue Biblique* 92:25-46.

McKane, W.
1970 *Proverbs: A New Approach.* Old Testament Library. Philadelphia: Westminster.

McKinlay, Judith
1999 To Eat or Not to Eat: Where is Wisdom in this Choice? *Semeia* 86:73-84.

Meinhold, Arndt
1992 Der Umgang mit dem Feind nach Spr 25,21f als Massstab für das Menschsein. Pp. 244-252 in *Alttestamentlicher Glaube und biblische Theologie.* Stuttgart: Kohlhammer.

Metlitzki, Dorothée
1986 "A Woman of Virtue": A Note on *Eshet Hayil. Orim* 1:23-26.

Millard, Alan R.
1975 'Its "To exult". *Journal of Theological Studies* 26:87-89.

Miller, Patrick D.
1970 Apotropaic Imagery in Proverbs 6:20-22. *Journal of Near Eastern Studies* 29.2:129-130.

Montgomery, David J.
2000 "A Bribe is a Charm": A Study of Proverbs 17:8. Pp. 134-149 in *The Way of Wisdom.* Editors, J. I. Packer and Sven K. Soderlund. Grand Rapids: Zondervan.

Moore, Rick D.
1994 A Home for the Alien: Worldly Wisdom and Covenantal Confession in Proverbs 30,1-9. *Zeitschrift für die alttestamentliche Wissenschaft* 106.1:96-107.

Moore, Erika
1994 The Domiestic Warrior." Unpublished manuscript.

Murphy, Roland E.
1966 The Kerygma of the Book of Proverbs. *Interpretation* 20:3-14.

1985 Wisdom and Creation. *Journal of Biblical Literature* 104:3-11.

1986 Wisdom's Song: Proverbs 1:20-33. *Catholic Biblical Quarterly* 48.3:456-460.

1987 Proverbs 22:1-9. *Interpretation* 41.4:398-402.

1988 Wisdom and Eros in Proverbs 1-9. *Catholic Biblical Quarterly* 50:600-603.

1998 *Proverbs.* Word Biblical Commentary 22. Nashville: Thomas Nelson.

Newsom, Carol A.
1989 Women and the Discourse of Patriarchal Wisdom: A Study of Proverbs 1-9. Pp. 142-160 in *Gender and Difference in Ancient Israel.* Editor, Peggy L. Day. Minneapolis: Fortress Press.

North, Francis Sparling
1965 Four Insatiables. *Vetus Testamentum* 15.2:281-282.

O'Connell, Robert H.

1991 Proverbs VII 16-17: A Case of Fatal Deception in a "Woman and a Window" Type Scene. *Vetus Testamentum* 41:235-239.

Origen

1936 *Origen on First Principles.* Translator, G. W. Butterworth. London: Society for Promoting Christian Knowledge.

Overland, Paul

2000 Did the Sage Draw from the Shema? A Study of Proverbs 3:1-12. *Catholic Biblical Quarterly* 62.3:424-440.

Peels, H. G. L.

1994 Passion or Justice? The Interpretation of *Beyôm Nāqām* in Proverbs vi 34. *Vetus Testamentum* 44.2:270-274.

Pleins, J. David

1987 Poverty in the Social World of the Wise. *Journal of the Study of the Old Testament* 37:61-78.

Plöger, Otto

1984 *Sprüche Salmos (Proverbia).* Neukirchen-Vluyn: Neukirchener Verlag.

Purdue, Leo G.

1994 *Wisdom and Creation: The Theology of Wisdom Literature.* Nashville: Abingdon.

Rad, Gerhard von

1972 *Wisdom in Israel.* Nashville: Abingdon.

Rendsburg, Gary A.

1997 Double Polysemy in Proverbs 31:19. Pp. 267-274 in *Humanism, Culture, and Language in the Near East.* Editors, Asma Afsaruddin and A. H. Mathias Zahniser. Winona Lake, IN: Eisenbrauns.

2001 Hebrew Philological Notes. *Hebrew Studies* 42:187-195.

Riess, Jana K.

1997 The Woman of Worth: Impressions of Proverbs 31:10-31. *Dialogue* 30:141-151.

Ryken, Leland, and Tremper Longman III

1993 *A Complete Literary Guide to the Bible.* Grand Rapids: Zondervan.

Scherer, Andreas

1997 Is the Selfish Man Wise? Considerations of Context in Proverbs 10.1-22.16 with Special Regard to Surety, Bribery and Friendship. *Journal for the Study of the Old Testament* 76:59-70.

Schwab, George

1995 The Proverbs and the Art of Persuasion. *Journal of Biblical Counseling* 14.1:6-17.

2001 Woman as the Object of Qohelet's Search. *Andrews University Seminary Studies* 39.1:73-84.

2002 *The Song of Songs' Cautionary Message Concerning Human Love.* Studies in Biblical Literature 41. New York: Peter Lang.

Scott, Robert B. Y.

1960 Wisdom in Creation: The 'Amôn of Proverbs 8:30. *Vetus Testamentum* 10.2:213-223.

1965 *Proverbs, Ecclesiastes.* Anchor Bible. New York: Doubleday.

Skehan, Patrick W.

1971 *Studies in Israelite Poetry and Wisdom.* Washington, DC: The Catholic Biblical Association of America.

Snell, Daniel C.

1983 "Taking Souls" in Proverbs 11:30. *Vetus Testamentum* 33.3:362-365.

1989 The Wheel in Proverbs 20:26. *Vetus Testamentum* 39.4:503-507.

1991 The Most Obscure Verse in Proverbs: Proverbs 26:10. *Vetus Testamentum* 41.3:350-356.

Stallman, Robert C.

2000 Divine Hospitality and Wisdom's Banquet in Proverbs 9:1-6. Pp. 117-133 in *The Way of Wisdom.* Editors, J. I. Packer and Sven K. Soderlund. Grand Rapids: Zondervan.

Steinmann, Andrew E.

2000 Proverbs 1-9 as a Solomonic Composition. *Journal of the Evangelical Theological Society* 43.4:659-674.

2001 Three Things . . . Four Things . . . Seven Things: The Coherence of Proverbs 30:11-33 and the Unity of Proverbs 30. *Hebrew Studies* 42:59-66.

Szlos, M. Beth

2000 A Portrait of Power: A Literary-Critical Study of the Depiction of the Woman in Proverbs 31:10-31. *Union Seminary Quarterly Review* 54:97-103.

Tepox, Alfredo

2001 The Importance of Becoming Wise: Proverbs 1.1-7. *Bible Translator* 52.2:216-222.

Thomas, D. Winton

1964 Meaning of *tshthkhth* in Proverbs 10:16. *Journal of Theological Studies* 15:295-296.

Torrey, Charles C.

1954 Proverbs, Chapter 30. *Journal of Biblical Literature* 73.2:93-96.

Toy, C. H.

1899 *Proverbs.* International Critical Commentary. Edinburgh: T&T Clark.

Van Leeuwen, Raymond C.

1986a Proverbs 25:27 Once Again. *Vetus Testamentum* 36.1:105-114.

1986b Proverbs 30:21-23 and the Biblical World Upside Down. *Journal of Biblical Literature* 105.4:599-610.

1986c A Technical Metallurgical Usage of *yskh. Zeitschrift für die alttestamentliche Wissenschaft* 98.1:112-113.

1988 *Context and Meaning in Proverbs 25–27.* Society of Biblical Literature Dissertation Series 96. Atlanta: Scholar's Press.

Vattioni, Francesco

1965 Ancora il Vento del Nord di Proverbi 25:23. *Biblica* 46.2:213-216.

Vawter, Bruce

1980 Prov 8:22: Wisdom and Creation. *Journal of Biblical Literature* 99:205-216.

Waegeman, Maryse

1992 *The Perfect Wife of Proverbia, 10,10-31.* Goldene Äpfel in Silbernen Schalen, 101-107. Frankfurt am Main: Peter Lang.

Waltke, Bruce K.

1979 The Book of Proverbs and Ancient Wisdom Literature. *Biblica Sacra* 136:221-238.

1987 The Authority of Proverbs: An Exposition of Proverbs 1:2-6. *Presbyterian* 13:65-78.

1996 The Dance between God and Humanity. Pp. 87-104 in *Doing Theology for the People of God.* Editors, Donald M. Lewis, Alister E. McGrath, and J. I. Packer. Downers Grove, IL: InterVarsity.

1998 Old Testament Interpretation Issues for Big Idea Preaching: Problematic Sources, Poetics, and Preaching the Old Testament, an Exposition of Proverbs 26:1-12. Pp. 41-52, 175-176 in *Big Idea of Biblical Preaching.* Editors, Keith Willhite and Scott M. Gibson. Grand Rapids: Baker.

2004 *The Book of Proverbs,* vol. 1. New International Commentary on the Old Testament. Grand Rapids: Eerdmans.

2005 *The Book of Proverbs,* vol. 2. New International Commentary on the Old Testament. Grand Rapids: Eerdmans.

Waltke, Bruce K., and M. O'Connor

1990 *Biblical Hebrew Syntax.* Winona Lake, IN: Eisenbrauns.

Wardlaw, Ralph

1982 *Lectures on the Book of Proverbs.* Minneapolis: Klock & Klock Christian Publishers. (Orig. pub. 1861.)

Whybray, Roger N.

1965 Proverbs 8:22-31 and Its Supposed Prototypes. *Vetus Testamentum* 15.4:504-514.

1994a *Proverbs.* The New Century Bible Commentary. Grand Rapids: Eerdmans.

1994b The Structure and Composition of Proverbs 22:17–24:22. Pp. 83-96 in *Crossing the Boundaries.* Editors, Stanley E. Porter, Paul Joyce, and David E. Orton. Leiden: Brill.

Williams, Daniel H.

1994 Proverbs 8:22-31. *Interpretation* 48:275-279.

Williams, Ronald

1990 The Sage in Egyptian Literature. Pp. 19-30 in *The Sage in Israel and the Ancient Near East.* Editors, John G. Gammie and Leo G. Perdue. Winona Lake, IN: Eisenbrauns.

Wolters, Al

1984 Nature and Grace in the Interpretation of Proverbs 31:10-31. *Calvin Theological Journal* 19:153-166.

1985 *Sôpiyyâ* (Prov 31:27) as Hymnic Participle and Play on Sophia. *Journal of Biblical Literature* 104.4:577-587.

1994 The Meaning of *kîsôr* (Prov 31:19). *Hebrew Union College Annual* 65:91-104.

2001 *The Song of the Valiant Woman.* Carlisle: Paternoster Press.

Yee, Gale A.

1982 An Analysis of Prov 8:22-31 according to Style and Structure. *Zeitschrift für die alttestamentliche Wissenschaft* 94:58-66.

1992 The Theology of Creation in Proverbs 8:22-31. Pp. 85-96 in *Creation in the Biblical Traditions.* Editors, Richard J. Clifford and John Joseph Collins. Washington, DC: Catholic Biblical Association of America.

Yoder, Christine

2003 The Woman of Substance: A Socioeconomic Reading of Proverbs 31:10-31. *Journal of Biblical Literature* 122.3:427-447.

Zalcman, Lawrence

2003 Prov 5,19c: shgykhwth my ybyn. *Zeitschrift fur die alttestamentliche Wissenschaft* 115.3:433-434.